Miscellaneous Statistical

Operations Management

Data Analysis & Decision Making

with Microsoft® Excel

S. Christian Albright
Kelley School of Business, Indiana University

Wayne L. Winston
Kelley School of Business, Indiana University

Christopher J. Zappe
Bucknell University

With Cases by

Mark Broadie
Graduate School of Business, Columbia University

Peter Kolesar
Graduate School of Business, Columbia University

Lawrence L. Lapin
San Jose State University

William D. Whisler
California State University, Hayward

SOUTH-WESTERN
CENGAGE Learning™

Australia • Brazil • Japan • Korea • Mexico • Singapore • Spain • United Kingdom • United States

SOUTH-WESTERN
CENGAGE Learning

Data Analysis & Decision Making with Microsoft® Excel, Revised Third Edition

S. Christian Albright,
Wayne L. Winston,
Christopher J. Zappe

VP/Editorial Director:
Jack W. Calhoun

Editor-in-Chief:
Alex von Rosenberg

Senior Acquisitions Editor:
Charles McCormick Jr.

Senior Developmental Editor:
Laura Bofinger

Editorial Assistant:
Bryn Lathrop

Marketing Communications Manager:
Libby Shipp

Marketing Manager:
Bryant Chrzan

Content Project Manager:
Emily Nesheim

Managing Media Editor:
Matt McKinney

Senior Manufacturing Coordinator:
Diane Gibbons

Production Service:
ICC Macmillan Inc.

Art Director:
Stacy Jenkins Shirley

Cover Designer:
Lou Ann Thesing/Kathy Heming

For product information and technology assistance, contact us at **Cengage Learning Academic Resource Center, 1-800-423-0563**

For permission to use material from this text or product, submit all requests online at **www.cengage.com/permissions** Further permissions questions can be emailed to **permissionrequest@cengage.com**

Library of Congress Control Number: 2008925260

Student Edition PKG ISBN-13: 978-0-324-66244-3
Student Edition PKG ISBN-10: 0-324-66244-0
Student Edition ISBN-13: 978-0-324-66247-4
Student Edition ISBN-10: 0-324-66247-5
Student CD-ROM ISBN-13: 978-0-324-66245-0
Student CD-ROM ISBN-10: 0-324-66245-9
Instructor's Edition PKG ISBN-13: 978-0-324-66348-8
Instructor's Edition PKG ISBN-10: 0-324-66348-X
Instructor's Edition ISBN-13: 978-0-324-66347-1
Instructor's Edition ISBN-10: 0-324-66347-1

South-Western Cengage Learning
5191 Natorp Boulevard
Mason, OH 45040
USA

Cengage Learning products are represented in Canada by Nelson Education, Ltd.

For your course and learning solutions, visit **academic.cengage.com**

Purchase any of our products at your local college store or at our preferred online store **www.ichapters.com**

Printed in the United States of America
1 2 3 4 5 6 7 12 11 10 09 08

S. Christian Albright got his B.S. degree in Mathematics from Stanford in 1968 and his Ph.D. in Operations Research from Stanford in 1972. Since then he has been teaching in the Operations & Decision Technologies Department in the Kelley School of Business at Indiana University (IU). He has taught courses in management science, computer simulation, statistics, and computer programming to all levels of business students: undergraduates, MBAs, and doctoral students. In addition, he has taught simulation modeling at General Motors and Whirlpool, and he has taught database analysis for the Army. He has published over 20 articles in leading operations research journals in the area of applied probability, and he has authored the books S*tatistics for Business and Economics, Practical Management Science, Spreadsheet Modeling and Applications*, *Data Analysis for Managers*, and *VBA for Modelers*. He also worked with the Palisade Corporation on the commercial version, *StatTools*, of his statistical StatPro add-in for Excel. His current interests are in spreadsheet modeling, the development of VBA applications in Excel, and programming in the .NET environment.

On the personal side, Chris has been married for 37 years to his wonderful wife, Mary, who retired several years ago after teaching 7th grade English for 30 years and is now working as a supervisor for student teachers at IU. They have one son, Sam, who is currently finishing a law degree at Penn Law School. Chris has many interests outside the academic area. They include activities with his family (especially traveling with Mary), going to cultural events at IU, playing golf, running and power walking, and reading. And although he earns his livelihood from statistics and management science, his *real* passion is for playing classical piano music.

Wayne L. Winston is Professor of Operations & Decision Technologies in the Kelley School of Business at Indiana University, where he has taught since 1975. Wayne received his B.S. degree in Mathematics from MIT and his Ph.D. degree in Operations Research from Yale. He has written the successful textbooks *Operations Research: Applications and Algorithms, Mathematical Programming: Applications and Algorithms, Simulation Modeling Using @RISK, Practical Management Science, Data Analysis and Decision Making,* and *Financial Models Using Simulation and Optimization*. Wayne has published over 20 articles in leading journals and has won many teaching awards, including the schoolwide MBA award four times. He has taught classes at Microsoft, GM, Ford, Eli Lilly, Bristol-Myers Squibb, Arthur Andersen, Roche, PricewaterhouseCoopers, and NCR. His current interest is in showing how spreadsheet models can be used to solve business problems in all disciplines, particularly in finance and marketing.

Wayne enjoys swimming and basketball, and his passion for trivia won him an appearance several years ago on the television game show *Jeopardy*, where he won two games. He is married to the lovely and talented Vivian. They have two children, Gregory and Jennifer.

Christopher J. Zappe earned his B.A. in Mathematics from DePauw University in 1983 and his M.B.A. and Ph.D. in Decision Sciences from Indiana University in 1987 and 1988, respectively. Between 1988 and 1993, he performed research and taught various decision sciences courses at the University of Florida in the College of Business Administration. Since 1993, Professor Zappe has been serving as an associate professor in the decision sciences area of the Department of Management at Bucknell University (Lewisburg, PA). He is currently serving a four-year term as associate dean of faculty in the College of Arts and Sciences. In this position, he specializes in faculty development in the area of teaching. Professor Zappe has taught undergraduate courses in business statistics, decision modeling and analysis, and computer simulation. He also developed and taught a number of interdisciplinary Capstone Experience courses and Foundation Seminars in support of the Common Learning Agenda at Bucknell. Moreover, he has taught advanced seminars in applied game theory, system dynamics, risk assessment, and mathematical economics. He has published articles in scholarly journals such as *Managerial and Decision Economics*, *OMEGA*, *Naval Research Logistics*, and *Interfaces*.

To my wonderful family

To my wonderful wife Mary—my best friend and constant companion. To Sam and Lindsay, and to our lovable Welsh corgi Bryn—the most avid and creative tennis ball player alive!   S.C.A

To my wonderful family   W.L.W.

To my wonderful family

Jeannie, Matthew, and Jack. And to my late sister, Jenny, and son, Jake, who live eternally in our loving memories.   C.J.Z.

Brief Contents

Contents

Preface

With today's technology, companies are able to *collect* tremendous amounts of data with relative ease. Indeed, many companies now have more data than they can handle. However, the data are usually meaningless until they are analyzed for trends, patterns, relationships, and other useful *information*. This book illustrates in a practical way a variety of statistical methods, from simple to complex, to help you analyze data sets and uncover important information. In many business contexts, data analysis is only the first step in the solution of a problem. Acting on the solution and the information it provides to make good decisions is a critical next step. Therefore, there is a heavy emphasis throughout this book on analytical methods that are useful in decision making. Again, the methods vary considerably, but the objective is always the same—to equip you with decision-making tools that you can *apply* in your business careers.

We recognize that the vast majority of students in this type of course are *not* majoring in a quantitative area. They are typically *business* majors in finance, marketing, operations management, or some other business discipline who will need to analyze data and make quantitative-based decisions in their jobs. We offer a hands-on, example-based approach and introduce fundamental concepts as they are needed. Our vehicle is spreadsheet software—specifically, Microsoft Excel. This is a package that most students already know and will undoubtedly use in their careers. Our MBA students at Indiana University are so turned on by the required course that is based upon this book that *almost all* of them (mostly finance and marketing majors) take at least one of our follow-up *elective* courses in spreadsheet modeling. We believe that students see value in statistics and quantitative analysis when the course is taught in a practical and example-based approach.

Rationale for writing this book

Data Analysis & Decision Making is different from the many fine textbooks written for statistics and management science. Our rationale for writing this book is based on three fundamental objectives.

1. **Integrated coverage and applications:** We want the book to unify the student's ability to approach business-related problems by integrating methods and applications that have been traditionally taught in separate courses, specifically Statistics and Management Science.

2. **Practical in approach:** We want the emphasis to be placed upon realistic business examples and the processes managers actually use to analyze business problems—not on abstract theory or computational methods.

3. **Spreadsheet-based:** We want the book to provide students with the skills to analyze business problems with tools they have access to and will use in their careers. To this end, we have adopted Excel and commercial spreadsheet add-ins.

Integrated coverage and applications

In the past, many Business Schools, including ours at Indiana University, have had a required statistics course, a required decision-making course, and a required management science course—or some subset of these. One current trend, however, is to have only one required course that covers the basics of statistics, some regression analysis, some decision making under uncertainty, some linear programming, some simulation, and possibly others. Essentially, we faculty in the quantitative area get one shot at teaching the business students, so we attempt to cover a *variety* of useful analytical methods. We are not necessarily arguing that this trend is ideal, but rather that it is a reflection of the reality at our university and, we suspect, at many others. After several years of teaching this course, we have found it to be a great opportunity to turn students on to the subject and to more advanced study.

Actually, this book is integrative in another important aspect. It not only integrates a number of analytical methods, but it also applies them to a wide variety of business problems—that is, it analyzes realistic examples from many business disciplines. We include examples, problems, and cases that deal with portfolio optimization, workforce scheduling, market share analysis, capital budgeting, new product analysis, and many others.

Practical in approach

Taking a cue from our *Practical Management Science* book, we want this book to be very example-based and practical. We strongly believe that students learn best by working through examples, and they appreciate the material most when the examples are realistic and interesting. Therefore, our approach in this book differs in two important ways from many competitors. First, there is just enough conceptual development to give students an understanding and appreciation for the issues raised in the examples. We often introduce important concepts, such as multicollinearity in regression, in the context of examples, rather than discussing them in the abstract. Our experience is that students gain greater intuition and understanding of the concepts and applications through this approach.

Second, we place virtually no emphasis on hand calculations. We believe it is more important for students to understand why they are conducting an analysis and what it means than to emphasize the tedious calculations associated with many analytical techniques. Therefore, we illustrate how powerful software can be used to create graphical and numerical outputs in a matter of seconds, freeing the rest of the time for in-depth interpretation of the output, sensitivity analysis, and alternative modeling approaches. In our own courses, we move directly into a discussion of examples, where we focus almost exclusively on interpretation and modeling issues and let the computer software perform the number crunching.

Spreadsheet-based

As we have demonstrated in our other texts, we are strongly committed to teaching spreadsheet-based, example-driven courses, regardless of whether the basic area is statistics or management science. We have found tremendous enthusiasm for this approach, both from students and from faculty around the world who have used our books. Students appear to learn and remember more, and they *appreciate* the material more. On the other side, instructors typically enjoy teaching more, and they usually receive immediate reinforcement through better teaching evaluations.

What we hope to accomplish in this book

Condensing the ideas in the above paragraphs, we hope to:

- Reverse negative student attitudes about statistics and quantitative methods by making them real, accessible, and interesting;

- Give students lots of hands-on experience with real problems and challenge them to develop their intuition, logic, and problem-solving skills;

- Expose students to real problems in many business disciplines and show them how these problems can be analyzed with quantitative methods;

- Develop spreadsheet skills, including experience with powerful spreadsheet add-ins that add immediate value in students' other courses and their future careers.

New in the original third edition

There are some significant changes from the first edition to the second. There are fewer changes from the second to the third, but we believe they make the book considerably better.

- **StatPro to StatTools:** Probably the most significant change is that we have moved to a different statistical add-in for Excel. The previous add-in, StatPro, has been redeveloped into a commercial product called StatTools by Palisade Corporation, and the educational version of StatTools is now the statistical add-in for the book. Although the functionality of the two add-ins is very similar—and users of StatPro will have no difficulty making the switch to StatTools—we have changed all of the explanations and screenshots to be consistent with StatTools.

- **Two simulation chapters:** Simulation has been expanded into two chapters, 16 and 17. The organization is similar to that of the optimization chapters, 14 and 15. In each case, the first chapter introduces the concepts and the add-in software, and it illustrates these with a few simple examples. The second chapter then presents a wide variety of business examples that can benefit from simulation or optimization. In addition, Chapter 16 includes more material (than in the second edition) on input probability distributions for simulation. We explain why, for example, someone might choose the triangular distribution instead of the normal distribution for some input variable. We also exploit the very useful @RISK program for viewing and learning about probability distributions. (@RISK is part of the Palisade suite that accompanies the book.)

- **Updated problem data:** Numerous problems, especially in the statistics chapters, are based on real data sets. Unfortunately, data sets get old rather quickly. Therefore, we revised dozens of data sets to make them as current as possible. Typically, the problems ask for the same information as in the previous edition, but the results are sometimes different.

- **Revised chapters:** Since the introduction of the second edition, we wrote another book called *Spreadsheet Modeling and Applications* with Duxbury, where we introduced a number of pedagogical features. In chapters where it was appropriate (Chapters 7 and 14–17), we introduce these same pedagogical features. For example, in each example in these chapters there is a "Where Do the Numbers Come From?" section that discusses how a company might obtain the inputs for the example. The changes are sometimes subtle, but we believe they will help students learn the material.

Reason for this revised edition

In 2007, Microsoft came out with its newest version of Office, Office 2007 (aka Office 12). This was not just another version with a few changes at the edges. It was a completely revamped package. Suddenly, many of the screenshots and instructions in our books were no longer correct because of the extensive user interface changes in Excel 2007. To add to the confusion, third-party developers of add-ins for Excel, particularly Palisade for our books, had to scramble to update their software for Excel 2007. We also had to scramble as the Fall semester of 2007 approached. By the time we obtained the updated software, even in beta version, it was too late to produce updates to our books by Fall 2007. Therefore, we put "changes" files on our Web site (at www.kelley.iu.edu/albrightbooks) to help many of you make the transition.

Of course, a more permanent solution was needed; hence, this revised edition. It is entirely geared to Excel 2007 and the updated add-ins for Excel 2007. If you have moved to Excel 2007, you should use this revised edition. If you are still using an earlier version of Excel, you should continue to use the original third edition. Almost all of the content in the two versions are identical. We changed as little as possible, mostly just the screenshots and accompanying explanations. For a couple of sections, namely, those on pivot tables in Chapter 2 and the new Excel tables in Chapter 4, the changes were so extensive that we rewrote these sections entirely.

Two other comments are in order. First, Palisade was in the midst of an extensive rewrite of its DecisionTools suite when Office 2007 came out. To get through the 2007–2008 academic year, Palisade developed a slightly revised version of its *old* DecisionTools suite (for example, version 4.5.7 of @RISK) that was compatible with Excel 2007, and we made that version available to users for the 2007–2008 year. Fortunately, their new version of the DecisionTools suite, version 5.0, is now out. Therefore, the educational version of it accompanies this book, and the screenshots and explanations are geared to it. We believe you will like its much friendlier interface.

Second, the example files on the CD-ROM inside the revised edition have been updated slightly. They still have the same content, but they are now in Excel 2007 format (.xlsx or .xlsm). Also, although we still provide templates and finished versions of all these example files (in different folders), we have appended "Finished" to the names of all the finished files. This should avoid the confusion of having the same name for two different files that some of you have commented on. Finally, we have included "Annotated" versions of these finished example files, plus a few "Extra" application files, to instructors. The annotated versions include our insights and suggestions for the examples. We hope these help you to teach the material even more effectively.

Software

This book is based entirely on Microsoft Excel, the spreadsheet package that has become the standard analytical tool in business. Excel is an extremely powerful package, and one of our goals is to convert *casual* users into *power* users who can take full advantage of its features. If we accomplish no more than this, we will be imparting a valuable skill for the business world. However, Excel has many specific analytical limitations. Therefore, this book includes several Excel add-ins that greatly enhance Excel's capabilities. As a group, these add-ins comprise what is arguably the most impressive assortment of spreadsheet-based software in any book on the market.

StatTools Statistical add-in. Excel is somewhat limited in its statistical capabilities, so we have relied on the StatPro add-in, developed by the first author, in the first two editions. Although this has proved successful, we are now fortunate to offer an educational version of StatTools™, a commercial product developed and tested by Palisade Corporation. This add-in, which Palisade based on StatPro, has a "cleaner" user interface than its predecessor, and it is every bit as powerful. We explain how to use it in the text, but there is fortunately almost no learning curve—it is *easy* to use. (For StatPro fans, this add-in is still available for free from the author's Web site at http://www.kelley.iu.edu/albrightbooks. However, this version is only for Excel 2003 or earlier; we are no longer supporting StatPro for Excel 2007 or later versions.)

DecisionTools add-in. The CD-ROM packaged with this book also contains the powerful DecisionTools™ Suite by Palisade Corporation. This suite includes four separate add-ins[*]:

- **@RISK**, the popular add-in for simulation;
- **PrecisionTree**, a graphical-based add-in for creating and analyzing decision trees;
- **TopRank**, an add-in for performing what-if analyses;
- **RISKOptimizer**, an add-in for performing optimization on simulation models.

StatTools™ and the DecisionTools™ Suite bundled with this book are a special version for students only. They are only slightly scaled down from the professional versions that sell for hundreds of dollars and are used by many leading companies. They function for two years when properly installed, and they have modest limitations on the size of data sets or models that can be analyzed. (Visit http://www.kelley.iu.edu/albrightbooks for specific details.) We make extensive use of @RISK and PrecisionTree in the chapters on simulation and decision making under uncertainty. We use StatTools extensively in many of the chapters.

SolverTable add-in. We also include SolverTable, a supplement to Excel's built-in Solver for optimization. If you have ever had difficulty trying to under-

---

[*]As we learned at the last minute, two other add-ins, Evolver and NeuralTools, are also included in the suite. However, they aren't used in the book.

stand Solver's sensitivity reports, then you will appreciate SolverTable. It works like Excel's data tables, except that for each input (or pair of inputs), the add-in runs Solver and reports the *optimal* output values. SolverTable is used extensively in the optimization chapters. The version of SolverTable included in this book has been revised for Excel 2007. (Although SolverTable is packaged with the book, it is also freely available at the first author's Web site at http://www.kelley.iu.edu/albrightbooks.)

Possible sequences of topics

Although we intend to use this book for our own required one-semester course, there is admittedly more material than can be covered adequately in one semester. We have tried to make the book as modular as possible, allowing an instructor to cover, say, simulation before linear programming or vice versa, or to omit either of these topics. The one exception is statistics. Due to the natural progression of statistical topics, the basic topics in the early chapters must be covered before the more advanced topics (regression and time series analysis) in the later chapters. With this in mind, here are several possible ways to cover the topics.

- A one-semester required course, with no statistics prerequisite (or where MBA students have forgotten whatever statistics they learned years ago). If statistics is the primary focus of the course, then Chapters 2, 3, 5, 6, 8–12, and possibly 4 (all statistical topics) should be covered. Depending on the time remaining, any of the topics in Chapters 7 (decision making under uncertainty), 13 (time series analysis), 14–15 (optimization), or 16–17 (simulation) can be covered in practically any order.

- A one-semester required course, with a statistics prerequisite. Assuming that students know the basic elements of statistics (up through hypothesis testing, say), then the material in Chapters 2, 3, 5, 6, and 8–10 can be reviewed *quickly*, primarily to illustrate how Excel and add-ins can be used to do the number crunching. Then the instructor can choose between any of the topics in Chapters 7, 11–12, 13, 14–15, or 16–17 (in practically any order) to fill the remainder of the course.

- A two-semester required sequence. Given the luxury of spreading the topics over two semesters, the entire book can be covered. The statistics topics in Chapters 2, 3, 5, 6, and 8–10 should be covered in chronological order before *other* statistical topics (regression and time series analysis), but the remaining chapters can be covered in practically any order.

Custom publishing

- If you want to use only a subset of the text, or add chapters from the authors' other texts or your own materials, you may do so through Cengage Custom Publishing. Contact your local Cengage Learning representative for more details.

Ancillaries

Each new copy of the book is bundled with the StatTools and DecisionTools Suite described earlier. In addition, the student CD-ROM included inside new copies of the book contains:

- Excel files for examples in the chapters (usually two versions of each—a template, or data-only version, and a finished version)
- Data files required for the problems and cases
- Excel Tutorial.docx, which contains a useful tutorial for getting up to speed in Excel 2007

Adopting instructors may obtain the *Instructors Resource* CD, which includes:

- Solution files (in Excel format) for all of the problems and cases in the book
- PowerPoint® presentation files for all of the examples in the book
- Test Bank in Word format

Additional ancillaries:

- The Book Companion Web site, **academic. cengage.com/decisionsciences/albright,** which includes software updates, errata,

additional problems and solutions, and additional resources for both students and faculty. The first author also maintains his own Web site at http://www.kelley.iu.edu/albrightbooks.

- A *Student Solutions* manual, on the IRCD, for students and with solutions to many of the odd-numbered problems (ISBN-10: 0-324-59518-2; ISBN-13: 978-0-324-59518-5).

Acknowledgments

The authors would like to thank several people who helped make this book a reality. First, the authors are indebted to Peter Kolesar, Mark Broadie, Lawrence Lapin, and William Whisler for contributing many excellent case studies that appear throughout the book.

There are more people who helped to produce this book than we can list here. However, there are a few special people whom we were happy (and lucky) to have on our team. First, we would like to thank our editor Charles McCormick. After developing a special relationship with our editor Curt Hinrichs on the first two editions of this book (and on other books), we were somewhat sorry to see Curt move to another position. But we quickly realized that Charles is also an extremely competent and caring editor, and we look forward to working with him on many projects in the future. We thank Charles for making the editor transition so smooth and painless.

We are also grateful to many of the professionals who worked behind the scenes to make this book a success: Bryant Chrzan, Marketing Manager; Bryn Lathrop, Editorial Assistant; Emily Nesheim, Content Project Manager; Stacy Shirley, Art Director; Laura Bofinger, Senior Developmental Editor; and Jill Traut, Project Manager at ICC Macmillan Inc.

S. Christian Albright

Wayne L. Winston

Christopher J. Zappe

January 2008

Introduction to Data Analysis and Decision Making

© Larry Downing/Reuters/Landov

USING QUANTITATIVE METHODS TO SOLVE REAL BUSINESS PROBLEMS

As you embark on your study of data analysis and decision making, you might question the usefulness of quantitative methods to the "real world." A front-page article in the December 31, 1997, edition of *USA Today* entitled "Higher Math Delivers Formula for Success" provides some convincing evidence of the applicability of the methods you will be learning. The subheading of the article, "Businesses turn to algorithms to solve complex problems," says it all. Today's business problems tend to be very complex. In the past, many managers and executives used a "by the seat of your pants" approach to solve problems—that is, they used their business experience, their intuition, and some thoughtful guesswork to obtain solutions. But common sense and intuition go only so far in the solution of the complex problems businesses now face. This is where data analysis and decision making—and the algorithms mentioned in the title of the article—are so useful. When the methods in this book are implemented in user-friendly computer software packages and are then applied to complex problems, the results can be amazing. Robert Cross, whose company, DFI Aeronomics, sells algorithm-based systems to airlines, states it succinctly: "It's like taking raw information and spinning money out of it."

The power of the methods in this book is that they are applicable to so many problems and environments. The article mentions the following "success stories" where quantitative analysis has been applied; others will be discussed throughout this book.

1. United Airlines installed one of DFI's systems, which cost between $10 million and $20 million. United expects the system to add $50 million to $100 million annually to its revenues.

2. The Gap clothing chain uses quantitative analysis to determine exactly how many employees should staff each store during the holiday rush.

3. Quantitative analysis has helped medical researchers test potentially dangerous drugs on fewer people with better results.

4. IBM obtained a $93-million contract to build a computer system for the Department of Energy that would do a once-impossible task: make exact real-time models of atomic blasts. It won the contract—and convinced the DOE that its system was cost effective—only by developing quantitative methods that would cut the processing time by half.

5. Hotels, airlines, and television broadcasters all use quantitative analysis to implement a new method called "yield management." In this method, different prices are charged to different customers, depending on their willingness to pay. The effect is that more customers are attracted, and revenues increase.

The article concludes by stating that Microsoft's Excel spreadsheet software contains a mini-optimization program called Solver. This is a key statement. Many of the algorithms that enable the successes discussed in the article are very complex mathematically. They are well beyond the grasp of the typical user, including most readers of this book. However, users no longer need to understand all of the details behind the algorithms. They need only to know how to model business problems so that appropriate algorithms can be applied and then how to apply them with user-friendly software. For example, we see in Chapters 14 and 15 how to apply Excel's Solver to a variety of complex problems. You will not learn the intricacies of how Solver does its optimization, but you *will* learn how to use Solver very productively. The same statement applies to the other methods discussed in this book. You might not understand exactly what is happening in the computer's "black box" as it performs its calculations, but you will learn how to become a very effective problem solver by taking advantage of powerful software. ■

1.1 INTRODUCTION

We are living in the age of technology. This has two important implications for everyone entering the business world. First, technology has made it possible to collect huge amounts of data. Retailers collect point-of-sale data on products and customers every time a transaction occurs; credit agencies have all sorts of data on people who have or would like to obtain credit; investment companies have a limitless supply of data on the historical patterns of stocks, bonds, and other securities; and government agencies have data on economic trends, the environment, social welfare, consumer product safety, and virtually everything else we can imagine. It has become relatively *easy* to collect the data. As a result, data are plentiful. However, as many organizations are now beginning to discover, it is quite a challenge to analyze and make sense of all the data they have collected.

A second important implication of technology is that it has given many more people the power and responsibility to analyze data and make decisions on the basis of quantitative analysis. Those entering the business world can no longer pass all of the quantitative analysis to the "quant jocks," the technical specialists who have traditionally done the number crunching. The vast majority of employees now have a desktop or laptop computer at their disposal, they have access to relevant data, and they have been trained in easy-to-use software, particularly spreadsheet and database software. For these employees, statistics and other quantitative methods are no longer forgotten topics they once learned in college. Quantitative analysis is now an integral part of their daily jobs.

A large amount of data already exists and will only increase in the future. Many companies already complain of swimming in a sea of data. However, enlightened companies are seeing this expansion as a source of competitive advantage. By using quantitative methods to uncover the *information* in the data and then acting on this information—again guided by quantitative analysis—they are able to gain advantages that their less enlightened competitors are not able to gain. Several pertinent examples of this follow.

■ Direct marketers analyze enormous customer databases to see which customers are likely to respond to various products and types of promotions. Marketers can then target different classes of customers in different ways to maximize profits—and give their customers what the customers want.

■ Hotels and airlines also analyze enormous customer databases to see what their customers want and are willing to pay for. By doing this, they have been able to devise very clever pricing strategies, where not everyone pays the same price for the same accommodations. For example, a business traveler typically makes a plane reservation closer to the time of travel than a vacationer. The airlines know this. Therefore, they reserve seats for these business travelers and charge them a higher price (for the same seats). The airlines profit, and the customers are happy.

■ Financial planning services have a virtually unlimited supply of data about security prices, and they have customers with widely differing preferences for various types of investments. Trying to find a match of investments to customers is a very challenging problem. However, customers can easily take their business elsewhere if good decisions are not made on their behalf. Therefore, financial planners are under extreme competitive pressure to analyze masses of data so that they can make informed decisions for their customers.

■ We all know about the pressures U.S. manufacturing companies have faced from foreign competition in the past couple of decades. The automobile companies, for example, have had to change the way they produce and market automobiles to stay in business. They have had to improve quality and cut costs by orders of magnitude. Although the struggle continues, much of the success they have had can be attributed to data analysis and wise decision making. Starting on the shop floor and moving up through the organization, these companies now measure almost everything they do, analyze these measurements, and then act on the information from these measurements.

We talk about companies analyzing data and making decisions. However, *companies* don't really do this; *people* do it. And who will these people be in the future? They will be *you*! We know from experience that students in all areas of business, at both the undergraduate and graduate level, will soon be *required* to describe large complex data sets, run regression analyses, make quantitative forecasts, create optimization models, and run simulations. You are the person who will soon be analyzing data and making important decisions to help gain your company a competitive advantage. And if you are *not* willing or able to do so, there will be plenty of other technically trained people who will be more than happy to replace you.

Our goal in this book is to teach you how to use a variety of quantitative methods to analyze data and make decisions. We plan to do so in a very hands-on way. We discuss a number of quantitative methods and illustrate their use in a large variety of realistic business problems. As you will see, this book includes many examples from finance, marketing, operations, accounting, and other areas of business. To analyze these examples, we take advantage of the Microsoft Excel spreadsheet package, together with a number of powerful Excel add-ins. In each example we will provide step-by-step details of the method and its implementation in Excel.

This is *not* a "theory" book. It is also not a book where you can lean comfortably back in your chair, prop your legs up on a table, and read about how *other* people use quantitative methods. It is a "get your hands dirty" book, where you will learn best by actively following the examples throughout the book at your own PC. In short, you will learn by doing. By the time you have finished, you will have acquired some very useful skills for today's business world.

1.2 AN OVERVIEW OF THE BOOK

This book is packed with quantitative methods and examples, probably more than can be covered in any single course. Therefore, we purposely intend to keep this introductory chapter brief so that you can get on with the analysis. Nevertheless, it is useful to introduce the methods you will be learning and the tools you will be using. In this section we provide an overview of the methods covered in this book and the software that is used to implement them. Then in the next section we preview some of the examples we cover in much more detail in later chapters. Finally, we present a brief discussion of models and the modeling process. Our primary purpose at this point is to stimulate your interest in what is to follow.

1.2.1 The Methods

This book is rather unique in that it combines topics from two separate fields: statistics and management science. In a nutshell, statistics is the study of data analysis, whereas management science is the study of model building, optimization, and decision making. In the academic arena these two fields traditionally have been separated, sometimes widely. Indeed, they are often housed in separate academic departments. However, from a user's standpoint it makes little sense to separate them. Both are useful in accomplishing what the title of this book promises: data analysis and decision making.

Therefore, we do not distinguish between the "statistics" and "management science" parts of this book. Instead, we view the entire book as a collection of useful quantitative methods that can be used to analyze data and help make business decisions. In addition, our choice of software helps to integrate the various topics. By using a single package, Excel, together with a number of add-ins, we see that the methods of statistics and management science are similar in many important respects. Most importantly, their combination gives us the power and flexibility to solve a wide range of business problems.

Three important themes run through this book. Two of them are in the title: **data analysis** and **decision making.** The third is **dealing with uncertainty.**[1] Each of these themes has subthemes. Data analysis includes data **description,** data **inference,** and the search for **relationships** in data. Decision making includes **optimization** techniques for problems with

---

[1]The fact that the uncertainty theme did not find its way into the title of this book does not detract from its importance. We just wanted to keep the title reasonably short!

no uncertainty, **decision analysis** for problems with uncertainty, and structured **sensitivity analysis**. Dealing with uncertainty includes **measuring** uncertainty and **modeling** uncertainty explicitly into the analysis. There are obvious overlaps between these themes and subthemes. When we make inferences from data and search for relationships in data, we must deal with uncertainty. When we use decision trees to help make decisions, we must deal with uncertainty. When we use simulation models to help make decisions, we must deal with uncertainty, and we often make inferences from the simulated data.

Figure 1.1 shows where you will find these themes and subthemes in the remaining chapters of this book. In the next few paragraphs we discuss the book's contents in more detail.

Figure 1.1

Themes and Subthemes

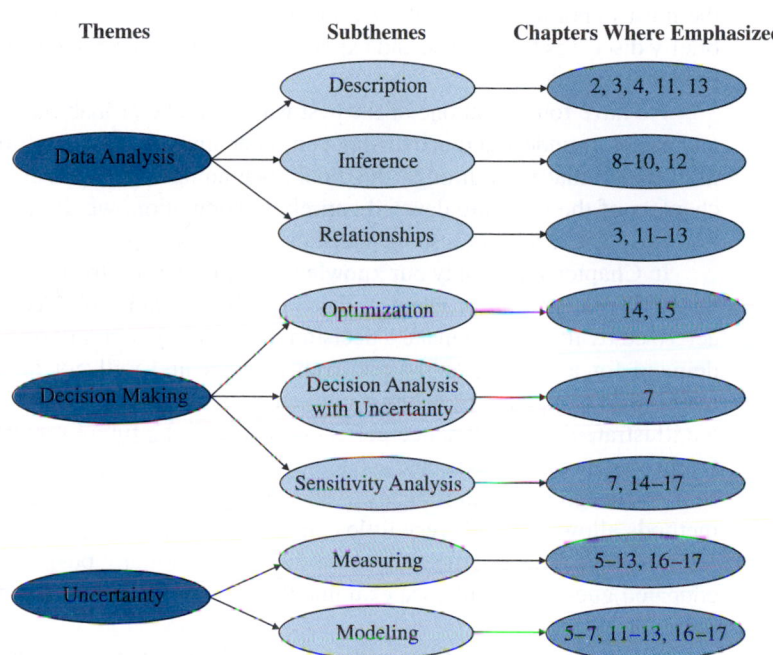

We begin in Chapters 2 and 3 by illustrating a number of ways to summarize the information in data sets. These include graphical and tabular summaries, as well as numerical summary measures such as means, medians, and standard deviations. The material in these two chapters is elementary from a mathematical point of view, but it is extremely important. As we stated at the beginning of this chapter, organizations are now able to collect huge amounts of raw data. The question then becomes, What does it all mean? Although there are very sophisticated methods for analyzing data sets, some of which we cover in later chapters, the "simple" methods in Chapters 2 and 3 are crucial for obtaining an initial understanding of the data. Fortunately, Excel and available add-ins now make what was once a very tedious task quite easy. For example, Excel's pivot tables for "slicing and dicing" data are an analyst's dream come true. You will be amazed at the complex analysis they enable you to perform—with almost no effort!

After the analysis in Chapters 2 and 3, we step back for a moment in Chapter 4 to see how we get the data we need in the first place. We know from experience that many students and businesspeople are able to perform appropriate statistical analysis once they have the data in a suitable form. Often the most difficult part, however, is getting the right data, in the right form, into a software package for analysis. Therefore, in Chapter 4 we present a number of extremely useful methods for doing this within Excel. Specifically, we discuss methods for using Excel's built-in filtering tools to perform queries on Excel data sets, for using Microsoft Query (part of Microsoft Office) to perform queries on *external* databases (such as Access) and bring the resulting data into Excel, for importing data directly into Excel from Web sites, and for "cleansing" data sets (getting rid of "bad" data values). This chapter provides tools that many analysts need but are usually not even aware of.

Uncertainty is a key aspect of most business problems. To deal with uncertainty, we need a basic understanding of probability. We provide this understanding in Chapters 5 and 6. Chapter 5 covers basic rules of probability and then discusses the extremely important concept of probability distributions. Chapter 6 follows up this discussion by focusing on two of the most important probability distributions, the normal and binomial distributions. It also briefly discusses the Poisson and exponential distributions, which have many applications in probability models.

We have found that one of the best ways to make probabilistic concepts "come alive" and easier to understand is by using computer simulation. Therefore, simulation is a common theme that runs through this book, beginning in Chapter 5. Although the final two chapters of the book are devoted entirely to simulation, we do not hesitate to use simulation early and often to illustrate statistical concepts.

In Chapter 7 we apply our knowledge of probability to decision making under uncertainty. These types of problems—faced by all companies on a continual basis—are characterized by the need to make a decision *now*, even though important information (such as demand for a product or returns from investments) will not be known until later. The material in Chapter 7 provides a rational basis for making such decisions. The methods we illustrate do not guarantee perfect outcomes—the future could unluckily turn out differently than we had expected—but they do enable us to proceed rationally and make the best of the given circumstances. Additionally, the software we use to implement these methods allows us, with very little extra work, to see how sensitive the optimal decisions are to inputs. This is crucial because the inputs to many business problems are, at best, educated guesses. Finally, we examine the role of risk aversion in these types of decision problems.

In Chapters 8, 9, and 10 we discuss sampling and statistical inference. Here the basic problem is to estimate one or more characteristics of a population. If it is too expensive or time consuming to learn about the *entire* population—and it usually is—we instead select a random sample from the population and then use the information in the sample to *infer* the characteristics of the population. We see this continually on news shows that describe the results of various polls. We also see it in many business contexts. For example, auditors typically sample only a fraction of a company's records. Then they infer the characteristics of the entire population of records from the results of the sample to conclude whether the company has been following acceptable accounting standards.

In Chapters 11 and 12 we discuss the extremely important topic of regression analysis, which is used to study relationships between variables. The power of regression analysis is its generality. Every part of a business has variables that are related to one another, and regression can often be used to estimate possible relationships between these variables. In managerial accounting, regression is used to estimate how overhead costs depend on direct labor hours and production volume. In marketing, regression is used to estimate how sales volume depends on advertising and other marketing variables. In finance, regression is used to estimate how the return of a stock depends on the "market" return. In real estate studies, regression is used to estimate how the selling price of a house depends on the assessed valuation of the house and characteristics such as the number of bedrooms and square footage. Regression analysis finds perhaps as many uses in the business world as any method in this book.

From regression, we move to times series analysis and forecasting in Chapter 13. This topic is particularly important for providing inputs into business decision problems. For example, manufacturing companies must forecast demand for their products to make sensible decisions about quantities to order from their suppliers. Similarly, fast-food restaurants must forecast customer arrivals, sometimes down to the level of 15-minute intervals, so that they can staff their restaurants appropriately.

There are many approaches to forecasting, ranging from simple to complex. Some involve regression-based methods, in which one or more time series variables are used to forecast the variable of interest, whereas other methods are based on extrapolation. In an extrapolation method the historical patterns of a time series variable, such as product demand or customer arrivals, are studied carefully and are then "extrapolated" into the future to obtain forecasts. A number of extrapolation methods are available. In Chapter 13 we study both regression and extrapolation methods for forecasting.

Chapters 14 and 15 are devoted to spreadsheet optimization, with emphasis on linear programming. We assume a company must make several decisions, and there are constraints that limit the possible decisions. The job of the decision maker is to choose the decisions such that all of the constraints are satisfied and an objective, such as total profit or total cost, is optimized. The solution process consists of two steps. First, we build a spreadsheet model that relates the decision variables to other relevant quantities by means of logical formulas. In this first step there is no attempt to find the *optimal* solution; all we want to do is relate all relevant quantities in a logical way. The second step is then to find the optimal solution. Fortunately, Excel contains a Solver add-in that performs this step. All we need to do is specify the objective, the decision variables, and the constraints; Solver then uses powerful algorithms to find the optimal solution. As with regression, the power of this approach is its generality. An enormous variety of problems can be solved by spreadsheet optimization.

Finally, Chapters 16 and 17 illustrate a number of computer simulation models. This is not our first exposure to simulation—it is used in a number of previous chapters to illustrate statistical concepts—but here it is studied in its own right. As we discussed previously, most business problems have some degree of uncertainty. The demand for a product is unknown, future interest rates are unknown, the delivery lead time from a supplier is unknown, and so on. Simulation allows us to build this uncertainty *explicitly* into spreadsheet models. Essentially, some cells in the model contain random values with given probability distributions. Every time the spreadsheet recalculates, these random values change, which causes "bottom-line" output cells to change as well. The trick then is to force the spreadsheet to recalculate many times and keep track of interesting outputs. In this way we can see which output values are most likely, and we can see best-case and worst-case results.

Spreadsheet simulations can be performed entirely with Excel's built-in tools. However, this can be quite tedious. Therefore, we use a spreadsheet add-in to streamline the process. In particular, we learn how the @RISK add-in can be used to run replications of a simulation, keep track of outputs, create useful charts, and perform sensitivity analyses. With the inherent power of spreadsheets and the ease-of-use of such add-ins as @RISK, spreadsheet simulation is becoming one of the most popular quantitative tools in the business world.

1.2.2 The Software

The topics we have just discussed are very important. Together, they can be used to solve a wide variety of business problems. However, they are not of much practical use unless we have the software to do the number crunching. Very few business problems are small enough to be solved with pencil and paper. They require powerful software.

The software included in new copies of this book, together with Microsoft Excel, provides you with a powerful software combination that you will not use for one course and then discard. This software is being used—and will continue to be used—by leading companies all over the world to solve large, complex problems. We firmly believe that the experience you obtain with this software, through working the examples and problems in this book, will give you a key competitive advantage in the marketplace.

It all begins with Excel. All of the quantitative methods that we discuss are implemented in Excel. Specifically, in this edition, we use Excel 2007. We cannot forecast the state of computer software in the long-term future, but as we are writing this book Excel is *the* most heavily used spreadsheet package on the market, and there is every reason to believe that this state will persist for many years. Most companies use Excel, most employees and most students have been trained in Excel, and Excel is a *very* powerful, flexible, and easy-to-use package.

Built-in Excel Features

Virtually everyone in the business world knows the basic features of Excel, but relatively few know many of its more powerful features. In short, relatively few people are the "power users" we expect you to become by working through this book. To get you started, the file **Excel Tutorial.docx** on the CD-ROM inside new copies of this book explains some of the "intermediate" features of Excel—features that we expect you to be able to use. These include the SUMPRODUCT, VLOOKUP, IF, NPV, and COUNTIF functions. They also include range names, data tables, the Paste Special command, the Goal Seek command, and a few others. Finally, although we assume you can perform routine spreadsheet tasks such as copying and pasting, we include a few tips to help you perform these tasks more efficiently.

Although the tutorial is presented in a Word file, it contains "embedded" Excel spreadsheets that allow you to practice spreadsheet techniques within Word.

In the body of the book we describe several of Excel's advanced features in more detail. In Chapters 2 and 3 we introduce pivot tables, the Excel tool that enables you to summarize data sets in an almost endless variety of ways. (Excel has many useful tools, but we personally believe that pivot tables are the most ingenious and powerful of all. We won't be surprised if you agree.) Beginning in Chapter 5, we introduce Excel's RAND function for generating random numbers. This function is used in all spreadsheet simulations (at least those that do not take advantage of an add-in).

Solver Add-in

In Chapters 14 and 15 we make heavy use of Excel's Solver add-in. This add-in, developed by Frontline Systems (not Microsoft), uses powerful algorithms—all behind the scenes—to perform spreadsheet optimization. Before this type of spreadsheet optimization add-in was available, specialized (nonspreadsheet) software was required to solve optimization problems. Now we can do it all within a familiar spreadsheet environment.

StatTools Add-in

Much of this book discusses basic statistical analysis. Here we needed to make an important decision as we developed the book. A number of excellent statistical software packages are on the market, including Minitab, SPSS, SAS, StatGraphics, and many others. Although there are now user-friendly Windows versions of these packages, they are *not* spreadsheet-based. We have found through our own experience that students resist the use of nonspreadsheet packages, regardless of their inherent quality, so we wanted to use Excel as our "statistics package." (We briefly discuss SPSS in Chapter 4, but it is not used anywhere else in the book.) Unfortunately, Excel's built-in statistical tools are rather limited, and the Analysis ToolPak (developed by a third party) that ships with Excel has significant limitations.

Therefore, we use an add-in called StatTools that accompanies this book. StatTools is powerful, easy to use, and capable of generating output quickly in an easily interpretable form. We do *not* believe you should have to spend hours each time you want to produce some statistical output. This might be a good learning experience the first time, but after that it acts as a strong incentive *not* to perform the analysis at all! We believe you should be able to generate output quickly and easily. This gives you the time to *interpret* the output, and it also allows you to try different methods of analysis.

A good illustration involves the construction of histograms, scatterplots, and time series graphs, discussed in Chapter 2. All of these extremely useful graphs can be created in a straightforward way with Excel's built-in tools. But by the time you perform all the necessary steps and "dress up" the charts exactly as you want them, you will not be very anxious to repeat the whole process again. StatTools does it all quickly and easily. (You still might want to "dress up" the resulting charts, but that's up to you.) Therefore, if we advise you in a later chapter, say, to look at several scatterplots as a prelude to a regression analysis, you can do so in a matter of seconds.

SolverTable Add-in

An important theme throughout this book is sensitivity analysis: How do outputs change when inputs change? Typically these changes are made in spreadsheets with a data table, a built-in Excel tool. However, data tables don't work in optimization models, where we would like to see how the *optimal* solution changes when certain inputs change. Therefore, we include an Excel add-in called SolverTable to perform this type of sensitivity analysis. It works almost exactly like Excel's data tables, and it is included with this book. In Chapters 14 and 15 we illustrate how to use SolverTable.

Decision Tools Suite

In addition to StatTools, SolverTable, and built-in Excel add-ins, we also have included in this book an educational version of Palisade Corporation's powerful Decision Tools suite. All of the programs in this suite are Excel add-ins—so the learning curve isn't very steep. There are four separate add-ins in this suite: @RISK, PrecisionTree, TopRank, and RISKOptimizer.[2] The first two are the most important for our purposes, but all are useful for certain tasks.

@RISK

The simulation add-in @RISK enables us to run as many replications of a spreadsheet simulation as we like. As the simulation runs, @RISK automatically keeps track of the outputs we select, and it then displays the results in a number of tabular and graphical forms. @RISK also enables us to perform a sensitivity analysis, so that we can see which inputs have the most effect on the outputs. Finally, @RISK provides a number of spreadsheet functions that enable us to generate random numbers from a variety of probability distributions.

PrecisionTree

The PrecisionTree add-in is used in Chapter 7 to analyze decision problems with uncertainty. The primary method for performing this type of analysis is to draw a decision tree. Decision trees are inherently graphical, and they have always been difficult to implement in spreadsheets, which are based on rows and columns. However, PrecisionTree does

---

[2]The Palisade suite has traditionally included two stand-alone programs, BestFit and RISKview. The functionality of both of these is now included in @RISK, so they have not been included in the suite. As this book is going to press, we have been told by Palisade that two new add-ins, NeuralTools and Evolver, will be added to the suite, but we haven't seen them yet, and they won't be discussed in the book.

this in a very clever and intuitive way. Equally important, once the basic decision tree has been built, it is easy to use PrecisionTree to perform a sensitivity analysis on the model inputs.

TopRank

Although we will not use the other Palisade add-ins as extensively as @RISK and PrecisionTree, they are all worth investigating. TopRank is a "what-if" add-in used for sensitivity analysis. It starts with any spreadsheet model, where a set of inputs are used, along with a number of spreadsheet formulas, to produce an output. TopRank then performs a sensitivity analysis to see which inputs have the largest effect on the output. For example, it might tell us which input affects after-tax profit the most: the tax rate, the risk-free rate for investing, the inflation rate, or the price charged by a competitor. Unlike @RISK, TopRank is used when uncertainty is not *explicitly* built into a spreadsheet model. However, it considers uncertainty implicitly by performing sensitivity analysis on the important model inputs.

RISKOptimizer

RISKOptimizer combines optimization with simulation. There are often times when we want to use simulation to model some business problem, but we also want to optimize a summary measure, such as a mean, of an output distribution. This optimization can be performed in a trial-and-error fashion, where we try a few values of the decision variable(s) and see which provides the best solution. However, RISKOptimizer provides a more automatic (and time-intensive) optimization procedure.

Software Guide

Figure 1.2 provides a guide to where these various add-ins appear throughout the book. We don't show Excel explicitly in this figure for the simple reason that Excel is used extensively in *all* chapters.

With Excel and the add-ins included in this book, you have a wealth of software at your disposal. The examples and step-by-step instructions throughout this book will help you to become a power user of this software. Admittedly, this takes plenty of practice and a willingness to experiment, but it is certainly within your grasp. When you are finished, we will not be surprised if you rate "improved software skills" as the most valuable thing you have learned from this book.

Figure 1.2

Software Guide

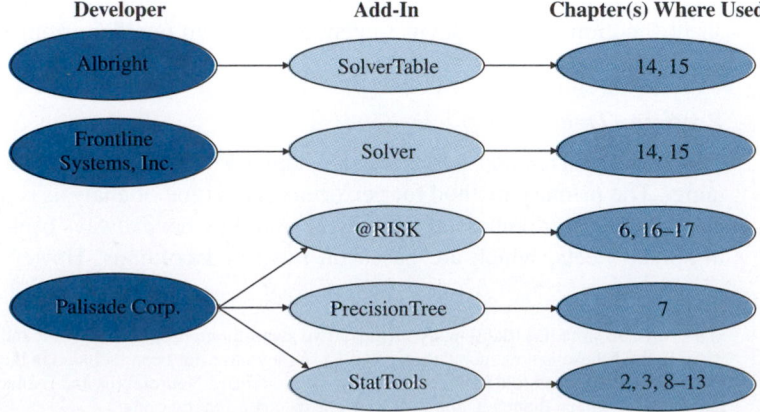

1.3 A SAMPLING OF EXAMPLES

Perhaps the best way to illustrate what you will be learning in this book is to preview a few examples from later chapters. Our intention here is not to teach you any methods; that will come later. We only want to indicate the types of problems you will learn how to solve. Each example below is numbered as in the chapter where it appears.

EXAMPLE	3.9

The Spring Mills Company produces and distributes a wide variety of manufactured goods. Because of its variety, it has a large number of customers. The company classifies these customers as small, medium, and large, depending on the volume of business each does with Spring Mills. Recently, Spring Mills has noticed a problem with its accounts receivable. It is not getting paid back by its customers in as timely a manner as it would like. This obviously costs Spring Mills money. If a customer delays a payment of $300 for 20 days, say, then the company loses potential interest on this amount. The company has gathered data on 280 customer accounts. For each of these accounts, the data set lists three variables: Size, the size of the customer (coded 1 for small, 2 for medium, 3 for large); Days, the number of days since the customer was billed; and Amount, the amount the customer owes. What information can we obtain from these data?

Objective   To use charts, summary measures, and pivot tables to understand data on accounts receivable at Spring Mills.

Solution

It is always a good idea to get a rough sense of the data first. We do this by calculating several summary measures for Days and Amount, a histogram of Amount, and a scatterplot of Amount versus Days. The next logical step is to see whether the different customer sizes have any effect on either Days, Amount, or the relationship between Days and Amount. There is obviously a lot going on here. We point out the following: (1) there are far fewer large customers than small or medium customers; (2) the large customers tend to owe considerably more than small or medium customers; (3) the small customers do not tend to be as long overdue as the medium or large customers; and (4) there is no relationship between Days and Amount for the small customers, but there is a definite positive relationship between these variables for the medium and large customers. If Spring Mills really wants to decrease its receivables, it might want to target the medium-size customer group, from which it is losing the most interest. Or it could target the large customers because they owe the most on average. The most appropriate action depends on the cost and effectiveness of targeting any particular customer group. However, the analysis presented here gives the company a much better picture of what's currently going on.

This example from Chapter 3 is a typical example of trying to make sense out of a large data set. Spring Mills has 280 observations on each of three variables. By realistic standards, this is not a large data set, but it still presents a challenge. We examine the data from a number of angles and present several tables and charts. For example, the scatterplots in Figures 1.3 through 1.5 clearly indicate that there is a *positive* relationship between the amount owed and the number of days since billing for the medium- and large-size customers, but that no such relationship exists for the small-size customers. As we will see, graphs such as these are very easy to construct in Excel, regardless of the size of the data set.

Figure 1.3 Scatterplot of Amount versus Days for Small-size Customers

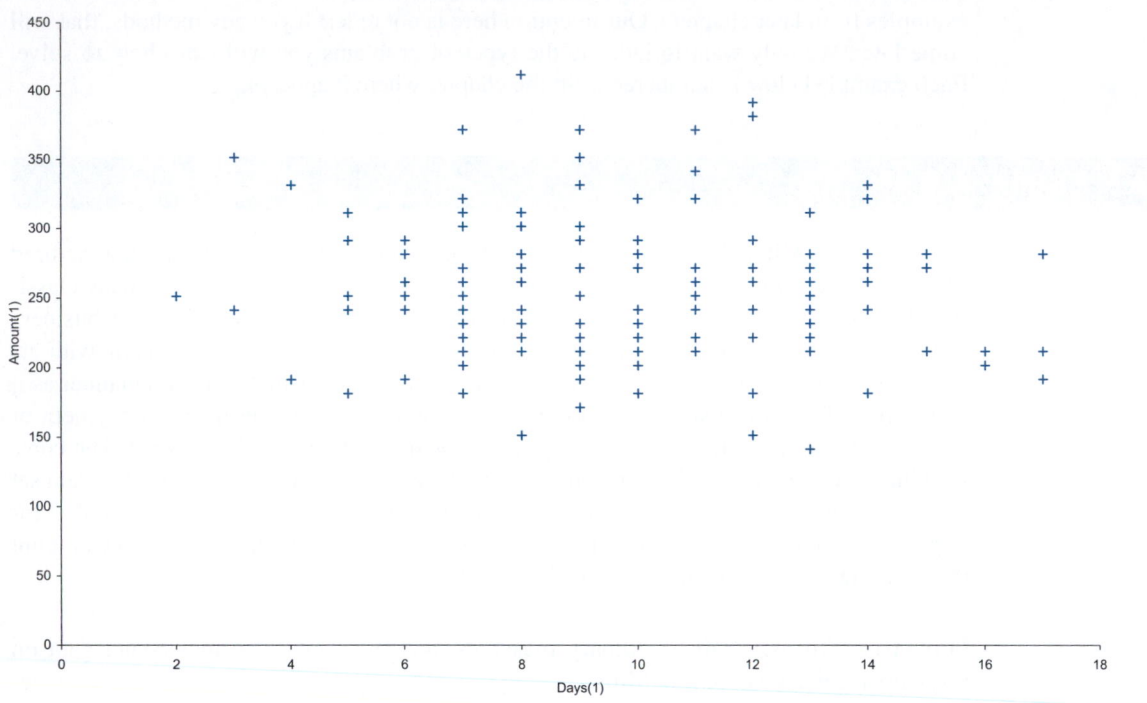

Scatterplot of Amount(1) vs Days(1)

Figure 1.4 Scatterplot of Amount versus Days for Medium-size Customers

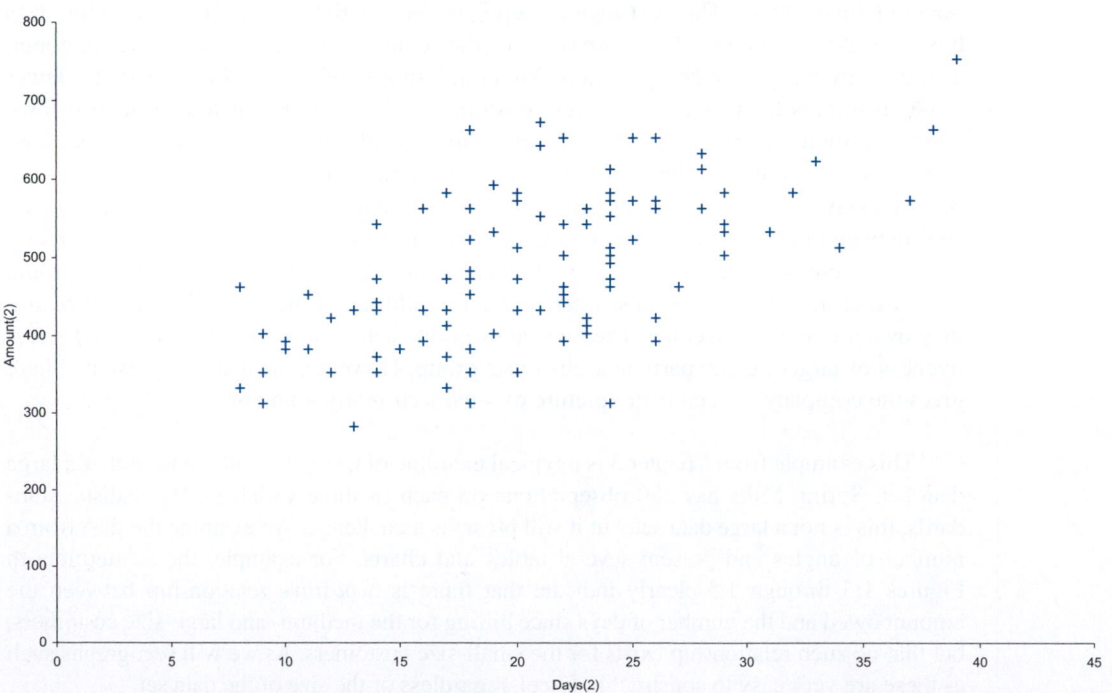

Scatterplot of Amount(2) vs Days(2)

Figure 1.5 Scatterplot of Amount versus Days for Large-size Customers

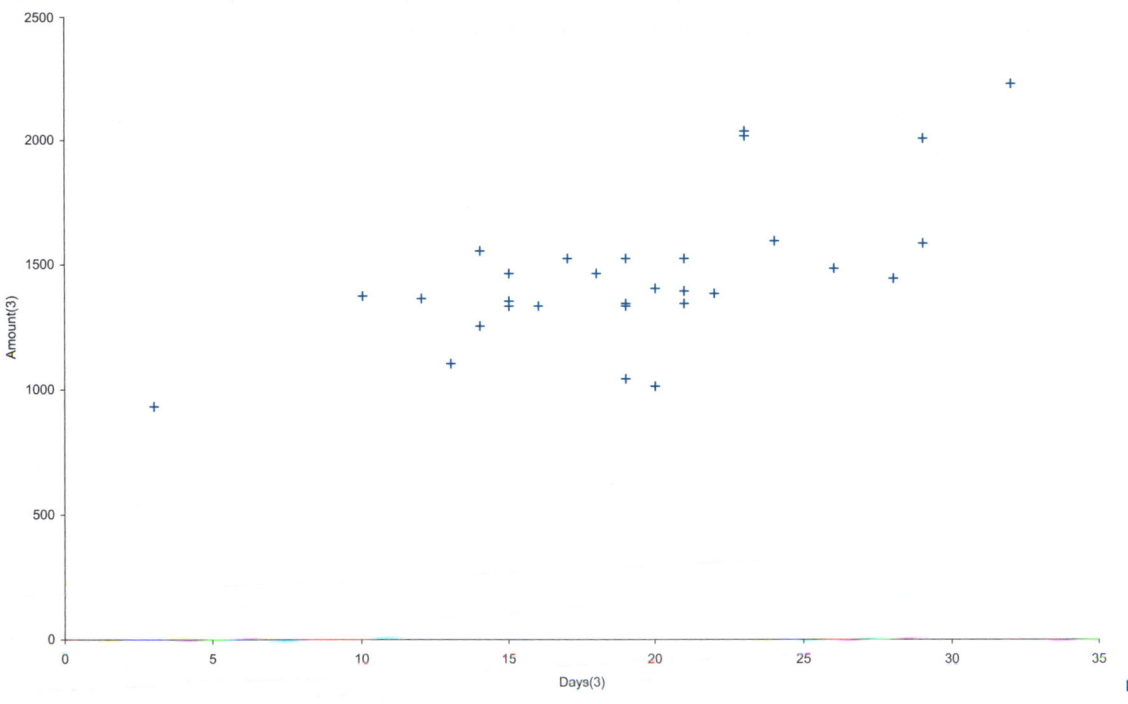

EXAMPLE **7.1**

SciTools Incorporated, a company that specializes in scientific instruments, has been invited to make a bid on a government contract. The contract calls for a specific number of these instruments to be delivered during the coming year. The bids must be sealed (so that no company knows what the others are bidding), and the low bid wins the contract. SciTools estimates that it will cost $5000 to prepare a bid and $95,000 to supply the instruments if it wins the contract. On the basis of past contracts of this type, SciTools believes that the possible low bids from the competition, if there is any competition, and the associated probabilities are those shown in Table 1.1. In addition, SciTools believes there is a 30% chance that there will be *no* competing bids.

Table 1.1 Probabilities of Low Bids from Competition

Low Bid	Probability
Less than $115,000	0.2
Between $115,000 and $120,000	0.4
Between $120,000 and $125,000	0.3
Greater than $125,000	0.1

Solution

This is a typical example of decision making under uncertainty, the topic of Chapter 7. SciTools has to make decisions *now* (whether to bid and, if so, how much to bid), without knowing what the competition is going to do. The company can't *assure* itself of a perfect outcome, but it can make a rational decision in light of the uncertainty it faces. We will see how decision trees, produced easily with the PrecisionTree add-in to Excel, not only lay out all of the elements of the problem in a logical manner but also indicate the best solution. The completed tree for this problem is in Figure 1.6, which indicates that SciTools should indeed prepare a bid, for the amount $115,000.

Figure 1.6 Decision Tree for SciTools

	A	B	C	D	E	F
14		No / FALSE / 0	0.0% / 0			
15						
16	SciTools Bidding	Bid?				
17		12200				
18				No / 30.0% / $20,000	30.0% / 15000	
19						
20			$115K / TRUE / 0	Competing bid? / 12200		
21						
22					Yes / 80.0% / $20,000	56.0% / 15000
23						
24				Yes / 70.0% / 0	Win bid? / 11000	
25						
26					No / 20.0% / 0	14.0% / -5000
27						
28		Yes / TRUE / -$5,000	How much to bid? / 12200			
29						
30				No / 30.0% / $25,000	0.0% / 20000	
31						
32			$120K / FALSE / 0	Competing bid? / 9500		
33						
34					Yes / 40.0% / $25,000	0.0% / 20000
35						
36				Yes / 70.0% / 0	Win bid? / 5000	
37						
38					No / 60.0% / 0	0.0% / -5000
39						
40				No / 30.0% / $30,000	0.0% / 25000	
41						
42			$125K / FALSE / 0	Competing bid? / 6100		
43						
44					Yes / 10.0% / $30,000	0.0% / 25000
45						
46				Yes / 70.0% / 0	Win bid? / -2000	
47						
48					No / 90.0% / 0	0.0% / -5000
49						

EXAMPLE 9.5

An auditor wants to determine the proportion of invoices that contain price errors—that is, prices that do not agree with those on an authorized price list. He checks 93 randomly sampled invoices and finds that two of them include price errors. What can he conclude, in terms of a 95% one-sided confidence interval, about the proportion of *all* invoices with price errors?

Solution

This is an important application of statistical inference in the auditing profession. Auditors try to determine what is true about a population (in this case, all of a company's invoices) by examining a relatively small sample from the population. The auditor wants an upper limit so that he is 95% confident that the overall proportion of invoices with errors is no greater than this upper limit. We show the spreadsheet solution in Figure 1.7, which shows that the auditor can be 95% confident that the overall proportion of invoices with errors is no greater than 6.6% (see cell B10).

Figure 1.7

Analysis of Auditing Example

	A	B	C	D	E	F
1	An exact one-sided confidence interval in auditing					
2						
3	Confidence level	95%				
4	Number of errors	2				
5	Sample size	93				
6						
7	Sample proportion	0.0215				
8						
9	Exact upper confidence limit for p			Goal seek condition		
10	Upper limit	0.066		0.050	=	0.05
11						
12	Large-sample upper confidence limit for p					
13	z-multiple	1.645				
14	Upper limit	0.046				

■

EXAMPLE 11.2

The Bendrix Company manufactures various types of parts for automobiles. The manager of the factory wants to get a better understanding of overhead costs. These overhead costs include supervision, indirect labor, supplies, payroll taxes, overtime premiums, depreciation, and a number of miscellaneous items such as charges for building depreciation, insurance, utilities, and janitorial and maintenance expenses. Some of these overhead costs are "fixed" in the sense that they do not vary appreciably with the volume of work being done, whereas others are "variable" and do vary directly with the volume of work. The fixed overhead costs tend to come from the supervision, depreciation, and miscellaneous categories, whereas the variable overhead costs tend to come from the indirect labor, supplies, payroll taxes, and overtime premiums categories. However, it is not easy to draw a clear line between the fixed and variable overhead components.

The Bendrix manager has tracked total overhead costs over the past 36 months. To help "explain" these, he has also collected data on two variables that are related to the amount of work done at the factory. These variables are

- *MachHrs*: number of machine hours used during the month
- *ProdRuns*: number of separate production runs during the month

The first of these is a direct measure of the amount of work being done. To understand the second, we note that Bendrix manufactures parts in fairly large batches. Each batch corresponds to a production run. Once a production run is completed, the factory must "set up" for the next production run. During this setup there is typically some downtime while the machinery is reconfigured for the part type scheduled for production in the next batch. Therefore, the manager believes both of these variables might be responsible (in different ways) for variations in overhead costs. Do scatterplots support this belief?

Solution

This is a typical regression example, in a cost-accounting setting. The manager is trying to see what type of relationship, if any, there is between overhead costs and the two explanatory variables: number of machine hours and number of production runs. The scatterplots requested appear in Figures 1.8 and 1.9. They do indeed indicate a positive and linear relationship between overhead and the two explanatory variables.

Figure 1.8   Scatterplot of Overhead versus Machine Hours

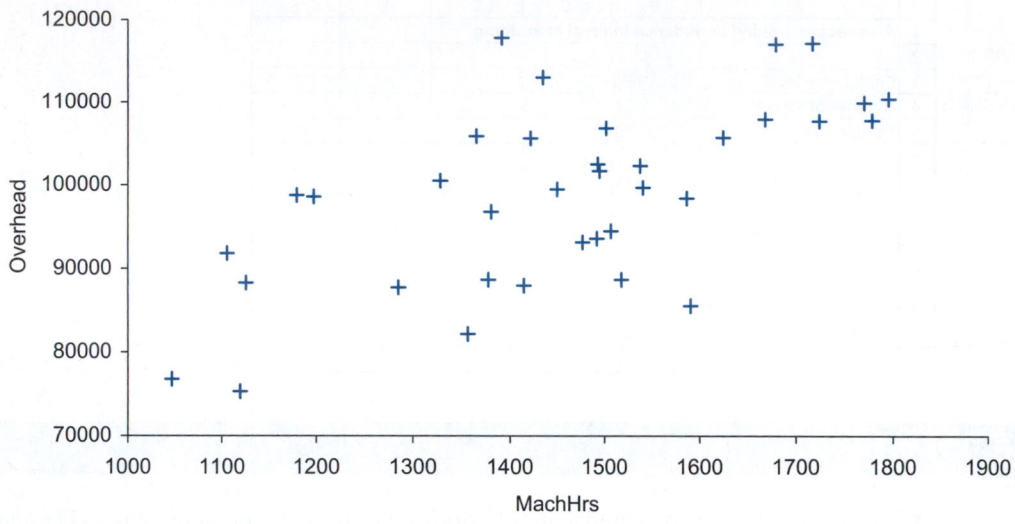

Correlation   - 0.632

Figure 1.9   Scatterplot of Overhead versus Production Runs

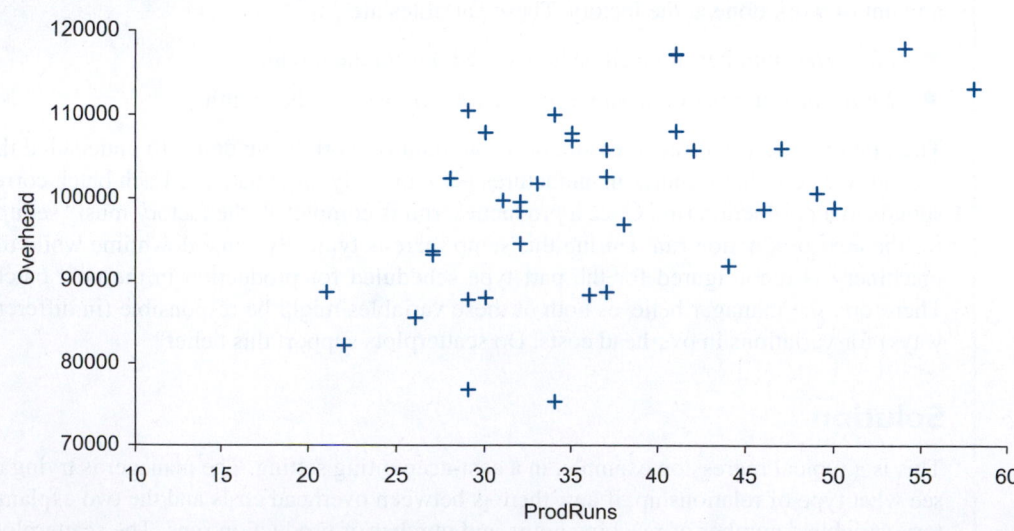

Correlation   0.521

However, regression goes well beyond scatterplots. It estimates an equation relating the variables. This equation can be determined from regression output such as that shown in Figure 1.10. This output implies the following equation for predicted overhead as a function of machine hours and production runs:

$$\text{Predicted Overhead} = 3997 + 43.54\text{MachHrs} + 883.62\text{ProdRuns}$$

Figure 1.10 Multiple Regression Output for Bendrix Example

	A	B	C	D	E	F	G
7		Multiple R	R-Square	Adjusted R-Square	StErr of Estimate	Durbin Watson	
8	*Summary*						
9		0.9308	0.8664	0.8583	4108.993	1.3131	
10							
11		Degrees of Freedom	Sum of Squares	Mean of Squares	F-Ratio	p-Value	
12	*ANOVA Table*						
13	Explained	2	3614020661	1807010330	107.0261	< 0.0001	
14	Unexplained	33	557166199.1	16883824.22			
15							
16		Coefficient	Standard Error	t-Value	p-Value	Lower Limit	Upper Limit
17	*Regression Table*						
18	Constant	3996.678	6603.651	0.6052	0.5492	-9438.551	17431.907
19	MachHrs	43.536	3.589	12.1289	< 0.0001	36.234	50.839
20	ProdRuns	883.618	82.251	10.7429	< 0.0001	716.276	1050.960

The positive coefficients of *MachHrs* and *ProdRuns* indicate the effects these variables have on overhead. We will not take the example any further at this point but will simply indicate that it is easy to generate the output in Figure 1.10 with StatTools. The challenge is learning how to interpret it. We spend plenty of time in Chapters 11 and 12 on interpretation issues. ∎

EXAMPLE 13.3

The file **PC Devices.xlsx** contains quarterly sales data (in millions of dollars) for a chip-manufacturing firm from the beginning of 1993 through the end of 2008. Are the company's sales growing exponentially through this entire period?

Solution

This example illustrates a regression-based trend curve, one of several possible forecasting techniques for a time series variable. A time series graph of the company's quarterly sales (through 2003 only) appears in Figure 1.11. It indicates that sales have been increasing steadily at an increasing rate. This is basically what an exponential trend curve implies. To estimate this curve we use regression analysis to obtain the following equation for predicted quarterly sales as a function of time:

$$\text{Predicted Sales} = 61.376e^{0.0663\text{Time}}$$

This equation implies that the company's sales are increasing by approximately 6.6% per quarter during this period, which translates to an annual percentage increase of about 29%! As we see in Chapter 13, this is the typical approach used in forecasting. We look at a time series graph to discover trends or other patterns in historical data and then use one of a variety of techniques to fit the observed patterns and extrapolate them into the future.

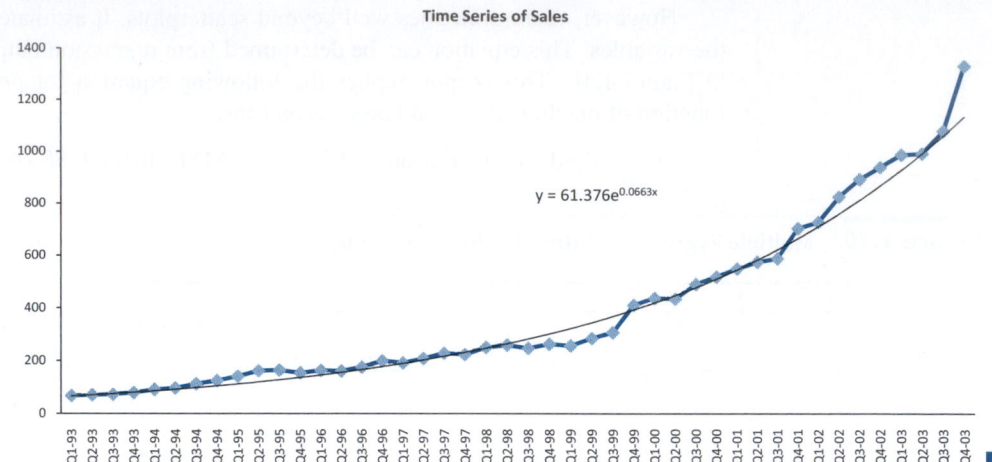

Time Series of Sales

$y = 61.376e^{0.0663x}$

EXAMPLE **15.6**

At the present time, the beginning of year 1, the Barney-Jones Investment Corporation has $100,000 to invest for the next 4 years. There are five possible investments, labeled A through E. The timing of cash outflows and cash inflows for these investments is somewhat irregular. For example, to take part in investment A, cash must be invested at the beginning of year 1, and for every dollar invested, there are returns of $0.50 and $1.00 at the beginnings of years 2 and 3. Similar information for the other investments are as follows, where all returns are per-dollar invested:

- Investment B: Invest at the beginning of year 2, receive returns of $0.50 and $1.00 at the beginnings of years 3 and 4.

- Investment C: Invest at the beginning of year 1, receive return of $1.20 at the beginning of year 2.

- Investment D: Invest at the beginning of year 4, receive return of $1.90 at the beginning of year 5.

- Investment E: Invest at the beginning of year 3, receive return of $1.50 at the beginning of year 4.

We assume that any amounts can be invested in these strategies and that the returns are the same for each dollar invested. However, to create a diversified portfolio, Barney-Jones decides to limit the amount put into any investment to $75,000. The company wants an investment strategy that maximizes the amount of cash on hand at the beginning of year 5. At the beginning of any year, it can invest only cash on hand, which includes returns from previous investments. Any cash not invested in any year can be put in a short-term money market account that earns 3% annually.

Solution

This is one of many optimization examples we present in Chapters 14 and 15. The typical situation is that a company such as Barney-Jones must make several decisions, subject to certain constraints, that optimize some objective. In this case, Barney-Jones needs to decide the amounts to invest, subject to some constraints, to maximize its ending cash 4 years from now. Our job is to formulate a spreadsheet model, similar to the one shown in Figure 1.12, that relates the various elements of the problem.

The investment amounts in row 26 are the decision variables, called "changing cells" in Excel's terminology. When we formulate the model, we can enter *any* values in these changing cells; we do not need to guess "good" values. Then we turn it over to Excel's Solver add-in. The Solver uses a powerful algorithm to find the optimal values in the changing cells—that is, the values that optimize the objective while satisfying the constraints. The values shown in Figure 1.12 are actually the optimal values. They imply that Barney-Jones can end with final cash of $286,792 by investing as indicated in row 26.

Figure 1.12   Investment Model

	A	B	C	D	E	F	G	H	I	J
1	Investments with irregular timing of returns							Range names used		
2								Cash_after_investing	=Model!$E$32:$E$35	
3	Inputs							Dollars_invested	=Model!$B$26:$F$26	
4	Initial amount to invest	$100,000						Final_cash	=Model!$B$38	
5	Maximum per investment	$75,000						Maximum_per_investment	=Model!$B$28:$F$28	
6	Interest rate on cash	3%								
7										
8	Cash outlays on investments (all incurred at beginning of year)									
9		Investment								
10	Year	A	B	C	D	E				
11	1	$1.00	$0.00	$1.00	$0.00	$0.00				
12	2	$0.00	$1.00	$0.00	$0.00	$0.00				
13	3	$0.00	$0.00	$0.00	$0.00	$1.00				
14	4	$0.00	$0.00	$0.00	$1.00	$0.00				
15										
16	Cash returns from investments (all incurred at beginning of year)									
17		Investment								
18	Year	A	B	C	D	E				
19	1	$0.00	$0.00	$0.00	$0.00	$0.00				
20	2	$0.50	$0.00	$1.20	$0.00	$0.00				
21	3	$1.00	$0.50	$0.00	$0.00	$0.00				
22	4	$0.00	$1.00	$0.00	$0.00	$1.50				
23	5	$0.00	$0.00	$0.00	$1.90	$0.00				
24										
25	Investment decisions									
26	Dollars invested	$64,286	$75,000	$35,714	$75,000	$75,000				
27		<=	<=	<=	<=	<=				
28	Maximum per investment	$75,000	$75,000	$75,000	$75,000	$75,000				
29										
30	Constraints on cash balance									
31	Year	Beginning cash	Returns from investments	Cash invested	Cash after investing					
32	1	$100,000	$0	$100,000	$0	>=	0			
33	2	$0	$75,000	$75,000	-$0	>=	0			
34	3	-$0	$101,786	$75,000	$26,786	>=	0			
35	4	$27,589	$187,500	$75,000	$140,089	>=	0			
36	5	$144,292	$142,500							
37										
38	Final cash	$286,792	←	Objective to maximize: final cash at beginning of year 5						

EXAMPLE   17.9

We assume that there are two dominant companies in the soft drink industry: "us" and "them." For this example, we will view everything from the point of view of "us." We start with a 45% market share. During each of the next 20 quarters, each company promotes its product to some extent. To make the model simple, we will assume that each company each quarter either promotes at a "regular" level or at a "blitz" level. Depending on each company's promotional behavior in a given month, the change in our market share from this month to the next is triangularly distributed, with parameters given in Table 1.2. For example, if we blitz and they don't, then we could lose as much as 1% market share, we could gain as much as 6% market share, and our most likely outcome is an increase of 2% market share. We want to develop a simulation model that allows us to gauge the long-term change in our market share for any pattern of blitzing employed by us and them.

Table 1.2 Parameters of Market Share Change Distributions

Blitzer	Minimum	Most Likely	Maximum
Neither	-0.03	0.00	0.03
Both	-0.05	0.00	0.05
Only us	-0.01	0.02	0.06
Only them	-0.06	-0.02	0.01

Solution

This is a typical example of computer simulation. We make a number of assumptions, build a spreadsheet model around these assumptions, explicitly incorporate uncertainty into some of the cells, and see how this uncertainty affects "bottom-line" outputs. The simulation model appears in Figure 1.13. Several cells in this model are random, including all of the numerical values in rows 21 through 24. Therefore, the numbers you see in this figure represent just one possible scenario of how market shares might evolve through time. By generating new random values, we see different scenarios.

Our job is to build the logic and randomness into the spreadsheet model. Then we can use Excel's built-in tools or an add-in such as @RISK to replicate the model and keep track of selected outputs. A typical result from @RISK appears in Figure 1.14. It shows a time series graph of how our market share might evolve, given a certain strategy of blitzing by our company and theirs.

Figure 1.13 Spreadsheet Simulation for Market Share Example

	A	B	C	D	E	F	G	H	S	T	U
1	**Market share model**										
2											
3	**Inputs**										
4	Our current market share	45%									
5											
6	Parameters of triangular distribution of change in our market share - depends on who has a big promotional campaign										
7		Minimum	Most likely	Maximum							
8	Neither	-0.03	0	0.03							
9	Both	-0.05	0	0.05							
10	Only us	-0.01	0.02	0.06							
11	Only them	-0.06	-0.02	0.01							
12											
13	Promotional campaigns (1 if promote, 0 if not) - enter any patterns you want to test in the following two rows										
14	Quarter	1	2	3	4	5	6	7	18	19	20
15	Us	0	1	0	1	0	1	0	1	0	1
16	Them	1	0	1	0	1	0	1	0	1	0
17											
18	**Simulation**										
19	Possible changes in our market share										
20	Quarter	1	2	3	4	5	6	7	18	19	20
21	Neither promote	0.60%	0.64%	-0.11%	-1.74%	-0.24%	-0.61%	0.12%	0.03%	-1.99%	-0.08%
22	Both promote	0.96%	-0.20%	-0.53%	1.91%	1.95%	-1.15%	1.62%	-2.04%	-1.24%	-0.43%
23	Only we promote	3.65%	0.70%	2.84%	0.19%	1.27%	3.07%	3.44%	1.23%	4.79%	-0.73%
24	Only they promote	-0.10%	-2.03%	-2.18%	-0.91%	-1.07%	-2.58%	0.05%	-3.85%	-0.13%	-4.06%
25											
26	Tracking our market share										
27	Beginning market share	45.00%	44.90%	45.61%	43.43%	43.62%	42.55%	45.62%	41.79%	43.02%	42.89%
28	Change in our market share	-0.10%	0.70%	-2.18%	0.19%	-1.07%	3.07%	0.05%	1.23%	-0.13%	-0.73%
29	Ending market share	44.90%	45.61%	43.43%	43.62%	42.55%	45.62%	45.67%	43.02%	42.89%	42.16%

Figure 1.14   Summary Chart of Our Market Share for One Set of Strategies

@RISK - Summary Trend

Market Share (B29 to U29)

— Mean

▮ +/- 1 Std. Dev.

▮ 5% - 95%

Close

1.4 MODELING AND MODELS

We have already used the term *model* several times in this chapter. In fact, we have shown several spreadsheet models in the previous section. Models and the modeling process are key elements throughout this book, so we explain them in more detail in this section.[3]

A model is an abstraction of a real problem. A model tries to capture the essence and key features of the problem without getting bogged down in relatively unimportant details. There are different types of models, and, depending on an analyst's preferences and skills, each can be a valuable aid in solving a real problem. We describe three types of models here: (1) graphical models, (2) algebraic models, and (3) spreadsheet models.

1.4.1 Graphical Models

Graphical models are probably the most intuitive and least quantitative type of model. They attempt to portray graphically how different elements of a problem are related—what affects what. A very simple graphical model appears in Figure 1.15. It is called an "influence diagram." (It can be constructed with the PrecisionTree add-in discussed in Chapter 7, but we will not use influence diagrams in this book.)

Figure 1.15

Influence Diagram for Souvenir Example

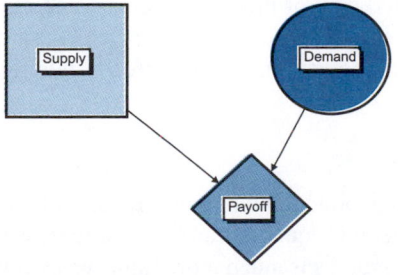

[3]Management scientists tend to use the terms *model* and *modeling* more than statisticians. However, many traditional statistics topics such as regression analysis and forecasting are clearly applications of modeling.

This particular influence diagram is for a company that is trying to decide how many souvenirs to order for the upcoming Olympics. The essence of the problem is that the company will order a certain supply, customers will request a certain demand, and the combination of supply and demand will yield a certain payoff for the company. The diagram indicates fairly intuitively what affects what. As it stands, the diagram does not provide enough quantitative details to enable us to "solve" the company's problem. But this is usually not the purpose of a graphical model. Instead, its purpose is usually to show the important elements of a problem and how they are related. For complex problems this can be very helpful and enlightening information for management.

1.4.2 Algebraic Models

Algebraic models are at the opposite end of the spectrum. By means of algebraic equations and inequalities, they specify a set of relationships in a very precise way, and their preciseness and lack of ambiguity are very appealing to people with a mathematical background. In addition, algebraic models can usually be stated concisely and with great generality.

A typical example is the "product mix" problem we discuss in Chapter 14. A company can make several products, each of which contributes a certain amount to profit and consumes certain amounts of several scarce resources. The problem is to select the product mix that maximizes profit subject to the limited availability of the resources. *All* product mix problems can be stated algebraically as follows:

$$\max \sum_{j=1}^{n} p_j x_j \tag{1.1}$$

$$\text{subject to} \sum_{j=1}^{n} a_{ij} x_j \leq b_i, \quad 1 \leq i \leq m \tag{1.2}$$

$$0 \leq x_j \leq u_j, \quad 1 \leq j \leq n \tag{1.3}$$

Here x_j is the amount of product j produced, u_j is an upper limit on the amount of product j that can be produced, p_j is the unit profit margin for product j, a_{ij} is the amount of resource i consumed by each unit of product j, b_i is the amount of resource i available, n is the number of products, and m is the number of scarce resources. This algebraic model states very concisely that we should maximize total profit [expression (1.1)], subject to consuming no more of the resources than is available [inequalities (1.2)], and all production quantities should be between 0 and the upper limits [inequalities (1.3)].

Algebraic models such as this appeal to mathematically trained analysts. They are concise, they spell out exactly which data are required (we would need to estimate the u_j's, the p_j's, the a_{ij}'s, and the b_i's from company data), they scale well (a problem with 500 products and 100 resource constraints is just as easy to state as one with only 5 products and 3 resource constraints), and many software packages accept algebraic models in essentially the same form as shown here, so that no "translation" is required. Indeed, algebraic models were the preferred type of model for years—and still are by many analysts. Their main drawback is that they require an ability to work with abstract mathematical symbols. Some people have this ability, but many perfectly intelligent people do not.

1.4.3 Spreadsheet Models

A fairly recent alternative to algebraic modeling is spreadsheet modeling. Instead of relating various quantities with algebraic equations and inequalities, we relate them in a spreadsheet with cell formulas. This process is much more intuitive to most people (at least in our experience). One of the primary reasons for this is the instant feedback available from spreadsheets. If you enter a formula incorrectly, it is often immediately obvious (from error messages or unrealistic numbers) that you have made an error, which you can then go back and fix. Algebraic models provide no such immediate feedback.

A specific comparison might help at this point. We already saw a general algebraic model of the product mix problem. Figure 1.16, taken from Chapter 14, illustrates a spreadsheet model for a specific example of this problem. The spreadsheet model should be fairly self-explanatory. All quantities in shaded cells are inputs to the model, the quantities in row 16 are the decision variables (they correspond to the x_j's in the algebraic model), and all other quantities are created through appropriate Excel formulas. To indicate constraints, we enter inequality signs in appropriate cells.

Figure 1.16   Optimal Solution for Product Mix Example

	A	B	C	D	E	F	G	H	I
1	Product mix model						Range names used		
2							Frames_produced	=Model!$B$16:$E$16	
3	Input data						Maximum_sales	=Model!$B$18:$E$18	
4	Hourly wage rate	$8.00					Profit	=Model!$F$32	
5	Cost per oz of metal	$0.50					Resources_available	=Model!$D$21:$D$23	
6	Cost per oz of glass	$0.75					Resources_used	=Model!$B$21:$B$23	
7									
8	Frame type	1	2	3	4				
9	Labor hours per frame	2	1	3	2				
10	Metal (oz.) per frame	4	2	1	2				
11	Glass (oz.) per frame	6	2	1	2				
12	Unit selling price	$28.50	$12.50	$29.25	$21.50				
13									
14	Production plan								
15	Frame type	1	2	3	4				
16	Frames produced	1000	800	400	0				
17		<=	<=	<=	<=				
18	Maximum sales	1000	2000	500	1000				
19									
20	Resource constraints	Resources used		Resources available					
21	Labor hours	4000	<=	4000					
22	Metal (oz.)	6000	<=	6000					
23	Glass (oz.)	8000	<=	10000					
24									
25	Revenue, cost summary								
26	Frame type	1	2	3	4	Totals			
27	Revenue	$28,500	$10,000	$11,700	$0	$50,200			
28	Costs of inputs								
29	Labor	$16,000	$6,400	$9,600	$0	$32,000			
30	Metal	$2,000	$800	$200	$0	$3,000			
31	Glass	$4,500	$1,200	$300	$0	$6,000			
32	Profit	$6,000	$1,600	$1,600	$0	$9,200			

Although a well-designed and well-documented spreadsheet model such as the one in Figure 1.16 is undoubtedly more intuitive for most people than its algebraic counterpart, the art of developing good spreadsheet models is not easy. Obviously, they must be *correct*. The formulas relating the various quantities must have the correct syntax, the correct cell references, and the correct logic. In complex models this can be quite a challenge.

However, correctness is not enough. If spreadsheet models are to be used in the business world, they must also be well designed and well documented. Otherwise, no one other than you (and maybe not even you after a few weeks have passed) will be able to understand what your models do or how they work. The strength of spreadsheets is their flexibility—you are limited only by your imagination. However, this flexibility can be a liability in spreadsheet modeling unless you plan the design of your models carefully.

Note the clear design in Figure 1.16. Most of the inputs are grouped at the top of the spreadsheet. All of the financial calculations are done at the bottom. When there are constraints, the two sides of the constraints are placed next to each other (as in the range B21:D23). Colored backgrounds (which appear on the screen but not in this book) are used for added clarity. Descriptive labels are used liberally. Excel itself imposes none of these "rules," but you should impose them on yourself.

We have made a conscious effort to establish good habits for you to follow throughout this book. We have designed and redesigned our spreadsheet models so that they are as clear as possible. This does not mean that you have to copy everything we do—everyone tends to develop their own spreadsheet style—but our models should give you something to emulate. Just remember that in the business world, you typically start with a *blank* spreadsheet. It is then up to you to develop a model that is not only correct but is also intelligible to you and to others. This takes a lot of practicing and a lot of editing, but it is a skill well worth developing.

1.4.4 The Seven-Step Modeling Process

Most of the modeling you will do in this book is only part of the overall modeling process typically done in the business world. We portray it as a seven-step process, as discussed here. Of course, not all problems require all seven steps. For example, the analysis of survey data might entail primarily steps 2 (data analysis) and 5 (decision making), without the formal model building discussed in steps 3 and 4.

The Modeling Process

1. **Define the problem.** Typically, a company does not develop a model unless it believes it has a problem. Therefore, the modeling process really begins by identifying an underlying problem. Perhaps the company is losing money, perhaps its market share is declining, or perhaps its customers are waiting too long for service. Any number of problems might be evident. However, as several people have warned [see Miser (1993) and Volkema (1995), for example], this step is not always as straightforward as it might appear. The company must be sure that it has identified the *right* problem before it spends time, effort, and money trying to solve it.

   For example, Miser cites the experience of an analyst who was hired by the military to investigate overly long turnaround times between fighter planes landing and taking off again to rejoin the battle. The military was convinced that the problem was caused by inefficient ground crews; if they were sped up, turnaround times would decrease. The analyst nearly accepted this statement of the problem and was about to do classical time-and-motion studies on the ground crew to pinpoint the sources of their inefficiency. However, by snooping around, he found that the problem obviously lay elsewhere. The trucks that refueled the planes were frequently late, which in turn was due to the inefficient way they were refilled from storage tanks at another location. Once this latter problem was solved—and its solution was embarrassingly simple—the turnaround times decreased to an acceptable level without any changes on the part of the ground crews. If the analyst had accepted the military's statement of the problem, the *real* problem might never have been located or solved.

2. **Collect and summarize data.** This crucial step in the process is often the most tedious. All organizations keep track of various data on their operations, but these data are often not in the form an analyst requires. They are also typically scattered in different places throughout the organization, in all kinds of different formats. Therefore, one of the first jobs of an analyst is to gather exactly the right data and summarize the

data appropriately—as we discuss in detail in Chapters 2 and 3—for use in the model. Collecting the data typically requires asking questions of key people (such as the accountants) throughout the organization, studying existing organizational databases, and performing time-consuming observational studies of the organization's processes. In short, it entails a lot of leg work.

3. **Develop a model.** This is the step we emphasize, especially in the latter chapters of the book. The form of the model varies from one situation to another. It could be a graphical model, an algebraic model, or a spreadsheet model. The key is that the model should capture the key elements of the business problem in such a way that it is understandable by all parties involved. This latter requirement is why we favor spreadsheet models, especially when they are well designed and well documented.

4. **Verify the model.** Here the analyst tries to determine whether the model developed in the previous step is an accurate representation of reality. A first step in determining how well the model fits reality is to check whether the model is valid for the current situation. This verification can take several forms. For example, the analyst could use the model with the company's current values of the input parameters. If the model's outputs are then in line with the outputs currently observed by the company, the analyst has at least shown that the model can duplicate the current situation.

A second way to verify a model is to enter a number of input parameters (even if they are not the company's current inputs) and see whether the outputs from the model are reasonable. One common approach is to use extreme values of the inputs to see whether the outputs behave as they should. If they do, then we have another piece of evidence that the model is reasonable.

If certain inputs are entered in the model, and the model's outputs are *not* as expected, there could be two causes. First, the model could simply be a poor representation of reality. In this case it is up to the analyst to refine the model until it provides reasonably accurate predictions. The second possible cause is that the model is fine but our intuition is not very good. In this case the fault lies with us, not the model.

A typical example of faulty intuition occurs with random sequences of 0's and 1's, such as might occur with successive flips of a fair coin. Most people expect that heads and tails will alternate and that there will be very few sequences of, say, four or more heads (or tails) in a row. However, a perfectly accurate simulation model of these flips will show, contrary to what most people expect, that fairly long runs of heads or tails are not at all uncommon. In fact, one or two long runs should be *expected* if there are enough flips.

The fact that outcomes sometimes defy intuition is an important reason why models are important. These models prove that our ability to predict outcomes in complex environments is often not very good.

5. **Select one or more suitable decisions.** Many, but not all, models are decision models. For any specific decisions, the model indicates the amount of profit obtained, the amount of cost incurred, the level of risk, and so on. If we believe the model is working correctly, as discussed in step 4, then we can use the model to see which decisions produce the *best* outputs.

6. **Present the results to the organization.** In a classroom setting you are typically finished when you have developed a model that correctly solves a particular problem. In the business world a correct model, even a useful one, is not always enough. An analyst typically has to "sell" the model to management. Unfortunately, the people in management are sometimes not as well trained in quantitative methods as the analyst, so they are not always inclined to trust complex models.

There are two ways to mitigate this problem. First, it is helpful to include relevant people throughout the company in the modeling process—from beginning to end—so that everyone has an understanding of the model and feels an ownership for it. Second, it helps to use a *spreadsheet* model whenever possible, especially if it is designed and documented properly. Almost everyone in today's business world is comfortable with spreadsheets, so spreadsheet models are more likely to be accepted.

7. **Implement the model and update it over time.** Again, there is a big difference between a classroom situation and a business situation. When you turn in a classroom assignment, you are typically finished with that assignment and can await the next one. In contrast, an analyst who develops a model for a company can usually not pack up his bags and leave. If the model is accepted by management, the company will then need to implement it company-wide. This can be very time consuming and politically difficult, especially if the model's prescriptions represent a significant change from the past. At the very least, employees must be trained how to use the model on a day-to-day basis.

In addition, the model will probably have to be updated over time, either because of changing conditions or because the company sees more potential uses for the model as it gains experience using it. This presents one of the greatest challenges for a model developer, namely, the ability to develop a model that *can* be modified as the need arises. Keep this in mind as you develop models throughout this book. Always try to make them as general as possible.

1.5 CONCLUSION

In this chapter we tried to convince you that the skills in this book are important for *you* to know as you enter the business world. The methods we discuss are no longer the sole province of the "quant jocks." By having a PC on your desk that is loaded with powerful software, you incur a responsibility to use this software to solve business problems. We have described the types of problems you will learn to solve in this book, along with the software you will use to solve them. We also discussed the modeling process, a theme that runs throughout this book. Now it's time for you to get started!

Cruise ship traveling has become big business. Many cruise lines are now competing for customers of all age groups and socioeconomic levels. They offer all types of cruises, from relatively inexpensive 3- to 4-day cruises in the Caribbean, to 12- to 15-day cruises in the Mediterranean, to several-month around-the-world cruises. Cruises have several features that attract customers, many of whom book 6 months or more in advance: (1) they offer a relaxing, everything-done-for-you way to travel; (2) they serve food that is plentiful, usually excellent, and included in the price of the cruise; (3) they stop at a number of interesting ports and offer travelers a way to see the world; and (4) they provide a wide variety of entertainment, particularly in the evening.

This last feature, the entertainment, presents a difficult problem for a ship's staff. A typical cruise might have well over 1000 passengers, including elderly singles and couples, middle-aged people with or without children, and young people, often honeymooners. These various types of passengers have varied tastes in terms of their after-dinner preferences in entertainment. Some want traditional dance music, some want comedians, some want rock music, some want movies, some want to go back to their cabins and read, and so on. Obviously, cruise entertainment directors want to provide the variety of entertainment their customers desire—within a reasonable budget—because satisfied customers tend to be repeat customers. The question is how to provide the right mix of entertainment.

On a cruise one of the authors and his wife took a few years ago, the entertainment was of high quality and there was plenty of variety. A seven-piece show band played dance music nightly in the largest lounge, two other small musical combos played nightly at two smaller lounges, a pianist played nightly at a piano bar in an intimate lounge, a group of professional singers and dancers played Broadway-type shows about twice weekly, and various professional singers and comedians played occasional single-night performances.[4] Although this entertainment was free to all of the passengers, much of it had embarrassingly low attendance. The nightly show band and musical combos, who were contracted to play nightly until midnight, often had less than a half dozen people in the audience—sometimes literally none. The professional singers, dancers, and comedians attracted larger audiences, but there were still plenty of empty seats. In spite of this, the cruise staff posted a weekly schedule, and they stuck to it regardless of attendance. In a short-term financial sense, it didn't make much difference. The performers got paid the same whether anyone was in the audience or not, the passengers had already paid (indirectly) for the entertainment as part of the cost of the cruise, and the only possible opportunity cost to the cruise line (in the short run) was the loss of liquor sales from the lack of passengers in the entertainment lounges. The morale of the entertainers was not great—entertainers love packed houses—but they usually argued, philosophically, that their hours were relatively short and they were still getting paid to see the world.

If you were in charge of entertainment on this ship, how would you describe the problem with entertainment: Is it a problem with deadbeat passengers, low-quality entertainment, or a mismatch between the entertainment offered and the entertainment desired? How might you try to solve the problem? What constraints might you have to work within? Would you keep a strict schedule such as the one followed by this cruise director, or would you play it more "by ear"? Would you gather data to help solve the problem? What data would you gather? How much would financial considerations dictate your decisions? Would they be long-term or short-term considerations? ∎

[4]There was also a moderately large onboard casino, but it tended to attract the same people every night, and it was always closed when the ship was in port.

Describing Data: Graphs and Tables

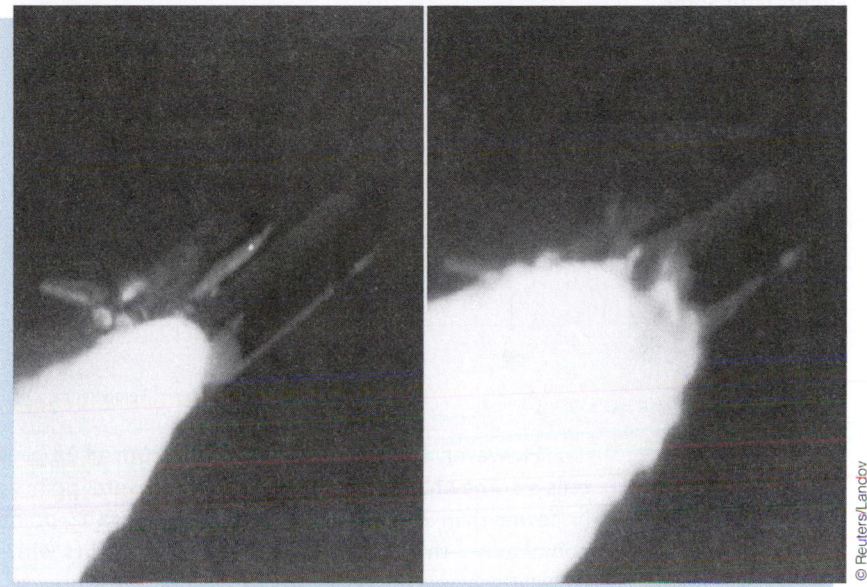

© Reuters/Landov

GRAPHICAL ANALYSIS OF THE CHALLENGER DISASTER

On the morning of January 28, 1986, the U.S. space shuttle *Challenger* exploded a few minutes after takeoff, killing all seven crew members. The physical cause of this tragic accident was found to be a failure in one of the O-rings located in a joint on the right-hand-side solid rocket booster. The Presidential Commission investigating the disaster concluded that the decision-making process leading up to the launch of *Challenger* was seriously flawed. Prior to the *Challenger* disaster, engineers from NASA and Morton Thiokol (the manufacturer of the shuttle's solid rocket motors) had observed evidence of in-flight damage to these O-rings. In spite of this evidence and the cold weather that adversely affected the performance of the O-ring seals, the *Challenger* was launched—and the outcome was disastrous.

This tragedy provides a dramatic example of how well-chosen graphs can make—or could have made—a huge difference. Data were available from previous shuttle flights on the ambient temperature of the solid rocket motor joints at launch and the number of joints observed to have suffered some form of damage. (These are included for your interest in the file **Challenger Disaster.xlsx**.) One set of data lists this information only for those seven previous flights where at least one joint suffered damage. Another set lists this information for all 23 previous flights. A scatterplot—one of the graph types we examine in this chapter—of the first set shows how two previous flights, one with a relatively cool temperature and one with a relatively warm temperature, each had two joints damaged. The other five flights, all with intermediate temperatures, each had a single joint damaged. This scatterplot appears in Figure 2.1. (Two of the points are identical, which explains why there appear to be only six points.) It contains virtually no evidence that damage is related to temperature. Perhaps the decision makers referred to this plot on launch day to confirm their go-ahead decision.

Figure 2.1

Scatterplot for Flights with Some Damage

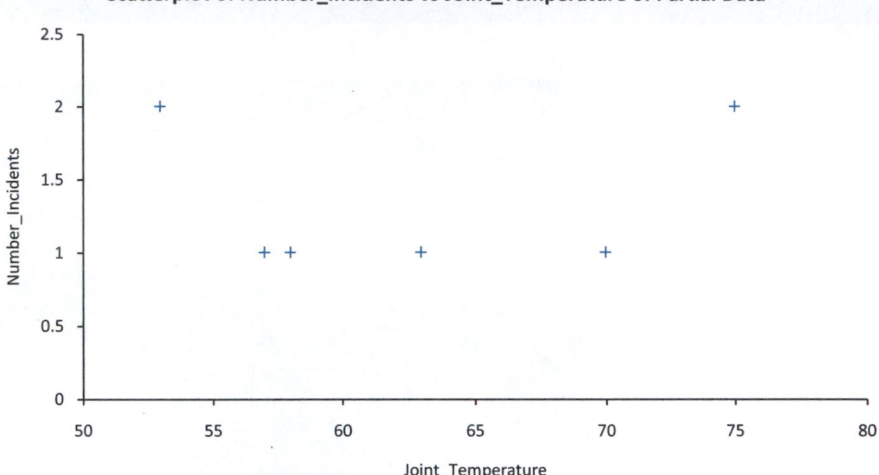

However, a scatterplot of the data from all 23 previous flights, shown in Figure 2.2, tells a somewhat different story. (Again, several points are identical, so there appear to be fewer than 23 points.) Note that the extra 16 points on this plot are all on the horizontal axis—that is, they all correspond to flights with no damage—and all correspond to relatively warm temperatures. In addition, it now becomes apparent that *most* of the flights with some damage occurred at relatively cool temperatures. The only exception is the point marked as a possible "outlier"—that is, a point outside the general pattern. If we ignore this potential outlier, a fairly clear pattern emerges: More damage tends to occur at low temperatures. Of course, this plot does not provide conclusive evidence that a shuttle launched at near-freezing temperatures, which the fateful launch experienced, was doomed to disaster. However, it provides a clear warning. If you had observed this plot and the freezing temperature on that January morning, would you have decided to go ahead with the launch? ■

Figure 2.2

Scatterplot for All Previous Flights

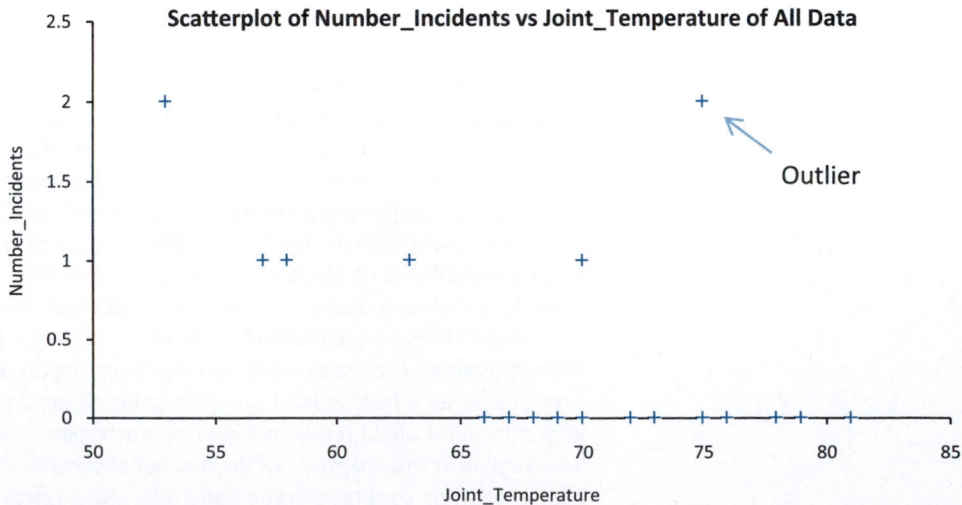

2.1 INTRODUCTION

The goal of this chapter and the next is very simple: to make sense out of data by constructing appropriate summary measures, tables, and graphs. Our purpose here is to take a set of data that at first glance has little meaning and to present the data in a form that makes sense to people. There are numerous ways to do this, limited only by your imagination, but there are several tools used most often: (1) a variety of graphs, including bar charts, pie charts, histograms, scatterplots, and time series graphs; (2) tables of summary measures (such as totals, averages, etc.) grouped by categories; and (3) numerical summary measures such as counts, percentages, averages, and measures of variability. These terms might not all be familiar at this point, but you have undoubtedly seen examples of them in newspapers, magazine articles, and books.

The material in these two chapters is *simple, complex,* and *important.* It is simple because there are no difficult mathematical concepts. With the possible exception of variance, covariance, and correlation, all of the numerical measures, tables, and graphs are natural and easy to understand. It used to be a tedious chore to produce them, but with the advances in statistical software, including add-ins for spreadsheet packages such as Excel, they can now be produced quickly and easily.

It is customary to refer to the raw numbers as data *and the output of a statistical analysis as* information. *We start with the data, and we hope to end with information that an organization can use for competitive advantage.*

If it's so easy, why do we also claim that the material in this chapter is complex? The data sets available to companies in today's computerized world tend to be extremely large and filled with "unstructured" data. As we will see, even in data sets that are quite small in comparison to those that real companies face, it is a challenge to summarize the data so that the important *information* stands out clearly. It is easy to produce summary measures, tables, and graphs, but our goal is to produce the most *appropriate* measures, tables, and graphs.

The typical employees of today—not just the managers and technical specialists—have a wealth of easy-to-use tools at their disposal, and it is frequently up to them to summarize data in a way that is both meaningful and useful to their constituents: people within their company, their company's suppliers, and their company's customers. It takes some training and practice to do this effectively.

Because today's companies are inundated with data, and because virtually every employee in the company must summarize data to some extent, the material in this chapter and Chapters 3 and 4 is arguably the most important material in this book. There is sometimes a tendency to race through the "descriptive statistics" chapters to get to the more "interesting" material in later chapters as quickly as possible. We want to resist this tendency. The material covered in these three chapters deserves close examination, and this takes some time.

Most of the material in this chapter and the next two could be covered in any order. This chapter involves graphs and tables. The next chapter covers numerical summary measures and another type of graph, the **box plot**, which utilizes several of the summary measures. Chapter 3 concludes with several examples that put the descriptive tools from both chapters to good use. Finally, in Chapter 4 we discuss ways of getting data from various sources, such as Access databases, into a format in Excel where they can be analyzed by the methods discussed in Chapters 2 and 3 (and later chapters).

2.2 BASIC CONCEPTS

We begin with a short discussion of several important concepts: populations and samples, variables and observations, and types of data.

2.2.1 Populations and Samples

First, we distinguish between a *population* and a *sample*. A **population** includes all of the entities of interest, whether they be people, households, machines, or whatever. The following are three typical populations:

- All potential voters in a presidential election
- All subscribers to cable television
- All invoices submitted for Medicare reimbursement by a nursing home

In these situations and many others it is virtually impossible to obtain information about all members of the population. For example, it is far too costly to ask all potential voters which presidential candidates they prefer. Therefore, we often try to gain insights into the characteristics of a population by examining a **sample**, or subset, of the population. In later chapters we examine populations and samples in some depth, but for now it is enough to know that we typically want samples to be *representative* of the population so that observed characteristics of the sample can be generalized to the population as a whole.

> A **population** includes all of the entities of interest in a study, whether they be people, households, machines, or whatever. A **sample** is a subset of the population, often randomly chosen and preferably representative of the population as a whole.

A famous example where a sample was *not* representative is the case of the *Literary Digest* fiasco of 1936. In the 1936 presidential election, subscribers to the *Literary Digest,* a highbrow literary magazine, were asked to mail in a ballot with their preference for president. Overwhelmingly, these ballots favored the Republican candidate, Alf Landon, over the Democratic candidate, Franklin D. Roosevelt. Despite this, FDR was a landslide winner. The discrepancy arose because the readers of the *Literary Digest* were not at all representative of most voters in 1936. Most voters in 1936 could barely make ends meet, let alone subscribe to a literary magazine. Thus, the typical lower-middle-income voter had almost no chance of being chosen in this sample.

Today, Gallup, Harris, and other pollsters make a conscious effort to ensure that their samples—which usually include about 1500 people—are representative of the population. (It is truly remarkable, for example, that a sample of 1500 voters can almost surely predict a candidate's actual percentage of votes correctly to within 3%. We explain why this is possible in Chapters 8 and 9.) The important point is that a representative sample of reasonable size can provide a lot of important information about the population of interest.

We use the terms *population* and *sample* a few times in this chapter, which is why we have defined them here. However, the distinction is not too important until later chapters. Our intent in this chapter is to focus entirely on the data in a given data set, not to generalize beyond it. Therefore, the given data set could be a population or a sample from a population. For now, the distinction is largely irrelevant.

2.2.2 Variables and Observations

To standardize data analysis, especially on a computer, it is customary to present the data in rows and columns. Each column represents a **variable**, and each row corresponds to an **observation**, that is, a member of the population or sample. The numbers of variables and observations vary widely from one data set to another, but they can all be put in this row–column format.

The terms *variables* and *observations* are fairly standard. However, alternative terms are often used. First, many people refer to *cases* instead of observations; that is, each row is a **case**. Second, if the data are stored in database packages such as Microsoft Access, the terms *fields* and *records* are typically used. **Fields** are the same as variables, so that each column corresponds to a field. **Records** are the same as observations (or cases), so that each row corresponds to a record.

A **variable** (or **field**) is an attribute, or measurement, on members of a population, such as height, gender, or salary. An **observation** (or **case** or **record**) is a list of all variable values for a single member of a population. A variable is usually listed in a column; an observation is usually listed in a row.

EXAMPLE | **2.1 DATA FROM ENVIRONMENTAL SURVEY**

The data set shown in Figure 2.3 represents 30 responses from a questionnaire concerning the president's environmental policies. (See the file **Questionnaire Data.xlsx**.) Identify the variables and observations.

Figure 2.3

Data from Environmental Survey

	A	B	C	D	E	F
1	Age	Gender	State	Children	Salary	Opinion
2	35	Male	Minnesota	1	$65,400	5
3	61	Female	Texas	2	$62,000	1
4	35	Male	Ohio	0	$63,200	3
5	37	Male	Florida	2	$52,000	5
6	32	Female	California	3	$81,400	1
7	33	Female	New York	3	$46,300	5
8	65	Female	Minnesota	2	$49,600	1
9	45	Male	New York	1	$45,900	5
10	40	Male	Texas	3	$47,700	4
11	32	Female	Texas	1	$59,900	4
12	57	Male	New York	1	$48,100	4
13	38	Female	Virginia	0	$58,100	3
14	37	Female	Illinois	2	$56,000	1
15	42	Female	Virginia	2	$53,400	1
16	38	Female	New York	2	$39,000	2
17	48	Male	Michigan	1	$61,500	2
18	40	Male	Ohio	0	$37,700	1
19	57	Female	Michigan	2	$36,700	4
20	44	Male	Florida	2	$45,200	3
21	40	Male	Michigan	0	$59,000	4
22	21	Female	Minnesota	2	$54,300	2
23	49	Male	New York	1	$62,100	4
24	34	Male	New York	0	$78,000	3
25	49	Male	Arizona	0	$43,200	5
26	40	Male	Arizona	1	$44,500	3
27	38	Male	Ohio	1	$43,300	1
28	27	Male	Illinois	3	$45,400	2
29	63	Male	Michigan	2	$53,900	1
30	52	Male	California	1	$44,100	3
31	48	Female	New York	2	$31,000	4

Objective   To illustrate variables and observations in a typical data set.

Solution

This data set provides observations on 30 people who responded to the questionnaire. Each observation lists the person's age, gender, state of residence, number of children, annual salary, and opinion of the president's environmental policies. These six pieces of information represent the variables. It is customary to include a row (row 3 in this case) that lists variable names. These variable names should be meaningful—and no longer than necessary. ■

2.2.3 Types of Data

There are several ways to categorize data, as we explain in the context of Example 2.1. We distinguish, for example, between *numerical* and *categorical* data. The basic distinction here is whether we intend to do any arithmetic on the data. It makes sense to do arithmetic on numerical data, but not on categorical data. Clearly, the Gender and State variables are categorical, and the Children and Salary variables are numerical. The Age and Opinion variables are more difficult to categorize. Age is expressed numerically, and we *might* want to perform some arithmetic on age (such as calculating the average age of the respondents). However, age could also be treated as a categorical variable, as we see shortly.

Three variables that appear to be numerical but are usually treated as categorical are phone numbers, zip codes, and Social Security numbers. Do you see why? Can you think of others?

> A variable is **numerical** if meaningful arithmetic can be performed on it. Otherwise, the variable is **categorical**.

The Opinion variable is expressed numerically, on a 1-to-5 **Likert** scale. These numbers are only "codes" for the categories "strongly disagree," "disagree," "neutral," "agree," and "strongly agree." We never intend to perform arithmetic on these numbers; in fact, it is not really appropriate to do so. Here, then, we treat the Opinion variable as categorical. Note, too, that there is a definite ordering of its categories, whereas there is no natural ordering of the categories for the Gender or State variables. When there is a natural ordering of categories, we classify the variable as **ordinal**. If there is no natural ordering, as with the Gender and State variables, we classify the variables as **nominal**. However, both ordinal and nominal variables are categorical.

> A categorical variable is **ordinal** if there is a natural ordering of its possible values. If there is no natural ordering, it is **nominal**.

Excel Tip *How do you remember, for example, that "1" stands for "strongly disagree" in the Opinion variable? You can enter a comment—a reminder to yourself and others—in any cell. This feature appears under the Insert menu. Alternatively, you can right-click on a cell and select the Insert Comment menu item. A small red tag appears in any cell with a comment. Moving the cursor over that cell causes the comment to appear. You will see numerous comments in the files that accompany this book.*

Categorical variables can be *coded* numerically or left uncoded. In Figure 2.3, Gender has not been coded, whereas Opinion has been coded. This is largely a matter of taste—so long as you realize that coding a truly categorical variable does not make it numerical and open to arithmetic operations. An alternative is shown in Figure 2.4. Now Gender has been coded (1 for males, 2 for females), and Opinion has not been coded. In addition, we have categorized the Age variable as "young" (34 years or younger), "middle-aged" (from 35 to 59 years), and "elderly" (60 years or older). The purpose of the study dictates whether age should be treated numerically or categorically; there is no right or wrong way.

Figure 2.4
Environmental Data Using a Different Coding

	A	B	C	D	E	F
1	Age	Gender	State	Children	Salary	Opinion
2	Middle-aged	1	Minnesota	1	$65,400	Strongly agree
3	Elderly	2	Texas	2	$62,000	Strongly disagree
4	Middle-aged	1	Ohio	0	$63,200	Neutral
5	Middle-aged	1	Florida	2	$52,000	Strongly agree
6	Young	2	California	3	$81,400	Strongly disagree
7	Young	2	New York	3	$46,300	Strongly agree
8	Elderly	2	Minnesota	2	$49,600	Strongly disagree
9	Middle-aged	1	New York	1	$45,900	Strongly agree
10	Middle-aged	1	Texas	3	$47,700	Agree
11	Young	2	Texas	1	$59,900	Agree
12	Middle-aged	1	New York	1	$48,100	Agree
13	Middle-aged	2	Virginia	0	$58,100	Neutral
14	Middle-aged	2	Illinois	2	$56,000	Strongly disagree
15	Middle-aged	2	Virginia	2	$53,400	Strongly disagree
16	Middle-aged	2	New York	2	$39,000	Disagree
17	Middle-aged	1	Michigan	1	$61,500	Disagree
18	Middle-aged	1	Ohio	0	$37,700	Strongly disagree
19	Middle-aged	2	Michigan	2	$36,700	Agree
20	Middle-aged	1	Florida	2	$45,200	Neutral
21	Middle-aged	1	Michigan	0	$59,000	Agree
22	Young	2	Minnesota	2	$54,300	Disagree
23	Middle-aged	1	New York	1	$62,100	Agree
24	Young	1	New York	0	$78,000	Neutral
25	Middle-aged	1	Arizona	0	$43,200	Strongly agree
26	Middle-aged	1	Arizona	1	$44,500	Neutral
27	Middle-aged	1	Ohio	1	$43,300	Strongly disagree
28	Young	1	Illinois	3	$45,400	Disagree
29	Elderly	1	Michigan	2	$53,900	Strongly disagree
30	Middle-aged	1	California	1	$44,100	Neutral
31	Middle-aged	2	New York	2	$31,000	Agree

Numerical variables can be classified as either *discrete* or *continuous*. The basic distinction is whether the data arise from counts or continuous measurements. The variable Children is clearly a count (that is, *discrete*), whereas the variable Salary is best treated as continuous. This distinction between discrete and continuous variables is sometimes important because it dictates the type of analysis that is most natural.

> A numerical variable is **discrete** if its possible values can be counted. A **continuous** variable is the result of an essentially continuous measurement.

Finally, data can be categorized as *cross-sectional* or *time series*. The opinion data in Example 2.1 are **cross-sectional**. A pollster evidently sampled a cross section of people at one particular point in time. In contrast, **time series** data occur when we track one or more variables through time. A typical example of a time series variable is the series of daily closing values of the Dow Jones Index. Very different types of analysis are appropriate for cross-sectional and time series data, as becomes apparent in this and later chapters.

> **Cross-sectional** data are data on a population at a distinct point in time. **Time series** data are data collected across time.

2.3 FREQUENCY TABLES AND HISTOGRAMS

A good place to start building a "toolkit" of descriptive methods is with *frequency tables* and their graphical analog, *histograms*. A **frequency table** indicates the numbers of observations in various categories. A **histogram** shows this same information graphically. We construct a frequency table and a histogram in the following example.

> A **frequency table** lists the numbers of observations of some variable in various categories. A **histogram** is a bar chart of these frequencies.

EXAMPLE | **2.2 DATA ON FAMOUS MOVIE STARS**

The file **Movie Stars.xlsx** contains information on 66 movie stars. (See Figure 2.5.) This data set contains the name of each actor and the following four variables:

- Gender
- Domestic Gross: average domestic gross of star's last few movies (in $ millions)
- Foreign Gross: average foreign gross of star's last few movies (in $ millions)
- Income: current amount the star asks for a movie (in $ millions)[1]

Figure 2.5

Data on Famous
Actors and Actresses

	A	B	C	D	E	F	G	H	I
1	Name	Gender	Domestic Gross	Foreign Gross	Income				
2	Angela BassettF	32	17	2.5					
3	Jessica Lange	F	21	27	2.5		All monetary values are in		
4	Winona Ryder	F	36	30	4		millions of dollars.		
5	Michelle Pfeiffer	F	66	31	10				
6	Whoopi Goldberg	F	32	33	10				
7	Emma Thompson	F	26	44	3				
8	Julia Roberts	F	57	47	12				
9	Sharon Stone	F	32	47	6				
10	Meryl Streep	F	34	47	4.5				
11	Susan Sarandon	F	38	49	3				
12	Nicole Kidman	F	55	51	4				
13	Holly Hunter	F	51	53	2.5				
14	Meg Ryan	F	43	55	8.5				
15	Andie Macdowell	F	26	75	2				
54	Harrison Ford	M	96	91	20				
55	Clint Eastwood	M	55	94	12.5				
56	Mel Gibson	M	91	95	19				
57	Bruce Willis	M	55	99	16.5				
58	Bill Pullman	M	38	103	6				
59	Liam Neeson	M	29	108	3				
60	Samuel Jackson	M	40	122	4.5				
61	Jim Carrey	M	122	123	15				
62	Morgan Freeman	M	77	123	6				
63	Arnold Schwarzenegger	M	108	124	20				
64	Brad Pitt	M	57	124	10				
65	Michael Douglas	M	68	137	18				
66	Robin Williams	M	92	180	15				
67	Tom Hanks	M	166	182	17.5				

---

[1]This data is slightly dated. If you can find similar, but more recent data, on the Web, we encourage you to use it. However, it's not easy to find how much movie stars make in particular movies.

Objective To use StatTools's Histogram procedure to plot the distribution of actors' incomes.

Solution

To obtain a frequency table for data that are essentially continuous, such as the Income variable, we must first choose appropriate categories. (These categories are usually called *bins*.) There is no set rule here. We want to have enough categories so that we can see a meaningful distribution, but we don't want so many categories that there are only a few observations per category. We provide some guidelines for choosing categories at the end of this example. However, many software packages, including StatTools, offer default categories that work well.

To create the histogram in Excel, we use the StatTools add-in that accompanies this book.

STEPS FOR CREATING A HISTOGRAM AND THE ASSOCIATED FREQUENCY TABLE

1 Before you initiate this and most other StatTools procedures, you must first define a **data set** within StatTools. This is a named set of data that StatTools can then analyze. To create a StatTools data set, place the cursor anywhere within the data range. (If you can imagine a rectangular range that contains the data, including the variable names at the top, the cursor should be somewhere—anywhere—within this range. If you forget to place it there, you will get a chance to select the data range manually later on.) Then select Manager from the StatTools ribbon. If the data set has not yet been named, you will be asked whether you want to create the data set. In this case, click on Yes to obtain the dialog box in Figure 2.6. Here you can change the name of the data set to something more meaningful, you can manually select the data range if StatTools's guess was not correct, and you can check the Apply Cell Formatting option to apply coloring and a border to the data range. In the bottom section of the dialog box, there are several options, but the defaults

Figure 2.6

Data Set Manager Dialog Box

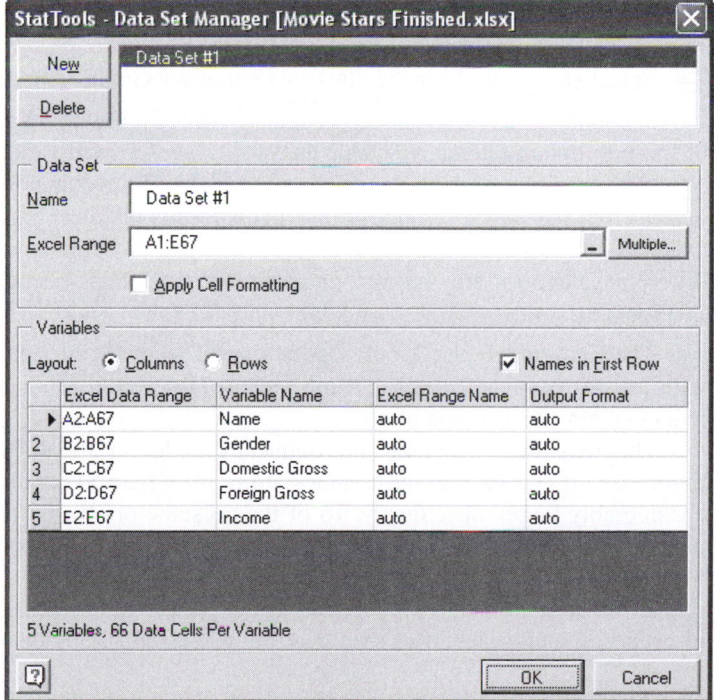

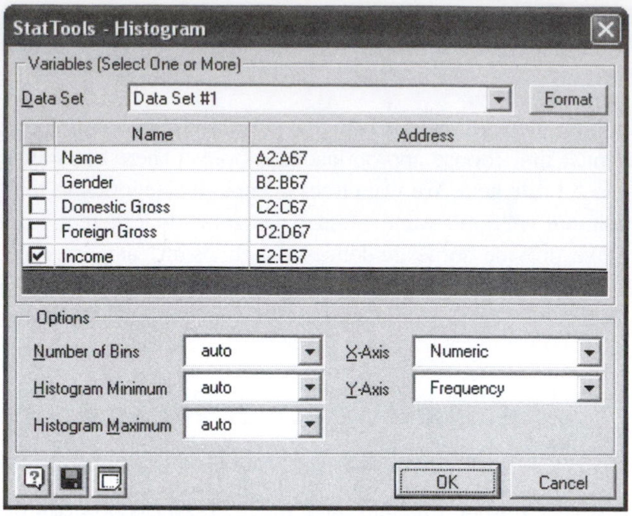

Figure 2.7

Histogram
Dialog Box

shown here are almost always appropriate. In particular, it is almost always a good idea to have your variables in columns, with variable names in the top row. Fill in the dialog box as shown to create a StatTools data set named **Data Set #1**. (If you check Apply Cell Formatting, you will recognize it as formatted because the variable names will be colored blue and there will be a double-black border around the data. This will remind you later on that this data range has been defined as a data set within StatTools.)

Excel Tip *There is a little-known key combination for selecting the rectangular region "surrounding" any cell in a data set: Ctrl-A. Try it. With the Movie Stars file open, put your cursor in any cell inside the data set, such as D12. Press Ctrl-A (both keys at once) to highlight the data range A1:E67. This is what StatTools does for you when it makes its guess in Step 1. (An alternative key combination that does the same thing is Ctrl-Shift-*.)*

2 Select Histogram from the StatTools Summary Graphs dropdown.

3 A list of variables in the data set appears. (See Figure 2.7.) You can select one or more of these to obtain a frequency table and histogram for each variable you select. For now, select the Income variable. Also, we suggest that you select the Numeric (not Categorical) option from the X-Axis dropdown list. (This results in "nicer" numbers on the horizontal axis, but you can experiment with both options.) At this point you could manually choose different categories for the histogram from the Options section, but for now, accept StatTools's automatic choices, and click on OK.

4 The histogram is placed on a separate worksheet with the name **Histogram**. (If a sheet with this name already exists, a name such as **Histogram (2)** is used. Of course, you can rename these sheets if you like.)

When we indicate a category such as "2–4," we mean that this includes the right endpoint, "4," and excludes the left endpoint, "2."

The resulting histogram and frequency table for the Income variable appear in Figure 2.8. It is clear that most values are in the $2- to $11-million range, but a few are considerably larger. Specifically, 16 of the 66 stars, or about 24%, make more than $11 million, and 7 of the 66, or about 10%, are in the highest income bracket, $17.75 million to $20 million.

If you aren't satisfied with this histogram (you want different categories, for example), just repeat the procedure, this time overriding StatTools's automatic categories.

Figure 2.8 Histogram of Movie Star Incomes

Histogram	Bin Min	Bin Max	Bin Midpoint	Freq.	Rel. Freq.	Prb. Density
Bin #1	2.000	4.250	3.125	17	0.2576	0.114
Bin #2	4.250	6.500	5.375	11	0.1667	0.074
Bin #3	6.500	8.750	7.625	13	0.1970	0.088
Bin #4	8.750	11.000	9.875	9	0.1364	0.061
Bin #5	11.000	13.250	12.125	5	0.0758	0.034
Bin #6	13.250	15.500	14.375	2	0.0303	0.013
Bin #7	15.500	17.750	16.625	2	0.0303	0.013
Bin #8	17.750	20.000	18.875	7	0.1061	0.047

Income / Data Set #1 (column header spanning Bin Min through Prb. Density)

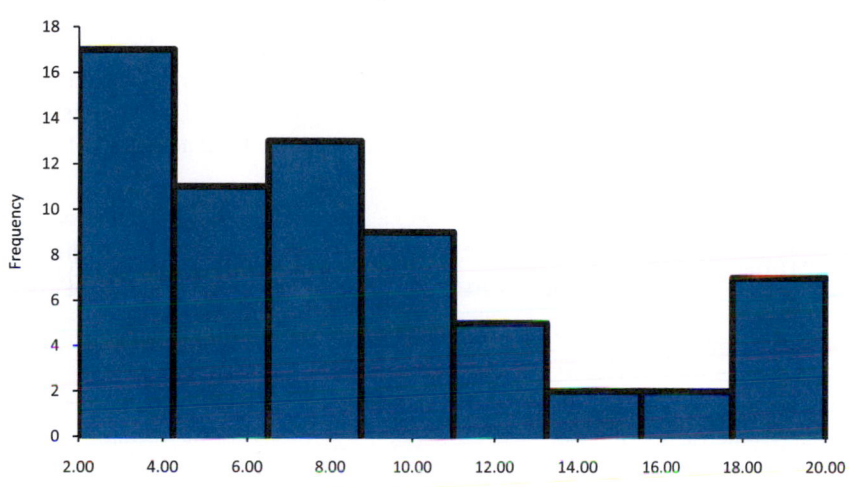

Histogram of Income

For a quick analysis, feel free to accept StatTools's automatic histogram options. However, don't be afraid to experiment with these options in defining your own bins. The goal is to make the histogram as meaningful and easy to read as possible.

Excel Tip *By default, StatTools puts all charts on separate worksheets. (You can change this default behavior by selecting the StatTools Settings button and changing the Placement setting on the Report tab. Note that any such change stays in effect for all later StatTools outputs until you change the setting again.) If you would rather have a chart on the same sheet as the data, it is easy to move it. Go to the chart's sheet, select the chart, select the Move Chart button from the Chart Tools Design ribbon and select the "As object in" option, with the desired worksheet selected in the box. The chart will automatically appear in the selected worksheet. The Move Chart option can also be used to place the chart on a separate "chart sheet" (a sheet with no rows and columns). To do this, select the "As new sheet" option in the Move Chart dialog box.*

Creating a histogram can be a tedious task, but an add-in such as StatTools makes it relatively easy. However, you must be prepared to fill in the dialog box in Figure 2.7—that is, you must be ready to specify the bins or accept the add-in's defaults. The following guidelines are useful.

PLANNING A HISTOGRAM

- Usually, choose about 8 to 15 categories. The more observations you have, the more categories you can afford to have.

- Try to select categories that "fill" the range of data. For example, it wouldn't make sense to have 10 categories of length $1000, starting with the category "less than $30,000," if most of the observations are in the $20,000 to $50,000 range. In this case all of the data would fall in the first few categories, virtually no data would fall in the higher categories, and the histogram would not tell a very interesting story.

- If you don't accept the add-in's defaults, it is customary to plan the categories so that the "breakpoints" between categories are nice, round numbers.

- Remember that there is not a single "right" answer. If your initial entries in the dialog box don't produce a very interesting histogram, try it again with new entries.

*The term **distribution** refers to the way the data are distributed in the various categories. It is common to refer to a positively skewed distribution, say, rather than a positively skewed histogram. However, either term can be used.*

2.3.1 Shapes of Histograms

Four different shapes of histograms are commonly observed: symmetric, positively skewed, negatively skewed, and bimodal. A histogram is **symmetric** if it has a single peak and looks approximately the same to the left and right of the peak. For reasons that become apparent in later chapters, symmetric histograms are very common. One is illustrated in the following example. (In each of the following examples, we have accepted StatTools's default bins.)

EXAMPLE | **2.3 DISTRIBUTION OF DIAMETERS OF ELEVATOR RAILS AT OTIS ELEVATOR**

Otis Elevator has measured the diameter (in inches) of 400 elevator rails. (See the Data1 sheet of the file **Elevator Rail Diameters 1.xlsx.**) The diameters range from a low of approximately 0.449 inch to a high of approximately 0.548 inch. Check that these diameters follow a symmetric distribution.

Objective   To illustrate a symmetric distribution of part diameters.

Solution

We use StatTools's Histogram procedure to create the histogram in Figure 2.9. Note that StatTools has chosen bin lengths of approximately 0.01 inch.

Figure 2.9

Symmetric Distribution of Diameters

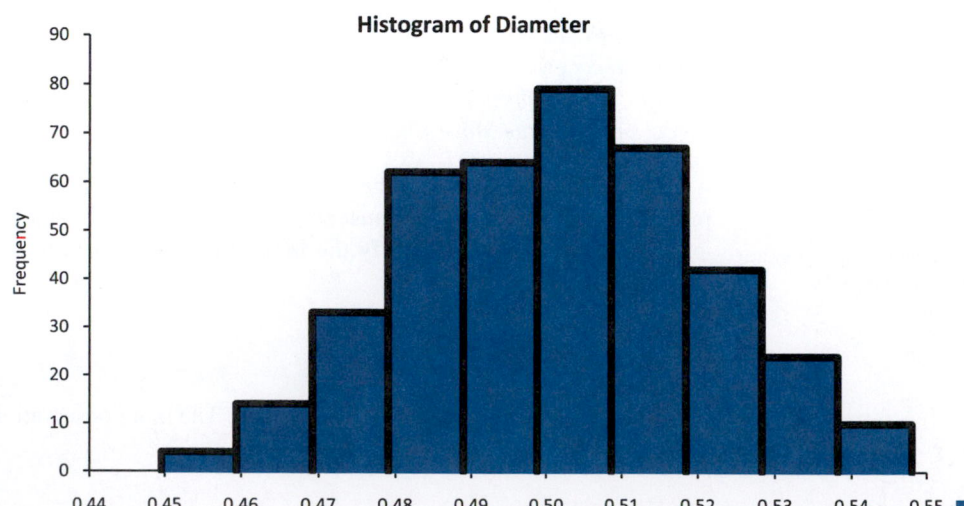

Clearly, the most likely diameters are between 0.48 and 0.52. Also, we see that the distribution of diameters is fairly symmetric. The diameters appear to follow the bell-shaped "normal" distribution, which we discuss in detail in Chapter 6.

A histogram is **skewed to the right** (or **positively** skewed) if it has a single peak and the values of the distribution extend farther to the right of the peak than to the left of the peak. One common example of positively skewed data is the following.

EXAMPLE	2.4 Distribution of Times Between Arrivals to a Bank

The file **Bank Arrivals.xlsx** is the time between customer arrivals—called *interarrival times*—for all customers arriving at a bank on a given day. Do these interarrival times appear to be positively skewed?

Objective   To illustrate a positively skewed distribution of times between customer arrivals to a bank.

Solution

For this data set, StatTools subdivides the data into intervals of 3 minutes. The resulting histogram appears in Figure 2.10. The interarrival times are clearly positively skewed. There is a "long tail" to the right of the peak, and none to the left. We also see that values over 15 minutes are quite unlikely. Evidently, there is usually very little time between consecutive customer arrivals. Now and then, however, there is a fairly large gap between arrivals. These occasional large gaps could be important for the bank. They could enable tellers to clear out long waiting lines.

Figure 2.10

Positively Skewed Distribution of Interarrival Times

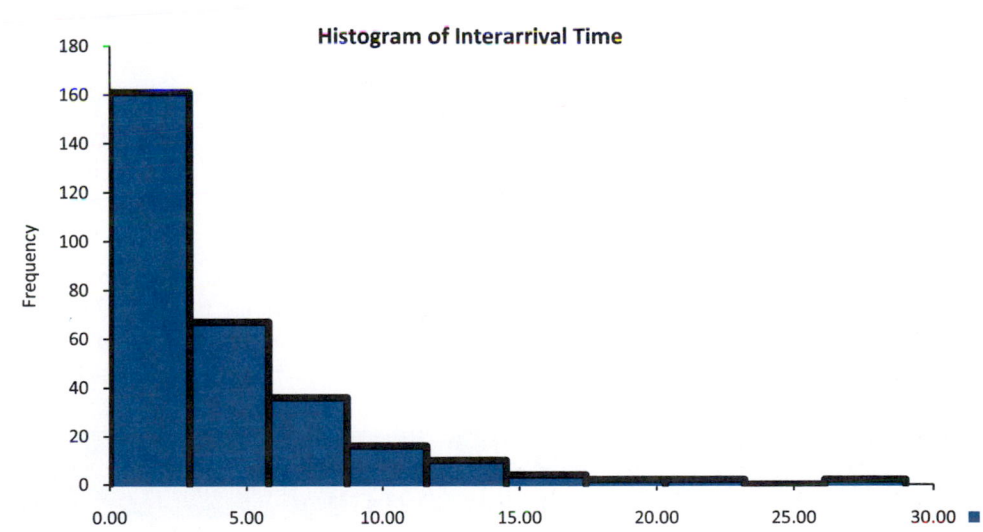

A histogram is **skewed to the left** (or **negatively** skewed) if its longer tail is on the left. Negatively skewed distributions are probably less common than positively skewed distributions, but the following example illustrates one situation where negative skewness often occurs.

2.5 DISTRIBUTION OF ACCOUNTING MIDTERM SCORES

The file **Midterm Scores.xlsx** lists the midterm scores for a large class of accounting students. Does the histogram indicate a negatively skewed distribution?

Objective To illustrate a negatively skewed distribution of scores on a midterm exam.

Solution

For this example StatTools uses bins of length 7 to create the histogram in Figure 2.11. This histogram shows that the most likely score is between 85 and 92. Clearly, the right tail can extend only to 100, whereas the left tail tapers off gradually. This leads to the obvious negative skewness. You've probably been in such classes, where most students do reasonably well but a few pull down the class average.

Figure 2.11

Negatively Skewed Distribution of Midterm Scores

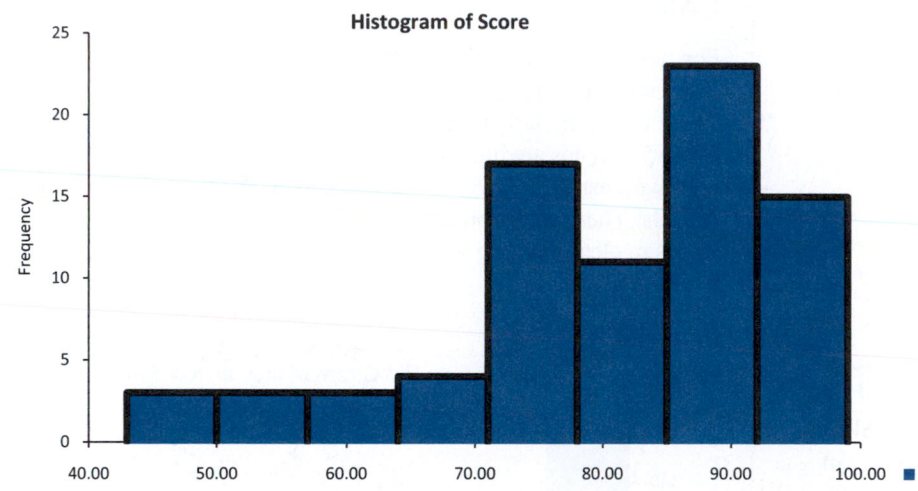

Histogram of Score

Some histograms have two or more peaks. This is often an indication that the data come from two or more distinct populations. Example 2.6 illustrates a situation where there are exactly *two* peaks, called a **bimodal distribution**.

2.6 DISTRIBUTION OF DIAMETERS OF ELEVATOR RAILS PRODUCED ON TWO MACHINES

The Data2 sheet of file **Elevator Rail Diameters.xlsx** lists the diameters of all elevator rails produced on a single day at Otis Elevator. Otis uses two machines to produce elevator rails. What do we learn from a histogram of these data?

Objective To illustrate a bimodal distribution of part diameters manufactured by two separate machines.

Solution

The diameters from the individual machines are listed in columns A and B of the Data2 sheet. We merge these into a single variable in column D. Figure 2.12 shows the histogram of the merged data in column D. This is an obvious bimodal distribution, and it provides clear evidence of two distinct populations. Evidently, rails from one machine average about 0.5 inch in diameter, whereas rails from the other average about 0.6 inch in diameter. (A closer look at the data confirms this.) In such a case it is better to construct a single histogram for each machine's production, as in Figures 2.13 and 2.14. (These are based on the data in columns A and B, respectively.) These show that each machine's distribution is reasonably symmetric, although the scales on their horizontal axes are quite different.

Figure 2.12

Bimodal
Distribution of
Diameters from
Both Machines

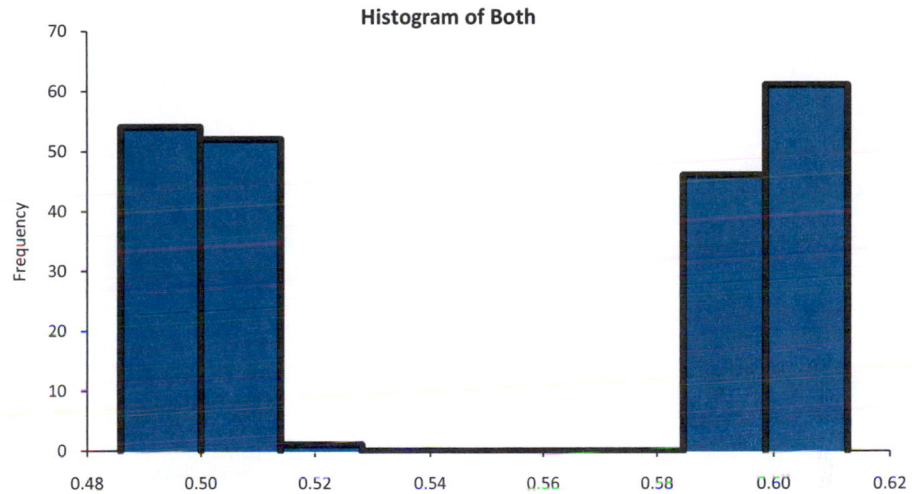

Figure 2.13

Distribution of
Diameters from
Machine 1

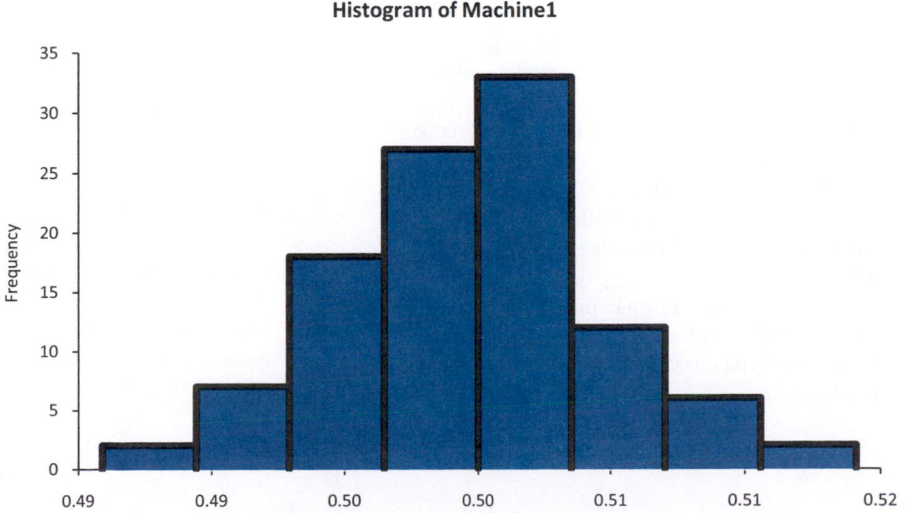

Figure 2.14
Distribution of
Diameters from
Machine 2

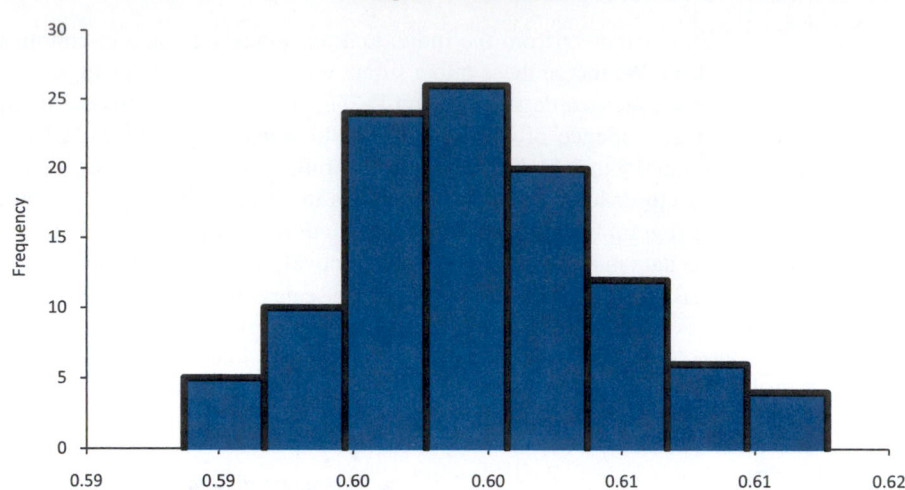

Histogram of Machine2

The bimodal histogram in Figure 2.12 provides a clear sign to management that there *are* two separate processes—and that possibly at least one of the two machines should be adjusted. ∎

PROBLEMS

Level A

1. A human resources manager at Beta Technologies, Inc., has collected current annual salary figures and related data for 52 of the company's full-time employees. The data are in the file **P02_01.xlsx**. These data include each selected employee's gender, age, number of years of relevant work experience prior to employment at Beta, the number of years of employment at Beta, the number of years of post-secondary education, and annual salary.

    a. Indicate the data type for each of the six variables included in this set.

    b. Create a frequency table and histogram for the ages of the employees included in this sample. How would you characterize the age distribution for these data?

    c. Create a frequency table and histogram for the salaries of the employees included in this sample. How would you characterize the salary distribution for these data?

2. A production manager is interested in determining the proportion of defective items in a typical shipment of one of the computer components that her company manufactures. The proportion of defective components is recorded for each of 500 randomly selected shipments collected during a 1-month period. The data are in the file **P02_02.xlsx**. Create a frequency table and histogram that will enable this production manager to begin to understand the variation of the proportion of defective components in the company's shipments.

3. *Business Week's Guide to the Best Business Schools* provides enrollment data on graduate business programs that they rate as the best in the United States. Specifically, this guide reports the percentages of women, minority, and international students enrolled in each of the top programs, as well as the total number of full-time students enrolled in each of these distinguished programs. The data are in the file **P02_03.xlsx**.

a. Create frequency tables and histograms for the distributions of each of the four variables included in this data set.

b. Compare the distributions of the proportions of women, minority, and international students enrolled in *Business Week's* top graduate business schools. What general conclusions can be drawn by comparing the histograms of these three distributions?

4. The manager of a local fast-food restaurant is interested in improving the service provided to customers who use the restaurant's drive-up window. As a first step in this process, the manager asks his assistant to record the time (in minutes) it takes to serve 200 different customers at the final window in the facility's drive-up system. The given 200 customer service times are all observed during the busiest hour of the day for this fast-food operation. The data are in the file **P02_04.xlsx**.

a. Create a frequency table and histogram for the distribution of observed customer service times.

b. Are shorter or longer service times more likely for these data?

5. A finance professor has just given a midterm examination in her corporate finance course. She is interested in learning how her class of 100 students performed on this exam. The data are in the file **P02_05.xlsx**.

a. Create a histogram of this distribution of exam scores (where the maximum possible score is 100).

b. Based on the histogram and associated frequency table, how would you characterize the group's performance on this test?

6. Five hundred households in a middle-class neighborhood were recently surveyed as a part of an economic development study conducted by the local government. For each of the 500 randomly selected households, the survey requested information on the following variables: family size, approximate location of the household within the neighborhood, an indication of whether those surveyed owned or rented their home, gross annual income of the first household wage earner, gross annual income of the second household wage earner (if applicable), monthly home mortgage or rent payment, average monthly expenditure on utilities, and the total indebtedness (excluding the value of a home mortgage) of the household. The data are in the file **P02_06.xlsx**.

a. Indicate the type of data for each of the eight variables included in this survey.

b. For each of the categorical variables in this survey, indicate whether the identified variable is *nominal* or *ordinal*. Explain your reasoning in each case.

c. Create a frequency table and histogram for each of the numerical variables in this data set. Indicate

whether each of these distributions is approximately *symmetric* or *skewed*. Which, if any, of these distributions are skewed to the right? Which, if any, are skewed to the left?

7. A real estate agent has gathered data on 150 houses that were recently sold in a suburban community. This data set includes observations for each of the following variables: the appraised value of each house (in thousands of dollars), the selling price of each house (in thousands of dollars), the size of each house (in hundreds of square feet), and the number of bedrooms in each house. The data are in the file **P02_07.xlsx**.

a. Indicate whether each of these four variables is *continuous* or *discrete*.

b. Create frequency tables and histograms for the appraised values and selling prices of the 150 houses included in the given sample. In what ways are these two distributions similar? In what ways are they different?

8. In a recent ranking of top graduate business schools in the United States published by *U.S. News & World Report*, data were provided on a number of attributes of recognized graduate programs. Specifically, the following variables were considered by *U.S. News & World Report* in establishing its overall ranking: each program's rating by peer institutions, each program's reputation rating by recruiters, the average undergraduate grade-point average for students enrolled in each program, the average GMAT score for students enrolled in each program, each program's acceptance rate, the average starting salary for recent graduates from each program, the proportion of graduates from each program who were employed at the time of graduation, the proportion of graduates from each program who were employed within three months of completing their graduate studies, the out-of-state tuition paid by affected full-time students in each program, and the total enrollment in each program. The data are listed in the file **P02_08.xlsx**.

a. Indicate the type of data for each of the 10 variables considered in the formulation of the overall ranking.

b. For each of the categorical variables in this set, indicate whether the identified variable is *nominal* or *ordinal*. Explain your reasoning in each case.

c. Create a frequency table and histogram for each of the numerical variables in this data set. Indicate whether each of these distributions is approximately *symmetric* or *skewed*. Which, if any, of these distributions are skewed to the right? Which, if any, are skewed to the left?

9. The operations manager of a toll booth, located at a major exit of a state turnpike, is trying to estimate the average number of vehicles that arrive at the toll booth during a 1-minute period during the peak of rush-hour traffic. To estimate this average throughput value, he records the number of vehicles that arrive at the toll booth over a 1-minute interval commencing at the same time for each of 365 normal weekdays. The data are in the file **P02_09.xlsx**.
   a. Create a histogram of the number of vehicles that arrive at this toll booth over the period of this study.
   b. Characterize this observed arrival distribution. Specifically, is it equally likely for smaller and larger numbers of vehicles to arrive during the chosen 1-minute period?

10. The SAT test score includes both verbal and mathematical components. The average scores on both the verbal and mathematical portions of the SAT have been computed for students taking this standardized test in each of the 50 states and the District of Columbia. Also, the proportion of high school graduates taking the test in each of the 50 states and the District of Columbia is recorded. The data are in the file **P02_10.xlsx**.
   a. Create a histogram for each of these three distributions of numerical values. Are these distributions essentially *symmetric* or are they *skewed*?
   b. Compare the distributions of the average verbal scores and average mathematical scores. In what ways are these two distributions similar? In what ways are they different?

11. In ranking metropolitan areas in the United States, David Savageau and Geoffrey Loftus, the authors of *Places Rated Almanac,* consider the average time (in minutes) it takes a citizen of each metropolitan area to travel to work and back home each day. The data are in the file **P02_11.xlsx**.
   a. Create a histogram for this distribution of daily commute times.
   b. Are shorter or longer average daily commute times generally more likely for citizens residing in these metropolitan areas?

12. The U.S. Department of Transportation regularly publishes the *Air Travel Consumer Report,* which provides a variety of performance measures of major U.S. commercial airlines. One dimension of performance reported is each airline's percentage of domestic flights arriving within 15 minutes of the scheduled arrival time at major airports throughout the country. The data are in the file **P02_12.xlsx**.
   a. Create a frequency table and histogram for each airline's distribution of percentage of on-time arrivals at the reporting airports. Indicate whether each distribution is skewed or not.
   b. Visually compare the histograms from part **a**. What general conclusions emerge from your visual comparisons regarding the on-time performance of these air carriers?

13. According to a survey conducted by Mercer Human Resource Consulting and published in *The Wall Street Journal* (May 2004), the typical salary of chief executive officers from 350 of the nation's largest U.S. public corporations increased by 3.8% to $950,000 in 2003. Furthermore, the typical annual bonus for CEOs increased by 6.7% to $1,100,000 in 2003. Given the data in **P02_13.xlsx**, create histograms to gain a clearer understanding of both the distributions of annual base salaries and of bonuses earned by the surveyed CEOs in fiscal 2003.

2.4 ANALYZING RELATIONSHIPS WITH SCATTERPLOTS

We are often interested in the relationship between two variables. A useful way to picture this relationship is to plot a point for each observation, where the coordinates of the point represent the values of the two variables. The resulting graph is called a **scatterplot**. By examining the scatter of points, we can usually see whether there is any relationship between the two variables and, if so, what type of relationship it is. We illustrate this method in the following example.

A **scatterplot** contains a point for each observation, based on the values of two selected variables. The resulting plot indicates the relationship, if any, between these two variables.

2.7 RELATIONSHIP BETWEEN INCOMES AND DOMESTIC GROSS FOR MOVIE STARS

The data in the **Movie Stars.xlsx** file may lead us to suppose that stars whose movies gross large amounts have the largest incomes. Is this actually true?

Objective   To use StatTools's Scatterplot procedure to illustrate the relationship between movie gross and income.

Solution

To analyze this, we plot each star's income on the vertical axis and the corresponding domestic gross on the horizontal axis. The resulting scatterplot appears in Figure 2.15. This graph can be obtained easily with StatTools. As with the histogram procedure, a StatTools data set must first be defined (through using the StatTools Data Set Manager). However, if you followed along with the histogram procedure for the movie stars data earlier in this chapter, a data set should already exist, and this initial step can be skipped. Then to create the scatterplot, select Scatterplot from the StatTools Summary Graphs dropdown, and fill in the resulting dialog box as in Figure 2.16, indicating that you want Income on the y-axis and Domestic Gross on the x-axis. (You can check or uncheck the Correlation option. We will discuss correlation in the next chapter.)

Figure 2.15

Scatterplot of Income versus Domestic Gross

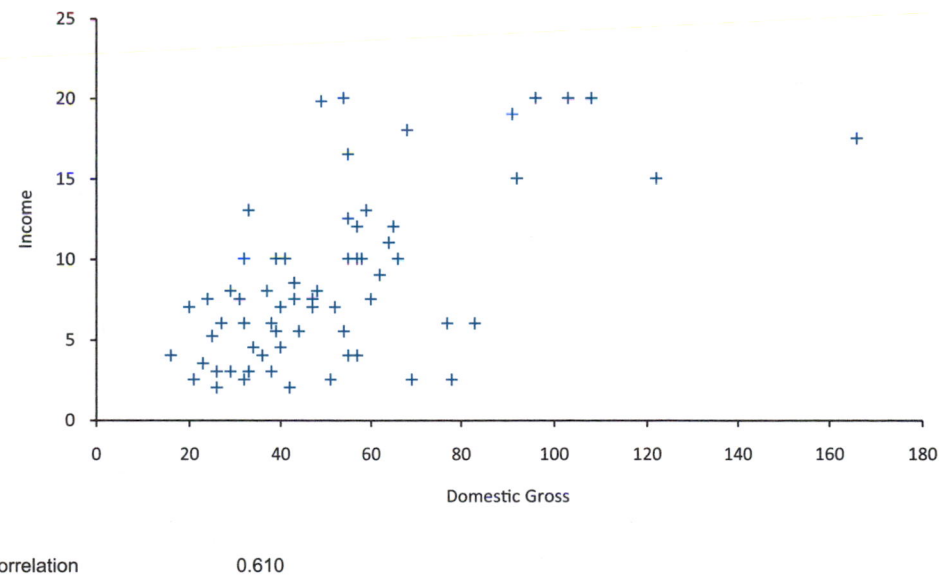

StatTools's scatterplot procedure automatically calculates the correlation between the two variables and shows it below the chart. Correlation will be explained in the next chapter.

Alternatively, you could create the graph with Excel's Chart Wizard, using an "X-Y" type of chart. However, we favor the ease of use of StatTools, along with its automatic formatting of the chart.

Figure 2.16

Scatterplot
Dialog Box

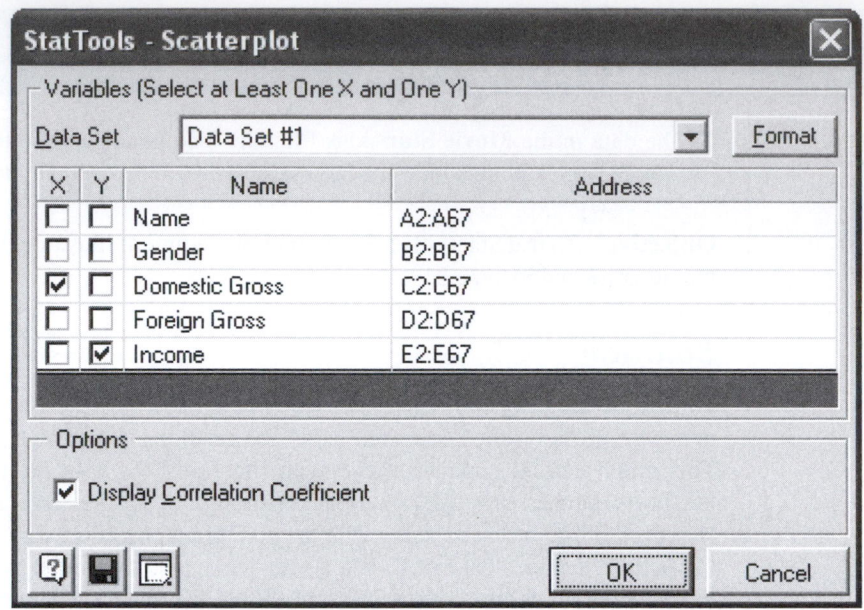

The message from Figure 2.15 is fairly clear. First, the points tend to move up and to the right. This means that stars in films with large domestic grosses tend to make the largest salaries. The correlation of 0.61 shown below the chart supports this conclusion. As we see in the next chapter, this implies a reasonably strong positive *linear* relationship between the two variables. ∎

For the sake of contrast, we now consider a relationship that is quite different.

EXAMPLE | **2.8 RELATIONSHIP BETWEEN SALES PRODUCTIVITY AND YEARS OF EXPERIENCE FOR SALESPEOPLE**

Suppose we are interested in the relationship between sales productivity and the number of years a salesperson has worked the territory. (The data, not shown here, are listed in the file **Sales Productivity.xlsx**.) Describe the relationship between sales and experience.

Objective To use a scatterplot to identify a nonlinear relationship between years of experience and sales.

Solution

Using StatTools's Scatterplot procedure, we construct the scatterplot shown in Figure 2.17. Note that as experience increases to around 14 years, sales increases, but at a decreasing rate. This indicates that there is a *nonlinear* relationship between sales and experience. Then beyond 14 years, additional experience appears to result in a sales decrease. Can you think of a reason why this might be the case? In Chapter 11 we learn how to estimate nonlinear relationships.

Figure 2.17

Scatterplot
Illustrating a
Nonlinear
Relationship

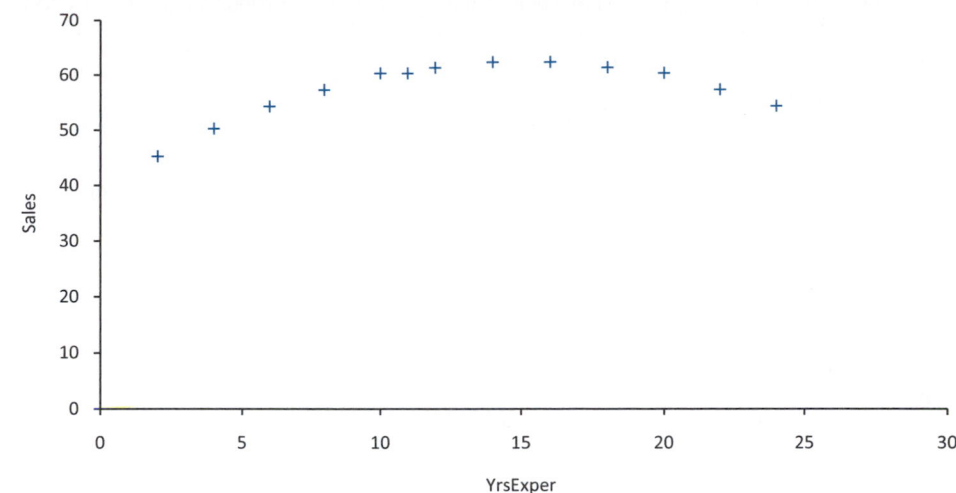

PROBLEMS

Level A

14. Explore the relationship between the selling prices and the appraised values of the 150 homes in the file **P02_07.xlsx** by generating a scatterplot.
    a. Is there evidence of a *linear* relationship between the selling price and appraised value? If so, characterize the relationship by indicating whether the relationship is positive or negative.
    b. For which of the two remaining variables, the size of the home or the number of bedrooms in the home, is the relationship with the home's selling price *stronger*? Justify your choice.

15. A human resources manager at Beta Technologies, Inc., is trying to determine the variable that best explains the variation in employee salaries for the data in the file **P02_01.xlsx**. Generate scatterplots to help this manager identify whether the employee's (a) gender, (b) age, (c) number of years of relevant work experience prior to employment at Beta, (d) number of years of employment at Beta, or (e) number of years of post-secondary education has the *strongest* linear relationship with annual salary.

16. Consider the enrollment data for *Business Week*'s top U.S. graduate business programs in the file **P02_03.xlsx**. Generate scatterplots to assess whether there is a systematic relationship between the total number of full-time students and each of the following: (a) the proportion of female students, (b) the proportion of minority students, and (c) the proportion of international students enrolled at these distinguished business schools.

17. What is the relationship between the number of short-term general hospitals and the number of general or family physicians in metropolitan areas? Explore this question by producing a scatterplot for these two variables using the data in the file **P02_17.xlsx**. Interpret your results.

18. Motorco produces electric motors for use in home appliances. One of the company's production managers is interested in examining the relationship between the dollars spent per month in inspecting finished motor products and the number of motors produced during that month that were returned by dissatisfied customers. He has collected the data in the file **P02_18.xlsx** to explore this relationship for the past 36 months. Create a scatterplot for these two variables and interpret it.

19. The *ACCRA Cost of Living Index* provides a useful and reasonably accurate measure of cost of living differences among many urban areas. Items on which the index is based have been carefully chosen to reflect the different categories of consumer expenditures. The

data are in the file **P02_19.xlsx**. Generate scatterplots to explore the relationship between the composite index and each of the various expenditure components.

   a. Which expenditure component has the *strongest* relationship with the composite index?

   b. Which expenditure component has the *weakest* relationship with the composite index?

20. Consider the proportions of U.S. domestic airline flights arriving within 15 minutes of the scheduled arrival times at the Philadelphia and Pittsburgh airports. The data are in the file **P02_20.xlsx**.

   a. Do you expect these two sets of performance measures to be *positively* or *negatively* associated with each other? Explain your reasoning.

   b. Compare your expectation to the actual relationship revealed by a scatterplot of the given data.

21. Examine the relationship between the average scores on the verbal and mathematical components of the SAT test across the 50 states and the District of Columbia by generating a scatterplot of the data in the file **P02_10.xlsx**. Also, explore the relationship between each of these variables and the proportion of high school graduates taking the SAT. Interpret each of these scatterplots.

22. Is there a strong relationship between a chief executive officer's annual compensation and her or his organization's recent profitability? Explore this question by creating relevant scatterplots for the survey data in the file **P02_13.xlsx**. In particular, create and interpret scatterplots for the change in the company's net income from 2002 to 2003 (see *Comp_NetInc03P* column) and the CEO's 2003 base salary, as well as

for the change in the company's net income from 2002 to 2003 and the CEO's 2003 bonus. Summarize your findings.

23. In response to a recent ranking of top graduate business schools in the United States published by *U.S. News & World Report,* the director of one of the recognized programs would like to know which variables are most strongly associated with a school's overall score. Ideally, she hopes to use an enhanced understanding of the ranking scheme to improve her program's score in future years and thus please both external and internal constituents. The data are in the file **P02_08.xlsx**.

   a. Use scatterplots to provide her with an indication of the measures that are most strongly related to the overall score in the *U.S. News & World Report* ranking.

   b. Generally, how can she and her administrative colleagues proceed to improve their program's ranking in future publications?

24. Consider the relationship between the size of the population and the average household income level for residents of U.S. towns. What do you expect the relationship between these two variables to be? Using the data in the file **P02_24.xlsx**, create and interpret the scatterplot for these two variables.

25. Based on the annual data in the file **P02_25.xlsx** from the U.S. Department of Agriculture, explore the relationship between the number of farms and the average size of a farm in the United States during the given time period. Specifically, create a scatterplot and interpret it.

2.5 TIME SERIES GRAPHS

When we are interested in forecasting future values of a time series, it is helpful to create a **time series graph**. This is essentially a scatterplot, with the time series variable on the vertical axis and time itself on the horizontal axis. To make patterns in the data more apparent, the points are usually connected with lines.

When we look at a time series graph, we usually look for two things:

■ Is there an observable trend? That is, do the values of the series tend to increase (an upward trend) or decrease (a downward trend) over time?

■ Is there a seasonal pattern? For example, do the peaks or valleys for quarterly data tend to occur every fourth observation? Or do soft drink sales peak in the summer months?

The following example illustrates the construction and interpretation of a time series graph.

2.9 TIME SERIES PATTERN OF QUARTERLY SALES REVENUE FOR FUN TOYS

The file **Toy Revenues.xlsx** lists quarterly sales revenues (in $ millions) for the Fun Toys Company during the years 2005 through 2008. The data are shown in Figure 2.18. Display these sales data in a time series graph and comment on whether trend and/or seasonality is present.

Figure 2.18

Revenue Data for Fun Toys

	A	B
1	Quarter	Revenue
2	Q1-2005	1026
3	Q2-2005	1056
4	Q3-2005	1182
5	Q4-2005	2861
6	Q1-2006	1172
7	Q2-2006	1249
8	Q3-2006	1346
9	Q4-2006	3402
10	Q1-2007	1286
11	Q2-2007	1317
12	Q3-2007	1449
13	Q4-2007	3893
14	Q1-2008	1462
15	Q2-2008	1452
16	Q3-2008	1631
17	Q4-2008	4200

You can probably spot the upward trend and the seasonal pattern in this data set by looking directly at the numbers in column B. However, such patterns are not usually so easy to detect, which is exactly why time series graphs are so useful.

Objective To use StatTools's Time Series Graph procedure to identify seasonality and an upward trend in sales.

Solution

To obtain the time series graph shown in Figure 2.19, first create a StatTools data set in the usual way (using the StatTools Data Set Manager), and then select the Time Series Graph option from Time Series and Forecasting on the StatTools ribbon to obtain the dialog box shown in Figure 2.20. This procedure allows us to plot one or more time series variables on the same chart. In this example there is only one variable, Revenue, to plot. We also have the option of selecting a variable for labeling the horizontal axis. Here we select Quarter (in column A) as the date variable. (If the "without Label" option is selected from the top drop-down list in the dialog box, the horizontal axis is labeled with consecutive integers, starting with 1.)

Figure 2.19   Time Series Graph of Revenue

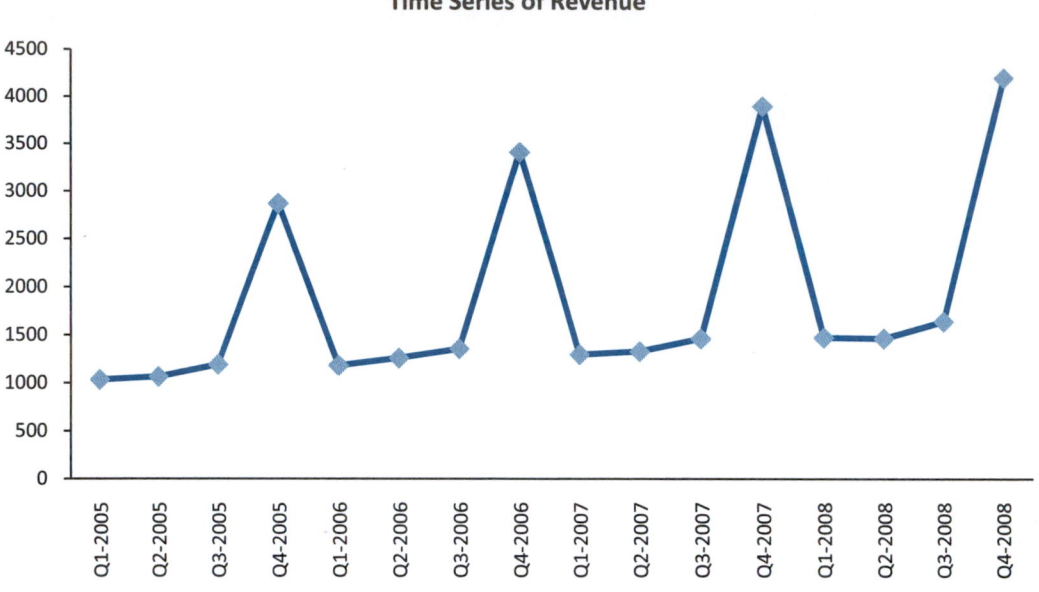

Time Series of Revenue

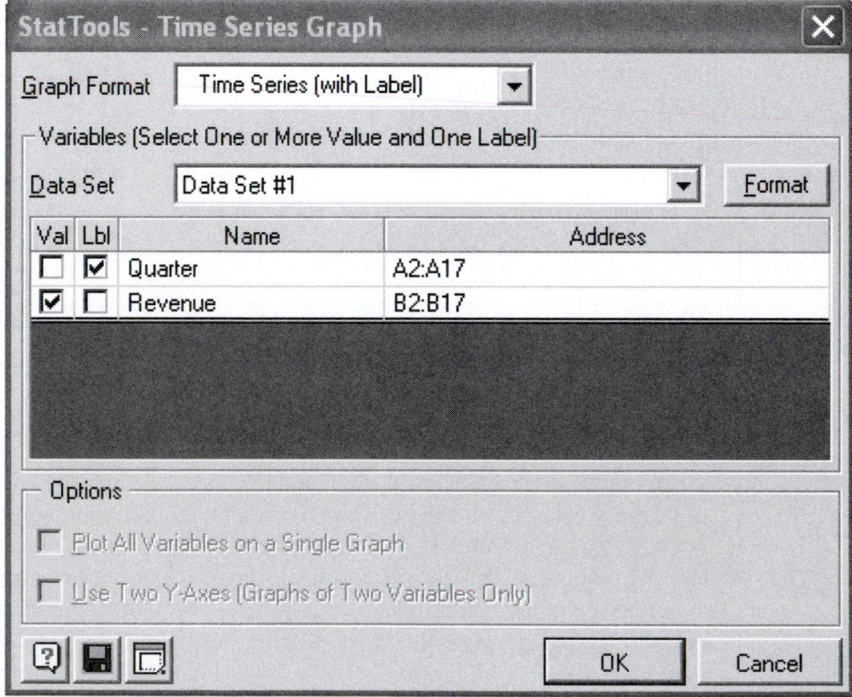

Figure 2.20

Time Series Graph
Dialog Box

The time series graph exhibits an obvious seasonal pattern. Fourth-quarter sales each year are much larger than the sales for the first three quarters. Of course, this is due to holiday sales. Focusing on the first three quarters of each successive year, we see a small upward trend in sales. This upward trend is also visible in the pattern of fourth quarters. The lesson from this graph is that if we want to forecast future quarterly sales for Fun Toys, we need to estimate the upward trend and seasonality of quarterly sales. ∎

Sometimes it is useful to plot two time series variables on the same chart to compare their time series behavior. This is simple to do in StatTools by selecting *two* time series variables to plot. However, if the data for these two variables are of completely different magnitudes, the graph will be dominated by the variable with the largest data; the graph of the other variable will barely be visible. Therefore, StatTools provides the option of using the *same* vertical scale for both variables or using *different* vertical scales. The following example illustrates the second option. (Note that this latter option is not available if you select to plot *more* than two series on the same chart.)

EXAMPLE | 2.10 TIME SERIES PATTERN OF SALES OF TWO PRODUCTS WITH DIFFERENT MAGNITUDES

Consider a company that sells two products. Product 1 is a much better seller than product 2. (See the file **Two Product Sales.xlsx**.) The monthly revenues from product 1 are typically above $100,000, whereas the revenues from product 2 are typically around $5000. How can the time series behavior of these revenues be shown on a single chart in a meaningful way?

Objective To illustrate how sales of two products with very different scales can be plotted in a single time series chart with StatTools.

Solution

The desired graph is shown in Figure 2.21. Note that it has two vertical scales. The scale on the left is appropriate for product 1, and the scale on the right is appropriate for product 2. We produced this chart in StatTools by selecting the Use Two Y-axes option in the Time Series Graph dialog box (see Figure 2.20). Note that this option is enabled only when you select exactly two variables to plot.

There are no obvious patterns (trend or seasonality) for the revenues of these two products. However, when they are both plotted on the same chart, we can see whether they move with one another. For example, in the last few months, revenues for product 1 increased, whereas revenues for product 2 decreased. Management might want to explore whether there is a reason for this.

Figure 2.21 Plotting Time Series Variables on Two Different Scales

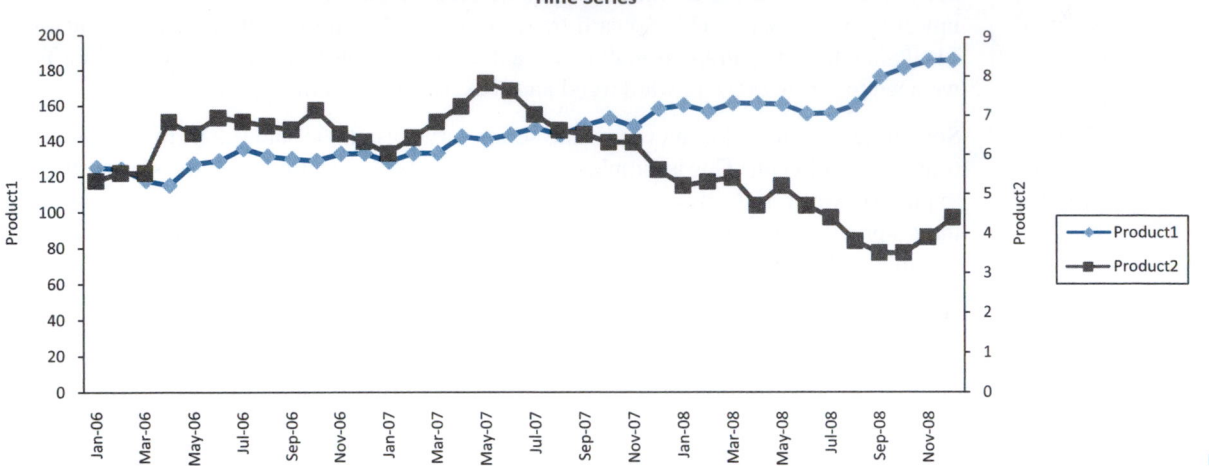

PROBLEMS

Level A

26. Consider the Consumer Price Index (CPI), which provides the annual percentage change in consumer prices. Annual data are in the file **P02_26.xlsx**.
   a. Create a time series graph for these data.
   b. What, if any, trend do you see in the CPI for the given time period?

27. Compare the trends of the percentage changes of annual new orders for all manufacturing, durable goods, and nondurable goods industries in the United States. Annual data are in the file **P02_27.xlsx**.
   a. Are the trends in these three times series similar?
   b. Can you explain the variation in each of these series over the given time period?

28. The Consumer Confidence Index (CCI) attempts to measure people's feelings about general business conditions, employment opportunities, and their own income prospects.
   a. Create a time series graph for the annual average values of the CCI for the data in the file **P02_28.xlsx**.
   b. Is it possible to say that U.S. consumers are more or less confident as time goes on?
   c. How would you explain recent variations in the overall trend of the CCI?

29. Consider the proportion of Americans under the age of 18 living below the poverty level for each of the years in the file **P02_29.xlsx**.

   a. Create and interpret a time series graph for these data.
   b. How successful have Americans been recently in their efforts to win "the war against poverty" for the nation's children?

30. Examine the trends in the annual average values of the discount rate, the federal funds rate, and the prime rate for the data in the file **P02_30.xlsx**. Can you discern any cyclical or other patterns in the times series graphs of these three key interest rates?

31. Consider the U.S. balance of trade for both goods and services (measured in millions of U.S. dollars) for the data in the file **P02_31.xlsx**.
   a. Create a times series graph for each of the three given time series.
   b. Characterize recent trends in the U.S. balance of trade figures using your time series graphs.

32. What is the recent trend in the number of mergers and acquisitions in the United States? Confirm your knowledge of this feature of U.S. business activity by creating a time series graph for the data in the file **P02_32.xlsx**.

33. The Federal Deposit Insurance Corporation provides annual data on the number of insured commercial banks and the number of commercial failures in the United States. The file **P02_33.xlsx** contains these data from 1980.
   a. Explore the relationship between these two time series by first creating and interpreting a

scatterplot. Is the revealed relationship consistent with your expectations?

    b. Create time series graphs for each of these variables and comment on recent trends in their behavior.

34. Is educational attainment in the United States on the rise? Explore this question by creating time series graphs for each of the variables in the file **P02_34.xlsx**. Comment on any observed trends in annual educational attainment of the general U.S. population over the given period.

35. Examine the trend of average annual interest rates on 30-year fixed mortgages in the United States for the data in the file **P02_35.xlsx**. What conclusion(s) can be drawn from an analysis of the time series graph generated from the given data?

36. What has happened to the total *number* and average *size* of farms in the United States during the second half of the 20th century? Answer this question by creating a time series graph of the data from the U.S. Department of Agriculture in the file **P02_25.xlsx**. Is the observed result consistent with your knowledge of the structural changes within the U.S. farming economy?

37. Consider the file **P02_37.xlsx**, which contains total monthly U.S. retail sales data for several recent years.

    a. Create a graph of this time series and comment on any observable trends, including a possible seasonal pattern, in the data.

    b. Based on your time series graph, make a qualitative projection about the total retail sales levels for the next 12 months. Specifically, in which months of the subsequent year do you expect retail sales levels to be *highest?* In which months of the subsequent year do you expect retail sales levels to be *lowest?*

38. Are there certain times of the year at which Americans typically purchase greater quantities of liquor? Investigate this question by creating a time series graph for the monthly retail sales data from U.S. liquor stores listed in the file **P02_38.xlsx**. Interpret the seasonal pattern revealed by your graph.

39. Examine the provided monthly time series data for total U.S. retail sales of building materials (which includes retail sales of building materials, hardware and garden supply stores, and mobile home dealers). The data are in the file **P02_39.xlsx**.

    a. Is there an observable trend in these data? That is, do the values of the series tend to increase or decrease over time?

    b. Is there a seasonal pattern in these data? If so, how do you explain this seasonal pattern?

40. In which months of the calendar year do U.S. gasoline service stations typically have their *lowest* retail sales levels? In which months of the calendar year do U.S. gasoline service stations typically have their *highest* retail sales levels? Create a time series graph for the monthly data in the file **P02_40.xlsx** to respond to these two questions.

2.6 EXPLORING DATA WITH PIVOT TABLES[2]

We now look at one of Excel's most powerful—and easy-to-use—tools, **pivot tables**. This tool provides an incredible amount of useful information about a data set. Pivot tables allow us to "slice and dice" data in a variety of ways. That is, they break the data down by categories so that we can see, for example, average sales by gender, by region of country, by time of day, or any combination of these. Sometimes pivot tables are used to simply display counts, such as the number of customers broken down by gender and region of country. These tables of counts, often called **contingency tables** or **crosstabs**, have been used by statisticians for years. However, Excel provides more variety and flexibility with its pivot tables than most statistical software packages have traditionally provided with their crosstabs options. In particular, crosstabs typically list only counts, whereas pivot tables can list counts, sums, averages, and other summary measures.[3]

It is easiest to understand pivot tables by means of examples, so we illustrate several possibilities in the following two examples. More examples of pivot tables appear in Section 3.9.

---

[2]The user interface for working with pivot tables has changed considerably in Excel 2007. Therefore, this section has been rewritten completely from the previous edition.

[3]To be fair, many other statistical software packages, such as SPSS and SAS, are now emulating Excel pivot tables.

2.11 EXAMINING CUSTOMER ORDERS AT ELECMART

The file **Elecmart.xlsx** (see Figure 2.22) contains data on 400 customer orders during a period of several months for Elecmart (a fictional company). This is a typical data set where pivot tables can be used to gain useful information. There are several categorical variables and several numeric variables. The categorical variables include the day of week, time of day, region of country, type of credit card used, gender of customer, and buy category of the customer (high, medium, or low) based on previous behavior. The date variable can also be treated as a categorical variable. The numeric variables include the number of items ordered, the total cost of the order, and the price of the highest-priced item purchased. The manager of Elecmart would like to summarize the data so that she can understand buying patterns of her customers. How can she use pivot tables to gain useful information?

Figure 2.22   Elecmart Data

	A	B	C	D	E	F	G	H	I	J
1	Date	Day	Time	Region	CardType	Gender	BuyCategory	ItemsOrdered	TotalCost	HighItem
2	6-Mar	Mon	Morning	West	ElecMart	Female	High	4	$136.97	$79.97
3	6-Mar	Mon	Morning	West	Other	Female	Medium	1	$25.55	$25.55
4	6-Mar	Mon	Afternoon	West	ElecMart	Female	Medium	5	$113.95	$90.47
5	6-Mar	Mon	Afternoon	NorthEast	Other	Female	Low	1	$6.82	$6.82
6	6-Mar	Mon	Afternoon	West	ElecMart	Male	Medium	4	$147.32	$83.21
7	6-Mar	Mon	Afternoon	NorthEast	Other	Female	Medium	5	$142.15	$50.90
8	7-Mar	Tues	Evening	West	Other	Male	Low	1	$18.65	$18.65
9	7-Mar	Tues	Evening	South	Other	Male	High	4	$178.34	$161.93
10	7-Mar	Tues	Evening	West	Other	Male	Low	2	$25.83	$15.91
11	8-Mar	Wed	Morning	MidWest	Other	Female	Low	1	$18.13	$18.13
12	8-Mar	Wed	Morning	NorthEast	ElecMart	Female	Medium	2	$54.52	$54.38
13	8-Mar	Wed	Afternoon	South	Other	Male	Medium	2	$61.93	$56.32
14	9-Mar	Thurs	Morning	NorthEast	ElecMart	Male	High	3	$147.68	$96.64
15	9-Mar	Thurs	Afternoon	NorthEast	Other	Male	Low	1	$27.24	$27.24
16	10-Mar	Fri	Morning	West	Other	Female	Low	3	$46.18	$44.27
17	10-Mar	Fri	Afternoon	West	Other	Male	Low	5	$107.44	$91.64

Objective   To use pivot tables to break down the customer order data by a number of categorical variables.

Solution

Pivot tables are perfect for breaking down data by categories. Many people call this "slicing and dicing" the data.

Before we dive into the details, we first preview the results we want to obtain. Pivot tables are useful for breaking down numeric variables by categories, or for counting observations in categories and possibly expressing the counts as percentages. So, for example, we might want to see how the average total cost for females differs from the similar average for males. Or we might simply want to see the percentage of the 400 sales made by females. Pivot tables allow us to find such averages and percentages *easily*.

We could undoubtedly find such averages or percentages without using pivot tables. For example, we could sort on gender and then find the average of the Female rows and the average of the Male rows. However, this takes time, and more complex breakdowns would be even more difficult and time-consuming. They are *all* easy and quick with pivot tables. Besides that, the resulting tables can be accompanied with corresponding charts that require virtually no extra effort to create. Pivot tables really are a manager's dream. Fortunately, with Excel they are also a manager's *reality*.[4]

[4]One recent Excel 2007 book by Bill Jelen (known as Mr. Excel) claims that although pivot tables have been around for years and represent Excel's arguably most powerful tool, they are used by only about 10% of business people. Fortunately, you will be in that 10%!

We begin by building a pivot table to find the sum of TotalCost broken down by time of day and region of country. Although we show this in a number of screen shots, just to help beginners get the knack of it, the process takes only a few seconds after you gain some experience with pivot tables.

To start, click on the PivotTable button from the Insert ribbon (see Figure 2.23). This produces the dialog box in Figure 2.24. The top section allows you to select a table range where the data set lives or an external data source. (We explore the latter option in Chapter 4.) The bottom section allows you to select the location where you want the results to be placed. If you start with the cursor inside the data set, then Excel's guess for the table range is usually correct, although you can override it if necessary. Make sure the range selected is A1:J401. This selected range should always include the variable names at the top of each column. Then click on OK. Note that with these settings, the pivot table will be placed in a new worksheet with a generic name such as Sheet1. We recommend that you rename it to something like Pivot Table 1.

This produces a blank pivot table, as shown in Figure 2.25. Also, assuming the cursor is within this blank pivot table, a PivotTable Tools tab is selected. This tab has two ribbons, Options and Design. The Options ribbon appears in Figure 2.26, and the Design ribbon appears in Figure 2.27. Each of these has a variety of buttons for manipulating pivot tables, some of which we will explore shortly. Finally, the Pivot Table Field List window in Figure 2.28 is visible. By default, it is docked at the right of the screen, but you can move it if you like.

Figure 2.23

PivotTable Button on the Insert Ribbon

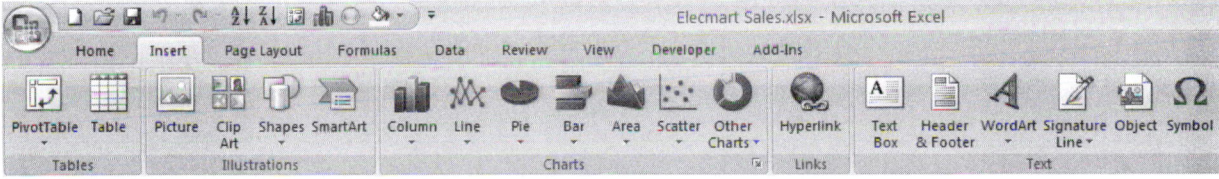

Figure 2.24

Create PivotTable Dialog Box

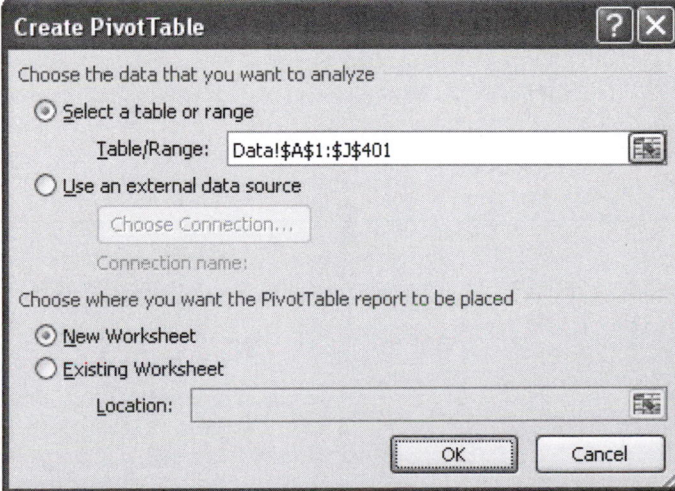

Figure 2.25

Blank Pivot Table

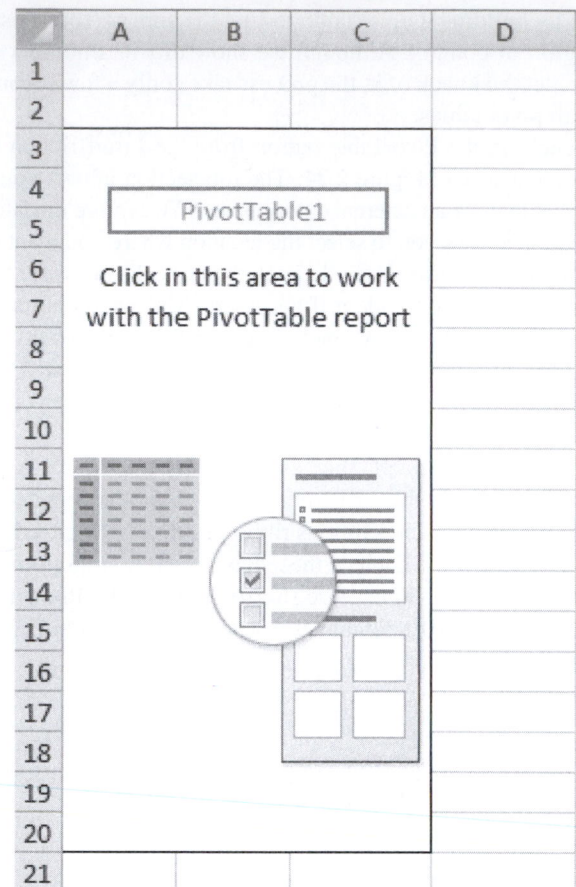

Figure 2.26

Pivot Table Options Ribbon

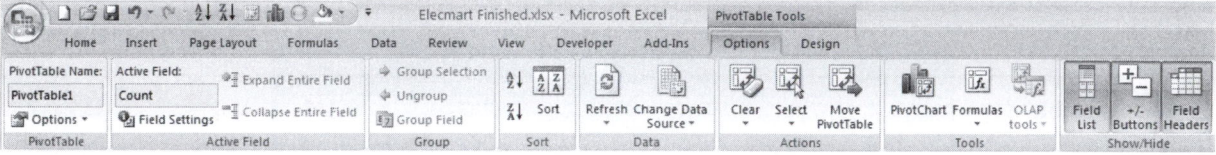

Figure 2.27

Pivot Table Design Ribbon

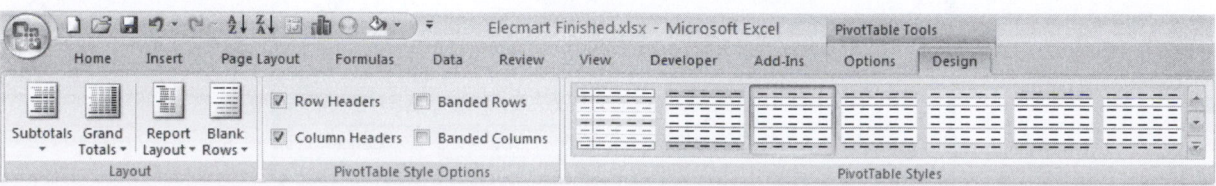

Figure 2.28

Pivot Table Field
List Window

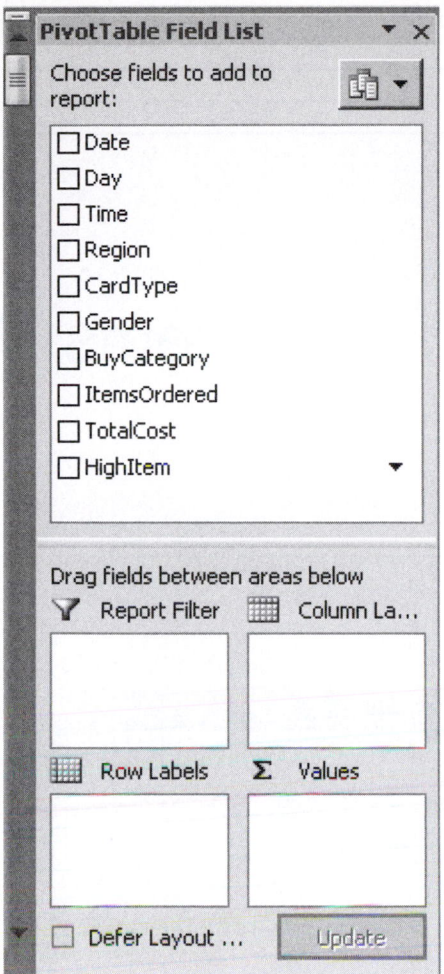

*The pivot table
ribbons and field
list window are
visible only when
your cursor is inside
the pivot table.*

Note that the two pivot table ribbons and the pivot table field list window are visible only when the active cell is within a pivot table. If you click outside the pivot table, say, in cell D1, all three of these will disappear. Don't worry. You can get them back by clicking anywhere inside the pivot table.

If you have used pivot tables in a previous version of Excel, the blank pivot table in Figure 2.25 will look strange. Here are two things to be aware of. First, if you open a file in the old .xls format (Excel 2003 or earlier) and go through the same steps as above, you will get an "old style" pivot table, as shown in Figure 2.29. Second, if you prefer the old style, especially for dragging and dropping, Excel 2007 lets you revert back to it. To do so, right-click on the pivot table, select Pivot Table Options, click on the Display tab, and check the Classic Pivot Table layout option (see Figure 2.30). You can use the new layout or the old one, whichever you prefer. We were always perfectly happy with the old layout, but Microsoft evidently got enough complaints from users that they revamped it to make it more user friendly.

The Field List window indicates that a pivot table has four areas. These are for Report Filter, Row Labels, Column Labels, and Values. They correspond to the four areas in Figure 2.29 where you can put fields. Here is the correspondence:

- Page Fields correspond to Report Filters
- Row Fields correspond to Row Labels

Figure 2.29

Old-Style Blank
Pivot Table

*The pivot table "look"
has changed consider-
ably from previous
versions of Excel, but
the functionality is
virtually the same.*

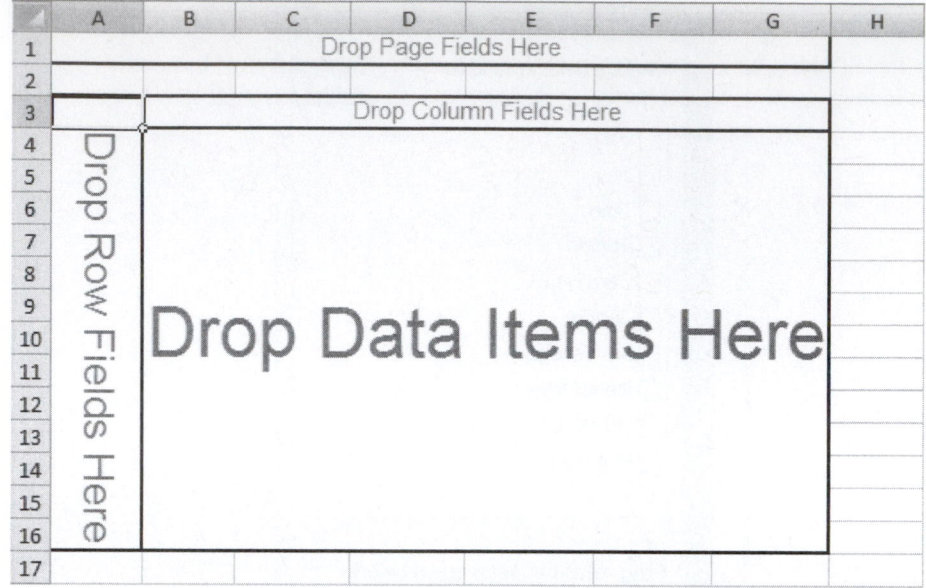

Figure 2.30

Switching to Classic
Pivot Table Layout

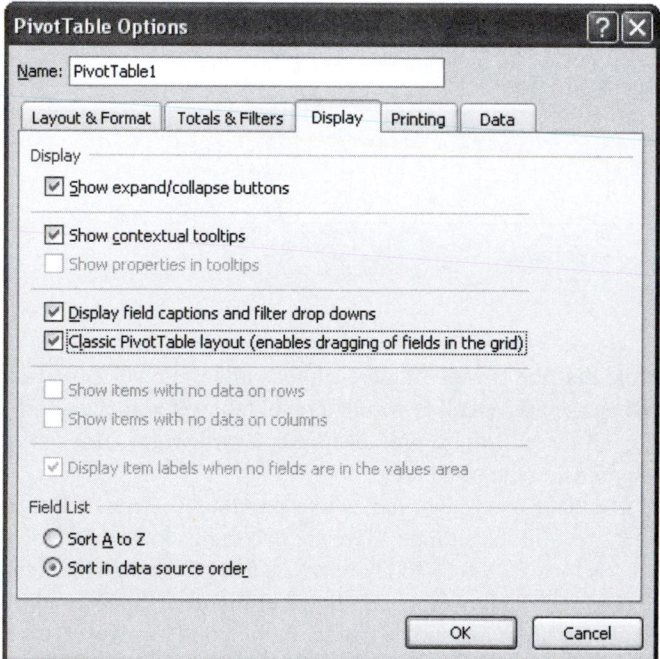

- Column Fields correspond to Column Labels
- Data Fields correspond to Values

Essentially, a Row field has categories that go down the left side of a pivot table, a Column field has categories that go across the top of a pivot table, a Page field lets you filter the whole pivot table by its categories, and a Data field includes the data you want to summarize. Typically (but not always), you will place categorical variables in the Page, Row, and/or Column areas, and you will place numeric variables in the Data area.

Figure 2.31

Sum of TotalCost by
Time and Region
(Compact Layout)

	A	B	C
1			
2			
3	Row Labels ▼	Sum of TotalCost	
4	⊟Afternoon	**24265.6**	
5	MidWest	3187.16	
6	NorthEast	8159.78	
7	South	5729.72	
8	West	7188.94	
9	⊟Evening	**18834.3**	
10	MidWest	2552.89	
11	NorthEast	5941.49	
12	South	3864.12	
13	West	6475.8	
14	⊟Morning	**18427.31**	
15	MidWest	3878.22	
16	NorthEast	5084.57	
17	South	3835.86	
18	West	5628.66	
19	**Grand Total**	**61527.21**	
20			

In the present example, select Time and Region for the Row fields and TotalCost for the Data field. To do this, check the Time, Region, and TotalCost boxes in the upper half of the Field List window. With no extra work whatsoever, you get the pivot table in Figure 2.31. It shows the sum of TotalCost, broken down by time of day and region of country. For example, the total cost of orders in the morning in the South was $3,835.86, and the total cost of orders in the morning (over all regions) was $18,427.31.

Excel uses two rules when you check variables in the top of the Field List window:

1 When you check a nonnumeric (text) variable or a date variable in the field list, it is added to the Row Labels area.

2 When you check a numeric variable in the field list, it is added to the Values area, and it is summarized with the Sum function.

This is exactly what happened when you checked Time, Region, and TotalCost. However, this is just the beginning. With very little work, you can do a lot more. Some of the possibilities are explained in the remainder of this example.

First, however, we discuss the new look of pivot tables in Excel 2007. Notice that the pivot table in Figure 2.31 has *both* row fields, Time and Region, in column A. This wasn't possible in old-style pivot tables, where the two row fields would have been in separate columns. Microsoft decided to offer this new layout because of its clean, streamlined look. In fact, you can now choose from three layouts: Compact, Outline, or Tabular. These are available from the Report Layout dropdown in the Layout group on the Design ribbon. When you create a pivot table (in an .xlsx file), you get the compact layout by default. If you'd rather have the tabular or outline layout, it is easy to switch to them. In particular, the tabular layout, shown in Figure 2.32, is closer to what you're used to in previous versions of Excel. (Outline layout, not shown here, is very similar to tabular layout, except for the placement of its subtotals.)

One significant advantage to using tabular (or outline) layout over compact layout is that you can see which fields are in the row and column areas. Take another look at the

Excel 2007 offers three different layout for pivot tables, but the differences are relatively minor. Ultimately, it's a matter of taste.

Figure 2.32

Sum of TotalCost by
Time and Region
(Tabular Layout)

	A	B	C	D
1				
2				
3	**Time** ▾	**Region** ▾	**Sum of TotalCost**	
4	⊟ **Afternoon**	MidWest	3187.16	
5		NorthEast	8159.78	
6		South	5729.72	
7		West	7188.94	
8	**Afternoon Total**		**24265.6**	
9	⊟ **Evening**	MidWest	2552.89	
10		NorthEast	5941.49	
11		South	3864.12	
12		West	6475.8	
13	**Evening Total**		**18834.3**	
14	⊟ **Morning**	MidWest	3878.22	
15		NorthEast	5084.57	
16		South	3835.86	
17		West	5628.66	
18	**Morning Total**		**18427.31**	
19	**Grand Total**		**61527.21**	
20				

pivot table in Figure 2.31. It is pretty obvious that categories such as afternoon and morning have to do with time of day, and that categories such as Midwest and South have to do with region of country. However, there are no labels that explicitly name the row fields. In contrast, the tabular layout in Figure 2.32 names them explicitly. For this reason, all screen shots of pivot tables from here on will show tabular layout.

Hiding Categories

The pivot table in Figure 2.31 shows all times of day for all regions, but this is not necessary. You can filter out any of the times or regions you don't want to see. To understand how this works, make sure the Options ribbon is visible. In the Active Field group, you will notice that one of the fields is designated as the active field. The active field corresponds to the location of your cursor. If your cursor is on a Time category, such as Evening, then Time is the active field. If your cursor is on a Region category such as NorthEast, then Region is the active field. If your cursor is on any of the numbers, then Sum of TotalCost is the active field.

Once you understand the active field concept, then the way Excel implements filtering makes sense. If Time is the active field and you click on the Row Labels dropdown, you see the dialog box in Figure 2.33. To see data only for Afternoon and Morning, say, uncheck the Select All box (to clear all boxes) and then check the Afternoon and Morning boxes. Similarly, if Region is the active field and you click on the Row Labels dropdown, you can check which regions you want to filter on. (If you're in tabular layout, it's more straightforward, because each row field then has its own dropdown.) For example, the pivot table in Figure 2.34 is obtained by filtering out the Evening and NorthEast categories. Note how the filter symbols appear in row 3 to indicate that some categories have been filtered out. Also, note that the updated subtotals for Morning and Afternoon and the updated grand total for all categories do *not* include the hidden categories.

Figure 2.33

Filtering on Time

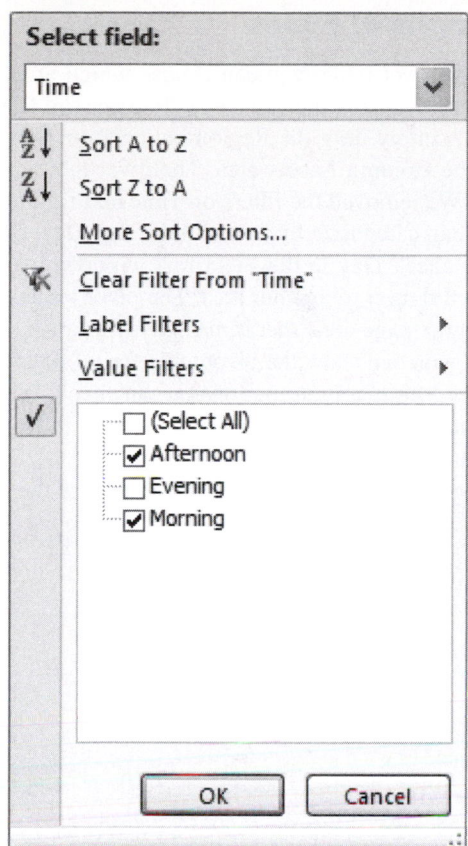

Figure 2.34

Pivot Table with
Hidden Categories

	A	B	C	D
1				
2				
3	**Time** 🔽	**Region** 🔽	**Sum of TotalCost**	
4	⊟**Afternoon**	MidWest	3187.16	
5		South	5729.72	
6		West	7188.94	
7	**Afternoon Total**		**16105.82**	
8	⊟**Morning**	MidWest	3878.22	
9		South	3835.86	
10		West	5628.66	
11	**Morning Total**		**13342.74**	
12	**Grand Total**		**29448.56**	
13				

Changing Locations of Fields

Changing the locations of fields in pivot tables has always been easy, and it continues to be easy in Excel 2007. We tend to favor dragging, but you can experiment with the various options.

Starting with the current pivot table, you can choose which area to place either Time or Region in; it does not *have* to be in the Row area. To place the Region variable in the column area, for example, simply drag the Region button from the Row Labels area of the Field List window to the Column Labels area. The pivot table changes automatically, as shown in Figure 2.35. (We removed the filters on Time and Region.)

Alternatively, you can categorize by a third field, say, Day, and locate it in a different area. As before, if you check Day in the Field List window, it goes to the Row area by default, but you can then drag it to another area. The pivot table in Figure 2.36 shows the result of placing Day in the page area, that is, using Day as a Report Filter. By clicking on the dropdown in row 1, you can show the pivot table for all days or any particular day. In fact, there is now a Show Multiple Items option you can check. We checked this option and then selected Friday and Saturday to obtain the pivot table in Figure 2.36. It reports data only for Fridays and Saturdays.

This ability to categorize by multiple fields and rearrange the fields as you like is a big reason why pivot tables are so powerful, useful—and easy to use.[5]

Figure 2.35

Putting Region in the Column Area

	A	B	C	D	E	F	G
1							
2							
3	**Sum of TotalCost**	**Region** ▾					
4	**Time** ▾	**MidWest**	**NorthEast**	**South**	**West**	**Grand Total**	
5	Afternoon	3187.16	8159.78	5729.72	7188.94	24265.6	
6	Evening	2552.89	5941.49	3864.12	6475.8	18834.3	
7	Morning	3878.22	5084.57	3835.86	5628.66	18427.31	
8	**Grand Total**	9618.27	19185.84	13429.7	19293.4	61527.21	
9							

Figure 2.36

Putting Day in the Page Area (and Filtering on Day)

	A	B	C	D	E	F	G
1	Day	(Multiple Items) ▾					
2							
3	**Sum of TotalCost**	**Region** ▾					
4	**Time** ▾	**MidWest**	**NorthEast**	**South**	**West**	**Grand Total**	
5	Afternoon	1978.13	4230.5	1426.74	2818.51	10453.88	
6	Evening	1358.56	2584.97	665.98	1334.55	5944.06	
7	Morning	1786.67	2253.85	1507.69	2406.81	7955.02	
8	**Grand Total**	5123.36	9069.32	3600.41	6559.87	24352.96	
9							

[5]Some people refer to switching field locations (Region to row, Time to column, say) as pivoting. This explains the origin of the term *pivot table*.

Changing Field Settings

Depending on which field is the active field, you can change various settings in a Field Settings dialog box. You can get to this dialog box in at least two ways. First, there is a Field Setting button in the Active Field group on the Options ribbon. Second, you can right-click on any of the pivot table cells and select the Field Settings item. The field settings are particularly useful for fields in the Data area, as we now explain.

For example, right-click on any number in the pivot table in Figure 2.36 and select Value Field Settings to obtain the dialog box in Figure 2.37. This allows you to choose which way you want to summarize the TotalCost variable—by Sum, Average, Count, or several others. You can also click on the Number Format button to choose from the usual number formatting options, and you can click on the Show Values As tab to display the data in various ways (more on this later). If you choose Average and format as currency with two decimals, the resulting pivot table appears as in Figure 2.38. Now each number is the average of TotalCost for all orders in its category combination. For example, the average of TotalCost for all Friday and Saturday morning orders in the South is $107.69, and the average of *all* Friday and Saturday orders in the South is $109.10.

The key to summarizing the data the way you want it summarized is the Value Field Settings dialog box. Get used to it, because you will use it often.

Figure 2.37

Value Field Settings
Dialog Box

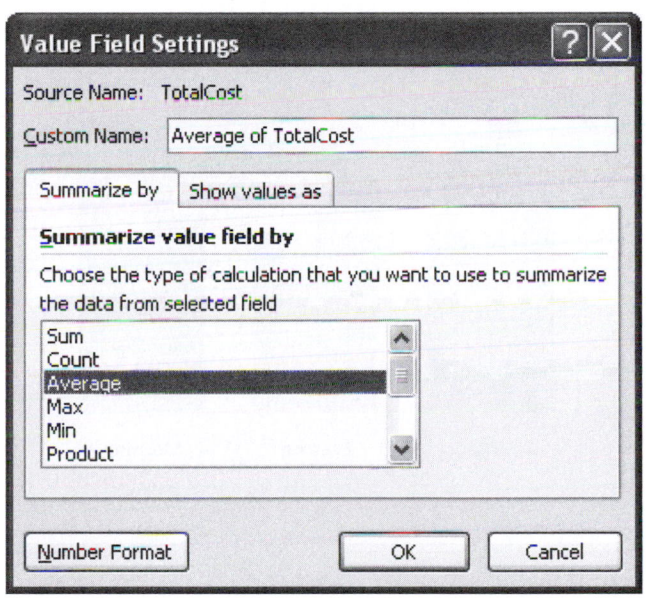

Figure 2.38

Pivot Table with Average of TotalCost

	A	B	C	D	E	F	G
1	Day	(Multiple Items)					
2							
3	Average of TotalCost	Region					
4	Time	MidWest	NorthEast	South	West	Grand Total	
5	Afternoon	$141.30	$192.30	$118.90	$156.58	$158.39	
6	Evening	$150.95	$161.56	$95.14	$111.21	$135.09	
7	Morning	$127.62	$150.26	$107.69	$150.43	$134.83	
8	**Grand Total**	**$138.47**	**$171.12**	**$109.10**	**$142.61**	**$144.10**	
9							

Creating Pivot Charts

Pivot charts are a wonderful extension of pivot tables. They not only "tell the story" graphically, but they update automatically when the pivot tables change.

It is easy to accompany pivot tables with pivot charts. These charts are not just the typical Excel charts; they adapt automatically to the underlying pivot table. If you make a change to the pivot table, such as pivoting the Row and Column fields, the pivot chart makes the same change automatically. To create a pivot chart, click anywhere inside the pivot table, select the PivotChart button on the Options ribbon (see Figure 2.26), and select a chart type. That's all there is to it! The resulting pivot chart (using the default column bar chart option) for the pivot table in Figure 2.38 appears in Figure 2.39. If you decide to pivot the Row and Column fields, the pivot chart changes automatically, as shown in Figure 2.40. Note that the categories on the horizontal axis are based on the Row field, and the categories in the legend are based on the Column field.

Note that when you activate a pivot chart, the PivotTable Tools tab changes to PivotChart Tools. This tab includes four ribbons for manipulating pivot charts: Design, Layout, Format, and Analyze (see Figure 2.41). There is not enough space here to discuss the many options on these ribbons. We simply state that they are intuitive and easy to use. As usual, don't be afraid to experiment.

Figure 2.39

Pivot Chart Based on Pivot Table

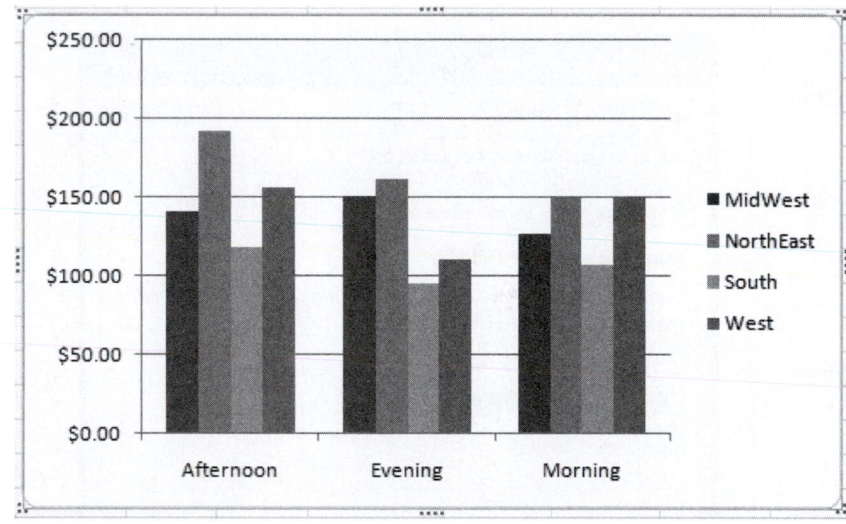

Figure 2.40

Pivot Chart after Pivoting Row and Column Fields

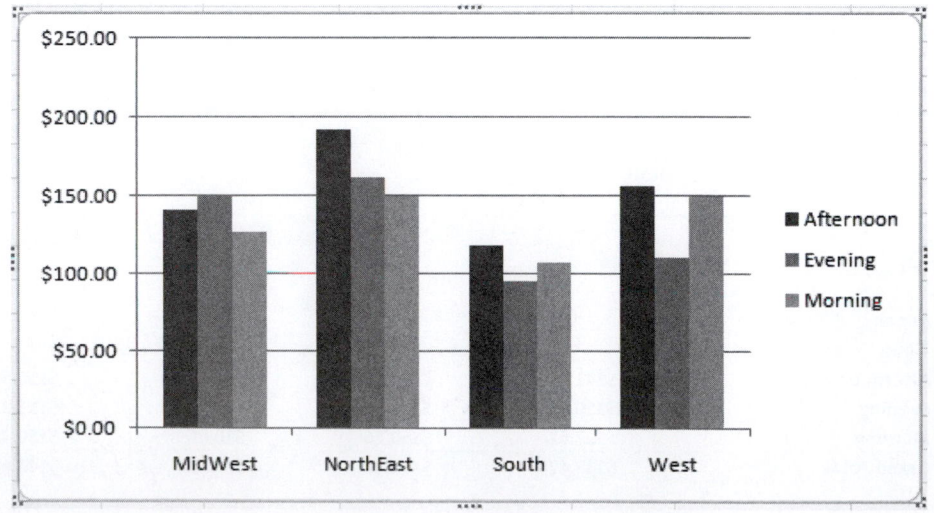

Figure 2.41

PivotChart Tools Ribbons

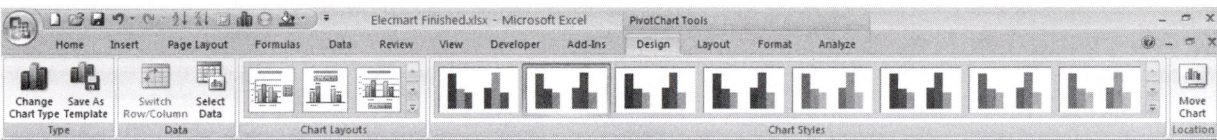

Multiple Variables in the Data Area

More than a single variable can be placed in the Data area. Alternatively, a given variable in the Data area can be summarized by more than one summarizing function. This can make for a rather busy pivot table, so we indicate our favorite way of doing it. Starting with the pivot table in Figure 2.38, drag the TotalCost item in the top of the Field List window (the item that's already checked) to the Values area. The bottom half of the Field List window should now appear as in Figure 2.42, and the pivot table should now appear as in Figure 2.43. Note in particular the Values button in the Column Labels area. This button controls the placement of the data in the pivot table. You have a number of options for this button: (1) leave it where it is, (2) drag it above the Time button, (3) drag it to the Row Labels area, below the Region button, or (4) drag it to the Row Labels area, above the Region button. You can experiment with these options, but we tend to prefer option (2), which leads to the pivot table in Figure 2.44.

In a similar manner, you can experiment with the buttons in the Values area. However, the effect here is less striking. If you drag the Sum of TotalCost button *above* the Average

Figure 2.42

Field List Window with Two Data Fields

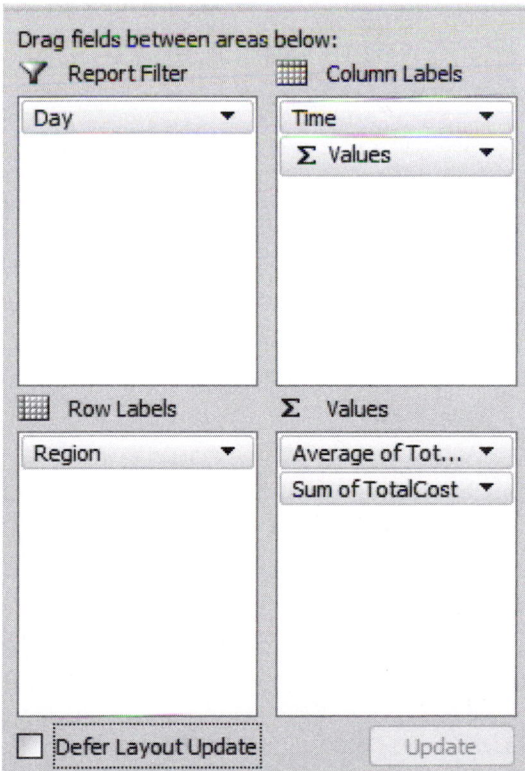

Figure 2.43

Pivot Table with Two Data Variables

	A	B	C	D	E	F	G	H	I	J
1	Day	(Multiple Items)								
2										
3		Time	Values							
4		Afternoon		Evening		Morning		Total Average of TotalCost	Total Sum of TotalCost	
5	Region	Average of TotalCost	Sum of TotalCost	Average of TotalCost	Sum of TotalCost	Average of TotalCost	Sum of TotalCost			
6	MidWest	$141.30	$1,978.13	$150.95	$1,358.56	$127.62	$1,786.67	$138.47	$5,123.36	
7	NorthEast	$192.30	$4,230.50	$161.56	$2,584.97	$150.26	$2,253.85	$171.12	$9,069.32	
8	South	$118.90	$1,426.74	$95.14	$665.98	$107.69	$1,507.69	$109.10	$3,600.41	
9	West	$156.58	$2,818.51	$111.21	$1,334.55	$150.43	$2,406.81	$142.61	$6,559.87	
10	Grand Total	$158.39	$10,453.88	$135.09	$5,944.06	$134.83	$7,955.02	$144.10	$24,352.96	
11										

Figure 2.44

Rearranged Pivot Table with Two Data Variables

	A	B	C	D	E	F	G	H	I	J
1	Day	(Multiple Items)								
2										
3		Values		Time						
4		Average of TotalCost			Sum of TotalCost			Total Average of TotalCost	Total Sum of TotalCost	
5	Region	Afternoon	Evening	Morning	Afternoon	Evening	Morning			
6	MidWest	$141.30	$150.95	$127.62	$1,978.13	$1,358.56	$1,786.67	$138.47	$5,123.36	
7	NorthEast	$192.30	$161.56	$150.26	$4,230.50	$2,584.97	$2,253.85	$171.12	$9,069.32	
8	South	$118.90	$95.14	$107.69	$1,426.74	$665.98	$1,507.69	$109.10	$3,600.41	
9	West	$156.58	$111.21	$150.43	$2,818.51	$1,334.55	$2,406.81	$142.61	$6,559.87	
10	Grand Total	$158.39	$135.09	$134.83	$10,453.88	$5,944.06	$7,955.02	$144.10	$24,352.96	
11										

Figure 2.45

Another Rearrangement of the Pivot Table with Two Data Variables

	A	B	C	D	E	F	G	H	I	J
1	Day	(Multiple Items)								
2										
3		Values		Time						
4		Sum of TotalCost			Average of TotalCost			Total Sum of TotalCost	Total Average of TotalCost	
5	Region	Afternoon	Evening	Morning	Afternoon	Evening	Morning			
6	MidWest	$1,978.13	$1,358.56	$1,786.67	$141.30	$150.95	$127.62	$5,123.36	$138.47	
7	NorthEast	$4,230.50	$2,584.97	$2,253.85	$192.30	$161.56	$150.26	$9,069.32	$171.12	
8	South	$1,426.74	$665.98	$1,507.69	$118.90	$95.14	$107.69	$3,600.41	$109.10	
9	West	$2,818.51	$1,334.55	$2,406.81	$156.58	$111.21	$150.43	$6,559.87	$142.61	
10	Grand Total	$10,453.88	$5,944.06	$7,955.02	$158.39	$135.09	$134.83	$24,352.96	$144.10	
11										

of TotalCost button, the effect is simply to switch the ordering of these summaries in the pivot table, as shown in Figure 2.45.

Summarizing by Count

The variable in the Data area, whatever it is, can be summarized by the Count function. This is useful when you want to know, for example, how *many* of the orders were placed by females in the South. When summarizing by Count, the key is to understand that the actual variable placed in the Data area is irrelevant, so long as you summarize it by the Count function. To illustrate, start with the pivot table in Figure 2.45, where TotalCost is summarized with the Sum function only (that is, get rid of the Average measure). Now right-click on any number in the pivot table, select Value Field Settings, and select the Count function (see Figure 2.46). The default Custom Name you will see in this dialog box, Count of TotalCost, is misleading, because TotalCost has nothing to do with the counts obtained. Therefore, we like to change this Custom Name label to Count, as shown. The resulting pivot table, with values formatted as Number with zero decimals, appears in Figure 2.47. For example, 27 of the 400 orders were placed in the morning in the South, and 115 of the 400 orders were placed in the NorthEast. (Do you now see why the counts have nothing to do with TotalCost?) This type of pivot table, with counts for various categories, has typically been called a *crosstabs* in the statistics literature.

When data are summarized by Count, there are a number of ways they can be displayed. The pivot table in Figure 2.47 shows "raw counts." Depending on the type of information you want, it might be more useful to display the counts as percentages. Three

Counts can be displayed in a number of ways. You should choose the way that best answers the question you are asking.

Figure 2.46

Field Settings Dialog Box with Count Selected

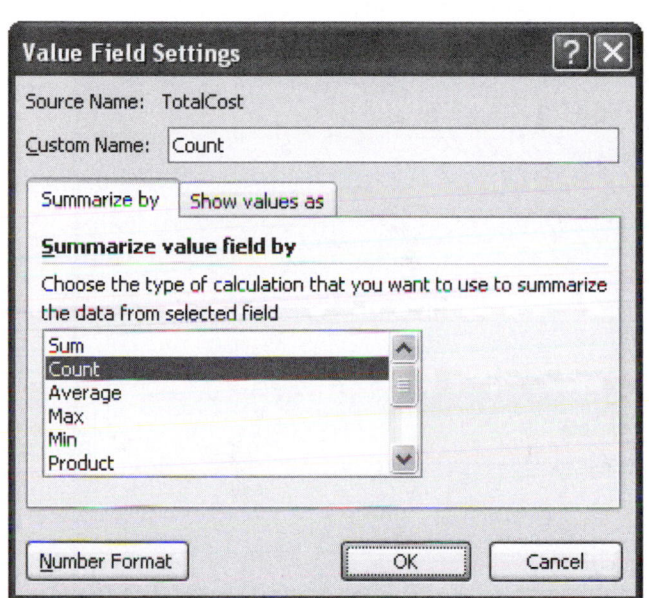

Figure 2.47

Pivot Table with Counts

	A	B	C	D	E	F
1						
2						
3	Count	Time ▾				
4	Region ▾	Afternoon	Evening	Morning	Grand Total	
5	MidWest	26	19	26	71	
6	NorthEast	48	34	33	115	
7	South	39	27	27	93	
8	West	41	42	38	121	
9	**Grand Total**	**154**	**122**	**124**	**400**	
10						

particular options are typically chosen: as percentages of total, as percentages of row, and as percentages of column. When shown as percentages of total, the percentages in the table sum to 100%; when shown as percentages of row, the percentages in *each* row sum to 100%; and when shown as percentages of column, the percentages in *each* column sum to 100%. Each of these options can be useful, depending on the question you are trying to answer. For example, if you want to know whether the daily pattern of orders varies from region to region, showing the counts as percentages of column is useful so that you can compare columns. But if you want to see whether the regional ordering pattern varies by time of day, showing the counts as percentages of row is useful so that you can compare rows.

To display the counts as percentages of some type, display the Value Field Settings dialog box (remember how?), select the Show Values As tab, and select the appropriate option (see Figure 2.48). The resulting pivot table and corresponding pivot chart appear in Figure 2.49. Apparently, the pattern of regional orders varies somewhat by time of day.

Sometimes it is useful to see the raw counts *and* the percentages. This can be done easily by dragging any variable to the Data area, summarizing it by Count, and displaying

Figure 2.48

Field Settings Dialog Box with Show Values As Options

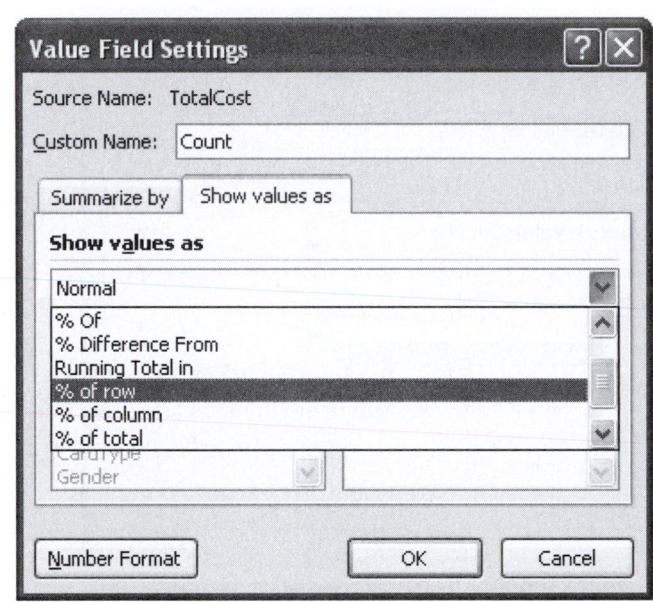

Figure 2.49

Pivot Table and Pivot Chart with Counts As Percentages of Rows

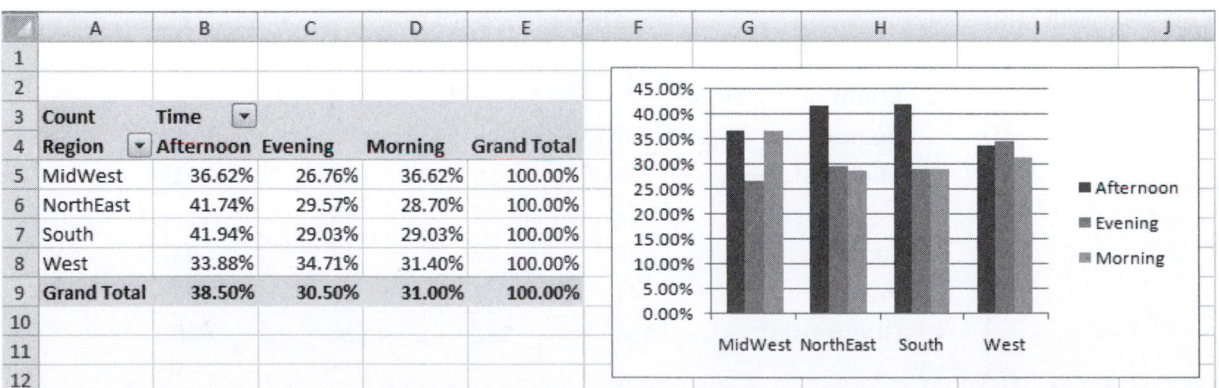

Figure 2.50

Pivot Table with Percentages of Rows and Raw Counts

	A	B	C	D	E	F	G	H	I	J
1										
2										
3		Time	Values							
4		Afternoon		Evening		Morning		Total Pct of Row	Total Raw Count	
5	Region	Pct of Row	Raw Count	Pct of Row	Raw Count	Pct of Row	Raw Count			
6	MidWest	36.62%	26	26.76%	19	36.62%	26	100.00%	71	
7	NorthEast	41.74%	48	29.57%	34	28.70%	33	100.00%	115	
8	South	41.94%	39	29.03%	27	29.03%	27	100.00%	93	
9	West	33.88%	41	34.71%	42	31.40%	38	100.00%	121	
10	Grand Total	38.50%	154	30.50%	122	31.00%	124	100.00%	400	
11										

it as "Normal." Figure 2.50 shows one possibility, where we have changed the Custom Names of the two Count variables to make them more meaningful.

Grouping

Categories in a Row or Column variable can be grouped. This is especially useful when a Row or Column variable has many distinct values. Because a pivot table creates a row or column for each distinct value, the results can be unwieldy. We present two possibilities. First, suppose you want to break Sum of TotalCost down by Date. Starting with a blank pivot table, check the Date and TotalCost variables in the pivot table Field List window. This creates a separate row for each distinct date in the data set—112 separate dates! This is too much detail, so it is useful to group on the Date variable. To do so, right-click on any date in column A and select the Group item. (Alternatively, Group options are available on the Options ribbon.) Accept the default selections in the Grouping dialog box (see Figure 2.51). The resulting pivot table appears in Figure 2.52.

As a second possibility for grouping, suppose you want to see how the Average of TotalCost varies by the amount of the highest priced item in the order. Place TotalCost in

Figure 2.51

Grouping Dialog Box

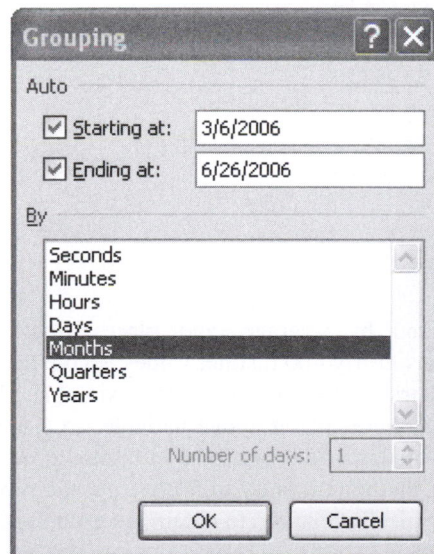

Figure 2.52

Pivot Table after Grouping by Month

	A	B	C
1			
2			
3	Date ▾	Sum of TotalCost	
4	Mar	$9,383.26	
5	Apr	$14,589.91	
6	May	$19,468.11	
7	Jun	$18,085.93	
8	**Grand Total**	**$61,527.21**	
9			

Figure 2.53

Grouping Dialog Box for a Non-Date Variable

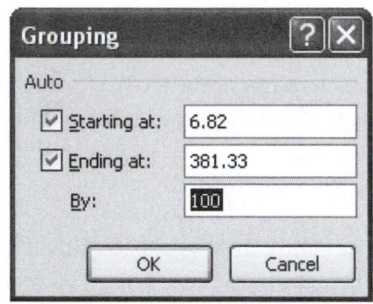

Figure 2.54

Pivot Table after Grouping on HighItem

	A	B	C
1			
2			
3	**HighItem** ▾	**Sum of TotalCost**	
4	6.82-56.82	$7,496.40	
5	56.82-106.82	$22,903.94	
6	106.82-156.82	$11,225.99	
7	156.82-206.82	$9,634.78	
8	206.82-256.82	$3,891.15	
9	256.82-306.82	$2,960.29	
10	306.82-356.82	$2,169.15	
11	356.82-406.82	$1,245.51	
12	**Grand Total**	**$61,527.21**	
13			

the Data area, summarized by Average, and place HighItem in the Row area. Unfortunately, HighItem has nearly 400 distinct values, so the resulting pivot table is virtually worthless. Again, the trick is to group on the Row variable. This time, however, there are no natural groupings as there are for a date variable, so it is up to you to create the groupings. Excel provides a suggestion, as shown in Figure 2.53, but you can override it. For example, by changing the bottom entry to 50, we get the pivot table in Figure 2.54. Some experimentation is typically required to obtain the grouping that presents the results in the most appropriate way. ∎

By now, we have illustrated the pivot table features that are most commonly used. Be aware, however, that there are *many* more features available. These include (but are not limited to) the following:

- Showing/hiding subtotals and grand totals (check the Layout options on the Design ribbon)

- Dealing with blank rows, that is, categories with no data (right-click on any number, choose PivotTable Options, and check the options on the Layout & Format tab)

- Displaying the data behind a given number in a pivot table (double-click on the number to get a new worksheet)

- Formatting a pivot table with various autoformat options (check the options on the Design ribbon)

- Sorting pivot tables in various ways (check the Sort options on the Options ribbon)

- Moving or renaming pivot tables (check the PivotTable and Action options on the Options ribbon)

- Refreshing pivot tables as the underlying data changes (check the Refresh dropdown on the Options ribbon)

- Creating pivot table formulas for calculated fields or calculated items (check the Formulas dropdown on the Options ribbon)

- Basing pivot tables on external databases (explained in Chapter 4)

Not only are these (and other) features available, but Excel usually provides more than one way to implement them. The suggestions above are just some of the ways they can be implemented. The key to learning pivot table features is to *experiment*. There are entire books written on pivot tables, but we don't recommend them. You can learn a lot more, and a lot quicker, by experimenting with data such as the Elecmart data. Don't be afraid to mess up. Pivot tables are very forgiving, and you can always start over!

We complete this section by providing one last quick example to illustrate how a pivot table can answer a business question in a matter of seconds.

EXAMPLE | 2.12 FROZEN LASAGNA TRIERS

The file **Lasagna Triers.xlsx** contains data on over 800 potential customers being tracked by a company that has been marketing a new frozen lasagna dinner. The file contains a number of demographics on these customers, as indicated in Figure 2.55: their

Figure 2.55 Lasagna Trier Data

	A	B	C	D	E	F	G	H	I	J	K	L	M
1	Person	Age	Weight	Income	PayType	CarValue	CCDebt	Gender	LiveAlone	DwellType	MallTrips	Nbhd	HaveTried
2	1	48	175	65500	Hourly	2190	3510	Male	No	Home	7	East	No
3	2	33	202	29100	Hourly	2110	740	Female	No	Condo	4	East	Yes
4	3	51	188	32200	Salaried	5140	910	Male	No	Condo	1	East	No
5	4	56	244	19000	Hourly	700	1620	Female	No	Home	3	West	No
6	5	28	218	81400	Salaried	26620	600	Male	No	Apt	3	West	Yes
7	6	51	173	73000	Salaried	24520	950	Female	No	Condo	2	East	No
8	7	44	182	66400	Salaried	10130	3500	Female	Yes	Condo	6	West	Yes
9	8	29	189	46200	Salaried	10250	2860	Male	No	Condo	5	West	Yes
10	9	28	200	61100	Salaried	17210	3180	Male	No	Condo	10	West	Yes
11	10	29	209	9800	Salaried	2090	1270	Female	Yes	Apt	7	East	Yes
12	11	29	171	46600	Salaried	16350	5520	Male	Yes	Home	11	West	Yes
13	12	30	243	24500	Salaried	5410	300	Male	No	Home	3	West	Yes
14	13	62	246	110900	Salaried	8410	730	Male	Yes	Condo	7	West	Yes
15	14	29	228	37200	Salaried	6420	700	Male	Yes	Apt	3	East	Yes
16	15	40	230	21800	Hourly	3230	1650	Male	No	Home	4	East	Yes
17	16	61	185	28900	Hourly	1300	1030	Male	Yes	Apt	2	South	No

age, weight, income, pay type, car value, credit card debt, gender, whether they live alone, dwelling type, monthly number of trips to the mall, and neighborhood. It also indicates whether they have tried the company's frozen lasagna. The company wants to understand why some potential customers are triers and others are not. Does gender make a difference? Does income make a difference? In general, what distinguishes triers from non-triers? How can the company use pivot tables to explore these questions?

Objective To use pivot tables to explore which demographic variables help to distinguish lasagna triers from non-triers.

Solution

Pivot tables, with counts, are a great way to discover which variables have the biggest effect on a Yes/No variable.

The key is to set up a pivot table that shows counts of triers and non-triers for different categories of any of the potential explanatory variables. For example, one such pivot table will show the percentages of triers and non-triers for males and females separately. If the percentages are different for males than for females, the company will know that gender is an important variable. On the other hand, if the percentages for males and females are about the same, the company will know that gender doesn't make much of a difference.

We set up the typical pivot table as shown in Figure 2.56. The Row variable is any demographic variable we want to investigate, in this case, Gender. The Column variable is HaveTried (Yes or No). The data variable can be *any* variable, as long as we express it as a count. Finally, we show these counts as percentage of row. This way we can easily look down column C to see whether the percentage in one category (Female) who have tried the product is any different from the percentage in another category (Male) who have tried the product. Specifically, we see that males are somewhat more likely to try the product than females: 60.9% versus 54.3%. We can also see this from the associated pivot chart.

Figure 2.56

Pivot Table and Pivot Chart for Examining the Effect of Gender

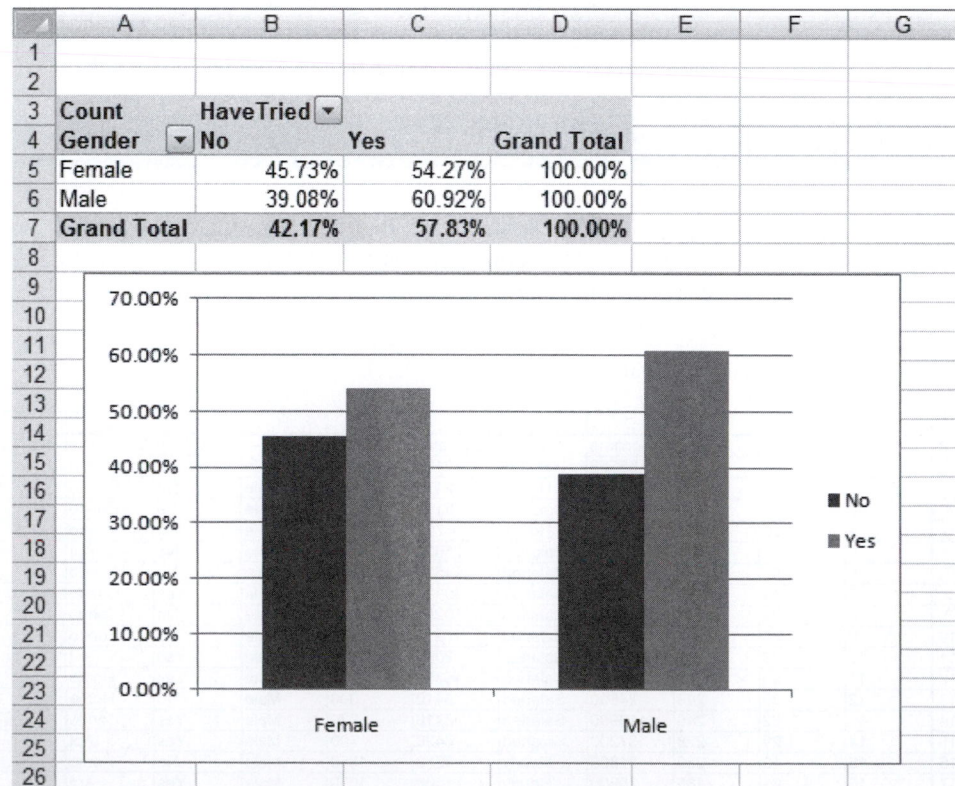

Figure 2.57

Pivot Table and Pivot Chart for Examining the Effect of LiveAlone

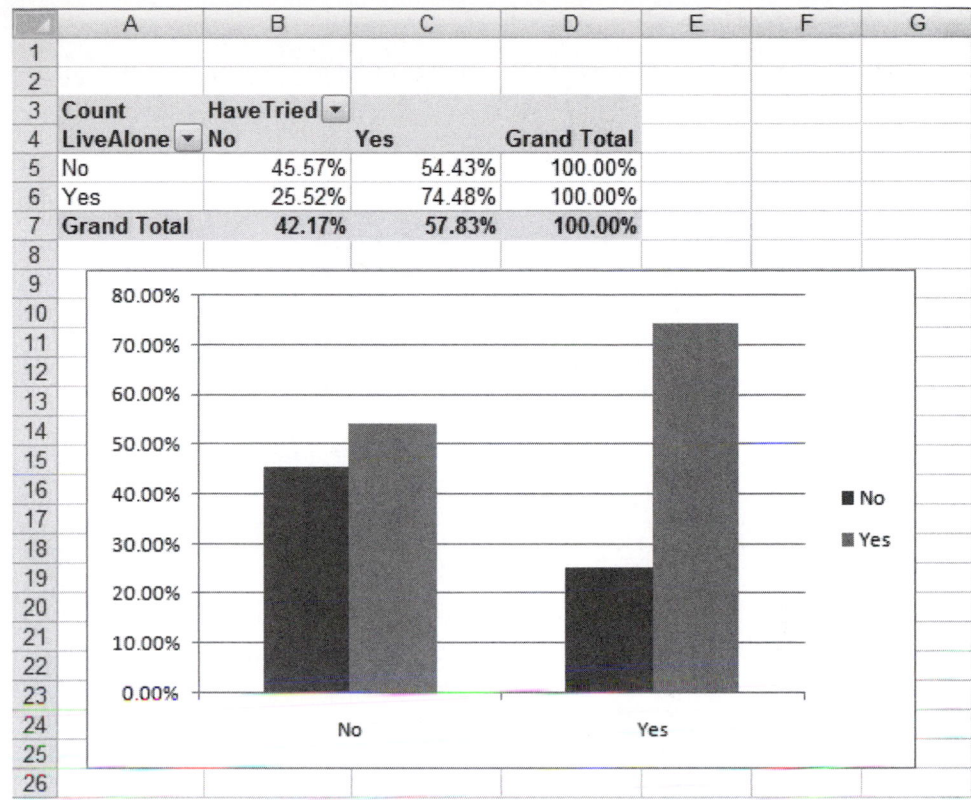

	A	B	C	D	E	F	G
1							
2							
3	Count	HaveTried ▾					
4	LiveAlone ▾	No	Yes	Grand Total			
5	No	45.57%	54.43%	100.00%			
6	Yes	25.52%	74.48%	100.00%			
7	Grand Total	42.17%	57.83%	100.00%			

Once this generic pivot table (and associated pivot chart) is set up, we can easily explore other demographic variables by swapping them for Gender. For example, Figure 2.57 indicates that people who live alone are (not surprisingly) *much* more likely to try this frozen microwave product than people who don't live alone. As another example, Figure 2.58 indicates that people with larger incomes are slightly more likely to try the product. There are two things to note about this income pivot table. First, because there are so many individual income values, we need to group on Income to obtain useful results. You can experiment with the grouping to get the most "meaningful" results. Second, you should be a bit skeptical about the last group, which has 100% triers. It is possible that there are only one or two people in this group. (It turns out that there are four.) For this reason, it is a good idea to show two pivot tables of the counts, one showing percentage of row and one showing the raw counts. This second pivot table is shown at the bottom of Figure 2.58.

The problem posed in this example is a common one in real business situations. We have one variable that indicates whether people are in one group or another (triers or non-triers), and we have a lot of variables that could potentially explain why some people are in one group and others are in the other group. There are a number of rather sophisticated techniques for attacking this problem, most of which are beyond the level of this book. However, we can go a long ways toward understanding which variables are important by the simple pivot table method illustrated here.

Figure 2.58
Pivot Table and Pivot Chart for Examining the Effect of Income

	A	B	C	D	E	F	G
1							
2							
3	Count	HaveTried ▼					
4	Income ▼	No	Yes	Grand Total			
5	0-49999	45.47%	54.53%	100.00%			
6	50000-99999	37.45%	62.55%	100.00%			
7	100000-149999	30.43%	69.57%	100.00%			
8	150000-199999	0.00%	100.00%	100.00%			
9	Grand Total	42.17%	57.83%	100.00%			
10							
11							

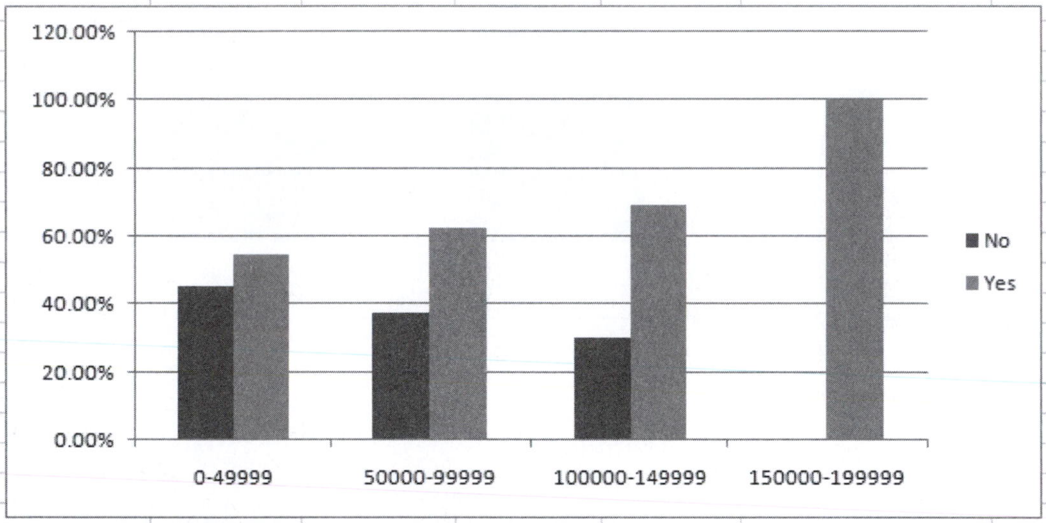

	A	B	C	D	E	F	G
29	Count	HaveTried ▼					
30	Income ▼	No	Yes	Grand Total			
31	0-49999	256	307	563			
32	50000-99999	91	152	243			
33	100000-149999	14	32	46			
34	150000-199999		4	4			
35	Grand Total	361	495	856			

PROBLEMS

Level A

41. Consider the Beta Technologies employee data in the file **P02_01.xlsx**. Create pivot tables or descriptive graphs to answer the following questions:

 a. What proportion of these full-time Beta employees are female?

 b. Is there evidence of salary discrimination against women at Beta Technologies? What are the limitations of the conclusion that you have drawn in answering this question?

 c. Is additional post-secondary education positively associated with higher average salaries at Beta?

 d. Is there evidence of salary discrimination against older employees at Beta Technologies? What are the limitations of the conclusion that you have drawn in answering this question?

42. Consider *Business Week's Guide to the Best Business Schools* enrollment data for top-rated graduate business programs in the United States in the file

P02_03.xlsx. Create pivot tables or descriptive graphs to answer the following questions:

a. Do graduate business programs with higher proportions of female student enrollments tend, on average, to have higher proportions of minority student enrollments?

b. Do graduate business programs with higher proportions of female student enrollments tend, on average, to have higher proportions of international student enrollments?

c. What, if any, are the limitations of the conclusions you have reached in responding to the previous questions?

43. Who has been most likely to access the Internet over the past decade? Consider the survey data collected from 1000 randomly selected Internet users, given in the file **P02_43.xlsx**. Create pivot tables to answer each of the following questions:

a. What proportion of these Internet users are men under the age of 30?

b. What proportion of these Internet users are single with no formal education beyond high school?

c. What proportion of these Internet users are currently employed? What is the average salary of the employed Internet users in this sample?

44. Is there a relationship between a state's number of classroom teachers and the average salary of classroom teachers in the state? Create one or more pivot tables using Excel to answer this question for the data in the file **P02_44.xlsx**. In addition to exploring the relationship between a state's total number of classroom teachers and their average annual salary, consider the same relationships for both elementary and secondary teachers.

45. Using the first data set in the file **P02_45.xlsx**, which was collected in 1994, create a pivot table that breaks down the 1000 randomly selected U.S. workers by sex *and* race. Develop a similar breakdown for those workers randomly selected in 1982. How have the proportions of U.S. workers in these various cross sections changed between 1982 and 1994?

46. Given data in the file **P02_13.xlsx** from a recent survey of chief executive officers from the largest U.S. public companies, create pivot tables to determine whether the levels of the 2003 annual salaries and bonuses earned by CEOs are related to the *types* of companies in which they serve.

47. Consider the data in the file **P02_12.xlsx** on various performance measures for the largest U.S. airlines. Create a pivot table and/or descriptive charts to determine whether the level of consumer complaints about an airline is associated with the number of reports of mishandled baggage filed by the airline's passengers. Summarize your findings.

Level B

48. What influences a metropolitan area's vulnerability to recession? Create pivot tables or descriptive graphs to explore this issue using the job statistics for selected towns in the United States in the file **P02_48.xlsx**. Be sure to consider the relative mix of new blue-collar jobs versus new white-collar jobs in attempting to explain an area's unemployment threat level.

49. Consider the data from an economic development study in the file **P02_06.xlsx**. Create pivot tables or descriptive graphs to answer the following questions:

a. What proportion of households in each of the four locations within this neighborhood own their homes?

b. What relationship, if any, exists between the primary household income level and family size?

c. What relationship, if any, exists between the primary household income level and the household's location within the neighborhood?

d. What relationship, if any, exists between the primary household income level and whether the household owns or rents their home?

50. Consider the relationship between the population size of selected metropolitan areas in the United States and the location's average annual rates for various forms of violent crime, including murder, rape, robbery, and aggravated assault. The data are in the file **P02_50.xlsx**. Use pivot tables or descriptive graphs to explore the relationship between a metro area's size and the area's level of violent criminal acts. Summarize your findings.

51. Using cost-of-living data from the *ACCRA Cost of Living Index* in the file **P02_19.xlsx**, examine the relationship between the geographical *location* of an urban area within the United States (e.g., northeast, southeast, midwest, northwest, or southwest) and its *composite* cost-of-living index. In other words, is the overall cost of living higher or lower for urban areas in particular geographical regions of the country? You will need to assign each urban area to one of any number of such geographical regions before you can produce pivot tables or other graphs before answering this question.

52. Consider the relationship between the size of the population and the average time (in minutes) it takes citizens of selected American communities to travel to work and back home each day. Using the data in the file **P02_11.xlsx**, create a pivot table to determine whether the population size is useful in explaining the variation of average commute times.

53. Consider the *U.S. News & World Report* rankings of top graduate business schools in the file **P02_08.xlsx**. Create pivot tables or descriptive graphs to answer the following questions:

a. Are higher average GMAT scores for enrolled students associated with higher average starting base salaries for recent graduates from these programs?

b. Are higher average undergraduate grade-point averages for enrolled students associated with higher average starting base salaries for recent graduates from these programs?

c. Are lower program acceptance rates associated with higher starting base salaries for recent graduates from these programs?

d. What are the limitations of the conclusions you have reached in answering these questions?

2.7 CONCLUSION

The graphs and tables we discussed in this chapter are extremely useful for describing data sets. The graphs show at a glance how a single variable is distributed, how two variables are related, or how a variable varies over time. The tables are also useful, not only in their own right but for providing the data needed to create graphs. We have paid special attention to the pivot table feature available in Excel. Pivot tables allow us to see relationships in a data set that would be very difficult to see in any other way. In fact, they are arguably the best kept secret in Excel, and their popularity will surely grow as business managers learn to take advantage of their power and flexibility.

Summary of Key Terms

Term	Explanation	Excel	Pages
Population	Includes all objects of interest in a study—people, households, machines, etc.		34
Sample	Representative subset of population, usually chosen randomly		34
Variable (or Field)	Attribute or measurement on members of a population, such as height, gender, or salary		34, 35
Case (or Observation or Record)	List of all variable values for a single member of a population		34
Data type	Several categorizations are possible: numerical versus categorical (with subcategories nominal, ordinal); discrete versus continuous; cross-sectional versus time series		36, 37
Frequency table	Contains counts of observations in specified categories		38
Histogram	Bar chart of frequencies from a frequency table	StatTools/ Summary Graphs/ Histogram	38
Distribution	General term for the way data are distributed, as indicated by a frequency table or histogram		42
Skewed distribution	Indicated by nonsymmetric shape of histogram. Skewed to the right (or positively skewed) means a long tail to the right. Skewed to the left (or negatively skewed) is the opposite		43
Bimodal distribution	Indicated by histogram with two peaks, often due to data from two distinct populations		44

(continued)

Term	Explanation	Excel	Pages
Scatterplot	Chart showing relationship between two variables, with a point for each observation	StatTools/ Summary Graphs/ Scatterplot	48
Time series graph	Chart showing behavior over time of a time series variable	StatTools/ Time Series & Forecasting/Time Series Graph	52
Pivot table (and Pivot table chart)	Table (and corresponding chart) in Excel that summarizes data broken down by one or more categorical variables	PivotTable from Insert ribbon	57
Contingency table (or Crosstabs)	Traditional statistical terms for pivot tables that list counts		57

PROBLEMS

Conceptual Exercises

C.1. An airline analyst wishes to estimate the proportion of all American adults who are still afraid to fly because of the terrorist attacks of September 11, 2001. To estimate this percentage, the analyst decides to survey 1500 Americans from across the nation. Identify the revelant sample and population in this case.

C.2. The number of children living in each of a large number of randomly selected households is an example of which data type? Be as specific as possible.

C.3. Does it make sense to construct a histogram for the state of residence of randomly selected individuals in a sample? Explain why or why not.

C.4. Characterize the likely shape of a histogram of the distribution of scores on a fairly easy midterm exam in a graduate statistics course.

C.5. A researcher is interested in determining whether there is a relationship between the number of room air-conditioning units sold each week and the time of year. What type of descriptive graph would be most useful in performing this analysis? Explain your choice.

Level A

54. Consider the economic development data in the file **P02_06.xlsx**.
   a. Create a scatterplot for each variable versus the size of the household's monthly home mortgage or rent payment.
   b. Which of the variables have a *positive* linear relationship with the size of the household's monthly home mortgage or rent payment?

   c. Which of the variables have a *negative* linear relationship with the size of the household's monthly home mortgage or rent payment?
   d. Which of the variables have essentially *no* linear relationship with the size of the household's monthly home mortgage or rent payment?

55. Consider the *Places Rated Almanac* metropolitan area rankings in the file **P02_55.xlsx**.
   a. Create scatterplots to discern the relationship between the metropolitan area's overall score and each of these numerical factors.
   b. Are the relationships revealed by the scatterplots consistent with your expectations? If not, can you explain any discrepancies between your findings and expectations?

56. The U.S. Bureau of Labor Statistics provides data on the year-to-year percentage changes in the wages and salaries of workers in private industries, including both white-collar and blue-collar occupations. Consider the data in the file **P02_56.xlsx**.
   a. Is there evidence of a strong relationship between the yearly changes in the wages and salaries of white-collar and blue-collar workers in the United States over the given time period? Describe the nature of any observed relationship between these two variables.
   b. Create time series graphs for each of the three time series and comment on any observed trends in these data.

57. The file **P02_57.xlsx** contains three years (1999–2001) of sales data for the Sky's the Limit Women's Apparel store. Each observation represents sales during a 4-week period. The first observation is sales during the first 4 weeks of 1999, and so on.

a. Does there appear to be any trend in sales?

b. Do sales appear to be seasonal? If so, discuss the nature of the seasonality.

58. For approximately 170 companies, the file **P02_58.xlsx** contains two pieces of information: a measure of the strength of the corporate culture (from 1 = High to 5 = Low), and the percentage net income growth from 1977 to 1988. Do these data indicate that a strong corporate culture is associated with financial success or weakness?

59. The file **P02_59.xlsx** contains quarterly sales revenues for Wal-Mart for several years. Construct a time series graph and discuss the trend and seasonal characteristics of Wal-Mart's sales.

60. Consider the data in the file **P02_60.xlsx**. In particular, columns B through D contain the following information about a sample of Bloomington residents: education level (completed high school only or completed college), income level (low or high), and whether the last purchased car was financed.

a. Using the data in columns B through D, determine how education and income influence the likelihood that a family finances a car.

b. Column A of this file contains the salaries of these Bloomington residents. Create a histogram of these salaries. (You can experiment with the appropriate categories.) Does the histogram appear to be bell shaped?

61. The file **P02_61.xlsx** contains the following information about a sample of Bloomington families: family size (large or small), number of cars owned by family (1, 2, 3, or 4), and whether family owns a foreign car.

a. Use these data to determine how family size and number of cars influence the likelihood that a family owns a foreign car.

b. Create a histogram with four bars, using the obvious categories, for the number of cars owned by a family. Interpret the histogram.

62. The file **P02_62.xlsx** contains monthly returns on Barnes and Noble stock for several years. Do monthly stock returns appear to be skewed or symmetric?

63. The file **P02_63.xlsx** contains annual returns for firms grouped by size. For example, in 1926, firms that ranked in the top 10% by size of sales returned an average of 14.9%, whereas firms that ranked in the bottom 10% by size returned an average of 26.1%. What do these data tell you about the relationship between firm size and average stock return? What are possible investment implications of this information?

64. The file **P02_64.xlsx** contains monthly returns on Mattel stock for several years. Create a histogram of these data and summarize what you learn from it.

65. It has been hypothesized that a reduction in the average length of the workweek in a country will reduce the

unemployment rate. The theory is that of job-sharing—if everybody works 5% less, the unemployed workers can pick up the reduced hours. Table 2.1 lists the percentage decrease in annual working hours per employee from 1975 to 1994 as well as the increase in unemployment rate for nine countries. Do these data support the hypothesis that job-sharing reduces unemployment? (Source: *The Economist,* November 25, 1995)

Table 2.1 Data on Workweeks and Unemployment

Country	% Decrease in Annual Working Hours per Employee	% Increase in Unemployment
United States	3.0%	−2.0%
Italy	5.3	5.0
Japan	7.0	0.0
Canada	6.6	5.0
Britain	9.4	5.0
Spain	10.8	15.0
Holland	12.5	0.5
Germany	12.5	3.0
France	12.8	9.0

66. Do countries with high rates of home ownership have higher or lower unemployment rates? The file **P02_66.xlsx** lists the 1996 home ownership percentage and unemployment rate for various countries. Discuss the relationship between home ownership and unemployment. Do you have any explanation for this relationship?

67. The SoftBus Company sells PC equipment and customized software to small companies to help them manage their day-to-day business activities. To understand its customers better, SoftBus recently sent questionnaires to a large number of prospective customers. Key personnel—those who would be using the software—were asked to fill out the questionnaire. SoftBus received 82 usable responses, as listed in the file **P02_67.xlsx**. The variables include the following information on the key person who filled out the questionnaire: gender, years of experience with this company, education level, whether the person owns a home PC, and the person's self-reported level of computer knowledge. Create pivot tables (as many as you believe are necessary) to help SoftBus understand these customers, and then write a short report that summarizes your findings.

68. The Comfy Company sells medium-priced patio furniture through a mail-order catalog. The company has operated primarily in the eastern United States but is now expanding to the Southwest. To get off to a good start, it plans to send potential customers a catalog with a discount coupon. However, Comfy is not sure how large a discount is necessary to entice customers to buy, so it experiments by sending catalogs to selected residents in six cities. Tucson and San Diego receive coupons for 5% off any furniture within the next 2 months, Phoenix and Santa Fe receive coupons for 10% off, and Riverside and Albuquerque receive coupons for 15% off. The data are in the file **P02_68.xlsx**. Develop one or more pivot tables to help the company determine the effect of the size of the coupon and whether this effect depends on the particular city. Write a short report that summarizes your findings.

69. You are a local Coca-Cola bottler. You want to determine whether sales of Coke and Diet Coke are more sensitive than the competition to changes in price. The file **P02_69.xlsx** contains weekly data on the price per can of Coke, Diet Coke, Pepsi, and Diet Pepsi, and the number of cans (in hundreds) sold of each product. Which of these products exhibits more price sensitivity?

70. Use the data in the file **P02_70.xlsx** to determine how the type of school (public or Catholic) that students attend affects their chance of graduating from high school.

71. It is well known that stock prices are a leading indicator of a recession. This means that several months before a recession begins, stock prices usually drop (foreshadowing a drop in the economy), and several months before a recession ends, stock prices usually increase (foreshadowing the end of the recession). Use the data in the file **P02_71.xlsx** to argue that the Dow Jones Index was a leading indicator for both the April 1960 through February 1961 recession and the December 1969 through November 1970 recession.

72. The file **P02_72.xlsx** contains information on monthly stock prices and trading volume for Wal-Mart. The data include date, low price for the month, high price for the month, closing price for the month, and number of shares traded during the month.
a. Create a time series graph of High, Low, and Close, all on the same graph. Are there any obvious time series patterns?
b. Create a time series graph of Volume. Are there any obvious time series patterns?
c. Create a scatterplot of Volume versus Close. Does there appear to be any relationship between these two variables?

73. The file **P02_73.xlsx** contains expense account data on a company's seven sales representatives for the past 4 months. Each row in the database includes a single expense record, which contains the rep's name, the month, the category (trip, entertaining client, or miscellaneous supplies), the amount claimed, and the amount reimbursed. (Only "legitimate" expenses are reimbursed.)
a. Create a pivot table to tabulate the number of expense records of each category by each

representative for the entire 4-month period. (For example, it should list the number of trips taken by Smith.) Use the data in the resulting pivot table to create an appropriate bar chart. (You can decide on the exact form of the chart.)
b. Create a pivot table to show the total amount spent each month by each rep. Use the resulting pivot table to create time series graphs, one for each rep.
c. Create a histogram of reimbursed amounts, for the entertaining clients and miscellaneous supplies categories only.

Level B

74. The annual base salaries for 200 students graduating from a reputable MBA program this year are of interest to those in the admissions office who are responsible for marketing the program to prospective students. The data are in the file **P02_74.xlsx**.
a. Create a frequency table and histogram for the given distribution of starting salaries. What does the histogram suggest about this distribution of starting salaries?
b. Is it possible to separate these salaries into two or more subgroups? If so, create a frequency distribution and histogram for each subset of starting salaries. Also, characterize the shape of each subgroup's distribution.
c. As an admissions officer of this MBA program, how would you proceed to use these findings to market the program to prospective students?

75. The percentage of private-industry jobs that are managerial has steadily declined in recent years as companies have found middle management a ripe area for cutting costs. How have women and various minority groups fared in gaining management positions during this period of corporate downsizing of the management ranks? Relevant data are listed in the file **P02_75.xlsx**. Create scatterplots and/or time series graphs using these data to make general comparisons across the various groups included in the set.

76. Chandler Enterprises produces Pentium chips. Five types of defects (labeled 1–5) have been known to occur. Chips are manufactured by two operators (A and B). Four machines (1–4) are used to manufacture chips. The file **P02_76.xlsx** contains data for a sample of defective chips including the type of defect, operator, machine, and day of the week. Use the data in this file to chart a course of action that would lead, as quickly as possible, to improved product quality. Use a pivot table to "stratify" the defects with respect to type of defect, day of the week, machine used, and operator working. You might even want to break the data down by machine and operator (or in some other way). You can assume that each operator and machine made an equal number of products.

77. You own a local McDonald's franchise and have done some market research to better understand your customers. For a random sample of Bloomington residents, the file **P02_77.xlsx** contains the income, gender, and number of days per week the resident goes to McDonald's. Use this information to determine how gender and income influence the frequency with which Bloomington residents attend McDonald's.

78. Students at Faber College apply to study either English or science. You have been assigned to determine whether Faber College discriminates against women in admitting students to the school of their choice. The file **P02_78.xlsx** contains the following data on Faber's students: gender, major applied for (English or science), and admission decision (yes or no). Assuming that women and men are equally qualified for each major, do the data indicate that the college discriminates against women? Make sure you use all available information.

79. You have been assigned to evaluate the quality of care given to heart attack patients at Emergency Room (ER) and Chicago Hope (CH). The file **P02_79.xlsx** contains the following patient data for the past month: hospital where patient was admitted (ER or CH), risk category (high or low, where high-risk people are less likely to survive than low-risk people), and patient's outcome (lived or died). Use the data to determine which hospital is doing a better job of caring for heart attack patients. Use all of the data.

80. The file **P02_80.xlsx** contains the monthly level of the Dow Jones Index for several decades. Do these data indicate any unusual seasonal patterns in stock returns? [*Hint*: You can extract the month (January, February, etc.) with the formula =TEXT(A4,"mmm") copied down any column.]

81. You sell station wagons and want to know how family size and salary influence the likelihood that a family will purchase a station wagon. You have surveyed some local families and discovered whether they own a station wagon, the size of the family (Large means at least five people, Small means no more than four people), and the family's salary (High means at least $80,000, Low means less than $80,000). The data are in the file **P02_81.xlsx**. Analyze these data to determine how salary and family size influence the likelihood that a family will purchase a station wagon.

82. The file **P02_82.xlsx** contains data on the diameter of an elevator rail, the operator who built the elevator rail, and the machine used to build the elevator rail. What can you learn from these data?

83. The file **P02_83.xlsx** contains daily returns and the daily level of the Standard and Poor's 500 stock index. Describe what you learn from these data.

84. Viscerex, a small chemical company, wants to determine how viscosity of liquid supplied to the company influences the level of impurities. The file **P02_84.xlsx** contains the following information: firm supplying the liquid to Viscerex, viscosity level of the liquid, and level of impurities in the liquid. Describe how viscosity affects the level of impurities.

85. Two major awards are given to daytime soap operas and their actors and actresses: the Daytime Emmys and the Soap Opera Digest Awards. The Daytime Emmys are voted on by members of the TV industry. The Soap Opera Digest Awards are voted on by soap opera viewers who are readers of *Soap Opera Digest*. The file **P02_85.xlsx** contains the number of awards of each type won by each daytime soap. Use these data to determine whether voters for Daytime Emmys and Soap Opera Digest Awards appear to be looking for the same qualities when they vote for awards.

86. In recent years economists and others have debated whether investment in information technology is good or bad for employment growth. Table 2.2 contains information technology (IT) investment as a percentage of total investment for eight countries during the 1980s. It also contains the average annual percentage change in employment during the 1980s. Explain how these data shed light on the question of whether IT investment creates or costs jobs. (Source: *The Economist*, September 28, 1996)

Table 2.2   Data on IT Investment

Country	IT Investment as % of Total Investment (1980s)	Annual Average % Change in Employment (1980–1989)
Netherlands	2.0%	1.3%
Italy	3.6	1.9
Germany	4.0	1.7
France	5.6	1.5
Canada	7.8	2.4
Japan	7.8	2.4
Britain	7.8	3.0
United States	11.9	3.4

87. Do countries with more income inequality have lower unemployment rates? Table 2.3 contains the following information for 10 countries during the period of 1980 to 1995: (1) change from 1980 to 1995 in ratio of the average wage of the top 10% of all wage earners to the median wage, and (2) change from 1980 to 1995 in unemployment rate. (Source: *The Economist*, August 17, 1996)

   a. Explain why the ratio of the average wage of the top 10% of all wage earners to the median measures income inequality.

b. Do these data help to confirm or contradict the hypothesis that increased wage inequality leads to lower unemployment levels?

c. What other data would you need to be more confident that increased income inequality leads to lower unemployment?

Table 2.3 Data on Income Inequality

Country	Change in Wage Inequality Ratio	Change in Unemployment Rate
Germany	−6.0%	6.0%
France	−3.5	5.6
Italy	1.0	5.2
Japan	0.0	0.6
Australia	5.0	2.4
Sweden	4.0	5.9
Canada	5.5	2.0
New Zealand	9.5	4.0
Britain	15.6	2.5
United States	15.8	−1.8

88. One magazine reported that a man's weight at birth has a significant impact on the chance that the man will suffer a heart attack during his life. Analyze the data in the file **P02_88.xlsx** to determine how birth weight influences the chances that a man will have a heart attack.

89. When Staples and Office Depot proposed merging in 1997, the Federal Trade Commission (FTC) rejected the merger. In analyzing the impact of the merger, the FTC looked at the prices of the following quantities:
- A Pentium 166 computer with 16 meg of RAM, 10-speed CD-ROM, and 2g hard drive (labeled Computer)
- A desk, filing cabinet, 10 reams of computer paper, and a laser printer (labeled Office)
- 10 notebooks, 5 boxes of pencils, a book bag, 10 boxes of crayons (labeled School)

The file **P02_89.xlsx** contains data on these variables for several cities. For example, the first city had both a Staples and an Office Depot, and a computer cost $1979.31. The second city had only a Staples, and the school supplies cost $179.86. Based on these data, can you explain why the FTC rejected the merger? (*Note*: The data in this file are fictitious but are consistent with the conclusions of the article.) (Source: Based on *The Economist*, May 3, 1998)

90. An important question in finance is whether the stock market is efficient. The market is efficient if knowledge of past changes in a stock's price tells us nothing about future changes in the stock's price. Here you will check whether daily price changes in IBM stock are consistent with efficient markets, using the data in the file **P02_90.xlsx**. Define an "up" day for IBM as a day when the return is greater than 0. A "down" day is when the return is less than or equal to 0. Does it appear that knowledge of whether IBM went up or down yesterday can help us predict whether it will go up or down today?

91. You work for a small travel agency and are about to do a mass mailing of a travel brochure. Your funds are limited, so you want to mail to the people who spend the most money on travel. The file **P02_91.xlsx** contains data for a random sample of 925 residents. These data include their gender, age, and amount spent on travel last year. Use these data to determine how gender and age influence a person's travel expenditures. Also make recommendations on the type of person to whom you should mail your brochure.

92 How has the distribution of family incomes changed in the United States during the past 20 years? The file **P02_92.xlsx** contains data for a sample of 499 family incomes (in real 2004 dollars). For each family, the 1984 and 2004 incomes are listed. Although these data are fictitious, they are consistent with what has actually happened to the U.S. family incomes over this period. Based on these data, discuss as completely as possible how the distribution of family income in the United States changed from 1984 to 2004.

Bank98 operates a main location and three branch locations in a medium-size city. All four locations perform similar services, and customers typically do business at the location nearest them. The bank has recently had more congestion—long waiting lines—than it (or its customers) would like. As part of a study to learn the causes of these long lines and to suggest possible solutions, all locations have kept track of customer arrivals during 1-hour intervals for the past 10 weeks. All branches are open Monday through Friday from 9 A.M. until 5 P.M. and on Saturday from 9 A.M. until noon. For each location, the file **Bank98 Arrivals.xlsx** contains the number of customer arrivals during each hour of a 10-week

period. The manager of Bank98 has hired you to make some sense out of these data. Specifically, your task is to present charts and/or tables that indicate how customer traffic into the bank locations varies by day of week and hour of day. There is also interest in whether any daily or hourly patterns you observe are stable across weeks. Although you don't have full information about the way the bank currently runs its operations—you know only its customer arrival pattern and the fact that it is currently experiencing long lines—you are encouraged to append any suggestions for improving operations, based on your analysis of the data. ■

Are people in the United States buying more cars than in the past? Are they buying more foreign cars relative to domestic cars? Are auto sales seasonal, with more sales occurring during some months than others? Does automobile production mirror sales very closely? These are some questions you have been asked to answer, using the data in the file **Automobiles.xlsx**. This file contains monthly data on U.S. sales of domestic and foreign cars since 1967. It also shows monthly production of domestic cars since 1993. The data are shown in two forms: not seasonally adjusted—the raw data—and

seasonally adjusted. (Although you will learn more about seasonal adjustment of time series data in Chapter 13, the basic idea is that this is a method for smoothing out seasonal ups and downs so that underlying trends can be seen more clearly.) You have been asked to prepare a report that explains any important patterns you observe in these data. Of course, your report should contain relevant charts and/or tables. Make sure your report indicates whether you are using seasonally adjusted data or raw data (or both) and why. ■

The best-selling book *The Millionaire Next Door* by Thomas J. Stanley and William D. Danko (Longstreet Press, 1996) presents some very interesting data on the characteristics of millionaires. We tend to believe that people with expensive houses, expensive cars, expensive clothes, country club memberships, and other outward indications of wealth are the millionaires. The authors define wealth, however, in terms of savings and investments, not consumer items. In this sense, they argue that people with a lot of expensive *things* and even large incomes often have surprisingly little wealth. These people tend to spend much of what they make on consumer items, often trying to keep up with, or impress, their peers. In contrast, the real millionaires, in terms of savings and investments, frequently come from "unglamorous" professions (particularly teaching!), own unpretentious homes and cars, dress in inexpensive clothes, and otherwise lead rather ordinary lives.

Consider the (hypothetical) data in the file **Social Climbers.xlsx**. For several hundred couples, it lists their education level, their annual combined salary, the market value of their home and cars, the amount of savings they have accumulated (in savings accounts, stocks, retirement accounts, and so on), and a self-reported "social climber index" on a scale of 1 to 10 (with 1 being very unconcerned about social status and material items and 10 being very concerned about these). Prepare a report based on these data, supported by relevant charts and/or tables, that might be used in a book such as *The Millionaire Next Door*. Although your report might be used in such a book, your conclusions can either support or contradict those of Stanley and Danko. ■

© Jeff Greenberg/Photo Edit, Inc.

PREDICTORS OF SUCCESSFUL MOVIES

The movie industry is a high-profile industry with a highly variable revenue stream. In 1998, U.S. moviegoers spent close to $7 billion at the box office alone. With this much money at stake, it is not surprising that movie studios are interested in knowing what variables are useful for predicting a movie's financial success. The article by Simonoff and Sparrow (2000) examines this issue for 311 movies released in 1998 and late 1997. (They obtained their data from a public Web site at http://www.imdb.com.) Although it is preferable to examine movie *profits,* the costs of making movies are virtually impossible to obtain. Therefore, the authors focused instead on revenues—specifically, the total U.S. domestic gross revenue for each film.

Simonoff and Sparrow obtained prerelease information on a number of variables that were thought to be possible predictors of gross revenue. (By "prerelease," we mean that this information is known about a film *before* the film is actually released.) These variables include: (1) the genre of the film, categorized as action, children's, comedy, documentary, drama, horror, science fiction, or thriller; (2) the Motion Picture Association of America (MPAA) rating of the film, categorized as G (general audiences), PG (parental guidance suggested), PG-13 (possibly unsuitable for children under 13), R (children not admitted unless accompanied by an adult), NC-17 (no one under 17 admitted), or U (unrated); (3) the country of origin of the movie, categorized as United States, English-speaking but non–United States, or non–English-speaking; (4) number of actors and actresses in the movie who were listed in *Entertainment Weekly's* lists of the 25 Best Actors and 25 Best Actresses, as of 1998; (5) number of actors and actresses in the movie who were among the top 20 actors and top 20 actresses in average box office gross per movie in their careers; (6) whether the movie was a sequel; (7) whether the movie was released before a holiday weekend; (8) whether the movie was released during the Christmas season; and (9) whether the movie was released during the summer season.

To get a sense of whether these variables are related to gross revenue, we could calculate a lot of summary measures and create numerous tables. However, we agree with Simonoff and Sparrow that the information is best presented in a series of *side-by-side box plots,* a type of graph we will introduce in this chapter. (See Figure 3.1.) These box plots are slightly different from the versions we describe in this book, but they accomplish exactly the same purpose. (There are two differences: First, their box plots are vertical; ours are horizontal. Second, their box plots capture an extra piece of information—the *widths* of their boxes are proportional to the square roots of the sample sizes, so that wide boxes correspond to categories with more movies. In contrast, the *heights* of our boxes carry no information about sample size.) Basically, each box and the lines and points extending above and below it indicate the distribution of gross revenues for any category. The box itself, from bottom to top, captures the middle 50% of the revenues in the category, the line in the middle of the box represents the median revenue, and the lines and dots indicate possible skewness and outliers.

These particular box plots indicate some interesting and possibly surprising information about the movie business. First, almost all of the box plots indicate a high degree of variability and positive skewness, where there are a few movies that gross extremely large amounts compared to the "typical" movies in the category. Second, genre certainly makes a difference. There are more comedies and dramas (wider boxes), but they typically gross considerably less than action, children's, and science fiction films. Third, the same is true of R-rated movies compared to movies rated G, PG, or PG-13—there are more of them, but they typically gross much less. Fourth, U.S. movies do considerably better than foreign movies. Fifth, it helps to have stars, although there are quite a few "sleepers" that succeed without having big-name stars. Sixth, sequels do better, presumably reflecting the success of the earlier films. Finally, the release date makes a big difference. Movies released before holidays, during the Christmas season, or during the summer season tend to have larger gross revenues. Indeed, as Simonoff and Sparrow discuss, movie studios compete fiercely for the best release dates.

Are these prerelease variables sufficient to predict gross revenues accurately? As we might expect from the amount of variability in most of the box plots in Figure 3.1, the answer is "no." Many intangible factors evidently determine the ultimate success of a movie, so that some, such as *There's Something About Mary,* do much better than expected, and others, such as *Godzilla,* do worse than expected. We revisit this movie data set in the chapter opener to Chapter 12. There, we see how Simonoff and Sparrow use "multiple regression" to predict gross revenue—with only limited success. ∎

Figure 3.1   Box Plots of Domestic Gross Revenues for 1998 Movies

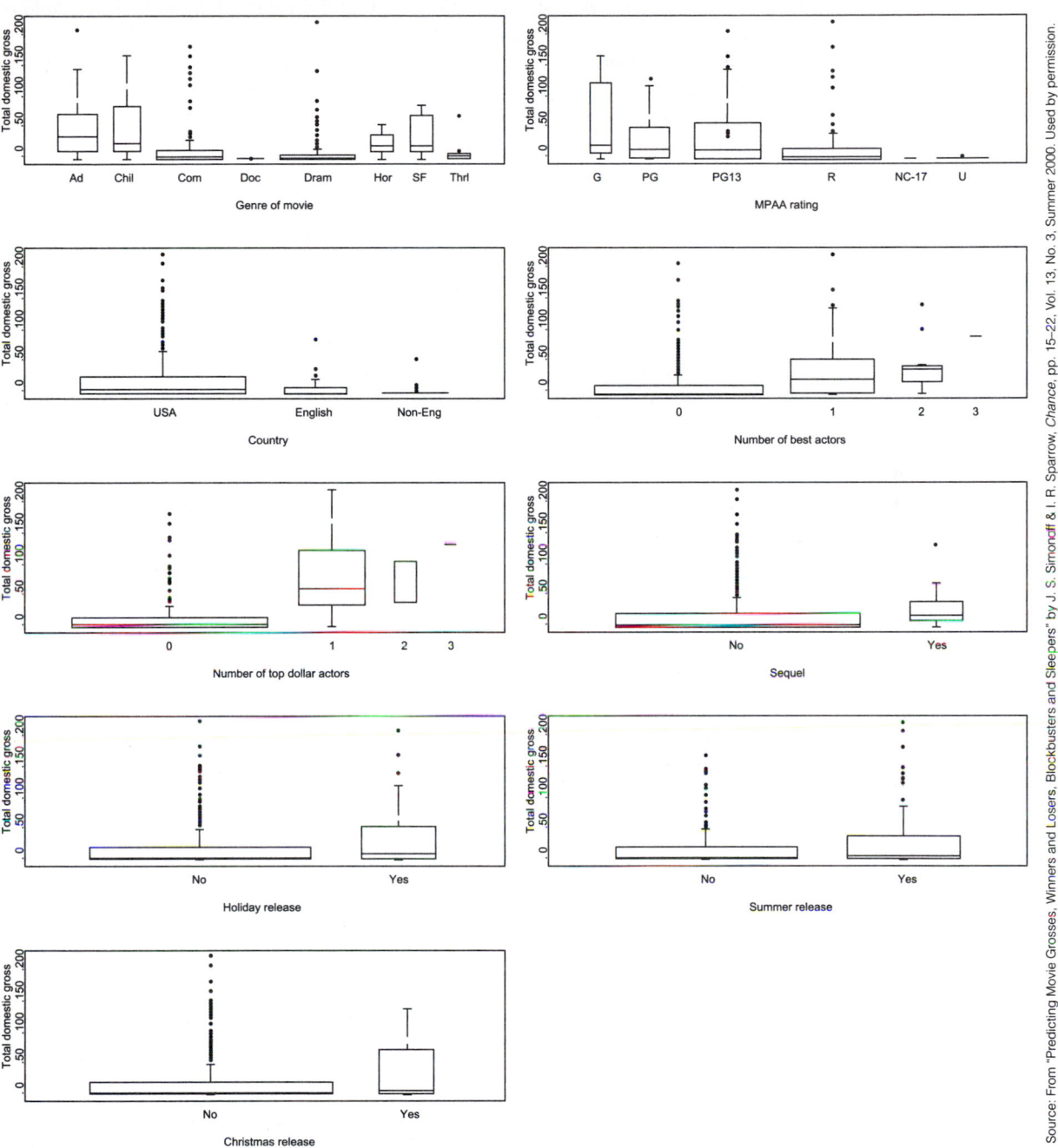

Source: From "Predicting Movie Grosses, Winners and Losers, Blockbusters and Sleepers" by J. S. Simonoff & I. R. Sparrow, *Chance*, pp. 15–22, Vol. 13, No. 3, Summer 2000. Used by permission.

3.1 INTRODUCTION

In Chapter 2 we summarize data mainly with tables and graphs. It is often useful to summarize data even further with a few well-chosen summary measures. In this chapter we learn the most frequently used numerical summary measures. These include measures for describing a single variable, such as the *mean*, *median*, and *standard deviation*, plus a couple of measures, *correlation* and *covariance*, for describing the potential relationship between two variables. Using these numerical summary measures, we then discuss an additional graph called a *box plot*. Box plots are useful for describing a single variable or comparing two or more related variables.

We conclude this chapter by examining three relatively complex examples. Here we are able to put all of the descriptive tools we have learned to good use. These examples are typical of the large-scale data sets business managers face on a continual basis. Only by looking at the data from a number of points of view can we discover the information and patterns hidden in the data.

3.2 MEASURES OF CENTRAL LOCATION

Most of the numerical summary measures we consider here are for a single variable. Each describes some aspect of the distribution of the variable. That is, each number describes one feature of the distribution that we see graphically in a histogram. We begin with measures of central location. The three most commonly used measures are the *mean*, *median*, and *mode*, each of which gives a slightly different interpretation to the term *central location*.

3.2.1 The Mean

The **mean** is the average of all values of a variable. If the data represent a sample from some larger population, we call this measure the **sample mean** and denote it by $\overline{X}$ (pronounced "x-bar"). If the data represent the entire population, we call it the **population mean** and denote it by μ. This distinction is not important in this chapter, but it will become relevant in later chapters when we discuss statistical inference. In either case the formula for the mean is given by equation (3.1).

The summation sign denoted by the Greek symbol sigma (Σ) is simply a shortcut for writing a sum, in this case $X_1 + X_2 + \cdots + X_n$. It is used extensively in statistical formulas.

Formula for the Mean

$$\text{Mean} = \frac{\sum_{i=1}^{n} X_i}{n} \qquad (3.1)$$

Here n is the number of observations and X_i is the value of observation i. Equation (3.1) simply says to add all the observations and divide by n, the number of observations.

To obtain the mean in Excel, we use the AVERAGE function on the appropriate range, as illustrated in the following example.

EXAMPLE | **3.1 SUMMARIZING STARTING SALARIES FOR BUSINESS UNDERGRADUATES**

The file **Starting Salaries.xlsx** lists starting salaries for 190 graduates from an undergraduate school of business. The data are in the range named Salary on a sheet called Data. Find the average of all salaries.

Objective   To use Excel's AVERAGE function to summarize salaries.

Solution

Figure 3.2 includes a number of summary measures produced by Excel's built-in functions. In particular, we calculate the mean salary by entering the formula

=**AVERAGE(Salary)**

in cell B6. It is nearly $30,000. (The other summary measures in Figure 3.2 are obtained using other Excel functions, as is discussed subsequently.)

Figure 3.2

Selected Summary Measures of Salary Data

	A	B	C
1	**Summary measures using Excel functions**		
2			
3	Count	190	
4	Minimum	$17,100	
5	Maximum	$38,200	
6	Average	$29,762	
7	Median	$29,850	
8	Lower quartile	$27,325	
9	Upper quartile	$32,300	
10	5-percentile	$23,690	
11	95-percentile	$35,810	
12	Range	$21,100	
13	Standard deviation	$3,707	
14	Variance	13743424	

When working with a set of data, the terms *mean* and *average* are synonymous.

The mean in Example 3.1 is a "representative" measure of central location because the distribution of salaries is nearly symmetric. (You can check this statement by constructing a histogram of salaries.) However, the mean is often misleading because of skewness. For example, if a few of the undergraduates got abnormally high salaries (over $100,000, say), these large values would tend to inflate the mean and make it unrepresentative of the majority of the salaries. In such cases, the median is often a more appropriate measure of central location.

3.2.2 The Median

Think of the difference between mean and median for some common variables: (1) all final exam scores for a large college course; (2) all household incomes in your state; (3) total yearly medical expenses for all households in your state. For these variables, which measure would probably be more "representative," the mean or median? Why?

The **median** is the "middle" observation when the data are arranged from smallest to largest. If there is an odd number of observations, the median is the middle observation. For example, if there are nine observations, the median is the fifth smallest (or fifth largest) observation. If there is an even number of observations, the median is usually defined to be the average of the two middle observations. For example, if there are 10 observations, the median is usually defined to be the average of the fifth and sixth smallest values.

We calculate the median salary in Example 3.1 by entering the formula

=**MEDIAN(Salary)**

in cell B7. (See Figure 3.2.) Its value is again approximately $30,000, almost the same as the mean. This is typical of symmetric distributions, but it is not true for skewed distributions. For example, if a few graduates received abnormally large salaries, the mean would be affected by them, but the median would not be affected at all. It would still represent the "middle" of the distribution.

> The **median** is the middle observation (for an odd number of observations) or the average of the middle two observations (for an even number of observations) after the observations have been sorted from low to high.

3.2.3 The Mode

The **mode** is the most frequently occurring value. If the values are essentially continuous, as with the salaries in Example 3.1, then the mode is essentially irrelevant. There is typically no *single* value that occurs more than once, or there are at best a few ties for the most frequently occurring value. In either case the mode is not likely to provide much information. However, the following example illustrates where the mode can be useful.

The **mode** is the most frequently occurring observation.

EXAMPLE | **3.2 SHOE SIZES PURCHASED AT A SHOE STORE**

The file **Shoe Sizes.xlsx** lists shoe sizes purchased at a shoe store. What is the store's best-seller?

Objective To use Excel's MODE function to find the best-selling shoe size.

Solution

Shoe sizes come in discrete increments, rather than a continuum, so it makes sense to find the mode, the size that is requested most often. This can be done with Excel's MODE function, which shows that size 11 is the most frequently purchased size. This is also apparent from the histogram in Figure 3.3, where the category for size 11 corresponds to the highest bar. (We deliberately overrode the default StatTools bins for this histogram. The trick is to ask StatTools for 15 bins, with minimum 6.25 and maximum 13.75. Then a typical bin has length 0.5, such as 10.25 to 10.75. Its midpoint, 10.5, is then the shoe size.)

Figure 3.3   Distribution of Shoe Sizes

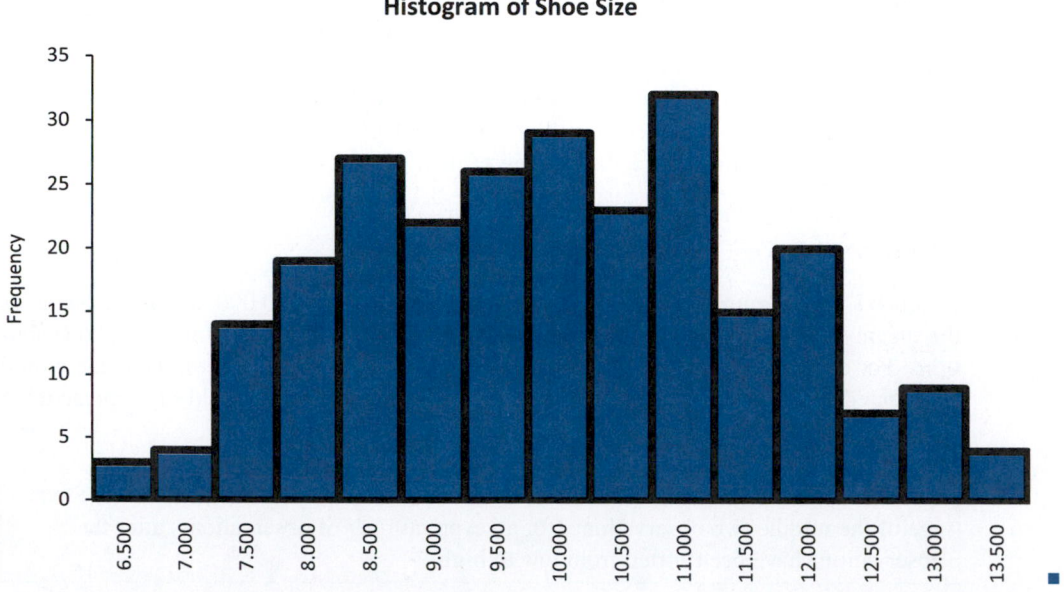

3.3 QUARTILES AND PERCENTILES

The median splits the data in half. It is sometimes called the 50th **percentile** because (approximately) half of the data are below the median. It is also called the second **quartile,** because if we divide the data into four parts, then the median separates the lower two parts from the upper two. We can also find other percentiles and quartiles. Some of these appear in Figure 3.2, which summarizes the salary data from Example 3.1.

For example, the 5th and 95th percentiles appear in cells B10 and B11. They are calculated with the formulas

=**PERCENTILE(Salary,.05)**

and

=**PERCENTILE(Salary,.95)**

The second argument of the PERCENTILE function must be a decimal between 0 and 1. In contrast, the second argument of the QUARTILE function must be an integer: 1, 2, or 3.

They say that 5% of all salaries are below $23,690 (so that 95% are above $23,690), and 95% of all salaries are below $35,810 (so that 5% are above $35,810). These two percentiles (and sometimes others) are frequently quoted.

Similarly, Figure 3.2 lists the lower and upper quartiles in cells B8 and B9. These are the 25th and 75th percentiles, so they can be calculated with the PERCENTILE function. They can also be calculated with the formulas

=**QUARTILE(Salary,1)**

and

=**QUARTILE(Salary,3)**

That is, they are the first and third quartiles. (The median is the second quartile.) In short, 25% of the salaries are below $27,325, 25% are above $32,300, and the other 50% are in between.

The difference between the first and third quartiles is called the **interquartile range** (IQR). It measures the spread between the largest and smallest of the middle half of the data. In the salary example the IQR is $4,975 (= $32,300 − $27,325). We come back to the IQR when we discuss box plots later in this chapter.

Excel Tip *Excel uses a rather obscure interpolation formula (which is not spelled out in its online help) for determining percentiles and quartiles. This can be particularly disconcerting—and wrong—for small data sets. For example, Excel reports that the 25th percentile (and the first quartile) of the 10 numbers 1, 2, 3, 4, 5, 6, 7, 8, 9, and 10 is 3.25. This does not appear to be consistent with our definition of the 25th percentile, which states that 25% of the numbers are below it and 75% are above it. As another example, it always reports the 25th percentile of 13 numbers as the fourth smallest of these numbers, which seems strange. Therefore, we recommend not putting too much reliance on Excel's PERCENTILE and QUARTILE functions for small data sets.*

3.4 MINIMUM, MAXIMUM, AND RANGE

Three other descriptive measures of a variable are its *minimum, maximum,* and *range.* The **minimum** is the smallest value, the **maximum** is the largest value, and the **range** is the difference between the maximum and minimum. These are listed in Figure 3.2 for the salary data. The minimum and maximum are calculated in cells B4 and B5 with the formulas

=MIN(Salary)

and

=MAX(Salary)

The range is then calculated in cell B12 with the formula

=B5-B4

We see that no salary is below $17,100, no salary is above $38,200, and all salaries are contained within an interval of length $21,100.

The minimum and maximum provide bounds on the data set, and the range provides a crude measure of the variability of the data. These measures are often worth reporting, but they can obviously be affected by one or two extreme values. The range, in particular, is usually not as good a measure of variability as the measures discussed next.

3.5 MEASURES OF VARIABILITY: VARIANCE AND STANDARD DEVIATION

To really understand a data set, we need to know more than measures of central location; we also need measures of variability. To see this, consider the following example.

EXAMPLE | 3.3 VARIABILITY OF ELEVATOR RAIL DIAMETERS AT OTIS ELEVATOR

Suppose Otis Elevator is going to stop manufacturing elevator rails. Instead, it is going to buy them from an outside supplier. Otis would like each rail to have a diameter of 1 inch. The company has obtained samples of 60 elevator rails from each supplier. These are listed in columns A and B of Figure 3.4. (See the file **Comparing Suppliers.xlsx**.) Which supplier should Otis prefer?

Figure 3.4 Two Samples with Different Amounts of Variability

	A	B	C	D	E	F	G	H	I
1	Supplier1	Supplier2					**Summary measures**		
2	0.986	0.973						Supplier1	Supplier2
3	0.990	1.041		Each value is the diameter of			Mean	1.000	1.000
4	1.018	0.975		an elevator rail in inches.			Median	1.000	1.000
5	1.022	1.049					Variance	0.000128	0.001354
6	1.002	0.975					Standard deviation	0.011	0.037
7	0.976	0.926							
8	0.992	1.036							
9	1.012	0.987							
10	0.997	1.016							
11	1.001	0.900							

Objective To calculate the variability for two suppliers and choose the one with the least variability.

Solution

Observe that the mean and median are both exactly 1 inch for each supplier. Based on these measures, the two suppliers are equally good and both are right on the mark. It is clear from a glance at the data, however, that supplier 1 is somewhat better than supplier 2. The reason is that supplier 2's rails exhibit more variability about the mean than supplier 1's rails. If we want rails to have a diameter of 1 inch, then variability around the mean is bad! ∎

The most commonly used measures of variability are the *variance* and *standard deviation.* The **variance** is essentially the average of the squared deviations from the mean. We say "essentially" because there are two versions of variance: the **population variance,** usually denoted by σ^2, and the **sample variance,** usually denoted by s^2. The formulas for them are given by equations (3.2) and (3.3). These formulas differ basically in their denominators. Also, their numerical values are practically the same when n, the number of observations, is large.

Formula for Population Variance

$$\sigma^2 = \frac{\sum_{i=1}^{n}(X_i - \mu)^2}{n}$$

(3.2)

Formula for Sample Variance

$$s^2 = \frac{\sum_{i=1}^{n}(X_i - \overline{X})^2}{n-1}$$

(3.3)

It is more common to quote the sample variance and the sample standard deviation than their population counterparts. However, for large n, the difference is practically irrelevant.

We say that each term in these sums is a squared deviation from the mean, where *deviation* means difference. Therefore, you can remember variance as the *average of the squared deviations from the mean.* This is not quite true for the sample variance (because of dividing by $n - 1$, not n), but it is nearly true. If we use the supplier 2 data in Figure 3.4 for illustration, the deviations from the mean are −0.027, 0.041, −0.025, 0.049, and so on; the squares of these deviations are 0.000733, 0.001676, 0.000628, 0.002394, and so on; and the sum of these 60 squares is 0.079912. Therefore, the population variance is 0.079912/60 = 0.001332, and the sample variance (the one quoted in the figure) is 0.079912/59 = 0.001354.

As their names imply, σ^2 is relevant if the data set includes the entire population, whereas s^2 is relevant for a sample from a population. Excel has a built-in function for each. To obtain σ^2 we use the VARP function; to obtain s^2 we use the VAR function. In this chapter we illustrate only the sample variance s^2.

The important part about either variance formula is that the variance tends to increase when there is more variability around the mean. Indeed, large deviations from the mean contribute heavily to the variance because they are *squared.* One consequence of this is that the variance is expressed in squared units (squared dollars, for example) rather than original units. Therefore, a more intuitive measure is the **standard deviation,** defined as the square root of the variance (3.4). The standard deviation is measured in original units, such as dollars, and, as we discuss shortly, it is much easier to interpret.

Relationship Between Standard Deviation and Variance

Standard deviation = $\sqrt{\text{Variance}}$

(3.4)

Of course, depending on which variance measure we use, we obtain the corresponding standard deviation, either σ (population) or *s* (sample). Excel has built-in functions for each of these; we use STDEVP for σ and STDEV for *s*. In this chapter we illustrate only *s*, but again, the difference is negligible when *n* is large.

The variances and standard deviations of the diameters from the two suppliers in Example 3.3 appear in Figure 3.4. To obtain them, enter the formulas

=VAR(A2:A61)

and

=STDEV(A2:A61)

in cells H5 and H6, and copy these for supplier 2 to cells I5 and I6. Because of the relationship between variance and standard deviation, we could also have used the formula

=SQRT(H5)

in cell H6, but we instead took advantage of the STDEV function.

As we mentioned previously, it is difficult to interpret these variances numerically because they are expressed in squared inches, not inches. All we can say is that the variance from supplier 2 is considerably larger than the variance from supplier 1. The standard deviations, on the other hand, are expressed in inches. The standard deviation for supplier 1 is approximately 0.011 inch, and supplier 2's standard deviation is approximately three times as large. This is a considerable disparity, as we explain next.

These rules are based on a theoretical distribution called the normal distribution, which we discuss in detail in Chapter 6. Remarkably, many data sets are at least approximately normally distributed, so that these empirical rules often provide very good approximations.

Interpretation of the Standard Deviation: Empirical Rules

Many data sets follow certain "empirical rules." In particular, suppose that a histogram of the data is approximately symmetric and "bell shaped." That is, heights of the bars rise to some peak and then decline. Such behavior is quite common, and it allows us to interpret the standard deviation intuitively. Specifically, we can state that

- approximately 68% of the observations are within 1 standard deviation of the mean, that is, within the interval $\overline{X} \pm s$;

- approximately 95% of the observations are within 2 standard deviations of the mean, that is, within the interval $\overline{X} \pm 2s$; and

- approximately 99.7%—almost all—of the observations are within 3 standard deviations of the mean, that is, within the interval $\overline{X} \pm 3s$.

We illustrate these empirical rules with the following example.

EXAMPLE	**3.4 DISTRIBUTION OF MONTHLY DOW RETURNS**

The file **DJI Index.xlsx** contains monthly closing prices for the Dow Jones Industrials index from January 1947 through January 1993. The monthly returns from the index are also shown, starting with the February 1947 value. Each return is the monthly percentage change (expressed as a decimal) in the index. How well do the empirical rules work for these data?

Objective To illustrate the empirical rules for Dow Jones monthly returns.

Solution

Figures 3.5 and 3.6 show time series graphs of the index itself and the monthly returns. Clearly, the index has been increasing fairly steadily over the period, whereas the returns exhibit no obvious trend. Whenever a series indicates a clear trend, most of the measures we have been discussing are less relevant. For example, the mean closing index for this period has at most historical interest. We are probably more interested in predicting the *future* of the Dow, and the historical mean (or standard deviation or variance) has little relevance for predicting the future.

Figure 3.5 Time Series Graph of Dow Closing Index

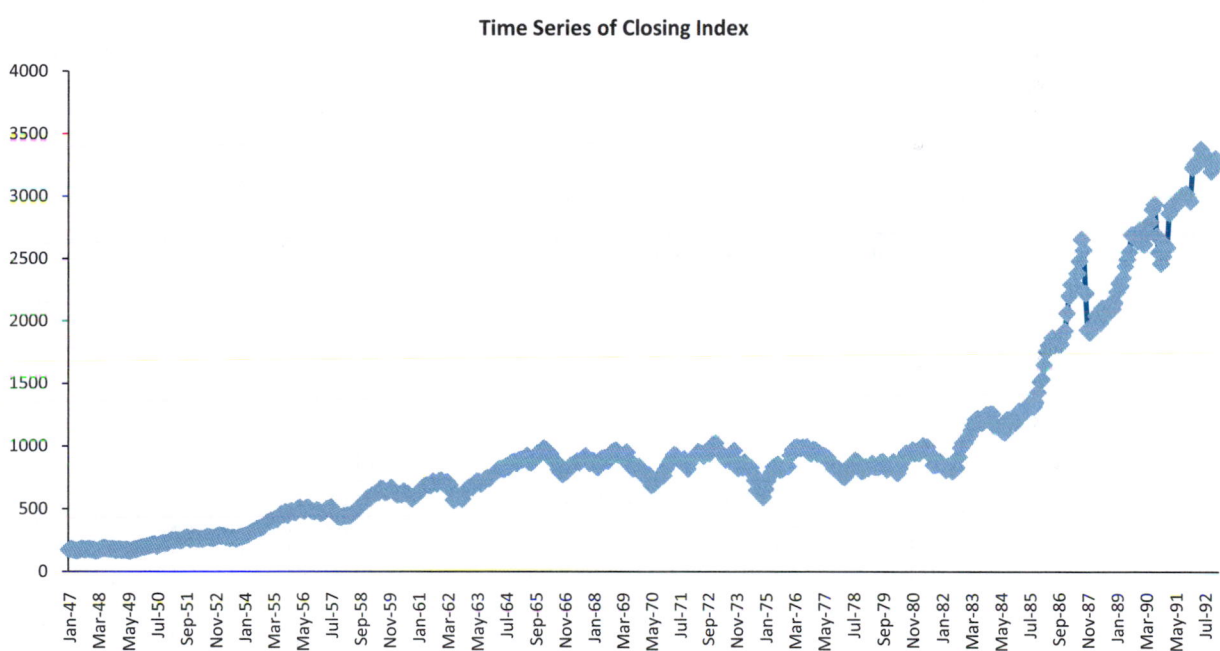

In contrast, the measures we have been discussing are relevant for the series of returns, which fluctuates around a stable mean. In Figure 3.7 we first calculate the mean and standard deviation of returns with the AVERAGE and STDEV functions in cells B4 and B5. These indicate an average return of about 0.59% and a standard deviation of about 3.37%. Therefore, the empirical rules (if they apply) imply, for example, that about 2/3 of all returns are within the interval 0.59% ± 3.37%, that is, from −2.78% to 3.95%.

Figure 3.6   Time Series Graph of Dow Returns

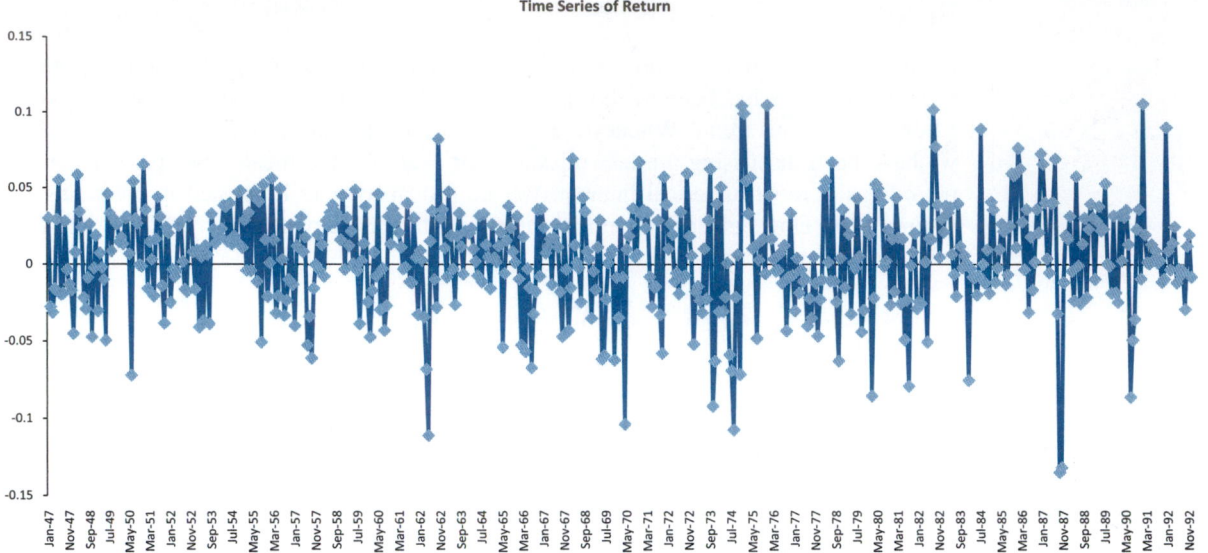

Figure 3.7

Empirical Rules for
Dow Jones Data

	A	B	C	D
1	**Checking empirical rules for returns**			
2				
3	Summary measures of returns			
4	Mean	0.0059		
5	Stdev	0.0337		
6				
7	Category	Upper limit	Frequency	
8	More than 3 stdevs below mean	-0.0951	5	
9	Between 2 and 3 stdevs below mean	-0.0614	13	
10	Between 1 and 2 stdevs below mean	-0.0278	57	
11	Between mean and 1 stdev below mean	0.0059	194	
12	Between mean and 1 stdev above mean	0.0395	217	
13	Between 1 and 2 stdevs above mean	0.0732	55	
14	Between 2 and 3 stdevs above mean	0.1069	11	
15	More than 3 stdevs above mean		0	
16				
17	Percentages within k stdevs of mean			
18	k	1	2	3
19	Actual	74.5%	94.7%	99.1%
20	From empirical rules	68.0%	95.0%	99.7%

We can use a frequency table to check whether the empirical rules apply to these returns. We first enter the upper limits of suitable categories in the range A8:A15. Although any categories could be chosen, it is convenient to choose values of the form $\overline{X} \pm ks$ as breakpoints for the categories, where the open-ended categories on either end are "more than 3 standard deviations from the mean." Here, k is a typical multiple of the standard deviation s. We let k have the values 1, 2, and 3. Then the upper limits of the categories can be calculated in column B by entering the formulas

=B4-3*B5

and

=B8+\$B\$5

in cells B8 and B9, and then copying this latter formula to the range B10:B14. In words, each breakpoint is 1 standard deviation higher than the previous one.

Next, we use the FREQUENCY function to fill in column C. Specifically, we highlight the range C8:C15, type the formula

=FREQUENCY(Return,Bins)

and press Ctrl-Shift-Enter. (Here, Return is the range name for the Returns variable, and Bins is the range name of the range B8:B14.)

The FREQUENCY function is an "array function" in Excel. We enter it with the Ctrl-Shift-Enter key combination.

Finally, we use the frequencies in column C to calculate the actual percentages of returns within k standard deviations of the mean for $k = 1$, $k = 2$, and $k = 3$, and we compare these with percentages from the empirical rules. (See rows 19 and 20.) The agreement between these percentages is not perfect—there are a few more observations within 1 standard deviation of the mean than the empirical rules predict—but in general the empirical rules work quite well. ∎

3.6 OBTAINING SUMMARY MEASURES WITH ADD-INS

In the past few sections we used Excel's built-in functions (AVERAGE, STDEV, and so on) to calculate a number of summary measures. A quicker way is to use the StatTools add-in. We illustrate the StatTools add-in in the following example.

EXAMPLE | **3.5 SUMMARIZING STARTING SALARIES FOR BUSINESS UNDERGRADUATES**

Refer again to the **Starting Salaries.xlsx** data set used in Example 3.1, and find a set of useful summary measures for the salaries.

Objective To use StatTools's One-Variable Summary Statistics procedure to calculate summary measures of salaries.

Solution

This is easy with StatTools's One-Variable Summary Statistics procedure. As usual, begin by creating a StatTools data set with the StatTools Data Set Manager. Then select One-Variable Summary from Summary Statistics on the StatTools ribbon, select all variables you want to summarize, and select the summary measures you want from the dialog box shown in Figure 3.8. (Here is a handy tip. When you first see the dialog box shown in Figure 3.8, it will probably have all of the options checked, which is probably more than you want. In this case, uncheck the options you don't want, and then click on the middle "Save" button on the lower left. This allows you to save your setup—the options you want for *future* analyses.)

Figure 3.8

One-Variable
Summary Statistics
Dialog Box

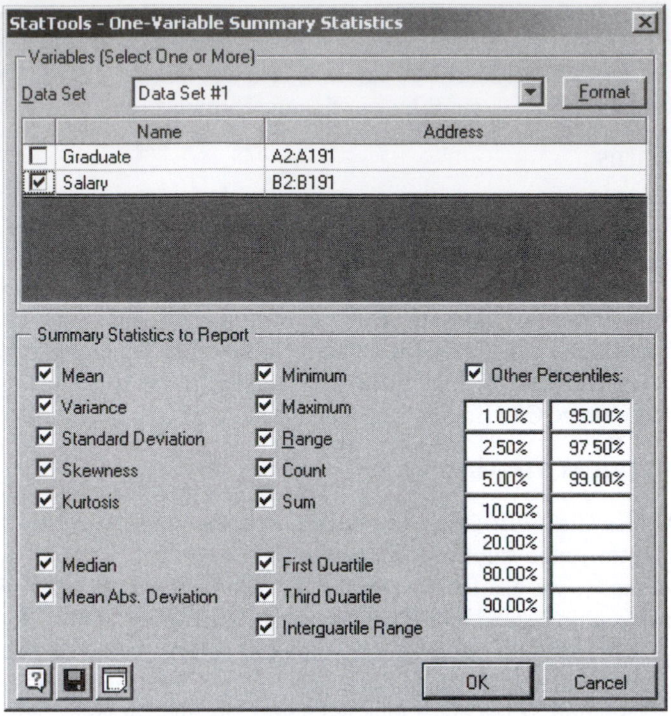

A typical output appears in Figure 3.9. It includes many of the summary measures we have discussed, plus a few more. The **mean absolute deviation** is similar to the variance, except that it is an average of the *absolute* (not squared) deviations from the mean. The **kurtosis** and **skewness** indicate the relative peakedness of the distribution and its skewness. These are relatively technical measures that we will not discuss here.

Figure 3.9

Selected Summary
Measures Using
StatTools Add-In

	A	B
7		Salary
8	*One Variable Summary*	Data Set #1
9	Mean	$29762.11
10	Variance	13743424.12
11	Std. Dev.	$3707.21
12	Skewness	-0.1663
13	Kurtosis	2.9291
14	Median	$29850.00
15	Mean Abs. Dev.	$2967.77
16	Minimum	$17100.00
17	Maximum	$38200.00
18	Range	$21100.00
19	Count	190
20	Sum	$5654800.00
21	1st Quartile	$27325.00
22	3rd Quartile	$32300.00
23	Interquartile Range	$4975.00
24	1.00%	$22168.00
25	2.50%	$22772.50
26	5.00%	$23690.00
27	10.00%	$25070.00
28	20.00%	$26800.00
29	80.00%	$33020.00
30	90.00%	$34620.00
31	95.00%	$35810.00
32	97.50%	$36510.00
33	99.00%	$36900.00

By clicking on any of the cells in column B of Figure 3.9, you see that StatTools provides *formulas* for the outputs, using its own built-in statistical functions. The effect is that if any of the original data change, the summary measures we just produced change automatically. Finally, note that all outputs are formatted with a certain number of decimal places by default. You can reformat them in a more appropriate manner if you like. ■

PROBLEMS

Level A

1. A human resources manager at Beta Technologies, Inc., is interested in compiling some statistics on full-time Beta employees. In particular, she is interested in summarizing age, number of years of relevant full-time work experience prior to coming to Beta, number of years of full-time work experience at Beta, number of years of post-secondary education, and salary. Find appropriate summary measures for these factors using data in the file **P02_01.xlsx**.

2. A production manager is interested in determining the typical proportion of defective items in a shipment of one of the computer components that her company manufactures. The spreadsheet provided in the file **P02_02.xlsx** contains the proportion of defective components for each of 500 randomly selected shipments collected during a 1-month period. Is the mean, median, or mode the most appropriate measure of central location for these data?

3. *Business Week's Guide to the Best Business Schools* provides enrollment data on graduate business programs that it rates as the best in the United States. Specifically, this guide reports the percentages of women, minority, and international students enrolled in each of the top programs, as well as the total number of full-time students enrolled in each program. Use the most appropriate measure(s) of central location to find the typical percentage of women, minority, and international students enrolled in these elite programs. These data are contained in the file **P02_03.xlsx**.

4. The manager of a local fast-food restaurant is interested in improving the service provided to customers who use the restaurant's drive-up window. As a first step in this process, the manager asks his assistant to record the time (in minutes) it takes to serve 200 customers at the final window in the facility's drive-up system. The 200 customer service times given in the file **P02_04.xlsx** are all observed during the busiest hour of the day for this fast-food operation.
   a. Compute the mean, median, and mode of this sample of customer service times.
   b. Which of these measures do you believe is the most appropriate one in describing this distribution? Explain the reasoning behind your choice.

5. A finance professor has just given a midterm examination in her corporate finance course. In particular, she is interested in learning how her class of 100 students performed on this exam. The 100 exam scores are given in the file **P02_05.xlsx**.
   a. What are the mean and median scores (out of 100 possible points) on this exam?
   b. Explain why the mean and median values are different for these data.

6. Compute the mean, median, and mode of the given set of average annual household income levels of citizens from selected U.S. metropolitan areas in the file **P03_06.xlsx**. What can you infer about the shape of this particular income distribution from the computed measures of central location?

7. The operations manager of a toll booth, located at a major exit of a state turnpike, is trying to estimate the typical number of vehicles that arrive at the toll booth during a 1-minute period during the peak of rush-hour traffic. In an effort to estimate this typical throughput value, he records the number of vehicles that arrive at the toll booth over a 1-minute interval commencing at the same time for each of 365 normal weekdays. These data are contained in the file **P02_09.xlsx**.
   a. Find the most appropriate measure of the given distribution's central location.
   b. Is this distribution of arrivals *skewed* somewhat? Explain.

8. The proportions of high school graduates annually taking the SAT test in each of the 50 states and the District of Columbia are provided in the file **P02_10.xlsx**.
   a. Compute the mean, median, and mode of this set of proportions.
   b. Which of these measures do you believe is the most appropriate one in describing this distribution? Explain the reasoning behind your choice.

9. Consider the average time (in minutes) it takes a citizen of each metropolitan area to travel to work and back home each day. Refer to the data given in the file **P02_11.xlsx**.
   a. Find the most representative average commute time across this distribution.

b. Does it appear that this distribution of average commute times is *approximately* symmetric? Explain why or why not.

10. Five hundred households in a middle-class neighborhood were recently surveyed as a part of an economic development study conducted by the local government. Specifically, for each of the 500 randomly selected households, the survey requested information on several variables, including the household's level of indebtedness (excluding the value of any home mortgage). These data are provided in the file **P02_06.xlsx**.
    a. Find the maximum and minimum debt levels for the households in this sample.
    b. Find the indebtedness levels at each of the 25th, 50th, and 75th percentiles.
    c. Compute and interpret the interquartile range for these data.

11. A real estate agent has gathered data on 150 houses that were recently sold in a suburban community. This data set includes observations for each of the following variables: the appraised value of each house (in thousands of dollars), the selling price of each house (in thousands of dollars), the size of each house (in hundreds of square feet), and the number of bedrooms in each house. Refer to the file **P02_07.xlsx** in answering the following questions.
    a. Find the house(s) at the 80th percentile of all sample houses with respect to *appraised value*.
    b. Find the house(s) at the 80th percentile of all sample houses with respect to *selling price*.
    c. Find the maximum and minimum sizes (measured in *square footage*) of all sample houses.
    d. What is the typical number of bedrooms in a recently sold house in this suburban community?

12. The U.S. Department of Transportation regularly publishes the *Air Travel Consumer Report,* which provides a variety of performance measures of major U.S. commercial airlines. One dimension of performance reported is each airline's percentage of domestic flights arriving within 15 minutes of the scheduled arrival time at major reporting airports throughout the country. Use these data, given in the file **P02_12.xlsx**, to answer the following questions:
    a. Which major U.S. airline has the *highest* third quartile on-time arrival percentage?
    b. Which major U.S. airline has the *lowest* first quartile on-time arrival percentage?
    c. Which major U.S. airline has the *largest* range of on-time arrival percentages?
    d. Which major U.S. airline has the *smallest* range of on-time arrival percentages?

13. Having computed measures of central location for various numerical attributes of full-time employees, a human resources manager at Beta Technologies, Inc., is now interested in compiling some statistics on the variability of sample data values about their respective means. Using the data provided in the file **P02_01.xlsx**, assist this manager by computing sample standard deviations for each of the following numerical variables: age, number of years of relevant full-time work experience prior to coming to Beta, number of years of full-time work experience at Beta, number of years of post-secondary education, and salary. For each variable, explain why the empirical rules apply or do not apply.

14. A production manager is interested in determining the variability of the proportion of defective items in a shipment of one of the computer components that her company manufactures. The spreadsheet provided in the file **P02_02.xlsx** contains the proportion of defective components for each of 500 randomly selected shipments collected during a 1-month period. Compute the sample standard deviation of these data. Discuss whether the empirical rules apply.

15. In an effort to provide more consistent customer service, the manager of a local fast-food restaurant would like to know the dispersion of customer service times about their average value for the facility's drive-up window. The file **P02_04.xlsx** contains 200 customer service times, all of which were observed during the busiest hour of the day for this fast-food operation.
    a. Find and interpret the variance and standard deviation of these sample values.
    b. Are the empirical rules applicable for these data? If so, apply these rules and interpret your results. If not, explain why the empirical rules are not applicable here.

16. Compute the standard deviation of the average annual household income levels of citizens from selected U.S. metropolitan areas in the file **P03_06.xlsx**. Is it appropriate to apply the empirical rules for these data? Explain.

17. The file **P02_26.xlsx** contains annual percentage changes in consumer prices. Are the empirical rules applicable in this case? If so, apply these rules and interpret your results.

18. The diameters of 100 rods produced by Rodco are listed in the file **P03_18.xlsx**. Based on these data, you can be approximately 99.7% sure that the diameter of a typical rod will be between what two numbers?

19. The file **P03_19.xlsx** contains the thickness (in centimeters) of some mica pieces. A piece meets specifications if it is between 7 and 15 centimeters in thickness.
    a. What fraction of mica pieces meet specifications?
    b. Do the empirical rules appear to be valid for these data?

Level B

20. A finance professor has just given a midterm examination in her corporate finance course. She is now interested in assigning letter grades to the scores earned by her 100 students who took this exam. The top 10% of all scores should receive a grade of A. The next 10% of all scores should be assigned a grade of B. The third 10% of all scores should receive a grade of C. The next 10% of all scores should be assigned a grade of D. All remaining scores should receive a grade of F. The 100 exam scores are given in the file **P02_05.xlsx**. Assist this instructor in assigning letter grades to these finance exam scores.

21. The operations manager of a toll booth, located at a major exit of a state turnpike, is trying to estimate the variability of the number of vehicles that arrive at the toll booth during a 1-minute period during the peak of rush-hour traffic. In an effort to estimate this measure of dispersion, he records the number of vehicles that arrive at the toll booth over a 1-minute interval commencing at the same time for each of 365 normal weekdays. These data are contained in the file **P02_09.xlsx**.
    a. Is the sample variance (or sample standard deviation) a reliable measure of dispersion for these data? Explain why or why not.
    b. If the sample variance (or sample standard deviation) is not a reliable measure of dispersion for these data, how can this operations manager most appropriately measure the variability of the values in this data set?

22. The file **P02_10.xlsx** contains the proportions of high school graduates annually taking the SAT test in each of the 50 states and the District of Columbia. Approximately 95% of these proportions fall between what two fractions?

23. The file **P03_23.xlsx** contains the salaries of all Indiana University business school professors.
    a. If you increased every professor's salary by $1000, what would happen to the mean and median salary?
    b. If you increased every professor's salary by $1000, what would happen to the sample standard deviation of the salaries?
    c. If you increased everybody's salary by 5%, what would happen to the sample standard deviation of the salaries?

24. The file **P03_24.xlsx** contains a sample of family incomes (in thousands of 1980 dollars) for a set of families sampled in 1980 and 1990. Assume that these families are representative of the whole United States. The Republicans claim that the country was better off in 1990 than 1980, because average income increased. Do you agree?

25. According to the Educational Testing Service, the scores of people taking the SAT were as listed in Table 3.1.
    a. Estimate the average and standard deviation of SAT scores for students whose families made at least $18,000 and for those whose families made no more than $6000. (*Hint*: Assume all scores in a group are concentrated at the group's midpoint.)
    b. Do these results have any implications for college admissions?

Table 3.1 Data on SAT Scores

Range	Number Having Family Income ≥$18,000	Number Having Family Income ≤$6000
200–250	325	1638
251–300	4212	7980
301–350	13,896	9622
351–400	26,175	8973
401–450	37,213	8054
451–500	41,412	6663
501–550	37,400	4983
551–600	28,151	3119
601–650	17,992	1626
651–700	9284	686
701–750	3252	239
751–800	415	17

26. The file **P03_26.xlsx** lists the fraction of U.S. men and women of various heights. Use these data to estimate the mean and standard deviation of the height of American men and women. (*Hint*: Assume all heights in a group are concentrated at the group's midpoint.)

27. The file **P03_27.xlsx** lists the fraction of U.S. men and women of various weights. Use these data to estimate the mean and standard deviation of the weights of U.S. men and women. (*Hint*: Assume all weights in a group are concentrated at the group's midpoint.)

3.7 MEASURES OF ASSOCIATION: COVARIANCE AND CORRELATION

All of the summary measures to this point involve a *single* variable. It is also useful to summarize the relationship between two variables. Specifically, we would like to summarize the type of behavior often observed in a scatterplot. Two such measures are *covariance* and *correlation*. We discuss them briefly here and in more depth in later chapters. Each measures the strength (and direction) of a *linear* relationship between two numerical variables. Intuitively, the relationship is "strong" if the points in a scatterplot cluster tightly around some straight line. If this straight line rises from left to right, then the relationship is *positive* and the measures are positive numbers. If it falls from left to right, then the relationship is *negative* and the measures are negative numbers.

If we want to measure the covariance or correlation between two variables X and Y—indeed, even if we just want to form a scatterplot of X versus Y—then X and Y must be "paired" variables. That is, they must have the same number of observations, and the X and Y values for any observation should be naturally paired. For example, each observation could be the height and weight for a particular person, the time in a store and the amount purchased for a particular customer, and so on.

With this in mind, let X_i and Y_i be the paired values for observation i, and let n be the number of observations. Then the covariance between X and Y, denoted by $Cov(X, Y)$, is given by equation (3.5):

Formula for Covariance

$$Cov(X, Y) = \frac{\sum_{i=1}^{n}(X_i - \overline{X})(Y_i - \overline{Y})}{n - 1}$$

(3.5)

Scatterplots that rise from lower left to upper right will tend to have positive covariance and correlation. Those that fall from upper left to lower right will tend to have negative covariance and correlation.

You probably will never have to use this formula directly—Excel has a built-in COVAR function that does it for you—but the formula does indicate what covariance is all about. It is essentially an average of products of deviations from means. If X and Y vary in the *same* direction, then when X is above (or below) its mean, Y will also tend to be above (or below) its mean. In either case, the product of deviations will be positive—a positive times a positive or a negative times a negative—so the covariance will be positive. The opposite is true when X and Y vary in *opposite* directions. Then the covariance will be negative.

The limitation of covariance as a descriptive measure is that it is affected by the *units* in which X and Y are measured. For example, we can inflate the covariance by a factor of 1000 simply by measuring X in dollars rather than in thousands of dollars. The correlation, denoted by $Corr(X, Y)$, remedies this problem. It is a *unitless* quantity defined by equation (3.6), where $Stdev(X)$ and $Stdev(Y)$ denote the standard deviations of X and Y. Again, you'll probably never have to use this formula for calculations—Excel does it for you with the built-in CORREL function—but it does show that to produce a unitless quantity, we need to divide the covariance by the product of the standard deviations.

Formula for Correlation

$$Corr(X, Y) = \frac{Cov(X, Y)}{Stdev(X) \times Stdev(Y)}$$

(3.6)

Statisticians use the symbol r for the correlation based on sample data. If they want to denote the correlation based on the entire population, they use the symbol ρ (rho).

The correlation is unaffected by the units of measurement of the two variables, and it is *always* between -1 and $+1$. The closer it is to either of these two extremes, the closer the points in a scatterplot are to some straight line, either in the negative or positive direction. On the other hand, if the correlation is close to 0, then the scatterplot is typically a "cloud" of points with no apparent relationship. However, it is also possible that the points are close to a *curve* and have a correlation close to 0. This is because correlation is relevant only for measuring *linear* relationships.

When there are more than two variables in a data set, it is often useful to create a table of covariances and/or correlations. Each value in the table then corresponds to a particular pair of variables. StatTools allows you to do this easily, as illustrated in the following example.

A survey questions members of 100 households about their spending habits. The data in the file **Household Expenses.xlsx** represent the salary, expenses for cultural activities, expenses for sports-related activities, and expenses for dining out for each household over the past year. Do these variables appear to be related linearly?

Objective To use StatTools's Correlation and Covariance procedure to measure the relationship between expenses in various categories.

Solution

Scatterplots of each variable versus each other variable answer the question quite nicely, but six scatterplots are required, one for each pair. To get a quick indication of possible linear relationships, we can use StatTools to obtain a table of correlations and/or covariances. To do so, make sure a StatTools data set has been created in the usual way, select Correlation and Covariance from Summary Statistics on the StatTools ribbon, select all four variables of interest, and choose to obtain correlations *and* covariances. Otherwise, accept all of StatTools's default settings. The tables of correlations and covariances appear in Figure 3.10.

Figure 3.10

Table of Correlations and Covariances

	A	B	C	D	E
7		Salary	Culture	Sports	Dining
8	*Correlation Table*	Data Set #1	Data Set #1	Data Set #1	Data Set #1
9	Salary	1.000	0.506	-0.081	0.558
10	Culture	0.506	1.000	-0.520	0.170
11	Sports	-0.081	-0.520	1.000	0.266
12	Dining	0.558	0.170	0.266	1.000
13					
14		Salary	Culture	Sports	Dining
15	*Covariance Table*	Data Set #1	Data Set #1	Data Set #1	Data Set #1
16	Salary	91130278.79	1105845.25	-221238.79	2590600.81
17	Culture	1105845.25	52315.39	-33946.99	18938.02
18	Sports	-221238.79	-33946.99	81427.23	36829.58
19	Dining	2590600.81	18938.02	36829.58	236187.67

The only relationships that stand out are the positive relationships between salary and cultural expenses and between salary and dining expenses, and the negative relationship between cultural and sports-related expenses. In contrast, there is very little linear relationship between salary and sports expenses or between dining expenses and either culture or sports expenses. To confirm these graphically, we show scatterplots of Salary versus Culture and Sports versus Culture in Figures 3.11 and 3.12. These indicate more intuitively what a correlation of approximately ±0.5 really means.

In general, we point out the following properties that are evident from Figure 3.10:

■ The correlation between a variable and itself is always 1.

■ The correlation between X and Y is the same as the correlation between Y and X. Therefore, it is sufficient to list the correlations below (or above) the diagonal in the table. (The same is true for covariances.) StatTools provides these options.

■ The covariance between a variable and itself is the *variance* of that variable.

- It is difficult to interpret the magnitudes of the covariances. These depend on the fact that the data are measured in dollars rather than, say, thousands of dollars. It is much easier to interpret the magnitudes of the correlations because they are scaled to be between −1 and +1.

Figure 3.11

Scatterplot Indicating a Positive Relationship

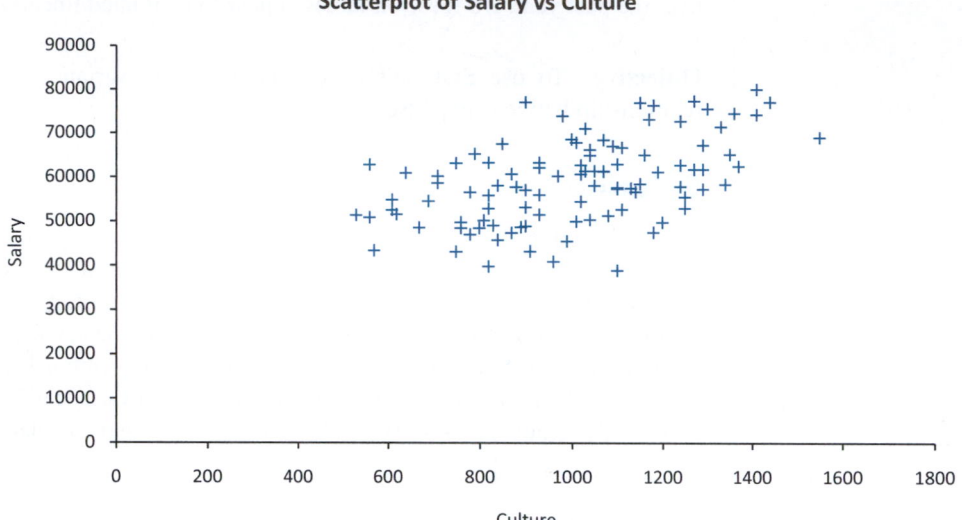

Figure 3.12

Scatterplot Indicating a Negative Relationship

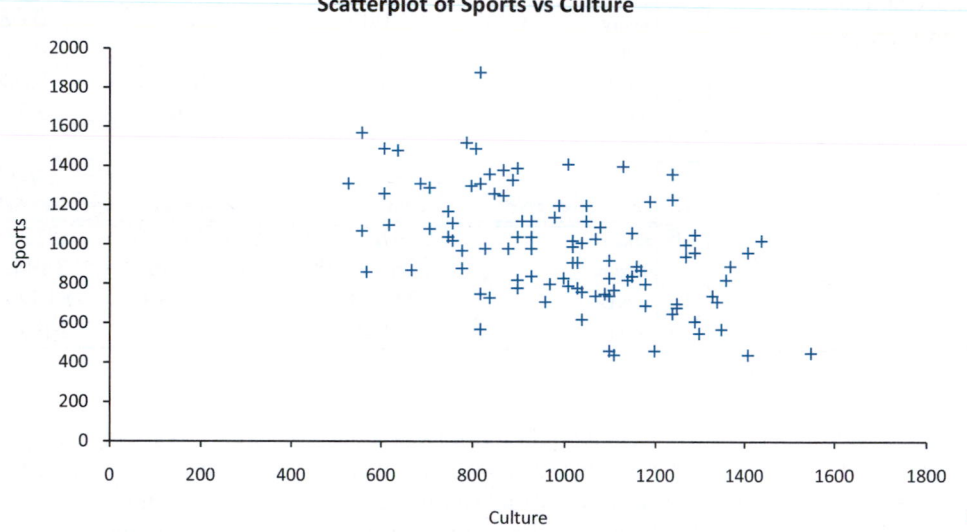

PROBLEMS

Level A

28. Explore the relationship between the selling prices and the appraised values of the 150 homes in the file **P02_07.xlsx** by computing a correlation.

a. Is there evidence of a *linear* relationship between the selling price and appraised value for these data? If so, characterize the relationship (i.e., indicate whether the relationship is a positive or negative one).

b. For which of the two remaining variables, the size of the home and the number of bedrooms in the home, is the relationship with the home's appraised value *stronger?* Justify your choice.

29. A human resources manager at Beta Technologies, Inc., is trying to determine the variable that best explains the variation of employee salaries using the sample of 52 full-time employees in the file **P02_01.xlsx**. Create a table of correlations to help this manager identify whether the employee's (a) gender, (b) age, (c) number of years of relevant work experience prior to employment at Beta, (d) the number of years of employment at Beta, or (e) the number of years of postsecondary education has the *strongest* linear relationship with annual salary.

30. Consider the enrollment data for *Business Week*'s top U.S. graduate business programs in the file **P02_03.xlsx**. Specifically, compute correlations to assess whether there is a linear relationship between the total number of full-time students and each of the following: (a) the proportion of female students, (b) the proportion of minority students, and (c) the proportion of international students enrolled at these distinguished business schools.

31. What is the relationship between the number of short-term general hospitals and the number of medical specialists in metropolitan areas? Explore this question by the correlation between these two variables using the data in the file **P02_17.xlsx**. Interpret your result.

32. Consider the economic development data in the file **P02_06.xlsx**.
   a. Calculate the correlation between each variable and the household's average monthly expenditure on utilities.
   b. Which of the variables have a *positive* linear relationship with the household's average monthly expenditure on utilities?
   c. Which of the variables have a *negative* linear relationship with the household's average monthly expenditure on utilities?
   d. Which of the variables have essentially *no* linear relationship with the household's average monthly expenditure on utilities?

33. Motorco produces electric motors for use in home appliances. One of the company's production managers is interested in examining the relationship between the dollars spent per month in inspecting finished motor products and the number of motors produced during that month that were returned by dissatisfied customers. He has collected the data in the file **P02_18.xlsx** to explore this relationship for the past 36 months. Calculate the correlation between these two variables, and interpret it for this production manager.

34. A large number of metropolitan areas in the United States have been ranked with consideration of the following aspects of life in each area: cost of living, transportation, jobs, education, climate, crime, arts, health, and recreation. The data are in the file **P02_55.xlsx**.
   a. Create a table of correlations to discern the relationship between the metropolitan area's overall score and each of these numerical factors.
   b. Which variables are most strongly associated with the overall score? Are you surprised by any of the results here?

35. The *ACCRA Cost of Living Index* provides a useful and reasonably accurate measure of cost-of-living differences among many urban areas. Items on which the index is based have been carefully chosen to reflect the different categories of consumer expenditures. The data are in the file **P02_19.xlsx**. Calculate a table of correlations to explore the relationship between the composite index and each of the various expenditure components.
   a. Which expenditure component has the *strongest* linear relationship with the composite index?
   b. Which expenditure component has the *weakest* linear relationship with the composite index?

36. Based on the annual data in the file **P02_25.xlsx** from the U.S. Department of Agriculture, determine whether a linear relationship exists between the number of farms and the average size of a farm in the United States during these years. Specifically, calculate an appropriate correlation and interpret it.

3.8 DESCRIBING DATA SETS WITH BOX PLOTS

We now introduce the *box plot,* a very useful graphical method for summarizing data. We saved box plots for this chapter because they are based on a number of summary measures we discussed in Section 3.2. **Box Plots** can be used in two ways: either to describe a single variable in a data set or to compare two (or more) variables. We illustrate these uses in the following examples.

EXAMPLE | **3.7 DISTRIBUTION OF MONTHLY DOW RETURNS**

Recall that the **DJI Index.xlsx** file lists the monthly returns on the Dow from February 1947 through January 1993. Use a box plot to summarize the distribution of these returns.

Objective   To use StatTools's Box Plot procedure to describe the distribution of monthly Dow returns.

Solution

Excel has no box plot option, but this option is included in the StatTools add-in. To create a box plot for Dow returns, make sure a StatTools data set has been created, select Box-Whisker Plot from Summary Graphs on the StatTools ribbon, click on the Format button and make sure the Unstacked option is selected, select the Return variable, and check the Include Key Describing Plot Elements option.[1] (We discuss the difference between the Stacked and Unstacked options in later sections.) The resulting box plot appears in Figure 3.13. Also, because you checked the Include Key option, the description of the box plot elements in Figure 3.14 is placed below the box plot. These elements are described next.

Figure 3.13   Box Plot of Dow Returns

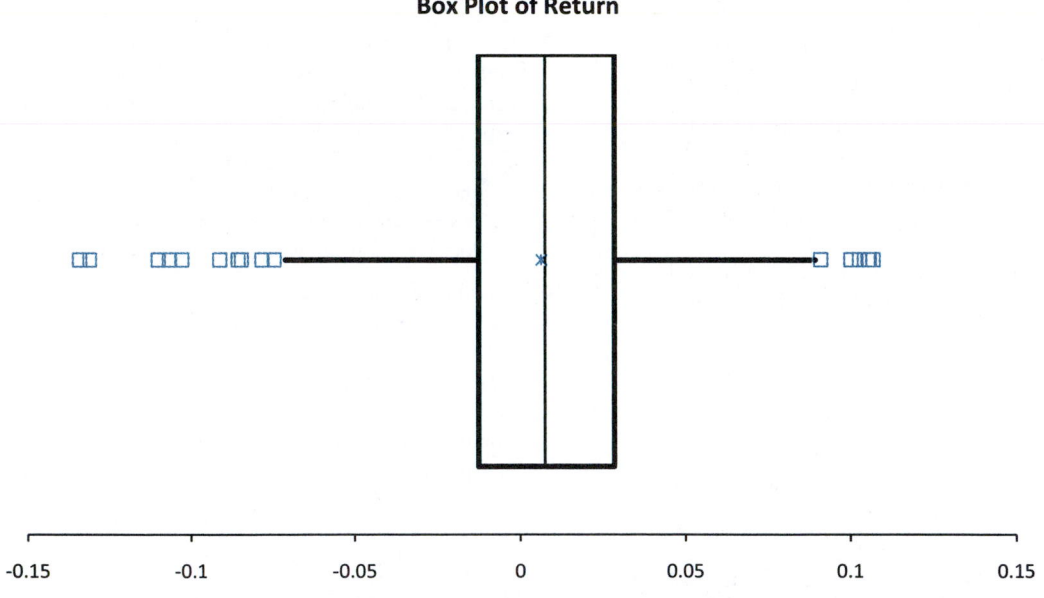

Box Plot of Return

-0.15   -0.1   -0.05   0   0.05   0.1   0.15

[1]Box plots are also called box-whisker plots to indicate the whiskers (lines) on either side of the box.

Figure 3.14

Elements of a
Box Plot

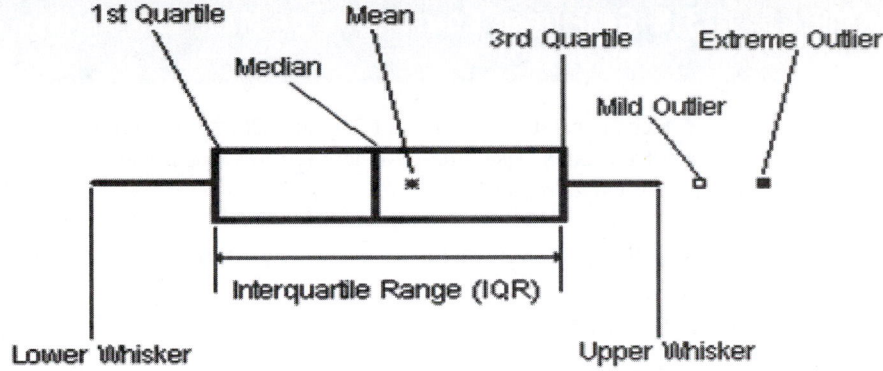

Whiskers extend to the furthest observations that are no more than 1.5 IQR from the edges of the box. Mild outliers are observations between 1.5 IQR and 3 IQR from the edges of the box. Extreme outliers are greater than 3 IQR from the edges of the box.

UNDERSTANDING A BOX PLOT

- The right and left of the box are at the third and first quartiles. Therefore, the length of the box equals the interquartile range (IQR), and the box itself represents the middle 50% of the observations. The height of the box has no significance. (Our box plot conventions are not the only ones, as we see in the chapter opener about movie revenues. However, the variations are primarily cosmetic.)

- The vertical line inside the box indicates the location of the median. The point inside the box indicates the location of the mean.

- Horizontal lines are drawn from each side of the box. They extend to the most extreme observations that are no farther than 1.5 IQRs from the box. They are useful for indicating variability and skewness.[2]

- Observations farther than 1.5 IQRs from the box are shown as individual points. If they are between 1.5 IQRs and 3 IQRs from the box, they are called **mild outliers** and are hollow. Otherwise, they are called **extreme outliers** and are solid.[3]

The box plot implies that the Dow returns are approximately symmetric on each side of the median, although the mean is slightly below the median. In addition, there are a few mild outliers but no extreme outliers. ∎

Box plots are probably most useful for comparing two populations graphically, as we illustrate in the following example.

---

[2]Some statistical software packages create vertical box plots rather than the horizontal type StatTools creates. However, the information is identical. Also, note that the generic chart in StatTools shown in Figure 3.14 is *not* drawn to scale. (The outliers should be farther out.)
[3]These conventions are due to the statistician John Tukey.

3.8 GRAPHICAL COMPARISON OF MALE AND FEMALE MOVIE STARS' INCOMES

Recall that the incomes of famous actors and actresses are listed in the file **Movie Stars.xlsx**. Use side-by-side box plots to compare the incomes of male and female actors and actresses.

Objective To use StatTools's Box Plot procedure to compare actors' incomes across gender.

Solution

This general problem of comparing two (or more) subpopulations is one of the most important problems in statistics, and the issue of a stacked versus unstacked setup almost always arises for such problems.

The data setup for this type of "comparison" problem can be in one of two forms: stacked or unstacked. The data are **stacked** if there is a categorical variable such as Gender that designates which gender each observation is in, and there is a numeric variable such as Income that lists the incomes for both genders. (In this case, StatTools dialog boxes have a "Cat" column for the categorical variable and a "Val" column for the numeric variable.) The data are **unstacked** if there is a *separate* Income column for each gender (one for males and one for females). As Figure 3.15 indicates, the data in the **Movie Stars.xlsx** file are in stacked form. Therefore, to obtain side-by-side box plots of male and female incomes, make sure a StatTools data set has been created, and select Box-Whisker Plot from the StatTools Summary Graphs dropdown. In the resulting dialog box, click on the Format button and make sure the Stacked option is checked. This gives you two columns of checkboxes. Select Gender as the "Cat" variable and Income as the "Val" variable. (This time you can leave the Include Key option unchecked. It always provides exactly the same output and is included only as a learning tool.)

Figure 3.15

Movie Star Data in Stacked Form

	A	B	C	D	E	F	G	H	I
1	Name	Gender	Domestic Gross	Foreign Gross	Income				
2	Angela Bassett	F	32	17	2.5				
3	Jessica Lange	F	21	27	2.5				
4	Winona Ryder	F	36	30	4		All monetary values are in		
5	Michelle Pfeiffer	F	66	31	10		millions of dollars.		
6	Whoopi Goldberg	F	32	33	10				
7	Emma Thompson	F	26	44	3				
8	Julia Roberts	F	57	47	12				
9	Sharon Stone	F	32	47	6				
10	Meryl Streep	F	34	47	4.5				
11	Susan Sarandon	F	38	49	3				
12	Nicole Kidman	F	55	51	4				
13	Holly Hunter	F	51	53	2.5				
14	Meg Ryan	F	43	55	8.5				
15	Andie Macdowell	F	26	75	2				
16	Jodie Foster	F	62	85	9				
17	Rene Russo	F	69	85	2.5				
18	Sandra Bullock	F	64	104	11				
19	Demi Moore	F	65	125	12				
20	Danny Glover	M	42	4	2				
21	Billy Crystal	M	52	14	7				

Excel Tip *Many statistical software packages require data to be in stacked form. StatTools allows data to be in either stacked or unstacked form. In addition, StatTools can convert from stacked to unstacked form, or vice versa.*

The resulting side-by-side box plots appear in Figure 3.16. It is clear that the female income box is considerably to the left of the male income box, although both have about the same IQR. Each box plot has three indications that the income distributions are skewed to the right: (1) the means are larger than the medians, (2) the medians are closer to the left sides of the boxes than to the right sides, and (3) the horizontal lines ("whiskers") extend farther to the right than to the left of the boxes. However, there are no outliers—not even the big stars like Harrison Ford or John Travolta!

Figure 3.16

Side-by-side Box Plots of Female and Male Incomes

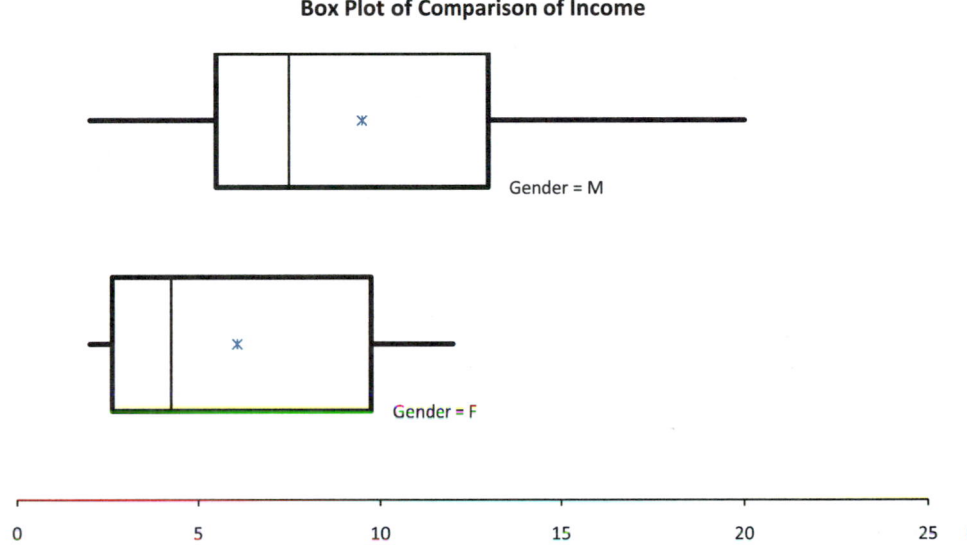

Box Plot of Comparison of Income

PROBLEMS

Level A

37. Consider the data in the file **P03_37.xlsx** on various performance measures for the largest U.S. airlines. Create box plots to summarize each of the given measures of airline performance. Are these four performance measures linearly associated with one another? Explain your findings.

38. In a recent ranking of top graduate business schools in the United States published by *U.S. News & World Report,* the average starting base salaries for recent graduates from recognized graduate programs were provided. These data are given in the file **P02_08.xlsx.** Create a box plot to characterize this distribution of average starting MBA salaries. Is this distribution essentially symmetric or skewed?

39. Consider the average annual rates for various forms of violent crime (including murder, rape, robbery, and aggravated assault) and the average annual rates for various forms of property-related crime (including

burglary, larceny-theft, and motor vehicle theft) in selected U.S. metropolitan areas. The data are provided in the file **P02_50.xlsx.** Create side-by-side box plots to compare the rates of these two general classes of crimes. Summarize your findings.

40. The annual average values of the Consumer Confidence Index are given in the file **P02_28.xlsx.** Create a box plot to find the middle 50% of this distribution of values. Characterize the nature and amount of the variability about the interquartile range for these data.

41. Consider the given set of average annual household income levels of citizens from selected U.S. metropolitan areas in the file **P03_06.xlsx.** What can you infer about the shape of this particular income distribution from a box plot of the given data? If applicable, note the presence of any outliers in this data set.

42. Using cost-of-living data from the *ACCRA Cost of Living Index* in the file **P02_19.xlsx,** create a box plot to summarize the *composite* cost-of-living index values.

43. In 1970 a lottery was held to determine who would be drafted and sent to Vietnam. For each date of the year, a ball was put into an urn. For instance, January 1 was number 305 and February 14 was number 4. Thus a person born on February 14 would be drafted before a person born on January 1. The file **P03_43.xlsx** contains the "draft number" for each date for the 1970 and 1971 lotteries. Do you notice anything unusual about the results of either lottery? What do you think might have caused this result? (*Hint*: Create a box plot for each month's numbers.)

3.9 APPLYING THE TOOLS

Now that you are equipped with a collection of tools for describing data, it's time to apply these tools to some serious data analysis. We examine three data sets in this section. Each of these is rather small by comparison with the data sets real companies often face, but they are large enough to make the analysis far from trivial. In each example we illustrate some of the output that might be obtained by the company involved, but you should realize that we are never really finished. With data sets as rich as these, there are always more numbers that could be calculated, more tables that could be formed, and more charts that could be created. We encourage you to take each analysis a few steps beyond what we present there.

Each example has a decision problem lurking behind it. If these data belonged to real companies, the companies would not only want to describe the data but they would want to use the information from their data analysis as a basis for decision making. We are not yet in a position to perform this decision making, but you should appreciate that the data analysis we perform here is really just the first step in an overall business analysis.

EXAMPLE | **3.9 ACCOUNTS RECEIVABLE AT SPRING MILLS**

The Spring Mills Company produces and distributes a wide variety of manufactured goods. Due to this variety, it has a large number of customers. The company classifies these customers as small, medium, and large, depending on the volume of business each does with Spring Mills. Recently, Spring Mills has noticed a problem with its accounts receivable. It is not getting paid back by its customers in as timely a manner as it would like. This obviously costs Spring Mills money. If a customer delays a payment of $300 for 20 days, say, then the company loses potential interest on this amount. The company has gathered data on 280 customer accounts. For each of these accounts, the data set lists three variables: Size, the size of the customer (coded 1 for small, 2 for medium, 3 for large); Days, the number of days since the customer was billed; and Amount, the amount the customer owes. (See the file **Accounts Receivable.xlsx**.) What information can we obtain from these data?

Appropriate charts let us see the big picture. StatTools makes it easy to create charts quickly and painlessly.

Objective To use charts, summary measures, and pivot tables to understand data on accounts receivable at Spring Mills.

Solution

It is always a good idea to get a rough sense of the data first. We do this by calculating several summary measures for Days and Amount, a histogram of Amount, and a scatterplot of Amount versus Days in Figures 3.17, 3.18, and 3.19. Figure 3.17 indicates positive skewness in the Amount variable—the mean is considerably larger than the median, probably because of some large amounts due. Also, the standard deviation of Amount is quite large. This positive skewness is confirmed by the histogram. The scatterplot suggests some suspicious behavior, with two distinct groups of points. (You can check that the upper group of points in the scatterplot corresponds to the large customers, whose amounts owed are uniformly greater than those in the other two groups.)

Figure 3.17

Summary Measures for the Combined Data

	A	B	C
7		**Days**	**Amount**
8	*One Variable Summary*	Data Set #1	Data Set #1
9	Mean	14.650	$464.29
10	Std. Dev.	7.221	$378.06
11	Median	13.000	$320.00
12	Minimum	2.000	$140.00
13	Maximum	39.000	$2220.00
14	Count	280	280
15	Sum	4102.000	$130000.00

Figure 3.18

Histogram of All Amounts Owed

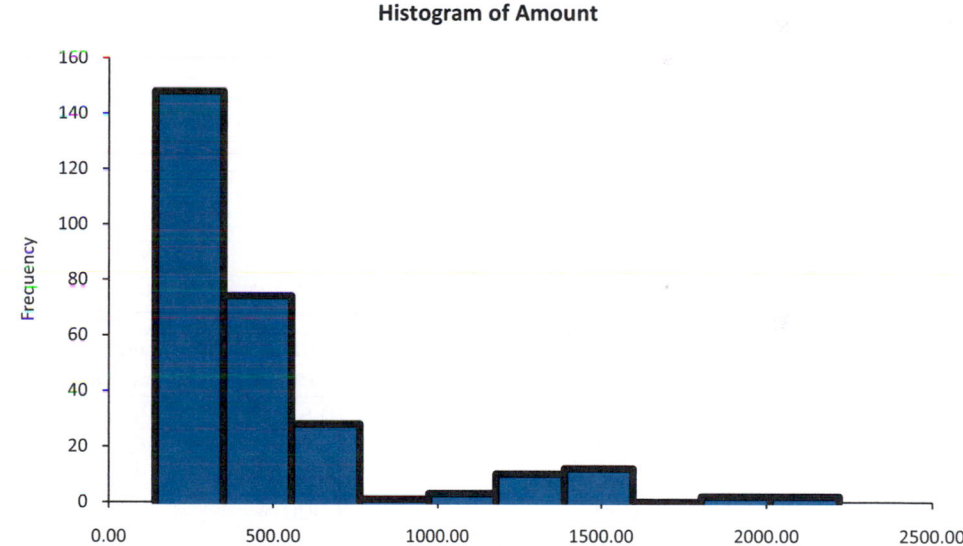

The next logical step is to see whether the different customer sizes have any effect on either Days, Amount, or the relationship between Days and Amount. To do this, it is useful to "unstack" the Days and Amount variables—that is, to create a new Days and Amount variable for *each* group of customer sizes. (To do this, use the Unstack option in the StatTools Utilities group.) For example, the Days and Amount variables for customers of size 1 are labeled Days(1) and Amount(1). (Note that some StatTools procedures can work with the stacked variables directly. Just make sure that when you run one of these StatTools procedures, you click on the Format button and check the Stacked option. However, this Stacked option isn't available for scatterplots, as in Figures 3.26–3.28. For these, we need the unstacked data.) Summary measures and a variety of charts based on these variables appear in Figures 3.20–3.28.

Figure 3.19 Scatterplot of Amount versus Days for All Customers

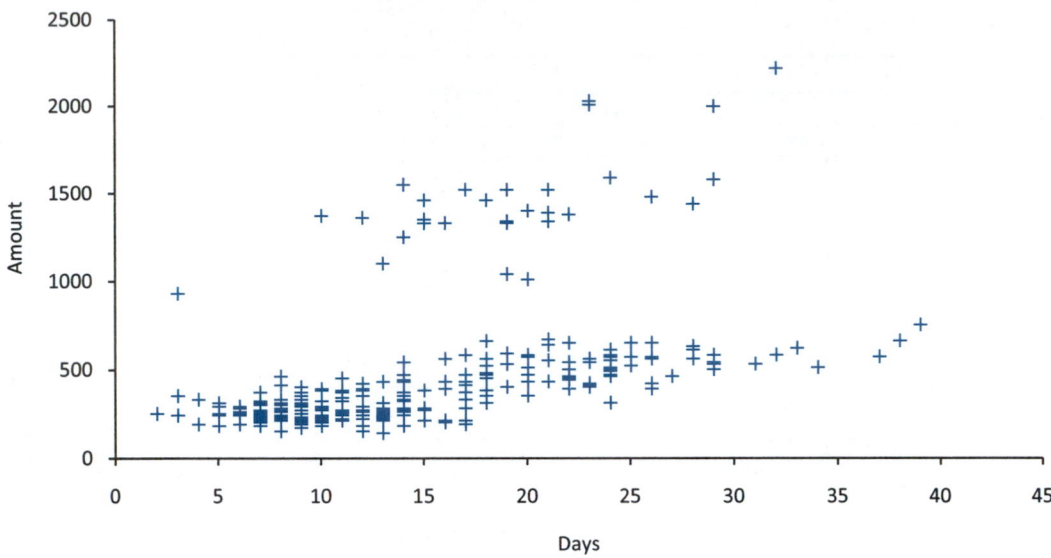

Figure 3.20 Summary Measures Broken Down by Size

	A	B	C	D
7		Days(1)	Days(2)	Days(3)
8	*One Variable Summary*	Data Set #2	Data Set #2	Data Set #2
9	Mean	9.800	20.550	19.233
10	Std. Dev.	3.128	6.622	6.191
11	Median	10.000	20.000	19.000
12	Minimum	2.000	8.000	3.000
13	Maximum	17.000	39.000	32.000
14	Count	150	100	30
15				
16		Amount(1)	Amount(2)	Amount(3)
17	*One Variable Summary*	Data Set #2	Data Set #2	Data Set #2
18	Mean	254.53	481.90	1454.33
19	Std. Dev.	49.28	99.15	293.89
20	Median	250.00	470.00	1395.00
21	Minimum	140.00	280.00	930.00
22	Maximum	410.00	750.00	2220.00
23	Count	150	100	30

Figure 3.21   Histogram of Amount for Small Customers

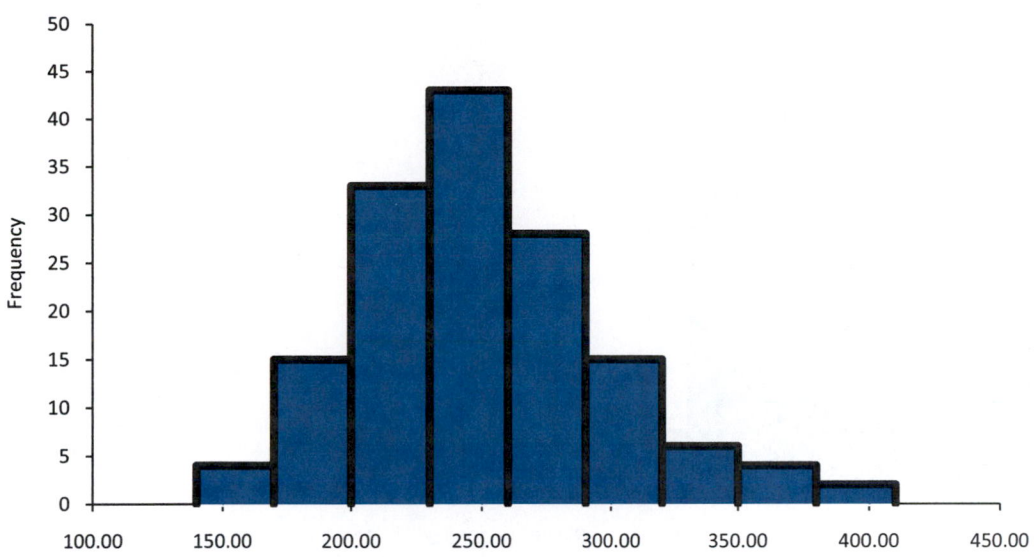

Histogram of Amount(1)

Figure 3.22   Histogram of Amount for Medium Customers

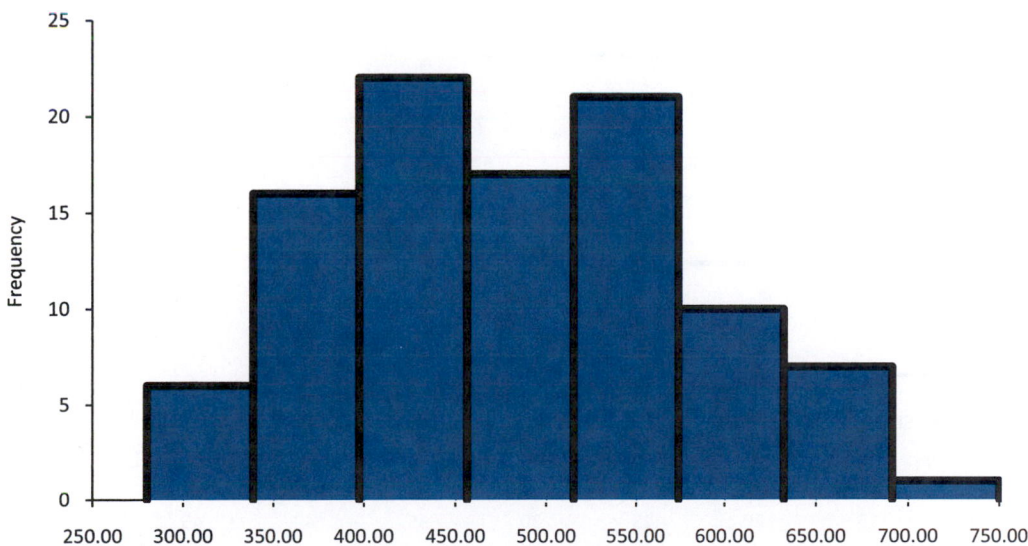

Histogram of Amount(2)

Figure 3.23   Histogram of Amount for Large Customers

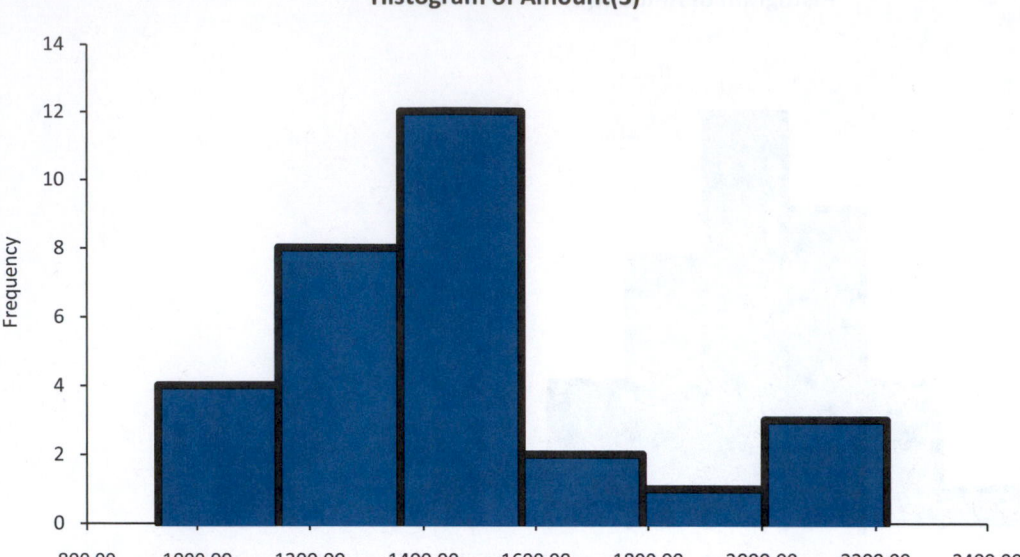

Histogram of Amount(3)

Figure 3.24   Box Plots of Days Owed by Different Size Customers

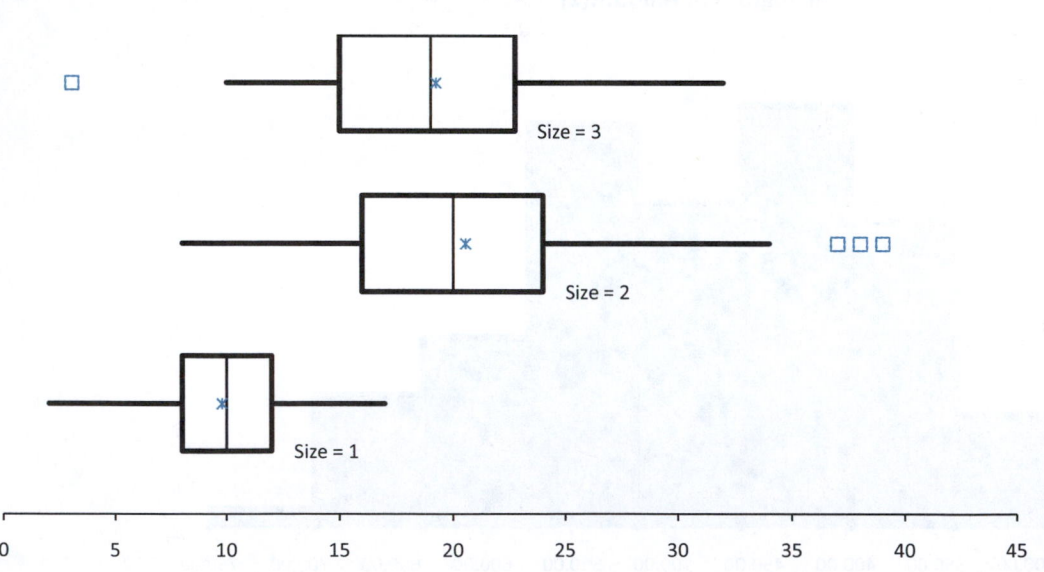

Box Plot of Comparison of Days

Figure 3.25 Box Plots of Amounts Owed by Different Size Customers

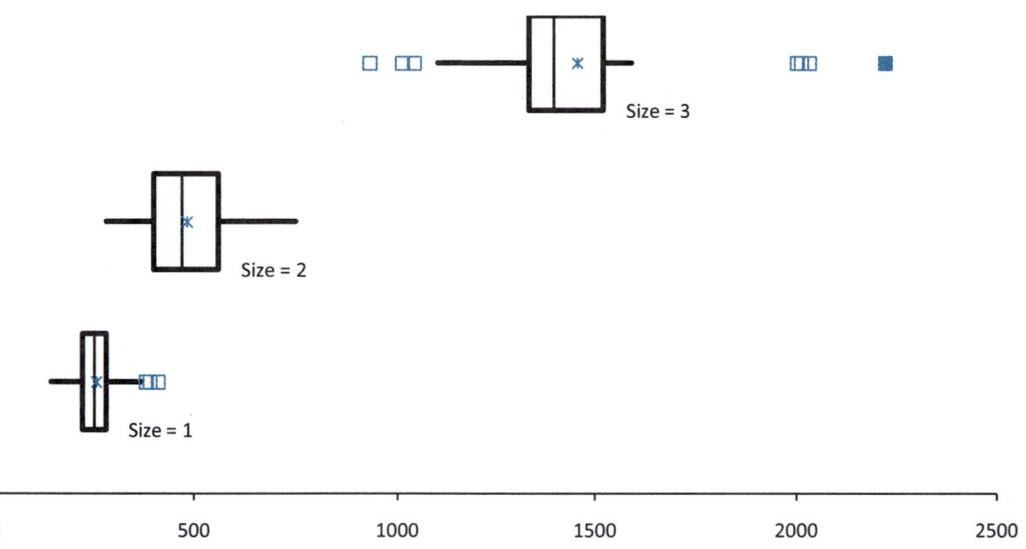

Box Plot of Comparison of Amount

Figure 3.26 Scatterplot of Amount versus Days for Small Customers

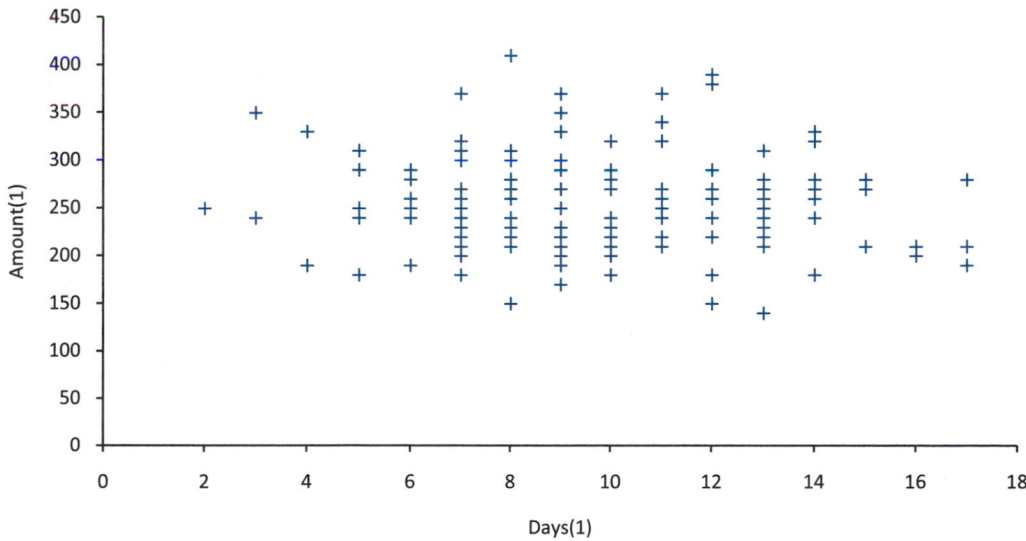

Scatterplot of Amount(1) vs Days(1)

Figure 3.27 Scatterplot of Amount versus Days for Medium Customers

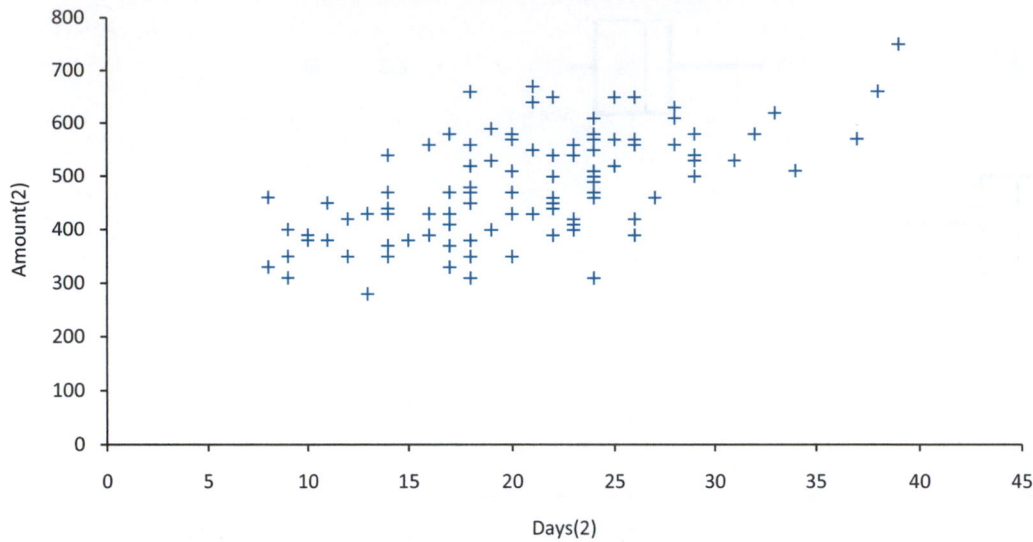

Figure 3.28 Scatterplot of Amount versus Days for Large Customers

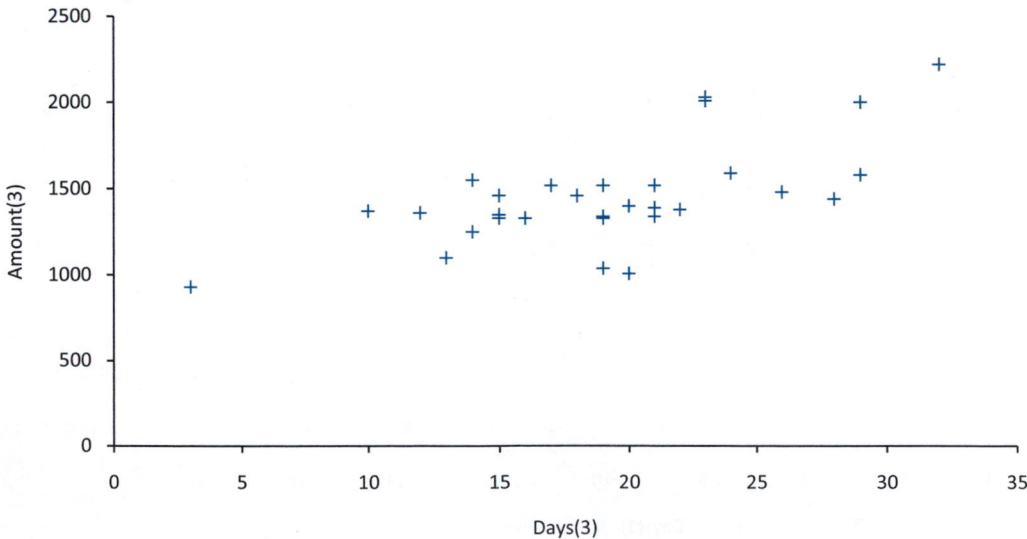

There is obviously a lot going on here, and most of it is clear from the charts. We point out the following: (1) there are far fewer large customers than small or medium customers; (2) the large customers tend to owe considerably more than small or medium customers; (3) the small customers do not tend to be as long overdue as the medium or large customers; and (4) there is no relationship between Days and Amount for the small customers, but there is a definite positive relationship between these variables for the medium and large customers.

We have now done the "obvious" analysis. There is still much more we can do, however. For example, suppose Spring Mills wants a breakdown of customers who owe at least $500. We first create a new variable called "Large?" next to the original variables that equals 1 for all amounts greater than or equal to $500 and equals 0 otherwise.[4] (See Figure 3.29 for some of the data.) We do this by entering the formula

=IF(D2>=$I$1,1,0)

in cell E2 and copying down. We then use a pivot table to create a *count* of the number of 1's in this new variable for each value of the Size variable.

Figure 3.29   Checking for Amounts at Least $500

	A	B	C	D	E	F	G	H	I
1	Account	Size	Days	Amount	Large?			Value to check	$500
2	1	1	7	$180	0				
3	2	1	8	$210	0				
4	3	1	10	$210	0				
5	4	1	8	$150	0				
6	5	1	9	$300	0				
7	6	1	5	$240	0				
8	7	1	4	$330	0				
9	8	1	10	$290	0				
10	9	1	5	$240	0				
11	10	1	13	$270	0				

Figure 3.30 shows the results. Actually, we created this pivot table twice, once (on top) showing counts as percentages of each column, and once showing them as percentages of each row. The top table shows, for example, that about 73% of all customers with amounts less than $500 are small customers. The bottom table shows, for example, that 45% of all medium-size customers owe at least $500. When you hear the expression "slicing and dicing the data," this is what it means. These two pivot tables are based on the *same* counts, but they portray them in slightly different ways. Neither is better than the other; each provides useful information.

Finally, we investigate the amount of interest Spring Mills is losing by the delays in its customers' payments. We assume that the company can make 12% annual interest on excess cash. Then we create a Lost variable for each customer size that indicates the amount of interest Spring Mills loses on each customer group. (See Figure 3.31.) The typical formula for lost interest in cell C10 is

=B10*A10*$C$7/365

[4]We could just as well enter the labels "yes" and "no" in the Large? column. However, it is common to use 0 to 1 values for such a variable.

Figure 3.30

Pivot Tables for Counts of Customers Who Owe More Than $500

	A	B	C	D
1				
2				
3	**Count**	**Large?** ▾		
4	**Size** ▾	**0**	**1**	**Grand Total**
5	1	73.17%	0.00%	53.57%
6	2	26.83%	60.00%	35.71%
7	3	0.00%	40.00%	10.71%
8	**Grand Total**	100.00%	100.00%	100.00%
9				
10	**Count**	**Large?** ▾		
11	**Size** ▾	**0**	**1**	**Grand Total**
12	1	100.00%	0.00%	100.00%
13	2	55.00%	45.00%	100.00%
14	3	0.00%	100.00%	100.00%
15	**Grand Total**	73.21%	26.79%	100.00%

Figure 3.31 Summary Measures of Lost Interest

	A	B	C	D	E	F	G	H	I	J	K	L	M	N
1	Days(1)	Amount(1)	Lost(1)	Days(2)	Amount(2)	Lost(2)	Days(3)	Amount(3)	Lost(3)		Annual rate	12%		
2	7	180	$0.41	17	470	$2.63	19	1330	$8.31					
3	8	210	$0.55	22	540	$3.91	20	1400	$9.21		Summary measures			
4	10	210	$0.69	28	560	$5.16	14	1550	$7.13			Lost(1)	Lost(2)	Lost(3)
5	8	150	$0.39	24	470	$3.71	15	1460	$7.20		Sum	$122.68	$338.65	$287.25
6	9	300	$0.89	26	650	$5.56	23	2030	$15.35		Pct of total	16.4%	45.2%	38.4%
7	5	240	$0.39	29	530	$5.05	19	1520	$9.49					
8	4	330	$0.43	21	550	$3.80	15	1330	$6.56					
9	10	290	$0.95	33	620	$6.73	17	1520	$8.50					
10	5	240	$0.39	16	430	$2.26	21	1390	$9.60					

This is the amount owed multiplied by the number of days owed multiplied by the interest rate, divided by the number of days in a year. Then we calculate sums of these amounts in row 5. Although Spring Mills is losing more per customer from the large customers, it is losing more in *total* from the medium-size customers—because there are more of them. This is shown graphically in Figure 3.32 with a pie chart of the sums in row 5. This pie chart shows, for example, that about 45% of the lost interest is due to the medium-size customers.

Figure 3.32

Pie Chart of Lost Interest by Customer Size

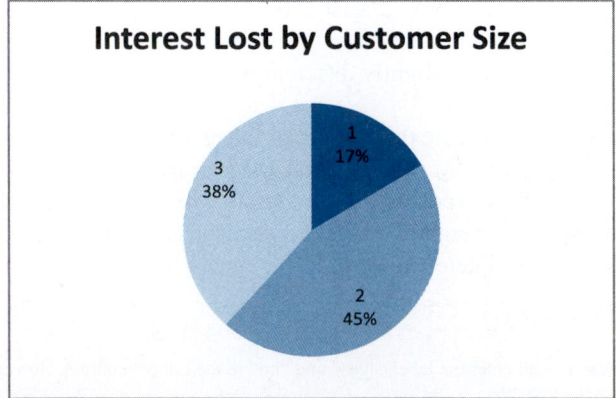

Interest Lost by Customer Size

If Spring Mills really wants to decrease its receivables, it might want to target the medium-size customer group, from which it is losing the most interest. Or it could target the large customers because they owe the most on average. The most appropriate action depends on the cost and effectiveness of targeting any particular customer group. However, the analysis presented here gives the company a much better picture of the current state of affairs. ■

EXAMPLE 3.10 CUSTOMER ARRIVAL AND WAITING PATTERNS AT R&P SUPERMARKET

The R&P Supermarket is open 24 hours a day, 7 days a week. Lately, it has been receiving a lot of complaints from its customers about excessive waiting in line for checking out. R&P has decided to investigate this situation by gathering data on arrivals, departures, and line lengths at the checkout stations. It has collected data in half-hour increments for an entire week—336 observations—starting at 8 A.M. on Monday morning and ending at 8 A.M. the following Monday.

Specifically, it has collected data on the following variables: InitialWaiting, the number waiting or being checked out at the beginning of a half-hour period; Arrivals, the number of arrivals to the checkout stations during a period; Departures, the number finishing the checkout process during a period; and Checkers, the number of checkout stations open during a period. (See the file **Customer Checkouts.xlsx**.)

The data set also includes time variables: Day, day of week; StartTime, clock time at the beginning of each half-hour period; and TimeInterval, a descriptive term for the time of day, such as Lunch rush for 11:30 A.M. to 1:30 P.M. (The comment in cell C1 of the data sheet spells these out.) Finally, the data set includes the *calculated* variable EndWaiting, the number waiting or being checked out at the end of a half-hour period. For any time period, it equals InitialWaiting plus Arrivals minus Departures; it also equals InitialWaiting for the *next* period. A partial listing of the data appears in Figure 3.33.

Figure 3.33

A Partial Listing of the Supermarket Checkout Data

	A	B	C	D	E	F	G	H	I
1	Day	StartTime	TimeInterval	InitialWaiting	Arrivals	Departures	EndWaiting	Checkers	TotalCustomers
2	Mon	8:00 AM	Morning rush	2	21	22	1	3	23
3	Mon	8:30 AM	Morning rush	1	25	18	8	3	26
4	Mon	9:00 AM	Morning	8	27	28	7	3	35
5	Mon	9:30 AM	Morning	7	21	23	5	3	28
6	Mon	10:00 AM	Morning	5	20	23	2	5	25
7	Mon	10:30 AM	Morning	2	36	31	7	5	38
8	Mon	11:00 AM	Morning	7	30	36	1	5	37
9	Mon	11:30 AM	Lunch rush	1	34	29	6	5	35
10	Mon	12:00 PM	Lunch rush	6	56	48	14	7	62
11	Mon	12:30 PM	Lunch rush	14	58	64	8	7	72
12	Mon	1:00 PM	Lunch rush	8	53	52	9	7	61
13	Mon	1:30 PM	Afternoon	9	30	36	3	5	39
14	Mon	2:00 PM	Afternoon	3	34	31	6	5	37
15	Mon	2:30 PM	Afternoon	6	36	37	5	5	42
16	Mon	3:00 PM	Afternoon	5	30	28	7	5	35
17	Mon	3:30 PM	Afternoon	7	29	34	2	5	36
18	Mon	4:00 PM	Afternoon	2	35	33	4	5	37
19	Mon	4:30 PM	Afternoon rush	4	32	25	11	5	36

The manager of R&P wants to analyze these data to discover any trends, particularly in the pattern of arrivals throughout a day or across the entire week. Also, the store currently uses a "by the seat of your pants" approach to opening and closing checkout stations each half hour. The manager would like to see how well the current approach is working. Of course, she would love to know the "best" strategy for opening and closing checkout stations—but this is beyond her (and our) capabilities at this point.

Objective To use charts, summary measures, and pivot tables to understand time patterns of arrivals and congestion at R&P Supermarket.

Solution

Obviously, time plays a crucial role in this example, so a good place to start is to create one or more time series graphs. The graph in Figure 3.34 shows the time series behavior of InitialWaiting (the lower line) and Arrivals during the entire week. (This looks much better on a PC monitor, where the two lines are in different colors.) There is almost *too* much clutter in this graph to see exactly what's happening, but it is clear that (1) Fridays and Saturdays are the busiest days; (2) the time pattern of arrivals is somewhat different—more spread out—during the weekends than during the weekdays; (3) there are fairly regular peak arrival periods during the weekdays; and (4) the number waiting is sometimes as large as 10 or 20, and the largest of these tend to be around the peak arrival times. You can decide whether it might be better (with less clutter) to separate this plot into two time series graphs, one for InitialWaiting and one for Arrivals. The advantage of the current plot is that we can match up time periods for the two variables.

Figure 3.34 Time Series Graph of InitialWaiting and Arrivals Variables

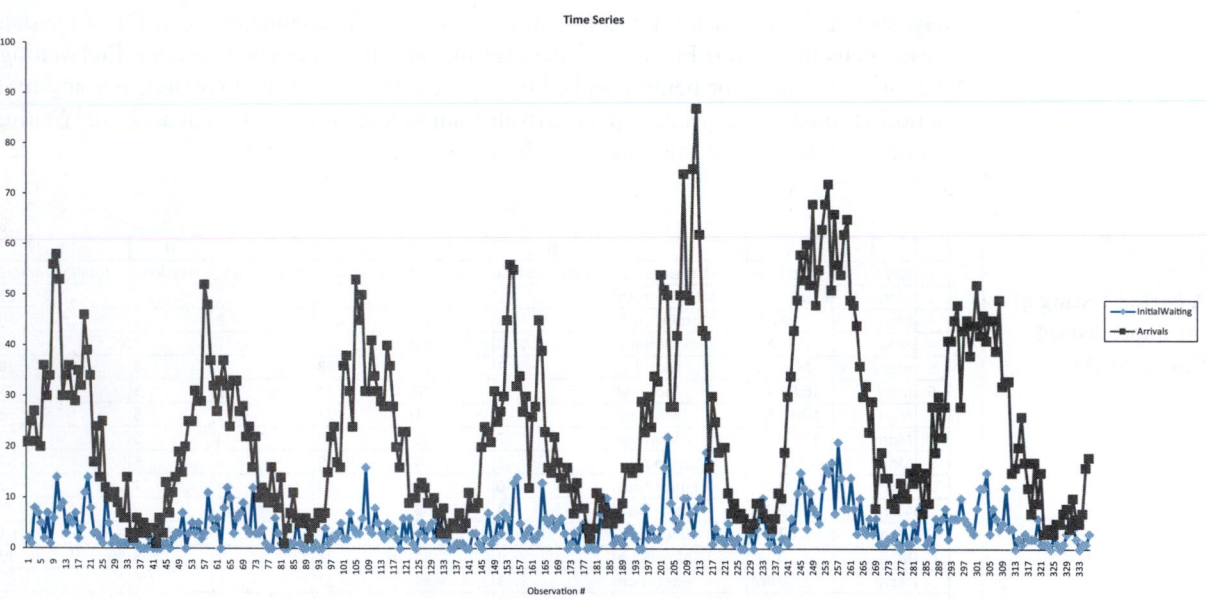

A similar time series graph appears in Figure 3.35. This shows Arrivals and Departures, although it is difficult to separate the two time series—they are practically on top of one another. Perhaps this is not so bad. It means that for the most part, the store is checking out customers approximately as quickly as they are arriving.

Figure 3.35 Time Series Graph of Arrivals and Departures Variables

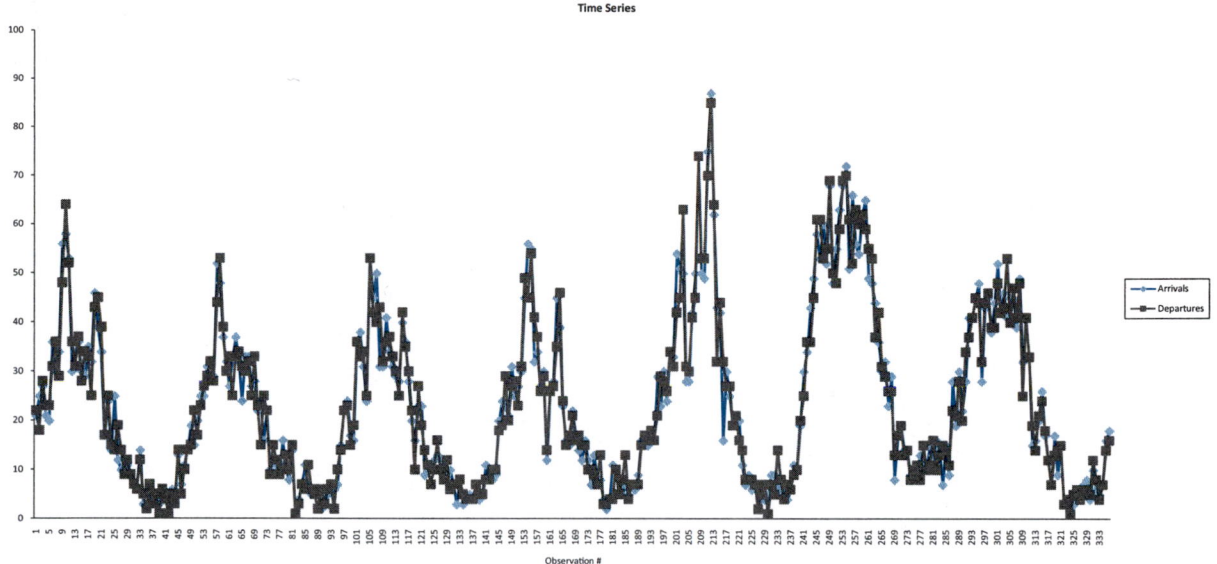

You can either create this chart automatically with the pivot chart option, or you can create it with StatTools from the data in the pivot table.

A somewhat more efficient way to obtain this time series behavior is with pivot tables. Figure 3.36 shows one possibility. To create this pivot table, we place the InitialWaiting variable in the Values area, express it as an average, place the StartTime variable in the Row area, and place the Day variable in the Report Filter area. (We also condensed the information from half-hour periods to hour-long periods by using the pivot table grouping option.) Finally, we create a time series graph from the data in the pivot table. Note how the variable in the Report Filter area works. For example, we obtain the graph in Figure 3.36 if we choose Monday in the Report Filter area (the drop-down list in cell B1). However, if we choose another day in cell B1, the data in the pivot table and the graph change automatically. So we can make comparisons across the days of the week with a couple of clicks of the mouse!

Similarly, the pivot table and corresponding column chart in Figure 3.37 indicate the average number of arrivals per half-hour period for each interval in the day. To obtain this output, we place the Arrival variable in the Values area, express it as an average, place the TimeInterval variable in the Row area, and place the Day variable in the Report Filter area. You can check that the pattern shown here for Friday is a bit different than for the other days—it has a significant bulge during the afternoon rush period.

The manager of R&P is ultimately interested in whether the "right" number of checkout stations are available throughout the day. Figures 3.38 and 3.39 provide some evidence.

Figure 3.36

Average
InitialWaiting by
Hour of Day

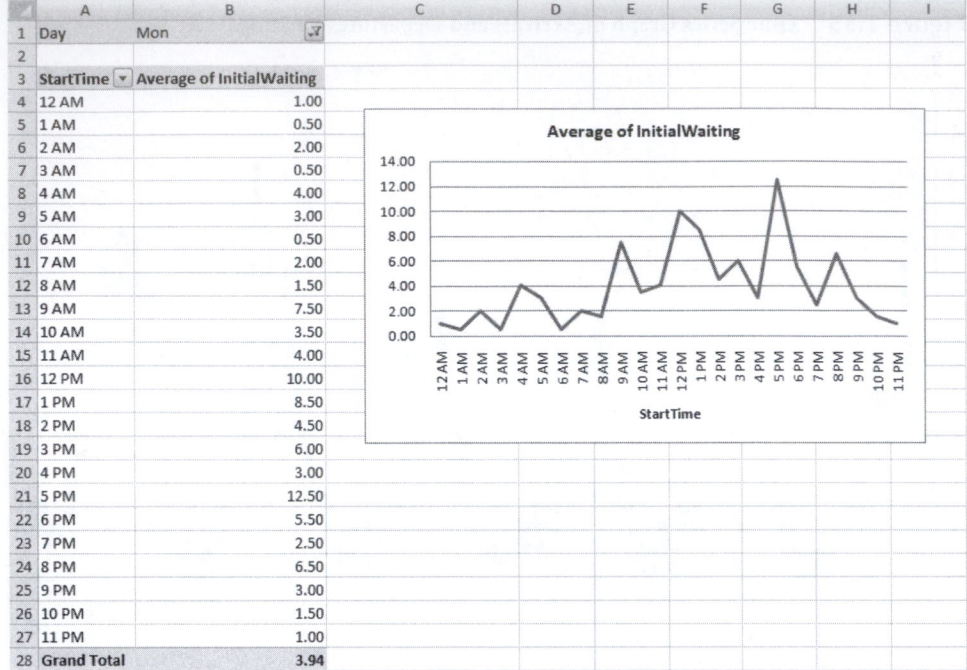

	A	B
1	Day	Mon
2		
3	StartTime	Average of InitialWaiting
4	12 AM	1.00
5	1 AM	0.50
6	2 AM	2.00
7	3 AM	0.50
8	4 AM	4.00
9	5 AM	3.00
10	6 AM	0.50
11	7 AM	2.00
12	8 AM	1.50
13	9 AM	7.50
14	10 AM	3.50
15	11 AM	4.00
16	12 PM	10.00
17	1 PM	8.50
18	2 PM	4.50
19	3 PM	6.00
20	4 PM	3.00
21	5 PM	12.50
22	6 PM	5.50
23	7 PM	2.50
24	8 PM	6.50
25	9 PM	3.00
26	10 PM	1.50
27	11 PM	1.00
28	Grand Total	3.94

Figure 3.37

Average Arrivals by
TimeInterval of Day

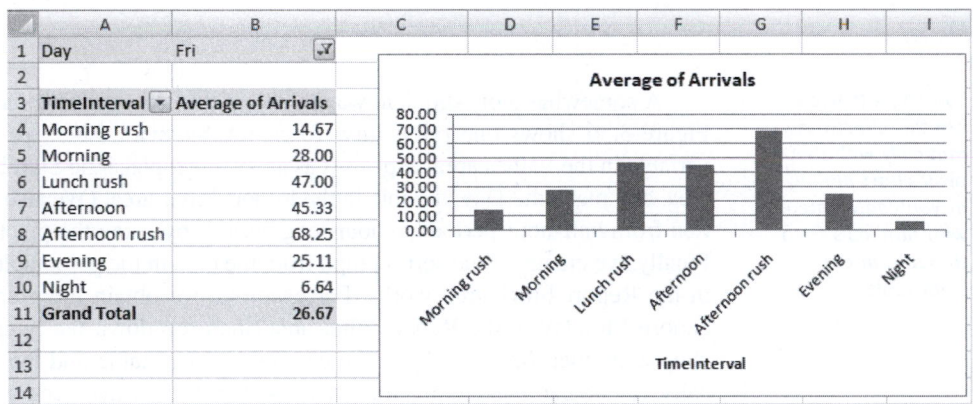

	A	B
1	Day	Fri
2		
3	TimeInterval	Average of Arrivals
4	Morning rush	14.67
5	Morning	28.00
6	Lunch rush	47.00
7	Afternoon	45.33
8	Afternoon rush	68.25
9	Evening	25.11
10	Night	6.64
11	Grand Total	26.67
12		
13		
14		

The first of these is a scatterplot of Checkers versus TotalCustomers. (We calculated the TotalCustomers variable as the sum of the InitialWaiting and the Arrivals variables to measure the total amount of work presented to the checkout stations in any half-hour period.) There is an obvious positive relationship between these two variables. Evidently, management is reacting as it should—it is opening more checkout stations when there is more traffic. The second scatterplot shows EndWaiting versus Checkers. There is again a definite upward trend. Periods when more checkout stations are open tend to be associated with periods where more customers still remain in the checkout process. Presumably, management is reacting with more open checkout stations in busy periods, but it is not reacting strongly enough.

Figure 3.38 Scatterplot of Checkers versus TotalCustomers

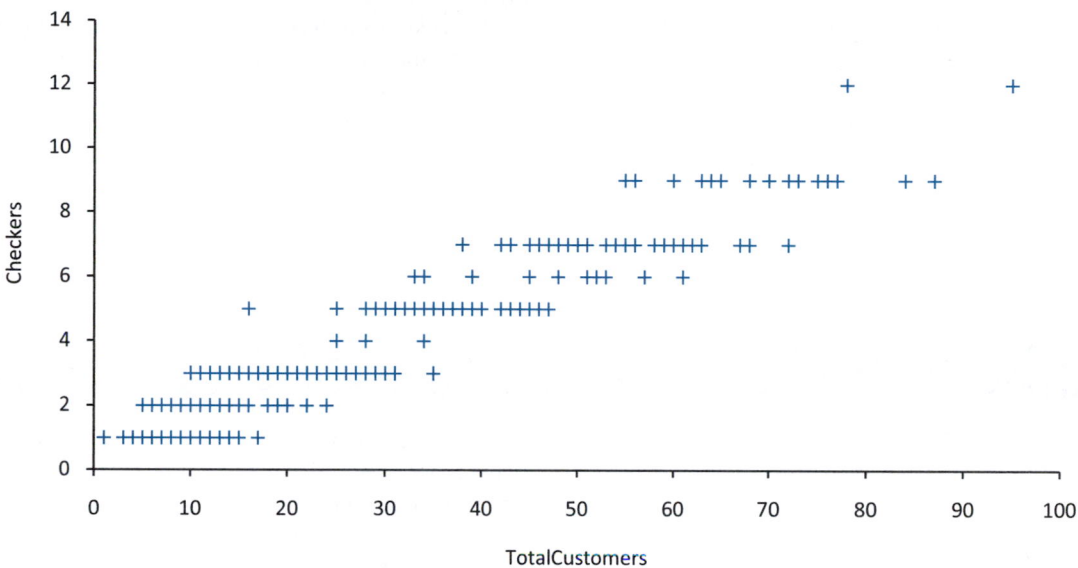

Figure 3.39 Scatterplot of EndWaiting versus Checkers

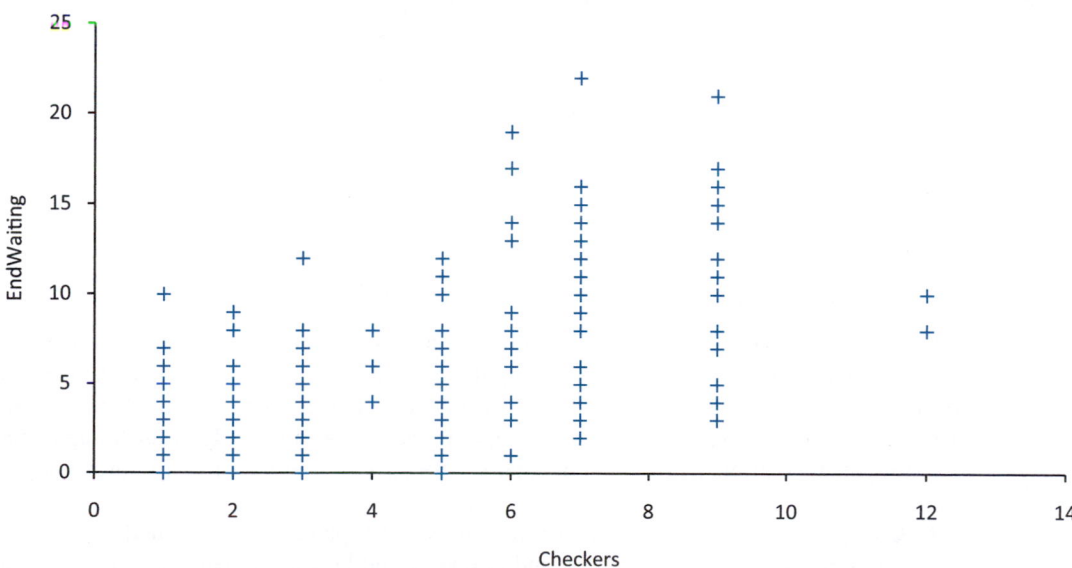

If you think you can solve the manager's problem just by fiddling with the numbers in the Checkers column, think again. There are two problems. First, there is a trade-off between the "cost" of having customers wait in line and the cost of paying extra checkout people. This is a difficult trade-off for any supermarket manager. Second, the number of departures is clearly related to the number of checkout stations open. (The relationship is a complex one that requires mathematical queuing theory to quantify.) Therefore, it doesn't make sense to change the numbers in the Checkers column without changing the numbers in the Departures (and hence the InitialWaiting and EndWaiting) columns in an appropriate way. This is *not* an easy problem! ∎

EXAMPLE 3.11 DEMOGRAPHIC AND CATALOG MAILING EFFECTS ON SALES AT HYTEX

The HyTex Company is a direct marketer of stereophonic equipment, personal computers, and other electronic products. HyTex advertises entirely by mailing catalogs to its customers, and all of its orders are taken over the telephone. The company spends a great deal of money on its catalog mailings, and it wants to be sure that this is paying off in sales. Therefore, HyTex has collected data on 1000 customers at the end of the current year. (See the file **Catalog Marketing.xlsx**.) For each customer the company has data on the following variables:

- Age: coded as 1 for 30 years or younger, 2 for 31 to 55 years, and 3 for 56 years or older
- Gender: coded as 1 for males, 0 for females
- OwnHome: coded as 1 if customer owns a home, 0 otherwise
- Married: coded as 1 if customer is currently married, 0 otherwise
- Close: coded as 1 if customer lives reasonably close to a shopping area that sells similar merchandise, 0 otherwise
- Salary: combined annual salary of customer and spouse (if any)
- Children: number of children living with customer
- History: coded as "NA" if customer had no dealings with the company before this year, 1 if customer was a low-spending customer last year, 2 if medium-spending, 3 if high-spending
- Catalogs: number of catalogs sent to the customer this year
- AmountSpent: total amount of purchases made by the customer this year

HyTex wants to analyze these data carefully to understand its customers better. Also, the company wants to see whether it is sending the catalogs to the right customers. Currently, each customer receives either 6, 12, 18, or 24 catalogs through the mail each year. However, the decision as to *who receives how many* has not really been thought out carefully. Is the current distribution of catalogs effective? Is there room for improvement?

Objective To use charts, summary measures, and pivot tables to understand the demographics of HyTex's customers, and to understand how these demographics, as well as the number of catalogs mailed, affect amounts spent.

Solution

This is the most difficult example we have faced so far, but it pales in comparison to the difficulty *real* direct marketing companies face. They have all sorts of data on millions of customers. How can they make sense of all these data? Using our relatively small data set, we will get the ball rolling. We challenge you to discover additional patterns in the data. Furthermore, we see only an indication of whether the current distribution of catalog mailings is effective. It is well beyond our abilities at this point to find a more effective catalog distribution policy.

HyTex is primarily interested in the AmountSpent variable, so it makes sense to create scatterplots of AmountSpent versus selected "explanatory" variables. We do this in Figures 3.40 to 3.42. Figure 3.40 shows AmountSpent versus Salary. It is clear that customers with higher salaries tend to spend more, although the variability in amounts spent increases significantly as salary increases. Figure 3.41 shows that there is some tendency toward higher spending among customers who receive more catalogs. But do the catalogs *cause* more spending, or are more catalogs sent to customers who would tend to spend more anyway? There is no way to answer this "cause-and-effect" question with the data the company has collected. Figure 3.42 shows the interesting tendency of customers with more children to spend less. Perhaps customers with more children are already spending so much on $100-plus athletic shoes that they have little left to spend on electronic equipment!

Figure 3.40   Scatterplot of AmountSpent versus Salary

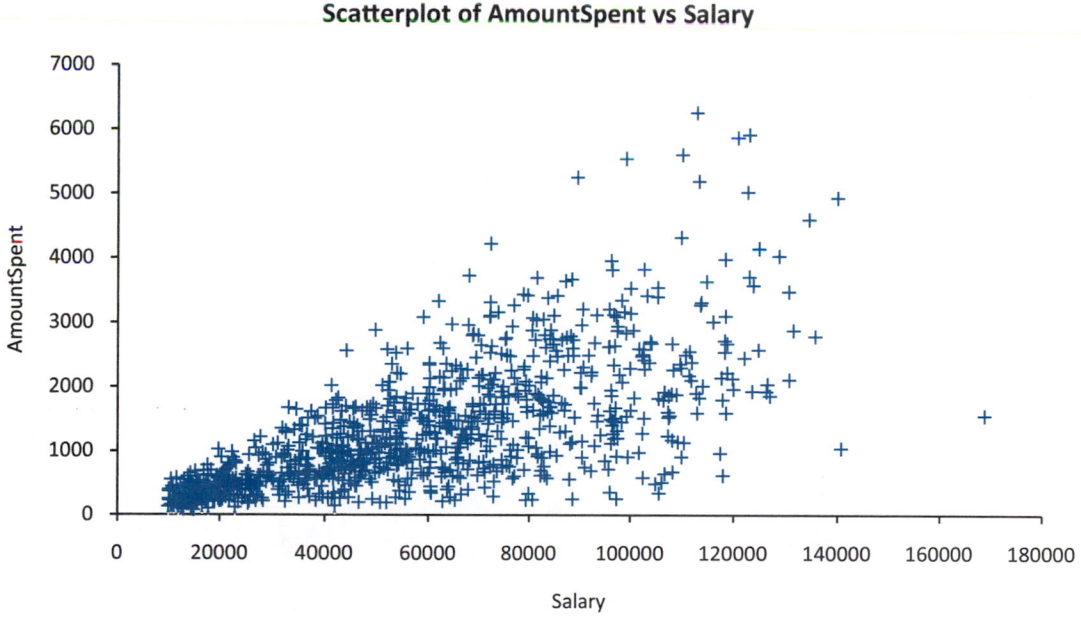

Figure 3.41   Scatterplot of AmountSpent versus Catalogs

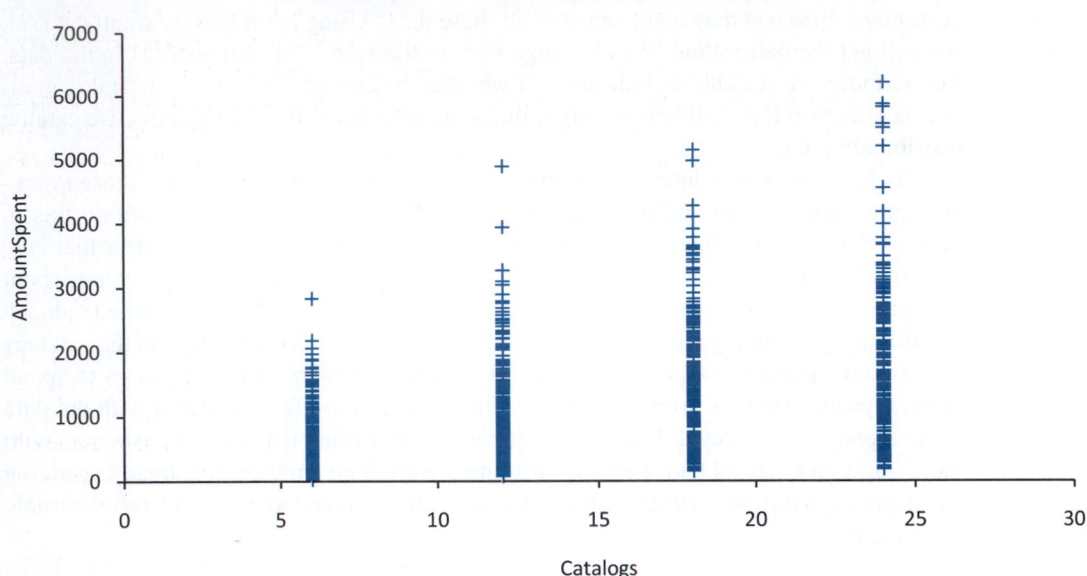

Figure 3.42   Scatterplot of AmountSpent versus Children

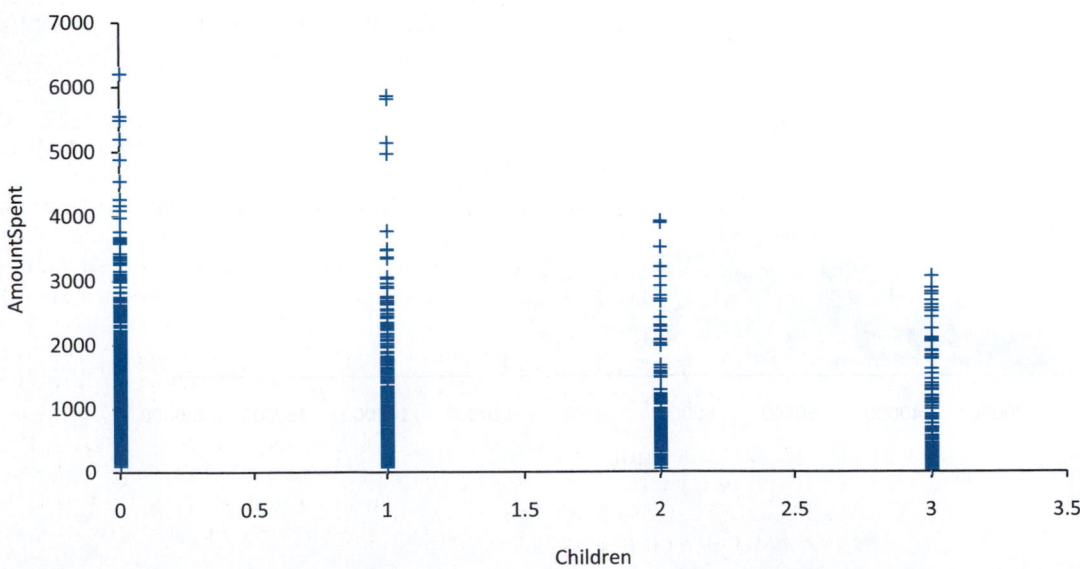

Pivot tables and accompanying charts are very useful in this type of situation. We show several. First, Figures 3.43 and 3.44 can be used to better understand the demographics of the customers. Each row of Figure 3.43 shows the percentages of an age group who own homes. By changing the Report Filter variables Married and Gender in cells B1 and B2, we can see how these percentages change for married women, unmarried men, and so on. You can check that these percentages remain relatively stable for the various groups. Specifically, a small percentage of the younger people own their own home, regardless of marital status or gender.

Figure 3.43

Percent Home Owners versus Age, Married, and Gender

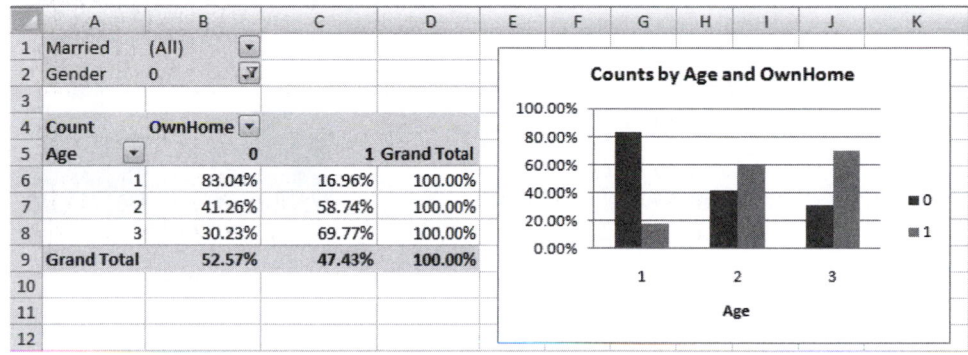

Figure 3.44 is similar. It shows the percentages of each age group who are married, for any combination of the Gender and OwnHome variables. Here the percentages change considerably for different settings of the page variables. For example, you can check that the married/unmarried split is quite different for women who don't own a home than for the male home owners shown in the figure.

Figure 3.44

Percent Married versus Age, OwnHome, and Gender

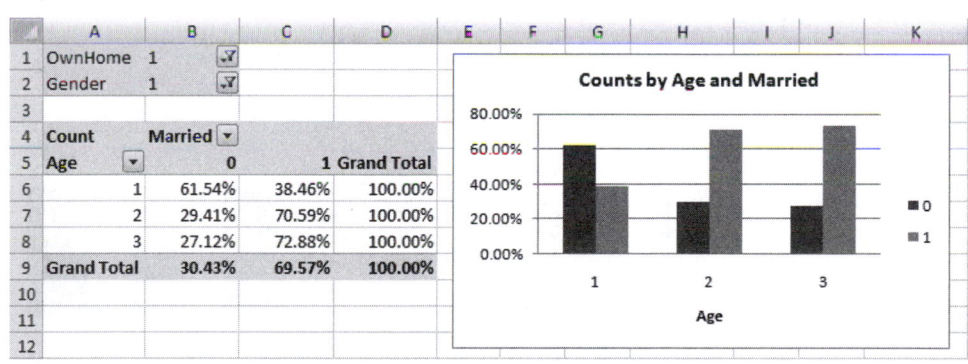

Excel Tip *We do not have to create a new pivot table and pivot chart to get those shown in Figure 3.44. Starting with the pivot table shown in Figure 3.43, we can simply drag the buttons in the PivotTable Field List to where we want them. Everything updates automatically, including the chart! The pivot table/pivot chart combinations for the rest of this example were created from the original pivot table/pivot chart combination in Figure 3.43 in the same way—that is, by dragging field buttons to the appropriate locations. What a time-saver!*

Figure 3.45 provides more demographic information. Now we show the average Salary broken down by Age and Gender, with Report Filter variables OwnHome and Married. You can check that the *shape* of the resulting chart is practically the same for any combination of the Report Filter variables. However, the heights of the bars change appreciably. For example, the average salaries are considerably larger for the married home owners shown in the figure than for unmarried customers who are not home owners.

Figure 3.45   Average Salary versus Age, Gender, Married, and OwnHome

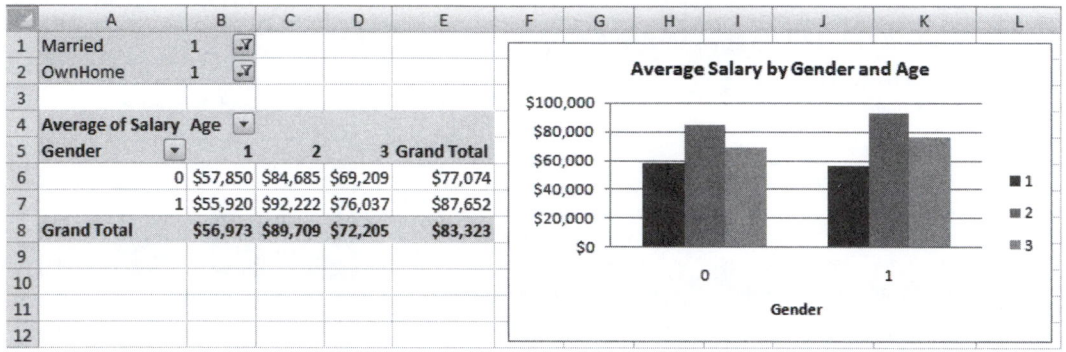

The pivot table and pivot chart in Figure 3.46 break the data down in another way. Each column in the pivot table shows the percentages in the various History categories for a particular number of children. Each of these columns corresponds to one of the bars in the "stacked" bar chart. Also, we have used Close as a Report Filter variable. Two interesting points emerge. First, customers with more children tend to be more heavily represented in the low-spending History category (and less heavily represented in the high-spending category). Also, as you can check by changing the setting of the Close variable from 1 to 0, the percentage of high-spenders among customers who live far from electronics stores is much higher than for those who live close to such stores.

Figure 3.46   Percentages in History Categories versus Children and Close

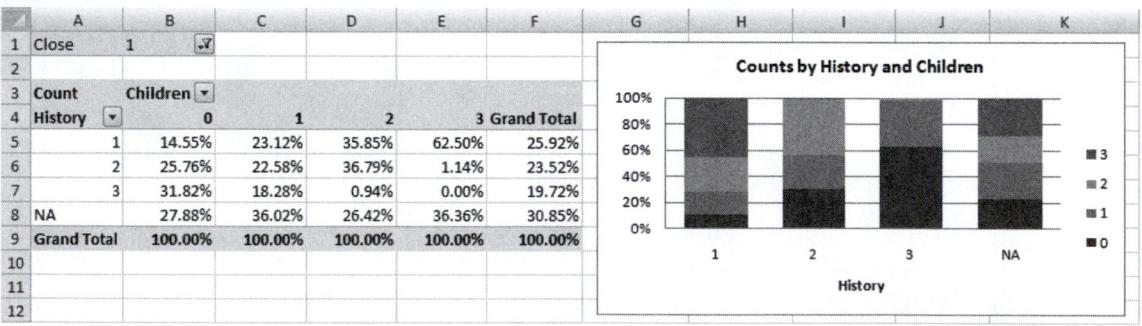

Although we are not told exactly how HyTex determined its catalog mailing distribution, Figure 3.47 provides an indication. Each row of the pivot table shows the percentages of a particular History category that were sent 6, 12, 18, or 24 catalogs. The company's distribution policy is still somewhat unclear—and there is probably hope for improvement—but it *did* evidently send more catalogs to high-spending customers and fewer to low-spending customers.

Figure 3.47 Catalog Distribution versus History

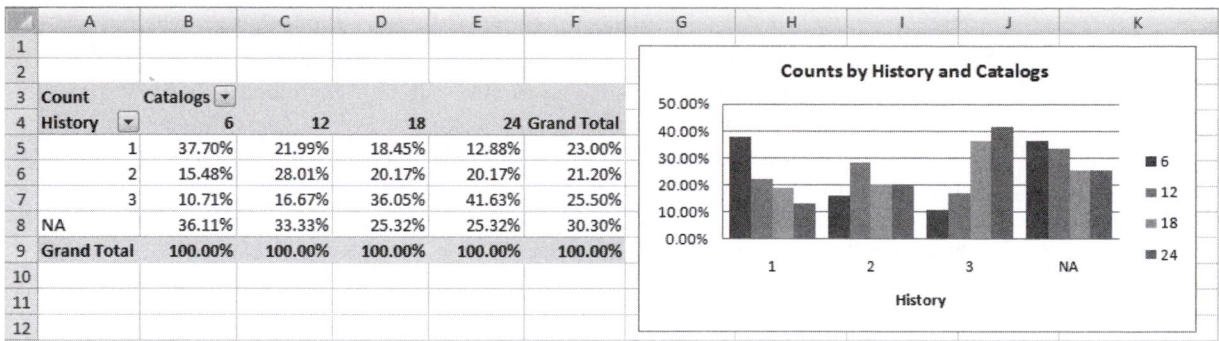

Finally, Figure 3.48 shows the average AmountSpent versus History and Catalogs, with a variety of demographic variables in the Report Filter area. There are so many possible combinations that it is difficult to discover all the existing patterns. However, one thing stands out loud and clear from the graph: the more catalogs customers receive, the more they tend to spend. In addition, if they were large spenders last year, they tend to be large spenders this year.

Figure 3.48 Average AmountSpent versus History, Catalogs, and Demographic Variables

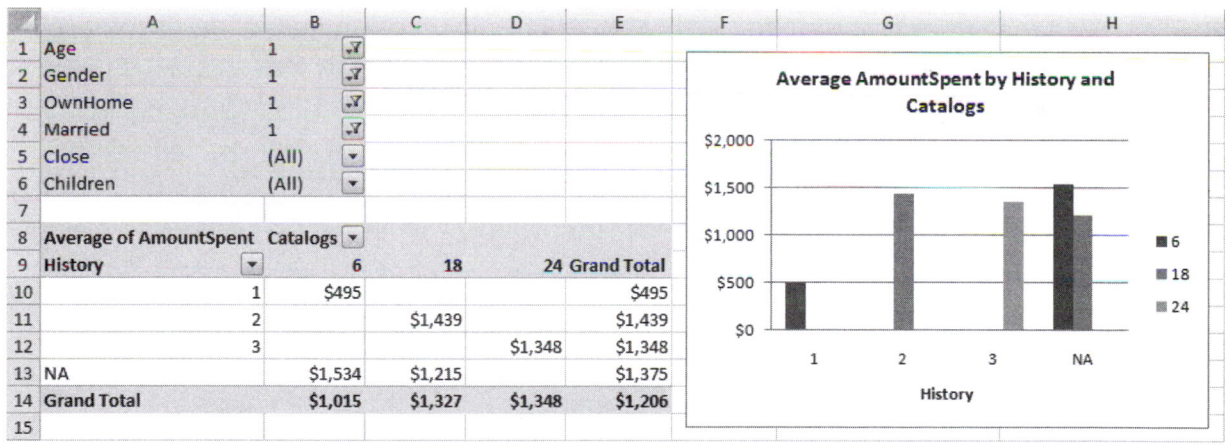

In a pivot table with this many combinations, there will almost certainly be some combinations with no observations. For example, it turns out that there are no young married males who were low-spenders last year and received 18 catalogs. In this case you see a blank in the corresponding pivot table cell. In addition, there are no young married male home owners who received 12 catalogs. If you try this combination, the whole "12" column of the pivot table disappears—and the corresponding bars disappear from the chart. ∎

3.10 CONCLUSION

This chapter and the previous chapter have illustrated the tremendous variety of descriptive measures you can obtain with Excel's built-in tools and add-ins such as StatTools. The *concepts* in these chapters are relatively simple. The key, therefore, is to have simple-to-use tools available to produce tables, graphs, and numerical summary measures in a matter of minutes (or even seconds). This is now possible, not only with statistical software packages but with spreadsheet packages, particularly Excel. These tools allow you to concentrate on presenting the data in the most appropriate way, so that interesting information hidden in the data is brought to the surface.

Summary of Key Terms

Term	Explanation	Excel	Pages	Equation Number
One-variable summary statistics	General term for measures that summarize distribution of a variable	StatTools/ Summary Statistics/ One-Variable Summary	101–102	
Mean $\bar{X}$ (for sample) μ (for population)	Average of observations	=AVERAGE(*range*)	92	3.1
Median	Middle observation after observations are sorted from low to high	=MEDIAN(*range*)	93	
Mode	Most frequently occurring observation	=MODE(*range*)	94	
Percentile	Value such that a specified percentage of observations are below it	=PERCENTILE(*range,pct*), where *pct* is decimal between 0 and 1	95	
Quartile	First quartile has 25% of observations below it. Third quartile has 25% of observations above it. Second quartile is the median	=QUARTILE(*range,n*), where *n* is 1, 2, or 3	95	
Interquartile range	Difference between third and first quartiles	=QUARTILE(*range*,3) − QUARTILE(*range*,1)	95	
Minimum	Smallest observation	=MIN(*range*)	95–96	
Maximum	Largest observation	=MAX(*range*)	95–96	
Range	Difference between largest and smallest observations	=MAX(*range*) − MIN(*range*)	95–96	
Variance s^2 (for sample) σ^2 (for population)	Measure of variability Basically, average of squared deviations from mean	=VAR(*range*) (for sample) =VARP(*range*) (for population)	96–98	3.2, 3.3
Standard deviation s (for sample) σ (for population)	Measure of variability in same units as observations Square root of variance	=STDEV(*range*) (for sample) =STDEVP(*range*) (for population)	96–98	3.4

(continued)

Term	Explanation	Excel	Pages	Equation Number
Empirical rules	They specify approximate percentages of observations within 1, 2, or 3 standard deviations of mean for bell-shaped distributions		98	
Measures of association	Measures of strength of linear relationship between two variables	StatTools/Summary Statistics/Correlation and Covariance	105–106	
Covariance	Measure of association, affected by units of measurement	=COVAR(range1,range2)	105–106	3.5
Correlation r (for sample) ρ (for population)	Measure of association, unaffected by units of measurement, always between -1 and $+1$	=CORREL(range1,range2)	105–106	3.6
Box plot	Chart that indicates the distribution of one or more variables; box captures middle 50% of data, lines and points indicate possible skewness and outliers	StatTools/Summary Graphs/Box-Whisker Plot	111	

PROBLEMS

Conceptual Exercises

C.1. Suppose that the histogram of a given income distribution is positively skewed. What does this fact imply about the relationship between the mean and median of this distribution?

C.2. "The midpoint of the line segment joining the first quartile and third quartile of any distribution is the median." Is this statement true or false? Explain your answer.

C.3. Explain why the standard deviation would likely *not* be a reliable measure of variability for a distribution of data that includes at least one extreme outlier.

C.4. "Two numerical variables are unrelated if the correlation between them is close to 0." Indicate whether this statement is true or false. Explain your choice.

C.5. Explain how a box plot could be used to determine whether the associated distribution of values is essentially symmetric.

Level A

44. The annual base salaries for 200 students graduating from a reputable MBA program this year (see the file **P02_74.xlsx**) are of interest to those in the admissions office who are responsible for marketing the program to prospective students. What salary level is *most*

indicative of those earned by students graduating from this MBA program this year?

45. In its annual ranking of top graduate business schools in the United States, *U.S. News & World Report* provides data on a number of attributes of recognized graduate programs (refer to the file **P02_08.xlsx**). One variable of interest is the annual out-of-state tuition paid by affected full-time students in each program.
   a. Find the annual out-of-state tuition levels at each of the 25th, 50th, and 75th percentiles.
   b. Identify the schools with the largest and smallest annual out-of-state tuitions. Does there appear to be a relationship between the program's overall ranking and its out-of-state tuition level?

46. Consider the Consumer Price Index, which provides the annual percentage change in consumer prices, for the period in the file **P02_26.xlsx**. Find and interpret the interquartile range of these annual percentage changes.

47. The Consumer Confidence Index (CCI) attempts to measure people's feelings about general business conditions, employment opportunities, and their own income prospects. The annual average values of the CCI are given in the file **P02_28.xlsx**.
   a. Fifteen percent of all years in this sample have annual CCI values that exceed what value?

b. Forty percent of all years in this sample have annual CCI values that are less than or equal to what value?

c. In which year of the given sample period were U.S. consumers *most* confident, as measured by the CCI?

d. In which year of the given sample period were U.S. consumers *least* confident, as measured by the CCI?

48. Consider the proportion of Americans under the age of 18 living below the poverty level for the data in the file **P02_29.xlsx**.

a. In which years of the sample has the poverty rate for American children exceeded the rate that defines the third quartile of these data?

b. In which years of the sample has the poverty rate for American children fallen below the rate that defines the first quartile of these data?

c. What is the typical poverty rate for American children during this period?

49. The annual averages of the discount rate, federal funds rate, and the prime rate are given in the file **P02_30.xlsx**. For each of these three key interest rates, determine the following:

a. Thirty percent of all years in the sample period have annual average rates that exceed what value?

b. Twenty-five percent of all years in the sample period have annual average rates that are less than or equal to what value?

c. What is the most typical annual average rate over the given sample period?

50. Given data in the file **P02_13.xlsx** from a recent survey of chief executive officers from 350 of the largest U.S. public companies, respond to the following questions:

a. Find the annual salary below which 75% of all given CEO salaries fall.

b. Find the annual bonus above which 55% of all given CEO bonuses fall.

c. Determine the range of the middle 50% of all given total annual compensation figures (i.e., of the amounts found in column *Sum03*).

51. The file **P02_44.xlsx** contains the number of classroom teachers and the average salary of classroom teachers for each of the 50 states and the District of Columbia. Which of the states paid their teachers average salaries that exceeded approximately 90% of all average salaries? Which of the states paid their teachers average salaries that exceeded only about 10% of all average salaries?

52. The annual base salaries for 200 students graduating from a reputable MBA program this year are given in the file **P02_74.xlsx**.

a. Do the empirical rules apply to these data? Explain.

b. If the empirical rules apply here, between what two numbers can we be about 68% sure that the salary of any one of these 200 students will fall?

53. Refer to the data given in the file **P02_11.xlsx**. Consider the average time (in minutes) it takes a citizen of each metropolitan area to travel to work and back home each day.

a. Find a reliable measure of the dispersion of these average commute times around the overall sample mean.

b. Between what two numbers can we be approximately 99.7% sure that any one of these average travel times will fall?

54. Is there a strong relationship between a chief executive officer's annual compensation and her or his organization's recent profitability? Explore this question by generating correlations for the survey data in the file **P02_13.xlsx**. In particular, compute and interpret correlation measures for the change in the company's net income from 2002 to 2003 (see *Comp_NetInc03P* column) and the CEO's 2003 base salary, as well as for the change in the company's net income from 2002 to 2003 and the CEO's 2003 bonus. Summarize your findings.

55. Create box plots to compare recent job growth rates with forecasted job growth rates for selected towns in the United States. These growth rates are all provided in the file **P03_55.xlsx**. Do you detect the presence of any outliers in either of these two distributions? Also, calculate the correlation between these two sets of job growth rates and interpret it.

56. The percentage of private-industry jobs that are managerial has steadily declined in recent years as companies have found middle management a ripe area for cutting costs. How have women and various minority groups fared in gaining management positions during this period of corporate downsizing of the management ranks? Relevant data are given in the file **P02_75.xlsx**. Create box plots using these data to make general comparisons across the various groups included in the set.

57. The U.S. Bureau of Labor Statistics provides data on the year-to-year percentage changes in the wages and salaries of workers in private industries, including both white-collar and blue-collar occupations. Consider the data in the file **P02_56.xlsx**. Create side-by-side box plots to summarize these distributions of annual percentage changes. Interpret the interquartile range for each of three distributions.

58. Explore the given distribution of the numbers of beds in short-term general hospitals in selected U.S. metropolitan areas by creating a box plot (refer to the data in the file **P02_17.xlsx**). Use your box plot to answer the following questions:

a. Is it more likely for these metropolitan areas to have larger or smaller numbers of hospital beds?

b. Is the mean or median the more accurate measure of central location in this case? Explain.

c. Characterize the variation of these values around the center of the data.

d. Do you detect the presence of any *extreme* outliers?

59. The file **P03_59.xlsx** contains the proportion of annual revenue spent on research and development (R&D) activities for each of 200 randomly selected high-technology firms. Characterize this distribution by computing numerical summary measures and creating a box plot. In particular, comment on the typical proportion of revenue dollars spent on R&D by these firms and the variation about the typical proportion value.

60. Consider various characteristics of the U.S. civilian labor force provided in the file **P03_60.xlsx**. In particular, examine the given unemployment rates across the United States to answer the following questions.
   a. Characterize the distribution of total unemployment rates. What is the most typical value? How are the other total unemployment rates distributed about the typical rate?
   b. Compare the distribution of total unemployment rate to those of the male unemployment rate and the female unemployment rate. How are these distributions similar? How are they different?
   c. Which is more strongly associated with the total unemployment rate in the United States: the male unemployment rate or the female unemployment rate?

61. The file **P03_61.xlsx** contains the sale price of gasoline in each of the 50 states.
   a. Compare the distributions of gasoline sale price data (one for each year). Specifically, do you find the mean and standard deviation of these distributions to be changing over time? If so, how do you explain the trends?
   b. In which regions of the country have gasoline prices changed the most?
   c. In which regions of the country have gasoline prices remained relatively stable?

62. Examine life expectations (in years) at birth for various countries across the world. These data are provided in the file **P03_62.xlsx**.
   a. Generate an estimate of the *typical* human's life span at birth using the 2002 data. What are the limitations of the method you have employed in estimating this world population parameter?
   b. Characterize the *variability* of the life spans at birth using the 2002 data. Is this distribution fairly symmetric or skewed? How do you know?
   c. How strongly are the 2002 life expectations associated with projections for births in 2025 and 2050? Explain why the degree of linear association between the 2002 data and each set of projections diminishes somewhat over time.

63. This problem focuses on the per capita circulation of daily newspapers in the United States. The file **P03_63.xlsx** contains these data.
   a. Compare the yearly distributions of daily newspaper per capita circulation over the period.
   b. Note any clear trends, both nationally and regionally, in the average value of and variability of per capita newspaper circulation during the given years.

64. Have the proportions of Americans receiving public aid changed in recent years? Explore this question through a careful examination of the data provided in the file **P03_64.xlsx**. In particular, generate numerical summary measures to respond to each of the following.
   a. Report any observed changes in the overall mean or median rates during the given time period.
   b. Can you find evidence of regional changes in the proportions of Americans receiving public aid? If so, summarize your specific findings.

65. The file **P03_65.xlsx** contains the measured weight (in ounces) of a particular brand of ready-to-eat breakfast cereal placed in each of 500 randomly selected boxes by one of five different filling machine operators. Quality assurance personnel at this company are interested in determining how well these five operators are performing their assigned task of *consistently* placing 15 ounces of cereal in each box.
   a. Employ descriptive graphs and summary measures to ascertain whether some or all of these operators are consistently missing the target weight of 15 ounces per box.
   b. If you were charged with selecting the "Outstanding Employee of the Month" from this set of filling machine operators, which operator would you select based on the given data? Defend your choice.

66. Electro produces voltage-regulating equipment in New York and ships the equipment to Chicago. The voltage held is measured in New York before each unit is shipped to Chicago. The voltage held by each unit is also measured when the unit arrives in Chicago. The file **P03_66.xlsx** contains a sample of voltage measurements at each city. A voltage regulator is considered acceptable if it can hold a voltage of between 25 and 75 volts.
   a. Using box plots and descriptive statistics, what can you learn about the voltage held by units before shipment and after shipment?
   b. What percentage of units are acceptable before and after shipping?
   c. Do you have any suggestions about how to improve the quality of Electro's regulators?
   d. Ten percent of all New York regulators have a voltage exceeding what value?
   e. Five percent of all New York regulators have a voltage less than or equal to what value?

67. The file **P03_67.xlsx** contains the individual scores of students in two different accounting sections who took the same exam. Comment on the differences between exam scores in the two sections.

68. The file **P03_68.xlsx** contains the monthly interest rates on 3-month government T-bills. For example, in January 1985, 3-month T-bills yielded 7.76% annual interest. To succeed in investments, it is important to understand the characteristics of the monthly changes in T-bill rates.
  a. Create a histogram of the monthly changes in interest rates. Choose categories so that you get an "interesting" histogram.
  b. Do the empirical rules hold for changes in monthly interest rates?
  c. Based on the given data, there is a 5% chance that during a given month T-bill rates will increase by less than what value? (A negative number is allowed here.)
  d. Based on the given data, there is a 10% chance that during a given month T-bill rates will increase by at least what value?
  e. Based on the given data, estimate the chances that T-bill rates during a given month will increase by more than 0.5%.

Level B

69. Data on the numbers of insured commercial banks in the United States are given in the file **P03_69.xlsx**.
  a. Compare these distributions of the numbers of U.S. commercial banks (one for each year). Are the mean and standard deviation of these numbers changing over time? If so, how do you explain the trends?
  b. What trends do you notice in the numbers of commercial banks *by region?* For example, how do the numbers of commercial banks appear to be changing in the northeastern United States over the given period? Summarize your findings for each region of the country.

70. Educational attainment in the United States is the focus of this problem. Employ descriptive methods with the data provided in the file **P03_70.xlsx** to characterize the educational achievements of Americans in the given year. Do your findings surprise you in some way?

71. Data on U.S. homeownership rates are given in the file **P03_71.xlsx**.
  a. Employ numerical summary measures to characterize the changes in homeownership rates across the country during this period.
  b. Do the trends appear to be uniform across the United States or are they unique to certain regions of the country? Explain.

72. Data on community hospital average daily cost are provided in the file **P03_72.xlsx**. Do the yearly distributions of average cost figures tend to become more or less variable over the given time period? Justify your answer with descriptive graphs and/or relevant summary measures.

73. The median sales price of existing one-family homes in selected metropolitan areas is the variable of interest in this exercise. Using the data contained in the file **P03_73.xlsx**, characterize the distribution of median sales prices of existing single-family homes in 1996. How is this distribution different from that for the median sales prices of such homes in 1992? Summarize the essential differences.

74. Are U.S. traffic fatalities related to the speed limit and/or road type? Consider the data found in the file **P03_74.xlsx**.
  a. Do the average number and/or variability in the number of traffic fatalities occurring on interstate highways tend to increase as the speed limit is raised above 55 miles per hour? Explain your answer.
  b. Do the average number and/or variability in the number of traffic fatalities occurring on noninterstate roads tend to increase as the speed limit rises above 35 miles per hour? Explain your answer.
  c. Do the average number and/or variability in the number of traffic fatalities occurring on a road with a posted speed limit of 55 miles per hour tend to change with the road type (i.e., interstate versus noninterstate highway)? Explain your answer.
  d. Based on these data, which combination of speed limit and road type appears to be most lethal for U.S. drivers?
  e. Based on these data, which combination of speed limit and road type appears to be safest for U.S. drivers?

75. Have greater or lesser proportions of Americans joined labor unions during the past two decades? Respond to this question by applying descriptive summary measures and graphical tools to the data provided in the file **P03_75.xlsx**. Interpret your output. What conclusions can you draw from an analysis of these data?

76. Consider the percentage of the U.S. population without health insurance coverage. The file **P03_76.xlsx** contains such percentages by state for 1998 through 2003.
  a. Describe the distribution of state percentages of Americans without health insurance coverage in the period 2002–2003. Be sure to employ both measures of central location and dispersion in developing your characterization of these data.
  b. Compare the 2002–2003 distribution with the corresponding set of percentages taken in 2001–2002. How are these two sets of figures similar? In what ways are they different?
  c. Compute a correlation measure for the given 2002–2003 and 2001–2002 sets of percentages. What does the correlation coefficient tell you in case?
  d. Based on your answers in parts **b** and **c** above, what would you expect to find upon analyzing similar data for 2003–2004?

77. Given data in the file **P02_13.xlsx** from a recent survey of chief executive officers from the largest U.S. public companies, apply your knowledge of numerical summary measures to determine whether the typical levels and variances of the 2003 annual salaries and bonuses earned by CEOs depend in part on the *types* of companies in which they serve.

78. Consider survey data collected from 1000 randomly selected Internet users, given in the file **P02_43.xlsx**.
   a. Use these data to formulate a profile of the typical *female* Internet user. Consider such attributes as age, education level, marital status, annual income, and family size in formulating your profile.
   b. Use these data to formulate a profile of the typical *married* Internet user. Consider such attributes as gender, age, education level, annual income, and family size in formulating your profile.
   c. Use these data to formulate a profile of the typical *high-income* (say, with an annual income in excess of $80,000) Internet user. Consider such attributes as gender, age, education level, marital status, and family size in formulating your profile.

79. Consider the economic development data in the file **P02_06.xlsx**.
   a. Use these data to formulate a profile of the typical household residing within each of the four neighborhood locations. Consider such attributes as family size, home ownership status, gross annual income(s) of household wage earner(s), monthly home mortgage or rent payment, average monthly expenditure on utilities, and the total indebtedness (excluding the value of a home mortgage) of the household in formulating your profile.
   b. Do differences arise in the mean or median income levels of those wage earners from households located in different quadrants of this neighborhood? If so, summarize these differences.
   c. Do differences arise in the mean or median monthly home mortgage or rent payment paid by households located in different quadrants of this neighborhood? If so, summarize these differences.
   d. Do differences arise in the mean or median debt levels of households located in different quadrants of this neighborhood? If so, summarize these differences.

80. A human resources manager at Beta Technologies, Inc., is interested in developing a profile of the highest paid full-time Beta employees based on the given resentative sample of 52 of the company's full-time workers in the file **P02_01.xlsx**. In particular, she is interested in determining the typical age, number of years of relevant full-time work experience prior to coming to Beta, number of years of full-time work experience at Beta, and number of years of post-secondary education for those employees in the *highest quartile* with respect to annual salary. Employ appropriate descriptive methods to help the human resources manager develop this desired profile.

81. Using cost-of-living data from the *ACCRA Cost of Living Index* (see the file **P02_19.xlsx**), examine the relationship between the geographical *location* of an urban area within the United States (e.g., northeast, southeast, midwest, northwest, or southwest) and its *composite* cost-of-living index. In other words, is the overall cost of living higher or lower and more or less variable for urban areas in particular geographical regions of the country? You must first assign the given urban areas systematically to one of several geographical regions before you can apply appropriate summary measures in responding to this question. Summarize your findings in detail.

82. The file **P03_82.xlsx** contains monthly interest rates on bonds that pay money a year after the day they are bought. It is often suggested that interest rates are more volatile (tend to change more) when interest rates are high. Do these data support this statement?

83. The file **P03_83.xlsx** contains data on 1000 of Marvak's best customers. Marvak is a direct-marketing firm that sells electronic items. It has collected these data to learn more about its customers. The variables are self-explanatory, although a few cell notes have been added in row 3. Your boss at Marvak would like you to do the following.
   a. She wants a breakdown of gender by age group. That is, she wants a pivot table that lists, for each age group, the percentages of females and males. She wants to be able to access this information easily (with a couple of clicks) for any values of Home and Married.
   b. She guesses that customers with larger salaries tend to spend more at Marvak. To check this, she wants you to append a new variable called SalaryCat to the data set that contains the four category labels in column J. A customer with salary below $30,000 is categorized as "LowSal"; between $30,000 and $70,000 as "MedSal"; between $70,000 and $120,000 as "HighSal"; and over $120,000 as "HugeSal." (By the way, no incomes are exactly equal to $30,000, $70,000, or $120,000.) You can use the lookup table in columns I and J to form this new *SalaryCat* column. Then create a pivot table that shows the average amount spent for each of the four salary categories, and comment briefly (on that sheet) whether your boss's conjecture appears to be correct.

84. The file **P03_84.txt** contains the largest 100 public companies in the world, as listed in *The Wall Street Journal* on September 24, 1992, ranked by market value. The rankings are shown for 1992, as well as for 1991. The following variables are included:
   - Company: name of company
   - Location: 1 for United States, 2 for Japan/Australia, 3 for Europe

- Bank: 1 if bank (or savings institution), 0 otherwise
- Rank92: rank according to market value in 1992
- Rank91: rank according to market value in 1991
- MarketVal: market value in millions of U.S. dollars (12/31/91 exchange rates used)
- Sales91: sales in 1991 in millions of U.S. dollars
- PctChSales: percent change in sales from 1990, based on home currency
- Profit91: profit in 1991 in millions of U.S. dollars
- PctChProfit: percent change in profit from 1990, based on home currency

a. This file is in ASCII (text) form, with blanks between the items and names (text data) in double quotes. Open this file in Excel. (There is no "import" command; you simply open the file.) Excel will recognize that this is a text file, and a "wizard" will lead you through the steps to open it properly into Excel format. The key is that it is "delimited" with blanks. Once the file is opened, look at it to make sure everything is lined up correctly. Then use the Save As command to save the file as an .XLS file. (Once you do this, the .TXT version is no longer needed.)

b. Note that percentage changes from 1990 to 1991 are given for sales and profits. Use formulas to create variables Sales90 and Profit90, the sales and profits for 1990. [*Hint*: For example, the formula for Sales90 is 100*Sales91/(100+PctChSales).]

c. Create a scatterplot of Profit91 (vertical axis) versus Profit90. Most of the points lie close to a line. For this problem, consider an outlier to be any point that is obviously not very close to this line. Which companies are the worst outliers in this sense? In business terms, what makes these companies outliers?

d. The companies designated "banks" are clearly different from the other companies in that their sales figures are much larger. For this question, consider only the subset of *nonbanks*. Define an outlier with respect to any variable as an observation that is at least 1.5 IQRs above the third quartile or below the first quartile. (This is the box plot definition of outliers.) How many outliers are there with respect to Sales91?

e. There is a variable that codes the location of the company: 1 for United States, 2 for Japan/Australia, 3 for Europe. With regard to Profit91, are there any obvious differences among these? (Use summary statistics and/or charts.)

f. The data in this file are somewhat dated. See if you can find similar, but up-to-date, data (possibly on the Web). Then do the same analysis on the new data.

85. The file **P03_85.xlsx** contains 1993 compensation data on the top 200 CEOs. The data include the CEO's name, company, total compensation, and the company's 5-year total return to shareholders (expressed as an annual rate). The data are sorted in descending order according to the 5-year return. (Source: *Fortune*, July 25, 1994)

a. How large must a total compensation be to qualify as an outlier on the high side according to the box plot definition of outliers? In column A of the spreadsheet, highlight the names of all CEOs whose total compensations are outliers. (You can highlight them by making them boldface, italicizing them, or painting them a different color, for example.)

b. Create a scatterplot of total compensation versus 5-year return. (Put total compensation on the horizontal axis.) Do the CEOs in this data set appear to be worth their pay?

c. The data in this file are somewhat dated. See if you can find similar, but up-to-date, data (possibly on the Web). Then do the same analysis on the new data.

86. The file **P03_86.xlsx** contains data on close to 1800 professional NFL football players. (In case you are not a pro football fan, there are two conferences in the NFL: the NFC and the AFC. Also, each player plays either on offense or defense.) The data for each player include his base salary, any bonus, and the total of the base salary and the bonus. For each part, do the requested analysis for the total salary.

a. Create histograms of the salaries for (1) all of the players, (2) all of the NFC players, and (3) all of the AFC players. Also, create tables of summary statistics for these three groups.

b. Proceed as in part **a**, but now make the distinction between offensive and defensive players instead of which conference they are in.

c. Repeat parts **a** and **b**, but now eliminate the quarterbacks (QB), who are often the highest paid players. Does it make a difference?

d. Use one or more pivot tables to break the data down in other interesting ways, such as by position. Your goal is to understand the salary structure in the NFL. Write up your results in a brief report.

87. The file **P03_87.xlsx** contains questionnaire data from a random sample of 200 TV viewers. (The variable name headings actually begin in row 25.) The questionnaire was taken by the local station XYZ, an affiliate of one of the three main networks. Like the local affiliates of the other two networks, XYZ's local dinnertime news program follows the national news program. The purpose of the questionnaire was to discover characteristics of the viewing public, presumably with the intention of doing something to increase XYZ's ratings. Your assignment is very open-ended—purposely so. Summarize any aspects of the data that you think are relevant—find means, proportions, scatterplots, pivot tables, whatever—to help XYZ management understand these viewers. (All 200 people watch both national and local news.)

The Dow Jones Industrial Average (DJI) is a composite index of 30 of the largest "blue-chip" companies in the United States. It is probably the most quoted index from Wall Street, partly because it is old enough that many generations of investors have become accustomed to quoting it, and partly because the U.S. stock market is the world's largest. Besides longevity, two other factors play a role in the Dow's widespread popularity: It is understandable to most people, and it reliably indicates the market's basic trend. As this edition was going to press, the Dow was hovering around 13,000, after having been above 14,000. It is difficult to predict where it might be when you read this.

Unlike most other market indexes that are weighted indexes (usually by market capitalization, that is, price times shares outstanding), the DJI is an unweighted index. It was originally an average, namely, the sum of the stock prices divided by the number of stocks. In fact, the very first average price of industrial stocks, on May 26, 1896, was 40.94. However, because of stock splits, the DJI is now calculated somewhat differently to preserve historical continuity. To calculate the DJI, the prices of the 30 stocks in the index are summed, and this sum is divided by a "divisor," which is currently slightly greater than 0.33 but varies over time.

The Dow originally consisted of 12 stocks in 1896 and increased to 20 in 1916. The 30-stock average made its debut in 1928, and the number has remained constant ever since. However, the 30 stocks comprising the Dow do not remain the same. For example, after the first edition of this book, SBC Communications, Home Depot, Honeywell International, Intel, Microsoft, and Citigroup have replaced Union Carbide, Sears Roebuck, Aluminum Company of America, Allied Signal, Chevron, and Traveler's Group in the select 30. Since then, more changes have been made. The editors of *The Wall Street Journal* select the components of the DJI. They take a broad view of what "industrial" means. In essence, it is almost any company that isn't in the transportation business and isn't a utility. In choosing a new company for the DJI, they look among substantial industrial companies with a history of successful growth and wide interest among investors. The components of the DJI are not changed often. It isn't a "hot stock" index, and the *Journal* editors believe that stability of composition enhances the trust that many people have in the averages. The most frequent reason for changing a stock is that something is happening to one of the components (for example, a company is being acquired).

Some people make predictions about where the stock market is headed based in part on their interpretation of DJI movements, as well as movements of the transportation and utilities averages. But indexes don't predict anything. They are doing their job if they accurately reflect where the market has been. However, there is a great deal of common ground between the economy and the market. Stock investors try to anticipate future profits, and corporate profits are a prime fuel for the U.S. economy. So, not surprisingly, the market frequently rises ahead of economic expansion and falls prior to economic slowdown or contraction. The trouble is that this relationship isn't perfectly correlated; there are other factors that move markets and still others that affect the economy. Moreover, many people make the mistake of calibrating their economic expectations to the DJI's movements. The result is, as Nobel-laureate economist Paul A. Samuelson put it, "The market has predicted nine of the last five recessions."

As indicated previously, the DJI is not the only market index. There are two other Dow Jones indexes, one for transportation (DJT), consisting of 20 stocks, and one for utilities (DJU), consisting of 15 stocks. An elaborate analytical system dubbed *Dow Theory* holds that the DJT must "confirm" the movement of the industrial average for a market trend to have staying power. If the industrials reach a new high, the transportations would need to reach a new high to "confirm" the broad trend. The trend reverses when both averages experience sharp downturns at around the same time. If they diverge—for example, if the industrial average keeps climbing while the transportations decline—watch out! The underlying fundamentals of the Dow Theory hold that the industrials make and the transportations take. If the transportations aren't taking what the industrials are making, it portends economic weakness and market problems. Similarly, according to analysts who study the averages, a rise in utility stock prices indicates that investors anticipate falling interest rates because utilities are big borrowers and their profits are enhanced by lower interest costs. But the utility average tends to decline when investors expect rising interest rates. Because of this interest-rate sensitivity, the utility average is regarded by some as a leading indicator for the stock market as a whole.

This information and other interesting facts about the Dow Jones averages are available http://www.dowjones.com. Other Web sites have data on the averages themselves. We wrote an Excel macro to allow you to download the historical data (daily, weekly, or monthly) from Yahoo's Web site for any of these indexes and the stocks they contain. The resulting data are in the files **DJI Closing Prices.xlsx**, **DJT Closing Prices.xlsx**, and **DJU Closing Prices.xlsx**. Each file contains a Stocks sheet with a list of the companies in the index and their ticker symbols, and a ClosingPrices sheet with approximately four years of weekly closing prices. (The files with the macros are also available. They are named **DJI Query.xlsm** and so on. You can run the macros to get more data or more recent data. However, we can't guarantee that the macros will continue to work if Yahoo changes its Web site, as it sometimes does.)

Use the tools you've learned in the past two chapters to analyze these data sets. Here are some suggested directions for analysis.

1. The return for any period is the percentage change in the price over that period. That is, the return is

$$\frac{p_{end} - p_{beg}}{p_{beg}}$$

where p_{end} is the ending price and p_{beg} is the beginning price. (The return also includes dividends, but you can ignore these here.) Are the weekly returns for the 30 stocks in the DJI highly correlated with each other? Are the weekly returns correlated with the DJI itself? Answer the same questions for the DJT; for the DJU.

2. How would you evaluate portfolios of any of these stocks over some period of time? How much better (or worse) are some portfolios?

3. As stated previously, some analysts believe that the DJU is a leading indicator of the market. Do the data bear this out, assuming we identify the DJI as "the market"? One way to answer this is with "cross-correlations," such as the correlation between the DJI today and the DJU a week ago. Alternatively, we could compare a time series graph of the DJI with a "shifted" version of the DJU.

4. Similarly, is there any relationship between the DJI and the DJT? ∎

Following up on Case Study 3.1, there are many market indexes other than the Dow Jones averages. These include broad U.S. indexes such as the Nasdaq Composite Index (mainly technology stocks), the NYSE Composite Index (an index of many stocks on the New York Stock Exchange), the S&P 500 index (an index of 500 of the largest U.S. companies), and others. There are also U.S. indexes for particular industries, such as the AMEX Biotechnology Index, and foreign indexes, such as the AMEX Japan Index. Weekly data (from the same source as in the previous case) for several of these indexes are listed in the file **Other Closing Indexes.xlsx**. In addition, weekly data for the components of various indexes are available in the files **DRG Closing Prices.xlsx**, **GOX Closing Prices.xlsx**, and a few others. Formulate and answer any interesting questions relating to these data and the Dow Jones data. In particular, do all of these indexes tend to move together, or do any tend to move in opposite directions? ■

CASE 3.3 Correct Interpretation of Means

A mean, as defined in this chapter, is a pretty simple concept—it is the average of a set of numbers. But even this simple concept can cause confusion if we aren't careful. The data in Figure 3.49 are typical of data presented by marketing researchers for a type of product, in this case, beer. Each value is an average of the number of six-packs of beer purchased per customer during a month. For the individual brands, the value is the average only for the customers who purchased at least one six-pack of that brand. For example, the value for Miller is the average number of six-packs purchased of *all* of these brands for customers who purchased at least one six-pack of Miller. In contrast, the "Any" average is the average number of six-packs purchased of these brands for all customers in the population.

Is there a paradox in these averages? On first glance, it might appear unusual, or even impossible, that the "Any" average is less than each brand average. Make up your own (small) data set, where you list a number of customers, along with the numbers of six-packs of each brand of beer each customer purchased, and calculate the averages for your data that correspond to those in Figure 3.49. Do you get the same result (that the "Any" average is lower than all of the others)? Are you *guaranteed* to get this result? Does it depend on the amount of brand loyalty in your population, where brand loyalty is greater when customers tend to stick to the same brand, rather than buying multiple brands? Write up your results in a concise report.

Figure 3.49 Average beer purchases

	A	B	C	D	E	F	G	H
1	Miller	Budweiser	Coors	Michelob	Heineken	Old Milwaukee	Rolling Rock	Any
2	6.77	6.62	6.64	7.11	7.29	7.30	7.17	4.71

■

© Digital Vision/Photodisc/Getty Images

FINDING INFORMATION WITH DATA MINING

The types of data analysis we discuss in this and other chapters of this book are crucial to the success of most companies in today's data-driven business world. However, the sheer volume of available data often defies traditional methods of data analysis. Therefore, a whole new set of methods—and accompanying software—have recently been developed under the name of *data mining*. **Data mining** attempts to discover the patterns, trends, and relationships among data, especially nonobvious and unexpected patterns. For example, the analysis might discover that people who purchase skim milk also tend to purchase whole wheat bread, or that cars built on Mondays before 10 A.M. on production line #5 using parts from suppliers ABC and XYZ have significantly more defects than average. This new knowledge can then be used for more effective management of a business.

A good introductory account of data mining appears in the article by Pass (1997). As he states, the place to start is with a *data warehouse*. Typically, a **data warehouse** is a huge database that is designed specifically to study patterns in data and is *not* the same as the databases companies use for their day-to-day operational activities. A data warehouse should (1) combine data from multiple sources to discover as many interrelationships as possible, (2) contain accurate and consistent data, (3) be structured to enable quick and accurate responses to a variety of queries, and (4) allow follow-up responses to specific, newly relevant questions. In short, a data warehouse represents a relatively new type of database, one that is specifically structured to enable data mining.

Once a data warehouse is in place, analysts can begin to mine the data with a collection of methodologies, techniques, and accompanying software. Some of the primary methodologies are *cluster analysis, linkage analysis, time series analysis,* and *categorization analysis.* **Cluster analysis** is used to identify associations among data points. For example, data mining software might search through credit card purchases to discover that meals charged on business-issued Gold Cards are typically purchased on weekdays and have an average value of more than $200. **Linkage analysis** is used to link two or more events together. It attempts to find items that are typically purchased together as part of a "market basket," such as beer and pretzels, yogurt and skim milk, or less obvious pairs. **Time series analysis** is used to relate events in time. Financial analysts, for example, might try to relate interest rate fluctuations or stock performance to a series of preceding events. **Categorization analysis**, which contains elements of the preceding three methodologies and is probably the most broadly applicable to different types of business problems, attempts to explain the influence that numerous factors have on one specific outcome. For example, given all information on a loan applicant, categorization analysis might attempt to predict whether the applicant will pay back a loan promptly.

In his article, Pass describes one successful application of data mining at Allders International, a company that operates duty-free outlets throughout Europe. Like many companies, Allders was deluged by paper-based reports and spreadsheets of data. In fact, meaningful information was usually obtained too late to be useful for day-to-day decision making. The introduction of data mining made an immediate impact, both on the bottom line and on employee morale. As one manager stated, "In one store we've been able to move the margin up by four points, by being able to identify why it wasn't performing as well as other outlets. We took out the lower margin lines, even though they might sell well, substituting them or adjusting their positioning." Data mining has enabled Allders to fine-tune its product line by identifying and eliminating the low-performing SKUs (stock keeping units). However, it has also identified apparently unprofitable items that still have an important role in pulling shoppers into the stores. The data warehouse is continually being made available to new users, and existing users expect to find new ways to exploit its power for competitive advantage.

We do not discuss the specific data-mining tools mentioned above in this book. However, the methods we discuss in this chapter are frequently necessary steps in data mining. Before we can mine the data for useful information and insights, we have to be able to get the data into a form suitable for analysis. This is exactly what we learn how to do here. ■

4.1 INTRODUCTION

We introduced several numerical and graphical methods for analyzing data statistically in the previous two chapters, and we examine many more statistical methods in later chapters. However, any statistical analysis, whether in Excel or any other software package, presumes that we have the appropriate data. This is a big presumption. Indeed, the majority of the time spent in many real-world statistical projects is devoted to getting the right data in the first place. Unfortunately, this aspect of data analysis is given very little, if any, attention in most statistics textbooks. We believe it is extremely important, so we devote this entire chapter to methods for getting the required data in the right form. The rest of this book then presents methods for *analyzing* the data.

Our basic assumption throughout most of this chapter is that the appropriate data exists somewhere. In particular, we do not cover methods for collecting data from scratch, such as using opinion polls, for example. This is a topic in itself and is better left to a specialized textbook in sampling methods. We assume that a data set already exists, either in an Excel file, in a database file (such as a Microsoft Access file), or on the Web. In the first case, where the data set already resides in an Excel file, we might need to **filter** the data, that is, extract a subset from the entire data set that satisfies specified conditions. For example, we might have customer data on all customers who have ordered from our company in the past year. However, we might want to analyze the subset of these customers who live in the East and have ordered at least three times with a total order amount of at least $500. Therefore, we will examine Excel's built-in capabilities for filtering the data to find only those customers who meet certain conditions. These tools are surprisingly easy to use. Once you know they exist, we expect that you will use them routinely.

Most of the large databases that companies collect are not stored in Excel. Instead, they reside in database packages, such as Microsoft Access, SQL Server, Oracle, and others. These packages are constructed to do certain tasks very well, such as data updating and report writing. However, they are not nearly as good as Excel at statistical data analysis—number crunching. Therefore, we show how to import data from a typical database package into Excel. The key here is to form a *query*, using the Microsoft Query package that ships with Office, that specifies exactly which data we want to import. This package not only presents a friendly user interface for creating the query, but it also finds the appropriate data from the database file and automatically imports it into Excel. Again, the entire process is surprisingly easy, even if you know practically nothing about database packages and database design.

Next, we briefly examine the possibility of importing data directly from the Web into Excel. Given that the amount of data on the Web is already enormous and is constantly growing, the ability to get it into Excel is valuable. As with importing data from a database file, we import data from the Web by creating a query and then running it in Excel. Unfortunately, the Web is still evolving, and sophisticated, easy-to-use tools for interfacing between the Web and Excel are still being developed. Nevertheless, we illustrate that the current possibilities are powerful and relatively straightforward. If you think that querying from a Web site is something only expert programmers can do, we hope to change your mind.

Often data sets are available on the Web, but the Web queries discussed in the previous paragraph cannot always be used to get the data into Excel. In optional Section 4.8, we illustrate one such situation, where the data from a large government survey are available to download from the Web, but only into *another* statistical package (SAS or SPSS). We do not cover either of these packages in this book, but if you really *must* analyze these data, you have no choice but to learn some fundamentals about these other statistical packages.

Finally, we cannot always assume that the data we obtain, from the Web or elsewhere, are "clean." There can be (and often are) many instances of "wrong" values—which can occur for all sorts of reasons—and unless we fix these at the beginning, the resulting statistical analysis can be seriously flawed. Therefore, we conclude this chapter by discussing a few techniques for cleansing data.

4.2 SOURCES OF DATA

There are numerous sources of data, more now than ever before. These include sources of *existing* data, as well as methods for creating *new* data. In this section we discuss these data sources in some generality. In the rest of this chapter, we examine specific methods for getting the data we need.

We begin by discussing sources of existing data, including (1) data stored in printed form (books, magazines, newspapers, and reports), (2) data stored in spreadsheet files, (3) data stored in database files, such as Access files, and (4) data available from Web sites. Of course, some of these overlap. For example, it is less common today to have a printed version of data that is not stored electronically in some form.

Some of these data sources are easy to obtain, and some require considerable work. Indeed, much of this chapter attempts to unravel the mysteries behind obtaining existing data from various sources. However, we cannot cover all situations, and the burden will often be on you, the analyst, to learn how to obtain data from existing sources. For example, most university libraries have access to online databases. These data are available to all students, but you will probably need to read some rather obscure manuals (or get help from a reference librarian) to obtain the data in a useful form.

Some data sources are freely available to everyone (over the Web, say), whereas some contain proprietary company data. Proprietary data are frequently stored by companies in **data warehouses**, huge databases that selected employees can obtain, say, over the company's intranet. These data are often unavailable to nonemployees—at any price. Other data sets are available, often over the Internet, for a fee. We frequently have found Web sites that contain exactly the data we need, only to be asked on the next screen for a credit card! As you will probably discover, some of these data sets are quite expensive.

Even if you find the data you need and are allowed to access it, getting the data into a form suitable for analysis is often a real challenge. Data are stored in a variety of formats, including plain text files (possibly delimited by tabs, commas, spaces, or some other character), Excel spreadsheets, relational databases (Access, SQL Server, and others), HTML tables on Web pages, binary format readable only by specific software packages (SPSS and SAS, for example), and others. It would be nice if all data sets were available in your favorite format (as Excel spreadsheets, say), but the world is not nearly so accommodating. As a data analyst, you will often be forced to learn new skills, including those discussed in this chapter, so that you can obtain the particular data you need.

In addition to the problem of getting data into the appropriate format, there is often a problem of *cleansing* the data. The simple fact is that you cannot always trust the integrity of the data you obtain from external sources. For example, there are often missing values in survey data, where respondents have refused to answer certain questions. To make things worse, these missing values are often not left blank but are instead coded as 9999 or some such value. Suppose you blindly accept these 9999 codes as "real" values and calculate, say, averages and standard deviations. You can only imagine how a few 9999's can affect the results! Data cleansing is tedious, especially for large data sets, but it is an absolute necessity when dealing with externally obtained data. We discuss some data-cleansing techniques in Section 4.9.

More data sets are available today than ever before, partly because of the Web and partly because of the relative ease with which companies can collect customer data (with point-of-sale scanners, for example). In addition, many companies (and academic researchers) continue to generate *new* data through *surveys* and *controlled experiments*. The techniques for doing this properly—both for design and implementation—take us well beyond the scope of this book. Indeed, entire books have been written about designing and implementing these data collection methods. We will limit our discussion to a brief overview.

4.2.1 Data from Surveys

In today's world, you can hardly exist without being intimately aware of surveys. We hear them discussed on the nightly news almost every day, we read about them in the newspapers, and most of us are asked to take part in them increasingly often through (uninvited) e-mail messages. Simply put, there are many organizations out there that want to know what we think, what products we buy, and what we do with our money. How do they design and implement these surveys?

Survey design is an art in itself. Part of it is common sense—don't ask poorly worded questions, and don't ask questions where the answers could be of no possible use. (We've seen plenty of both.) But phrasing questions in just the right way, and asking the right questions to elicit exactly the information we need is not easy. If you plan to conduct your own survey, we suggest that you read a book on survey design (or get help from a seasoned veteran) and perhaps run a pilot test on a small sample before you launch your survey on a large audience. Just remember that (1) people are reluctant to respond to one additional survey and probably do not consider your study as important as you do, and (2) you usually get only one chance—if your results come back as garbage, you probably won't have a chance to conduct the survey again.

When professional pollsters such as Gallup conduct surveys, whom do they survey? This is an extremely important issue. If the people selected are not "representative," the results of the survey can be biased in one direction or another. Typically, a *random* sample of some type is required. It is usually not sufficient, for example, to survey the first 50 people entering a supermarket on a given day. The rules for choosing random samples can be quite complex. For example, we discuss a large survey on substance abuse in Section 4.8 that was conducted by an agency within the U.S. Department of Health and Human Services. In an abstract to the study, the agency spelled out its sampling technique, about a third of which follows. (The full explanation can be found by following links from http://www.icpsr.umich.edu/SAMHDA.)

> *Multistage area probability sample design involving five selection stages: (1) primary sampling unit (PSU) areas (e.g., counties), (2) subareas within primary areas (e.g., blocks or block groups), (3) listing units within subareas, (4) age domains within sampled listing units, and (5) eligible individuals within sampled age domains. The 1998 NHSDA used the same 115 PSUs selected for the 1995 through 1997 NHSDAs, 6 supplemental PSUs from Arizona and California, and an additional 16 noncertainty PSUs from 13 purposely selected states. The 115 PSUs were selected to represent the nation's total eligible population, including areas of high Hispanic concentration.*

This quote illustrates the complexity of sample selection. We discuss several basic random sampling schemes in Chapter 8, but we only scratch the surface. To learn more about this topic—to see how the "pros" do it—you need to consult a book on survey sampling such as Levy and Lemeshow (1999).

4.2.2 Data from Controlled Experiments

Controlled experiments represent another popular method of obtaining new data. In a **controlled experiment**, a researcher purposely holds several variables (called *factors*) constant at prescribed levels and then sees how one or more selected variables vary as the experiment is run. For example, a tire manufacturer might run an experiment where selected tread designs are used at selected air pressures and selected outside temperatures. The experiment might be run by driving several cars with each tread design at each combination of pressure and temperature for 10,000 miles and recording the amount of tread deterioration. The objective is to see whether some tread designs perform better than others, and whether the answer to this depends on air pressure and external temperature. We say that the company *controls* for air pressure and temperature by explicitly incorporating them into the experiment.

Controlled experiments have long been used in the natural sciences. For example, we are all aware of medical experiments, involving animals or even human subjects, that attempt to measure the effectiveness of various drugs. More recently, many businesses, particularly those in manufacturing, have become aware of the usefulness of conducting controlled experiments such as the tire experiment mentioned previously. These experiments have frequently led to higher quality in manufactured products and lower manufacturing costs. Companies have learned that they can gain a lot of information about their products or processes through a well-designed experiment. As with survey design, the topic of controlled experiments is too large and complex to be covered in this book. However, we introduce the topic when we study analysis of variance (ANOVA) later in the book.

4.3 EXCEL TABLES FOR FILTERING, SORTING, AND SUMMARIZING[1]

In the previous two chapters, we introduced pivot tables for breaking down data by categories. In this section, we introduce a new addition to Excel 2007: tables. Tables were "sort of" available in previous versions of Excel, but they were never called *tables* before, and some of the really useful features of Excel 2007 tables are new.

At first, we weren't sure the new tables in Excel 2007 were a big deal. However, the more we work with them, the more we appreciate their useful features.

It is useful to begin with some terminology and history. In the two previous chapters, we examined data arranged in a rectangular range of rows and columns, where each row is a *record* and each column is a *field*, and there are field labels at the top of each column. Informally, we refer to such a range as a *data set*. In fact, this is the term used by StatTools. In previous versions of Excel, data sets were called *lists*, and Excel provided several tools for dealing with lists. In Excel 2007, recognizing the importance of data sets, Microsoft has made them much more prominent and has provided even better tools for analyzing them. Specifically, we now have the ability to designate a rectangular data set as a **table** and then employ a number of new and powerful tools for analyzing tables. These tools include formatting, sorting, filtering, and summarizing. We can even build formulas, using new table notation, that refer to parts of tables.

We illustrate Excel tables in the following example. Before proceeding, however, we mention one important caveat. Some of the tools discussed in this section *will not work* on an Excel file in the old .xls format. Therefore, we purposely illustrate them on files saved in the new .xlsx format.

EXAMPLE	4.1 HyTex's Customer Data

The file **Catalog Marketing.xlsx** contains the same data set that we discussed in Example 3.11 of the previous chapter. It contains data on 1000 customers of HyTex, a direct marketing company, for the current year. For convenience, we repeat the variable— or field—definitions here:

- Age: coded as 1 for 30 years or younger, 2 for 31 to 55 years, 3 for 56 years or older
- Gender: coded as 1 for males, 0 for females
- OwnHome: coded as 1 if customer owns a home, 0 otherwise
- Married: coded as 1 if customer is currently married, 0 otherwise
- Close: coded as 1 if customer lives reasonably close to a shopping area that sells similar merchandise, 0 otherwise
- Salary: combined annual salary of customer and spouse (if any)
- Children: number of children living with customer

[1]Because tables are new to Excel 2007, this section has been completely rewritten from the previous edition.

- History: coded as "NA" if customer had no dealings with the company before this year, 1 if customer was a low-spending customer last year, 2 if medium-spending, 3 if high-spending
- Catalogs: number of catalogs sent to the customer this year
- AmountSpent: total amount of purchases made by the customer this year

In addition, we have added three text fields, Region, State, and City where the customer resides, and we have added one date field, FirstPurchase, the date of the customer's first purchase with HyTex. In Chapter 3 we obtained information from this data set through a variety of charts and pivot tables. In this example and continuations of it, we see how HyTex can gain information about its customers through tables and filters.

Objective To illustrate Excel's tables for analyzing the HyTex data.

Solution

The data in range A1:N1001 is in the form of a data set: a rectangular range bounded by blank rows and columns, where each row is a record, each column is a field, and field headings appear in the top row. Therefore, it is a candidate for an Excel table. However, it doesn't benefit from the new table tools until we actually designate it as a table. To do so, select *any* cell in the data set, click on the Table button in the Tables group on the Insert ribbon (see Figure 4.1), and accept the default options. Two things happen. First, the data set is designated as a table, it is formatted nicely, and dropdown arrows appear next to each field heading, as shown in Figure 4.2. Second, a new Table Tools Design ribbon becomes available (see Figure 4.3). This ribbon is available any time the active cell is inside a table. Note that the table is named Table1 by default (if this is the first table). However, you can change this to a more descriptive name if you like.

Figure 4.1 Insert Ribbon with Table Button

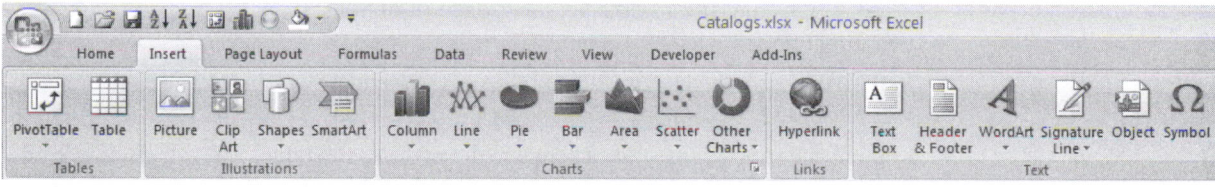

Figure 4.2 Table with Dropdowns

	A	B	C	D	E	F	G	H	I	J	K	L	M	N
1	A	Gend	OwnHor	Marri	Clo	Sala	Childr	Hist	Catal	Region	State	City	FirstPurcha	AmountSpe
2	1	0	0	0	1	$16,400	1	1	12	South	Florida	Orlando	10/23/2003	$218
3	2	0	1	1	0	$108,100	3	3	18	Midwest	Illinois	Chicago	5/25/2001	$2,632
4	2	1	1	1	1	$97,300	1	NA	12	South	Florida	Orlando	8/18/2007	$3,048
5	3	1	1	1	1	$26,800	0	1	12	East	Ohio	Cleveland	12/26/2004	$435
6	1	1	0	0	1	$11,200	0	NA	6	Midwest	Illinois	Chicago	8/4/2007	$106
7	2	0	0	0	1	$42,800	0	2	12	West	Arizona	Phoenix	3/4/2005	$759
8	2	0	0	0	1	$34,700	0	NA	18	Midwest	Kansas	Kansas City	6/11/2007	$1,615
9	3	0	1	1	0	$80,000	0	3	6	West	California	San Francisco	8/17/2001	$1,985
10	2	1	1	0	1	$60,300	0	NA	24	Midwest	Illinois	Chicago	5/29/2007	$2,091
11	3	1	1	1	0	$62,300	0	3	24	South	Florida	Orlando	6/9/2003	$2,644
12	2	1	0	1	1	$94,200	1	3	18	East	New York	Buffalo	4/27/2003	$1,211
13	2	1	1	1	0	$73,800	0	3	24	West	Utah	Salt Lake City	8/13/2003	$3,120
14	2	1	1	0	1	$45,900	2	1	12	South	Louisiana	New Orleans	6/2/2003	$416
15	2	1	0	0	0	$52,600	1	NA	18	East	New York	Buffalo	4/8/2007	$1,773

Figure 4.3 Table Tools Design Ribbon

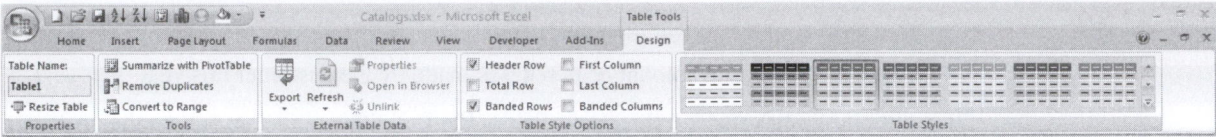

One nice feature of Excel tables is that the field names remain visible even when you scroll down the screen. Try it to see how it works. When you scroll down far enough that the field names would disappear, the column headers, A, B, C, and so on, change to the field names. Therefore, you no longer need to freeze panes or split the screen to see the field names. However, this works only when the active cell is within the table. If you click outside the table, the column headers revert back to A, B, C, and so on.

The dropdown arrows next to each field allow you to filter in many different ways. For example, click on the OwnHome dropdown, unselect the Select All option, and select the 1 option. This filters out all customers except those who own their own home. (If this reminds you of the filtering options for pivot tables, it should; the user interfaces are the same.) Filtering is discussed in much more detail in the next subsection. At this point, just be aware that filtering doesn't *delete* any records; it only hides them. There are three indications that the table has been filtered: (1) the row numbers are colored blue and some are missing; (2) a message appears at the bottom of the screen indicating that only 516 out of 1000 records are visible; and (3) there is a filter icon next to the OwnHome dropdown. It is easy to remove this filter by clicking on the OwnHome dropdown and selecting Clear Filter (but don't do so yet).

As indicated in Figure 4.3, there are various options you can apply to tables, including the following.

- A number of table styles are available for making the table attractive. You can experiment with these, including the various table styles and table style options. Note the dropdown in the Table Styles group. It gives you many more styles than the seven originally visible. In particular, at the top left of options, there is a "no color" style you might prefer.

- In the Tools group, you can click on Convert to Range. This undesignates the range as a table (and the dropdowns disappear).

- In the Properties group, you can change the name of the table. You can also click on the Resize Table button to expand or contract the table range. This is useful if new records or new fields are appended to the data range.

- A particularly useful option is the Total Row in the Table Style Options group. If you check this, a new row is appended to the bottom of the table (see Figure 4.4). It creates a sum formula in the rightmost column.[2] This sum includes *only* the nonhidden rows. To prove this to yourself, clear the OwnHome filter and check the sum. It increases to $1,216,768. This total row is quite flexible. First, you can summarize the last column by a number of summary measures, such as Max, Min, Count, and others. To do so, select cell N1002 and click on the dropdown that appears. Second, you can summarize other columns in the same way. For example, if you select cell F1002, a dropdown appears for Salary, and you can then summarize Salary with the same summarizing options.

This total row is one of the Excel table's best features. It allows you to summarize a filtered data set with a couple clicks.

---

[2]The actual formula is **=SUBTOTAL(109,[AmountSpent])**, where 109 is a code for summing. However, you never need to type any such formula; you can choose the summary function you want from the dropdown list.

Figure 4.4   Total Row

994	3	1	1	1	0	$59,700	0	3	18	Midwest	Ohio	Cincinnati	10/23/2004	$1,857
996	3	1	1	0	1	$41,900	0	2	6	South	Florida	Miami	7/7/2005	$654
997	2	0	1	0	1	$53,800	0	2	12	West	Washington	Seattle	8/14/2007	$843
999	2	1	1	1	1	$102,600	0	3	18	East	Pennsylvania	Philadelphia	8/9/2005	$2,546
1001	2	1	1	1	1	$102,500	1	3	24	West	Utah	Salt Lake City	3/9/2004	$2,464
1002 Total														$796,260

Excel tables have a lot of built-in intelligence. Although there is not enough space here to give a full account, you can try the following to see what we mean.

- In cell Q2 (a cell outside the table), enter a formula by typing an equals sign, pointing to cell N2, typing a divide sign (/), and finally pointing to cell F2. You do *not* get the usual formula **=N2/F2**. Instead you get **=Table1[[#This Row],[AmountSpent]]/Table1[[#This Row],[Salary]]**. This is certainly not the Excel syntax you are used to, and you probably won't use it often, but it makes sense.

- Similarly, you can expand the table with a new field, such as the ratio of AmountSpent to Salary. Start by typing the field name Ratio in cell O1. Then in cell O2, enter a formula exactly as you did in the previous bullet. You will notice two things. First, as soon as you type the new field name, column O becomes part of the table. Second, as soon as you enter the new formula in one cell, it is copied to all of column O. This is what we mean by table intelligence.

- We saved the best for last: expanding data sets. From the Table Tools Design tab, you can choose Summarize with PivotTable. When you do this, the usual PivotTable dialog appears, and the default range is the table name, such as Table1. The advantage of accepting Table1 as the range, rather than a fixed range such as A1:N1001, is that if the table expands in the future (more rows or more columns), all you need to do to make the pivot table adapt to the expansion is click on the Refresh button on the PivotTable Tools Options ribbon. Obviously, this is much easier than rebuilding the pivot table. This also works for charts. Let's say you have a monthly time series data set. You designate it as a table and then build a line chart from it. Later on, if you add new data to the bottom of the table, the chart will automatically include the new data. This is a great feature! ∎

This automatic expansion feature of Excel tables is arguably the feature users will appreciate most. Now, pivot tables and charts based on table data update automatically when data are added to the table.

Filters

We now discuss ways of filtering data sets, that is, finding records that match criteria we set. Before getting into details, there are two aspects of filtering you should be aware of. First, this section is concerned with the types of filters called AutoFilter in previous versions of Excel. The term AutoFilter implied that these were very simple filters, easily learned in a few minutes. If you wanted to do any complex filtering, you had to move beyond AutoFilter to Advanced Filters. Excel 2007 still has Advanced Filters, and we still provide examples of them in the next section. However, the term AutoFilter has been changed to Filter to indicate that these "easy" filters are now more powerful than the old AutoFilter. Fortunately, they are just as easy as AutoFilter.

Second, one way to filter is to create an Excel table, as indicated in the previous subsection. This automatically provides the dropdowns next to the field names that allow you to filter. Indeed, this is the way we will filter in this section: on an existing table. However, a designated table isn't required for filtering. You can filter on any rectangular data set with field names. There are actually three ways to do so. For each method, the active cell should be a cell inside the data set.

1. In the Editing group on the Home ribbon, click on the Filter button from the Sort & Filter dropdown.

2. In the Sort & Filter group on the Data ribbon, click on the Filter button.

3. Right-click on any cell in the table and choose the Filter option. You get several options, the most popular of which is Filter By Selected Cell's Value. The resulting behavior should be familiar to Access users. For example, if the selected cell has value 1 and is in the Children column, then only customers with a single child will remain visible.

The point is that Microsoft realizes how important filtering is to Excel users. Therefore, they have made filtering a very prominent and powerful tool in Excel 2007.

As far as we can tell, the two main advantages of filtering on a table, as opposed to the other three options we just listed, are the nice formatting (banded rows, for example) provided by tables, and more importantly, the totals row. If this totals row is showing, it summarizes *only* the visible records; the hidden rows are ignored.

We now continue Example 4.1 to illustrate a number of filtering possibilities. Unlike some thick "how to" Excel books, we won't lead you through a lot of descriptions and screenshots. Once you know the possibilities that are available, you will find them extremely easy to use.

EXAMPLE | **4.1 HyTex's Customer Data (continued)**

The HyTex company wants to analyze its customer data by applying one or more filters to the data. It has already designated the data set as an Excel table. What types of filters might be useful?

Objective To investigate the types of filters that might be applied to the HyTex data.

Solution

There is almost no limit to the filters we could apply, but here are a few possibilities.

- **Filter on one or more values in a field.** Click on the Catalogs dropdown. You will see five checkboxes, all checked: Select All, 6, 12, 18, and 24. To select one or more values, uncheck Select All and then check any values you want to filter on, such as 6 and 24. In this case, only customers who received 6 or 24 catalogs will remain visible. (In Excel 2003 and earlier, it wasn't possible to select more than one value this way. Now it's easy.)

- **Filter on more than one field.** With the Catalogs filter still in place, create a filter on some other field, such as customers with 1 child. When there are filters on multiple fields, only records that meet *all* of the criteria are visible, in this case, customers with 1 child who received 6 or 24 catalogs.

- **Filter on a continuous numerical field.** The Salary and AmountSpent fields are basically continuous fields, so it would not make much sense to filter on one or a few particular values. However, it does make sense to filter on ranges of values, such as all salaries greater than $75,000. This is easy. Click on the dropdown next to Salary and select Number Filters. You will see a number of obvious possibilities, including Greater Than.

- **Top 10 and Above/Below Average filters.** Continuing the previous bullet, the Number Filters include Top 10, Above Average, and Below Average options. These are particularly useful for managers who like to see the highs and the lows. The Above Average and Below Average filters do exactly what their names imply. The Top 10 filter is actually more flexible than its name implies. It can be used to select the top *n* items (where you can choose *n*), the bottom *n* items, the top *n* percent of items, or the bottom *n* percent of items. If a Top 10 filter is used on a text field, the ordering is alphabetical order. If it is used on a date field, the ordering is chronological order.

- **Filter on a text field.** If you click on the dropdown for a text field, such as Region, you can choose one or more of its values, such as East and South, to filter on. You can also select the Text Filters item, which provides a number of choices, including Begins With, Ends With, Contains, and others. For example, if there were an Address field, you could use the Begins With option to find all addresses that begin with P.O. Box.

- **Filter on a date field.** Excel 2007 has great built-in intelligence for filtering on dates. If you click on the FirstPurchase dropdown, you will see an item for each year (2001–2007) in the data set with plus signs next to them. By clicking on the plus signs, you can drill down to months and then days for as much control as you need. Figure 4.5 shows one possibility, where we have filtered out all dates except the last half of July 2007. In addition, if you click on the Date Filters item in this figure, you get a number of possibilities, such as Yesterday, Next Week, Last Month, and many others. There aren't many possibilities Microsoft hasn't thought of when it comes to dates.

Figure 4.5
Filtering on a Date Field

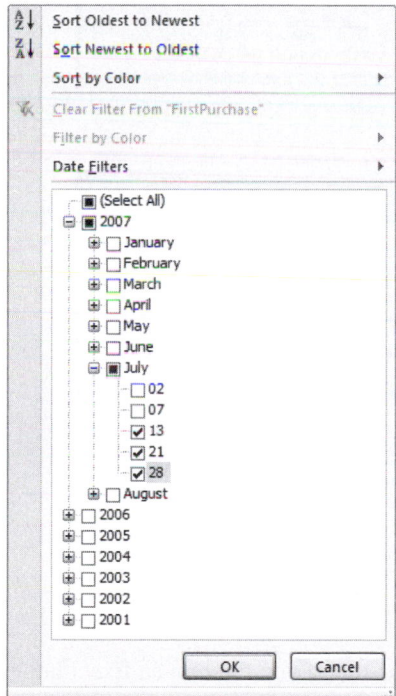

- **Filter on color or icon.** Excel 2007 has many ways to color cells or put icons in cells. Often the purpose is to denote the sizes of the numbers in the cells, such as red for small numbers and green for large numbers. We haven't covered the possibilities in this book, but you can experiment with Conditional Formatting on the Home ribbon. The point is that cells are often colored in certain ways or contain certain icons. Therefore, Excel 2007 allows you to filter on background color, font color, or icon. For example, if certain salaries are colored yellow, you can isolate them by filtering on yellow. We are not sure how often this feature will be used, but it's available and easy to use.

- **Use a custom filter.** If nothing else works, you can try a custom filter, available at the bottom of the Number Filters, Text Filters, and Date Filters lists. Figures 4.6 and 4.7 illustrate two possibilities. The first of these filters out all salaries between $25,000 and $75,000. Without a custom filter, this wouldn't be possible. The second uses the * wildcard to find regions ending in est (West and Midwest). Admittedly, this is an awkward way to perform this filter, but it indicates how flexible custom filters can be.

Figure 4.6
Custom Filter for Salary

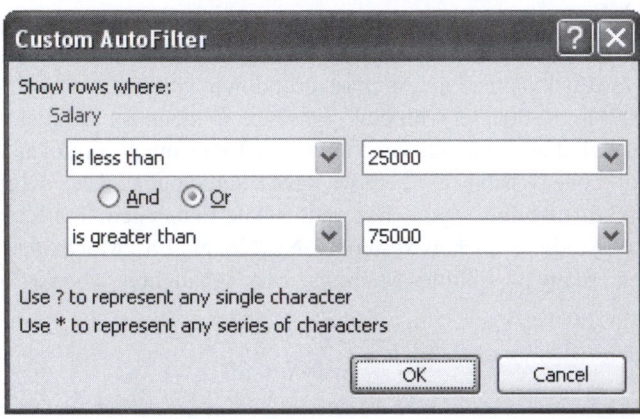

Figure 4.7
Custom Filter for Region

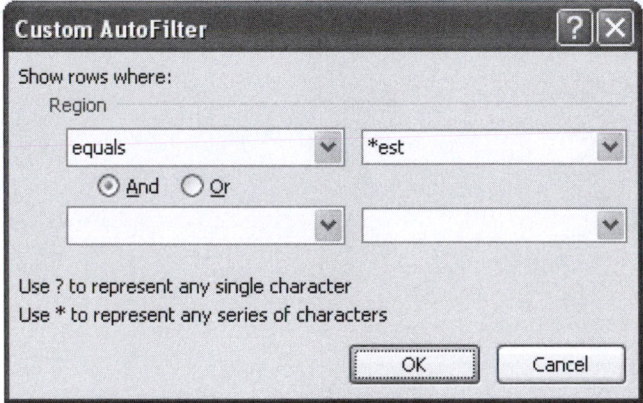

We remind you once again that if you filter on an Excel table and you have summary measures in a total row at the bottom of the table, these summary measures are based *only* on the filtered data; they ignore the hidden rows.

One final comment about filters is that when you click on the dropdown for any field, you always get three items at the top for *sorting,* not filtering (see Figure 4.5, for example). These allow you to perform the obvious sorts, from high to low or vice versa, and they even allow you to sort on color.

Now that you know the possibilities, here is one particular filter you can try. Suppose HyTex wants information about all middle-aged married customers with at least two children who have above average salaries, own their own home, and live in Indiana or Kentucky. We imagine that you can run this filter in a few seconds. The result, sorted in decreasing order of AmountSpent and shown in Figure 4.8, indicates that the average salary for these 10 customers is $84,750, and their average amount spent at HyTex is $1,471. (We summarized Salary and AmountSpent by average, not sum, in the totals row.)

Figure 4.8 Results from a Typical Filter

	A	B	C	D	E	F	G	H	I	J	K	L	M	N
1	A	Gend	OwnHor	Marri	Clo	Sala	Childr	Histo	Catalo	Region	State	City	FirstPurcha	AmountSpe
155	2	0	1	1	0	$96,800	3	NA		24	Midwest	Kentucky	Louisville	3/7/2007	$3,082
163	2	0	1	1	1	$62,200	3	NA		24	Midwest	Indiana	Indianapolis	6/17/2007	$2,119
245	2	1	1	1	0	$82,400	2	3		24	Midwest	Indiana	Indianapolis	11/25/2006	$2,035
370	2	1	1	1	0	$113,400	3	3		18	Midwest	Kentucky	Louisville	6/15/2006	$1,790
430	2	1	1	1	1	$113,000	2	2		18	Midwest	Kentucky	Louisville	3/3/2007	$1,554
570	2	1	1	1	1	$70,400	2	NA		12	Midwest	Indiana	Indianapolis	4/28/2007	$1,127
764	2	0	1	1	1	$85,500	2	2		18	Midwest	Kentucky	Louisville	6/7/2003	$895
790	2	1	1	1	1	$74,500	2	2		12	Midwest	Indiana	Indianapolis	4/12/2002	$824
804	2	0	1	1	1	$72,200	2	2		18	Midwest	Kentucky	Louisville	10/1/2003	$715
851	2	1	1	1	1	$77,100	2	2		6	Midwest	Indiana	Indianapolis	7/3/2006	$568
1002	Total					$84,750								$1,471

PROBLEMS

Level A

1. The file **P04_01.xlsx** contains a data set that represents 30 responses from a questionnaire concerning the president's environmental policies. Each observation lists the person's age, gender, state of residence, number of children, annual salary, and opinion of the president's environmental policies.

  a. Use an Excel filter to identify all respondents who are female, middle-age, and who have two children. What is the average salary of these respondents?

  b. Use an Excel filter to identify all respondents who are elderly and who strongly disagree with the president's environmental policies. What is the average salary of these respondents?

  c. Use an Excel filter to identify all respondents who strongly agree with the president's environmental policies. What proportion of these individuals are young?

2. A human resources manager at Beta Technologies, Inc., has collected current annual salary figures and related data for 52 of the company's full-time employees. The data are in the file **P04_02.xlsx**.

  a. Use an Excel filter to identify all employees who are male and who have exactly 4 years of post-secondary education. What is the average salary of these employees?

  b. Find the average salary of all *female* employees who have exactly 4 years of postsecondary education. How does this mean salary compare to the one obtained in part **a**?

  c. Use an Excel filter to identify all employees who have more than 4 years of postsecondary education. What proportion of these employees are male?

3. Five hundred households in a middle-class neighborhood were recently surveyed as part of an economic development study conducted by the local government. The data are in the file **P04_03.xlsx**. Use an Excel filter to answer the following questions:

  a. What are the average monthly home mortgage payment, average monthly utility bill, and average total debt (excluding the home mortgage) of all homeowners residing in the southeast sector of the city?

  b. What are the average monthly home mortgage payment, average monthly utility bill, and average total debt (excluding the home mortgage) of all homeowners residing in the northwest sector of the city? How do these results compare to those found in part **a**?

  c. What is the average annual income of the first household wage earners who rent their home (i.e., house or apartment)? How does this compare to the average annual income of the first household wage earners who own their home?

  d. What proportion of households surveyed contain a single person who owns his or her home?

4. The file **P04_04.xlsx** contains information on 66 movie stars. In particular, the data set contains the name of each actor and the following four variables: gender, domestic gross (average domestic gross of the star's last few movies, in millions of dollars), foreign gross (average foreign gross of the star's last few movies, in millions of dollars), and income (current amount the star asks for a movie, in millions of dollars). Use an Excel filter to answer the following questions:

a. Identify all stars whose average domestic gross exceeds 75 million dollars and whose average foreign gross exceeds 75 million dollars. Find the average income of these stars. What proportion of these stars are men?

b. Identify all stars whose average domestic gross is between 50 and 75 million dollars (inclusive) and whose average foreign gross is between 50 and 75 million dollars (inclusive). Find the average income of these stars. What proportion of these stars are women?

c. Identify all stars whose average domestic gross is less than 50 million dollars and whose average foreign gross is less than 50 million dollars. Find the average income of these stars. What proportion of these stars are men?

4.4 COMPLEX QUERIES WITH THE ADVANCED FILTER

The filtering options discussed in the previous section are useful for quick and simple queries, but they are primarily for queries of the form *Find all records where Field 1 satisfies certain conditions* **and** *Field 2 satisfies certain conditions* **and** *Field 3 satisfies certain conditions*, and so on. They cannot handle the following query: *Find all customers who are either male with salary above $40,000* **or** *female with at least 2 children*. Here there are two "and" queries (male *and* salary above $40,000, and female *and* at least 2 children), but they are combined with an "or." To perform a more complex query of this type, we need Excel's Advanced Filter tool, found under the Advanced button in the Sort & Filter group on the Data ribbon. However, we pay a price for being able to perform more complex queries. The price is that we must first construct a "criteria range." This criteria range essentially spells out the query. It consists of a top row of field names and one or more rows of conditions. Each row of conditions becomes an "or" part of the query. For example, the first row (right below the field names) might indicate that we want males with salary above $40,000, and the second row might indicate that we want females with at least 2 children. Then the query will return all records that match the conditions in *either* (or both) of these rows. There is no limit to the number of rows—sets of conditions—we can put in the criteria range, although it is typically a small number such as 1 or 2.

When we use the Advanced Filter tool, we must specify the original data range, the criteria range, and (optionally) a range where the results of the query will be placed. Also, the query is not automatically done "in-place," where the original database is replaced by the results of the query by hiding some of the rows. This is still an option, but we can also request that the results of the query be placed in any range we select. We demonstrate the procedure in the following continuation of Example 4.1.

EXAMPLE | **4.1 FILTERING HYTEX'S CUSTOMER DATA (CONTINUED)**

The Hytex Company would now like to perform more advanced queries on the data in the **Catalog Marketing.xlsx** file by using Excel's Advanced Filter tool. How might it proceed?

Objective To illustrate how Excel's Advanced Filter tool can be used to execute more complex "or" queries on the Hytex database.

Solution

We begin by copying the row of field names to any unused area of the data sheet. This might be right above the database (by first inserting some blank rows) or just to the right of the database. We chose the latter. This row becomes the top row of the criteria range. Then we (manually) enter conditions in the cells just below these field names. The key is that the conditions in a given row are "and" conditions, whereas conditions across rows are treated in an "or" manner, as described above. An example appears in Figure 4.9. The first row specifies that we want all customers who are married *and* have salary at least $80,000 *and* have at least 2 children. The second row specifies that we want all customers who have salary at least $100,000 *and* received at least 12 catalogs. Using the range P3:AC5 as the criteria range, the query will return records that match the conditions in either (or both) of rows 4 and 5. (Actually, the criteria range does not need to include field names not used in the query. For this particular query, the criteria range could be as in Figure 4.10. However, there is no harm in including all possible fields in the criteria range.)

Figure 4.9   Criteria Range with Two Sets of Conditions

	P	Q	R	S	T	U	V	W	X	Y	Z	AA	AB	AC
1	Criteria range (starts in row 3)													
2														
3	Age	Gender	OwnHome	Married	Close	Salary	Children	History	Catalogs	Region	State	City	stPurchase	ountSpent
4				1		>=80000	>=2							
5						>=100000			>=12					

Figure 4.10
An Alternative Form
of the Criteria Range

	P	Q	R	S
1	Criteria range (starts in row 3)			
2				
3	Married	Salary	Children	Catalogs
4	1	>=80000	>=2	
5		>=100000		>=12

Here are several example customers and an indication of whether they will be included in the query results:

1   Married, salary $85,000, 3 children, received 6 catalogs: included (satisfies conditions in row 4 but not row 5)

2   Married, salary $105,000, 2 children, received 18 catalogs: included (satisfies conditions in row 4 and row 5)

3   Unmarried, salary $120,000, 1 child, received 6 catalogs: not included (does not satisfy the conditions in either row)

4   Married, salary $120,000, 1 child, received 18 catalogs: included (satisfies the conditions in row 5 but not row 4)

Once the criteria range is created, we run the query by using the Advanced button on the Data ribbon. This brings up a dialog box, which we fill in as shown in Figure 4.11. If we select the top option (Filter the list, in-place), the query acts just like a filter from the previous section, so that records that do not match the conditions are temporarily hidden from view. We used the second option, which places the query results in a separate output range and keeps the original database intact. Two other points are worth mentioning. First, we

Figure 4.11

Dialog Box for
Advanced Filter

*If range names are
given to the data and
criteria ranges, they
can be used instead
of cell addresses in
the dialog box.*

need to specify only the top-left cell of the output range, here, cell AE1. Indeed, it would be difficult to specify the entire output range because we do not know how many records will match the query conditions! Second, if we check the box at the bottom, then any customers who meet the query conditions and are identical on all fields are listed only once in the output range. This is sometimes appropriate when we want to avoid duplicate records in the query results. Some of the results of this particular query appear in Figure 4.12.

Figure 4.12 Selected Query Results in the Output Range

	AE	AF	AG	AH	AI	AJ	AK	AL	AM	AN	AO	AP	AQ	AR
1	Age	Gender	OwnHome	Married	Close	Salary	Children	History	Catalogs	Region	State	City	FirstPurchase	AmountSpent
2	2	0	1	1	0	$108,100	3	3	18	Midwest	Illinois	Chicago	5/25/2001	$2,632
3	2	1	1	1	1	$95,800	3	1	12	Midwest	Missouri	St. Louis	2/1/2005	$678
4	2	1	1	1	1	$107,300	2	2	18	West	Washington	Seattle	10/31/2001	$1,566
5	2	1	1	1	0	$90,700	3	3	24	South	Florida	Miami	5/12/2003	$2,265
6	2	0	1	1	1	$81,700	3	1	24	East	Pennsylvania	Philadelphia	4/22/2004	$879
7	2	1	1	1	0	$96,800	2	3	18	Midwest	Illinois	Chicago	1/8/2002	$2,299
8	2	1	0	1	1	$117,700	1	3	12	West	Colorado	Denver	5/24/2001	$2,104
9	3	0	1	1	0	$118,000	3	1	12	South	Louisiana	New Orleans	1/8/2007	$581
10	3	0	1	1	0	$110,000	0	3	24	East	Ohio	Cleveland	10/1/2002	$5,564
11	3	1	1	1	1	$124,900	0	3	18	West	Utah	Salt Lake City	5/24/2007	$4,109

As another example, suppose we want the customers who are either (1) male with salary between $40,000 and $50,000, or (2) female with salary over $70,000. The problem here is that condition (1) includes an "and" condition (greater than $40,000 *and* less than $50,000) in the same field, Salary. How should this condition be entered in the criteria range? It is tempting to enter the label ">40000,<50000" in a cell under Salary, where we include both conditions, separated by a comma. However, this doesn't work! (We tried to see whether it would work, or what *would* work, in Excel's online help, but unfortunately there is very little we could find about specifying conditions for queries.) One solution— maybe you can find another—is to enter *two* Salary fields in the criteria range, as shown in Figure 4.13. There is no rule that every field name must be included in the criteria range. Only those names involved in the query are required. In addition, the same field name can be included more than once, evidently to deal with the situation we have posed. The criteria range, as set up in Figure 4.13, will return exactly the records we seek.

Figure 4.13

An "And" Condition
in the Salary Field

	AT	AU	AV
1	**Another criteria range**		
2			
3	Gender	Salary	Salary
4	1	>40000	<50000
5	0	>70000	

It is even possible to base the criteria on a formula. This is called a **computed query**. For example, suppose we want to locate all customers with salary at least $1000 greater than the median salary for all customers. Then in the criteria range, we can enter the formula

$$\text{=F2>(MEDIAN(\$F\$2:\$F\$1001)+1000)} \tag{4.1}$$

under any field name such as HighSalary. (We use F2 in this formula because it is the *first* cell with data in the Salary column.) Better yet, we can calculate the median salary plus $1000 in some unused cell (cell AX8, say) and replace formula (4.1) with the formula

$$\text{=F4>\$AX\$8} \tag{4.2}$$

(Note that the expression to the right of the first equals sign in either formula (4.1) or formula (4.2) is a *condition*. Therefore, the result of either formula is TRUE or FALSE.) The setup for this is shown in Figure 4.14. Cell AX4 contains formula (4.2), cell AX8 contains the formula

$$\text{=MEDIAN(F2:F1001)+1000}$$

and the criteria range is AX3:AX4. The resulting query returns 482 records (slightly less than 50% of all records)—exactly those with a salary greater than $54,700.

Figure 4.14

A Computed Query

	AX	AY	AZ	BA	BB
1	Criteria based on a formula				
2					
3	HighSalary				
4	FALSE	←	=F4>$AX$8		
5					
6					
7	Cutoff value				
8	$54,700	←	=MEDIAN(F2:F1001)+1000		

Guidelines for computed queries

- The column heading above a computed criterion must *not* be the same as a field name in the database. This is why we used the name HighSalary, not Salary, in the criteria range.

- References to cells outside the database range should be *absolute*. This is why we put dollar signs around AX8 in formula (4.2).

- References to cells inside the database range should be *relative*. This is why we made the leftmost F2 in formulas (4.1) and (4.2) relative. However, there is an exception to this rule, as shown in formula (4.1), where we made the range F2:F1001 absolute.

Once you understand the underlying logic, these last two rules—and the exception—make sense. As we see in Figure 4.14, the first salary, the one in cell F2, does *not* meet the criterion. This is why we see FALSE in cell AX4. However, when we run the query, Excel recognizes that the cell reference F2 in formula (4.2) is relative. Therefore, it substitutes *each* salary (first the one in cell F2, then the one in cell F3, and so on) into the formula in cell AX4 to check whether it meets the condition. This is why we want the left side of the inequality to be relative. However, because the median salary plus 1000 should remain fixed, we want the right side to be absolute. Finally, the reason we prefer formula (4.2) to formula (4.1) is that it is much faster. When we use formula (4.1), the median plus 1000 must be calculated 1000 times, once for each record in the database. When we use formula (4.2), the median plus 1000 is calculated only once. ∎

4.4.1 Tips for Forming Criteria

As this example has illustrated, Excel's Advanced Filter tool is very useful and relatively easy to use, provided that we know how to enter the conditions in the criteria range correctly. Unfortunately, this is not discussed in much detail in any online help we have been able to find. Here are some tips that might come in handy.

- For text fields such as last names or cities, entering a single letter such as *M* will return any text that starts with that letter. Similarly, entering any sequence of letters such as *Mon* will return any text that starts with this sequence—*Monday*, *Montana*, and so on. In addition, it is *not* case sensitive. We could enter *Mon* or *mon* with exactly the same results.

- A *formula* of the form ="=Smith" can be entered under a text field. This returns all records that match Smith exactly. Why might we do this? The reason is that if we enter only the name Smith (as a label, not a formula), it will return any name that starts with Smith, such as Smithsonian. So for an exact match, it is best to use a formula.

- To specify a "not equal" condition, use the characters <> (less than followed by greater than), as in <>10.

- Wildcards are permitted, exactly as in the previous section. The character "?" stands for any single character, and "*" stands for any series of characters.

- Be careful of putting the criteria range just to the right of the database range (as we did). If you then run the Advanced Filter with the default option of showing the results in-place (hiding the rows that don't match the criteria), the rows of your criteria range might be hidden as well! A useful alternative is to place the criteria range directly *above* the database range (with at least one blank row between them).

- Remember that only the fields involved in the conditions need to be entered in the criteria range. Also, as we saw in the example, the same field name can be entered more than once.

- Because it is so important, we state once more how Excel decides which records to return. For each row in the criteria range, Excel finds all records that match *all* of the conditions in that row. Then, if a record is a match for *any* of the rows in the criteria range, it is returned in the query results.

4.4.2 Database Functions

We have already worked with Excel's summary functions, including COUNT, COUNTA, SUM, AVERAGE, and STDEV.[3] There are similar functions for summarizing results from a database query. They all begin with the letter *D* (for database), as in DCOUNT, DCOUNTA, DSUM, DAVERAGE, and DSTDEV. Now that we have discussed criteria ranges, these database functions are easy to describe. They all take three arguments, as in

$$=\textbf{Dfunction}(\textit{database range,field name,criteria range})$$

Here, Dfunction is any of the database functions, such as DAVERAGE; *database range* is the range of the database, including the field labels at the top; *field name* is the name of a field we want to summarize, enclosed in double quotes; and *criteria range* is the criteria range, exactly as we discussed earlier in this section. We illustrate these functions in the following continuation of Example 4.1.

---

[3]Remember that COUNT returns the number of *numeric* values in a range, whereas COUNTA returns the number of *all nonblank* cells in a range.

EXAMPLE | **4.1 FILTERING HYTEX'S CUSTOMER DATA (CONTINUED)**

For HyTex's database of 1000 customers, we would like to calculate summary measures regarding the amount spent for all customers who are male, have a salary above $50,000, had a previous history with HyTex, and received at least 18 catalogs, or are female, have a salary above $60,000, had a previous history with HyTex, and received at least 12 catalogs.

Objective   To illustrate Excel's database summary functions on the Catalogs database.

Solution

The solution appears in Figure 4.15. The criteria range is formed in the usual way. It includes two criteria rows because of the "or" condition in the statement of the problem. Then we entered the database functions for count, sum, average, and standard deviation in cells BD7 through BD10 (and spelled them out as labels to the right for your convenience). There are two things to note. First, we can either enter the field name AmountSpent inside double quotes, or we can point to a cell (N1) with the AmountSpent label; we did the latter. Second, the query itself does not need to be performed explicitly. That is, we do not need to use the Advanced Filter as a first step. The database functions perform the query implicitly and report only the summary results. Alternatively, we could perform the query explicitly with the Advanced Filter tool and then use the *usual* Excel functions COUNT, SUM, AVERAGE, and STDEV on the results of the query. The summary results would be identical.

Figure 4.15

Excel's Database Functions

	BC	BD	BE	BF	BG	BH	BI
1	Criteria to use with D functions						
2							
3	Gender	Salary	History	Catalogs			
4	1	>50000	<>NA	>=18			
5	0	>60000	<>NA	>=12			
6							
7	Count	247	=DCOUNT($A$1:$N$1001,$N$1,$BC$3:$BF$5)				
8	Sum	504042.5	=DSUM($A$1:$N$1001,$N$1,$BC$3:$BF$5)				
9	Average	2040.658	=DAVERAGE($A$1:$N$1001,$N$1,$BC$3:$BF$5)				
10	Stdev	1067.994	=DSTDEV($A$1:$N$1001,$N$1,$BC$3:$BF$5)				

The "D" functions have been part of Excel for over a decade, and they continue to be available in Excel 2007. However, we suspect that with the Total row available for tables in Excel 2007, users will have less need to employ these "D" functions.

PROBLEMS

Level A

5. Recall that the file **P04_01.xlsx** contains 30 responses from a questionnaire concerning the president's environmental policies. Each observation lists the person's age, gender, state of residence, number of children, annual salary, and opinion of the president's environmental policies.
   a. Find all respondents who are either (1) middle-age men with at least one child and an annual salary of at least $50,000, or (2) middle-age women with two or fewer children and an annual salary of at least $30,000.
   b. Find the mean and median salaries of the respondents who meet the conditions specified above.
   c. What proportion of the respondents who satisfy the conditions specified above agree or strongly agree with the president's environmental policies?

6. Recall that the file **P04_04.xlsx** contains data on 66 movie stars.

a. Find all movie stars who are either (1) females with domestic gross between $40 million and $80 million (inclusive) and foreign gross between $40 million and $80 million (inclusive), or (2) males with domestic gross between $50 million and $90 million d(inclusive) and foreign gross between $50 million and $90 million (inclusive).

b. Find the mean and median incomes of the movie stars who meet the conditions specified in part **a**.

c. What proportion of the stars identified in part **a** earn incomes in excess of $10 million per movie?

7. A human resources manager at Beta Technologies, Inc., has collected current annual salary figures and related data for 52 of the company's full-time employees. The data are in the file **P04_02.xlsx**.

a. Identify all full-time employees who are either (1) females between the ages of 30 and 50 (inclusive) who have at least 5 years of prior work experience, at least 10 years of prior work experience at Beta, and at least 4 years of postsecondary education; or (2) males between the ages of 40 and 60 (inclusive) who have at least 6 years of prior work experience, at least 12 years of prior work experience at Beta, and at least 4 years of postsecondary education.

b. For those employees who meet the conditions specified in part **a**, compare the mean salary of the females with that of the males. Also, compare the median salary of the female employees with that of the male employees.

c. What proportion of the full-time employees identified in part **a** earn less than $50,000 per year?

8. Five hundred households in a middle-class neighborhood were recently surveyed as part of an economic development study conducted by the local government. The data are in the file **P04_03.xlsx**. Identify all of the households in the given data set that satisfy each of the following conditions:

a. The household owns their home and their monthly home mortgage payment is in the top quartile of the monthly payments for all households.

b. The household's typical monthly expenditure on utilities is within 2 standard deviations of the mean monthly expenditure on utilities for all households.

c. The household's total indebtedness (excluding home mortgage) is less than 10% of the household's primary annual income level.

4.5 IMPORTING EXTERNAL DATA FROM ACCESS

To this point, we have worked only with databases that already exist in Excel. Often, however, the data we need to analyze reside in an external source. In this section we discuss the situation where the data were created in a database package. Specifically, we consider data in Microsoft Access format. (This is the database package that is bundled with Microsoft Office.) Database packages such as Access, SQL Server, Oracle, and many others are extremely complex and powerful packages, and for database creation, querying, manipulation, and reporting, they have many advantages over spreadsheets. However, they are not nearly as powerful as spreadsheets for statistical analysis. Therefore, it is often necessary to import data from a database package—either all of it or just a subset of it, based on a query—into Excel, where we can then perform the statistical analysis. Fortunately, Microsoft has included a software package called Microsoft Query in its Office suite that makes the importing relatively easy. We will describe the process in this section.

4.5.1 A Brief Introduction to Relational Databases

First, we present some general concepts about database structure. The Excel "databases" we have discussed so far in this book are often called *flat files* or, more simply, *tables*. They are also called *single-table* databases, where **table** is the database term for a rectangular range of data, with columns corresponding to fields and rows corresponding to records.[4] For example, the data in the file **Catalog Marketing.xlsx** that we used in Example 4.1 reside in a single table. This table consists of 10 fields and 1000 records arranged in a rectangular range. Flat files are fine for relatively simple database applications, but they are not powerful enough for more complex applications. For the latter we need a **relational**

---

[4]Fortunately, Excel now uses the term *table* in exactly the same way as it has been used in database packages for years. However, Excel has no practical way for dealing with the multi-table databases discussed here.

database, a related set of tables, where each table is a rectangular arrangement of fields and records, and the tables are linked explicitly.

As a simple example, suppose you would like to keep track of information on all of the books you own. Specifically, you would like to keep track of data on each book (title, author, copyright date, whether you have read it, when you bought it, and so on), as well as data on each author (name, birthdate, awards won, number of books written, and so on). Now suppose you store *all* of these data in a flat file. Then if you own 10 books by Danielle Steele, say, you must fill in the identical personal information on Ms. Steele for *each* of the 10 records associated with her books. This is not only a waste of time, but it increases the chance of introducing errors as you enter the same information over and over.

A better solution is to create a Books table and an Authors table. In the Books table, each record would contain the data, including author name, for a particular book. It might also include an AuthorID field, where a unique number is associated with each author. Danielle Steele might have ID 001, John Grisham might have ID 002, and so on. The Authors table would have a *single* record for each author, and it would include the same AuthorID field. In this way, personal data on Danielle Steele would be entered only once. Similarly, for maintenance purposes, if any of her personal data changed, it would need to be updated in only one place: in her record of the Authors table.

The key to relating these two tables is the AuthorID field. In a database package such as Access, we explicitly draw a link between the AuthorID fields in the two tables.[5] This link allows a user to find data from the two tables easily. For example, suppose you see in the Authors table that John Updike's ID is 035. Then you can search through the Books table for all records with AuthorID 035. These correspond to the books you own by John Updike. Going the other way, if you see in the Books table that you own *The World According to Garp* by John Irving, who happens to have AuthorID 021, you can look up the (unique) record in the Authors table with AuthorID 021 to find personal information about John Irving.

The theory and implementation of relational databases is both lengthy and complex. Indeed, many books have been written about the topic. However, this brief introduction suffices for our purposes. As we see in examples, an Access database file (recognizable by the .mdb extension, or the .accdb extension in Access 2007) typically contains several related tables. They are related in the same basic way as the Books and Authors were related in the previous paragraph—through links of certain fields. These links will be apparent when we use Microsoft Query to import data from Access into Excel. Just keep in mind that we do not actually create Access databases. This would take us too far afield, given the goals of this book. In fact, we do not even require you to own Access. We simply assume that (1) an Access database exists, (2) we know the type of data it contains, and (3) we want to query it for information that we can import into Excel for eventual statistical analysis.

The linked fields are called keys. Specifically, the AuthorID field in the Authors table is called a primary key, and the AuthorID field in the Books table is called a foreign key. A primary key must contain unique values, whereas a foreign key can contain duplicate values. For example, there is only one Danielle Steele, but she has written several books.

4.5.2 Using Microsoft Query to Import Data from a Database Package

There are two ways to import Access data into Excel in Excel 2007. They are both found in the Get External Data group on the Data ribbon. (See Figure 4.16.) The first method uses the From Access button. This seems very natural, but it is limited to importing whole tables or saved queries. If you want to import only a single table, or if you have already saved a query in Access, then this is the method you should use because it is very easy. However, if you want to create a query "on the fly" that involves several Access tables, then you need to use the second method, which employs Microsoft Query.

---

[5]They do not actually have to have the same field name, such as AuthorIndex, but the indexes must match. For example, if 001 is Danielle Steele's index in one table, it must be her index in the other table.

Figure 4.16 Get External Data Group on Data Ribbon

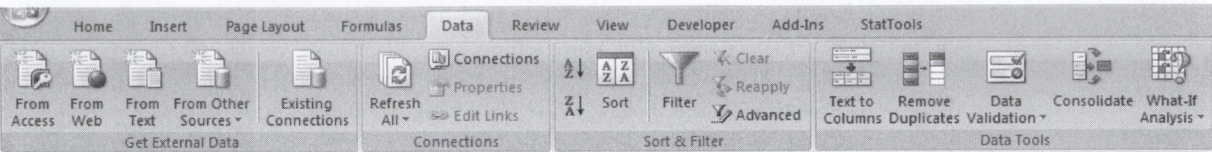

The Microsoft Query package allows you to import all or part of the data from many database packages into Excel—with very little work. You probably do not know you own this package. For example, if you click on the Windows Start button and then choose Programs, you will not find Microsoft Query on the list. However, it comes with Office, and you can use it. The only question is whether you installed it when you installed Office. To check, open a blank spreadsheet in Excel and select From Microsoft Query from the From Other Sources dropdown on the Data ribbon. If this doesn't work, then Microsoft Query is not installed. You will have to go through the Add/Remove part of the Office Setup program (with your Office CD-ROM) to install it.

Once Microsoft Query is installed, importing data from Access (or any other supported database package) is essentially a three-step process:

1. Define the source, so that Excel knows what type of database the data are in and where the data are located.

2. Use Microsoft Query to define a query.

3. Return the data to Excel.

We illustrate these three steps in the following example.

EXAMPLE | **4.2 FINE SHIRT COMPANY'S RELATIONAL DATA**

The Fine Shirt Company creates and sells shirts to its customers. These customers are retailers who sell the shirts to consumers. The company has created an Access database file **Shirt Orders.mdb** that has information on sales to its customers during the period of 1995 through 1999.[6] There are three related tables in this database: Customers, Orders, and Products. The Customers table has the following information on the company's seven customers:

- CustomerID (an index for the customer, from 1 to 7)
- Name
- Street
- City
- State
- Zip
- Phone

The Products table has the following information on the company's 10 products (types of shirts):

- ProductID (an index for the product, from 1 to 10)
- Description

---

[6]In Office 2003 and earlier, Access files had an .mdb extension. In Office 2007, the extension has changed to .accdb. Old .mdb files can be converted to the new .accdb format. However, Access 2007 has no problem reading .mdb files. Because we see no advantage to converting .mdb files to .accdb files, we have not done so.

- Gender (whether the product is made for females, males, or both)
- UnitPrice (the price to the retailer)

Finally, the bulk of the data are in the Orders table. This table has a record for each product ordered by each customer on each date during the 5-year period. There are 2245 records in this table. If a customer ordered more than one product on a particular date, there is a separate record for each product ordered. The fields in the Orders table are

- OrderID (an index for the order, from 1 to 2245)
- CustomerID (to link to the Customers table)
- ProductID (to link to the Products table)
- OrderDate
- UnitsOrdered (number of shirts of this type ordered)
- Discount (percentage discount, if any, for this order)

The Access file has a link between the CustomerID fields in the Customers and Orders tables, and a link between the ProductID fields in the Products and Orders tables. This way, the detailed information on customers and products must be entered only once. If we need any of this information for a particular order, we can find it through the links. For example, if a particular order shows that CustomerID and ProductID are 2 and 7, we can look up information about customer 2 and product 7 in the Customers and Products tables.

Access allows us to diagram the relationships between tables, as shown in Figure 4.17. This diagram shows the primary keys (the key symbols) and the links involving the CustomerID and ProductID fields. The 1 and ∞ signs on the links imply "many-to-one" relationships. Specifically, a given customer is included only once in the Customers table, but this same customer can be responsible for many orders in the Orders table. Similarly, a given product is included only once in the Products table, but it can be included in many orders in the Orders table.

Figure 4.17

Relationships Diagram

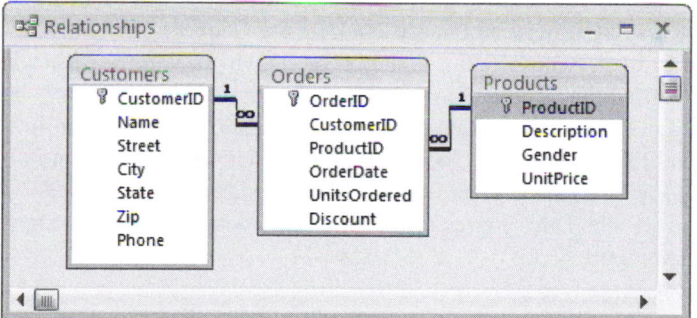

The company wants to perform a statistical analysis of the data on orders within Excel. How can it use Microsoft Query to import the data from Access into Excel?

Objective   To illustrate how Microsoft Query can be used to return the results of queries on the Shirt Orders database back into Excel.

Solution

Before going into the details, it is important to realize that the entire procedure is done within Excel and Microsoft Query, *not* Access. You need not even own Access to make the procedure work. All you need is the Access database file, in this case **Shirt Orders.mdb**.[7]

---

[7]We also note that this procedure can be done in the same way with databases from other database packages, such as SQL Server. We illustrate the procedure only for Access.

The first step of the procedure is to tell Excel what type of data you have and where it is located. In its terminology, you must define a "data source." To do so, open a blank spreadsheet in Excel and select the From Microsoft Query from the From Other Sources dropdown on the Data ribbon. This takes you to the Choose Data Source dialog box shown in Figure 4.18. Note that the list you see might not be the same as the one shown here. Each time you tell Excel about a new data source, it is added to the list shown. In any case, we want to add a new data source, so make sure the top item is highlighted. Also, make sure the bottom box is *not* checked. (We prefer *not* to use the Query Wizard, although you can experiment with it if you like.) Then click on OK.

Figure 4.18

Choose Data Source Dialog Box

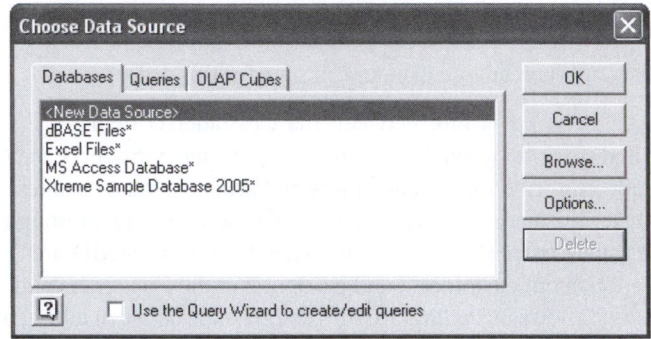

This takes you to the Create New Data Source dialog box. It should eventually be filled in as shown in Figure 4.19. Actually, there are three steps to filling it in. First, enter a descriptive title in line 1. (This does *not* need to be the same name as the Access file name.) Next, use the dropdown list in line 2 to select the appropriate driver, in this case the Microsoft Access Driver. (This is where you could specify another database package, such as SQL Server.) Finally, click on the Connect button in line 3 to bring up the ODBC Microsoft Access Setup dialog box shown in Figure 4.20, where you indicate which database *file* you want to use. To choose it, click on its Select button and browse for the **Shirt Orders.mdb** file. (Your file will almost certainly be in a different location than ours.) Once you have located this file, click on OK a couple of times to see the completed Create New Data Source dialog box, and click on OK once more to get back to the Choose Data Source dialog box, with your data source, Shirt Orders, now on the list. (See Figure 4.21.)

Figure 4.19

Create New Data Source Dialog Box

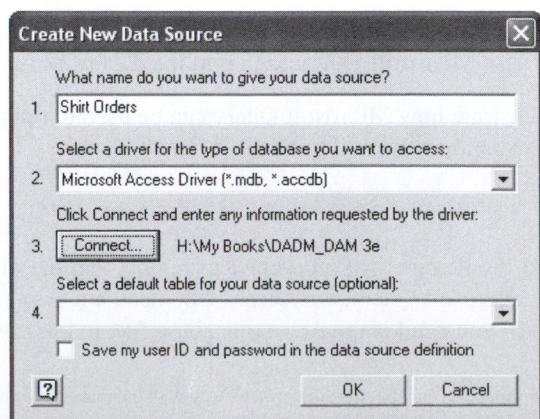

Figure 4.20

Dialog Box for
Selecting the
Appropriate
Database File

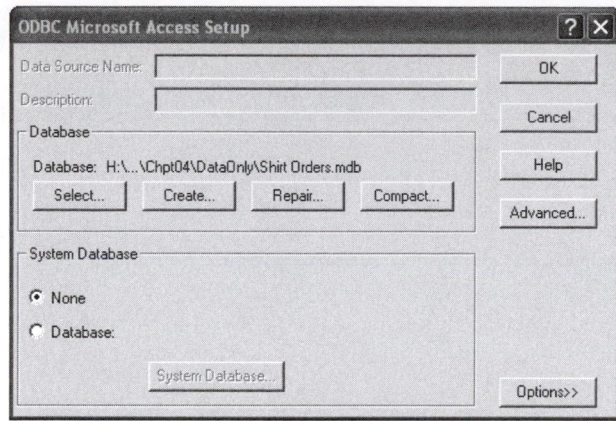

Figure 4.21

Choose Data Source
Dialog Box with the
New Entry

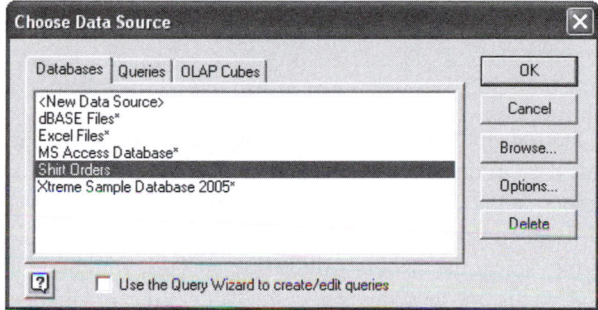

This completes step 1 of the overall procedure. You have defined a data source that you can now query. It is important to realize that once you have created this Shirt Orders source, you will not have to create it again. Specifically, if you want to run another query on this database at a later time, you can select the From Microsoft Query option, select the Shirt Orders source from the list, and proceed directly to the query itself, bypassing the actions described above.

At this point, you should be looking at the Choose Data Source dialog box shown in Figure 4.21—with Shirt Orders on the list. Make sure the Shirt Orders item is selected and the bottom checkbox is *unchecked*, and click on OK.[8] This brings up the Add Tables dialog box shown in Figure 4.22, in front of the Microsoft Query screen in shown Figure 4.23. This begins the second step of the overall procedure, where the query is defined. Essentially, we need to specify which tables are relevant for the query, which fields we want to return to Excel, and which records meet the criteria we spell out.

Figure 4.22

Add Tables
Dialog Box

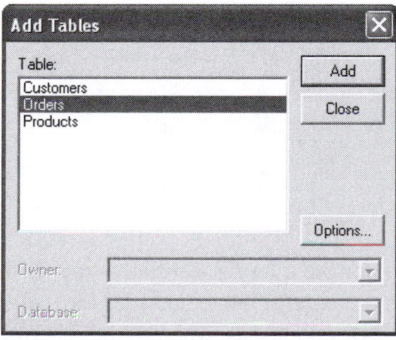

[8]If the bottom checkbox is checked, the Query Wizard will be launched when you click on OK. You can try this if you like, but we find it confusing and less useful than the method we described here.

Figure 4.23
Microsoft
Query Screen

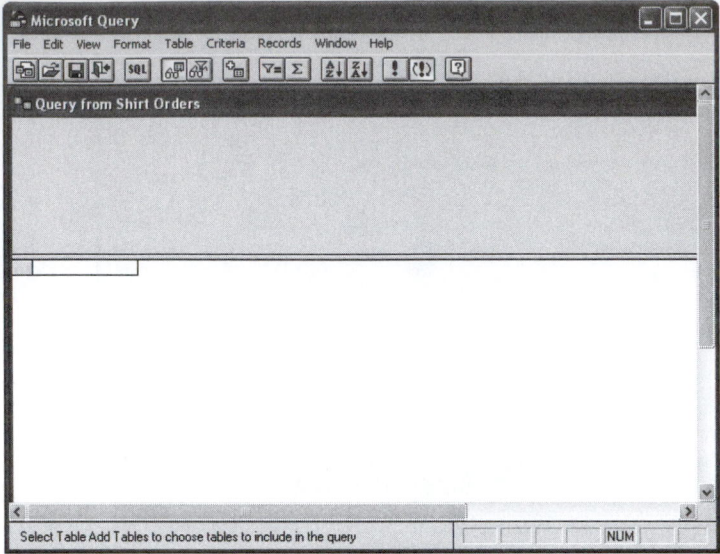

To get started, let's try a relatively easy single-table query. We will find all of the records from the Orders table where the order date is during the years 1997 or 1998, the product number is 3 or 5, and the number of units ordered is at least 100, and we will return to Excel all fields in the Orders table for these records. First, if the Add Tables dialog box is still showing, select the Orders table, click on Add, and then click on Close. (If the Add Tables dialog box is not showing, select the Add Tables menu item from the Table menu to make it show.) The table appears in the top pane of the screen. (See Figure 4.24). You can double-click on any of the fields in this table to add fields that will be returned by the query. If you double-click on the top item (the asterisk), all fields will be returned. For this query, double-click on the asterisk, and you should see a sampling of the data that will be returned in the bottom pane of the screen. Finally, click on the Show/Hide Criteria button on the toolbar (the button with the glasses and the funnel). This opens a middle pane on the screen, where you can enter criteria. The screen should now appear as in Figure 4.24.

Figure 4.24

Query Screen Before
Entering Criteria

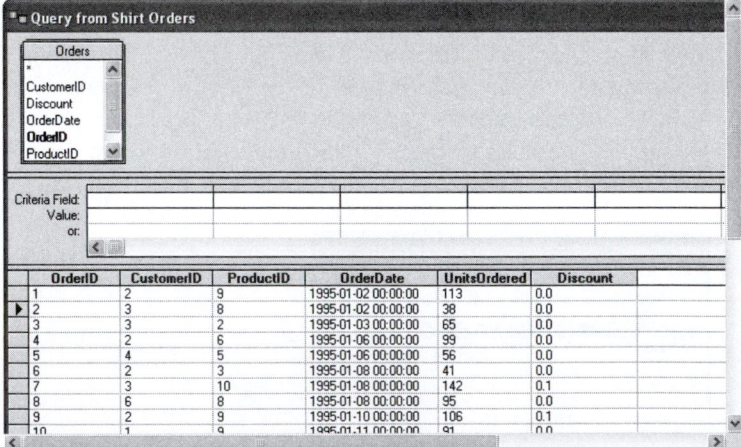

Now you enter the criteria for the query. Essentially, you fill in the middle pane of the Query screen like you filled in the criteria range in Excel for the Advanced Filter tool. Any conditions in a given row are "and" conditions, whereas those across rows are treated as "or" conditions. You can either type the conditions directly into the small "spreadsheet" in the middle pane—if you know the correct syntax—or select the Add Criteria menu item from the

Criteria menu. This latter option brings up the dialog box shown in Figure 4.25. After a bit of experimenting, you'll see how to enter conditions in this dialog box. Then when you click on the Add button, the condition appears in the middle pane of the screen. By examining the syntax of the conditions that are entered, you can quickly learn how to type in your own conditions directly. The final conditions for our query appear in Figure 4.26. (Note how dates are enclosed in # signs, and how the key words *Between* and *In* are used.)

Figure 4.25

Add Criteria
Dialog Box

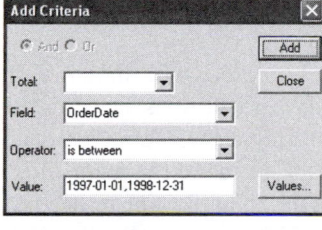

Figure 4.26

Criteria for
Single-Table Query

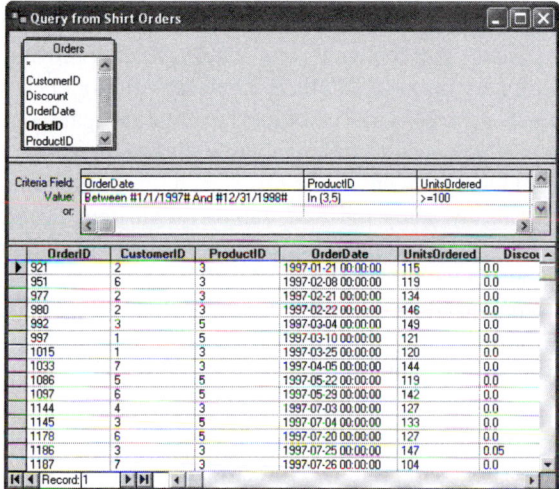

If you scroll down the records in the bottom pane of the screen, you will see that this query returns 69 of the 2245 records in the Orders table. The final step in our three-step process is to get these data back into Excel. This is easy. Simply select the Return Data to Microsoft Excel menu item from the File menu. This takes you back to Excel and brings up the dialog box in Figure 4.27, where you can specify the type of report you want and where you want the results. For now, we specify a Table, so that the Access data are "dumped" into an Excel table—the same type of table discussed at the beginning of this chapter. When you click on OK, the results appear in a few seconds, and you can now analyze them statistically using any tools we have discussed. However, there is more—these data are still linked to the query. This means you can refresh the data in Excel if the Access data change. To do so, make sure your cursor is inside the Excel table, and click on the Refresh button on the Table Tools Design ribbon (or the Refresh All button on the Data ribbon).

Figure 4.27

Import Data
Dialog Box

It is also possible to get back to Microsoft Query so that you can edit your query. Again, make sure your cursor is inside the Excel table, and click on the Connections button on the Data ribbon. This brings up a Workbook Connections dialog box. Click on Properties, then select the Definition tab, and finally, click on the Edit Query button.

One more possibility is to save the query itself. To do so, use the Save menu item from the File menu in the Microsoft Query screen with some suggestive file name such as Shirt Orders Query 1. The extension .dqy (for database query) is added by default. This allows you to run this query at any time from within Excel by selecting Existing Connections from the Data ribbon.

Let's now try a more ambitious query. We will find all of the records in the Orders table that correspond to orders for at least 80 units made by the customer Shirts R Us (customer number 3) for the product Long-sleeve Tunic (product number 6), and we will return the dates and units ordered for these orders. The main difference is that we now have to base the query on all three tables in the database. The reason is that the Orders table does not have "Shirts R Us"—it contains only customer *IDs*. Similarly, it doesn't know about "Long-sleeve Tunic." The trick is to use the links between the tables.

Make sure that Microsoft Query is closed before trying to create a new query.

Starting in Excel (with the cursor *not* inside the data previously returned), select the From Microsoft Query option. This time, however, simply click on the Shirt Orders data source that is already there—you do not need to create it again. (As before, clear the Query Wizard checkbox if you want to follow along with our directions.) This takes you directly into the Microsoft Query screen. Inside this screen, first add all three tables to the top pane of the Query screen by using the Add Tables menu item from the Tables menu. Next, double-click on the OrderDate and UnitsOrdered fields in the Orders table (because we want data in these two fields to be returned to Excel). Finally, fill out the criteria as shown in Figure 4.28. Note that the field names for the three criteria are from different tables. The Name field is from the Customers table, the Description field is from the Products table, and the UnitsOrdered field is from the Orders table. A good exercise is to think through the logic that Microsoft Query uses. From the Customers table, Microsoft Query finds that Shirts R Us corresponds to customer number 3. From the Products table, it finds that Long-sleeve Tunic corresponds to product number 6. Therefore, it searches the Orders table for all records where CustomerID is 3, ProductID is 6, and UnitsOrdered is at least 80. This returns 17 records, as shown in Figure 4.29.

Figure 4.28

Query Based on All
Three Tables

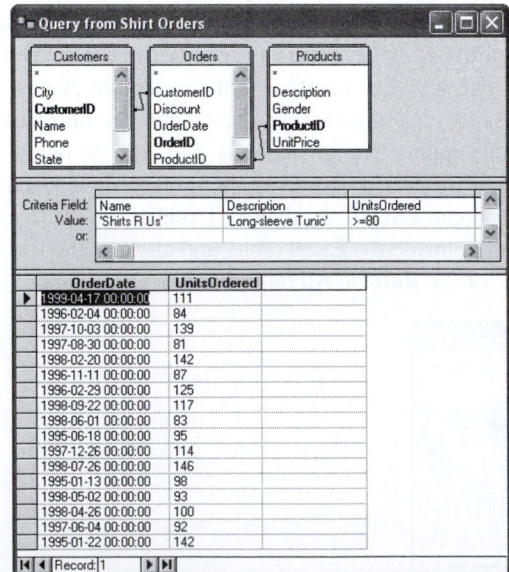

Figure 4.29

Data Returned
to Excel as a Table

	A	B
1	OrderDate	UnitsOrdered
2	4/17/1999 0:00	111
3	2/4/1996 0:00	84
4	10/3/1997 0:00	139
5	8/30/1997 0:00	81
6	2/20/1998 0:00	142
7	11/11/1996 0:00	87
8	2/29/1996 0:00	125
9	9/22/1998 0:00	117
10	6/1/1998 0:00	83
11	6/18/1995 0:00	95
12	12/26/1997 0:00	114
13	7/26/1998 0:00	146
14	1/13/1995 0:00	98
15	5/2/1998 0:00	93
16	4/26/1998 0:00	100
17	6/4/1997 0:00	92
18	1/22/1995 0:00	142

One last possibility we will illustrate is returning *calculated fields*. Suppose we want to return the *revenues* for all orders during 1998 or 1999 from Rags to Riches for shirts sold to females, where revenue is calculated as units ordered times unit price times 1 minus the discount. We form the query in the usual way, but in the bottom pane, we type the *expression* "UnitsOrdered*UnitPrice*(1-Discount)" as one of the field names. (*Note*: Unlike Excel, there is no equals sign to the left of the expression.) The resulting Query screen, assuming we want to return the fields Description, Gender, and OrderDate in addition to revenue, should appear as in Figure 4.30. When we return the data to Excel, the field name for revenue will be something like Expr1001. You can then change it to Revenue.

Figure 4.30

Query with a
Calculated Field

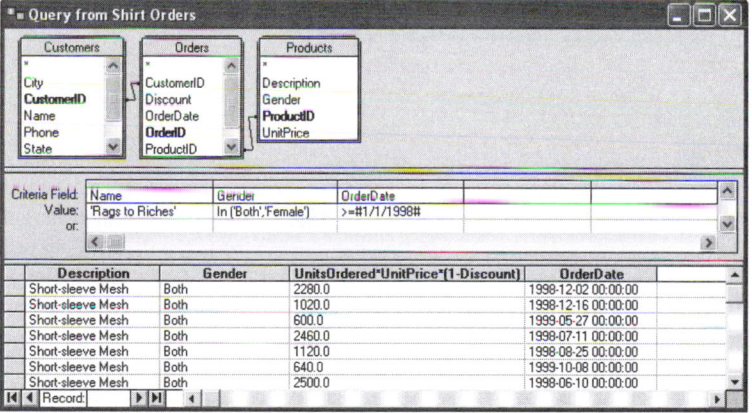

We reiterate that once the results of the query data are returned to Excel, you can then begin the statistical analysis of the data—creating summary measures, scatterplots, pivot tables, and so on. ∎

4.5.3 SQL Statements

Queries represent a large part of the power behind relational databases. Regardless of the particular database package, whether it be Access, SQL Server, or any of the others, the *types* of queries we create are all basically the same. We typically base the query on one or more tables and ask it to return selected fields with records that satisfy certain conditions. To standardize queries across packages, SQL (structured query language and pronounced "S-Q-L" or "sequel") was developed. Sitting behind each query you develop in a user-friendly interface such as the Microsoft Query screen is an SQL statement. Although these statements are beyond the scope of this book, you might like to take a look at them, just to see how the experts create queries. This is easy to do. Once you have created a query, click on the SQL button in the Query toolbar.

As an example, if you form the query shown in Figure 4.26 and click on the SQL button, you see the SQL statement in Figure 4.31. At first, this is probably intimidating. However, if you break it down into its parts, it isn't that bad. SQL has a number of key-words that are capitalized. This statement includes the keywords SELECT, FROM, WHERE, and AND. The SELECT part of the statement specifies which fields to return (where, in the case of multiple tables, the table name and a period precede the field name). The FROM part specifies which tables to base the query on. Finally, the WHERE part spells out the criteria, separated by ANDs. If you want to learn more about SQL, the best way is to create a query through the interface and then look at the corresponding SQL statement. Once you get used to SQL statements, you can edit a query by editing its SQL equivalent. If you get really proficient, you can even create a query from scratch by typing the appropriate SQL statement directly. (If you are interested, there are numerous books available for learning SQL. Just check out Amazon.com.)

Figure 4.31

SQL Statement

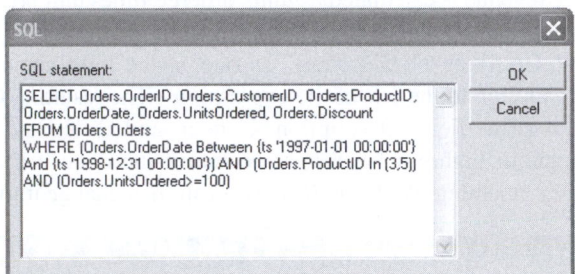

PROBLEMS

Level A

9. The Fine Shirt Company creates and sells shirts to its customers. These customers are retailers who sell shirts to customers. The company has created an Access database file **P04_09.mdb** that has information on sales to its customers over a five-year period (i.e., 2000-2004). There are three related tables in this data-base: Customers, Orders, and Products. These tables are described in detail in Example 4.2. Find all of the records from the Orders table where the order was placed in 2003 or 2004, the product number is 1 or 10, the customer is not 7, and the number of units ordered is at least 75. Return to Excel all fields in the Orders table for each of these records.

10. Continuing with the Fine Shirt Company database found in the file **P04_09.mdb**, find all of the records from the Orders table that correspond to orders for between 50 and 100 items made by the customer Rags to Riches for the product Short-sleeve Polo. Return to Excel the dates, units ordered, and discounts for each of these orders.

11. Continuing with the Fine Shirt Company database found in the file **P04_09.mdb**, find all of the records from the Orders table that correspond to orders for more than 75 items made by the customer Threads for products designed to be worn by women. Return to Excel the dates, units ordered, and product description for each of these orders.

Level B

12. Returning to the Fine Shirt Company, use the three tables contained in file **P04_09.mdb** to perform the following:

a. Find all of the records from the Orders table that correspond to orders placed in 2003 by the customer The Shirt on Your Back for shirts designed to be worn by *both* men and women. Return to Excel the fields OrderDate, Description, Gender, UnitsOrdered, UnitPrice, Discount, and a *calculated field* Revenue. Note that Revenue equals

UnitsOrdered*UnitPrice*(1-Discount)

b. Analyze the distribution of revenues associated with order records identified in part **a**. Be sure to consider measures of central location, variability, and skewness in characterizing this distribution.

c. Repeat parts **a** and **b** with the same criteria except that the analysis should now focus on the orders placed in 2004. Summarize the differences between the revenue distributions for 2003 and 2004.

13. Write the SQL statement to perform the query given in Problem 10.

14. Write the SQL statement to perform the query given in Problem 11.

4.6 CREATING PIVOT TABLES FROM EXTERNAL DATA

In the previous section you learned how to import data from external databases by using Microsoft Query. We now briefly discuss how external data can be used to create pivot tables.[9] The procedure is nearly the same as for creating pivot tables from an existing Excel database—the procedure we discussed in the previous two chapters. However, the data we now base the pivot table on are the result of a query on an external database. Fortunately, to develop this query, you do not have to learn anything new. You do it exactly as in the previous section. The following continuation of Example 4.2 illustrates the procedure.

EXAMPLE | **4.2 FINE SHIRT COMPANY'S RELATIONAL DATA (CONTINUED)**

The Fine Shirt Company would like to break down revenue from its various customers and products by using pivot tables. How should it proceed?

Objective   To illustrate how a pivot table can be created directly from data in the Shirt Orders database, using Microsoft Query.

Solution

If you want to base a pivot table on external data, you should go through Microsoft Query, *not* through the usual PivotTable button on the Insert menu.[10] To do so, get into Microsoft Query and spell out a query. We defined a sample query as shown in Figure 4.32 with *no* criteria—just a set of fields to return, one of which is calculated revenue—but you can impose criteria if you like. When you select the Return Data to Microsoft Excel menu item from Microsoft Query's File menu, you see the dialog box in Figure 4.27, where you can specify the type of report you want and where you want it. At this point, select PivotTable Report (or PivotChart and PivotTable Report), and you should be in familiar territory.

From here, you can create any pivot tables you desire. For example, we chose the settings in Figure 4.33, so that we can analyze the sum of revenue for any customer/product combination for any date(s). The only trick here involves the OrderDate field. The original pivot table contains a row for each date—over 1000 rows. We decided to group the data by quarter of year. To do this, right-click on any date in the original pivot table, select Group, and select *both* Quarter and Year. The resulting pivot table in Figure 4.34 (for long-sleeve products only) shows total revenue broken down by product, customer (using the Report Filter area at the top), and quarter of year. This is a lot of useful data with very little work! In addition, you have the option of obtaining corresponding pivot charts automatically.

---

[9]This section assumes you have read the previous section and know how to create pivot tables, as discussed in Chapters 2 and 3.

[10]If you do the latter, you will see an option to base the pivot table on external data and a Choose Connection button. However, this button leads only to saved query .dqy files. So unless you have already created such a file, this will lead to a dead end.

Figure 4.32

Specification of the Query

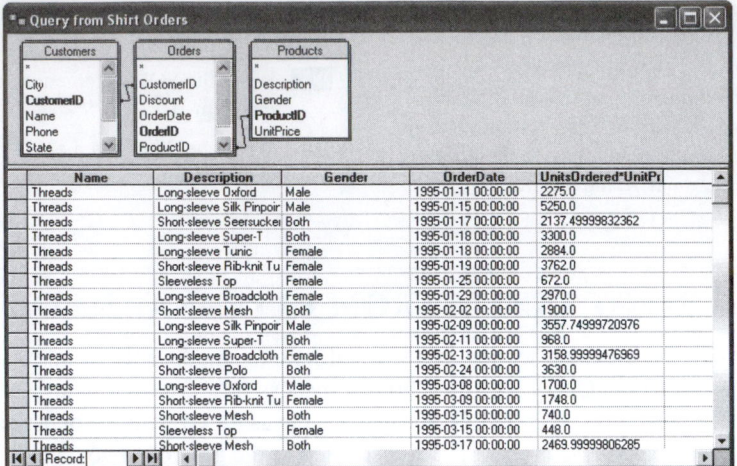

Figure 4.33

PivotTable Fields

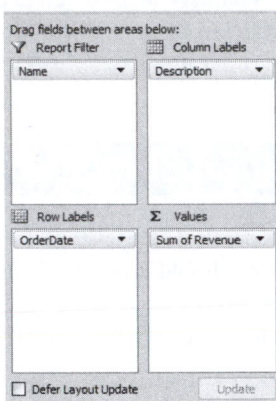

Figure 4.34   Pivot Table Results After Grouping by OrderDate

	Name	(All)						
	A	B	C	D	E	F	G	H
1	Name	(All)						
2								
3	Sum of Revenue		Description					
4	Years	OrderDate	Long-sleeve Broadcloth	Long-sleeve Oxford	Long-sleeve Silk Pinpoint	Long-sleeve Super-T	Long-sleeve Tunic	Grand Total
5	⊟1995	Qtr1	$25,396	$27,034	$40,161	$23,530	$39,487	$155,608
6		Qtr2	$33,880	$41,350	$29,148	$29,461	$27,930	$161,769
7		Qtr3	$23,598	$13,417	$41,501	$17,629	$20,649	$116,794
8		Qtr4	$24,550	$34,635	$58,964	$21,746	$17,478	$157,373
9	⊟1996	Qtr1	$14,915	$21,072	$40,455	$31,373	$33,597	$141,412
10		Qtr2	$21,122	$14,295	$29,797	$10,927	$26,810	$102,952
11		Qtr3	$26,136	$24,861	$45,570	$25,582	$17,305	$139,454
12		Qtr4	$31,369	$22,721	$28,826	$27,405	$38,828	$149,149
13	⊟1997	Qtr1	$17,485	$20,825	$30,940	$31,287	$29,445	$129,982
14		Qtr2	$24,461	$19,824	$45,288	$10,098	$26,502	$126,173
15		Qtr3	$33,758	$28,865	$43,526	$25,970	$33,400	$165,519
16		Qtr4	$26,419	$18,799	$36,050	$14,214	$19,901	$115,383
17	⊟1998	Qtr1	$14,215	$24,275	$35,821	$22,101	$27,462	$123,875
18		Qtr2	$33,257	$21,422	$25,056	$34,108	$19,270	$133,114
19		Qtr3	$33,965	$40,511	$28,360	$15,268	$29,863	$147,968
20		Qtr4	$19,678	$22,902	$48,365	$18,356	$18,231	$127,531
21	⊟1999	Qtr1	$26,198	$21,837	$21,791	$21,905	$14,335	$106,067
22		Qtr2	$35,510	$30,240	$24,001	$32,432	$31,437	$153,621
23		Qtr3	$10,827	$16,650	$43,568	$23,113	$30,974	$125,132
24		Qtr4	$25,369	$27,687	$34,207	$19,147	$17,122	$123,533
25	Grand Total		$502,108	$493,225	$731,397	$455,653	$520,024	$2,702,407

Like the query results we discussed in the previous section, pivot table results are linked to the query. This means that you can go back to Microsoft Query, edit the query, and return the data to Excel to update the pivot table. It is an amazingly intuitive and powerful tool!

Level A

15. The Fine Shirt Company would like to know how many units of each of its products were sold to each customer during each year of the period 2000–2004. Using the database given in the file **P04_09.mdb**, construct one or more pivot tables that provide Fine Shirt with the desired information.

16. The Fine Shirt Company would also like to know how many units of its products designed for each gender subset (i.e., men, women, and both genders) were sold to each customer during each quarter of the past 5 years (i.e., from the first quarter of 2000 through the fourth quarter of 2004). Using the database given in the file **P04_09.mdb**, create one or more pivot tables that provide Fine Shirt with the desired information.

Level B

17. The Fine Shirt Company would like to know what proportion of each customer's total dollar purchases in 2004 came from buying Short-sleeve Seersucker shirts. Furthermore, the company would like to compare this proportion to that of the most popular product, as measured by 2004 total dollar purchases, for each customer. Using the database given in the file **P04_09.mdb**, construct one or more pivot tables that provide Fine Shirt with the desired information. Summarize your findings.

4.7 WEB QUERIES

The chances are good that you have found interesting data on the Web that you would like to analyze in Excel. The question is how to import the data from the Web into Excel. Fortunately, this is possible with Excel's Web queries, a feature that was added to Excel in Office 97. It is still relatively primitive and will undoubtedly change as Office and the Web develop, but it provides powerful capabilities most users are completely unaware of. (We have already seen considerable changes in Excel's Web query feature, both from Excel 97 to Excel 2000, and from Excel 2000 to Excel XP and later. It is now better than ever—almost user-friendly!) We discuss Web queries briefly in this section, just to provide a glimpse of the possibilities. Hopefully, this will inspire you to try some things on your own.

To understand how it is possible to query a Web site from Excel, you should first understand at least a little of how Web pages are constructed. They are created with HTML (hypertext markup language), a text language that includes "tags" for displaying the various items you see on a typical Web page. One tag that is particularly useful for our purposes is the TABLE tag. When this tag is used as part of an HTML document, followed by data, it puts these data in a readable tabular form. Of course, the table might be surrounded by a lot of text and graphics, but the chances are that when we query a Web page from Excel, we are most interested in the table data and would like to ignore the surrounding stuff. Web queries allow us to do exactly this. They search for TABLE tags, find the corresponding data, and bring them into Excel in the usual row and column format.

We begin with a simple static Web query. We (the authors) have a Web server called http://www.kelley.iu.edu/albrightbooks that we control. (This means that unlike other ever-changing Web sites, this one will continue to behave as we describe here—probably!) There is an HTML page **Scores.htm** on this site, created just for this example, that contains a heading and a table of course scores for students in a fictitious course. To get the data in this table into Excel, use the following steps:

1. Make sure you have an active connection to the Web, and open a new workbook in Excel.

2. Select From Web from the Data ribbon.

3. Fill in this dialog box as shown in Figure 4.35. The most important part is the URL (the address of the page) at the top, which is

http://www.kelley.iu.edu/albrightbooks/scores.htm

You have to know this or browse the Web for it. We find it easiest to browse to the intended Web site, copy its URL, and paste it into the dialog box. Once you enter the URL and click on Go, you see the Web page with yellow arrows next to all of the tables. (Some of these will probably not look like "tables," but they all have the HTML <Table> tag.) You can click on any of these yellow arrows to change them to green checkmarks. The selected tables will then be imported into Excel.

4. After you click on OK, you will be asked where to place the results. We specified cell A1 of the blank worksheet.

Figure 4.35

Web Query Dialog Box

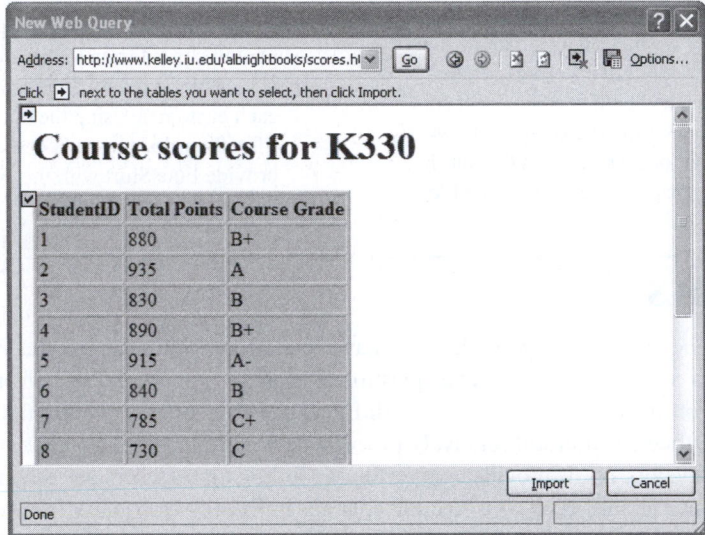

The results then appear as shown in Figure 4.36. This Web page has only one table, and its contents have been imported into Excel and are formatted nicely. In addition, a link to the Web page remains. This means that if the data on the Web page change, as they often do, you can refresh to obtain the latest data. To do so, put the cursor anywhere inside the Excel data and click on the Refresh All button on the Data ribbon.

Figure 4.36

Results of Web Query

	A	B	C
1	StudentID	Total Points	Course Grade
2	1	880	B+
3	2	935	A
4	3	830	B
5	4	890	B+
6	5	915	A-
7	6	840	B
8	7	785	C+
9	8	730	C
10	9	810	B-
11	10	905	A-
12	11	865	B
13	12	720	C-
14	13	895	B+
15	14	835	B
16	15	965	A

You can also save the definition of the query in an .iqy file. (You might want to save it so that you could give it to a friend or use it on a different PC.) To save it, make sure the cursor is inside the Excel table, click on the Connections button on the Data ribbon, then the Properties button, then the Definition tab, and finally the Edit Query button to get back to the Web Query definition in Figure 4.35. Now click on the Save Query button at the top, which allows you to save the query under some descriptive name, such as **Scores Web Query.iqy**. By default, Microsoft stores such queries in the C:\Documents and Setting*username*\ Application Data\Microsoft\Queries folder, although this might depend on your operating system. In any case, we suggest that you accept this default. Then you can run this query later on by clicking on Existing Connections on the Data ribbon and selecting your saved query file.

These saved query files are simply text files—very short text files, in fact. You can open one of them in Notepad to see how it is constructed. The one we saved (as **Scores Web Query.iqy**) for the previous query has the following lines:

```
WEB

1

http://www.kelley.iu.edu/albrightbooks/scores.htm

Selection=AllTables

Formatting=None

PreFormattedTextToColumns=True

ConsecutiveDelimitersAsOne=True

SingleBlockTextImport=False

DisableDateRecognition=False

DisableRedirections=False
```

The only required line in this file is the third one, which lists the URL of the Web page. The first two lines are optional, and the last seven, which indicate the settings from the New Web Query dialog box (Figure 4.35), including the advanced options, are also optional. We point this out because it is possible to create your Web query directly in Notepad as an .iqy file and then run it in Excel with the Existing Connections option.

In fact, Microsoft has included several .IQY files with Office to indicate some of the possibilities. On our PC, these files are located in the C:\Program Files\Microsoft Office\Office12\Queries folder, although this may differ depending on your operating system. One of these is **MSN MoneyCentral Investor Currency Rates.iqy**. Its contents (as seen in Notepad) follow:

```
WEB

1

http://moneycentral.msn.com/investor/external/excel/rates.asp

Selection=EntirePage

Formatting=All

PreFormattedTextToColumns=True

ConsecutiveDelimitersAsOne=True

SingleBlockTextImport=False
```

The third line is the key to the query. But what does it mean, and how would you know how to write it? Unfortunately, this is where Web queries get a bit complex, as we now explain.

This particular query is a static query, in that there are no prompts for information from the user. However, as another example, the sample file **MSN MoneyCentral Investor Stock Quotes.iqy** is a dynamic query. It includes the URL

```
http://moneycentral.msn.com/investor/external/excel/
quotes.asp?SYMBOL=["QUOTE",

"Enter stock, fund or other MoneyCentral Investor symbols separated by
commas."]
```

In this case, Quote is the name of a *parameter*, and the sentence following it is a prompt to the user. If you run this saved query in Excel (from Existing Connections), you will see the dialog box in Figure 4.37. You can enter any stock symbols you like, and the Web query will return data for these stocks.[11] Figure 4.38 shows a portion of the data returned for our choices.

Figure 4.37

Parameter
Dialog Box

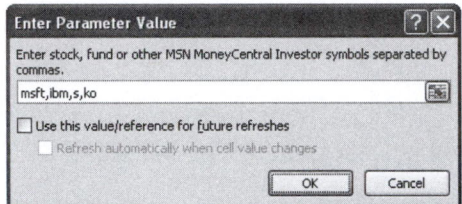

Figure 4.38 Results of Web Query

	A		B	C	D	E	F	G	H	I	J
1	**Stock Quotes Provided by MSN Money**										
2	Click here to visit MSN Money										
3					Last	Previous Close	High	Low	Volume	Change	% Change
4	Microsoft Corp		Chart	News	30.19	30.17	30.33	30.05	16,767,878	0.02	0.07%
5	IBM Ord Shs		Chart	News	117.18	117.81	118.37	117.04	1,744,047	-0.63	-0.53%
6	Sprint Nextel Corp		Chart	News	18	18.04	18.13	17.92	1,939,700	-0.04	-0.22%
7	Coca-Cola Co		Chart	News	57.72	57.8	58.19	57.7	474,800	-0.08	-0.13%

You can experiment with the sample queries Microsoft has supplied. However, what if you want to create your own Web query? What are the rules? The short answer is: It depends. We will not try to go through all of the details, but we will get you started. (Even Excel's online help on Web queries is pretty sketchy on the details.)

If you are lucky, you will find a page, such as our **Scores.htm** page referred to previously, that is static. There is no form to fill out, and the data are just there waiting to be downloaded to Excel. If you find such a page, you can proceed exactly as we did for the scores page, by entering its URL into the New Web Query dialog box shown in Figure 4.35.

More frequently, however, you will browse to a site that has a form you must fill out to indicate exactly what data you want. This form might have a text box where you type in a stock symbol, option buttons where you choose which years you are interested in, or other means of capturing user choices. Then when you submit this form, you get the data. In this type of situation, how do you know what URL to include in the New Web Query dialog box (or in an .iqy file)?

There are many possibilities, so you will need to experiment. Of course, you should also check out Excel's online help for Web queries, but as we stated previously, many of the details we would like to see there are missing. The following example illustrates how one possible Web query might be created.

The next example is optional. We admit that the procedure it describes is more complex than it ought to be. But this is the state of Web queries at the current time. If you absolutely need to import data you find on the Web into Excel, there is no guarantee that it will be easy, at least not yet.

---

[11] If you check the enabled box in Figure 4.37, you won't have to retype the stock symbols when you rerun or refresh this query. It will continue to use your initial choices. Also, as usual, we warn you that the screens you see might not match ours exactly because Web pages are in a continual state of flux.

EXAMPLE | 4.3 IMPORTING CONSUMER PRICE INDEX DATA FROM THE WEB

We found an interesting Web page on consumer price indexes for various commodities at the URL address http://146.142.4.24/cgi-bin/surveymost?ap. This page presents us with a number of choices, as shown in Figure 4.39. How can we construct a Web query that gives us a choice of which data to obtain and then downloads the requested data?

Figure 4.39

Consumer Price Index Web Page

Consumer Price Index

Average Price Data
(Select from list below)

☐ 500 kwh Electricity - APU000072621
☐ Utility Gas, 40 Therms - APU000072601
☐ Utility Gas, 100 Therms - APU000072611
☐ Fuel Oil, Per Gallon - APU000072511
☐ Gasoline, All Types - APU00007471A
☐ Gasoline, Unleaded Regular - APU000074714
☐ Bread, White - APU0000702111
☐ Ground Beef, All Types, Per Pound - APU0000703111
☐ Whole Chicken, Per Pound - APU0000706111
☐ Eggs, Large, Per Dozen - APU0000708111
☐ Milk, All Types, Per 1/2 gallon - APU0000709111
☐ Red Delicious Apples - APU0000711111
☐ Navel Oranges - APU0000711311
☐ Bananas - APU0000711211
☐ Tomatoes - APU0000712311
☐ Orange Juice, Frozen - APU0000713111
☐ Coffee, Ground Roast, All Sizes - APU0000717311
☐ Iceberg Lettuce - APU0000712211

[Retrieve data] [Reset form]

Objective   To illustrate how a Web query can be created to obtain dynamic data from the consumer price index site.

Solution

The key is to look at the HTML source code for the Web page. (This can be done with the View/Source menu item in Internet Explorer or the View/Page Source menu item in Firefox.) Somewhere in this page there is a <FORM> tag with the following line:

<FORM ACTION=http://data.bls.gov/cgi-bin/surveymost METHOD=POST>

There are two methods for sending a user's choices from a form to a Web server for processing: the POST method and the GET method. This form uses the POST method. For our Web query, this means that the information from the form—the parameter values—should be placed on a separate line in the .iqy file, right below the URL line. (With the GET method, they are placed on the *same* line as the URL, following a question mark.)

Regarding user inputs, we can see from the Web page itself that the user needs to specify the commodity (through a coded APU number). To get the proper syntax for the parameters line of the query, we search the HTML source code for INPUT tags. The following is a typical INPUT tag:

<INPUT TYPE=checkbox NAME=series_id VALUE=APU000072621> 500 kwh

Electricity

This indicates that the name of the commodity input is "series_id" and a typical value for this input is one of the APU numbers shown on the Web page. Another line is

<INPUT SIZE=0 TYPE=hidden NAME=survey VALUE=ap>

There are several other <INPUT> tags in the source code, but they are not necessary for our purposes.

Using this information, we type the following query into Notepad and save it in the file **Consumer Price Indexes.iqy**.

```
WEB

1

http://data.bls.gov/cgi-bin/surveymost?ap

series_id=["series_id","Select APU#"]&survey=ap

Selection=AllTables

Formatting=RTF

PreFormattedTextToColumns=True

ConsecutiveDelimitersAsOne=True

SingleBlockTextImport=False

DisableDateRecognition=False
```

The "series_id=" line is the tricky part. It is a sequence of "parameter name = parameter value" items (such as survey=ap) separated by ampersand (&) symbols. We know these parameter names from the <INPUT> lines in the source code. If we want to prompt the user for a parameter value, then we include a parameter name and a prompt to the right of the equals sign, enclosed in square brackets, as in =["series_id", "select APU#"].

If we run this query from Excel, using the Existing Connections option and then browsing to the .iqy file, we are presented with a dialog box prompting for the APU number, as shown in Figure 4.40. Unfortunately, users will typically not know what to enter in this dialog box. Who could remember which APU number corresponds to white bread, for example? Therefore, a nice touch is to manually enter the APU numbers and corresponding commodities in an Excel range.[12] We did this, as shown in Figure 4.41. (See the file **Consumer Price Index.xlsx**.) Now a user can respond to a dialog box by clicking on the appropriate APU-number cell, as we indicate in Figure 4.40.

Figure 4.40

Prompt for APU Number

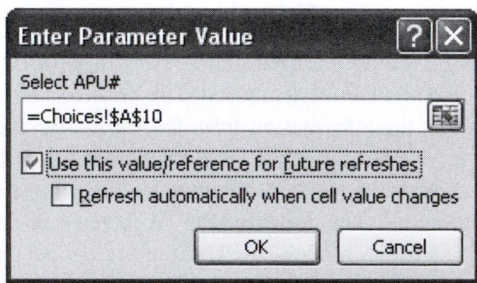

---

[12]If you are lucky, you might be able to cut and paste this information from the Web page into Excel instead of typing it.

Figure 4.41

Possible Choices
(Entered Manually)

	A	B	C	D	E
1	**Possible APU #'s**				
2	APU000072621	500 kwh Electricity			
3	APU000072601	Utility Gas, 40 Therms			
4	APU000072611	Utility Gas, 100 Therms			
5	APU000072511	Fuel Oil, Per Gallon			
6	APU00007471A	Gasoline, All Types			
7	APU000074714	Gasoline, Unleaded Regular			
8	APU0000702111	Bread, White			
9	APU0000703111	Ground Beef, All Types, Per Pound			
10	APU0000706111	Whole Chicken, Per Pound			
11	APU0000708111	Eggs, Large, Per Dozen			
12	APU0000709111	Milk, All Types, Per Gallon			
13	APU0000711111	Red Delicious Apples			
14	APU0000711311	Navel Oranges			
15	APU0000711211	Bananas			
16	APU0000712311	Tomatoes			
17	APU0000713111	Orange Juice, Frozen			
18	APU0000717311	Coffee, Ground Roast, All Sizes			
19	APU0000712211	Iceberg Lettuce			

Some of the results from one particular query (for whole chicken) appear in Figure 4.42. When we run this query, we keep our fingers crossed. We are usually not entirely sure what kind of data we will get because we are at the mercy of the Web site creator. Aside from some formatting, the data in Figure 4.42 look just about right.

Figure 4.42   Web Query Results

	A	B	C	D	E	F	G	H	I	J	K	L	M	N
16	**Series Id:** APU0000706111													
17	**Area:** U.S. city average													
18	**Item:** Chicken, fresh, whole, per lb. (453.6 gm)													
19														
20	**Year**	**Jan**	**Feb**	**Mar**	**Apr**	**May**	**Jun**	**Jul**	**Aug**	**Sep**	**Oct**	**Nov**	**Dec**	**Annual**
21	1997	1.016	1.008	1.009	1.002	1.007	0.993	1.005	0.988	0.992	0.984	1.018	1.001	
22	1998	1.022	1.007	1.032	1.029	1.032	1.016	1.033	1.059	1.074	1.076	1.084	1.06	
23	1999	1.072	1.064	1.057	1.057	1.026	1.041	1.045	1.043	1.08	1.055	1.078	1.053	
24	2000	1.059	1.046	1.064	1.069	1.052	1.069	1.089	1.086	1.087	1.09	1.065	1.078	
25	2001	1.091	1.09	1.103	1.101	1.095	1.106	1.102	1.11	1.107	1.115	1.133	1.109	
26	2002	1.091	1.111	1.11	1.11	1.094	1.066	1.077	1.035	1.074	1.027	1.044	1.048	
27	2003	1.004	1.031	1.049	1.053	1.031	1.033	1.027	1.023	1.022	1.022	1.068	1.05	
28	2004	1.062	1.06	1.1	1.12	1.039	1.06	1.077	1.092	1.078	1.078	1.039	1.03	
29	2005	1.026	1.038	1.061	1.07	1.052	1.075	1.067	1.042	1.056	1.062	1.059	1.061	
30	2006	1.062	1.045	1.047	1.054	1.034	1.055	1.04	1.048	1.063	1.038	1.049	1.057	
31	2007	1.033	1.039	1.064	1.115	1.118	1.134	1.13	1.145					

We are not sure how to rate the usefulness of Web queries at this stage. On the one hand, they vary from one Web site to another, and the data we obtain in Excel might or might not be in a form useful for statistical analysis. On the other hand, the Web itself is only about 15 years old, so the fact that we can get live data into Excel with a query file that contains only a few lines is pretty amazing. We suspect that the situation will only improve in the future, especially as Microsoft creates better tools for interfacing between Excel and the Web.

We should add that many Web sites have data that can be downloaded as a text file (probably with a .txt extension). This is quite different from what we have been describing so far. If you find one of these sites, you will have the option of downloading the file to a folder of your choice on your hard drive. Then you can open the file in Excel. Just make sure that the option in the "Files of type" box in the Open File dialog box is either All files or Text files. You will then be led through a Text Import Wizard that helps you get the data in the proper format in Excel. It is a fairly straightforward process, but you should always examine the resulting Excel data carefully to ensure that the columns are lined up correctly.

PROBLEMS

Level A

18. Import data of interest to you from the Web site at http://146.142.4.24/cgi-bin/surveymost?eb.

19. Import data of interest to you from the Web site at http://www.census.gov/.

20. Import data of interest to you from the Web site at http://wonder.cdc.gov/.

21. Import data of interest to you from the Web site at http://www.ers.usda.gov/.

22. Import data of interest to you from the Web site at http://nces.ed.gov/nationsreportcard/naepdata/.

23. Import data of interest to you from the Web site at http://www.bts.gov/.

4.8 OTHER DATA SOURCES ON THE WEB[13]

In the previous section we saw how it is sometimes possible to use Excel's Web query tool to import data on the Web into Excel. This works when we are lucky enough to find data *displayed* on a Web page in table form. However, there are many other types of data sources available on the Web—sometimes free and sometimes for a charge—and the number of these sources increases daily. It can often be quite a challenge to get these data into a form where they can be analyzed by the methods discussed in this book. We cannot hope in this section to discuss all of the possible data formats and available methods for extracting data from the Web. Instead, we will illustrate one possibility in the following example. As you read this example, you should imagine that your job depends on getting (and then analyzing) these data. Therefore, quitting because the process is too complex or because you don't know the required software is not an option!

EXAMPLE | **4.4 ACQUIRING DATA ON SUBSTANCE ABUSE**

An interesting article by Kovar (2000) discusses whether adolescents smoke as much as we tend to hear in the news media. To make her arguments, she analyzed data from a large national survey, the National Household Survey of Drug Abuse, funded by the Office of Applied Studies of the Substance Abuse and Mental Health Services Administration. As she indicates, the data are freely available from the Substance Abuse and Mental Health Data Archive (SAMHDA) Web site at http://www.icpsr.umich.edu/SAMHDA. Suppose you would like to analyze these survey data on your own. How should you proceed?

Objective To illustrate how to get the survey data from the SAMHDA Web site into a software package in a form suitable for statistical analysis.

Solution

The instructions we give in this example work correctly *now*. However, because the Web is in constant flux, we can only hope that nothing substantial will change by the time you try

[13]This section can be omitted without any loss of continuity.

them. First, we visit the SAMHDA Web site at http://www.icpsr.umich.edu/SAMHDA, and click on the Download Data Sets button. This takes us to a page, where we click on the National Survey on Drug Use and Health (NSDUH, formerly the NHSDA) link. This takes us to a page that briefly describes the purpose and history of the survey. From there, we click on the <u>Download Data</u> link that takes us to the page that lists yearly surveys (from 1979 on). There are four links for each survey, two of which are: <u>Description</u> and <u>Downloads</u>. The first of these takes us to an abstract of the survey. The second takes us to a page where we can download data. We now discuss each of these possibilities.

In a large survey such as this, it is extremely important to know the details of the survey: who did it, when it was done, and how it was done. Many of these details are listed in the abstract. For example, for the 2005 survey (the one we accessed), the investigator was the U.S. Department of Health and Human Services, Substance Abuse and Mental Health Services Administration, Office of Applied Studies. The intended population (the Universe) was "the civilian, noninstitutionalized population of the United States aged 12 and older, including residents of noninstitutional group quarters such as college dormitories, group homes, shelters, rooming houses, and civilians dwelling on military installations." The abstract also includes information on the data collection method, the sampling methodology, and other details. If you plan to do any serious analysis on these data, you should read the information in this abstract carefully.

Having read the abstract, we now follow the <u>Downloads</u> link to the download page. This page appears as in Figure 4.43. (You will need to log in as an anonymous guest.) After some experimenting, we filled it in as shown, requesting the data in SPSS format. When we clicked on Download, we got a large zip file, **10049556.zip**. Among other things, this zip file contains the two files we need: **04956-0001-Data.txt** and **04596-0001-Setup.sps**. We changed these file names to **Drug Use 2005.txt** and **Drug Use 2005.sps**.

Figure 4.43
Download Page from Web Site

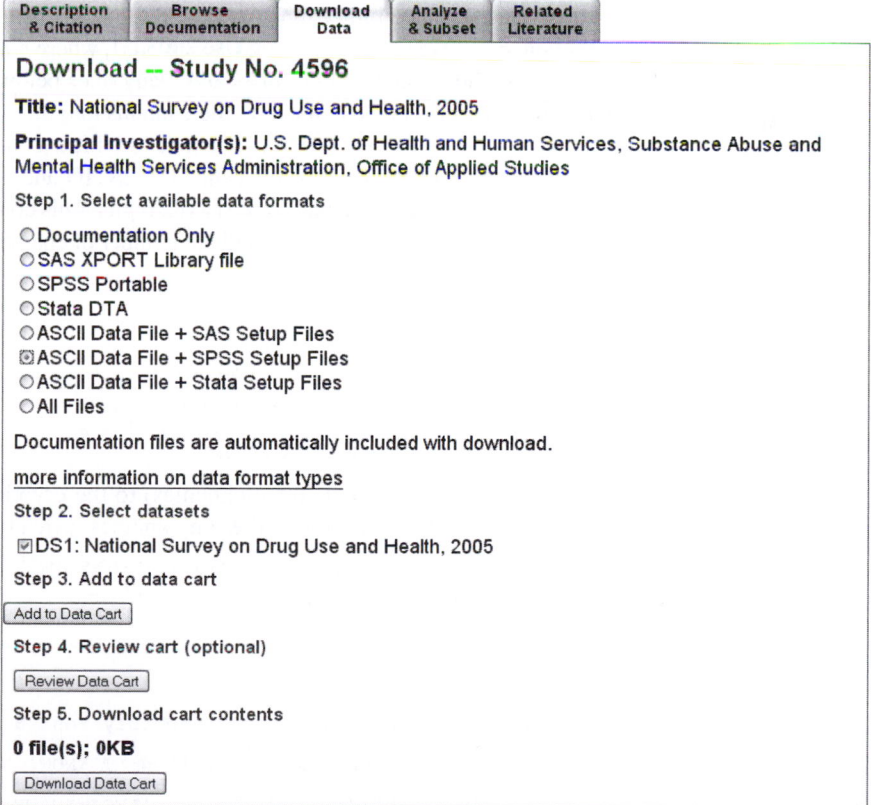

The .txt file is huge (over 344 MB), and at first glance it appears to be virtually useless. It is a plain text file with nothing but long lines of numbers—not even separated by delimiters such as tabs, spaces, or commas. How can anyone analyze a data set in this form!

This is where the .sps file comes into play. The survey agency has written *commands* for importing the data in the text file into a very common and powerful statistical package SPSS. (We could also have chosen to get the data into two other popular statistical packages, SAS and STATA.) Given that we are not covering this package in this book, you might imagine that we have hit a dead end at this stage. However, remember that your job might depend on analyzing such data sometime in the near future. We cannot afford to stop yet, so we will describe how to get the data into SPSS. (You or your instructor might want to try SAS or STATA instead.) If you have access to SPSS, you can follow along. Otherwise, you can read the following instructions to get the gist of the procedure.

SPSS is a Windows package with the usual menus and toolbars we are used to seeing in Windows packages. (The current version is 15.0.) However, SPSS still retains a command-driven language for performing various tasks, such as importing text data into the package. This is exactly what the .sps file contains: SPSS command lines for importing the data in the **Drug Use 2005.txt** file into SPSS. If you open the .sps file in a text editor such as WordPad, you will see a boxed-in explanation at the top, followed by a few command lines and interspersed with many data lines. The next few lines were taken from this file. We will briefly explain each of them.

```
* SPSS FILE HANDLE, DATA LIST COMMANDS.

FILE HANDLE DATA / NAME="data-filename" LRECL=6315.

DATA LIST FILE=DATA /

   CASEID 1-5 QUESTID 6-12 CIGEVER 13-14
```

Any line preceded by an asterisk is a "comment," which can be ignored. The next line indicates where the data are coming from. You should substitute the path and name of the data set for "data-filename." (We used *path***Drug Use 2005.txt**, where *path* is the path to the folder where we saved the file.) The next two lines (and many lines below these) describe the data setup. We mentioned previously that the data file contains long lines of digits. The command lines indicate how to "chop up" these digits. The first variable is called CASEID and contains the first 5 digits in each line. The second is called QUESTID and contains the next 7 digits. The third is called CIGEVER and contains the next 2 digits. This continues on and on. It turns out that there are well over 1000 variables, and the number of characters on each line is 6315.

```
* SPSS VARIABLE LABELS COMMAND.

VARIABLE LABELS

   CASEID "CASE IDENTIFICATION NUMBER"

   QUESTID "RESPONDENT IDENTIFICATION"

   CIGEVER "EVER SMOKED A CIGARETTE"
```

These lines give variable labels (or nicknames) to the cryptic variable names. When SPSS generates statistical output, it uses these nicknames instead of the variable names to label the output.

```
* SPSS VALUE LABELS COMMAND.

VALUE LABELS

   CIGEVER   1 'Yes' 2 'No' /

   CIGOFRSM  1 'Definitely Yes' 2 'Probably Yes' 3 'Probably Not'

            4 'Definitely Not'  94 'DON''T KNOW' 97 'REFUSED'

            98 'BLANK (NO ANSWER)' 99 'LEGITIMATE SKIP' /
```

The value labels explain the coding used. For example, the CIGEVER variable had two possible responses, coded 1 and 2. The value labels tell us what these codes really mean.

```
* SPSS MISSING VALUES COMMAND.

* MISSING VALUES

  CIGOFRSM (89 THRU HI)

  CIGWILYR (89 THRU HI)
```

Missing values are an extremely important issue, especially in survey data. Many respondents leave questions blank or respond in some unintended way. These command lines indicate which responses should be considered "missing." For example, any response to the variable CIGOFRSM that is coded 89 or higher should be considered "missing." However, because there is an asterisk next to the MISSING VALUES command, this command currently will be ignored. If you want the command to be active, you can just delete the asterisk—we did.

```
* Create SPSS system file

* SAVE outfile="spss-filename.sav".
```

These final two lines allow us to save the imported data in a special binary format with the SPSS extension .sav. (This is similar to saving Excel files in a format with the extension .xlsx.) Once the file is saved in this format, it is much easier to open in later SPSS sessions. You should replace **spss-filename.sav** with the path and filename you prefer. (We used *path***Drug Use 2005.sav**, where *path* is again the path to the folder where we want the data to be saved.) Also, this command is currently "commented out." Again, you should remove the asterisk in front of SAVE to make it active.

We're almost there. We have the data in a huge text file, and we have another text file of SPSS commands that will be used to import the data into SPSS. We now explain how to run these commands with the following four-step procedure.

Importing the data into SPSS

1 Make sure you have made the changes to the **Drug Use 2005.sps** file we indicated. (Delete the asterisks next to the MISSING VALUES and SAVE commands, and rename .txt and .sav files in the command lines appropriately.) Then double-click on this .sps file. This opens SPSS, and you can see the SPSS commands, exactly as you saw them in WordPad. (See Figure 4.44.)

2 Select the Run/All menu item.

Figure 4.44

SPSS Syntax
Window with
Commands
from .sps File

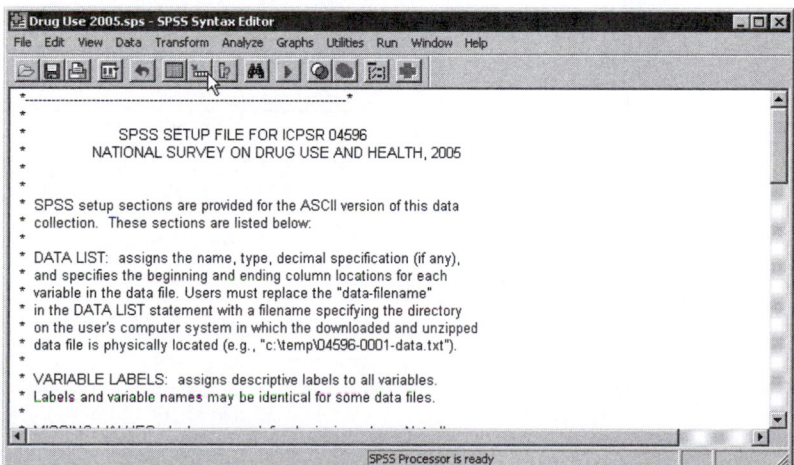

That's all there is to it. SPSS will now run the commands and import the data into a spreadsheet-like interface. It even saves the file in .sav format automatically for you. (Be prepared to wait a while, depending on the speed of your computer.) We will not pursue this example any further because we don't want to get into a lot of SPSS interface details. However, the following points should be helpful if you want to experiment on your own.

Helpful Hints for Using SPSS

- SPSS has two "sheets" with tabs just like Excel sheets. The Data View sheet, shown in Figure 4.45, allows you to look at the data in the usual row–column format. The Variable View sheet, shown in Figure 4.46, provides detailed information on all of the variables—a "data dictionary."

- The Analyze menu contains all of the statistical procedures. For example, the Analyze/Descriptive Statistics/Descriptives menu item is functionally similar to the Summary Statistics One-Variable Summary option in StatTools. However, SPSS contains *many* more statistical procedures than StatTools.

- The results from all SPSS procedures are placed in an output window. They can then be stored in an output file, with extension .spo, if desired.

Figure 4.45

SPSS Data
View Sheet

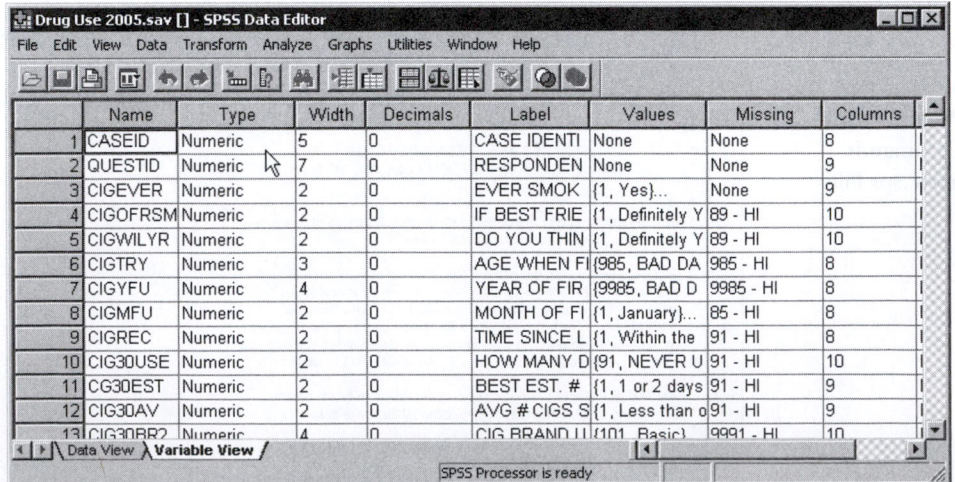

Figure 4.46

SPSS Variable View
Sheet

We conclude this example by putting everything in perspective. You might be annoyed at this point about having to learn about a new package (SPSS or SAS), but you have little choice if you really need to access this drug use data set. You might argue that we could avoid SPSS by importing the data text file directly into Excel. However, there is one big problem. We would need to use Excel's wizard for importing data from a text file. The wizard would ask us how to break these long lines into individual pieces, and it would also ask us for variable names. This would not be impossible, but it would be *extremely* tedious. We are better off taking advantage of what the survey agency has given us—SPSS (or SAS) command lines for quick and easy importing into a heavy-duty package.

The issues in this example are somewhat specific, but they are also quite general. They are specific in the sense that the details we discuss apply only to data sets for which the Web author has furnished SPSS command lines. We have no idea how many Web sites are set up this way, but we wouldn't be surprised if there are quite a few. The issues are general, however, in the sense that, as a user of Web data, you frequently will be confronted with a "new" situation. The data you need are out there, and you have access to them, but you must learn how to import them into some statistical package, Excel or otherwise, in a form suitable for analysis. The Web has suddenly provided a wealth of data for us to analyze, but obtaining the data often poses real challenges.

4.9 CLEANSING THE DATA

When you study statistics in a course, the data sets you analyze have usually been carefully prepared by the textbook author or your instructor. For that reason, they are usually in good shape—that is, they usually contain exactly the data you need, there are no missing data, and there are no "bad" entries (that might have been caused by keypunch errors, for example). Unfortunately, you cannot count on real-world data sets to be so perfect. This is especially the case when you obtain data from external sources such as the Web. There can be all sorts of problems with the data, and it is your responsibility to correct these problems before doing any serious analysis. This initial step, called *cleansing* the data, can be very tedious, but it can often prevent totally misleading results later on.

In this section we examine one data set that has a number of errors, all of which could very possibly occur in real data sets. We discuss methods for *finding* the problems and for *correcting* them. However, you should be aware of two things. First, the "errors" we consider here are only a few of those that could occur. Cleansing data requires real detective work to uncover all possible errors that might be present. Second, once an error is found, it is not always clear how to correct it. A case in point is missing data. For example, some respondents to a questionnaire, when asked for their annual income, might leave this box blank. How should we treat these questionnaires when we perform the eventual analysis? Should we delete them entirely, should we replace their blank incomes with the *average* income of all who responded to this question, or should we use a more complex rule to estimate the missing incomes? All three of these options have been suggested by statisticians, and all three have their pros and cons. Perhaps the safest method is to delete any questionnaires with missing data, so that we don't have to "guess" at the missing values, but then we might be throwing away a lot of potentially useful data. Our point is that some subjectivity and common sense must often be used when cleansing data sets.

EXAMPLE **4.5 CUSTOMER DATA WITH ERRORS**

The file **Data Cleansing.xlsx** has data on 1500 customers of a particular company. A portion of these data appears in Figure 4.47, where many of the rows have been hidden. How much of this data set is usable? How much needs to be cleansed?

Figure 4.47 Data Set with "Bad" Data

	A	B	C	D	E	F	G	H	I
1	Customer	SSN	Birthdate	Age	Region	CredCardUser	Income	Purchases	AmountSpent
2	1	539-84-9599	10/26/44	62	East	0	62900	4	2080
3	2	444-05-4079	01/01/32	67	West	1	23300	0	0
4	3	418-18-5649	08/17/73	25	East	1	48700	8	3990
5	4	065-63-3311	08/02/47	51	West	1	137600	2	920
6	5	059-58-9566	10/03/48	50	East	0	101400	2	1000
7	6	443-13-8685	03/24/60	39	East	0	139700	1	550
8	7	638-89-7231	12/02/43	55	South	1	50900	3	1400
9	8	202-94-6453	11/08/74	24	South	1	50500	0	0
10	9	266-29-0308	09/28/67	31	North	0	151400	2	910
11	10	943-85-8301	07/05/65	33	West	0	88300	2	1080
12	11	047-07-5332	11/13/64	34	North	0	120300	3	1390
1496	1495	632-29-6841	02/06/45	54	West	1	89700	2	1000
1497	1496	347-70-0762	09/28/65	33	West	0	71800	2	970
1498	1497	638-19-2849	07/31/30	68	South	0	121100	5	2540
1499	1498	670-57-4549	07/21/54	44	North	1	64000	4	2160
1500	1499	166-84-2698	10/30/66	32	South	0	91000	6	2910
1501	1500	366-03-5021	09/23/34	64	South	0	121400	1	530

Objective   To find and fix data errors in this company's data set.

You might think that a visual scan of column B (after sorting) would find the duplicates. However, with 1500 entries, it's easy to miss something. That's why we recommend entering the formulas in column J and using Excel's Find tool.

Solution

We purposely constructed this data set to have a number of "problems," all of which you might encounter in real data sets. We begin with the Social Security Number (SSN). Presumably, all 1500 customers are distinct people, so all 1500 SSNs should be different. How can you tell if they are? One simple way is as follows. First, sort on the SSN column. Once the SSNs are sorted, enter the formula

$$=IF(B3=B2,1,0)$$

in cell J3 and copy this formula down column J. This formula checks whether two adjacent SSNs are equal. Then enter the formula

$$=SUM(J3:J1501)$$

in cell J2 to see if there are any duplicate SSNs. (See Figure 4.48.) As we see, there are two pairs of duplicate SSNs. To find them, highlight the range from cell J3 down and select Find from the Find & Select dropdown on the Home ribbon, with the resulting dialog box filled in as shown in Figure 4.49. In particular, make sure the bottom box has Values selected.

Figure 4.48 Checking for Duplicate SSNs

	A	B	C	D	E	F	G	H	I	J
1	Customer	SSN	Birthdate	Age	Region	CredCardUser	Income	Purchases	AmountSpent	
2	681	001-05-3748	03/24/36	63	North	0	159700	1	530	2
3	685	001-43-2336	08/21/63	35	North	0	149300	4	1750	0
4	62	001-80-6937	12/27/54	44	West	1	44000	4	2020	0
5	787	002-23-4874	01/31/76	23	North	0	153000	3	1330	0
6	328	004-10-8303	10/19/76	22	West	1	49800	4	1940	0
7	870	004-39-9621	10/13/57	41	South	0	138900	2	1010	0
8	156	004-59-9799	06/12/38	60	North	0	79700	2	980	0
9	1481	005-06-4020	06/16/52	46	South	1	42700	6	2890	0

Figure 4.49

Dialog Box for Locating Duplicates

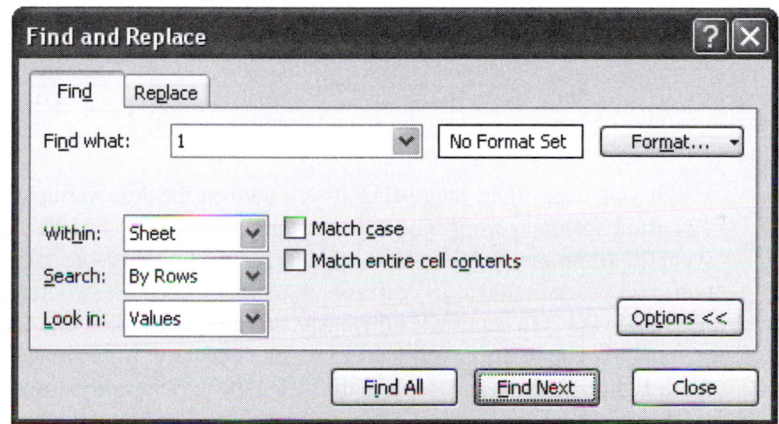

Then click on the Find Next button two times to find the offenders. Customers 369 and 618 each have SSN 283-42-4994, and customers 159 and 464 each have SSN 680-00-1375. At this point, the company should check the SSNs of these four customers (hopefully available from another source) and enter them correctly here. (You can now delete column J and sort on column A to bring the data set back to its original form.)

The Birthdate and Age columns present two interesting problems. When the birthdates were entered, they were entered in exactly the form shown (10/26/44, for example). Then the age was calculated by a somewhat complex formula, just as you would calculate your own age.[14] Are there any problems? First, sort on Birthdate. You'll see that the first 18 customers all have birthdate 05/17/27—quite a coincidence! (See Figure 4.50.) It turns out that Excel's dates are stored internally as integers, which you can see by formatting dates as numbers. So highlight these 18 birthdates and format them with the Number option (and zero decimals) to see what number they correspond to. It turns out to be 9999, the "code" some people use for missing values. Therefore, it is likely that these 18 customers were not born on 05/17/27 after all. Their birthdates were probably *missing* and simply entered as 9999, which were then formatted as dates. If birthdate is important for further analysis, these 18 customers should probably be deleted from the data set.

[14]In case you are interested in some of Excel's date functions, we left the formula for age in cell D2. (We replaced this formula by its values in the rest of column D; otherwise, Excel takes quite a while to recalculate it 1500 times!) This formula uses Excel's TODAY, YEAR, MONTH, and DAY functions. Check online help to learn more about these functions.

Figure 4.50 Suspicious Duplicate Birthdates

	A	B	C	D	E	F	G	H	I
1	Customer	SSN	Birthdate	Age	Region	CredCardUser	Income	Purchases	AmountSpent
2	64	205-84-3572	05/17/27	71	East	0	50500	1	490
3	429	279-23-7773	05/17/27	71	South	0	120300	4	2100
4	463	619-94-0553	05/17/27	71	East	0	62300	2	930
5	466	365-18-7407	05/17/27	71	East	0	155400	4	1900
6	486	364-94-9180	05/17/27	71	West	0	116500	2	1040
7	494	085-32-5438	05/17/27	71	East	0	103700	1	480
8	607	626-04-1182	05/17/27	71	South	1	75900	3	1540
9	645	086-39-4715	05/17/27	71	North	0	155300	5	2480
10	661	212-01-7062	05/17/27	71	West	0	147900	5	2450
11	730	142-06-2339	05/17/27	71	West	1	38200	1	510
12	754	891-12-9133	05/17/27	71	North	0	77300	4	1980
13	782	183-25-0406	05/17/27	71	West	0	51600	0	0
14	813	338-58-7652	05/17/27	71	East	1	47500	2	1020
15	1045	715-28-2884	05/17/27	71	South	0	82400	4	1850
16	1068	110-67-7322	05/17/27	71	North	0	138500	3	1400
17	1131	602-63-2343	05/17/27	71	North	1	67800	3	1520
18	1179	183-40-5102	05/17/27	71	East	0	44800	4	1940
19	1329	678-19-0332	05/17/27	71	West	0	83900	5	2710
20	174	240-78-9827	01/09/30	69	East	0	29900	2	960

The "code" used to denote missing data is not at all standard. Some people use 9999, others leave the entry blank, and others use some other code.

It gets even more interesting if you sort on the Age variable. You'll see that the first 12 customers after sorting have *negative* ages. (See Figure 4.51.) You have just run into a Y2K (year 2000) problem! These 12 customers were all born before 1930. Excel guesses that any two-digit year from 00 to 29 corresponds to the 21st century, whereas those from 30 to 99 correspond to the 20th century.[15] Obviously, this guess was a bad one for these 12 customers, and we should change their birthdates to the 20th century. An easy way to do so is to highlight these 12 birthdates, select Replace from the Find & Select dropdown, fill out the resulting dialog box as shown in Figure 4.52, and click on the Replace All button. This replaces any year that starts 202, as in 2028, with a year that starts 192. (Always be careful with the Replace All option. For example, if we had entered /20 and /19 in the "Find what:" and "Replace with:" boxes, we would not only have replaced the years, but the 20th *day* of any month would also have been replaced by the 19th day!) If you copy the formula for Age that was originally in cell D2 to all of column D, the ages should recalculate automatically as *positive* numbers.

Figure 4.51 Negative Ages: A Y2K Problem

	A	B	C	D	E	F	G	H	I
1	Customer	SSN	Birthdate	Age	Region	CredCardUser	Income	Purchases	AmountSpent
2	148	237-88-3817	08/11/29	-31	South	0	63800	8	3960
3	324	133-99-5496	05/13/28	-30	North	0	142500	2	1000
4	426	968-16-0774	09/29/28	-30	North	0	68400	2	1100
5	440	618-84-1169	10/19/28	-30	West	1	113600	1	470
6	1195	806-70-0226	10/14/28	-30	West	0	40600	4	1960
7	1310	380-84-2860	10/17/28	-30	West	0	91800	2	980
8	589	776-44-8345	04/16/27	-29	West	1	59300	2	1030
9	824	376-25-7809	11/02/27	-29	North	1	9999	2	1070
10	922	329-51-3208	03/21/28	-29	East	1	35400	6	3000
11	229	964-27-4755	01/29/27	-28	East	0	26700	1	450
12	1089	808-29-7482	02/28/27	-28	South	0	90000	5	2580
13	1037	594-47-1955	08/10/25	-27	East	1	128300	3	1510
14	23	943-09-9693	12/08/76	22	North	1	150500	0	0

---

[15]To make matters even worse, a *different* rule was used in earlier versions of MS Office. There is no guarantee that Microsoft will continue to use this same rule in *future* editions of Office. However, if we all enter 4-digit years from now on, as we should, it won't make any difference.

Figure 4.52
Dialog Box for Correcting the Y2K Problem

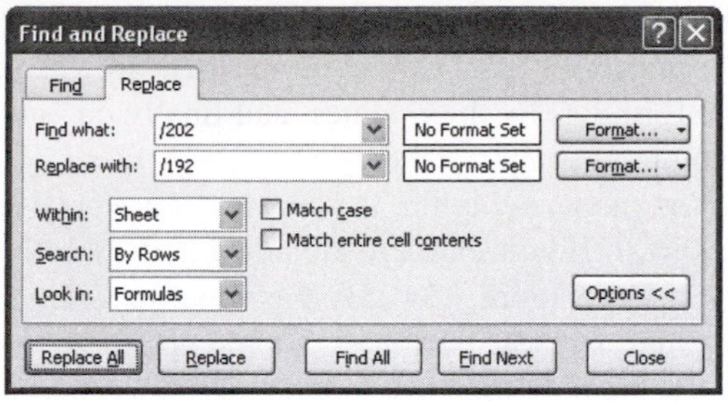

The Region variable presents a problem that can be very hard to find—because you usually are not looking for it. There are four regions: North, South, East, and West. If you sort on Region and starting scrolling down, you'll find a few Easts, a few Norths, a few Souths, and a few Wests, and then the Easts start again. Why aren't the Easts all together? If you look closely, you'll see that a few of the labels in these cells—those at the top after sorting—begin with a space. Whoever typed them inadvertently entered a space before the name. Does this matter? It certainly can. Suppose you create a pivot table, for example, with Region in the row area. You will get eight row categories, not four. (An example appears in Figure 4.53.) Therefore, you should get rid of the extra spaces. The most straightforward way is to use Replace from the Find & Select dropdown in the obvious way.

Figure 4.53
Pivot Table with Too Many Categories

	A	B
1		
2		
3	**Region**	**Sum of AmountSpent**
4	East	48550
5	North	36530
6	South	67289
7	West	35140
8	East	555909
9	North	514135
10	South	563585
11	West	520294
12	**Grand Total**	**2341432**

A slightly different problem occurs in the CredCardUser column, where 1 corresponds to credit card users and 0 corresponds to nonusers. A typical use of these numbers might be to find the proportion of credit card users, which we can find by entering the formula

The newest releases of Excel put a comment in such cells, warning that numbers have been formatted as text.

=AVERAGE(F2:F1501)

in some blank cell. This *should* give the proportion of 1's, but instead it gives an error (#DIV/0!). What's wrong? A clue is that the numbers in column F are left-justified, whereas numbers in Excel are usually right-justified. Here is what might have happened. Data on users and nonusers might initially have been entered as the labels Yes and No. Then to convert them to 1 and 0, someone might have entered the formula

The moral is to omit double quotes around numbers in IF statements. Use double quotes only around text.

=IF(F4="Yes","1","0")

The double quotes around 1 and 0 cause them to be interpreted as *text*, not *numbers*, and no arithmetic can be done on them. (In addition, text is typically left-justified, the telltale sign we observed.) Fortunately, Excel has a function called VALUE that converts text entries that look like numbers to numbers. So we should form a new column that uses this VALUE function on the entries in column F to convert them to numbers. (Specifically, we could create these VALUE formulas in a new column, then do a Copy and Paste-Special as Values to replace the formulas by their values, and finally cut and paste these values over the original text in column F.)

Next we turn to the Income column. If you sort on it, you'll see that most incomes go from $20,000 to $160,000. However, there are a few at the top that are much smaller, and there are a few 9999's. (See Figure 4.54.) By this time, you can guess that the 9999's correspond to missing values, so these customers should probably be deleted if Income is crucial to the analysis. The small numbers at the top take some educated guesswork. Because they range from 22 to 151, we might guess (and hopefully we could confirm) that the person who entered these data thought of them as "thousands" and simply omitted the trailing 000's. If this is indeed correct, we can fix them by multiplying each by 1000. (There is an easy way to do this. Enter the multiple 1000 in some blank cell, and press Ctrl-c to copy it. Next, highlight the range G2:G12, click on the Paste dropdown, select Paste Special, and check the Multiply option.)

Figure 4.54   Suspicious Incomes

	A	B	C	D	E	F	G	H	I
1	Customer	SSN	Birthdate	Age	Region	CredCardUser	Income	Purchases	AmountSpent
2	439	390-77-9781	06/03/70	37	West	0	22	8	4160
3	593	744-30-0499	05/04/60	47	East	0	25	5	2460
4	1343	435-02-2521	08/24/42	65	West	1	43	5	2600
5	925	820-65-4438	11/12/32	74	North	0	55	6	2980
6	1144	211-02-9333	08/13/34	73	North	0	71	9999	9999
7	460	756-41-9393	05/14/71	36	East	0	81	3	1500
8	407	241-86-3823	07/03/59	48	East	1	88	4	2000
9	833	908-76-1846	09/17/60	47	West	0	104	4	1970
10	233	924-59-1581	05/12/31	76	South	0	138	6	2950
11	51	669-39-4544	10/05/33	74	West	0	149	2	1010
12	816	884-27-5089	03/05/62	45	North	1	151	2	900
13	47	601-10-4503	12/19/48	58	East	1	9999	2	1020
14	270	985-78-7861	08/17/40	67	South	0	9999	2	940
15	447	856-77-6560	01/06/40	67	South	1	9999	0	0
16	518	378-83-7998	11/02/74	32	West	1	9999	2	940
17	527	906-06-0341	03/26/52	55	South	0	9999	3	1590

Finally, we examine the Purchases (number of separate purchases by a customer) and AmtSpent (total spent on all purchases) columns. First, sort on Purchases. You'll see the familiar 9999's at the bottom. In fact, each 9999 for Purchases has a corresponding 9999 for AmountSpent. This makes sense. If the number of purchases is unknown, the total amount spent is probably also unknown. We can effectively delete these 9999 rows by inserting a blank row right above them. Excel then automatically senses the boundary of the data. Essentially, a blank row or column imposes a separation from the "active" data. (See Figure 4.55.)

Figure 4.55   Separating Rows with Missing Data from the Rest

	A	B	C	D	E	F	G	H	I
1483	1427	182-48-9138	05/18/40	67	East	0	105000	9	4450
1484									
1485	1144	211-02-9333	08/13/34	73	North	0	71	9999	9999
1486	287	133-53-5943	09/22/35	72	North	1	20000	9999	9999
1487	1298	552-06-0509	10/12/37	70	North	0	23700	9999	9999
1488	375	867-63-6238	09/17/71	36	West	0	29900	9999	9999
1489	250	586-87-0627	06/24/52	55	East	1	53300	9999	9999
1490	14	614-59-6703	08/01/72	35	South	1	54400	9999	9999
1491	1106	102-74-2447	03/14/30	77	West	0	59300	9999	9999
1492	1121	637-23-3846	06/14/54	53	South	0	64000	9999	9999
1493	153	048-55-8930	09/05/34	73	West	1	64400	9999	9999
1494	980	967-97-4228	07/04/63	44	South	1	76800	9999	9999
1495	1061	377-29-0406	10/08/51	56	West	1	93000	9999	9999
1496	858	819-34-4450	05/26/59	48	South	1	101300	9999	9999
1497	432	572-79-9529	01/21/67	40	West	1	104500	9999	9999
1498	1438	452-69-6883	01/16/74	33	South	0	116400	9999	9999
1499	1125	394-20-9464	10/20/75	31	North	1	129400	9999	9999
1500	469	797-55-3419	09/16/61	46	North	1	132800	9999	9999
1501	443	087-21-2053	07/02/52	55	West	0	141200	9999	9999
1502	317	865-85-3875	12/19/31	75	South	0	149900	9999	9999

Now we examine the remaining data for these two variables. Presumably, there is a relationship between these variables, where the amount spent increases with the number of purchases. We can check this with a scatterplot of the (nonmissing) data, as shown in Figure 4.56. There is a clear upward trend for most of the points, but there are some suspicious outliers at the bottom of the plot. Again, we take an educated guess. Perhaps the *average spent per purchase*, rather than the total amount spent, was entered for a few of the customers. This would explain the abnormally small values. (It would also explain why these outliers are all at about the same height in the plot.) If we can locate these outliers on the data sheet, we should multiply each by the corresponding number of purchases (if our educated guess is correct). How do we find them on the data sheet? First, sort on AmountSpent, then sort on Purchases. This will arrange the amounts spent in increasing order for each value of Purchases. Then, using the scatterplot as a guide, scroll through each value of Purchases (starting with 2) and locate the abnormally low values of AmountSpent (which are all together). For example, Figure 4.57 indicates the suspicious values for 3 purchases. This procedure is a bit tedious, but it beats working with invalid data.

Figure 4.56

Scatterplot with Suspicious Outliers

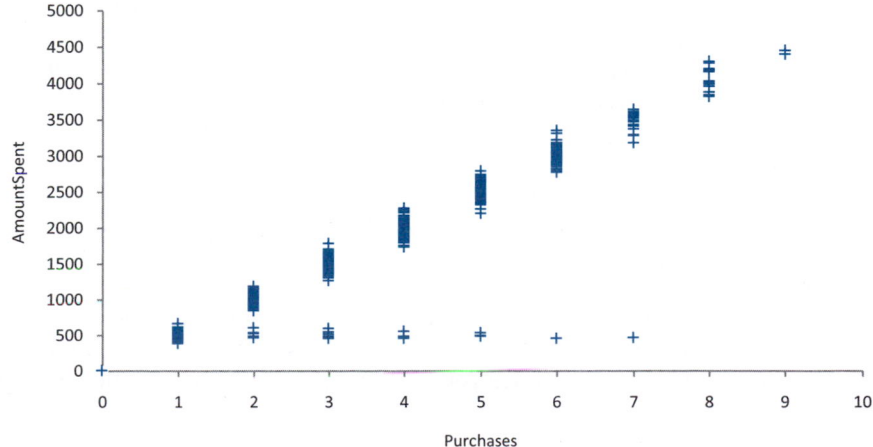

Figure 4.57   Suspicious Values of AmountSpent

	A	B	C	D	E	F	G	H	I
641	1455	169-31-5478	06/19/45	62	North	1	144600	2	1170
642	777	820-27-6346	07/04/36	71	West	0	155000	2	1180
643	259	731-52-6832	02/05/51	56	East	1	41700	3	450
644	121	345-16-5545	07/08/59	48	West	1	112700	3	450
645	109	280-07-3023	08/04/43	64	West	0	24300	3	460
646	1469	719-98-9028	03/15/69	38	North	1	91300	3	470
647	1331	745-63-6259	07/22/58	49	South	0	63700	3	480
648	1313	041-74-0192	12/04/59	47	East	0	25900	3	510
649	501	156-39-5201	08/15/38	69	East	0	111000	3	540
650	936	261-74-3204	10/01/37	70	West	0	65000	3	590
651	921	601-98-9218	05/06/38	69	South	1	131000	3	1260
652	294	728-06-3395	07/12/66	41	West	0	159800	3	1300
653	568	375-92-1009	01/13/59	48	North	1	73600	3	1310

PROBLEMS

Level A

24. The file **P04_01.xlsx** contains a data set that represents 30 responses from a questionnaire concerning the president's environmental policies. Each observation lists the person's age, gender, state of residence, number of children, annual salary, and opinion of the president's environmental policies. How much of this data set is usable? Cleanse all usable data.

25. The file **P04_05.xlsx** contains information on 66 movie stars. In particular, the data set contains the name of each actor and the following four variables: gender, domestic gross (average domestic gross of the star's last few movies, in millions of dollars), foreign gross (average foreign gross of the star's last few movies, in millions of dollars), and income (current amount the star asks for a movie, in millions of dollars). Are all of these data usable? Explain why or why not.

26. A human resources manager at Beta Technologies, Inc., has collected current annual salary figures and related data for 52 of the company's full-time employees. The data are in the file **P04_02.xlsx**. Specifically,

these data include each selected employee's gender, age, number of years of relevant work experience prior to employment at Beta, the number of years of employment at Beta, the number of years of post-secondary education, and annual salary. How much of this data set is usable? Cleanse all usable data.

27. Five hundred households in a middle-class neighborhood were recently surveyed as part of an economic development study conducted by the local government. Specifically, for each of the 500 randomly selected households, the survey requested information on the following variables: family size, approximate location of the household within the neighborhood, an indication of whether those surveyed owned or rented their home, gross annual income of the first household wage earner, gross annual income of the second household wage earner (if applicable), monthly home mortgage or rent payment, average monthly expenditure on utilities, and the total indebtedness (excluding the value of a home mortgage) of the household. The data are in the file **P04_03.xlsx**. Cleanse all usable data in this set.

4.10 CONCLUSION

This chapter has covered some very powerful tools for getting the right data into Excel. As with many other features of Excel, the tools we have discussed are fairly easy to use—once you know they exist. We believe that once you know that something can be done and have a general idea of how to do it, you can figure out the rest of the details. Indeed, as the software changes, you will be forced to learn the details on your own through experimenting and consulting online help. Therefore, as you look back on this chapter, focus on what *can* be done, not the nitty-gritty details. It *is* possible to create queries in Excel ranges so that we can find subsets of an Excel database that satisfy certain conditions. It *is* possible to create queries in Microsoft Query so that we can import data from many database packages into Excel. It *is* even possible to import data from Web pages into Excel by various methods. Once you realize these possibilities, you will be able to accomplish tasks that the majority of Excel users have never even tried.

Summary of Key Terms

Term	Explanation	Excel	Page
Data warehouse	A type of database used by companies to store large quantities of historical data for later statistical analysis		145
Filter	A way to query an Excel database	From Filter buttons	147
Survey	A questionnaire used to gather information from a sample of a population		148
Controlled experiment	An experiment where certain variables are deliberately set at specified levels to learn about their effects on one or more other variables		149
Query	An instruction to a database to return a subset of the data that satisfies specified conditions		158
Advanced Filter	Use for more complex queries	Advanced button on Data ribbon	158
Flat file	A single-table database		164
Table	A rectangular range of data, can be sorted or filtered in many useful ways	Table from Insert ribbon	164
Relational database	A database where the data are stored in related tables, which are related by primary and foreign key fields		164–165
Microsoft Query	Software that is packaged with Microsoft Office, used to get data from external databases and return the data to Excel	From Microsoft Query, under From Other Sources on Data ribbon	165
SQL	Structured Query Language, a general language used to specify database queries		173
Web query	A method for importing tables from selected Web pages into Excel	From Web on Data ribbon	177
SPSS, SAS, STATA	Three heavy-duty statistical software packages favored by many statisticians		186
Cleansing data	The process of removing errors—keypunch errors, Y2K errors, or any other types of errors—from a data set		189

PROBLEMS

Conceptual Exercises

C.1. What is the difference between a *survey* and a *census*?

C.2. An organizational behavior professor wonders whether the use of role-playing exercises will help her students learn how groups make decisions. She decides to conduct an experiment in which some students engage in role-playing exercises while others engage in a more traditional discussion about group decision making during recitation sections. This professor teaches two sections of her OB course: one at 8:00 A.M. to 9:30 A.M., and another at 1:00 A.M. to 2:30 P.M. on Tuesdays and Thursdays. To keep things simple, she decides that all students enrolled in the 8:00 A.M. section will be subjected to the role-playing pedagogy and those students enrolled in the 1:00 P.M. section will learn about how groups make decisions through one or more class discussions. Does the professor's plan for conducting this experiment appear to be sound? Explain why or why not.

C.3. Assume that a national insurance company has randomly selected 1500 of its customers to assess their attitudes toward the service they receive from the company's agents. Provide an example of how an analyst from this company might perform a query on the customer database in conducting this investigation.

C.4. Identify all flat files in the relational database described in Example 4.2.

C.5. Suppose that you collect a random sample of 250 salaries for the salespersons employed by a large PC manufacturer. Furthermore, assume that you find that two of these salaries are considerably higher than the others in the sample. In cleansing this data set, should you delete the unusual observations? Explain why or why not.

Level A

28. Consider the given survey data collected from 1000 randomly selected Internet users. The data are in the file **P04_28.xlsx**. Use filters to answer the following questions:
   a. What proportion of those surveyed are females who are married, employed, and have achieved more than a high school education?
   b. What proportion of those surveyed are males who are single, unemployed, and have achieved a high school education or less?
   c. Find the average annual income of the females who are married, employed, and have achieved more than a high school education.

   d. Find the average annual income of the males who are married, employed, and have achieved more than a high school education. How does this result compare to the average found in part **c**?

29. Consider the given survey data collected from 1000 randomly selected Internet users. The data are in the file **P04_28.xlsx**.
   a. Find all Internet users in the sample who are either (1) married men between the ages of 21 and 40 (inclusive) who are employed and have more than a high school education and two or fewer children, or (2) married women between the ages of 21 and 40 (inclusive) who are employed and have more than a high school education and at least one child.
   b. Characterize the distribution of annual incomes for the individuals who meet the conditions specified in part **a**. In particular, report the mean, median, and standard deviation for the resulting income distribution. Is this distribution skewed?
   c. For those Internet users who satisfy the conditions specified in part **a**, compare the mean salary of the men with that of the women. Also, compare the standard deviation of the salaries earned by the men with that of the salaries earned by the women.

30. ShirtCo is a direct competitor of the Fine Shirt Company described previously in Example 4.2. Like its rival, ShirtCo makes and sells shirts to its customers. The main difference is that ShirtCo focuses its efforts on the creation and production of specialty T-shirts. The company has created an Access database file **P04_30.mdb** that contains information on sales to its customers from 2001 through 2004. There are two related tables in this database: Sales and Customer. Each of the 2245 records in the Sales table contains the order number, customer number (1-7), order date, channel of sale (wholesale or retail), type of T-shirt product (Art, Dinosaurs, Environment, Humorous, Kids, Political, or Sports), units sold, list price, total invoice amount, and amount paid by customer. Each of the 7 records in the Customer table contains the customer number, the customer's name, street address, city, state, zip code, country, phone number, and the date of first contact. Find all of the records from the Sales table where the order was placed in 2003 or 2004, the sale channel was retail, the product type was not Kids, and the number of units ordered was at least 400. Return to Excel all fields in the sales table for each of these records.

31. Continuing with the ShirtCo database in the file **P04_30.mdb**, find all of the records from the Sales table that correspond to orders for over 500 items made by the customer Shirts R Us for the Environment, Humorous, and Political products. Return to Excel the dates, sale channel, product type, units ordered, and amounts paid for each of these orders.

32. ShirtCo would like to know the total amount spent by each of its customers on each of its products during each of the years 2001–2004. Using the database given in the file **P04_30.mdb**, construct one or more pivot tables that provide ShirtCo with the desired information.

33. ShirtCo would also like to know the proportions sold through each channel (i.e., wholesale versus retail) for each of its products during each quarter of the years 2001–2004. Using the database given in the file **P04_30.mdb**, construct one or more pivot tables that provide ShirtCo with the desired information.

34. Who is most likely to access the Internet today? Consider the given survey data collected from 1000 randomly selected Internet users. The data are in the file **P04_28.xlsx**. Are all of these data usable? Explain why or why not.

Level B

35. The file **P04_35.xlsx** contains 2003 compensation data for chief executive officers from 350 of the largest public companies in the United States.
  a. Find all executives whose annual salary in fiscal 2003 was at least $1,000,000 and whose company type was either Cyclical or Energy. Find the average bonus earned by these chief executive officers in fiscal 2003.
  b. Find all executives whose annual salary in fiscal 2003 was less than $750,000 and whose company type was either Non-Cyclical or Technology. Find the average bonus earned by these chief executive officers in fiscal 2003.
  c. Find all executives whose annual salary in fiscal 2003 was between $500,000 and $1,000,000 (inclusive) and whose company type was either Basic Materials or Financial. Find the average bonus earned by these chief executive officers in fiscal 2003.

36. Recall that the HyTex Company is a direct marketer of stereophonic equipment, personal computers, and other electronic products. The file **P04_36.xlsx** contains recent data on 1000 HyTex customers.
  a. Identify all customers in the sample who are 55 years of age or younger, female, single, and who have had at least some dealings with HyTex before this year. Find the average number of catalogs sent to these customers and the average amount spent by these customers this year. How strongly correlated are the numbers of catalogs sent and the amounts spent on HyTex purchases for these customers?

  b. Do any of the customers who satisfy the conditions stated in part **a** have salaries that fall in the bottom 10% of all 1000 combined salaries in the sample? If so, how many?
  c. Identify all customers in the sample who are more than 30 years of age or younger, male, homeowners, married, and who have had little if any dealings with HyTex before this year. Find the average combined household salary and the average amount spent by these customers this year. How strongly correlated are the combined household salaries and the amounts spent on HyTex purchases for these customers?
  d. Do any of the customers who satisfy the conditions stated in part **a** have salaries that fall in the top 10% of all 1000 combined salaries in the sample? If so, how many?

37. Recall that the HyTex Company is a direct marketer of stereophonic equipment, personal computers, and other electronic products. The file **P04_36.xlsx** contains recent data on 1000 HyTex customers.
  a. Identify all customers in the given sample who are either (1) homeowners between the ages of 31 and 55 who live reasonably close to a shopping area that sells similar merchandise, and who have a combined salary between $40,000 and $90,000 (inclusive) and a history of being a medium- or high-spender at HyTex; or (2) homeowners greater than the age of 55 who live reasonably close to a shopping area that sells similar merchandise, and who have a combined salary between $40,000 and $90,000 (inclusive) and a history of being a medium- or high-spender at HyTex.
  b. Characterize the subset of customers who satisfy the conditions specified in part **a**. In particular, what proportion of these customers are women? What proportion of these customers are married? On average, how many children do these customers have? Finally, how many catalogs do these customers typically receive, and how much do they typically spend each year at HyTex?
  c. In what ways are the customers who satisfy condition (1) in part **a** different from those who satisfy condition (2) in part **a**? Be as specific as possible.

38. Refer to Problem 37 with the data provided in the file **P04_36.xlsx**. Find all of the customers in the given sample who satisfy each of the following conditions:
  a. AmountSpent is at least $1000 greater than the median of AmountSpent for all customers.
  b. AmountSpent is more than two standard deviations above the mean of AmountSpent for all customers.
  c. Salary is no less than the 90th percentile of salaries for all customers.

39. ShirtCo is trying to determine who was its biggest customer in 2004, as measured by total units sold in 2004.

Once ShirtCo determines which customer was responsible for the maximum level of total unit sales, the company would then like to know the breakdown of this customer's 2004 total *expenditures* by product and channel. Using the database given in the file **P04_30.mdb**, construct pivot tables that provide ShirtCo with the desired information. Summarize your findings.

40. According to a survey conducted by Mercer Human Resource Consulting and published in *The Wall Street Journal* (May 2004), the typical salary of chief executive officers from 350 of the nation's largest U.S. public corporations increased by 3.8% to $950,000 in 2003. Furthermore, the typical annual bonus for CEOs increased by 6.7% to $1,100,000 in 2003. The data are given in the file **P04_35.xlsx**. Cleanse all usable data in this set.

41. The HyTex Company is a direct marketer of stereophonic equipment, personal computers, and other electronic products. HyTex advertises entirely by mailing catalogs to its customers, and all of its orders are taken over the telephone. The company spends a great deal of money on its catalog mailings and wants to be sure that this is paying off in sales. Therefore, it has collected data on 1000 customers at the end of the current year. For each customer it has data on the following variables: Age (coded as 1 for 30 years or younger, 2 for 31 to 55 years, 3 for 56 years or older), Gender (coded as 1 for males, and 2 for females), OwnHome (coded as 1 if customer owns a home, and 2 otherwise), Married (coded as 1 if customer is currently married, and 2 otherwise), Close (coded as 1 if customer lives reasonably close to a shopping area that sells similar merchandise, and 2 otherwise), Salary (combined annual salary of customer and spouse, if applicable), Children (number of children living with the customer), History (coded as "NA" if customer had no dealings with the company before this year, 1 if customer was a low-spending customer last year, 2 if medium-spending, and 3 if high-spending), Catalogs (number of catalogs sent to the customer this year), and AmountSpent (total amount of purchases made by the customer this year). These data are provided in the file **P04_36.xlsx**. Cleanse all unusable data in this file.

EduToys, Inc., sells a wide variety of educational toy products to its customers through its Web site. Jeannie Dobson, director of information services at EduToys, recently developed a relational database to store critical information that the management team needs to more effectively serve EduToys' customers. The database, which is provided in the file **EduToys.mdb**, consists of five related tables: Company, Customer, Inventory, Orders, and Toys.

The Company table consists of the following information on each of the 159 companies that manufacture and supply products to EduToys: identification number, name, and telephone number. The Customer table maintains the following data on each of the 307 customers who purchased at least one item from EduToys's electronic store during the first 10 months of operation (i.e., January–October 1998): identification number, last name, first name, age, gender, street address, city, state, zip code, and telephone number. The Inventory table consists of the following information on each of the 201 products that EduToys purchases from its various suppliers: identification number, name, quantity in current inventory, quantity on order, and expected delivery date of order. The Orders table records the following information for each of the customer transactions that took place during the first 10 months of 1998: transaction identification number, date, customer identification number, customer credit card number, product identification number, and quantity purchased. Finally, the Toys table maintains the following data on each of the products sold by EduToys: product identification number, company

(i.e., supplier) identification number, product name, type of product, appropriate age group for product, unit price, and detailed product description.

As part of your internship with EduToys, you have been asked by your supervisor to prepare a memorandum that responds to the following questions. Your supervisor encourages you to make extensive use of the database in completing this assignment. Also, she wants you to retain copies of all Excel spreadsheets that you prepare to generate the needed information.

1. How do EduToys's past customers break down by age and gender?

2. Which of EduToys's past customers have spent amounts that fall in the top 20% of all transactions (as measured in dollars)? Report the first name, last name, street address, city, state, and zip code for each of these customers.

3. Which products have generated sales revenues (in dollars) that fall in the top 25% of all such revenue contributions? Report the current inventory level, quantity on order, and supplier of each of these best-selling products.

4. How do the given 1998 sales (in dollars) break down by product type and product age group?

5. What proportion of all given transactions were conducted through the use of each type of credit card (including American Express, Discover, MasterCard, and Visa)?

6. What changes or additions would you recommend making to the present database? Provide the reasoning behind each of your recommendations. ■

Probability and Probability Distributions

© Tannen Maury/Bloomberg News/Landov

GAME AT MCDONALD'S

Several years ago McDonald's ran a campaign in which it gave game cards to its customers. These game cards made it possible for customers to win hamburgers, french fries, soft drinks, and other fast-food items, as well as cash prizes. Each card had 10 covered spots that could be uncovered by rubbing them with a coin. Beneath three of these spots were "zaps." Beneath the other seven spots were names of prizes, two of which were identical. (Some cards had variations of this pattern, but we'll use this type of card for purposes of illustration.) For example, one card might have two pictures of a hamburger, one picture of a Coke, one of french fries, one of a milk shake, one of $5, one of $1000, and three zaps. For this card the customer could win a hamburger. To win on any card, the customer had to uncover the two matching spots (which showed the potential prize for that card) before uncovering a zap; any card with a zap uncovered was automatically void. Assuming that the two matches and the three zaps were arranged randomly on the cards, what is the probability of a customer winning?

We'll label the two matching spots M_1 and M_2, and the three zaps Z_1, Z_2, and Z_3. Then the probability of winning is the probability of uncovering M_1 and M_2 before uncovering $Z_1, Z_2,$ or Z_3. In this case the relevant set of outcomes is the set of all orderings of $M_1, M_2, Z_1, Z_2,$ and Z_3, shown in the order they are uncovered. As far as the outcome of the game is concerned, the other five spots on the card are irrelevant. Then an outcome such as M_2, M_1, Z_3, Z_1, Z_2 is a winner, whereas M_2, Z_2, Z_1, M_1, Z_3 is a loser. Actually, the first of these would be declared a winner as soon as M_1 was uncovered, and the second would be declared a loser as soon as Z_2 was uncovered. However, we show the whole sequence of M's and Z's so that we can count outcomes correctly. We then find the probability of winning using the argument of equally likely outcomes. Specifically, we divide the number of outcomes that are winners by the total number of outcomes. It can be shown that the number of outcomes that are winners is 12, whereas the total number of outcomes is 120. Therefore, the probability of a winner is $12/120 = 0.1$.

This calculation, which showed that on the average, 1 out of 10 cards could be winners, was obviously important for McDonald's. Actually, this provides only an upper bound on the fraction of cards where a prize was awarded. The fact is that many customers threw their cards away without playing the game, and even some of the winners neglected to claim their prizes. So, for example, McDonald's knew that if they made 50,000 cards where a milk shake was the winning prize, somewhat less than 5000 milk shakes would be given away. Knowing approximately what their expected "losses" would be from winning cards, McDonald's was able to design the game (how many cards of each type to print) so that the expected extra revenue (from customers attracted to the game) would cover the expected losses. ∎

5.1 INTRODUCTION

A large part of the subject of statistics deals with uncertainty. Demands for products are uncertain, times between arrivals to a supermarket are uncertain, stock price returns are uncertain, changes in interest rates are uncertain, and so on. In these examples and many others, the uncertain quantity—demand, time between arrivals, stock price return, change in interest rate—is a numerical quantity. In the language of probability, such a numerical quantity is called a *random variable*. More formally, a **random variable** associates a numerical value with each possible random outcome.

Associated with each random variable is a **probability distribution** that lists all of the possible values of the random variable and their corresponding probabilities. A probability distribution provides very useful information. It not only tells us the possible values of the random variable, but also how likely they are. For example, it is useful to know that the possible demands for a product are, say, 100, 200, 300, and 400, but it is even more useful to know that the probabilities of these four values are, say, 0.1, 0.2, 0.4, and 0.3. Now we know, for example, that there is a 70% chance that demand will be at least 300.

It is often useful to summarize the information from a probability distribution with several well-chosen numerical summary measures. These include the mean, variance, and standard deviation, and, for distributions of more than one random variable, the covariance and correlation. As their names imply, these summary measures are much like the summary measures in Chapter 3. However, they are not identical. The summary measures in this chapter are based on probability distributions, not an observed data set. We use numerical examples to explain the difference between the two—and how they are related.

The purpose of this chapter is to explain the basic concepts and tools necessary to work with probability distributions and their summary measures. We begin by briefly discussing the basic rules of probability, which we need in this chapter and in several later chapters. We also introduce *computer simulation*, an extremely useful tool for illustrating important concepts in probability and statistics.

We conclude this chapter with a discussion of *weighted sums of random variables*. These are particularly useful in investment analysis, where we want to analyze portfolios of stocks or other securities. In this case the weights are the relative amounts invested in the securities, and the weighted sum represents the portfolio return. Our goal is to investigate the probability distribution of a weighted sum, particularly its summary measures.

Modeling uncertainty, as we will be doing in the next few chapters and later in Chapters 16 and 17, is sometimes difficult, depending on the complexity of the model, and it is easy to get so caught up in the details that you lose sight of the big picture. For this reason, we present the flow chart in Figure 5.1. (A colored version of this chart is available in the file **Modeling Uncertainty—Flow Chart.xlsx**.) Take a close look at the middle row of this chart. It indicates that we begin with inputs, some of which are uncertain quantities, we use Excel formulas to incorporate the logic of the model, we end with probability distributions of important outputs, which we can summarize in various ways, and we finally use this information to make decisions. The other boxes in the chart deal with implementation issues, particularly with software you have and can use to simplify the analysis. Read this chart carefully, and return to it as you proceed through the next few chapters and Chapters 16 and 17.

Figure 5.1   Flow Chart for Modeling Uncertainty

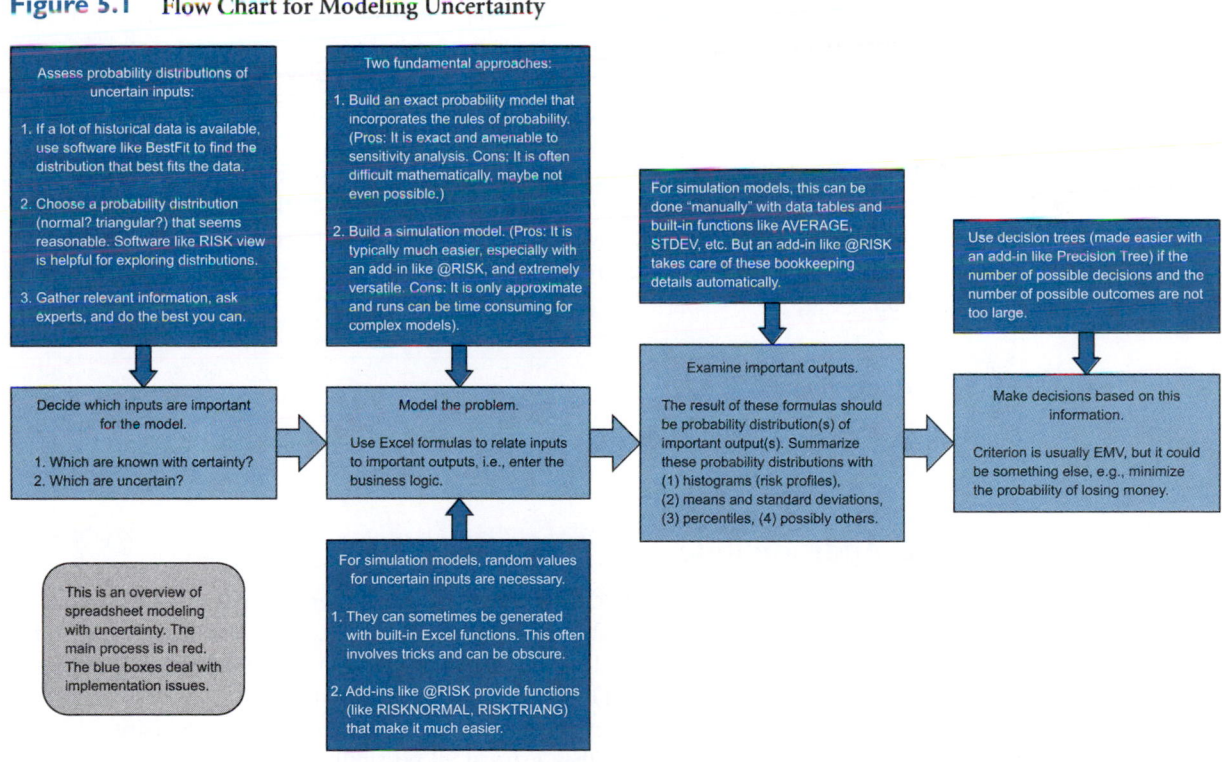

5.2 PROBABILITY ESSENTIALS

We begin with a brief discussion of probability. The concept of probability is one that we all encounter in everyday life. When a weather forecaster states that the chance of rain is 70%, she is making a probability statement. When we hear that the odds of the Miami Heat winning the NBA Championship are 2 to 1, this is also a probability statement. The *concept* of probability is quite intuitive. However, the *rules* of probability are not always as intuitive or easy to master. We examine the most important of these rules in this section.

> A **probability** is a number between 0 and 1 that measures the likelihood that some event will occur. An event with probability 0 cannot occur, whereas an event with probability 1 is certain to occur. An event with probability greater than 0 and less than 1 involves uncertainty, but the closer its probability is to 1, the more likely it is to occur.

As the examples in the preceding paragraph illustrate, we often express probabilities as percentages or odds. However, these can easily be converted to probabilities on a 0-to-1 scale. If the chance of rain is 70%, then the probability of rain is 0.7. Similarly, if the odds of the Heat winning are 2 to 1, then the probability of the Heat winning is 2/3 (or 0.6667).

5.2.1 Rule of Complements

The simplest probability rule involves the *complement* of an event. If A is any event, then the **complement of A**, denoted by $\overline{A}$ (or in some books by A^c), is the event that A does *not* occur. For example, if A is the event that the Dow Jones Index will finish the year at or above the 11,000 mark, then the complement of A is that the Dow will finish the year below 11,000.

If the probability of A is $P(A)$, then the probability of its complement, $P(\overline{A})$, is given by equation (5.1). Equivalently, the probability of an event and the probability of its complement sum to 1. For example, if we believe that the probability of the Dow finishing at or above 11,000 is 0.55, then the probability that it will finish the year below 11,000 is $1 - 0.55 = 0.45$.

> **Rule of Complements**
>
> $$P(\overline{A}) = 1 - P(A) \tag{5.1}$$

5.2.2 Addition Rule

We say that events are **mutually exclusive** if at most one of them can occur. That is, if one of them occurs, then none of the others can occur. For example, consider the following three events involving a company's annual revenue in some year: (1) revenue is less than \$1 million, (2) revenue is at least \$1 million but less than \$2 million, and (3) revenue is at least \$2 million. Clearly, only one of these events can occur. Therefore, they are mutually exclusive. They are also **exhaustive**, which means that they exhaust all possibilities—one of these three events *must* occur. Let A_1 through A_n be any n events. Then the *addition rule* of probability involves the probability that at least one of these events will occur. In general, this probability is quite complex, but it simplifies considerably when the events are mutually exclusive. In this case the probability that at least one of the events will occur is the sum of their individual probabilities, as shown in equation (5.2). Of course, when the events are mutually exclusive, "at least one" is equivalent to "exactly one." In addition, if the events A_1 through A_n are exhaustive, then the probability is 1. In this case we are certain that one of the events will occur.

Addition Rule for Mutually Exclusive Events
$$P(\text{at least one of } A_1 \text{ through } A_n) = P(A_1) + P(A_2) + \cdots + P(A_n) \qquad \text{(5.2)}$$

In a typical application, the events A_1 through A_n are chosen to partition the set of all possible outcomes into a number of mutually exclusive events. For example, in terms of a company's annual revenue, define A_1 as "revenue is less than \$1 million," A_2 as "revenue is at least \$1 million but less than \$2 million," and A_3 as "revenue is at least \$2 million." As we discussed previously, these three events are mutually exclusive and exhaustive. Therefore, their probabilities must sum to 1. Suppose these probabilities are $P(A_1) = 0.5$, $P(A_2) = 0.3$, and $P(A_3) = 0.2$. (Note that these probabilities *do* sum to 1.) Then the additive rule enables us to calculate other probabilities. For example, the event that revenue is at least \$1 million is the event that either A_2 or A_3 occurs. From the addition rule, its probability is

$$P(\text{revenue is at least \$1 million}) = P(A_2) + P(A_3) = 0.5$$

Similarly,

$$P(\text{revenue is less than \$2 million}) = P(A_1) + P(A_2) = 0.8$$

and

$$P(\text{revenue is less than \$1 million } \textit{or} \text{ at least \$2 million}) = P(A_1) + P(A_3) = 0.7$$

5.2.3 Conditional Probability and the Multiplication Rule

Probabilities are always assessed relative to the information currently available. As new information becomes available, probabilities often change. For example, if you read that Shaq pulled a hamstring muscle, your assessment of the probability that the Heat will win the NBA Championship would obviously change. A formal way to revise probabilities on the basis of new information is to use *conditional probabilities.*

Let A and B be any events with probabilities $P(A)$ and $P(B)$. Typically, the probability $P(A)$ is assessed without knowledge of whether B occurs. However, if we are *told* that B has occurred, then the probability of A might change. The new probability of A is called the **conditional probability** of A given B. It is denoted by $P(A|B)$. Note that there is still uncertainty involving the event to the left of the vertical bar in this notation; we do not know whether it will occur. However, there is no uncertainty involving the event to the right of the vertical bar; we *know* that it has occurred.

Conditional Probability
$$P(A|B) = \frac{P(A \text{ and } B)}{P(B)} \qquad \text{(5.3)}$$

Multiplication Rule
$$P(A \text{ and } B) = P(A|B)P(B) \qquad \text{(5.4)}$$

The **conditional probability formula** enables us to calculate $P(A|B)$ as shown in equation (5.3). The numerator in this formula is the probability that *both* A and B occur. This probability must be known to find $P(A|B)$. However, in some applications $P(A|B)$ and $P(B)$ are known. Then we can multiply both sides of the conditional probability formula by $P(B)$ to obtain the **multiplication rule** for $P(A$ and $B)$ in equation (5.4).

The conditional probability formula and the multiplication rule are both valid; in fact, they are equivalent. The one we use depends on which probabilities we know and which we want to calculate, as illustrated in the following example.

EXAMPLE | **5.1 ASSESSING UNCERTAINTY AT THE BENDRIX COMPANY**

The Bendrix Company supplies contractors with materials for the construction of houses. The company currently has a contract with one of its customers to fill an order by the end of July. However, there is some uncertainty about whether this deadline can be met, due to uncertainty about whether Bendrix will receive the materials it needs from one of its suppliers by the middle of July. Right now it is July 1. How can the uncertainty in this situation be assessed?

Objective   To apply several of the essential probability rules in determining the likelihood that Bendrix will meet its end-of-July deadline, given the information the company has at the beginning of July.

Solution

Let A be the event that Bendrix meets its end-of-July deadline, and let B be the event that Bendrix receives the materials from its supplier by the middle of July. The probabilities Bendrix is best able to assess on July 1 are probably $P(B)$ and $P(A|B)$. At the beginning of July, Bendrix might estimate that the chances of getting the materials on time from its supplier are 2 out of 3, that is, $P(B) = 2/3$. Also, thinking ahead, Bendrix estimates that *if* it receives the required materials on time, the chances of meeting the end-of-July deadline are 3 out of 4. This is a conditional probability statement, namely, that $P(A|B) = 3/4$. Then we can use the multiplication rule to obtain

$$P(A \text{ and } B) = P(A|B)P(B) = (3/4)(2/3) = 0.5$$

That is, there is a 50–50 chance that Bendrix will get its materials on time *and* meet its end-of-July deadline.

This uncertain situation is depicted graphically in the form of a *probability tree* in Figure 5.2. Note that Bendrix initially faces (at the leftmost branch of the tree diagram) the uncertainty of whether event B or its complement will occur. Regardless of whether event B takes place, Bendrix must next confront the uncertainty regarding event A. This uncertainty is reflected in the set of two parallel pairs of branches that model the possibility that either event A or its complement could occur next. Hence, there are four mutually exclusive outcomes regarding the two uncertain events in this situation, as shown on the right-hand side of Figure 5.2. Initially, we are interested in the first possible outcome, the joint occurrence of events A and B, found at the top of the probability tree diagram. Another way to compute the probability of *both* events B and A occurring is to multiply the probabilities associated with the branches along the path from the root of the tree (on the left-hand side) to the desired terminal point or outcome of the tree (on the right-hand side). In this case, we multiply the probability of B, corresponding to the first branch along the path of interest, by the conditional probability of *A* given *B*, associated with the second branch along the path of interest.

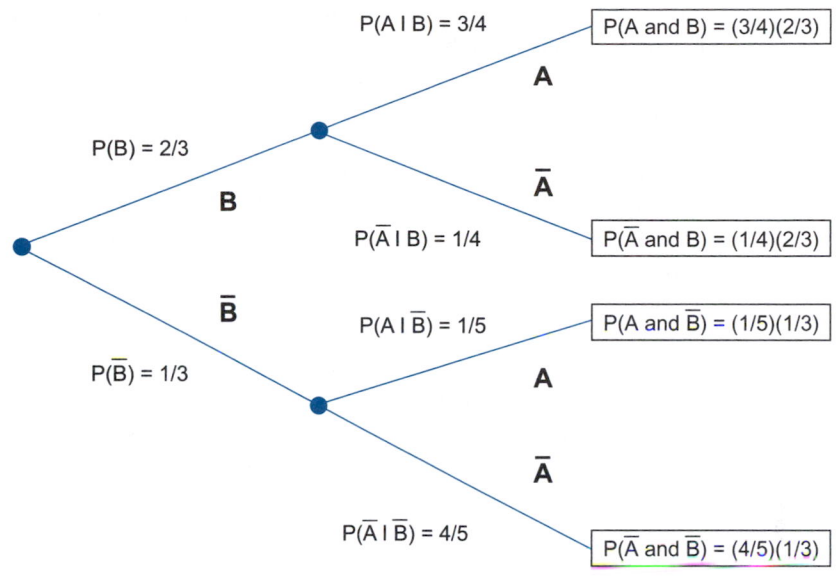

There are several other probabilities of interest in this example. First, let $\overline{B}$ be the complement of *B*; it is the event that the materials from the supplier do *not* arrive on time. We know that $P(\overline{B}) = 1 - P(B) = 1/3$ from the rule of complements. However, we do not yet know the conditional probability $P(A|\overline{B})$, the probability that Bendrix will meet its end-of-July deadline, given that it does not receive the materials from the supplier on time. In particular, $P(A|\overline{B})$ is *not* equal to $1 - P(A|B)$. (Can you see why?) Suppose Bendrix estimates that the chances of meeting the end-of-July deadline are 1 out of 5 if the materials do not arrive on time, that is, $P(A|\overline{B}) = 1/5$. Then a second use of the multiplication rule gives

$$P(A \text{ and } \overline{B}) = P(A|\overline{B})P(\overline{B}) = (1/5)(1/3) = 0.0667$$

In words, there is only 1 chance out of 15 that the materials will not arrive on time *and* Bendrix will meet its end-of-July deadline.

Again, we can use the probability tree for Bendrix in Figure 5.2 to compute the probability of the joint occurrence of the complement of event *B* and event *A*. This outcome is the third (from the top of the diagram) terminal point of the tree. To find the desired probability, we multiply the probabilities corresponding to the two branches included in this path from the left-hand side of the tree to the right-hand side. Of course, we confirm that the probability of interest is the product of the two relevant probabilities, namely, 1/5 and 1/3. Simply stated, probability trees can be quite useful in modeling and assessing such uncertain outcomes in real-life situations.

The bottom line for Bendrix is whether it will meet its end-of-July deadline. After mid-July, this probability is either $P(A|B) = 3/4$ or $P(A|\overline{B}) = 1/5$ because by this time, Bendrix will *know* whether the materials arrived on time. But on July 1, the relevant probability is $P(A)$—there is still uncertainty about whether *B* or $\overline{B}$ will occur. Fortunately, we can calculate $P(A)$ from the probabilities we already know. The logic is that *A* consists of the two mutually exclusive events (*A* and *B*) and (*A* and $\overline{B}$). That is, if *A* is to occur, it must occur with *B* or with $\overline{B}$. Therefore, using the *addition* rule for mutually exclusive events, we obtain

$$P(A) = P(A \text{ and } B) + P(A \text{ and } \overline{B}) = 1/2 + 1/15 = 17/30 = 0.5667$$

The chances are 17 out of 30 that Bendrix will meet its end-of-July deadline, given the information it has at the beginning of July. ∎

5.2.4 Probabilistic Independence

A concept that is closely tied to conditional probability is *probabilistic independence*. We just saw how the probability of an event A can depend on whether another event B has occurred. Typically, the probabilities $P(A)$, $P(A|B)$, and $P(A|\overline{B})$ are all different, as in Example 5.1. However, there are situations where all of these probabilities are equal. In this case we say that the events A and B are independent. This does *not* mean they are mutually exclusive. Rather, **probabilistic independence** means that knowledge of one event is of no value when assessing the probability of the other.

The main advantage to knowing that two events are independent is that the multiplication rule simplifies to equation (5.5). This follows by substituting $P(A)$ for $P(A|B)$ in the multiplication rule, which we are allowed to do because of independence. In words, the probability that both events occur is the product of their individual probabilities.

Multiplication Rule for Independent Events
$$P(A \text{ and } B) = P(A)P(B) \tag{5.5}$$

How can we tell whether events *are* probabilistically independent? Unfortunately, this issue usually cannot be settled with mathematical arguments; typically, we need empirical data to decide whether independence is reasonable. As an example, let A be the event that a family's first child is male, and let B be the event that its second child is male. Are A and B independent? We would argue that they aren't independent if we believe, say, that a boy is more likely to be followed by another boy than by a girl. We would argue that they are independent if we believe the chances of the second child being a boy are the same, regardless of the gender of the first child. (Note that neither argument has anything to do with boys and girls being equally likely.)

In any case, the only way to settle the argument is to observe many families with at least two children. If we observe, say, that 55% of all families with first child male also have the second child male, and only 45% of all families with first child female have the second child male, then we can make a good case for *nonindependence* of A and B.

5.2.5 Equally Likely Events

Much of what you know about probability is probably based on situations where outcomes are equally likely. These include flipping coins, throwing dice, drawing balls from urns, and other random mechanisms that are often discussed in books on probability. For example, suppose an urn contains 20 red marbles and 10 blue marbles. We plan to randomly select 5 marbles from the urn, and we are interested, say, in the probability of selecting at least 3 red marbles. To find this probability, we argue that because of randomness, every possible group of 5 marbles is equally likely to be chosen. Then we *count* the number of groups of 5 marbles that contain at least 3 red marbles, we count the total number of groups of 5 marbles that could be selected, and we set the desired probability equal to the ratio of these two counts.

Let us put this method of calculating probabilities into proper perspective. It is true that many probabilities, particularly in games of chance, *can* be calculated by using an equally likely argument. It is also true that probabilities calculated in this way satisfy all of the rules of probability, including the rules we have already discussed. However, many probabilities, especially those in business situations, *cannot* be calculated by equally likely arguments, simply because the possible outcomes are not equally likely. For example, just because we are able to identify five possible scenarios for a company's future, there is probably no reason whatsoever to conclude that each scenario has probability 1/5.

The bottom line is that we will have almost no need in this book to discuss counting rules for equally likely outcomes. If you dreaded learning about probability in terms of balls and urns, rest assured that you will *not* do so here!

5.2.6 Subjective Versus Objective Probabilities

In this section we ask a very basic question: Where do the probabilities in a probability distribution come from? A complete answer to this question could lead to a chapter by itself, so we only briefly discuss the issues involved. There are essentially two distinct ways to assess probabilities, *objectively* and *subjectively*. **Objective probabilities** are those that can be estimated from long-run proportions, whereas **subjective probabilities** cannot be estimated from long-run proportions. Some examples will make this distinction clearer.

Consider throwing two dice and observing the sum of the two sides that face up. What is the probability that the sum of these two sides is 7? We might argue as follows. Because there are $6 \times 6 = 36$ ways the two dice can fall, and because exactly 6 of these result in a sum of 7, the probability of a 7 is $6/36 = 1/6$. This is the equally likely argument we discussed previously that reduces probability to counting.

What if the dice are weighted in some way? Then the equally likely argument is no longer valid. We can, however, toss the dice many times and record the proportion of tosses that result in a sum of 7. This proportion is called a *relative frequency*.

The **relative frequency** of an event is the proportion of times the event occurs out of the number of times the random experiment is run. A relative frequency can be recorded as a proportion or a percentage.

A famous result called the **law of large numbers** states that this relative frequency, in the long run, will get closer and closer to the "true" probability of a 7. This is exactly what we mean by an objective probability. It is a probability that can be estimated as the long-run proportion of times an event occurs in a sequence of many identical experiments.

When it comes to flipping coins, throwing dice, and spinning roulette wheels, objective probabilities are certainly relevant. We don't need a person's *opinion* of the probability that a roulette wheel, say, will end up pointing to a red number; we can simply spin it many times and keep track of the proportion of times it points to a red number. However, there are many situations, particularly in business, that cannot be repeated many times—or even more than once—under identical conditions. In these situations objective probabilities make no sense (and equally likely arguments usually make no sense either), so we must resort to subjective probabilities. A subjective probability is one person's assessment of the likelihood that a certain event will occur. We assume that the person making the assessment uses all of the information available to make the most rational assessment possible.

This definition of subjective probability implies that one person's assessment of a probability might differ from another person's assessment of the *same* probability. For example, consider the probability that the Indianapolis Colts will win the next Super Bowl. If we ask a casual football observer to assess this probability, we'll get one answer, but if we ask a person with a lot of inside information about injuries, team cohesiveness, and so on, we might get a very different answer. Because these probabilities are *subjective*, people with different information typically assess probabilities in different ways.

Subjective probabilities are usually relevant for unique, one-time situations. However, most situations are not completely unique; we usually have some history to guide us. That is, historical relative frequencies can be factored into subjective probabilities. For example, suppose a company is about to market a new product. This product might be quite different in some ways from any products the company has marketed before, but it might also share some features with the company's previous products. If the company wants to assess the probability that the new product will be a success, it will certainly analyze the unique features of this product and the current state of the market to obtain a subjective assessment. However, the company will also look at its past successes and failures with reasonably similar products. If the proportion of successes with past products was 40%, say, then this value might be a starting point in the assessment of *this* product's probability of success.

All of the "given" probabilities in this chapter and later chapters can be placed somewhere on the objective-to-subjective continuum, usually closer to the subjective end. An important implication of this placement is that these probabilities are not cast in stone; they are only educated guesses. Therefore, it is always a good idea to run a **sensitivity analysis** (especially on a spreadsheet, where this is easy to do) to see how any "bottom-line" answers depend on the "given" probabilities. Sensitivity analysis is especially important in Chapter 7, when we study decision making under uncertainty.

PROBLEMS

Level A

1. In a particular suburb, 30% of the households have installed electronic security systems.
   a. If a household is chosen at random from this suburb, what is the probability that this household has not installed an electronic security system?
   b. If two households are chosen at random from this suburb, what is the probability that *neither* has installed an electronic security system?

2. Several major automobile producers are competing to have the largest market share for sport utility vehicles in the coming quarter. A professional automobile market analyst assesses that the odds of General Motors *not* being the market leader are 6 to 1. The odds against Chrysler and Ford having the largest market share in the coming quarter are similarly assessed to be 12 to 5 and 8 to 3, respectively.
   a. Find the probability that General Motors will have the largest market share for sport utility vehicles in the coming quarter.
   b. Find the probability that Chrysler will have the largest market share for sport utility vehicles in the coming quarter.
   c. Find the probability that Ford will have the largest market share for sport utility vehicles in the coming quarter.
   d. Find the probability that some other automobile manufacturer will have the largest market share for sport utility vehicles in the coming quarter.

3. The publisher of a popular financial periodical has decided to undertake a campaign in an effort to attract new subscribers. Market research analysts in this company believe that there is a 1 in 4 chance that the increase in the number of new subscriptions resulting from this campaign will be less than 3000, and there is a 1 in 3 chance that the increase in the number of new subscriptions resulting from this campaign will be between 3000 and 5000. What is the probability that the increase in the number of new subscriptions resulting from this campaign will be less than 3000 *or* more than 5000?

4. Suppose that 18% of the employees of a given corporation engage in physical exercise activities during the lunch hour. Moreover, assume that 57% of all employees are male, and 12% of all employees are males who engage in physical exercise activities during the lunch hour.
   a. If we choose an employee at random from this corporation, what is the probability that this person is a female who engages in physical exercise activities during the lunch hour?
   b. If we choose an employee at random from this corporation, what is the probability that this person is a female who does not engage in physical exercise activities during the lunch hour?

5. In a study designed to gauge married women's participation in the workplace today, the data provided in the file **P05_05.xlsx** are obtained from a sample of 750 randomly selected married women. Consider a woman

selected at random from this sample in answering the following questions.

    a. What is the probability that this randomly selected woman has a job outside the home?

    b. What is the probability that this randomly selected woman has at least one child?

    c. What is the probability that this randomly selected woman has a full-time job and no more than one child?

    d. What is the probability that this randomly selected woman has a part-time job or at least one child, but not both?

6. Suppose that we draw a single card from a standard deck of 52 playing cards.

    a. What is the probability that a diamond *or* club is drawn?

    b. What is the probability that the drawn card is not a 4?

    c. Given that a black card has been drawn, what is the probability that it is a spade?

    d. Let E_1 be the event that a black card is drawn. Let E_2 be the event that a spade is drawn. Are E_1 and E_2 independent events? Why or why not?

    e. Let E_3 be the event that a heart is drawn. Let E_4 be the event that a 3 is drawn. Are E_3 and E_4 independent events? Why or why not?

Level B

7. In a large accounting firm, the proportion of accountants with MBA degrees and at least 5 years of professional experience is 75% as large as the proportion of accountants with no MBA degree and less than 5 years of professional experience. Furthermore, 35% of the accountants in this firm have MBA degrees, and 45% have less than 5 years of professional experience. If one of the firm's accountants is selected at random, what is the probability that this accountant has an MBA degree or at least 5 years of professional experience, but not both?

8. A local beer producer sells two types of beer, a regular brand and a light brand with 30% fewer calories. The company's marketing department wants to verify that its traditional approach of appealing to local white-collar workers with light beer commercials and appealing to local blue-collar workers with regular beer commercials is indeed a good strategy. A randomly selected group of 400 local workers are questioned about their beer-drinking preferences, and the data in the file **P05_08.xlsx** are obtained.

    a. If a blue-collar worker is chosen at random from this group, what is the probability that she or he prefers light beer (to regular beer or no beer at all)?

    b. If a white-collar worker is chosen at random from this group, what is the probability that she or he prefers light beer (to regular beer or no beer at all)?

    c. If we restrict our attention to workers who like to drink beer, what is the probability that a randomly selected blue-collar worker prefers to drink light beer?

    d. If we restrict our attention to workers who like to drink beer, what is the probability that a randomly selected white-collar worker prefers to drink light beer?

    e. Does the company's marketing strategy appear to be appropriate? Explain why or why not.

9. Suppose that two dice are tossed. For each die, it is equally likely that 1, 2, 3, 4, 5, or 6 dots will show.

    a. What is the probability that the sum of the dots on the uppermost faces of the two dice will be 5 or 7?

    b. What is the probability that the sum of the dots on the uppermost faces of the two dice will be some number other than 4 or 8?

    c. Let E_1 be the event that the first die shows a 3. Let E_2 be the event that the sum of the dots on the uppermost faces of the two dice is 6. Are E_1 and E_2 independent events?

    d. Again, let E_1 be the event that the first die shows a 3. Let E_3 be the event that the sum of the dots on the uppermost faces of the two dice is 7. Are E_1 and E_3 independent events?

    e. Given that the sum of the dots on the uppermost faces of the two dice is 7, what is the probability that the first die showed 4 dots?

    f. Given that the first die shows a 3, what is the probability that the sum of the dots on the uppermost faces of the two dice is an even number?

5.3 DISTRIBUTION OF A SINGLE RANDOM VARIABLE

We now discuss the topic of most interest in this chapter, *probability distributions*. In this section we examine the probability distribution of a single random variable. In later sections we discuss probability distributions of two or more related random variables.

There are really two types of random variables: *discrete* and *continuous*. A **discrete random variable** has only a finite number of possible values, whereas a **continuous random variable** has a continuum of possible values.[1] As an example, consider demand for televisions.

[1]Actually, a more rigorous discussion allows a discrete random variable to have an infinite number of possible values, such as all positive integers. The only time this occurs in this book is when we discuss the Poisson distribution in Chapter 6.

Is this discrete or continuous? Strictly speaking, it is discrete because the number of televisions demanded must be an integer. However, because the number of possible demand values is probably quite large—all integers between 1000 and 5000, say—it might be easier to treat demand as a continuous random variable. On the other hand, for reasons of simplicity we might go the other direction and treat demand as discrete with only a few possible values, such as 1000, 2000, 3000, 4000, and 5000. This is obviously an approximation to reality, but it might suffice for all practical purposes.

Mathematically, there is an important difference between discrete and continuous probability distributions. Specifically, a proper treatment of continuous distributions, analogous to the treatment we will provide in this chapter, requires calculus—which we do not presume for this book. Therefore, we discuss only discrete distributions in this chapter. In later chapters we often *use* continuous distributions, particularly the bell-shaped normal distribution, but we simply state their properties without trying to derive them mathematically.

The essential properties of a discrete random variable and its associated probability distribution are quite simple. We discuss them in general and then analyze a numerical example. Let X be a random variable. (Usually, capital letters toward the end of the alphabet, such as X, Y, and Z, are used to denote random variables.)

To specify the probability distribution of X, we need to specify its possible values and their probabilities. We assume that there are k possible values, denoted $v_1, v_2, \ldots, v_k$. The probability of a typical value v_i is denoted in one of two ways, either $P(X = v_i)$ or $p(v_i)$. The first reminds us that this is a probability involving the random variable X, whereas the second is a simpler "shorthand" notation. Probability distributions must satisfy two criteria: (1) they mus be nonnegative, and (2) they must sum to 1. In symbols, we must have

$$\sum_{i=1}^{k} p(v_i) = 1, \quad p(v_i) \geq 0$$

A discrete distribution is simply a set of possible values and a corresponding set of nonnegative probabilities that sum to 1.

This is basically all there is to it: a list of possible values and a list of associated probabilities that sum to 1. Although this list of probabilities completely determines a probability distribution, it is sometimes useful to calculate *cumulative* probabilities. A **cumulative probability** is the probability that the random variable is *less than or equal to* some particular value. For example, assume that 10, 20, 30, and 40 are the possible values of a random variable X, with corresponding probabilities 0.15, 0.25, 0.35, and 0.25. Then a typical cumulative probability is $P(X \leq 30)$. From the addition rule it can be calculated as

$$P(X \leq 30) = P(X = 10) + P(X = 20) + P(X = 30) = 0.75$$

It is often convenient to summarize a probability distribution with two or three well-chosen numbers. The first of these is the *mean*, usually denoted μ. It is also called the *expected value* of X and denoted $E(X)$ (for *expected X*). The **mean** is a weighted sum of the possible values, weighted by their probabilities, as shown in equation (5.6). In much the same way that an average of a set of numbers indicates "central location," the mean indicates the center of the probability distribution. We see this more clearly when we analyze a numerical example.

Mean of a Probability Distribution, μ

$$\mu = E(X) = \sum_{i=1}^{k} v_i p(v_i) \tag{5.6}$$

To measure the variability in a distribution, we calculate its *variance* or *standard deviation*. The **variance**, denoted by σ^2 or Var(X), is a weighted sum of the squared deviations of the possible values from the mean, where the weights are again the probabilities. This is shown in equation (5.7). As in Chapter 3, the variance is expressed in the *square* of the units of X, such as dollars squared. Therefore, a more natural measure of variability is the **standard deviation**, denoted by s or Stdev(X). It is the square root of the variance, as indicated by equation (5.8).

Variance of a Probability Distribution, σ^2

$$\sigma^2 = \text{Var}(X) = \sum_{i=1}^{k} (v_i - E(X))^2 \, p(v_i) \qquad (5.7)$$

Standard Deviation of a Probability Distribution, σ

$$\sigma = \text{Stdev}(X) = \sqrt{\text{Var}(X)} \qquad (5.8)$$

We now consider a typical example.

EXAMPLE | 5.2 MARKET RETURN SCENARIOS FOR THE NATIONAL ECONOMY

In reality, there is a continuum of possible returns. Her assumption of only five possible returns is clearly an approximation to reality, but such an assumption is often made.

An investor is concerned with the market return for the coming year, where the market return is defined as the percentage gain (or loss, if negative) over the year. The investor believes there are five possible scenarios for the national economy in the coming year: rapid expansion, moderate expansion, no growth, moderate contraction, and serious contraction. Furthermore, she has used all of the information available to her to estimate that the market returns for these scenarios are, respectively, 0.23, 0.18, 0.15, 0.09, and 0.03. That is, the possible returns vary from a high of 23% to a low of 3%. Also, she has assessed that the probabilities of these outcomes are 0.12, 0.40, 0.25, 0.15, and 0.08. Use this information to describe the probability distribution of the market return.

Objective To compute the mean, variance, and standard deviation of the probability distribution of the market return for the coming year.

Solution

To make the connection between the general notation and this particular example, we let X denote the market return for the coming year. Then each possible economic scenario leads to a possible value of X. For example, the first possible value is $v_1 = 0.23$, and its probability is $p(v_1) = 0.12$. These values and probabilities appear in columns B and C of Figure 5.3.[2] (See the file **Market Return.xlsx**.) Note that the five probabilities sum to 1, as they should. This probability distribution implies, for example, that the probability of a market return at least as large as 0.18 is $0.12 + 0.40 = 0.52$ because it could occur as a result of rapid or moderate expansion of the economy. Similarly, the probability that the market return is 0.09 or less is $0.15 + 0.08 = 0.23$ because this could occur as a result of moderate or serious contraction of the economy.

---

[2]From here on, we often shade the given inputs in the spreadsheet figures blue so that you can immediately tell which cells contain inputs. This shading comes through clearly in the Excel files. On the printed page, the shading is a light blue.

Figure 5.3 Probability Distribution of Market Returns

	A	B	C	D	E	F	G	H
1	Mean, variance, and standard deviation of the market return					Range names Used		
2						Market_return	=Market!$C$4:$C$8	
3	Economic outcome	Probability	Market return	Sq dev from mean		Mean	=Market!$B$11	
4	Rapid Expansion	0.12	0.23	0.005929		Probability	=Market!$B$4:$B$8	
5	Moderate Expansion	0.40	0.18	0.000729		Sq_dev_from_mean	=Market!$D$4:$D$8	
6	No Growth	0.25	0.15	0.000009		Stdev	=Market!$B$13	
7	Moderate Contraction	0.15	0.09	0.003969		Variance	=Market!$B$12	
8	Serious Contraction	0.08	0.03	0.015129				
9								
10	Summary measures of return							
11	Mean	0.153						
12	Variance	0.002811						
13	Stdev	0.053						

The summary measures of this probability distribution appear in the range B11:B13. They can be calculated with the following steps.

PROCEDURE FOR CALCULATING SUMMARY MEASURES

1 **Mean return.** Calculate the mean return in cell B11 with the formula

=SUMPRODUCT(Market_return,Probability)

Excel Tip *Excel's SUMPRODUCT function is a gem, and you should use it whenever possible. It takes (at least) two arguments, which must be ranges of exactly the same size and shape. It sums the products of the values in these ranges. For example, =SUMPRODUCT(A1:A3,B1:B3) is equivalent to the formula =A1*B1+A2*B2+A3*B3. If the ranges contain only a few cells, there isn't much advantage to using SUMPRODUCT, but when the ranges are large, such as A1:A100 and B1:B100, SUMPRODUCT is the only viable choice.*

This formula illustrates the general rule in equation (5.6): The mean is the sum of products of possible values and probabilities.

2 **Squared deviations.** To get ready to compute the variance, calculate the squared deviations from the mean by entering the formula

=(C4-Mean)^2

in cell D4 and copying it down through cell D8.

3 **Variance.** Calculate the variance of the market return in cell B12 with the formula

=SUMPRODUCT(Sq_dev_from_mean,Probability)

As always, range names are not required, but they make the Excel formulas easier to read. You can use them or omit them, as you wish.

This illustrates the general formula for variance in equation (5.7): The variance is always a sum of products of squared deviations from the mean and probabilities.

4 **Standard deviation.** Calculate the standard deviation of the market return in cell B13 with the formula

=SQRT(Variance)

We see that the mean return is 15.3% and the standard deviation is 5.3%. What do these measures really mean? First, the mean, or *expected,* return does not imply that the most likely return is 15.3%, nor is this the value that the investor "expects" to occur. In fact, the value 15.3% is not even a possible market return (at least not according to the model). We can understand these measures better in terms of long-run averages. That is, if we could imagine the coming year being repeated many times, each time using the probability distribution in columns B and C to generate a market return, then the average of these market returns would be close to 15.3%, and their standard deviation—calculated as in Chapter 3—would be close to 5.3%. ∎

PROBLEMS

Level A

10. A fair coin (i.e., heads and tails are equally likely) is tossed three times. Let X be the number of heads observed in three tosses of this fair coin.
   a. Find the probability distribution of X.
   b. Find the probability that two or fewer heads are observed in three tosses.
   c. Find the probability that at least one head is observed in three tosses.
   d. Find the expected value of X.
   e. Find the standard deviation of X.

11. Consider a random variable with the following probability distribution: $P(X = 0) = 0.1$, $P(X = 1) = 0.2$, $P(X = 2) = 0.3$, $P(X = 3) = 0.3$, and $P(X = 4) = 0.1$.
   a. Find $P(X \leq 2)$.
   b. Find $P(1 < X \leq 3)$.
   c. Find $P(X > 0)$.
   d. Find $P(X > 3 | X > 2)$.
   e. Find the expected value of X.
   f. Find the standard deviation of X.

12. A study has shown that the probability distribution of X, the number of customers in line (including the one being served, if any) at a checkout counter in a department store, is given by $P(X = 0) = 0.25$, $P(X = 1) = 0.25$, $P(X = 2) = 0.20$, $P(X = 3) = 0.20$, and $P(X \geq 4) = 0.10$. Consider a newly arriving customer to the checkout line.
   a. What is the probability that this customer will not have to wait behind anyone?
   b. What is the probability that this customer will have to wait behind at least one customer?
   c. On average, behind how many other customers will the newly arriving customer have to wait?

13. A construction company has to complete a project no later than 3 months from now or there will be significant cost overruns. The manager of the construction company believes that there are four possible values for the random variable X, the number of months from now it will take to complete this project: 2, 2.5, 3, and 3.5.

The manager currently thinks that the probabilities of these four possibilities are in the ratio 1 to 2 to 4 to 2. That is, $X = 2.5$ is twice as likely as $X = 2$, $X = 3$ is twice as likely as $X = 2.5$, and $X = 3.5$ is half as likely as $X = 3$.
   a. Find the probability distribution of X.
   b. What is the probability that this project will be completed in less than 3 months from now?
   c. What is the probability that this project will *not* be completed on time?
   d. What is the expected completion time (in months) of this project from now?
   e. How much variability (in months) exists around the expected value you found in part **d**?

14. A corporate executive officer is attempting to arrange a meeting of his three vice presidents for tomorrow morning. He believes that each of these three busy individuals, independently of the others, has about a 60% chance of being able to attend the meeting.
   a. Find the probability distribution of X, the number of vice presidents who can attend the meeting.
   b. What is the probability that none of the three vice presidents can attend the meeting?
   c. If the meeting will be held tomorrow morning only if everyone can attend, what is the probability that the meeting will take place at that time?
   d. How many of the vice presidents should the CEO expect to be available for tomorrow morning's meeting?

Level B

15. Several students enrolled in a finance course subscribe to *Money* magazine. If two students are selected at random from this class, the probability that neither of the chosen students subscribes to *Money* is 0.81. Furthermore, the probability of selecting one student who subscribes and one student who does not subscribe to this magazine is 0.18. Finally, the probability of selecting two students who subscribe to *Money* is 0.01. Let X be the number of students who subscribe to *Money* magazine from the two selected at random. Find the mean and standard deviation of X.

16. The "house edge" in any game of chance is defined as

$$\frac{E(\text{player's loss on a bet})}{\text{Size of player's loss on a bet}}$$

For example, if a player wins $10 with probability 0.48 and loses $10 with probability 0.52 on any bet,

then the house edge is

$$\frac{-[10(0.48) - 10(0.52)]}{10} = 0.04$$

Give an interpretation to the house edge that relates to how much money the house is likely to win on average. Which do you think has a larger house edge: roulette or sports gambling? Why?

5.4 AN INTRODUCTION TO SIMULATION

In the previous section we asked you to imagine many repetitions of an event, with each repetition resulting in a different random outcome. Fortunately, we can do more than *imagine;* we can make it happen with computer *simulation.* Simulation is an extremely useful tool that can be used to incorporate uncertainty explicitly into spreadsheet models. As we see, a simulation model is the same as a regular spreadsheet model except that some cells include random quantities. Each time the spreadsheet recalculates, new values of the random quantities occur, and these typically lead to different "bottom-line" results. By forcing the spreadsheet to recalculate many times, a business manager is able to discover the results that are most likely to occur, those that are least likely to occur, and best-case and worst-case results. We use simulation in several places in this book to help explain difficult concepts in probability and statistics. We begin in this section by using simulation to explain the connection between summary measures of probability distributions and the corresponding summary measures from Chapter 3.

We continue to use the market return distribution in Figure 5.3 from Example 5.2. Because this is our first discussion of computer simulation in Excel, we proceed in some detail. Our goal is to simulate many returns (we arbitrarily choose 400) from this distribution and analyze the resulting returns. We want each simulated return to have probability 0.12 of being 0.23, probability 0.40 of being 0.18, and so on. Then, using the methods for summarizing data from Chapter 3, we calculate the average and standard deviation of the 400 simulated returns.

The method for simulating many market returns is straightforward once we know how to simulate a *single* market return. The key to this is Excel's RAND function, which generates a random number between 0 and 1. The RAND function has no arguments, so every time we call it, we enter RAND().[3] (Although there is nothing inside the parentheses next to RAND, the parentheses cannot be omitted.) That is, to generate a random number between 0 and 1 in any cell, we enter the formula

=RAND()

in that cell. The RAND function can also be used as part of another function. For example, we can simulate the result of a single flip of a fair coin by entering the formula

=IF(RAND()<=0.5,"Heads","Tails")

Random numbers generated with Excel's RAND function are said to be **uniformly distributed** between 0 and 1 because all decimal values between 0 and 1 are equally likely. These uniformly distributed random numbers can then be used to generate numbers from

---

[3]Before Excel 2007, RAND was the only built-in function for generating random numbers. There is a new function in Excel 2007, RANDBETWEEN. It generates a random integer within a given range. For example, =RANDBETWEEN(1,6) generates a random integer from 1 to 6, with all values equally likely. This could be used to simulate the roll of a single die.

any discrete distribution such as the market return distribution in Figure 5.3. To see how this is done, note first that there are five possible values in this distribution. Therefore, we divide the interval from 0 to 1 into five parts with lengths equal to the probabilities in the probability distribution. Then we see which of these parts the random number from RAND falls into and generate the associated market return. If the random number is between 0 and 0.12 (of length 0.12), we generate 0.23 as the market return; if the random number is between 0.12 and 0.52 (of length 0.40), we generate 0.18 as the market return; and so on. See Figure 5.4.

Figure 5.4 Associating RAND Values with Market Returns

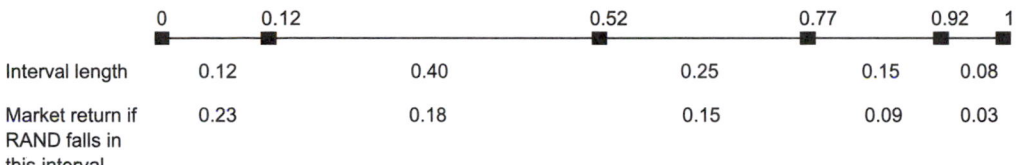

This procedure is accomplished most easily in Excel through the use of a *lookup table*. Lookup tables are useful when we want to compare a particular value to a set of values, and depending on where the particular value falls, assign a given "answer" or value from an associated list of values. In this case we want to compare a generated random number to values (between 0 and 1) falling in each of the five intervals shown in Figure 5.4, and then report the corresponding market return. This process is made relatively simple in Excel by applying the VLOOKUP function, as explained in the following steps.[4] (Refer to Figure 5.5 and the **Market Return.xlsx** file.)

Figure 5.5 Simulation of Market Returns

	A	B	C	D	E	F	G	H	I
1	Simulating market returns					Range names used			
2						LTable	=Simulation!$D$13:$E$17		
3	Summary statistics from simulation below					Simulated_market_return	=Simulation!$B$13:$B$412		
4	Average return	0.153							
5	Stdev of returns	0.054							
6									
7	Exact values from previous sheet (for comparison)								
8	Average return	0.153							
9	Stdev of returns	0.053							
10									
11	Simulation			Lookup table					
12	Random #	Simulated market return		Cum Prob	Return				
13	0.408942	0.18		0	0.23				
14	0.967120	0.03		0.12	0.18				
15	0.781840	0.09		0.52	0.15				
16	0.121152	0.18		0.77	0.09				
17	0.674945	0.15		0.92	0.03				
18	0.675920	0.15							
19	0.625830	0.15							
410	0.899577	0.09							
411	0.983381	0.03							
412	0.939450	0.03							

[4]This could also be accomplished with nested IF functions, but the resulting formula would be much more complex.

PROCEDURE FOR GENERATING RANDOM MARKET RETURNS IN EXCEL

1 **Lookup table.** Copy the possible returns to the range E13:E17. Then enter the *cumulative* probabilities next to them in the range D13:D17. To do this, enter the value 0 in cell D13. Then enter the formula

=D13+Market!B4

in cell D14 and copy it down through cell D17. (Note that the Market!B4 in this formula refers to cell B4 in the Market sheet, that is, cell B4 in Figure 5.3.) Each value in column D is the current probability plus the previous value. The table in this range, D13:E17, becomes the lookup range. For convenience, we have named this range LTable.

2 **Random numbers.** Enter random numbers in the range A13:A412. An easy way to do this is to highlight the range, then type the formula

=RAND()

and finally press Ctrl-Enter. Note that these random numbers are "live." That is, each time you do any calculation in Excel or press the recalculation key (the F9 key), these random numbers change.

Excel Tip *A quick way to enter a formula (or value) into a range of cells is to highlight the range, type in the formula (or value), and press Ctrl-Enter (both keys at once). This is equivalent to entering the formula in the first cell of the range in the usual way and then copying it to the rest of the range.*

3 **Market returns.** Generate the random market returns by referring the random numbers in column A to the lookup table. Specifically, enter the formula

=VLOOKUP(A13,LTable,2)

in cell B13 and copy it down through cell B412. This formula compares the random number in cell A13 to the cumulative probabilities in the first column of the lookup table and sees where it "fits," as illustrated in Figure 5.4. Then it returns the corresponding market return in the second column of the lookup table. (It uses the *second* column because we set the third argument of the VLOOKUP function to 2.)

Excel Tip *In general, the VLOOKUP function takes three arguments: (1) the value to be compared, (2) a table of lookup values, with the values to be compared against always in the leftmost column, and (3) the column number of the lookup table where we find the "answer." (It also takes a fourth optional argument, not needed here. You can look it up in online help.)*

4 **Summary statistics.** Summarize the 400 market returns by entering the formulas

=AVERAGE(Simulated_market_return)

and

=STDEV(Simulated_market_return)

in cells B4 and B5. For comparison, copy the average and standard deviation from the Market sheet in Figure 5.3 to cells B8 and B9.

Now let's step back and see what we've accomplished. The following points are relevant.

- Simulations such as this are very common, and we continue to use them to illustrate concepts in probability and statistics.

- The numbers you obtain will be different from the ones in Figure 5.5 because of the nature of simulation. The results depend on the particular random numbers that happen to be generated.

- The way we entered cumulative probabilities and then used a lookup table is generally the best way to generate random numbers from a discrete probability distribution. However, there is an easier way if a simulation add-in is available. We discuss this in Chapter 16.

- Each generated market return in the Simulated_market_return range is one of the five possible market returns. If you count the number of times each return appears and then divide by 400, the number of simulated values, you will see that the resulting fractions are *approximately* equal to the original probabilities. For example, the fraction of times the highest return 0.23 appears is about 0.12. This is the essence of what it means to simulate from a given probability distribution.

- The average and standard deviation in cells B4 and B5, calculated from the formulas in Chapter 3, are very close to the mean and standard deviation of the probability distribution in cells B8 and B9. Note, however, that these measures are calculated in entirely different ways. For example, the average in cell B4 is a simple average of 400 numbers, whereas the mean in cell B8 is a weighted sum of the possible market returns, weighted by their probabilities.

This last point allows us to interpret the summary measures of a probability distribution. Specifically, the mean and standard deviation of a probability distribution are approximately what we would obtain if we calculated the average and standard deviation, using the formulas from Chapter 3, of many simulated values from this distribution. In other words, the mean is the long-run average of the simulated values. Similarly, the standard deviation measures their variability.

You might ask whether this long-run average interpretation of the mean is relevant if the situation is going to occur only once. For example, the market return in the example is for "the coming year," and the coming year is going to occur only once. So what is the use of a long-run average? In this type of situation, the long-run average interpretation is probably *not* very relevant, but fortunately, there is another use of the expected value that we exploit in Chapter 7—namely, when a decision maker must choose among several actions that have uncertain outcomes, the preferred decision is often the one with the largest expected (monetary) value. This makes the expected value of a probability distribution extremely important in decision-making contexts.

PROBLEMS

Level A

17. A personnel manager of a large manufacturing plant is investigating the number of reported on-the-job accidents at the facility over the past several years. Let X be the number of such accidents reported during a 1-month period. Based on past records, the manager has established the probability distribution for X as shown in the file **P05_17.xlsx**.
  a. Generate 400 values of this random variable X with the given probability distribution using simulation.
  b. Compare the distribution of simulated values to the given probability distribution. Is the simulated distribution indicative of the given probability distribution? Explain why or why not.

18. A quality inspector picks a sample of 15 items at random from a manufacturing process known to produce 10% defective items. Let X be the number of defective items found in the random sample of 15 items. Assume that the condition of each item is independent of that of each of the other items in the sample. The probability distribution of X is provided in the file **P05_18.xlsx**.
  a. Generate 500 values of this random variable with the given probability distribution using simulation.
  b. Compute the mean and standard deviation of the distribution of simulated values. How do these summary measures compare to the mean and standard deviation of the given probability distribution?

19. The file **P05_19.xlsx** gives the probability distribution for the number of job applications processed at a small employment agency during a typical week.

a. Generate 400 values of this random variable with the given probability distribution using simulation.

b. Compute the mean and standard deviation of the distribution of simulated values. How do these summary measures compare to the mean and standard deviation of the given probability distribution?

c. Use your simulated distribution to find the probability that the weekly number of job applications processed will be within two standard deviations of the mean.

20. Consider a random variable with the following probability distribution: $P(X = 0) = 0.1$, $P(X = 1) = 0.2$, $P(X = 2) = 0.3$, $P(X = 3) = 0.3$, and $P(X = 4) = 0.1$.

a. Generate 400 values of this random variable with the given probability distribution using simulation.

b. Compare the distribution of simulated values to the given probability distribution. Is the simulated distribution indicative of the given probability distribution? Explain why or why not.

c. Compute the mean and standard deviation of the distribution of simulated values. How do these summary measures compare to the mean and standard deviation of the given probability distribution?

21. The probability distribution of X, the number of customers in line (including the one being served, if any) at a checkout counter in a department store, is given

by $P(X = 0) = 0.25$, $P(X = 1) = 0.25$, $P(X = 2) = 0.20$, $P(X = 3) = 0.20$, and $P(X = 4) = 0.10$.

a. Generate 500 values of this random variable with the given probability distribution using simulation.

b. Compare the distribution of simulated values to the given probability distribution. Is the simulated distribution indicative of the given probability distribution? Explain why or why not.

c. Compute the mean and standard deviation of the distribution of simulated values. How do these summary measures compare to the mean and standard deviation of the given probability distribution?

Level B

22. Betting on a football point spread works as follows. Suppose Michigan is favored by 17.5 points over Indiana. If you bet a "unit" on Indiana and Indiana loses by 17 or less, you win $10. If Indiana loses by 18 or more points, you lose $11. Find the mean and standard deviation of your winnings on a single bet. Assume that there is a 0.5 probability that you will win your bet and a 0.5 probability that you will lose your bet. Also simulate 1600 "bets" to estimate the average loss per bet. (*Note*: Do not be too disappointed if you are off by up to 50 cents. It takes many, say 10,000, simulated bets to get a really good estimate of the mean loss per bet because there is a lot of variability on each bet.)

5.5 DISTRIBUTION OF TWO RANDOM VARIABLES: SCENARIO APPROACH[5]

We now turn to the distribution of two related random variables. In this section we discuss the situation where the two random variables are related in the sense that they both depend on which of several possible scenarios occurs. In the next section we discuss a second way of relating two random variables probabilistically. These two methods differ slightly in the way they assign probabilities to different outcomes. However, for both methods there are two summary measures, *covariance* and *correlation,* that measure the relationship between the two random variables. As with the mean, variance, and standard deviation, covariance and correlation are similar to the measures with the same names from Chapter 3, but they are conceptually different. In Chapter 3, correlation and covariance were calculated from data; here they are calculated from a probability distribution.

If the random variables are X and Y, then we denote the covariance and correlation between X and Y by Cov(X, Y) and Corr(X, Y). These are defined by equations (5.9) and (5.10). Here, $p(x_i, y_i)$ in equation (5.9) is the probability that X and Y equal the values x_i and y_i, respectively; it is called a **joint probability**.

Formula for Covariance

$$\text{Cov}(X, Y) = \sum_{i=1}^{k} (x_i - E(X))(y_i - E(Y))p(x_i, y_i) \tag{5.9}$$

[5]The rest of this chapter can be skipped. Although it is useful material, it is not used in the rest of the book.

Formula for Correlation

$$\text{Corr}(X,\ Y) = \frac{\text{Cov}(X,\ Y)}{\text{Stdev}(X) \times \text{Stdev}(Y)} \qquad (5.10)$$

Although covariance and correlation based on a joint probability distribution are calculated differently than for known data, their interpretation is essentially the same as that discussed in Chapter 3. Each indicates the strength of a linear relationship between X and Y. That is, if X and Y tend to vary in the *same* direction, then both measures are positive. If they vary in *opposite* directions, both measures are negative. As before, the magnitude of the covariance is more difficult to interpret because it depends on the units of measurement of X and Y. However, the correlation is always between -1 and $+1$.

The following example illustrates the scenario approach, as well as covariance and correlation. Simulation is used to explain the relationship between the covariance and correlation as defined here and the similar measures from Chapter 3.

EXAMPLE   **5.3 ANALYZING A PORTFOLIO OF INVESTMENTS IN GM STOCK AND GOLD**

An investor plans to invest in General Motors (GM) stock and in gold. He assumes that the returns on these investments over the next year depend on the general state of the economy during the year. To keep things simple, he identifies four possible states of the economy: depression, recession, normal, and boom. Also, given the most up-to-date information he can obtain, he assumes that these four states have probabilities 0.05, 0.30, 0.50, and 0.15. For each state of the economy, he estimates the resulting return on GM stock and the return on gold. These appear in the shaded section of Figure 5.6. (See the file **GM vs Gold.xlsx**.) For example, if there is a depression, the investor estimates that GM stock will decrease by 20% and the price of gold will increase by 5%. The investor wants to analyze the joint distribution of returns on these two investments. He also wants to analyze the distribution of a portfolio of investments in GM stock and gold.

Objective   To obtain the relevant joint distribution and use it to calculate the covariance and correlation between returns on the two given investments.

As in the previous example, this assumption of discreteness is clearly an approximation to reality.

Solution

To obtain the joint distribution, we use the distribution of GM return, defined by columns B and C of the shaded region in Figure 5.6, and the distribution of gold return, defined by columns B and D. The scenario approach applies because a given state of the economy determines *both* GM and gold returns, so that only four pairs of returns are possible. For example, -0.20 is a possible GM return and 0.09 is a possible gold return, but they cannot occur simultaneously. The only possible *pairs* of returns, according to our assumptions, are -0.20 and 0.05; 0.10 and 0.20; 0.30 and -0.12; and 0.50 and 0.09. These possible pairs have the joint probabilities shown in column B.

To calculate means, variances, and standard deviations, we treat GM and gold returns separately. For example, the formula for the mean GM return in cell B10 is

=SUMPRODUCT(C4:C7,$B$4:$B$7)

The only new calculations in Figure 5.6 involve the covariance and correlation between GM and gold returns. To obtain these, we use the following steps.

Figure 5.6

Distribution of GM
and Gold Returns

	A	B	C	D	E
1	Calculating covariance and correlation between two random variables				
2					
3	Economic outcome	Probability	GM Return	Gold Return	
4	Depression	0.05	-0.20	0.05	
5	Recession	0.30	0.10	0.20	
6	Normal	0.50	0.30	-0.12	
7	Boom	0.15	0.50	0.09	
8					
9		GM	Gold		
10	Means	0.245	0.016		
11					
12		Deviations from means		Sq devs from means	
13		GM	Gold	GM	Gold
14	Depression	-0.45	0.03	0.1980	0.0012
15	Recession	-0.15	0.18	0.0210	0.0339
16	Normal	0.06	-0.14	0.0030	0.0185
17	Boom	0.26	0.07	0.0650	0.0055
18					
19		GM	Gold		
20	Variances	0.0275	0.0203		
21	Stdevs	0.166	0.142		
22					
23	Covariance	-0.0097			
24	Correlation	-0.410			

PROCEDURE FOR CALCULATING THE COVARIANCE AND CORRELATION

We could again use range names, but there would be too many of them. Besides, sometimes it is easier to copy formulas when range names are not used.

1 **Deviations between means.** The formula for covariance [equation (5.9)] is a weighted sum of deviations from means (not squared deviations), so we first need to calculate these deviations. To do this, enter the formula

=C4-B\$10

in cell B14 and copy it to the range B14:C17. Note how the use of the mixed relative/absolute address permits copying to the whole range.

2 **Covariance.** Calculate the covariance between GM and gold returns in cell B23 with the formula

=SUMPRODUCT(B14:B17,C14:C17,B4:B7)

Note the use of the SUMPRODUCT function in this formula. It usually takes two range arguments, but it is allowed to take more than two, all of which must have exactly the same dimension. This function multiplies corresponding elements from each of the three ranges and sums these products—exactly as prescribed by equation (5.9).

3 **Correlation.** Calculate the correlation between GM and gold returns in cell B24 with the formula

=B23/(B21*C21)

as prescribed by equation (5.10).

The negative covariance indicates that GM and gold returns tend to vary in opposite directions, although it is difficult to judge the strength of the relationship between them by the magnitude of the covariance. The correlation of -0.410, on the other hand, is also negative and indicates a moderately strong relationship. We can't rely too much on this correlation, however, because the relationship between GM and gold returns is *not* linear. From the values in the range C4:D7, we see that GM does better and better as the economy improves, whereas gold does better, then worse, then better.

Figure 5.7

Simulation of GM and Gold Returns

	A	B	C	D	E	F	G
1	Simulating GM and Gold returns						
2							
3	Summary measures from simulation below						
4		GM	Gold				
5	Means	0.241	0.019				
6	Stdevs	0.167	0.143				
7							
8	Covariance	-0.0100					
9	Correlation	-0.419					
10							
11	Exact results from previous sheet (for comparison)						
12		GM	Gold				
13	Means	0.245	0.016				
14	Stdevs	0.166	0.142				
15							
16	Covariance	-0.0097					
17	Correlation	-0.410					
18							
19	Simulation results				Lookup table for generating returns		
20	Random #	GM return	Gold return		CumProb	GM return	Gold return
21	0.9246150	0.50	0.09		0	-0.20	0.05
22	0.3945293	0.30	-0.12		0.05	0.10	0.20
23	0.7069285	0.30	-0.12		0.35	0.30	-0.12
24	0.2338176	0.10	0.20		0.85	0.50	0.09
25	0.1057734	0.10	0.20				
26	0.4402838	0.30	-0.12				
418	0.8915211	0.50	0.09				
419	0.8919036	0.50	0.09				
420	0.1530234	0.10	0.20				

This simulation is not necessary for the calculation of the covariance and correlation, but it provides some insight into their meaning.

A simulation of GM and gold returns sheds some light on the covariance and correlation measures. This simulation is shown in Figure 5.7. There are two keys to this simulation. First, we simulate the states of the economy, not—at least not directly—the GM and gold returns. For example, any random number between 0.05 and 0.35 implies a recession. The returns for GM and gold from a recession are then known to be 0.10 and 0.20. We implement this idea by entering a RAND function in cell A21 and then entering the formulas

=**VLOOKUP(A21,LTable,2)**

and

=**VLOOKUP(A21,LTable,3)**

in cells B21 and C21. These formulas are then copied down through row 420. This way, the *same* random number—hence the same scenario—is used to generate both returns in a given row, and the effect is that only four *pairs* of returns are possible.

Second, once we have the simulated returns in the range B21:C420, we can calculate the covariance and correlation of these numbers in cells B8 and B9 with the formulas[6]

=**COVAR(B21:B420,C21:C420)**

and

=**CORREL(B21:B420,C21:C420)**

[6]These formulas implement the covariance and correlation definitions from Chapter 3, not equations (5.9) and (5.10) of this chapter, because these formulas are based on given data.

Here, COVAR and CORREL are the built-in Excel functions discussed in Chapter 3 for calculating the covariance and correlation between pairs of numbers. A comparison of cells B8 and B9 with B16 and B17 shows that there is a reasonably good agreement between the covariance and correlation of the probability distribution [from equations (5.9) and (5.10)] and the measures based on the simulated values. This agreement is not perfect, but it typically improves as we simulate more pairs.

The final question in this example involves a portfolio consisting of GM stock and gold. The analysis appears in Figure 5.8. We assume that the investor has $10,000 to invest. He puts some fraction of this in GM stock (see cell B6) and the rest in gold. Of course, these fractions determine the total dollar values invested in row 7. The key to the analysis is the following. Because there are only four possible scenarios, there are only four possible portfolio returns. For example, if there is a recession, the GM and gold returns are 0.10 and 0.20, so the portfolio return (per dollar) is a weighted average of these returns, weighted by the fractions invested:

$$\text{Portfolio return in recession} = 0.6(0.10) + 0.4(0.20) = 0.14$$

Figure 5.8 Distribution of Portfolio Return

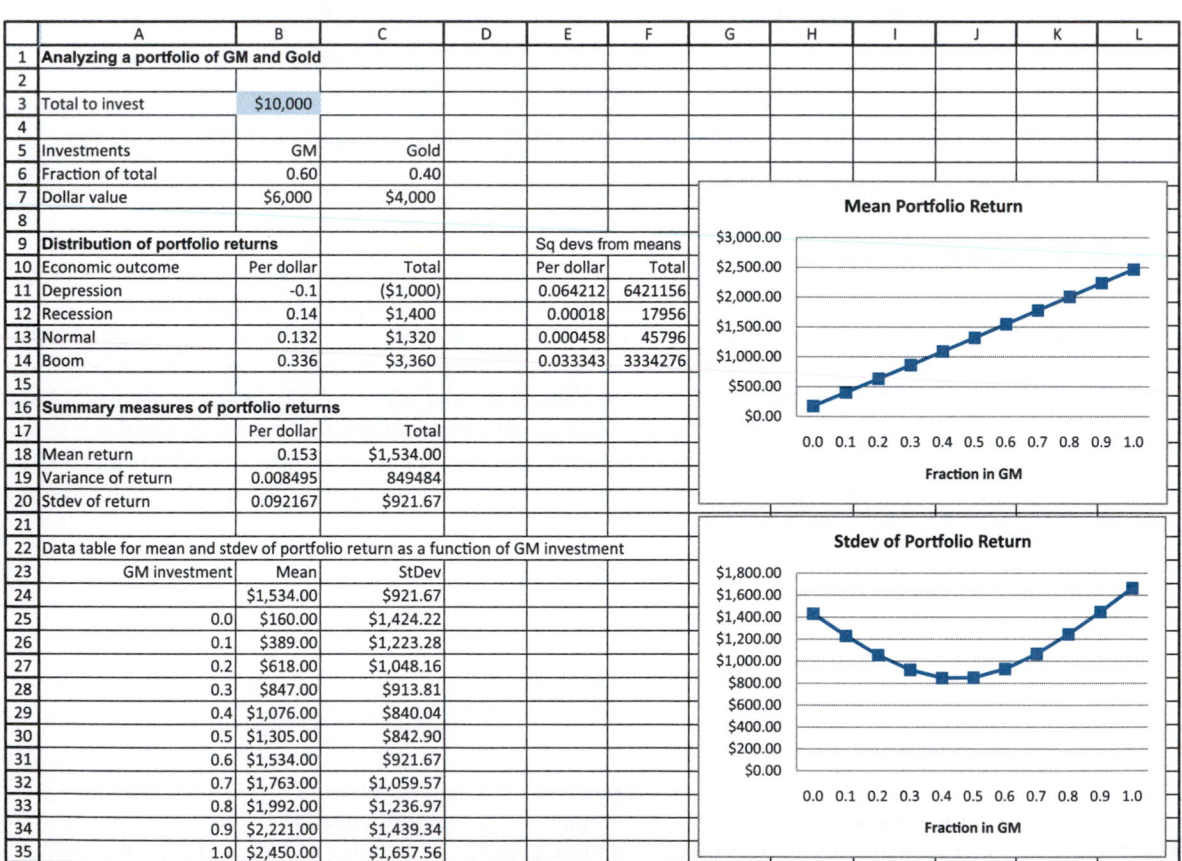

In this way, we can calculate the entire portfolio return distribution—either per dollar or total dollars—and then calculate its summary measures in the usual way. The details, which are similar to other spreadsheet calculations in this chapter, can be found in the **GM vs Gold.xlsx** file. In particular, the possible returns are listed in the ranges B11:B14 and C11:C14 of Figure 5.8, and the associated probabilities are the same as those used previously in this example. These lead to the summary measures in the range B18:C20. In particular, the investor's expected return per dollar invested is 0.153 and the standard deviation is 0.092. Based on a $10,000 investment, these translate to an expected total dollar return of $1534 and a standard deviation of $921.67.

Let's see how the expected portfolio return and the standard deviation of portfolio return change as the amount the investor puts into GM stock changes. To do this, we make sure that the value in cell B6 is a constant and that *formulas* are entered in cells C6, B7, and C7. In this way, these last three cells update automatically when the value in cell B6 changes—and the total investment amount remains $10,000. Then we form a data table in the range A24:C35 that calculates the mean and standard deviation of the total dollar portfolio return for each of several GM investment proportions in column A. (To do this, enter the formulas =C18 and =C20 in cells B24 and C24, highlight the range A24:C35, select Data Table from the What-If Analysis dropdown on the Data ribbon, and enter cell B6 as the column input cell. No row input cell is necessary.)

Recall that an Excel data table is used for "what-if" analysis. It allows us to vary an input over some range and see how one or more outputs change.

The graphs of the means and standard deviations from this data table are in Figure 5.8. They show that the expected portfolio return steadily increases as more and more is put into GM (and less is put into gold). However, the standard deviation, often used as a measure of risk, first decreases, then increases. This means there is a trade-off between expected return and risk as measured by the standard deviation. The investor could obtain a higher expected return by putting more of his money into GM, but past a fraction of approximately 0.4, the risk also increases. ■

PROBLEMS

Level A

23. The quarterly sales levels (in millions of dollars) of two U.S. retail giants are dependent on the general state of the national economy in the forthcoming months. The file **P05_23.xlsx** provides the probability distribution for the projected sales volume of each of these two retailers in the forthcoming quarter.
   a. Find the mean and standard deviation of the quarterly sales volume for each of these two retailers. Compare these two sets of summary measures.
   b. Find the covariance and correlation for the given quarterly sales volumes. Interpret your results.

24. The possible annual percentage returns of the stocks of Alpha, Inc. and Beta, Inc. are distributed as shown in the file **P05_24.xlsx**.
   a. What is the expected annual return of Alpha's stock? What is the expected annual return of Beta's stock?
   b. What is the standard deviation of the annual return of Alpha's stock? What is the standard deviation of the annual return of Beta's stock?
   c. On the basis of your answers to the questions in parts **a** and **b**, which of these two stocks would you prefer to buy? Defend your choice.
   d. Are the annual returns of these two stocks positively or negatively associated with each other? How might the answer to this question influence your decision to purchase shares of one or both of these companies?

25. The annual bonuses awarded to members of the management team and assembly-line workers of an automobile manufacturer depend largely on the corporation's sales performance during the preceding year. The file **P05_25.xlsx** contains the probability distribution of possible bonuses (measured in hundreds of dollars) awarded to white-collar and blue-collar employees at the end of the company's fiscal year.
   a. How much do a manager and an assembly-line worker expect to receive in their bonus check at the end of a typical year?
   b. For which group of employees within this organization does there appear to be more variability in the distribution of possible annual bonuses?
   c. How strongly associated are the bonuses awarded to the white-collar and blue-collar employees of this company at the end of the year? What are some possible implications of this result for the relations between members of the management team and the assembly-line workers in the future?

26. Consumer demand for small, economical automobiles depends somewhat on recent trends in the average price of unleaded gasoline. For example, consider the information given in the file **P05_26.xlsx** on the distributions of average annual sales of the Honda Civic and the Saturn SL in relation to the trend of the average price of unleaded fuel over the past 2 years.
   a. Find the annual mean sales levels of the Honda Civic and the Saturn SL.

b. For which of these two models are sales levels more sensitive to recent changes in the average price of unleaded gasoline?

c. Given the available information, how strongly associated are the annual sales volumes of these two popular compact cars? Provide a qualitative explanation of results.

Level B

27. Upon completing their respective homework assignments, marketing majors and accounting majors at a large state university enjoy hanging out at the local tavern in the evenings. The file **P05_27.xlsx** contains the distribution of number of hours spent by these students at the tavern in a typical week, along with typical cumulative grade-point averages (on a 4-point scale) for marketing and accounting students with common social habits.

a. Compare the means and standard deviations of the grade-point averages of the two groups of students. Does one of the two groups consistently perform better academically than the other? Explain.

b. Does academic performance, as measured by cumulative GPA, seem to be associated with the amount of time students typically spend at the local tavern? If so, characterize the observed relationship.

c. Find the covariance and correlation between the typical grade-point averages earned by the two subgroups of students. What do these measures of association indicate in this case?

5.6 DISTRIBUTION OF TWO RANDOM VARIABLES: JOINT PROBABILITY APPROACH

The previous section illustrated the scenario approach for specifying the joint distribution of two random variables. We first identify several possible scenarios, next specify the value of each random variable that will occur under each scenario, and then assess the probability of each scenario. For people who think in terms of scenarios—and this includes many business managers—this is a very appealing approach.

In this section we illustrate an alternative method for specifying the probability distribution of two random variables X and Y. We first identify the possible values of X and the possible values of Y. Let x and y be any two such values. Then we *directly* assess the joint probability of the pair (x, y) and denote it by $P(X = x$ and $Y = y)$ or more simply by $p(x, y)$. This is the probability of the joint event that $X = x$ and $Y = y$ both occur. As always, the joint probabilities must be nonnegative and sum to 1.

A joint probability distribution, specified by all probabilities of the form $p(x, y)$, provides a tremendous amount of information. It indicates not only how X and Y are related, but also how each of X and Y is distributed in its own right. In probability terms, the joint distribution of X and Y determines the *marginal distributions* of both X and Y, where each **marginal distribution** is the probability distribution of a *single* random variable. The joint distribution also determines the *conditional distributions* of X given Y, and of Y given X. The **conditional distribution** of X given Y, for example, is the distribution of X, given that Y is known to equal a certain value.

These concepts are best explained by means of an example, as we do next.

EXAMPLE | **5.4 UNDERSTANDING THE RELATIONSHIP BETWEEN DEMANDS FOR SUBSTITUTE PRODUCTS**

A company sells two products, product 1 and product 2, that tend to be substitutes for one another. That is, if a customer buys product 1, she tends not to buy product 2, and vice versa. The company assesses the joint probability distribution of demand for the two products during the coming month. This joint distribution appears in the shaded region of Figure 5.9. (See the Demand sheet of the file **Substitute Products.xlsx**.) The left and top margins of this table show the possible values of demand for the two products. Specifically, the company assumes that demand for product 1 can be from 100 to 400 (in increments of 100) and demand for product 2 can be from 50 to 250 (in increments of 50). Furthermore, each possible value of demand 1 can occur with each possible value of demand 2, with the joint probability given in the table. For example, the joint probability that demand 1 is 200 and demand 2 is 100 is 0.08. Given this joint probability distribution, describe more fully the probabilistic structure of demands for the two products.

Figure 5.9

Joint Probability Distribution of Demands

	A	B	C	D	E	F
1	Probability distribution of demands for substitute products					
2						
3				Demand for product 1		
4			100	200	300	400
5		50	0.015	0.040	0.050	0.035
6	Demand	100	0.030	0.080	0.075	0.025
7	for	150	0.050	0.100	0.100	0.020
8	product 2	200	0.045	0.100	0.050	0.010
9		250	0.060	0.080	0.025	0.010

Objective   To use the given joint probability distribution of demands to find the conditional distribution of demand for each product (given the demand for the other product) as well as to calculate the covariance and correlation between demands for these substitutes.

Solution

Let D_1 and D_2 denote the demands for products 1 and 2. We first find the marginal distributions of D_1 and D_2. These are the row and column sums of the joint probabilities in Figure 5.10. An example of the reasoning is as follows. Consider the probability $P(D_1 = 200)$. If demand for product 1 is to be 200, it must be accompanied by *some* value of D_2; that is, exactly one of the joint events ($D_1 = 200$ and $D_2 = 50$) through ($D_1 = 200$ and $D_2 = 250$) must occur. Using the addition rule for probability, we find the total probability of these joint events by summing the corresponding joint probabilities. The result is $P(D_1 = 200) = 0.40$, the column sum corresponding to $D_1 = 200$. Similarly, marginal probabilities for D_2 such as $P(D_2 = 150) = 0.27$ are the row sums, calculated in column G. Note that the marginal probabilities, either those in row 10 or those in column G, sum to 1, as they should. These marginal probabilities indicate how the demand for either product behaves in its own right, aside from any considerations of the *other* product.

The marginal distributions indicate that "in-between" values of D_1 or of D_2 are most likely, whereas extreme values in either direction are less likely. However, these marginal distributions tell us nothing about the *relationship* between D_1 and D_2. After all, products 1 and 2 are supposedly *substitute* products. The joint probabilities spell out this relationship, but they are rather difficult to interpret. A better way is to calculate the conditional distributions of D_1 given D_2, or of D_2 given D_1. We do this in rows 12 through 29 of Figure 5.10.

We first focus on the conditional distribution of D_1 given D_2, shown in rows 12 through 19. In each row of this table (rows 15–19), we fix the value of D_2 at the value in column B and calculate the conditional probabilities of D_1 given this fixed value of D_2. The conditional probability is the joint probability divided by the marginal probability of D_2. For example, the conditional probability that D_1 equals 200, given that D_2 equals 150, is

$$P(D_1 = 200 | D_2 = 150) = \frac{P(D_1 = 200 \text{ and } D_2 = 150)}{P(D_2 = 150)} = \frac{0.10}{0.27} = 0.37$$

This formula follows from the general conditional probability formula in Section 5.2.3.

These conditional probabilities can be calculated all at once by entering the formula

=C5/$G5

Figure 5.10

Marginal and
Conditional
Distributions and
Summary Measures

	A	B	C	D	E	F	G
1	Probability distribution of demands for substitute products						
2							
3				Demand for product 1			
4			100	200	300	400	
5		50	0.015	0.040	0.050	0.035	0.140
6	Demand	100	0.030	0.080	0.075	0.025	0.210
7	for	150	0.050	0.100	0.100	0.020	0.270
8	product 2	200	0.045	0.100	0.050	0.010	0.205
9		250	0.060	0.080	0.025	0.010	0.175
10			0.20	0.40	0.30	0.10	
11							
12	Conditional distribution of demand for product 1, given demand for product 2						
13				Demand for product 1			
14			100	200	300	400	
15		50	0.11	0.29	0.36	0.25	1.00
16	Demand	100	0.14	0.38	0.36	0.12	1.00
17	for	150	0.19	0.37	0.37	0.07	1.00
18	product 2	200	0.22	0.49	0.24	0.05	1.00
19		250	0.34	0.46	0.14	0.06	1.00
20							
21	Conditional distribution of demand for product 2, given demand for product 1						
22				Demand for product 1			
23			100	200	300	400	
24		50	0.08	0.10	0.17	0.35	
25	Demand	100	0.15	0.20	0.25	0.25	
26	for	150	0.25	0.25	0.33	0.20	
27	product 2	200	0.23	0.25	0.17	0.10	
28		250	0.30	0.20	0.08	0.10	
29			1.00	1.00	1.00	1.00	
30							
31		Product 1	Product 2				
32	Means	230.00	153.25				
33							
34	Squared deviations from means (along left and top)						
35	and products of deviations from mean (in body)						
36			16900.0	900.0	4900.0	28900.0	
37		10660.6	13422.5	3097.5	-7227.5	-17552.5	
38		2835.6	6922.5	1597.5	-3727.5	-9052.5	
39		10.6	422.5	97.5	-227.5	-552.5	
40		2185.6	-6077.5	-1402.5	3272.5	7947.5	
41		9360.6	-12577.5	-2902.5	6772.5	16447.5	
42							
43		Product 1	Product 2				
44	Variances	8100.00	4176.94				
45	Stdevs	90.00	64.63				
46							
47	Covariance	-1647.50					
48	Correlation	-0.283					

in cell C15 and copying it to the range C15:F19. (Make sure you see why only column G, not row 5, is held absolute in this formula.) We can also check that each row of this table is a probability distribution in its own right by summing across rows. The row sums shown in column G are all equal to 1, as they should be.

Similarly, the conditional distribution of D_2 given D_1 is in rows 21 through 29. Here, each column represents the conditional probability distribution of D_2 given the fixed value of D_1 in row 23. These probabilities can be calculated by entering the formula

=C5/C$10

in cell C24 and copying it to the range C24:F28. Now the column sums shown in row 29 are 1, indicating that each column of the table represents a probability distribution.

Various summary measures can now be calculated. We show some of them in Figure 5.10. The following steps present the details.

PROCEDURE FOR CALCULATING SUMMARY MEASURES

1 **Expected values.** The expected demands in cells B32 and C32 follow from the marginal distributions. To calculate these, enter the formulas

=SUMPRODUCT(C4:F4,C10:F10)

and

=SUMPRODUCT(B5:B9,G5:G9)

in these two cells. Note that each of these is based on equation (5.6) for an expected value, that is, a sum of products of possible values and their (marginal) probabilities.

2 **Variances and standard deviations.** These measures of variability are also calculated from the marginal distributions by appealing to equation (5.7). We first find squared deviations from the means, then calculate the weighted sum of these squared deviations, weighted by the corresponding marginal probabilities. For example, to find the variance of D_1, enter the formula

=(C4-$B$32)^2

in cell C36 and copy it across to cell F36. Then enter the formula

=SUMPRODUCT(C36:F36,C10:F10)

in cell B44, and take its square root in cell B45.

3 **Covariance and correlation.** The formulas for covariance and correlation are the same as before [see equations (5.9) and (5.10)]. However, we proceed somewhat differently than in Example 5.3. Now we form a complete table of products of deviations from means in the range C37:F41. To do so, enter the formula

=(C$4-$B$32)*($B5-$C$32)

in cell C37 and copy it to the range C37:F41. Then calculate the covariance in cell B47 with the formula

=SUMPRODUCT(C37:F41,C5:F9)

Finally, calculate the correlation in cell B48 with the formula

=B47/(B45*C45)

Now let's step back and see what we have. If we are interested in the behavior of a single demand only, say, D_1, then the relevant quantities are the marginal probabilities in row 10 and the mean and standard deviation of D_1 in cells B32 and B45. However, we are often more interested in the joint behavior of D_1 and D_2. The best way to see this behavior is in the conditional probability tables. For example, compare the probability distributions in rows 15 through 19. As the value of D_2 increases, the probabilities for D_1 tend to shift to the left. That is, as demand for product 2 increases, demand for product 1 tends to decrease. This is only a *tendency*. When D_2 equals its largest value, there is still some chance that D_1 will be large, but this probability is fairly small.

This behavior can be seen more clearly from the graph in Figure 5.11. Each line in this graph corresponds to one of the rows 15 through 19. The legend represents the different values of D_2. We see that when D_2 is large, D_1 tends to be small, although again, this is only a tendency, not a perfect relationship. When economists say that the two products are substitutes for one another, this is the type of behavior they imply.

Figure 5.11

Conditional
Distributions of
Demand 1, Given
Demand 2

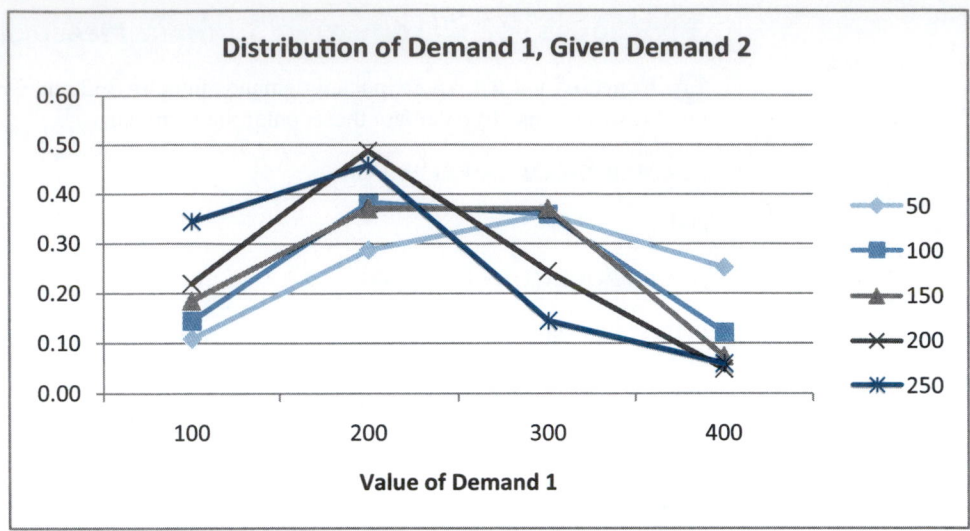

By symmetry, the conditional distribution of D_2 given D_1 shows the same type of behavior. This is illustrated in Figure 5.12, where each line represents one of the columns C through F in the range C24:F28 and the legend represents the different values of D_1.

Figure 5.12

Conditional
Distributions of
Demand 2, Given
Demand 1

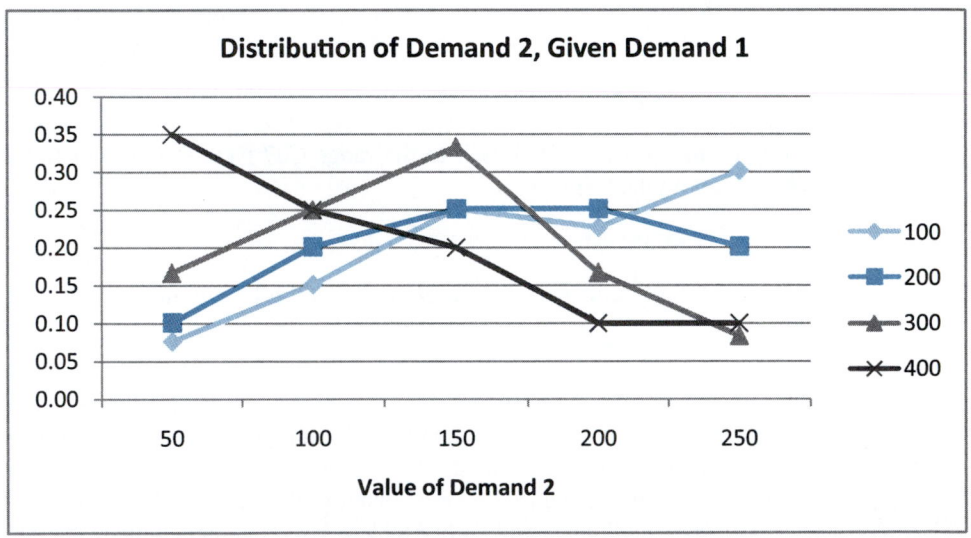

The information in these graphs is confirmed—to some extent, at least—by the covariance and correlation between D_1 and D_2. In particular, their negative values indicate that demands for the two products tend to move in opposite directions. Also, the rather small magnitude of the correlation, -0.283, indicates that the relationship between these demands is far from perfect. When D_1 is large, there is still a reasonably good chance that D_2 will be large, and when D_1 is small, there is still a reasonably good chance that D_2 will be small. ∎

How to Assess Joint Probability Distributions

In the scenario approach from Section 5.5, only one probability for each scenario has to be assessed. In the joint probability approach, a whole table of joint probabilities must be assessed. This can be quite difficult, especially when there are many possible values for each of the random variables. In Example 5.4 it requires $4 \times 5 = 20$ joint probabilities that not only sum to 1 but imply the "substitute product" behavior we want.

Assessing the joint probability distribution of two (or more) random variables is never easy for a manager, but the suggestions here can be helpful.

One approach is to proceed *backward* from the way we proceeded in the example. Instead of specifying the joint probabilities and then deriving the marginal and conditional distributions, we can specify either set of marginal probabilities and either set of conditional probabilities, and then use these to *calculate* the joint probabilities. The reasoning is based on the multiplication rule for probability in the form given by equation (5.11).

Joint Probability Formula
$$P(X = x \text{ and } Y = y) = P(X = x | Y = y)P(Y = y) \tag{5.11}$$

In words, the joint probability on the left is the conditional probability that $X = x$ given $Y = y$, multiplied by the marginal probability that $Y = y$. Of course, the roles of X and Y can be reversed, yielding the alternative formula in equation (5.12). We choose the formula that makes the probabilities on the right-hand side easiest to assess.

Alternative Joint Probability Formula
$$P(X = x \text{ and } Y = y) = P(Y = y | X = x)P(X = x) \tag{5.12}$$

The advantage of this procedure over assessing the joint probabilities directly is that it is probably *easier* and *more intuitive* for a business manager. The manager has more control over the relationship between the two random variables, as determined by the conditional probabilities she assesses.

PROBLEMS

Level A

28. Let X and Y represent the number of Dell and Compaq desktop computers, respectively, sold per month at a local computer store. The file **P05_28.xlsx** contains the probabilities of various combinations of monthly sales volumes of these competitors.
   a. Find the marginal distributions of X and Y. Interpret your findings.
   b. Calculate the expected monthly desktop computer sales volumes for Dell and Compaq at this computer store.
   c. Calculate the standard deviations of the monthly desktop computer sales volumes for Dell and Compaq at this computer store.
   d. Construct and interpret the conditional distribution of X given Y.
   e. Construct and interpret the conditional distribution of Y given X.
   f. Find and interpret the correlation between X and Y.

29. The joint probability distribution of the weekly demand for two brands of diet soda is provided in the file **P05_29.xlsx**. In particular, let D_1 and D_2 represent the weekly demand (in hundreds of 2-liter bottles) for brand 1 and brand 2, respectively, in a small town in central Pennsylvania.
   a. Find the mean and standard deviation of this community's weekly demand for each brand of diet soda.
   b. What is the probability that the weekly demand for each brand will be at least 1 standard deviation above its mean?
   c. What is the probability that at least one of the two weekly demands will be at least 1 standard deviation above its mean?
   d. What is the correlation between the weekly demands for these two brands of diet soda? What does this measure of association tell you about the relationship between these two products?

30. A local pharmacy has two checkout stations available to its customers: a regular checkout station and an express checkout station. Customers with six or fewer items are assumed to join the express line. Let X and Y be the numbers of customers in the regular checkout line and the express checkout line, respectively, at the busiest time of a typical day. Note that these numbers include the customer(s) being served, if any. The joint distribution for X and Y is given in the file **P05_30.xlsx**.

a. Find the marginal distributions of X and Y. What does each of these distributions tell you?

b. Calculate the conditional distribution of X given Y. What is the practical benefit of knowing this conditional distribution?

c. What is the probability that no one is waiting or being served in the regular checkout line?

d. What is the probability that no one is waiting or being served in the express checkout line?

e. What is the probability that no more than two customers are waiting in both lines combined?

f. On average, how many customers would we expect to see in each of these two lines during the busiest time of day at the pharmacy?

31. Suppose that the manufacturer of a particular product assesses the joint distribution of price P per unit and demand D for its product in the upcoming quarter as provided in the file **P05_31.xlsx**.

a. Find the expected price and demand level in the upcoming quarter.

b. What is the probability that the price of this product will be above its mean in the upcoming quarter?

c. What is the probability that the demand for this product will be below its mean in the upcoming quarter?

d. What is the probability that demand for this product will exceed 2500 units during the upcoming quarter, given that its price will be less than $40?

e. What is the probability that demand for this product will be fewer than 3500 units during the upcoming quarter, given that its price will be greater than $30?

f. Compute the correlation between price and demand. Is the result consistent with your expectations? Explain.

Level B

32. The recent weekly trends of two particular stock prices, P_1 and P_2, can best be described by the joint probability distribution shown in the file **P05_32.xlsx**.

a. What is the probability that the price of stock 1 will not increase in the upcoming week?

b. What is the probability that the price of stock 2 will change in the upcoming week?

c. What is the probability that the price of stock 1 will not decrease, given that the price of stock 2 will remain constant in the upcoming week?

d. What is the probability that the price of stock 2 will change, given that the price of stock 1 will change in the upcoming week?

e. Why is it impossible to find the correlation between the typical weekly movements of these two stock prices from the information given? Nevertheless, does it appear that they are positively or negatively related? Why? What are the implications of this result for choosing an investment portfolio that may or may not include these two particular stocks?

33. Two service elevators are used in parallel by employees of a three-story hotel building. At any point in time when both elevators are stationary, let X_1 and X_2 be the floor numbers at which elevators 1 and 2, respectively, are currently located. The joint probability distribution of X_1 and X_2 is given in the file **P05_33.xlsx**.

a. What is the probability that these two elevators are not stationed on the same floor?

b. What is the probability that elevator 2 is located on the third floor?

c. What is the probability that elevator 1 is not located on the first floor?

d. What is the probability that elevator 2 is located on the first floor, given that elevator 1 is not stationed on the first floor?

e. What is the probability that a hotel employee approaching the first-floor elevators will find at least one available for service?

f. Repeat part **e** for a hotel employee approaching each of the second- and third-floor elevators.

g. How might this hotel's operations manager respond to your findings for each of the previous questions?

5.7 INDEPENDENT RANDOM VARIABLES

A very important special case of joint distributions is when the random variables are **independent**. Intuitively, this means that any information about the values of any of the random variables is worthless in terms of predicting any of the others. In particular, if there are only two random variables X and Y, then information about X is worthless in terms of predicting Y, and vice versa. Usually, random variables in real applications are *not* independent; they are usually related in some way, in which case we say they are **dependent**.

However, we often make an assumption of independence in mathematical models to simplify the analysis.

The most intuitive way to express independence of X and Y is to say that their conditional distributions are equal to their marginals. For example, the conditional probability that X equals any value x, given that Y equals some value y, equals the marginal probability that X equals x—and this statement is true for *all* values of x and y. In words, knowledge of the value of Y has no effect on probabilities involving X. Similarly, knowledge of the value of X has no effect on probabilities involving Y.

An equivalent way of stating the independence property is that for all values x and y, the events $X = x$ and $Y = y$ are probabilistically independent in the sense of Section 5.2.4. This leads to the important property that *joint probabilities equal the product of the marginals,* as shown in equation (5.13). This follows from equation (5.11) and also because conditionals equal marginals under independence. Equation (5.13) might not be as intuitive, but it is very useful, as illustrated in the following example.

> **Joint Probability Formula for Independent Random Variables**
> $$P(X = x \text{ and } Y = y) = P(X = x)P(Y = y) \tag{5.13}$$

EXAMPLE

5.5 ANALYZING THE SALES OF TWO POPULAR PERSONAL DIGITAL ASSISTANTS

A local office supply and equipment store, Office Station, sells several different brands of personal digital assistants (PDAs). One of the store's managers has studied the daily sales of its two most popular personal digital assistants, the Palm M505 and the Palm Vx, over the past quarter. In particular, she has used historical data to assess the joint probability distribution of the sales of these two products on a typical day. The assessed distribution is shown in Figure 5.13 (see the file **PDA Sales.xlsx**). The manager would like to use this distribution to determine whether there is support for the claim that the sales of the Palm Vx are often made at the expense of Palm M505 sales, and vice versa.

Figure 5.13

Joint Probability
Distribution of Sales

	A	B	C	D	E	F
1	Assessed probability distribution of sales of two popular PDAs					
2						
3				Daily sales of Palm Vx		
4			0	1	2	3
5		0	0.01	0.03	0.06	0.09
6	Daily sales of	1	0.02	0.06	0.12	0.09
7	Palm M505	2	0.03	0.12	0.06	0.09
8		3	0.04	0.09	0.06	0.03

Objective To use the assessed joint probability distribution to find the conditional distribution of daily sales of each PDA (given the sales of the other PDA), and to determine whether the daily sales of these two products are *independent* random variables.

Solution

As in the solution of Example 5.4, we begin by applying the addition rule for probability to find the marginal probability distribution of sales for each of the two personal digital assistants, as shown in Figure 5.14. By summing the corresponding joint probabilities recorded in the various rows and columns of C5:F8, we find the marginal probability that Office Station sells exactly 0, 1, 2, or 3 units of a particular PDA per day. For example, the sum of the joint

Figure 5.14

Marginal and
Conditional
Distributions
of Sales

	A	B	C	D	E	F	G
1	Assessed probability distribution of sales of two popular PDAs						
2							
3				Daily sales of Palm Vx			
4			0	1	2	3	
5		0	0.01	0.03	0.06	0.09	0.19
6	Daily sales of	1	0.02	0.06	0.12	0.09	0.29
7	Palm M505	2	0.03	0.12	0.06	0.09	0.30
8		3	0.04	0.09	0.06	0.03	0.22
9			0.10	0.30	0.30	0.30	
10							
11	Conditional distribution of sales of Palm Vx, given sales of Palm M505						
12				Daily sales of Palm Vx			
13			0	1	2	3	
14		0	0.05	0.16	0.32	0.47	1
15	Daily sales of	1	0.07	0.21	0.41	0.31	1
16	Palm M505	2	0.10	0.40	0.20	0.30	1
17		3	0.18	0.41	0.27	0.14	1
18							
19	Conditional distribution of sales of Palm M505, given sales of Palm Vx						
20				Daily sales of Palm Vx			
21			0	1	2	3	
22		0	0.10	0.10	0.20	0.30	
23	Daily sales of	1	0.20	0.20	0.40	0.30	
24	Palm M505	2	0.30	0.40	0.20	0.30	
25		3	0.40	0.30	0.20	0.10	
26			1	1	1	1	

probabilities in the range C5:F5 indicates that P(daily sales of Palm M505 = 0) = 0.19, and the sum of the joint probabilities in the range C5:C8 indicates that the P(daily sales of Palm Vx = 0) = 0.10. The marginal probabilities for Palm M505 sales calculated in G5:G8, as well as the marginal probabilities for Palm Vx sales calculated in C9:F9, sum exactly to 1, as they should.

Before constructing the conditional distribution of sales for each product, we check whether these two random variables are independent. Let M and V denote the daily sales for the Palm M505 and Palm Vx, respectively. We know from equation (5.13) that $P(M = m$ and $V = v) = P(M = m)P(V = v)$ for all values of m and v if M and V are independent. However, we have already discovered in computing the marginal probabilities that $P(M = 0)P(V = 0) = (0.19)(0.10) = 0.019$, whereas $P(M = 0$ and $V = 0) = 0.01$ from the table. In other words, the joint probability that Office Station sells no units of each product does not equal the product of the marginal probabilities that this office supply store sells no units of these products. This inequality rules out the possibility that M and V are independent random variables. If you are not yet convinced of this conclusion, compare the products of other marginal probabilities with corresponding joint probabilities in Figure 5.14. You can verify that equation (5.13) fails to hold for virtually all of the different combinations of sales levels.

We now construct and interpret the conditional distribution of daily sales of each PDA. We first focus on the conditional distribution of V given M, shown in rows 11 through 17 of Figure 5.14. In each row of this table (located in rows 14–17), we fix the value of M at the value in column B and calculate the conditional probabilities of V given this fixed value of M. These conditional probabilities can be calculated all at once by entering the formula

= C5/\$G5

in cell C14 and copying it to the range C14:F17. We can verify that each row of this table is a probability distribution in its own right by summing across rows. The row sums shown in the range G14:G17 are all equal to the required value of 1.

Similarly, the conditional distribution of M given V is in rows 19 through 26 of Figure 5.14. In each column of this table (located in columns C–F), we fix the value of V at the value in row 21 and calculate the conditional probabilities of M given this fixed value of V. All of these conditional probabilities can be calculated at once by entering the formula

= C5/C$9

in cell C22 and copying it to the range C22:F25. Note that the column sums shown in row 26 are 1, indicating that each column of the table represents a probability distribution.

What can the Office Station manager infer by examining these conditional probability distributions? Observe in the first table (the one located in rows 14–17) that the likelihood of achieving the *highest* daily sales level of the Palm Vx *decreases* as the given daily sales level of the Palm M505 increases. This same table reveals that the probability of experiencing the *lowest* daily sales level of the Palm Vx *increases* as the given daily sales level of the Palm M505 increases. Furthermore, by closely examining the second table (the one located in rows 22–25), we see that the likelihood of achieving the *highest* daily sales level of the Palm M505 *decreases* as the given daily sales level of the Palm Vx increases. This same table reveals that the probability of experiencing the *lowest* daily sales level of the Palm M505 *increases* as the given daily sales level of the Palm Vx increases.

Thus, there is considerable support for the claim that the sales of the Palm Vx are often made at the expense of Palm M505 sales, and vice versa. This result makes sense in light of our previous finding that the daily sales of these two products are *not* independent of one another. In other words, by knowing the sales level of one of these PDAs, the manager has a better understanding of the likelihood of achieving particular results regarding sales of the other product. ∎

PROBLEMS

Level A

34. The file **P05_34.xlsx** shows the conditional distribution of the daily number of accidents at a given intersection during the winter months, X_2, given the amount of snowfall (in inches) for the day, X_1. The marginal distribution of X_1 is provided in the bottom row of the table.
   a. Are X_1 and X_2 independent random variables? Explain why or why not.
   b. What is the probability of observing no accidents at this intersection on a winter day with no snowfall?
   c. What is the probability of observing no accidents at this intersection on a randomly selected winter day?
   d. What is the probability of observing at least two accidents at this intersection on a randomly selected winter day on which the snowfall is at least 3 inches?
   e. What is the probability of observing less than 4 inches of snowfall on a randomly selected day in this area?

35. A sporting goods store sells two competing brands of exercise bicycles. Let X_1 and X_2 be the numbers of the two brands sold on a typical day at this store. Based on available historical data, the conditional probability distribution of X_1 given X_2 is assessed as shown in the file **P05_35.xlsx**. The marginal distribution of X_2 is given in the bottom row of the table.
   a. Are X_1 and X_2 independent random variables? Explain why or why not.
   b. What is the probability of observing the sale of one brand 1 bicycle and one brand 2 bicycle on the same day at this sporting goods store?
   c. What is the probability of observing the sale of at least one brand 1 bicycle on a given day at this sporting goods store?
   d. What is the probability of observing no more than two brand 2 bicycles on a given day at this sporting goods store?
   e. Given that no brand 2 bicycles are sold on a given day, what is the likelihood of observing the sale of at least one brand 1 bicycle at this sporting goods store?

36. The file **P05_28.xlsx** contains the probabilities of various combinations of monthly sales volumes of Dell (X) and Compaq (Y) desktop computers at a local computer store. Are the monthly sales of these two competitors independent of each other? Explain your answer.

37. Let D_1 and D_2 represent the weekly demand (in hundreds of 2-liter bottles) for brand 1 diet soda and brand 2 diet soda, respectively, in a small central Pennsylvania town. The joint probability distribution of the weekly demand for these two brands of diet soda is provided in the file **P05_29.xlsx**. Are D_1 and D_2 independent random variables? Explain why or why not.

38. The file **P05_31.xlsx** contains the joint probability distribution of price P per unit and demand D for a particular product in the upcoming quarter.
    a. Are P and D independent random variables? Explain your answer.
    b. If P and D are *not* independent random variables, which joint probabilities result in the same *marginal* probabilities for P and D as given in the file but make P and D independent of each other?

Level B

39. You know that in 1 year you are going to buy a house. (In fact, you've already selected the neighborhood, but right now you're finishing your graduate degree, and you're engaged to be married this summer, so you're delaying the purchase for a year.) The annual interest rate for fixed-rate 30-year mortgages is currently 7.00%, and the price of the type of house you're considering is $120,000. However, things may change. Using your knowledge of the economy (and a crystal ball), you estimate that the interest rate might increase or decrease by as much as 1 percentage point. Also, the price of the house might increase by as much as $10,000—it certainly won't decrease! You assess the probability distribution of the interest rate change as shown in the file **P05_39.xlsx**. The probability distribution of the increase in the price of the house is also shown in this file. Finally, you assume that the two random events (change in interest rate, change in house price) are probabilistically independent. This means that the probability of any joint event, such as an interest increase of 0.50% and a price increase of $5000, is the product of the individual probabilities.
    a. Using Excel's PMT function, find the expected monthly house payment (using a 30-year fixed-rate mortgage) if there is no down payment. Find the variance and standard deviation of this monthly payment.
    b. Repeat part **a**, but assume that the down payment is 10% of the price of the house (so that you finance only 90%).

5.8 WEIGHTED SUMS OF RANDOM VARIABLES

In this section we will analyze summary measures of weighted sums of random variables. An extremely important application of this topic is in financial investments. The example in this section illustrates such an application. However, there are many other applications of weighted sums of random variables, both in business and elsewhere. It is a topic well worth learning.

It is common (but not required) to use capital letters to denote random variables and lowercase letters to denote constants.

Before proceeding to the example, we lay out the main concepts and results. Let $X_1, X_2, ..., X_n$ be any n random variables (which could be independent or dependent), and let $a_1, a_2, ..., a_n$ be any n constants. We form a new random variable Y that is the weighted sum of the X's:

$$Y = a_1 X_1 + a_2 X_2 + \cdots + a_n X_n$$

In general, it is too difficult to obtain the complete probability distribution of Y, so we will be content to obtain its summary measures, namely, the mean $E(Y)$ and the variance $\text{Var}(Y)$. Of course, we can then calculate $\text{Stdev}(Y)$ as the square root of $\text{Var}(Y)$.

The mean is the easy part. We substitute the mean of each X into the formula for Y to obtain $E(Y)$. This appears in equation (5.14).

> **Expected Value of a Weighted Sum of Random Variables**
> $$E(Y) = a_1 E(X_1) + a_2 E(X_2) + \cdots + a_n E(X_n) \qquad (5.14)$$

Using summation notation, we can write this more compactly as

$$E(Y) = \sum_{i=1}^{n} a_i E(X_i)$$

The variance is not as straightforward. Its value depends on whether the X's are independent or dependent. If they are independent, then Var(Y) is a weighted sum of the variances of the X's, using the *squares* of the a's as weights, as shown in equation (5.15).

Variance of a Weighted Sum of Independent Random Variables

$$\text{Var}(Y) = a_1^2 \text{Var}(X_1) + a_2^2 \text{Var}(X_2) + \cdots + a_n^2 \text{Var}(X_n) \tag{5.15}$$

Using summation notation, this becomes

$$\text{Var}(Y) = \sum_{i=1}^{n} a_i^2 \text{Var}(X_i)$$

If the X's are not independent, the variance of Y is more complex and requires covariance terms. In particular, for every pair X_i and X_j, there is an extra term in equation (5.15): $2a_i a_j \text{Cov}(X_i, X_j)$. The general result is best written in summation notation, as shown in equation (5.16).

Variance of a Weighted Sum of Dependent Random Variables

$$\text{Var}(Y) = \sum_{i=1}^{n} a_i^2 \text{Var}(X_i) + \sum_{i<j} 2a_i a_j \text{Cov}(X_i, X_j) \tag{5.16}$$

The first summation is the variance when the X's are independent. The second summation indicates that we should add the covariance term for all pairs of X's that have nonzero covariances. Actually, this equation is *always* valid, regardless of independence, because the covariance terms are all zero when the X's are independent.

Special Cases of Expected Value and Variance

- **Sum of independent random variables.** Here we assume the X's are independent and the weights are all 1, that is,

$$Y = X_1 + X_2 + \cdots + X_n$$

  Then the mean of the sum is the sum of the means, and the variance of the sum is the sum of the variances:

$$E(Y) = E(X_1) + E(X_2) + \cdots + E(X_n)$$
$$\text{Var}(Y) = \text{Var}(X_1) + \text{Var}(X_2) + \cdots + \text{Var}(X_n)$$

- **Difference between two independent random variables.** Here we assume X_1 and X_2 are independent and the weights are $a_1 = 1$ and $a_2 = -1$, so that we can write Y as

$$Y = X_1 - X_2$$

  Then the mean of the difference is the difference between means, but the variance of the difference is the *sum* of the variances (because $a_2^2 = (-1)^2 = 1$):

$$E(Y) = E(X_1) - E(X_2)$$
$$\text{Var}(Y) = \text{Var}(X_1) + \text{Var}(X_2)$$

- **Sum of two dependent random variables.** In this case we make no independence assumption and set the weights equal to 1, so that $Y = X_1 + X_2$. Then the mean of the sum is again the sum of the means, but the variance of the sum includes a covariance term:

$$E(Y) = E(X_1) + E(X_2)$$

$$\text{Var}(Y) = \text{Var}(X_1) + \text{Var}(X_2) + 2\text{Cov}(X_1, X_2)$$

- **Difference between two dependent random variables.** This is the same as the second case, except that the X's are no longer independent. Again, the mean of the difference is the difference between means, but the variance of the difference now includes a covariance term, and because of the negative weight $a_2 = -1$, the sign of this covariance term is negative:

$$E(Y) = E(X_1) - E(X_2)$$

$$\text{Var}(Y) = \text{Var}(X_1) + \text{Var}(X_2) - 2\text{Cov}(X_1, X_2)$$

- **Linear Function of a Random Variable.** Suppose that Y can be written as

$$Y = a + bX$$

for some constants a and b. In this special case the random variable Y is said to be a *linear function* of another random variable X. Then the mean, variance, and standard deviation of Y can be calculated from the similar quantities for X with the following formulas:

$$E(Y) = a + bE(X)$$

$$\text{Var}(Y) = b^2\,\text{Var}(X)$$

$$\text{Stdev}(Y) = b\,\text{Stdev}(X)$$

In particular, if Y is a constant multiple of X (that is, if $a = 0$), then the mean and standard deviation of Y are the same multiple of the mean and standard deviation of X.

We now put these concepts to use in an investment example.

| EXAMPLE | 5.6 DESCRIBING INVESTMENT PORTFOLIO RETURNS |

In fact, all of the correlations are positive, which probably indicates that each stock tends to vary in the same direction as some underlying economic indicator. Also, the diagonal entries in the correlation matrix are all 1 because any stock return is perfectly correlated with itself.

An investor has $100,000 to invest, and she would like to invest it in a portfolio of eight stocks. She has gathered historical data on the returns of these stocks and has used the historical data to estimate means, standard deviations, and correlations for the stock returns. These summary measures appear in rows 12, 13, and 17 through 24 of Figure 5.15. (See the file **Portfolio Analysis.xlsx**.)

For example, the mean and standard deviation of stock 1 are 0.101 and 0.124. These imply that the historical annual returns of stock 1 averaged 10.1% and the standard deviation of the annual returns was 12.4%. Also, the correlation between the annual returns on stocks 1 and 2, for example, is 0.32 (see either cell C17 or B18, which necessarily contain the same value). This value, 0.32, indicates a moderate positive correlation between the historical annual returns of these stocks.

Figure 5.15 Input Data for Investment Example

	A	B	C	D	E	F	G	H	I	J
1	Calculating mean, variance, and stdev for a weighted sum of random variables									
2										
3			Assumptions:							
4			1. Random variables are one-year returns from various stocks.							
5			2. Weights are amounts invested in stocks.							
6			3. Weighted sum is return from portfolio.							
7	Given quantities									
8		Stock1	Stock2	Stock3	Stock4	Stock5	Stock6	Stock7	Stock8	Total
9	Weights	$10,500	$16,300	$9,600	$9,300	$9,500	$15,400	$14,300	$15,100	$100,000
10										
11		Stock1	Stock2	Stock3	Stock4	Stock5	Stock6	Stock7	Stock8	
12	Means	0.101	0.073	0.118	0.099	0.118	0.091	0.096	0.123	
13	Stdevs	0.124	0.119	0.134	0.141	0.158	0.159	0.113	0.174	
14										
15	Correlations between stock returns									
16		Stock1	Stock2	Stock3	Stock4	Stock5	Stock6	Stock7	Stock8	
17	Stock1	1.000	0.320	0.370	0.610	0.800	0.610	0.550	0.560	
18	Stock2	0.320	1.000	0.410	0.780	0.430	0.800	0.950	0.480	
19	Stock3	0.370	0.410	1.000	0.330	0.860	0.380	0.340	0.700	
20	Stock4	0.610	0.780	0.330	1.000	0.680	0.500	0.500	0.670	
21	Stock5	0.800	0.430	0.860	0.680	1.000	0.580	0.420	0.540	
22	Stock6	0.610	0.800	0.380	0.500	0.580	1.000	0.920	0.340	
23	Stock7	0.550	0.950	0.340	0.500	0.420	0.920	1.000	0.650	
24	Stock8	0.560	0.480	0.700	0.670	0.540	0.340	0.650	1.000	

Although these summary measures have been obtained from historical data, the investor believes they are relevant for predicting *future* returns. Now she would like to analyze a portfolio of these stocks, using the investment amounts shown in row 9. What is the mean annual return from this portfolio? What are its variance and standard deviation?

Objective   To determine the mean annual return of this investor's portfolio, and to quantify the risk associated with the total dollar return from the given weighted sum of annual stock returns.

Solution

This is a typical weighted sum model. The random variables, the X's, are the annual returns from the stocks; the weights, the a's, are the dollar amounts invested in the stocks; and the summary measures of the X's are given in rows 12, 13, and 17 through 24 of Figure 5.15. Be careful about units, however. Each X_i represents the return on a *single* dollar invested in stock i, whereas Y, the weighted sum of the X's, represents the *total* dollar return. So a typical value of an X might be 0.105, whereas a typical value of Y might be $10,500.

We can immediately apply equation (5.14) to obtain the mean return from the portfolio. This appears in cell B38 of Figure 5.16, using the formula

=SUMPRODUCT(Weights,Means)

Figure 5.16 Calculations for Investment Example

	A	B	C	D	E	F	G	H	I	J	K	L	M
1	Calculating mean, variance, and stdev for a weighted sum of random variables										Range names used		
2											Covariances	=Model!$B$28:$I$35	
3			Assumptions:								Means	=Model!$B$12:$I$12	
4			1. Random variables are one-year returns from various stocks.								Stdevs	=Model!$B$13:$I$13	
5			2. Weights are amounts invested in stocks.								Variance	=Model!$B$39	
6			3. Weighted sum is return from portfolio.								Weights	=Model!$B$9:$I$9	
7	Given quantities												
8		Stock1	Stock2	Stock3	Stock4	Stock5	Stock6	Stock7	Stock8	Total			
9	Weights	$10,500	$16,300	$9,600	$9,300	$9,500	$15,400	$14,300	$15,100	$100,000			
10													
11		Stock1	Stock2	Stock3	Stock4	Stock5	Stock6	Stock7	Stock8				
12	Means	0.101	0.073	0.118	0.099	0.118	0.091	0.096	0.123				
13	Stdevs	0.124	0.119	0.134	0.141	0.158	0.159	0.113	0.174				
14													
15	Correlations between stock returns												
16		Stock1	Stock2	Stock3	Stock4	Stock5	Stock6	Stock7	Stock8				
17	Stock1	1.000	0.320	0.370	0.610	0.800	0.610	0.550	0.560				
18	Stock2	0.320	1.000	0.410	0.780	0.430	0.800	0.950	0.480				
19	Stock3	0.370	0.410	1.000	0.330	0.860	0.380	0.340	0.700				
20	Stock4	0.610	0.780	0.330	1.000	0.680	0.500	0.500	0.670				
21	Stock5	0.800	0.430	0.860	0.680	1.000	0.580	0.420	0.540				
22	Stock6	0.610	0.800	0.380	0.500	0.580	1.000	0.920	0.340				
23	Stock7	0.550	0.950	0.340	0.500	0.420	0.920	1.000	0.650				
24	Stock8	0.560	0.480	0.700	0.670	0.540	0.340	0.650	1.000				
25													
26	Covariances between stock returns (variances of stock returns are on the diagonal)												
27		Stock1	Stock2	Stock3	Stock4	Stock5	Stock6	Stock7	Stock8				
28	Stock1	0.0154	0.0047	0.0061	0.0107	0.0157	0.0120	0.0077	0.0121				
29	Stock2	0.0047	0.0142	0.0065	0.0131	0.0081	0.0151	0.0128	0.0099				
30	Stock3	0.0061	0.0065	0.0180	0.0062	0.0182	0.0081	0.0051	0.0163				
31	Stock4	0.0107	0.0131	0.0062	0.0199	0.0151	0.0112	0.0080	0.0164				
32	Stock5	0.0157	0.0081	0.0182	0.0151	0.0250	0.0146	0.0075	0.0148				
33	Stock6	0.0120	0.0151	0.0081	0.0112	0.0146	0.0253	0.0165	0.0094				
34	Stock7	0.0077	0.0128	0.0051	0.0080	0.0075	0.0165	0.0128	0.0128				
35	Stock8	0.0121	0.0099	0.0163	0.0164	0.0148	0.0094	0.0128	0.0303				
36													
37	Summary measures of portfolio												
38	Mean	$10,056.40											
39	Variance	124992021											
40	Stdev	$11,179.98											

We are not quite ready to calculate the variance of the portfolio return. The reason is that the input data include standard deviations and correlations for the X's, not the variances and covariances required in equation (5.16).[7] But the variances and covariances are related to standard deviations and correlations by

$$\text{Var}(X_i) = (\text{Stdev}(X_i))^2 \tag{5.17}$$

and

$$\text{Cov}(X_i, X_j) = \text{Stdev}(X_i) \times \text{Stdev}(X_j) \times \text{Corr}(X_i, X_j) \tag{5.18}$$

---

[7]This was intentional. It is often easier for an investor to assess standard deviations and correlations because they are more intuitive measures.

We can form a table of variances and covariances of the X's in the range B28:I35, using equations (5.17) and (5.18), in one step with a careful use of the HLOOKUP (horizontal lookup) function. To do so, highlight the range B28:I35, type the formula

=HLOOKUP($A28,$B$11:$I$13,3,FALSE)*B17*HLOOKUP(B$27,$B$11:$I$13,3,FALSE)

and press Ctrl-Enter. (Be careful with relative and absolute addresses.) Note how the HLOOKUP functions find the appropriate standard deviations from row 13 for use in the covariance formula. Each diagonal element of the covariance range is a variance, and the elements off the diagonal are covariances.

Now we are ready to use equation (5.16) to calculate the portfolio variance in cell B39. Although Equation (5.16) looks intimidating, it can be implemented fairly easily with Excel's matrix multiplication function, MMULT, and its TRANSPOSE function. To do so, enter the following formula in cell B39 and then press Ctrl-Shift-Enter (all three keys at once):

=MMULT(Weights,MMULT(Covariances,TRANSPOSE(Weights)))

(This formula, called an *array formula,* is somewhat advanced, but it is a very handy shortcut for implementing Equation (5.16). Section 15.8.3 provides more information about matrix multiplication and the MMULT function in general.) Finally, calculate the standard deviation of the portfolio return in cell B40 as the square root of the variance.

The results in Figure 5.16 indicate that the investor has an expected return of slightly more than $10,000 (or 10%) from this portfolio. However, the standard deviation of approximately $11,200 is sizable. This standard deviation is a measure of the portfolio's risk. Investors always want a large mean return, but they also want low risk. Moreover, they realize that the only way to obtain a higher mean return is usually to accept more risk. You can experiment with the spreadsheet for this example to see how the mean and standard deviation of portfolio return vary with the investment amounts. Just enter new weights in row 9 (keeping the sum equal to $100,000) and see how the values in B49 through B51 change. ■

PROBLEMS

Level A

40. A typical consumer buys a random number (X) of polo shirts when he shops at a men's clothing store. The distribution of X is given by the following probability distribution: $P(X = 0) = 0.30$, $P(X = 1) = 0.30$, $P(X = 2) = 0.20$, $P(X = 3) = 0.10$, and $P(X = 4) = 0.10$.
  a. Find the mean and standard deviation of X.
  b. Assuming that each shirt costs $35, let Y be the total amount of money (in dollars) spent by a customer when he visits this clothing store. Find the mean and standard deviation of Y.
  c. Compute the probability that a customer's expenditure will be more than 1 standard deviation above the mean expenditure level.

41. Based on past experience, the number of customers who arrive at a local gasoline station during the noon hour to purchase fuel is best described by the probability distribution given in the file **P05_41.xlsx**.
  a. Find the mean, variance, and standard deviation of this random variable.

b. Find the probability that the number of arrivals during the noon hour will be within 1 standard deviation of the mean number of arrivals.

c. Suppose that the typical customer spends $15 on fuel upon stopping at this gasoline station during the noon hour. Compute the mean and standard deviation of the total gasoline revenue earned by this gas station during the noon hour.

d. What is the probability that the total gasoline revenue will be less than the mean value found in part **c**?

e. What is the probability that the total gasoline revenue will be more than 2 standard deviations above the mean value found in part **c**?

42. Let X be the number of defective items found by a quality inspector in a random batch of 15 items from a particular manufacturing process. The probability distribution of X is provided in the file **P05_18.xlsx**. This firm earns $500 profit from the sale of each *acceptable* item in a given batch. In the event that an item is found to be *defective,* it must be reworked at a cost of $100 before it can be sold, thus reducing its per-unit profit to $400.

a. Find the mean and standard deviation of the profit earned from the sale of all items in a given batch.

b. What is the probability that the profit earned from the sale of all items in a given batch is within 2 standard deviations of the mean profit level? Is this result consistent with the empirical rules from Chapter 3? Explain.

43. The probability distribution for the number of job applications processed at a small employment agency during a typical week is given in the file **P05_19.xlsx**.

a. Assuming that it takes the agency's administrative assistant 2 hours to process a submitted job application, on average how many hours in a typical week will the administrative assistant spend processing incoming job applications?

b. Find an interval with the property that the administrative assistant can be approximately 95% sure that the total amount of time he spends each week processing incoming job applications will be in this interval.

44. Consider a financial services salesperson whose annual salary consists of both a fixed portion of $25,000 and a variable portion that is a commission based on her sales performance. In particular, she estimates that her monthly sales commission can be represented by a random variable with mean $5000 and standard deviation $700.

a. What annual salary can this salesperson expect to earn?

b. Assuming that her sales commissions in different months are independent random variables, what is the standard deviation of her annual salary?

c. Between what two annual salary levels can this salesperson be approximately 95% sure that her true total earnings will fall?

45. A film-processing shop charges its customers 18 cents per print, but customers may refuse to accept one or more of the prints for various reasons. Assume that this shop does not charge its customers for refused prints. The number of prints refused per 24-print roll is a random variable with mean 1.5 and standard deviation 0.5.

a. What are the mean and standard deviation of the amount that customers pay for the development of a typical 24-print roll?

b. Assume that this shop processes 250 24-print rolls of film in a given week. If the numbers of refused prints on these rolls are independent random variables, what are the mean and standard deviation of the weekly film processing revenue of this shop?

c. Find an interval such that the manager of this film shop can be approximately 95% sure that the weekly processing revenue will be contained within the interval.

46. Suppose the monthly demand for Thompson televisions has a mean of 40,000 and a standard deviation of 20,000. Determine the mean and standard deviation of the annual demand for Thompson TVs. Assume that demand in any month is probabilistically independent of demand in any other month. (Is this assumption realistic?)

47. Suppose there are five stocks available for investment and each has an annual mean return of 10% and a standard deviation of 4%. Assume the returns on the stocks are independent random variables.

a. If you invest 20% of your money in each stock, determine the mean, standard deviation, and variance of the annual dollar return on your investments.

b. If you invest $100 in a single stock, determine the mean, standard deviation, and variance of the annual return on your investment.

c. How do the answers to parts **a** and **b** relate to the phrase, "Don't put all your eggs in one basket"?

48. An investor puts $10,000 into each of four stocks, labeled A, B, C, and D. The file **P05_48.xlsx** contains the means and standard deviations of the annual returns of these four stocks. Assuming that the returns of these four stocks are independent of each other, find the mean and standard deviation of the total amount that this investor earns in 1 year from these four investments.

Level B

49. Consider again the investment problem described in the previous problem. Now, assume that the returns of the four stocks are no longer independent of one another. Specifically, the correlations between all pairs of stock returns are given in the file **P05_49.xlsx**.

a. Find the mean and standard deviation of the total amount that this investor earns in 1 year from these four investments. Compare these results to those you found in the previous problem. Explain the differences in your answers.

   b. Suppose that this investor now decides to place $15,000 each in stocks B and D, and $5000 each in stocks A and C. How do the mean and standard deviation of the total amount that this investor earns in 1 year change from the allocation used in part **a**? Provide an intuitive explanation for the changes you observe here.

50. A supermarket chain operates five stores of varying sizes in Harrisburg, Pennsylvania. Profits (represented as a percentage of sales volume) earned by these five stores are 2.75%, 3%, 3.5%, 4.25%, and 5%, respectively. The means and standard deviations of the daily sales volumes at these five stores are given in the file **P05_50.xlsx**. Assuming that the daily sales volumes are independent of each other, find the mean and standard deviation of the total *profit* that this supermarket chain earns in 1 day from the operation of its five stores in Harrisburg.

51. A manufacturing company constructs a 1-cm assembly by snapping together four parts that average 0.25 cm in length. The company would like the standard deviation of the length of the assembly to be 0.01 cm. Its engineer, Peter Purdue, believes that the assembly will meet the desired level of variability if each part has a standard deviation of 0.01/4 = 0.0025 cm. Instead, show Peter that you can do the job by making each part have a standard deviation of $0.01/\sqrt{4} = 0.005$ cm. This could save the company a lot of money because not as much precision is needed for each part.

52. The weekly demand function for one of a given firm's products can be represented by $Q = 200 - 5p$, for

$p = 1, 2, \ldots, 40$, where Q is the number of units purchased (in hundreds) at a sales price of p (in dollars). Assume that the probability distribution of the sales price is given by $P(p = k) = .025$, for $k = 1, 2, \ldots, 40$. (In words, each price is equally likely.)

   a. Find the mean and standard deviation of p. Interpret these measures in this case.

   b. Find the mean and standard deviation of Q. Interpret these measures in this case.

   c. Assuming that it costs this firm $10 to manufacture and sell each unit of the given product, define π to be the firm's weekly contribution to profit from the sale of this product (measured in dollars). Express π as a function of the quantity purchased, Q.

   d. Find the expected weekly contribution to the firm's profit from the sale of this product. Also, compute the standard deviation of the weekly contribution to the firm's profit from the sale of this product.

53. A retailer purchases a batch of 1000 fluorescent light-bulbs from a wholesaler at a cost of $2 per bulb. The wholesaler agrees to replace each defective bulb with one that is guaranteed to function properly for a charge of $0.20 per bulb. The retailer sells the bulbs at a price of $2.50 per bulb and gives his customers free replacements if they bring defective bulbs back to the store. Let X be the number of defective bulbs in a typical batch, and assume that the mean and standard deviation of X are 50 and 10, respectively.

   a. Find the mean and standard deviation of the profit (in dollars) the retailer makes from selling a batch of lightbulbs.

   b. Find an interval with the property that the retailer can be approximately 95% sure that his profit will be in this interval.

5.9 CONCLUSION

This chapter has introduced some very important concepts, including the basic rules of probability, random variables, probability distributions, and summary measures of probability distributions. We have also shown how computer simulation can be used to help explain some of these concepts. Many of the concepts presented in this chapter will be used in later chapters, so it is important to learn them now. In particular, we rely heavily on probability distributions in Chapter 7 when we discuss decision making under uncertainty. There we learn how the expected value of a probability distribution is the primary criterion for making decisions. We also continue to use computer simulation in later chapters to help explain difficult statistical concepts.

Summary of Key Terms

Term	Explanation	Excel	Pages	Equation Number
Random variable	Associates a numerical value with each possible outcome of a random phenomenon		206	
Probability	A number between 0 and 1 that measures the likelihood that some event will occur		208	
Rule of complements	The probability of any event A and the probability of its complement—the event that A does *not* occur—sum to 1	Must be done manually	208	5.1
Mutually exclusive events	Events where only one of them can occur		208	
Exhaustive events	Events where at least one of them must occur		208	
Addition rule for mutually exclusive events	The probability that at least one of a set of mutually exclusive events will occur is the sum of their probabilities	Must be done manually	209	5.2
Conditional probability formula	Updates the probability of an event, given the knowledge that another related event has occurred	Must be done manually	209	5.3
Multiplication rule for two events	Formula for the probability that two events *both* occur	Must be done manually	209	5.4
Probabilistic independence	Events where knowledge that one of them has occurred is of no value when assessing the probability that the other will occur; allows for simplification of the multiplication rule	Must be done manually	212	5.5
Relative frequency	The proportion of times the event occurs out of the number of times the random experiment is run		213	
Mean (or expected value) of a probability distribution	A measure of central tendency—the weighted sum of the possible values of a random variable, weighted by their probabilities	Must be done manually	216	5.6
Variance of a probability distribution	A measure of variability: the weighted sum of the squared deviations of the possible values of a random variable from the mean, weighted by the probabilities	Must be done manually	217	5.7
Standard deviation of a probability distribution	A measure of variability: the square root of the variance	Must be done manually	217	5.8
Simulation	An extremely useful tool that can be used to incorporate uncertainty explicitly into spreadsheet models		220	
Uniformly distributed random numbers	Random numbers such that all decimal values between 0 and 1 are equally likely	**=RAND()**	220	
Uniformly distributed random integers	Random integers such that all integers between two given values are equally likely	**=RAND-BETWEEN(1,6), for example**	220	

(continued)

Term	Explanation	Excel	Pages	Equation Number
Covariance for a joint probability distribution	A measure of the relationship between two jointly distributed random variables	Must be done manually	224	5.9
Correlation for a joint probability distribution	A measure of the relationship between two jointly distributed random variables, scaled to be between -1 and $+1$	Must be done manually	225	5.10
Multiplication rule for random variables	Formula for a joint probability as the product of a marginal probability and a conditional probability	Must be done manually	235	5.11, 5.12
Independent random variables	Random variables where information about one of them is of no value in terms of predicting the other		236	
Multiplication rule for independent random variables	The joint probability is the product of the marginal probabilities.	Must be done manually	237	5.13
Expected value of a weighted sum of random variables	Useful for finding the expected value of Y, where $Y = a_1 X_1 + a_2 X_2 + \cdots + a_n X_n$	Must be done manually	240	5.14
Variance of a weighted sum of independent random variables	Useful for finding the variance of Y, where $Y = a_1 X_1 + a_2 X_2 + \cdots + a_n X_n$ and the X's are independent of one another	Must be done manually	241	5.15
Variance of a weighted sum of dependent random variables	Useful for finding the variance of Y, where $Y = a_1 X_1 + a_2 X_2 + \cdots + a_n X_n$ and the X's are *not* independent of one another	Must be done manually	241	5.16
Covariance in terms of standard deviations and correlation	Used to calculate covariance when only information on correlations and standard deviations is given	Must be done manually	244	5.18

PROBLEMS

Conceptual Exercises

C1. Suppose that you want to find the probability that event *A* or event *B* will occur in the case where these two events are *not* mutually exclusive. Explain how you would proceed to calculate the probability that at least one of these two events will occur.

C2. "If two events are mutually exclusive, then they must *not* be independent events." Is this statement true or false? Explain your choice.

C3. Is the number of passengers who show up for a particular commercial airline flight a discrete or a continuous random variable? Is the time between flight arrivals at a major airport a discrete or a continuous random variable? Explain your answers.

C4. Suppose that officials in the federal government are trying to determine the likelihood of a major smallpox epidemic in the United States within the next 12 months. Is this an example of an objective probability or a subjective probability? Explain your choice.

C5. What is another term for the covariance between a random variable and itself?

Level A

54. A business manager who needs to make many phone calls has estimated that when she calls a client, the probability that she will reach the client right away is 60%. If she does not reach the client on the first call, the probability that she will reach the client with a subsequent call in the next hour is 20%.

a. Find the probability that the manager will reach her client in two or fewer calls.

b. Find the probability that the manager will reach her client on the second call but not on the first call.

c. Find the probability that the manager will be unsuccessful on two consecutive calls.

55. Suppose that a marketing research firm sends questionnaires to two different companies. Based on historical evidence, the marketing research firm believes that each company, independently of the other, will return the questionnaire with probability 0.40.

a. What is the probability that *both* questionnaires will be returned?

b. What is the probability that *neither* of the questionnaires will be returned?

c. Now, suppose that this marketing research firm sends questionnaires to *ten* different companies. Assuming that each company, independently of the others, returns its completed questionnaire with probability 0.40, how do your answers to parts **a** and **b** change?

56. Based on past sales experience, an appliance store stocks five window air conditioner units for the coming week. No orders for additional air conditioners will be made until next week. The weekly consumer demand for this type of appliance has the probability distribution given in the file **P05_56.xlsx**.

a. Let X be the number of window air conditioner units left at the end of the week (if any), and let Y be the number of special stockout orders required (if any), assuming that a special stockout order is required each time there is a demand and no unit is available in stock. Find the probability distributions of X and Y.

b. Find the expected value of X and the expected value of Y.

c. Assume that this appliance store makes a $40 profit on each air conditioner sold from the weekly available stock, but the store loses $10 for each unit sold on a special stockout order basis. Let Z be the profit that the store earns in the upcoming week from the sale of window air conditioners. Find the probability distribution of Z.

d. Find the expected value of Z.

57. Simulate 400 weekly consumer demands for window air conditioner units with the probability distribution given in the file **P05_56.xlsx**. How does your simulated distribution compare to the given probability distribution? Explain any differences between these two distributions.

58. The probability distribution of the weekly demand (in hundreds of reams) of copier paper used in the duplicating center of a corporation is provided in the file **P05_58.xlsx**.

a. Find the mean and standard deviation of this distribution.

b. Find the probability that weekly copier paper demand will be at least 1 standard deviation above the mean.

c. Find the probability that weekly copier paper demand will be within 1 standard deviation of the mean.

59. Consider the probability distribution of the weekly demand (in hundreds of reams) of copier paper used in a corporation's duplicating center, as shown in the file **P05_58.xlsx**.

a. Generate 500 values of this random variable with the given probability distribution using simulation.

b. Compute the mean and standard deviation of the simulated values.

c. Use your simulated distribution to find the probability that weekly copier paper demand will be within 1 standard deviation of the mean.

60. The probability distribution of the weekly demand (in hundreds of reams) of copier paper used in the duplicating center of a corporation is provided in the file **P05_58.xlsx**. Assuming that it costs the duplicating center $5 to purchase a ream of paper, find the mean and standard deviation of the weekly copier paper cost for this corporation.

61. The instructor of an introductory organizational behavior course believes that there might be a relationship between the number of writing assignments (X) she makes in the course and the final grades (Y) earned by students enrolled in this class. She has taught this course with varying numbers of writing assignments for many semesters now. She has compiled relevant historical data in the file **P05_61.xlsx** for you to review.

a. Convert the given frequency table to a table of conditional probabilities of final grades (Y) earned by students enrolled in this class, given the number of writing assignments (X) made in the course. Comment on your constructed table of conditional probabilities. Generally speaking, what does this table tell you?

b. Given that this instructor makes only one writing assignment in the course, what is the expected final grade earned by the typical student?

c. How much variability exists around the conditional mean grade you found in part **b**? Furthermore, what proportion of all relevant students earn final grades within 2 standard deviations of this conditional mean?

d. Given that this instructor makes more than one writing assignment in the course, what is the expected final grade earned by the typical student?

e. How much variability exists around the conditional mean grade you found in part **d**? What proportion of all relevant students earn final grades within 2 standard deviations of this conditional mean?

f. Compute the covariance and correlation between X and Y. What does each of these measures tell you?

In particular, is this organizational behavior instructor correct in believing that there is a systematic relationship between the number of writing assignments made and final grades earned in her classes?

62. The file **P05_62.xlsx** contains the joint probability distribution of recent weekly trends of two particular stock prices, P_1 and P_2.
    a. Are P_1 and P_2 independent random variables? Explain why or why not.
    b. If P_1 and P_2 are *not* independent random variables, which joint probabilities result in the same *marginal* probabilities for P_1 and P_2 as given in this file but make P_1 and P_2 independent of each other?

63. Consider two service elevators used in parallel by employees of a three-story hotel building. At any point in time when both elevators are stationary, let X_1 and X_2 be the floor numbers at which elevators 1 and 2, respectively, are currently located. The file **P05_33.xlsx** contains the joint probability distribution of X_1 and X_2.
    a. Are X_1 and X_2 independent random variables? Explain your answer.
    b. If X_1 and X_2 are *not* independent random variables, which joint probabilities result in the same *marginal* probabilities for X_1 and X_2 as given in this file but make X_1 and X_2 independent of each other?

64. A roulette wheel contains the numbers 0, 00, and 1, 2, . . . , 36. If you bet $1 on a single number coming up, you earn $35 if the number comes up and lose $1 if the number does not come up. Find the mean and standard deviation of your winnings on a single bet.

65. Assume that there are four equally likely states of the economy: boom, low growth, recession, and depression. Also, assume that the percentage annual return you obtain when you invest a dollar in gold or the stock market is shown in the file **P05_65.xlsx**.
    a. Find the covariance and correlation between the annual return on the market and the annual return on gold. Interpret your answers.
    b. Suppose you invest 40% of your money in the market and 60% of your money in gold. Determine the mean and standard deviation of the annual return on your portfolio.
    c. Obtain your part **b** answer by determining the actual return on your portfolio in each state of the economy and determining the mean and variance directly without using any formulas involving covariances or correlations.
    d. Suppose you invested 70% of your money in the market and 30% in gold. Without doing any calculations, determine whether the mean and standard deviation of your portfolio would increase or decrease from your answer in part **b**. Give an intuitive explanation to support your answers.

66. You are considering buying a share of Ford stock with the possible returns for the next year as shown in the

file **P05_66.xlsx**. Determine the mean, variance, and standard deviation of the annual return on Ford stock.

67. Suppose there are three states of the economy: boom, moderate growth, and recession. The annual return on GM and Ford stock in each state of the economy is shown in the file **P05_67.xlsx**.
    a. Calculate the mean, standard deviation, and variance of the annual return on each stock assuming the probability of each state is 1/3.
    b. Calculate the mean, standard deviation, and variance of the annual return on each stock assuming the probabilities of the three states are 1/4, 1/4, and 1/2.
    c. Calculate the covariance and correlation between the annual return on GM and Ford stocks assuming the probability of each state is 1/3.
    d. Calculate the covariance and correlation between the annual return on GM and Ford stocks assuming the probabilities of the three states are 1/4, 1/4, and 1/2.
    e. You have invested 25% of your money in GM and 75% in Ford. Assuming that each state is equally likely, determine the mean and variance of your portfolio's return.
    f. Now check your answer to part **e** by directly computing for each state the return on your portfolio and use the formulas for mean and variance of a random variable. For example, in the boom state, your portfolio earns 0.25(0.25) + 0.75(0.32).

68. You have placed 30% of your money in investment A and 70% of your money in investment B. The annual returns on investments A and B depend on the state of the economy as shown in the file **P05_68.xlsx**. Determine the mean and standard deviation of the annual return on your investments.

69. There are three possible states of the economy during the next year (states 1, 2, and 3). The probability of each state of the economy and the percentage annual return on IBM and Disney stocks are as shown in the file **P05_69.xlsx**.
    a. Find the correlation between the annual return on IBM and Disney. Interpret this correlation.
    b. If you put 80% of your money in IBM and 20% in Disney, find the mean and standard deviation of your annual return.

70. The return on a portfolio during a period is defined by

$$\frac{PV_{end} - PV_{beg}}{PV_{beg}}$$

where PV_{beg} is the portfolio value at the beginning of a period and PV_{end} is the portfolio value at the end of the period. Suppose there are two stocks in which we can invest, stock 1 and stock 2. During each year there is a 50% chance that each dollar invested in stock 1 will turn into $2 and a 50% chance that each dollar invested in stock 1 will turn into $0.50. During each year there is a 50% chance that each dollar invested in stock 2 will turn into $2 and a 50% chance that each dollar invested in stock 2 will turn into $0.50.

  a. If you invest all your money in stock 1, determine the expected value, variance, and standard deviation of your 1-year return.

  b. Assume the returns on stocks 1 and 2 are independent random variables. If you put half your money into each stock, determine the expected value, variance, and standard deviation of your 1-year return.

  c. Can you give an intuitive explanation of why the variance and standard deviation in part **b** are smaller than the variance and standard deviation in part **a**?

  d. Use simulation to check your answers to part **b**. Use at least 1000 trials.

71. Each year the employees at Zipco receive a $0, $2000, or $4500 salary increase. They also receive a merit rating of 0, 1, 2, or 3, with 3 indicating outstanding performance and 0 indicating poor performance. The joint probability distribution of salary increase and merit rating is listed in the file **P05_71.xlsx**. For example, 20% of all employees receive a $2000 increase and have a merit rating of 1. Find the correlation between salary increase and merit rating. Then interpret this correlation.

72. Suppose X and Y are independent random variables. The possible values of X are -1, 0, and 1; the possible values of Y are 10, 20, and 30. You are given that $P(X = -1 \text{ and } Y = 10) = 0.05$, $P(X = 0 \text{ and } Y = 30) = 0.20$, $P(Y = 10) = 0.20$, and $P(X = 0) = 0.50$. Determine the joint probability distribution of X and Y.

73. You are involved in a risky business venture where three outcomes are possible: (1) you will lose not only your initial investment ($5000) but an additional $3000; (2) you will just make back your initial investment (for a net gain of $0); or (3) you will make back your initial investment plus an extra $10,000. The probability of (1) is half as large as the probability of (2), and the probability of (3) is one-third as large as the probability of (2).

  a. Find the individual probabilities of (1), (2), and (3). (They should sum to 1.)

  b. Find the expected value of your net gain (or loss) from this venture. Find its variance and standard deviation.

Level B

74. Imagine that you are trying to predict what will happen to the price of gasoline (regular unleaded) and the price of natural gas for home heating during the next month. Assume you believe that the price of either will stay the same, go up by 5%, or go down by 5%. Assess the joint probabilities of these possibilities, that is, assess nine

probabilities that sum to 1 and are "realistic." Do you believe it is easier to assess the marginal probabilities of one and the conditional probabilities of the other, or to assess the joint probabilities directly? (*Note*: There is no "correct" answer, but there are unreasonable answers—those that do not reflect reality.)

75. Consider an individual selected at random from a sample of 750 married women (see the data in the file **P05_05.xlsx**) in answering each of the following questions.

  a. What is the probability that this woman does not work outside the home, given that she has at least one child?

  b. What is the probability that this woman has no children, given that she works part time?

  c. What is the probability that this woman has at least two children, given that she does not work full time?

76. Suppose that 8% of all managers in a given company are African American, 13% are women, and 17% have earned an MBA degree from a top-10 graduate business school. Let A, B, and C be, respectively, the events that a randomly selected individual from this population is African American, is a woman, and has earned an MBA from a top-10 graduate business school.

  a. Would you expect A, B, and C to be independent events? Explain why or why not.

  b. Assuming that A, B, and C *are* independent events, compute the probability that a randomly selected manager from this company is a white male and has earned an MBA degree from a top-10 graduate business school.

  c. If A, B, and C are *not* independent events, could you calculate the probability requested in part **b** from the information given? What further information would you need?

77. Consider again the supermarket chain described in Problem 50. Now, assume that the daily sales of the five stores are no longer independent of one another. In particular, the file **P05_77.xlsx** contains the correlations between all pairs of daily sales volumes.

  a. Find the mean and standard deviation of the total profit that this supermarket chain earns in 1 day from the operation of its five stores in Harrisburg. Compare these results to those you found in Problem 50. Explain the differences in your answers.

  b. Find an interval such that the regional sales manager of this supermarket chain can be approximately 95% sure that the total daily profit earned by its stores in Harrisburg will be contained within the interval.

78. A manufacturing plant produces two distinct products, X and Y. The cost of producing one unit of X is $18 and that of Y is $22. Assume that this plant incurs a weekly setup cost of $24,000 regardless of the number of units of X or Y produced. The means and standard deviations of the weekly production levels of X and Y are given in the **P05_78.xlsx**.

a. Assuming that the weekly production levels of X and Y are independent, compute the mean and standard deviation of this plant's total weekly production cost. Between what two total cost figures can we be about 68% sure that this plant's actual total weekly production cost will fall?

b. How do your answers in part **a** change when you discover that the correlation between the weekly production levels of X and Y is actually 0.29? Explain the differences in the two sets of results.

79. The typical standard deviation of the annual return on a stock is 20% and the typical mean return is about 12%. The typical correlation between the annual returns of two stocks is about 0.25. Mutual funds often put an equal percentage of their money in a given number of stocks. By choosing a large number of stocks, they hope to diversify away the risk involved with choosing particular stocks. How many stocks does an investor need to own to diversify away the risk associated with individual stocks? To answer this question, use the above information about "typical" stocks to determine the mean and standard deviation for the following portfolios:

- Portfolio 1: Half your money in each of 2 stocks
- Portfolio 2: 20% of your money in each of 5 stocks
- Portfolio 3: 10% of your money in each of 10 stocks
- Portfolio 4: 5% of your money in each of 20 stocks
- Portfolio 5: 1% of your money in each of 100 stocks

What do your answers tell you about the number of stocks a mutual fund needs to invest in to diversify? (*Hint*: You will need to consider a square range. For portfolio 2, for example, it will be a square range with 25 cells, 5 on the diagonal and 20 off the diagonal. Each diagonal term makes the same contribution to the variance and each off-diagonal term makes the same contribution to the variance.)

80. You are ordering milk for Mr. D's supermarket and you are determined to please! Milk is delivered once a week (at midnight Sunday). The mean and standard deviation of the number of gallons of milk demanded each day are given in the file **P05_80.xlsx**. Determine the mean and standard deviation of the weekly demand for milk. What assumption must you make to determine the weekly standard deviation? Presently you are ordering 1000 gallons per week. Is this a sensible order quantity? Assume all milk spoils after 1 week.

81. At the end of 1995, Wall Street's best estimates of the means, standard deviations, and correlations for the 1996 returns on stocks, bonds, and T-bills were as shown in the file **P05_81.xlsx**. Stocks have the highest average return and the most risk, whereas T-bills have the lowest average return and the least risk. Find the mean and standard deviation for the return on your 1996 investments for the three asset allocations listed in this file. For example, portfolio 1 allocates 53% of all assets to stocks, 6% to bonds, and 41% to T-bills. (This is what most Wall Street firms did.) Based on your results, can you explain why nobody in 1996 should have allocated all their assets to bonds? (*Note*: T-bills are 90-day government issues; the bonds are 10-year government bonds.)

82. The annual returns on stocks 1 and 2 for three possible states of the economy are given in the file **P05_82.xlsx**.

a. Find and interpret the correlation between stocks 1 and 2.

b. Consider another stock (stock 3) that always yields an annual return of 10%. Suppose you invest 60% of your money in stock 1, 10% in stock 2, and 30% in stock 3. Determine the standard deviation of the annual return on your portfolio. (*Hint*: You do not need Excel to compute the variance of stock 3 and the covariance of stock 3 with the other two stocks!)

83. The application at the beginning of this chapter describes the campaign McDonald's used several years ago, where customers could win various prizes.

a. Verify the figures that are given in the description. That is, argue why there are 10 winning outcomes and 120 total outcomes.

b. Suppose McDonald's had designed the cards so that each card had two zaps and three pictures of the winning prize (and again five pictures of other irrelevant prizes). The rules are the same as before: To win, the customer must uncover all three pictures of the winning prize before uncovering a zap. Would there be more or fewer winners with this design? Argue by calculating the probability that a card is a winner.

c. Going back to the original game (as in part **a**), suppose McDonald's printed 1 million cards, each of which was eventually given to a customer. Assume that the (potential) winning prizes on these were: 500,000 Cokes worth $0.40 each, 250,000 french fries worth $0.50 each, 150,000 milk shakes worth $0.75 each, 75,000 hamburgers worth $1.50 each, 20,000 cards with $1 cash as the winning prize, 4000 cards with $10 cash as the winning prize, 800 cards with $100 cash as the winning prize, and 200 cards with $1000 cash as the winning prize. Find the expected amount (the dollar equivalent) that McDonald's gave away in winning prizes, assuming everyone played the game and claimed the prize if they won. Find the standard deviation of this amount.

The results we obtain when we work with conditional probabilities can be quite unintuitive, even paradoxical. This case is similar to one described in an article by Blyth (1972) and is usually referred to as Simpson's paradox. [Two other examples of Simpson's paradox are described in the articles by Westbrooke (1998) and Appleton et al. (1996).] Essentially, Simpson's paradox says that even if one treatment has a better effect than another on *each* of two separate subpopulations, it can have a *worse* effect on the population as a whole.

Suppose that the population is the set of managers in a large company. We categorize the managers as those with an MBA degree (the B's) and those without an MBA degree (the $\overline{B}$'s). These categories are the two "treatment groups." We also categorize the managers as those who were hired directly out of school by this company (the C's) and those who worked with another company first (the $\overline{C}$'s). These two categories form the two "subpopulations." Finally, we use as a measure of effectiveness those managers who have been promoted within the past year (the A's).

Assume the following conditional probabilities are given:

$$P(A|B \text{ and } C) = 0.10, P(A|\overline{B} \text{ and } C) = 0.05 \quad \textbf{(5.19)}$$

$$P(A|B \text{ and}(\overline{C}) = 0.35, P(A|\overline{B} \text{ and } \overline{C}) = 0.20 \quad \textbf{(5.20)}$$

$$P(C|B) = 0.90, P(C|\overline{B}) = 0.30 \quad \textbf{(5.21)}$$

Each of these can be interpreted as a proportion. For example, the probability $P(A|B \text{ and } C)$ implies that

10% of all managers who have an MBA degree and were hired by the company directly out of school were promoted last year. Similar explanations hold for the other probabilities.

Joan Seymour, the head of personnel at this company, is trying to understand these figures. From the probabilities in equation (5.19), she sees that among the subpopulation of workers hired directly out of school, those with an MBA degree are twice as likely to be promoted as those without an MBA degree. Similarly, from the probabilities in equation (5.20), she sees that among the subpopulation of workers hired after working with another company, those with an MBA degree are *almost* twice as likely to be promoted as those without an MBA degree. The information provided by the probabilities in equation (5.21) is somewhat different. From these, she sees that employees with MBA degrees are three times as likely as those without MBA degrees to have been hired directly out of school.

Joan can hardly believe it when a whiz-kid analyst uses these probabilities to show—correctly—that

$$P(A|B) = 0.125, P(A|\overline{B}) = 0.155 \quad \textbf{(5.22)}$$

In words, those employees *without* MBA degrees are more likely to be promoted than those with MBA degrees. This appears to go directly against the evidence in equations (5.19) and (5.20), both of which imply that MBAs have an advantage in being promoted. Can you derive the probabilities in equation (5.22)? Can you shed any light on this "paradox"? ■

Normal, Binomial, Poisson, and Exponential Distributions

© Photodisc/Getty Images

CHALLENGING CLAIMS OF *The Bell Curve*

One of the most controversial books of the past decade is *The Bell Curve* (Herrnstein and Murray, 1994). The authors are the late Richard Herrnstein, a psychologist, and Charles Murray, an economist, both of whom had extensive training in statistics. The book is a scholarly treatment of differences in intelligence, measured by IQ, and its effect on socioeconomic status (SES). The authors argue, by appealing to many past studies and presenting many statistics and graphs, that there are significant differences in IQ among different groups of people, and that these differences are at least partially responsible for differences in SES. Specifically, their basic claims are that (1) there is a quantity, intelligence, that can be measured by an IQ test; (2) the distribution of IQ scores is essentially a symmetric bell-shaped curve; (3) IQ scores are highly correlated with various indicators of success; (4) IQ is determined predominantly by genetic factors and less so by environmental factors; and (5) African Americans score significantly lower—about 15 points lower—on IQ than whites.

Although the discussion of this latter point takes up a relatively small part of the book, it has generated by far the most controversy. Many criticisms of the authors' racial thesis have been based on emotional arguments. However, it can also be criticized on entirely statistical grounds, as Barnett (1995) has done.[1] Barnett never states that the analysis by Herrnstein and Murray is *wrong*. He merely states that (1) the assumptions behind some of the analysis are at best questionable, and (2) some of the crucial details are not made as explicit as they should have been. As he states, "The issue is not that *The Bell Curve* is demonstrably wrong, but that it falls so far short of being demonstrably right. The book does not meet the burden of proof we might reasonably expect of it."

For example, Barnett takes issue with the claim that the genetic component of IQ is, in the words of Herrnstein and Murray, "unlikely to be smaller than 40 percent or higher than 80 percent." Barnett asks what it would mean if genetics made up, say, 60 percent of IQ. His only clue from the book is in an endnote, which implies this definition: If a large population of genetically identical newborns grew up in randomly chosen environments, and their IQs were measured once they reached adulthood, then the variance of these IQs would be 60 percent less than the variance for the entire population. The key word is *variance*. As Barnett notes, however, this statement implies that the corresponding drop in *standard deviation* is only 37 percent. That is, even if all members of the population were exactly the same genetically, differing environments would create a standard deviation of IQs 63 percent as large as the standard deviation that exists today. If this is true, it is hard to argue, as Herrnstein and Murray have done, that environment plays a minor role in determining IQ.

Because the effects of different racial environments are so difficult to disentangle from genetic effects, Herrnstein and Murray try at one point to bypass environmental influences on IQ by matching blacks and whites from similar environments. They report that blacks in the top decile of SES have an average IQ of 104, but that whites within that decile have an IQ 1 standard deviation higher. Even assuming that they have their facts straight, Barnett criticizes the vagueness of their claim. What standard deviation are they referring to: the standard deviation of the entire population or the standard deviation of only the people in the upper decile of SES? The latter is certainly much smaller than the former. Should we assume that the "top-decile blacks" are in the top decile of the black population or of the overall population? If the latter, then the matched comparison between blacks and whites is flawed because the wealthiest 10 percent of whites have far more wealth than the wealthiest 10 percent of blacks. Moreover, even if the reference is to the pooled national population, the matching is imperfect. It is possible that the blacks in this pool could average around the ninth percentile, whereas the whites could average around the fourth percentile, with a significant difference in income between the two groups.

The problem is that Herrnstein and Murray never state these details explicitly. Therefore, we have no way of knowing—without collecting and analyzing all of the data ourselves—whether their results are essentially correct. As Barnett concludes his article, "I believe that *The Bell Curve*'s statements about race would have been better left unsaid even if they were definitely true. And they are surely better left unsaid when, as we have seen, their meaning and accuracy [are] in doubt." ∎

---

[1]Arnold Barnett is a professor in operations research at MIT's Sloan School of Management and specializes in data analyses about issues of health and safety.

6.1 INTRODUCTION

In the previous chapter we discussed probability distributions in general. In this chapter we investigate several specific distributions that commonly occur in a variety of business applications. The first of these is a continuous distribution called the *normal* distribution, which is characterized by a symmetric bell-shaped curve and is the cornerstone of statistical theory. The second distribution is a discrete distribution called the *binomial* distribution. It is relevant when we sample from a population with only two types of members or when we perform a series of independent, identical "experiments" with only two possible outcomes. The other two distributions we will discuss briefly are the *Poisson* and *exponential* distributions. These are often used when we are counting events of some type through time, such as arrivals to a bank. In this case, the Poisson distribution, which is discrete, describes the *number* of arrivals in any period of time, whereas the exponential distribution, which is continuous, describes the *times* between arrivals.

The main goals in this chapter are to present the properties of these distributions, give some examples of when they apply, and see how to perform calculations involving them. Regarding this last objective, analysts have traditionally used special tables to look up probabilities or values for the distributions in this chapter. However, we will see how these tasks can be simplified with the statistical functions available in Excel. Given the availability of these Excel functions, the traditional tables are no longer necessary.

We cannot overemphasize the importance of these distributions. Almost all of the statistical results we will learn in later chapters are based on either the normal distribution or the binomial distribution. The Poisson and exponential distributions play a less important role in this book, but they are nevertheless extremely important in many management science applications. Therefore, it is essential that you become familiar with these distributions before proceeding.

6.2 THE NORMAL DISTRIBUTION

The single most important distribution in statistics is the normal distribution. It is a *continuous* distribution and is the basis of the familiar symmetric bell-shaped curve. The normal distribution is defined by its mean and standard deviation. By changing the mean, we can shift the normal curve to the right or left. By changing the standard deviation, we can make the curve more or less spread out. Therefore, there are really many normal distributions, not just a single normal distribution.

6.2.1 Continuous Distributions and Density Functions

We first take a moment to discuss continuous probability distributions in general. In the previous chapter we discussed discrete distributions, characterized by a list of possible values and their probabilities. The same idea holds for continuous distributions such as the normal distribution, but the mathematics becomes more complex. Now instead of a list of possible values, there is a *continuum* of possible values, such as all values between 0 and 100 or all values greater than 0. Instead of assigning probabilities to each individual value in the continuum, we "spread" the total probability of 1 over this continuum. The key to this spreading is called a *probability density function,* which acts like a histogram. The higher the value of the density function, the more likely this region of the continuum is.

Probability Density Function

A **probability density function,** usually denoted by $f(x)$, specifies the probability distribution of a continuous random variable X. The higher $f(x)$ is, the more likely x is. Also, the total area between the graph of $f(x)$ and the horizontal axis, which represents the total probability, is equal to 1. Finally, $f(x)$ is nonnegative for all possible values of X.

As an example, consider the density function—*not* a normal density function—shown in Figure 6.1. It indicates that all values in the continuum from 25 to 100 are possible, but that the values near 70 are most likely. (This density function might correspond to scores on an exam.) To be a bit more specific, because the height of the density at 70 is approximately twice the height of the curve at 84 or 53, a value near 70 is approximately twice as likely as a value near 84 or a value near 53. In this sense, the height of the density function indicates *relative* likelihoods.

Figure 6.1

A Skewed Density Function

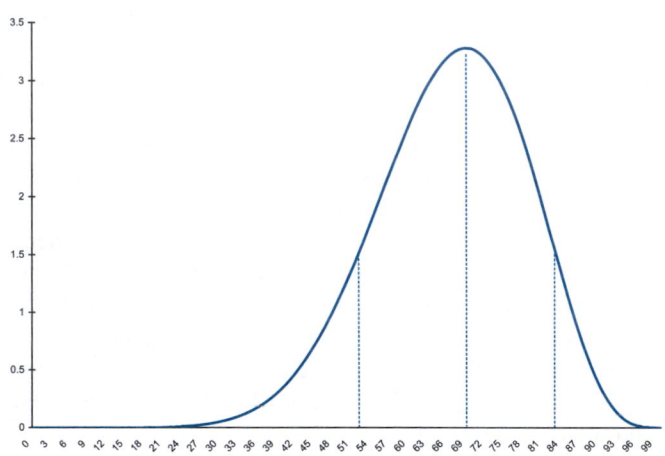

For continuous distributions, probabilities are areas under the density function. These probabilities can often be calculated with special Excel functions. They can be calculated even more easily with the RISKview add-in, which we discuss in Chapter 16.

To find probabilities from a density function, we need to calculate areas under the curve. For example, the area of the designated region in Figure 6.2 represents the probability of a score between 65 and 75. Also, the area under the *entire* curve is 1 because the total probability of all possible values is always 1. Unfortunately, this is about as much as we can say without calculus. Integral calculus is necessary to find areas under curves. Fortunately, statistical tables have been constructed to find such areas for a number of well-known density functions, including the normal. Even better, Excel functions have been developed to find these areas—without the need for bulky tables. We take advantage of these Excel functions as we study the normal distribution (and other distributions).

Figure 6.2

Probability as the Area Under the Density

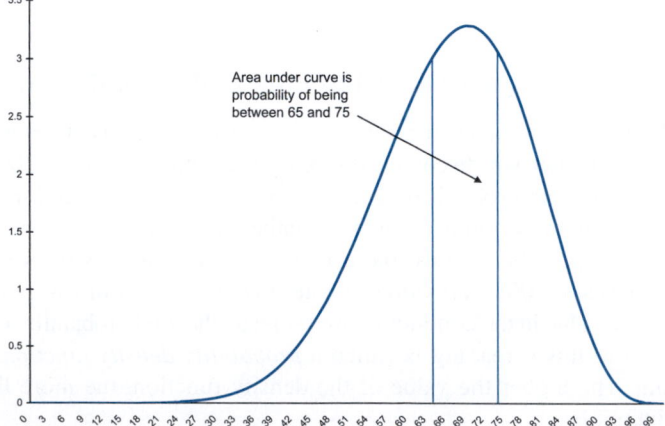

Area under curve is probability of being between 65 and 75

What about the mean and standard deviation (or variance) of a continuous distribution? As before, the mean is a measure of central tendency of the distribution, and the standard deviation (or variance) measures the variability of the distribution. Again, however, calculus is generally required to calculate these quantities. We will simply list their values (which *were* obtained through calculus) for the normal distribution and any other continuous distributions where we need them. By the way, the mean for the density in Figure 6.1 is slightly *less* than 70—it is always to the left of the peak for a left-skewed distribution and to the right of the peak for a right-skewed distribution—and the standard deviation is approximately 15.

6.2.2 The Normal Density

The normal distribution is a continuous distribution with possible values ranging over the *entire* number line—from "minus infinity" to "plus infinity." However, only a relatively small range has much chance of occurring. The normal density function is actually quite complex, in spite of its "nice" bell-shaped appearance. For the sake of completeness, we list the formula for the normal density function in equation (6.1). Here, μ and σ are the mean and standard deviation of the distribution.

Normal Probability Density Function

$$f(x) = \frac{1}{\sqrt{2\pi}\sigma} e^{-(x-\mu)^2/(2\sigma^2)} \quad \text{for } -\infty < x < +\infty \tag{6.1}$$

The curves in Figure 6.3 illustrate several normal density functions for different values of μ and σ. The mean μ can be any number: negative, positive, or zero. As we see, the effect of increasing or decreasing the mean μ is to shift the curve to the right or the left. On the other hand, the standard deviation σ must be a *positive* number. It controls the spread of the normal curve. When σ is small, the curve is more peaked; when σ is large, the curve is more spread out. For shorthand, we use the notation $N(\mu, \sigma)$ to refer to the normal distribution with mean μ and standard deviation σ. For example, $N(-2, 1)$ refers to the normal distribution with mean -2 and standard deviation 1.

Figure 6.3

Several Normal Density Functions

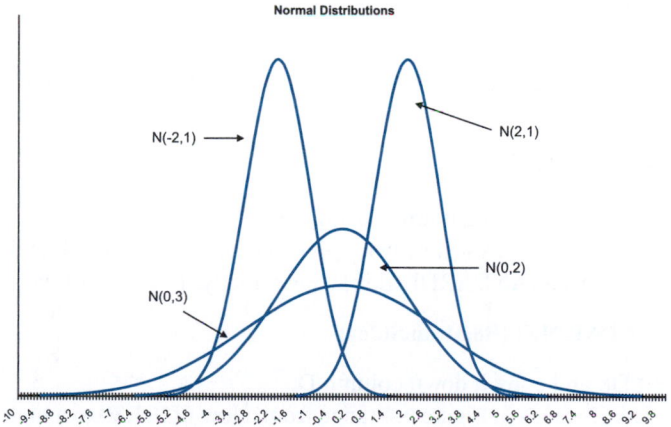

Normal Distributions

6.2.3 Standardizing: Z-Values

There are infinitely many normal distributions, one for each pair μ and σ. We single out one of these for special attention, the *standard normal* distribution. The **standard normal** distribution has mean 0 and standard deviation 1, so we can denote it by $N(0,1)$. It is also referred to as the **Z distribution.** Suppose the random variable X is normally distributed with mean μ and standard deviation σ. We define the random variable Z by equation (6.2). This operation is called *standardizing*. That is, to **standardize** a variable, we subtract its mean and then divide the difference by the standard deviation. When X is normally distributed, the standardized variable is $N(0, 1)$.

Standardizing a Normal Random Variable

$$Z = \frac{X - \mu}{\sigma}$$

(6.2)

One reason for standardizing is to measure variables with different means and/or standard deviations on a single scale. For example, suppose several sections of a college course are taught by different instructors. Because of differences in teaching methods and grading procedures, the distributions of scores in these sections might differ, possibly by a wide margin. However, if each instructor calculates his or her mean and standard deviation and then calculates a Z-value for each student, the distributions of the Z-values should be approximately the same in each section.

It is also easy to interpret a Z-value. It is the number of standard deviations to the right or the left of the mean. If Z is positive, the original value (in this case, the original score) is to the *right* of the mean; if Z is negative, the original score is to the *left* of the mean. For example, if the Z-value for some student is 2, then this student's score is 2 standard deviations above the mean. If the Z-value for another student is -0.5, then this student's score is 0.5 standard deviation below the mean. We illustrate Z-values in the following example.

EXAMPLE | **6.1 STANDARDIZING RETURNS FROM MUTUAL FUNDS**

The annual returns for 30 mutual funds appear in Figure 6.4. (See the file **Standardizing.xlsx.**) Find and interpret the Z-values of these returns.

Objective   To use Excel to standardize annual returns of various mutual funds.

Solution

The 30 annual returns appear in column B of Figure 6.4. Their mean and standard deviation are calculated in cells B4 and B5 with the AVERAGE and STDEV functions. The corresponding Z-values are calculated in column C by entering the formula

=**(B8-Mean)/Stdev**

in cell C8 and copying it down column C.

There is an equivalent way to calculate these Z-values in Excel. We do this in column D, using Excel's STANDARDIZE function directly. To use this function, enter the formula

=**STANDARDIZE(B8,Mean,Stdev)**

in cell D8 and copy it down column D.

The Z-values in Figure 6.4 range from a low of -1.80 to a high of 2.19. Specifically, the return for stock 1 is about 1.80 standard deviations below the mean, whereas the return for fund 17 is about 2.19 standard deviations above the mean. As we will see shortly, these values are typical: Z-values are usually in the range from -2 to $+2$ and values beyond -3 or $+3$ are very uncommon. (Recall the *empirical* rules that we first discussed in Chapter 3.) Also, the Z-values automatically have mean 0 and standard deviation 1, as we see in cells C5 and C6 by using the AVERAGE and STDEV functions on the Z-values in column C (or D).

Figure 6.4

Mutual Fund
Returns and
Z-Values

	A	B	C	D	E	F	G	H
1	Standardizing mutual fund returns							
2								
3	Summary statistics from returns below				Calculated two different ways - the second with the Standardize function			
4	Mean	0.091						
5	Stdev	0.047						
6								
7	Fund	Annual return	Z value	Z value		Range names used		
8	1	0.007	-1.8047	-1.8047		Annual_return	=Data!$B$8:$B$37	
9	2	0.080	-0.2363	-0.2363		Mean	=Data!$B$4	
10	3	0.082	-0.1934	-0.1934		Stdev	=Data!$B$5	
11	4	0.123	0.6875	0.6875				
12	5	0.022	-1.4824	-1.4824				
13	6	0.054	-0.7949	-0.7949				
14	7	0.109	0.3867	0.3867				
15	8	0.097	0.1289	0.1289				
16	9	0.047	-0.9453	-0.9453				
17	10	0.021	-1.5039	-1.5039				
18	11	0.111	0.4297	0.4297				
19	12	0.180	1.9121	1.9121				
20	13	0.157	1.4180	1.4180				
21	14	0.134	0.9238	0.9238				
22	15	0.140	1.0528	1.0528				
23	16	0.107	0.3438	0.3438				
24	17	0.193	2.1914	2.1914				
25	18	0.156	1.3965	1.3965				
26	19	0.095	0.0859	0.0859				
27	20	0.039	-1.1172	-1.1172				
28	21	0.034	-1.2246	-1.2246				
29	22	0.064	-0.5801	-0.5801				
30	23	0.071	-0.4297	-0.4297				
31	24	0.079	-0.2578	-0.2578				
32	25	0.088	-0.0645	-0.0645				
33	26	0.077	-0.3008	-0.3008				
34	27	0.125	0.7305	0.7305				
35	28	0.094	0.0645	0.0645				
36	29	0.078	-0.2793	-0.2793				
37	30	0.066	-0.5371	-0.5371				

6.2.4 Normal Tables and Z-Values[2]

A common use for Z-values and the standard normal distribution is in calculating proba-bilities and percentiles by the "traditional" method. This method is based on a table of the standard normal distribution found in many statistics textbooks. Such a table is given in Figure 6.5. The body of the table contains probabilities. The left and top margins contain possible values. Specifically, suppose we want to find the probability that a standard nor-mal random variable is less than 1.35. We locate 1.3 along the left and 0.05—for the sec-ond decimal in 1.35—along the top, and then read into the table to find the probability 0.9115. In words, the probability is about 0.91 that a standard normal random variable is less than 1.35.

Alternatively, if we are given a probability, we can use the table to find the value with this much probability to the left of it under the standard normal curve. We call this a *percentile* calculation. For example, if the probability is 0.75, we can find the 75th per-centile by locating the probability in the table closest to 0.75 and then reading to the left and up. With interpolation, the required value is approximately 0.675. In words, the proba-bility of being to the left of 0.675 under the standard normal curve is approximately 0.75.

[2]If you intend to rely on Excel functions for normal calculations, you can skip this subsection.

Figure 6.5 Normal Probabilities

z	0.00	0.01	0.02	0.03	0.04	0.05	0.06	0.07	0.08	0.09
0.0	0.5000	0.5040	0.5080	0.5120	0.5160	0.5199	0.5239	0.5279	0.5319	0.5359
0.1	0.5398	0.5438	0.5478	0.5517	0.5557	0.5596	0.5636	0.5675	0.5714	0.5753
0.2	0.5793	0.5832	0.5871	0.5910	0.5948	0.5987	0.6026	0.6064	0.6103	0.6141
0.3	0.6179	0.6217	0.6255	0.6293	0.6331	0.6368	0.6406	0.6443	0.6480	0.6517
0.4	0.6554	0.6591	0.6628	0.6664	0.6700	0.6736	0.6772	0.6808	0.6844	0.6879
0.5	0.6915	0.6950	0.6985	0.7019	0.7054	0.7088	0.7123	0.7157	0.7190	0.7224
0.6	0.7257	0.7291	0.7324	0.7357	0.7389	0.7422	0.7454	0.7486	0.7517	0.7549
0.7	0.7580	0.7611	0.7642	0.7673	0.7704	0.7734	0.7764	0.7794	0.7823	0.7852
0.8	0.7881	0.7910	0.7939	0.7967	0.7995	0.8023	0.8051	0.8078	0.8106	0.8133
0.9	0.8159	0.8186	0.8212	0.8238	0.8264	0.8289	0.8315	0.8340	0.8365	0.8389
1.0	0.8413	0.8438	0.8461	0.8485	0.8508	0.8531	0.8554	0.8577	0.8599	0.8621
1.1	0.8643	0.8665	0.8686	0.8708	0.8729	0.8749	0.8770	0.8790	0.8810	0.8830
1.2	0.8849	0.8869	0.8888	0.8907	0.8925	0.8944	0.8962	0.8980	0.8997	0.9015
1.3	0.9032	0.9049	0.9066	0.9082	0.9099	0.9115	0.9131	0.9147	0.9162	0.9177
1.4	0.9192	0.9207	0.9222	0.9236	0.9251	0.9265	0.9279	0.9292	0.9306	0.9319
1.5	0.9332	0.9345	0.9357	0.9370	0.9382	0.9394	0.9406	0.9418	0.9429	0.9441
1.6	0.9452	0.9463	0.9474	0.9484	0.9495	0.9505	0.9515	0.9525	0.9535	0.9545
1.7	0.9554	0.9564	0.9573	0.9582	0.9591	0.9599	0.9608	0.9616	0.9625	0.9633
1.8	0.9641	0.9649	0.9656	0.9664	0.9671	0.9678	0.9686	0.9693	0.9699	0.9706
1.9	0.9713	0.9719	0.9726	0.9732	0.9738	0.9744	0.9750	0.9756	0.9761	0.9767
2.0	0.9772	0.9778	0.9783	0.9788	0.9793	0.9798	0.9803	0.9808	0.9812	0.9817
2.1	0.9821	0.9826	0.9830	0.9834	0.9838	0.9842	0.9846	0.9850	0.9854	0.9857
2.2	0.9861	0.9864	0.9868	0.9871	0.9875	0.9878	0.9881	0.9884	0.9887	0.9890
2.3	0.9893	0.9896	0.9898	0.9901	0.9904	0.9906	0.9909	0.9911	0.9913	0.9916
2.4	0.9918	0.9920	0.9922	0.9925	0.9927	0.9929	0.9931	0.9932	0.9934	0.9936
2.5	0.9938	0.9940	0.9941	0.9943	0.9945	0.9946	0.9948	0.9949	0.9951	0.9952
2.6	0.9953	0.9955	0.9956	0.9957	0.9959	0.9960	0.9961	0.9962	0.9963	0.9964
2.7	0.9965	0.9966	0.9967	0.9968	0.9969	0.9970	0.9971	0.9972	0.9973	0.9974
2.8	0.9974	0.9975	0.9976	0.9977	0.9977	0.9978	0.9979	0.9979	0.9980	0.9981
2.9	0.9981	0.9982	0.9982	0.9983	0.9984	0.9984	0.9985	0.9985	0.9986	0.9986
3.0	0.9987	0.9987	0.9987	0.9988	0.9988	0.9989	0.9989	0.9989	0.9990	0.9990
3.1	0.9990	0.9991	0.9991	0.9991	0.9992	0.9992	0.9992	0.9992	0.9993	0.9993
3.2	0.9993	0.9993	0.9994	0.9994	0.9994	0.9994	0.9994	0.9995	0.9995	0.9995
3.3	0.9995	0.9995	0.9995	0.9996	0.9996	0.9996	0.9996	0.9996	0.9996	0.9997
3.4	0.9997	0.9997	0.9997	0.9997	0.9997	0.9997	0.9997	0.9997	0.9997	0.9998

We can perform the same kind of calculations for *any* normal distribution if we first standardize. As an example, suppose that X is normally distributed with mean 100 and standard deviation 10. We will find the probability that X is less than 115 and the 85th percentile of this normal distribution. To find the probability that X is less than 115, we first standardize the value 115. The corresponding Z-value is

Z = (115 − 100)/10 = 1.5

Now we look up 1.5 in the table (1.5 row, 0.00 column) to obtain the probability 0.9332. For the percentile question we first find the 85th percentile of the standard normal distribution. Interpolating, we obtain a value of approximately 1.037. Then we set this value equal to a standardized value:

Z = 1.037 = (X − 100)/10

Finally, we solve for X to obtain 110.37. In words, there is a probability 0.85 of being to the left of 110.37 in the $N(100, 10)$ distribution.

There are some obvious drawbacks to using the standard normal table for probability calculations. The first is that there are holes in the table—we often have to interpolate. A second drawback is that the standard normal table takes different forms in different textbooks. These differences are rather minor, but they can easily cause confusion. Finally, the table requires us to perform calculations. For example, we might have to standardize. More importantly, we often have to use the symmetry of the normal distribution to find probabilities that are not in the table. As an example, to find the probability that Z is less than -1.5, we must go through some mental gymnastics. First, by symmetry this is the same as the probability that Z is greater than 1.5. Then, because only left-tail probabilities are tabulated, we must find the probability that Z is less than 1.5 and subtract this probability from 1. The chain of reasoning is

$$P(Z < -1.5) = P(Z > 1.5) = 1 - P(Z < 1.5) = 1 - 0.9332 = 0.0668$$

This is not too difficult, given a bit of practice, but it is easy to make a mistake. Spreadsheet functions make the whole procedure much easier and less prone to errors.

6.2.5 Normal Calculations in Excel

Two types of calculations are typically made with normal distributions: finding probabilities and finding percentiles. Excel makes each of these fairly simple. The functions used for normal probability calculations are NORMDIST and NORMSDIST. The main difference between these is that the one with the "S" (for standardized) applies only to $N(0, 1)$ calculations, whereas NORMDIST applies to *any* normal distribution. On the other hand, percentile calculations, where we supply a probability and require a value, are often called *inverse* calculations. Therefore, the Excel functions for these are named NORMINV and NORMSINV. Again, the "S" in the second of these indicates that it applies only to the standard normal distribution.

The NORMDIST and NORMSDIST functions give left-tail probabilities, such as the probability that a normally distributed variable is *less than* 35. The syntax for these functions is

=NORMDIST(x,μ,σ,1)

and

=NORMSDIST(x)

Here, x is a number we supply, and μ and σ are the mean and standard deviation of the normal distribution. The last argument "1" in the NORMDIST function is used to obtain the *cumulative* normal probability, the only kind we'll ever need. (This 1 is a bit of a nuisance to remember, but it's necessary.) Note that NORMSDIST takes only one argument (because μ and σ are known to be 0 and 1), so it is easier to use—when it applies.

The NORMINV and NORMSINV functions return values for user-supplied probabilities. For example, if we supply the probability 0.95, these functions return the 95th percentile. Their syntax is

=NORMINV(p,μ,σ)

and

=NORMSINV(p)

where p is a probability we supply. These are analogous to the NORMDIST and NORMSDIST functions (except there is no fourth argument "1" in the NORMINV function).

We illustrate these Excel functions in the following example.[3]

---

[3]Actually, we already illustrated the NORMSDIST function; it was used to create the body of Figure 6.5. In other words, you can use it to build your own normal probability table!

EXAMPLE **6.2 BECOMING FAMILIAR WITH NORMAL CALCULATIONS IN EXCEL**

Use Excel to calculate the following probabilities and percentiles for the standard normal distribution: (a) $P(Z < -2)$, (b) $P(Z > 1)$, (c) $P(-0.4 < Z < 1.6)$, (d) the 5th percentile, (e) the 75th percentile, and (f) the 99th percentile. Then for the $N(75, 8)$ distribution, find the following probabilities and percentiles: (a) $P(X < 70)$, (b) $P(X > 73)$, (c) $P(75 < X < 85)$, (d) the 5th percentile, (e) the 60th percentile, and (f) the 97th percentile.

Objective To calculate probabilities and percentiles for standard normal and nonstandard normal random variables in Excel.

Solution

The solution appears in Figure 6.6. (See the file **Normal Calculations.xlsx**.) The $N(0, 1)$ calculations are in rows 7 through 14; the $N(75, 8)$ calculations are in rows 23 through 30. For your convenience, the formulas used in column B are spelled out in column D (as labels). Note that the standard normal calculations use the normal functions with the "S" in the middle; the rest use the normal functions without the "S"—and require more arguments.

Figure 6.6 Normal Calculations with Excel Functions

	A	B	C	D	E	F	G	H	I
1	Normal probability calculations								
2									
3	Examples with standard normal								
4									
5	Probability calculations								
6	Range	Probability		Formula					
7	Less than -2	0.0228		=NORMSDIST(-2)					
8	Greater than 1	0.1587		=1-NORMSDIST(1)					
9	Between -.4 and 1.6	0.6006		=NORMSDIST(1.6)-NORMSDIST(-0.4)					
10									
11	Percentiles								
12	5th	-1.645		=NORMSINV(0.05)					
13	75th	0.674		=NORMSINV(0.75)					
14	99th	2.326		=NORMSINV(0.99)					
15									
16	Examples with nonstandard normal								
17				Range names used:					
18	Mean	75		Mean	=Normal!$B$18				
19	Stdev	8		Stdev	=Normal!$B$19				
20									
21	Probability calculations								
22	Range	Probability		Formula					
23	Less than 70	0.2660		=NORMDIST(70,Mean,Stdev,1)					
24	Greater than 73	0.5987		=1-NORMDIST(73,Mean,Stdev,1)					
25	Between 75 and 85	0.3944		=NORMDIST(85,Mean,Stdev,1)-NORMDIST(75,Mean,Stdev,1)					
26									
27	Percentiles								
28	5th	61.841		=NORMINV(0.05,Mean,Stdev)					
29	60th	77.027		=NORMINV(0.6,Mean,Stdev)					
30	97th	90.046		=NORMINV(0.97,Mean,Stdev)					

Note the following for normal *probability* calculations:

■ For "less than" probabilities, use NORMDIST or NORMSDIST directly. (See rows 7 and 23.)

- For "greater than" probabilities, subtract the NORMDIST or NORMSDIST function from 1. (See rows 8 and 24.)
- For "between" probabilities, subtract the two NORMDIST or NORMSDIST functions. For example, in row 9 the probability of being between -0.4 and 1.6 is the probability of being less than 1.6 minus the probability of being less than -0.4.

The percentile calculations are even more straightforward. In most percentile problems we want to find the value with a certain probability to the *left* of it. In this case we use the NORMINV or NORMSINV function with the specified probability as the first argument. See rows 12 through 14 and 28 through 30. ∎

There are a couple of variations of percentile calculations. First, suppose we want the value with probability 0.05 to the *right* of it. This is the same as the value with probability 0.95 to the left of it, so we use NORMINV or NORMSINV with probability argument 0.95. For example, the value with probability 0.4 to the right of it in the $N(75, 8)$ distribution is 77.027. (See cell B29 in Figure 6.6.)

As a second variation, suppose we want to find an interval of the form $-x$ to x, for some positive number x, with (1) probability 0.025 to the left of $-x$, (2) probability 0.025 to the right of x, and (3) probability 0.95 between $-x$ and x. This is a very common problem in statistical inference. In general, we want a probability (such as 0.95) to be in the middle of the interval so that half of the remaining probability (0.025) is in each of the tails. (See Figure 6.7.) Then the required x can be found with NORMINV or NORMSINV, using probability argument 0.975, because there must be a total probability of 0.975 to the left of x.

For example, if the relevant distribution is the standard normal, then the required value of x is 1.96, found with the function NORMSINV(0.975). Similarly, if we want probability 0.90 in the middle and probability 0.05 in each tail, the required x is 1.645, found with the function NORMSINV(0.95). Remember these two numbers, 1.96 and 1.645. They occur frequently in statistical applications.

Figure 6.7

Typical Normal
Probabilities

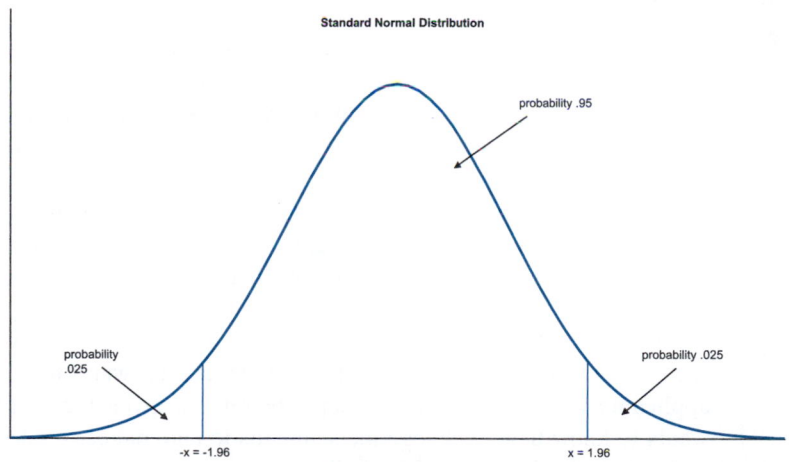

Standard Normal Distribution

probability .95

probability
.025

probability .025

$-x = -1.96$ $x = 1.96$

6.2.6 Empirical Rules Revisited

Chapter 3 introduced three empirical rules that apply to many data sets. Namely, about 68% of the data fall within 1 standard deviation of the mean, about 95% fall within 2 standard deviations of the mean, and almost all fall within 3 standard deviations of the mean. For these rules to hold with real data, the distribution of the data must be at least approximately symmetric and bell shaped. Let's look at these rules more closely.

Let X be normally distributed with mean μ and standard deviation σ. To perform a probability calculation on X, we can first standardize X and then perform the calculation on the standardized variable Z. Specifically, we will find the probability that X is within k standard deviations of its mean for $k = 1$, $k = 2$, and $k = 3$. In general, this probability is $P(\mu - k\sigma < X < \mu + k\sigma)$. But by standardizing the values $\mu - k\sigma$ and $\mu + k\sigma$, we obtain the equivalent probability $P(-k < Z < k)$, where Z has a $N(0, 1)$ distribution. This latter probability can be calculated in Excel with the formula

=NORMSDIST(k)−NORMSDIST(−k)

The normal distribution is the basis for the empirical rules introduced in Chapter 3.

By substituting the values 1, 2, and 3 for k, we find the following probabilities:

$P(-1 < Z < 1) = 0.6827$
$P(-2 < Z < 2) = 0.9545$
$P(-3 < Z < 3) = 0.9973$

As we see, there is virtually no chance of being beyond 3 standard deviations from the mean, the chances are about 19 out of 20 of being within 2 standard deviations of the mean, and the chances are about 2 out of 3 of being within 1 standard deviation of the mean. These probabilities are the basis for the empirical rules in Chapter 3. These rules more closely approximate reality as the histograms of observed data become more bell shaped.

6.3 APPLICATIONS OF THE NORMAL DISTRIBUTION

In this section we apply the normal distribution to a variety of business problems.

EXAMPLE 6.3 PERSONNEL TESTING AT ZTEL

The personnel department of ZTel, a large communications company, is reconsidering its hiring policy. Each applicant for a job must take a standard exam, and the hire or no-hire decision depends at least in part on the result of the exam. The scores of all applicants have been examined closely. They are approximately normally distributed with mean 525 and standard deviation 55.

The current hiring policy occurs in two phases. The first phase separates all applicants into three categories: automatic accepts, automatic rejects, and "maybes." The automatic accepts are those whose test scores are 600 or above. The automatic rejects are those whose test scores are 425 or below. All other applicants (the "maybes") are passed on to a second phase where their previous job experience, special talents, and other factors are used as hiring criteria. The personnel manager at ZTel wants to calculate the percentage of applicants who are automatic accepts or rejects, given the current standards. She also wants to know how to change the standards to automatically reject 10% of all applicants and automatically accept 15% of all applicants.

Objective To determine test scores that can be used to accept or reject job applicants at ZTel.

Solution

Let X be the test score of a typical applicant. Then the distribution of X is $N(525, 55)$. If we find a probability such as $P(X \le 425)$, we can interpret this as the probability that a typical applicant is an automatic reject, or we can interpret it as the percentage of *all* applicants who are automatic rejects. Given this observation, the solution to ZTel's problem appears in Figure 6.8. (See the file **Personnel Decisions.xlsx**.) The probability that a typical applicant is automatically accepted is 0.0863, found in cell B10 with the formula

=1−NORMDIST(B7,Mean,Stdev,1)

Figure 6.8

Calculations for Personnel Example

	A	B	C	D	E	F
1	**Personnel Decisions**					
2				Range names used:		
3	Mean of test scores	525		Mean	=Model!$B$3	
4	Stdev of test scores	55		Stdev	=Model!$B$4	
5						
6	**Current Policy**					
7	Automatic accept point	600				
8	Automatic reject point	425				
9						
10	Percent accepted	8.63%		=1-NORMDIST(B7,Mean,Stdev,1)		
11	Percent rejected	3.45%		=NORMDIST(B8,Mean,Stdev,1)		
12						
13	**New Policy**					
14	Percent accepted	15%				
15	Percent rejected	10%				
16						
17	Automatic accept point	582		=NORMINV(1-B14,Mean,Stdev)		
18	Automatic reject point	455		=NORMINV(B15,Mean,Stdev)		

Similarly, the probability that a typical applicant is automatically rejected is 0.0345, found in cell B11 with the formula

=NORMDIST(B8,Mean,Stdev,1)

Therefore, ZTel automatically accepts about 8.6% and rejects about 3.5% of all applicants under the current policy.

To find new cutoff values that reject 10% and accept 15% of the applicants, we need the 10th and 85th percentiles of the $N(525, 55)$ distribution. These are 455 and 582 (rounded to the nearest integer), respectively, found in cells B17 and B18 with the formulas

=NORMINV(1-B14,Mean,Stdev)

and

=NORMINV(B15,Mean,Stdev)

To accomplish its objective, ZTel needs to raise the automatic rejection point from 425 to 455 and lower the automatic acceptance point from 600 to 582. ∎

EXAMPLE | **6.4 QUALITY CONTROL AT PAPERSTOCK COMPANY**

The PaperStock Company runs a manufacturing facility that produces a paper product. The fiber content of this product is supposed to be 20 pounds per 1000 square feet. (This is typical for the type of paper used in grocery bags, for example.) Because of random variations in the inputs to the process, however, the fiber content of a typical 1000-square-foot roll varies according to a $N(\mu, \sigma)$ distribution. The mean fiber content (μ) can be controlled—that is, it can be set to any desired level by adjusting an instrument on the machine. The variability in fiber content, as measured by the standard deviation σ, is 0.1 pound when the process is "good," but it sometimes increases to 0.15 pound when the machine goes "bad." A given roll of this product must be rejected if its actual fiber content is less than 19.8 pounds or greater than 20.3 pounds. Calculate the probability that a given roll is rejected, for a setting of $\mu = 20$, when the machine is "good" and when it is "bad."

Objective To determine the machine settings that result in paper of acceptable quality at PaperStock Company.

Solution

Let X be the fiber content of a typical roll. The distribution of X will be either $N(20, 0.1)$ or $N(20, 0.15)$, depending on the status of the machine. In either case, the probability that the roll must be rejected can be calculated as shown in Figure 6.9. (See the file **Paper Machine Settings.xlsx**.) The formula for rejection in the "good" case appears in cell B12:

=NORMDIST(B8,Mean,Stdev_good,1)+(1-NORMDIST(B9,Mean,Stdev_good,1))

Figure 6.9 Calculations for Paper Quality Example

	A	B	C	D	E	F	G	H	I	J
1	Paper Machine Settings			Range names used:						
2				Mean	=Model!$B$3					
3	Mean	20		Stdev_bad	=Model!$B$5					
4	Stdev in good case	0.1		Stdev_good	=Model!$B$4					
5	Stdev in bad case	0.15								
6										
7	Reject region									
8	Lower limit	19.8								
9	Upper limit	20.3								
10										
11	Probability of reject									
12	in good case	0.024		=NORMDIST(B8,Mean,Stdev_good,1)+(1-NORMDIST(B9,Mean,Stdev_good,1))						
13	in bad case	0.114		=NORMDIST(B8,Mean,Stdev_bad,1)+(1-NORMDIST(B9,Mean,Stdev_bad,1))						
14										
15	Data table of rejection probability as a function of the mean and good standard deviation									
16					Standard deviation					
17		0.024	0.1	0.11	0.12	0.13	0.14	0.15		
18		19.7	0.841	0.818	0.798	0.779	0.762	0.748		
19		19.8	0.500	0.500	0.500	0.500	0.500	0.500		
20		19.9	0.159	0.182	0.203	0.222	0.240	0.256		
21	Mean	20	0.024	0.038	0.054	0.072	0.093	0.114		
22		20.1	0.024	0.038	0.054	0.072	0.093	0.114		
23		20.2	0.159	0.182	0.203	0.222	0.240	0.256		
24		20.3	0.500	0.500	0.500	0.500	0.500	0.500		
25		20.4	0.841	0.818	0.798	0.779	0.762	0.748		

It is the sum of two probabilities: the probability of being to the left of the lower limit and the probability of being to the right of the upper limit. These probabilities of rejection are represented graphically in Figure 6.10. A similar formula for the "bad" case appears in cell B13, using Stdev_bad in place of Stdev_good.

Figure 6.10

Rejection Regions
for Paper Quality
Example

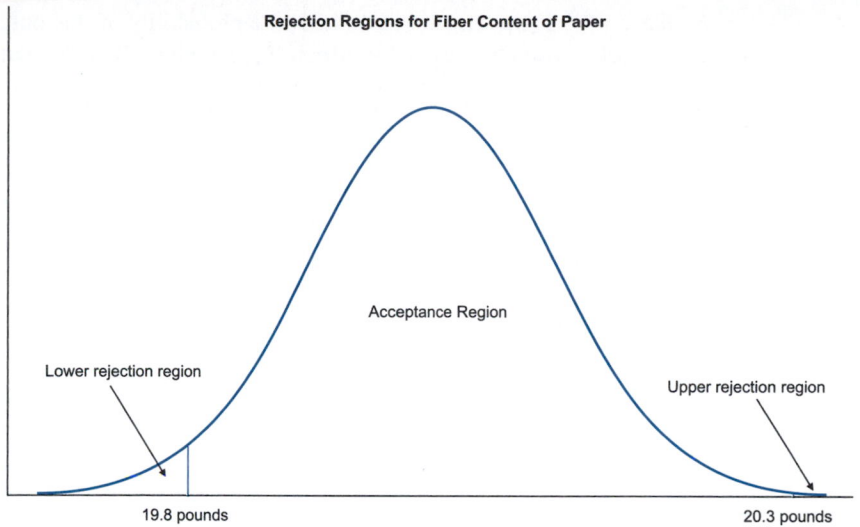

We see that the probability of a rejected roll in the "good" case is 0.024; in the "bad" case it is 0.114. That is, when the standard deviation increases by 50% from 0.1 to 0.15, the percentage of rolls rejected more than quadruples, from 2.4% to 11.4%.

It is certainly possible that the true process mean and "good" standard deviation will not always be equal to the values we've assumed in cells B3 and B4. Therefore, it is useful to see how sensitive the rejection probability is to these two parameters. We do this with a two-way data table, as shown in Figure 6.9. The tabulated values show that the probability of rejection varies greatly even for small changes in the key inputs. In particular, a combination of a badly centered mean and a large standard deviation can make the probability of rejection very large. ■

To form this data table, enter the formula =B12 in cell B17, highlight the range B17:H25, and create a data table with row input cell B4 and column input cell B3.

E X A M P L E | **6.5 ANALYZING AN INVESTOR'S AFTER-TAX PROFIT**

Howard Davis invests $10,000 in a certain stock on January 1. By examining past movements of this stock and consulting with his broker, Howard estimates that the annual return from this stock, X, is normally distributed with mean 10% and standard deviation 4%. Here X (when expressed as a decimal) is the profit Howard receives per dollar invested. It means that on December 31, his $10,000 will have grown to $10,000(1 + X)$ dollars. Because Howard is in the 33% tax bracket, he will then have to pay the Internal Revenue Service 33% of his profit. Calculate the probability that Howard will have to pay the IRS at least $400. Also, calculate the dollar amount such that Howard's after-tax profit is 90% certain to be less than this amount; that is, calculate the 90th percentile of his after-tax profit.

Objective To determine the after-tax profit Howard Davis can be 90% certain of earning.

Solution

Howard's before-tax profit is $10,000X$ dollars, so the amount he pays the IRS is $0.33(10,000X)$, or $3300X$ dollars. We want the probability that this is at least $400. Because

$3300X > 400$ is the same as $X > 4/33$, the probability of this outcome can be found as in Figure 6.11. (See the file **Tax on Stock Return.xlsx**.) It is calculated with the formula

=1-NORMDIST(400/(Amount_invested*Tax_rate),Mean,Stdev,1)

in cell B8. As we see, Howard has about a 30% chance of paying at least $400 in taxes.

To answer the second question, note that the after-tax profit is 67% of the before-tax profit, or $6700X$ dollars, and we want its 90th percentile. If this percentile is x, then we know that $P(6700X < x) = 0.90$, which is the same as $P(X < x/6700) = 0.90$. In words, we want the 90th percentile of the X distribution to be $x/6700$. From cell B10 of Figure 6.11, we see that the 90th percentile is 15.13%, so the required value of x is $1,013. Note that the *mean* after-tax profit is $670 (67% of the mean before-tax profit of 0.10 multiplied by $10,000). Of course, Howard might get lucky and make more than this, but he is 90% certain that his after-tax profit will be no greater than $1013. ■

Figure 6.11   Calculations for Taxable Returns Example

	A	B	C	D	E	F	G	H	I
1	Tax on Stock Return								
2				Range names used:					
3	Amount invested	$10,000		Amount_invested	=Model!$B$3				
4	Mean	10%		Mean	=Model!$B$4				
5	Stdev	4%		Stdev	=Model!$B$5				
6	Tax rate	33%		Tax_rate	=Model!$B$6				
7									
8	Probability he pays at least $400 in taxes	0.298		=1-NORMDIST(400/(Amount_invested*Tax_rate),Mean,Stdev,1)					
9									
10	90th percentile of stock return	15.13%		=NORMINV(0.9,Mean,Stdev)					
11	90th percentile of after-tax return	$1,013		=(1-Tax_rate)*Amount_invested*B10					

It is sometimes tempting to model every continuous random variable with a normal distribution. This can be dangerous for at least two reasons. First, not all random variables have a *symmetric* distribution. Some are skewed to the left or the right, and for these the normal distribution can be a poor approximation. The second problem is that many random variables in real applications must be *nonnegative,* and the normal distribution allows the possibility of negative values. The following example shows how assuming normality can get us into trouble if we aren't careful.

EXAMPLE   **6.6 PREDICTING FUTURE DEMAND FOR MICROWAVE OVENS AT HIGHLAND COMPANY**

The Highland Company is a retailer that sells microwave ovens. The company wants to model its demand for microwaves over the next 12 years. Using historical data as a guide, it assumes that demand in year 1 is normally distributed with mean 5000 and standard deviation 1500. It assumes that demand in every subsequent year is normally distributed with mean equal to the *actual* demand from the previous year and standard deviation 1500. For example, if demand in year 1 turns out to be 4500, then the *mean* demand in year 2 is 4500. This assumption appears plausible because it leads to correlated demands. For example, if demand is high one year, it will tend to be high the next year. Investigate the ramifications of this model, and suggest models that might be more realistic.

Objective To construct and analyze a spreadsheet model for microwave oven demand over the next 12 years using Excel's NORMINV function, and to show how "normal" models can lead to nonsensical outcomes unless we are careful.

Solution

The best way to analyze this model is with simulation, much as we did in Chapter 5. To do this, we must be able to simulate normally distributed random numbers in Excel. We can do this with the NORMINV function. Specifically, to generate a normally distributed number with mean μ and standard deviation σ, we use the formula

$$=\text{NORMINV}(\text{RAND}(),\mu,\sigma)$$

Because this formula uses the RAND function, it generates a *different* random number each time it is used—and each time the spreadsheet recalculates.[4]

The spreadsheet in Figure 6.12 shows a simulation of yearly demands over a 12-year period. (See the file **Oven Demand Simulation.xlsx**.) To simulate the demands in row 15, we enter the formula

Figure 6.12 One Set of Demands for Model 1 in the Microwave Example

$$=\text{NORMINV}(\text{RAND}(),\text{B6},\text{B7})$$

in cell B15. Then we enter the formula

$$=\text{NORMINV}(\text{RAND}(),\text{B15},\$\text{B}\$11)$$

[4]To see why this formula makes sense, note that the RAND function in the first argument generates a uniformly distributed random value between 0 and 1. Therefore, the effect of the function is to generate a random *percentile* from the normal distribution.

in cell C15 and copy it across row 15. (Note how the mean demand in any year is the *simulated* demand from the previous year.) As the accompanying time series graph of these demands indicates, the model seems to be performing well.

However, the simulated demands in Figure 6.12 are only one set of possible demands. Remember that each time the spreadsheet recalculates, all of the random numbers change.[5] Figure 6.13 shows a different set of random numbers generated by the *same* formulas. Clearly, the model is not working well in this case—some demands are negative, which makes no sense. The problem is that if the actual demand is low in one year, there is a fair chance that the next normally distributed demand will be negative. You can check (by recalculating many times) that the demand sequence is *usually* all positive, but every now and then you'll get a nonsense sequence as in Figure 6.13. We need a new model!

One way to modify the model is to let the standard deviation and mean move together. That is, if the mean is low, then the standard deviation will also be low. This minimizes the chance that the *next* random demand will become negative. Besides, this type of model is probably more realistic. If demand in one year is low, there is likely to be less variability in next year's demand. Figure 6.14 illustrates one way to model this changing standard deviation.

Figure 6.13   Another Set of Demands for Model 1 in the Microwave Example

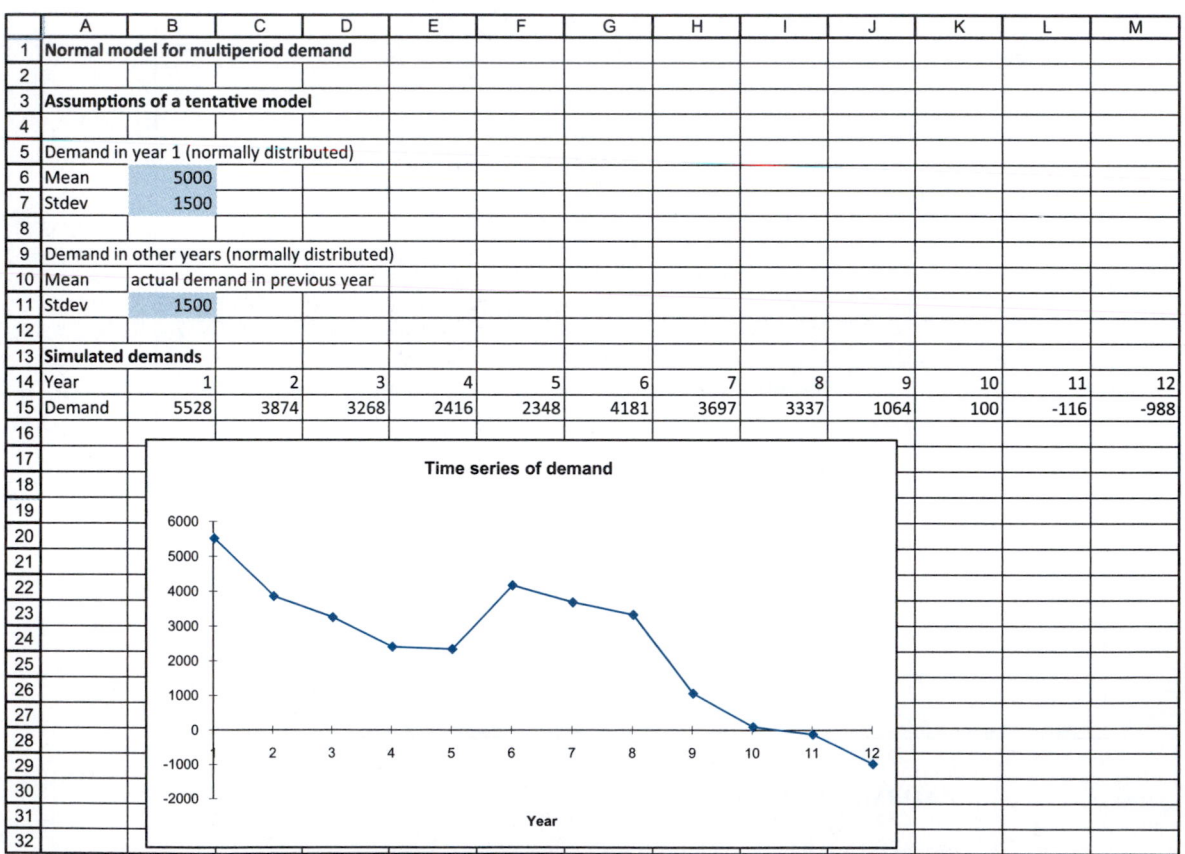

	A	B	C	D	E	F	G	H	I	J	K	L	M
1	Normal model for multiperiod demand												
2													
3	Assumptions of a tentative model												
4													
5	Demand in year 1 (normally distributed)												
6	Mean	5000											
7	Stdev	1500											
8													
9	Demand in other years (normally distributed)												
10	Mean	actual demand in previous year											
11	Stdev	1500											
12													
13	Simulated demands												
14	Year	1	2	3	4	5	6	7	8	9	10	11	12
15	Demand	5528	3874	3268	2416	2348	4181	3697	3337	1064	100	-116	-988

Figure 6.14 Generated Demands for Model 2 in Microwave Example

	A	B	C	D	E	F	G	H	I	J	K	L	M
1	Normal model for multiperiod demand												
2													
3	Assumptions of a "safer" model												
4													
5	Demand in year 1 (normally distributed)												
6	Mean	5000											
7	Stdev	1500											
8													
9	Demand in other years (normally distributed)												
10	Mean	actual demand in previous year											
11	Stdev	1500 times ratio of previous year's actual demand to year 1's mean demand											
12													
13	Simulated demands												
14	Year	1	2	3	4	5	6	7	8	9	10	11	12
15	Demand	6521	6255	8239	6856	9638	7045	7122	4877	7212	10681	5211	4211
16													
17													

We let the standard deviation of demand in any year (after year 1) be the original standard deviation, 1500, multiplied by the ratio of the expected demand for this year to the expected demand in year 1. For example, if demand in some year is 500, then the expected demand next year is 500, and the standard deviation of next year's demand is reduced to 1500(500/5000) = 150. The only change to the spreadsheet model is in row 15, where we enter

=NORMINV(RAND(),B15,$B$7*B15/$B$6)

in cell C15 and copy it across row 15. Now the chance of a negative demand is practically negligible because this would require a value more than 3 standard deviations below the mean.

The model in Figure 6.14 is still not foolproof. By recalculating many times, we can still generate a negative demand now and then. To be even safer, we can "truncate" the demand distribution at some nonnegative value such as 250, as shown in Figure 6.15. Now we generate a random demand as in the previous model, but if this randomly generated value is below 250, we set the demand equal to 250. This is done by entering the formulas

=MAX(NORMINV(RAND(),B8,B9),D5)

and

=MAX(NORMINV(RAND(),B17,$B$9*B17/$B$8),$D$5)

in cells B17 and C17 and copying this latter formula across row 17. Whether this is the way the demand process works for Highland's microwaves is an open question, but at least we have prevented demands from ever becoming negative—or even falling below 250. Moreover, this type of truncation is a common way of modeling when we want to use a normal distribution but for physical reasons cannot allow the random quantities to become negative.

Figure 6.15 Generated Demands for a Truncated Model in Microwave Example

	A	B	C	D	E	F	G	H	I	J	K	L	M
1	Normal model for multiperiod demand												
2													
3	Assumptions of an even "safer" model												
4													
5	Minimum demand in any year			250									
6													
7	Demand in year 1 (truncated normal)												
8	Mean	5000											
9	Stdev	1500											
10													
11	Demand in other years (truncated normal)												
12	Mean	actual demand in previous year											
13	Stdev	1500 times ratio of previous year's actual demand to year 1's mean demand											
14													
15	Simulated demands												
16	Year	1	2	3	4	5	6	7	8	9	10	11	12
17	Demand	4087	1956	2274	2846	1947	1458	1969	1887	1572	2695	2483	1088
18													
19													
20													
21													
22													
23													
24													
25													
26													
27													
28													
29													
30													
31													
32													

Before leaving this example, we challenge your intuition. In the final model in Figure 6.15, the demand in any year (say, year 6) is, aside from the truncation, normally distributed with a mean and standard deviation that depend on the previous year's demand. Does this mean that if we recalculate many times and keep track of the year 6 demand each time, the resulting histogram of these year 6 demands will be normally distributed? Perhaps surprisingly, the answer is a clear "no." We show the evidence in Figures 6.16 and 6.17. In Figure 6.16 we use a data table to obtain 400 replications of demand in year 6 (in column B). Then we use StatTools's histogram procedure to create a histogram of these simulated demands in Figure 6.17. It is clearly skewed to the right and *nonnormal.*

What causes this distribution to be nonnormal? It is *not* the truncation. Truncation has a relatively minor effect because most of the demands don't need to be truncated anyway. The real reason is that the distribution of year 6 demand is only normal *conditional* on the demand in year 5. That is, if we fix the demand in year 5 at any level and then replicate year 6 demand many times, the resulting histogram *is* normally shaped. But we don't fix the year 5 demand. It varies from replication to replication, and this variation causes the skewness in Figure 6.17. Admittedly, the reason for this skewness is not obvious from an intuitive standpoint, but simulation makes it easy to demonstrate.

Figure 6.16

Replication of Demand in Year 6

	A	B	C	D	E
36	Replication	Demand			
37		4476		Average	4916
38	1	1635		Stdev	3956
39	2	8229			
40	3	3582			
41	4	11282			
42	5	2845			
43	6	3942			
44	7	5700			
45	8	12273			
433	396	8919			
434	397	4587			
435	398	10003			
436	399	5012			
437	400	3944			

Figure 6.17 Histogram of Year 6 Demands

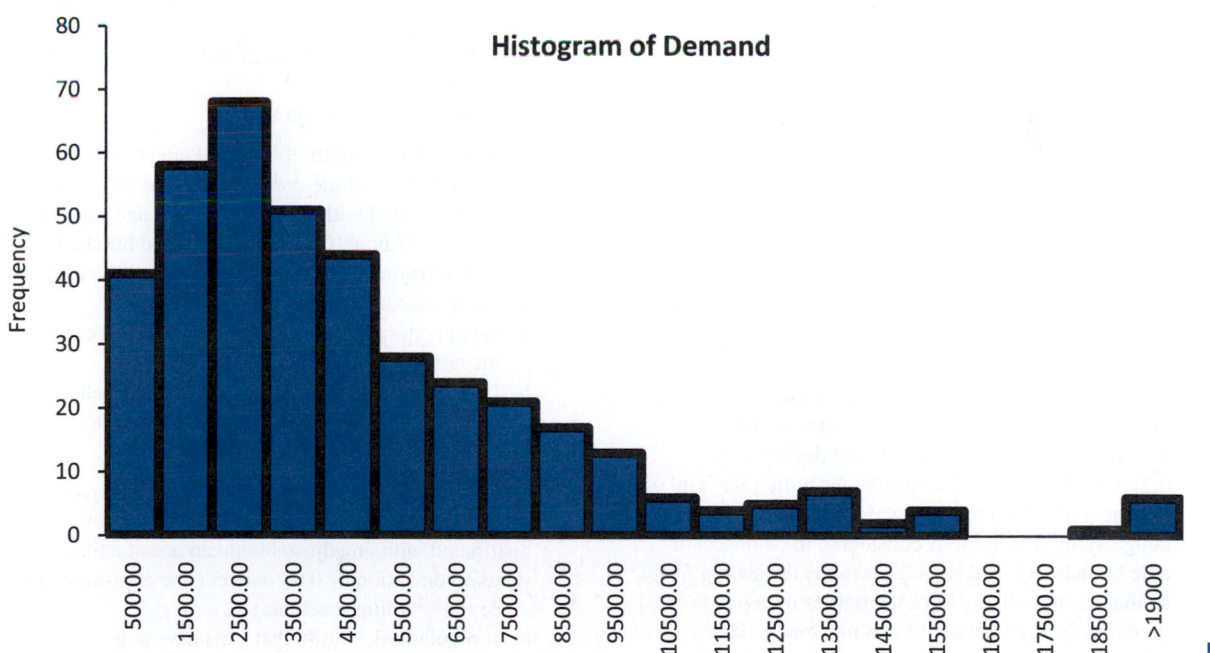

Level A

1. The grades on the midterm examination given in a large managerial statistics class are normally distributed with mean 75 and standard deviation 9. The instructor of this class wants to assign an A grade to the top 10% of the scores, a B grade to the next 10% of the scores, a C grade to the next 10% of the scores, a D grade to the next 10% of the scores, and an F grade to all scores below the 60th percentile of this distribution. For each possible letter grade, find the lowest acceptable score within the established range. For example, the lowest acceptable score for an A is the score at the 90th percentile of this normal distribution.

2. Suppose it is known that the distribution of purchase amounts by customers entering a popular retail store is approximately normal with mean $25 and standard deviation $8.
   a. What is the probability that a randomly selected customer spends less than $35 at this store?
   b. What is the probability that a randomly selected customer spends between $15 and $35 at this store?
   c. What is the probability that a randomly selected customer spends more than $10 at this store?
   d. Find the dollar amount such that 75% of all customers spend no more than this amount.
   e. Find the dollar amount such that 80% of all customers spend at least this amount.
   f. Find two dollars amounts, equidistant from the mean of $25, such that 90% of all customer purchases are between these values.

3. A machine used to regulate the amount of a certain chemical dispensed in the production of a particular type of cough syrup can be set so that it discharges an average of μ milliliters (ml) of the chemical in each bottle of cough syrup. The amount of chemical placed into each bottle of cough syrup is known to have a normal distribution with a standard deviation of 0.250 ml. If this machine discharges more than 2 ml of the chemical when preparing a given bottle of this cough syrup, the bottle is considered to be unacceptable by industry standards. Determine the setting for μ so that no more than 1% of the bottles of cough syrup prepared through the use of this machine will be rejected.

4. The weekly demand for Ford car sales follows a normal distribution with mean 50,000 cars and standard deviation 14,000 cars.
   a. There is a 1% chance that Ford will sell more than what number of cars during the next year?

   b. What is the probability that Ford will sell between 2.4 and 2.7 million cars during the next year?

5. Warren Dinner has invested in nine different investments. The returns on the different investments are probabilistically independent, and each return follows a normal distribution with mean $500 and standard deviation $100.
   a. There is a 1% chance that the total return on the nine investments is less than what value? (Use the fact that the sum of independent normal random variables is normally distributed, with mean equal to the sum of the individual means, and variance equal to the sum of the individual variances.)
   b. What is the probability that Warren's total return is between $4000 and $5200?

6. Scores on an exam appear to follow a normal distribution with $\mu = 60$ and $\sigma = 20$. The instructor wishes to give a grade of D to students scoring between the 10th and 30th percentiles on the exam. For what range of scores should a D be given?

7. Suppose the weight of a typical American male follows a normal distribution with $\mu = 180$ lb and $\sigma = 30$ lb. Also, suppose 91.92% of all American males weigh more than I weigh.
   a. What fraction of American males weigh more than 225 pounds?
   b. How much do I weigh?

8. Assume that the length of a typical televised baseball game, including all the commercial timeouts, is normally distributed with mean 2.45 hours and standard deviation 0.37 hour. Consider a televised baseball game that begins at 2:00 in the afternoon. The next regularly scheduled broadcast is at 5:00.
   a. What is the probability that the game will cut into the next show, that is, go past 5:00?
   b. If the game is over before 4:30, another half-hour show can be inserted into the 4:30–5:00 slot. What is the probability of this occurring?

9. The amount of a soft drink that goes into a typical 12-ounce can varies from can to can. It is normally distributed with an adjustable mean μ and a fixed standard deviation of 0.05 ounce. (The adjustment is made to the filling machine.)
   a. If regulations require that cans have at least 11.9 ounces, what is the smallest mean μ that can be used so that at least 99.5% of all cans meet the regulation?
   b. If the mean setting from part **a** is used, what is the probability that a typical can has at least 12 ounces?

Level B

10. The manufacturer of a particular bicycle model has the following costs associated with the management of this product's inventory. In particular, the company currently maintains an inventory of 1000 units of this bicycle model at the beginning of each year. If X units are demanded each year and X is less than 1000, the excess supply, $1000 - X$ units, must be stored until next year at a cost of $50 per unit. If X is greater than 1000 units, the excess demand, $X - 1000$ units, must be produced separately at an extra cost of $80 per unit. Assume that the annual demand (X) for this bicycle model is normally distributed with mean 1000 and standard deviation 75.
    a. Find the expected annual cost associated with managing potential shortages or surpluses of this product. (*Hint*: Use simulation to approximate the answer. An exact solution using probability arguments is beyond the level of this book.)
    b. Find two annual total cost levels, equidistant from the expected value found in part **a**, such that 95% of all costs associated with managing potential shortages or surpluses of this product are between these values. (Continue to use simulation.)
    c. Comment on this manufacturer's annual production policy for this bicycle model in light of your findings in part **b**.

11. Matthew's Bakery prepares peanut butter cookies for sale every morning. It costs the bakery $0.25 to bake each peanut butter cookie, and each cookie is sold for $0.50. At the end of the day, leftover cookies are discounted and sold the following day at $0.10 per cookie. The daily demand (in dozens) for peanut butter cookies at this bakery is known to be normally distributed with mean 50 and standard deviation 15. The manager of Matthew's Bakery is trying to determine how many dozen peanut butter cookies to make each morning to maximize the product's contribution to bakery profits. Use simulation to find a very good, if not optimal, production plan.

12. Suppose that a particular production process fills detergent in boxes of a given size. Specifically, this process fills the boxes with an amount of detergent (in ounces) that is adequately described by a normal distribution with mean 50 and standard deviation 0.5.
    a. Simulate this production process for the filling of 500 boxes of detergent. Compute the mean and standard deviation of your simulated sample weights. How do your sample statistics compare to the theoretical population parameters in this case? How well do the empirical rules apply in describing the variation in the weights of the detergent in your simulated detergent boxes?
    b. A box of detergent is rejected by quality control personnel if it is found to contain less than

49 ounces or more than 51 ounces of detergent. Given these quality standards, what proportion of all boxes are rejected? What step(s) could the supervisor of this production process take to reduce this proportion to 1%?

13. It is widely known that many drivers on interstate highways in the United States do not observe the posted speed limit. Assume that the actual rates of speed driven by U.S. motorists are normally distributed with mean μ mph and standard deviation 5 mph. Given this information, answer each of the following independent questions.
    a. If 40% of all U.S. drivers are observed traveling at 65 mph or more, what is the mean μ?
    b. If 25% of all U.S. drivers are observed traveling at 50 mph or less, what is the mean μ?
    c. Suppose now that the mean μ and standard deviation σ of this distribution are both unknown. Furthermore, it is observed that 40% of all U.S. drivers travel at less than 55 mph and 10% of all U.S. drivers travel at more than 70 mph. What must μ and σ be?

14. The lifetime of a certain manufacturer's washing machine is normally distributed with mean 4 years. Only 15% of all these washing machines last at least 5 years. What is the standard deviation of the lifetime of a washing machine made by this manufacturer?

15. You have been told that the distribution of regular unleaded gasoline prices over all gas stations in Indiana is normally distributed with mean $2.95 and standard deviation $0.075, and you have been asked to find two dollar values such that 95% of all gas stations charge somewhere between these two values. Why is each of the following an acceptable answer: between $2.776 and $3.081, or between $2.802 and $3.097? Can you find any other acceptable answers? Which of the many possible answers would you prefer if you are asked to obtain the *shortest* interval?

16. When we create box plots, we place the sides of the "box" at the first and third quartiles, and the difference between these (the length of the box) is called the interquartile range (IQR). A mild outlier is then defined as an observation that is between 1.5 and 3 IQRs from the box, and an extreme outlier is defined as an observation that is more than 3 IQRs from the box.
    a. If the data are normally distributed, what percentage of values will be mild outliers? What percentage will be extreme outliers? Why don't the answers depend on the mean and/or standard deviation of the distribution?
    b. Check your answers in part **a** with simulation. Simulate a large number of normal random numbers (you can choose any mean and standard deviation), and count the number of mild and extreme outliers with appropriate IF functions. Do these match, at least approximately, your answers to part **a**?

17. A fast-food restaurant sells hamburgers and chicken sandwiches. On a typical weekday the demand for hamburgers is normally distributed with mean 313 and standard deviation 57; the demand for chicken sandwiches is normally distributed with mean 93 and standard deviation 22.

  a. How many hamburgers must the restaurant stock to be 98% sure of not running out on a given day?

  b. Answer part **a** for chicken sandwiches.

  c. If the restaurant stocks 400 hamburgers and 150 chicken sandwiches for a given day, what is the probability that it will run out of hamburgers or chicken sandwiches (or both) that day? Assume that the demand for hamburgers and the demand for chicken sandwiches are probabilistically independent.

  d. Why is the independence assumption in part **c** probably not realistic? Using a more realistic assumption, do you think the probability requested in part **c** would increase or decrease?

18. Suppose that the demands for a company's product in weeks 1, 2, and 3 are each normally distributed. The means are 50, 45, and 65. The standard deviations are 10, 5, and 15. Assume that these three demands are probabilistically independent. This means that if you observe one of them, it doesn't help you to predict the others. Then it turns out that total demand for the 3 weeks is also normally distributed. Its mean is the sum of the individual means, and its variance is the sum of the individual variances. (Its standard deviation, however, is not the sum of the individual standard deviations; square roots don't work that way.)

  a. Suppose that the company currently has 180 units in stock, and it will not be receiving any more shipments from its supplier for at least 3 weeks. What is the probability that it will stock out during this 3-week period?

  b. How many units should the company currently have in stock so that it can be 98% certain of not stocking out during this 3-week period? Again, assume that it won't receive any more shipments during this period.

6.4 THE BINOMIAL DISTRIBUTION

The normal distribution is undoubtedly the most important probability distribution in statistics. Not far behind in order of importance is the *binomial* distribution. The binomial distribution is a discrete distribution that can occur in two situations: (1) whenever we sample from a population with only two types of members (males and females, for example), and (2) whenever we perform a sequence of identical experiments, each of which has only two possible outcomes.

Imagine any experiment that can be repeated many times under identical conditions. It is common to refer to each repetition of the experiment as a *trial*. We assume that the outcomes of successive trials are probabilistically independent of one another and that each trial has only two possible outcomes. We label these two possibilities generically as success and failure. In any particular application the outcomes might be Democrat/Republican, defective/nondefective, went bankrupt/remained solvent, and so on. The probability of a success on each trial is p, and the probability of a failure is $1 - p$. The number of trials is n.

Binomial Distribution

Consider a situation in which there are n independent, identical trials, where the probability of a success on each trial is p and the probability of a failure is $1 - p$. Define X to be the random number of successes in the n trials. Then X has a **binomial** distribution with parameters n and p.

For example, the binomial distribution with parameters 100 and 0.3 is the distribution of the number of successes in 100 trials when the probability of success is 0.3 on each trial. A simple example that you can keep in mind throughout this section is the number of heads you would see if you flipped a coin n times. Assuming the coin is well balanced, the relevant distribution is binomial with parameters n and $p = 0.5$. This coin-flipping example is often used to illustrate the binomial distribution because of its simplicity, but we will see that the binomial distribution also applies to many important business situations.

To understand how the binomial distribution works, consider the coin-flipping example with $n = 3$. If X represents the number of heads in three flips of the coin, then the possible values of X are 0, 1, 2, and 3. We can find the probabilities of these values by considering the eight possible outcomes of the three flips: (T,T,T), (T,T,H), (T,H,T), (H,T,T), (T,H,H), (H,T,H), (H,H,T), and (H,H,H). Because of symmetry (the well-balanced property of the coin), each of these eight possible outcomes must have the same probability, so each must have probability 1/8. Next, note that one of the outcomes has $X = 0$, three outcomes have $X = 1$, three outcomes have $X = 2$, and one outcome has $X = 3$. Therefore, the probability distribution of X is

$$P(X = 0) = 1/8, P(X = 1) = 3/8, P(X = 2) = 3/8, P(X = 3) = 1/8$$

This is a special case of the binomial distribution, with $n = 3$ and $p = 0.5$. In general, where n can be any positive integer and p can be any probability between 0 and 1, there is a rather complex formula for calculating $P(X = k)$ for any integer k from 0 to n. Instead of presenting this formula, we will discuss how to calculate binomial probabilities in Excel. We do this with the BINOMDIST function. The general form of this function is

=BINOMDIST(k,n,p,cum)

The middle two arguments are as stated previously: the number of trials n and the probability of success p on each trial. The first parameter k is an integer number of successes that we specify. The last parameter, *cum*, is either 0 or 1. It is 1 if we want the probability of *less than or equal to k* successes, and it is 0 if we want the probability of *exactly k* successes. We illustrate typical binomial calculations in the following example.

EXAMPLE **6.7 BATTERY LIFE EXPERIMENT**

Suppose 100 identical batteries are inserted in identical flashlights. Each flashlight takes a single battery. After 8 hours of continuous use, we assume that a given battery is still operating with probability 0.6 and has failed with probability 0.4. Let X be the number of successes in these 100 trials, where a success means that the battery is still functioning. Find the probabilities of the following events: (a) exactly 58 successes, (b) no more than 65 successes, (c) less than 70 successes, (d) at least 59 successes, (e) greater than 65 successes, (f) between 55 and 65 successes (inclusive), (g) exactly 40 failures, (h) at least 35 failures, and (i) less than 42 failures. Then find the 95th percentile of the distribution of X.

Objective To use Excel's BINOMDIST and CRITBINOM functions for calculating binomial probabilities and percentiles in the context of batteries in flashlights.

Solution

Figure 6.18 shows the solution to all of these problems. (See the file **Binomial Calculations.xlsx**.) The probabilities requested in parts (a) through (f) all involve the number of successes X. The key to these is the wording of phrases such as "no more than," "greater than," and so on. In particular, we have to be careful to distinguish between probabilities such as $P(X < k)$ and $P(X \leq k)$. The latter includes the possibility of having $X = k$ and the former does not.

Figure 6.18 Typical Binomial Calculations

	A	B	C	D	E	F	G	H	I	J
1	Binomial Probability Calculations									
2				Range names used:						
3	Number of trials	100		NTrials	=BinomCalcs!$B$3					
4	Probability of success on each trial	0.6		PSuccess	=BinomCalcs!$B$4					
5										
6	Event	Probability		Formula						
7	Exactly 58 successes	0.0742		=BINOMDIST(58,NTrials,PSuccess,0)						
8	No more than 65 successes	0.8697		=BINOMDIST(65,NTrials,PSuccess,1)						
9	Less than 70 successes	0.9752		=BINOMDIST(69,NTrials,PSuccess,1)						
10	At least 59 successes	0.6225		=1-BINOMDIST(58,NTrials,PSuccess,1)						
11	Greater than 65 successes	0.1303		=1-BINOMDIST(65,NTrials,PSuccess,1)						
12	Between 55 and 65 successes (inclusive)	0.7386		=BINOMDIST(65,NTrials,PSuccess,1)-BINOMDIST(54,NTrials,PSuccess,1)						
13										
14	Exactly 40 failures	0.0812		=BINOMDIST(40,NTrials,1-PSuccess,0)						
15	At least 35 failures	0.8697		=1-BINOMDIST(34,NTrials,1-PSuccess,1)						
16	Less than 42 failures	0.6225		=BINOMDIST(41,NTrials,1-PSuccess,1)						
17										
18	Finding the 95th percentile (trial and error)									
19	Trial values	CumProb								
20	65	0.8697		=BINOMDIST(A20,NTrials,PSuccess,1)						
21	66	0.9087		(Copy down)						
22	67	0.9385								
23	68	0.9602								
24	69	0.9752								
25	70	0.9852								
26				Formula in cell A27:						
27	68	0.95		=CRITBINOM(NTrials,PSuccess,B27)						

With this in mind, we can translate the probabilities requested in (a) through (f) to the following:

a. $P(X = 58)$

b. $P(X \le 65)$

c. $P(X < 70) = P(X \le 69)$

d. $P(X \ge 59) = 1 - P(X < 59) = 1 - P(X \le 58)$

e. $P(X > 65) = 1 - P(X \le 65)$

f. $P(55 \le X \le 65) = P(X \le 65) - P(X < 55) = P(X \le 65) - P(X \le 54)$

Note how we have converted each of these so that it includes only terms of the form $P(X = k)$ or $P(X \le k)$ (for suitable values of k). These are the types of probabilities that can be handled directly by the BINOMDIST function. The answers appear in the range B7:B12, and the corresponding formulas are shown (as labels) in column D.

The probabilities requested in (g) through (i) involve *failures* rather than successes. But because each trial results in either a success or a failure, the number of failures is also binomially distributed, with parameters n and $1 - p = 0.4$. So in rows 14 through 16, we calculate the requested probabilities in exactly the same way, except that we substitute 1-PSuccess for PSuccess in the third argument of the BINOMDIST function.

Finally, to calculate the 95th percentile of the distribution of X, we proceed by trial and error. For each value k from 65 to 70, we have calculated the probability $P(X \le k)$ in column B with the BINOMDIST function. Note that there is no value k such that $P(X \le k) = 0.95$ exactly. We see that $P(X \le 67)$ is slightly less than 0.95, and $P(X \le 68)$ is slightly greater than 0.95. Therefore, the meaning of the "95th percentile" is a bit ambiguous. If we want the largest value k such that $P(X \le k) \le 0.95$, then this k is 67. If instead we want the smallest value k such that $P(X \le k) \ge 0.95$, then this value is 68. The latter interpretation is the one usually accepted for binomial percentiles.

In fact, Excel has another built-in function, CRITBINOM, for finding this value of k. We illustrate it in row 27 of Figure 6.18. Now we enter the requested probability, 0.95, in cell B27 and the formula

=CRITBINOM(NTrials,PSuccess,B27)

in cell A27. It returns 68, the smallest value k such that $P(X \le k) \ge 0.95$ for this binomial distribution. ∎

6.4.1 Mean and Standard Deviation of the Binomial Distribution

It can be shown that the mean and standard deviation of a binomial distribution with parameters n and p are given by the following equations.

$$E(X) = np \tag{6.3}$$

$$\text{Stdev}(X) = \sqrt{np(1 - p)} \tag{6.4}$$

The formula for the mean is quite intuitive. For example, if you observe 100 trials, each with probability of success 0.6, your best guess for the number of successes is clearly $100(0.6) = 60$. The standard deviation is less obvious but still very useful. It indicates how far the actual number of successes might deviate from the mean. In this case the standard deviation is $\sqrt{100(0.6)(0.4)} = 4.90$.

Fortunately, the empirical rules discussed in Chapter 3 also apply, at least approximately, to the binomial distribution. That is, there is about a 95% chance that the actual number of successes will be within 2 standard deviations of the mean, and there is almost no chance that the number of successes will be more than 3 standard deviations from the mean. So for this example, it is very likely that the number of successes will be in the range of approximately 50 to 70, and it is very unlikely that there will be fewer than 45 or more than 75 successes.

This reasoning is extremely useful. It gives us a rough estimate of the number of successes we are likely to observe. Suppose we randomly sample 1000 parts from an assembly line and, based on historical performance, we know that the percentage of parts with some type of defect is about 5%. Translated into a binomial model, we assume that each of the 1000 parts, independently of the others, has some type of defect with probability 0.05. Would we be surprised to see, say, 75 parts with a defect? The mean is $1000(0.05) = 50$ and the standard deviation is $\sqrt{1000(0.05)(0.95)} = 6.89$. Therefore, the number of parts with defects is 95% certain to be within $50 \pm 2(6.89)$, or approximately from 36 to 64. Because 75 is slightly beyond 3 standard deviations from the mean, it is highly unlikely that we would observe 75 (or more) parts with defects.

6.4.2 The Binomial Distribution in the Context of Sampling

We now discuss how the binomial distribution applies to sampling from a population with two types of members. Let's say these two types are men and women, although in applications they might be Democrats versus Republicans, users of our product versus nonusers, and so on. We will assume that the population has N members, of whom N_M are men and N_W are women (where $N_M + N_W = N$). If we sample n of these randomly, we are typically interested in the composition of the sample. We might expect that the number of men in the sample is binomially distributed with parameters n and $p = N_M/N$, the fraction of men in the population. However, this depends on how the sampling is performed.

If sampling is done **without replacement**, then each member of the population can be sampled only once. That is, once a person is sampled, his or her name is struck from the list and cannot be sampled again. If sampling is done **with replacement**, then it is possible, although maybe not likely, to select a given member of the population any number of times. Most real-world sampling is performed *without* replacement. There is no point in obtaining information from the same person more than once. However, *the binomial model applies only to sampling with replacement*. Because the composition of the remaining population keeps changing as the sampling progresses, the binomial model can provide only an approximation if sampling is done without replacement. If there is no replacement, the value of *p*, the proportion of men in this case, does *not* stay constant, a requirement of the binomial model. The appropriate distribution for sampling without replacement is called the **hypergeometric** distribution, a distribution we will not discuss in detail here.

If *n* is small relative to *N*, however, the binomial distribution is a very good approximation to the hypergeometric distribution and can be used even if sampling is performed without replacement. A rule of thumb is that if *n* is no greater than 10% of *N*, that is, no more than 10% of the population is sampled, then the binomial model can be used safely. Of course, most national polls sample considerably less than 10% of the population. In fact, they often sample only a few thousand people from the hundreds of millions in the entire population. The bottom line is that in most real-world sampling contexts, the binomial model is perfectly adequate.

6.4.3 The Normal Approximation to the Binomial

If n is large and p is not too close to 0 or 1, the binomial distribution is bell shaped and can be approximated well by the normal distribution.

If we graph the binomial probabilities, we see an interesting phenomenon—namely, the graph begins to look symmetric and bell shaped when *n* is fairly large and *p* is not too close to 0 or 1. An example is illustrated in Figure 6.19 with the parameters $n = 30$ and $p = 0.4$. Generally, if $np > 5$ and $n(1 - p) > 5$, the binomial distribution can be approximated well by a normal distribution with mean np and standard deviation $\sqrt{np(1 - p)}$.

One practical consequence of the normal approximation to the binomial is that the empirical rules can be applied. That is, when the binomial distribution is approximately symmetric and bell shaped, we know the chances are about 2 out of 3 that the number of successes will be within 1 standard deviation of the mean. Similarly, there is about a 95% chance that the number of successes will be within 2 standard deviations of the mean, and the number of successes will almost surely be within 3 standard deviations of the mean. Here, the mean is np and the standard deviation is $\sqrt{np(1 - p)}$.

Figure 6.19

Bell-shaped Binomial Distribution

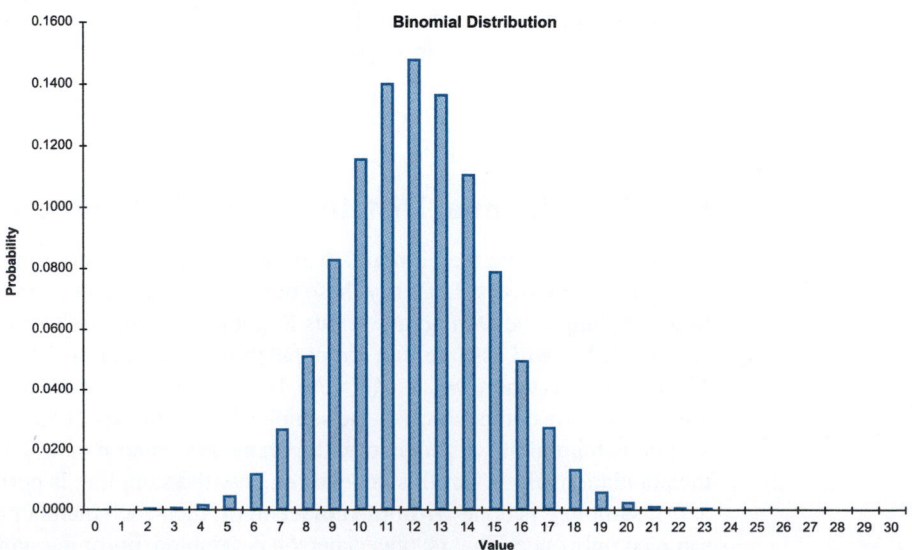

6.5 APPLICATIONS OF THE BINOMIAL DISTRIBUTION

The binomial distribution finds many applications in the business world and elsewhere. We discuss a few typical applications in this section.

EXAMPLE | **6.8 IS THIS MUTUAL FUND REALLY A WINNER?**

An investment broker at the Michaels & Dodson Company claims that he has found a real winner. He has tracked a mutual fund that has beaten a standard market index in 37 of the past 52 weeks. Could this be due to chance, or has he *really* found a winner?

Objective　To determine the probability of a mutual fund outperforming a standard market index at least 37 out of 52 weeks.

Solution

The broker is no doubt tracking a lot of mutual funds, and he is probably reporting on the best of these. Therefore, we will check whether the best of *many* mutual funds could do at least this well purely by chance. To do this, we first specify what we mean by "purely by chance." This means that each week, a given fund has a 50–50 chance of beating the market index, independently of performance in other weeks. In other words, the number of weeks where a given fund outperforms the market index is binomially distributed with $n = 52$ and $p = 0.5$. With this in mind, cell B6 of Figure 6.20 shows the probability that a given fund does at least as well—beats the market index at least 37 out of 52 weeks—as the reported fund. (See the **Beating the Market.xlsx** file.) Because $P(X \geq 37) = 1 - P(X \leq 36)$, the relevant formula is

=1-BINOMDIST(B3-1,B4,0.5,1)

Obviously, this probability, 0.00159, is quite small. A single fund isn't likely to beat the market this often purely by chance.

However, the probability that the *best* of many mutual funds does at least this well is much larger. To calculate this probability, let's assume that 400 funds are being tracked, and let Y be the number of these that beat the market at least 37 of 52 weeks. Then Y is also binomially distributed, with parameters $n = 400$ and $p = 0.00159$, the probability calculated previously. We want to know whether *any* of the 400 funds beats the market at least 37 of 52 weeks, so we calculate $P(Y \geq 1) = 1 - P(Y = 0)$. We do this in cell B9 with the formula

=1-BINOMDIST(0,B8,B6,1)

(Can you see why the fourth argument could be 0 *or* 1?) The resulting probability is nearly 0.5—that is, there is nearly a 50–50 chance that at least one of 400 funds will do as well as the reported fund. This certainly casts doubt on the broker's claim that he has found a real winner. Perhaps his star fund just got lucky and will perform no better than average in succeeding weeks.

To see how the probability in cell B9 depends on the level of success of the reported fund (the value in cell B3) and the number of mutual funds being tracked (in cell B8), we create a two-way data table in the range B13:G18. (The formula in cell B13 is =B9, the row input cell is B3, and the column input cell is B8.) As we saw, beating the market 37 times out of 52 is no big deal with 400 funds, but beating it 40 times out of 52, even with 600 funds, is something worth reporting. The probability of this happening purely by chance is only 0.038, or less than 1 out of 25.

Figure 6.20

Binomial
Calculations for
Investment Example

	A	B	C	D	E	F	G
1	**Beating the market**						
2							
3	Weeks beating market index	37					
4	Total number of weeks	52					
5							
6	Probability of doing at least this well by chance	0.00159		=1-BINOMDIST(B3-1,B4,0.5,1)			
7							
8	Number of mutual funds	400					
9	Probability of at least one doing at least this well	0.471		=1-BINOMDIST(0,B8,B6,1)			
10							
11	Two-way data table of the probability in B9 as a function of values in B3 and B8						
12				Number of weeks beating the market index			
13		0.471	36	37	38	39	40
14	Number of mutual funds	200	0.542	0.273	0.113	0.040	0.013
15		300	0.690	0.380	0.164	0.060	0.019
16		400	0.790	0.471	0.213	0.079	0.025
17		500	0.858	0.549	0.258	0.097	0.031
18		600	0.904	0.616	0.301	0.116	0.038

The next example requires a normal calculation to find a probability p, which is then used in a binomial calculation.

EXAMPLE 6.9 ANALYZING DAILY SALES AT DIGGLY WIGGLY SUPERMARKET

Customers at the Diggly Wiggly Supermarket spend varying amounts. Historical data show that the amount spent per customer is normally distributed with mean $85 and standard deviation $30. If 500 customers shop in a given day, calculate the mean and standard deviation of the number who spend at least $100. Then calculate the probability that at least 30% of all customers spend at least $100.

Objective To use the normal *and* binomial distributions to calculate the typical number of customers who spend at least $100 per day and the probability that at least 30% of all 500 daily customers spend at least $100.

Solution

Both questions involve the number of customers who spend at least $100. Because the amounts spent are normally distributed, the probability that a typical customer spends at least $100 is found with the NORMDIST function. This probability, 0.309, appears in cell B7 of Figure 6.21. (See the file **Supermarket Spending.xlsx**.) We calculate it with the formula

=1-NORMDIST(100,B4,B5,1)

This probability is then used as the parameter p in a binomial model. The mean and standard deviation of the number who spend at least $100 are calculated in cells B13 and B14 as np and $\sqrt{np(1-p)}$, using $n = 500$, the number of shoppers, and $p = 0.309$. The expected number who spend at least $100 is slightly greater than 154, and the standard deviation of this number is slightly greater than 10.

Figure 6.21   Calculations for Supermarket Example

	A	B	C	D	E	F
1	**Supermarket spending**					
2						
3	Amount spent per customer (normally distributed)					
4	Mean	$85				
5	StDev	$30				
6						
7	Probability that a customer spends at least $100	0.309		=1-NORMDIST(100,B4,B5,1)		
8						
9						
10	Number of customers	500				
11						
12	Mean and stdev of number who spend at least $100					
13	Mean	154.27		=B10*B7		
14	StDev	10.33		=SQRT(B10*B7*(1-B7))		
15						
16	Probability at least 30% spend at least $100	0.676		=1-BINOMDIST(0.3*B10-1,B10,B7,1)		

To answer the second question, note that 30% of 500 customers is 150 customers. Then the probability that at least 30% of the customers spend at least $100 is the probability that a binomially distributed random variable, with $n = 500$ and $p = 0.309$, is at least 150. We calculate this binomial probability, which turns out to be about 2/3, in cell B16 with the formula

=1-BINOMDIST(0.3*B10-1,B10,B7,1)

Note that the first argument calculates to 149. This is because the probability of *at least* 150 customers is 1.0 minus the probability of less than or equal to 149 customers. ∎

EXAMPLE | **6.10 OVERBOOKING BY AIRLINES**

This example presents a simplified version of calculations used by airlines when they overbook flights. They realize that a certain percentage of ticketed passengers will cancel at the last minute. Therefore, to avoid empty seats, they sell more tickets than there are seats, hoping that just about the right number of passengers show up. We will assume that the no-show rate is 10%. In binomial terms, we are assuming that each ticketed passenger, independently of the others, shows up with probability 0.90 and cancels with probability 0.10.

For a flight with 200 seats, the airline wants to find how sensitive various probabilities are to the number of tickets it issues. In particular, it wants to calculate (a) the probability that more than 205 passengers show up, (b) the probability that more than 200 passengers show up, (c) the probability that at least 195 seats will be filled, and (d) the probability that at least 190 seats will be filled. The first two of these are "bad" events from the airline's perspective; they mean that some customers will be bumped from the flight. The last two events are "good" in the sense that the airline wants most of the seats to be occupied.

Objective   To assess the benefits and drawbacks of issuing various numbers of tickets on an airline flight with 200 seats.

Solution

To solve the airline's problem, we use the BINOMDIST function and a data table. The solution appears in Figure 6.22. (See the file **Airline Overbooking.xlsx**.) We first enter a possible number of tickets issued in cell B6 and, for this number, calculate the required probabilities in row 10. For example, the formulas in cells B10 and D10 are

$=$1-BINOMDIST(205,NTickets,1-PNoShow,1)

and

$=$1-BINOMDIST(194,NTickets,1-PNoShow,1)

Figure 6.22

Binomial Calculations for Overbooking Example

	A	B	C	D	E	F
1	Airline overbooking			Range names used:		
2				NTickets	=Overbooking!$B$6	
3	Number of seats	200		PNoShow	=Overbooking!$B$4	
4	Probability of no-show	0.1				
5						
6	Number of tickets issued	215				
7						
8	Required probabilities					
9		More than 205 show up	More than 200 show up	At least 195 seats filled	At least 190 seats filled	
10		0.001	0.050	0.421	0.820	
11						
12	Data table showing sensitivity of probabilities to number of tickets issued					
13	Number of tickets issued	More than 205 show up	More than 200 show up	At least 195 seats filled	At least 190 seats filled	
14		0.001	0.050	0.421	0.820	
15	206	0.000	0.000	0.012	0.171	
16	209	0.000	0.001	0.064	0.384	
17	212	0.000	0.009	0.201	0.628	
18	215	0.001	0.050	0.421	0.820	
19	218	0.013	0.166	0.659	0.931	
20	221	0.064	0.370	0.839	0.978	
21	224	0.194	0.607	0.939	0.995	
22	227	0.406	0.802	0.981	0.999	
23	230	0.639	0.920	0.995	1.000	
24	233	0.822	0.974	0.999	1.000	

Note that the condition "more than" requires a slightly different calculation than "at least." The probability of more than 205 is 1.0 minus the probability of less than or equal to 205, whereas the probability of at least 195 is 1.0 minus the probability of less than or equal to 194. Also, note that we are treating a "success" as a passenger who shows up. Therefore, the third argument of each BINOMDIST function is 1.0 minus the no-show probability.

To see how sensitive these probabilities are to the number of tickets issued, we create a one-way data table at the bottom of the spreadsheet. It is *one-way* because there is only one *input,* the number tickets issued, even though four output probabilities are tabulated. (To create the data table, list several possible numbers of tickets issued along the side in column A and create links to the probabilities in row 10 in row 14. That is, enter the formula $=$B10 in cell B14 and copy it across row 14. Then form a data table using the range A14:E24, no row input cell, and column input cell B6.)

The results are as expected. As the airline issues more tickets, there is a larger chance of having to bump passengers from the flight, but there is also a larger chance of filling most seats. In reality, the airline has to make a trade-off between these two, taking its various costs and revenues into account. ∎

The following is another simplified example of a real problem that occurs every time we watch election returns on TV. This problem is of particular interest in light of the highly unusual events that took place during election night television coverage of the U.S. presidential election in 2000, where the networks declared Gore an early winner in at least one state that he eventually lost. The basic question is how soon the networks can declare one of the candidates the winner, based on early voting returns. Our example is somewhat unrealistic because it ignores the possibility that early tabulations might be biased one way or the other. For example, the earliest reporting precincts might be known to be more heavily in favor of the Democrat than the population in general. Nevertheless, the example explains why the networks are able to make conclusions based on such seemingly small amounts of data.

| EXAMPLE | 6.11 PROJECTING ELECTION WINNERS FROM EARLY RETURNS |

We assume that there are N voters in the population, of whom N_R will vote for the Republican and N_D will vote for the Democrat. The eventual winner will be the Republican if $N_R > N_D$ and will be the Democrat otherwise, but we won't know which until all of the votes are tabulated. (To simplify the example, we assume there are only two candidates and that the election will *not* end in a tie.) Let's suppose that a small percentage of the votes have been counted and the Republican is currently ahead 540 to 460. On what basis can the networks declare the Republican the winner, especially when there are millions of voters in the population?

Objective   To use a binomial model to determine whether early returns reflect the eventual winner of an election between two candidates.

Solution

Let $n = 1000$ be the total number of votes that have been tabulated. If X is the number of Republican votes so far, $X = 540$. Now we pose the following question. If the Democrat were going to be the eventual winner, that is, $N_D > N_R$, and we randomly sampled 1000 voters from the population, how likely is it that at least 540 of these voters would be in favor of the Republican? If this is very *unlikely*, then the only reasonable conclusion is that the Democrat will *not* be the eventual winner. This is the reasoning the networks use to declare the Republican the winner.

We use a binomial model to see how unlikely the event "at least 540 out of 1000" is, assuming that the Democrat will be the eventual winner. We need a value for p, the probability that a typical vote is for the Republican. This probability should be the proportion of voters in the entire population who favor the Republican. All we know is that this probability is less than 0.5, because we have assumed that the Democrat will eventually win. In Figure 6.23, we show how the probability of at least 540 out of 1000 varies with values of p less than, but close to, 0.5. (See the file **Election Returns.xlsx**.)

We enter a trial value of 0.49 for p in cell B3 and then calculate the required probability in cell B9 with the formula

=1-BINOMDIST(B6-1,B5,B3,1)

Then we use this to create the data table at the bottom of the spreadsheet. This data table tabulates the probability of the given lead (at least 540 out of 1000) for various values of p less than 0.5. As shown in the last few rows, even if the eventual outcome were going to be a virtual tie—with the Democrat slightly ahead—there would still be very little chance of the Republican being at least 80 votes ahead so far. But because the Republican *is* currently ahead by 80 votes, the networks feel safe in declaring the Republican the winner.

Figure 6.23

Binomial
Calculations for
Voting Example

	A	B	C	D	E	F
1	Election returns					
2						
3	Population proportion for Republican	0.49				
4						
5	Votes tabulated so far	1000				
6	Votes for Republican so far	540				
7						
8	Binomial probability of at least this many votes for Republican					
9		0.0009		=1-BINOMDIST(B6-1,B5,B3,1)		
10						
11	Data table showing sensitivity of this probability to population proportion for Republican					
12	Population proportion for Republican	Probability				
13		0.0009				
14	0.490	0.0009				
15	0.492	0.0013				
16	0.494	0.0020				
17	0.496	0.0030				
18	0.498	0.0043				
19	0.499	0.0052				

The final example in this section challenges the two assumptions of the binomial model. So far, we have assumed that the outcomes of successive trials (1) have the same probability p of success and (2) are probabilistically independent. There are many situations where either or both of these assumptions are questionable. For example, consider successive items from a production line, where each item either meets specifications (a success) or doesn't (a failure). If the process deteriorates over time, at least until it receives maintenance, then the probability p of success could slowly decrease. Even if p remains constant, defective items could come in bunches (because of momentary inattentiveness on the part of a worker, say), which would invalidate the independence assumption.

If an analyst believes that the binomial assumptions are invalid, then an alternative model must be specified that reflects reality more closely. This is not easy—all kinds of *nonbinomial* assumptions can be imagined. Furthermore, even when we make such assumptions, there are probably no simple formulas to use, such as the BINOMDIST formulas we have been using. Simulation might be the only alternative, as we illustrate in the following example.

EXAMPLE 6.12 STREAK SHOOTING IN BASKETBALL

Do basketball players shoot in streaks? This question has been debated by thousands of basketball fans, and it has even been studied statistically by several academic researchers. Most fans believe the answer is "yes," arguing that players clearly alternate between hot streaks where they can't miss and cold streaks where they can't hit the broad side of a barn. This situation does not fit a binomial model where, say, a "450 shooter" has a 0.450 probability of making each shot and a 0.550 probability of missing, independently of other shots. If the binomial model does not apply, what model might be appropriate, and how could it be used to calculate a probability such as the probability of making at least 13 shots out of 25 attempts?[6]

---

[6]There are obviously a lot of extenuating circumstances surrounding any shot: the type of shot (layup versus jump shot), the type of defense, the score, the time left in the game, and so on. For this example we focus on a pure jump shooter who is more or less unaffected by the various circumstances in the game.

Objective To formulate a nonbinomial model of basketball shooting, and to use it to find the probability of a 0.450 shooter making at least 13 out of 25 shots.

Solution

This problem is quite open-ended. There are numerous alternatives to the binomial model that could capture the "streakiness" most fans believe in, and the one we suggest here is by no means definitive. We challenge you to develop others.

The model we propose assumes that this shooter makes 45% of his shots in the long run. The probability that he makes his first shot in a game is 0.45. In general, consider his nth shot. If he has made his last k shots, we assume the probability of making shot n is 0.45 $+ kd_1$. On the other hand, if he has missed his last k shots, we assume the probability of making shot n is $0.45 - kd_2$. Here, d_1 and d_2 are small values (0.01 and 0.02, for example) that indicate how much the shooter's probability of success increases or decreases depending on his current streak. The model implies that the shooter gets better the more shots he makes and worse the more he misses.

To implement this model, we use simulation as shown in Figure 6.24. (See the file **Basketball Simulation.xlsx**.) Actually, we first do a "baseline" binomial calculation in cell B9, using the parameters $n = 25$ and $p = 0.450$. The formula in cell B9 is

=1-BINOMDIST(12,B7,B3,1)

If the player makes each shot with probability 0.45, independently of the other shots, then the probability that he will make over half of his 25 shots is 0.306—about a 30% chance.

The simulation in the range A17:D41 shows the results of 25 random shots according to the *nonbinomial* model we have assumed. Column B indicates the length of the current streak, where a negative value indicates a streak of misses and a positive value indicates a streak of makes. Column C indicates the probability of a make on the current shot, and column D contains 1's for makes and 0's for misses. Here are step-by-step instructions for developing this range.

1 **First shot.** Enter the formulas

=B3

and

=IF(RAND()<C17,1,0)

in cells C17 and D17 to determine the outcome of the first shot.

2 **Second shot.** Enter the formulas

=IF(D17=0,-1,1)

=IF(B18<0,$B$3+B18*$B$5,$B$3+B18*$B$4)

and

=IF(RAND()<C18,1,0)

in cells B18, C18, and D18. The first of these indicates that by the second shot, the shooter will have a streak of one make or one miss. The second formula is the important one. It indicates how the probability of a make changes depending on the current streak. The third formula simulates a make or a miss, using the probability in cell C18.

Figure 6.24 Simulation of Basketball Shooting Model

	A	B	C	D	E	F	G	H	I
1	Basketball shooting simulation								
2									
3	Long-run average	0.45							
4	Increment d1 after a make	0.015							
5	Increment d2 after a miss	0.015							
6									
7	Number of shots	25							
8									
9	Binomial probability of at least 13 out of 25	0.306							
10									
11	Summary statistics from simulation below			Compare these		Fraction of reps with at least 13 from table below			
12	Number of makes	12				0.304			
13	At least 13 makes?	0							
14									
15	Simulation of makes and misses using nonbinomial model					Data table to replicate 25 shots many times			
16		Shot	Streak	P(make)	Make?		Rep	At least 13?		
17		1	NA	0.45	0			0		
18		2	-1	0.435	1		1	0		
19		3	1	0.465	0		2	0		
20		4	-1	0.435	1		3	0		
21		5	1	0.465	0		4	1		
22		6	-1	0.435	0		5	1		
23		7	-2	0.42	0		6	0		
24		8	-3	0.405	1		7	1		
25		9	1	0.465	1		8	0		
26		10	2	0.48	0		9	0		
27		11	-1	0.435	1		10	1		
28		12	1	0.465	1		11	1		
29		13	2	0.48	1		12	1		
30		14	3	0.495	0		13	0		
31		15	-1	0.435	1		14	1		
32		16	1	0.465	0		15	1		
33		17	-1	0.435	0		16	1		
34		18	-2	0.42	1		17	1		
35		19	1	0.465	0		18	0		
36		20	-1	0.435	0		19	0		
37		21	-2	0.42	1		20	0		
38		22	1	0.465	0		21	0		
39		23	-1	0.435	0		22	1		
40		24	-2	0.42	1		23	0		
41		25	1	0.465	1		24	1		
42							25	0		
43							26	0		
265							248	1		
266							249	0		
267							250	0		

3 **Length of streak on third (and succeeding) shots.** Enter the formula

=IF(AND(B18<0,D18=0),B18-1, IF(AND(B18<0,D18=1),1,

IF(AND(B18>0,D18=0),−1,B18+1)))

in cell B19 and copy it down column B. This nested IF formula checks for all four combinations of the previous streak (negative or positive, indicated in cell B18) and the most recent shot (make or miss, indicated in cell D18) to see whether the current streak continues by one or a new streak starts.

4 **Results of remaining shots.** The logic for the formulas in columns C and D is the same for the remaining shots as for shot 2, so copy the formulas in cells C18 and D18 down their respective columns.

5 **Summary of 25 shots.** Enter the formulas

=SUM(D17:D41)
  and

=IF(B12>=13,1,0)

in cells B12 and B13 to summarize the results of the 25 simulated shots. In particular, the value in cell B13 is 1 only if at least 13 of the shots are successes.

What about the *probability* of making at least 13 shots with this nonbinomial model? So far, we have simulated one set of 25 shots and have reported whether at least 13 of the shots are successes. We need to replicate this simulation many times and report the fraction of the replications where at least 13 of the shots are successes. We do this with a data table in columns F and G.

To create this table, enter the replication numbers 1 through 250 (you could use any number of replications) in column F. Then put a link to B13 in cell G17 by entering the formula = B13 in this cell. Essentially, we are recalculating this value 250 times, each with different random numbers. To do this, highlight the range F17:G267, and create a data table with no row input cell and *any blank cell* (such as F17) as the column input cell. This causes Excel to recalculate the basic simulation 250 times, each time with different random numbers. Finally, enter the formula

=AVERAGE(G18:G267)

in cell F12 to calculate the fraction of the replications with at least 13 makes out of 25 shots.

After finishing all of this, you'll note that the spreadsheet is "live" in the sense that if you press the F9 recalculation key, all of the simulated quantities change—new random numbers. In particular, the estimate in cell F12 of the probability of at least 13 makes out of 25 shots changes. It is sometimes less than the binomial probability in cell B9 and sometimes greater. In general, the two probabilities are roughly the same. The bottom line? Even if the world doesn't behave exactly as the binomial model indicates, probabilities of various events can often be approximated fairly well by binomial probabilities—which saves us the trouble of developing and working with more complex models! ∎

PROBLEMS

Level A

19. In a typical month, an insurance agent presents life insurance plans to 40 potential customers. Historically, one in four such customers chooses to buy life insurance from this agent. Based on the relevant binomial distribution, answer the following questions:
  a. What is the probability that exactly 5 customers will buy life insurance from this agent in the coming month?
  b. What is the probability that no more than 10 customers will buy life insurance from this agent in the coming month?

  c. What is the probability that at least 20 customers will buy life insurance from this agent in the coming month?
  d. Determine the mean and standard deviation of the number of customers who will buy life insurance from this agent in the coming month.
  e. What is the probability that the number of customers who buy life insurance from this agent in the coming month will lie within 2 standard deviations of the mean?
  f. What is the probability that the number of customers who buy life insurance from this agent in the coming month will lie within 3 standard deviations of the mean?

20. Continuing the previous exercise, use the normal approximation to the binomial to answer each of the questions posed in parts **a** through **f**. How well does the normal approximation perform in this case? Explain.

21. Many vehicles used in space travel are constructed with redundant systems to protect flight crews and their valuable equipment. In other words, backup systems are included within many vehicle components so that if one or more systems fail, backup systems will assure the safe operation of the given component and thus the entire vehicle. For example, consider one particular component of the U.S. space shuttle that has n duplicated systems (i.e., one original system and $n - 1$ backup systems). Each of these systems functions, independently of the others, with probability 0.98. This shuttle component functions successfully provided that *at least* one of the n systems functions properly.
    a. Find the probability that this shuttle component functions successfully if $n = 2$.
    b. Find the probability that this shuttle component functions successfully if $n = 4$.
    c. What is the minimum number n of duplicated systems that must be incorporated into this shuttle component to ensure at least a 0.9999 probability of successful operation?

22. Suppose that a popular hotel for vacationers in Orlando, Florida, has a total of 300 identical rooms. Like many major airline companies, this hotel has adopted an overbooking policy in an effort to maximize the usage of its available lodging capacity. Assume that each potential hotel customer holding a room reservation, independently of other customers, cancels the reservation or simply does not show up at the hotel on a given night with probability 0.15.
    a. Find the largest number of room reservations that this hotel can book and still be at least 95% sure that everyone who shows up at the hotel will have a room on a given night.
    b. Given that the hotel books the number of reservations found in answering part **a**, find the probability that at least 90% of the available rooms will be occupied on a given night.
    c. Given that the hotel books the number of reservations found in answering part **a**, find the probability that at most 80% of the available rooms will be occupied on a given night.
    d. How does your answer to part **a** change as the required assurance rate increases from 95% to 97%? How does your answer to part **a** change as the required assurance rate increases from 95% to 99%?
    e. How does your answer to part **a** change as the cancellation rate varies between 5% and 25% (in increments of 5%)? Assume now that the required assurance rate is held fixed at 95%.

23. A production process manufactures items with weights that are normally distributed with mean 15 pounds and standard deviation 0.1 pound. An item is considered to be defective if its weight is less than 14.8 pounds or greater than 15.2 pounds. Suppose that these items are currently produced in batches of 1000 units.
    a. Find the probability that at most 5% of the items in a given batch will be defective.
    b. Find the probability that at least 90% of the items in a given batch will be acceptable.
    c. How many items would have to be produced in a batch to guarantee that a batch consists of no more than 1% defective items?

24. Past experience indicates that 30% of all individuals entering a certain store decide to make a purchase. Using (a) the binomial distribution and (b) the normal approximation to the binomial, find that probability that 10 or more of the 30 individuals entering the store in a given hour will decide to make a purchase. Compare the results obtained using the two different approaches. Under what conditions will the normal approximation to this binomial probability become even more accurate?

25. Suppose that the number of ounces of soda put into a Pepsi can is normally distributed with $\mu = 12.05$ ounces and $\sigma = 0.03$ ounce.
    a. Legally, a can must contain at least 12 ounces of soda. What fraction of cans will contain at least 12 ounces of soda?
    b. What fraction of cans will contain less than 11.9 ounces of soda?
    c. What fraction of cans will contain between 12 and 12.08 ounces of soda?
    d. One percent of all cans will weigh more than what value?
    e. Ten percent of all cans will weigh less than what value?
    f. Pepsi controls the mean weight in a can by setting a timer. For what mean should the timer be set so that only 1 in 1000 cans will be underweight?
    g. Every day Pepsi produces 10,000 cans. The government inspects 10 randomly chosen cans each day. If at least two are underweight, Pepsi is fined $10,000. Given that $\mu = 12.05$ ounces and $\sigma = 0.03$ ounce, what is the probability that Pepsi will be fined on a given day?

26. Suppose that 52% of all registered voters prefer John Kerry to George Bush. (You may substitute the names of the current presidential candidates!)
    a. In a random sample of 100 voters, what is the probability that the sample will indicate that Kerry will win the election (that is, there will be more votes in the sample for Kerry)?
    b. In a random sample of 100 voters, what is the probability that the sample will indicate that Bush will win the election?

c. In a random sample of 100 voters, what is the probability that the sample will indicate a dead heat (50–50)?

d. In a random sample of 100 voters, what is the probability that between 40 and 60 (inclusive) voters will prefer Kerry?

27. Assume that, on average, 95% of all ticket-holders show up for a flight. If a plane seats 200 people, how many tickets should be sold to make the chance of an overbooked flight as close as possible to 5%?

28. Suppose that 60% of all people prefer Coke to Pepsi. We randomly choose 500 people and ask them if they prefer Coke to Pepsi. What is the probability that our survey will (erroneously) indicate that Pepsi is preferred by more people than Coke?

29. A firm's office contains 150 PCs. The probability that a given PC will not work on a given day is 0.05.
   a. On a given day what is the probability that exactly one computer will not be working?
   b. On a given day what is the probability that at least two computers will not be working?
   c. What assumptions do your answers in parts **a** and **b** require?

30. Suppose that 4% of all tax returns are audited. In a group of n tax returns, consider the probability that at most two returns are audited. How large must n be before this probability will be less than 0.01?

31. Suppose that the height of a typical American female is normally distributed with $\mu = 64$ inches and $\sigma = 4$ inches. We observe the height of 10 American females.
   a. What is the probability that exactly half the women will be under 58 inches tall?
   b. Let X be the number of the 10 women who are under 58 inches tall. Determine the mean and standard deviation of X.

32. Consider a large population of shoppers, each of whom spends a certain amount during their current shopping trip; the distribution of these amounts is normally distributed with mean $55 and standard deviation $15. We randomly choose 25 of these shoppers. What is the probability that at least 15 of them spend between $45 and $75?

Level B

33. Many firms utilize sampling plans to control the quality of manufactured items ready for shipment. To illustrate the use of a sampling plan, suppose that a particular company produces and ships electronic computer chips in lots, each consisting of 1000 chips. This company's sampling plan specifies that quality control personnel will randomly sample 50 chips from each lot and accept the lot for shipping if the number of defective chips is less than 5. The lot will be rejected if the number of defective chips is 5 or more.

a. Find the probability of accepting a lot as a function of the actual fraction of defective chips. In particular, let the actual fraction of defective chips in a given lot equal any of 0.02, 0.04, 0.06, 0.08, 0.10, 0.12, 0.14, 0.16, 0.18. Then compute the lot acceptance probability for each of these lot defective fractions.

b. Construct a graph showing the probability of lot acceptance for each of the 9 lot defective fractions. Interpret your graph.

34. Continuing the previous exercise, repeat parts **a** and **b** under a revised sampling plan that calls for accepting a given lot if the number of defective chips found in the random sample of 50 chips is *not greater than* 5. Summarize any notable differences between the two graphs you have constructed in completing part **b** of this and the previous exercise.

35. Comdell Computer receives computer chips from Chipco. Each batch sent by Chipco is inspected as follows: 35 chips are tested and the batch passes inspection if at most one defective chip is found in the set of 35 tested chips. Past history indicates an average of 1% of all chips produced by Chipco are defective. Comdell has received 10 batches this week. What is the probability that at least 9 of the batches will pass inspection?

36. A standardized test consists entirely of multiple-choice questions, each with 5 possible choices. You want to ensure that a student who randomly guesses on each question will obtain an expected score of zero. How would you accomplish this?

37. In the current tax year, suppose that 5% of the millions of individual tax returns are fraudulent. That is, they contain errors that were purposely made to cheat the government.
   a. Although these errors are often well concealed, let's suppose that a thorough IRS audit will uncover them. If a random 250 tax returns are audited, what is the probability that the IRS will uncover at least 15 fraudulent returns?
   b. Answer the same question as in part **a**, but this time assume there is only a 90% chance that a given fraudulent return will be spotted as such if it is audited.

38. Suppose you work for a survey research company. In a typical survey, you mail questionnaires to 150 companies. Of course, some of these companies might decide not to respond. We'll assume that the nonresponse rate is 45%; that is, each company's probability of not responding, independently of the others, is 0.45. If your company requires at least 90 responses for a "valid" survey, find the probability that it will get this many. Use a data table to see how your answer varies as a function of the nonresponse rate (for a reasonable range of response rates surrounding 45%).

39. Continuing the previous problem, suppose your company does this survey in two "waves." It mails the 150 questionnaires and waits a certain period for the responses. As before, assume that the nonresponse rate is 45%. However, after this initial period, your company follows up (by telephone, say) on the nonrespondents, asking them to please respond. Suppose that the nonresponse rate on this second "wave" is 70%; that is, each original nonrespondent now responds with probability 0.3, independently of the others. Your company now wants to find the probability of obtaining at least 110 responses total. It turns out that this is a very difficult probability to calculate directly. So instead, approximate it with simulation.

40. A person claims that she is a fortune teller. Specifically, she claims that she can predict the direction of the change (up or down) in the Dow Jones Industrial Average for the next 10 days (such as U, U, D, U, D, U, U, D, D, D). (You can assume that she makes all 10 predictions right now, although that won't affect your answer to the question.) Obviously, you are skeptical, thinking that she is just guessing, so you'll be surprised if her predictions are accurate. Which would surprise you more: (1) she predicts at least 8 out of 10 correctly, or (2) she predicts at least 6 out of 10 correctly on each of 4 separate occasions? Answer by assuming that (1) she really is guessing and (2) each day the Dow is equally likely to go up or down.

6.6 THE POISSON AND EXPONENTIAL DISTRIBUTIONS

The final two distributions in this chapter are called the *Poisson* and *exponential* distributions. In most statistical applications, including those in the rest of this book, these distributions play a much less important role than the normal and binomial distributions. For this reason we will not analyze them in as much detail. However, in many applied management science models, the Poisson and exponential distributions are as important as any other distributions, discrete or continuous. For example, much of the study of probabilistic inventory models, queuing models, and reliability models relies heavily on these two distributions.

6.6.1 The Poisson Distribution

The **Poisson distribution** is a discrete distribution. It usually applies when we are interested in the *number* of events occurring within a specified period of time or space. Its possible values are all of the nonnegative integers: 0, 1, 2, and so on—there is no upper limit. Even though there is an infinite number of possible values, this causes no real problems because the probabilities of all sufficiently large values are essentially 0.

The Poisson distribution is characterized by a single parameter, usually labeled λ (Greek lambda), which must be positive. By adjusting the value of λ, we are able to produce different Poisson distributions, all of which have the same basic shape as in Figure 6.25. That is, they first increase, then decrease. It turns out that λ is easy to interpret. It is both the mean and the variance of the Poisson distribution. Therefore, the standard deviation is $\sqrt{\lambda}$.

Figure 6.25

Typical Poisson Distribution

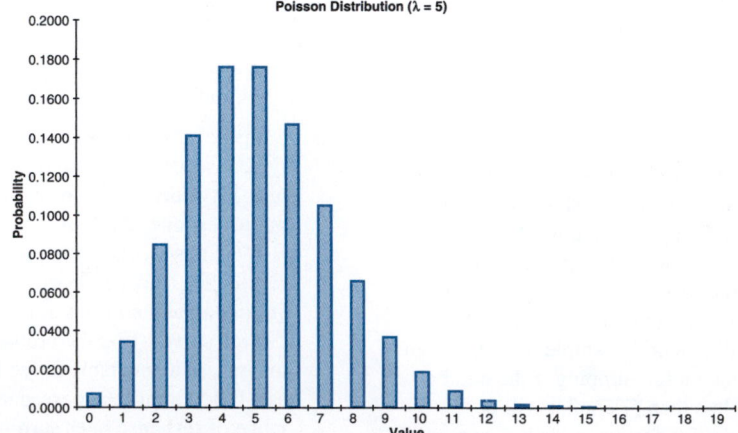

Typical Examples of the Poisson Distribution

1. A bank manager is studying the arrival pattern to the bank. Then the events are customer arrivals, the number of arrivals in an hour is Poisson distributed, and λ represents the expected number of arrivals per hour.

2. An engineer is interested in the lifetime of a type of battery. A device that uses this type of battery is operated continuously. When the first battery fails, it is replaced by a second; when the second fails, it is replaced by a third, and so on. The events are battery failures, the number of failures that occur in a month is Poisson distributed, and λ represents the expected number of failures per month.

3. A retailer is interested in the number of units of a product demanded in a particular unit of time such as a week. Then the events are customer demands, the number of units demanded in a week is Poisson distributed, and λ is the expected number of units demanded per week.

4. In a quality control setting, the Poisson distribution is often relevant for describing the number of defects in some unit of space. For example, when paint is applied to the body of a new car, any minor blemish is considered a defect. Then the number of defects on the hood, say, might be Poisson distributed. In this case, λ is the expected number of defects per hood.

These examples are representative of the many situations where the Poisson distribution has been applied. For the obvious reason, the parameter λ is often called a rate—arrivals per hour, failures per month, and so on. If we change the unit of time, we simply modify the rate accordingly. For example, if the number of arrivals to a bank in a single hour is Poisson distributed with rate $\lambda = 30$, then the number of arrivals in a half-hour period is Poisson distributed with rate $\lambda = 15$.

We can use Excel to calculate Poisson probabilities much as we did with binomial probabilities. The relevant function is the POISSON function. It takes the form

=POISSON(k,λ,cum)

The third argument *cum* works exactly as in the binomial case. If it is 0, the function returns $P(X = k)$; if it is 1, the function returns $P(X \leq k)$. As examples, if $\lambda = 5$, POISSON(7,5,0) returns the probability of exactly 7, POISSON(7,5,1) returns the probability of less than or equal to 7, and 1-POISSON(3,5,1) returns the probability of greater than 3.

The following example shows how a manager or consultant might use the Poisson distribution.

| EXAMPLE | **6.13 MANAGING INVENTORY OF TELEVISIONS AT KRIEGLAND** |

Kriegland is a department store that sells various brands of color television sets. One of the manager's biggest problems is to decide on an appropriate inventory policy for stocking television sets. On the one hand, he wants to have enough in stock so that customers receive their requests right away, but on the other hand, he does not want to tie up too much money in inventory that sits on the storeroom floor.

Most of the difficulty results from the unpredictability of customer demand. If this demand were constant and known, the manager could decide on an appropriate inventory policy fairly easily. But the demand varies widely from month to month in a random manner. All the manager knows is that the historical average demand per month is approximately 17. Therefore, he decides to call in a consultant. The consultant immediately suggests using a probability model. Specifically, she attempts to find the probability distribution of demand in a typical month. How might she proceed?

Objective   To model the probability distribution of monthly demand for color television sets with a particular Poisson distribution.

Solution

Let X be the demand in a typical month. The consultant knows that there are many possible values of X. For example, if historical records show that monthly demands have always been between 0 and 40, the consultant knows that almost all of the probability should be assigned to the values 0 through 40. However, she does not relish the thought of finding 41 probabilities, $P(X = 0)$ through $P(X = 40)$, that sum to 1 and reflect historical frequencies. Instead, she discovers from the manager that the histogram of demands from previous months is shaped much like the graph in Figure 6.25. That is, it rises to some peak, then falls.

Figure 6.26   Poisson Calculations for Television Example

	A	B	C	D	E	F	G	H	I	J	K
1	Poisson distribution for monthly demand										
2				Range name used:							
3	Mean monthly demand (λ)	17		Mean	=Sheet1!$B$3						
4											
5	Representative probability calculations										
6	Less than or equal to 20	0.805		=POISSON(20,Mean,1)							
7	Between 10 and 15 (inclusive)	0.345		=POISSON(15,Mean,1)-POISSON(9,Mean,1)							
8											
9	Individual probabilities										
10	Value	Prob									
11	0	0.000		=POISSON(A11,MeanDem,0)							
12	1	0.000									
13	2	0.000									
14	3	0.000									
15	4	0.000									
16	5	0.000									
17	6	0.001									
18	7	0.003									
19	8	0.007									
20	9	0.014									
21	10	0.023									
22	11	0.036									
23	12	0.050									
24	13	0.066									
25	14	0.080									
26	15	0.091									
27	16	0.096									
28	17	0.096									
29	18	0.091									
30	19	0.081									
31	20	0.069									
32	21	0.056									
33	22	0.043									
34	23	0.032									
35	24	0.023									
36	25	0.015									
37	26	0.010									
38	27	0.006									
39	28	0.004									
40	29	0.002									
41	30	0.001									
42	31	0.001									
43	32	0.000									
44	33	0.000									
45	34	0.000									
46	35	0.000									
47	36	0.000									
48	37	0.000									
49	38	0.000									
50	39	0.000									
51	40	0.000									

Poisson Distribution with λ=17

Knowing that a Poisson distribution has this same basic shape, the consultant decides to model the monthly demand with a Poisson distribution. To choose a particular Poisson distribution, all she has to do is choose a value of λ, the mean demand per month. Because the historical average is approximately 17, she chooses $\lambda = 17$. Now she can test the Poisson model by calculating probabilities of various events and asking the manager whether these probabilities are a reasonable approximation to reality.

For example, the Poisson probability that monthly demand is less than or equal to 20, $P(X \leq 20)$, is 0.805 [using the Excel function POISSON(20,17,1)], and the probability that demand is between 10 and 15 inclusive, $P(10 \leq X \leq 15)$, is 0.345 [using POISSON(15,17,1)-POISSON(9,17,1)]. Figure 6.26 illustrates various probability calculations and shows the graph of the individual Poisson probabilities. (See the file **Poisson Demand Distribution.xlsx**.)

If the manager believes that these probabilities and other similar probabilities are reasonable, then the *statistical* part of the consultant's job is finished. Otherwise, she must try a different Poisson distribution—a different value of λ—or perhaps a different type of distribution altogether. ∎

6.6.2 The Exponential Distribution

Suppose that a bank manager is studying the pattern of customer arrival at her branch location. As indicated previously in this section, the number of arrivals in an hour at a facility such as a bank is often well described by a Poisson distribution with parameter λ, where λ represents the expected number of arrivals per hour. An alternative way to view the uncertainty in the arrival process is to consider the *times* between customer arrivals. The most common probability distribution used to model these times, often called *interarrival times,* is the *exponential* distribution.

In general, the *continuous* random variable X has an **exponential** distribution with parameter λ (with $\lambda > 0$) if the probability density function for X has the form $f(x) = \lambda e^{-\lambda x}$ for $x > 0$. This exact form is not as important as the shape of the graph it implies, as shown in Figure 6.27. Because this density function decreases continually from left to right, its most likely value is $x = 0$. Alternatively, if we collect many observations from an exponential distribution and draw a histogram of the observed values, then we expect it to resemble the smooth curve shown in Figure 6.27, with the tallest bars to the left. The mean and standard deviation of this distribution are easy to remember. They are both equal to the *reciprocal* of the parameter λ. For example, an exponential distribution with parameter $\lambda = 0.1$ has mean and standard deviation both equal to 10.

Figure 6.27

Exponential Density Function

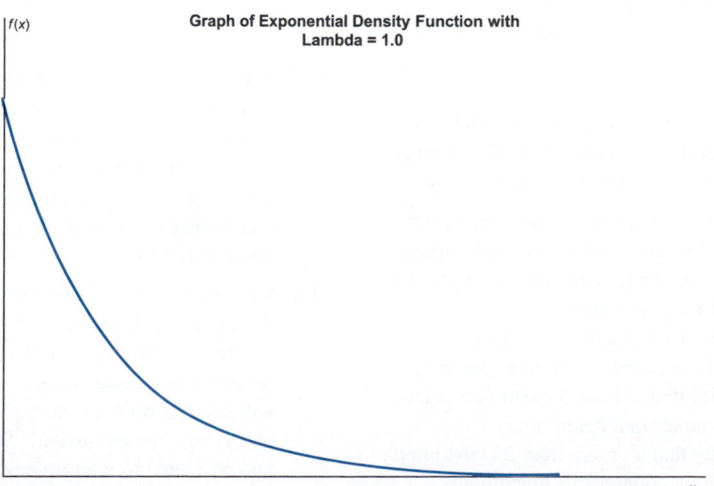

$f(x)$

Graph of Exponential Density Function with Lambda = 1.0

x

As with the normal distribution, we usually want probabilities to the left or right of a given value. For any exponential distribution, we can calculate the probability to the left of a given value $x > 0$ with Excel's EXPONDIST function. In particular, this function takes the form

=EXPONDIST(x, λ, 1)

For example, if $x = 0.5$ and $\lambda = 5$ (so that the mean equals $1/5 = 0.2$), then the probability of being less than 0.5 can be found with the formula

=EXPONDIST(0.5, 5, 1)

This returns the probability 0.918. Of course, the probability of being greater than 0.5 is then $1 - 0.918 = 0.082$.

Returning to the bank manager's analysis of customer arrival data, when the times between arrivals are exponentially distributed, we sometimes hear that "arrivals occur according to a Poisson process." This is because there is a close relationship between the exponential distribution, which measures *times* between events such as arrivals, and the Poisson distribution, which counts the *number* of events in a certain length of time. The details of this relationship are beyond the level of this book, so we will not explore the topic further. It is sufficient for our purposes to say, for example, that if customers arrive at a facility according to a Poisson process with rate 6 per hour, then we know the corresponding times between arrivals are exponentially distributed with mean $1/\lambda = 1/6$ hour.

PROBLEMS

Level A

41. The annual number of industrial accidents occurring in a particular manufacturing plant is known to follow a Poisson distribution with mean 12.
  a. What is the probability of observing exactly 12 accidents at this plant during the coming year?
  b. What is the probability of observing no more than 12 accidents at this plant during the coming year?
  c. What is the probability of observing at least 15 accidents at this plant during the coming year?
  d. What is the probability of observing between 10 and 15 accidents (inclusive) at this plant during the coming year?
  e. Find the smallest integer k such that we can be at least 99% sure that the annual number of accidents occurring at this plant will be less than k.

42. Suppose that the number of customers arriving each hour at the only checkout counter in a local pharmacy is approximately Poisson distributed with an expected arrival rate of 20 customers per hour.
  a. Find the probability that exactly 10 customers arrive at this checkout counter in a given hour.
  b. Find the probability that at least 5 customers arrive at this checkout counter in a given hour.
  c. Find the probability that no more than 25 customers arrive at this checkout counter in a given hour.

  d. Find the probability that between 10 and 30 customers (inclusive) arrive at this checkout counter in a given hour.
  e. Find the largest integer k such that we can be at least 95% sure that the number of customers arriving at this checkout counter in a given hour will be greater than k.
  f. Recalling the relationship between the Poisson and exponential distributions, find the probability that the time between two successive customer arrivals is more then 4 minutes. Find the probability that it is less than 2 minutes.

43. Suppose the number of points scored by the Indiana University basketball team in 1 minute follows a Poisson distribution with $\lambda = 1.5$. In a 10-minute span of time, what is the probability that Indiana University scores exactly 20 points? (Use the fact that if the rate per minute is λ, then the rate in t minutes is λt.)

44. Suppose that the times between arrivals at a bank during the peak period of the day are exponentially distributed with a mean of 45 seconds. If you just observed an arrival, what is the probability that you will need to wait for more than a minute before observing the next arrival? What is the probability you will need to wait at least 2 minutes?

Level B

45. Consider a Poisson random variable X with parameter $\lambda = 2$.

   a. Find the probability that X is within 1 standard deviation of its mean.

   b. Find the probability that X is within 2 standard deviations of its mean.

   c. Find the probability that X is within 3 standard deviations of its mean.

   d. Do the empirical rules we learned previously seem to be applicable in working with the Poisson distribution where $\lambda = 2$? Explain why or why not.

   e. Repeat parts **a through d** for the case of a Poisson random variable where $\lambda = 20$.

46. Based on historical data, the probability that a major league pitcher pitches a no-hitter in a game is about 1/1300.

   a. Use the binomial distribution to determine the probability that in 650 games 0, 1, 2, or 3 no-hitters will be pitched. (Find the separate probabilities of these four events.)

   b. Repeat part **a** using the Poisson approximation to the binomial. This approximation says that if n is large and p is small, a binomial distribution with parameters n and p is approximately Poisson with $\lambda = np$.

6.7 FITTING A PROBABILITY DISTRIBUTION TO DATA WITH @RISK[7]

The normal, binomial, Poisson, and exponential distributions are four of the most commonly used distributions in real applications. However, many other discrete and continuous distributions are also used. These include the uniform, triangular, Erlang, lognormal, gamma, Weibull, and others. How do we know which to choose for any particular application? Often we can answer this by seeing which of several potential distributions fits a given set of data most closely. Essentially, we compare a histogram of the data with the theoretical probability distributions available and see which gives the best fit.

@RISK, one of the Palisade add-ins in the Decision Tools suite, makes this fairly easy, as we illustrate in the following example. (Many other features of the @RISK add-in are discussed in depth in Chapters 16 and 17.)

EXAMPLE 6.14 ASSESSING A DISTRIBUTION OF SUPERMARKET CHECKOUT TIMES

A supermarket has collected checkout times on over 100 customers. (See the file **Checkout Times.xlsx**.) As shown in Figure 6.28, the times vary from 40 seconds to 279 seconds, with the mean and median right around 2 minutes.

Figure 6.28

Supermarket Checkout Times

	A	B	C	D	E	F	G
1	Customer	Time			*Summary measures for selected variables*		
2	1	131				Time	
3	2	101			Count	113.000	
4	3	178			Mean	159.239	
5	4	246			Median	155.000	
6	5	207			Standard deviation	52.609	
7	6	155			Minimum	40.000	
8	7	95			Maximum	279.000	
9	8	105					
10	9	168					
11	10	92					
12	11	112					
13	12	163					
111	110	138					
112	111	279					
113	112	90					
114	113	155					

[7]In the previous edition, we showed how to do this with Palisade's stand-alone program BestFit. Because @RISK incorporates all the functionality of BestFit, and because BestFit is not included in the current version of the Palisade suite, we now illustrate the procedure with @RISK.

The supermarket manager would like to check whether these data are normally distributed or whether some other distribution fits them better. How can he tell?

Objective   To use @RISK to determine which probability distribution fits the given data best.

Solution

To open @RISK, go to the Windows Start button, find the Palisade group, and click on @RISK. If Excel is already open, this opens @RISK on top of it. If Excel isn't it open, this launches Excel and @RISK. You will know @RISK is open when you see the @RISK tab and the associated ribbon in Figure 6.29. For now, we are interested only in the Distribution Fitting item. From here, we can go in one of two ways. We can test the fit of a *given* distribution, or we can find the best-fitting distribution from a number of candidates. We illustrate both.

Figure 6.29   @RISK Ribbon

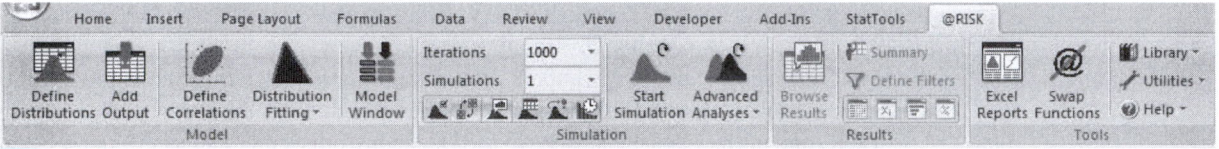

Because the supermarket manager wants to know whether the data could come from a normal distribution, we check this possibility first. To do so, select Fit Manager from the Distribution Fitting dropdown. The first step is to define a data set, as we have in Figure 6.30. The second step is to click on the Distributions to Fit tab and select the Normal distribution, as shown in Figure 6.31. To see how well a normal distribution fits the data, all you need to do is click on the Fit button. This produces the output shown in Figure 6.32, with a normal curve superimposed on the histogram of the data. A visual examination of this graph is often sufficient to tell whether the fit is any "good." (We would judge this fit to be "fair," but not great.)

@RISK provides several numerical measures of the goodness of fit, which you can find by clicking on the dropdown next to Fit Ranking at the top left in the figure. We won't pursue the technical details, but we will simply mention that each test value measures "goodness of fit" in a slightly different way. For each of these measures, the larger the test value is, the *worse* the fit is. They can then be used to compare fits; the distribution with the lowest test values is the winner.

Figure 6.30

Defining a Data Set

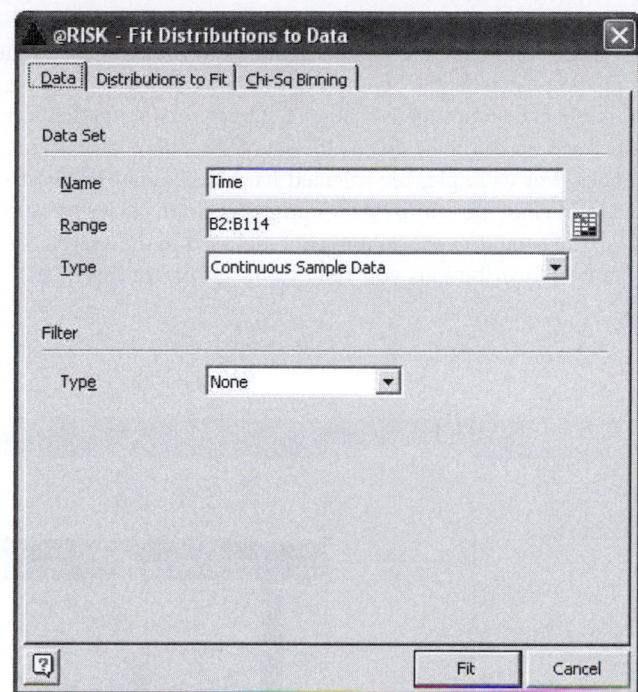

Figure 6.31

Selecting the
Distribution(s)
to Fit

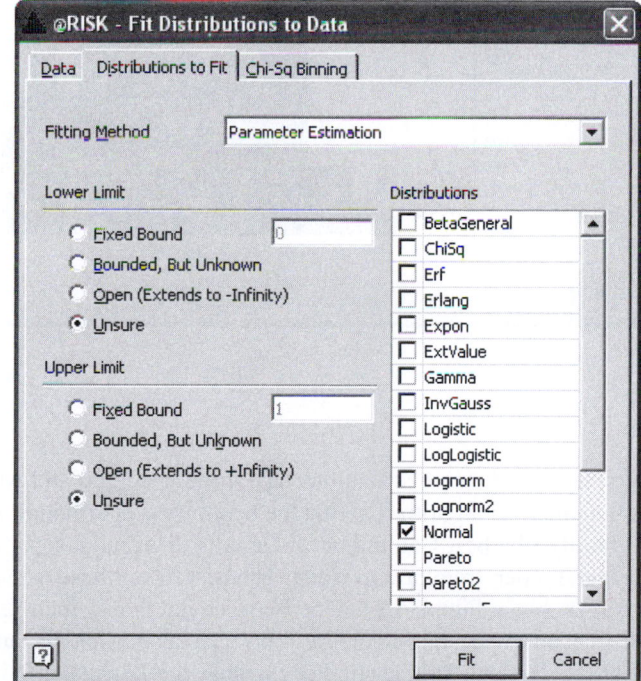

We next see which of several possible distributions fit the data best. To do this, get back into Fit Manager and click on the Distributions to Fit tab. (See Figure 6.33.) On the left we have made some "reasonable" choices about the checkout data. We have specified that the lowest possible checkout time is 0 but we are not sure about the upper limit on the checkout times. When we make such choices, the set of possible distributions that are checked on the right changes. For example, the selected list here contains only distributions with a lower limit of 0. (Note that the normal distribution does *not* satisfy these conditions.) We can then uncheck any distributions we do not want included in the search for the best fit. (You might want to uncheck distributions you've never heard of, for instance!)

Figure 6.32

Normal Fit to the Data

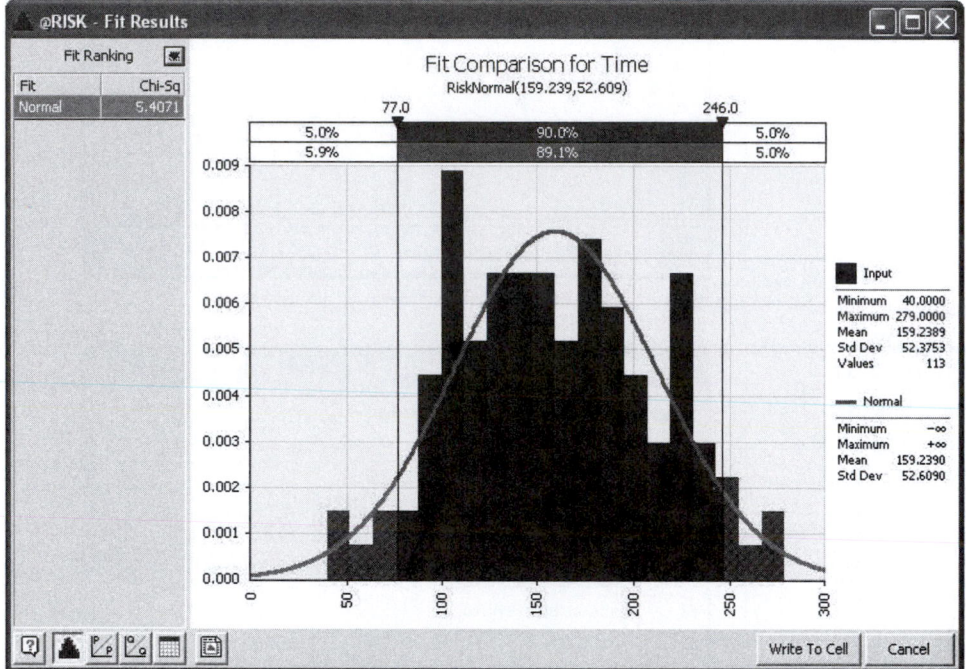

Once these candidate distributions have been specified and we click on Fit, @RISK performs a numerical algorithm to find the best-fitting distribution from each selected distribution family (the best Gamma of all Gamma distributions, for example) and displays them in ranked order, from best to worst. The best fit for these data is the BetaGeneral distribution, as shown in Figure 6.34. (The BetaGeneral family includes skewed distributions, although this one appears symmetric.) We can also click on any of the "runner up" distributions to see how well they fit. For example, the Triangular fit is shown in Figure 6.35. Obviously, this fit is not nearly as good as the BetaGeneral fit.

Figure 6.33
Selecting
Distributions to Fit

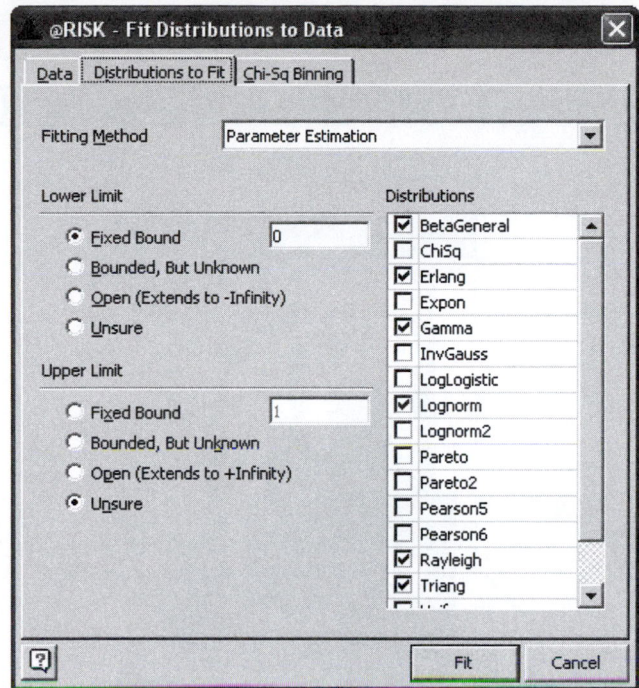

Figure 6.34 BetaGeneral Fit to the Data

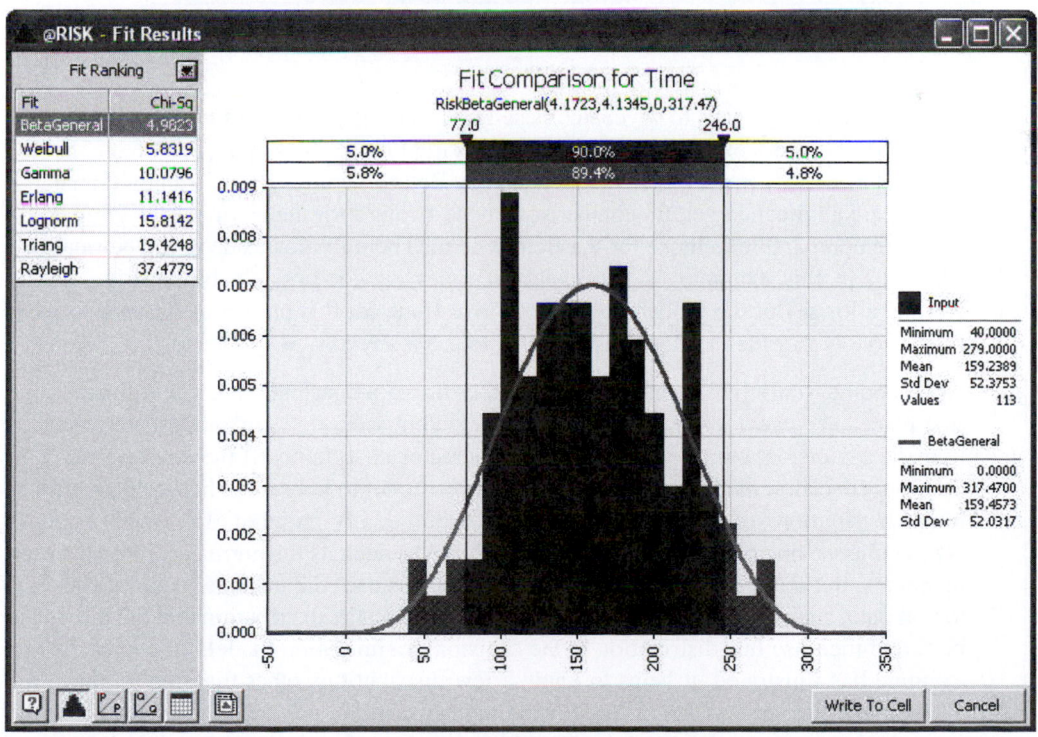

6.7 Fitting a Probability Distribution to Data with @RISK   **303**

Figure 6.35 Triangular Fit to the Data

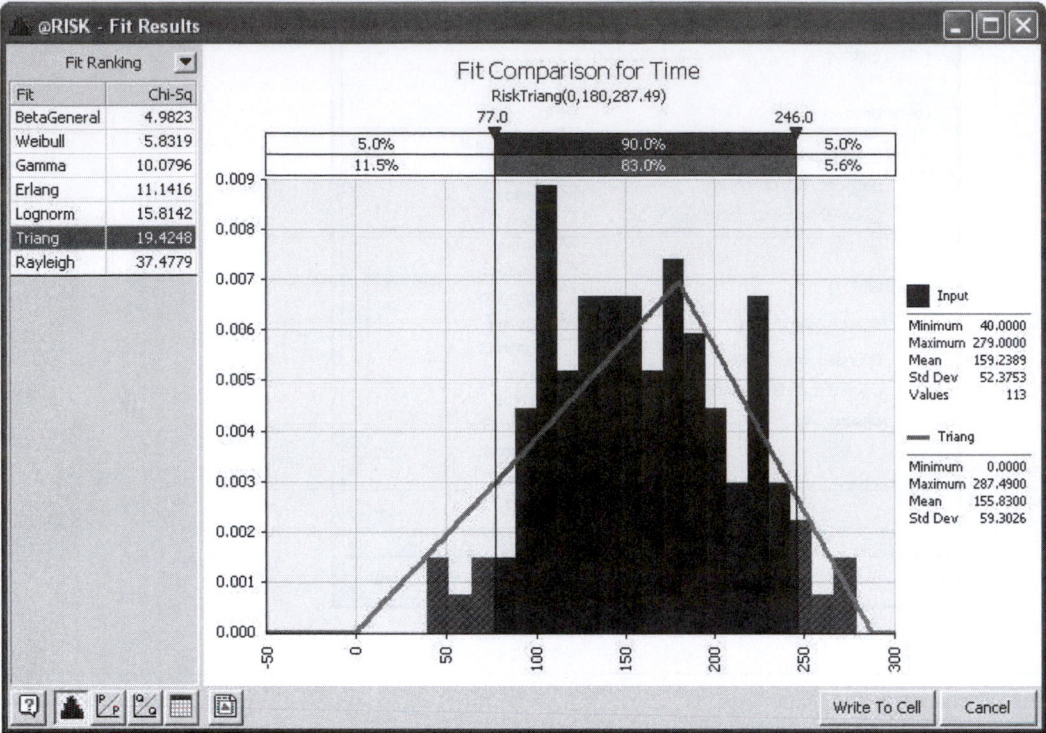

It is not always easy to "eyeball" these graphs and judge which fit is best. This is the reason for the goodness-of-fit measures. Comparing Figures 6.34 and 6.35, we see that the Triangular fit is considerably worse than the BetaGeneral—its test values (some not shown) are all much larger. By comparison, the test values for the Normal fit in Figure 6.32 are quite comparable to those for the BetaGeneral. The only downside to the Normal distribution, in this example, is that checkout times cannot possibly be negative, as the Normal allows. But the probability of a negative value for this particular Normal distribution is so low that the manager might decide to use it anyway. ■

At this point, you might wonder why we bother fitting a distribution to a set of data in the first place. The usual reason is given in the following scenario. Suppose a manager needs to make a decision, but there is at least one source of uncertainty. If the manager wants to develop a decision model or perhaps a simulation model to help solve his problem, probability distributions of all uncertain outcomes are typically required. The manager could always choose one of the "well-known" distributions, such as the normal, for all uncertain outcomes, but these might not reflect reality well. Instead, the manager could gather historical data, such as those in the preceding example, find the distribution that fits these data best, and then use this distribution in the decision or simulation model. Of course, as this example has illustrated, it helps to know a few distributions other than the normal—the Weibull and the gamma, for instance. Although we will not pursue these in this book, the more distributions you have in your "tool kit," the more effectively you can model.

Level A

47. A production manager is interested in determining the proportion of defective items in a typical shipment of one of the computer components that her company manufactures. The proportion of defective components is recorded for each of 500 randomly selected shipments collected during a 1-month period. The data are in the file **P02_02.xlsx**. Use @RISK to determine which probability distribution best fits these data.

48. The manager of a local fast-food restaurant is interested in improving the service provided to customers who use the restaurant's drive-up window. As a first step in this process, the manager asks his assistant to record the time (in minutes) it takes to serve 200 different customers at the final window in the facility's drive-up system. The given 200 customer service times are all observed during the busiest hour of the day for this fast-food operation. The data are in the file **P02_04.xlsx**. Use @RISK to determine which probability distribution best fits these data.

49. The operations manager of a toll booth, located at a major exit of a state turnpike, is trying to estimate the average number of vehicles that arrive at the toll booth during a 1-minute period during the peak of rush-hour traffic. In an effort to estimate this average throughput value, he records the number of vehicles that arrive at the toll booth over a 1-minute interval commencing at the same time for each of 365 normal weekdays. The data are in the file **P02_09.xlsx**. Use @RISK to determine which probability distribution best fits these data.

50. A finance professor has just given a midterm examination in her corporate finance course and is interested in learning how her class of 100 students performed on this exam. The data are in the file **P02_05.xlsx**. Use @RISK to determine which probability distribution best fits these data.

6.8 CONCLUSION

We have covered a lot of ground in this chapter, and much of the material, especially that on the normal distribution, will be used in later chapters. The normal distribution is the cornerstone for much of statistical theory. As we see when we study statistical inference and regression, an assumption of normality is behind most of the procedures we use. Therefore, it is important to understand the properties of the normal distribution and how to work with it in Excel. The binomial, Poisson, and exponential distributions, although not used as frequently as the normal distribution in this book, are also extremely important. The examples we have discussed indicate how these distributions can be used in a variety of business situations.

Although we have attempted to stress *concepts* in this chapter, we have also described the details necessary to work with these distributions in Excel. Fortunately, these details are not too difficult to master once you understand Excel's built-in functions such as NORMDIST, NORMINV, and BINOMDIST. Figures 6.6 and 6.18 provide typical examples of these functions. We suggest that you keep a copy of these figures handy.

Summary of Key Terms

Term	Explanation	Excel	Page	Equation Number
Probability density function	Specifies the probability distribution of a continuous random variable		258	
Normal distribution	A continuous distribution with possible values ranging over the *entire* number line; its density function is a symmetric bell-shaped curve		259	6.1
Standardizing a normal random variable	Transforms any normal distribution with mean μ and standard deviation σ to the *standard* normal distribution with mean 0 and standard deviation 1	STANDARDIZE	260	6.2
Normal calculations in Excel	Useful for finding probabilities and percentiles for nonstandard and standard normal distributions	NORMDIST, NORMSDIST, NORMINV, NORMSINV	263	
Empirical rules for normal distribution	About 68% of the data fall within 1 standard deviation of the mean, about 95% of the data fall within 2 standard deviations of the mean, and almost all fall within 3 standard deviations of the mean.		265	
Binomial distribution	The distribution of the number of successes in n independent, identical trials, where each trial has probability p of success	BINOMDIST CRITBINOM	278	
Mean and standard deviation of a binomial distribution	The mean and standard deviation of a binomial distribution with parameters n and p are np and $[np(1-p)]^{1/2}$, respectively.		281	6.3, 6.4
Normal approximation to the binomial distribution	If $np > 5$ and $n(1-p) > 5$, the binomial distribution can be approximated well by a normal distribution with mean np and standard deviation $[np(1-p)]^{1/2}$.		282	
Poisson distribution	A discrete probability distribution that often describes the number of events occurring within a specified period of time or space; mean and variance both equal the parameter λ	POISSON	294	
Exponential distribution	A continuous probability distribution useful for measuring *times* between events such as customer arrivals to a service facility; mean and standard deviation both equal $1/\lambda$	EXPONDIST	297	
Relationship between Poisson and exponential distributions	Exponential distribution measures *times* between events; Poisson distribution counts the *number* of events in a certain period of time.		298	
@RISK	An Excel add-in for finding how well a specified distribution fits a set of data, or for finding the distribution that best fits a set of data	Distribution Fitting item on @RISK ribbon	299	

PROBLEMS

Conceptual Exercises

C.1 Explain why the probability that a continuous random variable equals any particular value must be zero.

C.2 What is the relationship between the mean and standard deviation of any normal distribution? Explain.

C.3 A New York Yankees fan would like to determine the probability that his beloved team will sweep the National League Championship team in the first four games of this year's World Series. Explain, in words, how the fan should proceed to assess this probability. Be sure to state all assumptions that the fan needs to make to proceed with the approach you prescribe.

C.4 A production manager would like to determine the probability that a particular production process yields more than 3 defective items per hour. Explain, in words, how the manager should proceed to assess this probability. Be sure to state all assumptions that the manager needs to make to proceed with the approach you prescribe.

C.5 State the major similarities and differences between the *normal* distribution and the *exponential* distribution.

Level A

51. Suppose the annual return on XYZ stock follows a normal distribution with mean 0.12 and standard deviation 0.30.
   a. What is the probability that XYZ's value will decrease during a year?
   b. What is the probability that the return on XYZ during a year will be at least 20%?
   c. What is the probability that the return on XYZ during a year will be between −6% and 9%?
   d. There is a 5% chance that the return on XYZ during a year will be greater than what value?
   e. There is a 1% chance that the return on XYZ during a year will be less than what value?
   f. There is a 95% chance that the return on XYZ during a year will be between what two values (equidistant from the mean)?

52. Assume the annual mean return on Disney stock is around 15% and the annual standard deviation is around 25%. Assume the annual and daily returns on Disney stock are normally distributed.
   a. What is the probability that Disney will lose money during a year?
   b. There is a 5% chance that Disney will earn a return of at least what value during a year?
   c. There is a 10% chance that Disney will earn a return of less than or equal to what value during a year?
   d. What is the probability that Disney will earn at least 35% during a year?

   e. Assume there are 252 trading days in a year. What is the probability that Disney will lose money on a given day? [*Hint:* Let Y be the annual return on Disney and Xi be the return on Disney on day i. Then (approximately) $Y = X_1 + X_2 + \cdots + X_{252}$. Use the fact that the sum of independent normal random variables is normally distributed, with mean equal to the sum of the individual means, and variance equal to the sum of the individual variances.]

53. Suppose Comdell Computer receives its disk drives from Diskco. On average, 4% of all floppy disk drives received by Comdell are defective.
   a. Dell has adopted the following policy. It samples 50 disk drives in each shipment and accepts the shipment if all disk drives in the sample are nondefective. What fraction of batches will Comdell accept?
   b. Suppose instead that the batch is accepted if at most 1 disk drive in the sample is defective. What fraction of batches will Comdell accept?
   c. What is the probability that a sample of size 50 will contain at least 10 defectives?

54. A family is considering a move from a midwestern city to a city in California. The distribution of housing costs where the family currently lives is normal with mean $105,000 and standard deviation $18,200. The distribution of housing costs in the California city is normal with mean $235,000 and standard deviation $30,400. The family's current house is valued at $110,000.
   a. What percentage of houses in the family's current city cost less than theirs?
   b. If the family buys a $200,000 house in the new city, what percentage of houses there will cost less than theirs?
   c. What price house will the family need to buy to be in the same percentile (of housing costs) in the new city as they are in the current city?

55. The number of traffic fatalities in a typical month in a given state has a normal distribution with mean 125 and standard deviation 31.
   a. If a person in the highway department claims that there will be at least m fatalities in the next month with probability 0.95, what value of m makes this claim true?
   b. If the claim is that there will be no more than n fatalities in the next month with probability 0.98, what value of n makes this claim true?

56. It can be shown that a sum of independent normally distributed random variables is also normally distributed. Do *all* functions of normal random variables lead to normal random variables? Consider the following.

SuperDrugs is a chain of drugstores with three similar-size stores in a given city. The sales in a given week for any of these stores is normally distributed with mean $15,000 and standard deviation $3000. At the end of each week, the sales figure for the store with the largest sales among the three stores is recorded. Is this maximum value normally distributed? To answer this question, simulate a weekly sales figure at each of the three stores and calculate the maximum. Then replicate this maximum 500 times with a data table and create a histogram of the 500 maximum values. Does it appear to be normally shaped? Whatever this distribution looks like, use your simulated values to estimate its mean and standard deviation.

Level B

57. When we sum 30 or more independent random variables, the sum of the random variables will usually be approximately normally distributed, even if each individual random variable is not normally distributed. Use this fact to estimate the probability that a casino will be behind after 90,000 roulette bets, given that it wins $1 or loses $35 on each bet with probabilities 37/38 and 1/38.

58. The daily demand for six-packs of Coke at Mr. D's supermarket follows a normal distribution with mean 120 and standard deviation 30. Every Monday the Coke delivery driver delivers Coke to Mr. D's. If Mr. D's wants to have only a 1% chance of running out of Coke by the end of the week, how many should Mr. D's order for the week? Assume orders are placed on Sunday at midnight. (Assume also that demands on different days are probabilistically independent. Use the fact that the sum of independent normal random variables is normally distributed, with mean equal to the sum of the individual means, and variance equal to the sum of the individual variances.)

59. Many companies use sampling to determine whether a batch should be accepted. An (n, c) sampling plan consists of inspecting n randomly chosen items from a batch and accepting the batch if c or fewer sampled items are defective. Suppose a company uses a (100, 5) sampling plan to determine whether a batch of 10,000 computer chips is acceptable.
   a. The "producer's risk" of a sampling plan is the probability that an acceptable batch will be rejected by a sampling plan. Suppose the customer considers a batch with 3% defectives acceptable. What is the producer's risk for this sampling plan?
   b. The "consumer's risk" of a sampling plan is the probability that an unacceptable batch will be accepted by a sampling plan. Our customer says

that a batch with 9% defectives is unacceptable. What is the consumer's risk for this sampling plan?

60. Suppose that if a presidential election were held today, 52% of all voters would vote for Kerry over Bush. (You may substitute the names of the current presidential candidates!) This problem shows that even if there are 100 million voters, a sample of several thousand is enough to determine the outcome, even in a fairly close election.
   a. If we were to randomly sample 1500 voters, what is the probability that the sample would indicate (correctly) that Kerry is preferred to Bush?
   b. If we were to randomly sample 6000 voters, what is the probability that the sample would indicate (correctly) that Kerry is preferred to Bush?

61. The Coke factory fills bottles of soda by setting a timer on a filling machine. It has generally been observed that the distribution of the number of ounces the machine puts into a bottle is normal with standard deviation 0.05 ounces. The company wants 99.9% of all its bottles to have at least 16 ounces of soda. To what amount should the mean amount put in each bottle be set? (The company does not want to fill any more than is necessary!)

62. The time it takes me to swim 100 yards in a race is normally distributed with mean 62 seconds and standard deviation 2 seconds. In my next five races, what is the probability that I will swim under a minute exactly twice?

63. We assemble a large part by joining two smaller parts together. In the past, the smaller parts we have produced have a mean length of 1 inch and a standard deviation of 0.01 inch. Assume that the lengths of the smaller parts are normally distributed.
   a. What fraction of the larger parts are longer than 2.05 inches? (Use the fact that the sum of independent normal random variables is normally distributed, with mean equal to the sum of the individual means, and variance equal to the sum of the individual variances.)
   b. What fraction of the larger parts are between 1.96 inches and 2.02 inches long?

64. (Suggested by Sam Kaufmann, Indiana University MBA who runs Harrah's Lake Tahoe Casino.) A high roller has come to the casino to play 300 games of craps. For each game of craps played there is a 0.493 probability that the high roller will win $1 and a 0.507 probability that the high roller will lose $1. After 300 games of craps, what is the probability that the casino will be behind more than $10?

65. (Suggested by Sam Kaufmann, Indiana University MBA who runs Harrah's Lake Tahoe Casino.) A high roller comes to the casino intending to play 500 hands of blackjack for $1 a hand. On each hand,

the high roller will win $1 with probability 0.48 and lose $1 with probability 0.52. After the 500 hands, what is the probability that the casino has lost more than $40?

66. Bottleco produces 100,000 12-ounce bottles of soda per year. By adjusting a timer, Bottleco can adjust the mean number of ounces placed in a bottle. No matter what the mean, the standard deviation of the number of ounces in a bottle is 0.05. Soda costs $0.05 per ounce. Any bottle weighing less than 12 ounces will incur a $10 fine for being underweight. Determine a setting for the mean number of ounces per bottle of soda that will minimize the expected cost per year of producing soda. Your answer should be accurate within 0.001 ounce. Does the number of bottles produced per year influence your answer?

67. The weekly demand for televisions at Lowland Appliance is normally distributed with mean 400 and standard deviation 100. Each time an order for TVs is placed, it arrives exactly 4 weeks later. That is, TV orders have a 4-week lead time. Lowland doesn't want to run out of TVs during any more than 1% of all lead times. How low should Lowland let its TV inventory drop before it places an order for more TVs? (*Hint*: How many standard deviations above the mean lead-time demand must the reorder point be for there to be a 1% chance of a stockout during the lead time? Use the fact that the sum of independent normal random variables is normally distributed, with mean equal to the sum of the individual means, and variance equal to the sum of the individual variances.)

68. An elevator rail is assumed to meet specifications if its diameter is between 0.98 and 1.01 inches. Each year we make 100,000 elevator rails. For a cost of $10/\sigma^2$ per year we can rent a machine that produces elevator rails whose diameters have a standard deviation of σ. (The idea is that we must pay more for smaller variances.) Any machine will produce rails having a mean diameter of 1 inch. Any rail that does not meet specifications must be reworked (at a cost of $12). Assume that the diameter of an elevator rail follows a normal distribution.
   a. What standard deviation (within 0.001 inch) will minimize our annual cost of producing elevator rails? You do not need to try standard deviations in excess of 0.02 inch.
   b. For your answer in part **a**, one elevator rail in 1000 will be at least how many inches in diameter?

69. A 20-question true–false examination is given. Each correct answer is worth 5 points. Consider an unprepared student who randomly guesses on each question.
   a. If no points are deducted for incorrect answers, what is the probability that the student will score at least 60 points?

   b. If 5 points are deducted for each incorrect answer, what is the probability that the student will score at least 60 points?
   c. If 5 points are deducted for each incorrect answer, what is the probability that the student will receive a negative score?

70. The percentage of examinees who took the GMAT (Graduate Management Admission) exam from June 1992 to March 1995 and scored below each total score is given in the file **P06_70.xlsx**. For example, 96% of all examinees scored 690 or below. The mean GMAT score for this time period was 497 and the standard deviation was 105. Does it appear that GMAT scores can accurately be approximated by a normal distribution? (Source: 1995 GMAT Examinee Interpretation Guide)

71. What caused the crash of TWA Flight 800 in 1996? Physics Professors Hailey and Helfand of Columbia University believe there is a reasonable possibility that a meteor hit Flight 800. They reason as follows. On a given day, 3000 meteors of a size large enough to destroy an airplane hit the earth's atmosphere. Around 50,000 flights per day, averaging 2 hours in length, have been flown from 1950 to 1996. This means that at any given point in time, planes in flight cover approximately two-billionths of the world's atmosphere. Determine the probability that at least one plane in the last 47 years has been downed by a meteor. (*Hint*: Use the Poisson approximation to the binomial. This approximation says that if n is large and p is small, a binomial distribution with parameters n and p is approximately Poisson distributed with $\lambda = np$.)

72. In the decade 1982 through 1991, 10 employees working at the Amoco Company chemical research center were stricken with brain tumors. The average employment at the center was 2000 employees. Nationwide, the average incidence of brain tumors in a single year is 20 per 100,000 people. If the incidence of brain tumors at the Amoco chemical research center were the same as the nationwide incidence, what is the probability that at least 10 brain tumors would have been observed among Amoco workers during the decade 1982 through 1991? What do you conclude from your analysis? (Source: AP wire service report, March 12, 1994)

73. Claims arrive at random times to an insurance company. The daily amount of claims is normally distributed with mean $1570 and standard deviation $450. Total claims on different days each have this distribution, and they are probabilistically independent of one another.
   a. Find the probability that the amount of total claims over a period of 100 days is at least $150,000. (Use the fact that the sum of independent normally distributed random variables is normally distributed, with mean equal to the sum of the individual means

and variance equal to the sum of the individual variances.)

b. If the company receives premiums totaling $165,000, find the probability that the company will net at least $10,000 for the 100-day period.

74. A popular model for stock prices is the following. If p_0 is the current stock price, then the price, p_k, k periods from now (where a period could be a day, week, or any other convenient unit of time, and k is any positive integer) is given by

$$p_k = p_0\exp((\mu - 0.5\sigma^2)k + sZ\sqrt{k})$$

Here, exp is the exponential function (EXP in Excel), μ is the mean percentage growth rate per period of the stock, σ is the standard deviation of the growth rate per period, and Z is a normally distributed random variable with mean 0 and standard deviation 1. Both μ and σ are typically estimated from actual stock price data, and they are typically expressed in decimal form, such as $\mu = 0.01$ for a 1% mean growth rate. Suppose a period is defined as a month, the current price of the stock (as of the end of December 2004) is $75, $\mu = 0.006$, and $\sigma = 0.028$. Use simulation to obtain 500 possible stock price changes from the end of December 2004 to the end of December 2007. (Note that you can simulate a given change in one line and then copy it down.) Create a histogram of these changes to see whether the stock price change is at least approximately normally distributed. Also, use the simulated data to estimate the mean price change and the standard deviation of the change.

75. Continuing the previous problem (with the same parameters), use simulation to generate the ending stock prices for each month in 2005. (Use $k = 1$ to get January's price from December's, use $k = 1$ again to get February's price from January's, and so on.) Then use a data table to replicate the ending December 2005 stock price 500 times. Create a histogram of these 500 values. Do they appear to resemble a normal distribution?

76. Your company is running an audit on the Sleaze Company. Because Sleaze has a bad habit of overcharging its customers, the focus of your audit is on checking whether the billing amounts on its invoices are correct. We'll assume that each invoice is for too high an amount with probability 0.06 and for too low an amount with probability 0.01 (so that the probability of a correct billing is 0.93). Also, we assume that the outcome for any invoice is probabilistically independent of the outcomes for other invoices.

a. If you randomly sample 200 of Sleaze's invoices, what is the probability that you will find at least 15 invoices that overcharge the customer? What is the probability you won't find any that undercharge the customer?

b. Find an integer k such that the probability is at least 0.99 that you will find at least k invoices that overcharge the customer. (*Hint*: Use trial and error with the BINOMDIST function to find k.)

77. Continuing the previous problem, suppose that when Sleaze overcharges a customer, the distribution of the amount overcharged (expressed as a percentage of the correct billing amount) is normally distributed with mean 15% and standard deviation 4%.

a. What percentage of overbilled customers are charged at least 10% more than they should pay?

b. What percentage of *all* customers are charged at least 10% more than they should pay?

c. If your auditing company samples 200 randomly chosen invoices, what is the probability that it will find at least 5 where the customer was overcharged by at least 10%?

78. Let X be normally distributed with a given mean and standard deviation. Sometimes you want to find two values a and b such that $P(a < X < b)$ is equal to some specific probability such as 0.90 or 0.95. There are many answers to this problem, depending on how much probability you put in each of the two tails. For this question, assume the mean and standard deviation are $\mu = 100$ and $\sigma = 10$, and that we want to find a and b such that $P(a < X < b) = 0.90$.

a. Find a and b so that there is probability 0.05 in each tail.

b. Find a and b so that there is probability 0.025 in the left tail and 0.075 in the right tail.

c. The "usual" answer to the general problem is the answer from part **a**, that is, where you put equal probability in the two tails. It turns out that this is the answer that minimizes the length of the interval from a to b. That is, if you solve the problem: min $(b - a)$, subject to $P(a < X < b) = 0.90$, you'll get the same answer as in part **a**. Verify this using Excel's Solver.

79. Your manufacturing process makes parts such that each part meets specifications with probability 0.98. You need a batch of 250 parts that meet specifications. How many parts must you produce to be at least 99% certain of producing at least 250 parts that meet specifications?

80. The Excel functions discussed in this chapter are useful for solving a lot of probability problems, but there are other problems that, even though they are similar to normal or binomial problems, cannot be solved with these functions. In cases like this, computer simulation can often be used. Here are a couple of such problems for you to simulate. For each example, use 500 replications of the experiment.

a. You observe a sequence of parts from a manufacturing line. These parts use a component that is supplied by one of two suppliers. The probability that a given part uses a component supplied by supplier 1 is 0.6; it is supplied by supplier 2 with probability 0.4. Each part made with a component from supplier 1 works properly with probability 0.95, and each part made with a component from supplier 2 works properly with probability 0.98. Assuming that 30 of these parts are made, we want the probability that at least 29 of them work properly.

b. Here we look at a more generic example such as coin flipping. That is, there is a sequence of trials where each trial is a success with probability p and a failure with probability $1 - p$. A "run" is a sequence of consecutive successes or failures. For most of us, intuition says that there should not be "long" runs. Test this by finding the probability that there is at least 1 run of length at least 6 in a sequence of 15 trials. (The run could be of 0's or 1's.) You can use any value of p you like—or try different values of p.

81. As any credit-granting agency knows, there are always some customers who default on credit charges. Typically, customers are grouped into relatively homogeneous categories, so that customers within any category have approximately the same chance of defaulting on their credit charges. Here we'll look at one particular group of customers. We'll assume each of these customers has (1) probability 0.07 of defaulting on his or her current credit charges, and (2) total credit charges that are normally distributed with mean $350 and standard deviation $100. We'll also assume that if a customer defaults, 20% of his or her charges can be recovered. The other 80% are written off as bad debt.

a. What is the probability that a typical customer in this group will default and produce a write-off of more than $250 in bad debt?

b. If there are 500 customers in this group, what are the mean and standard deviation of the number of customers who will meet the description in part **a**?

c. Again assuming there are 500 customers in this group, what is the probability that at least 25 of them will meet the description in part **a**?

d. Suppose now that nothing is recovered from a default—the whole amount is written off as bad debt. Show how to simulate the total amount of bad debt from 500 customers in just two cells, one with a binomial calculation, the other with a normal calculation.

82. You have a device that uses a single battery, and you operate this device continuously, never turning it off. Whenever a battery fails, you replace it with a brand new one immediately. Suppose the lifetime of a typical battery has an exponential distribution with mean 205 minutes. If you operate the device, starting with a new battery, until you have observed 25 battery failures, what is the probability that at least 15 of these 25 batteries lived at least 3.5 hours?

83. In the previous problem, we ran the "experiment" until there are a certain number of failures and then answered a question about the times between failures. In this problem, we take a different point of view. We run the experiment for a certain amount of time and then ask a question about the number of failures during this time. Specifically, suppose you operate the device from the previous problem continuously for 3 days, making battery changes when necessary. Find the probability that you will observe at least 25 failures. (*Hint*: Do a Poisson calculation using an appropriate λ for the number of failures in a 3-day period.)

The EuroWatch Company assembles expensive wristwatches and then sells them to retailers throughout Europe. The watches are assembled at a plant with two assembly lines. These lines are intended to be identical, but line 1 uses somewhat older equipment than line 2 and is typically less reliable. Historical data have shown that each watch coming off line 1, independently of the others, is free of defects with probability 0.98. The similar probability for line 2 is 0.99. Each line produces 500 watches per hour. The production manager has asked you to answer the following questions.

1. She wants to know how many defect-free watches each line is likely to produce in a given hour. Specifically, find the smallest integer k (for each line separately) such that you can be 99% sure that the line will not produce more than k defective watches in a given hour.

2. EuroWatch currently has an order for 500 watches from an important customer. The company plans to fill this order by packing slightly more than 500 watches, all from line 2, and sending this package off to the customer. Obviously, EuroWatch wants to send as few watches as possible, but it wants to be 99% sure that when the customer opens the package, there are at least 500 defect-free watches. How many watches should be packed?

3. EuroWatch has another order for 1000 watches. Now it plans to fill this order by packing slightly more than one hour's production from each line. This package will contain the *same* number of watches from each line. As in the previous question, EuroWatch wants to send as few watches as possible, but it again wants to be 99% sure that when the customer opens the package, there are at least 1000 defect-free watches. The question of how many watches to pack is unfortunately quite difficult because the total number of defect-free watches is *not* binomially distributed. (Why not?) Therefore, the manager asks you to solve the problem with simulation (and some trial and error). (*Hint*: It turns out that it's much faster to simulate small numbers than large numbers, so simulate the number of watches with defects, not the number without defects.)

4. Finally, EuroWatch has a third order for 100 watches. The customer has agreed to pay $50,000 for the order—that is, $500 per watch. If EuroWatch sends more than 100 watches to the customer, its revenue doesn't increase; it can never exceed $50,000. Its unit cost of producing a watch is $450, regardless of which line it is assembled on. The order will be filled entirely from a single line, and EuroWatch plans to send slightly more than 100 watches to the customer.

5. If the customer opens the shipment and finds that there are fewer than 100 defect-free watches (which we'll assume the customer has the ability to do), then he'll pay only for the defect-free watches—EuroWatch's revenue will decrease by $500 per watch short of the 100 required—and on top of this, EuroWatch will be required to make up the difference at an expedited cost of $1000 per watch. The customer won't pay a dime for these expedited watches. (If expediting is required, EuroWatch will make sure that the expedited watches are defect-free. It doesn't want to lose this customer entirely!)

6. You have been asked to develop a spreadsheet model to find EuroWatch's expected profit for any number of watches it sends to the customer. You should develop it so that it responds correctly, regardless of which assembly line is used to fill the order and what the shipment quantity is. (*Hints*: Use the BINOMDIST function, with last argument 0, to fill up a column of probabilities for each possible number of defective watches. Next to each of these, calculate EuroWatch's profit. Then use a SUMPRODUCT to obtain the expected profit. Finally, you can assume that EuroWatch will never send more than 110 watches. It turns out that this large a shipment is not even close to optimal.) ∎

Many states supplement their tax revenues with state-sponsored lotteries. Most of them do so with a game called lotto. Although there are various versions of this game, they are all basically as follows. People purchase tickets that contain r distinct numbers from 1 to m, where r is generally 5 or 6 and m is generally around 50. For example, in Virginia, the state discussed in this case, $r = 6$ and $m = 44$. Each ticket costs $1, about 39 cents of which is allocated to the total jackpot.[8] There is eventually a drawing of $r = 6$ distinct numbers from the $m = 44$ possible numbers. Any ticket that matches these 6 numbers wins the jackpot.

There are two interesting aspects of this game. First, the current jackpot includes not only the revenue from this round of ticket purchases but any jackpots carried over from previous drawings because of no winning tickets. Therefore, the jackpot can build from one drawing to the next, and in celebrated cases it has become huge. Second, if there is more than one winning ticket—a distinct possibility—the winners share the jackpot equally. (This is called the "parimutuel" effect.) So, for example, if the current jackpot is $9 million and there are three winning tickets, then each winner receives $3 million.

It can be shown that for Virginia's choice of r and m, there are approximately 7 million possible tickets (7,059,052 to be exact). Therefore, any ticket has about one chance out of 7 million of being a winner. That is, the probability of winning with a single ticket is $p = 1/7,059,052$—not very good odds! If n people purchase tickets, then the number of winners is binomially distributed with parameters n and p. Because n is typically very large and p is small, the number of winners has approximately a Poisson distribution with rate $\lambda = np$. (This makes ensuing calculations somewhat easier.) For example, if 1 million tickets are purchased, then the number of winning tickets is approximately Poisson distributed with $\lambda = 1/7$.

In 1992, an Australian syndicate purchased a huge number of tickets in the Virginia lottery in an attempt to assure itself of purchasing a winner. It

worked! Although the syndicate wasn't able to purchase all 7 million possible tickets (it was about 1.5 million shy of this), it did purchase a winning ticket, and there were no other winners. Therefore, the syndicate won a 20-year income stream worth approximately $27 million, with a net present value of approximately $14 million. This easily covered the cost of the tickets it purchased. Two questions come to mind: (1) Is this "hogging" of tickets unfair to the rest of the public? (2) Is it a wise strategy on the part of the syndicate (or did it just get lucky)?

To answer the first question, consider how the lottery changes for the general public with the addition of the syndicate. To be specific, suppose the syndicate can invest $7 million and obtain *all* of the possible tickets, making itself a sure winner. Also, suppose n people from the general public purchase tickets, each of which has 1 chance out of 7 million of being a winner. Finally, let R be the jackpot carried over from any previous lotteries. Then the total jackpot on this round will be $[R + 0.39(7,000,000 + n)]$ because 39 cents from every ticket goes toward the jackpot. The number of winning tickets for the public will be Poisson distributed with $\lambda = n/7,000,000$. However, any member of the public who wins will *necessarily* have to share the jackpot with the syndicate, which is a sure winner. Use this information to calculate the expected amount the public will win. Then do the same calculation when the syndicate does *not* play. (In this case the jackpot will be smaller, but the public won't have to share any winnings with the syndicate.) For values of n and R that you can select, is the public better off with or without the syndicate? Would you, as a general member of the public, support a move to outlaw syndicates from "hogging" the tickets?

---

[8]Of the remaining 61 cents, the state takes about 50 cents. The other 11 cents is used to pay off lesser prize winners whose tickets match some, but not all, of the winning 6 numbers. To keep this case relatively simple, however, we will ignore these lesser prizes and concentrate only on the jackpot.

The second question is whether the syndicate is wise to buy so many tickets. Again assume that the syndicate can spend $7 million and purchase each possible ticket. (Would this be possible in reality?) Also, assume that n members of the general public purchase tickets, and that the carryover from the previous jackpot is R. The syndicate is thus assured of having a winning ticket, but is it assured of covering its costs? Calculate the expected net benefit (in terms of net present value) to the syndicate, using any reasonable values of n and R, to see whether the syndicate can expect to come out ahead.

Actually, the analysis suggested in the previous paragraph is not complete. There are at least two complications to consider. The first is the effect of taxes. Fortunately for the Australian syndicate, it did not have to pay federal or state taxes on its winnings, but a U.S. syndicate wouldn't be so lucky. Second, the jackpot from a $20 million jackpot, say, is actually paid in 20 annual $1 million payments. The Lottery Commission pays the winner $1 million immediately and then purchases 19 "strips" (bonds with the interest not included) maturing at 1-year intervals with face value of $1 million each. Unfortunately, the lottery prize does not offer the liquidity of the Treasury issues that back up the payments. This lack of liquidity could make the lottery less attractive to the syndicate. ∎

Decision Making under Uncertainty

DECISION AND RISK ANALYSIS AT DU PONT

Formal decision analysis in the face of uncertainty frequently occurs at the most strategic levels of a company's planning process and typically involves teams of high-level managers from all areas of the company. This is certainly the case with Du Pont, as reported by two internal decision analysis experts, Krumm and Rolle (1992), in their article "Management and Application of Decision and Risk Analysis in Du Pont." Du Pont's formal use of decision analysis began in the 1960s, but because of a lack of computing power and distrust of the method by senior-level management, it never really got a foothold. However, by the mid-1980s things had changed considerably. The company was involved in a faster-moving, more uncertain environment; more people throughout the company were empowered to make decisions; and these decisions had to be made more quickly. In addition, the computing power had arrived to make large-scale quantitative analysis feasible. Since that time, Du Pont has embraced formal decision-making analysis in all its businesses, and the trend is almost certain to continue.

The article describes a typical example of decision analysis within the company. One of Du Pont's businesses, Business Z (so-called for reasons of confidentiality), was stagnating. It was not set up to respond quickly to changing customer demands, and its financial position was declining due to lower prices and market share. A decision board and a project team were empowered to turn things around. The project team developed a detailed timetable to accomplish three basic steps: frame the problem, assess uncertainties and perform the analysis, and implement the recommended decision. The first step involved setting up a "strategy table" to list the possible strategies and the factors that would affect or be affected by them. The three basic strategies were (1) a base-case strategy (continue operating as is), (2) a product differentiation strategy (develop new products), and (3) a cost leadership strategy (shut down the plant and streamline the product line).

In the second step, the team asked a variety of experts throughout the company for their assessments of the likelihood of key uncertain events. In the analysis step the team then used all of the information gained to determine the strategy with the largest expected net present value. Two important aspects of this analysis step were the extensive use of sensitivity analysis (many what-if questions) and the emergence of new "hybrid" strategies that dominated the strategies that had been considered to that point. In particular, the team finally decided on a product differentiation strategy that also decreased costs by shutting down some facilities in each plant.

When it was time for the third step, implementation, the decision board needed little convincing. Because all of the key people had been given the opportunity to provide input to the process, everyone was convinced that the right strategy had been selected. All that was left was to put the plan in motion and monitor its results. The results were impressive. Business Z made a complete turnaround, and its net present value increased by close to $200 million. Besides this tangible benefit, there were definite intangible benefits from the overall process. As Du Pont's vice president for finance said, "The D&RA [decision and risk analysis] process improved communication within the business team as well as between the team and corporate management, resulting in rapid approval and execution. As a decision maker, I highly value such a clear and logical approach to making choices under uncertainty and will continue to use D&RA whenever possible." ■

7.1 INTRODUCTION

In this chapter we provide a formal framework for analyzing decision problems that involve uncertainty. We discuss the following:

- criteria for choosing among alternative decisions
- how probabilities are used in the decision-making process
- how early decisions affect decisions made at a later stage
- how a decision maker can quantify the value of information
- how attitudes toward risk can affect the analysis

Throughout, we employ a powerful graphical tool—a decision tree—to guide the analysis. A decision tree enables the decision maker to view all important aspects of the problem at once: the decision alternatives, the uncertain outcomes and their probabilities, the economic consequences, and the chronological order of events. We show how to implement decision trees in Excel by taking advantage of a very powerful and flexible add-in from Palisade called PrecisionTree.

Many examples of decision making under uncertainty exist in the business world, including the following.

- Companies routinely place bids for contracts to complete a certain project within a fixed time frame. Often these are sealed bids, where each company presents a bid for completing the project in a sealed envelope. Then the envelopes are opened, and the low bidder is awarded the bid amount to complete the project. Any particular company in the bidding competition must deal with the uncertainty of the other companies' bids. The trade-off is between bidding low to win the bid and bidding high to make a larger profit.

■ Whenever a company contemplates introducing a new product into the market, there are a number of uncertainties that affect the decision, probably the most important being the customers' reaction to this product. If the product generates high customer demand, the company will make a large profit. But if demand is low—and, after all, the vast majority of new products do poorly—the company might not even recoup its development costs. Because the level of customer demand is critical, the company might try to gauge this level by test marketing the product in one region of the country. If this test market is a success, the company can then be more optimistic that a full-scale national marketing of the product will also be successful. But if the test market is a failure, the company can cut its losses by abandoning the product.

■ Borison (1995) describes an application of formal decision analysis by Oglethorpe Power Corporation (OPC), a Georgia-based electricity supplier. The basic decision OPC faced was whether to build a new transmission line to supply large amounts of electricity to parts of Florida and, if the company decided to build it, how to finance this project. OPC had to deal with several sources of uncertainty: the cost of building new facilities, the demand for power in Florida, and various market conditions, such as the spot price of electricity.

■ Utility companies must make many decisions that have significant environmental and economic consequences. [Balson et al. (1992) provide the probabilities of such consequences.] For these companies it is not necessarily enough to conform to federal or state environmental regulations. Recent court decisions have found companies liable—for huge settlements—when accidents occurred, even though the companies followed all existing regulations. Therefore, when utility companies decide, say, whether to replace equipment or mitigate the effects of environmental pollution, they must take into account the possible environmental consequences (such as injuries to people) as well as economic consequences (such as lawsuits). An aspect of these situations that makes decision analysis particularly difficult is that the potential "disasters" are often extremely improbable; hence, their probabilities are difficult to assess accurately.

7.2 ELEMENTS OF A DECISION ANALYSIS

Although decision making under uncertainty occurs in a wide variety of contexts, all problems have three common elements: (1) the set of decisions (or strategies) available to the decision maker, (2) the set of possible outcomes and the probabilities of these outcomes, and (3) a value model that prescribes monetary values for the various decision–outcome combinations. Once these elements are known, the decision maker can find an "optimal" decision, depending on the optimality criterion chosen.

Before moving on to realistic business problems, we discuss the basic elements of any decision analysis for a very simple problem. We assume that a decision maker must choose among three decisions, labeled $D1$, $D2$, and $D3$. Each of these decisions has three possible outcomes, labeled $O1$, $O2$, and $O3$.

Payoff Tables

At the time the decision must be made, the decision maker does *not* know which outcome will occur. However, once the decision is made, the outcome will eventually be revealed, and a corresponding payoff will be received. This payoff might actually be a cost, in which case it is indicated as a negative value. The listing of payoffs for all decision–outcome pairs is called the **payoff table**.[1] For our simple decision problem, this payoff table appears in Table 7.1. For example, if the decision maker chooses decision $D2$ and outcome $O3$ then occurs, a payoff of $40 is received.

> A **payoff table** lists the payoff for each decision–outcome pair. Positive values correspond to "rewards" (or "gains") and negative values correspond to "costs" (or "losses").

Table 7.1   Payoff Table for Simple Decision Problem

		Outcome		
		O1	O2	O3
Decision	D1	10	10	10
	D2	−10	20	40
	D3	−30	30	70

A decision maker gets to decide which row of the payoff table she wants. However, she does not get to choose the column.

This table shows that the decision maker can play it safe by choosing decision $D1$. This provides a sure $10 payoff. With decision $D2$, rewards of $20 or $40 are possible, but a loss of $10 is also possible. Decision $D3$ is even riskier; the possible loss is greater, and the maximum gain is also greater. Which decision would you choose? Would your choice change if the values in the payoff table were really measured in *thousands* of dollars? The answers to these questions are what this chapter is all about. We need a criterion for making choices, and we need to evaluate this criterion so that we can identify the "best" decision. As we will see, it is customary to use one particular criterion for decisions involving "moderate" amounts of money.

Before proceeding, there is one very important point we need to emphasize. In any decision-making problem where there is uncertainty, the "best" decision can have less than optimal results—that is, we can be unlucky. Regardless of which decision we choose, we might get an outcome that, in hindsight, makes us wish we had made a different decision. For example, if we make decision $D3$, hoping for a large reward, we might get outcome $O1$, in which case we will wish we had chosen decision $D1$ or $D2$. Or if we choose decision $D2$, hoping to limit possible losses, we might get outcome $O3$, in which case we will wish we had chosen decision $D3$. The point is that decision makers must make rational decisions, based on the information they have when the decisions must be made, and then live with the consequences. "Second guessing" these decisions, just because of bad luck with the outcomes, is not appropriate.

Possible Decision Criteria

What do we mean by a "best" decision? We will eventually settle on one particular criterion for making decisions, but we first explore some possibilities. With respect to Table 7.1, one possibility is to choose the decision that maximizes the *worst* payoff. This criterion, called the **maximin** criterion, is appropriate for a very conservative (or pessimistic) decision maker. The worst payoffs for the three decisions are the minimums in the three rows: 10, −10, and −30. The maximin decision maker chooses the decision corresponding to the best of these: decision $D1$ with payoff 10. Clearly, such a criterion tends to avoid large losses, but

---

[1]In situations where all monetary consequences are costs, it is customary to list these costs in a **cost table**. In this case, all monetary values are shown as *positive* costs.

it fails to even consider large rewards. Hence, it is typically *too* conservative and is not commonly used.

> The **maximin** criterion finds the worst payoff in each row of the payoff table and chooses the decision corresponding to the maximum of these.

The maximin and maximax criteria make sense in some situations, but they are generally not used in real decision-making situations.

At the other extreme, the decision maker might choose the decision that maximizes the *best* payoff. This criterion, called the **maximax** criterion, is appropriate for a risk taker (or optimist). The best payoffs for the three decisions are the maximums in the three rows: 10, 40, and 70. The maximax decision maker chooses the decision corresponding to the best of these: decision $D3$ with payoff 70. This criterion looks tempting because it focuses on large gains, but its very serious downside is that it ignores possible losses. Because this type of decision making could eventually bankrupt a company, the maximax criterion is also seldom used.

> The **maximax** criterion finds the best payoff in each row of the payoff table and chooses the decision corresponding to the maximum of these.

Expected Monetary Value (EMV)

We have introduced the maximin and maximax criteria because (1) they are occasionally used to make decisions, and (2) they illustrate that there are several "reasonable" criteria for making decisions. In fact, there are a number of other possible criteria available that we will not discuss. Instead, we now focus on a criterion that is generally regarded as the preferred criterion in most decision problems. It is called the **expected monetary value**, or **EMV**, criterion. To motivate the EMV criterion, we first note that the maximin and maximax criteria make no reference to how *likely* the various outcomes are. However, decision makers typically have at least some idea of these likelihoods, and they ought to use this information in the decision-making process. After all, if outcome $O1$ in our problem is extremely unlikely, then the pessimist who uses maximin is being overly conservative. Similarly, if outcome $O3$ is quite unlikely, then the optimist who uses maximax is taking an unnecessary risk.

The EMV approach assesses probabilities for each outcome of each decision and then calculates the *expected* payoff from each decision based on these probabilities. This expected payoff, or EMV, is a weighted average of the payoffs in any given row of the payoff table, weighted by the probabilities of the outcomes. We calculate the EMV for each decision, and we choose the decision with the largest EMV.

> The **expected monetary value**, or **EMV**, for any decision is a weighted average of the possible payoffs for this decision, weighted by the probabilities of the outcomes. Using the EMV criterion, we choose the decision with the largest EMV. This is sometimes called "playing the averages."

Where do the probabilities come from? This is a difficult question to answer in general because it depends on each specific situation. In some cases the current decision problem is similar to those a decision maker has faced many times in the past. Then the probabilities can be estimated from the knowledge of previous outcomes. If a certain type of outcome occurred, say, in about 30% of previous situations, we might estimate its current probability as 0.30.

However, there are many decision problems that have no parallels in the past. In such cases, a decision maker must use whatever information is available, plus some intuition, to assess the probabilities. For example, if the problem involves a new product decision, and one possible outcome is that a competitor will introduce a similar product in the coming year, the decision maker will have to rely on any knowledge of the market and the competitor's situation to assess the probability of this outcome. It is important to note that this assessment can be very subjective. Two decision makers could easily assess the probability of the *same* outcome as 0.30 and 0.45, depending on their information and feelings, and neither could be considered "wrong." This is the nature of assessing probabilities subjectively in real business situations.

With this general framework in mind, let's assume that our decision maker assesses the probabilities of the three outcomes in Table 7.1 as 0.4, 0.4, and 0.2.[2] Then it is simple to calculate the EMV for each decision as the sum of products of payoffs and probabilities:

$$\text{EMV for } D1: \quad 10(0.4) + 10(0.4) + 10(0.2) = 10$$

$$\text{EMV for } D2: \quad -10(0.4) + 20(0.4) + 40(0.2) = 12$$

$$\text{EMV for } D3: \quad -30(0.4) + 30(0.4) + 70(0.2) = 14$$

These calculations lead to the optimal decision: Choose decision $D3$ because it has the largest EMV.

It is important to understand what the EMV of a decision represents—and what it doesn't represent. For example, the EMV of 14 for decision $D3$ does *not* mean that we expect to gain \$14 from this decision. The payoff table indicates that the result from $D3$ will be a loss of \$30, a gain of \$30, or a gain of \$70; it will *never* be a gain of \$14. The EMV is only a weighted average of the possible payoffs. As such, it can be interpreted in one of two ways. First, suppose we can imagine the situation occurring many times, not just once. If we use decision $D3$ each time, then *on average*, we will make a gain of about \$14. About 40% of the time we will lose \$30, about 40% of the time we will gain \$30, and about 20% of the time we will gain \$70. These average to \$14. For this reason, using the EMV criterion is sometimes referred to as "playing the averages."

But what if the current situation is a "one-shot deal," which will *not* occur many times in the future? Then the second interpretation of EMV is still relevant. It states that the EMV is a "sensible" criterion for making decisions under uncertainty. This is actually a point that has been debated in intellectual circles for years—what is the best criterion for making decisions? However, researchers have generally concluded that EMV makes sense, even for one-shot deals, as long as the monetary values are not too large. For situations where the monetary values are extremely large, we will introduce an alternative criterion in the last section of this chapter. Until then, however, we will use EMV.

This is the gist of decision making uncertainty. We develop a payoff table, we assess probabilities of outcomes, we calculate EMVs, and we choose the decision with the largest EMV. However, before proceeding to examples, it is useful to introduce a few other concepts: *sensitivity analysis*, *decision trees*, and *risk profiles*.

Sensitivity Analysis

Some of the quantities in a decision analysis, particularly the probabilities, are often intelligent guesses at best. It is important, especially in real-world business problems, to accompany any decision analysis with a sensitivity analysis. Here we systematically vary inputs to the problem to see how (or if) the outputs—the EMVs and the best decision—change. For our simple decision problem, this is easy to do in a spreadsheet. We first develop the spreadsheet model shown in Figure 7.1. (See the file **Simple Decision Problem.xlsx**.)

---

[2]We always express probabilities as numbers between 0 and 1 that sum to 1. However, they are often expressed in more intuitive, but equivalent, ways. For example, we might assess that outcomes $O1$ and $O2$ are equally likely and that each of these is twice as likely as outcome $O3$. This assessment leads to the same probabilities: 0.4, 0.4, and 0.2.

Figure 7.1

Spreadsheet Model
of Simple Decision
Problem

	A	B	C	D	E	F
1	Simple decision problem under uncertainty					
2						
3			Outcome			
4			O1	O2	O3	EMV
5	Decision	D1	10	10	10	10
6		D2	-10	20	40	12
7		D3	-30	30	70	14
8	Probability		0.4	0.4	0.2	

*Usually, the most
important information
from a sensitivity
analysis is whether
the optimal decision
continues to be
optimal as one or more
inputs change.*

After entering the payoff table and probabilities, we calculate the EMVs in column F as a sum of products, using the formula

=SUMPRODUCT(C5:E5,$C$8:$E$8)

in cell F5 and copying it down. Then it is easy to change any of the inputs and see whether the optimal decision continues to be D3. For example, you can check that if the probabilities change only "slightly" to 0.5, 0.4, and 0.1, the EMVs change to 10, 7, and 4. Now D3 is the worst decision and D1 is the best, so that it appears that the optimal decision is quite sensitive to the assessed probabilities. As another example, if the probabilities remain the same but the last payoff for D2 changes from 40 to 55, then its EMV changes to 16, and D2 becomes the best decision.

Given a simple spreadsheet model, it is easy to make a number of "ad hoc" changes to inputs, as we have done here, to answer specific sensitivity questions. However, it is often useful to conduct a more systematic sensitivity analysis, and we see how to do this later in the chapter. The important thing to realize at this stage is that a sensitivity analysis is not an "afterthought" to the overall analysis; it is a key component of the analysis.

Decision Trees

The decision problem we have been analyzing is very basic. We make a decision, we then observe an outcome, we receive a payoff, and that is the end of it. Many decision problems are of this basic form, but many are more complex. In these more complex problems, we make a decision, an outcome is observed, we make a second decision, a second outcome is observed, and so on. A graphical tool called a **decision tree** has been developed to represent decision problems. Decision trees can be used for any decision problems, but they are particularly useful for the more complex types. They clearly show the sequence of events (decisions and outcomes), as well as probabilities and monetary values. The decision tree for our simple problem appears in Figure 7.2. This tree is based on one we drew by hand and calculated with a hand calculator. We urge you to try this on your own, at least once. However, later in the chapter we introduce an Excel add-in that automates the procedure.

Figure 7.2

Decision Tree for
Simple Decision
Problem

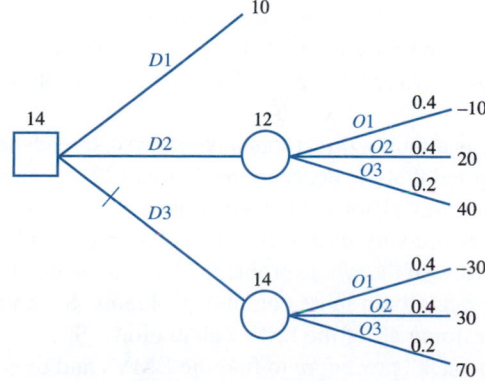

To understand this decision tree, we need to introduce a number of decision tree conventions that have become standard.

Decision Tree Conventions

1. Decision trees are composed of **nodes** (circles, squares, and triangles) and **branches** (lines).

2. The nodes represent points in time. A **decision node** (a square) represents a time when the decision maker makes a decision. A **probability node** (a circle) represents a time when the result of an uncertain outcome becomes known. An **end node** (a triangle) indicates that the problem is completed—all decisions have been made, all uncertainty has been resolved, and all payoffs and costs have been incurred. (When people draw decision trees by hand, they often omit the actual triangles, as we have done in Figure 7.2. However, we still refer to the right-hand tips of the branches as the end nodes.)

3. Time proceeds *from left to right*. This means that any branches leading into a node (from the left) have already occurred. Any branches leading out of a node (to the right) have not yet occurred.

4. Branches leading out of a decision node represent the possible decisions; the decision maker can choose the preferred branch. Branches leading out of probability nodes represent the possible outcomes of uncertain events; the decision maker has no control over which of these will occur.

5. Probabilities are listed on probability branches. These probabilities are *conditional* on the events that have already been observed (those to the left). Also, the probabilities on branches leading out of any probability node must sum to 1.

6. Monetary values are shown to the right of the end nodes. (As we discuss shortly, some monetary values are also placed next to the branches where they occur in time.)

7. EMVs are calculated through a "folding-back" process, discussed next. They are shown above the various nodes. It is then customary to mark the optimal decision branch(es) in some way. We have marked ours with a small notch.

The decision tree in Figure 7.2 follows these conventions. The decision node comes first (to the left) because the decision maker must make a decision *before* observing the uncertain outcome. The probability nodes then follow the decision branches, and the probabilities appear above their branches. (Actually, there is no need for a probability node after the *D*1 branch because the monetary value is 10 for each outcome.) The ultimate payoffs appear next to the end nodes, to the right of the probability branches. The EMVs above the probability nodes are for the various decisions. For example, if we go along the *D*2 branch, the EMV is 12. The maximum of the EMVs is written above the decision node. Because it corresponds to *D*3, we put a notch on the *D*3 branch to indicate that this decision is optimal.

This decision tree is almost a direct translation of the spreadsheet model in Figure 7.1. Indeed, it might be argued that the decision tree is overkill for such a simple problem; the spreadsheet model provides all of the information we need—in a more compact form. However, decision trees are very useful in business problems. First, they provide a manager with a graphical view of the whole problem. This can be useful in its own right for the insights it provides, especially in more complex problems. Second, the decision tree provides a framework for doing all of the EMV calculations. Specifically, it allows us to use the following "folding-back" procedure to find the EMVs and the optimal decision.

The folding-back process is a systematic way of calculating EMVs in a decision tree and thereby identifying the optimal decision strategy.

This is exactly what we did in Figure 7.2. At each probability node, we calculated EMVs in the usual way and wrote them above the nodes. Then at the decision node, we took the maximum of the three EMVs and wrote it above this node. Although this procedure entails more work for more complex decision trees, the same two steps—taking EMVs at probability nodes and taking maximums at decision nodes—are the only ones required. In addition, we introduce an Excel add-in in the next section that does the calculations for us.

Risk Profiles

In our small example each decision leads to three possible monetary payoffs with various probabilities. In more complex problems, the number of outcomes could be larger, maybe considerably larger. It is then useful to represent the probability distribution of the monetary values for any decision graphically. Specifically, we show a bar chart, where the bars are located at the possible monetary values, and the heights of the bars correspond to the probabilities. In decision-making contexts, this type of chart is called a **risk profile**. By looking at the risk profile for a particular decision, we see the risks and rewards involved. By comparing risk profiles for different decisions, we gain more insight into their relative strengths and weaknesses.

> The **risk profile** for a decision is a bar chart that represents the probability distribution of monetary outcomes for this decision.

The risk profile for decision $D3$ appears in Figure 7.3. It shows that a loss of $30 and a gain of $30 are equally likely with probability 0.4 each, and that a gain of $70 has probability 0.2. The risk profile for decision $D2$ would be similar, except that its bars would be over the values -10, 20, and 40, and the risk profile for decision $D1$ would be a single bar of height 1 over the value 10. (The file **Simple Decision Problem.xlsx** provides instructions for constructing such a chart with Excel 2007 tools.)

Figure 7.3

Risk Profile for Decision $D3$

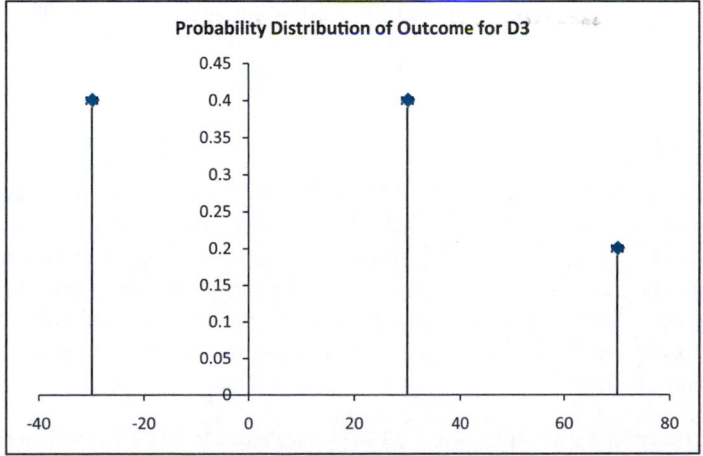

Note that the EMV for any decision is a summary measure from the complete risk profile—it is the *mean* of the corresponding probability distribution. Therefore, when we

<p><em>A risk profile shows the complete probability distribution of monetary outcomes, but we typically use only its mean, the EMV, for making decisions.</em></p>

use the EMV criterion for making decisions, we are not using *all* of the information in the risk profiles; we are comparing only their means. Nevertheless, risk profiles can be useful as extra information for making decisions. For example, a manager who sees too much risk in the risk profile of the EMV-maximizing decision might choose to override this decision and instead choose a somewhat less risky alternative.

We now apply all of these concepts to the following example.

EXAMPLE

7.1 BIDDING FOR A GOVERNMENT CONTRACT AT SCITOOLS

SciTools Incorporated, a company that specializes in scientific instruments, has been invited to make a bid on a government contract. The contract calls for a specific number of these instruments to be delivered during the coming year. The bids must be sealed (so that no company knows what the others are bidding), and the low bid wins the contract. SciTools estimates that it will cost $5000 to prepare a bid and $95,000 to supply the instruments if it wins the contract. On the basis of past contracts of this type, SciTools believes that the possible low bids from the competition, if there is any competition, and the associated probabilities are those shown in Table 7.2. In addition, SciTools believes there is a 30% chance that there will be *no* competing bids. What should SciTools bid to maximize its EMV?

Table 7.2   Data for Bidding Example

Low Bid	Probability
Less than $115,000	0.2
Between $115,000 and $120,000	0.4
Between $120,000 and $125,000	0.3
Greater than $125,000	0.1

Objective   To develop a decision model that finds the EMV for various bidding strategies and indicates the best bidding strategy.

WHERE DO THE NUMBERS COME FROM?

The company has probably done a thorough cost analysis to estimate its cost to prepare a bid and its cost to manufacture the instruments if it wins the contract. Its estimates of whether, or how, the competition will bid are probably based on previous bidding experience and some subjectivity. This is discussed in more detail next.

Solution

Let's examine the three elements of SciTools' problem. First, SciTools has two basic strategies: submit a bid or do not submit a bid. If SciTools submits a bid, then it must decide how much to bid. Based on SciTools' cost to prepare the bid and its cost to supply the instruments, there is clearly no point in bidding less than $100,000—SciTools wouldn't make a profit even if it won the bid. Although any bid amount over $100,000 might be considered, the data in Table 7.2 suggest that SciTools might limit its choices to $115,000, $120,000, and $125,000.[3]

---

[3]The problem with a bid such as $117,000 is that the data in Table 7.2 make it impossible to calculate the probability of SciTools winning the contract if it bids this amount. Other than this, however, there is nothing that rules out such "in-between" bids.

The next element of the problem involves the uncertain outcomes and their probabilities. We have assumed that SciTools knows exactly how much it will cost to prepare a bid and how much it will cost to supply the instruments if it wins the bid. (In reality, these are probably only estimates of the actual costs, and a follow-up study could treat these costs as additional uncertain quantities.) Therefore, the only source of uncertainty is the behavior of the competitors—will they bid, and if so, how much? From SciTools' standpoint, this is difficult information to obtain. The behavior of the competitors depends on (1) how many competitors are likely to bid and (2) how the competitors assess *their* costs of supplying the instruments. Nevertheless, we will assume that SciTools has been involved in similar bidding contests in the past and can, therefore, predict competitor behavior from past competitor behavior. The result of such prediction is the assessed probability distribution in Table 7.2 and the 30% estimate of the probability of no competing bids.

The last element of the problem is the value model that transforms decisions and outcomes into monetary values for SciTools. The value model is straightforward in this example. If SciTools decides not to bid, then its monetary value is $0—no gain, no loss. If it makes a bid and is underbid by a competitor, then it loses $5000, the cost of preparing the bid. If it bids B dollars and wins the contract, then it makes a profit of B minus $100,000— that is, B dollars for winning the bid, minus $5000 for preparing the bid and $95,000 for supplying the instruments. For example, if it bids $115,000 and the lowest competing bid, if any, is greater than $115,000, then SciTools wins the bid and makes a profit of $15,000.

Developing the Payoff Table

The corresponding payoff table, along with probabilities of outcomes, appears in Table 7.3. At the bottom of the table, we list the probabilities of the various outcomes. For example, the probability that the competitors' low bid is less than $115,000 is 0.7 (the probability of at least one competing bid) multiplied by 0.2 (the probability that the lowest competing bid is less than $115,000).

Table 7.3   Payoff Table for SciTools Bidding Example

		No bid	<115	>115, <120	>120, <125	>125
			Competitors' Low Bid ($1000s)			
SciTools' Bid	**No**	0	0	0	0	0
($1000s)	**bid**					
	115	15	−5	15	15	15
	120	20	−5	−5	20	20
	125	25	−5	−5	−5	25
Probability		0.3	0.7(0.2) = 0.14	0.7(0.4) = 0.28	0.7(0.3) = 0.21	0.7(0.1) = 0.07

It is sometimes possible to simplify payoff tables to better understand the essence of the problem. In the present example, if SciTools bids, then the only necessary information about the competitors' bid is whether it is lower or higher than SciTools' bid. That is, SciTools really only cares whether it wins the contract. Therefore, an alternative way of presenting the payoff table is shown in Table 7.4. (See the file **SciTools Bidding Decision 1.xlsx** for these and other calculations. However, we urge you to work this problem on a piece of paper with a hand calculator, just for practice with the concepts.)

Table 7.4 Alternative Payoff Table for SciTools Bidding Example

		Monetary Value		Probability That SciTools Wins
		SciTools Wins	SciTools Loses	
	No Bid	NA	0	0.00
SciTools' Bid ($1000s)	**115**	15	−5	0.86
	120	20	−5	0.58
	125	25	−5	0.37

The Monetary Value columns of this table indicate the payoffs to SciTools, depending on whether it wins or loses the bid. The rightmost column shows the probability that SciTools wins the bid for each possible decision. For example, if SciTools bids $120,000, then it wins the bid if there are no competing bids (probability 0.3) *or* if there are competing bids but the lowest of these is greater than $120,000 [probability 0.7(0.3 + 0.1) = 0.28]. In this case the total probability that SciTools wins the bid is 0.3 + 0.28 = 0.58.

Developing the Risk Profiles

From Table 7.4 we can obtain risk profiles for each of SciTools' decisions. Again, this risk profile simply indicates all possible monetary values and their corresponding probabilities in a bar chart. For example, if SciTools bids $120,000, there are two monetary values possible, a profit of $20,000 and a loss of $5000, and their probabilities are 0.58 and 0.42, respectively. The corresponding risk profile, shown in Figure 7.4, is a bar chart with two bars, one above −$5000 with height 0.42 and one above $20,000 with height 0.58. On the other hand, if SciTools decides not to bid, there is a sure monetary value of $0—no profit, no loss. The risk profile for the "no bid" decision, not shown here, is even simpler. It has a single bar above $0 with height 1.

Figure 7.4

Risk Profile for a Bid of $120,000

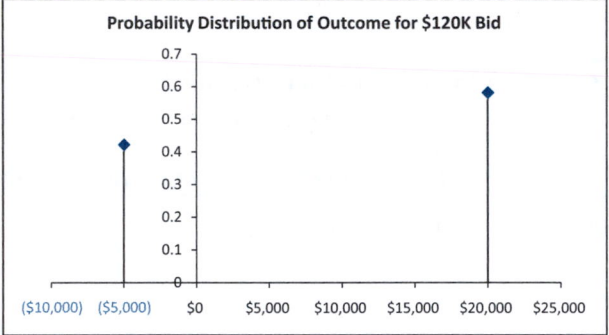

Calculating EMVs

The EMVs for SciTools' problem are listed in Table 7.5. As always, each EMV (other than the EMV of $0 for not bidding) is a sum of products of monetary outcomes and probabilities. These EMVs indicate that if SciTools uses the EMV criterion for making its decision, it should bid $115,000. The EMV from this bid, $12,200, is the largest of the EMVs.

Table 7.5 EMVs for SciTools Bidding Example

Alternative	EMV Calculation	EMV
No bid	0(1)	$0
Bid $115,000	15,000(0.86) + (−5000)(0.14)	$12,200
Bid $120,000	20,000(0.58) + (−5000)(0.42)	$9500
Bid $125,000	25,000(0.37) + (−5000)(0.63)	$6100

As discussed previously, it is very important to understand what an EMV implies and what it does not imply. If SciTools bids $115,000, its EMV is $12,200. However, SciTools will definitely *not* earn a profit of $12,200. It will earn $15,000 or it will lose $5000. The EMV of $12,200 represents only a weighted average of these two possible values. Nevertheless, it is the value that we use as our decision criterion.

Developing the Decision Tree

The corresponding decision tree for this problem is shown in Figure 7.5. This is a direct translation of the payoff table and EMV calculations. The company first makes a bidding decision, it then observes what the competition bids, if anything, and it finally receives a payoff. The folding-back process is equivalent to the calculations shown in Table 7.5.

Figure 7.5

Decision Tree for SciTools Bidding Example

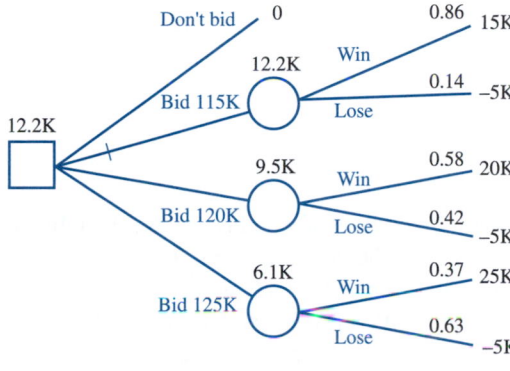

It is common to place monetary values below the branches where they occur in time.

As long as we follow the decision tree conventions, there are often equivalent ways to structure a decision tree. One alternative for this example that might be more intuitive appears in Figure 7.6. This tree shows exactly how the problem unfolds. The company first decides whether to bid at all. If the company does not make a bid, the profit is a sure $0. Otherwise, the company then decides how much to bid. Note that if the company decides to bid, it incurs a sure cost of $5000, so we place this cost under the Bid branch. This is a common procedure, to place the monetary values on the branches where they occur in time, and it is followed by the PrecisionTree add-in we examine in the next section. Once the company decides how much to bid, it then observes whether there is any competition. If there isn't any, the company wins the bid for sure and makes a corresponding profit. Otherwise, if there is competition, the company eventually discovers whether it wins or loses the bid, with the corresponding probabilities and payoffs. Note that we place these payoffs below the branches where they occur in time. Also, we place the *cumulative* payoffs at the ends of the branches. Each cumulative payoff is the sum of all payoffs on branches that lead to that end node.

Folding Back the Decision Tree

The folding-back procedure is bit more complex than it was for the smaller tree in Figure 7.5. To illustrate, we have numbered the nodes in Figure 7.6 for reference. The EMVs above a selected few of these nodes are calculated as follows:

- Node 7: EMV = 20000(0.40) + (−5000)(0.60) = $5000 (uses monetary values from end nodes)
- Node 4: EMV = 20000(0.30) + (5000)(0.70) = $9500 (uses monetary value from an end node and the EMV from node 7)
- Node 2: EMV = max(12200, 9500, 6100) = $12,200 (uses EMVs from nodes 3, 4, and 5)
- Node 1: EMV = max(0, 12200) = $12,200 (uses monetary value from an end node and EMV from node 2)

Figure 7.6

Equivalent Decision
Tree for SciTools
Bidding Example

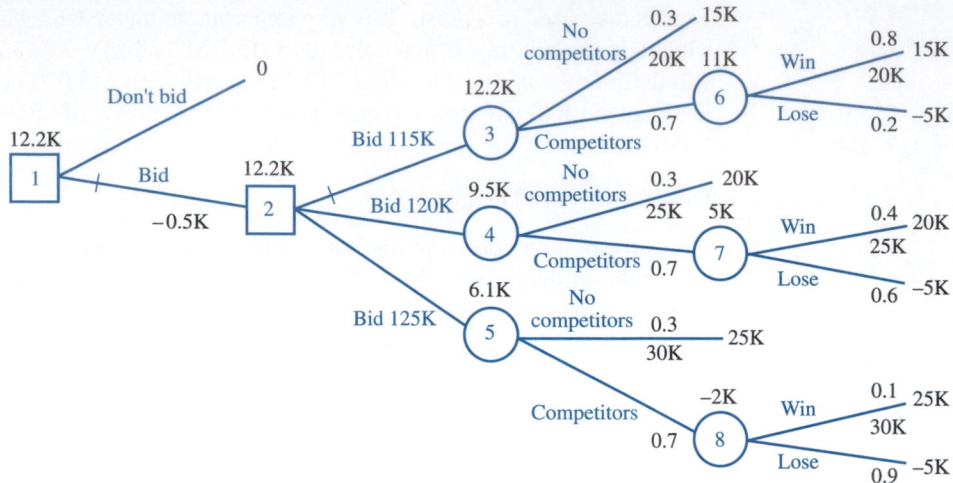

The results are the same, regardless of whether we use the table of EMVs in Table 7.5, the decision tree in Figure 7.5, or the decision tree in Figure 7.6 because they all calculate the same EMVs in equivalent ways. In each case, we see that the company should bid $115,000, with a resulting EMV of $12,200. Of course, this decision is not *guaranteed* to produce a good outcome for the company. For example, the competition could bid less than $115,000, in which case SciTools would be out $5000. Alternately, the competition could bid over $120,000, in which case SciTools would be kicking itself for not bidding $120,000 and getting an extra $5000 in profit. Unfortunately, in problems with uncertainty, we can virtually never guarantee that the optimal decision will produce the best result. All we can guarantee is that the EMV-maximizing decision is the most rational decision, given what we know when we must make the decision.

Sensitivity Analysis

The next step in the SciTools decision analysis is to perform a sensitivity analysis. We will eventually see that PrecisionTree, an Excel add-in that helps automate the decision-making process, has some powerful sensitivity analysis tools. However, it is also possible to use Excel data tables. One example is shown in Figure 7.7. (See the finished version of the file **SciTools Bidding Decision 1.xlsx**.) We first calculate the EMVs in column G, exactly as described previously. Then we find the maximum of these in cell B21, and we use the following nested IF formula in cell B22 to find the decision from column B that achieves this maximum:

=IF(G16=B21,B16,IF(G17=B21,B17,IF(G18=B21,B18,B19)))

This long formula simply checks which EMV in column G matches the maximum EMV in cell B21 and returns the corresponding decision from column B.

Once we have the formulas in cells B21 and B22 set up, the data table is easy. In Figure 7.7 we have allowed the probability of no competing bid to vary from 0.2 to 0.7. The data table shows how the optimal EMV increases over this range. Also, its third column shows that the $115,000 bid is optimal for small values of the input, but that $125,000 becomes optimal for larger values. The main point here is that if we set up a spreadsheet model that links all of the EMV calculations to the inputs, it is easy to use data tables to perform sensitivity analyses on selected inputs.

Figure 7.7 Sensitivity Analysis with a Data Table

	A	B	C	D	E	F	G
1	SciTools Bidding Example						
2							
3	Inputs						
4	Cost to prepare a bid	$5,000		Range names used:			
5	Cost to supply instruments	$95,000		BidCost	=Data!$B$4		
6				PrNoBid	=Data!$B$7		
7	Probability of no competing bid	0.3		ProdCost	=Data!$B$5		
8	Comp bid distribution (if they bid)						
9	<$115K	0.2					
10	$115K to $120K	0.4					
11	$120K to $125K	0.3					
12	>$125K	0.1					
13							
14	EMV analysis		Monetary outcomes		Probabilities		
15			SciTools wins	SciTools loses	SciTools wins	SciTools loses	EMV
16		No bid	NA	0	0	1	$0
17	SciTools' Bid	$115,000	$15,000	-$5,000	0.86	0.14	$12,200
18		$120,000	$20,000	-$5,000	0.58	0.42	$9,500
19		$125,000	$25,000	-$5,000	0.37	0.63	$6,100
20							
21	Maximum EMV	$12,200					
22	Best decision	$115,000					
23							
24	Data table for sensitivity analysis						
25	Probability of no competing bid	Maximum EMV	Best decision				
26		$12,200	$115,000				
27	0.2	$11,800	$115,000				
28	0.3	$12,200	$115,000				
29	0.4	$12,600	$115,000				
30	0.5	$13,000	$115,000				
31	0.6	$14,200	$125,000				
32	0.7	$16,900	$125,000				

PROBLEMS

Level A

1. In the simple 3-decision, 3-outcome example, we found that decision $D3$ is the EMV-maximizing decision for the probabilities we used. See whether you can find probabilities that make decision $D1$ the best. See if you can find probabilities that make decision $D2$ the best. Qualitatively, how can you explain the results? That is, which types of probabilities tend to favor the various decisions?

2. Using a data table in Excel, perform a sensitivity analysis on the simple 3-decision, 3-outcome example. Specifically, continue to assume that outcomes $O1$ and $O2$ are equally likely, each with probability p. Because the probabilities of all outcomes must sum to 1, the probability of outcome $O3$ must be $1 - 2p$. Let p vary from 0 to 0.5, in increments of 0.05. How does the optimal EMV vary? How does the optimal decision vary? Why can't p be greater than 0.5?

3. For the simple 3-decision, 3-outcome example, are there any probabilities that make the EMV criterion equivalent to the maximin criterion? Are there any probabilities that make the EMV criterion equivalent to the maximax criterion? Explain.

4. In the SciTools example, which decision would a maximin decision maker choose? Which decision would a maximax decision maker choose? Would you defend either of these criteria for this particular example? Explain.

5. In the SciTools example, suppose that we make two changes: All references to $115,000 change to $110,000, and all references to $125,000 change to $130,000. Rework the EMV calculations and the decision tree. What is the best decision and its corresponding EMV?

6. In the SciTools example, the probabilities for the low bid of competitors, given that there is at least one competing bid, are currently 0.2, 0.4, 0.3, and 0.1. Let the second of these be p, and let the others sum to $1 - p$ but keep the same ratios to one another: 2 to 3 to 1. Use a one-way data table to see how (or whether) the optimal decision changes as p varies from 0.1 to 0.7 in increments of 0.05. Explain your results.

7. In the SciTools example, use a two-way data table to see how (or whether) the optimal decision changes as the bid cost and the company's production cost change simultaneously. Let the bid cost vary from $2000 to $8000 in increments of $1000, and let the production cost vary from $90,000 to $105,000 in increments of $2500. Explain your results.

Level B

8. A decision d is said to be **dominated** by another decision D if, for every outcome, the payoff from D is better than (or no worse than) the payoff from d.
    a. Explain why you would never choose a dominated decision, using the maximin criterion; using the maximax criterion; using the EMV criterion.
    b. Are any of the decisions in the simple 3-decision, 3-outcome example dominated by any others? What about in the SciTools example?

9. Besides the maximin, maximax, and EMV criteria, there are other possible criteria for making decisions. One possibility involves "regret." The idea behind regret is that if we make any decision and then some outcome occurs, we look at that outcome's column in the payoff table to see how much more we could have made if we had chosen the best payoff in that column. For example, if the decision we make and the outcome we observe lead to a $50 payoff, and if the highest payoff in this outcome's column is $80, then our regret is $30. We don't want to look back and see how much more we could have made, if only we had made a different decision. Therefore, we calculate the regret for each cell in the payoff table (as the maximum payoff in that column minus the payoff in that cell),

calculate the maximum regret in each row, and choose the row with the smallest maximum regret. This is called the minimax regret criterion.
    a. Apply this criterion to the simple 3-decision, 3-outcome example. Which decision do you choose?
    b. Repeat part **a** for the SciTools example.
    c. In general, discuss potential strengths and weaknesses of this decision criterion.

10. Referring to the previous problem, another possible criterion is called **expected regret**. Here we calculate the regret for each cell, take a weighted average of these regrets in each row, weighted by the probabilities of the outcomes, and choose the decision with the smallest expected regret.
    a. Apply this criterion to the simple 3-decision, 3-outcome example. Which decision do you choose?
    b. Repeat part **a** for the SciTools example.
    c. The expected regret criterion is actually *equivalent* to the EMV criterion, in that they always lead to the same decisions. Argue why this is true.

11. In the SciTools example, you might argue that there is a *continuum* of possible low competitor bids (given that there is at least one competing bid), not just four possibilities. In fact, assume the low competitor bid in this case is normally distributed with mean $118,000 and standard deviation $4500. Also, assume that SciTools will still either not bid or bid $115,000, $120,000, or $125,000. Use Excel's NORMDIST function to find the EMV for each of SciTools' alternatives. Which is the best decision now? Why can't this be represented in a decision tree?

7.3 THE PRECISIONTREE ADD-IN

Decision trees present a challenge for Excel. We must somehow take advantage of Excel's calculating capabilities (to calculate EMVs, for example) and its graphical capabilities (to depict the decision tree). Fortunately, there is a powerful add-in, PrecisionTree, developed by Palisade Corporation, that makes the process relatively straightforward. This add-in not only enables us to draw and label a decision tree, but it performs the folding-back procedure automatically and then allows us to perform sensitivity analysis on key input parameters.

The first thing you must do to use PrecisionTree is to "add it in." You do this in two steps. First, you must install the Palisade Decision Tools suite (or at least the PrecisionTree program) with the Setup program on the CD-ROM that accompanies this book. Of course, you need to do this only once. Then to run PrecisionTree, there are two options (we usually use the first):

- If Excel is not currently running, you can launch Excel *and* PrecisionTree by clicking on the Windows Start button and selecting the PrecisionTree item from the Palisade Decision Tools group in the list of Programs.

- If Excel is currently running, the procedure in the previous bullet will launch PrecisionTree on top of Excel.

You will know that PrecisionTree is ready for use when you see its tab and the associated ribbon (shown in Figure 7.8). If you want to unload PrecisionTree *without* closing Excel, you can do so from its Utilities dropdown.

Figure 7.8 PrecisionTree Ribbon

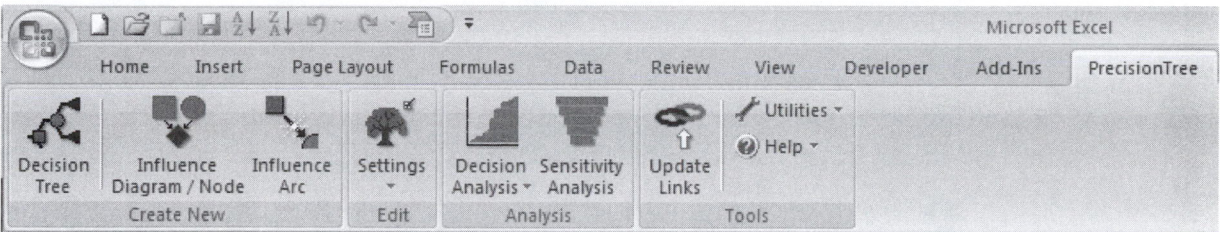

The Decision Tree Model

PrecisionTree is quite easy to use—at least its most basic items are. We will lead you through the steps for the SciTools example. Figure 7.9 shows the results of this procedure, just so that you can see what you are working toward. (See the file **SciTools Bidding Decision 2.xlsx**.) However, we recommend that you work through the steps on your own, starting with a blank spreadsheet.

Figure 7.9 Completed Tree from PrecisionTree

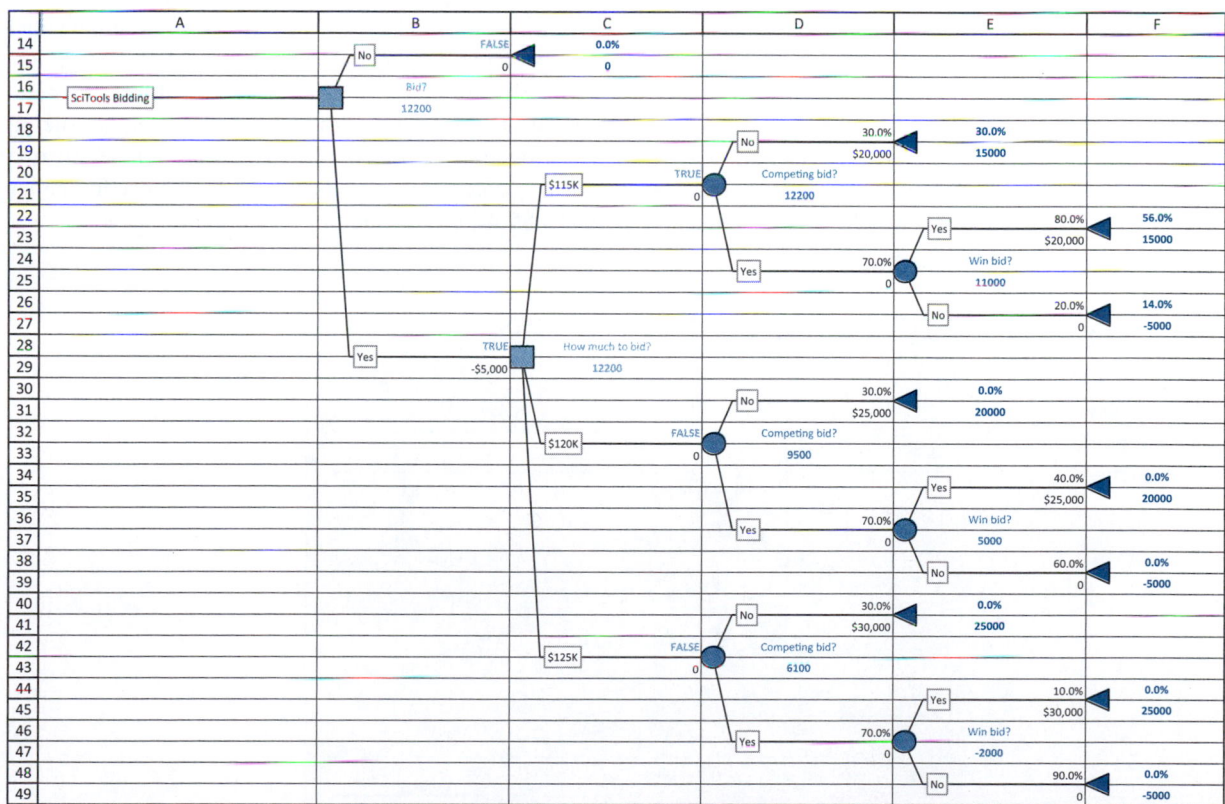

1 Inputs. Enter the inputs shown in columns A and B of Figure 7.10.

Figure 7.10

Inputs for SciTools
Bidding Example

	A	B	C	D	E
1	SciTools Bidding Decision				
2					
3	Inputs			Range names used:	
4	Cost to prepare a bid	$5,000		BidCost	=Model!$B$4
5	Cost to supply instruments	$95,000		PrNoBid	=Model!$B$7
6				ProductionCost	=Model!$B$5
7	Probability of no competing bid	0.3			
8	Comp bid distribution (if they bid)				
9	<$115K	0.2			
10	$115K to $120K	0.4			
11	$120K to $125K	0.3			
12	>$125K	0.1			

2 New tree. Click on the Decision Tree button on the PrecisionTree ribbon, and then select cell A14 below the input section to start a new tree. You will immediately see a dialog box where, among other things, you can name the tree. Type in a descriptive name for the tree, such as SciTools Bidding, and click on OK. You should now see the beginnings of a tree, as shown in Figure 7.11.

Figure 7.11

Beginnings of a
New Tree

	A	B	C
14	SciTools Bidding	100.0%	
15		0	

3 Decision nodes and branches. From here on, keep the tree in Figure 7.9 in mind. This is the finished product we eventually want. To obtain decision nodes and branches, select the (only) triangle end node to open the dialog box in Figure 7.12. Click on the green square to indicate that we want a decision node, and fill in the dialog box as shown. By default, you get two branches, which is what you want in this case. However, if you wanted more than two branches, you would click on the Branches tab and then on Add to get additional branches. The tree expands as shown in Figure 7.13. The boxes that say "branch" show the default labels for these branches. Click on either of them to open another dialog box where you can provide a more descriptive name for the branch. Do this to label the two branches "No" and "Yes." Also, you can enter the immediate payoff or cost for either branch right below it. Because there is a $5000 cost of bidding, enter the formula

=-BidCost

Figure 7.12

Dialog Box for
Adding a New
Decision Node
and Branches

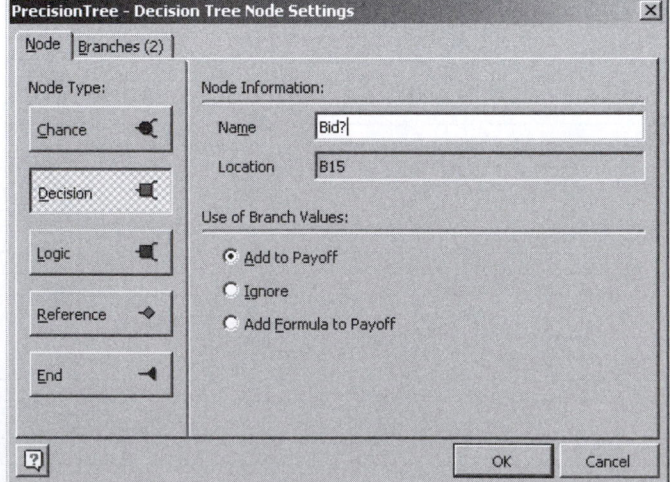

below the "Yes" branch in cell B19. (It is negative to reflect a *cost*.) The tree should now appear as in Figure 7.14.

PrecisionTree Tip: *Allowable Entries*

On your computer screen, you will note the color-coding PrecisionTree uses. If you investigate any colored (nonblack) cells, you will see strange formulas that PrecisionTree uses for its own purposes. You should not modify these formulas. You should enter your own probabilities and monetary values only in the black cells.

Figure 7.13

Tree with Initial Decision Node and Branches

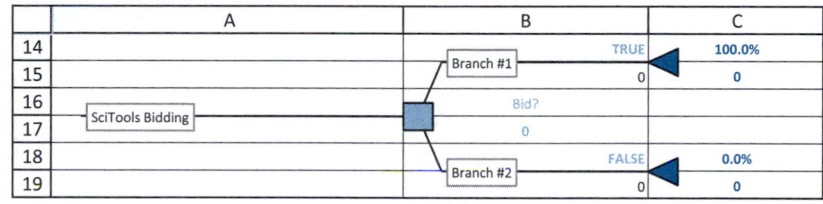

Figure 7.14

Decision Tree with Decision Branches Labeled

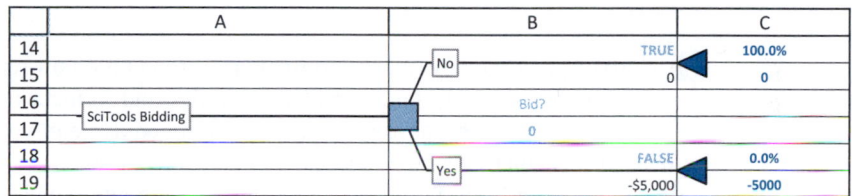

4 **More decision branches.** The top branch is completed; if SciTools does not bid, there is nothing left to do. So click on the bottom end node (the triangle), following SciTools' decision to bid, and proceed as in the previous step to add and label the decision node and three decision branches for the amount to bid. (Again, refer to Figure 7.9.) The tree to this point should appear as in Figure 7.15. Note that there are no monetary values below these decision branches because no *immediate* payoffs or costs are associated with the bid amount decision.

Figure 7.15

Tree with All Decision Nodes and Branches

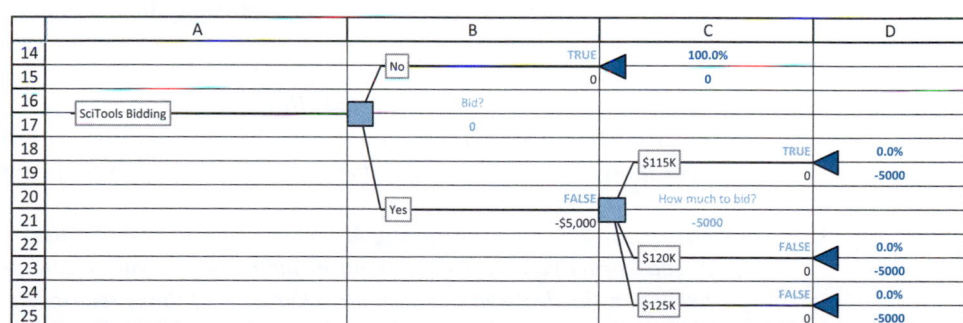

5 **Probability nodes and branches.** We now need a probability node and branches from the rightmost end nodes to capture whether the competition bids. Click on the top one of these end nodes to bring up the same dialog box as in Figure 7.12. Now, however, click on the red circle box to indicate that we want a probability node. Label it "Any competing bid?", accept two branches, and click on OK. Then label the two branches "No" and "Yes." Next, repeat this procedure to form another probability node (with two branches) following the "Yes" branch, call it "Win bid?", and label its branches as shown in Figure 7.16.

Figure 7.16   Decision Tree with One Set of Probability Nodes and Branches

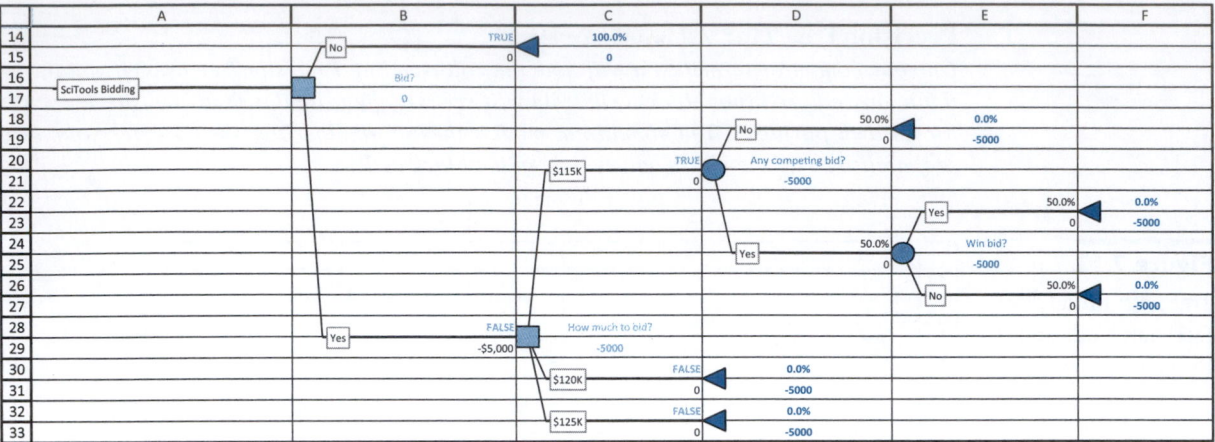

6 **Copying probability nodes and branches.** You could now repeat the same procedure from the previous step to build probability nodes and branches following the other bid amount decisions, but because they are structurally equivalent, you can save a lot of work by using PrecisionTree's copy and paste feature. Right-click on the leftmost probability node and click on Copy SubTree. Then right-click on either end node below and click on Paste SubTree. Do this again with the other end node. Decision trees can get very "bushy," but this copy and paste feature can make them much less tedious to construct.

7 **Labeling probability branches.** You should now have the decision tree shown in Figure 7.17. It is structurally the same as the completed tree in Figure 7.9, but the probabilities and monetary values on the probability branches are incorrect. Note that each probability branch has a value above and below the branch. The value above is the probability (the default values make the branches equally likely), and the value below is the monetary value (the default values are 0). We can enter any values or formulas in these cells, exactly as we do in typical Excel worksheets. As usual, it is a good practice to refer to input cells in these formulas whenever possible. In addition, range names can be used instead of cell addresses.

PrecisionTree Tip: *Sum of Probabilities*
PrecisionTree does not enforce the rule that probabilities on branches leading out of a node must sum to 1. You must enforce this rule with appropriate formulas.

PrecisionTree Tip: *Entering Monetary Values, Probabilities*
A good practice is to calculate all of the monetary values and probabilities that will be needed in the decision tree in some other area of the spreadsheet. Then the values needed next to the tree branches can be created with simple "linking" formulas.

We will get you started with the probability branches following the decision to bid $115,000. First, enter the probability of no competing bid in cell D18 with the formula

=PrNoBid

and enter its complement in cell D24 with the formula

=1-D18

Figure 7.17 Structure of Completed Tree

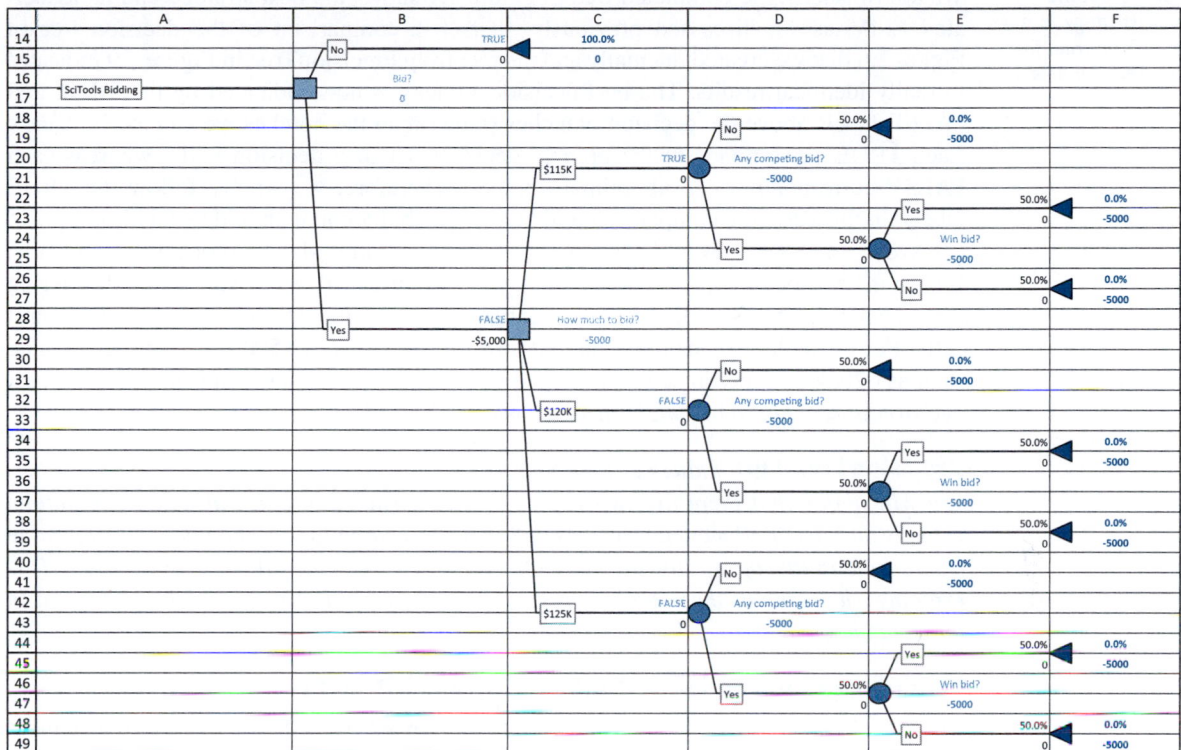

Next, enter the probability that SciTools wins the bid in cell E22 with the formula

=SUM(B10:B12)

and enter its complement in cell E26 with the formula

=1-E22

(Remember that SciTools wins the bid only if the competition bids higher, and in this part of the tree, SciTools is bidding $115,000.) For the monetary values, enter the formula

=115000-ProdCost

in the two cells, D19 and E23, where SciTools wins the contract. Note that we already subtracted the cost of the bid in cell B29, so we should *not* do so again. This would be double-counting, and you should always avoid it in decision trees.

8 **Enter the other formulas on probability branches.** Using the previous step and Figure 7.9 as a guide, enter formulas for the probabilities and monetary values on the other probability branches, those following the decision to bid $120,000 or $125,000.

PrecisionTree Tip: *Copying Subtrees*
Take advantage of PrecisionTree's copying capability to speed up the tree-building process. However, it is generally a good idea to fill the subtree as much as possible (with labels, probabilities, and monetary values) before copying. In that way, the copies will require less work. Note that formulas on the subtree are copied in the usual Excel way (with regard to relative and absolute references), so that the formulas on the copies often have to be adjusted slightly. In this example, we could have sped up the process slightly by completing step 7 before copying. Then step 8 would entail only a few formula adjustments on the copied subtrees.

Interpreting the Decision Tree

To find the optimal decision strategy in any PrecisionTree tree, follow the TRUE labels.

We are finished! The completed tree in Figure 7.9 shows the best strategy and its associated EMV, as we discussed previously. In fact, a comparison of the decision tree in Figure 7.6 that we created manually and the tree from PrecisionTree in Figure 7.9 indicates virtually identical results. The best decision strategy is now indicated by the TRUE and FALSE labels above the decision branches (rather than the notches we entered by hand). Each TRUE corresponds to the optimal decision out of a decision node, whereas each FALSE corresponds to a suboptimal decision. Therefore, we simply follow the TRUE labels. In this case, the company should bid, and its bid amount should be $115,000.

Note that we never have to perform the folding-back procedure manually. PrecisionTree does it for us. Essentially, the tree is completed as soon as we finish entering the relevant inputs. In addition, if we change any of the inputs, the tree reacts automatically. For example, try changing the bid cost in cell B4 from $5000 to some large value such as $20,000. You will see that the tree calculations update automatically, and the best decision is then *not* to bid, with an associated EMV of $0.

PrecisionTree Tip: *Values at End Nodes*

You will notice that there are two values following each triangle end node. The bottom value is the sum of all monetary values on branches leading to this end node. The top value is the probability of getting to this end node when the optimal strategy is used. This explains why many of these probabilities are 0; the optimal strategy would never lead to these end nodes.

Policy Suggestion and Risk Profile for Optimal Strategy

The Policy Suggestion shows only the subtree corresponding to the optimal decision strategy.

Once the decision tree is completed, PrecisionTree has several tools we can use to gain more information about the decision analysis. First, we can see a subtree (called a Policy Suggestion) for the *optimal* decision. To do so, click on the Decision Analysis dropdown on the PrecisionTree ribbon and fill in the resulting dialog box as shown in Figure 7.18. (You can experiment with other options.) The Policy Suggestion option allows us to see only that part of the tree that corresponds to the best decision, as shown in Figure 7.19.

We can also obtain a graphical risk profile of the optimal decision. To get it, select Risk Profile from the Decision Analysis dropdown, and fill in the resulting dialog box as shown in Figure 7.20. (Again, you can experiment with the other options.) As the risk profile in Figure 7.21 indicates, there are only two possible monetary outcomes if SciTools bids $115,000. It either wins $15,000 or loses $5000, and the former is much more likely. (The associated probabilities are 0.86 and 0.14, respectively.) This graphical information is even more useful when there are a larger number of possible monetary outcomes. We can see what they are and how likely they are.

Figure 7.18

Dialog Box for Information About Optimal Decision

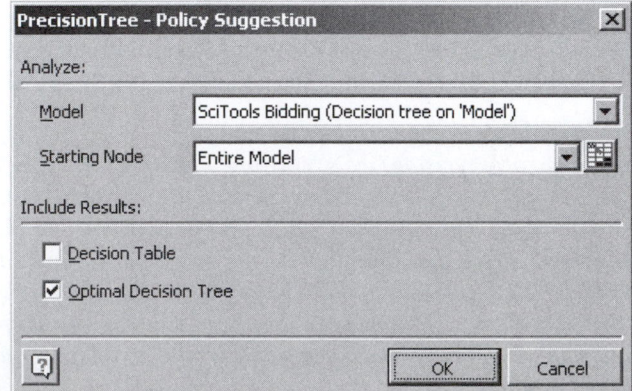

Figure 7.19 Subtree for Optimal Decision

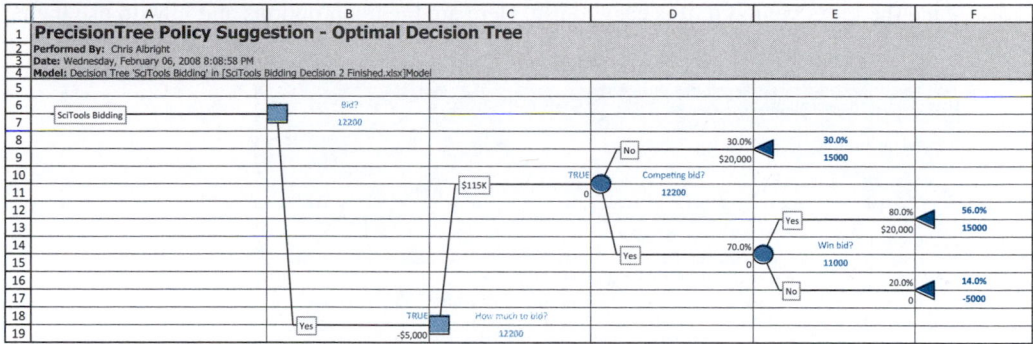

Figure 7.20

Risk Profile Dialog
Box

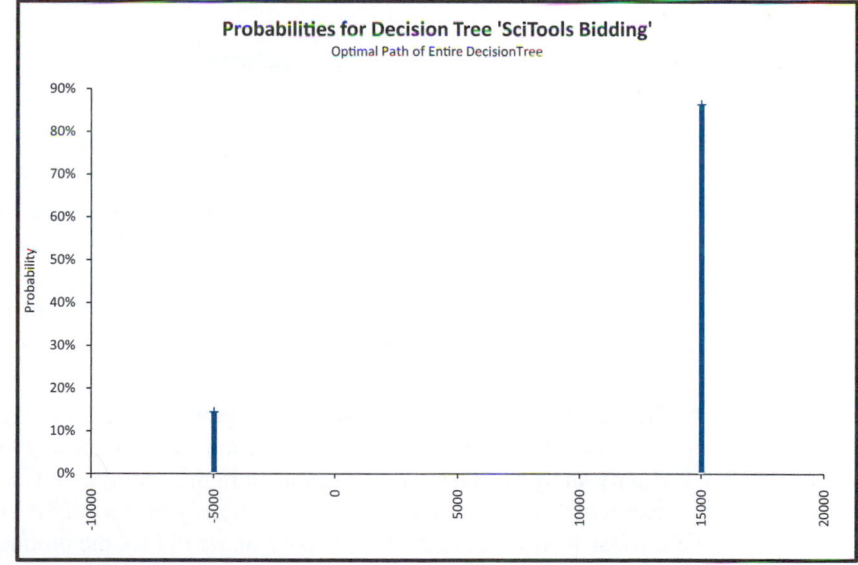

Figure 7.21

Risk Profile of
Optimal Decision

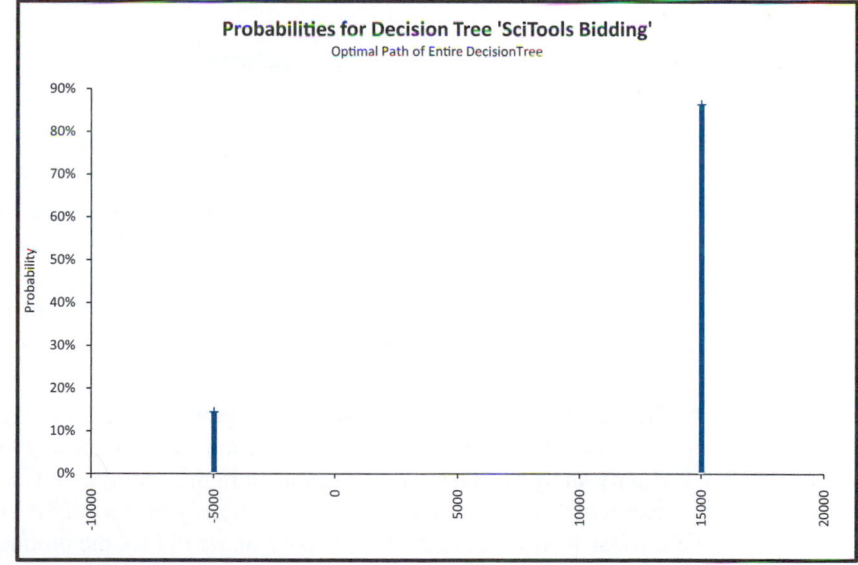

Sensitivity Analysis

We have already stressed the importance of a follow-up sensitivity analysis to any decision problem, and PrecisionTree makes this relatively easy to perform. First, we can enter any values into the input cells and watch how the tree changes. But we can obtain more systematic information by clicking on PrecisionTree's Sensitivity Analysis button. This brings up the dialog box in Figure 7.22. This dialog is fairly "busy," but once you understand the ideas behind it, it is easy to use. Here are the main options and how to use them.

Figure 7.22

Sensitivity Analysis
Dialog Box

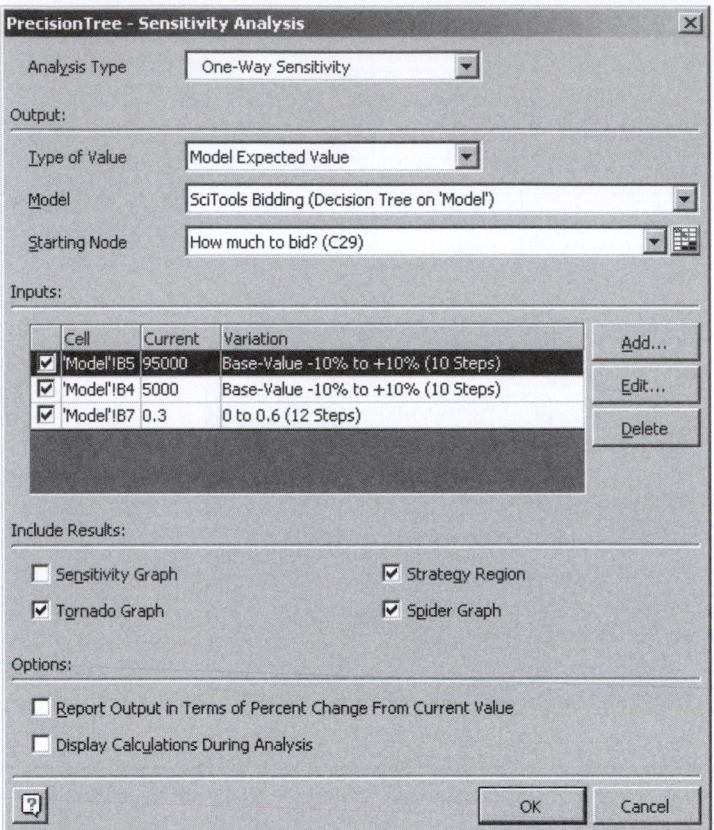

It takes some practice and experimenting to get used to PrecisionTree's sensitivity analysis tools. However, they are powerful and worth learning.

- The Analysis Type dropdown allows you to vary one input (One-Way Sensitivity) or two inputs (Two-Way Sensitivity) simultaneously.

- The Starting Node dropdown lets you choose any node in the tree, and the sensitivity analysis is then performed for the EMV *from that node to the right.* In other words, it assumes you have gotten to that node and are now interested in what will happen from then on. The node selected in the figure, C29, is the left-most node, so by selecting it, we perform a sensitivity analysis for the EMV of the entire tree. This is the most common setting.

- The Inputs section is where you can add inputs to vary. You can add as many as you like, and whichever inputs are then checked are the ones included in a particular sensitivity analysis. When you add an input to this section, you can specify the range over which you want it to vary. For example, you can vary it by plus or minus 10% in 10 steps from a selected base value, as we did for the production cost in cell B5, or you can vary it from 0 to 0.6 in 12 steps, as we did for the probability of no competing bids in cell B7.

- The Include Results checkboxes provide up to four types of charts you can select, depending on the type of sensitivity analysis. (The bottom two options are disabled for a two-way sensitivity analysis.) You can experiment with these options, but we'll illustrate our favorites shortly.

When we click on Run Analysis, PrecisionTree varies each of the checked inputs in the middle section, one at a time if we select the One-Way option, and presents the results in new worksheets. By default, these new worksheets are placed in a new workbook. If you'd rather have them in the same workbook as the model, click on the PrecisionTree Utilities dropdown, select Application Settings, and select Active Workbook from the Replace Reports In option. (This is a global setting. It will take effect for all future PrecisionTree analyses.)

Strategy Region Chart

In strategy region charts, we are especially interested in where (or whether) lines cross. This is where decisions change.

Figure 7.23 illustrates a strategy region chart from a one-way analysis. This chart shows how the EMV varies with the production cost for *both* of the original decisions (bid or don't bid). This type of chart is useful for seeing whether the optimal decision *changes* over the range of the input variable. It does so only if the two lines cross. In this particular graph it is clear that the "Bid" decision dominates the "No bid" decision over the production cost range we selected.

Figure 7.23

EMV versus Production Cost for Each of Two Decisions

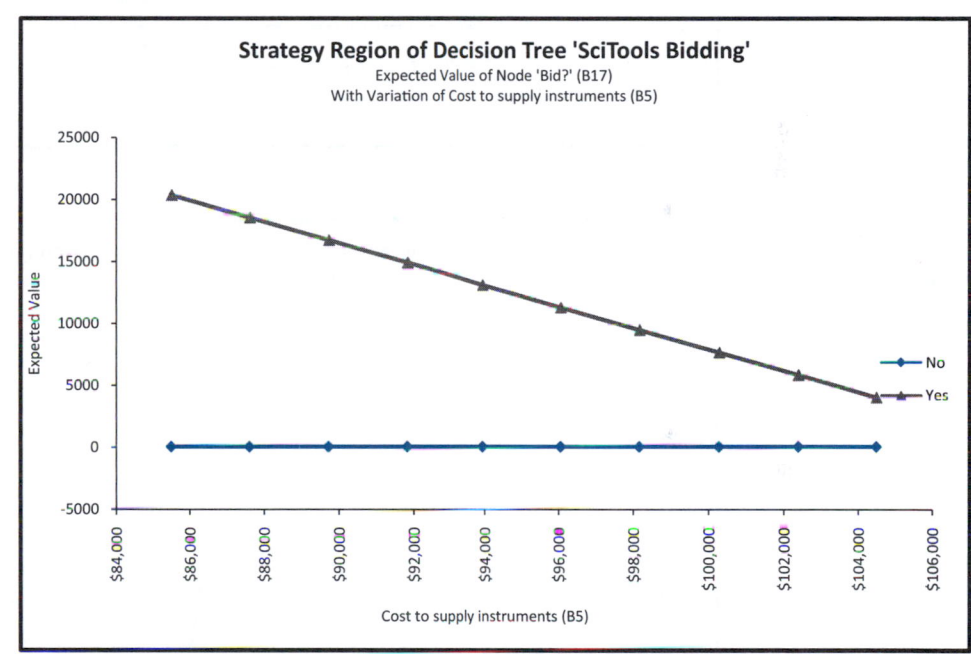

Strategy Region of Decision Tree 'SciTools Bidding'
Expected Value of Node 'Bid?' (B17)
With Variation of Cost to supply instruments (B5)

Tornado Chart

A tornado chart shows how sensitive the EMV of the *optimal* decision is to each of the selected inputs over the specified ranges. (See Figure 7.24.) The length of each bar shows the change in the EMV in either direction, so inputs with longer bars have a greater effect on the selected EMV. (If you checked the next-to-bottom checkbox in Figure 7.22, the lengths of the bars would indicate *percentage* changes from the base value.) The bars are always arranged from longest on top to shortest on the bottom—hence the name *tornado* chart. Here we see that production cost has the largest effect on EMV, and bid cost has the smallest effect.

Spider Chart

Finally, a spider chart shows how much the optimal EMV varies in magnitude for various percentage changes in the input variables. (See Figure 7.25.) The steeper the slope of the line, the more the EMV is affected by a particular input. We again see that the production cost has a relatively large effect, whereas the other two inputs have relatively small effects.

Figure 7.24

Tornado Chart for
SciTools Example

*Tornado charts and
spider charts indicate
which inputs the
selected EMV is most
sensitive to.*

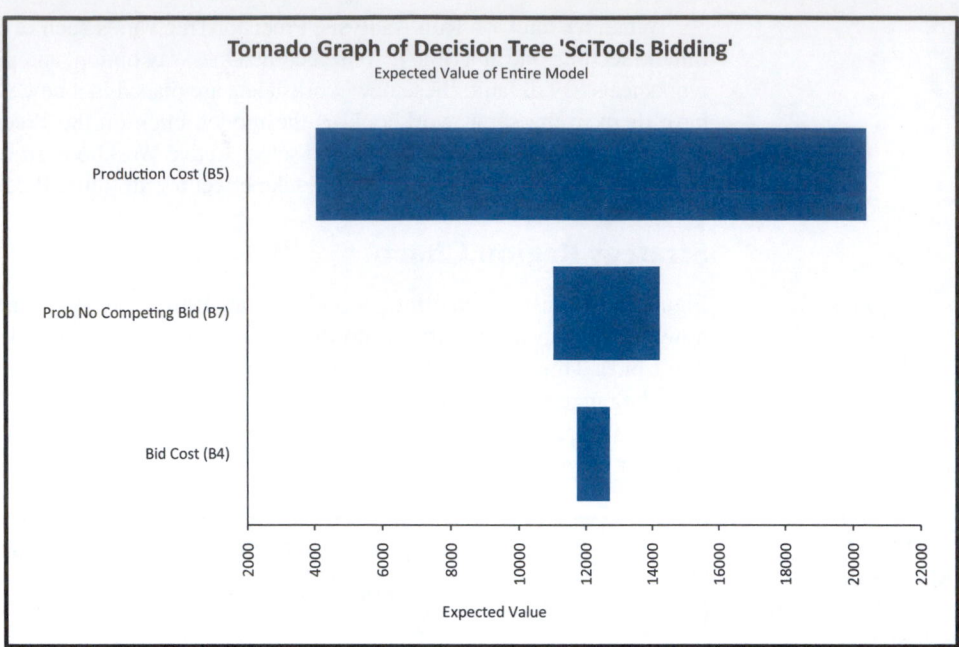

Figure 7.25

Spider Chart for
SciTools Example

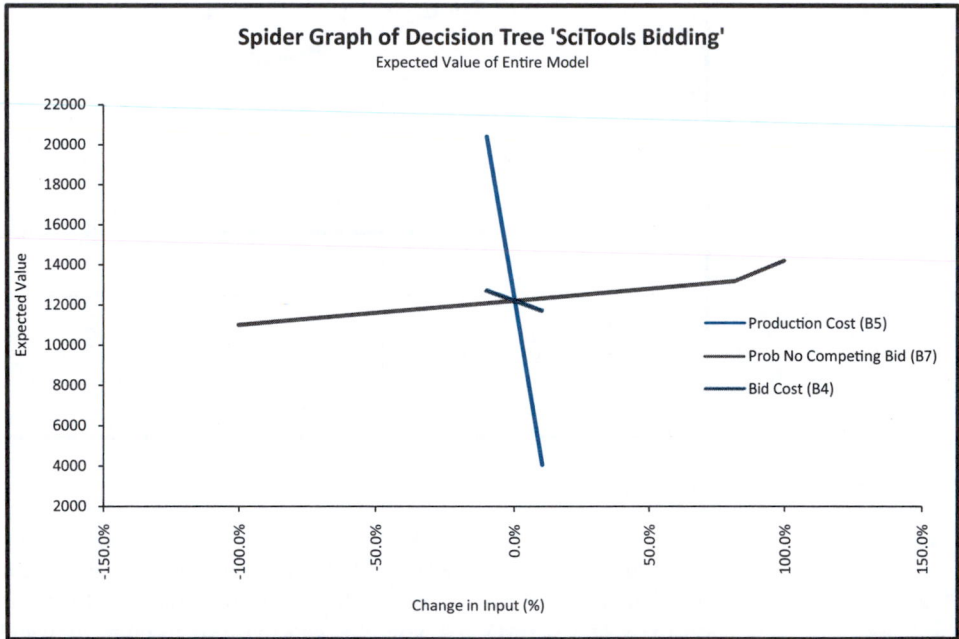

Another Sensitivity Chart

Each time we click on the Sensitivity Analysis button, we can run a different sensitivity analysis. For example, we might want to choose cell C29 as the cell to analyze. This is the optimal EMV for the problem, given that the company has decided to place a bid. One interesting chart from this analysis is the strategy region chart in Figure 7.26. It indicates how the EMV varies with the probability of no competing bid for *each* of the three bid amount decisions. As we see, the $115,000 bid is best for most of the range, but when the probability of no competing bid is sufficiently large (about 0.55), the $120,000 bid becomes best.

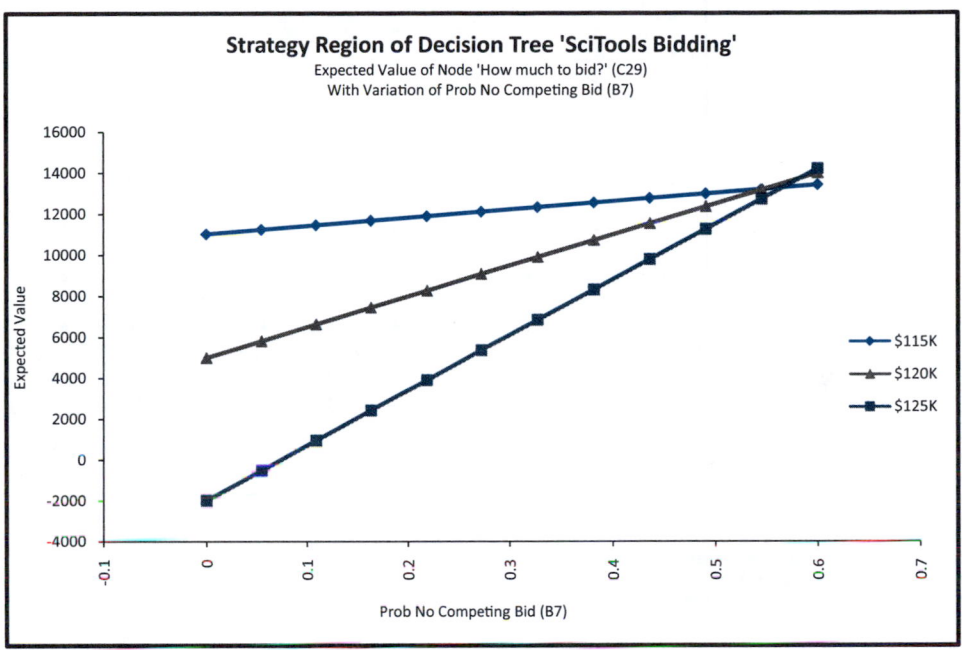

Figure 7.26

Strategy Region Chart for Another EMV Cell

Two-Way Sensitivity Chart

A one-way sensitivity analysis varies only one input at a time. A two-way analysis varies two inputs simultaneously.

Another interesting option is to run a two-way analysis. Then we see how the selected EMV varies as each *pair* of inputs vary simultaneously. We analyzed the EMV in cell C29 with this option, using the same inputs as before. A typical result is shown in Figure 7.27. For each of the possible values of production cost and the probability of no competitor bid, this chart indicates which bid amount is optimal. (By choosing cell C29, we are assuming SciTools will bid; the question is only how much.) As we see, the optimal bid amount remains $115,000 unless the production cost *and* the probability of no competing bid are both large. Then it becomes optimal to bid $120,000 or $125,000. This makes sense intuitively. As the chance of no competing bid increases and a larger production cost must be recovered, it seems reasonable that SciTools should increase its bid.

We reiterate that a sensitivity analysis is always an important component of any real-world decision analysis. If we had to construct decision trees by hand—with paper and pencil—a sensitivity analysis would be virtually out of the question. We would have to recompute everything each time through. Therefore, one of the most valuable features of the PrecisionTree add-in is that it enables us to perform sensitivity analyses in a matter of seconds.

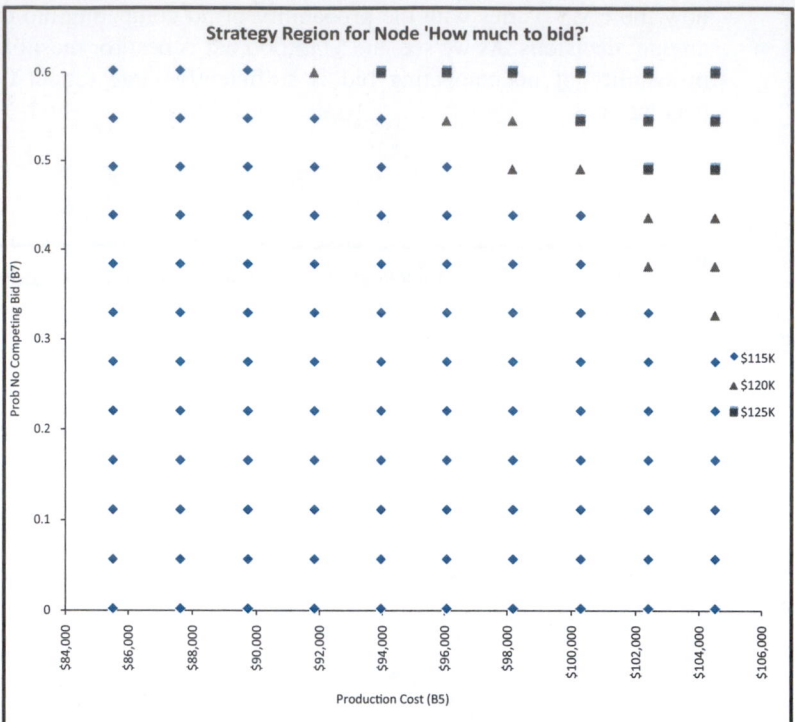

Figure 7.27

Two-Way Sensitivity
Analysis

PROBLEMS

Level A

12. In a tree built with PrecisionTree, there are two blue values at each end node, the top one of which is a probability. Why are so many of these probabilities 0 in the finished tree in Figure 7.9? What do the remaining (positive) probabilities represent?

13. In the SciTools example, we saw that there are two equivalent decision tree structures, shown in Figures 7.5 and 7.6. Use PrecisionTree to create the first of these, and verify that it yields the same EMVs and the same optimal decision as the tree we developed in this section.

14. For the completed decision tree in Figure 7.9, the monetary values in black are those we enter. The monetary values in color are calculated automatically by PrecisionTree. For this particular example, explain exactly how these latter values are calculated (remember the folding-back process) and what they represent. These include the blue values at the end nodes, the red

values at the probability nodes, and the green values at the decision nodes.

15. For the SciTools example, once you build the tree as in Figure 7.9 and then run a one-way sensitivity analysis with the dialog box filled in as in Figure 7.22, you obtain three strategy charts. (Try it.) Explain exactly what each of these charts represents. (For this problem, you can ignore the tornado and spider charts.)

16. The tornado chart in Figure 7.24 and the spider chart in Figure 7.25 show basically the same information in slightly different forms. Explain in words exactly what information they provide.

17. Explain in words what information a two-way sensitivity chart, such as the one in Figure 7.27, provides. Demonstrate how you could provide this same information without PrecisionTree's sensitivity tools, using only data tables. (You can still utilize the tree built with PrecisionTree.)

7.4 BAYES' RULE

So far, the examples have required a single decision. We now examine multistage problems, where the decision maker must make at least two decisions that are separated in time, such as when a company must first decide whether to buy information that will help it make a second decision. In multistage decision problems we typically have alternating sets of decision nodes and probability nodes. The decision maker makes a decision, some uncertain outcomes are observed, the decision maker makes another decision, more uncertain outcomes are observed, and so on. Before we can analyze such problems, we must resolve one important probability issue.

In a multistage decision tree, all probability branches at the *right* of the tree are conditional on outcomes that have occurred earlier, to their left. Therefore, the probabilities on these branches are of the form $P(A|B)$, read "A given B," where A is an event corresponding to a current probability branch, and B is an event that occurs *before* event A in time. However, it is sometimes more natural to *assess* conditional probabilities in the opposite order, that is, $P(B|A)$. Whenever this is the case, we must use **Bayes' rule** to obtain the probabilities needed on the tree. Essentially, Bayes' rule is a mechanism for revising probabilities as new information becomes available.

To develop Bayes' rule, let A_1 through A_n be any outcomes. Without any further information, we believe the probabilities of the A's are $P(A_1)$ through $P(A_n)$. These are called **prior probabilities**. We then have the possibility of gaining some information. There are several information outcomes we might observe, a typical one of which is labeled B. We assume the probabilities of B, given that any of the A's will occur, are known. These probabilities, labeled $P(B|A_1)$ through $P(B|A_n)$, are often called **likelihoods**. Because an information outcome might influence our thinking about the probabilities of the A's, we need to find the conditional probability $P(A_i|B)$ for each outcome A_i. This is called the **posterior probability** of A_i. This is where Bayes' rule enters the picture. It states that we can calculate posterior probabilities using the following formula.

Bayes' rule

$$P(A_i|B) = \frac{P(B|A_i)P(A_i)}{P(B|A_1)P(A_1) + \cdots + P(B|A_n)P(A_n)} \qquad \textbf{(7.1)}$$

In words, Bayes' rule says that the posterior is the likelihood times the prior, divided by a sum of likelihoods times priors. As a side benefit, the denominator in Bayes' rule is also useful in multistage decision trees. It is the probability $P(B)$ of the information outcome:

Denominator of Bayes' rule

$$P(B) = P(B|A_1)P(A_1) + \cdots + P(B|A_n)P(A_n) \qquad \textbf{(7.2)}$$

In the case where there are only two A's, which we relabel as A and Not A, Bayes' rules takes the following form:

Bayes' rule for two outcomes

$$P(A|B) = \frac{P(B|A)P(A)}{P(B|A)P(A) + P(B|\text{Not } A)P(\text{Not } A)} \qquad \textbf{(7.3)}$$

We illustrate the mechanics of Bayes' rule in the following example. [See Feinstein (1990) for a real application of this example.]

7.2 DRUG TESTING COLLEGE ATHLETES

If an athlete is tested for a certain type of drug usage (steroids, say), then the test result will be either positive or negative. However, these tests are never perfect. Some athletes who are drug free test positive, and some who are drug users test negative. The former are called **false positives**; the latter are called **false negatives**. We assume that 5% of all athletes use drugs, 3% of all tests on drug-free athletes yield false positives, and 7% of all tests on drug users yield false negatives. Suppose a typical athlete is tested. If this athlete tests positive, are we sure that he is a drug user? If he tests negative, are we sure he does not use drugs?

Objective To use Bayes' rule to revise the probability of being a drug user, given the positive or negative results of the test.

WHERE DO THE NUMBERS COME FROM?

The estimate that 5% of all athletes are drug users is probably based on a well-known national average. The error rates from the tests are undoubtedly known from extensive experience with the tests. (However, we are not claiming that the numbers used here match reality.)

Solution

Let D and ND denote that a randomly chosen athlete is or is not a drug user, and let $T+$ and $T-$ indicate a positive or negative test result. (The outcomes D and ND correspond to A and Not A in equation (7.3), where either $T+$ or $T-$ corresponds to B.) We are given the following probabilities. First, because 5% of all athletes are drug users, we know that $P(D) = 0.05$ and $P(ND) = 0.95$. These are the prior probabilities. They represent the chance that an athlete is or is not a drug user *prior* to the results of a drug test.

Second, from the information on the accuracy of the drug test, we know the conditional probabilities $P(T+|ND) = 0.03$ and $P(T-|D) = 0.07$. In addition, a drug-free athlete tests either positive or negative, and the same is true for a drug user. Therefore, we also have the probabilities $P(T-|ND) = 0.97$ and $P(T+|D) = 0.93$. These four conditional probabilities of test results given drug user status are the likelihoods of the test results.

Given these priors and likelihoods, we want posterior probabilities such as $P(D|T+)$, the probability that an athlete who tests positive is a drug user, and $P(ND|T-)$, the probability that an athlete who tests negative is drug free. They are called posterior probabilities because they are assessed *after* the drug test results.

Using Bayes' rule for two outcomes, equation (7.3), we find

$P(D|T+)$

$$= \frac{P(T+|D)P(D)}{P(T+|D)P(D) + P(T+|ND)P(ND)} = \frac{(0.93)(0.05)}{(0.93)(0.05) + (0.03)(0.95)} = 0.620$$

and

$P(ND|T-)$

$$= \frac{P(T-|ND)P(ND)}{P(T-|D)P(D) + P(T-|ND)P(ND)} = \frac{(0.97)(0.95)}{(0.07)(0.05) + (0.97)(0.95)} = 0.996$$

In words, if the athlete tests positive, there is still a 38% chance that he is *not* a drug user, but if he tests negative, we are virtually sure he is not a drug user. The denominators of these two formulas are the probabilities of the test results. We find them from equation (7.2):

$$P(T+) = 0.93(0.05) + 0.03(0.95) = 0.075$$

and

$$P(T-) = 0.07(0.05) + 0.97(0.95) = 0.925$$

The first Bayes' rule result might surprise you. After all, there is only a 3% chance of a false positive, so if you observe a positive test result, you should be pretty sure that the athlete is a drug user, right? The reason the first posterior probability is "only" 0.620 is that very few athletes in the population are drug users—only 5%. Therefore, we need a lot of evidence to convince us that a particular athlete is a drug user, and a positive test result from a somewhat inaccurate test is not enough evidence to be totally convincing. On the other hand, a negative test result simply adds confirmation to what we already suspected— that a typical athlete is *not* a drug user. This is why $P(ND|T-)$ is so close to 1.

A More Intuitive Calculation

If you have trouble understanding or implementing Bayes' rule, you are not alone. At least one study has shown that even trained medical specialists have trouble with this type of calculation. Most of us do not think intuitively about conditional probabilities. However, there is an equivalent and more intuitive way to obtain the same result.

This alternative procedure, using counts instead of probabilities, is equivalent to Bayes' rule and is probably more intuitive.

Imagine that there are 100,000 athletes. Because 5% of all athletes are drug users, we assume 5000 of our athletes use drugs and the other 95,000 do not. Now we administer the test to all of them. We expect 3%, or 2850, of the nonusers to test positive (because the false-positive rate is 3%), and we expect 93%, or 4650, of the drug users to test positive (because the false-negative rate is 7%). Therefore, we observe a total of 2850 + 4650 = 7500 positives. If we choose one of these athletes at random, what is the probability that we choose a drug user? It is clearly

$$P(D|T+) = 4650/7500 = 0.620$$

This is the same result we got using Bayes' rule! So if you have trouble with Bayes' rule using probabilities, you can use this alternative method of using *counts*. (By the way, the 100,000 value is irrelevant. We could have used 10,000, 50,000, 1,000,000, or any other convenient value.)

Spreadsheet Implementation of Bayes' Rule

It is fairly easy to implement Bayes' rule in a spreadsheet, as illustrated in Figure 7.28 for the drug example. (See the file **Bayes Rule.xlsx**.[4])

---

[4]The Bayes2 sheet in this file illustrates how Bayes' rule can be used when there are more than two possible test results and/or drug user categories.

Figure 7.28

Bayes' Rule for
Drug-Testing
Example

	A	B	C	D	E	F
1	Illustration of Bayes' rule using drug example					
2						
3	Prior probabilities of drug user status					
4		User	Non-user			
5		0.05	0.95	1		
6						
7	Likelihoods of test results, given drug user status					
8		User	Non-user			
9	Test positive	0.93	0.03			
10	Test negative	0.07	0.97			
11		1	1			
12						
13	Unconditional probabilities of test results (denominators of Bayes' rule)					
14	Test positive	0.075				
15	Test negative	0.925				
16		1				
17						
18	Posterior probabilities of drug user status (Bayes' rule)					
19		User	Non-user			
20	Test positive	0.620	0.380	1		
21	Test negative	0.004	0.996	1		

The given priors and likelihoods are listed in the ranges B5:C5 and B9:C10. We first use equation (7.2) to calculate the denominators for Bayes' rule, the unconditional probabilities of the two possible test results, in the range B14:C15. Because each of these is a sum of products of priors and likelihoods, the formula in cell B14 is

=SUMPRODUCT($B$5:$C$5,B9:C9)

and this is copied to cell B15. Then we use equation (7.1) to calculate the posterior probabilities in the range B20:C21. Because each of these is a product of a prior and a likelihood, divided by a denominator, the formula in cell B20 is

=B$5*B9/$B14

and this is copied to the rest of the B20:C21 range. The various 1's in the margins of Figure 7.28 are row sums or column sums that must equal 1. We show them only as checks of our logic.

As we have noted, a positive drug test still leaves a 38% chance that the athlete is *not* a drug user. Is this a valid argument for not requiring drug testing of athletes? We will explore this question in a continuation of the drug-testing example in the next section. ∎

PROBLEMS

Level A

18. For each of the following, use a one-way data table to see how the posterior probability of being a drug user, given a positive test, varies as the indicated input varies. Write a brief explanation of your results.
 a. Let the input be the prior probability of being a drug user, varied from 0.01 to 0.10 in increments of 0.01.
 b. Let the input be the probability of a false positive from the test, varied from 0 to 0.10 in increments of 0.01.
 c. Let the input be the probability of a false negative from the test, varied from 0 to 0.10 in increments of 0.01.

19. In the drug testing, assume there are three possible test results: positive, negative, and inconclusive. For a drug user, the probabilities of these outcomes are 0.65, 0.06, and 0.29. For a nonuser, they are 0.03, 0.72, and 0.25. Use Bayes' rule to find a table of all posterior probabilities. (The prior probability of being a drug user is still 0.05.) Then answer the following.
 a. What is the posterior probability that the athlete is a drug user, given that her test results are positive? given that her test results are negative? given that her drug results are inconclusive?
 b. What is the probability of observing a positive test result? a negative test result? an inconclusive test result?

20. Referring to the previous problem, find the same probabilities through the counting argument explained in this section. Start with 100,000 athletes and divide them into the various categories.

Level B

21. The terms *prior* and *posterior* are relative. Assume that the drug test has been performed, and the outcome is positive, which leads to the posterior probabilities in row 20 of Figure 7.28. Now assume there is a *second* test, independent of the first, that can be used as a

follow-up. We assume that its false-positive and false-negative rates are 0.02 and 0.06.

a. Use the posterior probabilities from row 20 as *prior* probabilities in a second Bayes' rule calculation. (Now *prior* means prior to the second test.) If the athlete also tests positive in this second test, what is the posterior probability that he is a drug user?

b. We assumed that the two tests are independent. Why might this not be realistic? If they are not independent, what kind of additional information would we need about the likelihoods of the test results?

7.5 MULTISTAGE DECISION PROBLEMS

In this section we investigate multistage decision problems. In many such problems the first-stage decision is whether to purchase information that will help make a better second-stage decision. In this case the information, if obtained, typically changes the probabilities of later outcomes. To revise the probabilities once the information is obtained, we often need to apply Bayes' rule, as discussed in the previous section. In addition, we typically want to learn how much the information is worth. After all, information usually comes at a price, so we want to know whether the information is worth its price. This leads to an investigation of the value of information, an important theme of this section.

We begin with a continuation of the drug-testing example from the previous section. If drug tests are not completely reliable, should they be used? As we will see, it all depends on the "costs."[5]

EXAMPLE | **7.3 DRUG TESTING COLLEGE ATHLETES**

The administrators at State University are trying to decide whether to institute mandatory drug testing for athletes. They have the same information about priors and likelihoods as in Example 7.2, but they now want to use a decision tree approach to see whether the benefits outweigh the costs.[6]

Objective To use a multistage decision framework to see whether mandatory drug testing can be justified, given a somewhat unreliable test and a set of "reasonable" monetary values.

WHERE DO THE NUMBERS COME FROM?

We already discussed the source of the probabilities in Example 7.2. The monetary values we need are discussed in detail here.

Solution

We have already discussed the uncertain outcomes and their probabilities. Now we need to discuss the decision alternatives and the monetary values—the other two elements of a

---

[5]It might also depend on whether there is a second type of test that could help confirm the findings of the first test. However, we will not consider such a test.
[6]Again, see Feinstein (1990) for an enlightening discussion of this drug-testing problem at a real university.

decision analysis. We will assume that there are only two alternatives: perform drug testing on all athletes or don't perform any drug testing. In the former case we assume that if an athlete tests positive, this athlete is then barred from athletics.

Assessing the Monetary Values

The "monetary" values are more difficult to assess. They include

- the benefit B from correctly identifying a drug user and barring this person from athletics
- the cost C_1 of the test itself for a single athlete (materials and labor)
- the cost C_2 of falsely accusing a nonuser (and barring this person from athletics)
- the cost C_3 of not identifying a drug user and allowing this person to participate in athletics
- the cost C_4 of violating a nonuser's privacy by performing the test

Real decision problems often involve nonmonetary benefits and costs. These must be assessed, relative to one another, before rational decisions can be made.

It is clear that only C_1 is a direct monetary cost that is easy to measure. However, the other "costs" and the benefit B are real, and they must be compared on some scale to enable administrators to make a rational decision. We will do so by comparing everything to the cost C_1, to which we assign value 1. (This does not mean that the cost of testing an athlete is necessarily \$1; it just means that we express all other monetary values as multiples of C_1.) Clearly, there is a lot of subjectivity involved in making these comparisons, so sensitivity analysis on the final decision tree is a must.

Developing a Benefit–Cost Table

Before developing this decision tree, it is useful to form a benefit–cost table for both alternatives and all possible outcomes. Because we will eventually maximize expected *net benefit*, all benefits in this table have a positive sign and all costs have a negative sign. These net benefits are listed in Table 7.6. The first two columns are relevant if no tests are performed; the last four are relevant when testing is performed. For example, if a positive test is obtained for a nonuser and this athlete is barred from athletics, there are three costs: the cost of the test (C_1), the cost of falsely accusing the athlete (C_2), and the cost of violating the athlete's privacy (C_4). The other entries are obtained similarly.

Table 7.6   Net Benefit for Drug-Testing Example

	Don't Test		Perform Test			
Ultimate decision	D	ND	D and $T+$	ND and $T+$	D and $T-$	ND and $T-$
Bar from athletics	B	$-C_2$	$B-C_1$	$-(C_1+C_2+C_4)$	$B-C_1$	$-(C_1+C_2+C_4)$
Don't bar from athletics	$-C_3$	0	$-(C_1+C_3)$	$-(C_1+C_4)$	$-(C_1+C_3)$	$-(C_1+C_4)$

Developing the Decision Tree Model

The decision model, developed with PrecisionTree and shown in Figures 7.29 and 7.30, is now fairly straightforward. (See the file **Drug Testing Decision.xlsx**.) We first enter all of the benefits and costs in an input section. These, together with the Bayes' rule calculations from Example 7.2, appear at the top of the spreadsheet in Figure 7.29. Then we use PrecisionTree in the usual way to build the tree in Figure 7.30 and enter the links to the values and probabilities.

348   Chapter 7   Decision Making under Uncertainty

Figure 7.29 Inputs and Bayes' Rule Calculations for Drug-Testing Example

	A	B	C	D	E	F
1	Drug testing decision					
2						
3	Benefits			Given probabilities		
4	Identifying user	25		Prior probabilities		
5					User	Non-user
6	Costs				0.05	0.95
7	Test cost	1				
8	Barring non-user	50		Conditional probabilities of test results		
9	Not identifying user	20			User	Non-user
10	Violation of privacy	2		Positive	0.93	0.03
11				Negative	0.07	0.97
12	Key probabilities					
13	PrUser	0.05		Bayesian revision		
14	PrFalseNegative	0.07		Unconditional probabilities of test results		
15	PrFalsePositive	0.03		Positive	0.075	
16				Negative	0.925	
17						
18				Posterior probabilities		
19					User	Non-user
20				Positive	0.620	0.380
21				Negative	0.004	0.996

Figure 7.30 Decision Tree for Drug-Testing Example

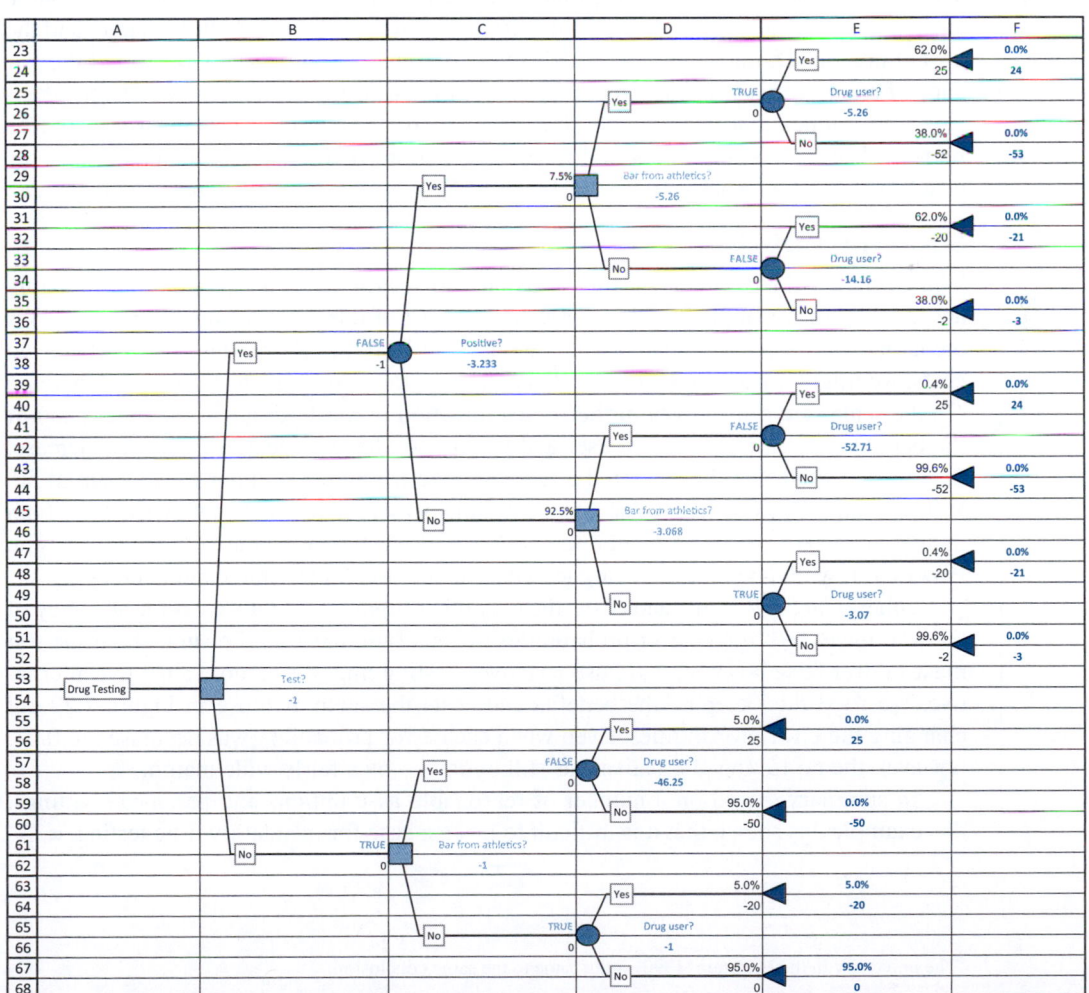

It is important to understand the timing (from left to right) in this decision tree. If drug testing is performed, the result of the drug test is observed first (a probability node). Each test result leads to an action (bar from sports or don't), and then the eventual benefit or cost depends on whether the athlete uses drugs (again a probability node). You might argue that the university never knows for certain whether the athlete uses drugs, but we must include this information in the tree to get the correct benefits and costs. On the other hand, if no drug testing is performed, then there is no intermediate test result node or branch.

We require Bayes' rule because it yields exactly those probabilities that are needed in the decision tree.

Make sure you understand which probabilities are used in the tree. In the lower part, where we don't test, the probabilities are the prior probabilities. We have no test information in this case. In the upper part, where we test, the probabilities for the user and nonuser branches are posterior probabilities, given the results of the test. The reason is that by the time we get to these nodes, the results of the test have already been observed. However, the probabilities for the test results are *unconditional* probabilities, the denominators in Bayes' rule. They are not conditional probabilities such as $P(T+ | D)$ because we condition only on information to the *left* of any given branch. In other words, by the time we get to the test result branches, we do not yet know whether the athlete is a user.

Discussion of the Solution

Now we move on to the solution. First, we discuss the benefits and costs shown in Figure 7.29. These were chosen fairly arbitrarily, but with some hope of reflecting reality. The largest cost is falsely accusing (and then barring) a nonuser. This is 50 times as large as the cost of the test. The benefit of identifying a drug user is only half this large, and the cost of not identifying a user is 40% as large as barring a nonuser. The violation of the privacy of a nonuser is twice as large as the cost of the test. Based on these values, the decision tree implies that drug testing should *not* be performed (and no athletes should be barred). The EMVs for testing and for not testing are both negative, indicating that the costs outweigh the benefits for each, but the EMV for not testing is slightly *less* negative.[7]

Sensitivity Analysis

What would it take to change this decision? We begin with the assumption, probably accepted by most people in our society, that the cost of falsely accusing a nonuser (C_2) is the largest of the benefits and costs in the range B4:B10. In fact, because of possible legal costs, we might argue that C_2 is *more* than 50 times the cost of the test. But if we increase C_2, the scales are tipped even further in the direction of not testing. On the other hand, if the benefit B from identifying a user and the cost C_3 for not identifying a user increase, then testing might be the preferred alternative. We tried this, keeping C_2 constant at 50. When B and C_3 both had value 45, no testing was still optimal, but when they both increased to 50—the same magnitude as C_2—then testing won out by a small margin. However, it would be difficult to argue that B and C_3 are of the same magnitude as C_2.

Other than the benefits and costs, the only other input we might vary is the accuracy of the test, measured by the error probabilities in cells B14 and B15. Presumably, if the test makes fewer false positives and false negatives, testing might be a more attractive alternative. We tried this, keeping the benefits and costs the same as those in Figure 7.29 but changing the error probabilities. Even when each error probability was decreased to 0.01, however, the no-testing alternative was still optimal—by a fairly wide margin.

In summary, based on a number of reasonable assumptions and parameter settings, this example has shown that it is difficult to make a case for mandatory drug testing. ∎

---

[7]The university in the Feinstein (1990) study came to the same conclusion.

The Value of Information

The drug-testing decision problem represents a typical multistage decision problem. We first decide whether to obtain some information that could be useful—the results of a drug test. If we decide not to obtain the information, we make a decision right away (bar the athlete or don't), based on prior probabilities. If we do decide to obtain the information, then we first observe the information and *then* make the final decision, based on posterior probabilities.

The questions we ask now are: How much is the information worth, and if it costs a given amount, should we purchase it? Presumably, information that will help us make our ultimate decision should be worth something, but it might not be clear how much the information is worth. In addition, even if the information is worth something, it might not be worth as much as its actual price. Fortunately, the answers to our questions are embedded in the decision tree itself.

We will find the values of two types of information: sample information and perfect information. **Sample information** is the information from the experiment itself. For example, it is the information from the (less than perfect) drug test. **Perfect information**, on the other hand, is information from a perfect test—that is, a test that will tell us with certainty which ultimate outcome will occur. In the drug example, this would correspond to a test that never makes mistakes. Admittedly, perfect information is almost never available at any price, but finding its value is still useful because it provides an upper bound on the value of *any* information. For example, if perfect information is valued at $2000, then *no* information can possibly be worth more than $2000.

We will find the **expected value of sample information**, or **EVSI**, and the **expected values of perfect information**, or **EVPI**. They are defined as follows:

The **EVSI** is the most we would be willing to pay for the sample information.

Formula for EVSI

EVSI = EMV with (free) sample information − EMV without information   (7.4)

The **EVPI** is the most we would be willing to pay for the perfect information.

Formula for EVPI

EVPI = EMV with (free) perfect information − EMV without information   (7.5)

Information that has no effect on the ultimate decision is worthless.

We first make one important general point about the value of information. Suppose we have an ultimate decision to make. Before making this decision, we obtain information, supposedly to help us make the ultimate decision. But suppose we make the *same* ultimate decision, regardless of the information we obtain—the same decision we would have made in the absence of information. Can you guess the value of this information? It is zero! The information cannot be worth anything if it never leads to a different decision than we would have made without the information. The moral is that if you plan to pay something for information, you are wasting your money unless you use this information to influence your decision making.

We will see how the value of information can be evaluated in the following typical multistage decision problem.

EXAMPLE | 7.4 MARKETING A NEW PRODUCT AT ACME

The Acme Company is trying to decide whether to market a new product. As in many new-product situations, there is considerable uncertainty about whether the new product will eventually "catch on." Acme believes that it might be wise to introduce the product in a regional test market before introducing it nationally. Therefore, the company's first decision is whether to conduct the test market.

Acme estimates that the net cost of the test market is $100,000. We assume this is mostly fixed costs, so that the same cost is incurred regardless of the test market results. If Acme decides to conduct the test market, it must then wait for the results. Based on the results of the test market, it can then decide whether to market the product nationally, in which case it will incur a fixed cost of $7 million. On the other hand, if the original decision is *not* to run a test market, then the final decision—whether to market the product nationally—can be made without further delay. Acme's unit margin, the difference between its selling price and its unit variable cost, is $18. We assume this is relevant only for the national market.

Acme classifies the results in either the test market or the national market as great, fair, or awful. Each of these results in the national market is accompanied by a forecast of total units sold. These sales volumes (in 1000s of units) are 600 (great), 300 (fair), and 90 (awful). In the absence of any test market information, Acme estimates that probabilities of the three national market outcomes are 0.45, 0.35, and 0.20, respectively.

In addition, Acme has the following historical data from products that were introduced into both test markets and national markets.

- Of the products that eventually did great in the national market, 64% did great in the test market, 26% did fair in the test market, and 10% did awful in the test market.

- Of the products that eventually did fair in the national market, 18% did great in the test market, 57% did fair in the test market, and 25% did awful in the test market.

- Of the products that eventually did awful in the national market, 9% did great in the test market, 48% did fair in the test market, and 43% did awful in the test market.[8]

The company wants to use a decision tree approach to find the best strategy. It also wants to find the expected value of the information provided by the test market.

Objective To develop a decision tree to find the best strategy for Acme, to perform a sensitivity analysis on the results, and to find EVSI and EVPI.

WHERE DO THE NUMBERS COME FROM?

The fixed costs of the test market and the national market are probably accurate estimates, based on planned advertising and overhead expenses. The unit margin is just the difference between the anticipated selling price and the known unit cost of the product. The sales volume estimates are clearly an approximation to reality because the sales from any new product would form a continuum of possible values. Here, the company has "discretized" the problem into three possible outcomes for the national market, and it has estimated the sales for each of these outcomes. As for the probabilities of national market results given test market results, these are probably based on results from previous products that went through test markets and then national markets.

---

[8]You can question why the company ever marketed products nationally after awful test market results, but we will assume that, for whatever reason, the company made a few such decisions—and that a few even turned out to be winners.

This is clearly an approximation of the real problem. In the real problem there would be a continuum of possible outcomes, not just three.

Solution

We begin by discussing the three basic elements of this decision problem: the possible strategies, the possible outcomes and their probabilities, and the value model. The possible strategies are clear. Acme must first decide whether to run a test market. Then it must decide whether to introduce the product nationally. However, it is important to realize that if Acme decides to run a test market, it can base the national market decision on the results of the test market. In this case its final strategy will be a **contingency plan**, where it conducts the test market, then introduces the product nationally if it receives sufficiently positive test market results and abandons the product if it receives sufficiently negative test market results. The optimal strategies from many multistage decision problems involve similar contingency plans.

> In a **contingency plan**, later decisions can depend on earlier decisions and information received.

Bayes' rule is required whenever the probabilities in the statement of the problem are in the "wrong order" for what we need in the tree.

Regarding the uncertain outcomes and their probabilities, we note that the given prior probabilities of national market results in the absence of test market results will be needed in one part of the tree: where Acme decides not to run a test market. However, the historical percentages we quoted are really likelihoods of test market results, given national market results. For example, one of these is $P(\text{Great test market} \mid \text{Great national market}) = 0.64$. Such probabilities are the opposite of what we need in the tree. This is because the event to the right of the given sign, "great national market," occurs in time *after* the event to the left of the given sign, "great test market." This is a sure sign that Bayes' rule is required.

The required posterior probabilities of national market results, given test market results, are calculated directly from Bayes' rule, equation (7.1). For example, if NG, NF, and NA represent great, fair, and awful national market results, respectively, and if TG, TF, and TA represent similar events for the test market, than one typical example of a posterior probability calculation is

$$P(NG|TF) = \frac{P(TF|NG)P(NG)}{P(TF|NG)P(NG) + P(TF|NF)P(NF) + P(TF|NA)P(NA)}$$

$$= \frac{0.26(0.45)}{0.26(0.45) + 0.57(0.35) + 0.48(0.20)} = \frac{0.117}{0.4125} = 0.2836$$

This is a reasonable result. In the absence of test market information, we believe the probability of a great national market is 0.45. However, after a test market with only fair results, we revise the probability of a great national market down to 0.2836. The other posterior probabilities are calculated similarly. In addition, the denominator in this calculation, 0.4125, is the unconditional probability of a fair test market. We will need such test market probabilities in the tree.

Finally, the monetary values in the tree are straightforward. There are fixed costs of test marketing or marketing nationally, which are incurred as soon as these "go ahead" decisions are made. From that point, if we market nationally, we observe the sales volumes and multiply them by the unit margin to obtain the selling profits.

Implementing Bayes' Rule

The inputs and Bayes' rule calculations are shown in Figure 7.31. (See file **Acme Marketing Decisions.xlsx**.) We perform the Bayes' rule calculations exactly as in the drug example. To calculate the unconditional probabilities for test market results, the denominators for Bayes' rule from equation (7.2), enter the formula

=SUMPRODUCT($B$17:$D$17,B21:D21)

in cell G16 and copy it down to cell G18. To calculate the posterior probabilities from equation (7.1), enter the formula

=B$17*B21/$G16

in cell G22 and copy it to the range G22:I24.

Figure 7.31 Inputs and Bayes' Rule Calculations for Acme Marketing Example

	A	B	C	D	E	F	G	H	I	J	K	L	M	N
1	Acme marketing decisions													
2														
3	Inputs													
4	Fixed costs ($1000s)													
5	Test market	100												
6	National market	7000												
7														
8	Unit margin (either market)	$18												
9														
10	Possible quantities sold (1000s of units) in national market													
11	Great	600												
12	Fair	300												
13	Awful	90												
14							Bayes' rule calculations							
15	Prior probabilities of national market results					Unconditional probabilities of test mkt results (denominators of Bayes' rule)							
16		Great	Fair	Awful		Great	0.3690							
17		0.45	0.35	0.20		Fair	0.4125							
18						Awful	0.2185							
19	Likelihoods of test market results (along side), given national market results (along top) from historical data													
20		Great	Fair	Awful		Posterior probabilities of national mkt results (along top), given test mkt results (along side)							
21	Great	0.64	0.18	0.09			Great	Fair	Awful				
22	Fair	0.26	0.57	0.48		Great	0.7805	0.1707	0.0488				
23	Awful	0.10	0.25	0.43		Fair	0.2836	0.4836	0.2327				
24						Awful	0.2059	0.4005	0.3936				

DEVELOPING THE DECISION TREE MODEL

The tree is now straightforward to build and label, as shown in Figure 7.32. Note that the fixed costs of test marketing and marketing nationally appear on the decision branches where they occur in time, so that only the selling profits need to be placed on the probability branches. For example, the formula for the selling profit in cell D33 is

=B8*B11.

Pay particular attention to the probabilities on the branches. The top group are the prior probabilities from the range B17:D17. In the bottom group, the probabilities on the left are unconditional probabilities of test market results from the range G16:G18, and those on the right are posterior probabilities of national market results from the range G22:I24. Again, this corresponds to the standard decision tree convention, where all probabilities on the tree are conditioned on any events that have occurred to the left of them.

Discussion of the Solution

To interpret this tree, note that each value just below each node name is an EMV. (These are colored red or green in Excel.) For example, the 796.76 in cell B41 is the EMV for the entire decision problem. It means that Acme's best EMV from acting optimally is $796,760. As another example, the 74 in cell D35 means that if Acme ever gets to that point—there is no test market and the product is marketed nationally—then the EMV is $74,000. Actually, this is the expected selling profit minus the $7 million fixed cost, so the expected selling profit, given that no information from a test market has been obtained, is $7,074,000.

Figure 7.32   Decision Tree for Acme Marketing Example

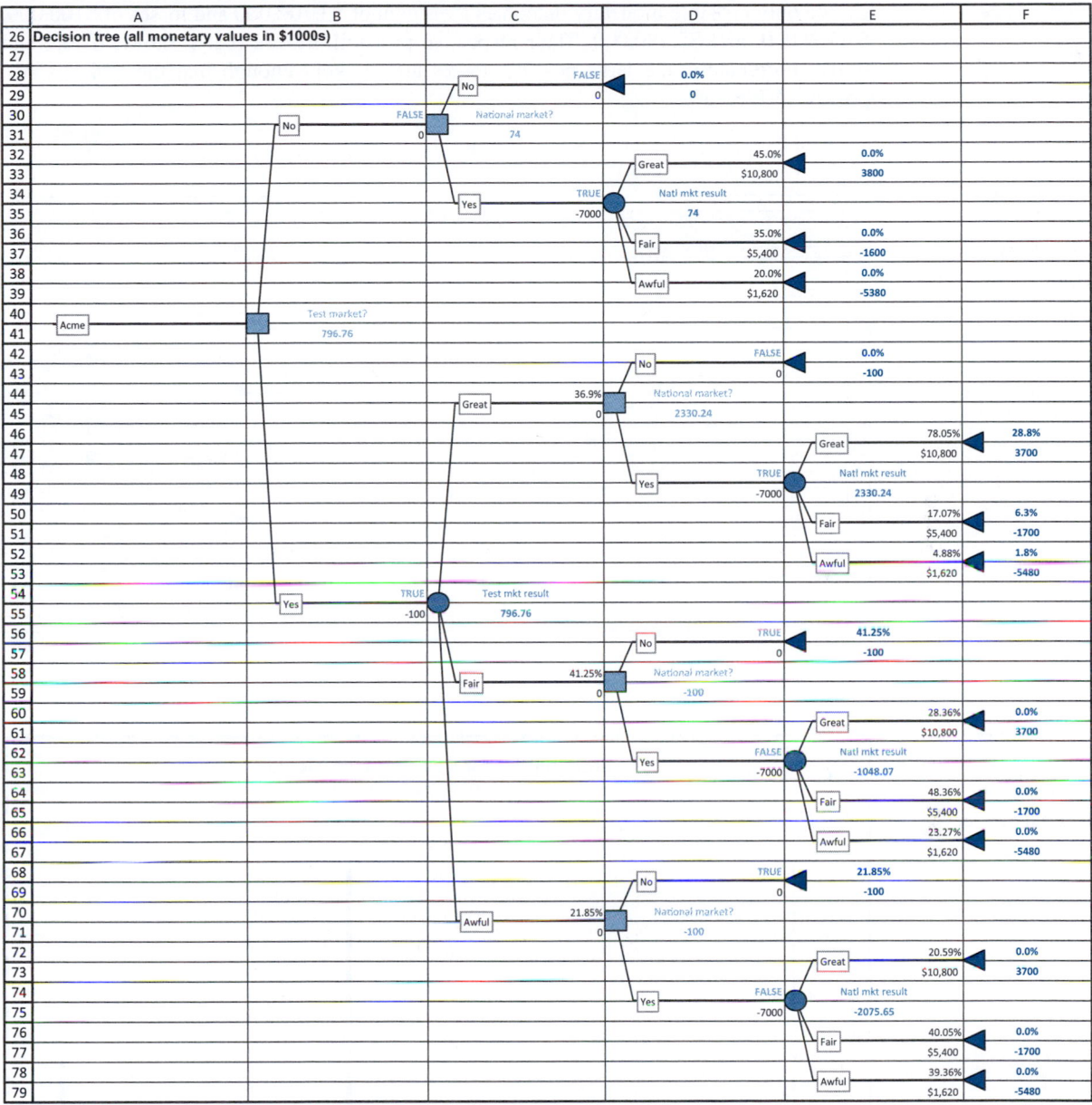

We can also see Acme's optimal strategy by following the TRUE branches from left to right. Acme should first run a test market. If the test market result is great, then the product should be marketed nationally. However, if the test market result is fair or awful, the product should be abandoned. In these cases the prospects from a national market look bleak, so Acme should cut its losses. (And there *are* losses. In these latter two cases, Acme has already spent $100,000 on the test market and has nothing to show for it.)

Once we have done the work to build the tree, we can reap the benefits of PrecisionTree's tools. For example, its policy suggestion and risk profile outputs are given in Figures 7.33 and 7.34. The policy suggestion shows only the part of the tree corresponding to the optimal strategy. Note that there are two values at each end node. The bottom number is the combined monetary value if we proceed along this sequence of branches, and the top number is the probability of this sequence of branches. This information leads directly to probability distribution in the risk profile. For this optimal strategy, the only possible monetary outcomes are a gain of $3,700,000 and losses of $100,000, $1,700,000, and $5,480,000. Their respective probabilities are 0.288, 0.631, 0.063, and 0.018. Fortunately, the large possible losses are unlikely enough that the EMV is still positive, $796,760.

Figure 7.33

Policy Suggestion (Optimal Strategy Branches)

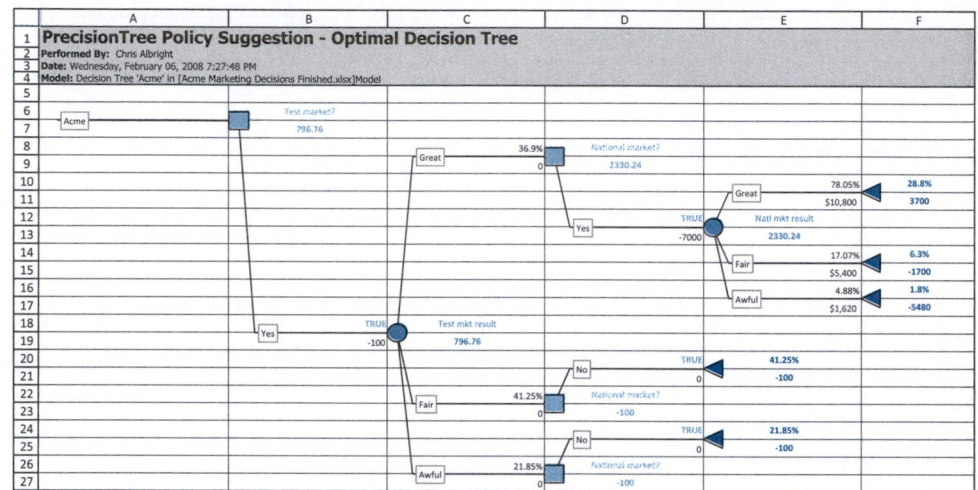

Figure 7.34

Risk Profile of Optimal Strategy

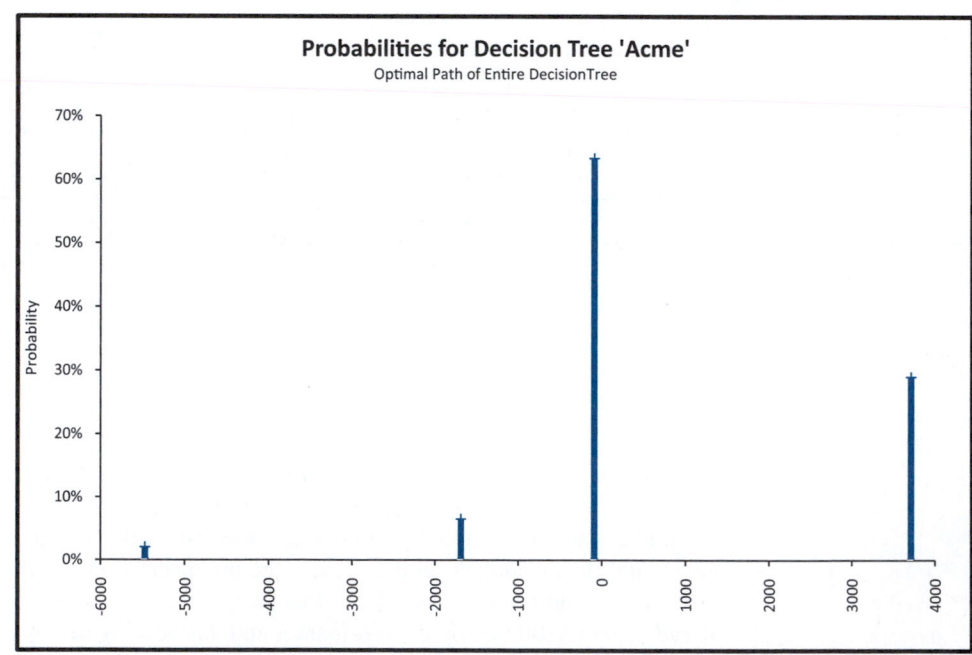

You might argue that the large potential losses and the slightly higher than 70% chance of *some* loss should persuade Acme to abandon the product right away—without a test market. However, this is what "playing the averages" with EMV is all about. Because the EMV of this optimal strategy is greater than 0, the EMV from abandoning the product right away, Acme should go ahead with this optimal strategy if the company is indeed an EMV maximizer. In Section 7.6 we see how this reasoning could change if Acme is a risk-averse decision maker—as it might be with multimillion dollar losses looming in the future!

Sensitivity Analysis

There are several sensitivity analyses we can perform on this model. We investigate how things change when the unit margin, currently $18, varies from $8 to $28. This could change our decision about whether to run a test market or to market nationally.

Sensitivity analysis is often important for the insights it provides. It makes us ask, "Why do these results occur?"

We first analyze the overall EMV in cell B41, setting up the sensitivity dialog box as in Figure 7.35. The resulting chart is shown in Figure 7.36. The chart indicates that for small unit margins, it is better *not* to run a test market. The top line, at value 0, corresponds to abandoning the product altogether, whereas the bottom line, at value −100, corresponds to running a test market and then abandoning the product regardless of the results. Similarly, for large unit margins, it is also best not to run a test market. Again, the top line is 100 above the bottom line. However, the reasoning now is different. For large unit margins, the company should market nationally *regardless* of test market results, so there is no reason to spend money on a test market. Finally, for intermediate unit margins, as in our original model, the chart shows that it is best to test market. We hope you agree that this one single chart provides a lot of information and insight!

Figure 7.35

Dialog Box for
Sensitivity Analysis

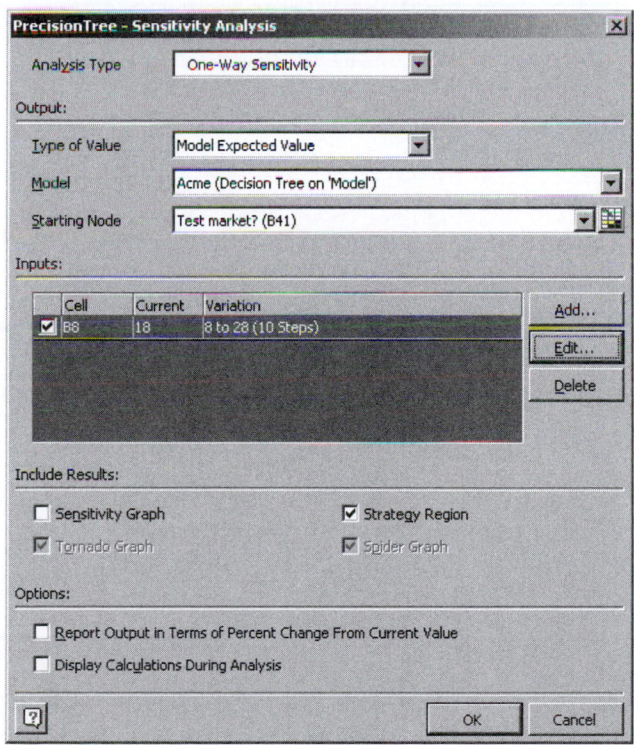

By changing the cell to analyze in Figure 7.35, we can gain additional insight. For example, if no test market is available, the EMV for deciding nationally right away, in cell C31, is relevant. The resulting chart is in Figure 7.37. As we see, it is a contest between getting zero profit from abandoning the product and getting a linearly increasing profit from marketing nationally. The breakpoint appears to be slightly below $18. If the unit margin is above this value, Acme should market nationally; otherwise, it should abandon the product.

Figure 7.36

Sensitivity Analysis
on Overall Profit

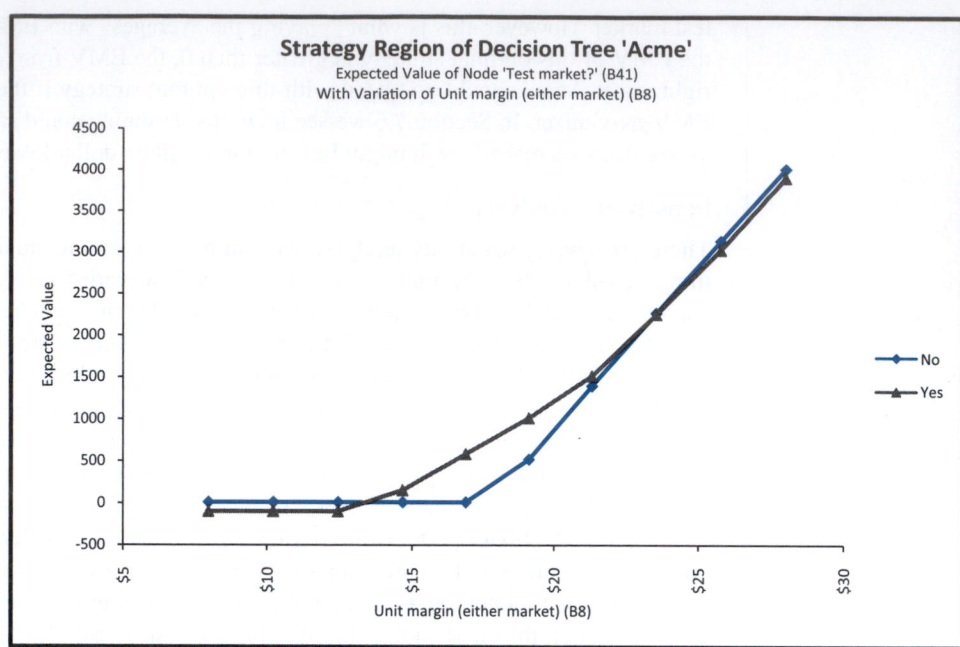

Figure 7.37

Sensitivity Analysis
for Deciding
Nationally Right
Away

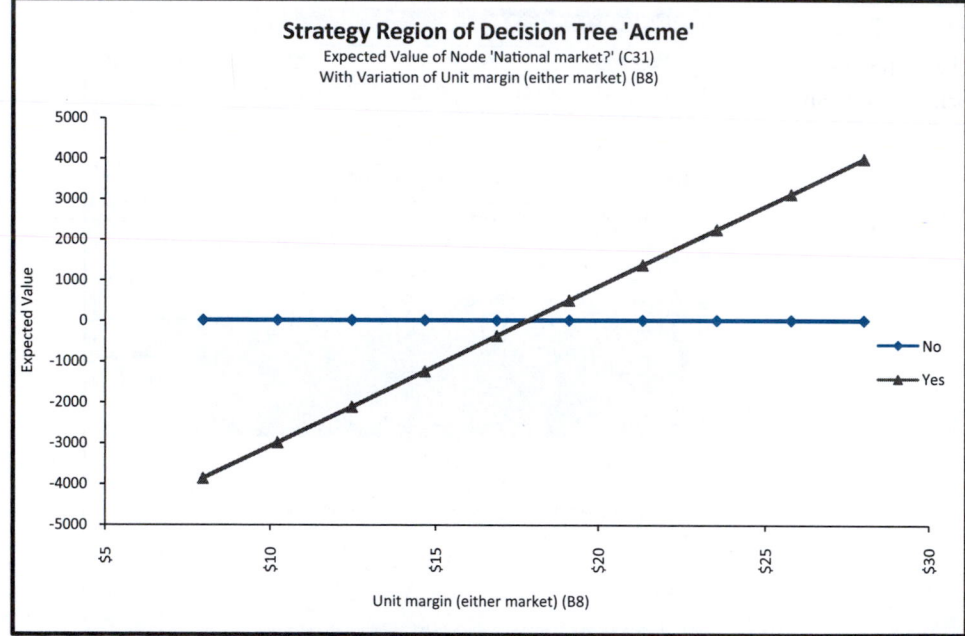

We can also choose to analyze any of the EMVs in cells D45, D59, or D71. Each of these is relevant in the case where we have run the test market, we have observed the test market results, and we are about to decide whether to market nationally. For example, if we choose D71 as the cell to analyze, we obtain the chart in Figure 7.38. It indicates that there are indeed situations—where the unit margin is about $26 or more—when the company should market nationally, even though the test market is awful. In contrast, the chart in Figure 7.39, where we analyze cell D45, indicates the opposite behavior. It shows that if the unit margin is low enough—about $13.50 or less—the company should abandon the product nationally, even though the test market results are great. These are very useful insights.

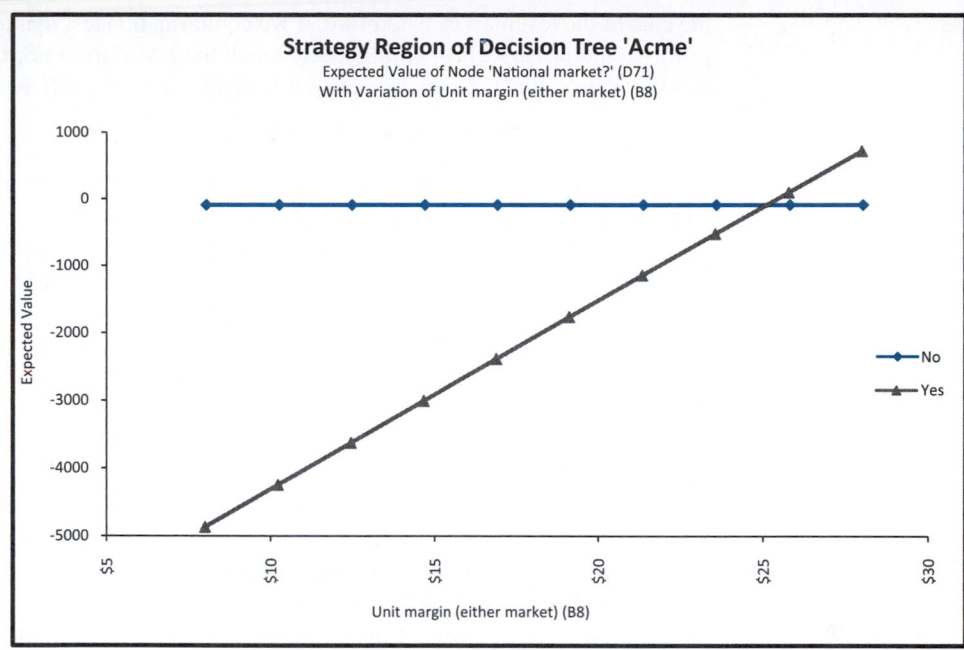

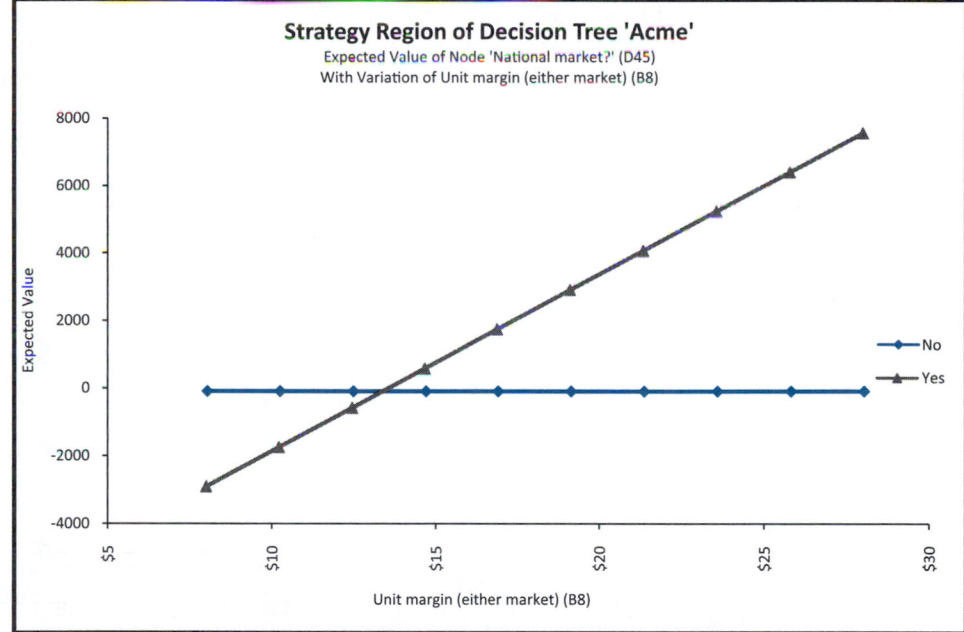

Expected Value of Sample Information

The role of the test market in this example is to provide information in the form of more accurate probabilities of national market results. Information usually costs something, as it does in Acme's problem. Currently, the fixed cost of the test market is $100,000, which is evidently not too much to pay because Acme's best strategy is to run the test market. However, we might ask how much this test market is really worth. This is the expected value of sample information, or EVSI, and it is simple to obtain from the tree. From Figure 7.32, we see that the EMV from test marketing is $796,760—$100,000 of which is the cost of the test market. Therefore, if we could run this test market for free, the expected profit would be $896,760. On the other hand, the EMV from not running a test market is $74,000 (see cell C31 in the tree). From equation (7.4), the difference is EVSI:

$$\text{EVSI} = \$896,760 - \$74,000 = \$822,760$$

You can check that if you put any value less than 822.76 in cell B5, the test market fixed cost cell, the decision to test market will continue to be best.

Intuitively, this test market is worth something because it changes the optimal decision. With no test market information, the best decision is to market nationally. (See the top part of the tree in Figure 7.32.) However, with the test market information, the ultimate decision depends on the test market results. Specifically, Acme should market nationally only if the test market result is great. This is what makes information worth something—its outcome affects the optimal decision.

Expected Value of Perfect Information

We did a lot of work to find EVSI. We had to assess various conditional probabilities, use Bayes' rule, and then build a fairly complex decision tree. In general, Acme might have many sources of information it could obtain that would help it make its national decision; the test market we analyzed is just one of them. The question, then, is how much such information *could* be worth. This is answered by EVPI, the expected value of perfect information. It provides an upper bound on how much *any* information could be worth, and it is relatively easy to calculate.

Our perfect information envelope is obviously a fiction, but it helps to explain how perfect information works.

Imagine that Acme could purchase an envelope that has the true national market result—great, fair, or awful—written inside. Once opened, this envelope would remove all uncertainty, and Acme could make the correct decision. EVPI is what this envelope is worth. To calculate it, we build the tree in Figure 7.40. The key here is that the nodes are reversed in time. We first open the envelope to discover what is inside. This corresponds to the probability node. Then we make the "easy" decision. Given the cost parameters, it is easy to see that Acme should market nationally only if the contents of the envelope reveal that the national market will be great. Otherwise, Acme should abandon the product right away.

Figure 7.40

Decision Tree for Evaluating EVPI

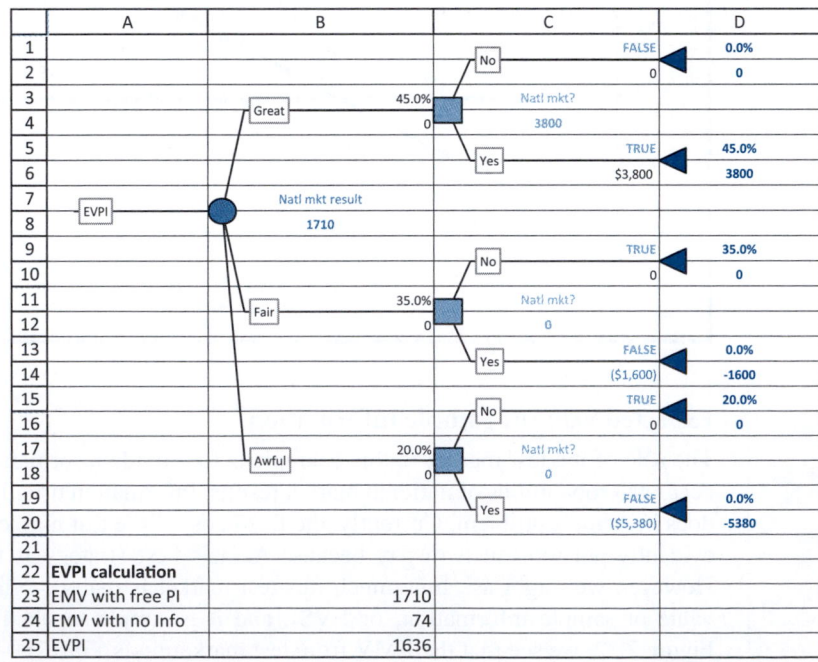

The EVPI calculation is now straightforward. If we get the envelope (perfect information) for free, the tree in Figure 7.40 indicates that the EMV is $1,710,000. If we have no information, the EMV is, as before, $74,000. Therefore, from equation (7.5),

$$\text{EVPI} = \$1,710,000 - \$74,000 = \$1,636,000$$

No sample information, test market or otherwise, could possibly be worth more than this. So if some hotshot market analyst offers to provide "extremely reliable" market information to Acme for, say, $1.8 million, Acme knows this information cannot be worth the cost. ∎

PROBLEMS

Level A

22. In deciding whether to perform mandatory drug testing, we claimed that it is difficult to justify such testing under reasonable conditions. Check this yourself in the following questions.
    a. Drug testing ought to be more attractive if the test is more reliable. Keeping the costs the same as in the example, use PrecisionTree's two-way sensitivity tool to see whether the optimal decision (test or not test) changes as the probability of a false positive and the probability of a false negative both change. You can let them vary through some reasonable ranges. How do you explain the results?
    b. Repeat part a, but first double the two monetary values that make the test more attractive: the benefit of identifying a user and the cost of not identifying a user. How do your results differ from those in part a?
    c. In this part, keep the probabilities of false positives and false negatives the same, but let the benefits and costs vary. Specifically, let the benefit of identifying a user and the cost of not identifying a user be of the form 25a and 20a, where a is some factor that you will vary. Similarly, let the cost of barring a nonuser and the cost of violating privacy be of the form 50b and 2b. The cost of the test is still 1. (The idea is that large values of a and/or small values of b will make the testing more attractive.) Use PrecisionTree's two-way sensitivity tool to see whether the optimal decision (test or not test) changes for a reasonable range of values of a and b. Discuss your results.

23. In the drug testing decision, find and interpret EVSI and EVPI. Here, "sample" information refers to the information from the imperfect drug test, whereas "perfect" information refers to completely reliable information on whether the athlete uses drugs.

24. Explain in general why EVSI is independent of the actual cost of the information. For example, in the

Acme problem EVSI is the same regardless of whether the actual cost of the test market is $100,000, $200,000, or any other value. Then explain how EVSI, together with the actual cost of the information, leads to the decision about whether to purchase the information.

25. Following up on the previous problem, the "expected net gain from information" is defined as the expected amount we gain by having access to the information, at its given cost, as opposed to not having access to the information. Explain how you would calculate this in general. What is its value for the Acme problem?

26. Prior probabilities are often educated guesses at best, so it is worth performing a sensitivity analysis on their values. However, we must make sure that we vary them so that all probabilities are nonnegative and sum to 1. For the Acme problem, perform the following sensitivity analyses on the three prior probabilities and comment on the results.
    a. Vary the probability of great in a one-way sensitivity analysis from 0 to 0.6 in increments of 0.1. Do this in such a way that the probabilities of the two other outcomes, fair and awful, stay in the same ratio as they are currently, 7 to 4.
    b. Vary the probabilities of great and fair independently in a two-way sensitivity analysis. You can choose the ranges over which these vary, but you must ensure that the three prior probabilities continue to be nonnegative and sum to 1. (For example, you couldn't choose ranges where the probabilities of great and fair could be 0.6 and 0.5.)

27. In the Acme problem, perform a sensitivity analysis on the quantity sold from a great national market (the value in cell B11). Let this value vary over a range of values *greater than* the current value of 600, so that a great national market is even more attractive than before. Does this ever change the optimal strategy? In what way?

28. Using trial and error on the prior probabilities in the Acme problem, find values of them that make EVSI equal to 0. These are values where Acme will make the same decision, regardless of the test market results it observes.

Level B

29. We related EVPI to the value of an envelope that contains the true ultimate outcome. We can extend this concept to "less than perfect" information. For example, in the Acme problem suppose that we could purchase information that would tell us, with certainty, that one of the following two outcomes will occur: (1) the national market will be great, or (2) the national market will not be great. Notice that outcome (2) doesn't tell us whether the national market will be fair or awful; it just tells us that it won't be great. How much should Acme be willing to pay for such information?

30. The concept behind EVPI is that we purchase perfect information (the envelope), we then open the envelope to see which outcome occurs, and then we make an easy decision. We do *not*, however, get to choose what information the envelope contains. Sometimes a company can pay, not to obtain information, but to influence the outcome. Consider the following version of the Acme problem. There is no possibility of a test market, so that Acme must decide right away whether to market nationally. However, suppose Acme can pay to change the probabilities of the national market outcomes from their current values, 0.45, 0.35, and 0.20, to the new values p, $(7/11)(1 - p)$, and $(4/11)(1 - p)$, for some p. (In this way, the probabilities of fair and awful stay in the same ratio as before, 7 to 4, but by making p large, the probability of great increases.)

    a. How much should Acme be willing to pay for the change if $p = 0.6$? If $p = 0.8$? If $p = 0.95$?

    b. Are these types of changes realistic? Answer by speculating on the types of actions Acme might be able to take to make the probability of a great national market higher. Do you think such actions would cost more or less than what Acme should be willing to pay for them (from part **a**)?

7.6 INCORPORATING ATTITUDES TOWARD RISK

Rational decision makers are sometimes willing to violate the EMV maximization criterion when large amounts of money are at stake. These decision makers are willing to sacrifice some EMV to reduce risk. Are you ever willing to do so personally? Consider the following scenarios.

■ You have a chance to enter a lottery where you will win $100,000 with probability 0.1 or win nothing with probability 0.9. Alternatively, you can receive $5000 for certain. How many of you—truthfully—would take the certain $5000, even though the EMV of the lottery is $10,000? Or change the $100,000 to $1,000,000 and the $5000 to $50,000 and ask yourself whether you'd prefer the sure $50,000!

■ You can either buy collision insurance on your expensive new car or not buy it, where the insurance costs a certain premium and carries some deductible provision. If you decide to pay the premium, then you are essentially paying a certain amount to avoid a gamble: the possibility of wrecking your car and not having it insured. You can be sure that the premium is greater than the expected cost of damage; otherwise, the insurance company would not stay in business. Therefore, from an EMV standpoint you should not purchase the insurance. But how many of you drive without this type of insurance?

These examples, the second of which is certainly realistic, illustrate situations where rational people do not behave as EMV maximizers. Then how do they act? This question has been studied extensively by many researchers, both mathematically and behaviorally. Although the answer is still not agreed upon universally, most researchers agree that if certain basic behavioral assumptions hold, people are **expected utility** maximizers—that is, they choose the alternative with the largest expected utility. Although we do not go deeply into the subject of expected utility maximization, the discussion in this section acquaints you with the main ideas.

Utility Functions

We begin by discussing an individual's **utility function**. This is a mathematical function that transforms monetary values—payoffs and costs—into **utility values**. Essentially, an individual's utility function specifies the individual's preferences for various monetary payoffs and costs and, in doing so, it automatically encodes the individual's attitudes toward risk. Most individuals are **risk averse**, which means intuitively that they are willing to sacrifice some EMV to avoid risky gambles. In terms of the utility function, this means that every extra dollar of payoff is worth slightly less to the individual than the previous dollar, and every extra dollar of cost is considered slightly more costly (in terms of utility) than the previous dollar. The resulting utility functions are shaped as shown in Figure 7.41. Mathematically, these functions are said to be **increasing** and **concave**. The increasing part means that they go uphill—everyone prefers more money to less money. The concave part means that they increase at a decreasing rate. This is the risk-averse behavior.

Figure 7.41

Risk-Averse Utility Function

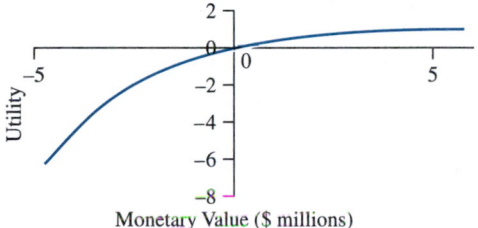

There are two aspects of implementing utility maximization in a real decision analysis. First, we must obtain an individual's (or company's) utility function. This is a time-consuming task that typically involves many trade-offs. It is usually carried out by experts in the field, and we do not discuss the details of the process here. Second, we must use the resulting utility function to find the best decision. This second step is relatively straightforward. We simply substitute utility values for monetary values in the decision tree and then fold back as usual. That is, we calculate expected *utilities* at probability branches and take maximums (of expected utilities) at decision branches. We will look at a numerical example later in this section.

Exponential Utility

As we have indicated, utility assessment is tedious. Even in the best of circumstances, when a trained consultant attempts to assess the utility function of a single person, the process requires the person to make a series of choices between hypothetical alternatives involving uncertain outcomes. Unless the person has some training in probability, these choices will probably be difficult to understand, let alone make, and it is unlikely that the person will answer *consistently* as the questioning proceeds. The process is even more difficult when a company's utility function is being assessed. Because the company executives involved typically have different attitudes toward risk, it is difficult for these people to reach a consensus on a common utility function.

For these reasons classes of "ready-made" utility functions have been developed. One important class is called **exponential utility** and has been used in many financial investment analyses. An exponential utility function has only one adjustable numerical parameter, called the **risk tolerance**, and there are straightforward ways to discover the most appropriate value of this parameter for a particular individual or company. So the advantage of using an exponential utility function is that it is relatively easy to assess. The drawback is that exponential utility functions do not capture all types of attitudes toward risk. Nevertheless, their ease of use has made them popular.

An exponential utility function has the following form:

Exponential utility

$$U(x) = 1 - e^{-x/R} \qquad (7.6)$$

Here x is a monetary value (a payoff if positive, a cost if negative), $U(x)$ is the utility of this value, and $R > 0$ is the risk tolerance. As the name suggests, the risk tolerance measures how much risk the decision maker will accept. The larger the value of R, the less risk averse the decision maker is. That is, a person with a large value of R is more willing to take risks than a person with a small value of R.

In terms of exponential utility, the **risk tolerance** is a single number that specifies an individual's aversion to risk. The higher the risk tolerance, the less risk averse the individual is.

To assess a person's (or company's) exponential utility function, we need only to assess the value of R. There are a couple of tips for doing this. First, it has been shown that the risk tolerance is approximately equal to that dollar amount R such that the decision maker is indifferent between the following two options:

- Option 1: Obtain no payoff at all.

- Option 2: Obtain a payoff of R dollars or a loss of $R/2$ dollars, depending on the flip of a fair coin.

For example, if you are indifferent between a bet where you win $1000 or lose $500, with probability 0.5 each, and not betting at all, then your R is approximately $1000. From this criterion it certainly makes intuitive sense that a wealthier person (or company) ought to have a larger value of R. This has been found in practice.

Finding the appropriate risk tolerance value for any company or individual is not necessarily easy, but it is easier than assessing an entire utility function from scratch.

A second tip for finding R is based on empirical evidence found by Ronald Howard, a prominent decision analyst. Through his consulting experience with large companies, he discovered tentative relationships between risk tolerance and several financial variables: net sales, net income, and equity. [See Howard (1988).] Specifically, he found that R was approximately 6.4% of net sales, 124% of net income, and 15.7% of equity for the companies he studied. For example, according to this prescription, a company with net sales of $30 million should have a risk tolerance of approximately $1.92 million. Howard admits that these percentages are only guidelines. However, they do indicate that larger and more profitable companies tend to have larger values of R, which means that they are more willing to take risks involving large dollar amounts.

We illustrate the use of the expected utility criterion, and exponential utility in particular, with the following example.

EXAMPLE | **7.5 DECIDING WHETHER TO ENTER RISKY VENTURES AT VENTURE LIMITED**

Venture Limited is a company with net sales of $30 million. The company currently must decide whether to enter one of two risky ventures or invest in a sure thing. The gain from the latter is a sure $125,000. The possible outcomes for the less risky venture are a $0.5 million loss, a $0.1 million gain, and a $1 million gain. The probabilities of these outcomes are 0.25, 0.50, and 0.25, respectively. The possible outcomes of the more risky venture are a $1 million loss, a $1 million gain, and a $3 million gain. The probabilities of these outcomes are 0.35, 0.60, and 0.05, respectively. If Venture Limited must decide on exactly one of these alternatives, what should it do?

Objective To see how the company's risk averseness, determined by its risk tolerance in an exponential utility function, affects its decision.

WHERE DO THE NUMBERS COME FROM?

The outcomes for each of the risky alternatives probably form a continuum of possible values. However, as in example 7.4, the company has "discretized" these into a few possibilities, and it has made intelligent estimates of the monetary consequences and probabilities of these discrete possibilities.

Solution

Don't worry about the actual utility values (for example, whether they are positive or negative). Only the relative magnitudes matter in terms of decision making.

We assume that Venture Limited has an exponential utility function. Also, based on Howard's guidelines, we assume that the company's risk tolerance is 6.4% of its net sales, or $1.92 million. (We will perform a sensitivity analysis on this parameter later on.) We can substitute into equation (7.6) to find the utility of any monetary outcome. For example, the gain from the riskless alternative (in $1000s) is 125, and its utility is

$$U(125) = 1 - e^{-125/1920} = 1 - 0.9370 = 0.0630$$

As another example, the utility of a $1 million loss is

$$U(-1000) = 1 - e^{-(-1000)/1920} = 1 - 1.6834 = -0.6834$$

These are the values we use (instead of monetary values) in the decision tree.

DEVELOPING THE DECISION TREE MODEL

Fortunately, PrecisionTree takes care of all the details. After we build a decision tree and label it (with monetary values) in the usual way, we click on the name of the tree (the box on the far left of the tree) to open the dialog box in shown in Figure 7.42. We then fill in the information under the Utility Function tab as shown in the figure. This says to use an exponential utility function with risk tolerance 1920, the value in cell B5.[9] (As indicated in the spreadsheet, we are measuring all monetary values in $1000s.) It also indicates that we want expected utilities (as opposed to EMVs) to appear in the decision tree.

The tree is built and labeled (with monetary values) exactly as before. PrecisionTree then takes care of calculating the expected utilities.

The completed tree for this example is shown in Figure 7.43. (See the file **Using Exponential Utility.xlsx**.) We build it in exactly the same way as usual and link probabilities and monetary values to its branches in the usual way. For example, there is a link in cell C22 to the monetary value in cell B12. However, the expected values shown in the tree (those shown in color on a computer screen) are expected *utilities*, and the optimal decision is the one with the largest expected utility. In this case the expected utilities for the riskless option, investing in the less risky venture, and investing in the more risky venture are 0.0630, 0.0525, and 0.0439, respectively. Therefore, the optimal decision is to take the riskless option.

[9]This is a definite improvement over the previous version of PrecisionTree. The "*R*" value is now linked to a cell, so that it is easy to perform sensitivity analysis on *R*.

Figure 7.42

Dialog Box for
Specifying the
Exponential Utility
Criterion

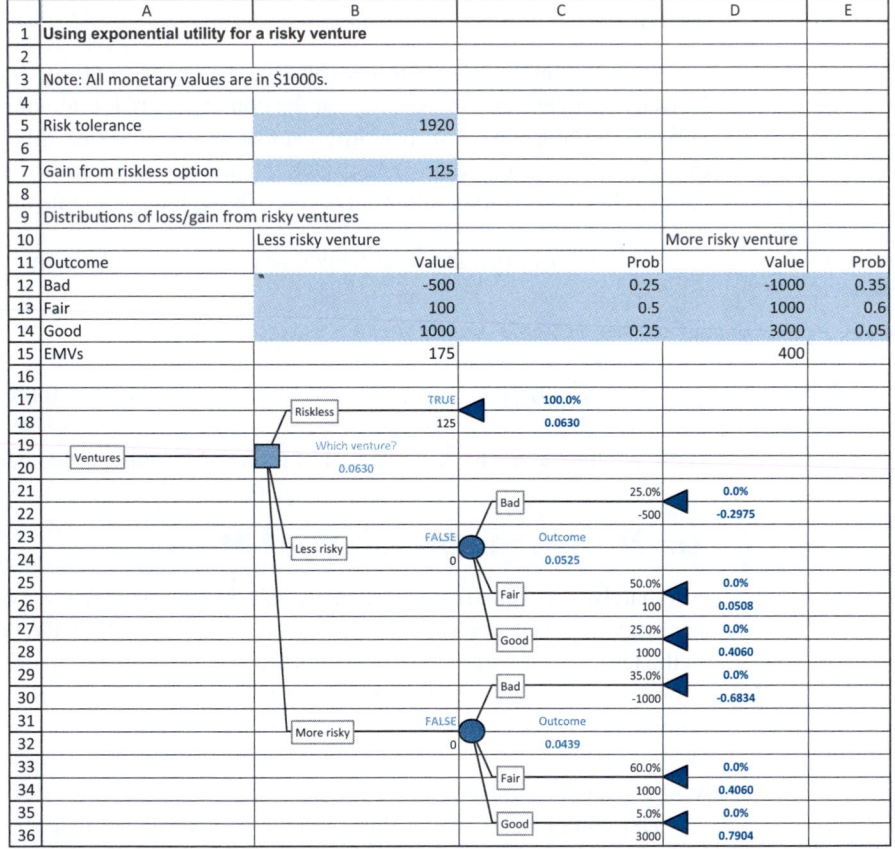

Figure 7.43

Decision Tree for
Risky Venture
Example

	A	B	C	D	E
1	**Using exponential utility for a risky venture**				
2					
3	Note: All monetary values are in $1000s.				
4					
5	Risk tolerance	1920			
6					
7	Gain from riskless option	125			
8					
9	Distributions of loss/gain from risky ventures				
10		Less risky venture		More risky venture	
11	Outcome	Value	Prob	Value	Prob
12	Bad	-500	0.25	-1000	0.35
13	Fair	100	0.5	1000	0.6
14	Good	1000	0.25	3000	0.05
15	EMVs	175		400	
16					
17		TRUE	100.0%		
18	Riskless	125	0.0630		
19	Ventures	Which venture?			
20		0.0630			
21			25.0%	0.0%	
22		Bad	-500	-0.2975	
23		FALSE	Outcome		
24	Less risky	0	0.0525		
25		Fair	50.0%	0.0%	
26			100	0.0508	
27		Good	25.0%	0.0%	
28			1000	0.4060	
29		Bad	35.0%	0.0%	
30			-1000	-0.6834	
31		FALSE	Outcome		
32	More risky	0	0.0439		
33		Fair	60.0%	0.0%	
34			1000	0.4060	
35		Good	5.0%	0.0%	
36			3000	0.7904	

Discussion of the Solution

*A risk-averse
decision maker
typically gives up
EMV to avoid
risk—when the
stakes are large
enough.*

As we see from the tree, the riskless option is best in terms of the expected utility criterion; it has the largest expected utility. However, note that the EMVs of the three decisions are $125,000, $175,000, and $400,000. (The latter two of these are calculated in row 15 as the usual "sumproduct" of monetary values and probabilities.) So from an EMV point of view, the more risky venture is definitely best. In fact, the ordering of the three alternatives using the EMV criterion is exactly the *opposite* of the ordering using expected utility. But Venture Limited is sufficiently risk averse, and the monetary values are sufficiently large, that the company is willing to sacrifice $275,000 of EMV to avoid risk.

Sensitivity Analysis

How sensitive is the optimal decision to the key parameter, the risk tolerance? We can answer this by changing the risk tolerance and watching how the decision tree changes. You can check that when the company becomes *more* risk tolerant, the more risky venture eventually becomes optimal. In fact, this occurs when the risk tolerance increases to approximately $2.210 million. In the other direction, of course, when the company becomes *less* risk tolerant, the riskless decision continues to be optimal. (The "middle" decision, the less risky alternative, is evidently not optimal for *any* value of the risk tolerance.) The bottom line is that the "optimal" decision depends entirely on the attitudes toward risk of Venture Limited's top management. ■

Is Expected Utility Maximization Used?

The previous discussion indicates that utility maximization is a fairly involved task. The question, then, is whether the effort is justified. Theoretically, expected utility maximization might be interesting to researchers, but is it really used in the business world? The answer appears to be: not very often. For example, one recent article on the practice of decision making [see Kirkwood (1992)] quotes Ronald Howard—the same person we quoted previously—as having found risk aversion to be of practical concern in only 5% to 10% of business decision analyses. This same article quotes the president of a Fortune 500 company as saying, "Most of the decisions we analyze are for a few million dollars. It is adequate to use expected value (EMV) for these."

PROBLEMS

Level A

31. For the risky venture example, create a line chart that includes three series—that is, three lines (or curves). Each line should show the expected utility of a particular decision for a sequence of possible risk tolerance values. (You'll have to create the data for the chart "manually," by changing the risk tolerance, recording the three expected utilities somewhere on the spreadsheet, changing the risk tolerance again, and so on.) This chart should make it clear when the more risky option becomes optimal and whether the less risky option is ever optimal.

32. In the risky venture example, the more risky alternative, in spite of its dominating EMV, is not preferred by a decision maker with risk tolerance $1.92 million. Now suppose everything stays the same except for the best monetary outcome of the more risky alternative (the value in cell D14). How much larger must this value be for the decision maker to prefer the more risky alternative? What is the corresponding EMV at that point?

33. In the risky venture example, suppose there is no riskless alternative; the only two possible decisions are the less risky venture and the more risky venture. Explore which of these is the preferred alternative for a range of risk tolerances. Can you find a "cutoff point" for the risk tolerance such that the less risky venture is preferred for risk tolerances below the cutoff and the more risky venture is preferred otherwise?

Level B

34. Do the absolute magnitudes of the monetary outcomes matter in the risky venture example? Consider the following two possibilities. In each case, multiply all monetary values in the example by a factor of A. (For example, double them if $A = 2$.) For each part, briefly explain your findings.

    a. Currently, an EMV-maximizer would choose the most risky venture. Would this continue to be the case for any factor A?

    b. Currently, an expected utility maximizer with risk tolerance $1.92 million prefers the riskless alternative. Would this continue to be the case for any factor A greater than 1? What about when A is less than 1? You can answer by using trial and error on A.

    c. Referring to the dialog box in Figure 7.42, there is a Display dropdown with three options: expected value (EMV), expected utility, and certainty equivalent. The latter is defined for any gamble as the sure monetary amount a risk-averse person would take as a trade for the risky gamble. For example, you can check that the certainty equivalent for the more risky alternative is 86.2017 (in thousands of dollars). Explain what this really means by calculating the utility of 86.2017 manually and comparing it to the *expected* utility from the more risky venture (as shown on the tree). How does this explain why the decision maker prefers the riskless alternative to the more risky venture?

7.7 CONCLUSION

In this chapter we have discussed methods that can be used in decision-making problems where uncertainty is a key element. Perhaps the most important skill you can gain from this chapter is the ability to approach decision problems with uncertainty in a systematic manner. This systematic approach requires you to list all possible decisions or strategies, list all possible uncertain outcomes, assess the probabilities of these outcomes (possibly with the aid of Bayes' rule), calculate all necessary monetary values, and finally do the necessary calculations to obtain the best decision. If large dollar amounts are at stake, you might also need to perform a utility analysis, where the decision maker's attitudes toward risk are taken into account. Once the basic analysis has been completed, using "best guesses" for the various parameters of the problem, you should perform a sensitivity analysis to see whether the best decision continues to be best within a range of problem parameters.

Summary of Key Terms

Term	Explanation	Excel	Page
Payoff (or cost) table	A table that lists the payoffs (or costs) for all combinations of decisions and uncertain outcomes		318
Maximin criterion	The pessimist's criterion; find the worst possible payoff for each decision, and choose the decision with the best of these		319
Maximax criterion	The optimist's criterion; find the best possible payoff for each decision, and choose the decision with the best of these		319
Expected monetary value (EMV)	The weighted average of the possible payoffs from a decision, weighted by their probabilities		319
EMV criterion	Choose the decision with the maximum EMV		319
Decision tree	A graphical device for illustrating all of the aspects of the decision problem and for finding the optimal decision (or decision strategy)		321
Folding-back procedure	Calculation method for decision tree; starting at the right, take EMVs at probability nodes, maximums of EMVs at decision nodes		323
Risk profile	Chart that represents the probability distribution of monetary outcomes for any decision		323
PrecisionTree add-in	Useful Excel add-in developed by Palisade for building and analyzing decision trees in Excel	Has its own ribbon	330

(continued)

Term	Explanation	Excel	Page
PrecisionTree strategy region chart	Useful for seeing how the optimal decision changes as selected inputs vary	Use PrecisionTree Sensitivity Analysis button	339
PrecisionTree tornado and spider charts	Useful for seeing which inputs affect a selected EMV the most	Use PrecisionTree Sensitivity Analysis button	339
Bayes' rule	Formula for updating probabilities as new information becomes available; prior probabilities are transformed into posterior probabilities		342
Expected value of sample information (EVSI)	The most the (imperfect) sample information (such as the results of a test market) would be worth		351
Expected value of perfect information (EVPI)	The most perfect information on some uncertain outcome would be worth; represents an upper bound on *any* EVSI		351
Contingency plan	A decision strategy where later decisions depend on earlier decisions and outcomes observed in the meantime		353
Expected utility criterion	Chooses the decision that maximizes the expected utility; typically sacrifices EMV to avoid risk when large monetary amounts are at stake		362
Utility function	A mathematical function that encodes an individual's (or company's) attitudes toward risk		363
Exponential utility function, risk tolerance	A popular class of utility functions, where only a single parameter, the risk tolerance, has to be specified		363

PROBLEMS

Level A

35. The SweetTooth Candy Company knows it will need 10 tons of sugar 6 months from now to implement its production plans. Jean Dobson, SweetTooth's purchasing manager, has essentially two options for acquiring the needed sugar. She can either buy the sugar at the going market price when she needs it, 6 months from now, or she can buy a futures contract now. The contract guarantees delivery of the sugar in 6 months but the cost of purchasing it will be based on today's market price. Assume that possible sugar futures contracts available for purchase are for 5 tons or 10 tons only. No futures contracts can be purchased or sold in the intervening months. Thus, SweetTooth's possible decisions are to (1) purchase a futures contract for 10 tons of sugar now, (2) purchase a futures contract for 5 tons of sugar now and purchase 5 tons of sugar in 6 months, or (3) purchase all 10 tons of needed sugar in 6 months. The price of sugar bought now for delivery in 6 months is $0.0851 per pound. The transaction costs for 5-ton and 10-ton futures contracts are $65 and $110, respectively. Finally, Ms. Dobson has assessed the probability distribution for the possible prices of sugar 6 months from now (in dollars per pound). The file **P07_35.xlsx** contains these possible prices and their corresponding probabilities.

a. Given that SweetTooth wants to acquire the needed sugar in the least costly way, formulate a cost table that specifies the cost (in dollars) associated with each possible decision and possible sugar price in the future.

b. Use PrecisionTree to identify the decision that minimizes SweetTooth's expected cost of meeting its sugar demand.

c. Perform a sensitivity analysis on the optimal decision and summarize your findings. In response to which model inputs is the expected cost value most sensitive?

36. Carlisle Tire and Rubber, Inc., is considering expanding production to meet potential increases in the demand for one of its tire products. Carlisle's alternatives are to construct a new plant, expand the existing plant, or do nothing in the short run. The market for this particular tire product may expand, remain stable, or contract. Carlisle's marketing department estimates the probabilities of these market outcomes as 0.25, 0.35, and 0.40, respectively. The file P07_36.xlsx contains Carlisle's estimated payoff (in dollars) table.

a. Use PrecisionTree to identify the strategy that maximizes this tire manufacturer's expected profit.

b. Perform a sensitivity analysis on the optimal decision and summarize your findings. In response to which model inputs is the expected profit value most sensitive?

37. A local energy provider offers a landowner $180,000 for the exploration rights to natural gas on a certain site and the option for future development. This option, if exercised, is worth an additional $1,800,000 to the landowner, but this will occur only if natural gas is discovered during the exploration phase. The landowner, believing that the energy company's interest in the site is a good indication that gas is present, is tempted to develop the field herself. To do so, she must contract with local experts in natural gas exploration and development. The initial cost for such a contract is $300,000, which is lost forever if no gas is found on the site. If gas is discovered, however, the landowner expects to earn a net profit of $6,000,000. Finally, the landowner estimates the probability of finding gas on this site to be 60%.

a. Formulate a payoff table that specifies the landowner's payoff (in dollars) associated with each possible decision and each outcome with respect to finding natural gas on the site.

b. Use PrecisionTree to identify the strategy that maximizes the landowner's expected net earnings from this opportunity.

c. Perform a sensitivity analysis on the optimal decision and summarize your findings. In response to which model inputs is the expected profit value most sensitive?

38. Techware Incorporated is considering the introduction of two new software products to the market. In particular, the company has four options regarding these two proposed products: introduce neither product, introduce product 1 only, introduce product 2 only, or introduce both products. Research and development costs for products 1 and 2 are $180,000 and $150,000, respectively. Note that the first option entails no costs because research and development efforts have not yet begun. The success of these software products depends on the trend of the national economy in the coming year and on the consumers' reaction to these products. The company's revenues earned by introducing product 1 only, product 2 only, or both products in various states of the national economy are given in the

file **P07_38.xlsx**. The probabilities of observing a strong, fair, and weak trend in the national economy in the coming year are 0.30, 0.50, and 0.20, respectively.

a. Formulate a payoff table that specifies Techware's net revenue (in dollars) for each possible decision and each outcome with respect to the trend in the national economy.

b. Use PrecisionTree to identify the strategy that maximizes Techware's expected net revenue from the given marketing opportunities.

c. Perform a sensitivity analysis on the optimal decision and summarize your findings. In response to which model inputs is the expected net revenue value most sensitive?

39. Consider an investor with $10,000 available to invest. He has the following options regarding the allocation of his available funds: (1) he can invest in a risk-free savings account with a guaranteed 3% annual rate of return; (2) he can invest in a fairly safe stock, where the possible annual rates of return are 6%, 8%, or 10%; or (3) he can invest in a more risky stock, where the possible annual rates of return are 1%, 9%, or 17%. Note that the investor can place all of his available funds in any one of these options, or he can split his $10,000 into two $5000 investments in any two of these options. The joint probability distribution of the possible return rates for the two stocks is given in the file **P07_39.xlsx**.

a. Formulate a payoff table that specifies this investor's return (in dollars) in 1 year for each possible decision and each outcome with respect to the two stock returns.

b. Use PrecisionTree to identify the strategy that maximizes the investor's expected earnings in 1 year from the given investment opportunities.

c. Perform a sensitivity analysis on the optimal decision and summarize your findings. In response to which model inputs is the expected earnings value most sensitive?

40. A buyer for a large department store chain must place orders with an athletic shoe manufacturer 6 months prior to the time the shoes will be sold in the department stores. In particular, the buyer must decide on November 1 how many pairs of the manufacturer's newest model of tennis shoes to order for sale during the upcoming summer season. Assume that each pair of this new brand of tennis shoes costs the department store chain $45 per pair. Furthermore, assume that each pair of these shoes can then be sold to the chain's customers for $70 per pair. Any pairs of these shoes remaining unsold at the end of the summer season will be sold in a closeout sale next fall for $35 each. The probability distribution of consumer demand for these tennis shoes (in hundreds of pairs) during the upcoming summer season has been assessed by market research specialists and is provided in the file

P07_40.xlsx. Finally, assume that the department store chain must purchase these tennis shoes from the manufacturer in lots of 100 pairs.

   a. Formulate a payoff table that specifies the contribution to profit (in dollars) from the sale of the tennis shoes by this department store chain for each possible purchase decision (in hundreds of pairs) and each outcome with respect to consumer demand.

   b. Use PrecisionTree to identify the strategy that maximizes the department store chain's expected profit earned by purchasing and subsequently selling pairs of the new tennis shoes.

   c. Perform a sensitivity analysis on the optimal decision and summarize your findings. In response to which model inputs is the expected earnings value most sensitive?

41. Each day the manager of a local bookstore must decide how many copies of the community newspaper to order for sale in her shop. She must pay the newspaper's publisher $0.40 for each copy, and she sells the newspapers to local residents for $0.50 each. Newspapers that are unsold at the end of day are considered worthless. The probability distribution of the number of copies of the newspaper purchased daily at her shop is provided in the file **P07_41.xlsx.** Employ a decision tree to find the bookstore manager's profit-maximizing daily order quantity.

42. Two construction companies are bidding against one another for the right to construct a new community center building in Lewisburg, Pennsylvania. The first construction company, Fine Line Homes, believes that its competitor, Buffalo Valley Construction, will place a bid for this project according to the distribution shown in the file **P07_42.xlsx.** Furthermore, Fine Line Homes estimates that it will cost $160,000 for its own company to construct this building. Given its fine reputation and long-standing service within the local community, Fine Line Homes believes that it will likely be awarded the project in the event that it and Buffalo Valley Construction submit exactly the same bids. Employ a decision tree to identify Fine Line Homes' profit-maximizing bid for the new community center building.

43. Suppose that you have sued your employer for damages suffered when you recently slipped and fell on an icy surface that should have been treated by your company's physical plant department. Specifically, your injury resulting from this accident was sufficiently serious that you, in consultation with your attorney, decided to sue your company for $500,000. Your company's insurance provider has offered to settle this suit with you out of court. If you decide to reject the settlement and go to court, your attorney is confident that you will win the case but is uncertain about the amount the court will award you in damages. He has

provided his assessment of the probability distribution of the court's award to you in the file **P07_43.xlsx.** Let S be the insurance provider's proposed out-of-court settlement (in dollars). For which values of S will you decide to accept the settlement? For which values of S will you choose to take your chances in court? Of course, you are seeking to maximize the expected payoff from this litigation.

44. Suppose that one of your colleagues has $2000 available to invest. Assume that all of this money must be placed in one of three investments: a particular money market fund, a stock, or gold. Each dollar your colleague invests in the money market fund earns a virtually guaranteed 6% annual return. Each dollar he invests in the stock earns an annual return characterized by the probability distribution provided in the file **P07_44.xlsx.** Finally, each dollar he invests in gold earns an annual return characterized by the probability distribution given in the file.

   a. If your colleague must place all of his available funds in a single investment, which investment should he choose to maximize his expected earnings over the next year?

   b. Suppose now that your colleague can place all of his available funds in one of these three investments as before, or he can invest $1000 in one alternative and $1000 in another. Assuming that he seeks to maximize his expected total earnings in 1 year, how should he allocate his $2000?

45. Consider a population of 2000 individuals, 800 of whom are women. Assume that 300 of the women in this population earn at least $60,000 per year, and 200 of the men earn at least $60,000 per year.

   a. What is the probability that a randomly selected individual from this population earns less than $60,000 per year?

   b. If a randomly selected individual is observed to earn less than $60,000 per year, what is the probability that this person is a man?

   c. If a randomly selected individual is observed to earn at least $60,000 per year, what is the probability that this person is a woman?

46. Yearly automobile inspections are required for residents of the state of Pennsylvania. Suppose that 18% of all inspected cars in Pennsylvania have problems that need to be corrected. Unfortunately, Pennsylvania state inspections fail to detect these problems 12% of the time. On the other hand, an inspection never detects a problem when there is no problem. Consider a car that is inspected and is found to be free of problems. What is the probability that there is indeed something wrong that the inspection has failed to uncover?

47. Consider again the landowner's decision problem described in Problem 37. Suppose now that, at a cost of $90,000, the landowner can request that a soundings test be performed on the site where natural gas is believed to be present. The company that conducts the soundings concedes that 30% of the time the test will indicate that no gas is present when it actually is. When natural gas is not present in a particular site, the soundings test is accurate 90% of the time.

a. Given that the landowner pays for the soundings test and the test indicates that gas is present, what is the landowner's revised estimate of the probability of finding gas on this site?

b. Given that the landowner pays for the soundings test and the test indicates that gas is not present, what is the landowner's revised estimate of the probability of not finding gas on this site?

c. Should the landowner request the given soundings test at a cost of $90,000? Explain why or why not. If not, when (if ever) would the landowner choose to obtain the soundings test?

48. The chief executive officer of a firm in a highly competitive industry believes that one of her key employees is providing confidential information to the competition. She is 90% certain that this informer is the vice president of finance, whose contacts have been extremely valuable in obtaining financing for the company. If she decides to fire this vice president and he is the informer, she estimates that the company will gain $500,000. If she decides to fire this vice president but he is not the informer, the company will lose his expertise and still have an informer within the staff; the CEO estimates that this outcome would cost her company about $2.5 million. If she decides not to fire this vice president, she estimates that the firm will lose $1.5 million regardless of whether he actually is the informer (because in either case the informer is still with the company). Before deciding whether to fire the vice president for finance, the CEO could order lie detector tests. To avoid possible lawsuits, the lie detector tests would have to be administered to all company employees, at a total cost of $150,000. Another problem she must consider is that the available lie detector tests are not perfectly reliable. In particular, if a person is lying, the test will reveal that the person is lying 95% of the time. Moreover, if a person is not lying, the test will indicate that the person is not lying 85% of the time.

a. To minimize the expected total cost of managing this difficult situation, what strategy should the CEO adopt?

b. Should the CEO order the lie detector tests for all of her employees? Explain why or why not.

c. Determine the maximum amount of money that the CEO should be willing to pay to administer lie detector tests.

49. A customer has approached a bank for a $100,000 1-year loan at a 12% interest rate. If the bank does not approve this loan application, the $100,000 will be invested in bonds that earn a 6% annual return. Without additional information, the bank believes that there is a 4% chance that this customer will default on the loan, assuming that the loan is approved. If the customer defaults on the loan, the bank will lose $100,000. At a cost of $1000, the bank can thoroughly investigate the customer's credit record and supply a favorable or unfavorable recommendation. Past experience indicates that in cases where the customer did not default on the approved loan, the probability of receiving a favorable recommendation on the basis of the credit investigation was 0.80. Furthermore, in cases where the customer defaulted on the approved loan, the probability of receiving a favorable recommendation on the basis of the credit investigation was 0.25.

a. What course of action should the bank take to maximize its expected profit?

b. Compute and interpret the expected value of sample information (EVSI) in this decision problem.

c. Compute and interpret the expected value of perfect information (EVPI) in this decision problem.

50. A company is considering whether to market a new product. Assume, for simplicity, that if this product is marketed, there are only two possible outcomes: success or failure. The company assesses that the probabilities of these two outcomes are p and $1 - p$, respectively. If the product is marketed and it proves to be a failure, the company will lose $450,000. If the product is marketed and it proves to be a success, the company will gain $750,000. Choosing not to market the product results in no gain or loss for the company. The company is also considering whether to survey prospective buyers of this new product. The results of the consumer survey can be classified as favorable, neutral, or unfavorable. In similar cases where proposed products proved to be market successes, the likelihoods that the survey results were favorable, neutral, and unfavorable were 0.6, 0.3, and 0.1, respectively. In similar cases where proposed products proved to be market failures, the likelihoods that the survey results were favorable, neutral, and unfavorable were 0.1, 0.2, and 0.7, respectively. The total cost of administering this survey is C dollars.

a. Let $p = 0.4$. For which values of C, if any, would this company choose to conduct the consumer survey?

b. Let $p = 0.4$. What is the largest amount that this company would be willing to pay for perfect information about the potential success or failure of the new product?

c. Let $p = 0.5$ and $C = \$15,000$. Find the strategy that maximizes the company's expected earnings in this situation. Does the optimal strategy involve conducting the consumer survey? Explain why or why not.

51. The U.S. government is attempting to determine whether immigrants should be tested for a contagious

disease. Let's assume that the decision will be made on a financial basis. Furthermore, assume that each immigrant who is allowed to enter the United States and has the disease costs the country $100,000. Also, each immigrant who is allowed to enter the United States and does not have the disease will contribute $10,000 to the national economy. Finally, assume that x percent of all potential immigrants have the disease. The U.S. government can choose to admit all immigrants, admit no immigrants, or test immigrants for the disease before determining whether they should be admitted. It costs T dollars to test a person for the disease; the test result is either positive or negative. A person who does not have the disease *always* tests negative. However, 20% of all people who *do* have the disease test negative. The government's goal is to maximize the expected net financial benefits per potential immigrant.

   a. Let $x = 10$ (i.e., 10%). What is the largest value of T at which the U.S. government will choose to test potential immigrants for the disease?

   b. How does your answer to the question in part **a** change when x increases to 15?

   c. Let $x = 10$ and $T = \$100$. Find the government's optimal strategy in this case.

   d. Let $x = 10$ and $T = \$100$. Compute and interpret the expected value of perfect information (EVPI) in this decision problem.

52. The senior executives of an oil company are trying to decide whether to drill for oil in a particular field in the Gulf of Mexico. It costs the company $300,000 to drill in the selected field. Company executives believe that if oil is found in this field its estimated value will be $1,800,000. At present, this oil company believes that there is a 48% chance that the selected field actually contains oil. Before drilling, the company can hire a geologist at a cost of $30,000 to prepare a report that contains a recommendation regarding drilling in the selected field. There is a 55% chance that the geologist will issue a favorable recommendation and a 45% chance that the geologist will issue an unfavorable recommendation. Given a favorable recommendation from the geologist, there is a 75% chance that the field actually contains oil. Given an unfavorable recommendation from the geologist, there is a 15% chance that the field actually contains oil.

   a. Assuming that this oil company wishes to maximize its expected net earnings, determine its optimal strategy through the use of a decision tree.

   b. Compute and interpret EVSI for this decision problem.

   c. Compute and interpret EVPI for this decision problem.

53. A local certified public accountant must decide which of two copying machines to purchase for her expanding business. The cost of purchasing the first machine is $3100, and the cost of maintaining the first machine

each year is uncertain. The CPA's office manager believes that the annual maintenance cost for the first machine will be $0, $150, or $300 with probabilities 0.325, 0.475, and 0.20, respectively. The cost of purchasing the second machine is $3000, and the cost of maintaining the second machine through a guaranteed maintenance agreement is $225 per year. Before the purchase decision is made, the CPA can hire an experienced copying machine repairperson to evaluate the quality of the first machine. Such an evaluation would cost the CPA $100. If the repairperson believes that the first machine is satisfactory, there is a 65% chance that its annual maintenance cost will be $0 and a 35% chance that its annual maintenance cost will be $150. If, however, the repairperson believes that the first machine is unsatisfactory, there is a 60% chance that its annual maintenance cost will be $150 and a 40% chance that its annual maintenance cost will be $300. The CPA's office manager believes that the repairperson will issue a satisfactory report on the first machine with probability 0.50.

   a. Provided that the CPA wishes to minimize the expected total cost of purchasing and maintaining one of these two machines for a 1-year period, which machine should she purchase? When, if ever, would it be worthwhile for the CPA to obtain the repairperson's review of the first machine?

   b. Compute and interpret EVSI for this decision problem.

   c. Compute and interpret EVPI for this decision problem.

54. FineHair is developing a new product to promote hair growth in cases of male pattern baldness. If FineHair markets the new product and it is successful, the company will earn $500,000 in additional profit. If the marketing of this new product proves to be unsuccessful, the company will lose $350,000 in development and marketing costs. In the past, similar products have been successful 60% of the time. At a cost of $50,000, the effectiveness of the new restoration product can be thoroughly tested. If the results of such testing are favorable, there is an 80% chance that the marketing efforts of this new product will be successful. If the results of such testing are not favorable, there is a mere 30% chance that the marketing efforts of this new product will be successful. FineHair currently believes that the probability of receiving favorable test results is 0.60.

   a. Identify the strategy that maximizes FineHair's expected net earnings in this situation.

   b. Compute and interpret EVSI for this decision problem.

   c. Compute and interpret EVPI for this decision problem.

55. Hank is considering placing a bet on the upcoming showdown between the Penn State and Michigan football teams in State College. The winner of this contest will represent the Big Ten Conference in the Rose

Bowl on New Year's Day. Without any additional information, Hank believes that Penn State has a 0.475 chance of winning this big game. If he wins the bet, he will win $500; if he loses the bet, he will lose $550. Before placing his bet, he may decide to pay his friend Al, who happens to be a football sportswriter for the *Philadelphia Enquirer*, $50 for Al's expert prediction on the game. Assume that Al predicts that Penn State will win similar games 55% of the time, and that Michigan will win similar games 45% of the time. Furthermore, Hank knows that when Al predicts that Penn State will win, there is a 70% chance that Penn State will indeed win the football game. Finally, when Al predicts that Michigan will win, there is a 20% chance that Penn State will proceed to win the upcoming game.

a. To maximize his expected profit from this betting opportunity, how should Hank proceed?
b. Compute and interpret EVSI for this decision problem.
c. Compute and interpret EVPI for this decision problem.

56. A product manager at Clean & Brite (C&B) seeks to determine whether her company should market a new brand of toothpaste. If this new product succeeds in the marketplace, C&B estimates that it could earn $1,800,000 in future profits from the sale of the new toothpaste. If this new product fails, however, the company expects that it could lose approximately $750,000. If C&B chooses not to market this new brand, the product manager believes that there would be little, if any, impact on the profits earned through sales of C&B's other products. The manager has estimated that the new toothpaste brand will succeed with probability 0.50. Before making her decision regarding this toothpaste product, the manager can spend $75,000 on a market research study. Such a study of consumer preferences will yield either a positive recommendation with probability 0.50 or a negative recommendation with probability 0.50. Given a positive recommendation to market the new product, the new brand will eventually succeed in the marketplace with probability 0.75. Given a negative recommendation regarding the marketing of the new product, the new brand will eventually succeed in the marketplace with probability 0.25.

a. To maximize expected profit, what course of action should the C&B product manager take?
b. Compute and interpret EVSI for this decision problem.
c. Compute and interpret EVPI for this decision problem.

57. Ford is going to produce a new vehicle, the Pioneer, and wants to determine the amount of annual capacity it should build. Ford's goal is to maximize the profit from this vehicle over the next 10 years. Each vehicle

will sell for $13,000 and incur a variable production cost of $10,000. Building 1 unit of annual capacity will cost $3000. Each unit of capacity will also cost $1000 per year to maintain, even if the capacity is unused. Demand for the Pioneer is unknown but marketing estimates the distribution of annual demand to be as shown in the file **P07_57.xlsx**. Assume that the number of units sold during a year is the minimum of capacity and annual demand.

a. Explain why a capacity of 1,300,000 is not a good choice.
b. Which capacity level should Ford choose?

58. Pizza King (PK) and Noble Greek (NG) are competitive pizza chains. PK believes there is a 25% chance that NG will charge $6 per pizza, a 50% chance NG will charge $8 per pizza, and a 25% chance that NG will charge $10 per pizza. If PK charges price p_1 and NG charges price p_2, PK will sell $100 + 25(p_2 - p_1)$ pizzas. It costs PK $4 to make a pizza. PK is considering charging $5, $6, $7, $8, or $9 per pizza. To maximize its expected profit, what price should PK charge for a pizza?

59. Many decision problems have the following simple structure. A decision maker has two possible decisions, 1 and 2. If decision 1 is made, a *sure* cost of c is incurred. If decision 2 is made, there are two possible outcomes, with costs c_1 and c_2 and probabilities p and $1 - p$. We assume that $c_1 < c < c_2$. The idea is that decision 1, the riskless decision, has a "moderate" cost, whereas decision 2, the risky decision, has a "low" cost c_1 or a "high" cost c_2.

a. Find the decision maker's cost table, that is, the cost for each possible decision and each possible outcome.
b. Calculate the expected cost from the risky decision.
c. List as many scenarios as you can think of that have this structure. (Here's an example to get you started. Think of insurance, where you pay a sure premium to avoid a large possible loss.)

60. A nuclear power company is deciding whether to build a nuclear power plant at Diablo Canyon or at Roy Rogers City. The cost of building the power plant is $10 million at Diablo and $20 million at Roy Rogers City. If the company builds at Diablo, however, and an earthquake occurs at Diablo during the next 5 years, construction will be terminated and the company will lose $10 million (and will still have to build a power plant at Roy Rogers City). Without further expert information the company believes there is a 20% chance that an earthquake will occur at Diablo during the next 5 years. For $1 million, a geologist can be hired to analyze the fault structure at Diablo Canyon. She will predict either that an earthquake will occur or that an earthquake will not occur. The geologist's past record indicates that she will predict an earthquake on

95% of the occasions for which an earthquake will occur and no earthquake on 90% of the occasions for which an earthquake will not occur. Should the power company hire the geologist? Also, calculate and interpret EVSI and EVPI.

61. Consider again Techware's decision problem described in Problem 38. Suppose now that Techware's utility function of net revenue x (measured in dollars), earned from the given marketing opportunities, is $U(x) = 1 - e^{-x/350000}$.

    a. Find the course of action that maximizes Techware's expected utility. How does this optimal decision compare to the optimal decision with an EMV criterion? Explain any difference in the two optimal decisions.

    b. Repeat part **a** when Techware's utility function is $U(x) = 1 - e^{-x/50000}$.

62. Consider again the bank's customer loan decision problem in Problem 49. Suppose now that the bank's utility function of profit x (in dollars) is $U(x) = 1 - e^{-x/150000}$. Find the strategy that maximizes the bank's expected utility in this case. How does this optimal strategy compare to the optimal decision with an EMV criterion? Explain any difference in two optimal strategies.

Level B

63. Mr. Maloy has just bought a new $30,000 sport utility vehicle. As a reasonably safe driver, he believes that there is only about a 5% chance of being in an accident in the forthcoming year. If he is involved in an accident, the damage to his new vehicle depends on the severity of the accident. The probability distribution for the range of possible accidents and the corresponding damage amounts (in dollars) are given in the file **P07_63.xlsx**. Mr. Maloy is trying to decide whether he is willing to pay $170 each year for collision insurance with a $300 deductible. Note that with this type of insurance, he pays the *first* $300 in damages if he causes an accident and the insurance company pays the remainder.

    a. Formulate a payoff table that specifies the cost (in dollars) associated with each possible decision and type of accident.

    b. Use PrecisionTree to identify the strategy that minimizes Mr. Maloy's annual expected cost.

    c. Perform a sensitivity analysis on the optimal decision and summarize your findings. In response to which model inputs is the expected earnings value most sensitive?

64. The purchasing agent for a microcomputer manufacturer is currently negotiating a purchase agreement for a particular electronic component with a given supplier. This component is produced in lots of 1000, and the cost of purchasing a lot is $30,000. Unfortunately, past experience indicates that this supplier has occasionally shipped defective components to its customers. Specifically, the proportion of defective components supplied by this supplier is described by the probability distribution given in the file **P07_64.xlsx**. While the microcomputer manufacturer can repair a defective component at a cost of $20 each, the purchasing agent is intrigued to learn that this supplier will now assume the cost of replacing defective components in excess of the first 100 faulty items found in a given lot. This guarantee may be purchased by the microcomputer manufacturer prior to the receipt of a given lot at a cost of $1000 per lot. The purchasing agent is interested in determining whether it is worthwhile for her company to purchase the supplier's guarantee policy.

    a. Formulate a payoff table that specifies the microcomputer manufacturer's total cost (in dollars) of purchasing and repairing (if necessary) a complete lot of components for each possible decision and each outcome with respect to the proportion of defective items.

    b. Use PrecisionTree to identify the strategy that minimizes the expected total cost of achieving a complete lot of satisfactory microcomputer components.

    c. Perform a sensitivity analysis on the optimal decision and summarize your findings. In response to which model inputs is the expected earnings value most sensitive?

65. A home appliance company is interested in marketing an innovative new product. The company must decide whether to manufacture this product essentially on its own or employ a subcontractor to manufacture it. The file **P07_65.xlsx** contains the estimated probability distribution of the cost of manufacturing 1 unit of this new product (in dollars) under the alternative that the home appliance company produces the item on its own. This file also contains the estimated probability distribution of the cost of purchasing 1 unit of this new product (in dollars) under the alternative that the home appliance company commissions a subcontractor to produce the item.

    a. Assuming that the home appliance company seeks to minimize the expected unit cost of manufacturing or buying the new product, use PrecisionTree to see whether the company should make the new product or buy it from a subcontractor.

    b. Perform a sensitivity analysis on the optimal expected cost. Under what conditions, if any, would the home appliance company select an alternative different from the one you identified in part **a**?

66. A grapefruit farmer in central Florida is trying to decide whether to take protective action to limit damage to his crop in the event that the overnight temperature falls to a level well below freezing. He is concerned that if the temperature falls sufficiently low and he fails to make an effort to protect his grapefruit trees, he runs the risk of losing his entire crop, which is worth approximately $75,000. Based on the latest forecast issued by the National Weather Service, the farmer estimates that there is a 60% chance that he will lose his entire crop if it is left unprotected. Alternatively, the farmer can insulate his fruit by spraying water on all of the trees in his orchards. This action, which would likely cost the farmer C dollars, would prevent total devastation but might not completely protect the grapefruit trees from incurring some damage as a result of the unusually cold overnight temperatures. The file **P07_66.xlsx** contains the assessed distribution of possible damages (in dollars) to the insulated fruit in light of the cold weather forecast. Of course, this farmer seeks to minimize the expected total cost of coping with the threatening weather.

a. Find the maximum value of C below which the farmer will choose to insulate his crop in hopes of limiting damage as result of the unusually cold weather.

b. Set C equal to the value identified in part **a**. Perform sensitivity analysis to determine under what conditions, if any, the farmer might be better off not spraying his grapefruit trees and taking his chances in spite of the threat to his crop.

67. A retired partner from Goldman Sachs has 1 million dollars available to invest in particular stocks or bonds. Each investment's annual rate of return depends on the state of the economy in the forthcoming year. The file **P07_67.xlsx** contains the distribution of returns for these stocks and bonds as a function of the economy's state in the coming year. This investor wants to allocate her $1 million to maximize her expected total return 1 year from now.

a. If $X = Y = 15\%$, find the optimal investment strategy for this investor.

b. For which values of X (where $10\% < X < 20\%$) and Y (where $12.5\% < Y < 17.5\%$), if any, will this investor prefer to place all of her available funds in the given stocks to maximize her expected total return 1 year from now?

c. For which values of X (where $10\% < X < 20\%$) and Y (where $12.5\% < Y < 17.5\%$), if any, will this investor prefer to place all of her available funds in the given bonds to maximize her expected total return 1 year from now?

68. A city in Ohio is considering replacing its fleet of gasoline-powered automobiles with electric cars. The manufacturer of the electric cars claims that this municipality will experience significant cost savings over the life of the fleet if it chooses to pursue the conversion. If the manufacturer is correct, the city will save about $1.5 million dollars. If the new technology employed within the electric cars is faulty, as some

critics suggest, the conversion to electric cars will cost the city $675,000. A third possibility is that less serious problems will arise and the city will break even with the conversion. A consultant hired by the city estimates that the probabilities of these three outcomes are 0.30, 0.30, and 0.40, respectively. The city has an opportunity to implement a pilot program that would indicate the potential cost or savings resulting from a switch to electric cars. The pilot program involves renting a small number of electric cars for 3 months and running them under typical conditions. This program would cost the city $75,000. The city's consultant believes that the results of the pilot program would be significant but not conclusive; she submits the values in the file **P07_68.xlsx**, a compilation of probabilities based on the experience of other cities, to support her contention. For example, the first row of her table indicates that given that a conversion to electric cars actually results in a savings of $1.5 million, the conditional probabilities that the pilot program will indicate that the city saves money, loses money, and breaks even are 0.6, 0.1, and 0.3, respectively.

a. What actions should this city take to maximize the expected savings?

b. Should the city implement the pilot program at a cost of $75,000?

c. Compute and interpret EVSI for this decision problem.

69. A manufacturer must decide whether to extend credit to a retailer who would like to open an account with the firm. Past experience with new accounts indicates that 45% are high-risk customers, 35% are moderate-risk customers, and 20% are low-risk customers. If credit is extended, the manufacturer can expect to lose $60,000 with a high-risk customer, make $50,000 with a moderate-risk customer, and make $100,000 with a low-risk customer. If the manufacturer decides not to extend credit to a customer, the manufacturer neither makes nor loses any money. Prior to making a credit extension decision, the manufacturer can obtain a credit rating report on the retailer at a cost of $2000. The credit agency concedes that its rating procedure is not completely reliable. In particular, the credit rating procedure will rate a low-risk customer as a moderate-risk customer with probability 0.10 and as a high-risk customer with probability 0.05. Furthermore, the given rating procedure will rate a moderate-risk customer as a low-risk customer with probability 0.06 and as a high-risk customer with probability 0.07. Finally, the rating procedure will rate a high-risk customer as a low-risk customer with probability 0.01 and as a moderate-risk customer with probability 0.05.

a. Find the strategy that maximizes the manufacturer's expected net earnings.

b. Should the manufacturer routinely obtain credit rating reports on those retailers who seek credit approval? Why or why not?

c. Compute and interpret EVSI for this decision problem.

70. A television network earns an average of $1.6 million each season from a hit program and loses an average of $400,000 each season on a program that turns out to be a flop. Of all programs picked up by this network in recent years, 25% turn out to be hits and 75% turn out to be flops. At a cost of C dollars, a market research firm will analyze a pilot episode of a prospective program and issue a report predicting whether the given program will end up being a hit. If the program is actually going to be a hit, there is a 90% chance that the market researchers will predict the program to be a hit. If the program is actually going to be a flop, there is a 20% chance that the market researchers will predict the program to be a hit.

a. Assuming that $C = \$160,000$, identify the strategy that maximizes this television network's expected profit in responding to a newly proposed television program.

b. What is the maximum value of C that this television network should be willing to incur in choosing to hire the market research firm?

c. Compute and interpret EVPI for this decision problem.

71. A publishing company is trying to decide whether to publish a new business law textbook. Based on a careful reading of the latest draft of the manuscript, the publisher's senior editor in the business textbook division assesses the distribution of possible payoffs earned by publishing this new book. The file **P07_71.xlsx** contains this probability distribution. Before making a final decision regarding the publication of the book, the editor can learn more about the text's potential for success by thoroughly surveying business law instructors teaching at universities across the country. Historical frequencies based on similar surveys administered in the past are also provided in this file.

a. Find the strategy that maximizes the publisher's expected payoff (in dollars).

b. What is the most (in dollars) that the publisher should be willing to pay to conduct a new survey of business law instructors?

c. If the actual cost of conducting the given survey is less than the amount identified in part **a**, what should the publisher do?

d. Assuming that a survey could be constructed that provides "perfect information" to the publisher, how much should the company be willing to pay to acquire and implement such a survey?

72. Sharp Outfits is trying to decide whether to ship some customer orders now via UPS or wait until after the threat of another UPS strike is over. If Sharp Outfits decides to ship the requested merchandise now and the UPS strike takes place, the company will incur $60,000 in delay and shipping costs. If Sharp Outfits decides to

ship the customer orders via UPS and no strike occurs, the company will incur $4000 in shipping costs. If Sharp Outfits decides to postpone shipping its customer orders via UPS, the company will incur $10,000 in delay costs regardless of whether UPS goes on strike. Let p represent the probability that UPS will go on strike and impact Sharp Outfits' shipments.

a. For which values of p, if any, does Sharp Outfits minimize its expected total cost by choosing to postpone shipping its customer orders via UPS?

b. Suppose now that, at a cost of $1000, Sharp Outfits can purchase information regarding the likelihood of a UPS strike in the near future. Based on similar strike threats in the past, the probability that this information indicates the occurrence of a UPS strike is 27.5%. If the purchased information indicates the occurrence of a UPS strike, the chance of a strike actually occurring is 0.105/0.275. If the purchased information does not indicate the occurrence of a UPS strike, the chance of a strike actually occurring is 0.680/0.725. Provided that $p = 0.15$, what strategy should Sharp Outfits pursue to minimize its expected total cost?

c. Continuing part **b**, compute and interpret EVSI when $p = 0.15$.

d. Continuing part **b**, compute and interpret the EVPI when $p = 0.15$.

73. An investor has $10,000 in assets and can choose between two different investments. If she invests in the first investment opportunity, there is an 80% chance that she will increase her assets by $590,000 and a 20% chance that she will increase her assets by $190,000. If she invests in the second investment opportunity, there is a 50% chance that she will increase her assets by $1.19 million and a 50% chance that she will increase her assets by $1000. This investor has an exponential utility function for final assets with a risk tolerance parameter equal to $600,000. Which investment opportunity will she prefer?

74. City officials in Fort Lauderdale, Florida, are trying to decide whether to evacuate coastal residents in anticipation of a major hurricane that may make landfall near their city within the next 48 hours. Based on previous studies, it is estimated that it will cost approximately $1 million to evacuate the residents living along the coast of this major metropolitan area. However, if city officials choose not to evacuate their residents and the storm strikes Fort Lauderdale, there would likely be some deaths as a result of the hurricane's storm surge along the coast. Although city officials are reluctant to place an economic value on the loss of human life resulting from such a storm, they realize that it may ultimately be necessary to do so to make a sound judgment in this situation. Prior to making the evacuation decision, city officials consult hurricane experts at the National Hurricane Center in

Coral Gables regarding the accuracy of past predictions. They learn that in similar past cases, hurricanes that were *predicted* to make landfall near a particular coastal location actually did so 60% of the time. Moreover, they learn that in past similar cases hurricanes that were predicted *not* to make landfall near a particular coastal location actually did so 20% of the time. Finally, in response to similar threats in the past, weather forecasters have issued predictions of a major hurricane making landfall near a particular coastal location 40% of the time.

a. Let L be the economic valuation of the loss of human life resulting from a coastal strike by the hurricane. Employ a decision tree to help these city officials make a decision that minimizes the expected cost of responding to the threat of the impending storm as a function of L. To proceed, you might begin by choosing an initial value of L and then perform sensitivity analysis on the optimal decision by varying this model parameter. Summarize your findings.

b. For which values of L will these city officials *always* choose to evacuate the coastal residents, regardless of the Hurricane Center's prediction?

75. A homeowner wants to decide whether he should install an electronic heat pump in his home. Given that the cost of installing a new heat pump is fairly large, the homeowner would like to do so only if he can count on being able to recover the initial expense over *five* consecutive years of cold winter weather. After reviewing historical data on the operation of heat pumps in various kinds of winter weather, he computes the expected annual costs of heating his home during the winter months with and without a heat pump in operation. These cost figures are shown in the file **P07_75.xlsx**. The probabilities of experiencing a mild, normal, colder than normal, and severe winter are $0.2(1 - x), 0.5(1 - x), 0.3(1 - x)$, and x, respectively.

a. Given that $x = 0.1$, what is the most that the homeowner is willing to pay for the heat pump?

b. If the heat pump costs $500, how large must x be before the homeowner decides it is economically worthwhile to install the heat pump?

c. Given that $x = 0.1$, compute and interpret EVPI when the heat pump costs $500.

d. Repeat part c when $x = 0.15$.

76. Many men over 50 take the PSA blood test. The purpose of the PSA test is to detect prostate cancer early. Dr. Rene Labrie of Quebec conducted a study to determine whether the PSA test can actually prevent cancer deaths. In 1989, Dr. Labrie randomly divided all male registered voters between 45 and 80 in Quebec City into two groups. Two-thirds of the men were asked to be tested for prostate cancer and one-third were not asked. Eventually, 8137 men were screened for prostate cancer (PSA plus digital rectal exam) in 1989; 38,056 men were not screened. By 1997 only 5 of the screened men had died of prostate cancer whereas 137

of the men who were not screened had died of prostate cancer (*Source: New York Times*, May 19, 1998).

a. Discuss why this study seems to indicate that screening for prostate cancer saves lives.

b. Despite the results of this study, many doctors are not convinced that early screening for prostate cancer saves lives. Can you see why they doubt the conclusions of the study?

77. Sarah Chang is the owner of a small electronics company. In 6 months, a proposal is due for an electronic timing system for the next Olympic Games. For several years, Chang's company has been developing a new microprocessor, a critical component in a timing system that would be superior to any product currently on the market. However, progress in research and development has been slow, and Chang is unsure about whether her staff can produce the microprocessor in time. If they succeed in developing the microprocessor (probability p_1), there is an excellent chance (probability p_2) that Chang's company will win the $1 million Olympic contract. If they do not, there is a small chance (probability p_3) that she will still be able to win the same contract with an alternative, inferior timing system that has already been developed. If she continues the project, Chang must invest $200,000 in research and development. In addition, making a proposal (which she will decide whether to do after seeing whether the R&D is successful or not) requires developing a prototype timing system at an additional cost. This additional cost is $50,000 if R&D is successful (so that she can develop the new timing system), and it is $40,000 if R&D is unsuccessful (so that she needs to go with the older timing system). Finally, if Chang wins the contract, the finished product will cost an additional $150,000 to produce.

a. Develop a decision tree that can be used to solve Chang's problem. You can assume in this part of the problem that she is using EMV (of her net profit) as a decision criterion. Build the tree so that she can enter any values for p_1, p_2, and p_3 (in input cells) and automatically see her optimal EMV and optimal strategy from the tree.

b. If $p_2 = 0.8$ and $p_3 = 0.1$, what value of p_1 makes Chang indifferent between abandoning the project and going ahead with it?

c. How much would Chang be willing to pay the Olympic organization (now) to guarantee her the contract in the case where her company is successful in developing the contract? (This guarantee is in force only if she is successful in developing the product.) Assume $p_1 = 0.4, p_2 = 0.8$, and $p_3 = 0.1$.

d. Suppose now that this a "big" project for Chang. Therefore, she decides to use expected utility as her criterion, with an exponential utility function. Using some trial and error, see which risk tolerance changes her initial decision from "go ahead" to "abandon" when $p_1 = 0.4, p_2 = 0.8$, and $p_3 = 0.1$.

78. Suppose an investor has the opportunity to buy the following contract, a stock call option, on March 1. The contract allows him to buy 100 shares of ABC stock at the end of March, April, or May at a guaranteed price of $50 per share. He can "exercise" this option at most once. For example, if he purchases the stock at the end of March, he can't purchase more in April or May at the guaranteed price. The current price of the stock is $50. Each month, we assume the stock price either goes up by a dollar (with probability 0.6) or goes down by a dollar (with probability 0.4). If the investor buys the contract, he is hoping that the stock price will go up. The reasoning is that if he buys the contract, the price goes up to $51, and he buys the stock (that is, he exercises his option) for $50, then he can turn around and sell the stock for $51 and make a profit of $1 per share. On the other hand, if the stock price goes down, he doesn't have to exercise his option; he can just throw the contract away.

    a. Use a decision tree to find the investor's optimal strategy (that is, when he should exercise the option), *assuming* he purchases the contract.

    b. How much should he be willing to pay for such a contract?

79. The Ventron Engineering Company has just been awarded a $2 million development contract by the U.S. Army Aviation Systems Command to develop a blade spar for its Heavy Lift Helicopter program. The blade spar is a metal tube that runs the length of and provides strength to the helicopter blade. Due to the unusual length and size of the Heavy Lift Helicopter blade, Ventron is unable to produce a single-piece blade spar of the required dimensions, using existing extrusion equipment and material. The engineering department has prepared two alternatives for developing the blade spar: (1) sectioning or (2) an improved extrusion process. Ventron must decide which process to use. (Backing out of the contract at any point is not an option.) The risk report has been prepared by the engineering department. The information from it is explained next.

    The sectioning option involves joining several shorter lengths of extruded metal into a blade spar of sufficient length. This work will require extensive testing and rework over a 12-month period at a total cost of $1.8 million. Although this process will definitely produce an adequate blade spar, it merely represents an extension of existing technology.

    To improve the extrusion process, on the other hand, it will be necessary to perform two steps: (1) improve the material used, at a cost of $300,000, and (2) modify the extrusion press, at a cost of $960,000. The first step will require 6 months of work, and if this first step is successful, the second step will require another 6 months of work. If both steps are successful, the blade spar will be available at that time, that is, a year from now. The engineers estimate that the probabilities of succeeding in steps 1 and 2 are 0.9 and 0.75, respectively. However, if either step is unsuccessful (which will be known only in 6 months for step 1 and in a year for step 2), Ventron will have no alternative but to switch to the sectioning process—and incur the sectioning cost on top of any costs already incurred.

    Development of the blade spar must be completed within 18 months to avoid holding up the rest of the contract. If necessary, the sectioning work can be done on an accelerated basis in a 6-month period, but the cost of sectioning will then increase from $1.8 million to $2.4 million. Frankly, the Director of Engineering, Dr. Smith, wants to try developing the improved extrusion process. This is not only cheaper (if successful) for the current project, but its expected side benefits for future projects could be sizable. Although these side benefits are difficult to gauge, Dr. Smith's best guess is an additional $2 million. (Of course, these side benefits are obtained only if both steps of the modified extrusion process are completed successfully.)

    a. Develop a decision tree to maximize Ventron's EMV. This includes the revenue from this project, the side benefits (if applicable) from an improved extrusion process, and relevant costs. You don't need to worry about the time value of money; that is, no discounting or NPVs are required. Summarize your findings in words in the spreadsheet.

    b. What value of side benefits would make Ventron indifferent between the two alternatives?

    c. How much would Ventron be willing to pay, right now, for perfect information about both steps of the improved extrusion process? (This information would tell Ventron, right now, the ultimate success and failure outcomes of both steps.)

80. Based on Balson et al. (1992). An electric utility company is trying to decide whether to replace its PCB transformer in a generating station with a new and safer transformer. To evaluate this decision, the utility needs information about the likelihood of an incident, such as a fire, the cost of such an incident, and the cost of replacing the unit. Suppose that the total cost of replacement as a present value is $75,000. If the transformer is replaced, there is virtually no chance of a fire. However, if the current transformer is retained, the probability of a fire is assessed to be 0.0025. If a fire occurs, then the cleanup cost could be high ($80 million) or low ($20 million). The probability of a high cleanup cost, given that a fire occurs, is assessed at 0.2.

    a. If the company uses EMV as its decision criterion, should it replace the transformer?

    b. Perform a sensitivity analysis on the key parameters of the problem that are difficult to assess, namely, the probability of a fire, the probability of a high cleanup cost, and the high and low cleanup costs. Does the optimal decision from part **a** remain optimal for a "wide" range of these parameters?

    c. Do you believe EMV is the correct criterion to use in this type of problem involving environmental accidents?

The Jogger Shoe Company is trying to decide whether to make a change in its most popular brand of running shoes. The new style would cost the same to produce, and it would be priced the same, but it would incorporate a new kind of lacing system that (according to its marketing research people) would make it more popular.

There is a fixed cost of $300,000 of changing over to the new style. The unit contribution to before-tax profit for either style is $8. The tax rate is 35%. Also, because the fixed cost can be depreciated and will therefore affect the after-tax cash flow, we need a depreciation method. We assume it is straight-line depreciation.

The current demand for these shoes is 190,000 pairs annually. The company assumes this demand will continue for the next 3 years if the current style is retained. However, there is uncertainty about demand for the new style, if it is introduced. The company models this uncertainty by assuming a normal distribution in year 1, with mean 220,000 and standard deviation 20,000. The company also assumes that this demand, whatever it is, will remain constant for the next 3 years. However, if demand in year 1 for the new style is sufficiently low, the company can always switch back to the current style and realize an annual demand of 190,000. The company wants a strategy that will maximize the expected net present value (NPV) of total cash flow for the next 3 years, where a 15% interest rate is used for the purpose of calculating NPV. ■

CASE 7.2 WESTHOUSER PAPER COMPANY

The Westhouser Paper Company in the state of Washington currently has an option to purchase a piece of land with good timber forest on it. It is now May 1, and the current price of the land is $2.2 million. Westhouser does not actually need the timber from this land until the beginning of July, but its top executives fear that another company might buy the land between now and the beginning of July. They assess that there is 1 chance out of 20 that a competitor will buy the land during May. If this does not occur, they assess that there is 1 chance out of 10 that the competitor will buy the land during June. If Westhouser does not take advantage of its current option, it can attempt to buy the land at the beginning of June or the beginning of July, provided that it is still available.

Westhouser's incentive for delaying the purchase is that its financial experts believe there is a good chance that the price of the land will fall significantly in one or both of the next 2 months. They assess the possible price decreases and their probabilities in Table 7.7 and Table 7.8. Table 7.7 shows the probabilities of the possible price decreases during May. Table 7.8 lists the *conditional* probabilities of the possible price decreases in June, *given* the price decrease in May. For example, it indicates that if the price decrease in May is $60,000, then the possible price decreases in June are $0, $30,000, and $60,000 with respective probabilities 0.6, 0.2, and 0.2.

If Westhouser purchases the land, it believes that it can gross $3 million. (This does not count the cost of purchasing the land.) But if it does not purchase the land, Westhouser believes that it can make $650,000 from alternative investments. What should the company do?

Table 7.7 Distribution of Price Decrease in May

Price Decrease	Probability
$0	0.5
$60,000	0.3
$120,000	0.2

Table 7.8 Distribution of Price Decrease in June

Price Decrease in May					
$0		$60,000		$120,000	
June Decrease	Probability	June Decrease	Probability	June Decrease	Probability
$0	0.3	$0	0.6	$0	0.7
$60,000	0.6	$30,000	0.2	$20,000	0.2
$120,000	0.1	$60,000	0.2	$40,000	0.1

Biotechnical Engineering specializes in developing new chemicals for agricultural applications. The company is a pioneer in using the sterile-male procedure to control insect infestations. It operates several laboratories around the world where insects are raised and then exposed to extra-large doses of radiation, making them sterile. As an alternative to chlorinated hydrocarbon pesticides, such as DDT, the sterile-male procedure has been used more frequently with a good track record of success, most notably with the Mediterranean Fruitfly (or Medfly).

That pest was controlled in California through the release of treated flies on the premise that the sterile male flies would compete with fertile wild males for mating opportunities. Any female that has mated with a sterile fly will lay eggs that do not hatch. The California Medfly campaigns required about five successive releases of sterile males—at intervals timed to coincide with the time for newly hatched flies to reach adulthood—before the Medfly was virtually eliminated. (Only sterile flies were subsequently caught in survey traps.) The effectiveness of the sterile-male procedure was enhanced by the release of malathion poisonous bait just a few days before each release, cutting down on the number of viable wild adults.

More recently, Biotechnical Engineering has had particular success in using genetic engineering to duplicate various insect hormones and pheromones (scent attractants). Of particular interest is the application of such methods against the Gypsy Moth, a notorious pest that attacks trees. The company has developed synthetic versions of both hormones and pheromones for that moth. It has a synthetic sexual attractant that male moths can detect at great distances. Most promising is the synthetic juvenile hormone.

The juvenile hormone controls moth metamorphosis, determining the timing for the transformation of a caterpillar into a chrysalis and then into an adult. Too much juvenile hormone wreaks havoc with this process, causing caterpillars to turn into freak adults that cannot reproduce.

Biotechnical Engineering has received a government contract to test its new technology in an actual eradication campaign. The company will participate in a small-scale campaign against the Gypsy Moth in the state of Oregon. Because the pest is so damaging, Dr. June Scribner, the administrator in charge, is considering using DDT as an alternative procedure. Of course, that banned substance is only available for government emergency use because of the environmental damage it may cause. In addition to spraying with DDT, two other procedures may be employed: (1) using Biotechnical's scent lure, followed by release of sterile males, and (2) spraying with the company's juvenile hormone to prevent larvae from developing into adults. Dr. Scribner wants to select the method that yields the best expected payoff, described below.

Although both of the newer procedures are known to work under laboratory conditions, there is some uncertainty about successful propagation of the chemicals in the wild and about the efficacy of the sterile-male procedure with moths.

If the scent-lure program is launched at a cost of $5 million, Biotechnical claims that it will have a 50–50 chance of leaving a low number of native males versus a high number. Once the results of that phase are known, a later choice must be made to spray with DDT or to release sterile males; the cost of the sterilization and delivery of the insects to the countryside is an additional $5 million. But if this two-phase program is successful, the net present value of the worth of trees saved is $30 million, including the benefit of avoiding all other forms of environmental damage. The indigenous moth population would be destroyed, and a new infestation could occur only from migrants. Biotechnical's experience with other eradication programs indicates that if the scent lure leaves a small native male population, there is a 90% chance for a successful eradication by using sterile males; otherwise, there is only a 10% chance for success by using sterile males. A failure results in no savings.

[10]This case was written by Lawrence L. Lapin, San Jose State University.

The cost of synthesizing enough juvenile hormone is $3 million. Biotechnical maintains that the probability that the hormone can be effectively disseminated is only 0.20. If it works, the worth of the trees saved and environmental damage avoided will be $50 million. This greater level of savings is possible because of the permanent nature of the solution because a successful juvenile hormone can then be applied wherever the moths are known to exist, virtually eliminating the pest from the environment. But if the hormone does not work, the DDT must still be used to save the trees.

DDT constitutes only a temporary solution, and the worth of its savings in trees is far less than the worth of either of the esoteric eradication procedures—if they prove successful. To compare alternatives, Dr. Scribner proposes using the net advantage (crop and environmental savings, minus cost) relative to where she would be were she to decide to use DDT at the outset or were she to be forced to spray with it later. (Regardless of the outcome, Biotechnical will be reimbursed for all expenditures. The decision is hers, not the company's.)

Questions

1. Under Biotechnical's proposal, the selection of DDT without even trying the other procedures would lead to a neutral outcome for the government, having zero payoff. Discuss the benefits of Dr. Scribner's proposed payoff measure.

2. Construct Dr. Scribner's decision tree diagram, using the proposed payoff measure.

3. What action will maximize Dr. Scribner's expected payoff?

4. Dr. Scribner is concerned about the assumed 50–50 probability for the two levels of surviving native males following the scent-lure program.

   a. Redo the decision tree analysis to find what action will maximize Dr. Scribner's expected payoff when the probability of low native males is, successively, (1) 0.40 or (2) 0.60 instead.

   b. How is the optimal action affected by the probability level assumed for the low native male outcome?

5. Dr. Scribner is concerned about the assumed 0.20 probability for the dissemination success of the juvenile hormone.

   a. Keeping all other probabilities and cash flows at their original levels, redo the decision tree analysis to find what action will maximize Dr. Scribner's expected payoff when the probability of juvenile hormone success is, successively, (1) 0.15 or (2) 0.25 instead.

   b. How is the optimal action affected by the probability level assumed for the juvenile hormone's success?

6. Dr. Scribner is concerned about the assumed probability levels for the success of the sterile-male procedure.

   a. Keeping all other probabilities and cash flows at their original levels, redo the decision tree analysis to find what action will maximize Dr. Scribner's expected payoff when the sterile-male success probabilities are instead as follows:

      (1) 80% for low native males and 5% for high native males

      (2) 70% for low native males and 15% for high native males

   b. How is the optimal action affected by the probability level assumed for the success of the sterile-male procedure?

7. Dr. Scribner is concerned about the assumed levels for the net present value of the worth of trees saved and damage avoided. She believes these amounts are only accurate within a range of ±10%.

   a. Keeping all other probabilities and cash flows at their original levels, redo the decision tree analysis to find what action will maximize Dr. Scribner's expected payoff when the two net present values are instead, successively, (1) 10% lower or (2) 10% higher than originally assumed.

   b. How is the optimal action affected by the level assumed for the net present values of the savings from using one of the two esoteric Gypsy Moth eradication procedures? ■

PART

3

Statistical Inference

CHAPTER
8

Sampling and Sampling Distributions

©Photodisc/Getty Images

CHOOSING SAMPLES OF CUSTOMERS TO RECEIVE MAILINGS

In the first half of this chapter, we discuss methods for selecting random samples. The purpose of these samples is to discover characteristics of a population, such as the proportion who favor the president's economic policy. By selecting a random sample of perhaps 1000 people out of a population of millions, we can make fairly accurate inferences about the population as a whole, at savings of much time and money.

A different type of sample has recently become the focus of many direct response marketers, companies that mail advertisements for their products directly to prospective customers. The experience of one such company, the Franklin Mint (FM) of Philadelphia, is described in Zahavi (1995). The FM markets expensive collectibles, ranging from famous Precision Car models to the Sword of Francis Drake, to a relatively small, but avid, collector population. The FM relies entirely on its mailings to prospective customers for sales. However, it is important for the company to mail ads for any particular products to the right customers; otherwise, mailing costs can seriously erode profits. This is especially the case when, on average, the response rate to products in this type of market is less than one-half percent—that is, no more than 1 person out of every 200 who receive a mailing actually purchases a product.

Until recently, companies such as the FM used relatively subjective rules to choose the sample of customers to receive mailings. However, these companies now have an abundance of data about their customers, and they are

387

beginning to use sophisticated statistical methods to locate the customers who are most likely to purchase any particular type of product. In essence, they build a probability model that relates the probability of purchasing to (1) the customer's purchase history; (2) demographic variables (many of which can be acquired from outside vendors and appended to the customer's record); and (3) the product attributes, such as theme, material, artist, sponsor, and product code. The most challenging part of the model is to identify the best predictor variables from the hundreds available, but techniques (and software) are now available to perform this task efficiently.

Direct marketers such as the FM have found that this is a situation where even a small amount of explanatory power from a statistical model can make a big difference in the bottom line. No model can correctly identify exactly who will respond positively to an ad and who will not, but if the model can identify customer samples where the response rate to mailings is even a little higher than it was, the ratio of mailing costs to eventual sales can decrease significantly. For example, the FM installed its system (called AMOS) in 1992 and realized an increase in profit of approximately 7.5% in 3 years; undoubtedly, it has increased even more since then. As Zahavi states, "Looking beyond the FM, the implications of using AMOS-like systems to support the decision-making process in the database marketing industry are likely to be quite substantial, which, given the size of the industry, could run well in excess of several hundred million dollars a year!" ■

8.1 INTRODUCTION

In a typical statistical inference problem we want to discover one or more characteristics of a given population. For example, we might want to know the proportion of toothpaste customers who have tried, or intend to try, a particular brand. Or we might want to know the average amount owed on credit card accounts for a population of customers at a shopping mall. Generally, the population is large and/or spread out, and it is difficult, maybe even impossible, to contact each member. Therefore, we identify a sample of the population and then obtain information from the members of the sample.

There are two main objectives of this chapter. The first is to discuss the sampling schemes that are generally used in real sampling applications. We focus on several types of *random* samples and see why these are preferable to nonrandom samples. The second objective is to see how the information from a sample of the population—for example, 1% of the population—can be used to infer the properties of the entire population. The key here is the concept of *sampling distributions*. We focus on the sampling distribution of the sample mean, and we see how a famous mathematical result called the *central limit theorem* is the key to the analysis.

8.2 SAMPLING TERMINOLOGY

We begin by introducing some of the terminology that is used in sampling. In any sampling problem there is a relevant *population*. A **population** is the set of all members about which a study intends to make inferences, where an **inference** is a statement about a numerical characteristic of the population, such as an average income or the proportion of incomes below $50,000. It is important to realize that a population is defined in relationship to any particular study. Any analyst planning a survey should first decide which population the conclusions of the study will concern, so that a sample can be chosen from *this* population.

The relevant **population** contains all members about which a study intends to make inferences.

For example, if a marketing researcher plans to use a questionnaire to infer consumers' reactions to a new product, she must first decide which population of consumers is of interest—all consumers, consumers over 21 years old, consumers who do most of their shopping in shopping malls, or others. Once the relevant consumer population has been designated, a sample from this population can then be surveyed. However, inferences made from the study pertain only to this *particular* population.

Before we can choose a sample from a given population, we typically need a list of all members of the population. This list is called a **frame**, and the potential sample members are called **sampling units**. Depending on the context, sampling units could be individual people, households, companies, cities, or others.

> A **frame** is a list of all members, called **sampling units**, in the population.

In this chapter we assume that the population is finite and consists of N sampling units. We also assume that a frame of these N sampling units is available. Unfortunately, there are situations where a complete frame is practically impossible to obtain. For example, if we want to survey the attitudes of all unemployed teenagers in Chicago, it is practically impossible to obtain a complete frame of them. In this situation all we can hope to obtain is a partial frame, from which the sample can be selected. If the partial frame omits any significant segments of the population—which a complete frame would include—then the resulting sample could be biased. For instance, if we use the Yellow Pages of a Los Angeles telephone book to choose a sample of restaurants, we automatically omit all restaurants that do not advertise in the Yellow Pages. Depending on the purposes of the study, this could be a serious omission.

There are two basic types of samples: *probability samples* and *judgmental samples*. A **probability sample** is a sample in which the sampling units are chosen from the population by means of a random mechanism such as a random number table. In contrast, no formal random mechanism is used to select a **judgmental sample**. In this case the sampling units are chosen according to the sampler's judgment.

> The members of a **probability sample** are chosen according to a random mechanism, whereas the members of a **judgmental sample** are chosen according to the sampler's judgment.

We do not discuss judgmental samples. The reason is very simple—there is no way to measure the accuracy of judgmental samples because the rules of probability do not apply to them. In other words, if we estimate some population characteristic from the observations in a judgmental sample, there is no way to tell how accurate this estimate is. In addition, it is very difficult to choose a representative sample from a population *without* using some random mechanism. Because our judgment is usually not as good as we think, judgmental samples are likely to contain our own built-in biases. Therefore, we focus exclusively on probability samples from here on.

8.3 METHODS FOR SELECTING RANDOM SAMPLES

In this section we discuss the types of random samples that are used in real sampling applications. Different types of sampling schemes have different properties. There is typically a trade-off between cost and accuracy. Some sampling schemes are cheaper and easier to administer, whereas others cost more but provide more accurate information. We discuss some of these issues, but anyone who intends to make a living in survey sampling needs to learn much more about the topic than we can cover here.

8.3.1 Simple Random Sampling

The simplest type of sampling scheme is appropriately called *simple random sampling*. Consider a population of size N and suppose we want to sample n units from this population. Then a **simple random sample** of size n has the property that every possible sample of size n has the same probability of being chosen. Simple random samples are the easiest to understand, and their statistical properties are fairly straightforward. Therefore, we will focus primarily on simple random samples in the rest of this book. However, as we discuss shortly, more complex random samples are often used in real applications.

> A **simple random sample** of size n is one where each possible sample of size n has the same chance of being chosen.

We illustrate a simple random sample for a small population. Suppose the population size is $N = 5$, and we label the five members of the population as a, b, c, d, and e. Also, suppose we want to sample $n = 2$ of these members. Then the possible samples are (a, b), (a, c), (a, d), (a, e), (b, c), (b, d), (b, e), (c, d), (c, e), and (d, e). That is, there are 10 possible samples—the number of ways two members can be chosen from five members. Then a *simple* random sample of size $n = 2$ has the property that each of these 10 possible samples has an equal probability, 1/10, of being chosen.

One other property of simple random samples can be seen from this example. If we focus on any member of the population, say, member b, we note that b is a member of 4 of the 10 samples. Therefore, the probability that b is chosen in a simple random sample is 4/10, or 2/5. In general, any member has the same probability n/N of being chosen in a simple random sample. If you are one of 100,000 members of a population, then the probability that you will be selected in a simple random sample of size 100 is 100/100,000, or 1 out of 1000.

There are several ways simple random samples can be chosen, all of which involve random numbers. One approach that works well for our small example with $N = 5$ and $n = 2$ is to generate a single random number with the RAND function in Excel. We divide the interval from 0 to 1 into 10 equal subintervals of length 1/10 each and see into which of these subintervals the random number falls. We then choose the corresponding sample. For example, suppose the random number is 0.465. This is in the fifth subinterval, that is, the interval from 0.4 to 0.5, so we choose the fifth sample, (b, c).

For those who have not yet covered the simulation sections of previous chapters, the RAND function in Excel generates numbers that are distributed randomly and uniformly between 0 and 1.

Clearly, this method is consistent with simple random sampling—each of the samples has the same chance of being chosen—but it is prohibitive when n and N are large. In this case there are too many possible samples to list. Fortunately, there is another method that can be used. The idea is simple. We sort the N members of the population randomly, using Excel's RAND function to generate random numbers for the sort. Then we include the first n members from the sorted sequence in the random sample. We illustrate this procedure in the following example.

EXAMPLE | **8.1 SELECTING A SAMPLE OF FAMILIES TO ANALYZE ANNUAL INCOMES**

Consider the frame of 40 families with annual incomes shown in column B of Figure 8.1. (See the file **Random Sampling.xlsm**.) We want to choose a simple random sample of size 10 from this frame. How can this be done? And how do summary statistics of the chosen families compare to the corresponding summary statistics of the population?

Objective To illustrate how Excel's random number function, RAND, can be used to generate simple random samples.

Figure 8.1

Population
Income Data

	A	B	C	D
1	**Simple random sampling**			
2				
3	**Summary statistics**			
4		Mean	Median	Stdev
5	Population	$39,985	$38,500	$7,377
6	Sample			
7				
8	**Population**			
9	Family	Income		
10	1	$43,300		
11	2	$44,300		
12	3	$34,600		
13	4	$38,000		
14	5	$44,700		
15	6	$45,600		
16	7	$42,700		
17	8	$36,900		
18	9	$38,400		
19	10	$33,700		
20	11	$44,100		
21	12	$51,500		
22	13	$35,900		
23	14	$35,600		
24	15	$43,000		
47	38	$46,900		
48	39	$37,300		
49	40	$41,000		

Solution

The idea is very simple. We first generate a column of random numbers in column C. Then we sort the rows according to the random numbers and choose the first 10 families in the sorted rows. The following procedure produces the results in Figure 8.2. (See the first sheet in the finished version of the file.)

Figure 8.2

Selecting a Simple
Random Sample

	A	B	C	D	E	F
1	**Simple random sampling**					
2						
3	**Summary statistics**					
4		Mean	Median	Stdev		
5	Population	$39,985	$38,500	$7,377		
6	Sample	$41,490	$42,850	$5,323		
7						
8	**Population**			**Random sample**		
9	Family	Income		Family	Income	Random #
10	1	$43,300		1	$43,300	0.04545
11	2	$44,300		2	$44,300	0.1496768
12	3	$34,600		12	$51,500	0.23527
13	4	$38,000		7	$42,700	0.2746325
14	5	$44,700		13	$35,900	0.3003506
15	6	$45,600		15	$43,000	0.3197393
16	7	$42,700		6	$45,600	0.3610983
17	8	$36,900		3	$34,600	0.3852641
18	9	$38,400		9	$38,400	0.4427564
19	10	$33,700		14	$35,600	0.4447877
20	11	$44,100		5	$44,700	0.4505899
21	12	$51,500		40	$41,000	0.4597361
22	13	$35,900		11	$44,100	0.5621297
23	14	$35,600		4	$38,000	0.5860911
24	15	$43,000		38	$46,900	0.7192539
47	38	$46,900		39	$37,300	0.8644119
48	39	$37,300		8	$36,900	0.9059098
49	40	$41,000		10	$33,700	0.9637509

1 **Random numbers next to a copy.** Copy the original data to columns D and E. Then enter the formula

=RAND()

in cell F10 and copy it down column F.

2 **Replace with values.** To enable sorting we must first "freeze" the random numbers—that is, replace their formulas with values. To do this, copy the range F10:F49 and select Paste Values from the Paste dropdown on the Home ribbon.

3 **Sort.** Sort on column F in ascending order. Then the 10 families with the 10 smallest random numbers are the ones in the sample. (These are shaded in the figure.)

4 **Means.** Use the AVERAGE, MEDIAN, and STDEV functions in row 6 to calculate summary statistics of the first 10 incomes in column E. Similar summary statistics for the population have already been calculated in row 5. (Cell D5 uses the STDEVP function because this is the *population* standard deviation.)

To obtain more random samples of size 10 (for comparison), we would need to go through this process repeatedly. To save you the trouble of doing so, we wrote a macro to automate the process. (See the Automated sheet in the **Random Samples.xlsm** file.) This sheet looks essentially the same as the sheet in Figure 8.2, except that there is a button to run the macro and only the required data remain on the spreadsheet. Try clicking on this button. (Don't forget to enable the macro first.) Each time you do so, you will get a different random sample—and different summary measures in row 6. By doing this many times and keeping track of the sample summary data, you can see how the summary measures vary from sample to sample. We have much more to say about this variation later in this chapter. ■

The procedure described in Example 8.1 can be used in Excel to select a simple random sample of any size from any population. All we need is a frame, a list of the population values. Then it is just a matter of inserting random numbers, freezing them, and sorting on the random numbers.

Perhaps surprisingly, simple random samples are used infrequently in real applications. There are several reasons for this.

- Because each sampling unit has the same chance of being sampled, simple random sampling can result in samples that are spread over a large geographical region. This can make sampling extremely expensive, especially if personal interviews are used.

- Simple random sampling requires that all sampling units be identified prior to sampling. Sometimes this is infeasible.

- Simple random sampling can result in underrepresentation or overrepresentation of certain segments of the population. For example, if the primary—but not sole—interest is in the graduate student subpopulation of university students, a simple random sample of *all* university students might not provide enough information about the graduate students.

Despite this, most of the statistical analysis in this book assumes simple random samples. The analysis is considerably more complex for other types of random samples and is discussed in more advanced books on sampling.

8.3.2 Using StatTools to Generate Simple Random Samples

The method described in Example 8.1 is simple but somewhat tedious, especially if we want to generate more than one random sample. (Even the macro described at the end of the example works only for that particular file.) Fortunately, a more general method is available in StatTools. This procedure generates any number of simple random samples of any specified sample size from a given data set. It can be found under Data Utilities on the StatTools ribbon.

| EXAMPLE | 8.2 SAMPLING FROM ACCOUNTS RECEIVABLE AT SPRING MILLS COMPANY |

The file **Accounts Receivable.xlsx** contains 280 accounts receivable for the Spring Mills Company (the same data we discussed in Example 3.9). There are three variables:

- Size: customer size (small, medium, large), depending on its volume of business with Spring Mills
- Days: number of days since the customer was billed
- Amount: amount of the bill

Generate 25 random samples of size 15 each from the small customers only, calculate the average amount owed in each random sample, and construct a histogram of these 25 averages.

Objective   To illustrate StatTools's method of choosing simple random samples, and how sample means are distributed.

Solution

We proceed in several steps. First, because we want random samples of the small customers only and the data are already sorted on Size, we first create a StatTools data set of the small customers only. (It will be the range A1:D151.) Then we use the Random Sample item from StatTools Utilities to generate 25 samples of size 15 each of the Amount variable. (The Random Sample dialog box should be filled out as shown in Figure 8.3.) These will appear on a new Random Sample sheet, as shown in Figure 8.4 (with many columns hidden). Each of these columns is a random sample of 15 Amount values.

Figure 8.3

Random Sample
Dialog Box

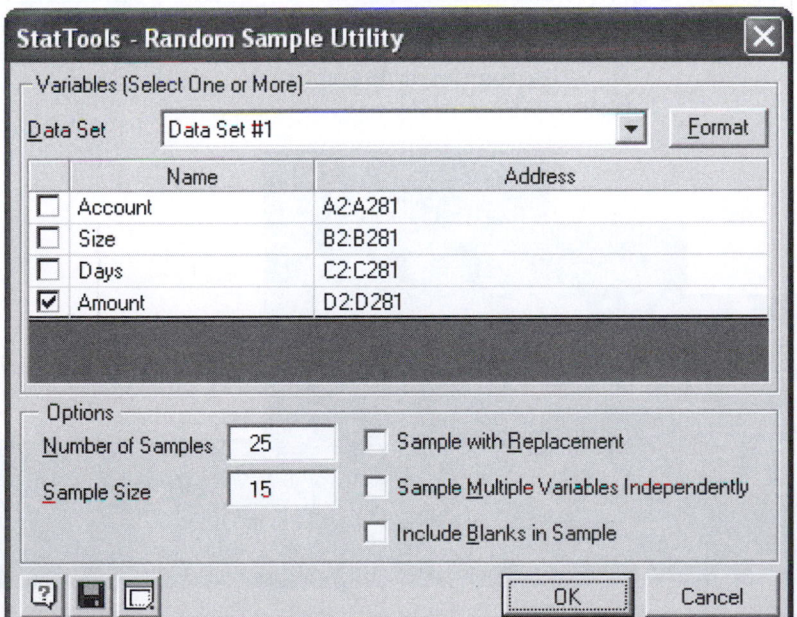

Figure 8.4
Randomly
Generated Samples

	A	B	C	D	X	Y	Z
1		Amount(1)	Amount(2)	Amount(3)	Amount(23)	Amount(24)	Amount(25)
2		260	200	290	250	240	260
3		230	240	260	220	210	290
4		250	310	240	240	230	300
5		280	250	290	260	220	240
6		210	210	330	270	200	250
7		310	270	210	280	220	270
8		280	270	290	220	240	270
9		260	190	260	290	410	250
10		280	240	370	210	300	230
11		240	190	290	260	260	240
12		210	240	260	240	270	250
13		270	240	260	210	210	150
14		240	240	230	240	210	180
15		220	300	240	250	250	310
16		260	320	240	210	280	200
17	Average	253.333	247.333	270.667	243.333	250.000	246.000

Next, we insert a new column A, as shown in Figure 8.4, and we calculate the averages in row 17 for each sample with Excel's AVERAGE function. Finally, because we want a histogram of the averages in row 17, we define a second StatTools data set of the data in row 17 of Figure 8.4 but, for a change, we specify that the only variable for this data set is in a *row,* not a column. (This is an option in the StatTools Data Set Manager.) We can then create a histogram of these 25 averages in the usual way. It appears in Figure 8.5.

The histogram in Figure 8.5 indicates the variability of sample means we might obtain by selecting many *different* random samples of size 15 from this particular population of small customer accounts. This histogram, which is approximately bell shaped, approximates the sampling distribution of the sample mean. We come back to this important idea when we study sampling distributions in Section 8.4.

Figure 8.5   Histogram of 25 Sample Averages

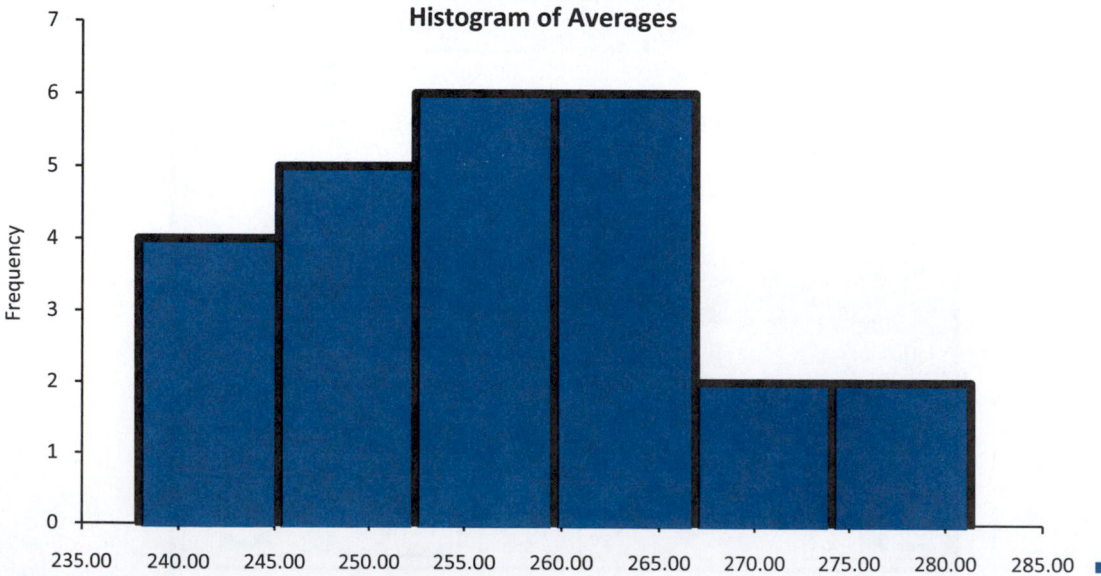

In the next several subsections we describe sampling plans that are often used. These plans differ from simple random sampling both in the way the samples are chosen and in the way the data analysis is performed. However, we will barely touch on this latter issue. The details are quite complicated and are better left to a book devoted entirely to sampling. [See, for example, the excellent book by Levy and Lemeshow (1999).]

8.3.3 Systematic Sampling

Suppose you are asked to select a random sample of 250 names from the white pages of a telephone book. Let's also say that there are 55,000 names listed in the white pages. A *systematic sample* provides a convenient way to choose the sample, as follows. First, we calculate the **sampling interval** as the population size divided by the sample size: $55,000/250 = 220$. Conceptually, we can think of dividing the book into 250 "blocks" with 220 names per block. Next, we use a random mechanism to choose a number between 1 and 220. Say this number is 131. Then we choose the 131st name and every 220th name thereafter. So we would choose the 131st name, the 351st name, the 571st name, and so on. The result is a systematic sample of size $n = 250$.

> In **systematic sampling**, one of the first k members is selected randomly, and then every kth member after this one is selected. The value k is called the **sampling interval** and equals the ratio N/n, where N is the population size and n is the desired sample size.

Clearly, systematic sampling is different from simple random sampling because not every sample of size 250 has a chance of being chosen. In fact, there are only 220 different samples possible (depending on the first number chosen), and each of these is equally likely. Nevertheless, systematic sampling is generally similar to simple random sampling in its statistical properties. The key is the relationship between the ordering of the sampling units in the frame (the white pages of the telephone book in this case) and the purpose of the study.

Systematic random samples are typically chosen because of their convenience.

If the purpose of the study is to analyze personal incomes, say, then there is probably no relationship between the alphabetical ordering of names in the telephone book and personal income. However, there are situations where the ordering of the sampling units is not random, which could make systematic sampling more or less appealing. For example, suppose that a company wants to sample randomly from its customers, and its customer list is in decreasing order of order volumes. That is, the largest customers are at the top of the list and the smallest are at the bottom. Then systematic sampling might be more representative than simple random sampling because it guarantees a wide range of customers in terms of order volumes.

However, some type of cyclical ordering in the list of sampling units can lead to very *unrepresentative* samples. As an extreme, suppose a company has a list of daily transactions and it decides to draw a systematic sample with the sampling interval equal to 7. Then if the first sampled day is Monday, all other days in the sample will be Mondays! This could clearly bias the sample. Except for obvious examples like this one, however, systematic sampling can be an attractive alternative to simple random sampling and is often used because of its convenience.

8.3.4 Stratified Sampling

Suppose we can identify various subpopulations within the total population. We call these subpopulations **strata**. Then instead of taking a simple random sample from the entire population, it might make more sense to select a simple random sample from each stratum separately. This sampling method is called **stratified sampling**. It is a particularly useful approach when there is considerable variation *between* the various strata but relatively little variation *within* a given stratum.

> In **stratified sampling**, the population is divided into relatively homogeneous subsets called **strata**, and then random samples are taken from each of the strata.

Stratified samples are typically chosen because they provide more accurate estimates of population parameters for a given sampling cost.

There are several advantages to stratified sampling. One obvious advantage is that we obtain separate estimates within each stratum—which we would not obtain if we took a simple random sample from the entire population. Even if we eventually plan to pool the samples from the individual strata, it cannot hurt to have the total sample broken down into separate samples initially.

A more important advantage of stratified sampling is that the accuracy of the resulting population estimates can be increased by using appropriately defined strata. The trick is to define the strata so that there is less variability within the individual strata than in the population as a whole. We want strata such that there is relative homogeneity within the strata, but relative heterogeneity among the strata, with respect to the variable(s) being analyzed. By choosing the strata in this way, we can generally obtain more accuracy for a given sampling cost than we could obtain from a simple random sample at the same cost. Alternatively, we can achieve the same level of accuracy at a lower sampling cost.

The key to using stratified sampling effectively is selecting the appropriate strata. Suppose a company that advertises its product on television wants to estimate the reaction of viewers to the advertising. Here the population consists of all viewers who have seen the advertising. But what are the appropriate strata? The answer depends on the company's objectives and its product. The company could stratify the population by gender, by income, by amount of television watched, by the amount of the product class consumed, and probably others. Without knowing more specific information about the company's objectives, it is impossible to say which of these stratification schemes is most appropriate.

Suppose that we have identified I nonoverlapping strata in a given population. Let N be the total population size, and let N_i be the population size of stratum i, so that

$$N = N_1 + N_2 + \cdots + N_I$$

To obtain a stratified random sample, we must choose a total sample size n, and we must choose a sample size n_i from each stratum i, such that

$$n = n_1 + n_2 + \cdots + n_I$$

We can then select a simple random sample of the specified size from *each* stratum exactly as in Example 8.1.

However, how do we choose the individual sample sizes n_1 through n_I, given that the total sample size n has been chosen? For example, if we decide to sample 500 customers in total, how many should come from each stratum? There are many ways that we could choose numbers n_1 through n_I that sum to n, but probably the most popular method is to use *proportional sample sizes*. The idea is very simple. If one stratum has, say, 15% of the total population, then we select 15% of the total sample from this stratum. For example, if the total sample size is $n = 500$, we select $0.15(500) = 75$ members from this stratum.

> With **proportional sample sizes**, the proportion of a stratum in the sample is the same as the proportion of that stratum in the population.

The advantage of proportional sample sizes is that they are very easy to determine. The disadvantage is that they ignore differences in variability among the strata. To illustrate, suppose that we are attempting to estimate the population mean amount paid annually per student for textbooks at a large university. We identify three strata: undergraduates, master's students, and doctoral students. Their population sizes are 20,000, 4000, and 1000, respectively. Therefore, the proportions of students in these strata are $20,000/25,000 = 0.80$, $4000/25,000 = 0.16$, and $1000/25,000 = 0.04$. If the total sample size is $n = 150$, then the sample should include 120 undergraduates, 24 master's students, and 6 doctoral students if proportional sample sizes are used.

However, let σ_i be the standard deviation of annual textbook payments in stratum i, and suppose that $\sigma_1 = \$50$, $\sigma_2 = \$120$, and $\sigma_3 = \$180$. Thus, there is considerably more variation in the amounts paid by doctoral students than by undergraduates, with the master's students in the middle. If we are interested in estimating the mean amount spent per student, then despite its small sample size, the doctoral sample is likely to have a large effect on the accuracy of our estimate of the mean. This is because of its relatively large standard deviation. In contrast, we might not need to sample as heavily from the undergraduate population because of its relatively small standard deviation. In general, strata with less variability can afford to be sampled less heavily than proportional sampling calls for, and the opposite is true for strata with larger variability. In fact, there are *optimal* sample size formulas that take the σ_i's into account, but we do not present them here.

In the following example we illustrate how stratified sampling can be accomplished with Excel by using random numbers.

EXAMPLE | **8.3 STRATIFIED SAMPLING FROM THE SMALLTOWN POPULATION OF SEARS CREDIT CARD HOLDERS**

The file **Stratified Sampling.xlsx** contains a frame of all 1000 people in the city of Smalltown who have Sears credit cards. Sears is interested in estimating the average number of *other* credit cards these people own, as well as other information about their use of credit. The company decides to stratify these customers by age, select a stratified sample of size 100 with proportional sample sizes, and then contact these 100 people by phone. How might Sears proceed?

Objective To illustrate how stratified sampling, with proportional sample sizes, can be implemented in Excel.

Solution

First, Sears has to decide exactly how to stratify by age. Their reasoning is that different age groups probably have different attitudes and behavior regarding credit. After some preliminary investigation, they decide to use three age categories: 18–30, 31–62, and 63–80. (We assume that no one in the population is younger than 18 or older than 80.)

Figure 8.6 shows how the calculations might then proceed. We begin with the following inputs: (1) the total sample size in cell C3, (2) the definitions of the strata in rows 6 through 8, and (3) the customer data in the range A11:B1010. To see which age category each customer is in, we enter the formula

=IF(B11<=$D$6,1,IF(B11<=$D$7,2,3))

in cell C11 and then copy it down column C.

Figure 8.6 Selecting a Stratified Sample

	A	B	C	D	E	F	G	H	I	J	K	L	M	N
1	Stratified sampling by Sears													
2														
3	Total sample size		100											
4														
5	Strata based on age					Counts	Sample size							
6	Stratum 1	18	to	30		132	13							
7	Stratum 2	31	to	62		766	77							
8	Stratum 3	63	to	80		102	10							
9														
10	Customer	Age	Category		Customer(1)	Age(1)	Customer(2)	Age(2)	Customer(3)	Age(3)		Customer(1)	Age(1)	Random #
11	1	49	2		11	23	1	49	4	66		124	22	0.0017915
12	2	39	2		13	24	2	39	12	63		371	22	0.009226
13	3	55	2		15	30	3	55	38	75		563	27	0.009469
14	4	66	3		20	29	5	52	40	64		521	25	0.0159193
15	5	52	2		26	30	6	37	42	71		790	29	0.0170073
16	6	37	2		34	26	7	34	53	63		122	27	0.0181953
17	7	34	2		43	25	8	34	64	71		475	25	0.0209581
18	8	34	2		55	25	9	33	68	66		520	27	0.0285292
19	9	33	2		56	28	10	36	95	64		544	28	0.030113
20	10	36	2		60	21	14	47	102	76		919	29	0.047836
21	11	23	1		62	28	16	59	117	63		281	20	0.0500385
22	12	63	3		67	27	17	31	127	67		404	28	0.0611028
23	13	24	1		79	30	18	34	128	71		802	20	0.0670667
24	14	47	2		80	29	19	35	130	74		322	29	0.0895438
25	15	30	1		87	23	21	47	138	63		412	26	0.0941503
26	16	59	2		99	26	22	31	149	67		797	29	0.0974123
27	17	31	2		101	22	23	54	168	72		409	27	0.0996534
28	18	34	2		116	25	24	41	178	69		116	25	0.1083134
29	19	35	2		119	25	25	38	181	70		652	24	0.1123277
30	20	29	1		122	27	27	44	187	63		390	24	0.1131511

Next, it is useful to "unstack" the data into three groups, one for each age category, as shown in columns E through J. For example, columns E and F list the customer numbers and ages for all customers in the first age category. It is easy to unstack the data in columns A through C with StatTools. After identifying the A10:C1010 range as a StatTools data set, use the Unstack option in StatTools Utilities, select Category as the "Cat" variable, and select Customer and Age as the "Val" variables to unstack. You can then move the unstacked data to a different location, as in Figure 8.6.

Once the variables are unstacked, we can calculate the information in the range F6:G8 by entering the formulas

=COUNTIF(ST_Category, 1)

and

=ROUND($B$3*F6/1000,0)

in cells F6 and G6, with similar formulas for the other two categories. (ST_Category is the range name StatTools gives to the Category data in column C.) In words, if Sears wants to use proportional sample sizes, then it should sample 13, 77, and 10 customers from the three age categories. The formula for proportional sample sizes might lead to fractional values, so we use Excel's ROUND function to round to integers.

Finally, we can proceed as in Example 8.1 for each of the three categories separately. Figure 8.6 illustrates the selection of 13 customers from age category 1. We copy the data in columns E and F to columns L and M, append a column of random numbers with the RAND function in column N, freeze these random numbers (with Copy and Paste Values), sort on the random number column, and choose the first 13 customers. (The finished version of the file shows similar calculations for the other two age categories to the right of column N.) Note that if we wanted a *different* sample of 13 from age category 1, all we would need to do is generate new random numbers in column N with the RAND function, freeze them, and sort again. ■

8.3.5 Cluster Sampling

Suppose that a company is interested in various characteristics of households in a particular city. The sampling units are households. We could select a random sample of households by one of the sampling methods already discussed. However, it might be more convenient to proceed somewhat differently. We could first divide the city into city blocks and consider the city blocks as sampling units. We could then select a simple random sample of city blocks and then sample all of the households in the chosen blocks. In this case the city blocks are called **clusters** and the sampling scheme is called **cluster sampling**.

> In **cluster sampling**, the population is separated into clusters, such as cities or city blocks, and then a random sample of the clusters is selected.

Cluster analysis is typically more convenient and less costly than other random sampling methods.

The primary advantage of cluster sampling is sampling convenience (and possibly less cost). If an agency is sending interviewers to interview heads of household, it is much easier for them to concentrate on particular city blocks than to contact households throughout the city. The downside, however, is that the inferences drawn from a cluster sample can be less accurate, for a given sample size, than for other sampling plans.

Consider the following scenario. A nationwide company wants to survey its salespeople with regard to management practices. It decides to randomly select several sales districts (the clusters) and then interview all salespeople in the selected districts. It is likely that in any particular sales district the attitudes toward management are somewhat similar. This overlapping information means that the company is probably not getting the maximum amount of information per sampling dollar spent. Instead of sampling 20 salespeople from a given district who all have similar attitudes, it might be better to sample 20 salespeople from different districts who have a wider variety of attitudes. Nevertheless, the relative convenience of cluster sampling sometimes outweighs these statistical considerations.

Selecting a cluster sample is straightforward. The key is to define the sampling units as the *clusters*—the city blocks, for example. Then we can select a simple random sample of clusters exactly as in Example 8.1. Once the clusters are selected, we typically sample all of the population members in each selected cluster.

8.3.6 Multistage Sampling Schemes

The cluster sampling scheme just described, where a sample of clusters is chosen and then all of the sampling units within each chosen cluster are taken, is called a **single-stage** sampling scheme. Real applications are often more complex than this, resulting in **multistage** sampling schemes. For example, the Gallup organization uses multistage sampling in its nationwide surveys. A random sample of approximately 300 locations is chosen in the first stage of the sampling process. City blocks or other geographical areas are then randomly sampled from the first-stage locations in the second stage of the process. This is followed by a systematic sampling of households from each second-stage area. A total of about 1500 households comprise a typical Gallup poll.

We do not pursue the topic of multistage sampling schemes in this book. However, you should realize that real-world sampling procedures can be very complex.

PROBLEMS

Level A

1. Consider the frame of 52 full-time employees of Beta Technologies, Inc. Beta's human resources manager has collected current annual salary figures and related data for these employees. The data are in the file **P02_01.xlsx**. In particular, these data include each selected employee's gender, age, number of years of relevant work experience prior to employment at Beta, the number of years of employment at Beta, the number of years of postsecondary education, and annual salary.
   a. Compute the mean, median, and standard deviation of the annual salaries for the 52 employees in the given frame.
   b. Use Excel to choose a simple random sample of size 15 from this frame.
   c. Compute the mean, median, and standard deviation of the annual salaries for the 15 employees included in your simple random sample. Compare these statistics with your computed descriptive measures for the frame obtained in part **a**. Is your simple random sample representative of the frame with respect to the annual salary variable?

2. A manufacturing company's quality control personnel have recorded the proportion of defective items for each of 500 monthly shipments of one of the computer components that the company produces. The data are in the file **P02_02.xlsx**. The quality control department manager does not have sufficient time to review all of these data. Rather, she would like to examine the proportions of defective items for a simple random sample of 50 shipments.
   a. Use Excel to generate such a random sample from the given frame.
   b. What are the advantages and disadvantages of the sampling method requested by this quality control manager?

3. The manager of a local fast-food restaurant is interested in improving the service provided to customers who use the restaurant's drive-up window. As a first step in this process, the manager asks his assistant to record the time (in minutes) it takes to serve a large number of customers at the final window in the facility's drive-up system. The given frame of 200 customer service times are all observed during the busiest hour of the day for this fast-food operation. The data are in the file **P02_04.xlsx**.

   a. Compute the mean, median, and standard deviation of the customer service times in the given frame.
   b. Use Excel to choose a simple random sample of size 20 from this frame.
   c. Compute the mean, median, and standard deviation of the service times for the 20 customers included in your simple random sample. Compare these statistics with your computed descriptive measures for the frame obtained in part **a**.

4. A finance professor has just given a midterm examination in her corporate finance course, and she is interested in learning how her large class of 100 students peformed on this exam. The data are in the file **P02_05.xlsx**.
   a. Using these 100 students as the frame, generate a simple random sample of size 10 with Excel.
   b. Compare the mean of the scores in the frame with that of the scores contained in the simple random sample.

5. Consider a frame consisting of 500 households in a middle-class neighborhood that was the recent focus of an economic development study conducted by the local government. Specifically, for each of the 500 households, information was gathered on each of the following variables: family size, location of the household within the neighborhood, an indication of whether those surveyed owned or rented their home, gross annual income of the first household wage earner, gross annual income of the second household wage earner (if applicable), monthly home mortgage or rent payment, average monthly expenditure on utilities, and the total indebtedness (excluding the value of a home mortgage) of the household. The data are in the file **P02_06.xlsx**.
   a. Compute the mean, median, and standard deviation of the monthly home mortgage or rent payments of all households in the given frame.
   b. Use Excel to choose a simple random sample of size 25 from this frame.
   c. Compute the mean, median, and standard deviation of the monthly home mortgage or rent payments for the 25 households included in your simple random sample. Compare these statistics with your computed descriptive measures for the frame obtained in part **a**.

6. A real estate agent has received data on 150 houses that were recently sold in a suburban community. Included

in this data set are observations for each of the following variables: the appraised value of each house (in thousands of dollars), the selling price of each house (in thousands of dollars), the size of each house (in hundreds of square feet), and the number of bedrooms in each house. The data are in the file **P02_07.xlsx**. Suppose that this real estate agent wishes to examine a representative subset of these 150 houses. Use Excel to assist her by finding a simple random sample of size 10 from this frame.

7. Consider the given set of average annual household income levels of citizens of selected U.S. metropolitan areas in the file **P03_06.xlsx**. Use Excel to obtain a simple random sample of size 15 from this frame.

8. The operations manager of a toll booth located at a major exit of a state turnpike is trying to estimate the average number of vehicles that arrive at the toll booth during a 1-minute period during the peak of rush-hour traffic. In an effort to estimate this average throughput value, he records the number of vehicles that arrive at the toll booth over a 1-minute interval commencing at the same time for each of 365 normal weekdays. The data are provided in the file **P02_09.xlsx**. Choose a simple random sample of size 20 from the given frame of 365 values to help the operations manager estimate the average throughput value.

9. In ranking metropolitan areas in the United States, the *Places Rated Almanac* considers the average time (in minutes) it takes a citizen of each metropolitan area to travel to work and back home each day. The data are in the file **P02_11.xlsx**. Use Excel to obtain a simple random sample of 20 average commute times from the given set of such values.

10. Given data in the file **P02_13.xlsx** from a recent survey of chief executive officers from the largest U.S. public companies, choose a simple random sample of 25 executives and find the mean, median, and standard deviation of the bonuses awarded to them in fiscal year 2003. How do these sample statistics compare to the mean, median, and standard deviation of the bonuses given to all executives included in the frame?

11. A lightbulb manufacturer wants to know the number of defective bulbs contained in a typical box shipped by the company. Production personnel at this company have recorded the number of defective bulbs found in each of the 1000 boxes shipped during the past week. These data are provided in **P08_11.xlsx**. Using this shipment of boxes as a frame, select a simple random sample of 50 boxes and compute the mean number of defective bulbs found in a box.

12. Consider the frame of 52 full-time employees of Beta Technologies, Inc. Beta's human resources manager has collected current annual salary figures and related data for these employees. The data are in the file **P02_01.xlsx**.

a. Compute the mean, median, and standard deviation of the annual salaries for the 52 employees in the given frame.

b. Use Excel to choose a systematic sample of size 13 from this frame.

c. Compute the mean, median, and standard deviation of the annual salaries for the 13 employees included in your systematic sample. Compare these statistics with your computed descriptive measures for the frame obtained in part **a**. Is your systematic sample representative of the frame with respect to the annual salary variable?

13. A manufacturing company's quality control personnel have recorded the proportion of defective items for each of 500 monthly shipments of one of the computer components that the company produces. The data are in the file **P02_02.xlsx**. The quality control department manager does not have sufficient time to review all of these data. Rather, she would like to examine the proportions of defective items for a systematic sample of 50 shipments.

a. Use Excel to generate such a systematic sample from the given frame.

b. What are the advantages and disadvantages of the sampling method requested by this quality control manager?

14. The manager of a local fast-food restaurant is interested in improving the service provided to customers who use the restaurant's drive-up window. As a first step in this process, the manager asks his assistant to record the time (in minutes) it takes to serve a large number of customers at the final window in the facility's drive-up system. The given frame of 200 customer service times are all observed during the busiest hour of the day for this fast-food operation. The data are in the file **P02_04.xlsx**.

a. Compute the mean, median, and standard deviation of the customer service times in the given frame.

b. Use Excel to choose a systematic sample of size 20 from this frame.

c. Compute the mean, median, and standard deviation of the service times for the 20 customers included in your systematic sample. Compare these statistics with your computed descriptive measures for the frame obtained in part **a**.

15. A finance professor has just given a midterm examination in her corporate finance course. In particular, she is interested in learning how her large class of 100 students performed on this exam. The data are in the file **P02_05.xlsx**.

a. Using these 100 students as the frame, generate a systematic sample of size 10 with Excel.

b. Compare the mean of the scores in the frame with that of the scores included in the systematic sample.

16. Consider a frame consisting of 500 households in a middle-class neighborhood that was the recent focus

of an economic development study conducted by the local government. The data are in the file **P02_06.xlsx**.

    a. Compute the mean, median, and standard deviation of the monthly home mortgage or rent payments of all households in the given frame.

    b. Use Excel to choose a systematic sample of size 25 from this frame.

    c. Compute the mean, median, and standard deviation of the monthly home mortgage or rent payments for the 25 households included in your systematic sample. Compare these statistics with your computed descriptive measures for the frame obtained in part **a**.

17. A real estate agent has received data on 150 houses that were recently sold in a suburban community. Included in this data set are observations for each of the following variables: the appraised value of each house (in thousands of dollars), the selling price of each house (in thousands of dollars), the size of each house (in hundreds of square feet), and the number of bedrooms in each house. The data are in the file **P02_07.xlsx**. Suppose that this real estate agent wishes to examine a representative subset of these 150 houses. Use Excel to assist her by finding a systematic sample of size 10 from this frame.

18. Consider the given set of average annual household income levels of citizens of selected U.S. metropolitan areas in the file **P03_06.xlsx**. Use Excel to obtain a systematic sample of size 25 from this frame.

19. The operations manager of a toll booth located at a major exit of a state turnpike is trying to estimate the average number of vehicles that arrive at the toll booth during a 1-minute period during the peak of rush-hour traffic. In an effort to estimate this average throughput value, he records the number of vehicles that arrive at the toll booth over a 1-minute interval commencing at the same time for each of 365 normal weekdays. The data are provided in the file **P02_09.xlsx**. Choose a systematic sample of size 20 from the given frame of 365 values to help the operations manager estimate the average throughput value.

20. Consider the average time (in minutes) it takes citizens of each of the metropolitan areas across the United States to travel to work and back home each day. The data are in the file **P02_11.xlsx**. Use Excel to obtain a systematic sample of 25 average commute times from the given set of such values.

21. Consider the data on Beta Technologies employees in the file **P02_01.xlsx**.

    a. Compute the mean, median, and standard deviation of the annual salaries for the 52 employees in the given frame.

    b. Assuming that the human resources manager wishes to stratify these employees by the number

of years of postsecondary education, select such a stratified sample of size 15 with approximately proportional sample sizes.

    c. Compute the mean, median, and standard deviation of the annual salaries for the 15 employees included in your stratified sample. Compare these statistics with your computed descriptive measures for the frame obtained in part **a**. Is your stratified sample representative of the frame with respect to the annual salary variable?

22. Consider the economic development data in the file **P02_06.xlsx**.

    a. Compute the mean, median, and standard deviation of the gross annual income of the first wage earner of all households in the given frame.

    b. Given that researchers have decided to stratify the given households by location within the neighborhood, choose a stratified sample of size 25 with proportional sample sizes.

    c. Compute the mean, median, and standard deviation of the gross annual income of the first wage earner of the 25 households included in your stratified sample. Compare these statistics with your computed descriptive measures for the frame obtained in part **a**.

    d. Explain how economic researchers could apply cluster sampling in selecting a sample of size 25 from this frame. What are the advantages and disadvantages of employing cluster sampling in this case?

23. Consider the data on real estate sales in the file **P02_07.xlsx**.

    a. Suppose that this real estate agent wishes to examine a representative subset of these 150 houses that has been stratified by the number of bedrooms. Use Excel to assist her by finding such a stratified sample of size 15 with proportional sample sizes.

    b. Explain how the real estate agent could apply cluster sampling in selecting a sample of size 15 from this frame. What are the advantages and disadvantages of employing cluster sampling in this case?

24. Given the data in the file **P02_13.xlsx** from a recent survey of chief executive officers from the largest U.S. public companies, choose a sample of 25 executives stratified by company type with proportional sample sizes. Next, find the mean, median, and standard deviation of the salaries earned by the selected CEOs in fiscal year 2003. How do these sample statistics compare to the mean, median, and standard deviation of the salaries earned by all executives included in the frame?

Level B

25. The employee benefits manager of a small private university would like to know the proportion of its full-time employees who prefer adopting each of three available health care plans in the forthcoming annual enrollment period. A reliable frame of the university's employees and their tentative health care preferences are given in **P08_25.xlsx**.

a. Compute the proportion of the employees in the given frame who favor *each* of the three plans (i.e., plans A, B, and C).

b. Use Excel to choose a sample of 45 employees stratified by employee classification with proportional sample sizes.

c. Compute the proportion of the 45 employees in the stratified sample who favor each health plan. Compare these sample proportions to the corresponding values obtained in part **a**. Explain any differences between the corresponding values.

d. What are the advantages and disadvantages of employing stratified sampling in this particular case?

e. Explain how the benefits manager could apply cluster sampling in selecting a sample of size 30 from this frame. What are the advantages and disadvantages of employing cluster sampling in this case?

26. The file **P02_17.xlsx** reports the number of short-term general hospitals in each of a large number of U.S. metropolitan areas. Suppose that you are a sales manager for a major pharmaceutical producer and are interested in estimating the average number of such hospitals in *all* metropolitan areas across the entire country. Assuming that you do not have access to the data for each metropolitan location, you decide to select a sample that will be representative of all such areas.

a. Choose a simple random sample of 30 metropolitan areas from the given frame. Compute the mean number of short-term general hospitals for the metropolitan areas included in your sample.

b. Do you believe that simple random sampling is the best approach to obtaining a representative subset of the metropolitan areas in the given frame? Explain. If not, how might you proceed to select a better sample of size 30 using the data provided in the file? Compute the mean number of short-term general hospitals for the metropolitan areas included in your revised sample. How does this

sample mean compare to that computed from your simple random sample in part **a**?

27. As human resources manager of a manufacturing plant, you are quite concerned about recent reports of sexual and racial harassment from the production workers within the organization. In an effort to gain a better understanding of the apparent problems, you decide that it would be wise to interview a cross section of your employees about this and other issues in the workplace.

a. Using the frame of employees provided in the file **P08_27.xlsx**, select a subset of 30 production workers stratified by sex with proportional sample sizes.

b. Next, select another subset of 30 workers stratified by race with proportional sample sizes.

c. Finally, select one more subset of 30 workers stratified by *both* sex and race (e.g., black women, white men, Asian women, Hispanic men, etc.) with proportional sample sizes.

d. Explain how the human resources manager could apply cluster sampling in selecting a sample of size 30 from this frame. What are the advantages and disadvantages of employing cluster sampling in this case?

28. Is the overall cost of living higher or lower for urban areas in particular geographical regions of the United States?

a. Begin by first selecting 40 urban areas from the given frame provided in the file **P08_28.xlsx**. The urban areas you select should be stratified by geographical location within the United States (e.g., northeast, southeast, midwest, northwest, or southwest) and should reflect proportional sample sizes. Note that you will first need to assign the given urban areas to one of any number of such geographical regions before you can generate a stratified sample.

b. Explain how you could apply cluster sampling in selecting a sample of size 40 from this frame. What are the advantages and disadvantages of employing cluster sampling in this case?

8.4 AN INTRODUCTION TO ESTIMATION

The purpose of any random sample is to estimate properties of a population from the data observed in the sample. The following is a good example to keep in mind. Suppose a government agency wants to know the average household income, where this average is taken over the population of all households in Atlanta. Then this unknown average is the population parameter of interest, and the government is likely to estimate it by sampling several "representative" households in Atlanta and reporting the average of their incomes.

The mathematical procedures appropriate for performing this estimation depend on which properties of the population are of interest and which type of random sampling scheme is used. Because the details are considerably more complex when a more complex sampling scheme such as multistage sampling is used, we will focus on *simple* random samples, where the mathematical details are relatively straightforward. Details for other sampling schemes such as stratified sampling can be found in Levy and Lemeshow (1999). However, even for more complex sampling schemes, the *concepts* are the same as those we discuss here; only the details change.

Throughout most of this section, we focus on the population mean of some variable such as household income. Our goal is to estimate this population mean by using the data in a randomly selected sample. We first discuss the types of errors that can occur in this estimation problem.

8.4.1 Sources of Estimation Error

There are two basic sources of errors that can occur when we sample randomly from a population: *sampling error* and all other sources, usually lumped together as *nonsampling error*. Sampling error results from "unlucky" samples. As such, the term *error* is somewhat misleading. Suppose, for example, that the mean grade-point average (GPA) in a large class of 400 students is 2.85. The instructor wants to know this mean but doesn't want to ask *each* student for his or her GPA. Therefore, the instructor asks a random sample of 20 students for their GPAs, and it turns out that the sample mean for these 20 students is 2.97. If the instructor then infers that the mean of *all* GPAs is 2.97, the resulting sampling error is the difference between the reported value and the true value, 0.12. Note that the instructor hasn't done anything "wrong." This sampling error is essentially due to bad luck.

> **Sampling error** is the inevitable result of basing an inference on a random sample rather than on the entire population.

We see shortly how to measure the potential sampling error involved. The point here is that the resulting estimation error is not caused by anything we're doing wrong—we might just get unlucky.

Nonsampling error is quite different and can occur for a variety of reasons. We discuss a few of them.

- Perhaps the most serious type of nonsampling error is **nonresponse bias**. This occurs when a portion of the sample fails to respond to the survey. Anyone who has ever conducted a questionnaire, whether by mail, by phone, or any other method, knows that the percentage of nonrespondents can be quite large. The question is whether this introduces estimation error. If the nonrespondents *would* have responded similarly to the respondents, had they responded, we don't lose much by not hearing from them. However, because the nonrespondents don't respond, we typically have no way of knowing whether they differ in some important respect from the respondents. Therefore, unless we are able to persuade the nonrespondents to respond—through a follow-up phone call, for example—we must guess at the amount of nonresponse bias.

- Another source of nonsampling error is **nontruthful responses**. This is particularly a problem when we ask sensitive questions in a questionnaire. For example, if the questions "Have you ever had an abortion?" or "Do you regularly use cocaine?" are asked, most people will answer "no," regardless of whether the true answer is "yes" or "no."

There is a way of getting at such sensitive information, called the **randomized response** technique. Here the investigator presents each respondent with two questions, one of which is the sensitive question. The other is innocuous, such as, "Were you born in the summer?" The respondent is asked to decide randomly which of the two questions to answer—by flipping a coin, say—and then answer the chosen question truthfully. The investigator sees only the answer (yes or no), not the result of the coin flip. That is, the investigator doesn't know which question is being answered. However, by using probability theory, it is possible for the investigator to infer from many such responses the percentage of the population whose truthful answer to the sensitive question is "yes."

- Another type of nonsampling error is **measurement error**. This occurs when the responses to the questions do not reflect what the investigator had in mind. It might result from poorly worded questions, questions the respondents don't fully understand, questions that require the respondents to supply information they don't have, and so on. Undoubtedly, there have been times when you were filling out a questionnaire and said to yourself, "OK, I'll answer this as well as I can, but I know it's not what they want to know."

- One final type of nonsampling error is **voluntary response bias**. This occurs when the subset of people who respond to a survey differ in some important respect from all potential respondents. For example, suppose a population of students are surveyed to see how many hours they study per night. If the students who respond are predominantly those who get the best grades, the resulting sample mean number of hours will be biased on the high side.

From this discussion and your own experience with questionnaires, you should realize that the potential for nonsampling error is enormous. However, unlike sampling error, it cannot be measured with probability theory. It can be controlled only by using appropriate sampling procedures and designing good survey instruments. We do not pursue this topic any further here. If you are interested, however, you can learn about methods for controlling nonsampling error, such as proper questionnaire design, from books on marketing research.

8.4.2 Key Terms in Sampling

We now set the stage for the rest of this chapter, as well as for several later chapters. Suppose there is some numerical population parameter we would like to know. This parameter could be a population mean, a population proportion, the difference between two population means, the difference between two population proportions, or many others. Unless we measure each member of the population—that is, we take a complete census—we cannot learn the exact value of this population parameter. Therefore, we instead take a random sample of some type and try to *estimate* the population parameter from the data in the sample.

We typically begin by calculating a **point estimate** (or, simply, an **estimate**) from the sample data, a "best guess" of the population parameter. The difference between the point estimate and the true value of the population parameter is called the **estimation error** (or **sampling error**). We then try to use probability theory to gauge the magnitude of the estimation error. The key to this is the **sampling distribution** of the point estimate, which is defined as the distribution of the point estimates we would see from *all* possible samples (of a given sample size) from the population. Often we report the accuracy of the point estimate with an accompanying *confidence interval*. A **confidence interval** is an interval around the point estimate, calculated from the sample data, where we strongly believe the true value of the population parameter lies.

A **point estimate** is a single numeric value, a "best guess" of a population parameter, based on the data in a sample.

The **estimation error** (or **sampling error**) is the difference between the point estimate and the true value of the population parameter being estimated.

The **sampling distribution** of any point estimate is the distribution of the point estimates we would see from *all* possible samples (of a given sample size) from the population.

A **confidence interval** is an interval around the point estimate, calculated from the sample data, where we strongly believe the true value of the population parameter lies.

Additionally, there are two other key terms you should know. First, consider the *mean* of the sampling distribution of a point estimate. It is the average value of the point estimates we would see from all possible samples. When this mean is equal to the true value of the population parameter, we say that the point estimate is **unbiased**. Otherwise, we say that it is **biased**. Naturally, we prefer unbiased estimates. They sometimes miss on the low side and sometimes on the high side, but on average they tend to be right on target.

An **unbiased estimate** is a point estimate such that the mean of its sampling distribution is equal to the true value of the population parameter being estimated.

Unbiased estimates are desirable because they average out to the correct value. However, this isn't enough. We do not want point estimates from different samples to vary wildly from sample to sample. If they did, we couldn't rely much on an estimate from any particular sample. Therefore, we measure the standard deviation of the sampling distribution of the estimate, which indicates how much point estimates from different samples vary. In the context of sampling, this standard deviation is called the **standard error** of the estimate. Ideally, we want estimates that have *small* standard errors.

The **standard error** of an estimate is the standard deviation of the sampling distribution of the estimate. It measures how much estimates vary from sample to sample.

The terms in this subsection are relevant for practically any population parameter we might want to estimate. In the following subsection we discuss them in the context of estimating a population mean.

8.4.3 Sampling Distribution of the Sample Mean

In this section we discuss the estimation of the population mean from some population. For example, we might be interested in the mean household income for all families in a particular city, the mean diameter of all parts from a manufacturing process, the mean pollution count over all cities in the world with a population of at least 100,000, and so on. We label the unknown population mean by μ.

The point estimate of μ we use, based on a sample from the population, is the sample mean $\overline{X}$, the average of the observations in the sample. There are *other* possible point estimates for a population mean besides the sample mean. We could use the sample median, the *trimmed mean* (where we average all but the few most extreme observations), and others. However, it turns out that the "natural" estimate, the sample mean, has very good theoretical properties, so it is the point estimate used most often.

How accurate is $\overline{X}$ in estimating μ? That is, how large does the estimation error $\overline{X} - \mu$ tend to be? As we discussed in the previous subsection, the sampling distribution of the sample mean $\overline{X}$ provides the key. Before describing this sampling distribution in some generality, we provide some insight into it by revisiting the population of 40 incomes in Example 8.1. There we showed how to generate a single random sample of size 10. For the particular sample we generated (see Figure 8.2), the sample mean was $38,750. Because we know that the population mean of all 40 incomes is $39,985, the estimation error based on this particular sample is the difference $38,750 − $39,985, or $1235 on the low side.

However, this is only one of many possible samples. To see other possibilities, we used StatTools's procedure for generating random samples to generate 100 random samples of size 10 from the population of 40 incomes. We then calculated the sample mean for each random sample and created a histogram of these sample means, shown in Figure 8.7. Although this is not *exactly* the sampling distribution of the sample mean (because there are many more than 100 possible samples of size 10 from a population of size 40), it indicates how the possible sample means are distributed. They are most likely to be near the population mean ($39,985), they are very unlikely to be more than about $3000 from this population mean, and the distribution is approximately bell shaped.

The insights in the previous paragraph can be generalized. It turns out that the sampling distribution of the sample mean has the following properties, regardless of the underlying population. First, it is an unbiased estimate of the population mean, as indicated in equation (8.1). The sample means from some samples will be too low, and those from other samples will be too high, but on the average, they will be just right.

Unbiased Property of Sample Mean

$$E(\overline{X}) = \mu \tag{8.1}$$

The second property involves the variability of the $\overline{X}$ estimate. Recall that the standard deviation of an estimate, called the standard error, indicates how much the estimates vary from sample to sample. The standard error of $\overline{X}$ is given in equation (8.2). Here, $\text{SE}(\overline{X})$ is our abbreviation for the standard error of $\overline{X}$, σ is the standard deviation of the population, and n is the sample size. We see that the standard error is large when the observations in the population are spread out (large σ), but that the standard error can be reduced by taking a larger sample.[1]

Figure 8.7
Approximate Sampling Distribution of Sample Mean

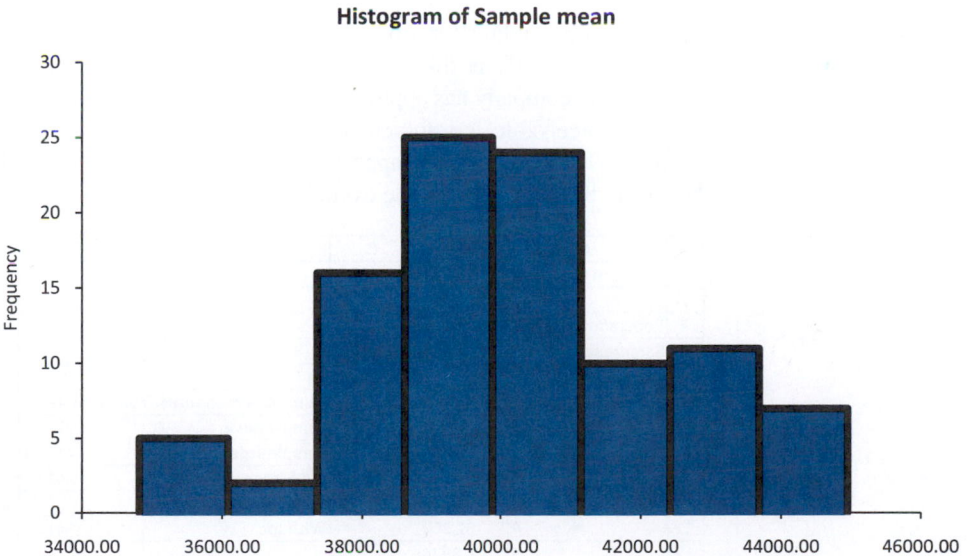

---

[1]This formula for $\text{SE}(\overline{X})$ assumes that the sample size n is small relative to the population size N. As a rule of thumb, we assume that n is no more than 5% of N. Later we provide a "correction" to this formula when n is a larger percentage of N.

Standard Error of Sample Mean

$$\text{SE}(\overline{X}) = \sigma/\sqrt{n} \qquad\qquad (8.2)$$

There is one problem with the standard error in equation (8.2). Its value depends on another unknown population parameter, σ. Therefore, it is customary to approximate the standard error by substituting the *sample* standard deviation, s, for σ. This leads to equation (8.3).

Approximate Standard Error of Sample Mean

$$\text{SE}(\overline{X}) = s/\sqrt{n} \qquad\qquad (8.3)$$

As we discuss in the next subsection, the shape of the sampling distribution of $\overline{X}$ is approximately normal. Therefore, we can use the standard error exactly as we have used standard deviations in previous chapters to obtain confidence intervals of the population mean.[2] Specifically, if we go out 2 standard errors on either side of the sample mean, as shown in expression (8.4), we are 95% confident of capturing the population mean. Alternatively, we are 95% confident that the estimation error will be no greater than 2 standard errors in magnitude.

Confidence Interval for Population Mean

$$\overline{X} \pm 2s/\sqrt{n} \qquad\qquad (8.4)$$

The following example illustrates a typical use of sample information.

EXAMPLE

8.4 ESTIMATING THE MEAN OF ACCOUNTS RECEIVABLE FOR A FURNITURE RETAILER

An internal auditor for a furniture retailer wants to estimate the average of all accounts receivable, where this average is taken over the population of all customer accounts. Because the company has approximately 10,000 accounts, an exhaustive enumeration of all accounts receivable is impractical. Therefore, the auditor randomly samples 100 of the accounts. The observed data appear in Figure 8.8. (See the file **Auditing Receivables.xlsx**.) What can the auditor conclude from this sample?

Figure 8.8

Sampling in
Auditing Example

	A	B	C	D	E
1	Random sample of accounts receivable				
2					
3	Population size	10000			
4	Sample size	100			
5					
6	Sample of receivables			Summary measures from sample	
7	Account	Amount		Sample mean	$278.92
8	1	$85		Sample stdev	$419.21
9	2	$1,061		Std Error of mean	$41.92
10	3	$0			
11	4	$1,260		With fpc	$41.71
12	5	$924			
13	6	$129			
105	98	$657			
106	99	$86			
107	100	$0			

[2]Strictly speaking, as we discuss in the next chapter, this is an approximate 95% confidence interval for the mean.

Objective To illustrate the meaning of standard error of the mean in a sample of accounts receivable.

Solution

The receivables for the 100 sampled accounts appear in column B. This is the only information available to the auditor, so he must base all conclusions on these sample data. We calculate the sample mean and sample standard deviation in cells E7 and E8 with the formulas

=AVERAGE(B8:B107)

and

=STDEV(B8:B107)

Then we use equation (8.3) to calculate the (approximate) standard error of the mean in cell E9 with the formula

=E8/SQRT(B4)

The auditor should interpret these values as follows. First, the sample mean \$279 can be used to estimate the unknown population mean. It provides a best guess for the average of the receivables from all 10,000 accounts. In fact, because the sample mean is an unbiased estimate of the population mean, there is no reason to suspect that \$279 either underestimates or overestimates the population mean. Second, the standard error \$42 provides a measure of accuracy of the \$279 estimate. Specifically, there is about a 95% chance that the estimate differs by no more than 2 standard errors (about \$84) from the true (but unknown) population mean. Therefore, the auditor can be 95% certain that the mean from all 10,000 accounts is within the interval \$279 ± \$84, that is, between \$195 and \$363. ∎

It is important to distinguish between the sample standard deviation s and the standard error of the mean, approximated by $s/\sqrt{n}$. The sample standard deviation in the auditing example, \$419, measures the variability in *individual* receivables in the sample (or in the population). By scrolling down column B, we see that there are some very low amounts (many zeros) and some fairly large amounts. This variability is indicated by the rather large sample standard deviation s. However, this value does not measure the accuracy of the sample mean as an estimate of the population mean. To judge *its* accuracy, we need to divide s by the square root of the sample size n. The resulting standard error, about \$42, is much smaller than the sample standard deviation. It indicates that we can be about 95% certain that the sampling error is no greater than \$84.

The Finite Population Correction We mentioned that equation (8.2) [or equation (8.3)] for the standard error of $\overline{X}$ is appropriate when the sample size n is small relative to the population size N. Generally, "small" means that n is no more than 5% of N. In most realistic samples this is certainly true. For example, political polls are typically based on samples of approximately 1000 people from the entire U.S. population.

There are situations, however, when we sample more than 5% of the population. In this case the formula for the standard error of the mean should be modified with a *finite population correction,* or *fpc,* factor. Then the modified standard error of the mean appears in equation (8.5), where the *fpc* is given by equation (8.6). Note that this factor is always less than 1 (when $n > 1$) and it decreases as n increases. Therefore, the standard error of the mean decreases—and the accuracy increases—as n increases.

> **Standard Error of Mean with Finite Population Correction Factor**
>
> $$\mathrm{SE}(\overline{X}) = fpc \times (s/\sqrt{n}) \tag{8.5}$$

> **Finite Population Correction Factor**
>
> $$fpc = \sqrt{\frac{N-n}{N-1}} \tag{8.6}$$

To see how the *fpc* varies with *n* and *N*, consider the values in Table 8.1. Rather than listing *n*, we have listed the percentage of the population sampled, that is, $n/N \times 100\%$. It is clear that when 5% or less of the population is sampled, the *fpc* is very close to 1 and can safely be ignored. In this case we can use $s/\sqrt{n}$ as the standard error of the mean. Otherwise, we should use the modified formula in equation (8.5).

Table 8.1 Finite Population Correction Factors

N	% Sampled	fpc
100	5%	0.980
100	10%	0.953
10,000	1%	0.995
10,000	5%	0.975
10,000	10%	0.949
1,000,000	1%	0.995
1,000,000	5%	0.975
1,000,000	10%	0.949

If less than 5% of the population is sampled, as is often the case, the fpc can safely be ignored.

In the auditing example, $n/N = 100/100,000 = 0.1\%$. This suggests that the *fpc* can safely be omitted. We illustrate this in cell E11 of Figure 8.8, which uses the formula from equation (8.5):

=SQRT((B3-B4)/(B3-1))*E9

Clearly, it makes no practical difference in this example whether we use the *fpc* or not. The standard error, rounded to the nearest dollar, is $42 in either case.

Virtually all standard error formulas used in sampling include an *fpc* factor. However, because it is rarely necessary—the sample size is usually very small relative to the population size—we omit it from here on.

8.4.4 The Central Limit Theorem

Our discussion to this point has concentrated primarily on the mean and standard deviation of the sampling distribution of the sample mean. In this section we discuss this sampling distribution in more detail. Because of an important theoretical result called the *central limit theorem*, we know that this distribution is approximately *normal* with mean μ and standard deviation $\sigma/\sqrt{n}$. This theorem is the reason why the normal distribution appears in so many statistical results. We can state the theorem as follows.

> For any population distribution with mean μ and standard deviation σ, the sampling distribution of the sample mean $\overline{X}$ is approximately normal with mean μ and standard deviation $\sigma/\sqrt{n}$, and the approximation improves as *n* increases.

The important part of this result is the *normality* of the sampling distribution. We know, without any conditions placed upon the sample size n, that the mean and standard deviation are μ and $\sigma/\sqrt{n}$. However, the central limit theorem also implies normality, provided that n is reasonably large.

How large must n be for the approximation to be valid? Most analysts suggest $n \geq 30$ as a rule of thumb. However, this depends on the population distribution. If the population distribution is very *nonnormal*—extremely skewed or bimodal, for example—then the normal approximation might not be accurate unless n is considerably greater than 30. On the other hand, if the population distribution is already approximately symmetric, then the normal approximation is quite good for n considerably less than 30. In fact, in the special case where the population distribution itself is normal, the sampling distribution of $\overline{X}$ is *exactly* normal for *any* value of n.

The central limit theorem is not a simple concept to grasp. To help explain it, we employ simulation in the following example.

EXAMPLE | **8.5 AVERAGE WINNINGS FROM SPINNING A WHEEL OF FORTUNE**

Suppose you have the opportunity to play a game with a "wheel of fortune" (similar to a popular television game show). When you spin a large wheel, it is equally likely to stop in any position. Depending on where it stops, you win anywhere from $0 to $1000. Let's suppose your winnings are actually based on not one, but n spins of the wheel. For example, if $n = 2$, your winnings are based on the average of two spins. If the first spin results in $580 and the second spin results in $320, then you win the average, $450. How does the distribution of your winnings depend on n?

Objective To illustrate the central limit theorem in the context of winnings in a game of chance.

Solution

First, we need to discuss what this experiment has to do with random sampling. Here, the population is the set of all outcomes we could obtain from a *single* spin of the wheel—that is, all dollar values from $0 to $1000. Each spin results in one randomly sampled dollar value from this population. Furthermore, because we have assumed that the wheel is equally likely to land in any position, all possible values in the continuum from $0 to $1000 have the same chance of occurring. The resulting population distribution is called the **uniform distribution** on the interval from $0 to $1000. (See Figure 8.9, where the 1 on the horizontal axis corresponds to $1000.) It can be shown (with calculus) that the mean and standard deviation of this uniform distribution are $\mu = \$500$ and $\sigma = \$289$.[3]

Figure 8.9

Uniform Distribution

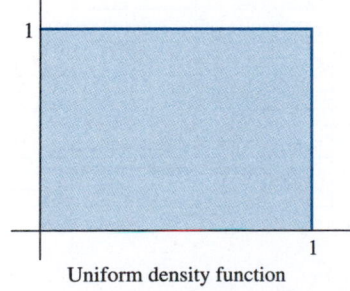

Uniform density function

---

[3]In general, if a distribution is uniform on the interval from a to b, then its mean is the midpoint $(a + b)/2$ and its standard deviation is $(b - a)/\sqrt{12}$.

Before we go any further, take a moment to test your own intuition. If you play this game once and your winnings are based on the average of n spins, how likely is that you will win at least $600 if $n = 1$? if $n = 3$? if $n = 10$? (The answers are 0.4, 0.27, and 0.14, respectively, where the last two answers are approximate and are based on the central limit theorem or on our simulations. So you are much less likely to "win big" if your winnings are based on the average of many spins.)

Now we analyze the distribution of winnings based on the average of n spins. We do so by means of a sequence of simulations in Excel, for $n = 1$, $n = 2$, $n = 3$, $n = 6$, and $n = 10$. (See the file **Wheel of Fortune Simulation.xlsx**, which is set up to work for any number of spins up to 10.) For each simulation we consider 1000 replications of an experiment. Each replication of the experiment simulates n spins of the wheel and calculates the average—that is, the winnings—from these n spins. Based on these 1000 replications, we can then calculate the average winnings, the standard deviation of winnings, and a histogram of winnings for each n. These will show clearly how the distribution of winnings depends on n.

The values in Figure 8.10 and the histogram in Figure 8.11 show the results for $n = 1$. Here there is no averaging—we spin the wheel once and win the amount shown. To replicate this experiment 1000 times and collect statistics, we proceed as follows.

1 **Random outcomes.** To generate outcomes uniformly distributed between $0 and $1000, enter the formula

=IF(B$9<=$B$6,$B$3+($B$4-$B$3)*RAND(),"")

in cell B11 and copy it to the entire range B11:K1010. The effect of this formula, given the values in cells B3 and B4, is to generate a random number between 0 and 1 and multiply it by $1000. The effect of the IF part is to fill up as many Outcome columns as there are spins in cell B6 and to leave the rest blank.

2 **Winnings.** Calculate the winnings in each row in column L as the average of the outcomes of the spins in that row. (Note that the AVERAGE function ignores blanks.)

3 **Summary measures.** Calculate the average and standard deviation of the 1000 winnings in column L with the AVERAGE and STDEV functions. These values appear in cells L4 and L5.

4 **Frequency table and histogram.** Use the StatTools Histogram procedure to create a histogram of the values in column L.

Figure 8.10
Simulation of Winnings from a Single Spin

	A	B	C	D	E	F	G	H	I	J	K	L
1	Wheel of fortune simulation											
2												
3	Minimum winnings	$0									Summary measures of winnings	
4	Maximum winnings	$1,000									Mean	$506
5											Stdev	$294
6	Number of spins	1										
7												
8	Simulation of spins											
9	Spin	1	2	3	4	5	6	7	8	9	10	
10	Replication	Outcome	Outcome	Outcome	Outcome	Outcome	Outcome	Outcome	Outcome	Outcome	Outcome	Winnings
11	1	$678										$678
12	2	$127										$127
13	3	$287										$287
14	4	$623										$623
15	5	$883										$883
16	6	$884										$884
17	7	$700										$700
18	8	$973										$973
19	9	$860										$860
20	10	$32										$32

Figure 8.11

Histogram of
Simulated Winnings
from a Single Spin

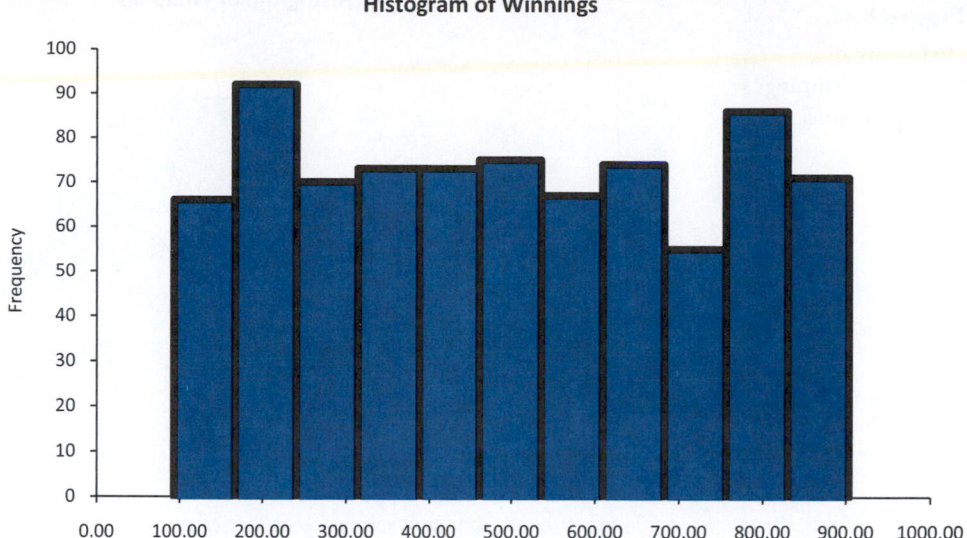

Histogram of Winnings

Note the following from Figures 8.10 and 8.11.

- The sample mean of the winnings (cell L4) is very close to the population mean, $500.
- The standard deviation of the winnings (cell L5) is very close to the population standard deviation, $289.
- The histogram is nearly flat.

These properties should come as no surprise. When $n = 1$, the "sample mean" is a single observation—that is, no averaging takes place. Therefore, the sampling distribution of the sample mean is *equivalent* to the flat population distribution in Figure 8.9.

But what happens when $n > 1$? Figure 8.12 shows the results for $n = 2$. All you need to do is change the number of spins in cell B6, and everything updates automatically. The average winnings is again very close to $500, but the standard deviation of winnings is much lower. In fact, it is close to $\sigma/\sqrt{2} = 289/\sqrt{2} = \$204$, exactly as theory predicts. In addition, the histogram of winnings is no longer flat. It is triangularly shaped—symmetric, but not yet bell shaped.

To develop similar simulations for $n = 3$, $n = 6$, $n = 10$, or any other n, just change the number of spins in cell B6. The resulting histograms appear in Figures 8.13 through 8.15. They clearly show two effects of increasing n: (1) the histogram becomes more bell shaped, and (2) there is less variability. However, the mean stays right at $500. This behavior is exactly what the central limit theorem predicts. In fact, because the population distribution is symmetric in this example—it is flat—we see the effect of the central limit theorem for n much less than 30; it is already evident for n as low as 6.

Figure 8.12

Histogram of
Simulated Winnings
from Two Spins

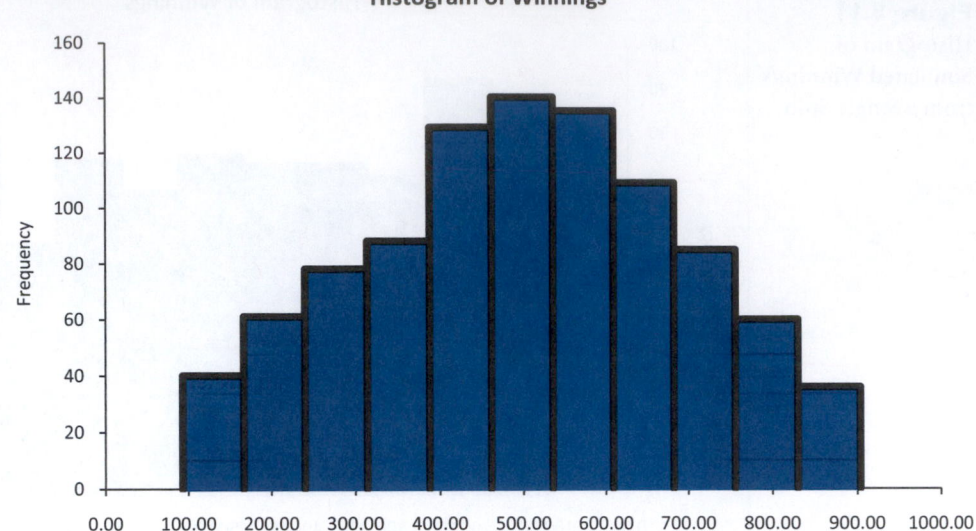

Figure 8.13

Histogram of
Simulated Winnings
from Three Spins

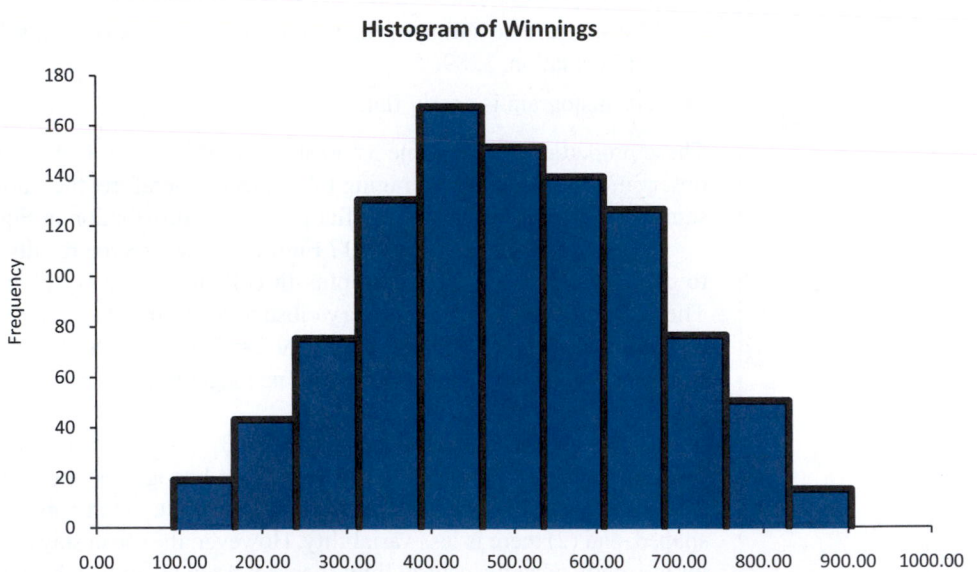

Figure 8.14
Histogram of
Simulated Winnings
from Six Spins

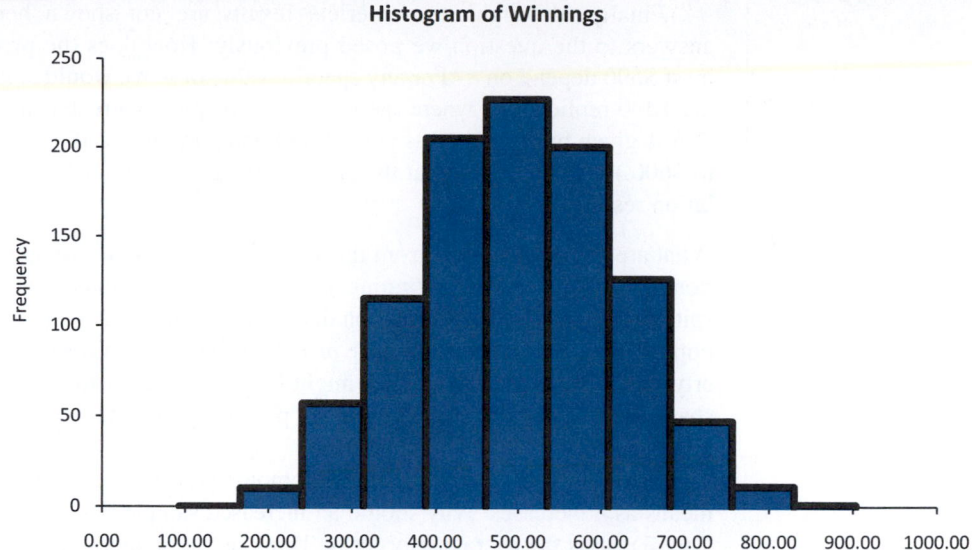

Figure 8.15
Histogram of
Simulated Winnings
from Ten Spins

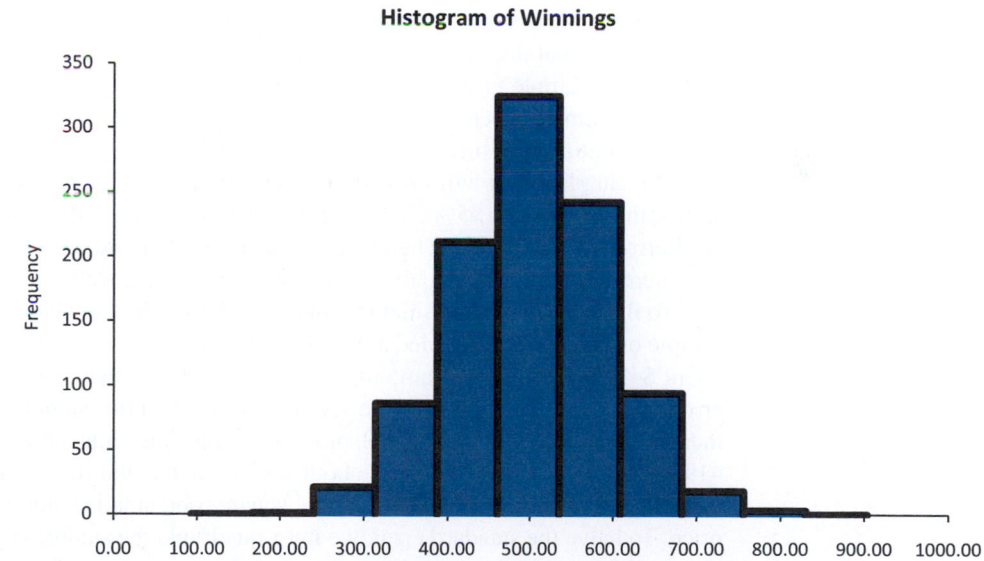

Finally, although the numerical results are not shown here, we could find the answers to the question we posed previously: How does the probability of winning at least $600 depend on n? For any specific value of n, we would simply find the fraction of the 1000 replications where the average of n spins is greater than $600. (This information is given by StatTools as part of its histogram output if you set one of the bin limits to $600.) You can check that the answers we gave previously are supported by the simulation results. ∎

What are the main lessons from this example? For one, we see that the sampling distribution of the sample mean (winnings) is bell shaped when n is reasonably large. This is in spite of the fact that the population distribution is flat—far from bell shaped. Actually, the population distribution could have *any* shape, not just uniform, and the bell-shaped property would still hold (although n might have to be larger than in the example). This bell-shaped normality property allows us to perform probability calculations, as we will see in subsequent examples.

Equally important, this example demonstrates the *decreased variability* in the sample means as n increases. Why should an increased sample size lead to decreased variability? The reason is the averaging process. Think about obtaining a winnings of $750 based on the average of two spins. All we need is two lucky spins. In fact, one really lucky spin and an average spin will do. But think about obtaining a winnings of $750 based on the average of *10* spins. Now we need a *lot* of really lucky spins—and virtually no unlucky ones. The point is that we are much less likely to obtain a really large (or really small) sample mean when n is large than when n is small. This is exactly what we mean when we say that the variability of the sample means decreases with increasing sample size.

This decreasing variability is predicted by the formula for the standard error of the mean, $\sigma/\sqrt{n}$. As n increases, the standard error obviously decreases. This is what drives the behavior in Figures 8.12 through 8.15. In fact, using $\sigma = \$289$, the standard errors for $n = 2$, $n = 3$, $n = 6$, and $n = 10$ are $204, $167, $118, and $91, respectively.

Finally, what does this decreasing variability have to do with estimating a population mean with a sample mean? Very simply, it means that the sample mean tends to be a more *accurate* estimate when the sample size is large. Because of the approximate normality from the central limit theorem, we know from Chapter 6 that there is about a 95% chance that the sample mean will be within 2 standard errors of the population mean. In other words, there is about a 95% chance that the sampling error will be no greater than two standard errors in magnitude. Therefore, because the standard error decreases as the sample size increases, the sampling error is likely to decrease as well.

To illustrate this, reconsider the auditor in Example 8.4. The standard error based on a sample of size $n = 100$ yielded a sample standard deviation of $419 and a standard error of about $42. Therefore, the sampling error has a 95% chance of being less than 2 standard errors, or $84, in magnitude. If the auditor believes that this sampling error is too large and therefore randomly samples 300 more accounts, then the new standard error will be $419/\sqrt{400} \approx \$21$. Now there is about a 95% chance that the sampling error will be no more than $42. Note that because of the square root, small standard errors come at a high price. To halve the standard error, we must quadruple the sample size!

8.4.5 Sample Size Determination

The problem of determining the appropriate sample size in any sampling context is not an easy one, but it must be faced in the planning stages, *before* any sampling is done. We focus here on the relationship between sampling error and sample size. As we discussed previously, the sampling error tends to decrease as the sample size increases, so the desire to minimize sampling error encourages us to select larger sample sizes. We should note, however, that several other factors encourage us to select *smaller* sample sizes. The ultimate sample size selection must achieve a trade-off between these opposing forces.

What are these other factors? First, there is the obvious cost of sampling. Larger sample sizes require larger costs. Sometimes, a company or agency might have a budget for a given sampling project. If the sample size required to achieve an "acceptable" sampling error is 500, say, but the budget allows for a sample size of only 300, budget considerations will probably prevail.

Another problem caused by large sample sizes is timely collection of the data. Suppose a retailer wants to collect sample data from its customers to decide whether to run an advertising blitz in the coming week. Obviously, the retailer needs to collect these data quickly if they are to be of any use, and a large sample could require too much time to collect.

Finally, a more subtle problem caused by large sample sizes is the increased chance of *nonsampling* error, such as nonresponse bias. As we discussed previously in this chapter, there are many potential sources of nonsampling error, and they are usually very difficult to quantify. However, they are likely to increase as the sample size increases. Arguably, the potential increase in *sampling* error from a smaller sample could be more than offset by a decrease in nonsampling error, especially if the cost saved by the smaller sample size is used to reduce the sources of nonsampling error—more follow-up of nonrespondents, for example.

Nevertheless, the determination of sample size is usually driven by sampling error considerations. If we want to estimate a population mean with a sample mean, then the key is the standard error of the mean, given by

$$\text{SE}(\overline{X}) = \sigma/\sqrt{n}$$

We know from the central limit theorem that if n is reasonably large, there is about a 95% chance that the magnitude of the sampling error will be no more than 2 standard errors. Because σ is fixed in the formula for $\text{SE}(\overline{X})$, we can choose n to make $2\text{SE}(\overline{X})$ acceptably small.

We postpone further discussion of sample size selection until the next chapter, where we discuss in detail how it can be used to control confidence interval length.

8.4.6 Summary of Key Ideas for Simple Random Sampling

To this point, we have covered some very important concepts. Because we build on these concepts in later chapters, we summarize them here.

Key Concepts of Simple Random Sampling

- To estimate a population mean with a simple random sample, we use the sample mean as a "best guess." This estimate is called a *point estimate*. That is, $\overline{X}$ is a point estimate of μ.

- The accuracy of the point estimate is measured by its standard error. It is the standard deviation of the sampling distribution of the point estimate. The standard error of $\overline{X}$ is approximately $s/\sqrt{n}$, where s is the sample standard deviation.

- A *confidence interval* (with 95% confidence) for the population mean extends to approximately 2 standard errors on either side of the sample mean.

- From the *central limit theorem*, the sampling distribution of $\overline{X}$ is approximately normal when n is reasonably large.

- There is approximately a 95% chance that any particular $\overline{X}$ will be within 2 standard errors of the population mean μ.

- The sampling error can be reduced by increasing the sample size n. Appropriate sample size formulas for controlling confidence interval length are given in the next chapter.

PROBLEMS

Level A

29. A manufacturing company's quality control personnel have recorded the proportion of defective items for each of 500 monthly shipments of one of the computer components that the company produces. The data are in the file **P02_02.xlsx**. The quality control department manager does not have sufficient time to review all of these data. Rather, she would like to examine the proportions of defective items for a sample of these shipments.
   a. Use Excel to generate a simple random sample of size 25 from the given frame.
   b. Compute a point estimate of the population mean from the sample selected in part **a**. What is the sampling error in this case? Assume that the population consists of the proportion of defective items for each of the given 500 monthly shipments.
   c. Determine a good approximation to the standard error of the mean in this case.
   d. Repeat parts **b** and **c** after generating a simple random sample of size 50 from the given frame.

30. The manager of a local fast-food restaurant is interested in improving the service provided to customers who use the restaurant's drive-up window. As a first step in this process, the manager asks his assistant to record the time (in minutes) it takes to serve a large number of customers at the final window in the facility's drive-up system. The given frame of 200 customer service times are all observed during the busiest hour of the day for this fast-food operation. The data are in the file **P02_04.xlsx**.
   a. Use Excel to generate a simple random sample of size 10 from this frame.
   b. Compute a point estimate of the population mean from the sample selected in part **a**. What is the sampling error in this case? Assume that the population consists of the given 200 customer service times.
   c. Determine a good approximation to the standard error of the mean in this case.
   d. Repeat parts **b** and **c** after generating a simple random sample of size 20 from the given frame.

31. Consider the given set of average annual household income levels of citizens of selected U.S. metropolitan areas in the file **P03_06.xlsx**.
   a. Use Excel to obtain a simple random sample of size 15 from this frame.
   b. Compute a point estimate of the population mean from the sample selected in part **a**. What is the sampling error in this case? Assume that the population consists of all average annual household income levels in the given frame.
   c. Determine a good approximation to the standard error of the mean in this case.

   d. Repeat parts **b** and **c** after generating a simple random sample of size 30 from the given frame.

32. The operations manager of a toll booth located at a major exit of a state turnpike is trying to estimate the average number of vehicles that arrive at the toll booth during a 1-minute period during the peak of rush-hour traffic. In an effort to estimate this average throughput value, he records the number of vehicles that arrive at the toll booth over a 1-minute interval commencing at the same time for each of 365 normal weekdays. The data are provided in the file **P02_09.xlsx**.
   a. Choose a simple random sample of size 18 from the given frame to help the operations manager estimate the average throughput value.
   b. Compute a point estimate of the population mean from the sample selected in part **a**. What is the sampling error in this case? Assume that the population consists of the numbers of vehicle arrivals over the 365 weekdays in the given frame.
   c. Determine a good approximation to the standard error of the mean in this case.
   d. Repeat parts **b** and **c** after generating a simple random sample of size 36 from the given frame.

33. Continuing the previous problem with the same data file, answer the following questions.
   a. What sample size would be required for the operations manager to be approximately 95% sure that his estimate of the average throughput value is within 1 unit of the true mean? Assume that his best estimate of the population standard deviation σ is 1.7 arrivals per minute.
   b. How does the answer to part **a** change if the operations manager wants his estimate to be within 0.75 unit of the actual population mean? Explain the difference in your answers to parts **a** and **b**.

34. A lightbulb manufacturer wants to estimate the average number of defective bulbs contained in a box shipped by the company. Production personnel at this company have recorded the number of defective bulbs found in each of the 1000 boxes shipped during the past week. These data are provided in **P08_11.xlsx**.
   a. What sample size would be required for the production personnel to be approximately 95% sure that their estimate of the average number of defective bulbs per box is within 0.25 unit of the true mean? Assume that their best estimate of the population standard deviation σ is 0.9 defective bulb per box.
   b. How does the answer to part **a** change if the production personnel want their estimate to be within 0.40 unit of the actual population mean? Explain the difference in your answers to parts **a** and **b**.

418   Chapter 8   Sampling and Sampling Distributions

35. Senior management of a certain consulting services firm is concerned about a growing decline in the organization's productivity. In an effort to understand the depth and extent of this problem, management would like to estimate the average number of hours its employees spend on work-related activities in a typical week. The frame of virtually all of the firm's full-time employees, including the employees' self-reported amounts of time typically devoted to work activities each week, is provided in **P08_35.xlsx**.

    a. What sample size would be required for management to be approximately 95% sure that its estimate of the average number of hours the employees spend on work-related activities in a typical week is within 6 hours of the true mean? Assume that management's best estimate of the population standard deviation σ is 10 hours per week.

    b. How does the answer to part **a** change if management want its estimate to be within 3 hours of the actual population mean? Explain the difference in your answers to parts **a** and **b**.

36. Elected officials in a small Florida town are preparing the annual budget for their community. Specifically, they would like to estimate how much their constituents living in this town are typically paying each year in real estate taxes. Given that there are more than 3000 homeowners in this small community, officials have decided to sample a representative subset of taxpayers and thoroughly study their tax payments. The latest frame of homeowners is given in **P08_36.xlsx**.

    a. What sample size would be required for elected officials to be approximately 95% sure that their estimate of the average annual real estate tax payment made by homeowners in their community is within $100 of the true mean? Assume that their best estimate of the population standard deviation σ is $535.

    b. Choose a simple random sample of the size found in part **a**.

    c. Compute the observed sampling error based on the sample you have drawn from the population given in the file. How does the actual sampling error compare to the maximum probable absolute error established in part **a**? Explain.

Level B

37. Continuing Problem 29, what proportion of the given 500 monthly shipments contain fractions of defective components within 1 standard deviation of the mean (based on the original simple random sample of size 25)? What proportion of the 500 monthly shipments contain fractions of defective components within 2 standard deviations of the mean (again, based on the original simple random sample of size 25)?

38. Continuing Problem 30, what proportion of the given 200 customer service times are within 2 standard deviations of the mean (based on the original simple random sample of size 10)? What proportion of the 200 customer service times are within 3 standard deviations of the mean (again, based on the original simple random sample of size 10)?

39. Continuing Problem 31, what proportion of the given average annual household income levels are within 2 standard deviations of the mean (based on the original simple random sample of size 15)? What proportion of the given average annual household income levels are within 2 standard deviations of the mean (now, based on the second simple random sample of size 30)?

40. Continuing Problem 32, what proportion of the numbers of vehicle arrivals over the given 365 weekdays are within 2 standard deviations of the mean (based on the original simple random sample of size 18)? What proportion of the given numbers of vehicle arrivals are within 2 standard deviations of the mean (now, based on the second simple random sample of size 36)?

41. Wal-Mart buyers seek to purchase adequate supplies of various brands of toothpaste to meet the ongoing demands of its customers. In particular, Wal-Mart is interested in estimating the proportion of its customers who favor the country's leading brand of toothpaste, Crest. The file **P08_41.xlsx** contains the toothpaste brand preferences of 2000 Wal-Mart customers, obtained recently through the administration of a customer survey.

    a. Use Excel to choose a simple random sample of size 100 from the given frame.

    b. Using the sample found in part **a**, compute a point estimate (called the sample proportion, $\hat{p}$) of the true proportion of Wal-Mart customers who prefer Crest toothpaste. What is the sampling error in this case? Assume that the population consists of the preferences of all customers in the given frame.

    c. Given that the standard error of the sampling distribution of the sample proportion $\hat{p}$ is approximately $\sqrt{\hat{p}(1-\hat{p})/n}$, compute a good approximation to the standard error of the sample proportion in this case.

    d. Repeat parts **b** and **c** after generating a simple random sample of size 50 from the given frame. How do you explain the differences in your results?

42. A finance professor has just given a midterm examination in her corporate finance course. The 100 scores are provided in **P02_05.xlsx**.

    a. Generate an appropriate histogram for the given distribution of 100 examination scores. Characterize this distribution. Also, compute the mean and standard deviation of the given scores.

b. Repeatedly choose simple random samples of size 2 from the original distribution given in the file. Record the sample mean for each of 100 sampling repetitions and generate an appropriate histogram of the resulting sampling distribution. Characterize this sampling distribution and compute its mean and standard deviation.

c. Repeatedly choose simple random samples of size 5 from the original distribution given in the file. Record the sample mean for each of 100 sampling repetitions and generate an appropriate histogram of the resulting sampling distribution. Characterize this sampling distribution and compute its mean and standard deviation.

d. Repeatedly choose simple random samples of size 10 from the original distribution given in the file. Record the sample mean for each of 100 sampling repetitions and generate an appropriate histogram of the resulting sampling distribution. Characterize this sampling distribution and compute its mean and standard deviation.

e. Explain the changes in your constructed sampling distributions as the sample size was increased from $n = 2$ to $n = 10$. In particular, how does the sampling distribution you constructed in part **d** compare to the original distribution (where $n = 1$) you described in part **a**?

43. The annual base salaries for 200 students graduating from a reputable MBA program this year are of interest to those in the admissions office who are responsible for marketing the program to prospective students. These salaries are given in the file **P02_74.xlsx**.

a. Generate an appropriate histogram for the given distribution of 200 annual salaries. Characterize this distribution. Also, compute the mean and standard deviation of the given salaries.

b. Repeatedly choose simple random samples of size 3 from the original distribution given in the file. Record the sample mean for each of 100 sampling repetitions and generate an appropriate histogram of the resulting sampling distribution. Characterize

this sampling distribution and compute its mean and standard deviation.

c. Repeatedly choose simple random samples of size 6 from the original distribution given in the file. Record the sample mean for each of 100 sampling repetitions and generate an appropriate histogram of the resulting sampling distribution. Characterize this sampling distribution and compute its mean and standard deviation.

d. Repeatedly choose simple random samples of size 12 from the original distribution given in the file. Record the sample mean for each of 100 sampling repetitions and generate an appropriate histogram of the resulting sampling distribution. Characterize this sampling distribution and compute its mean and standard deviation.

e. Explain the changes in your constructed sampling distributions as the sample size was increased from $n = 3$ to $n = 12$. In particular, how does the sampling distribution you constructed in part **d** compare to the original distribution (where $n = 1$) you described in part **a**?

44. A market research consultant hired by the Pepsi-Cola Co. is interested in determining the proportion of consumers who favor Pepsi-Cola over Coke Classic in a particular urban location. A frame of customers from the market under investigation is provided in **P08_44.xlsx**.

a. What sample size would be required for the market research consultant to be approximately 95% sure that her estimate of the proportion of consumers who favor Pepsi-Cola in the given urban location is within 0.20 of the true proportion? Assume that her best estimate of the population proportion parameter p is 0.45. [*Hint:* The required sample size formula in this case is given by $n = 4p(1 - p)/B^2$, where p is the population proportion parameter and B is the specified error, in this case 0.20.]

b. How does the answer to part **a** change if the market research consultant wants her estimate to be within 0.15 of the actual population proportion? Explain the difference in your answers to parts **a** and **b**.

8.5 CONCLUSION

This chapter has provided the fundamental concepts behind statistical inference. We discussed ways to obtain random samples from a population; how to calculate a point estimate of a particular population parameter, the population mean; and how to measure the accuracy of this point estimate. The key idea is the sampling distribution of the estimate and specifically its standard deviation, called the standard error of the estimate. From the central limit theorem, we saw that the sampling distribution of the sample mean is approximately normal, which implies that the sample mean will be within 2 standard errors of the population mean in approximately 95% of all random samples. In the next two chapters we build on these important concepts.

Summary of Key Terms

Term	Symbol	Explanation	Excel	Page	Equation Number
Population		Contains all members about which a study intends to make inferences		388	
Frame		A list of all members of the population		389	
Sampling units		Potential members of a sample from a population		389	
Probability sample		Any sample that is chosen by using a random mechanism		389	
Judgmental sample		Any sample that is chosen according to a sampler's judgment rather a random mechanism		389	
Simple random sample		A sample where each member of the population has the same chance of being chosen	StatTools/ Data Utilities/ Random Sample	390	
Systematic sample		A sample where one of the first k members is selected randomly, and then every kth member after this one is selected		395	
Stratified sample		A sample where the population is divided into relatively homogeneous subsets called strata, and then random samples are taken from each of the strata		396	
Proportional sample sizes (in stratified sampling)		Occurs when the proportion of each stratum selected is the same from stratum to stratum		397	
Cluster sampling		A sample where the population is separated into clusters, such as cities or city blocks, and then a random sample of the clusters is selected		399	
Sampling error		The inevitable result of basing an inference on a sample rather than on the entire population		404	
Nonsampling error		Any type of estimation error that is not sampling error, including nonresponse bias, nontruthful responses, measurement error, and voluntary response bias		404	
Point estimate		A single numeric value, a "best guess" of a population parameter, based on the data in a sample		405	
Estimation error		Difference between the estimate of a population parameter and the true value of the parameter		405	

(continued)

Term	Symbol	Explanation	Excel	Page	Equation Number
Sampling distribution		The distribution of the point estimates we would see from *all* possible samples (of a given sample size) from the population		406	
Confidence interval		An interval around the point estimate, calculated from the sample data, where we strongly believe the true value of the population parameter lies		406	
Unbiased estimate		An estimate where the mean of its sampling distribution equals the value of the parameter being estimated		406	
Standard error of an estimate		The standard deviation of the sampling distribution of the estimate		406	
Mean of sample mean	$E(\overline{X})$	Indicates property of unbiasedness of sample mean		407	8.1
Standard error of sample mean	$SE(\overline{X})$	Indicates how sample means from different samples vary		408	8.2, 8.3
Confidence interval for population mean		We are very confident that the population mean is within this interval		408	8.4
Finite population correction	*fpc*	A correction for the standard error when the sample size is fairly large relative to the population size		410	8.5, 8.6
Central limit theorem		States that the distribution of the sample mean is approximately normal for sufficiently large sample sizes		410	

PROBLEMS

Conceptual Exercises

C.1. Suppose that you want to know the opinions of American secondary school teachers about establishing a national test for high school graduation. You obtain a list of the members of the National Education Association (the largest teachers' union) and mail a questionnaire to 3000 teachers chosen at random from this list. In all, 1529 teachers return the questionnaire. Identify the relevant *population* and *frame* in this case.

C.2. A sportswriter wants to know how strongly the residents of Indianapolis, Indiana, support the local minor league baseball team, the Indianapolis Indians. She stands outside the stadium before a game and interviews the first 30 people who enter the stadium. Suppose that the newspaper asks you to comment on the approach taken by this sportswriter in performing the survey of local opinion. How do you respond?

C.3. A large corporation has 4520 male and 1167 female employees. The organization's equal employment opportunity officer wants to poll the opinions of a random sample of employees. To give adequate attention to the opinions of female employees, exactly how should the EEO officer sample from the given population? Explain in detail.

C.4. Suppose that you want to estimate the mean monthly gross income of all households in your local community. You decide to estimate this population parameter by calling 150 randomly selected residents and asking each individual to report the household's monthly income. Assume that you use the local phone directory as the frame in selecting the households to be included in your sample. What are some possible sources of error that might arise in your effort to estimate this population mean?

C.5. What is the difference between a *standard deviation* and a *standard error*?

Level A

45. The annual base salaries for 200 students graduating from a reputable MBA program this year are of interest to those in the admissions office who are responsible for marketing the program to prospective students. The data are in the file **P02_74.xlsx**. Use Excel to choose 10 simple random samples of size 15 from the given frame. For each simple random sample you obtain, compute the mean annual salary. Are these sample means equivalent? Explain why or why not.

46. A market research consultant hired by the Pepsi-Cola Co. is interested in determining who favors the Pepsi-Cola brand over Coke Classic in a particular urban location. A frame of customers from the market under investigation is provided in **P08_44.xlsx**.
   a. Compute the proportion of the customers in the given frame who favor Pepsi.
   b. Use Excel to choose a simple random sample of size 30 from the given frame.
   c. Compute the proportion of the 30 customers in the random sample who favor Pepsi. Compare this sample proportion to the value obtained in part **a**. Explain any difference between the two values.
   d. What are the advantages and disadvantages of employing simple random sampling in this particular case?

47. The employee benefits manager of a small private university would like to know the proportion of its full-time employees who prefer adopting each of three available health care plans in the forthcoming annual enrollment period. A reliable frame of the university's employees and their tentative health care preferences are given in **P08_25.xlsx**.
   a. Compute the proportion of the employees in the given frame who favor *each* of the three plans (i.e., plans A, B, and C).
   b. Use Excel to choose a simple random sample of size 45 from the given frame.
   c. Compute the proportion of the 45 employees in the random sample who favor each health plan. Compare these sample proportions to the corresponding values obtained in part **a**. Explain any differences between the corresponding values.
   d. What are the advantages and disadvantages of employing simple random sampling in this particular case?

48. Senior management of a certain consulting services firm is concerned about a growing decline in the organization's productivity. In an effort to understand the depth and extent of this problem, management would like to determine the average number of hours its employees spend on work-related activities in a typical week. The frame of virtually all of the firm's full-time employees, including the employees' self-reported amounts of time typically devoted to work activities each week, is provided in **P08_35.xlsx**.
   a. Select a simple random sample of size 100 from the given frame.
   b. Compute the mean and standard deviation of the weekly number of hours worked by all employees in the frame. Also, compute the mean and standard deviation of the weekly number of hours worked by employees in the simple random sample. How do these two sets of descriptive measures compare?

49. Elected officials in a small Florida town are preparing the annual budget for their community. Specifically, they would like to know how much their constituents living in this town are typically paying each year in real estate taxes. Given that there are more than 3000 homeowners in this small community, officials have decided to sample a representative subset of taxpayers and thoroughly study their tax payments. The latest frame of homeowners is given in **P08_36.xlsx**. Note that this file contains the real estate tax payment made by each homeowner last year.
   a. Compute the average real estate tax payment made by the homeowners included in the frame. Is the overall mean a valid measure of central tendency in this case?
   b. Use Excel to choose a simple random sample of 150 homeowners from the given frame.
   c. Compute the average real estate tax payment for the 150 homeowners in the random sample. Compare this sample mean to the corresponding summary measure obtained in part **a**.
   d. Is the sample mean computed in part **c** a good estimate of the average real estate tax payment made by homeowners living in this small town? Explain why or why not.

50. Auditors of a particular bank are interested in comparing the reported value of customer savings account balances with their own findings regarding the actual value of such assets. Rather than reviewing the records of each savings account at the bank, the auditors decide to examine a representative sample of savings account balances. The frame from which they will sample is given in the file **P08_50.xlsx**.
   a. Assist the bank's auditors by selecting a simple random sample of 100 savings accounts.
   b. Explain how the auditors might use the simple random sample identified in part **a** to estimate the value of *all* savings accounts balances within this bank.

51. The manager of a local supermarket wants to know the average amount (in dollars) customers spend at his store on Fridays. He would like to study the buying behavior of each customer who makes a purchase at the store on a typical Friday. However, the manager's assistant, who is currently enrolled in a managerial statistics course at a local college, urges the manager to save his scarce time and money by studying a sample of customer purchases. The available frame of relevant customer purchases is provided in file **P08_51.xlsx**.
   a. Compute the average purchase amount made by the customers included in the given frame.
   b. Use Excel to choose a simple random sample of 25 customers from the given frame.
   c. Compute the average purchase amount made by the 25 customers in the random sample. Compare this sample mean to the corresponding summary measure obtained in part **a**.
   d. Is the sample mean a good estimate of the overall population mean in this case? Explain why or why not.

52. The annual base salaries for 200 students graduating from a reputable MBA program this year are of interest to those in the admissions office who are responsible for marketing the program to prospective students. The data are in the file **P02_74.xlsx**. Use Excel to choose 15 systematic samples of size 10 from the given frame. For each systematic sample you obtain, compute the mean annual salary. Are these sample means equivalent? Explain why or why not.

53. Given the data in the file **P02_13.xlsx** from a recent survey of chief executive officers from the largest U.S. public companies, choose a systematic sample of 25 executives and find the mean, median, and standard deviation of the bonuses awarded to them in fiscal year 2003. How do these sample statistics compare to the mean, median, and standard deviation of the bonuses given to all executives included in the frame?

54. A market research consultant hired by the Pepsi-Cola Co. is interested in determining who favors the Pepsi-Cola brand over Coke Classic in a particular urban location. A frame of customers from the market under investigation is provided in **P08_44.xlsx**.
   a. Compute the proportion of the customers in the given frame who favor Pepsi.
   b. Use Excel to choose a systematic sample of size 30 from the given frame.
   c. Compute the proportion of the 30 customers in the systematic sample who favor Pepsi. Compare this sample proportion to the value obtained in part **a**. Explain any difference between the two values.
   d. What are the advantages and disadvantages of employing systematic sampling in this particular case?

55. A lightbulb manufacturer wants to know the number of defective bulbs contained in a typical box shipped by the company. Production personnel at this company have recorded the number of defective bulbs found in each of the 1000 boxes shipped during the past week. These data are provided in **P08_11.xlsx**. Using this shipment of boxes as a frame, select a systematic sample of 50 boxes and compute the mean number of defective bulbs found in a box.

56. The employee benefits manager of a small private university would like to know the proportion of its full-time employees who prefer adopting each of three available health care plans in the forthcoming annual enrollment period. A reliable frame of the university's employees and their tentative health care preferences are given in **P08_25.xlsx**.
   a. Compute the proportion of the employees in the given frame who favor *each* of the three plans (i.e., plans A, B, and C).
   b. Use Excel to choose a systematic sample of size 47 from the given frame.
   c. Compute the proportion of the 47 employees in the systematic sample who favor each health plan. Compare these sample proportions to the corresponding values obtained in part **a**. Explain any differences between the corresponding values.
   d. What are the advantages and disadvantages of employing systematic sampling in this particular case?

57. Senior management of a certain consulting services firm is concerned about a growing decline in the organization's productivity. In an effort to understand the depth and extent of this problem, management would like to determine the average number of hours their employees spend on work-related activities in a typical week. The frame of virtually all of the firm's full-time employees, including the employees' self-reported amounts of time typically devoted to work activities each week, is provided in **P08_35.xlsx**.
   a. Select a systematic sample of size 100 from the given frame.
   b. Compute the mean and standard deviation of the weekly number of hours worked by all employees in the frame. Also, compute the mean and standard deviation of the weekly number of hours worked by employees in the systematic sample. How do these two sets of descriptive measures compare?

58. Elected officials in a small Florida town are preparing the annual budget for their community. Specifically, they would like to know how much their constituents living in this town are typically paying each year in real estate taxes. Given that there are more than 3000 homeowners in this small community, officials have decided to sample a representative subset of taxpayers and thoroughly study their tax payments. The

latest frame of homeowners is given in **P08_36.xlsx**. Note that this file contains the real estate tax payment made by each homeowner last year.

  a. Use Excel to choose a systematic sample of 150 homeowners from the given frame.

  b. Compute the average real estate tax payment for the 150 homeowners in the systematic sample.

  c. Is the sample mean computed in part **b** a good estimate of the average real estate tax payment made by homeowners living in this small town? Explain why or why not.

59. Auditors of a particular bank are interested in comparing the reported value of customer savings account balances with their own findings regarding the actual value of such assets. Rather than reviewing the records of each savings account at the bank, the auditors decide to examine a representative sample of savings account balances. The frame from which they will sample is given in the file **P08_50.xlsx**.

  a. Assist the bank's auditors by selecting a systematic sample of 151 savings accounts.

  b. Explain how the auditors might use the systematic sample identified in part **a** to estimate the value of *all* savings accounts balances within this bank.

60. The manager of a local supermarket wants to know the average amount (in dollars) customers spend at his store on Fridays. He would like to study the buying behavior of each customer who makes a purchase at the store on a typical Friday. However, the manager's assistant, who is currently enrolled in a managerial statistics course at a local college, urges the manager to save his scarce time and money by studying a sample of customer purchases. The available frame of relevant customer purchases is provided in file **P08_51.xlsx**.

  a. Compute the average purchase amount made by the customers included in the given frame.

  b. Use Excel to choose a systematic sample of 43 customers from the given frame.

  c. Compute the average purchase amount made by the 43 customers in the systematic sample. Compare this sample mean to the corresponding summary measure obtained in part **a**.

  d. Is the sample mean a good estimate of the overall population mean in this case? Explain why or why not.

61. Elected officials in a small Florida town are preparing the annual budget for their community. Specifically, they would like to know how much their constituents living in this town are typically paying each year in real estate taxes. Given that there are more than 3000 homeowners in this small community, officials have decided to sample a representative subset of taxpayers and thoroughly study their tax payments. The latest frame of homeowners is given in **P08_36.xlsx**. Note that this file contains the real estate tax payment made by each homeowner last year.

  a. Compute the average real estate tax payment made by the homeowners included in the frame. Is the overall mean a valid measure of central tendency in this case?

  b. Use Excel to choose a sample of 150 homeowners stratified by neighborhood with proportional sample sizes.

  c. Compute the average real estate tax payment for the 150 homeowners in the stratified sample. Compare this sample mean to the corresponding summary measure obtained in part **a**.

  d. Is the sample mean computed in part **c** a good estimate of the average real estate tax payment made by homeowners living in this small town? Explain why or why not.

  e. Explain how the elected officials could apply cluster sampling in selecting a sample of size 150 from this frame. What are the advantages and disadvantages of employing cluster sampling in this case?

62. Auditors of a particular bank are interested in comparing the reported value of customer savings account balances with their own findings regarding the actual value of such assets. Rather than reviewing the records of each savings account at the bank, the auditors decide to examine a representative sample of savings account balances. The frame from which they will sample is given in the file **P08_50.xlsx**.

  a. What sample size would be required for the auditors to be approximately 95% sure that their estimate of the average savings account balance at this bank is within $100 of the true mean? Assume that their best estimate of the population standard deviation σ is $500.

  b. Choose a simple random sample of the size found in part **a**.

  c. Compute the observed sampling error based on the sample you have drawn from the population given in the file. How does the actual sampling error compare to the error ($100) specified in part **a**? Explain.

63. The manager of a local supermarket wants to estimate the average amount customers spend at his store on Fridays. He would like to study the buying behavior of each customer who makes a purchase at the store on a typical Friday. However, the manager's assistant, who is currently enrolled in a managerial statistics course at a local college, urges the manager to save his scarce time and money by studying a sample of customer purchases. The available frame of relevant customer purchases is provided in file **P08_51.xlsx**.

  a. What sample size would be required for the supermarket manager to be approximately 95% sure that his estimate of the average customer expenditure on Fridays is within $25 of the true mean? Assume that his best estimate of the population standard deviation σ is $72.

b. Choose a simple random sample of the size found in part **a**.

c. Compute the observed sampling error based on the sample you have drawn from the population given in the file. How does the actual sampling error compare to the error ($25) specified in part **a**? Explain.

64. *The Hite Report* was Sheri Hite's survey of the attitudes of American women toward sexuality. She sent out more than 100,000 surveys; each contained multiple-choice and open-ended questions. These surveys were given to women's groups and announced in church newsletters. Ads were also placed in women's magazines. A total of 3019 surveys were returned. Sheri Hite's findings challenged much conventional wisdom about sexuality. She found that most women were unhappy in their romantic relationships (some for reasons that are too graphic for this book!). How would you criticize Hite's methodology? A later poll, by the way, contradicted many of her findings.
  a. Give two criticisms of Hite's sampling methodology.
  b. Despite these criticisms, what value might you see in Hite's results?

65. A market research consultant hired by the Pepsi-Cola Co. is interested in determining who favors the Pepsi-Cola brand over Coke Classic in a particular urban location. A frame of customers from the market under investigation is provided in **P08_44.xlsx**.
  a. Compute the proportion of the consumers in the given frame who favor Pepsi.
  b. Use Excel to choose a sample of size 30 stratified by gender with proportional sample sizes.
  c. Compute the proportion of the 30 consumers in the stratified sample who favor Pepsi. Compare this sample proportion to the value obtained in part **a**. Explain any difference between the two values.
  d. What are the advantages and disadvantages of employing stratified sampling in this particular case?

Level B

66. Repeat the previous problem, but now stratify the consumers in the given frame by *age* rather than by gender. How does this modification affect your answers to the questions posed in parts **b** and **c**? Finally, stratify the consumers by both gender *and* age (e.g., all females over 60) with proportional sample sizes. How does this change affect your answers to the questions posed in parts **b** and **c**? Which approach to stratification appears to give the best results in estimating the actual proportion of the customers in the given frame who favor Pepsi?

67. Wal-Mart buyers seek to purchase adequate supplies of various brands of toothpaste to meet the ongoing demands of their customers. In particular, Wal-Mart is interested in knowing the proportion of its customers who favor such leading brands of toothpaste as Aquafresh, Colgate, Crest, and Mentadent. The file **P08_41.xlsx** contains the toothpaste brand preferences of 2000 Wal-Mart customers, obtained recently through the administration of a customer survey.
  a. Determine the proportion of Wal-Mart customers who favor each major brand of toothpaste.
  b. Assuming that the given data constitute an appropriate frame, choose a simple random sample of 100 of these customers.
  c. Calculate the proportion of Wal-Mart customers in the random sample who favor each major brand of toothpaste. Compare these sample proportions to the corresponding values found in part **a**. How do you explain any disparities between corresponding proportions for customers included in the sample and those in the frame?

68. Suppose that you are an entrepreneur interested in establishing a new Internet-based sports information service. Furthermore, suppose that you have gathered basic demographic information on a large number of Internet users. Assume that these 1000 individuals were carefully selected through stratified sampling. These data are stored in the file **P02_43.xlsx**.
  a. To assess potential interest in your proposed enterprise, you would like to conduct telephone interviews with a representative subset of the 1000 Internet users you surveyed previously. How would you proceed to stratify the given frame of 1000 individuals to choose 50 for telephone interviews? Explain your approach and implement it to select a useful sample of size 50.
  b. Explain how the entrepreneur could apply cluster sampling to obtain a sample of size 50 from this frame. What are the advantages and disadvantages of employing cluster sampling in this case?

69. A market research consultant hired by the Pepsi-Cola Co. is interested in determining the proportion of consumers who favor Pepsi-Cola over Coke Classic in a particular urban location. A frame of customers from the market under investigation is provided in **P08_44.xlsx**.
  a. Use Excel to choose a simple random sample of size 30 from the given frame.
  b. Using the sample found in part **a**, compute a point estimate (called the sample proportion, $\hat{p}$) of the true proportion of consumers who favor Pepsi-Cola in this market. What is the sampling error in this case? Assume that the population consists of the preferences of all consumers in the given frame.
  c. Given that the standard error of the sampling distribution of the sample proportion $\hat{p}$ is approximately $\sqrt{\hat{p}(1 - \hat{p})/n}$, compute a good approximation to the standard error of the sample proportion in this case.
  d. Repeat parts **b** and **c** after generating a simple random sample of size 15 from the given frame. How do you explain the differences in your computed results?

70. The employee benefits manager of a small private university would like to estimate the proportion of full-time employees who prefer adopting the first (i.e., plan A) of three available health care plans in the forthcoming annual enrollment period. A reliable frame of the university's employees and their tentative health care preferences are given in **P08_25.xlsx**.

   a. Use Excel to choose a simple random sample of size 45 from the given frame.

   b. Using the sample found in part **a**, compute a point estimate (called the sample proportion, $\hat{p}$) of the true proportion of university employees who prefer plan A. What is the sampling error in this case? Assume that the population consists of the preferences of all employees in the given frame.

   c. Given that the standard error of the sampling distribution of the sample proportion p is approximately $\sqrt{\hat{p}(1-\hat{p})/n}$, compute a good approximation to the standard error of the sample proportion in this case.

   d. Repeat parts **b** and **c** after generating a simple random sample of size 25 from the given frame. How do you explain the differences in your computed results?

71. Auditors of a particular bank are interested in comparing the reported value of customer savings account balances with their own findings regarding the actual value of such assets. Rather than reviewing the records of each savings account at the bank, the auditors decide to examine a representative sample of savings account balances. The frame from which they will sample is given in the file **P08_50.xlsx**.

   a. Generate an appropriate histogram for the given distribution of savings account balances. Characterize this distribution. Also, compute the mean and standard deviation of the given scores.

   b. Repeatedly choose simple random samples of size 2 from the original distribution given in the file. Record the sample mean for each of 500 sampling repetitions and generate an appropriate histogram of the resulting sampling distribution. Characterize this sampling distribution and compute its mean and standard deviation.

   c. Repeatedly choose simple random samples of size 5 from the original distribution given in the file. Record the sample mean for each of 500 sampling repetitions and generate an appropriate histogram of the resulting sampling distribution. Characterize this sampling distribution and compute its mean and standard deviation.

   d. Repeatedly choose simple random samples of size 10 from the original distribution given in the file. Record the sample mean for each of 500 sampling repetitions and generate an appropriate histogram of the resulting sampling distribution. Characterize this sampling distribution and compute its mean and standard deviation.

   e. Explain the changes in your constructed sampling distributions as the sample size was increased from $n = 2$ to $n = 10$. In particular, how does the sampling distribution you constructed in part **d** compare to the original distribution (where $n = 1$) you described in part **a**?

72. A lightbulb manufacturer wants to estimate the number of defective bulbs contained in a typical box shipped by the company. Production personnel at this company have recorded the number of defective bulbs found in each of the 1000 boxes shipped during the past week. These data are provided in **P08_11.xlsx**.

   a. Generate an appropriate histogram for the given distribution of 1000 numbers of defective bulbs. Characterize this distribution. Also, compute the mean and standard deviation of the given numbers.

   b. Repeatedly choose simple random samples of size 3 from the original distribution given in the file. Record the sample mean for each of 100 sampling repetitions and generate an appropriate histogram of the resulting sampling distribution. Characterize this sampling distribution and compute its mean and standard deviation.

   c. Repeatedly choose simple random samples of size 6 from the original distribution given in the file. Record the sample mean for each of 100 sampling repetitions and generate an appropriate histogram of the resulting sampling distribution. Characterize this sampling distribution and compute its mean and standard deviation.

   d. Repeatedly choose simple random samples of size 12 from the original distribution given in the file. Record the sample mean for each of 100 sampling repetitions and generate an appropriate histogram of the resulting sampling distribution. Characterize this sampling distribution and compute its mean and standard deviation.

   e. Explain the changes in your constructed sampling distributions as the sample size was increased from $n = 3$ to $n = 12$. In particular, how does the sampling distribution you constructed in part **d** compare to the original distribution (where $n = 1$) you described in part **a**?

73. The employee benefits manager of a small private university would like to estimate the proportion of full-time employees who prefer adopting the first (i.e., plan A) of three available health care plans in the forthcoming annual enrollment period. A reliable frame of the university's employees and their tentative health care preferences are given in **P08_25.xlsx**.

   a. What sample size would be required for the benefits manager to be approximately 95% sure that her estimate of the proportion of full-time university employees who prefer adopting plan A is within 0.15 of the true proportion? Assume that her best estimate of the population proportion parameter p is 1/3.

[*Hint*: The required sample size formula in this case is given by $n = 4p(1 - p)/B^2$, where p is the population proportion parameter and B is the specified error, in this case, 0.15.]

b. How does the answer to part **a** change if the benefits manager wants her estimate to be within 0.25 of the actual population proportion? Explain the difference in your answers to parts **a** and **b**.

74. Suppose the monthly unpaid balance on a Citicorp MasterCard is normally distributed with a mean of $1200 and standard deviation of $240. We want to show that the sample mean $\overline{X}$ is an unbiased estimate of the population mean μ, and the sample variance s^2 is an unbiased estimate of the population variance σ^2. Note that you can generate observations from CITICORP accounts by using the formula =NORMINV(RAND(),1200,240). Develop a simulation as follows:

■ Generate 50 samples of five credit card balances each. Do *not* freeze the random numbers.
■ Calculate $\overline{X}$ and s^2 for each sample.
■ Show that the $\overline{X}$'s average to a value near the actual mean of $1200.
■ Show that the s^2's average to a value near the true value $\sigma^2 = 240^2$.

75. (Based on an actual case) Indiana audits nursing homes to see whether and how much the nursing home has overbilled Medicaid. Here is how they do it. Nurseco has 70 homes in Indiana. The state randomly samples one invoice per nursing home and determines Nurseco's liability as follows. Suppose nursing home 1 has billed Medicaid $100,000. If the one surveyed invoice at nursing home 1 indicates Nurseco has overbilled by 40%, then Nurseco would have to return 40%

(or $40,000) that it has collected from the state. What is wrong with this approach? Assuming all nursing homes have overbilled at a similar rate, can you suggest a better plan to determine how much money should be returned to the state?

76. The central limit theorem states that when many independent random variables are summed, the result follows a normal distribution even if the individual random variables in the sum do not. To illustrate this idea, simulate 500 samples of size 15 from the uniform (0, 1) distribution (generated with the RAND function). Are the 500 sums (where each is a sum of 15 values) normally distributed? Show by constructing a histogram and also by checking the empirical rules.

77. Assume a very large normally distributed population of scores on a test with mean 70 and standard deviation 7.

a. Find an interval that includes 95% of the population.
b. Suppose you randomly sample a single member from this population. Find an interval so that you are 95% confident that this member's score will be in the interval.
c. Now suppose you sample 30 members randomly from this population. Find an interval so that you are 95% confident that the average of these members' scores will be in the interval.
d. Finally, suppose you sample 300 members randomly from this population. Find an interval so that you are 95% confident that the average of these members' scores will be in the interval.
e. Explain intuitively why the answers to parts **a** through **d** are not all the same.

The file **Videos.xlsx** contains a large database on 10,000 customer transactions for a fictional chain of video stores in the United States. Each row corresponds to a different customer and lists (1) a customer ID number (1–10,000); (2) the state where the customer lives; (3) the city where the customer lives; (4) the customer's gender; (5) the customer's favorite type of movie (drama, comedy, science fiction, or action); (6) the customer's next favorite type of movie; (7) the number of times the customer has rented movies in the past year; and (8) the total dollar amount the customer has spent on movie rentals during the past year. The data are sorted by state, then city, then gender. We assume that this database represents the entire population of customers for this video chain. (Of course, national chains would have significantly larger customer populations, but this database is large enough to illustrate the ideas.)

Imagine that only the data in columns A through D are readily available for this population. The company is interested in summary statistics of the data in columns E through H, such as the percentage of customers whose favorite movie type is drama or the average amount spent annually per customer, but it will have to do some work to obtain the data in columns E through H for any particular customer.

Therefore, the company wants to perform sampling. The question is: What form of sampling—simple random sampling, systematic sampling, stratified sampling, cluster sampling, or even some type of multistage sampling—is most appropriate?

Your job is to investigate the possibilities and to write a report on your findings. For any sampling method, any sample size, and any quantity of interest (such as average dollar amount spent annually), you should be concerned with sampling cost and accuracy. One way to judge the latter is to generate several random samples from a particular method and calculate the mean and standard deviation of your point estimates from these samples. For example, you might generate 10 systematic samples, calculate the average amount spent (an $\overline{X}$) for each sample, and then calculate the mean and standard deviation of these 10 $\overline{X}$'s. If your sampling method is accurate, the mean of the $\overline{X}$'s should be close to the population average, and the standard deviation should be small. By doing this for several sampling methods and possibly several sample sizes, you can experiment to see what is most cost efficient for the company. You can make any reasonable assumptions about the cost of sampling with any particular method. ■

Confidence Interval Estimation

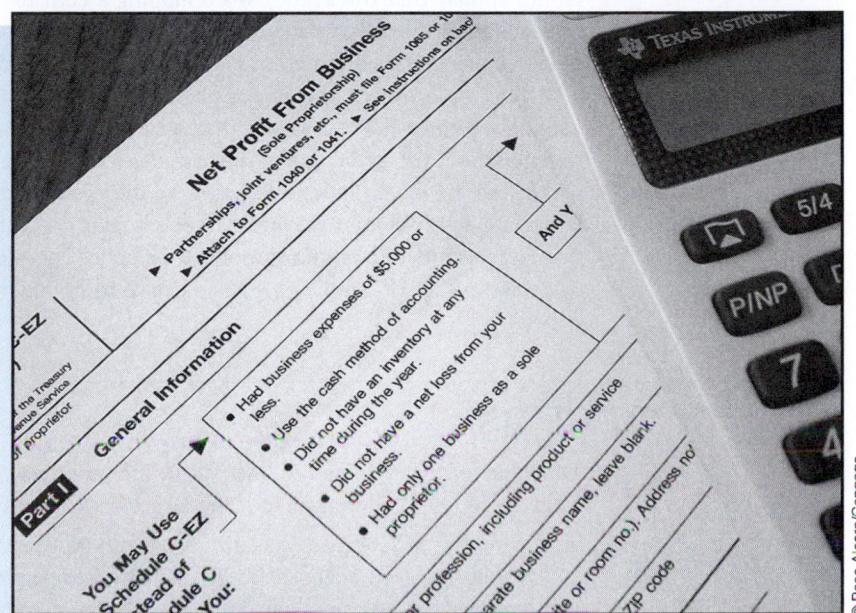

© Rose Alcorn/Cengage

ESTIMATING A COMPANY'S TOTAL TAXABLE INCOME

In Example 8.4 from the previous chapter, we illustrated how sampling can be used in auditing. We see another illustration of sampling in auditing in Example 9.5 of this chapter. In both examples, the point of the sampling is to discover some property (such as a mean or a proportion) from a large population of a company's accounts by examining a small fraction of these accounts and projecting the results to the population. The article by Press (1995) offers an interesting variation on this problem. He poses the question of how a government revenue agency should assess a business taxpayer's income for tax purposes on the basis of a sample audit of the company's business transactions. A sample of the company's transactions will indicate a taxable income for each sampled transaction. The methods of this chapter will be applied to the sample information to obtain a confidence interval for the total taxable income owed by the company.

Suppose for the sake of illustration that this confidence interval extends from $1,000,000 to $2,200,000 and is centered at $1,600,000. In words, the government's best guess of the company's taxable income is $1,600,000, and it is fairly confident that the true taxable income is between $1,000,000 and $2,200,000. How much tax should it assess the company? Press argues that the agency would like to maximize its revenue while minimizing the risk that the company will be assessed more than it really owes. This last assumption, that the government does not want to *overassess* the company, is crucial. By making several reasonable assumptions, he is able to argue that the agency should base the tax on the *lower* limit of the confidence interval, in this case, $1,000,000.[1]

On the other hand, if the agency were indifferent between overcharging and undercharging, then it would base the tax on the midpoint, $1,600,000, of the confidence interval. Using this strategy, the agency would overcharge in about half the cases and undercharge in the other half. This would certainly be upsetting to companies—it would appear that the agency were flipping a coin to decide whether to overcharge or undercharge! (Today this strategy is most commonly used by state agencies, but it is being challenged, and the courts will have to make a decision.)

If the government agency does indeed decide to base the tax on the *lower* limit of the confidence interval, Press argues that it can still increase its tax revenue—by increasing the sample size of the audit. When the sample size increases, the confidence interval shrinks in width, and the lower limit, which governs the agency's tax revenue, almost surely increases. But there is some point at which larger samples are not warranted, for the simple reason that larger samples cost more money to obtain. Therefore, there is an optimal size that will balance the cost of sampling with the desire to obtain more tax revenue. ■

9.1 INTRODUCTION

This chapter expands on the ideas from the previous chapter. Given an observed data set, we want to make inferences to some larger population. Two typical examples follow:

■ A mail-order company has accounts with thousands of customers. The company would like to infer the average time its customers take to pay their bills, so it randomly samples a relatively small number of its customers, sees how long these customers take to pay their bills, and draws inferences about the entire population of customers.

■ A manufacturing company is considering two compensation schemes to implement for its workers. It believes that these two different compensation schemes might provide different incentives and hence result in different worker productivity. To see whether this is true, the company randomly assigns groups of workers to the two different compensation schemes for a period of 3 months and observes their productivity. Then it attempts to infer whether any differences observed in the experiment can be generalized to the overall worker population.

In each of these examples, there is an unknown population parameter a company would like to estimate. In the mail-order example the unknown parameter is the mean length of time customers take to pay their bills. Its true value could be discovered only by learning how long *every* customer in the entire population takes to pay its bills. This might not be possible, given the large number of customers. In the manufacturing example the unknown parameter is really a mean difference, the difference between the mean productivities with the two different compensation schemes. This mean difference could be discovered only by subjecting each worker to each compensation scheme and measuring their resulting productivities. This procedure would almost certainly be impossible from a practical standpoint. Therefore, in these examples the companies involved are likely to select random samples and base their estimates of the unknown population parameters on sample data.

---

[1] In case this sounds overly generous on the government's part, the result is based on two important assumptions: (1) the confidence interval is a 90% confidence interval, and (2) the agency is 19 times more concerned about overassessing than about underassessing.

The inferences we draw in this chapter are always based on an underlying probability model, which means that some type of random mechanism must generate the given data. Two random mechanisms are generally used. The first involves sampling randomly from a larger population, as we discussed in the previous chapter. This is the mechanism responsible for generating the sample of customers in the mail-order example. Regardless of whether the sample is a simple random sample or a more complex random sample, such as a stratified sample, the fact that it is *random* allows us to use the rules of probability to make inferences about the population as a whole.

The second commonly used random mechanism is called a **randomized experiment**. The compensation scheme example just described is a typical randomized experiment. Here we select a set of subjects (employees), randomly assign them to two different **treatment groups** (compensation schemes), and then compare some quantitative measure (productivity) across the groups. The fact that the subjects are *randomly* assigned to the two treatment groups is useful for two reasons. First, it allows us to rule out a number of factors that might have led to differences across groups. For example, assuming that males and females are randomly spread across the two groups, we can rule out gender as the cause of any observed group differences. Second, the random selection allows us to use the rules of probability to infer whether observed differences can be generalized to all employees.

We actually introduced 95% confidence intervals for the mean in the previous chapter. We generalize this method in the current chapter.

Generally, statistical inferences are of two types: *confidence interval estimation* and *hypothesis testing*. The first of these is the subject of the current chapter; we study hypothesis testing in the next chapter. They differ primarily in their point of view. For example, the mail-order company might sample 100 customers and find that they average 15.5 days before paying their bills. In **confidence interval estimation**, we use the data to obtain a point estimate and a confidence interval around this point estimate. In this example the point estimate is 15.5 days. It is a best guess for the mean bill-paying time in the entire customer population. Then, using the methods in this chapter, the company might find that a 95% confidence interval for the mean bill-paying time in the population is from 13.2 days to 17.8 days. The company is now 95% certain that the true mean bill-paying time in the population is within this interval.

Hypothesis testing takes a different point of view. Here we wish to check whether the observed data provide support for a particular hypothesis. In the compensation scheme example, suppose the manager believes that workers will have higher productivity if they are paid by salary than by an hourly wage. He runs the 3-month randomized experiment described previously and finds that the salaried workers produce on average eight more parts per day than the hourly workers. Now he must make one of two conclusions. Either salaried workers are in general no more productive than hourly workers and the ones in the experiment just got lucky, or salaried workers really *are* more productive. We learn in the next chapter how to decide which of these conclusions is more reasonable.

There are only a few key ideas in this chapter, and the most important of these, *sampling distributions*, was introduced in the previous chapter. It is important to concentrate on these key ideas and not get bogged down in formulas or numerical calculations. Statistical software such as the StatTools add-in is generally available to take care of these calculations. The job of a businessperson is much more dependent on knowing which methods to use in which situations and how to interpret computer output than on memorizing and plugging into formulas.

9.2 SAMPLING DISTRIBUTIONS

As we soon learn, most confidence intervals are of the form in expression (9.1). For example, when estimating a population mean, the point estimate is the sample mean, the standard error is the sample standard deviation divided by the square root of the sample size, and the multiple is approximately equal to 2. To learn why it works this way, we must first learn a bit about sampling distributions. Then in the next section we put this knowledge to use.

Typical Form of Confidence Interval

$$\text{Point Estimate} \pm \text{Multiple} \times \text{Standard Error} \qquad (9.1)$$

In the previous chapter we introduced the sampling distribution of the sample mean $\overline{X}$ and saw how it was related to the central limit theorem. In general, whenever we make inferences about one or more population parameters, such as a mean or the difference between two means, we always base this inference on the sampling distribution of a point estimate, such as the sample mean. Although the *concepts* of point estimates and sampling distributions are no different from those in the previous chapter, there are some new details we need to learn.

We again begin with the sample mean $\overline{X}$. From the central limit theorem we know that if the sample size n is reasonably large, then for *any* population distribution, the sampling distribution of $\overline{X}$ is approximately normally distributed with mean μ and standard deviation $\sigma/\sqrt{n}$, where μ and σ are the population mean and standard deviation. An equivalent statement is that the standardized quantity Z defined in equation (9.2) is approximately normal with mean 0 and standard deviation 1.

Standardized Z-Value

$$Z = \frac{\overline{X} - \mu}{\sigma/\sqrt{n}} \qquad (9.2)$$

Typically, we use this fact to make inferences about an unknown population mean μ. There is one problem, however—we usually do not know the population standard deviation σ. This parameter, σ, is called a **nuisance parameter** because we need its value even though it is typically not the parameter of primary interest. The solution appears to be straightforward: Replace the nuisance parameter σ by its sample estimate s in the formula for Z and proceed from there. However, when we replace σ by the sample standard deviation s, we introduce a new source of variability, and the sampling distribution is no longer normal. It is instead called the *t* **distribution**, a close relative of the normal distribution that appears in a variety of statistical applications.

9.2.1 The *t* Distribution

We first set the stage for this new sampling distribution. We are interested in estimating a population mean μ with a sample of size n. We assume the population distribution is normal with unknown standard deviation σ. We intend to base inferences on the standardized value of $\overline{X}$, where σ is replaced by the sample standard deviation s. Then the standardized value in equation (9.3) has a *t* **distribution with** $n - 1$ **degrees of freedom**.

Standardized Value

$$t = \frac{\overline{X} - \mu}{s/\sqrt{n}} \qquad (9.3)$$

The "degrees of freedom" is a numerical parameter of the *t* distribution that defines the precise shape of the distribution. Each time we encounter a *t* distribution, we will specify its degrees of freedom. In this particular sampling context, where we are basing inferences about μ on the sampling distribution of $\overline{X}$, the degrees of freedom turns out to be 1 less than the sample size n.

The t distribution looks very much like the standard normal distribution. It is bell shaped and is centered at 0. The only difference is that it is slightly more spread out, and this increase in spread is greater for *small* degrees of freedom. In fact, when n is large, so that the degrees of freedom is large, the t distribution and the standard normal distribution are practically indistinguishable. This is illustrated in Figure 9.1. With 5 degrees of freedom, it is possible to see the increased spread in the t distribution. With 30 degrees of freedom, the t and standard normal curves are practically the same curve.

Figure 9.1

The t and Standard Normal Distributions

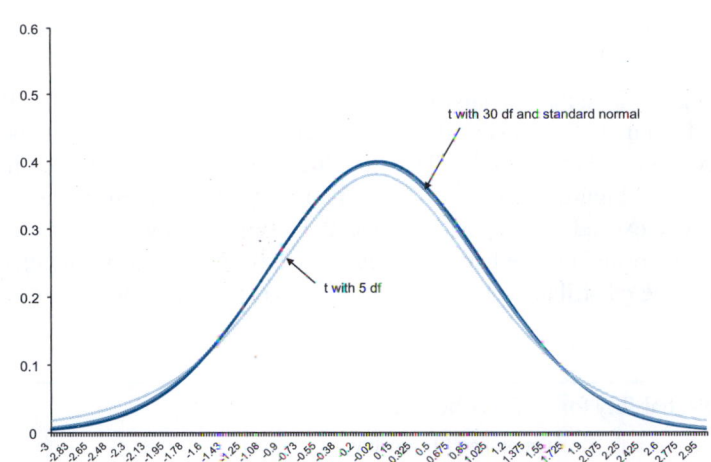

The t distribution and the standard normal distribution are practically the same when the degrees of freedom parameter is large.

The t-value in equation (9.3) is very much like a typical Z-value such as in equation (9.2). That is, the t-value represents the number of standard errors by which the sample mean differs from the population mean. For example, if a t-value is 2.5, then the sample mean is 2.5 standard errors above the population mean. In contrast, if a t-value is -2.5, then the sample mean is 2.5 standard errors below the population mean. Also, t-values greater in magnitude than 3 are very unexpected because of the same property we saw with the normal distribution: It is very unlikely for a random value to be more than 3 standard deviations away from its mean. (In this case the random value is a sample mean, and the standard deviation is the standard error of the mean.)

> A **t-value** indicates the number of standard errors by which a sample mean differs from a population mean.

Because of this interpretation, t-values are perfect candidates for the "multiple" in expression (9.1), as we soon see. First, however, we will briefly examine two Excel functions that help us work with the t distribution in Excel.

In Chapter 6 we learned how to use Excel's NORMSDIST and NORMSINV functions to calculate probabilities or percentiles from the standard normal distribution. There are similar Excel functions for the t distribution: TDIST and TINV. Unfortunately, these functions are somewhat more difficult to master than their normal counterparts. To make the transition easier, it helps to know that these functions are generally used to find (1) the probability beyond a certain value, either in one or both tails, or (2) the value that has a certain (usually small) probability beyond it, in either one or both tails.

EXAMPLE | 9.1 GASOLINE PRICES IN THE UNITED STATES

Suppose a government agency randomly samples 30 gas stations from the population of all gas stations in the United States. Its goal is to estimate the mean price for a gallon of premium unleaded gasoline. What is the probability that the sample mean price will be at least 2 standard errors above the population mean price? What is the probability that the sample mean price will differ by at least 2 standard errors from the population mean price?

Objective To use Excel's TDIST function to analyze differences between a sample mean and a population mean for gasoline prices.

Solution

First, we note that the answers to these questions do *not* depend on the values of the sample and population means or the standard error of the mean. They depend only on finding the probability that a "standardized" *t*-value is beyond some value, as illustrated in Figures 9.2 and 9.3. Figure 9.2 shows a one-tailed probability, where we are interested in whether a *t*-value exceeds some positive value, 2. Figure 9.3 shows a two-tailed probability, where we are interested in whether the *magnitude* of a *t*-value, positive or negative, exceeds 2. In each case the *t* distribution has $30 - 1 = 29$ degrees of freedom.

Figure 9.2 One-Tailed Probability for a *t* Distribution

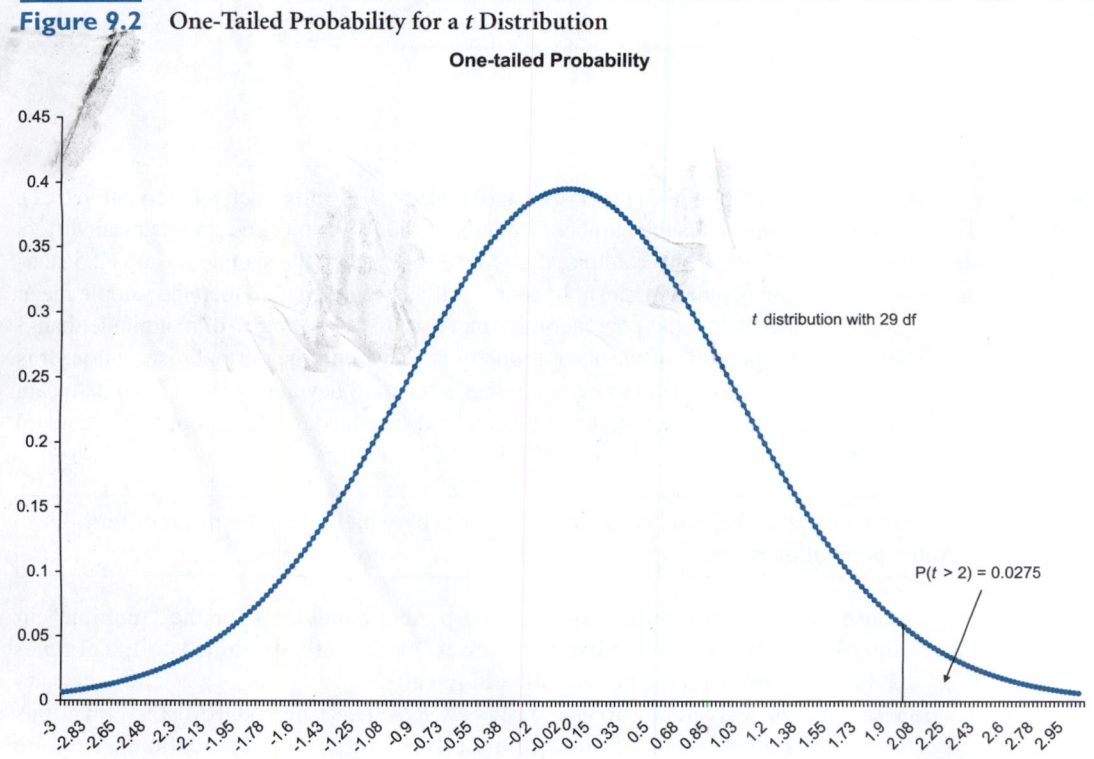

The calculations are in Figure 9.4. (See the file **t Calculations.xlsx**.) We answer the first question in rows 7 and 8. We want the probability that a *t*-value with 29 degrees of freedom exceeds 2. We find this with the formula spelled out in row 8. The first argument of TDIST is

the value we want to exceed, the second is the degrees of freedom, and the third is the number of tails (1 or 2). We see that the probability of the sample mean exceeding the population mean by this much—2 standard errors—is only 0.0275. The answer to the second question is exactly twice this probability. We find it with the formula spelled out in row 12. The only difference is that the third argument is now 2.

Figure 9.3 Two-Tailed Probability for a *t* Distribution

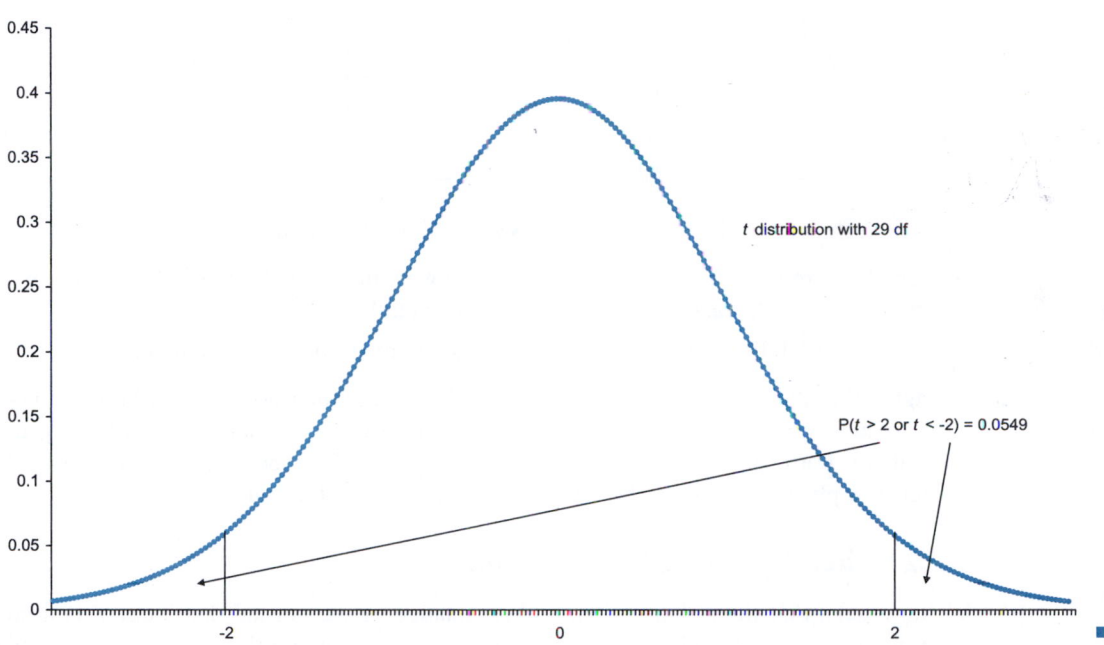

In general, here are the technical details for using the TDIST function properly:

- Its first argument must be nonnegative.
- Unlike the NORMSDIST function, TDIST returns the probability to the *right* of the first argument (if the third argument is 1).
- Its third argument is either 1 or 2 and indicates the number of tails. By using 1 for this argument, we get the probability in the right-hand tail only. If we use 2 for the third argument, we obtain the probability of greater than the first argument or less than its negative.

Before proceeding, we mention the "inverse" problem, also illustrated in Figure 9.4. Instead of specifying a *t*-value and asking for the probability of exceeding this value, we can specify a probability and ask for the *t*-value that has this much probability beyond it. Again, this can be a one-tailed or a two-tailed problem. Rows 15 and 16 illustrate the one-tailed problem, whereas rows 18 and 19 illustrate the two-tailed problem. Each of these uses Excel's TINV function to find the appropriate *t*-value, as spelled out by the formulas in the figure. As we see, the *t*-value 1.699 has probability 0.05 to its right (when there are 29 degrees of freedom), whereas the *t*-values ±2.045 have total probability 0.05 beyond them, or 0.025 in each tail.

Figure 9.4

Excel Functions for
the *t* Distribution

	A	B	C	D	E
1	**Using the TDIST and TINV functions for the t distribution**				
2					
3	Sample size	30			
4	Degrees of freedom	29			
5					
6	One-tailed probability				
7	t-value	2		Formulas	
8	Probability in right tail	0.0275		=TDIST(B7,B4,1)	
9					
10	Two-tailed probability				
11	t-value	2			
12	Probability in both tails	0.0549		=TDIST(B11,B4,2)	
13					
14	TINV calculations				
15	Probability in right tail	0.05			
16	t-value	1.699		=TINV(2*B15,B4)	
17					
18	Probability in both tails	0.05			
19	t-value	2.045		=TINV(B18,B4)	

The technical details for using the TINV function properly are as follows:

- The first argument is the total probability we want in both tails—half of this goes in the right-hand tail and half goes in the left-hand tail.
- Unlike the TDIST function, there is no third argument for the TINV function.

We agree that these differences between the *t* distribution and normal distribution functions are more complex than they ought to be, but this is the way Microsoft decided to program them. Fortunately, the StatTools add-in simplifies the process for most statistical inference applications. It does the *t* distribution calculations for you.

9.2.2 Other Sampling Distributions

We have seen that the *t* distribution, a close relative of the normal distribution, is used when we want to make inferences about a population mean and the population standard deviation is unknown. Throughout this chapter (and later chapters) we see other contexts where the *t* distribution appears. The theme is always the same—one or more means are of interest, and one or more standard deviations are unknown.

The *t* (and normal) distributions are not the only sampling distributions we encounter. Two other close relatives of the normal distribution that appear in various contexts are the *chi-square* and *F distributions*. These are used primarily to make inferences about variances (or standard deviations), as opposed to means. We omit the details of these distributions for now, but you can look forward to seeing them in the near future.

PROBLEMS

Level A

1. Compute the following probabilities using Excel:
   a. $P(t_{10} \geq 1.75)$, where t_{10} has a *t* distribution with 10 degrees of freedom.
   b. $P(t_{100} \geq 1.75)$, where t_{100} has a *t* distribution with 100 degrees of freedom. How do you explain the difference between this result and the one obtained in part **a**?

   c. $P(Z \geq 1.75)$, where Z is a standard normal random variable. Compare this result to the results obtained in parts **a** and **b**. How do you explain the differences in these probabilities?
   d. $P(t_{20} \leq -0.80)$, where t_{20} has a *t* distribution with 20 degrees of freedom.
   e. $P(t_3 \leq -0.80)$, where t_3 has a *t* distribution with 3 degrees of freedom. How do you explain the difference between this result and the result obtained in part **d**?

2. Determine the following quantities using Excel:

    a. $P(-2.00 \leq t_{10} \leq 1.00)$, where t_{10} has a t distribution with 10 degrees of freedom.

    b. $P(-2.00 \leq t_{100} \leq 1.00)$, where t_{100} has a t distribution with 100 degrees of freedom. How do you explain the difference between this result and the one obtained in part **a**?

    c. $P(-2.00 \leq Z \leq 1.00)$, where Z is a standard normal random variable. Compare this result to the results obtained in parts **a** and **b**. How do you explain the differences in these probabilities?

    d. Find the 68th percentile of the t distribution with 20 degrees of freedom.

    e. Find the 68th percentile of the t distribution with 3 degrees of freedom. How do you explain the difference between this result and the result obtained in part **d**?

3. Determine the following quantities using Excel:

    a. Find the value of x such that $P(t_{10} > x) = 0.75$, where t_{10} has a t distribution with 10 degrees of freedom.

    b. Find the value of y such that $P(t_{100} > y) = 0.75$, where t_{100} has a t distribution with 100 degrees of freedom. How do you explain the difference between this result and the result obtained in part **a**?

    c. Find the value of z such that $P(Z > z) = 0.75$, where Z is a standard normal random variable. Compare this result to the results obtained in parts **a** and **b**. How do you explain the differences in the values of x, y, and z?

4. The NORMSDIST and NORMSINV functions in Excel give you probabilities and Z-values, respectively, for the standard normal distribution. The analogous functions for the t distribution are TDIST and TINV. However, they do not work exactly the same as the normal functions. Try the following:

    a. You have a t distribution with 15 degrees of freedom (df), and you want the probability to the right of the value 1.074. From t tables included in many statistics books, this probability is 0.15. Verify that you can get the answer in Excel with =TDIST(1.074,15,1), where the last "1" means one tail only.

    b. This is the same as part **a**, but now you want the probability to the left of -1.074 or the right of 1.074, that is, the combined probability in both tails. Verify that you can get the answer in Excel with =TDIST(1.074,15,2), where the last "2" means two tails.

    c. You have a t distribution with 15 df, and you want the t-value with probability 0.05 to the right of it. From t tables, this t-value is 1.753. Verify that you can get the answer in Excel with =TINV(0.10,15). (The tricky part here is that the first argument, 0.10, is double the original probability you asked for. This is hard to remember!)

    d. This is the same as part **c**, but now you want the t-value, call it t, such that probability 0.025 is to the right of t, and probability 0.025 is to the left of $-t$. The t tables show that t is 2.131. Verify that you can get the answer in Excel with =TINV(0.05,15). (Here you can see the trick in part **c** better. You use the *combined* probability in both tails as the first argument in TINV.)

9.3 CONFIDENCE INTERVAL FOR A MEAN

We now come to the focal point of this chapter: using results about sampling distributions to construct confidence intervals. As explained in the introduction to this chapter, we assume that data have been generated by some random mechanism, either by observing a random sample from some population or by performing a randomized experiment. We want to use these data to infer the values of one or more population parameters such as the mean, the standard deviation, or a proportion. For each such parameter we use the data to calculate a point estimate, which can be considered a "best guess" for the unknown parameter. We then calculate a confidence interval around the point estimate to gauge its accuracy. This is exactly how we went out 2 standard errors on either side of the point estimate to form confidence intervals in the previous chapter. However, we expand on this procedure in this chapter.

We begin by deriving a confidence interval for a population mean μ, and we discuss its interpretation. Although the particular details pertain to a specific parameter, the mean, the same ideas carry over to estimation of other parameters as well, as we see in later sections. As usual, we use $\overline{X}$, the sample mean, as the point estimate of μ.

To obtain a confidence interval for μ, we first specify a **confidence level**, usually 90%, 95%, or 99%. We then use the sampling distribution of the point estimate to determine the *multiple* of the standard error we need to go out on either side of the point estimate to achieve the given confidence level. If the confidence level is 95%, the value used most frequently in applications, then the multiple is approximately 2. More precisely, it is a t-value. That is, a typical confidence interval for μ is of the form in expression (9.4), where $\text{SE}(\overline{X}) = s/\sqrt{n}$.

Confidence Interval for Population Mean
$$\overline{X} \pm t\text{-multiple} \times \text{SE}(\overline{X}) \qquad\qquad (9.4)$$

To obtain the correct t-multiple, let α be 1 minus the confidence level (expressed as a decimal). For example, if the confidence level is 90%, then $\alpha = 0.10$. Then the appropriate t-multiple is the value that cuts off probability $\alpha/2$ in each tail of the t distribution with $n - 1$ degrees of freedom. For example, if $n = 30$ and the confidence level is 95%, we see from cell B19 of Figure 9.4 that the correct t-value is 2.045. The corresponding 95% confidence interval for μ is then

$$\overline{X} \pm 2.045(s/\sqrt{n})$$

If the confidence level is instead 90%, the appropriate t-value is 1.699 (to see this, change the probability in cell B18 to 0.10), and the resulting 90% confidence interval is

$$\overline{X} \pm 1.699(s/\sqrt{n})$$

If the confidence level is 99%, the appropriate t-value is 2.756 (to see this, change the probability in cell B18 to 0.01), and the resulting 99% confidence interval is

$$\overline{X} \pm 2.756(s/\sqrt{n})$$

Confidence interval widths increase when we ask for higher confidence levels, but they tend to decrease when we use larger sample sizes.

Note that as the confidence level increases, the width of the confidence interval also increases. Because we naturally want confidence intervals to be as narrow as possible, this presents a trade-off. We can either have less confidence and a narrow interval, or we can have more confidence and a wide interval. However, we can also take a larger sample. As n increases, the standard error $s/\sqrt{n}$ decreases, and the length of the confidence interval tends to decrease for *any* confidence level. (Why won't it decrease for sure? The larger sample *might* result in a larger value of s that could offset the increase in n.)

The following example illustrates confidence interval estimation for a population mean. It uses the One-Sample procedure in StatTools to perform the calculations. However, by examining the resulting Excel formulas, you can check that all it is really doing is (1) calculating the sample mean, (2) calculating the standard error of the sample mean, $s/\sqrt{n}$, (3) finding the appropriate t-multiple, and (4) combining these to form the confidence interval via expression (9.4).

EXAMPLE | **9.2 CUSTOMER RESPONSE TO A NEW SANDWICH**

A fast-food restaurant recently added a new sandwich to its menu. To estimate the popularity of this sandwich, a random sample of 40 customers who ordered the sandwich were surveyed. Each of these customers was asked to rate the sandwich on a scale of 1 to 10, 10 being the best. The results of this survey appear in column B of Figure 9.6. (See the file **Satisfaction Ratings.xlsx**.) The manager wants to estimate the mean satisfaction rating over the entire population of customers by using a 95% confidence interval. How should she proceed?

Objective To use StatTools's One-Sample procedure to obtain a 95% confidence interval for the mean satisfaction rating of the new sandwich.

Solution

We use StatTools's One-Sample procedure on the Satisfaction variable. To do so, make sure a StatTools data set has been created, and select Confidence Interval from the StatTools Statistical Inference dropdown. Fill in the resulting dialog box as shown in Figure 9.5. In particular, select One-Sample Analysis as the Analysis type. (We see other types later in the chapter.) You should obtain the output shown in Figure 9.6. (*Note*: To get the output to be next to the data, select Settings from the StatTools ribbon, and, under the Report tab, select Query for Starting Cell as the Placement option.)

Figure 9.5

Dialog Box for One-Sample Confidence Interval

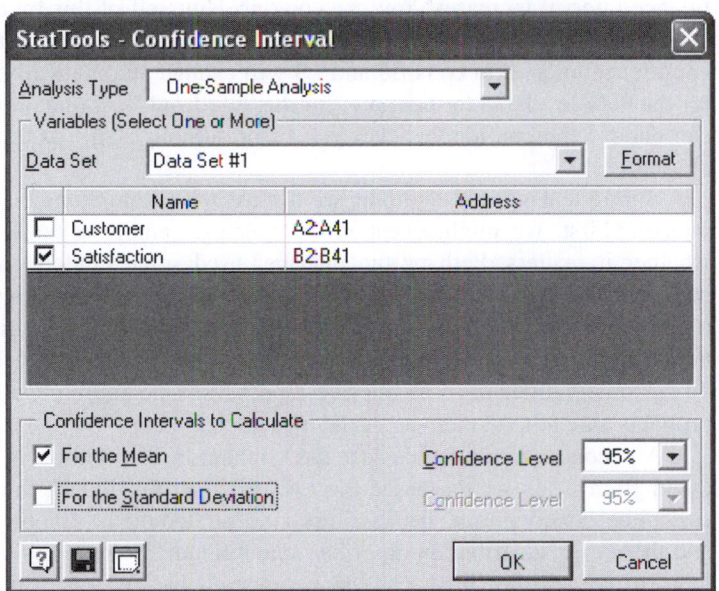

Figure 9.6

Analysis of New Sandwich Data

	A	B	C	D	E
1	Customer	Satisfaction			**Satisfaction**
2	1	7		*Conf. Intervals (One-Sample)*	**Data Set #1**
3	2	5		**Sample Size**	40
4	3	5		**Sample Mean**	6.250
5	4	6		**Sample Std Dev**	1.597
6	5	8		**Confidence Level (Mean)**	95.0%
7	6	7		**Degrees of Freedom**	39
8	7	6		**Lower Limit**	5.739
9	8	7		**Upper Limit**	6.761
10	9	10			
11	10	7			
12	11	9			
13	12	5			
14	13	5			
15	14	8			
16	15	8			
17	16	6			
40	39	5			
41	40	4			

To understand where these numbers come from, take a look at the formulas in column E.

The principal results are that (1) the best guess for the population mean rating is 6.250, the sample average in cell E4, and (2) a 95% confidence interval for the population mean rating extends from 5.739 to 6.761, as seen in cells E8 and E9. The manager can be 95% confident that the true mean rating over all customers who might try the sandwich is within this confidence interval.

The degrees of freedom for the t distribution is 1 less than the sample size, as shown in cell E7. The formulas for the confidence interval limits, in cells E8 and E9, are equivalent to the general formula in equation (9.4), but they use special StatTools functions to calculate the t-multiples.

We stated previously that as the confidence level increases, the length of the confidence interval increases. You can convince yourself of this by entering different confidence levels, such as 90% or 99%, in cell E6. The lower and upper limits of the confidence interval in cells E8 and E9 will change automatically, getting closer together for the 90% level and farther apart for the 99% level. Just remember that you, the analyst, can choose the confidence level you favor, although 95% is the level most commonly chosen.

Before leaving this example, we discuss the assumptions that lead to the confidence interval. First, we might question whether the sample is really a *random* sample—or whether it matters. Perhaps the manager used some random mechanism to select the customers to be surveyed. More likely, however, she simply surveyed 40 consecutive customers who tried the sandwich on a given day. This is called a **convenience sample** and is not really a random sample. However, unless there is some reason to believe that these 40 customers differ in some relevant aspect from the entire population of customers, it is probably safe to treat them as a random sample.

A second assumption is that the population distribution is *normal*. We made this assumption when we discussed the t distribution. Obviously, the population distribution *cannot* be exactly normal because it is concentrated on the 10 possible satisfaction ratings, and the normal distribution describes a continuum. However, this is probably not a problem for two reasons. First, confidence intervals based on the t distribution are **robust** to violations of normality. This means that the resulting confidence intervals are valid for any populations that are *approximately* normal. Second, the normal population assumption is less crucial for larger sample sizes because of the central limit theorem. For n as large as 40, the results should be valid.

Finally, it is important to recognize what this confidence interval tells us and what it doesn't. In the entire population of customers who ordered this sandwich, there is a distribution of satisfaction ratings. Some fraction rate it as 1, some rate it as 2, and so on. All we are trying to determine here is the *average* of all these ratings. Based on our analysis, we can be 95% confident that this (still unknown) average is between 5.739 and 6.761. However, this confidence interval doesn't tell us other characteristics of the population of ratings that might be of interest, such as the proportion of customers who rate the sandwich 6 or higher. It tells us only about the *mean* rating. Later in this chapter, we see how to find a confidence interval for a proportion, which allows us to analyze another important characteristic of a population distribution. ∎

In the sandwich example we said that the manager can be 95% confident that the true mean rating is between 5.739 and 6.761. What does this statement really mean? Contrary to what you might expect, it does *not* mean that the true mean lies between 5.739 and 6.761 with probability 0.95. Either the true mean is inside this interval or it is not. The true meaning of a 95% confidence interval is based on the *procedure* used to obtain it. Specifically, if we use this procedure on a large number of random samples, all from the same population, then approximately 95% of the resulting confidence intervals will be "good" ones that include the true mean, and the other 5% will be "bad" ones that do not include the true mean. Of course, when we have only a single sample, as in the sandwich example, we have no way of knowing whether our confidence interval is one of the good ones or one of the bad ones, but we can be 95% confident that we obtained one of the good intervals.

Because this is such an important concept, we illustrate it in Figure 9.7 with simulation. (See the file **Confidence Interval Simulation.xlsx**.) The data in column B are generated randomly from a normal distribution with the *known* values of μ and σ in cells B3 and B4. Next, we invoke StatTools's One-Sample Confidence Interval procedure to calculate a 95% confidence interval for the true value of μ, exactly as in the sandwich example. However, we now know whether the true value of μ is within the interval, so we record a 1 in cell H6 if it is and a 0 otherwise. This requires the formula

$$=IF(AND(B3>=D13,B3<=D14),1,0)$$

Figure 9.7 Simulation Demonstration of Confidence Intervals

	A	B	C	D	E	F	G	H
1	Interpretation of a "95% confidence interval"							
2				This simulation uses a *normal* population for illustration. But you could generate the random				
3	Population mean	100		sample from another distribution (e.g., triangular) to see if the confidence intervals are still				
4	Population stdev	20		valid, i.e, if the % in cell H7 is about 95%.				
5								
6	Random sample			Random sample			Mean captured?	1
7	61.47		Conf. Intervals (One-Sample)	Data Set #1			% of CI's capturing mean	95.0%
8	90.67		Sample Size	30				
9	115.94		Sample Mean	103.94			Data table to replicate confidence interval	
10	128.39		Sample Std Dev	16.66			Replication	Mean captured?
11	101.11		Confidence Level (Mean)	95.0%				1
12	124.82		Degrees of Freedom	29			1	1
13	92.88		Lower Limit	97.72			2	1
14	121.72		Upper Limit	110.16			3	1
15	117.49						4	1
16	100.24		Graphical representation				5	1
17	115.04		Limit	Height			6	1
18	87.97		97.72	1			7	0
19	108.06		110.16	1			8	1
20	114.35						9	1
21	100.74		Mean	Height			10	1
22	90.80		100	1			11	1
23	83.30						12	1
24	121.87						13	1
25	84.70						14	1
26	82.66						15	1
27	110.82						16	1
28	110.04						17	1
29	84.71						18	1
30	111.35						19	1
31	117.51						20	1
32	138.46						21	1
33	99.58						22	1
34	103.16						23	1
35	94.50						24	1
36	103.79						25	1
37							26	1
38							27	1

Finally, we use a data table to replicate the simulated results 1000 times.[2] Specifically, we enter the formula

=G6

in cell G11 and build a data table (only a few rows of which are shown) in the range F11:G1011, leaving the row input cell box empty and using any blank cell as the column input cell. Then we calculate the fraction of values in the range G12:G1011 that are 1's in cell G7 with the AVERAGE function.

We see that 942 of the simulated confidence intervals (each based on a *different* random sample of size 30) contain the true mean 100. In theory, we would expect 950 of the 1000 intervals to cover the true mean, and this is almost exactly what we obtained. Of course, in a particular application you might unluckily obtain the fifth sample (in row 31). However, without knowing that the true mean is 100, you would have no way of knowing that you obtained a "bad" interval!

We also show this graphically in the file. (See Figure 9.7.) The small square in this graph is positioned at the known mean and never changes. The blue line represents a particular confidence interval. Put your cursor below this chart in, say, cell C35, and press the Delete key. (This forces a recalculation without recalculating the whole data table.) The position of the blue line will change. About 95% of the time, the blue line will straddle the small square—the confidence interval will include the true mean—but about 1 time out of 20, it will not. This also illustrates the meaning of a "95% confidence interval."

PROBLEMS

Level A

5. A manufacturing company's quality control personnel have recorded the proportion of defective items for each of 500 monthly shipments of one of the computer components that the company produces. The data are in the file **P02_02.xlsx**. The quality control department manager does not have sufficient time to review all of these data. Rather, she would like to examine the proportions of defective items for a sample of these shipments.
  a. Use Excel to generate a simple random sample of size 25 from the given frame.
  b. Using the sample generated in part **a**, construct a 95% confidence interval for the mean proportion of defective items over all monthly shipments. Assume that the population consists of the proportion of defective items for each of the given 500 monthly shipments.
  c. Interpret the 95% confidence interval constructed in part **b**.
  d. Does the 95% confidence interval contain the actual population mean in this case? If not, explain why not. What proportion of many similarly constructed confidence intervals should include the true population mean value?

6. Consider the given set of average annual household income levels of citizens of selected U.S. metropolitan areas in the file **P03_06.xlsx**.
  a. Use Excel to obtain a simple random sample of size 15 from this frame.
  b. Using the sample generated in part **a**, construct a 99% confidence interval for the mean average annual household income level of citizens in the selected U.S. metropolitan areas. Assume that the population consists of all average annual household income levels in the given frame.
  c. Interpret the 99% confidence interval constructed in part **b**.
  d. Does the 99% confidence interval contain the actual population mean? If not, explain why not. What proportion of many similarly constructed confidence intervals should include the true population mean value?

7. The file **P03_86.xlsx** contains data on all NFL players as of 2000. Because this file contains all players, you can calculate the *population* mean if we define "population" as all 2000 NFL salaries. However, proceed as in Chapter 8 to select a random sample of size 50 from this population. Based on this random sample, calculate a 95% confidence interval for the mean NFL

---

[2]It can take quite a while to simulate 1000 samples of size 30 in this data table. Therefore, it is a good idea to set the recalculation mode to "automatic except tables." (To find this option, click on the Office button, then Excel Options, and then the Formulas tab.) That way, the data table recalculates only if you explicitly tell it to (by pressing the F9 key).

salary in 2000. Does it contain the population mean? Repeat this procedure several times until you find a random sample where the population mean is *not* included in the confidence interval.

8. The file **P09_08.xlsx** contains data on repetitive task times for each of two workers. John has been doing this task for months, whereas Fred has just started. Each time listed is the time (in seconds) to perform a routine task on an assembly line. The times shown are in chronological order.
   a. Find a 95% confidence interval for the mean time it takes John to perform the task. Do the same for Fred.
   b. Do you believe both of the confidence intervals in part **a** are valid and/or useful? Why or why not? Which of the two workers would you rather have (assuming time is the only issue)?

9. The manager of a local fast-food restaurant is interested in improving the service provided to customers who use the restaurant's drive-up window. As a first step in this process, the manager asks his assistant to record the time (in minutes) it takes to serve a large number of customers at the final window in the facility's drive-up system. The given frame of 200 customer service times are all observed during the busiest hour of the day for

this fast-food operation. The data are in the file **P02_04.xlsx**.
   a. Use Excel to generate a simple random sample of size 10 from this frame.
   b. Using the sample generated in part **a**, construct a 90% confidence interval for the mean service time of all customers arriving during the busiest hour of the day at this fast-food operation. Assume that the population consists of the given 200 customer service times.
   c. Interpret the 90% confidence interval constructed in part **b**.

Level B

10. Continuing the previous problem, use Excel to generate 100 simple random samples of size 10 from the frame given in the file **P02_04.xlsx**. Then use each of these random samples to construct a 90% confidence interval for the mean service time of all customers arriving during the busiest hour of the day at this fast-food operation. How many of the 100 constructed confidence intervals actually contain the true value of the population mean in this case? Is this result consistent with your expectations? Explain.

9.4 CONFIDENCE INTERVAL FOR A TOTAL[3]

There are situations where a population mean is not the population parameter of most interest. A good example is the auditing example discussed in the previous chapter (Example 8.4). Rather than estimating the mean amount of receivables *per account,* the auditor might be more interested in the *total* amount of all receivables, summed over all accounts. In this section we provide a point estimate and a confidence interval for a population total.

First, we introduce some notation. Let T be a population total we want to estimate, such as the total of all receivables, and let $\hat{T}$ be a point estimate of T based on a simple random sample of size n from a population of size N. We need a reasonable formula for $\hat{T}$; that is, we need to know how to calculate a point estimate of T. For the population total T, it is reasonable to sum all of the values in the sample, denoted T_S, and then "project" this total to the population with equation (9.5), where the second equality follows because the sample total T_S divided by the sample size n is the sample mean $\overline{X}$.

Point Estimate for Population Total

$$\hat{T} = \frac{N}{n} T_S = N\overline{X} \tag{9.5}$$

Actually, equation (9.5) is quite intuitive. Suppose there are 1000 accounts in the population, we sample 50 of them, and we observe a sample total of $5000. Then, because we sampled only 1/20 of the population, a natural estimate of the population total is $20 \times \$5000 = \$100,000$.

Like the sample mean $\overline{X}$, the estimate $\hat{T}$ has a sampling distribution. The mean and standard deviation of this sampling distribution are given in equations (9.6) and (9.7), where σ is again the population standard deviation.

---

[3]This section can be omitted without any loss of continuity.

Because σ is usually unknown, we use s instead of σ to obtain the approximate standard error of $\hat{T}$ given in equation (9.8). The second equality follows because $s/\sqrt{n}$ is the standard error of $\overline{X}$.

Note from equation (9.6) that $\hat{T}$ is an unbiased estimate of the population total T. Therefore, it has no tendency to either overestimate or underestimate T.

From equations (9.5) and (9.8), we see that the point estimate of T is the point estimate of the mean multiplied by N, and the standard error of this point estimate is the standard error of the sample mean multiplied by N. This has a very nice consequence. We can form a confidence interval for T with the following two-step procedure:

1. Find a confidence interval for the sample mean in the usual way.

2. Multiply each endpoint of the confidence interval by the population size N.

We illustrate this procedure in the following example.

EXAMPLE | **9.3 ESTIMATING TOTAL TAX REFUNDS**

Suppose the Internal Revenue Service would like to estimate the total net amount of refund due to a particular set of 10,000 taxpayers. Each taxpayer will either receive a refund, in which case the net refund is positive, or will have to pay an amount due, in which case the net refund is negative. Therefore the *total* net amount of refund is a natural quantity of interest; it is the net amount the IRS will have to pay out (or receive, if negative). Find a 95% confidence interval for this total using the refunds from a random sample of 500 taxpayers in the file **IRS Refunds.xlsx**.

Objective   To use StatTools's One-Sample Confidence Interval procedure, with an appropriate modification, to find a 95% confidence interval for the total (net) amount the IRS must pay out to these 10,000 taxpayers.

Solution

The solution appears in Figure 9.8. Although there is no explicit StatTools procedure for dealing with population totals, we can take advantage of the close relationship between the confidence interval for a mean and the confidence interval for a total. That is, we first use StatTools to find a 95% confidence interval for the population mean. This output appears in rows 6–13. The average refund per taxpayer in the sample is slightly less than \$300 (cell E6), and the standard error of this sample mean (not shown explicitly) is about \$26. The confidence interval for the mean (in cells E10 and E11) extends from \$244 to \$346. This part of the output analyzes the average refund for a single taxpayer.

Figure 9.8

Confidence Interval
for a Population
Total

	A	B	C	D	E
1	Customer	Refund		Population size	10000
2	1	$70			
3	2	$1,190			Refund
4	3	$220		Conf. Intervals (One-Sample)	Data Set #1
5	4	($280)		Sample Size	500
6	5	$260		Sample Mean	$294.98
7	6	$370		Sample Std Dev	$581.31
8	7	$450		Confidence Level (Mean)	95.0%
9	8	$210		Degrees of Freedom	499
10	9	$1,150		Lower Limit	$243.90
11	10	$270		Upper Limit	$346.06
12	11	$470			
13	12	($10)		Confidence interval for population total	
14	13	($160)		Confidence level	95.0%
15	14	$2,430		Point estimate	$2,949,800
16	15	$140		Standard error	$259,970
17	16	($190)		Lower limit	$2,439,028
18	17	($810)		Upper limit	$3,460,572
19	18	($20)			
20	19	$300			
21	20	($280)			
497	496	$50			
498	497	$790			
499	498	$190			
500	499	$1,840			
501	500	($20)			

Now all we need to do is project these results to the entire population. We do this in the range E15:E18 by multiplying each of the values in the previous paragraph by the population size, 10,000. The IRS can be 95% confident that it will need to pay out somewhere between 2.44 and 3.46 million dollars to these 10,000 taxpayers. ■

PROBLEMS

Level A

11. The operations manager of a toll booth located at a major exit of a state turnpike is trying to estimate the total number of vehicles that arrive at the toll booth during a 1-minute period during the peak of rush-hour traffic. In an effort to estimate this total throughput value, he records the number of vehicles that arrive at the toll booth over a 1-minute interval commencing at the same time for each of 50 normal weekdays. The data are provided in the file **P09_11.xlsx**. Construct a 95% confidence interval for the total number of vehicles that arrive at the toll booth during a 1-minute period during the peak of rush-hour traffic for 1000 normal weekdays. What does this interval reveal about the actual throughput value of interest?

12. A lightbulb manufacturer wants to estimate the total number of defective bulbs contained in all of the boxes shipped by the company during the past week. Production personnel at this company have recorded the number of defective bulbs found in each of 50 randomly selected boxes shipped during the past week. These data are provided in the file **P09_12.xlsx**. Construct a 99% confidence interval for the total number of defective bulbs contained in the 1000 boxes shipped by this company during the past week.

Interpret this confidence interval for the production personnel at this company.

13. Auditors of a particular bank are interested in comparing the reported value of all 2265 customer savings account balances with their own findings regarding the actual value of such assets. Rather than reviewing the records of each savings account at the bank, the auditors decide to examine a representative sample of savings account balances. The frame from which they will sample is given in the file **P08_50.xlsx**.

   a. Select a simple random sample consisting of 100 savings account balances from the given frame.

   b. Using the sample generated in part **a**, construct a 90% confidence interval for the total value of all savings account balances within this bank. Assume that the population consists of all savings account balances in the given frame.

   c. Interpret the 90% confidence interval constructed in part **b**.

Level B

14. Continuing the previous problem, use StatTools to generate 50 simple random samples of size 100 from the frame given in **P08_50.xlsx**. Then use each of these random samples to construct a 90% confidence interval for the total value of all 2265 savings account balances within this bank. How many of the 50 constructed confidence intervals actually contain the true total value in this case? Is this result consistent with your expectations? Explain.

9.5 CONFIDENCE INTERVAL FOR A PROPORTION

How often have you heard on the evening news a survey finding such as, "52% of the public agree with the president's handling of the economy, with a sampling error of plus or minus 3%"? Surveys are often used to estimate proportions, such as the proportion of the public who agree with the president's handling of the economy. We will now see how to form a confidence interval for any population proportion p.

The basic procedure is very similar to what we described for a population mean. We find a point estimate, the standard error of this point estimate, and a multiple that depends on the confidence level. Then the confidence level has the same form as in expression (9.1):

$$\text{point estimate} \pm \text{multiple} \times \text{standard error}$$

In the news example the point estimate is 52% and the "multiple $\times$ standard error" is 3%. Therefore, the confidence interval extends from 49% to 55%. Although the news show doesn't state the confidence level explicitly, it is 95% by convention. In words, we can be 95% confident that the percentage of the public who agree with the president's handling of the economy is somewhere between 49% and 55%.

The theory that leads to this result is fairly straightforward. Let A be any property that members of a population either have or do not have. As examples, A might be the property that

- a person agrees with the president's handling of the economy;
- a person has purchased a company's product at least once within the past 3 months;
- the diameter of a part is with specification limits;
- a customer's account is at least 2 months overdue; or
- a customer's rating of a new sandwich is at least 6 on a 10-point scale.

In each of these examples, we are interested in the proportion p of the population that have property A. We sample n members randomly and let $\hat{p}$ be the sample proportion of members with property A. For example, if 10 out of 50 sampled members have property A, then $\hat{p} = 10/50 = 0.2$. Then we use $\hat{p}$ as a point estimate of p.

It can be shown that for sufficiently large n, the sampling distribution of $\hat{p}$ is approximately normal with mean p and standard deviation $\sqrt{p(1-p)/n}$. Because p is the unknown parameter, we substitute $\hat{p}$ for p in this standard deviation to obtain the following approximate standard error of $\hat{p}$:

Finally, the multiple we use to obtain a confidence interval for p is a Z-value. It is the standard normal value that cuts off an appropriate probability in each tail. For example, the z-multiple for a 95% confidence interval is 1.96 because this value cuts off probability 0.025 in each tail of the standard normal distribution. In general, the confidence interval has the form in expression (9.10):

Confidence Interval for a Proportion

$$\hat{p} \pm z\text{-multiple} \times \sqrt{\frac{\hat{p}(1 - \hat{p})}{n}} \qquad (9.10)$$

This confidence interval is based on the assumption of a large sample size. A rule of thumb for checking the validity of this assumption is the following. Let p_L and p_U be the lower and upper limits of the confidence interval. Then the sample size is sufficiently large—and the confidence interval is valid—if $np_L > 5$, $n(1 - p_L) > 5$, $np_U > 5$, and $n(1 - p_U) > 5$.

We illustrate the procedure in the following example.

EXAMPLE

9.4 ESTIMATING THE RESPONSE TO A NEW SANDWICH

The fast-food manager from Example 9.2 has already sampled 40 customers to estimate the population mean rating of its new sandwich. Recall that each rating is on a 1-to-10 scale, 10 being the best. The manager would now like to use the same sample to estimate the proportion of customers who rate the sandwich at least 6. Her thinking is that these are the customers who are likely to purchase the sandwich on subsequent visits.

Objective To illustrate the procedure for finding a confidence interval for the proportion of customers who rate the new sandwich at least 6 on a 10-point scale.

Solution

The solution appears in Figure 9.9. (See the file **Satisfaction Ratings.xlsx**.) StatTools does not yet have a procedure for calculating confidence intervals for proportions, but this example illustrates how a few Excel functions accomplish the job. We first count the number of ratings that are at least 6 in cell E4. The easiest way to do this is with the formula

=COUNTIF(B2:B41,">=6")

Excel's COUNTIF function is useful for counting the number of cells in some range that satisfy some condition.

(The quotes around the condition are required.) Then we calculate the sample proportion in cell E5 with the formula

=E4/E1

The rest is simply a matter of implementing equation (9.9) and expression (9.10). Specifically, the standard error formula in cell E9 is

=SQRT(E5*(1-E5)/E1)

and the formula for the lower limit of the confidence interval, in cell E11, is

=E5-E10*E9

Figure 9.9

Analysis of a
Proportion for New
Sandwich Data

	A	B	C	D	E
1	Customer	Satisfaction		Sample size	40
2	1	7			
3	2	5		Ratings at least 6	
4	3	5		Number	25
5	4	6		Proportion	0.625
6	5	8			
7	6	7		Confidence interval calculations	
8	7	6		Confidence level	95%
9	8	7		Standard error	0.077
10	9	10		z-multiple	1.960
11	10	7		Lower limit	0.475
12	11	9		Upper limit	0.775
13	12	5			
14	13	5			
40	39	5			
41	40	4			

Of course, the formula for the upper limit is the same except with a plus sign.

Then using the confidence interval limits, $p_L = 0.475$ and $p_U = 0.775$, we can check the assumption of large sample size. With $n = 40$, you can check that np_L, $n(1 - p_L)$, np_U, and $n(1 - p_U)$ are all well above 5, so that the validity of this confidence interval is established.

The output is fairly good news for the manager. Based on this sample of size 40, she can be 95% confident that the percentage of all customers who would rate the sandwich 6 or higher is somewhere between 47.5% and 77.5%. Of course, she realizes that this is a very wide interval, so there is still a lot of uncertainty about the *true* population proportion. To reduce the length of this interval, she would need to sample more customers—quite a few more customers. Typically, confidence intervals for proportions are fairly wide unless n is quite large. ∎

We explore this final statement a bit more. Referring again to news shows, you have probably noticed that they almost always quote a sampling error of plus or minus 3%. In words, the "plus or minus" part of their 95% confidence interval is 3%, or 0.03. How large a sample size must they use to achieve this? We know that the "plus or minus" part of the confidence interval is 1.96 times the standard error of $\hat{p}$, so we must have

$$1.96 \times \sqrt{\hat{p}(1 - \hat{p})/n} = 0.03$$

Now, the quantity $\hat{p}(1 - \hat{p})$ is fairly constant for values of $\hat{p}$ between 0 and 1, provided that $\hat{p}$ isn't too close to 0 or 1. To get a reasonable estimate of the required n, we assume $\hat{p} = 0.5$. Then we have

$$1.96 \times \sqrt{(0.5)(0.5)/n} = 0.03$$

Solving for n, we obtain $n = [(1.96)(0.5)/0.03]^2 \approx 1067$.

This is a rather remarkable result. To obtain a 95% confidence interval of this length for a population proportion, where the population consists of millions of people, only about 1000 people need to be sampled. The remarkable fact is that this small a sample can provide such accurate information about such a large population.

One of many business applications of confidence intervals for proportions is in auditing. Auditors typically use **attribute sampling** to check whether certain procedures are being followed correctly. The term "attribute" implies that each item checked is done

450 Chapter 9 Confidence Interval Estimation

either correctly or incorrectly—there is no "in between." Examples of items not done correctly might include (1) an invoice copy that is not initialed by an accounting clerk, (2) an invoice quantity that does not agree with the quantity on the shipping document, (3) an invoice price that does not agree with the price on an authorized price list, and (4) an invoice with a clerical inaccuracy. Typically, an auditor focuses on one of these types of errors and then estimates the proportion of items with this type of error.

Because auditors are concerned primarily with how *large* the proportion of errors might be, they usually calculate **one-sided** confidence intervals for proportions. Instead of using sample data to find lower and upper limits p_L and p_U of a confidence interval, they automatically use $p_L = 0$ and then determine an upper limit p_U such that the 95% confidence interval is from 0 to p_U. A simple modification of the confidence interval in formula (9.10) provides the result in equation (9.11), where the z-multiple is chosen so that the entire probability (0.05 for a 95% interval) is in the right-hand tail. For a 95% confidence level, the relevant z-multiple is 1.645.

Upper Limit of a One-Sided Confidence Interval for a Proportion

$$p_U = \hat{p} + z\text{-multiple} \times \sqrt{\hat{p}(1 - \hat{p})/n}$$

(9.11)

One further complication occurs, however. This formula for p_U relies on the large-sample approximation of the normal distribution to the binomial distribution. Auditors typically use an *exact* procedure to find p_U that is based directly on the binomial distribution. We illustrate how this is done in the following example.

EXAMPLE | **9.5 AUDITING FOR PRICE ERRORS**

An auditor wants to check the proportion of invoices that contain price errors—that is, prices that do not agree with those on an authorized price list. He checks 93 randomly sampled invoices and finds that 2 of them include price errors. What can he conclude, in terms of a one-sided 95% confidence interval, about the proportion of all invoices with price errors?

Objective To find the upper limit of a one-sided 95% confidence interval for the proportion of errors in the context of attribute sampling in auditing.

Solution

The results appear in Figure 9.10. (See the file **One-Sided Confidence Interval.xlsx**.) The sample proportion is $p = 2/93 = 0.0215$ and the upper confidence limit based on the large-sample approximation is 0.046. This latter value is calculated in cell B14 with the formula

=B7+B13*SQRT(B7*(1-B7)/B5)

However, the fact that $np_U = 93(0.046) = 4.278$ is less than 5 indicates that the large-sample approximation might not be very accurate.

A more accurate procedure, based on the binomial distribution, appears in row 10. It turns out that if p_U is the appropriate upper confidence limit, then p_U satisfies the equation

$$P(X \leq k) = \alpha$$

(9.12)

Figure 9.10

Analysis of Auditing
Example

	A	B	C	D	E	F
1	An exact one-sided confidence interval in auditing					
2						
3	Confidence level	95%				
4	Number of errors	2				
5	Sample size	93				
6						
7	Sample proportion	0.0215				
8						
9	Exact upper confidence limit for p			Goal seek condition		
10	Upper limit	0.066		0.050	=	0.05
11						
12	Large-sample upper confidence limit for p					
13	z-multiple	1.645				
14	Upper limit	0.046				

Here, X is binomially distributed with parameters n and p_U, k is the observed number of errors, and α is 1 minus the confidence level. There is no way to find p_U directly (by means of a formula) from equation (9.12). However, we can use Excel's Goal Seek tool. First, we enter *any* trial value of p_U in cell B10 and the binomial formula

=BINOMDIST(B4,B5,B10,1)

in cell D10. (This formula calculates $P(X \leq k)$ from the trial value in cell B10.) Then we use Goal Seek from the What-If Analysis dropdown on the Data ribbon, with cell D10 as the Set cell, 0.05 as the target value, and cell B10 as the Changing cell. (See Figure 9.11.)

Figure 9.11

Settings in Goal Seek
Dialog Box

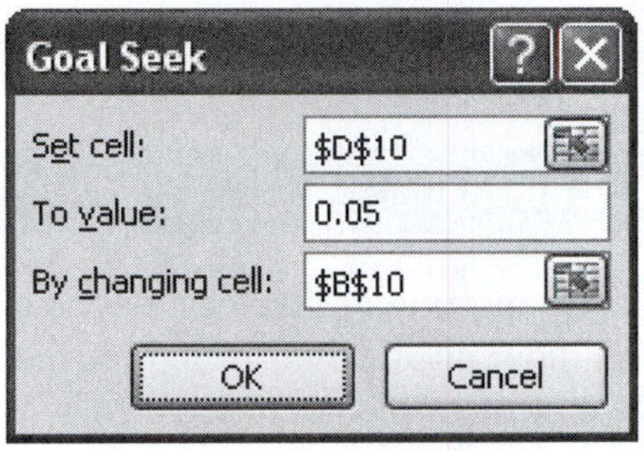

Goal Seek	? X
Set cell:	$D$10
To value:	0.05
By changing cell:	$B$10
OK	Cancel

The resulting value of p_U is 0.066. This is considerably different (from the auditor's point of view) from the 0.046 value found from the large-sample approximation. It allows the auditor to state with 95% confidence that the percentage of invoices with price errors is no greater than 6.6%, based on the 2 errors out of 93 observed in the sample. ■

PROBLEMS

Level A

15. Wal-Mart buyers seek to purchase adequate supplies of various brands of toothpaste to meet the ongoing demands of its customers. In particular, Wal-Mart is interested in estimating the proportion of its customers who favor the country's leading brand of toothpaste, Crest. The file **P09_15.xlsx** contains the toothpaste brand preferences of 200 Wal-Mart customers, obtained recently through the administration of a customer survey. Construct a 95% confidence interval for the proportion of all Wal-Mart customers who prefer Crest toothpaste. Interpret this confidence interval for the buyers at Wal-Mart.

16. The employee benefits manager of a small private university would like to estimate the proportion of full-time employees who prefer adopting the first (i.e., plan A) of three available health care plans in the coming annual enrollment period. A reliable frame of the university's employees and their tentative health care preferences are given in the file **P08_25.xlsx**.
   a. Use Excel to choose a simple random sample of size 45 from the given frame.

b. Using the sample found in part **a,** construct a 99% confidence interval for the proportion of university employees who prefer plan A. Assume that the population consists of the preferences of all employees in the given frame.

c. Interpret the 99% confidence interval constructed in part **b.**

17. A market research consultant hired by the Pepsi-Cola Co. is interested in determining the proportion of consumers who favor Pepsi-Cola over Coke Classic in a particular urban location. A random sample of 250 consumers from the market under investigation is provided in **P09_17.xlsx.** Construct a 90% confidence interval for the proportion of all consumers in this market who prefer Pepsi. Interpret this confidence interval for Pepsi-Cola's market researchers.

Level B

18. Continuing Problem 16, select simple random samples of 30 individuals from *each* of the given employee classifications (i.e., administrative staff, support staff, and faculty). Construct a 99% confidence interval for the proportion of employees who prefer adopting plan A for each of the three classifications. Do you see evidence of significant differences among these three interval estimates? Summarize your findings.

19. Continuing Problem 17, separate the given random sample of consumers (provided in the file **P09_17.xlsx**) into two gender subgroups: *males* and *females.* Construct 90% confidence intervals for the proportion of male consumers who prefer Pepsi and the proportion of female consumers who prefer Pepsi. Do you see evidence of a significant difference between the preferences of males and females in this case? Repeat this same process with the *age* attribute of the given consumers. In other words, separate the given sample of consumers by age (i.e., *under 20, between 20 and 40, between 40 and 60,* and *over 60*). Construct a 90% confidence interval for the proportion of consumers in each age category favoring Pepsi. Summarize your findings.

9.6 CONFIDENCE INTERVAL FOR A STANDARD DEVIATION[4]

In Section 9.3 we focused primarily on estimation of a population *mean.* Our concern with the population standard deviation σ was in its role as a nuisance parameter. That is, we needed an estimate of σ to estimate the standard error of the sample mean. However, there are cases where the variability in the population, measured by σ, is of interest in its own right. We briefly describe a procedure for obtaining a confidence interval for σ in this section.

The theory is somewhat more complex than for the case of the mean. As you might expect, we use the sample standard deviation s as a point estimate of σ. However, the sampling distribution of s is not symmetric—in particular, it is not the normal distribution or the t distribution. Rather, the appropriate sampling distribution is a right-skewed distribution called the **chi-square** distribution. Like the t distribution, the chi-square distribution has a degrees of freedom parameter, which (for this procedure) is again $n - 1$.

Tables of the chi-square distribution, for selected degrees of freedom, appear in many statistics books, but the necessary information can be obtained more easily with Excel's CHIDIST and CHIINV functions. The CHIDIST function takes the form

$$=\text{CHIDIST}(v, df)$$

This function returns the probability to the right of value v when the degrees of freedom parameter is df. Similarly, the CHIINV function takes the form

$$=\text{CHIINV}(p, df)$$

It returns the value with probability p to the right of it when the degrees of freedom parameter is df.

We do not present the rather complex confidence interval formulas for σ. However, we point out that because of the skewness of the sampling distribution of s, a confidence interval for σ is *not* centered at s. That is, the confidence interval is *not* the point estimate

---

[4]This section can be omitted without any loss of continuity.

plus or minus a multiple of a standard error. Instead, *s* is always closer to the left endpoint of the confidence interval than to the right endpoint, as indicated in Figure 9.12.

Figure 9.12

Confidence Interval for a Standard Deviation

Lower limit   Sample stdev *s*   Upper limit

The StatTools One-Sample Confidence Interval procedure enables us to obtain a confidence interval for a population standard deviation as easily as for a mean. We illustrate this in the following example.

EXAMPLE   **9.6 ANALYZING VARIABILITY IN DIAMETERS OF MACHINE PARTS**

A machine produces parts that are supposed to have diameter 10 centimeters. However, due to inherent variability, some diameters are greater than 10 and some are less. The production supervisor is concerned about two things. First, he is concerned that the mean diameter might not be 10 centimeters. Second, he is worried about the extent of variability in the diameters. Even if the mean is on target, excessive variability implies that many of the parts will fail to meet specifications. To analyze the process, he randomly samples 50 parts during the course of a day and measures the diameter of each part to the nearest millimeter. The results are shown in columns A and B of Figure 9.13. (See the file **Part Diameters.xlsx**.) Should he be concerned about the results from this sample?

Figure 9.13   Analysis of Parts Data

	A	B	C	D	E	F	G	H	I
1	Part	Diameter			Diameter				
2	1	10.031		*Conf. Intervals (One-Sample)*	Data Set #1				
3	2	10.011		**Sample Size**	50				
4	3	10.003		**Sample Mean**	9.996				
5	4	10.025		**Sample Std Dev**	0.034				
6	5	10.048		**Confidence Level (Mean)**	95.0%				
7	6	10.014		**Degrees of Freedom**	49				
8	7	10.030		**Lower Limit**	9.986				
9	8	10.008		**Upper Limit**	10.005				
10	9	10.049		**Confidence Level (Std Dev)**	95.0%				
11	10	9.995		**Degrees of Freedom**	49				
12	11	9.965		**Lower Limit**	0.029				
13	12	10.003		**Upper Limit**	0.043				
14	13	9.959							
15	14	10.013		**Proportion of unusable parts**					
16	15	10.012		**Maximum deviation for usability**	0.065				
17	16	10.005		**Assumed mean**	10				
18	17	9.921		**Assumed standard deviation**	0.043				
19	18	9.930		**Proportion unusable**	0.131				
20	19	9.990							
21	20	9.948		**Twoway data table for finding proportion unusable as a function of mean and stdev**					
22	21	10.077			Assumed standard deviation				
23	22	9.959			0.131	0.029	0.034	0.043	
24	23	10.000		Assumed mean	9.986	0.041	0.080	0.149	
25	24	9.998			9.996	0.025	0.060	0.130	
26	25	9.983			10.005	0.026	0.061	0.131	
27	26	9.995							
49	48	10.009							
50	49	9.973							
51	50	9.970							

Objective To use StatTools's One-Sample Confidence Interval procedure to find a confidence interval for the standard deviation of part diameters, and to see how variability affects the proportion of unusable parts produced.

Solution

Because the manager is concerned about the mean *and* the standard deviation of diameters, we obtain 95% confidence intervals for both. This is easy to do with StatTools's One-Sample Confidence Interval procedure. We go through the same dialog boxes as before, except that we now check the boxes for both confidence interval options—mean and standard deviation. The top part of the output in Figure 9.13 (through cell E9) provides a 95% confidence interval for the mean. This confidence interval extends from 9.986 cm to 10.005 cm. Therefore, there is probably not too much cause for concern about the mean. The supervisor can be fairly confident that the mean diameter of all parts is close to 10 cm.

The bottom part of the output (the range E10:E13) provides a 95% confidence interval for the standard deviation of diameters. This interval extends from 0.029 cm to 0.043 cm. Is this good news or bad news? It depends. Let's say that a part is unusable if its diameter is more than 0.065 cm from the target. Let's also assume the true mean is right on target and that the standard deviation is at the *upper* end of the confidence interval, that is, $\sigma = 0.043$ cm. Finally, we assume that the population distribution of diameters is normal. Then the calculation in cell E19 shows that 13.1% of the parts will be unusable! The formula in cell E19 is

=NORMDIST(10-E16,E17,E18,1)+(1-NORMDIST(10+E16,E17,E18,1))

It adds the normal probabilities of being below or above the usable range.

To pursue this analysis one step further, we form a two-way data table in the range E23:H26. The assumed means we use in column E are the lower confidence limit, the sample mean, and the upper confidence limit. Similarly, the assumed standard deviations in row 23 are the lower confidence limit, the sample standard deviation, and the upper confidence limit. To form the table, enter the formula =E19 in cell E23, highlight the range E23:H26, and create a data table with cells E18 and E17 as the row and column input cells.

Each value in the body of the data table is the resulting proportion of unusable parts. Obviously, a mean close to the target and a small standard deviation are best, but even this best-case scenario results in 2.5% unusable parts (see cell F25). However, a mean off target and a large standard deviation can lead to as many as 14.9% unusable parts (see cell H24). In any case, the message for the supervisor should be clear—he must work to reduce the underlying variability in the process. This variability is hurting him much more than an off-target mean. ∎

PROBLEMS

Level A

20. Consider a frame consisting of 500 households in a middle-class neighborhood that was the recent focus of an economic development study conducted by the local government. Specifically, for each of the 500 households, information was gathered on the total indebtedness (excluding the value of a home mortgage) of the household and each of several other variables. The data are in the file **P02_06.xlsx**.
  a. Use Excel to choose a simple random sample of size 25 from this frame.
  b. Using the sample generated in part **a**, construct a 95% confidence interval for the standard deviation of the total indebtedness of all households in the given neighborhood.

c. Interpret the 95% confidence interval constructed in part **b**.

d. Does the 95% confidence interval contain the actual value of the population standard deviation in this case? If not, explain why not. What proportion of many similarly constructed confidence intervals should include the true population standard deviation?

21. Senior management of a certain consulting services firm is concerned about a growing decline in the organization's weekly number of billable hours. Ideally, the organization expects each professional employee to spend *at least* 40 hours per week on work. In an effort to understand this problem better, management would like to estimate the standard deviation of the number of hours their employees spend on work-related activities in a typical week. The frame of virtually all of the firm's full-time employees, including the employees' self-reported amounts of time typically devoted to work activities each week, is provided in the file **P08_35.xlsx**.

a. Select a simple random sample of size 100 from the given frame.

b. Using the sample generated in part **a**, construct a 99% confidence interval for the standard deviation of the number of hours this organization's employees spend on work-related activities in a typical week.

c. Given the target range of 40 to 60 hours of work per week, should senior management be concerned about the number of hours their employees are currently devoting to work? Explain why or why not.

Level B

22. A manufacturing company's quality control personnel have recorded the proportion of defective items for each of 500 randomly selected shipments of one of the computer components that the company produces. The data are in the file **P09_22.xlsx**. The quality control department manager would like to use this random sample to estimate the mean and standard deviation of the proportion of defective items in the company's shipments. She is concerned that some shipments of this computer component contain an unacceptably high proportion of defective items. In particular, her company cannot tolerate a defective rate higher than 5% for any of its shipments.

a. Use the given random sample to construct 95% confidence intervals for the mean and standard deviation of the proportion of defective items in the company's shipments. Interpret each of these interval estimates.

b. Assuming the proportion of defective computer components in a given shipment is *normally* distributed, what is the probability that a randomly selected shipment will be unacceptable? Based on information derived from the confidence intervals constructed in part **a**, compute this probability for various combinations of the mean and standard deviation. You might want to generate a two-way data table to compute this probability for various combinations of the mean and standard deviation of the defective rate in the company's shipments.

9.7 CONFIDENCE INTERVAL FOR THE DIFFERENCE BETWEEN MEANS

One of the most important applications of statistical inference is the comparison of two population means. There are many applications to business, including the following.

Applications of Statistical Inference to Business

- Men and women shop at a retail clothing store. The manager would like to know how much more (or less), on average, a woman spends on a typical purchase occasion than a man.

- Two airline companies fly similar routes. A consumer organization would like to check how much the average delay differs between the two airlines, where delay is defined as the actual arrival time at the destination minus the scheduled arrival time.

Statisticians call these general types of problems "comparison problems." They are among the most important types of problems attacked by statistical methods.

- A supermarket chain mails coupons for various products to its customers in one city. Its customers in another city receive no such coupons. The chain would like to check how much the average amount spent on these products differs between the two sets of customers over the next couple of months.

- A computer company has a customer service center that responds to customers' questions and complaints. The center employs two types of people: those who have had a recent course in dealing with customers (but little actual experience) and those with a lot of experience dealing with customers (but no formal course). The company would like to know how these two types of employees differ with respect to the average number of customer complaints of poor service in the last 6 months.

- A consulting company hires business students directly out of undergraduate school. The new hires all take a problem-solving test. They then go through an intensive 3-month training program, after which they take another similar problem-solving test. The company wants to know how much the average test score improves after the training program.

- A car dealership often deals with husband–wife pairs shopping for cars. To check whether husbands react differently than their wives to the sales presentation, husbands and wives are asked (separately) to rate the quality of the sales presentation. The dealership wants to know how much husbands differ from their wives in terms of average ratings.

Each of these examples deals with a difference between means from two populations. However, the first four examples differ in one important respect from the last two. In the last two examples there is a natural *pairing* across the two samples. In the first of these, each employee takes a test before a course and then a test after the course, so that each employee is naturally paired with himself or herself. In the final example, husbands and wives are naturally paired with one another. There is no such pairing in the first four examples. Instead, we assume that the samples in these first four examples are chosen *independently* of one another. For statistical reasons we need to distinguish these two cases, *independent samples* and *paired samples*, in the discussion that follows.

9.7.1 Independent Samples

The framework for this situation is the following. We are interested in some quantity, such as dollars spent or airplane delay, for each of two populations. The population means are μ_1 and μ_2, and the population standard deviations are σ_1 and σ_2. We take random samples of sizes n_1 and n_2 from the populations to estimate the difference between means, $\mu_1 - \mu_2$. A point estimate of this difference is the natural one, the difference between sample means, $\overline{X}_1 - \overline{X}_2$. Starting with this estimate, we want to form a confidence interval for the unknown population mean difference, $\mu_1 - \mu_2$.

It turns out that the appropriate sampling distribution of this estimate is again the t distribution, now with $n_1 + n_2 - 2$ degrees of freedom.[5] Therefore, a confidence interval for $\mu_1 - \mu_2$ is given by expression (9.13). The t-multiple is the value that cuts off the appropriate probability (depending on the confidence level) in each tail of the t distribution with $n_1 + n_2 - 2$ degrees of freedom. For example, if the confidence level is 95% and $n_1 = n_2 = 30$, then the appropriate t-multiple is 2.002, which is found in Excel with the function TINV(0.05,58).

Confidence Interval for Difference Between Means

$$\overline{X}_1 - \overline{X}_2 \pm t\text{-multiple} \times \mathrm{SE}(\overline{X}_1 - \overline{X}_2) \qquad (9.13)$$

The standard error, $\mathrm{SE}(\overline{X}_1 - \overline{X}_2)$, is more involved. We must first make the assumption that the population standard deviations are equal, that is, $\sigma_1 = \sigma_2$. (We shortly present an alternative procedure when it is clear that the population standard deviations are *not*

---

[5]This assumes that either the population distributions are normal or that the sample sizes are reasonably large, conditions that are at least approximately met in a wide variety of applications.

equal.) Then an estimate of this common standard deviation is provided by the "pooled" estimate from both samples, labeled s_p:

Pooled Estimate of Common Standard Deviation

$$s_p = \sqrt{\frac{(n_1 - 1)s_1^2 + (n_2 - 1)s_2^2}{n_1 + n_2 - 2}}$$

Here, s_1 and s_2 are the sample standard deviations from the two samples. This pooled estimate is somewhere between s_1 and s_2, with the relative sample sizes determining its exact value. Then the standard error of $\overline{X}_1 - \overline{X}_2$ is given by equation (9.14):

Standard Error of Difference Between Sample Means

$$\text{SE}(\overline{X}_1 - \overline{X}_2) = s_p\sqrt{\frac{1}{n_1} + \frac{1}{n_2}}$$ (9.14)

Fortunately, the StatTools Two-Sample Confidence Interval procedure takes care of all these calculations, as illustrated in the following example.

EXAMPLE | **9.7 RELIABILITY OF TREADMILL MOTORS AT THE SURESTEP COMPANY**

The SureStep Company manufactures high-quality treadmills for use in exercise clubs. SureStep currently purchases its motors for these treadmills from supplier A. However, it is considering a change to supplier B, which offers a slightly lower cost. The only question is whether supplier B's motors are as reliable as supplier A's. To check this, SureStep installs motors from supplier A on 30 of its treadmills and motors from supplier B on another 30 of its treadmills. It then runs these treadmills under typical conditions and, for each treadmill, records the number of hours until the motor fails. The data from this experiment appear in Figure 9.14. (See the file **Treadmill Motors.xlsx**.) What can SureStep conclude?

Objective To use StatTools's Two-Sample Confidence Interval procedure to find a confidence interval for the difference between mean lifetimes of motors, and to see how this confidence interval can help SureStep choose the better supplier.

Solution

In any comparison problem it is a good idea to look initially at side-by-side box plots of the two samples. These appear in Figure 9.15. These show that (1) the distributions of times until failure are skewed to the right for each supplier, (2) the mean for supplier A is somewhat greater than the mean for supplier B, and (3) there are several mild outliers. There seems to be little doubt that supplier A's motors will last longer on average than supplier B's—or is there? A confidence interval for the mean difference allows us to see whether the differences apparent in the box plots can be generalized to *all* motors from the two suppliers.

We find this confidence interval by using the StatTools Two-Sample Confidence Interval procedure. To do so, select Confidence Interval from the StatTools Statistical Inference dropdown, and fill in the resulting dialog box as shown in Figure 9.16. Specifically, make sure the Analysis Type dropdown list shows Two-Sample Analysis,

Figure 9.14 Analysis of Treadmill Motors Data

	A	B	C	D	E	F
					Supplier A	Supplier B
1	Supplier A	Supplier B				
2	1358	658		*Sample Summaries*	Data Set #1	Data Set #1
3	793	404		Sample Size	30	30
4	587	735		Sample Mean	748.80	655.67
5	608	457		Sample Std Dev	283.88	259.99
6	472	431				
7	562	658			Equal	Unequal
8	879	453		*Conf. Intervals (Difference of Means)*	Variances	Variances
9	575	488		Confidence Level	95.0%	95.0%
10	1293	522		Sample Mean Difference	93.13	93.13
11	1457	1247		Standard Error of Difference	70.281	70.281
12	705	1095		Degrees of Freedom	58	58
13	623	430		Lower Limit	-47.549	-47.549
14	725	726		Upper Limit	233.815	233.815
15	569	793				
16	424	498				
17	436	502		*Equality of Variances Test*		
18	1250	589		Ratio of Sample Variances	1.1923	
19	493	975		p-Value	0.6390	
20	485	808				
21	462	456				
29	791	846				
30	684	732				
31	666	507				

and click on the Format button to make sure the Unstacked option is checked. We obtain the output in Figure 9.14. The top part of the output summarizes the two samples. It shows that the sample means differ by approximately 93 hours and that the sample standard deviations are of roughly the same magnitude.

Excel Tip *The data are "unstacked" because there are separate columns for supplier A's times and supplier B's times. The Format button in the StatTools dialog box allows you to select the appropriate option: Stacked or Unstacked.*

The confidence interval calculations appear in the range E9:E14. Here we see that the difference between sample means is 93.133 hours, the standard error of the sample mean difference is 70.281 hours, and a 95% confidence interval for the mean difference extends from -47.549 to 233.815 hours. Not only is this interval quite wide, but it extends from a negative value to a positive value. If SureStep had to make a guess, it would say that supplier A's motors last longer on average than supplier B's. But because of the negative part of the confidence interval, there is still a possibility that the opposite is true.

Should SureStep continue with supplier A? This depends on the trade-off between the cost of the motors and warranty costs (and any other relevant costs). Because the warranty probably depends on whether a motor lasts a certain amount of time, warranty costs probably depend on a *proportion* (the proportion that fail before 500 hours, say) rather than a mean. Therefore, we postpone further discussion of this issue until we discuss differences between proportions in Section 9.8.

Figure 9.15

Box Plots for
Treadmill Motors
Data

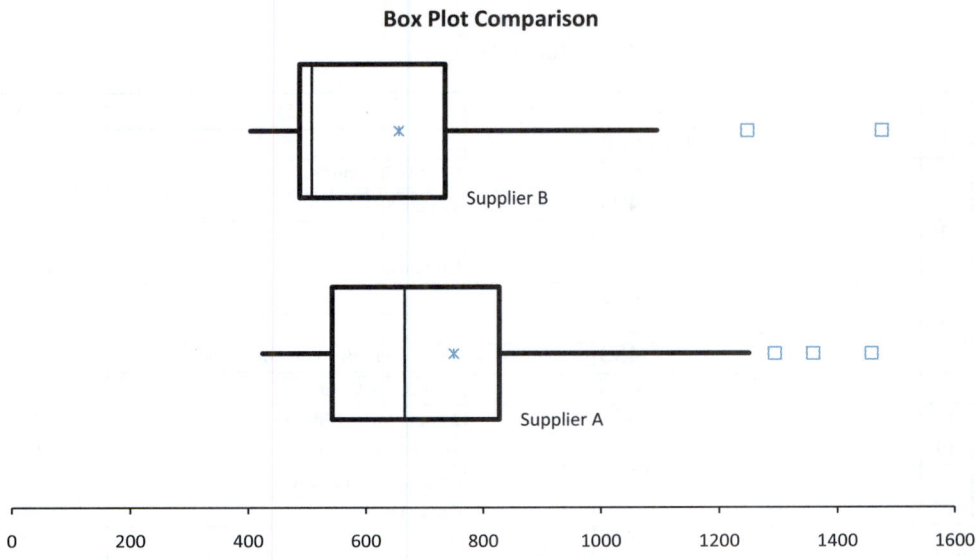

Figure 9.16

Dialog Box for Two-
Sample Procedure

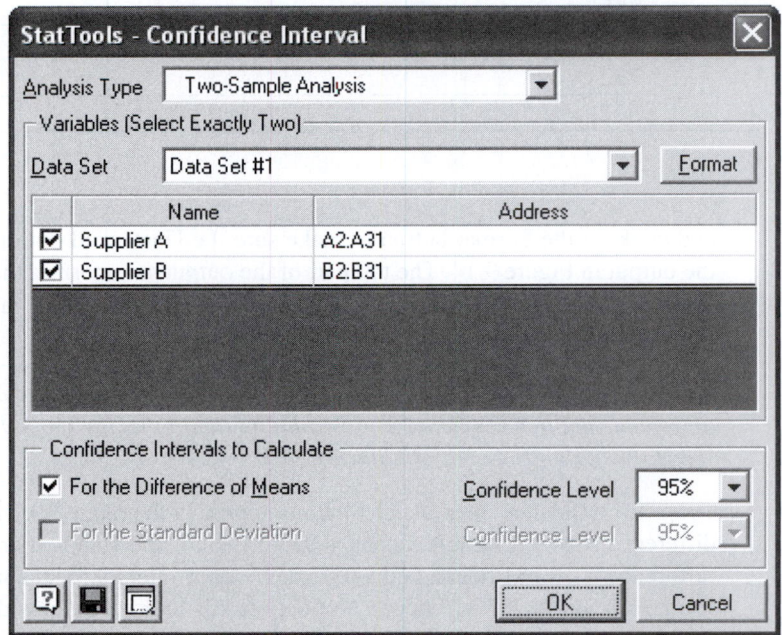

Equal-Variance Assumption

This two-sample analysis makes the strong assumption that the standard deviations (or variances) from the two populations are equal. How can we tell if they are equal, and what do we do if they are not equal?

To check whether they are equal, we should first look at the two sample standard deviations. If they are of widely different magnitudes, this certainly casts doubt on the equal-variance assumption. The sample standard deviations in the treadmill example, 283.88 and 259.98, are of similar magnitudes and present no clear evidence of unequal population variances. A statistical test for equality of two population variances is automatically shown at the bottom of the StatTools Two-Sample output. Because we have not yet discussed hypothesis testing, however, we postpone discussion of this test for now. Suffice it to say that it presents no evidence of unequal variances for this example.

If we do have reason to believe that the population variances are unequal, then a slightly different procedure can be used to calculate a confidence interval for the difference between means. The appropriate standard error of $\overline{X}_1 - \overline{X}_2$ is now

$$\text{SE}(\overline{X}_1 - \overline{X}_2) = \sqrt{s_1^2/n_1 + s_2^2/n_2}$$

and the degrees of freedom used to find the t-multiple is given by a complex expression that we do not present here.

StatTools always calculates the results in both columns. When they are nearly the same, as they often are, it makes no practical difference which you quote.

StatTools's Two-Sample procedure automatically calculates the confidence interval under this unequal-variance assumption. For the treadmill example you can see the results in the range F9:F14 of Figure 9.14. In this example they are exactly the same as the results (in column E) when we make the equal-variance assumption. This is a consequence of equal sample sizes and roughly equal sample variances. In general, the two results will differ appreciably only when the sample sizes *and* the sample variances differ considerably across samples. In any case, the appropriate results to use are those on the right (column F) if there is reason to suspect unequal population variances and those on the left (column E) otherwise.

We next revisit the R&P Supermarket data in Example 3.10 from Chapter 3. We again make a comparison between two means, this time the mean number of customers left in line during rush times versus normal times. There are two objectives in this example. First, it provides one more illustration of the two-sample procedure, now with unequal sample sizes. Perhaps more importantly, it illustrates that not all data sets come "ready-made" for performing a particular analysis. We have to do some data manipulation before we can invoke StatTools's Two-Sample procedure. Indeed, this is sometimes the most time-consuming part of statistical analysis in real applications—getting the data ready for the analysis.

EXAMPLE | **9.8 ANALYZING CUSTOMER WAITING AT R&P SUPERMARKET**

As in Example 3.10, the manager of the R&P Supermarket has collected a week's worth of data on customer arrivals, departures, and waiting. There are 48 observations per day, each taken at the end of a half-hour period. The data appear in the file **Customer Checkouts.xlsx**. The various times of day are listed in the TimeInterval variable. (See Figure 9.17.) They include Morning Rush, Morning, Lunch Rush, Afternoon, Afternoon Rush, Evening, and Night. (The comment in cell C3 explains exactly which time intervals these refer to.) There is also a variable, EndWaiting, that records the number of customers still being served or waiting in line at the end of each half-hour period.

The manager would like to check whether the average value of EndWaiting differs during rush periods from normal, non-night periods. She is concerned that there might be excessive waiting during rush periods, in which case she might need to add more checkout people during these times. She plans to exclude the night period from the analysis because she knows from experience that customers very seldom need to wait during the night.

Figure 9.17 Original Data for Supermarket Example

	A	B	C	D	E	F	G	H	I
1	Day	StartTime	TimeInterval	InitialWaiting	Arrivals	Departures	EndWaiting	Checkers	TotalCustomers
2	Mon	8:00 AM	Morning rush	2	21	22	1	3	23
3	Mon	8:30 AM	Morning rush	1	25	18	8	3	26
4	Mon	9:00 AM	Morning	8	27	28	7	3	35
5	Mon	9:30 AM	Morning	7	21	23	5	3	28
6	Mon	10:00 AM	Morning	5	20	23	2	5	25
7	Mon	10:30 AM	Morning	2	36	31	7	5	38
8	Mon	11:00 AM	Morning	7	30	36	1	5	37
9	Mon	11:30 AM	Lunch rush	1	34	29	6	5	35
10	Mon	12:00 PM	Lunch rush	6	56	48	14	7	62
11	Mon	12:30 PM	Lunch rush	14	58	64	8	7	72
12	Mon	1:00 PM	Lunch rush	8	53	52	9	7	61
13	Mon	1:30 PM	Afternoon	9	30	36	3	5	39
14	Mon	2:00 PM	Afternoon	3	34	31	6	5	37
15	Mon	2:30 PM	Afternoon	6	36	37	5	5	42
16	Mon	3:00 PM	Afternoon	5	30	28	7	5	35
17	Mon	3:30 PM	Afternoon	7	29	34	2	5	36
18	Mon	4:00 PM	Afternoon	2	35	33	4	5	37
19	Mon	4:30 PM	Afternoon rush	4	32	25	11	5	36

Objective To use StatTools's Two-Sample Confidence Interval procedure to find a confidence interval for the difference between mean waiting times during the supermarket's rush periods versus its normal periods.

Solution

Starting with the data set in its original form, we need to perform two main steps:

1 Rename the seven time intervals (Morning rush, Morning, and so on) so that there are only three: Rush, Normal, and Night.

2 Perform the statistical comparison between the EndWaiting variables for the Rush and Normal periods.

The finished version of the file contains the results of step 1 in the NewData sheet and the results of step 2 in the Analysis sheet. If you want to follow along, hands-on, with the step-by-step procedure, you should use the "data only" version of the **Customer Checkouts.xlsx** file and perform the following steps.

1 **Copy sheet:** Create a copy of the Data sheet by pressing the Ctrl key and dragging the Data sheet tab to the right. Double-click on the new sheet tab and rename it Renamed Data.

2 **Rename time intervals:** To rename the time intervals on the Renamed Data sheet, use Excel's Find and Replace feature. Click on column C's tab to select the entire column, and then select Replace from the Find & Select dropdown on the Home ribbon. Type **Morning rush** in the "Find what:" box, type **Rush** in the "Replace with:" box, and click on the Replace All button. Repeat this for the other time intervals to be renamed. That is, replace Lunch rush and Afternoon rush by Rush, and replace Morning, Afternoon, and Evening by Normal. Figure 9.18 shows some of the results.

3 **Create box plots:** Define a StatTools data set from the data on the Renamed Data sheet, and use StatTools's Box Plot procedure to create side-by-side box plots of the EndWaiting variable. Select the Stacked option, and select TimeInterval as the "Cat" variable and EndWaiting as the "Val" variable. (See Figure 9.19.)

Figure 9.18 Supermarket Data with Time Categories Renamed

	A	B	C	D	E	F	G	H	I
1	Day	StartTime	TimeInterval	InitialWaiting	Arrivals	Departures	EndWaiting	Checkers	TotalCustomers
2	Mon	8:00 AM	Rush	2	21	22	1	3	23
3	Mon	8:30 AM	Rush	1	25	18	8	3	26
4	Mon	9:00 AM	Normal	8	27	28	7	3	35
5	Mon	9:30 AM	Normal	7	21	23	5	3	28
6	Mon	10:00 AM	Normal	5	20	23	2	5	25
7	Mon	10:30 AM	Normal	2	36	31	7	5	38
8	Mon	11:00 AM	Normal	7	30	36	1	5	37
9	Mon	11:30 AM	Rush	1	34	29	6	5	35
10	Mon	12:00 PM	Rush	6	56	48	14	7	62
11	Mon	12:30 PM	Rush	14	58	64	8	7	72
12	Mon	1:00 PM	Rush	8	53	52	9	7	61
13	Mon	1:30 PM	Normal	9	30	36	3	5	39
14	Mon	2:00 PM	Normal	3	34	31	6	5	37
15	Mon	2:30 PM	Normal	6	36	37	5	5	42
16	Mon	3:00 PM	Normal	5	30	28	7	5	35
17	Mon	3:30 PM	Normal	7	29	34	2	5	36
18	Mon	4:00 PM	Normal	2	35	33	4	5	37
19	Mon	4:30 PM	Rush	4	32	25	11	5	36

Figure 9.19

Box Plots for Supermarket Example

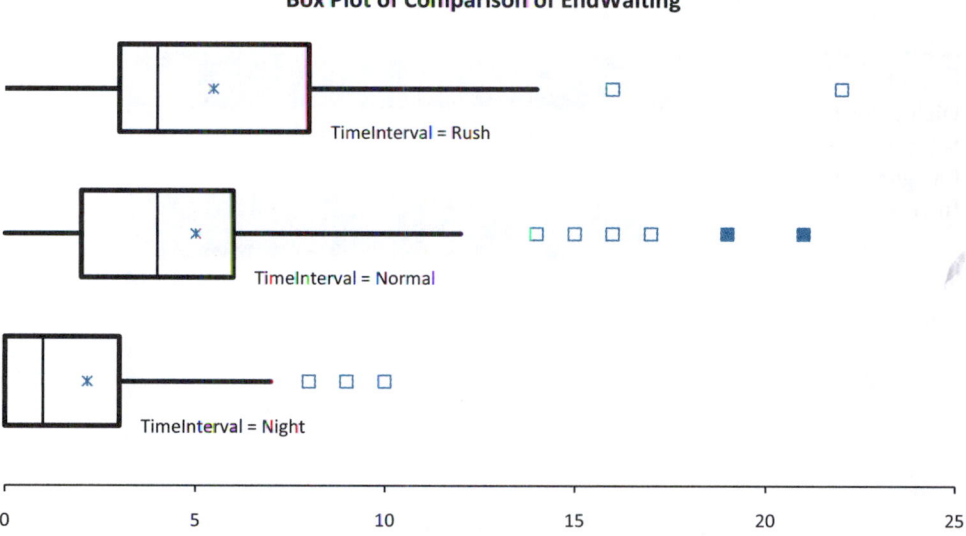

4 **Perform Two-Sample Analysis:** Select Confidence Interval from the StatTools Statistical Inference dropdown using this data set. In the resulting dialog box, select the Stacked option, and again select TimeInterval as the "Cat" variable and EndWaiting as the "Val" variable. Because there are three categories for TimeInterval, StatTools will then ask you which two of these you want to base the difference on. Select Normal and Rush. StatTools then analyzes the difference "Normal minus Rush." If you checked the Analyze in Reverse Order option, StatTools would analyze the opposite difference, "Rush minus Normal." (See the StatTools dialog boxes in Figures 9.20 and 9.21.)

Figure 9.20

Two-Sample
Dialog Box

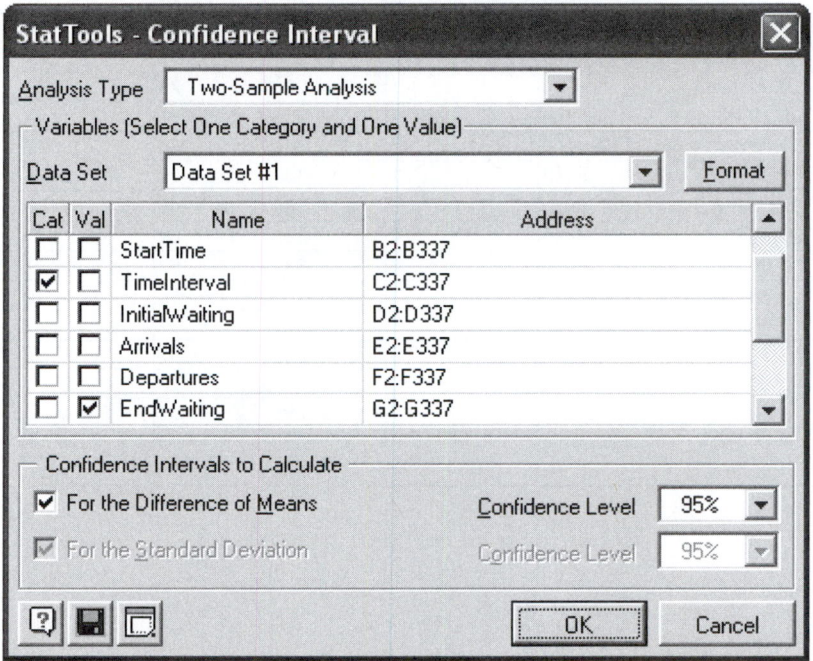

Figure 9.21

Dialog Box for
Selecting Two
Categories of
Interest

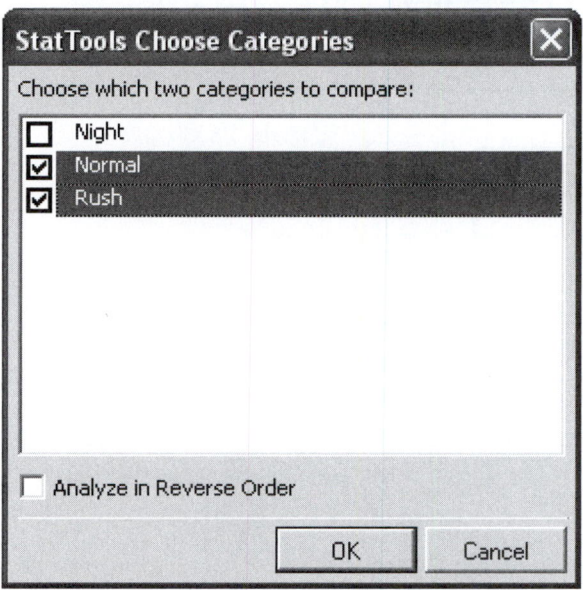

The side-by-side box plots in Figure 9.19 show that (1) the distribution of EndWaiting is definitely skewed to the right for each time interval, with a number of outliers, and

(2) the mean value of EndWaiting is slightly larger for Rush than for Normal, with Night a distant third. Given the nature of the data, it should not really be surprising that the data are skewed to the right with a number of outliers. When the supermarket gets busy, waiting lines can really build. All it takes is one or two really long checkout times to produce an excessively large value of EndWaiting, and this is evidently what happened at R&P.

The output from the two-sample procedure appears in Figure 9.22. The sample means of EndWaiting are 5.480 and 5.014 for the Rush and Normal periods, the sample standard deviations are 4.284 and 4.293, and these are based on sample sizes of 98 and 140 half-hour periods. These summary statistics provide some evidence of a difference between population means but very little evidence of different population variances. This latter statement means that we can use the results in column L, not column M (although they are practically identical). We see that a point estimate for the mean difference (Normal minus Rush) is -0.465 and that a 95% confidence interval for this mean difference extends from -1.578 to 0.648.

Figure 9.22

Analysis of Supermarket Data

	K	L	M
1		**EndWaiting (Normal)**	**EndWaiting (Rush)**
2	*Sample Summaries*	Data Set #1	Data Set #1
3	Sample Size	140	98
4	Sample Mean	5.014	5.480
5	Sample Std Dev	4.293	4.284
6			
7		**Equal**	**Unequal**
8	*Conf. Intervals (Difference of Means)*	**Variances**	**Variances**
9	Confidence Level	95.0%	95.0%
10	Sample Mean Difference	-0.465	-0.465
11	Standard Error of Difference	0.565	0.565
12	Degrees of Freedom	236	209
13	Lower Limit	-1.578	-1.579
14	Upper Limit	0.648	0.648
15			
16			
17	*Equality of Variances Test*		
18	Ratio of Sample Variances	1.0042	
19	p-Value	0.9912	

What can the manager conclude from this analysis? Should she add extra checkout people during rush periods? This is difficult to answer because it obviously involves a trade-off between the cost of extra checkout people and the "cost" of making customers wait in line. Also, we have no way of knowing, at least not from the present analysis, how much effect extra checkout people would have on waiting. However, the manager does know from this analysis that the mean difference between rush and normal periods is rather minor. Specifically, because the confidence interval extends from a negative value to a positive value, there is a good possibility that the *true* mean difference could be *positive*. That is, the mean for normal times could be *larger* than the mean for rush times. Therefore, the results of this analysis do not provide a strong incentive for the manager to change the current system. ■

9.7.2 Paired Samples

When the samples we want to compare are paired in some natural way, such as a pretest or posttest for each person or husband–wife pairs, there is a more appropriate form of analysis than the two-sample procedure we've been discussing. Consider the example where each new employee takes a test, then receives a 3-month training course, and finally takes another similar test. There is likely to be a fairly strong correlation between the pretest and posttest scores. Employees who score relatively low on the first test are likely to score relatively low on the second test, and employees who score relatively high on the first test are likely to score relatively high on the second test. The two-sample procedure does not take this correlation into account and therefore ignores important information. The paired procedure described in this section, on the other hand, uses this information to advantage.

The procedure itself is very straightforward. We do not directly analyze two separate variables (pretest scores and posttest scores, say); we analyze their *differences*. For each pair in the sample, we calculate the difference between the two scores for the pair. Then we perform a *one*-sample analysis, as in Section 9.3, on these differences. Actually, StatTools's Paired-Sample procedure does the differencing *and* the ensuing one-sample analysis automatically, as described in the following example.

EXAMPLE

9.9 HUSBAND AND WIFE REACTIONS TO SALES PRESENTATIONS AT STEVENS HONDA–BUICK

The Stevens Honda–Buick automobile dealership often sells to husband–wife pairs. The manager would like to check whether the sales presentation is viewed any more or less favorably by the husbands than the wives. If it is, then some new training might be recommended for its salespeople. To check for differences, a random sample of husbands and wives are asked (separately) to rate the sales presentation on a scale of 1 to 10, 10 being the most favorable rating. The results appear in Figure 9.23. (See the **Sales Presentation Ratings.xlsx** file.) What can the manager conclude from these data?

Figure 9.23

Data for Sales Presentation Example

	A	B	C
1	Pair	Husband	Wife
2	1	6	3
3	2	7	8
4	3	8	5
5	4	6	4
6	5	8	5
7	6	7	6
8	7	8	5
9	8	6	7
10	9	7	8
31	30	7	3
32	31	7	5
33	32	5	1
34	33	7	5
35	34	7	4
36	35	10	5

Objective To use StatTools's Paired-Sample Confidence Interval procedure to find a confidence interval for the mean difference between husbands' and wives' ratings of sales presentations.

Solution

We illustrate two ways to perform the analysis. Normally, we would use only the second of these, but the first sheds some light on the procedure. For the first method, make a copy of the Data sheet and call it OneSample. Then manually form a new variable in column D called Difference by entering the formula

=B2-C2

in cell D2 and copying it down column D. (See Figure 9.24.) This new variable is, for each couple, the husband's rating minus the wife's rating. Next, with the cursor anywhere in the resulting data set, select Confidence Interval from the StatTools Statistical Inference drop-down, select One-Sample Analysis as the Analysis Type, and select the Difference variable. This produces the output shown in Figure 9.24. We see that the sample mean Husband minus Wife difference is 1.629 and that a 95% confidence interval for this difference extends from 1.057 to 2.200.

Figure 9.24 One-Sample Analysis of Differences for Sales Presentation Data

	A	B	C	D	E	F	G
1	Pair	Husband	Wife	Difference			Difference
2	1	6	3	3		Conf. Intervals (One-Sample)	OneSampleData
3	2	7	8	-1		Sample Size	35
4	3	8	5	3		Sample Mean	1.629
5	4	6	4	2		Sample Std Dev	1.664
6	5	8	5	3		Confidence Level (Mean)	95.0%
7	6	7	6	1		Degrees of Freedom	34
8	7	8	5	3		Lower Limit	1.057
9	8	6	7	-1		Upper Limit	2.200
10	9	7	8	-1			
11	10	7	5	2			
34	33	7	5	2			
35	34	7	4	3			
36	35	10	5	5			

To perform this analysis more efficiently, again make a copy of the Data sheet and call it PairedSample. After creating a StatTools data set from the data on this sheet, select Confidence Interval from the StatTools Statistical Inference dropdown, and fill in the resulting dialog box as shown in Figure 9.25. Specifically, select Paired-Sample Analysis as the Analysis Type. We obtain the output in Figure 9.26. The results are exactly the same as before. This is because StatTools's Paired-Sample procedure performs a one-sample analysis on the differences—and it saves you the work of creating the differences.

Figure 9.27 shows side-by-side box plots of the husband and wife scores. These box plots are not as useful here as in the two-sample procedure because we lose sight of which husbands are paired with which wives. A more useful box plot is of the differences, shown in Figure 9.28. Here we see that the sample mean difference is positive, but even more importantly, we see that the vast majority of husband scores are greater than the corresponding wife scores. There is little doubt that most husbands tend to react more favorably to the sales presentations than their wives. Perhaps the salespeople need to be somewhat more sensitive to their female customers!

Figure 9.25

Dialog Box for
Paired-Sample
Analysis

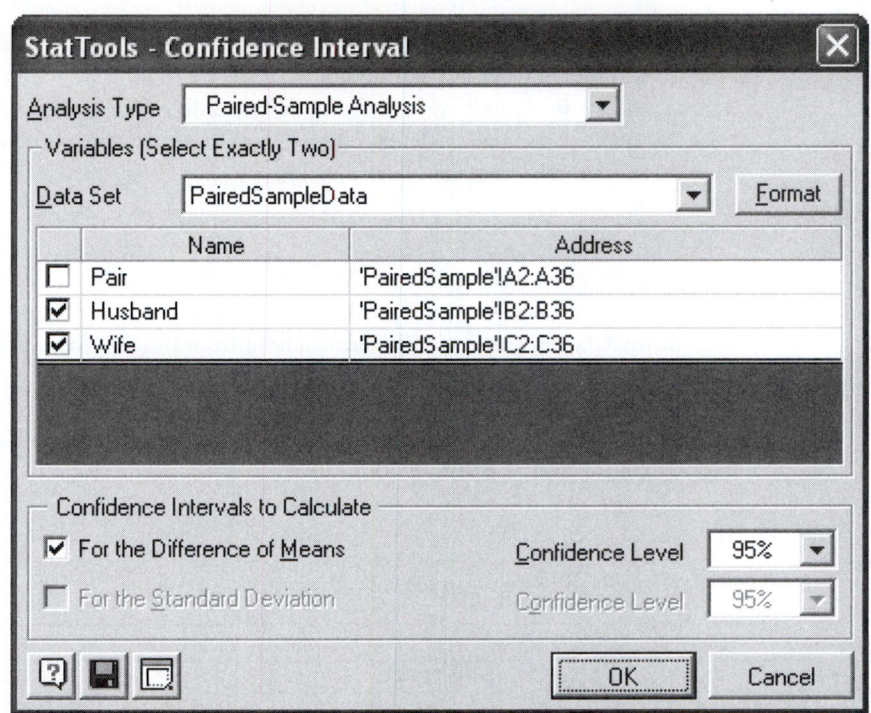

Figure 9.26 Paired-Sample Analysis of Sales Presentation Data

	A	B	C	D	E	F
1	Pair	Husband	Wife			
2	1	6	3		*Conf. Intervals (Paired-Sample)*	Husband - Wife
3	2	7	8		Sample Size	35
4	3	8	5		Sample Mean	1.629
5	4	6	4		Sample Std Dev	1.664
6	5	8	5		Confidence Level	95.0%
7	6	7	6		Degrees of Freedom	34
8	7	8	5		Lower Limit	1.057
9	8	6	7		Upper Limit	2.200
10	9	7	8			
11	10	7	5			
33	32	5	1			
34	33	7	5			
35	34	7	4			
36	35	10	5			

Figure 9.27   Side-by-side Box Plots for Sales Presentation Data

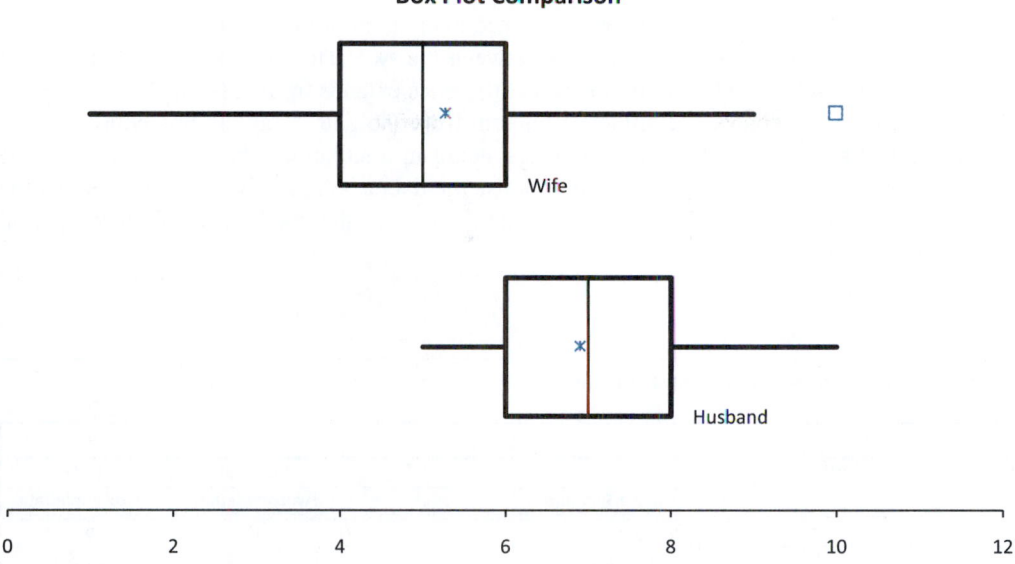

Box Plot Comparison

Wife

Husband

| 0 | 2 | 4 | 6 | 8 | 10 | 12 |

Figure 9.28   Single Box Plot of Differences for Sales Presentation Data

Box Plot of Difference

| -3 | -2 | -1 | 0 | 1 | 2 | 3 | 4 | 5 | 6 |

Before leaving this example, let's see what would have happened if we had used the two-sample procedure on the Husband and Wife variables. The results appear in Figure 9.29. Because there is a considerable difference between the sample standard deviations, we should probably use the confidence interval output in column G, not column F, although there is not much difference between the two. The important point is that the resulting confidence interval for the mean difference extends from 0.895 to 2.362, which is somewhat *wider* than the confidence interval from the paired-sample procedure. This is typical. When we use the two-sample procedure in a situation where the paired-sample procedure is more appropriate, we do not use the data as efficiently. The effect is that the standard error of the difference tends to be larger, and the resulting confidence interval tends to be wider.

Figure 9.29   Two-Sample Analysis of Sales Presentation Data

	A	B	C	D	E	F	G
						Husband	Wife
1	Pair	Husband	Wife				
2	1	6	3		*Sample Summaries*	TwoSampleData	TwoSampleData
3	2	7	8		Sample Size	35	35
4	3	8	5		Sample Mean	6.914	5.286
5	4	6	4		Sample Std Dev	1.222	1.792
6	5	8	5				
7	6	7	6			Equal	Unequal
8	7	8	5		*Conf. Intervals (Difference of Means)*	Variances	Variances
9	8	6	7		Confidence Level	95.0%	95.0%
10	9	7	8		Sample Mean Difference	1.629	1.629
11	10	7	5		Standard Error of Difference	0.367	0.367
12	11	6	3		Degrees of Freedom	68	60
13	12	5	4		Lower Limit	0.897	0.895
14	13	8	5		Upper Limit	2.360	2.362
15	14	7	8				
16	15	7	5				
17	16	7	6		*Equality of Variances Test*		
18	17	6	5		Ratio of Sample Variances	0.4649	
19	18	5	4		p-Value	0.0285	
20	19	6	5				
34	33	7	5				
35	34	7	4				
36	35	10	5				

Why is the paired-sample procedure appropriate here? It is *not* just because husbands and wives naturally come in pairs. It is because they tend to react similarly to one another. You can check that the correlation between the husbands' scores and their wives' scores is 0.442. (Use Excel's CORREL function on the Husband and Wife variables.) This is far from perfect correlation, but it is large enough to warrant using the paired-sample procedure. ∎

In general, the paired-sample procedure is appropriate when the samples are naturally paired in some way *and* there is a reasonably large positive correlation between the pairs. In this case the paired-sample procedure makes more efficient use of the data and generally results in narrower confidence intervals.

PROBLEMS

Level A

23. The director of a university's career development center is interested in comparing the starting annual salaries of male and female students who recently graduated from the university and commenced full-time employment. The director has formed pairs of male and female graduates with the same major and similar grade-point averages. Specifically, she has collected a random sample of 50 such pairs and has recorded the starting annual salary of each person. These data are provided in the file **P09_23.xlsx**. Construct a 99% confidence interval for the mean difference between similar male and female graduates of this university. Interpret your result.

24. A real estate agent has collected a random sample of 75 houses that were recently sold in a suburban community. She is particularly interested in comparing the appraised value and recent selling price of the houses in this particular market. The values of these two variables for each of the 75 randomly chosen houses are provided in the file **P09_24.xlsx**. Using the sample data, generate a 95% confidence interval for the mean difference between the appraised values and selling prices of the houses sold in this suburban community. Interpret the constructed interval estimate for the real estate agent.

Level B

25. A company employs two shifts of workers. Each shift produces a type of gasket where the thickness is the critical dimension. The average thickness and the standard deviation of thickness for shift 1, based on a random sample of 30 gaskets, are 10.53 mm and 0.14 mm. The similar figures for shift 2, based on a random sample of 25 gaskets, are 10.55 mm and 0.17 mm. Let $\mu_1 - \mu_2$ be the mean difference in thickness between shifts 1 and 2.
  a. Find a 95% confidence interval for $\mu_1 - \mu_2$.
  b. Based on your answer to part **a**, are you convinced that the gaskets from shift 2 are, on average, wider than those from shift 1? Why or why not?
  c. How would your answers to parts **a** and **b** change if the sample sizes were instead 300 and 250?

26. Consider a random sample of 100 households from a middle-class neighborhood that was the recent focus of an economic development study conducted by the local government. Specifically, for each of the 100 households, information was gathered on each of the following variables: family size, location of the household within the neighborhood, an indication of whether those surveyed owned or rented their home, gross annual income of the first household wage earner, gross annual income of the second household wage earner (if applicable), monthly home mortgage or rent payment, average monthly expenditure on utilities, and the total indebtedness (excluding the value of a home mortgage) of the household. The data are in the file **P09_26.xlsx**.
  a. Separate the households in the sample by the *location* of their residence within the given community. For each of the four locations, use the sample information to generate a 90% confidence interval for the mean annual income of all relevant first household wage earners. Compare these four interval estimates. You might also consider generating box plots of the primary wage earner variable for households in each of the four given locations.
  b. Generate a 90% confidence interval for the difference between the mean annual income levels of the first household wage earners in the first (i.e., SW) and second (i.e., NW) sectors of this community. Generate similar 90% confidence intervals for the differences between the mean annual income levels of primary wage earners from all other pairs of locations (i.e., first and third, first and fourth, second and third, second and fourth, and third and fourth). Summarize your findings.

27. Given data in the file **P02_13.xlsx** from a recent survey of chief executive officers from the largest U.S. public companies, construct 95% confidence intervals for the differences in the mean levels of fiscal year 2003 salaries earned by executives from *Technology* companies and those from each of the other company types. For instance, construct a 95% confidence interval for the difference in the mean 2003 salaries of executives from *Technology* and *Basic Materials* companies. What conclusions can you draw from the 95% confidence intervals you have generated?

9.8 CONFIDENCE INTERVAL FOR THE DIFFERENCE BETWEEN PROPORTIONS

The final confidence interval we examine is a confidence interval for the difference between two population proportions. As in the previous section, this "comparison" procedure finds many real applications. Several potential business applications are the following:

Applications of Confidence Interval Comparisons to Business

- When an appliance store is about to run a sale, it sometimes sends selected customers a mailing to notify them of the sale. On other occasions it includes a coupon for 5% off the sale price in these mailings. The store's manager would like to know whether the inclusion of coupons affects the proportion of customers who respond.

- A manufacturing company has two plants that produce identical products. The company wants to know how much the proportion of out-of-spec products differs across the two plants.

- A pharmaceutical company has developed a new over-the-counter sleeping pill. To judge its effectiveness, the company runs an experiment where one set of randomly chosen people takes the new pill and another set takes a placebo. (Neither set knows which type of pill they are taking.) The company judges the effectiveness of the new pill by comparing the proportions of people who fall asleep within a certain amount of time with the new pill and with the placebo.

- An advertising agency would like to check whether men are more likely than women to switch TV channels when a commercial comes on. The agency runs an experiment where the channel switching behavior of randomly chosen men and women can be monitored, and it collects data on the proportion of viewers who switch channels on at least half of the commercial times. The agency then compares these proportions across gender.

The basic form of analysis in each of these examples is the same as in the two-sample analysis for differences between means. However, instead of comparing two means, we now compare two proportions.

Formally, let p_1 and p_2 represent the two unknown population proportions, and let $\hat{p}_1$ and $\hat{p}_2$ be the two sample proportions, based on samples of sizes n_1 and n_2. Then the point estimate of the difference between proportions, $p_1 - p_2$, is the difference between sample proportions, $\hat{p}_1 - \hat{p}_2$. If we assume that the sample sizes are reasonably large, then the sampling distribution of $\hat{p}_1 - \hat{p}_2$ is approximately normal.[6]

Therefore, a confidence interval for $p_1 - p_2$ is given by expression (9.15). Here, the z-multiple is the usual value from the standard normal distribution that cuts off the appropriate probability in each tail (1.96 for a 95% confidence interval, for example). Also, the standard error of $\hat{p}_1 - \hat{p}_2$ is given by equation (9.16).

Confidence Interval for Difference Between Proportions

$$\hat{p}_1 - \hat{p}_2 \pm z\text{-multiple} \times \text{SE}(\hat{p}_1 - \hat{p}_2) \tag{9.15}$$

Standard Error of Difference Between Sample Proportions

$$\text{SE}(\hat{p}_1 - \hat{p}_2) = \sqrt{\frac{\hat{p}_1(1 - \hat{p}_1)}{n_1} + \frac{\hat{p}_2(1 - \hat{p}_2)}{n_2}} \tag{9.16}$$

The following example illustrates this procedure.

---

[6]This large-sample assumption is valid as long as $n_i \hat{p}_i > 5$ and $n_i(1 - \hat{p}_i) > 5$ for $i = 1$ and $i = 2$.

EXAMPLE | 9.10 SALES RESPONSE TO COUPONS FOR DISCOUNTS ON APPLIANCES

An appliance store is about to run a big sale. It selects 300 of its best customers and randomly divides them into two sets of 150 customers each. It then mails a notice of the sale to all 300 customers but includes a coupon for an extra 5% off the sale price to the second set of customers only. As the sale progresses, the store keeps track of which of these customers purchase appliances. The resulting data appear in Figure 9.30. (See the file **Coupon Effectiveness.xlsx**.) What can the store's manager conclude about the effectiveness of the coupons?

Figure 9.30

Analysis of Coupon Data

	A	B	C	D
1	Effectiveness of coupons in promoting a sale			
2				
3		Purchased	Didn't purchase	Total
4	Received coupon	55	95	150
5	Didn't receive coupon	35	115	150
6				
7	Sample proportions who purchased			
8	Received coupon	0.3667		
9	Didn't receive coupon	0.2333		
10				
11	Difference between sample proportions	0.1333		
12	Standard error of difference	0.0524		
13				
14	Confidence level	95%		
15	z-multiple	1.960		
16				
17	Confidence interval for difference between proportions			
18	Lower limit	0.0307		
19	Upper limit	0.2359		

Objective   To illustrate how to find a confidence interval for the difference between proportions of customers purchasing appliances with and without 5% discount coupons.

Solution

First, note that the data have been arranged in a "contingency" table, much like the pivot tables we discussed in Chapters 2 and 3.[7] Of the 150 customers who received coupons, 55 purchased an appliance. Of the 150 who did not receive coupons, only 35 purchased an appliance. These translate to the sample proportions 0.3667 and 0.2333, calculated in cells B8 and B9 with the formulas

=B4/D4

and

=B5/D5

By subtraction, these lead directly to the sample difference between proportions, 0.1333, in cell B11. The standard error of this difference is calculated in cell B12 with the formula

=SQRT(B8*(1-B8)/D4+B9*(1-B9)/D5)

---

[7]StatTools doesn't have a procedure for solving this problem when the data are in the form of a contingency table. However, the finished version of the **Coupon Effectiveness.xlsx** file can be used as a "template" for all such problems.

Also, the z-multiple for the confidence interval is calculated in cell B15 with the formula

=NORMSINV(B14+(1-B14)/2)

Finally, the limits of the confidence interval for the difference are calculated in cells B18 and B19 with the formulas

=B11-B15*B12

and

=B11+B15*B12

Because the confidence limits are both positive, we can conclude that the effect of coupons is almost surely to *increase* the proportion of buyers. Our best guess is that the increase is about 13% (from 23.3% to 36.7%). How can the store manager interpret this mean difference? He can use it to estimate the extra business he will receive by including coupons as opposed to not including them. The confidence interval implies that for every 100 customers, the coupons will probably induce an extra 3 to 23 customers to purchase an appliance who otherwise would not have made a purchase.

However, the difference between proportions does not directly indicate the difference in *profit* from including coupons. This is because the customers with coupons pay 5% less than the customers without them. Suppose, for example, that the average purchase amount without a coupon is $400, $50 of which is profit for the store. For every 100 customers who receive a mailing with no coupon, the store can expect to make about

$$\$50(0.2333)(100) = \$1166.50$$

in profit. If these 100 customers receive coupons, the expected profit becomes

$$\$30(0.3667)(100) = \$1100.10$$

because these customers pay only $380 on average, $30 of which is profit to the store. Therefore, it appears that if the sample proportions in cells B8 and B9 are anywhere near the true proportions, the store will make *less* profit by including coupons than by not including them. ∎

We now revisit Example 9.7, where the SureStep Company is trying to decide which of two suppliers to buy its treadmill motors from. We now compare the two suppliers with regard to warranty costs by analyzing the difference between relevant proportions.

EXAMPLE 9.11 ANALYZING WARRANTIES ON TREADMILL MOTORS AT SURESTEP COMPANY

As before, the SureStep Company is trying to decide whether to switch from supplier A to supplier B for the motors in its treadmills. Let's suppose that each treadmill carries a 3-month warranty on the motor. If the motor fails within 3 months, SureStep will supply the customer with a new motor at no cost. This includes installation of the new motor at SureStep's expense. Based on the normal usage at most exercise clubs, SureStep translates the 3-month warranty period into approximately 500 hours of treadmill use. Therefore, using the data from Example 9.7 (in the **Treadmill Warranty.xlsx** file, the same data as in the **Treadmill Motors.xlsx** file), it would like to compare the proportion of motors failing before 500 hours across the two suppliers.

Objective To illustrate how to find a confidence interval for the difference between proportions of motors failing within the warranty period for the two suppliers.

Solution

The analysis is almost exactly the same as in the previous example, so we will omit most of the detailed formulas. However, in this case we must first find the counts (numbers of failures within warranty) in cells E4 and F4 of Figure 9.31. The easiest way to do this is to use Excel's COUNTIF function. For example, the formula in cell E4 is

=COUNTIF(A2:A31,"<500")

Figure 9.31
Analysis of Treadmill Warranty Data

	A	B	C	D	E	F	G
1	Supplier A	Supplier B		Failure within warranty period (500 hours)			
2	1358	658			Supplier A	Supplier B	
3	793	404		Sample size	30	30	
4	587	735		Number	6	11	
5	608	457		Proportion	0.200	0.367	
6	472	431					
7	562	658		Confidence interval for difference calculations			
8	879	453		Difference (B-A)	0.167		
9	575	488		StErr	0.114		
10	1293	522					
11	1457	1247		Confidence level	95%		
12	705	1095		z-multiple	1.960		
13	623	430					
14	725	726		Lower limit	-0.057		
15	569	793		Upper limit	0.391		
16	424	498					
17	436	502					
18	1250	589					
19	493	975					
20	485	808					
21	462	456					
22	765	731					
23	854	491					
24	634	487					
25	1109	503					
26	800	465					
27	883	1475					
28	522	508					
29	791	846					
30	684	732					
31	666	507					

We see that the point estimate for the difference in proportions is 0.167 and that a 95% confidence interval for this difference extends from −0.057 to 0.391. Keep in mind that this difference is the proportion for supplier B minus the proportion for supplier A.

This is fairly convincing, but not conclusive, evidence that a higher proportion of supplier B motors will fail under warranty. It says that if 100 motors from each supplier were tested, as many as 39 more B motors than A motors might fail before 500 hours—but as many as 5 or 6 more A motors than B motors might fail before 500 hours. In other words, there is still a little uncertainty about which supplier makes the more reliable motors, even though the weight of the evidence favors supplier A.

What does this mean in terms of costs? And should SureStep change suppliers? As we just saw, the confidence interval implies that more motors are likely to fail under warranty if SureStep changes to supplier B, but B's motors cost less. A cost analysis might go as follows. Suppose that each motor from supplier A costs SureStep $500, whereas supplier B offers them for $475 apiece. Let's follow 100 motors sent to exercise clubs for a period of 3 months. If these are from supplier A, they cost $500 apiece, and approximately 20% (see cell E5) will fail within the warranty period. Of course, each failure costs SureStep another $500. Therefore, the expected cost to SureStep is

$$\$500(100) + \$500(20\%)(100) = \$60,000$$

On the other hand, if these 100 motors come from supplier B, the unit cost is only $475, but approximately 36.7% of them will fail within the warranty period. Therefore, the expected cost is

$$= \$475(100) + \$475(36.7\%)(100) = \$64,933$$

Based on this analysis, the cheaper motors from supplier B are likely to cost more in the long run, so SureStep should probably not switch suppliers. (By the way, we omitted the cost of installing the motors from the analysis. This would have made supplier A look even better.) ∎

PROBLEMS

Level A

28. A market research consultant hired by the Pepsi-Cola Co. is interested in estimating the difference between the proportions of female and male consumers who favor Pepsi-Cola over Coke Classic in a particular urban location. A random sample of 250 consumers from the market under investigation is provided in the file **P09_17.xlsx**. After separating the 250 randomly selected consumers by *gender,* construct a 95% confidence interval for the difference between these two proportions. Of what value might this interval estimate be to marketing managers at the Pepsi-Cola Co.?

Level B

29. Continuing the previous problem, marketing managers at the Pepsi-Cola Co. have asked their market research consultant to explore further the difference between the proportions of women and men who prefer drinking Pepsi over Coke Classic. Specifically, Pepsi managers would like to know whether the difference between the proportions of female and male consumers who favor Pepsi varies by the *age* of the consumers. Use the random sample of 250 consumers provided in the file **P09_17.xlsx** to assess whether estimates of this difference vary across the four given age categories: under 20, between 20 and 40, between 40 and 60, and over 60. Employ a 95% confidence level in generating each of the *four* required interval estimates. Summarize your findings in detail. Finally, what recommendations would you make to the marketing managers in light of your statistical findings?

30. The employee benefits manager of a small private university would like to estimate differences in the proportions of various groups of full-time employees who prefer adopting the third (i.e., plan C) of three available health care plans in the forthcoming annual enrollment period. A reliable frame of the university's employees and their tentative health care preferences are given in the file **P08_25.xlsx**.
    a. First, select a simple random sample of 25 employees from *each* of three employee classifications: administrative staff, support staff, and faculty.
    b. Use the three simple random samples obtained in part **a** to generate three 90% confidence intervals for the differences in the proportions of employees within respective classifications who favor plan C in the coming year. For instance, the first such confidence interval should estimate the difference between the proportion of administrative employees who favor plan C and the proportion of the support staff who prefer plan C.
    c. Interpret each of your constructed confidence intervals. How might the benefits manager use the information you have derived from the three random samples of university employees?

31. Consider a random sample of 100 households from a middle-class neighborhood that was the recent focus of an economic development study conducted by the local government. Specifically, for each of the 100 randomly selected households, information was gathered on each of the following variables: family size, location of the household within the neighborhood, an indication of whether those surveyed owned or rented their home, gross annual income of the first household

wage earner, gross annual income of the second household wage earner (if applicable), monthly home mortgage or rent payment, average monthly expenditure on utilities, and the total indebtedness (excluding the value of a home mortgage) of the household. The data are provided in the file **P09_26.xlsx**.

Researchers would like to use the available sample information to discern whether home ownership rates vary by household *location*. For example, is there a nonzero difference between the proportions of individuals who own their homes (as opposed to those who rent their homes) in households located in the first (i.e., SW) and second (i.e., NW) sectors of this community? Use the given sample to construct a 99% confidence interval that estimates this potential difference in home ownership rates as well as those of other combinations of household locations. Interpret and summarize your results. (*Hint*: To be complete, you should construct and interpret a total of *six* 99% confidence intervals.)

9.9 CONTROLLING CONFIDENCE INTERVAL LENGTH

In this section we discuss the most widely used methods for achieving a confidence interval of a specified length. Confidence intervals are a function of three things: (1) the data in the sample, (2) the confidence level, and (3) the sample size(s). We briefly discuss the role of the first two in terms of their effect on confidence interval length and then discuss the effect of sample size in more depth.

The data in the sample directly affect the length of a confidence interval through their determination of the sample standard deviation(s). It might appear that because of *random* sampling, we have no control over the sample data, but this is not entirely true. In the case of surveys from a population, there are random sampling plans that can reduce the amount of variability in the sample and hence reduce confidence interval length. Indeed, this is the primary reason for using the stratified sampling procedure we discussed in the previous chapter.

Variance reduction is also possible in randomized experiments. There is a whole area of statistics called **experimental design** that suggests how to perform experiments to obtain the most information from a given amount of sample data. Although this is often aimed at scientific and medical research, it is also appropriate in business contexts. For example, the automobile dealership in Example 9.9 was wise to use *paired* husband–wife data rather than two independent samples of men and women. The pairing leads to a potential reduction in variability and hence a narrower confidence interval.

The confidence level has a clear effect on confidence interval length. As the confidence level increases, the length of the confidence interval increases as well. For example, a 99% confidence interval is always longer than a 95% confidence interval, assuming that they are both based on the same data. However, we rarely use the confidence level to control the length of the confidence interval. Instead, we usually choose the confidence level based on convention, and 95% is by far the most commonly used value. For example, it is the default level built into most software packages, including the StatTools add-in. We can override this default (by choosing 90% or 99%, for example), but we don't usually do so simply to control the confidence interval length.

The most obvious way to control confidence interval length is to choose the sample size(s) appropriately. In the rest of this section, we see how this can be done. For each parameter we discuss, our goal is to make the length of a confidence interval sufficiently narrow. Because each confidence interval we have discussed (with the exception of the confidence interval for a standard deviation) is a point estimate plus or minus some quantity, we focus on the "plus or minus" part, called the *half-length* of the interval. (See Figure 9.32.) The usual approach is to specify the half-length B we would like to obtain. Then we find the sample size(s) necessary to achieve this half-length.

Figure 9.32
Half-Length of a
Confidence Interval

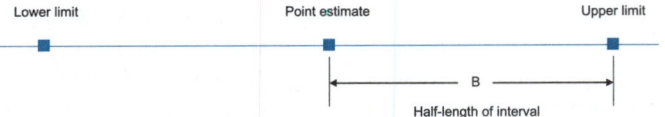

9.9.1 Sample Size for Estimation of the Mean

We begin with a confidence interval for the mean. From Section 9.3, we know that its formula is

$$\overline{X} \pm t\text{-multiple} \times s/\sqrt{n}$$

We want to make the half-length of this interval equal to some prescribed value B. For example, if we want the confidence interval to be of the form $\overline{X} \pm 5$, we use $B = 5$. Actually, we aren't able to achieve this half-length B exactly, but we are able to approximate it.

By setting

$$t\text{-multiple} \times s/\sqrt{n} = B$$

and solving for n, we obtain

$$n = \left(\frac{t\text{-multiple} \times s}{B} \right)^2$$

Keep in mind that the sample size must be determined before the data are observed.

Unfortunately, sample size selection must be done *before* a sample is observed. Therefore, no value of s is yet available. Also, because the t-multiple depends on n (through the degrees of freedom parameter), it is not clear which t-multiple to use.

The usual way out of this dilemma is to replace s by some reasonable estimate σ_{est} of the population standard deviation σ, and to replace the t-multiple with the corresponding z-multiple from the standard normal distribution. The latter replacement is justified because Z-values and t-values are practically equal unless n is very small. The resulting sample size formula is given in equation (9.17). This formula generally results in a noninteger value of n, in which case the practice is to round n *up* to the next larger integer.

> **Sample Size Formula for Estimating a Mean**
> $$n = \left(\frac{z\text{-multiple} \times \sigma_{\text{est}}}{B} \right)^2 \qquad (9.17)$$

The following example, an extension of Example 9.2, shows how to implement equation (9.17).

EXAMPLE | **9.12 SAMPLE SIZE SELECTION FOR ESTIMATING REACTION TO NEW SANDWICH**

The fast-food manager in Example 9.2 surveyed 40 customers, each of whom rated a new sandwich on a scale 1 to 10. Based on the data, a 95% confidence interval for the mean rating of all potential customers extended from 5.739 to 6.761, for a half-length of $(6.761 - 5.739)/2 = 0.511$. How large a sample would be needed to reduce this half-length to approximately 0.3?

Objective To find the sample size of customers required to achieve a sufficiently narrow confidence for the mean rating of the new sandwich.

Solution

Formula (9.17) for n uses three inputs: the z-multiple, which is 1.96 for a 95% confidence level; the prescribed confidence interval half-length B, which is 0.3 for this example; and an estimate σ_{est} of the standard deviation. This final quantity must be guessed, but based on the given sample of size 40, we can use the observed sample standard deviation, 1.597, from Example 9.2. Therefore, formula (9.17) yields

$$n = \left(\frac{1.96(1.597)}{0.3} \right)^2 = 108.86$$

which we round up to $n = 109$. The claim, then, is that if the manager surveys 109 customers, a 95% confidence interval will have approximate half-length 0.3. Its *exact* half-length will differ slightly from 0.3 because the standard deviation from the sample will almost surely not equal 1.597.

The StatTools add-in has a Sample Size Selection procedure that performs this sample size calculation. It can be used anywhere in a spreadsheet. There doesn't even have to be a data set. Just select the StatTools/Statistical Inference/Sample Size Selection menu item, select the parameter to analyze (in this case the mean), and enter the requested values. In this case the requested values are the confidence level (95), the half-length of the interval (0.3), and an estimate of the standard deviation (1.597). (See Figure 9.33, where the choices on the right depend on which parameter is selected on the left.) This produces the output shown in Figure 9.34, which indicates that a sample size of 109 is required.

Figure 9.33

Sample Size Selection Dialog Box

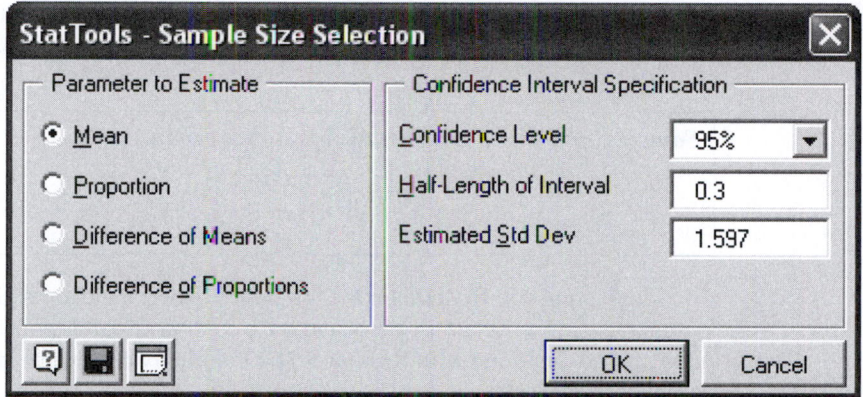

Figure 9.34

Sample Size for a Mean

	A	B
3	*Sample Size for Mean*	
4	Confidence Level	95.00%
5	Half-length of Interval	0.30
6	Std Dev (estimate)	1.5970
7	Sample Size	109

What if the manager is at the planning stage and doesn't have a "preliminary" sample of size 40? What standard deviation estimate should she use for σ_{est} (because the value

1.597 is no longer available)? This is not an easy question to answer, but because of the role of σ_{est} in equation (9.17), it is crucial for the determination of n. The manager basically has three choices: (1) she can base her estimate of the standard deviation on historical data, assuming relevant historical data are available; (2) she can take a small preliminary sample (of size 20, say) just to get an estimate of the standard deviation; or (3) she can simply guess a value for the standard deviation. We do not recommend the third option, but there are cases in which it is the only feasible option available. ∎

We have demonstrated the use of equation (9.17) for a sample mean. In the same way, it can also be used in the paired-sample procedure. In this case the resulting value of n refers to the number of *pairs* that should be included in the sample, and σ_{est} refers to an estimate of the standard deviation of the *differences* (husband scores minus wife scores, for example).

9.9.2 Sample Size for Estimation of Other Parameters

The sample-size analysis for the mean carries over with very few changes to other parameters. We discuss three other parameters in this section: a *proportion*, the *difference between two means*, and the *difference between two proportions*. In each case the required confidence interval can be obtained by setting the half-length equal to a prescribed value B and solving for n.

There are two points worth mentioning. First, the confidence interval for the difference between means uses a *t*-multiple. As we did for the mean, we replace this by a *z*-multiple, which is perfectly acceptable in most situations. Second, the confidence intervals for differences between means or proportions require *two* sample sizes, one for each sample. The formulas below assume that each sample uses the *same* sample size, denoted by n.

The sample size formula for a proportion p is given by equation (9.18). Here, p_{est} is an estimate of the population proportion p. A *conservative* value of n can be obtained by using $p_{est} = 0.5$. It is conservative in the sense that the sample size obtained by using $p_{est} = 0.5$ guarantees a confidence interval half-length no greater than B, regardless of the true value of p.

> **Sample Size Formula for Estimating a Proportion**
>
> $$n = \left(\frac{z\text{-multiple}}{B}\right)^2 p_{est}(1 - p_{est}) \qquad (9.18)$$

The sample size formula for the difference between means is given by equation (9.19). Here, σ_{est} is an estimate of the standard deviation of *each* population, where we again make the assumption (as in Section 9.7.1) that the two populations have a *common* standard deviation σ.

> **Sample Size Formula for Estimating the Difference Between Means**
>
> $$n = 2\left(\frac{z\text{-multiple} \times \sigma_{est}}{B}\right)^2 \qquad (9.19)$$

Finally, the sample size formula for the difference between proportions is given by equation (9.20). Here, p_{1est} and p_{2est} are estimates of the two unknown population proportions p_1 and p_2. As in the case of a single proportion, we obtain a conservative value of n by using the estimates $p_{1est} = p_{2est} = 0.5$.

Sample Size Formula for Estimating the Difference Between Proportions

$$n = \left(\frac{z\text{-multiple}}{B}\right)^2 [p_{1est}(1 - p_{1est}) + p_{2est}(1 - p_{2est})] \quad \textbf{(9.20)}$$

EXAMPLE 9.13 Sample Size Selection for Estimating the Proportion Who Have Tried a New Sandwich

Suppose that the fast-food manager from the previous example wants to estimate the proportion of customers who have tried its new sandwich. It wants a 90% confidence interval for this proportion to have half-length 0.05. For example, if the sample proportion turns out to be 0.42, then a 90% confidence interval should be (approximately) 0.42 ± 0.05. How many customers need to be surveyed?

Objective To find the sample size of customers required to achieve a sufficiently narrow confidence interval for the proportion of customers who have tried the new sandwich.

Solution

If the manager has "no idea" what the proportion is, then she can use $p_{est} = 0.5$ in equation (9.18) to obtain a conservative value of n. The appropriate z-multiple is now 1.645 because this value cuts off probability 0.05 in each tail of the standard normal distribution. Therefore, the required value of n is

$$n = \left(\frac{1.645}{0.05}\right)^2 (0.5)(1 - 0.5) \simeq 271$$

On the other hand, if the manager is "pretty sure" that the proportion who have tried the new sandwich is around 0.3, she can use $p_{est} = 0.3$ instead. This time we use StatTools and enter the values 90 (confidence level), 0.05 (desired half-length), and 0.3 (estimate of the proportion). We receive the output shown in Figure 9.35.

Figure 9.35
Sample Size for a Proportion

	A	B
10	***Sample Size for Proportion***	
11	**Confidence Level**	90.00%
12	**Half-length of Interval**	0.05
13	**Proportion (estimate)**	0.3000
14	**Sample Size**	228

Again remember that lower confidence levels result in narrower confidence intervals.

These calculations indicate that if we have more specific information about the unknown proportion, we can get by with a smaller sample size—in this case 228 rather than 271. Also, note that we selected a 90% confidence level rather than the usual 95% level. There is a trade-off here. Using 90% rather than 95% obviously gives us less confidence in the result, but it requires a smaller sample size. You can check that the required sample sizes for a 95% confidence level increase from 271 and 228 to 385 and 323. ■

9.14 SAMPLE SIZE SELECTION FOR ANALYZING CUSTOMER COMPLAINTS ABOUT POOR SERVICE

A computer company has a customer service center that responds to customers' questions and complaints. The center employs two types of people: those who have had a recent course in dealing with customers (but little actual experience) and those with a lot of experience dealing with customers (but no formal course). The company wants to estimate the difference between these two types of employees in terms of the average number of customer complaints regarding poor service in the last 6 months. The company plans to obtain information on a randomly selected sample of each type of employee, using equal sample sizes. How many employees should be in each sample to achieve a 95% confidence interval with approximate half-length 2?

Objective   To see how many employees in each experimental group must be sampled to achieve a sufficiently narrow confidence interval for the difference between the mean numbers of complaints.

Solution

We use equation (9.19) with z-multiple 1.96 and $B = 2$. However, this formula also requires a value for σ_{est}, an estimate of the (assumed) common standard deviation for each group of employees, and there is no obvious estimate available. The manager might use the following argument. Based on a brief look at complaint data, he believes that some employees receive as few as 6 complaints over a 6-month period, whereas others receive as many as 36 (about 6 per month). Now he can estimate σ_{est} by arguing that all observations are likely to be within 3 standard deviations of the mean, so that the range of data—minimum to maximum—is about 6 standard deviations. Therefore, he sets

$$6\sigma_{est} = 36 - 6 = 30$$

and obtains $\sigma_{est} = 5$. Using this value in equation (9.19), the required sample size is

$$n = 2\left(\frac{1.96(5)}{2}\right)^2 \approx 49$$

The StatTools Sample Size Selection procedure confirms this value. Here, we enter the values 95 (confidence level), 2 (desired half-length), and 5 (estimated standard deviation). We receive the output in Figure 9.36.

Figure 9.36

Sample Size for a Difference Between Means

	A	B
17	*Sample Size for Difference of Means*	
18	Confidence Level	95.00%
19	Half-length of Interval	2.00
20	Common Std Dev (estimate)	5.0000
21	Sample Size	49

Some analysts prefer the estimate

$$4\sigma_{est} = 36 - 6 = 30$$

that is, $\sigma_{est} = 7.5$, arguing that the quoted range (6 to 36) might not include "extreme" values and hence might extend to only 2 standard deviations on either side of the mean. By using this estimate of the standard deviation, you can check that the required sample size increases from 49 to 109. The important point here is that the estimate of the standard deviation can have a dramatic effect on the required sample size. (And don't forget that this size sample must be taken from *each* group of employees.) ∎

The final example in this section illustrates what can happen when we ask for extremely accurate confidence intervals.

<table>
<tr><td>EXAMPLE</td><td>9.15 SAMPLE SIZE SELECTION FOR ANALYZING PROPORTIONS OF OUT-OF-SPEC PRODUCTS</td></tr>
</table>

A manufacturing company has two plants that produce identical products. The production supervisor wants to know how much the proportion of out-of-spec products differs across the two plants. He suspects that the proportion of out-of-spec products in each plant is in the range of 3% to 5%, and he wants a 99% confidence interval to have approximate half-length 0.005 (or 0.5%). How many items should he sample from each plant?

Objective To see how many products in each plant must be sampled to achieve a sufficiently narrow confidence interval for the difference between the proportions of out-of-spec products.

Solution

Here we use equation (9.20) with z-multiple 2.576 (the value that cuts off probability 0.005 in each tail of the standard normal distribution), $B = 0.005$, and $p_{1est} = p_{2est} = 0.05$. The reasoning for the latter is that the supervisor believes each proportion is around 3% to 5%, and we obtain the most conservative (largest) sample size by using the larger 5% value. Then the required sample size is

$$n = \left(\frac{2.576}{0.005}\right)^2 [0.05(0.95) + 0.05(0.95)] \approx 25{,}213$$

This sample size (from *each* sample) is almost certainly prohibitive, so the supervisor decides he must lower his goals. One way is to decrease the confidence level, say, from 99% to 95%. Another way is to increase the desired half-length from 0.005 to, say, 0.025. We implemented both of these changes in the StatTools Sample Size Selection procedure by entering the values 95 (confidence level), 0.025 (desired half-length), and 0.05 and 0.05 (estimates of the proportions). The resulting output is shown in Figure 9.37. Even now the required sample size is 584. Obviously, narrow confidence intervals for differences between proportions can require very large sample sizes.

Figure 9.37

Sample Size for a Difference Between Proportions

	A	B
24	**Sample Size for Difference of Proportions**	
25	Confidence Level	95.00%
26	Half-length of Interval	0.03
27	Proportion 1 (estimate)	0.0500
28	Proportion 2 (estimate)	0.0500
29	Sample Size	584

∎

PROBLEMS

Level A

32. Elected officials in a small Florida town are preparing the annual budget for their community. Specifically, they would like to estimate how much their constituents living in this town are typically paying each year in real estate taxes. Given that there are over 3000 homeowners in this small community, officials have decided to sample a representative subset of taxpayers and thoroughly study their tax payments. The latest frame of homeowners is given in the file **P08_36.xlsx**.
   a. What sample size would be required to generate a 95% confidence interval for the community's mean annual real estate tax payment with a half-length of $100? Assume that the best estimate of the population standard deviation σ is $535.
   b. Choose a simple random sample of the size found in part **a** from the frame in the file. Construct a 95% confidence interval for the population mean. What is the half-length of this interval estimate? Is the half-length consistent with your expectations? Explain.
   c. Now suppose that elected officials want to construct a 95% confidence interval with a half-length of $75. What sample size would be required to achieve this objective? Again, assume that the best estimate of the population standard deviation σ is $535. Explain the difference between your result her7e and the result you obtained in part **a**.

33. You have been assigned to determine whether more people prefer Coke or Pepsi. Assume that roughly half the population prefers Coke and half prefers Pepsi. How large a sample would you need to take to ensure that you could estimate, with 95% confidence, the fraction of people preferring Coke within 2% of the actual value?

34. You are trying to estimate the average amount a family spends on food during a year. In the past the standard deviation of the amount a family has spent on food during a year has been approximately $1000. If you want to be 99% sure that you have estimated average family food expenditures within $50, how many families do you need to survey?

35. In past years, approximately 20% of all U.S. families purchased potato chips at least once a month. We are interested in determining the fraction of all U.S. families that currently purchase potato chips at least once a month. How many families must we survey if we want to be 99% sure that our estimate of the fraction of U.S. families currently purchasing potato chips at least once a month is accurate within 2%?

36. Continuing Problem 32, suppose that elected officials in this community would like to estimate the proportion of taxpayers whose annual real estate tax payments exceed $2000.
   a. What sample size would be required to generate a 99% confidence interval for this proportion with a half-length of 0.10? Assume for now that the relevant population proportion p is close to 0.50.
   b. Assume now that officials discover old tax records that suggest that approximately 30% of all property owners in this community pay more than $2000 annually in real estate taxes. What sample size would now be required to generate a 99% confidence interval for this proportion with a half-length of 0.10?
   c. Explain the difference in your answers to parts **a** and **b**.
   d. Choose a simple random sample of the size found in part **b** from the frame given in the file **P08_36.xlsx**. Use this sample to evaluate the revised assumption that approximately 30% of all property owners in this community pay more than $2000 annually in real estate taxes.

Level B

37. Continuing the previous problem, suppose that elected officials in this town would like to estimate the difference between the proportions, labeled p_2 and p_6, of taxpayers living in the *second* neighborhood whose annual real estate tax payments exceed $2000 and those living in the *sixth* neighborhood whose annual real estate tax payments exceed $2000.
   a. What sample size (randomly selected from a frame of all taxpayers residing in each neighborhood) would be required to generate a 90% confidence interval for this difference between proportions with a half-length of 0.10? Assume for now that p_2 and p_6 are both close to 0.5.
   b. Choose a simple random sample of the size found in part **a** from the frame of all taxpayers residing in the second neighborhood. Also, choose a simple random sample of the size found in part **a** from the frame of all taxpayers residing in the sixth neighborhood. Use these samples to evaluate the assumption that p_2 and p_6 are both close to 0.5.
   c. Use the samples obtained in part **b** to generate revised estimates of p_2 and p_6. Repeat part **a** with these revised estimates of p_2 and p_6. Explain the difference between your original and revised responses to the question posed in part **a**.

9.10 CONCLUSION

When we want to estimate a population parameter from sample data, one of the most useful ways to do so is to report a point estimate and a corresponding confidence interval. This confidence interval gives us a quick sense of where the true parameter lies. It essentially quantifies the amount of uncertainty in the point estimate. Obviously, we prefer narrow confidence intervals. We have seen that the length of a confidence interval is determined by the variability in the data, the confidence level, usually set at 95%, and the sample size(s). We have also seen how sample size formulas can be used at the planning stage to achieve confidence intervals that are sufficiently narrow. Finally, we have seen how confidence intervals can be calculated from mathematical formulas or with statistical software such as the StatTools add-in. The advantage of software is that it enables us to concentrate on the important issues for business applications: which confidence intervals are appropriate, how to interpret them, and how to control their length.

Summary of Key Terms

Term	Explanation	Excel	Page	Equation Number
Confidence interval	An interval that, with a stated level of confidence, is likely to capture a population parameter		434	9.1
t distribution	The sampling distribution of the standardized sample mean when the sample standard deviation is used in place of the population standard deviation	=TDIST(*value*, *df*, 1 or 2) =TINV(*prob,df*)	434	9.3
Confidence level	Percentage (usually 90%, 95%, or 99%) that indicates how confident we are that the interval will capture the true population parameter		439	
Confidence interval for a mean	Interval that is likely to capture a population mean	StatTools/ Statistical Inference/ Confidence Interval	440	9.4
Confidence interval for a total	Interval that is likely to capture the total of all observations in a population	Can be derived from StatTools/ Statistical Inference/ Confidence Interval	445	9.8
Confidence interval for a proportion	Interval that is likely to capture the proportion of all population members that satisfy a specified property	Must be done manually	448	9.10
Confidence interval for a standard deviation	Interval that is likely to capture a population standard deviation	StatTools/ Statistical Inference/ Confidence Interval	453	
Chi-square distribution	Skewed distribution useful for estimating standard deviations	=CHIDIST(*value,df*) =CHIINV(*prob,df*)	453	

(continued)

Term	Explanation	Excel	Page	Equation Number
Confidence interval for difference between means with independent samples	Interval that is likely to capture the difference between two population means when the samples are independent of one another	StatTools/ Statistical Inference/ Confidence Interval	456–458	9.13, 9.14
Confidence interval for difference between means with paired samples	Interval that is likely to capture the difference between two population means when the samples are paired in a natural way	StatTools/ Statistical Inference/ Confidence Interval	466	
Confidence interval for difference between proportions	Interval that is likely to capture the difference between similarly defined proportions from two populations	Must be done manually	471–472	9.15, 9.16
Sample size formulas	Formulas that specify the sample size(s) required to obtain sufficiently narrow confidence intervals	StatTools/Statistical Inference/Sample Size Selection	478–481	9.17–9.20

PROBLEMS

Conceptual Exercises

C.1 Under what conditions, if any, is it *not* possible for us to assume that the sampling distribution of the sample mean is approximately normally distributed?

C.2 When, if ever, would it be appropriate to use the standard normal distribution as a substitute for the t distribution with $n - 1$ degrees of freedom in estimating a population mean?

C.3. "Assuming that all else remains constant, the width of a confidence interval for a population mean increases whenever the confidence level and sample size increase simultaneously." Is this statement true or false? Explain your choice.

C.4. Assuming that all else remains constant, what happens to the width of a 95% confidence interval for a population parameter when the sample size is reduced by half? You can assume that the resulting sample size is still quite large. Justify your answer.

C.5. "The probability is 0.99 that a 99% confidence interval contains the true value of the relevant population parameter." Is this statement true or false? Explain your choice.

Level A

38. A sample of 9 quality control managers with more than 20 years experience have an average salary of $68,000 and a sample standard deviation of $19,000.
   a. You can be 95% confident that the mean salary for all quality managers with at least 20 years of experience is between what two numbers? What

assumption are you making about the distribution of salaries?
   b. What size sample would be needed to ensure that we could estimate the true mean salary of all quality managers with more than 20 years of experience and have only 1 chance in 100 of being off by more than $500?

39. Political polls typically sample randomly from the U.S. population to investigate the percentage of voters who favor some candidate or issue. The number of people polled is usually on the order of 1000. Suppose that one such poll asks voters how they feel about the President's handling of environmental issues. The results show that 575 out of the 1280 people polled say they either "approve" or "strongly approve" of the President's handling. Find a 95% confidence interval for the proportion of the entire voter population who "approve" or "strongly approve" of the President's handling. If the same sample proportion were found in a sample twice as large—that is 1150 out of 2560— how would this affect the confidence interval? How would the confidence interval change if the confidence level were 90% instead of 95%?

40. Referring to the previous problem, we often hear the results of such a poll in the news. In fact, the newscasters usually report something such as, "44.9% of the population approve or strongly approve of the President's handling of the environment. The margin of error in this result is plus or minus 3%." Where does this 3% comes from? If the pollsters want the margin of error to be plus or minus 3%, how does this lead to a sample size of approximately 1000?

41. The widths of 100 elevator rails have been measured. The sample mean and standard deviation of the elevator rails are 2.05 inches and 0.01 inch.

    a. Construct a 95% confidence interval for the average width of an elevator rail. Do we need to assume that the width of elevator rails follows a normal distribution?

    b. How large a sample of elevator rails would we have to measure to ensure that we could estimate, with 95% confidence, the average diameter of an elevator rail within 0.01 inch?

42. We want to determine the percentage of Fortune 500 CEOs who think Indiana University (IU) deserves its current *Business Week* rating. We mail a questionnaire to all 500 CEOs and 100 respond. Exactly half of the respondents believe IU does deserve its ranking.

    a. Construct a 99% confidence interval for the fraction of Fortune 500 CEOs who believe IU deserves its ranking.

    b. Suppose again that we want to estimate the fraction of Fortune 500 CEOs who believe IU deserves its ranking. Our goal is to have only a 5% chance of having our estimate be in error by more than 0.02. What size sample do we need to take?

43. The SEC requires companies to file annual reports concerning their financial status. It is impossible to audit every account receivable. Suppose we audit a random sample of 49 accounts receivable invoices and find a sample average of $128 and a sample standard deviation of $53.

    a. Find a 99% confidence interval for the mean size of an accounts receivable invoice. Does your answer require that the sizes of the accounts receivable invoices follow a normal distribution?

    b. How large a sample do we need if we want to be 99% sure that we can estimate the mean invoice size within $5?

44. An opinion poll surveyed 900 people and reported that 52% believe the White House broke campaign financing laws.

    a. Compute a 95% confidence interval for the population proportion of people who believe the White House broke campaign financing laws. Does the result of the poll convince you that a *majority* of citizens favor that viewpoint?

    b. Suppose 10,000 (not 900) people are surveyed and 52% believe that the White House broke campaign financing laws. Would you now be convinced that a majority of citizens believe the White House broke campaign financing laws? Why is your answer different than in part **a**?

    c. How many people would you have to survey to be 99% confident that you can estimate the fraction of people who believe the White House has broken a campaign financing law to within 1%?

45. Sometimes you are given summary data, not the original data, and are asked for a confidence interval. In this case it is probably easier to calculate it using a hand calculator. Try it in the following examples.

    a. A sample of 35 jazz CD recordings has been examined. The average playing time of these 35 recordings is 54.7 minutes, and the standard deviation is 6.8 minutes. Find a 95% confidence interval for the mean playing time of all jazz recordings in the population from which this was a sample.

    b. You are told that a random sample of 130 people from Indiana has been given cholesterol tests, and 47 of these people had levels over the "safe" count of 180. Find a 95% confidence interval for the population proportion of people with cholesterol levels over 180.

Level B

46. We know that IQs are normally distributed with a mean of 100 and standard deviation of 15. Suppose we did not know this, and we took 100 random samples of four people's IQs and, for each sample, constructed a 95% confidence interval for the mean IQ. We expect that approximately 95 of these intervals would contain the true mean IQ (100) and approximately five of these intervals would not contain the true mean. Use simulation in Excel to see whether this is the case.

47. In Section 9.9, we gave a sample size formula for confidence interval estimation of a mean. If the confidence level is 95%, then (because the z-multiple is about 2), this formula is essentially

$$n = \frac{4\sigma^2}{B^2}$$

However, this formula is based on the assumption that the sample size n will be small relative to the population size N. If this is *not* the case, the appropriate formula is

$$n = \frac{N\sigma^2}{\sigma^2 + (N - 1)B^2/4}$$

Now suppose we want to find a 95% confidence interval for a population mean. Based on preliminary (or historical) data, we believe that the population standard deviation is approximately 15. We want the confidence interval to have length 4. That is, we want the confidence interval to be of the form $X \pm 2$. What sample size is required if $N = 400$? if $N = 800$? if $N = 10,000$? if $N = 100,000,000$? How would you summarize these findings in words?

48. The Ritter Manufacturing Company has kept track of machine hours and overhead costs at its main manufacturing plant for the past 52 weeks. The data appear in the file **P09_48.xlsx**. Ritter has studied these data to understand the relationship between machine hours and overhead costs. Although the relationship is far from perfect, Ritter believes it can obtain a fairly accurate prediction of overhead costs from machine hours through the equation

Estimated Overhead = 746.5078 + 3.3175MachHrs

By substituting any observed value of MachHrs into this equation, Ritter obtains an estimated value of Overhead, which is always somewhat different from the true value of Overhead. The difference is called the prediction error.

a. Find a 95% confidence interval for the mean prediction error. Do the same for the *absolute* prediction error. (*Hint*: For example, the prediction error in week 1, actual overhead minus predicted overhead, is −94.53. The absolute prediction error is the absolute value, 94.53.)

b. A close examination of the data suggests that week 45 is a possible outlier. Illustrate this by creating a box plot of the prediction errors. In what sense would you say week 45 is an outlier? See whether week 45 has much effect on the confidence intervals from part **a** by recalculating these confidence intervals, this time with week 45 deleted. Discuss your findings briefly.

Problems 49 through 58 are related to the data in the file **P09_49.xlsx**. This file contains data on 400 customers' orders from ElecMart, a company that sells electronic appliances by mail order. The variables are:

- Date: date of order
- Day: day (Monday–Sunday) of order
- Time: time of day (morning, afternoon, evening) order was placed
- Region: region of country (Northeast, Midwest, South, West) customer is from
- CardType: whether order is paid for by ElecMart's own credit card or another type of credit card
- Gender: gender of customer
- BuyCategory: level of customer's previous order volume from ElecMart (high, medium, low)
- ItemsOrdered: number of items ordered on this order
- TotalCost: total cost of this order
- HighItem: cost of most expensive item on this order

You can consider the data as a random sample from all of ElecMart's orders.

49. Find a 95% confidence interval for the mean total cost of all customer orders. Then do this separately for each of the four regions. Create side-by-side box plots of total cost for the four regions. Does the positive skewness in these box plots invalidate the confidence interval procedure used?

50. Find a 95% confidence interval for the proportion of all customers whose order is for more than $100. Then do this separately for each of three times of day.

51. Find a 95% confidence interval for the proportion of all customers whose orders contain at least 3 items *and* cost at least $100 total.

52. Find a 95% confidence interval for the difference between the mean amount of the highest cost item purchased for the High customer category and the similar mean for the Medium customer category. Do the same for the difference between the Medium and Low customer categories. Because of the way these customer categories are defined, you would probably expect these mean differences to be positive. Is this what the data indicate?

53. Of the subpopulation of customers who order in the evening, consider the proportion who are female. Similarly, of the subpopulation of customers who order in the morning, consider the proportion who are female. Find a 95% confidence interval for the difference between these two proportions.

54. Find a 95% confidence interval for the difference between the proportion of female customers who order during the evening and the proportion of male customers who order during the evening.

55. Find a 95% confidence interval for the difference between the mean total order cost for West customers and Northeast customers. Do the same for the other combinations: West versus Midwest, West versus South, Northeast versus South, Northeast versus Midwest, and South versus Midwest.

56. Find a 95% confidence interval for the difference between the mean cost per item for female orders and the similar mean for males.

57. Let $p_{E,F}$ be the proportion of female orders that are paid for with the ElecMart credit card, and let $p_{E,M}$ be the similar proportion for male orders.
a. Find a 95% confidence interval for $p_{E,F}$; for $p_{E,M}$; for the difference $p_{E,F} - p_{E,M}$.
b. Let $p_{E,F,Wd}$ be the proportion of female orders on weekdays that are paid for with the ElecMart credit card, and let $p_{E,F,We}$ be the similar proportion for weekends. Define $p_{E,M,Wd}$ and $p_{E,M,We}$ similarly for males. Find a 95% confidence interval for the difference $(p_{E,F,Wd} - p_{E,M,Wd}) - (p_{E,F,We} - p_{E,M,We})$. Interpret this difference in words. Might it be of any interest to ElecMart?

58. Suppose these 400 orders are a sample of the 4295 orders made during this time period, and suppose 2531 of these orders were placed by females. Find a 95% confidence interval for the total paid for all 4295 orders. Do the same for all 2531 orders placed by females. Do the same for all 1764 orders placed by males.

Problems 59 through 64 are related to the data in the file **P09_59.xlsx**. This file contains data on 91 billings from Rebco, a company that sells plumbing supplies to retailers. The three variables in the file are as follows:

- CustSize: small, medium, or large, depending on the volume of business the customer does with Rebco
- Days: number of days from when Rebco billed the customer until Rebco got paid
- Amount: amount of the bill

You can consider the data as a random sample from all of Rebco's billings.

59. Find a 95% confidence interval for the mean amount of all Rebco's bills. Do the same for each customer size separately.

60. Find a 95% confidence interval for the mean number of days it takes Rebco's customers (as a combined group) to pay their bills. Do the same for each customer size separately. Create a box plot for the variable Days, based on all 91 billings. Also, create side-by-side box plots for Days for the three separate customer sizes. Do any of these suggest problems with the validity of the confidence intervals?

61. Find a 95% confidence interval for the proportion of all large customers who pay bills of at least $1000 at least 15 days after they are billed.

62. Find a 95% confidence interval for the proportion of all bills paid within 15 days. Find a 95% confidence interval for the difference between the proportion of large customers who pay within 15 days and the similar proportion of medium-size customers. Find a 95% confidence interval for the difference between the proportion of medium-size customers who pay within 15 days and the similar proportion of small customers.

63. Suppose a bill is considered late if it is paid after 20 days. In this case its "lateness" is the number of days over 20. For example, a bill paid 23 days after billing has a lateness of 3, whereas a bill paid 18 days after billing has a lateness of 0. Find a 95% confidence interval for the mean amount of lateness for all customers. Find similar confidence intervals for each customer size separately.

64. Suppose Rebco can earn interest at the rate of 0.011% daily on excess cash. The company realizes that it could earn extra interest if its customers would pay their bills more promptly.
   a. Find a 95% confidence interval for the mean amount of interest it could gain if each of its customers would pay exactly 1 day more promptly. Find similar confidence intervals for each customer class separately.
   b. Suppose these 91 billings represent a random sample of the 965 billings Rebco generates during the year. Find a 95% confidence interval for the total amount of extra interest it could gain by getting each of these 965 billings to be paid 2 days more promptly.

65. The file **P09_65.xlsx** contains data on the first 100 customers who entered a two-teller bank on Friday. All variables in this file are times, measured in minutes. These variables are as follows:
   - ArriveTime: arrival time of customer (measured from the time the bank's doors opened)
   - ServiceTime: amount of time customer spent with a teller
   - WaitTime: amount of time customer spent waiting in line
   - BankTime: amount of time customer spent in the bank (waiting plus in service)
   a. Find a 95% confidence interval for the mean amount of time a customer spends in service with a teller.
   b. The bank is most interested in mean waiting times because customers get upset when they have to spend a lot of time waiting in line. Use the usual procedure to calculate a 95% confidence interval for the mean waiting time per customer.
   c. Your answer in part **b** is not valid! (It is much too narrow. It makes you believe you have a much more accurate estimate of the mean waiting time than you really have.) We made two implicit assumptions when we stated the confidence interval procedure for a mean: (1) The individual observations all come from the same distribution, and (2) the individual observations are probabilistically independent. Why are both of these, particularly (2), violated for the customer waiting times? [*Hint*: For (1), how do the first few customers differ from "typical" customers? For (2), if you are behind someone in line who has to wait a long time, what about your own waiting time?]
   d. Following up on (2) of part **c**, you might expect waiting times of successive customers to be autocorrelated, that is, correlated with each other. Large waiting times tend to be followed by large waiting times, and small by small. Check this with StatTools's Autocorrelation procedure, under the StatTools/Time Series & Forecasting/Autocorrelation menu item. An autocorrelation of a certain lag, say, lag 2, is the correlation in waiting times between a customer and the customer two behind her. Do these successive waiting times appear to be autocorrelated? (A *valid* confidence interval for the mean waiting time takes autocorrelations into account—but it is considerably more difficult to calculate.)

Problems 66 through 68 are related to the data in the file **P09_66.xlsx**. The SoftBus Company sells PC equipment and customized software to small companies to help them manage their day-to-day business activities. Although SoftBus spends time with all customers to understand their needs, the customers are eventually on their own to use the equipment and software intelligently. To understand its customers better, SoftBus recently sent questionnaires to a large number of prospective customers. Key personnel—those who would be using the software—were asked to fill out the questionnaire. SoftBus received 82 usable responses, as shown in the file. The variables are as follows:

■ Gender: gender of key person
■ YrsExper: years of experience of key person with this company
■ Education: level of education of key person
■ OwnPC: whether key person owns his or her own home PC
■ PCKnowledge: key person's self-reported level of computer knowledge

You can assume that these employees represent a random sample of all of SoftBus's prospective customers.

66. Construct a histogram of the PCKnowledge variable. [Because there are only five possible responses (1–5), this histogram should have only five bars.] Repeat this separately for those who own a PC and those who do not. Then find a 95% confidence interval for the mean value of PCKnowledge for all of SoftBus's prospective customers; of all its prospective customers who own PCs; of all its prospective customers who do not own PCs. The PCKnowledge variable obviously can't be exactly normally distributed because it has only five possible values. Do you think this invalidates the confidence intervals?

67. SoftBus believes it can afford to spend much less time with customers who own PCs and score at least 4 on PCKnowledge. We call these the "PC-savvy" customers. On the other hand, SoftBus believes it will have to spend a lot of time with customers who do not own a PC and score 2 or less on PCKnowledge. We call these the "PC-illiterate" customers.

   a. Find a 95% confidence interval for the proportion of all prospective customers who are PC-savvy. Find a similar interval for the proportion who are PC-illiterate.
   b. Repeat part a twice, once for the subpopulation of customers who have at least 12 years of experience and once for the subpopulation who have less than 12 years of experience.
   c. Again repeat part a twice, once for the subpopulation of customers who have no more than a high school diploma and once for the subpopulation who have more than a high school diploma.
   d. Find a 95% confidence interval for the difference between the proportion of all customers with some

college education who are PC-savvy and the similar proportion of all customers with no college education. Repeat this, substituting "PC-savvy" with "PC-illiterate."
   e. Discuss any insights you gain from parts a through d that might be of interest to SoftBus.

68. Following up on the previous problem, SoftBus believes its profit from each prospective customer depends on the customer's level of PC knowledge. It divides the customers into three classes: PC-savvy, PC-illiterate, and all others (where the first two classes are as defined in the previous problem). As a rough guide, SoftBus figures it can gain profit P_1 from each PC-savvy customer, profit P_3 from each PC-illiterate company, and profit P_2 from each of the others.

   a. What values of P_1, P_2, and P_3 seem "reasonable"? For example, would you expect $P_1 < P_2 < P_3$ or the opposite?
   b. Using any reasonable values for P_1, P_2, and P_3, find a 95% confidence interval for the mean profit per customer that SoftBus can expect to obtain.

Problems 69 through 72 are related to the data in the file **P09_69.xlsx**. The Comfy Company sells medium-priced patio furniture through a mail-order catalog. It has operated primarily in the East but is now expanding to the Southwest. To get off to a good start, it plans to send potential customers a catalog with a discount coupon. However, Comfy is not sure how large a discount is needed to entice customers to buy. It experiments by sending catalogs to selected residents in six cities. Tucson and San Diego receive coupons for 5% off any furniture within the next 2 months, Phoenix and Santa Fe receive coupons for 10% off, and Riverside and Albuquerque receive coupons for 15% off. The variables are as follows:

■ City: city where customer lives
■ Discount: discount offered (5%, 10%, 15%)
■ ItemsPurch: number of items purchased with the discount
■ TotPaid: total paid (after subtracting the discount) for the items

69. Find a 95% confidence interval for the proportion of customers who will purchase at least one item if they receive a coupon for 5% off. Repeat for 10% off; for 15% off.

70. Find a 95% confidence interval for the proportion of customers who will purchase at least one item and pay at least $500 total if they receive a coupon for 5% off. Repeat for 10% off; for 15% off.

71. Comfy wonders whether the customers who receive larger discounts are buying more expensive items. Recalling that the value in the TotPaid column is *after* the discount, find a 95% confidence interval for the difference between the mean *original price per item*

for customers who purchase something with the 5% coupon and the similar mean for customers who purchase something with the 10% coupon. Repeat with 5% and 10% replaced by 10% and 15%. What can you conclude?

72. Comfy wonders whether there are differences across cities that receive the *same* discount.
   a. Find a 95% confidence interval for the difference between the mean amount spent in Tucson and the similar mean in San Diego. (These means should include the "0 purchases.") Repeat this for the difference between Phoenix and Santa Fe; between Riverside and Albuquerque. Does city appear to make a difference?
   b. Repeat part **a**, but instead of analyzing differences between means, analyze differences between proportions of customers who purchase something. Does city appear to make a difference?

Problems 73 through 76 are related to the data in the files **P09_73a.xlsx** and **P09_73b.xlsx**. The Niyaki Company sells VCRs through a number of retail stores. On one popular model, there is a standard warranty that covers parts for the first 6 months and labor for the first year. Customers are always asked whether they wish to purchase an extended service plan for $25 that extends the original warranty 2 more years—that is, to 30 months on parts and 36 months on service. To get a better understanding of warranty costs, the company has gathered data on 70 VCRs purchased. The variables in the **P09_73a.xlsx** file are as follows:
   ■ ExtendedPlan: whether customer purchased the extended service plan
   ■ FailureTime: time (months) until the *first* failure of the unit
   ■ PartsCost: cost of parts to repair the unit
   ■ LaborCost: cost of labor to repair the unit

The latter two costs are tracked only for repairs covered by warranty. [Otherwise, the customer bears the cost(s).] The variables in the **P09_73b.xlsx** file are similar, but they also include information of *subsequent* failures of the units (that occur during the warranty period).

73. Construct a histogram of the time until first failure for this type of VCR. Then find a 95% confidence interval for the mean time until failure for this type of VCR. Does the shape of the histogram invalidate the confidence interval? Why or why not?

74. Find a 95% confidence interval for the proportion of customers who purchase the extended service plan. Find a 95% confidence interval for the proportion of all customers who would benefit by purchasing the extended service plan.

75. Find a 95% confidence interval for Niyaki's mean net warranty cost per unit sold (net of the $25 paid for the plan for those who purchase it). You can assume that this mean is for the *first* failure only; subsequent failures of the same units are ignored here.

76. This problem follows up on the previous two problems with the data in the **P09_73b.xlsx** file. Here Niyaki did more investigation on the same 70 customers. It tracked subsequent failures and costs (if any) that occurred within the warranty period. (Note that only two customers had three failures within the warranty period, and parts weren't covered for either on the third failure. Also, no one had more than three failures within the warranty period.)
   a. With these data, find the confidence intervals requested in the previous two problems.
   b. Suppose that Niyaki sold this VCR model to 12,450 customers during the year. Find a 95% confidence interval for its total net cost due to warranties from all of these sales.

Harrigan University is a liberal arts university in the Midwest that attempts to attract the highest quality students, especially from its region of the country. It has gathered data on 178 applicants who were accepted by Harrigan (a random sample from all acceptable applicants over the past several years). The data are in the file **University Admissions.xlsx**. The variables are as follows:

- Accepted: whether the applicant accepts Harrigan's offer to enroll
- MainRival: whether the applicant enrolls at Harrigan's main rival university
- HSClubs: number of high school clubs applicant served as an officer
- HSSports: number of varsity letters applicant earned
- HSGPA: applicant's high school GPA
- HSPctile: applicant's percentile (in terms of GPA) in his or her graduating class
- HSSize: number of students in applicant's graduating class
- SAT: applicant's combined SAT score
- CombinedScore: a combined score for the applicant used by Harrigan to rank applicants

The derivation of the combined score is a closely kept secret by Harrigan, but it is basically a weighted average of the various components of high school performance and SAT. Harrigan is concerned that it is not getting enough of the best students, and worse yet, it is concerned that many of these best students are going to Harrigan's main rival. Solve the following problems and then, based on your analysis, comment on whether Harrigan appears to have a legitimate concern.

1. Find a 95% confidence interval for the proportion of all acceptable applicants who accept Harrigan's invitation to enroll. Do the same for all acceptable applicants with a combined score less than 330; with a combined score between 330 and 375; with a combined score greater than 375. (Note that 330 and 375 are approximately the first and third quartiles of the Score variable.)

2. Find a 95% confidence interval for the proportion of all acceptable students with a combined score less than the median (356) who choose Harrigan's rival over Harrigan. Do the same for those with a combined score greater than the median.

3. Find 95% confidence intervals for the mean combined score, the mean high school GPA, and the mean SAT score of all acceptable students who accept Harrigan's invitation to enroll. Do the same for all acceptable students who choose to enroll elsewhere. Then find 95% confidence intervals for the differences between these means, where each difference is a mean for students enrolling at Harrigan minus the similar mean for students enrolling elsewhere.

4. Harrigan is interested (as are most schools) in getting students who are involved in extracurricular activities (clubs and sports). Does it appear to be doing so? Find a 95% confidence interval for the proportion of all students who decide to enroll at Harrigan who have been officers of at least two clubs. Find a similar confidence interval for those who have earned at least four varsity letters in sports.

5. The combined score Harrigan calculates for each student gives some advantage to students who rank highly in a *large* high school relative to those who rank highly in a small high school. Therefore, Harrigan wonders whether it is relatively more successful in attracting students from large high schools than from small high schools. Develop one or more confidence intervals for relevant parameters to shed some light on this issue. ■

Demand for systems analysts in the consulting industry is greater than ever. Graduates with a combination of business and computer knowledge—some even from liberal arts programs—are getting great offers from consulting companies. Once these people are hired, they frequently switch from one company to another as competing companies lure them away with even better offers. One consulting company, D&Y, has collected data on a sample of systems analysts they hired with an undergraduate degree several years ago. The data are in the file **Employee Retention.xlsx**. The variables are as follows:

- StartSal: employee's starting salary at D&Y
- OnRoadPct: percentage of time employee has spent on the road with clients
- StateU: whether the employee graduated from State University (D&Y's principal source of recruits)
- CISDegree: whether the employee majored in Computer Information Systems (CIS) or a similar computer-related area
- Stayed3Yrs: whether the employee stayed at least 3 years with D&Y
- Tenure: tenure of employee at D&Y (months) if he or she moved before 3 years

D&Y is trying to learn everything it can about retention of these valuable employees. You can help by solving the following problems and then, based on your analysis, presenting a report to D&Y.

1. Although starting salaries are in a fairly narrow band, D&Y wonders whether they have anything to do with retention.

a. Find a 95% confidence interval for the mean starting salary of all employees who stay at least 3 years with D&Y. Do the same for those who leave before 3 years. Then find a 95% confidence interval for the difference between these means.

b. Among all employees whose starting salary is below the median ($37,750), find a 95% confidence interval for the proportion who stay with D&Y for at least 3 years. Do the same for the employees with starting salaries above the median. Then find a 95% confidence interval for the difference between these proportions.

2. D&Y wonders whether the percentage of time on the road might influence who stays and who leaves. Repeat the previous problem, but now do the analysis in terms of percentage of time on the road rather than starting salary. (The median percentage of time on the road is 54%.)

3. Find a 95% confidence interval for the mean tenure (in months) of all employees who leave D&Y within 3 years of being hired. Why is it not possible with the given data to find a confidence interval for the mean tenure at D&Y among *all* systems analysts hired by D&Y?

4. State University's students, particularly those in its nationally acclaimed CIS area, have traditionally been among the best of D&Y's recruits. But are they relatively hard to retain? Find one or more relevant confidence intervals to help you make an argument one way or the other. ∎

CASE 9.3 DELIVERY TIMES AT SNOWPEA RESTAURANT

The SnowPea Restaurant is a Chinese carryout/delivery restaurant. Most of SnowPea's deliveries are within a 10-mile radius, but it occasionally delivers to customers more than 10 miles away. SnowPea employs a number of delivery people, four of whom are relatively new hires. The restaurant has recently been receiving customer complaints about excessively long delivery times. Therefore, SnowPea has collected data on a random sample of deliveries by its four new delivery people during the peak dinner time. The data are in the file **Delivery Times.xlsx**. The variables are as follows:

- Deliverer: which person made the delivery
- PrepTime: time from when order was placed until delivery person started driving it to the customer
- TravelTime: time to drive from SnowPea to customer
- Distance: distance (miles) from SnowPea to customer

Solve the following problems and then, based on your analysis, write a report that makes reasonable recommendations to SnowPea management.

1. SnowPea is concerned that one or more of the new delivery people might be slower than others.
   a. Let μ_{Di} and μ_{Ti} be the mean delivery time and mean total time for delivery person i, where the total time is the sum of the delivery and prep times. Find 95% confidence intervals for each of these means for each delivery person. Although these might be interesting, give two reasons why they are not really fair measures for comparing the efficiency of the delivery people.
   b. Responding to the criticisms in part **a**, find a 95% confidence interval for the mean speed of delivery for each delivery person, where speed is measured as miles per hour during the trip from SnowPea to the customer. Then find 95% confidence intervals for the mean difference in speed between each pair of delivery people.

2. SnowPea would like to advertise that it can achieve a total delivery time of no more than M minutes for all customers within a 10-mile radius. On all orders that take more than M minutes, SnowPea will give the customers a $10 certificate on their next purchase.
   a. Assuming for now that the delivery people in the sample are representative of all of SnowPea's delivery people, find a 95% confidence interval for the proportion of deliveries (within the 10-mile limit) that will be on time if $M = 25$ minutes; if $M = 30$ minutes; if $M = 35$ minutes.
   b. Suppose SnowPea makes 1000 deliveries within the 10-mile limit. For each of the values of M in part **a**, find a 95% confidence interval for the total dollar amount of certificates it will have to pay for being late.

3. The policy in the previous problem is simple to state and simple to administer. However, it is somewhat unfair to customers who live close to SnowPea—they will never get $10 certificates! A fairer, but more complex, policy is the following. SnowPea first analyzes the data and finds that total delivery times can be predicted fairly well with the equation

   Predicted Delivery Time = 14.8 + 2.06Distance

   (This is based on regression analysis, the topic of Chapters 11 and 12.) Also, most of these predictions are within 5 minutes of the actual delivery times. Therefore, whenever SnowPea receives an order over the phone, it looks up the customer's address in its computerized geographical database to find distance, calculates the predicted delivery time based on this equation, rounds this to the nearest minute, adds 5 minutes, and guarantees this delivery time or else a $10 certificate. It does this for *all* customers, even those beyond the 10-mile limit.
   a. Assuming again that the delivery people in the sample are representative of all of SnowPea's delivery people, find a 95% confidence interval for the proportion of all deliveries that will be within the guaranteed total delivery time.
   b. Suppose SnowPea makes 1000 deliveries. Find a 95% confidence interval for the total dollar amount of certificates it will have to pay for being late. ■

Ralph Butts, manager of Woodland Operations for Intergalactica Papelco's Southeastern Region, had to decide this morning whether to approve the Bodfish Lot logging contract that was sitting on his desk. Accompanying the contract was a cruise report that gave Mr. Butts the results of a sample survey of the timber on the Bodfish Lot. Was there enough timber to make logging operations worthwhile?

The Pluto Mill of Intergalactica Papelco is located on the River Styxx in Median, Michigan. The scale of operations at Pluto is enormous. Just one of its several $500 million, football-field-long, 4-story-high paper machines has the capability to produce a 20-mile-long, 16-foot-wide, 20-ton reel of paper every hour. Such a machine is run nonstop 24 hours a day for as many of the 365 days in the year that mill maintenance can keep it up and producing paper within specified quality levels. In total, the Pluto Mill produces about 400,000 tons of white paper a year. Because it takes about a ton of wood to produce a ton of paper, a huge quantity of cordwood logs suitable for chipping and pulping must be supplied continually to keep the mill operating. Intergalactica Papelco runs a large-scale logistics, planning, and procurement operation to provide the Pluto Mill with the requisite species, quantity, and quality of wood in a timely fashion.

The Pluto Mill sits on 500 acres of land in the midst of a region in which the huge Intergalactica Papelco owns over a quarter of a million acres of forest. Although this wholly-owned forest is the single largest supplier of wood to the mill, more than 60% of the wood used at Pluto is purchased from independent landowners and loggers under contract. Supplying contract wood dependably on such an enormous scale involves frequent purchasing decisions by the Intergalactica Woodlands Operations as to which independent woodlots have sufficient wood volume and quality to support economical logging operations. A prospective seller enters into a tentative agreement with Intergalactica on the basis of market price and a visual scan of the woodlot. The final decision about whether to proceed with the logging is usually based on sampling estimates of the total wood volume on the lot.

A recent case in point was the Bodfish Lot in Henryville, Arkansas, whose owner approached Intergalactica with a proposal for logging during the 1991 to 1992 season. Aerial photographs indicated that the land was sufficiently promising to warrant a "cruise" to estimate the total volume of wood. (*Cruising* is a term used in the forestry industry to describe a systematic procedure for estimating the quantity, quality, variety, and value of the wood on a plot of land. Indeed, standard cruising methods have been developed and disseminated by the U.S. Department of Agriculture and Forestry Service.) Estimation based on limited sampling is essential. Even for the modest-size Bodfish Lot, with 586 acres of forested land, it would be practically impossible to measure every tree on the lot.

For the Bodfish Lot cruise it was decided to sample 89 distinct 1/7-acre plots for actual measurement. Although the plots were chosen "systematically," the sample was, Intergalactica hoped, still effectively "random." Indeed, *no* consistent attempt was made to select the plots from areas of heavy tree growth, large-diameter trees, heavy spruce concentration, and so on. In fact, the opposite was true: The regular spacing of the sampling grid more or less guaranteed a good cross section of the entire lot. This was what is called in forestry industry jargon a "standard line plot cruise." The total lot was 700 acres in area. The plots were spaced at 8-chain intervals apart on a rectangular grid drawn in advance at the Intergalactica Woodlands Field Office at One Rootmean Square in the town of Covariance, Illinois. The aerial photographs showed that, of the Bodfish Lot's 700 total acres, 586 acres were forested. The total volume estimate, to be done separately for each species, was to be based on the average for the 89 sampled plots on these 586 acres.

A circular area two-person cruise was then initiated. Typically, about 10 plots could be cruised in one day. The foresters counted the entire number of cordwood trees over 6 inches in diameter within each 1/7-acre circle. Then, back in the office in

[8]This case was contributed by Peter Kolesar from Columbia University.

Covariance, the number of trees on each plot was entered into a computer according to species, diameter, and possible end product. The file **Bodfish Trees.xlsx** contains this tabulation from the cruise notes of the counts for spruce, hard maple, and beech of the number of cordwood trees on the 89 sampled plots. (In the actual database, 13 different species of trees were recorded, and Intergalactica would have decided which trees were more suitable for lumber, plywood, or pulping applications.)

With these data, Intergalactica now had to decide whether to contract to log the lot. Ralph Butts, manager of Woodlands Operations, knew that even though Intergalactica would pay on the basis of the weight received at the mill, he needed at least 31,000 cordwood size trees on the lot to make operations economical. More detailed knowledge of the amount of timber by species would help the Pluto Mill make the crucial blending decisions that affect the cost and quality of the resulting wood pulp.

This was just one of several hundred similiar contracts to be made over the coming year. Butts was concerned with the rising cost of cruising in the Southeastern Region. Was the Bodfish Lot cruise excessive, he wondered? Could he get by in the future with considerably smaller samples? Suppose that only a half or a quarter of the plots on Bodfish had been cruised? ■

Hypothesis Testing

©Mike Powell/ALLSPORT/Getty Images

OFFICIAL SPONSORS OF THE OLYMPICS

Hypothesis testing is one of the most frequently used tools in academic research, including research in the area of business. Many studies pose interesting questions, stated as hypotheses, and then test these with appropriate statistical analysis of experimental data. One such study is reported in McDaniel and Kinney (1996). They investigate the effectiveness of "ambush marketing" in prominent sports events such as the Olympic Games. Many companies pay significant amounts of money, perhaps $10 million, to become official sponsors of the Olympics. Ambushers are their competitors who pay no such fees but nevertheless advertise heavily during the Olympics, with the intention of linking their own brand image to the event in the minds of consumers. The question McDaniel and Kinney investigate is whether consumers are confused into thinking that the ambushers are the official sponsors.

At the time of the 1994 Winter Olympics in Lillehammer, Norway, the researchers ran a controlled experiment using 215 subjects ranging in age from 19 to 49 years old. Approximately half of the subjects—the "control group"—viewed a 20-minute tape of a women's skiing event in which several actual commercials for official sponsors in four product categories were interspersed. (The categories were fast food, automobile, credit card, and insurance; the official sponsors were McDonald's, Chrysler, VISA, and John Hancock.) The other half—the "treatment group"—watched the same tape but with commercials for competing ambushers. (The ambushers were Wendy's, Ford, American Express, and Northwestern Mutual, all of which advertised during the 1994 Olympics.) After watching the tape, each subject was asked to fill out a questionnaire. This questionnaire asked subjects to recall the official Olympics sponsors in each product category, to rate their attitudes toward the products, and to state their intentions to purchase the products.

McDaniel and Kinney tested several hypotheses. First, they tested the hypothesis that there would be no difference between the control and treatment groups in terms of which products they would recall as official Olympics sponsors. The experimental evidence allowed them to reject this hypothesis decisively. For example, the vast majority of the control group, who watched the McDonald's commercial, recalled McDonald's as being the official sponsor in the fast-food category. But a clear majority of the treatment group, who watched the Wendy's commercial, recalled Wendy's as being the official sponsor in this category. Evidently, Wendy's commercial was compelling.[1]

Because the ultimate objective of commercials is to increase purchases of a company's brand, the researchers also tested the hypothesis that viewers of official sponsor commercials would rate their intent to purchase that brand *higher* than viewers of ambusher commercials would rate their intent to purchase the ambusher brand. After all, isn't this why the official sponsors were paying large fees to be "official" sponsors? However, except for the credit card category, the data did *not* support this hypothesis. VISA viewers did indeed rate their intent to use VISA higher than American Express viewers rated their intent to use American Express. But in the other three product categories, the ambusher brand came out ahead of the official brand in terms of intent to purchase (although the differences were not statistically significant).

There are at least two important messages this research should convey to business. First, if a company is going to spend a lot of money to become an official sponsor of an event such as the Olympic Games, it must create a more vivid link in the mind of consumers between its product and the event. Otherwise, the company might be wasting its money. Second, ambush marketing is very possibly a wise strategy. By seeing enough of the ambushers' commercials during the event, consumers get confused into thinking that the ambusher is an "official" sponsor. In addition, previous research in the area suggests that consumers do not view ambushers negatively for using an ambushing strategy. ■

10.1 INTRODUCTION

Hypothesis testing is a form of decision making under uncertainty, where we decide which of two competing hypotheses to accept, based on sample data. However, in contrast to the methods discussed in Chapter 7, it is performed in a very specific way, as described in this chapter.

When we want to make inferences about a population on the basis of sample data, we can perform the analysis in either of two ways. We can proceed as in the previous chapter, where we calculate a point estimate of a population parameter and then form a confidence interval around this point estimate. In this way we bring no preconceived ideas to the analysis but instead let the data "speak for themselves" in telling us where the true parameter is likely to be.

In contrast, an analyst often has a particular theory, or hypothesis, that he or she would like to test. This hypothesis might be that a new packaging design will produce more sales than the current design, that a new drug will have a higher cure rate for a given disease than any drug currently on the market, that people who smoke cigarettes are more susceptible to heart disease than nonsmokers, and so on. In this case the analyst typically collects sample data and checks whether the data provide enough evidence to support the hypothesis.

The hypothesis that the analyst is attempting to prove is called the **alternative hypothesis.** It is also frequently called the **research hypothesis.** The opposite of the

---

[1]Whereas the McDonald's commercial featured the five-ringed Olympics logo and had an Olympics theme, the Wendy's commercial used a humorous approach built around the company's founder, Dave Thomas, and his dream of winning gold in Olympics bobsled competition.

alternative hypothesis is called the **null hypothesis.** It usually represents the current thinking or status quo. That is, the null hypothesis is usually the accepted theory that the analyst is trying to *disprove*. In the previous examples the null hypotheses are:

- The new packaging design is no better than the current design.
- The new drug has a cure rate no higher than other drugs on the market.
- Smokers are no more susceptible to heart disease than nonsmokers.

The burden of proof is traditionally on the alternative hypothesis. It is up to the analyst to provide enough evidence in support of the alternative; otherwise, the null hypothesis will continue to be accepted. A slight amount of evidence in favor of the alternative is usually not enough. For example, if a slightly higher percentage of people are cured with a new drug in a sequence of clinical tests, this still might not be enough evidence to warrant introducing the new drug to the market. In general, we reject the null hypothesis—and accept the alternative—only if the results of the hypothesis test are "statistically significant," a concept we will explain in this chapter.

> The **null hypothesis** is usually the current thinking, or "status quo." The **alternative, or research, hypothesis** is usually the hypothesis a researcher wants to prove. The burden of proof is on the alternative hypothesis.

As we see in this chapter, confidence interval estimation and hypothesis testing use data in much the same way and they often report basically the same results, only from different points of view. There continues to be a debate (largely among academic researchers) over which of these two procedures is more useful. We believe that in a business context, confidence interval estimation is more useful and enlightening than hypothesis testing. However, hypothesis testing continues to be a key aspect of statistical analysis. Indeed, statistical software packages routinely include the elements of standard hypothesis tests in their outputs. We see this, for example, when we study regression analysis in Chapters 11 and 12. Therefore, it is essential to understand the fundamentals of hypothesis testing so that we can interpret this output intelligently.

10.2 CONCEPTS IN HYPOTHESIS TESTING

Before we plunge into the details of specific hypothesis tests, it is useful to discuss the *concepts* behind hypothesis testing. There are a number of concepts and statistical terms involved, all of which lead eventually to the key concept of statistical significance. To make this discussion somewhat less abstract, we place it in the context of the following example.

EXAMPLE | **10.1 EXPERIMENTING WITH A NEW PIZZA STYLE AT THE PEPPERONI PIZZA RESTAURANT**

The manager of the Pepperoni Pizza Restaurant has recently begun experimenting with a new method of baking its pepperoni pizzas. He personally believes that the new method produces a better-tasting pizza, but he would like to base a decision on whether to switch from the old method to the new method on customer reactions. Therefore, he performs an experiment. For 100 randomly selected customers who order a pepperoni pizza for home delivery, he includes both an old-style and a free new-style pizza in the order. All he asks is that these customers rate the *difference* between pizzas on a −10 to +10 scale, where −10 means that they strongly favor the old style, +10 means they strongly favor the new style, and 0 means they are indifferent between the two styles. Once he gets the ratings from the customers, how should he proceed?

We begin by stating that Example 10.1 is used primarily to explain hypothesis-testing concepts. We do *not* mean to imply that the manager would, or should, use a hypothesis-testing procedure to decide whether to switch from the old method to the new method. First, hypothesis testing does not take costs into account. If the new method of making pizzas uses more expensive cheese, for example, then hypothesis testing would ignore this important aspect of the decision problem. Second, even if the costs of the two pizza-making methods are equivalent, the manager might base his decision on a simple point estimate and possibly a confidence interval. For example, if the sample mean rating is 1.8 and a 95% confidence interval for the mean rating extends from 0.3 to 3.3, this in itself might be enough evidence to make the manager switch to the new method.

We come back to these ideas—basically, that hypothesis testing is not necessarily the best procedure to use in a business decision-making context—throughout this chapter. However, with these caveats in mind, we discuss how the manager *might* proceed by using hypothesis testing. ■

10.2.1 Null and Alternative Hypotheses

As we stated in the introduction to this chapter, the hypothesis the manager is trying to prove is called the alternative, or research, hypothesis, whereas the "status quo" is called the null hypothesis. In this example the manager would personally like to prove that the new method provides better-tasting pizza, so this becomes the alternative hypothesis. The opposite, that the old-style pizzas are at least as good as the new-style pizzas, becomes the null hypothesis. We assume he judges which of these is true on the basis of the mean rating over the entire customer population, labeled μ. If it turns out that $\mu \leq 0$, then the null hypothesis is true. Otherwise, if $\mu > 0$, the alternative hypothesis is true. The hypotheses are summarized in the box.

Hypotheses for Pizza Example

Null hypothesis: $\mu \leq 0$

Alternative hypothesis: $\mu > 0$

where μ is the mean population rating.

Usually, the null hypothesis is labeled H_0 and the alternative hypothesis is labeled H_a. Therefore, in our example we can specify these as $H_0 : \mu \leq 0$ and $H_a : \mu > 0$. This is typical. The null and alternative hypotheses divide all possibilities into two nonoverlapping sets, exactly one of which must be true. In our case either the mean rating is less than or equal to 0, or it is positive. Exactly one of these possibilities *must* be true, and the manager intends to use sample data to learn which of them is true.

Traditionally, hypothesis testing has been phrased as a decision-making problem, where an analyst decides either to accept the null hypothesis or reject it, based on the sample evidence. In our example, accepting the null hypothesis means deciding that the new-style pizza is not really better than the old-style pizza and presumably discontinuing the new style. In contrast, rejecting the null hypothesis means deciding that the new-style pizza is indeed better than the old-style pizza and presumably switching to the new style.

10.2.2 One-Tailed Versus Two-Tailed Tests

The form of the alternative hypothesis can be either *one-tailed* or *two-tailed,* depending on what the analyst is trying to prove. The pizza manager's alternative hypothesis is

one-tailed because he is hoping to prove that the customers' ratings are, on average, greater than 0. The only sample results that can lead to rejection of the null hypothesis are those in a particular direction, namely, those where the sample mean rating is *positive*. On the other hand, if the manager sets up his rating scale in the reverse order, so that *negative* ratings favor the new-style pizza, then the test is still one-tailed, but now only negative sample means lead to rejection of the null hypothesis.

In contrast, a **two-tailed** test is one where results in either of two directions can lead to rejection of the null hypothesis. A slight modification of the pizza example where a two-tailed alternative might be appropriate is the following. Suppose the manager currently uses two methods for producing pepperoni pizzas. He is thinking of discontinuing one of these methods if it appears that customers, on average, favor one method over the other. Therefore, he runs the same experiment as before, but now the hypotheses he tests are $H_0: \mu = 0$ versus $H_a: \mu \neq 0$, where μ is again the mean rating across the customer population. In this case *either* a large positive sample mean *or* a large negative sample mean will lead to rejection of the null hypothesis—and presumably to discontinuing one of the production methods. The difference between these two types of tests is summarized in the box.

A **one-tailed alternative** is one that is supported only by evidence in a single direction.

A **two-tailed alternative** is one that is supported by evidence in either direction.

It is important to realize that the analyst, not the data, determines the type of alternative hypothesis. The hypothesis depends entirely on what the analyst wants to prove, and it should be formed before the data are collected.

Once the hypotheses are set up, it is easy to detect whether the test is one-tailed or two-tailed. One-tailed alternatives are phrased in terms of ">" or "<" whereas two-tailed alternatives are phrased in terms of "≠". The real question is whether to set up hypotheses for a particular problem as one-tailed or two-tailed. There is no *statistical* answer to this question. It depends entirely on what we are trying to prove. If the pizza manager is trying to prove that the new-style pizza is better than the old-style pizza—only results on "one side" will lead to a switch—a one-tailed alternative is appropriate. However, if he is trying to decide whether to discontinue either of two existing production methods—where results on "either side" will lead to a switch—then a two-tailed alternative is appropriate.

10.2.3 Types of Errors

Regardless of whether the manager decides to accept or reject the null hypothesis, it *might* be the wrong decision. He might incorrectly reject the null hypothesis when it is true ($\mu \leq 0$), and he might incorrectly accept the null hypothesis when it is false ($\mu > 0$). In the tradition of hypothesis testing, these two types of errors have acquired the names *type I* and *type II errors*. In general, we commit a **type I error** when we incorrectly *reject* a null hypothesis that is true. We commit a **type II error** when we incorrectly *accept* a null hypothesis that is false. These ideas appear graphically in Figure 10.1.

Figure 10.1

Types of Errors in Hypothesis Testing

		Truth	
		H_0 is true	H_a is true
Decision	Reject H_0	Type I error	No error
	Do not reject H_0	No error	Type II error

The pizza manager commits a type I error if he concludes, based on sample evidence, that the new-style pizza is better (and switches to it) when in fact the entire customer population would, on average, favor the old-style pizza. In contrast, he commits a type II error if he concludes, again based on sample evidence, that the new style is no better (and discontinues it) when in fact the entire customer population would, on average, favor the new style.

> **Possible Errors in Pizza Example**
> Type I error: Switching to new style when it is no better than old style
> Type II error: Staying with old style when new style is better

Although we might be inclined to regard these two types of errors as equally serious or costly, type I errors have traditionally been regarded as the more serious of the two. Therefore, the hypothesis-testing procedure favors caution in terms of rejecting the null hypothesis. The thinking is that if we reject the null hypothesis and it is really true, then we commit a type I error—which is bad. Given this rather conservative way of thinking, we are inclined to accept the null hypothesis unless the sample evidence provides strong support for the alternative hypothesis. Unfortunately, we can't have it both ways. By accepting the null hypothesis, we risk committing a type II error.

Type I errors are usually considered more "costly," although this can lead to conservative decision making.

This is exactly the dilemma the pizza manager faces. If he wants to avoid a type I error (where he switches to the new style but really shouldn't), then he will require fairly convincing evidence from the survey that he *should* switch. If he observes *some* evidence to this effect, such as a sample mean rating of $+1.5$ and a 95% confidence interval that extends from -0.3 to $+3.3$, say, this evidence might not be strong enough to make him switch. However, if he decides not to switch, he risks committing a type II error.

10.2.4 Significance Level and Rejection Region

The analyst gets to choose the significance level α. It is traditionally chosen to be 0.05, but it is occasionally chosen to be 0.01 or 0.10.

The real question, then, is how strong the evidence in favor of the alternative hypothesis must be to reject the null hypothesis. Two approaches to this problem are commonly used. In the first, the analyst prescribes the probability of a type I error that he is willing to tolerate. This type I error probability is usually denoted by α and is most commonly set equal to 0.05, although $\alpha = 0.01$ and $\alpha = 0.10$ are also frequently used. The value of α is called the **significance level** of the test. Then, given the value of α, we use statistical theory to determine a *rejection region*. If the sample evidence falls into the **rejection region,** we reject the null hypothesis; otherwise, we accept it. The rejection region is chosen precisely so that the probability of a type I error is at most α. Sample evidence that falls into the rejection region is called **statistically significant at the α level**. For example, if $\alpha = 0.05$, we say that the evidence is statistically significant at the 5% level. These terms are summarized in the following boxes.

> The **rejection region** is the set of sample data that leads to the rejection of the null hypothesis.

> The **significance level,** α, determines the size of the rejection region. Sample results in the rejection region are called **statistically significant** at the α level.

It is important to understand the effect of varying α. If α is small, such as 0.01, then the probability of a type I error is small. Therefore, we require a lot of sample evidence in favor of the alternative hypothesis to reject the null hypothesis. Equivalently, the rejection region in this case is small. In contrast, when α is larger, such as 0.10, the rejection region is larger, and it is easier to reject the null hypothesis.

10.2.5 Significance from *p*-values

A second approach, and one that is currently more popular, is to avoid the use of an α level and instead simply report "how significant" the sample evidence is. We do this by means of a *p-value*. The idea is quite simple—and very important. Suppose in the pizza example that the true mean rating (if it could be observed) is μ = 0. In other words, the customer population, on average, judges the two styles of pizza to be equal. Now suppose that the sample mean rating is +2.5. The manager has two options at this point. (Remember that he doesn't know that μ = 0; he only observes the sample.) He can conclude that (1) the null hypothesis is true—the new-style pizza is not preferred over the old style—and he just observed an unusual sample, or (2) the null hypothesis is *not* true—customers do prefer the new-style pizza—and the sample he observed is a typical one.

The *p*-value of the sample quantifies this. The **p-value** is the probability of seeing a random sample at least as extreme as the observed sample, given that the null hypothesis is true. Here, "extreme" is relative to the null hypothesis. For example, a sample mean rating of +3.5 from the pizza customers is more extreme evidence than a sample mean rating of +2.5. Each provides some evidence against the null hypothesis, but the former provides stronger, more extreme evidence.

> The **p-value of a sample** is the probability of seeing a sample with at least as much evidence in favor of the alternative hypothesis as the sample actually observed. The smaller the *p*-value, the more evidence there is in favor of the alternative hypothesis.

Let's suppose that the pizza manager collects data from the 100 sampled customers and finds that the *p*-value for the sample is 0.03. This means that *if* the entire customer population, on average, judges the two types of pizza to be approximately equal, then only 3 random samples out of 100 would provide as much evidence in support of the new style as the observed sample. So should he conclude that the null hypothesis is true and he just happened to observe an unusual sample, or should he conclude that the null hypothesis is *not* true? There is no clear statistical answer to this question; it depends on how convinced the manager must be before switching. But we can say in general that smaller *p*-values indicate more evidence in support of the alternative hypothesis. If a *p*-value is sufficiently small, then almost any decision maker will conclude that rejecting the null hypothesis (and accepting the alternative) is the most "reasonable" decision.

How small is a "small" *p*-value? This is largely a matter of semantics, but Figure 10.2 indicates the attitude of many analysts. If a *p*-value is less than 0.01, it provides "convincing" evidence that the alternative hypothesis is true. After all, fewer than 1 sample out of 100 would provide such support for the alternative hypothesis if it weren't true. If the *p*-value is between 0.01 and 0.05, there is "strong" evidence in favor of the alternative hypothesis. Unless the consequences of making a type I error are really serious, we are likely to reject the null hypothesis in this case.

Figure 10.2

Evidence in Favor of the Alternative Hypothesis

The interval between 0.05 and 0.10 is a "gray area." If a scientific researcher were trying to prove a research hypothesis and observed a *p*-value between 0.05 and 0.10, she would probably be reluctant to publish her results as "proof" of the alternative hypothesis, but she would probably be encouraged to continue her research and collect more sample evidence. Finally, p-values larger than 0.10 are generally interpreted as weak or no evidence in support of the alternative.

There is a strong connection between the α-level approach and the p-value approach. Namely, we can reject the null hypothesis at a specified level of significance α only if the p-value from the sample is less than or equal to α. Equivalently, the sample evidence is statistically significant at a given α level only if its p-value is less than or equal to α. For example, if the p-value from a sample is 0.03, then we can reject the null hypothesis at the 10% and the 5% significance levels, but we cannot reject it at the 1% level. The p-value essentially states *how* significant a given sample is.

> Sample evidence is statistically significant at the α level only if the p-value is less than α.

If you remember only one thing from this chapter, remember that a p-value measures how unlikely the observed sample results would be, given that the null hypothesis is true. Therefore, a low p-value provides evidence for rejecting the null hypothesis and accepting the alternative.

The advantage of the p-value approach is that the analyst doesn't have to choose a significance value α ahead of time. Because it is far from obvious what value of α we should choose in any particular situation, this is certainly an advantage. Another compelling advantage is that p-values for standard hypothesis tests are routinely included in most statistical software output. In addition, all p-values can be interpreted in basically the same way: A small p-value provides support for the alternative hypothesis.

10.2.6 Type II Errors and Power

A type II error occurs when the alternative hypothesis is true but there isn't enough evidence in the sample to reject the null hypothesis. This type of error is traditionally considered less important than a type I error, but it can lead to serious consequences in real situations. For example, in medical trials on a proposed new cancer drug, a type II error occurs if the new drug is really superior to existing drugs but experimental evidence is not sufficiently conclusive to warrant marketing the new drug. For patients suffering from cancer, this is a serious error!

As we stated previously, the alternative hypothesis is typically the hypothesis a researcher wants to prove. If it is in fact true, the researcher wants to be able to reject the null hypothesis and hence avoid a type II error. The probability that she is able to do so is called the **power** of the test—that is, the power is 1 minus the probability of a type II error. There are several ways to achieve high power, the most popular of which is to increase sample size. By sampling more members of the population, we are better able to see whether the alternative is really true and hence avoid a type II error if it is true. As in the previous chapter, there are formulas that specify the sample size required to achieve a certain power for a given set of hypotheses. We will not pursue these in this book, but you should be aware that they exist. The definition of power is summarized in the following box.

> The **power** of a test is 1 minus the probability of a type II error. It is the probability that we reject the null hypothesis when the alternative hypothesis is true.

10.2.7 Hypothesis Tests and Confidence Intervals

When we present the results of hypothesis tests, we often include confidence intervals in the output. This gives us two complementary ways to interpret the data. However, there is a more formal connection between the two, at least for two-tailed tests. Let α be the stated significance level of the test. We will state the connection for the most commonly used level, $\alpha = 0.05$, although it extends to any α value. The connection is that we can reject the null hypothesis at the 5% significance level if and only if a 95% confidence interval does *not* include the hypothesized value of the parameter.

> **Using a Confidence Interval to Perform a Two-Tailed Hypothesis Test**
>
> Reject the null hypothesis if and only if the hypothesized value does *not* lie inside a confidence interval for the parameter.

As an example, consider the test of $H_0: \mu = 0$ versus $H_a: \mu \neq 0$. Suppose a 95% confidence interval for μ extends from 1.35 to 3.42; that is, it does *not* include the hypothesized value 0. Then we can reject H_0 at the 5% significance level, and we know that the p-value from the sample must be less than 0.05. On the other hand, if a 95% confidence interval for μ extends, say, from -1.25 to 2.31 (negative to positive), then we can't reject the null hypothesis at the 5% significance level, and the p-value must be greater than 0.05.

There is also a correspondence between one-tailed hypothesis tests and "one-sided" confidence intervals, but we do not pursue it here.

10.2.8 Practical versus Statistical Significance

We have stated that statistically significant results are those that produce sufficiently small p-values. In other words, statistically significant results are those that provide strong evidence in support of the alternative hypothesis. We frequently hear about studies, particularly in the medical sciences, that produce statistically significant results. For example, we might hear that mice injected with one kind of drug develop "significantly more" cancer cells than mice injected with a second kind of drug.

The point of this section is that such results are not necessarily significant in the sense of being *important*. They might be significant only in the statistical sense. An example of what could happen is the following. An education researcher wants to see whether quantitative SAT scores differ, on average, across gender. He sets up the hypotheses $H_0: \mu_M = \mu_F$ versus $H_a: \mu_M \neq \mu_F$, where μ_M and μ_F are the mean quantitative SAT scores for males and females, respectively. He then randomly samples scores from 4000 males and 4000 females and finds the male and female sample averages to be 521 and 524. He also finds that the sample standard deviation for each group is about 50. Based on these numbers, the p-value for the sample data is approximately 0.007. (We see how to make this calculation later in the chapter.) Therefore, he claims that the results are "significant proof" that males do score differently (lower) than females.

If you read these results in a newspaper, your immediate reaction might be, "Who cares?" After all, the difference between 521 and 524 is certainly not very large from a practical point of view. So why does the education researcher get to make his claim? Here's what is going on. The chances are that the means μ_M and μ_F are not *exactly* equal. There is bound to be some difference between genders over the entire population. If the researcher takes large enough samples—and 4000 is plenty large—he is almost certain to obtain enough evidence to "prove" that the means are not equal. That is, he will almost surely obtain *statistically* significant results. However, the difference he finds, as in the numbers we quoted, might be of little *practical* significance. No one really cares whether females score 3 points higher or lower than males. If the difference were on the order of 30 to 40 points, then we might be interested.

Extremely large samples can easily lead to statistically significant results that are not practically important. In contrast, small samples can fail to produce statistically significant results that might indeed be practically important.

As this example illustrates, there is always a possibility of statistical significance but not practical significance with large sample sizes. To be fair, we should also mention the opposite case, which typically occurs with small sample sizes. Here we fail to obtain statistical significance even though the truth about the population(s), if it were known, would be of practical significance. Let's assume that a medical researcher wants to test whether a new form of treatment produces a higher cure rate for a deadly disease than the best treatment currently on the market. Due to expenses, the researcher is able to run a controlled experiment on only a relatively small number of patients with the disease. Unfortunately, the results of the experiment are inconclusive. They show some evidence that the new treatment works better, but the *p*-value for the test is only 0.25.

In the scientific community these results would not be enough to warrant a switch to the new treatment. However, it is certainly possible that the new treatment, if it were used on a large number of patients, would provide a "significant" improvement in the cure rate—where "significant" now means *practical* significance. In this type of situation, we could easily fail to discover practical significance because the sample sizes are not large enough to detect it statistically.

From here on, when we use the term "significant," we mean *statistically* significant. However, you should always keep the ideas in this section in mind. A statistically significant result is not necessarily of practical importance. Conversely, a result that fails to meet the criterion for statistical significance is not necessarily one that should be ignored.

10.3 HYPOTHESIS TESTS FOR A POPULATION MEAN

Now that we have covered the general concepts behind hypothesis testing and the principal sampling distributions, the mechanics of hypothesis testing are fairly straightforward. We discuss in some detail how the procedure works for a population mean. Then in later sections we illustrate similar hypothesis tests for other parameters.

As with confidence intervals, the key to the analysis is the sampling distribution of the sample mean. We know that if we subtract the true mean μ from the sample mean and divide the difference by the standard error $s/\sqrt{n}$, the result has a t distribution with $n - 1$ degrees of freedom. In a hypothesis-testing context, the true mean to use is the null hypothesis value, specifically, the borderline value between the null and alternative hypotheses. This value is usually labeled μ_0, where the subscript reminds us that it is based on the *null* hypothesis.

To run the test, we calculate the *test statistic* in equation (10.1). This *t*-value indicates how many standard errors the sample mean is from the null value, μ_0. If the null hypothesis is true, or more specifically, if $\mu = \mu_0$, this test statistic has a t distribution with $n - 1$ degrees of freedom. The *p*-value for the test is the probability beyond the test statistic in both tails (for a two-tailed alternative) or in a single tail (for a one-tailed alternative) of the t distribution.

Test Statistic for Test of Mean

$$t\text{-value} = \frac{\bar{X} - \mu_0}{s/\sqrt{n}}$$

(10.1)

We illustrate the procedure by continuing the pizza manager's problem in Example 10.1.

EXAMPLE | **10.1 EXPERIMENTING WITH A NEW PIZZA STYLE AT THE PEPPERONI PIZZA RESTAURANT (CONTINUED)**

Recall that the manager of the Pepperoni Pizza Restaurant is running an experiment to test the hypotheses $H_0: \mu \leq 0$ versus $H_a: \mu > 0$, where μ is the mean rating in the entire customer population. Here, each customer rates the difference between an old-style pizza and a new-style pizza on a scale from -10 to $+10$, where negative ratings favor the old style and positive ratings favor the new style. The ratings for 40 randomly selected customers and several summary statistics appear in Figure 10.3. (See the file **Pizza Ratings.xlsx**.) Is there sufficient evidence from these sample data for the manager to reject H_0?

Figure 10.3

Data and Summary
Measures for Pizza
Example

	A	B	C	D	E
1	Customer	Rating			Rating
2	1	-7		*One Variable Summary*	Data Set #1
3	2	7		**Mean**	2.100
4	3	-2		**Std. Dev.**	4.717
5	4	4		**Count**	40
6	5	7			
7	6	6			
8	7	0			
9	8	2			

Objective To use a one-sample t test to see whether consumers prefer the new-style pizza to the old style.

Solution

From the summary statistics, we see that the sample mean is $\overline{X} = 2.10$ and the sample standard deviation is $s = 4.717$. This positive sample mean provides some evidence in favor of the alternative hypothesis, but given the rather large value of s and the box plot of ratings shown in Figure 10.4, which indicates a lot of negative ratings, does it provide *enough* evidence to reject H_0?

Figure 10.4

Box Plot for Pizza
Data

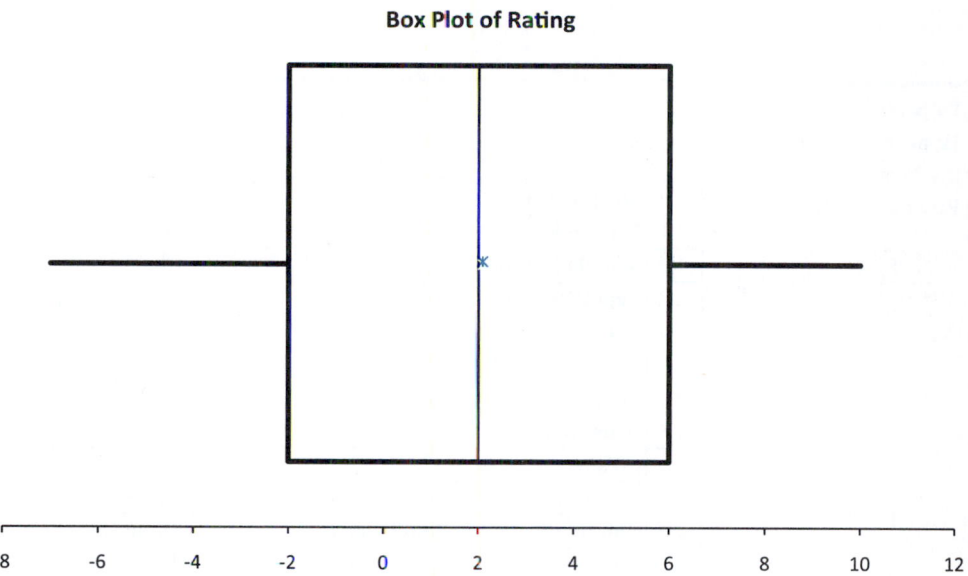

Box Plot of Rating

To run the test, we calculate the test statistic, using the borderline null hypothesis value $\mu_0 = 0$, and report how much probability is beyond it in the right tail of the appropriate t distribution. We use the *right* tail because the alternative is one-tailed of the "greater than" variety. The test statistic is

$$t\text{-value} = \frac{2.10 - 0}{4.717/\sqrt{40}} = 2.816$$

This t-value indicates that the sample mean is over 2.8 standard errors to the right of the null value, 0. Intuitively, this provides a lot of evidence in favor of the alternative—we are quite unlikely to see a sample mean 2.8 standard errors to right of a "true" mean. The probability beyond this value in the right tail of a t distribution with $n - 1 = 39$ degrees of freedom is approximately 0.004, which can be found in Excel with the function TDIST(2.816,39,1). (Recall that the first argument is the t-value, the second is the degrees of freedom, and the third is the number of tails.)

This probability, 0.004, is the p-value for the test. It indicates that these sample results would be *very* unlikely if the null hypothesis is true. The manager has two choices at this point. He can conclude that the null hypothesis is true and he obtained a very unlikely sample, or he can conclude that the alternative hypothesis is true—and presumably switch to the new-style pizza. This second conclusion certainly appears to be the more reasonable of the two.

Another way of interpreting the results of the test is in terms of traditional significance levels. We can reject H_0 at the 1% significance level because the p-value is less than 0.01. Of course, we can also reject H_0 at the 5% level or the 10% level because the p-value is also less than 0.05 and 0.10. But as we discussed previously, the p-value is a preferred way of reporting the results because it indicates exactly *how* significant these sample results are.

The StatTools One-Sample Hypothesis Test procedure can be used to perform this analysis easily, with the results shown in Figure 10.5. To use it, make sure a StatTools data set has been created, and select Hypothesis Test from the StatTools Statistical Inference dropdown. Then fill out the resulting dialog box as shown in Figure 10.6. In particular, make sure the Analysis Type is One-Sample Analysis and the Alternative Hypothesis Type is the "Greater Than" choice.

Figure 10.5

Hypothesis Test for the Mean for the Pizza Example

	D	E
8		Rating
9	Hypothesis Test (One-Sample)	Data Set #1
10	Sample Size	40
11	Sample Mean	2.100
12	Sample Std Dev	4.717
13	Hypothesized Mean	0
14	Alternative Hypothesis	> 0
15	Standard Error of Mean	0.746
16	Degrees of Freedom	39
17	t-Test Statistic	2.8159
18	p-Value	0.0038
19	Null Hypoth. at 10% Significance	Reject
20	Null Hypoth. at 5% Significance	Reject
21	Null Hypoth. at 1% Significance	Reject

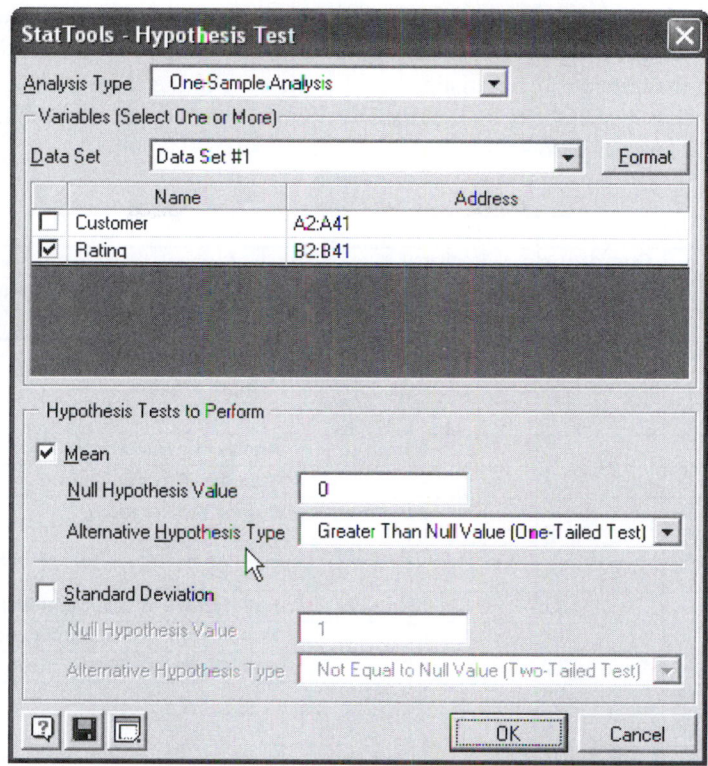

Figure 10.6

One-Sample
Hypothesis Test
Dialog Box

Most of the output in Figure 10.5 should be familiar: It mirrors the calculations we did previously, and you can check the formulas in the output cells to ensure that you understand the procedure. We note the following. First, the value in cell E13, 0, is the null hypothesis value μ_0 at the borderline between H_0 and H_a; it is the value specified in the dialog box in Figure 10.6. Second, take a look at the note entered in cell D9. (This note isn't visible in Figure 10.5, but it can be seen in the completed file.) It reminds us that this test is based on normality of the underlying population distribution and/or a sufficiently large sample size. If these conditions are not satisfied (which is not a problem for this example), then other more appropriate tests are available. Finally, StatTools compares the p-value to the three traditional significance levels, 1%, 5%, and 10%, and interprets significance in terms of these. As indicated in cells E19, E20, and E21, we can reject the null hypothesis in favor of the alternative at each of these three significance levels.

Before leaving this example, we ask one last question. Should the manager switch to the new-style pizza on the basis of these sample results? We would probably recommend "yes." There is no indication that the new-style pizza costs any more to make than the old-style pizza, and the sample evidence is fairly convincing that customers, on average, prefer the new-style pizza. Therefore, unless there are reasons for not switching that we haven't mentioned here, we recommend the switch. However, if it costs more to make the new-style pizza, hypothesis testing is *not* the best way to perform the decision analysis. We return to this theme throughout this chapter. ■

Example 10.1 illustrates how to run and interpret any one-tailed hypothesis for the mean, assuming the alternative is of the "greater than" variety. If the alternative is still one-tailed but of the "less than" variety, there is virtually no change. We illustrate this in Figure 10.7, where the ratings have been reversed in sign. That is, we multiplied each rating by -1, so that negative ratings now favor the new-style pizza. The hypotheses are now $H_0\!:\mu \geq 0$ versus $H_a\!:\mu < 0$ because a negative mean now supports the new style. The only difference in running the analysis with StatTools is that we select the "Less Than" choice for the Alternative Analysis Type in Figure 10.6. As Figure 10.7 indicates, we obtain the negative of the previous test statistic, -2.816, and exactly the same p-value, 0.004. This is now the probability in the *left* tail of the t distribution, but the interpretation of the results is exactly the same as before.

Figure 10.7

Hypothesis Test with Reverse Coding

	A	B	C	D	E
1	Customer	Rating			Rating
2	1	7		*Hypothesis Test (One-Sample)*	Data Set #2
3	2	-7		Sample Size	40
4	3	2		Sample Mean	-2.100
5	4	-4		Sample Std Dev	4.717
6	5	-7		Hypothesized Mean	0
7	6	-6		Alternative Hypothesis	< 0
8	7	0		Standard Error of Mean	0.746
9	8	-2		Degrees of Freedom	39
10	9	-8		t-Test Statistic	-2.8159
11	10	-2		p-Value	0.0038
12	11	-3		Null Hypoth. at 10% Significance	Reject
13	12	4		Null Hypoth. at 5% Significance	Reject
14	13	-8		Null Hypoth. at 1% Significance	Reject
15	14	5			
16	15	-7			
17	16	5			

The analysis of two-tailed tests for the mean is also quite similar to the analysis in Example 10.1. We illustrate a typical two-tailed test in the following example.

EXAMPLE | **10.2 MEASURING STUDENT REACTION TO A NEW TEXTBOOK**

A large required chemistry course at State University has been using the same textbook for a number of years. Over the years, the students have been asked to rate this textbook on 10-point scale, and the average rating has been stable at about 5.2. This year, the faculty decided to experiment with a new textbook. After the course, 50 randomly selected students were asked to rate this new textbook, also on a scale of 1 to 10. The results appear in column B of Figure 10.8. Can we conclude that the students like this new textbook any more or less than the previous textbook?

Objective   To use a one-sample t test to see whether students like the new textbook any more or less than the old textbook.

Solution

The first question is whether the test should be one-tailed or two-tailed. Of course, the faculty have chosen the new textbook with the expectation that it will be preferred by the students, but it is very possible that students will like it *less* than the previous textbook. (Students are notoriously unpredictable in their acceptance of textbooks.) Therefore, we set this up as a two-tailed test—that is, the alternative hypothesis is that the mean rating of the new textbook is either less than *or* greater than the mean rating, 5.2, of the previous textbook. Formally, we write the hypotheses as H_0: $\mu = 5.2$ versus H_a: $\mu \neq 5.2$.

Figure 10.8   Test of Two-Tailed Alternative

	A	B	C	D	E	F
1	Student	Rating		Mean rating of previous textbook (on a 1-10 scale)		5.2
2	1	6				
3	2	3			Rating	
4	3	6		*Hypothesis Test (One-Sample)*	Data Set #1	
5	4	7		Sample Size	50	
6	5	6		Sample Mean	5.680	
7	6	10		Sample Std Dev	1.953	
8	7	6		Hypothesized Mean	5.2	
9	8	8		Alternative Hypothesis	<> 5.2	
10	9	7		Standard Error of Mean	0.276	
11	10	10		Degrees of Freedom	49	
12	11	3		t-Test Statistic	1.738	
13	12	6		p-Value	0.088	
14	13	4		Null Hypoth. at 10% Significance	Reject	
15	14	6		Null Hypoth. at 5% Significance	Don't Reject	
16	15	8		Null Hypoth. at 1% Significance	Don't Reject	
17	16	10				
18	17	5			Rating	
19	18	4		*Conf. Intervals (One-Sample)*	Data Set #1	
20	19	6		Sample Size	50	
21	20	4		Sample Mean	5.680	
22	21	6		Sample Std Dev	1.953	
23	22	6		Confidence Level (Mean)	95.0%	
24	23	4		Degrees of Freedom	49	
25	24	5		Lower Limit	5.125	
26	25	7		Upper Limit	6.235	
27	26	8				
28	27	7				
29	28	5				

The test is run (and the StatTools One-Sample Hypothesis Test procedure can be used) almost exactly as with a one-tailed test. The only difference is that we specify the "Not Equal" choice for the Alternative Hypothesis Type, and the Null Hypothesis Value is now 5.2, the historical average rating. (See Figure 10.9.) We calculate the t-distributed test statistic in the same way as before:

$$t\text{-value} = \frac{\overline{X} - 5.2}{s/\sqrt{n}} = \frac{5.680 - 5.2}{1.953/\sqrt{50}} = 1.738$$

The p-value is then the probability beyond -1.738 in the left tail *and* beyond $+1.738$ in the right tail of a t distribution with $n - 1 = 49$ degrees of freedom. The effect is to double the one-tailed p-value. From the output (cell E13) in Figure 10.8, we see that the two-tailed p-value is 0.088.

This moderately small p-value provides some evidence, but not convincing evidence, that the mean rating of the new textbook is different from the old mean rating of 5.2. Specifically, the output indicates that the null hypothesis can be rejected at the 10% level, but

Figure 10.9

Dialog Box for
Two-Tailed
Hypothesis Test

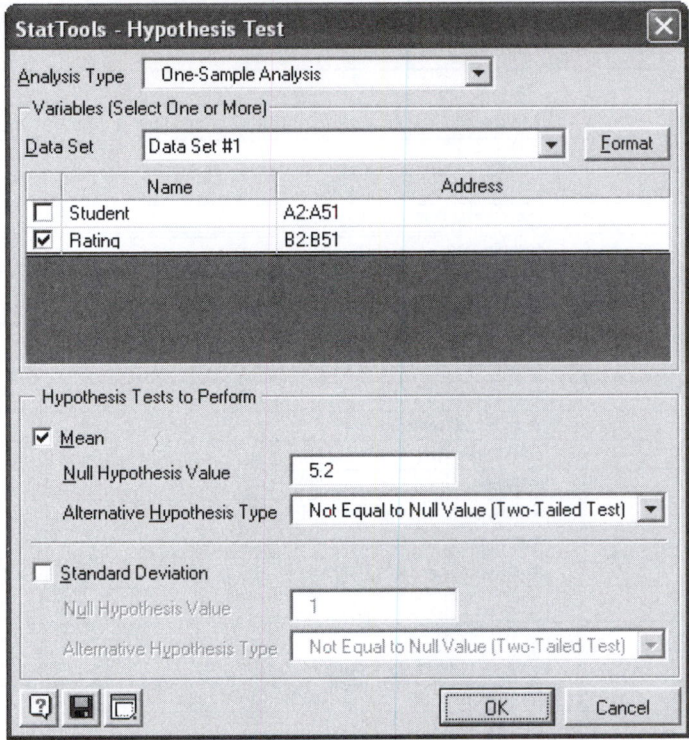

not at the 5% or 1% levels. If the *p*-value were lower (which might occur if more students were sampled), the evidence would be more conclusive. As in Example 10.1, we can now ask whether the faculty should continue to use the new textbook. Here again, it is probably not a decision that hypothesis testing, at least by itself, should determine. The students *appear* to favor the new textbook, if only by a small margin. If the faculty also favor it, we see no reason for not continuing to use it.

Because this is a two-tailed test, we could also perform the test by appealing to confidence intervals. A 95% confidence interval for the mean rating of the new textbook, also shown in Figure 10.8, extends from 5.125 to 6.235. Because this interval *does* include the old mean rating of 5.2, we cannot reject the null hypothesis at the 5% significance level. This is in agreement with the *p*-value of the test, which is greater than 0.05. However, you can check that a 90% confidence interval for the mean does *not* include 5.2. Therefore, we can reject the null hypothesis at the 10% level. This too is in agreement with the *p*-value, which is less than 0.10. ∎

PROBLEMS

Level A

1. Suppose a firm producing lightbulbs wants to know whether it can claim that its lightbulbs typically last more than 1000 burning hours. Hoping to find support for this claim, the firm collects a random sample of 100 lightbulbs and records the lifetime (in hours) of each. The sample data are contained in the file **P10_01.xlsx**.

a. Using a 5% significance level, can this lightbulb manufacturer claim that its bulbs typically last more than 1000 hours? Explain your answer.

b. Using a 1% significance level, can this lightbulb manufacturer claim that its bulbs typically last more than 1000 hours? Explain your answer.

2. A manufacturer is interested in determining whether it can claim that the boxes of detergent it sells contain, on average, more than 500 grams of detergent. From past experience the manufacturer knows that the amount of detergent in the boxes is approximately normally distributed. The firm selects a random sample of 100 boxes and records the amount of detergent (in grams) in each box. These data are provided in the file **P10_02.xlsx**. Formulate an appropriate hypothesis test and report a *p*-value. Do you find statistical support for the manufacturer's claim? Explain.

3. A producer of steel cables wants to know whether the steel cables it produces have an average breaking strength of 5000 pounds. An average breaking strength of less than 5000 pounds would not be adequate, and to produce steel cables with an average breaking strength in excess of 5000 pounds would unnecessarily increase production costs. The producer collects a random sample of 64 steel cable pieces. The breaking strength for each of these cable pieces is recorded in the file **P10_03.xlsx**.
   a. Using a 5% significance level, what statistical conclusion can the producer reach regarding the average breaking strength of its steel cables? Explain your answer.
   b. Using a 1% significance level, what statistical conclusion can the producer reach regarding the average breaking strength of its steel cables? Explain your answer.

4. A U.S. Navy recruiting center knows from past experience that the heights of its recruits are normally distributed with mean 68 inches. The recruiting center wants to test the claim that the average height of this year's recruits is greater than 68 inches. To do this, recruiting personnel take a random sample of 64 recruits from this year and record their heights (in inches). The data are provided in the file **P10_04.xlsx**.
   a. On the basis of the available sample information, do the recruiters find support for the given claim at the 1% significance level? Explain.
   b. Use the sample data to construct a 95% confidence interval for the average height of this year's recruits. Based on this confidence interval, what conclusion should recruiting personnel reach regarding the given claim?

5. Suppose that we wish to test $H_0: \mu = 10$ versus $H_a: \mu > 10$ at the $\alpha = 0.05$ significance level. Furthermore, suppose that we observe values of the sample mean and sample standard deviation when $n = 40$ that do *not* lead to the rejection of H_0. Is it true that we might reject H_0 if we observed the same values of the sample mean and sample standard deviation from a sample with $n > 40$? Why or why not?

Level B

6. A study is performed in a large southern town to determine whether the average weekly grocery bill per four-person family in the town is significantly different from the national average. A random sample of the weekly grocery bills of four-person families in this town is given in the file **P10_06.xlsx**.
   a. Assume that the national average weekly grocery bill for a four-person family is $100. Is the sample evidence statistically significant? If so, at what significance levels can you reject the null hypothesis?
   b. For which values of the sample mean (i.e., average weekly grocery bill) would you decide to reject the null hypothesis at the $\alpha = 0.01$ significance level? For which values of the sample mean would you decide to reject the null hypothesis at the $\alpha = 0.10$ level?

7. An aircraft manufacturer needs to buy aluminum sheets with an average thickness of 0.05 inch. The manufacturer knows that significantly thinner sheets would be unsafe and considerably thicker sheets would be too heavy. A random sample of 100 sheets from a potential supplier is collected. The thickness of each sheet in this sample is measured (in inches) and recorded in the file **P10_07.xlsx**.
   a. Based on the results of an appropriate hypothesis test, should the aircraft manufacturer buy aluminum sheets from this supplier? Explain why or why not.
   b. For which values of the sample mean (i.e., average thickness) would the aircraft manufacturer decide to buy sheets from this supplier? Assume that $\alpha = 0.05$ in answering this question.

8. Suppose that we observe a random sample of size n from a normally distributed population. If we are able to reject $H_0: \mu = \mu_0$ in favor of a two-tailed alternative hypothesis at the 10% significance level, is it true that we can definitely reject H_0 in favor of the appropriate one-tailed alternative at the 5% significance level? Why or why not?

10.4 HYPOTHESIS TESTS FOR OTHER PARAMETERS

Just as we developed confidence intervals for a variety of parameters, we can develop hypothesis tests for other parameters. They are based on the same sampling distributions we discussed in the previous chapter, and they are run and interpreted exactly as the tests for the mean in the previous section. In each case we use sample data to calculate a test statistic that has a well-known sampling distribution. Then we calculate a corresponding *p*-value to measure the support for the alternative hypothesis. Beyond this, only the details change, as we illustrate in this section.

10.4.1 Hypothesis Tests for a Population Proportion

To test a population proportion p, recall that the sample proportion $\hat{p}$ has a sampling distribution that is approximately normal when the sample size is reasonably large. Specifically, the standardized value

$$\frac{\hat{p} - p}{\sqrt{p(1-p)/n}}$$

is approximately distributed as a standard normal random variable Z.

Let p_0 be the borderline value of p between the null and alternative hypotheses. Then we substitute p_0 for p to obtain the test statistic in equation (10.2). The *p*-value of the test is found by seeing how much probability is beyond this test statistic in the tail (or tails) of the standard normal distribution.[2] A rule of thumb for checking the large-sample assumption of this test is to check whether $np_0 > 5$ and $n(1 - p_0) > 5$.

Test Statistic for Test of Proportion

$$z\text{-value} = \frac{\hat{p} - p_0}{\sqrt{p_0(1-p_0)/n}} \qquad\qquad (10.2)$$

We illustrate this test of proportion in the following example.

EXAMPLE | **10.3 CUSTOMER COMPLAINTS AT WALPOLE APPLIANCE COMPANY**

The Walpole Appliance Company has a customer service department that handles customer questions and complaints. This department's processes are set up to respond quickly and accurately to customers who phone in their concerns. However, there is a sizable minority of customers who prefer to write letters. Traditionally, the customer service department has not been very efficient in responding to these customers.

Letter writers first receive a mailgram asking them to call customer service (which is exactly what letter writers wanted to avoid in the first place!), and when they do call, the customer service representative who answers the phone typically has no knowledge of the customer's problem. As a result, the department manager estimates that 15% of letter writers have not obtained a satisfactory response within 30 days of the time their letters were first received. The manager's goal is to reduce this value by at least half, that is, to 7.5% or less.

To do so, she changes the process for responding to letter writers. Under the new process, these customers now receive a prompt and courteous form letter that responds to their problem. (This is possible because the vast majority of concerns can be addressed by one of several form letters.) Each form letter states that if the customer still has problems, he or she can call the department. The manager also files the original letters so that if customers do call back, the representative who answers will be able to find their letters quickly and respond intelligently. With this new process in place, the manager has tracked

---

[2]Do not confuse the unknown proportion p with the *p*-value of the test. They are logically different concepts and just happen to share the same letter p.

400 letter writers and has found that only 23 of them are classified as "unsatisfied" after a 30-day period. Does it appear that the manager has achieved her goal?

Objective To use a test for a proportion to see whether the new process of responding to complaint letters results in an acceptably low proportion of unsatisfied customers.

Solution

The manager's goal is to reduce the proportion of unsatisfied customers after 30 days from 0.15 to 0.075 or less. Because the burden of proof is on her to "prove" that she has accomplished this goal, we set up the hypotheses as $H_0: p \geq 0.075$ versus $H_a: p < 0.075$, where p is the proportion of all letter writers who are still unsatisfied after 30 days. The sample proportion she has observed is $\hat{p} = 23/400 = 0.0575$. This is obviously less than 0.075, but is it *enough* less to reject the null hypothesis?

The test statistic for the data, using the borderline value $p_0 = 0.075$, is

$$z\text{-value} = \frac{0.0575 - 0.075}{\sqrt{0.075(1 - 0.075)/400}} = -1.329$$

This value appears in cell B10 of Figure 10.10. You can already guess that the results will not be statistically significant. This Z-value indicates that the observed proportion is only about 1.33 standard errors below the null proportion, which isn't all that large a difference. (See the file **Customer Complaints.xlsx**. Although StatTools does not have a procedure for testing proportions, this file serves as a template for all such tests.) Note that we first find the denominator (the standard error of $\hat{p}$) in cell B8 with the formula

=SQRT(B3*(1-B3)/B6)

Figure 10.10

Analysis of New Process for Letter Writers

	A	B	C
1	Test of a proportion: responding to customer complaint letters		
2			
3	Target proportion with new procedure	0.075	
4			
5	Number of unsatisfied customers after 30 days	23	
6	Number of customers sampled	400	
7	Sample proportion	0.0575	
8	Standard error of sample proportion	0.01317	
9			
10	z test statistic	-1.329	
11	p value for a one-tailed test	0.092	
12			
13	Confidence interval for true proportion		
14	Confidence level	95%	
15	Standard error	0.012	
16	z-multiple	1.960	
17	Lower limit	0.035	
18	Upper limit	0.080	

The corresponding p-value, 0.092, is found with the formula

=NORMSDIST(B10)

in cell B11. It is the probability to the *left* of -1.329 in the standard normal distribution. Also, because $np_0 = 400(0.075) = 30 > 5$ and $n(1 - p_0) = 400(0.925) > 5$, this test is valid; that is, the sample size is large enough for the normal approximation to hold.

The *p*-value in cell B11 might not be as low as you expected—or as low as the manager would like. In spite of the fact that the sample proportion appears to be well below the target proportion of 0.075, the evidence in support of the alternative hypothesis is not overwhelming. In statistical terminology, the results are significant at the 10% level, but not at the 5% or 1% levels.

We also show a 95% confidence interval for the unknown proportion *p* in Figure 10.10. For example, the formula in cell B17 is

=B7-B16*SQRT(B7*(1-B7)/B6)

This confidence interval extends from 0.035 to 0.080. It includes the target value, 0.075, but just barely. In this sense it also provides some support for the argument that the manager has indeed achieved her goal.[3]

Analysts might disagree on whether a hypothesis test or a confidence interval is the more appropriate way to present these results. However, we see them as complementary and do not necessarily favor one over the other. The bottom line is that they both provide some, but not totally conclusive, evidence that the manager has achieved her goal. ■

10.4.2 Hypothesis Tests for Differences Between Population Means

This comparison problem—comparing two population means—is one of the most important problems analyzed with statistical methods. It can be analyzed with confidence intervals, hypothesis tests, or both.

We now discuss the comparison problem, where we test the difference between two population means. As in the previous chapter, the form of the analysis depends on whether the two samples are independent or paired. For variety, we begin with the paired case.

If the samples are paired, then the test proceeds exactly as in Section 10.3, using the differences as the single variable of analysis. That is, if $\overline{D}$ is the sample mean difference between *n* pairs, D_0 is the hypothesized difference (the borderline value between H_0 and H_a), and s_D is the sample standard deviation of the differences, then the test is based on the test statistic in equation (10.3). If D_0 is the true mean difference, then this test statistic has a *t* distribution with $n - 1$ degrees of freedom. The validity of the test also requires that *n* be reasonably large and/or the population of *differences* be approximately normally distributed.

> **Test Statistic for Paired Samples Test of Difference Between Means**
> $$t\text{-value} = \frac{\overline{D} - D_0}{s_D/\sqrt{n}} \tag{10.3}$$

If the samples are independent and the population standard deviations are equal, then the two-sample theory discussed in Section 9.7 is relevant. It leads to the test statistic in equation (10.4). Here, $\overline{X}_1$ and $\overline{X}_2$ are the two sample means, D_0 is the hypothesized difference, n_1 and n_2 are the sample sizes, and s_p is the same pooled estimate of the common population standard deviation as in the previous chapter:

$$s_p = \sqrt{\frac{(n_1 - 1)s_1^2 + (n_2 - 1)s_2^2}{n_1 + n_2 - 2}}$$

---

[3]Note that the standard error in cell B8 for the hypothesis test uses the target proportion 0.075. In contrast, the standard error for the confidence interval uses the sample proportion 0.0575. The sampling distribution for a hypothesis test always uses the borderline value between H_0 and H_a. But because confidence intervals aren't connected to any hypotheses, their standard errors must rely on sample data. In most cases the two standard errors are practically the same.

If D_0 is the true mean difference, then this test statistic has a t distribution with $n_1 + n_2 - 2$ degrees of freedom. The validity of this test again requires that the sample sizes be reasonably large and/or the populations be approximately normally distributed.

Test Statistic for Independent Samples Test of Difference Between Means

$$t\text{-value} = \frac{(\bar{X}_1 - \bar{X}_2) - D_0}{s_p \sqrt{1/n_1 + 1/n_2}}$$

(10.4)

Fortunately, these formulas are implemented automatically by StatTools's procedures. We begin by illustrating an example of the paired-sample t test.

EXAMPLE | **10.4 MEASURING THE EFFECTS OF TRADITIONAL AND NEW STYLES OF SOFT-DRINK CANS**

Beer and soft-drink companies have recently become very concerned about the style of their cans. There are cans with fluted and embossed sides and cans with six-color graphics and holograms. Coca-Cola is even experimenting with a contoured can, shaped like the old-fashioned Coke bottle minus the neck. Evidently, these companies believe the style of the can makes a difference to consumers, which presumably translates into higher sales.

Assume that a soft-drink company is considering a style change to its current can, which has been the company's trademark for many years. To determine whether this new style is popular with consumers, the company runs a number of focus group sessions around the country. At each of these sessions, randomly selected consumers are allowed to examine the new and traditional styles, exchange ideas, and offer their opinions. Eventually, they fill out a form where, among other items, they are asked to respond to the following items, each on a scale of 1 to 7, 7 being the best:

- Rate the attractiveness of the traditional-style can (AO).
- Rate the attractiveness of the new-style can (AN).
- Rate the likelihood that you would buy the product with the traditional-style can (WBO).
- Rate the likelihood that you would buy the product with the new-style can (WBN).

What can the company conclude from these data? (See the file **Soft-Drink Cans.xlsx**.) Are hypothesis tests appropriate?

Objective To use paired-sample t tests for differences between means to see whether consumers rate the attractiveness, and their likelihood to purchase, higher for a new-style can than for the traditional-style can.

Solution

First, it is a good idea to examine summary statistics for the data. The averages from each survey item are shown at the bottom of Figure 10.11. They indicate some support for the new-style can. Also, we might expect the ratings for a given consumer to be correlated. This turns out to be the case, as shown by the relatively large positive correlations in Figure 10.12. These large positive correlations indicate that if we want to examine differences between survey items, a paired-sample procedure will make the most efficient use of the data. Of course, a paired-sample procedure also makes sense because each consumer answers each item on the form. (If this is confusing, think about the following alternative setup. We have four *separate* groups of consumers. The first group responds to item 1 only, the second group responds to item 2 only, and so on. Then the responses to the various items are in no way paired, and an *independent-sample* procedure would be used instead. However, this experimental design would not be as efficient as the paired design in terms of making the best use of a given amount of data.)

Figure 10.11

Data on Soft-Drink Cans

	A	B	C	D	E	F	G	H	I	J
1	Consumer	AO	AN	WBO	WBN	AO-AN	WBO-WBN	AN-WBN	AO-WBO	(AN-WBN)-(AO-WBO)
2	1	5	7	4	1	-2	3	6	1	5
3	2	7	7	6	6	0	0	1	1	0
4	3	6	7	7	6	-1	1	1	-1	2
5	4	1	3	1	1	-2	0	2	0	2
6	5	3	4	1	1	-1	0	3	2	1
7	6	7	7	7	7	0	0	0	0	0
8	7	5	7	4	6	-2	-2	1	1	0
9	8	6	7	6	7	-1	-1	0	0	0
10	9	5	7	6	6	-2	0	1	-1	2
11	10	5	4	4	6	1	-2	-2	1	-3
12	11	1	3	1	1	-2	0	2	0	2
13	12	2	1	1	3	1	-2	-2	1	-3
14	13	6	6	6	6	0	0	0	0	0
15	14	4	5	3	3	-1	0	2	1	1
16	15	2	5	1	1	-3	0	4	1	3
17	16	6	7	7	7	-1	0	0	-1	1
18	17	4	5	2	1	-1	1	4	2	2
179	178	5	4	4	3	1	1	1	1	0
180	179	3	4	1	3	-1	-2	1	2	-1
181	180	3	5	6	7	-2	-1	-2	-3	1
182										
183	Averages	4.41	4.95	3.86	4.34					

Figure 10.12

Correlations for Soft-Drink Can Data

	A	B	C	D	E
7					
8	*Correlation Table*	AO	AN	WBO	WBN
9	AO	1.000			
10	AN	0.740	1.000		
11	WBO	0.746	0.595	1.000	
12	WBN	0.594	0.401	0.774	1.000

There are several differences of interest. The two most obvious are the difference between the attractiveness ratings of the two styles and the difference between the likelihoods of buying the two styles—that is, column B minus column C and column D minus column E. A third difference of interest is the difference between the attractiveness ratings of the new style and the likelihoods of buying the new can—that is, column C minus column E. This difference indicates whether perceptions of the new-style can are likely to translate into sales. Finally, a fourth difference that might be of interest is the difference between the third difference (column C minus column E) and the similar difference for the old style (column B minus column D). This checks whether the translation of perceptions into sales is any different for the two styles of cans.

All of these differences appear next to the original data in Figure 10.13. In terms of the original data, they are labeled as:

- Diff1: AO − AN
- Diff2: WBO − WBN

- Diff3: AN − WBN
- Diff4: AO − WBO
- Diff5: (AN − WBN) − (AO − WBO)

Figure 10.13 Original and Difference Variables for Soft-Drink Can Data

	A	B	C	D	E	F	G	H	I	J
1	Consumer	AO	AN	WBO	WBN	AO-AN	WBO-WBN	AN-WBN	AO-WBO	(AN-WBN)-(AO-WBO)
2	1	5	7	4	1	-2	3	6	1	5
3	2	7	7	6	6	0	0	1	1	0
4	3	6	7	7	6	-1	1	1	-1	2
5	4	1	3	1	1	-2	0	2	0	2
6	5	3	4	1	1	-1	0	3	2	1
7	6	7	7	7	7	0	0	0	0	0
8	7	5	7	4	6	-2	-2	1	1	0
9	8	6	7	6	7	-1	-1	0	0	0
10	9	5	7	6	6	-2	0	1	-1	2
11	10	5	4	4	6	1	-2	-2	1	-3
12	11	1	3	1	1	-2	0	2	0	2
13	12	2	1	1	3	1	-2	-2	1	-3

We generate these differences in columns F through J. (Actually, StatTools's Paired-Sample procedure generates the required differences internally when it tests these differences. We manually inserted the differences in Figure 10.13 so that we can see them explicitly.)

For each of the differences, Diff1, Diff2, Diff3, and Diff5, we test the mean difference over all potential consumers with a paired-sample analysis. (We actually run the one-sample procedure on the difference variables.) Exactly as in the previous chapter, we treat each difference variable as a *single* sample and run the same t test as in Section 10.3 on this sample. (This means that the differences in columns F through J of Figure 10.13 should be included in the StatTools data set.) In each case the hypothesized difference, D_0, is 0. The only question is whether to run one-tailed or two-tailed tests. We propose that the tests for Diff1, Diff2, and Diff5 be two-tailed tests and that the test on Diff3 be a one-tailed test with the alternative of the "greater than" variety. The reasoning is that the company probably has little idea which way the differences Diff1, Diff2, and Diff5 will go (positive or negative), whereas it expects that Diff3 will be positive on average. That is, the company expects that consumers' ratings of the attractiveness of the new design will, on average, be larger than their likelihoods of purchasing the product. However, any of these hypotheses could be run as one-tailed or two-tailed tests. It depends on the prior beliefs of the company. In any case, to change a one-tailed p-value to a two-tailed p-value, all we need to do is multiply by 2. Similarly, we can change two-tailed p-values to one-tailed p-values by dividing by 2.

The results from the four tests appear in Figures 10.14 and 10.15. (These outputs also include 99% confidence intervals for the corresponding mean differences.) We obtained each output for Diff1, Diff2, and Diff3 by selecting Confidence Interval or Hypothesis Test from the StatTools Statistical Inference dropdown, used on the appropriate difference variable and the One-Sample analysis type.[4]

Figure 10.14 Analysis of Diff1 and Diff2 Variables

	A	B	C	D	E
7		**AO-AN**			**WBO-WBN**
8	*Conf. Intervals (One-Sample)*	Data Set #1		*Conf. Intervals (One-Sample)*	Data Set #1
9	Sample Size	180		Sample Size	180
10	Sample Mean	-0.539		Sample Mean	-0.478
11	Sample Std Dev	1.351		Sample Std Dev	1.347
12	Confidence Level (Mean)	99.0%		Confidence Level (Mean)	99.0%
13	Degrees of Freedom	179		Degrees of Freedom	179
14	Lower Limit	-0.801		Lower Limit	-0.739
15	Upper Limit	-0.277		Upper Limit	-0.216
16					
17		**AO-AN**			**WBO-WBN**
18	*Hypothesis Test (One-Sample)*	Data Set #1		*Hypothesis Test (One-Sample)*	Data Set #1
19	Sample Size	180		Sample Size	180
20	Sample Mean	-0.539		Sample Mean	-0.478
21	Sample Std Dev	1.351		Sample Std Dev	1.347
22	Hypothesized Mean	0		Hypothesized Mean	0
23	Alternative Hypothesis	<> 0		Alternative Hypothesis	<> 0
24	Standard Error of Mean	0.1007		Standard Error of Mean	0.1004
25	Degrees of Freedom	179		Degrees of Freedom	179
26	t-Test Statistic	-5.3514		t-Test Statistic	-4.7578
27	p-Value	< 0.0001		p-Value	< 0.0001
28	Null Hypoth. at 10% Significance	Reject		Null Hypoth. at 10% Significance	Reject
29	Null Hypoth. at 5% Significance	Reject		Null Hypoth. at 5% Significance	Reject
30	Null Hypoth. at 1% Significance	Reject		Null Hypoth. at 1% Significance	Reject

Figure 10.15 Analysis of Diff3 and Diff5 Variables

	A	B	C	D	E
7		**AN-WBN**			**(AN-WBN)-(AO-WBO)**
8	*Conf. Intervals (One-Sample)*	Data Set #1		*Conf. Intervals (One-Sample)*	Data Set #1
9	Sample Size	180		Sample Size	180
10	Sample Mean	0.611		Sample Mean	0.061
11	Sample Std Dev	2.213		Sample Std Dev	2.045
12	Confidence Level (Mean)	99.0%		Confidence Level (Mean)	99.0%
13	Degrees of Freedom	179		Degrees of Freedom	179
14	Lower Limit	0.182		Lower Limit	-0.336
15	Upper Limit	1.041		Upper Limit	0.458
16					
17		**AN-WBN**			**(AN-WBN)-(AO-WBO)**
18	*Hypothesis Test (One-Sample)*	Data Set #1		*Hypothesis Test (One-Sample)*	Data Set #1
19	Sample Size	180		Sample Size	180
20	Sample Mean	0.611		Sample Mean	0.061
21	Sample Std Dev	2.213		Sample Std Dev	2.045
22	Hypothesized Mean	0		Hypothesized Mean	0
23	Alternative Hypothesis	> 0		Alternative Hypothesis	<> 0
24	Standard Error of Mean	0.1650		Standard Error of Mean	0.1524
25	Degrees of Freedom	179		Degrees of Freedom	179
26	t-Test Statistic	3.7046		t-Test Statistic	0.4010
27	p-Value	0.0001		p-Value	0.6889
28	Null Hypoth. at 10% Significance	Reject		Null Hypoth. at 10% Significance	Don't Reject
29	Null Hypoth. at 5% Significance	Reject		Null Hypoth. at 5% Significance	Don't Reject
30	Null Hypoth. at 1% Significance	Reject		Null Hypoth. at 1% Significance	Don't Reject

[4]Because this can be a source of confusion, we repeat again that when you want to run a paired-sample analysis in StatTools, you can do it by creating the differences manually and then using the One-Sample option, or you can choose the Paired-Sample option and select the two original variables you want to difference, in which case StatTools creates the difference variable internally for you. The results are identical.

Results of the analysis of soft-drink can style

■ From the output for the Diff1 variable (AO − AN) in Figure 10.14, there is over-whelming evidence that consumers, on average, rate the attractiveness of the new design higher than the attractiveness of the current design. The t-distributed test statistic is −5.351, calculated as

$$\frac{-0.539 - 0}{0.101} = -5.351$$

and the corresponding p-value for a two-tailed test of the mean difference is (to three decimal places) 0.000. A 99% confidence interval for the mean difference extends from −0.801 to −0.277. Note that this 99% confidence interval does *not* include the hypothesized value 0. This is consistent with the fact that the two-tailed p-value is less than 0.01. (Recall the relationship between confidence intervals and two-tailed hypothesis tests from Section 10.2.7.)

■ The results are basically the same for the difference between consumers' likelihoods of buying the product with the two styles. (See the output for the Diff2 variable, WBO–WBN, in Figure 10.14.) Again, consumers are definitely more likely, on average, to buy the product with the new-style can. A 99% confidence interval for the mean difference extends from −0.739 to −0.216.

■ The company's hypothesis that consumers' ratings of attractiveness of the new-style can are greater, on average, than their likelihoods of buying the product with this style can is confirmed. (See the output for the Diff3 variable, AN–WBN, in Figure 10.15.) The test statistic for this one-tailed test is 3.705 and the corresponding p-value is 0.000. A 99% confidence interval for the mean difference extends from 0.182 to 1.041.

■ There is no evidence that the difference between attractiveness ratings and the likelihood of buying is any different for the new-style can than for the current-style can. (See the output for the Diff5 variable, (AN–WBN)–(AO–WBO), in Figure 10.15.) The test statistic for a two-tailed test of this difference is 0.401 and the corresponding p-value, 0.689, isn't even close to any of the traditional significance levels. Furthermore, a 99% confidence interval for the mean difference extends from a negative value, −0.336, to a positive value, 0.458.

These results are further confirmed by histograms of the difference variables such as those shown in Figures 10.16 and 10.17. (Box plots could be used, but we prefer histograms when the variables include only a few possible integer values.) The histogram of the Diff1 variable in Figure 10.16 shows many more negative differences than positive differences. This leads to the large negative test statistic and the all-negative confidence interval. In contrast, the histogram of the Diff5 variable in Figure 10.17 is almost perfectly symmetric around 0 and hence provides no evidence that the mean difference is nonzero.

This example illustrates once again how hypothesis tests and confidence intervals provide complementary information, although the confidence intervals are arguably more useful here. The hypothesis test for the first difference, for example, shows that the average rating for the new style is undoubtedly larger than for the current style. This is useful information, but it might be even more useful to know *how much* larger the average for the new style is. A confidence interval provides this information.

Figure 10.16   Histogram of the Diff1 Variable

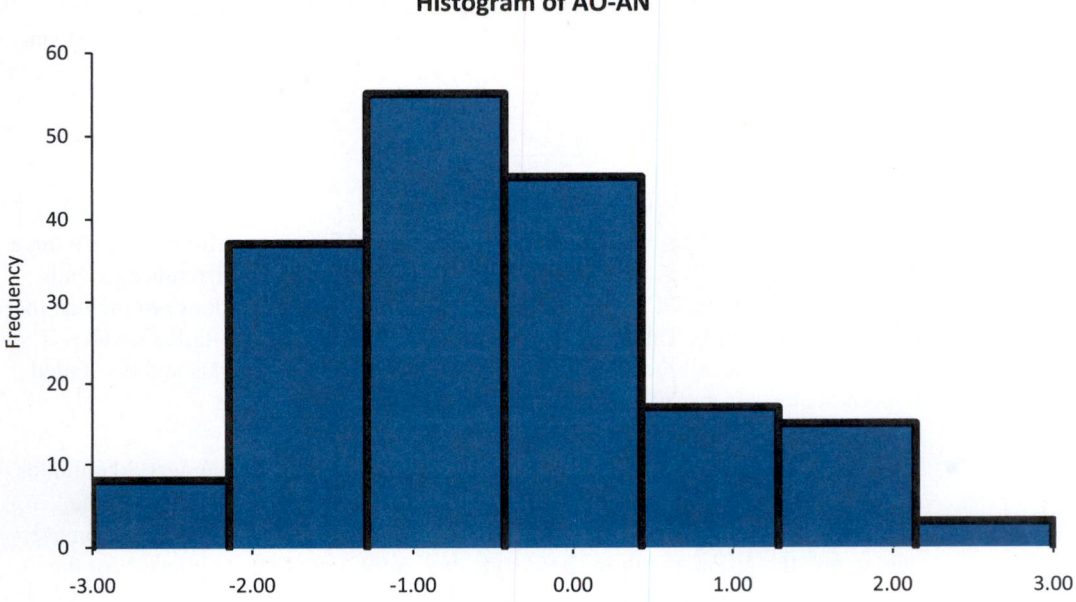

Histogram of AO-AN

Figure 10.17   Histogram of the Diff5 Variable

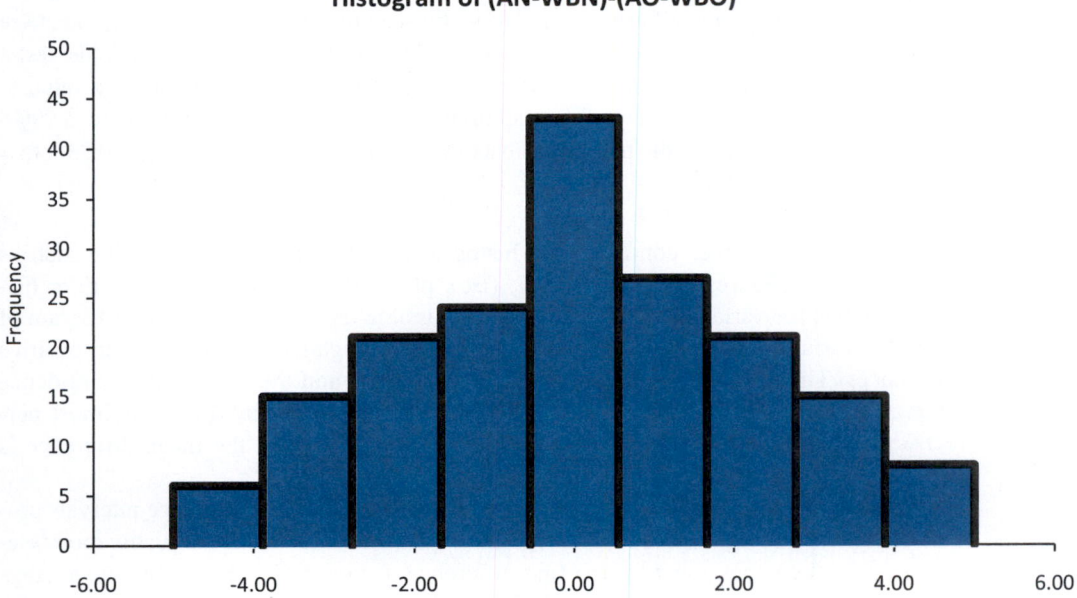

Histogram of (AN-WBN)-(AO-WBO)

We conclude this example by recalling the distinction between practical significance and statistical significance. Due to the extremely low p-values, the results in Figure 10.14, for example, leave no doubt as to statistical significance. But this could be due to the large sample size. That is, if the true mean differences are even slightly different from 0, large samples will almost surely discover this and report small p-values. The soft-drink company, on the other hand, is more interested in knowing whether the observed differences are of any practical importance. This is not a statistical question. It is a question of what differences are important for the *business*. We suspect that the company would indeed be quite impressed with the observed differences in the sample—and might very well switch to the new-style can. ■

The following example illustrates the independent two-sample t test. We can tell that a paired-sample procedure is not appropriate because there is no attempt to match the observations in the two samples in any way. Indeed, this would be impossible because the sample sizes are not equal.

<table>
<tr><td>EXAMPLE</td><td>10.5 PRODUCTIVITY DUE TO EXERCISE AT INFORMATRIX SOFTWARE COMPANY</td></tr>
</table>

Many companies are now installing exercise facilities at their plants. The goal is not only to provide a bonus (free use of exercise equipment) for their employees, but to make the employees more productive by getting them in better shape. One such company, the Informatrix Software Company, installed exercise equipment on site a year ago. To check whether it is having a beneficial effect on employee productivity, the company has gathered data on a sample of 80 randomly chosen employees, all between the ages of 30 and 40 and all with similar job titles and duties. The company observed which of these employees use the exercise facility regularly (at least three times per week on average). This group included 23 of the 80 employees in the sample. The other 57 employees were asked whether they exercise regularly elsewhere, and 6 of them replied that they do. The remaining 51, who admitted to being nonexercisers, were then compared to the combined group of 29 exercisers.

The comparison was based on the employees' productivity over the year, as rated by their supervisors. Each rating was on a scale of 1 to 25, 25 being the best. To increase the validity of the study, neither the employees nor the supervisors were told that a study was in progress. In particular, the supervisors did not know which employees were involved in the study or which were exercisers. The data from the study appear in Figure 10.18. (See the file **Exercise & Productivity.xlsx**.) Do these data support the company's (alternative) hypothesis that exercisers outperform nonexercisers on average? Can the company infer that any difference between the two groups is due to exercise?

Objective To use a two-sample t test for the difference between means to see whether regular exercise increases worker productivity.

Solution

Side-by-side box plots are typically a good way to begin the analysis when comparing two populations.

To see whether there is any indication of a difference between the two groups, we create side-by-side box plots of the Rating variable. These appear in Figure 10.19. Although there is a great deal of overlap between the two distributions, the distribution for the exercisers is somewhat to the right of that for the nonexercisers. Also, the variances of the two distributions appear to be roughly the same, although there is a bit more variation in the nonexerciser distribution.

Figure 10.18

Data for Study on
Effectiveness of
Exercise

	A	B	C
1	Employee	Exerciser	Rating
2	1	Yes	14
3	2	No	7
4	3	No	15
5	4	Yes	15
6	5	No	13
7	6	No	16
8	7	No	19
9	8	No	14
10	9	Yes	14
11	10	No	9
12	11	Yes	23
13	12	No	23
14	13	No	15
15	14	Yes	8
16	15	No	24
17	16	No	18
18	17	Yes	12
19	18	No	19
20	19	Yes	16
21	20	Yes	14

Figure 10.19

Box Plots for
Exercise Data

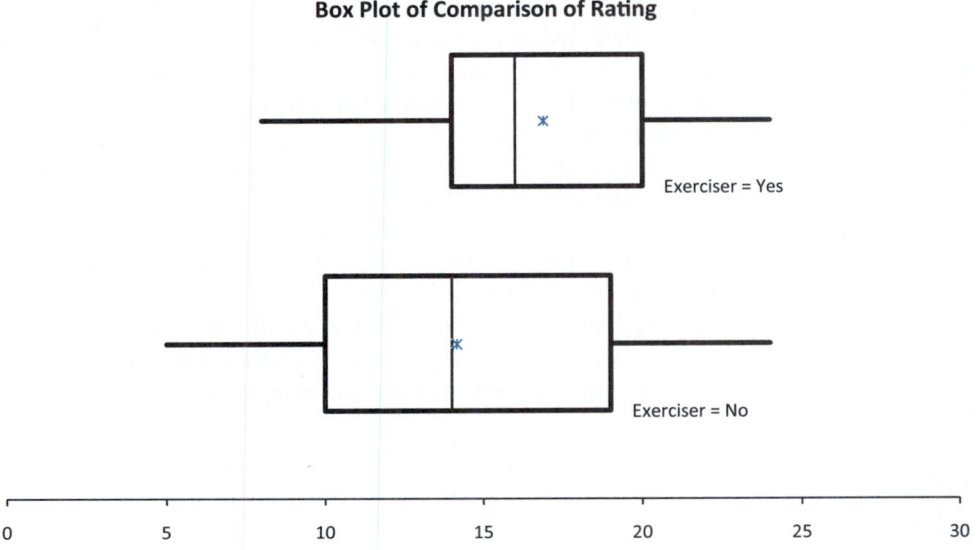

Box Plot of Comparison of Rating

Exerciser = Yes

Exerciser = No

A formal test on the mean difference uses the hypotheses $H_0: \mu_1 - \mu_2 \geq 0$ versus $H_a: \mu_1 - \mu_2 < 0$, where μ_1 and μ_2 are the mean ratings for the nonexerciser and exerciser populations. We use a one-tailed test, with the alternative of the "less than" variety, because the company expects higher ratings, on average, for the exercisers. The output for this test, along with a 95% confidence interval for $\mu_1 - \mu_2$, appears in Figure 10.20. We obtain the right part (the hypothesis test) by filling out the StatTools Hypothesis Test dialog box as shown in Figure 10.21. Specifically, select Two-Sample Analysis as the Analysis Type, click on the Format button and make sure the Stacked option is checked, select Exerciser as the "Cat" variable and Rating as the "Val" variable, and choose the "Less Than" Alternative Hypothesis Type.[5]

Figure 10.20

Analysis of Exercise Data

	A	B	C
7		Rating (No)	Rating (Yes)
8	Sample Summaries	Data Set #1	Data Set #1
9	Sample Size	51	29
10	Sample Mean	14.137	16.862
11	Sample Std Dev	5.307	4.103
12			
13		Equal	Unequal
14	Conf. Intervals (Difference of Means)	Variances	Variances
15	Confidence Level	95.0%	95.0%
16	Sample Mean Difference	-2.725	-2.725
17	Standard Error of Difference	1.142	1.064
18	Degrees of Freedom	78	71
19	Lower Limit	-4.998	-4.847
20	Upper Limit	-0.452	-0.603
32			
33		Equal	Unequal
34	Hypothesis Test (Difference of Means)	Variances	Variances
35	Hypothesized Mean Difference	0	0
36	Alternative Hypothesis	< 0	< 0
37	Sample Mean Difference	-2.725	-2.725
38	Standard Error of Difference	1.142	1.064
39	Degrees of Freedom	78	70
40	t-Test Statistic	-2.387	-2.560
41	p-Value	0.0097	0.0063
42	Null Hypoth. at 10% Significance	Reject	Reject
43	Null Hypoth. at 5% Significance	Reject	Reject
44	Null Hypoth. at 1% Significance	Reject	Reject
45			
46			
47	Equality of Variances Test		
48	Ratio of Sample Variances	1.6725	
49	p-Value	0.1454	

If we can assume that the population standard deviations are at least approximately equal (and the values in cells B11 and C11 suggest that this assumption is plausible), then the output in the range B37:B44 is relevant. It shows that the observed sample mean difference, -2.725, is indeed negative. That is, the exercisers in the sample outperformed the nonexercisers by 2.725 rating points on average. The output also shows that (1) the standard error of the sample mean difference is 1.142, (2) the test statistic is -2.387, and (3) the p-value for a one-tailed test is 0.010. In words, the data provide enough evidence to reject the null hypothesis at the 1% significance level (as well as at the 5% and 10% levels). It is clear that exercisers perform better, in terms of mean ratings, than nonexercisers. A 95% confidence for this mean difference is all negative; it extends from -4.998 to -0.452.

[5]The Stacked versus Unstacked issue is the same as we have seen before. The data in this file are stacked because there are two long columns that list a categorical variable, Exerciser, and a numeric variable, Rating.

Figure 10.21

Dialog Box for
Two-Sample
Analysis

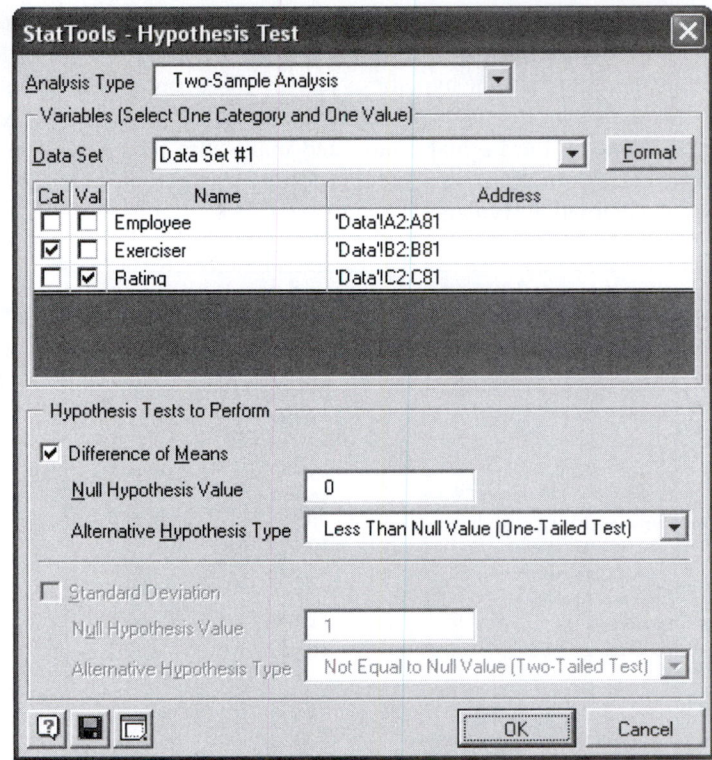

This answers the first question we posed, but it doesn't answer the second. There is no way to be sure that the higher ratings for the exercisers are a direct result of exercise. It could be that employees who exercise are naturally more ambitious and hard-working people, and that this extra drive is responsible for *both* their exercising and their higher ratings. This study is an **observational study** because the company simply observes two randomly selected groups of employees and analyzes the results. It does not explicitly control for other factors, such as personality, that might be responsible for differences in ratings. Therefore, it can never be sure that there is a cause–effect relationship between exercise and performance ratings. All it can state is that exercisers appear, on average, to be more productive than nonexercisers—for whatever reason.

We are almost finished with this example, but not quite. What about the output in column C, and the test in rows 48 and 49? The test we just performed and the confidence interval we reported are based on the assumption of equal population standard deviations (or variances). As we discuss in Section 9.7.1, if this assumption is violated, then a slightly different form of analysis should be performed, and its results are reported in column C. As we see, the results are very similar to those in column B, although the *p*-value is slightly lower and the confidence interval is slightly narrower.

The test reported in rows 48 and 49 is a formal test of the hypothesis $H_0: \sigma_1^2/\sigma_2^2 = 1$ versus $H_a: \sigma_1^2/\sigma_2^2 \neq 1$, where the parameter being tested is the *ratio* of the two population variances. (The details behind this test are explained in the following subsection.) If we can reject this null hypothesis on the basis of a low *p*-value in cell B49, then we are fairly certain that the equal-variance assumption is *not* valid and that we should use the output in column C. Otherwise, we can use the output in column B. The *p*-value in cell B49, 0.1454, suggests that the evidence *against* equal population variances is far from overwhelming. Of course, the similarity of the outputs in columns B and C implies, especially from a practical point of view, that it doesn't really make much difference. In other examples it could be more critical. ∎

10.4.3 Hypothesis Test for Equal Population Variances

As we just saw, the two-sample procedure for a difference between population means depends on whether we can assume equal population variances.[6] Therefore, it is natural to test first for equal variances. We phrase this latter test in terms of the *ratio* of population variances, σ_1^2/σ_2^2. The null hypothesis is that this ratio is 1 (equal variances), whereas the alternative is that it is not 1 (unequal variances). The test statistic for this test is the ratio of sample variances:

$$F\text{-value} = s_1^2/s_2^2$$

Assuming that the population variances are equal, this test statistic has an F distribution with $n_1 - 1$ and $n_2 - 1$ degrees of freedom.

The F distribution is a distribution of positive values and is always skewed to the right. It typically appears in tests of equal variances.

The F distribution, named after the famous statistician R. A. Fisher, is another sampling distribution that arises frequently in statistical studies. (We see it again when we study regression analysis in Chapters 11 and 12.) Because it always describes a ratio, there are two degrees of freedom parameters, one for the numerator and one for the denominator, and the numerator degrees of freedom is always quoted first.

Tables of the F distribution, for selected degrees of freedom, appear in many statistics books, but the necessary information can be obtained more easily with Excel's FDIST and FINV functions. The FDIST function takes the form

=**FDIST**(*v*,*df*1,*df*2)

This function returns the probability to the right of value v when the degrees of freedom are *df*1 and *df*2. Similarly, the FINV function takes the form

=**FINV**(*p*,*df*1,*df*2)

It returns the value with probability p to the right of it when the degrees of freedom are *df*1 and *df*2.

When StatTools tests for equal variances, it first calculates the ratio of variances. (See cell B48 in Figure 10.20.) It then implements the F test to calculate the corresponding p-value (in cell B49). For our purposes, the most important thing is the conclusion we draw from the test. If the p-value is small, we can conclude that the population variances are *not* equal. Otherwise, we can accept an equal-variance assumption. The p-value for the exercise data, 0.1454, provides *some* evidence of unequal variances, but the evidence is certainly not overwhelming.

10.4.4 Hypothesis Tests for Differences Between Population Proportions

One of the most common uses of hypothesis testing is to test whether two population proportions are equal. Let p_1 and p_2 be the two population proportions, and let $\hat{p}_1$ and $\hat{p}_2$ be the corresponding sample proportions, based on sample sizes n_1 and n_2. The goal is to test

---

[6]The test in this section is traditionally stated in terms of variances, as we do here. It could also be stated in terms of standard deviations because equal variances imply equal standard deviations.

whether the sample proportions differ enough to conclude that the *population* proportions are not equal. To base a test on the difference $\hat{p}_1 - \hat{p}_2$, we need its standard error. If the null hypothesis is true and $p_1 = p_2$, then it can be shown that the standard error of $\hat{p}_1 - \hat{p}_2$ is given by equation (10.5), where $\hat{p}_c$ is the pooled proportion from the two samples combined. For example, if $\hat{p}_1 = 20/85$ and $\hat{p}_2 = 34/115$, then $\hat{p}_c = (20 + 34)/(85 + 115) = 54/200$. (The reason we use this pooled estimate is that if the null hypothesis is true and the two population proportions are equal, then it makes sense to base an estimate of this common proportion on the *combined* sample of data.)

Standard Error for Difference Between Sample Proportions

$$\text{SE}(\hat{p}_1 - \hat{p}_2) = \sqrt{\hat{p}_c(1 - \hat{p}_c)(1/n_1 + 1/n_2)} \qquad \text{(10.5)}$$

Given this standard error, the rest is straightforward. Assuming that the sample sizes are reasonably large, the test statistic in equation (10.6) has (approximately) a standard normal distribution. Therefore, the corresponding *p*-value for the test can be found with Excel's NORMSDIST function, as illustrated in the next example.

Test Statistic for Difference Between Proportions

$$z\text{-value} = \frac{\hat{p}_1 - \hat{p}_2}{\text{SE}(\hat{p}_1 - \hat{p}_2)} \qquad \text{(10.6)}$$

EXAMPLE | **10.6 EMPLOYEE EMPOWERMENT AT ARMCO COMPANY**

The ArmCo Company, a large manufacturer of automobile parts, has several plants in the United States. For years, ArmCo employees have complained that their suggestions for improvements in the manufacturing processes are ignored by upper management. In the spirit of employee empowerment, ArmCo management at the Midwest plant decided to initiate a number of policies to respond to employee suggestions. For example, a mailbox was placed in a central location, and employees were encouraged to drop suggestions into this box. No such initiatives were taken at the other ArmCo plants. As expected, there was a great deal of employee enthusiasm at the Midwest plant shortly after the new policies were implemented, but the question was whether life would revert to normal and the enthusiasm would dampen with time.

To check this, 100 randomly selected employees at the Midwest plant and 300 employees from other plants were asked to fill out a questionnaire 6 months after the implementation of the new policies at the Midwest plant. Employees were instructed to respond to each item on the questionnaire by checking either a "yes" box or a "no" box. Two specific items on the questionnaire were the following:

- Management at this plant is generally responsive to employee suggestions for improvements in the manufacturing processes.

- Management at this plant is more responsive to employee suggestions now than it used to be.

The results of the questionnaire for these two items appear in rows 5 and 6 of Figure 10.22. (See the file **Empowerment 1.xlsx**.) Does it appear that the policies at the Midwest plant are appreciated? Should ArmCo implement these policies in its other plants?

Figure 10.22

Results for Employee Empowerment Example

	A	B	C	D	E	F	G
1	Employee empowerment results						
2							
3	Item 1: Management responds				Item 2: Things have improved		
4		Midwest	Other			Midwest	Other
5	Yes	39	93		Yes	68	159
6	No	61	207		No	32	141
7	Totals	100	300		Totals	100	300
8							
9	Sample proportion yes	0.39	0.31		Sample proportion yes	0.68	0.53
10	Pooled proportion yes	0.33			Pooled proportion yes	0.5675	
11							
12	Difference between proportions	0.08			Difference between proportions	0.15	
13	Standard error of difference	0.054			Standard error of difference	0.057	
14	Test statistic	1.473			Test statistic	2.622	
15	p-value	0.070			p-value	0.004	
16							
17	Confidence interval for difference				Confidence interval for difference		
18	Confidence level	95%			Confidence level	95%	
19	Standard error of difference	0.056			Standard error of difference	0.055	
20	z-multiple	1.960			z-multiple	1.960	
21	Lower confidence limit	-0.029			Lower confidence limit	0.043	
22	Upper confidence limit	0.189			Upper confidence limit	0.257	

Objective To use a test for the difference between proportions to see whether a program of accepting employee suggestions is appreciated by employees.

Solution

For either questionnaire item we let p_1 be the proportion of "yes" responses we would obtain at the Midwest plant if the questionnaire were given to all of its employees. We define p_2 similarly for the other plants. Management certainly hopes to find a larger proportion of "yes" responses (to either item) at the Midwest plant than at the other plants, so the appropriate test is one-tailed, with the hypotheses set up as $H_0: p_1 - p_2 \leq 0$ versus $H_a: p_1 - p_2 > 0$. (We could also write these as $H_0: p_1 \leq p_2$ versus $H_a: p_1 > p_2$, but this has no effect on the test.)

The data from this type of questionnaire are usually given as *counts* of "yes" and "no" responses, as in Figure 10.22, but these easily translate into sample proportions. (As we stated in Example 10.3, StatTools has no procedure for testing differences between proportions, but the finished file for this example can be used as a template for any such test.) For the first questionnaire item (see columns B and C), the sample proportions of "yes" responses are $\hat{p}_1 = 39/100 = 0.39$ and $\hat{p}_2 = 93/300 = 0.31$, for a difference of $\hat{p}_1 - \hat{p}_2 = 0.08$. The standard error of this difference, under the assumption that $p_1 = p_2$, uses the pooled proportion $\hat{p}_c = (39 + 93)/(100 + 300) = 0.33$. This produces a standard error of 0.054, calculated in cell B13 with the formula

=SQRT(B10*(1-B10)*(1/B7+1/C7))

Then the test statistic is $0.08/0.054 = 1.473$, and the corresponding *p*-value for the test is the probability to the right of 1.473 in the standard normal distribution. Its value is 0.070, found in cell B15 with the formula

=1-NORMSDIST(B14)

A similar analysis for the second questionnaire item (see columns F and G) leads to a sample difference of $0.68 - 0.53 = 0.15$ and a *p*-value of 0.004.

These results should be fairly good news for management. There is moderate, but not overwhelming, support for the hypothesis that management at the Midwest plant is more responsive than at the other plants, at least as perceived by employees. There is convincing support for the hypothesis that things have improved more at the Midwest plant than at the other plants. Corresponding 95% confidence intervals for the differences between proportions appear in rows 21 and 22. Because they are almost completely positive, they reinforce the hypothesis-test findings. Moreover, they provide a range of plausible values for the differences between the population proportions.

The only real downside to these findings, from Midwest management's point of view, is the sample proportion $\hat{p}_1$ for the first item. Only 39% of the sampled employees at that plant believe that management generally responds to their suggestions, even though 68% believe things are better than they used to be. A reasonable conclusion by ArmCo management is that they are on the right track at the Midwest plant, and the policies initiated there ought to be initiated at other plants, but more must be done at *all* plants. ∎

PROBLEMS

Level A

9. In the past, 60% of all undergraduate students enrolled at State University earned their degrees within 4 years of matriculation. A random sample of 36 students from the class that matriculated in the fall of 1998 was recently selected to test whether there has been a change in the proportion of students who graduate within 4 years. Administrators found that 15 of these 36 students graduated in the spring of 2002 (i.e., 4 academic years after matriculation).
   a. Given the sample outcome, construct a 95% confidence interval for the relevant population proportion. Does this interval estimate suggest that there has been in a change in the proportion of students who graduate within 4 years? Why or why not?
   b. Given the sample outcome, construct a 99% confidence interval for the relevant population proportion. Does this interval estimate suggest that there has been in a change in the proportion of students who graduate within 4 years? Why or why not?

10. Continuing the previous problem, suppose now that State University administrators want to test the claim made by faculty that the proportion of students who graduate within 4 years at State University has fallen *below* the historical value of 60% this year. Use the given sample proportion to test this claim. Report a *p*-value and interpret it in the context of this statistical hypothesis test.

11. The director of admissions of a distinguished (i.e., top-20) MBA program is interested in studying the proportion of entering students in similar graduate business programs who have achieved a composite score on the Graduate Management Admissions Test (GMAT) in excess of 630. In particular, the admissions director believes that the proportion of students entering top-rated programs with such composite GMAT scores is now 50%. To test this hypothesis, he has collected a random sample of MBA candidates entering his program in the fall of 2004. He believes that these students' GMAT scores are indicative of the scores earned by their peers in his program and in competitors' programs. The GMAT scores for these 25 individuals are given in the file **P10_11.xlsx**. Test the admission director's claim at the 5% significance level and report your findings. Does your conclusion change when the significance level is increased to 10%?

12. A market research consultant hired by the Pepsi-Cola Co. is interested in determining the proportion of consumers who favor Pepsi-Cola over Coke Classic in a particular urban location. A random sample of 250 consumers from the market under investigation is provided in the file **P09_17.xlsx**.
   a. Construct a 99% confidence interval for the proportion of all consumers in this market who prefer Pepsi over Coke. Interpret this confidence interval for Pepsi's market researchers.
   b. Does the confidence interval in part **a** support the claim made by one of Pepsi-Cola's marketing managers that more than half of the consumers in this urban location favor Pepsi over Coke? Explain your answer.
   c. Comment on the sample size used by the market research consultant. Specifically, is the sample unnecessarily large? Why or why not?

13. The CEO of a medical supply company is committed to expanding the proportion of highly qualified women in the organization's staff of salespersons. He claims that the proportion of women in similar sales positions across the country in 2002 is less than 50%. Hoping to find support for his claim, he directs his assistant to collect a random sample of salespersons employed by his company, which is thought to be representative of sales staffs of competing organizations in the industry. These data are listed in the file **P10_13.xlsx**. Test this manager's claim using the given sample data and report a p-value. Do you find statistical support for his hypothesis that the proportion of women in similar sales positions across the country is less than 50%?

14. Management of a software development firm would like to establish a wellness program during the lunch hour to enhance the physical and mental health of its employees. Before introducing the wellness program, management must first be convinced that a sufficiently large majority of its employees are not already exercising at lunchtime. Specifically, it plans to initiate the program only if less than 40% of its personnel take time to exercise prior to eating lunch. To make this decision, management has surveyed a random sample of 100 employees regarding their midday exercise activities. The results of the survey are given in the file **P10_14.xlsx**.
    a. Using a 10% significance level, is there sufficient evidence for managers of this organization to initiate a corporate wellness program? Why or why not?
    b. Using a 1% significance level, is there sufficient evidence for managers of this organization to initiate a corporate wellness program? Why or why not?

15. The managing partner of a major consulting firm is trying to assess the effectiveness of expensive computer skills training given to all new entry-level professionals. In an effort to make such an assessment, she administers a computer skills test immediately before and after the training program to each of 40 randomly chosen employees. The pretraining and posttraining scores of these 40 individuals are recorded in the file **P10_15.xlsx**.
    a. Using a 10% level of significance, do the given sample data support the claim that the organization's training program is increasing the new employee's working knowledge of computing?
    b. Using a 1% level of significance, do the given sample data support the claim that the organization's training program is increasing the new employee's working knowledge of computing?

16. A large buyer of household batteries wants to decide which of two equally priced brands to purchase. To do this, he takes a random sample of 100 batteries of each brand. The lifetimes, measured in hours, of the randomly chosen batteries are recorded in the file **P10_16.xlsx**.
    a. Using the given sample data, generate a 95% confidence interval for the difference between the mean lifetimes of brand 1 and brand 2 batteries. Based on this confidence interval, which brand should the buyer purchase?

    b. Using the given sample data, generate a 99% confidence interval for the difference in the mean lifetimes of brand 1 and brand 2 batteries. Based on this confidence interval, which brand should the buyer purchase?
    c. How can your analyses in parts **a** and **b** be related to hypothesis testing?

17. The managers of a chemical manufacturing plant are interested in determining whether recent safety training workshops have reduced the weekly number of reported safety violations at the facility. The management team has randomly selected weekly safety violation reports for each of 25 weeks prior to the safety training and 25 weeks after the safety workshops. These data are provided in the file **P10_17.xlsx**. Given this evidence, is it possible to conclude that the safety workshops have been effective in reducing the number of safety violations reported per week? Report a p-value and interpret your findings for the management team.

18. A real estate agent has collected a random sample of 75 houses that were recently sold in a suburban community. She is particularly interested in comparing the appraised value and recent selling price of the houses in this particular market. The values of these two variables for each of the 75 randomly chosen houses are provided in the file **P09_24.xlsx**. Using these sample data, test whether there exists a statistically significant mean difference between the appraised values and selling prices of the houses sold in this suburban community. Report a p-value. For which levels of significance is it appropriate to conclude that *no* difference exists between these two values?

19. The owner of two submarine sandwich shops located in Gainesville, Florida, would like to know how the mean daily sales of the first shop (located in the downtown area) compares to that of the second shop (located on the southwest side of town). In particular, he would like to know whether the mean daily sales levels of these two restaurants are essentially equal. He records the sales (in dollars) made at each location for 30 randomly chosen days. These sales levels are given in the file **P10_19.xlsx**. Construct a 99% confidence level for the mean difference between the daily sales of restaurant 1 and restaurant 2. Use this confidence interval to answer the following questions:
    a. Is it possible to conclude that a statistically significant mean difference exists at the 1% level of significance? Explain why or why not.
    b. Is it possible to conclude that a statistically significant mean difference exists at the 5% level of significance? Explain why or why not.
    c. Is it possible to conclude that a statistically significant mean difference exists at the 10% level of significance? Explain why or why not.

20. Suppose that an investor wants to compare the risks associated with two different stocks. One way to measure the risk of a given stock is to measure the variation in the stock's daily price changes. The investor obtains a random sample of 25 daily price changes for stock 1 and 25 daily price changes for stock 2. These data are provided in the file **P10_20.xlsx**. Show how this investor can compare the risks associated with the two stocks by testing the null hypothesis that the variances of the stocks are equal. Use $\alpha = 0.10$ and interpret the results of the statistical test.

21. A manufacturing company is interested in determining whether a significant difference exists between the variance of the number of units produced per day by one machine operator and the similar variance for another machine operator. The file **P10_21.xlsx** contains the number of units produced by operator 1 and operator 2, respectively, on each of 25 days. Note that these two sets of days are not necessarily the same, so you can assume that the two samples are *independent* of one another.
   a. Do these sample data indicate a statistically significant difference at $\alpha = 0.10$? Explain your answer.
   b. If your conclusion in part **a** were incorrect, would you have committed a type I or type II error? Explain.
   c. At which values of α could you *not* reject the null hypothesis?

22. A large buyer of household batteries wants to decide which of two equally priced brands to purchase. To do this, he takes a random sample of 100 batteries of each brand. The lifetimes, measured in hours, of the batteries are recorded in the file **P10_16.xlsx**. Before testing for the difference between the mean lifetimes of these two batteries, he must first determine whether the underlying population variances are equal.
   a. Perform a test for equal population variances. Report a p-value and interpret its meaning.
   b. Based on your conclusion in part **a,** which test statistic should be used in performing a test for the existence of a difference between population means?

23. Do undergraduate business students who major in finance earn, on average, higher annual starting salaries than their peers who major in marketing? Before addressing this question through a statistical hypothesis test, we should determine whether the variances of annual starting salaries of the two types of majors are equal. The file **P10_23.xlsx** contains the starting salaries of 50 randomly selected finance majors and 50 randomly chosen marketing majors.
   a. Perform a test for equal population variances. Report a p-value and interpret its meaning.
   b. Based on your conclusion in part **a,** which test statistic should be used in performing a test for the existence of a difference between population means?

24. The CEO of a medical supply company is committed to expanding the proportion of highly qualified women in the organization's large staff of salespersons. Given the recent hiring practices of his human resources director, he claims that the company has increased the proportion of women in sales positions throughout the organization between 2000 and 2005. Hoping to find support for his claim, he directs his assistant to collect random samples of the salespersons employed by the company in 2000 and 2005. These data can be found in the file **P10_13.xlsx**. Test the CEO's claim using the given sample data and report a p-value. Do you find statistical support for the efficacy of his committed strategy to hiring a greater proportion of female salespersons?

25. The director of admissions of a distinguished (i.e., top-20) MBA program is interested in studying the proportion of entering students in similar graduate business programs who have achieved a composite score on the Graduate Management Admissions Test (GMAT) in excess of 630. In particular, the admissions director believes that the proportion of students entering top-rated programs with such composite GMAT scores is higher in 2004 than it was in 1994. To test this hypothesis, he has collected random samples of MBA candidates entering his program in the fall of 2004 and in the fall of 1994. He believes that these students' GMAT scores are indicative of the scores earned by their peers in his program and in competitors' programs. The GMAT scores for the randomly selected students entering in each year are given in the file **P10_11.xlsx**. Test the admission director's claim at the 5% significance level and report your findings. Does your conclusion change when the significance level is increased to 10%?

26. Managers of a software development firm have established a wellness program during the lunch hour to enhance the physical and mental health of their employees. Now, they would like to see whether the wellness program has increased the proportion of employees who exercise regularly during the lunch hour. To make this assessment, the managers surveyed a random sample of 100 employees about their noontime exercise habits *before* the wellness program was initiated. Later, *after* the program was initiated, another 100 employees were independently chosen and surveyed about their lunchtime exercise habits. The results of these two surveys are given in the file **P10_14.xlsx**.
   a. Construct a 99% confidence interval for the difference in the proportions of employees who exercise regularly during their lunch hour before and after the implementation of the corporate wellness program.
   b. Does the confidence interval found in part **a** support the belief that the wellness program has increased the proportion of employees who exercise regularly

during the lunch hour? If so, at which levels of significance is this claim supported?

c. Would your results in parts **a** and **b** differ if the *same* 100 employees surveyed before the program were also surveyed after the program? Explain.

Level B

27. An Environmental Protection Agency official asserts that more than 80% of the plants in the northeast region of the United States meet air pollution standards. An antipollution advocate does not believe the EPA's claim. She takes a random sample of 64 plants in the northeast region and finds that 56 meet the federal government's pollution standards.

a. Does the sample information support the EPA's claim at the 5% level of significance?

b. For which values of the sample proportion (based on a sample size of 64) would the sample data support the EPA's claim? Assume that $\alpha = 0.05$.

c. Would the conclusion found in part **a** change if the sample proportion remained constant but the sample size increased to 124? Explain why or why not.

28. A television network decides to cancel one of its shows if it is convinced that less than 14% of the viewing public are watching this show.

a. If a random sample of 1500 households with televisions is selected, what sample proportion values will lead to this show's cancellation? Assume a 5% significance level.

b. What is the probability that this show will be canceled if 13.4% of all viewing households are watching it?

29. An economic researcher would like to know whether he can reject the null hypothesis, at the $\alpha = 0.10$ level, that no more than 20% of the households in Pennsylvania make more than $70,000 per year.

a. If 200 Pennsylvania households are chosen at random, how many of them would have to be earning more than $70,000 per year for the researcher to reject the null hypothesis?

b. Assuming that the true proportion of all Pennsylvania households with annual incomes of at least $70,000 is 0.217, find the probability of *not* rejecting a *false* null hypothesis when the sample size is 200.

30. Senior partners of an accounting firm are concerned about recent complaints by some female managers that they are paid less than their male counterparts. In response to these charges, the partners ask their human resources director to record the salaries of female and male managers with equivalent education, work experience, and job performance. A random sample of these pairs of managers is provided in the file **P10_30.xlsx**.

a. Do these data support the claim made by some female managers within this organization? Report and interpret a *p*-value.

b. Assuming a 5% significance level, which values of the sample mean difference between the female and male salaries would support the claim of discrimination against female managers?

31. Do undergraduate business students who major in finance earn, on average, higher annual starting salaries than their peers who major in marketing? Address this question through a statistical hypothesis test. The file **P10_23.xlsx** contains the starting salaries of 50 randomly selected finance majors and 50 randomly selected marketing majors.

a. Is it appropriate to perform a paired-comparison *t* test in this case? Explain why or why not.

b. Perform an appropriate hypothesis test with a 1% significance level. Summarize your findings.

c. How large would the difference between the mean starting salaries of finance and marketing majors have to be before you could conclude that finance majors earn more on average? Employ a 1% significance level in answering this question.

32. Consider a random sample of 100 households from a middle-class neighborhood that was the recent focus of an economic development study conducted by the local government. Specifically, for each of the 100 households, information was gathered on each of the following variables: family size, location of the household within the neighborhood, an indication of whether those surveyed owned or rented their home, gross annual income of the first household wage earner, gross annual income of the second household wage earner (if applicable), monthly home mortgage or rent payment, average monthly expenditure on utilities, and the total indebtedness (excluding the value of a home mortgage) of the household. The data are in the file **P09_26.xlsx**.

Test for the existence of a significant difference between the mean indebtedness levels of the households in the first (i.e., SW) and second (i.e., NW) sectors of this community. Perform similar hypothesis tests for the differences between the mean indebtedness levels of households from all other pairs of locations (i.e., first and third, first and fourth, second and third, second and fourth, and third and fourth). Summarize your findings.

33. Elected officials in a small Florida town are preparing the annual budget for their community. They would like to determine whether their constituents living across town are typically paying the same amount in real estate taxes each year. Given that there are over 3000 homeowners in this small community, officials have decided to sample a representative subset of taxpayers and thoroughly study their tax payments.

A randomly selected set of 170 homeowners is given in the file **P10_33.xlsx**. Specifically, the elected officials would like to test for the existence of a statistical difference between the mean real estate tax bill paid by residents of the *first* neighborhood of this town and each of the remaining five neighborhoods (i.e., neighborhoods 2–6).

a. Before conducting any hypothesis tests on the difference between various pairs of mean real estate tax payments, perform a test for equal population variances for each pair of neighborhoods. For each pair, report a *p*-value and interpret its meaning.

b. Based on your conclusions in part **a,** which test statistic should be used in performing a test for the existence of a difference between population means in each pair?

c. Given your conclusions in part **b,** appropriately perform each of the tests for the existence of a difference between mean real estate tax payments in each pair of neighborhoods. For each pair, report a *p*-value and interpret its meaning.

34. Suppose that you sample two normal populations independently. The variances of these two populations are σ_1^2 and σ_2^2. You take random samples of sizes n_1 and n_2 and observe sample variances of s_1^2 and s_2^2.

a. If $n_1 = n_2 = 21$, how large must the fraction s_1/s_2 be before you can reject the null hypothesis that σ_1^2 is no greater than σ_2^2 at the 5% significance level?

b. Answer part **a** when $n_1 = n_2 = 41$.

c. If s_1 is 25% greater than s_2, approximately how large must n_1 and n_2 be if you are able to reject the null hypothesis in part **a** at the 5% significance level? Assume that n_1 and n_2 are equal.

35. Two teams of workers assemble automobile engines at a manufacturing plant in Michigan. Quality control personnel inspect a random sample of the teams' assemblies and judge each assembly to be acceptable or unacceptable. A random sample of 127 assemblies from team 1 shows 12 unacceptable assemblies. A similar random sample of 98 assemblies from team 2 shows 5 unacceptable assemblies.

a. Construct a 90% confidence interval for the difference between the proportions of unacceptable assemblies generated by the two teams.

b. Based on a review of the confidence interval found in part **a,** is there sufficient evidence to conclude, at the 10% significance level, that the two teams differ with respect to their proportions of unacceptable assemblies?

c. For which values of the difference between these two sample proportions could you conclude that a statistically significant difference exists? Assume that $\alpha = 0.10$.

36. A market research consultant hired by the Pepsi-Cola Co. is interested in determining whether there is a difference between the proportions of female and male consumers who favor Pepsi-Cola over Coke Classic in a particular urban location. A random sample of 250 consumers from the market under investigation is provided in the file **P09_17.xlsx**.

a. After separating the 250 randomly selected consumers by *gender,* perform the statistical test and report a *p*-value. At which levels of α will the market research consultant conclude that there is essentially no difference between the proportions of female and male consumers who prefer Pepsi to Coke in this urban area?

b. Marketing managers at the Pepsi-Cola Co. have asked their market research consultant to explore further the potential differences in the proportions of women and men who prefer drinking Pepsi to Coke Classic. Specifically, Pepsi managers would like to know whether the potential difference between the proportions of female and male consumers who favor Pepsi varies by the *age* of the consumers. Using the same random sample of consumers as in part **a,** assess whether this difference varies across the four given age categories: under 20, between 20 and 40, between 40 and 60, and over 60. Employ a 10% significance level in performing each of the *six* required hypothesis tests. Summarize your conclusions in detail. Finally, what recommendations would you make to the marketing managers in light of your statistical findings?

37. The employee benefits manager of a small private university would like to determine whether differences exist in the proportions of various groups of full-time employees who prefer adopting the second (i.e., plan B) of three available health care plans in the forthcoming annual enrollment period. A reliable frame of the university's employees and their tentative health care preferences are given in the file **P08_25.xlsx**.

a. First, select a simple random sample of 25 employees from *each* of three employee classifications: administrative staff, support staff, and faculty.

b. Use the three simple random samples obtained in part **a** to perform tests for differences in the proportions of employees within respective classifications who favor plan B in the coming year. For instance, the first such test should examine the potential difference between the proportion of administrative employees who favor plan B and the proportion of the support staff who prefer plan B.

c. Report a *p*-value for each of your hypothesis tests and interpret your results. How might the benefits manager use the information you have derived from these statistical tests?

38. Consider a random sample of 100 households from a middle-class neighborhood that was the recent focus of an economic development study conducted by the local

government. Specifically, for each of the 100 randomly selected households, information was gathered on each of the following variables: family size, location of the household within the neighborhood, an indication of whether those surveyed owned or rented their home, gross annual income of the first household wage earner, gross annual income of the second household wage earner (if applicable), monthly home mortgage or rent payment, average monthly expenditure on utilities, and the total indebtedness (excluding the value of a home mortgage) of the household. The data are provided in the file **P09_26.xlsx**.

Researchers would like to use the available sample information to discern whether home ownership rates vary by household *location*. For example, is there a nonzero difference between the proportions of individuals who own their homes (as opposed to those who rent their homes) in households located in the first (i.e., SW) and second (i.e., NW) sectors of this community? Use the given sample to perform a test for the existence of a difference in home ownership rates in these two sectors as well as for those of other pairs of household locations. Assume that $\alpha = 0.05$. Interpret and summarize your results. (*Hint:* To be complete, you should construct and interpret a total of six hypothesis tests.)

39. For testing the difference between two proportions, we use $\sqrt{\hat{p}_c(1 - \hat{p}_c)(1/n_1 + 1/n_2)}$ as the approximate standard error of $\hat{p}_1 - \hat{p}_2$, where $\hat{p}_c$ is the pooled sample proportion. Explain why this is reasonable when the null-hypothesized value of $p_1 - p_2$ is zero. Why would this not be a good approximation when the null-hypothesized value of $p_1 - p_2$ is a nonzero number? What would you recommend using for the standard error of $\hat{p}_1 - \hat{p}_2$ in that case?

10.5 TESTS FOR NORMALITY

In this section we discuss several tests for normality. As we have already seen, many statistical procedures are based on the assumption that population data are normally distributed. The tests in this section allow us to test this assumption. The null hypothesis is that the population is normally distributed, whereas the alternative is that the population distribution is not normal. Therefore, the burden of proof is on showing that the population distribution is *not* normal. Unless there is sufficient evidence to this effect, we will accept the normal assumption.

The first test we discuss is called a *chi-square goodness-of-fit* test. It is quite intuitive. We form a histogram of the sample data and compare this to the *expected* bell-shaped histogram we would observe if the data were normally distributed with the same mean and standard deviation as the sample. If the two histograms are sufficiently similar, we accept the null hypothesis of normality. Otherwise, we reject it.

The chi-square test for normality makes a comparison between the observed histogram and a histogram based on normality.

The test is based on a numerical measure of the difference between the two histograms. Let C be the number of categories in the histogram, and let O_i be the observed number of observations in category i. Also, let E_i be the expected number of observations in category i if the population were normal with the same mean and standard deviation as the sample. Then we use the goodness-of-fit measure in equation (10.7) as a test statistic. If the null hypothesis of normality is true, this test statistic has (approximately) a chi-square distribution with $C - 3$ degrees of freedom. Because *large* values of the test statistic indicate a poor fit—the O_i's do not match up well with the E_i's—the p-value for the test is the probability to the right of the test statistic in the chi-square distribution with $C - 3$ degrees of freedom.

Test Statistic for Chi-Square Test of Normality

$$\chi^2\text{-value} = \sum_{i=1}^{C} (O_i - E_i)^2 / E_i \qquad (10.7)$$

(Here, χ is the Greek letter chi.)

Although it is possible to perform this test manually, it is certainly preferable to use StatTools, as we demonstrate in the following example.

10.7 DISTRIBUTION OF METAL STRIP WIDTHS IN MANUFACTURING

A company manufactures strips of metal that are supposed to have width 10 centimeters. For purposes of quality control, the manager plans to run some statistical tests on these strips. However, realizing that these statistical procedures assume normally distributed widths, he first tests this normality assumption on 90 randomly sampled strips. How should he proceed?

Objective To use the chi-square goodness-of-fit test to see whether the metal strip widths are normally distributed.

Solution

The sample data appear in Figure 10.23, where each width is measured to three decimal places. (See the file **Testing Normality.xlsx**.) A number of summary measures also appear.

Figure 10.23

Data for Testing Normality

	A	B	C	D	E
1	Part	Width			Width
2	1	9.990		One Variable Summary	Data Set #1
3	2	10.031		Mean	9.999
4	3	9.985		Std. Dev.	0.010
5	4	9.983		Median	9.998
6	5	10.004		Minimum	9.970
7	6	10.000		Maximum	10.031
8	7	9.992		Count	90
9	8	9.996		1st Quartile	9.993
10	9	9.997		3rd Quartile	10.006
11	10	9.993		5.00%	9.983
12	11	9.991		95.00%	10.014
13	12	9.991			
14	13	10.006			
15	14	9.998			
16	15	9.995			
17	16	9.989			
18	17	9.987			

To run the test, we select Chi-square Test from the StatTools Normality Tests drop-down, which leads to basically the same dialog box as in StatTools's Histogram procedure. As with the Histogram procedure, you can specify your own bins, or you can accept StatTools's default bins. We do the latter.[7] The resulting histograms in Figure 10.24 provide visual evidence of the goodness of fit. The left bars represent the observed frequencies (the O_i's), and the right bars represent the expected frequencies for a normal distribution (the E_i's). The normal fit to the data appears to be quite good.

The output in Figure 10.25 confirms this statistically. Each value in column E is an E_i, calculated as the total number of observations multiplied by the normal probability of being in the corresponding category. Column F contains the individual $(O_i - E_i)^2/E_i$ terms, and cell B11 contains their sum, the chi-square test statistic. The corresponding p-value in cell B12, is 0.5206.

[7]You might try defining the bins differently and rerunning the test. The category definitions *can* make a difference in the results.

Figure 10.24 Observed and Normal Histograms

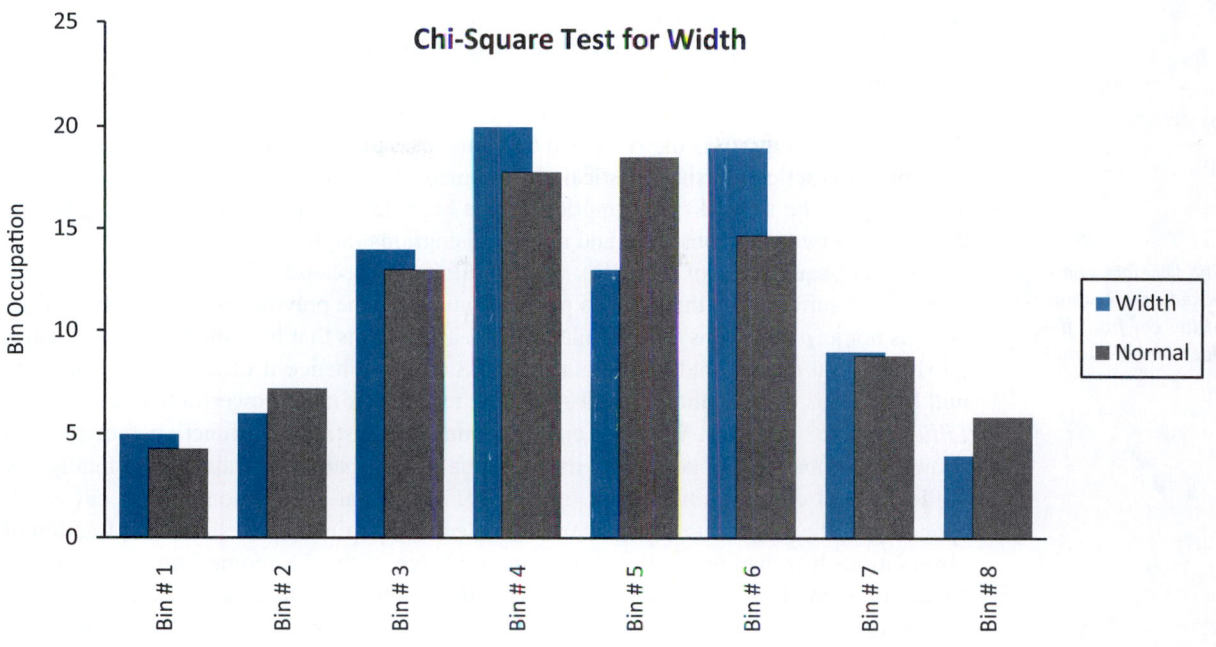

Chi-Square Test for Width

Figure 10.25 Chi-square Test of Normality

	A	B	C	D	E	F
7		Width				
8	*Chi-Square Test*	Data Set #1				
9	Mean	9.999256				
10	Std Dev	0.009728				
11	Chi-Square Stat.	4.2027				
12	P-Value	0.5206				
13						
14						
15	*Chi-Squared Bins*	BinMin	BinMax	Actual	Normal	Distance
16	Bin # 1	-Inf	9.983000	5	4.2630	0.1274
17	Bin # 2	9.983000	9.988167	6	7.1827	0.1948
18	Bin # 3	9.988167	9.993333	14	12.9751	0.0810
19	Bin # 4	9.993333	9.998500	20	17.7934	0.2736
20	Bin # 5	9.998500	10.003667	13	18.5249	1.6477
21	Bin # 6	10.003667	10.008833	19	14.6421	1.2970
22	Bin # 7	10.008833	10.014000	9	8.7859	0.0052
23	Bin # 8	10.014000	+Inf	4	5.8328	0.5759

This large *p*-value provides no evidence whatsoever of nonnormality. It implies that if we repeated this procedure on many random samples, each taken from a population known to be normal, we would obtain a fit at least this poor in over 50% of the samples. Stated differently, only fewer than 50% of the fits would be *better* than the one we observed. Therefore, whatever statistical procedures the manager intends to use, he doesn't need to worry about the normality assumption. ∎

We make three comments about this chi-square procedure. First, the test *does* depend on which (and how many) bins we use for the histogram. Reasonable choices are likely to lead to the same conclusion, but this is not guaranteed. Second, the test is not very effective unless the sample size is large, say, at least 80 or 100. Only then can we begin to see the true shape of the histogram and judge accurately whether it is normal. Finally, the test tends to be *too* sensitive if the sample size is really large. In this case any little "bump" on the observed histogram is likely to lead to a conclusion of nonnormality. This is one more example of practical versus statistical significance. With a large sample size we might be able to reject the normality assumption with a high degree of certainty, but the practical difference between the observed and normal histograms might be unimportant.

The Lilliefors test is based on a comparison of the cdf from the data and a normal cdf.

The chi-square test of normality is an intuitive one because it is based on histograms. However, it suffers from the first two points discussed in the previous paragraph. In particular, it is not as *powerful* as other available tests. This means that it is often unable to distinguish between normal and nonnormal distributions, and hence it often fails to reject the null hypothesis of normality when it should be rejected. A more powerful test is called the *Lilliefors test*.[8] This test is based on the cumulative distribution function (cdf), which shows the probability of being less than or equal to any particular value. Specifically, the **Lilliefors test** compares two cdf's: the cdf from a normal distribution and the cdf corresponding to the given data. This latter cdf, called the **empirical cdf,** shows the fraction of observations less than or equal to any particular value. If the data come from a normal distribution, then the normal and empirical cdf's should be quite close. Therefore, the Lilliefors test compares the *maximum vertical distance* between the two cdf's and compares it to specially tabulated values. If this maximum vertical distance is sufficiently large, the null hypothesis of normality is rejected.

To run the Lilliefors test for the Width variable in Example 10.7, we select Lilliefors Test from the StatTools Normality Tests dropdown. StatTools then shows the numerical outputs in Figure 10.26 and the corresponding graph in Figure 10.27 of the normal and empirical cdf's. The numeric output indicates that the maximum vertical distance between the two curves is 0.0513. It also provides a number of "CVal" values for comparison. If the test statistic is larger than any of these, we can reject the null hypothesis of normality at the corresponding significance level. In this case, however, the test statistic is relatively small—not nearly large enough to reject the normal hypothesis at any of the usual significance levels. This conclusion agrees with the one based on the chi-square goodness-of-fit test (as well as the closeness of the two curves in Figure 10.27). Nevertheless, you should be aware that the two tests do not agree on *all* data sets.

Figure 10.26

Lilliefors Test Results

	A	B
7		Width
8	*Lilliefors Test Results*	Data Set #1
9	Sample Size	90
10	Sample Mean	9.999256
11	Sample Std Dev	0.009728
12	Test Statistic	0.0513
13	CVal (15% Sig. Level)	0.0810
14	CVal (10% Sig. Level)	0.0856
15	CVal (5% Sig. Level)	0.0936
16	CVal (2.5% Sig. Level)	0.0998
17	CVal (1% Sig. Level)	0.1367

[8]This is actually a special case of the more general and widely known **Kolmogorov-Smirnoff** (or **K-S**) **test.**

Figure 10.27 Normal and Empirical Cumulative Distribution Functions

Normal and Empirical Cumulative Distributions of Width

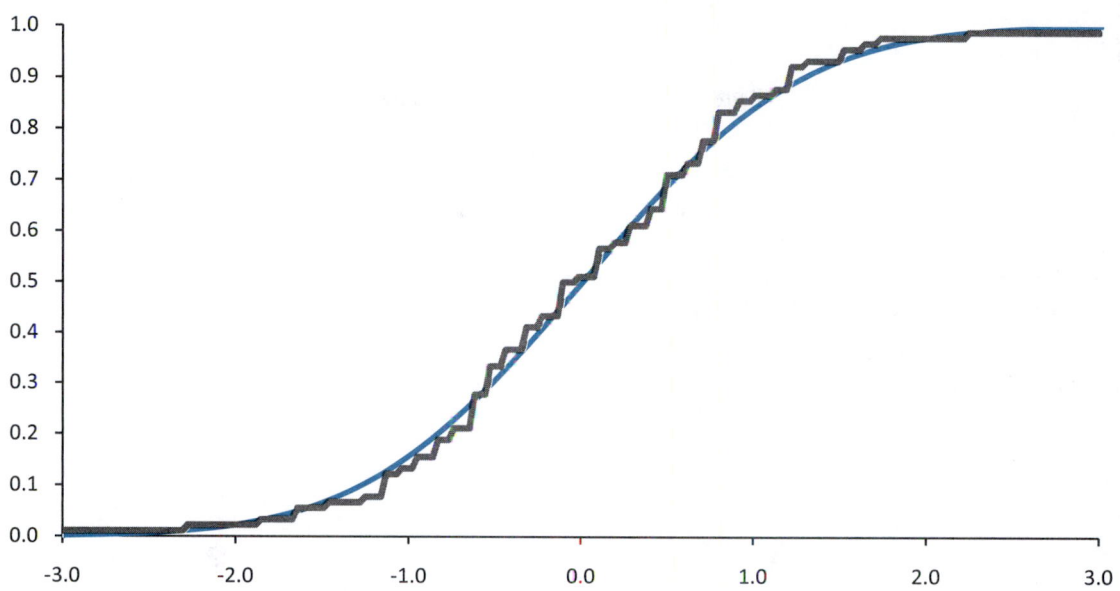

If data are normally distributed, the points on the corresponding Q-Q plot should be close to a 45° line.

    We conclude this section with a popular, but informal, test of normality. This is based on a plot called a *quantile-quantile* (or *Q-Q*) *plot*. Although the technical details for forming this plot are somewhat complex, it is basically a scatterplot of the standardized values from the data set versus the values we would expect if the data were perfectly normally distributed (with the same mean and standard deviation as in the data set). If the data are, in fact, normally distributed, then the points in this plot will tend to cluster around a 45° line. Any large deviations from a 45° line signal some type of nonnormality. Again, however, this is not a *formal* test of normality. A Q-Q plot is usually used only to obtain a general idea of whether the data are normally distributed and, if they are not, what type of nonnormality exists. For example, if points on the right of the plot are well *above* a 45° line, this is an indication that the largest observations in the data set are larger than we would expect from a normal distribution. Therefore, these points might be high-end outliers and/or a signal of positive skewness.

    To obtain a Q-Q plot for the Width variable in Example 10.7, we select Q-Q Normal Plot from the StatTools Normality Tests dropdown (and check each option at the bottom of the dialog box). The Q-Q plot for the Width data in Example 10.7 appears in Figure 10.28. Although the points in this Q-Q plot do not all lie *exactly* on a 45° line, they are about as close to doing so as we can expect from real data. Therefore, there is no reason to question the normal hypothesis for these data—the same conclusion we reached with the chi-square and Lilliefors tests. (Note that in the StatTools Q-Q plot dialog box, you can elect to plot using *standardized* Q-values. We used this option in Figure 10.28. The plot with *unstandardized* Q-values, not shown here, provides virtually the same information. The only difference is in the scale of the vertical axis.)

Figure 10.28   Q-Q Plot with Standardized Q-Values

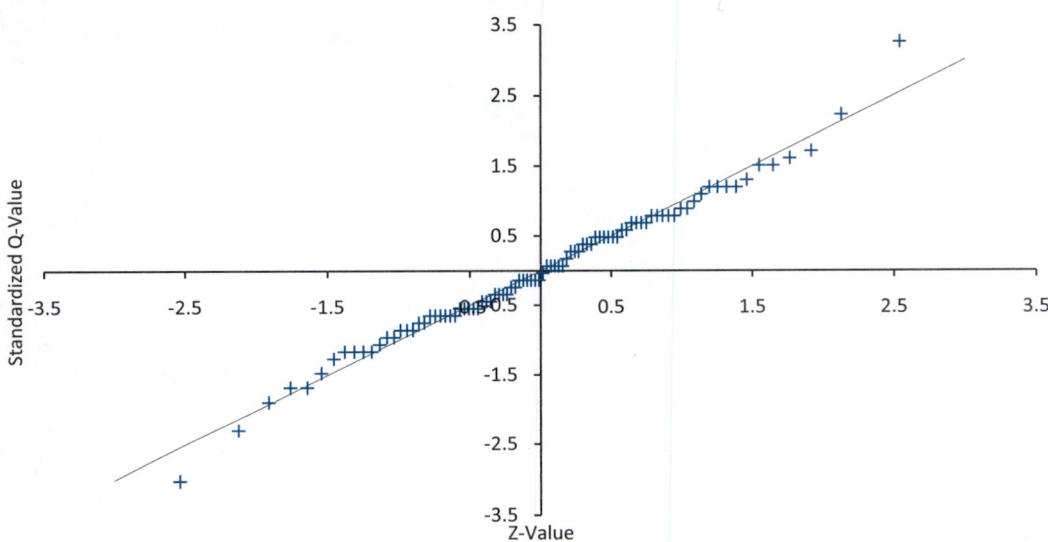

Q-Q Normal Plot of Width

PROBLEMS

Level A

40. A finance professor has just given a midterm examination in her corporate finance course. In particular, she is interested in determining whether the distribution of 100 exam scores is normally distributed. The data are in the file **P02_05.xlsx**. Perform a chi-square goodness-of-fit test. Report and interpret the computed *p*-value. What can you conclude about normality?

41. The annual base salaries for 100 students graduating from a reputable MBA program this year are of interest to those in the admissions office who are responsible for marketing the program to prospective students. The data are in the file **P10_41.xlsx**. Are these salaries normally distributed? Perform a chi-square goodness-of-fit test. Report and interpret the computed *p*-value.

42. The manager of a local fast-food restaurant is interested in improving the service provided to customers who use the restaurant's drive-up window. As a first step in this process, the manager asks his assistant to record the time (in minutes) it takes to serve 100 different customers at the final window in the facility's drive-up system. The given 100 customer service times are all observed during the busiest hour of the day for this fast-food operation. The data are in the file **P10_42.xlsx**. Prior to performing some statistical tests on these data, the manager's assistant must know whether the given customer service times are normally distributed. Perform a chi-square goodness-of-fit test. Report and interpret the computed *p*-value.

43. A manufacturer is interested in determining whether it can claim that the boxes of detergent it sells contain, on average, more than 500 grams of detergent. From past experience the manufacturer assumes that the amount of detergent in the boxes is normally distributed. The firm takes a random sample of 100 boxes and records the amount of detergent (in grams) in each box. Based on the data in the file **P10_02.xlsx**, is it still reasonable for the manufacturer to assume that the amount of detergent in these boxes is normally distributed? Perform a chi-square goodness-of-fit test. Report and interpret the computed *p*-value.

44. An aircraft manufacturer needs to buy aluminum sheets with an average thickness of 0.05 inch. The manufacturer collects a random sample of 100 sheets from a potential supplier. The thickness of each sheet in this sample is measured (in inches) and recorded in the file **P10_07.xlsx**. Are these measurements normally distributed? Using a 5% significance level, perform a chi-square goodness-of-fit test. Summarize your results.

45. A U.S. Navy recruiting center knows from past experience that the mean height of its recruits is 68 inches. The recruiting center wants to test the claim that the average height of this year's recruits is greater than 68 inches. To do this, recruiting personnel take a random sample of 64 recruits from the past year and record their heights (in inches). These data are provided in the file **P10_04.xlsx**. Before conducting an appropriate statistical test, the recruiters would like to check whether the given distribution of heights is normally distributed.

    a. On the basis of the available information, do the recruiters find support for the normality assumption at the 10% significance level? Explain.

    b. On the basis of the available information, do the recruiters find support for the normality assumption at the 1% significance level? Explain.

Level B

46. The chi-square test for normality discussed in this section is far from perfect. If the sample is too small, the test tends to accept the null hypothesis of normality for any population distribution even remotely bell shaped; that is, it is not **powerful** in detecting nonnormality. On the other hand, if the sample is very large, it will tend to reject the null hypothesis of normality for *any* data set.[9] Check this by using simulation. Simulate data from a normal distribution to illustrate that if the sample size is sufficiently large, there is a good chance that the null hypothesis will (wrongly) be rejected. Then simulate data from a nonnormal distribution (uniform or triangular, say) to illustrate that if the sample size is fairly small, there is a good chance that the null hypothesis will (wrongly) not be rejected. Summarize your findings in a short report.

10.6 CHI-SQUARE TEST FOR INDEPENDENCE

The test we discuss in this section, like one of the tests for normality from the previous section, uses the name "chi-square." However, this test, called the *chi-square test for independence*, has an entirely different objective. It is used in situations where a population is categorized in two different ways. For example, we might categorize people by their smoking habits and their drinking habits. The question then is whether these two attributes are *independent* in a probabilistic sense. They are **independent** if information on a person's drinking habits is of no use in predicting the person's smoking habits (or vice versa). In this particular example, however, we might suspect that these attributes are **dependent.** In particular, we might suspect that heavy drinkers are more likely (than non-heavy drinkers) to be heavy smokers, and we might suspect that nondrinkers are more likely (than drinkers) to be nonsmokers. The chi-square test for independence enables us to test this empirically.

Rejecting independence does not tell us the form of dependence. To see this, we must look more closely at the data.

    The null hypothesis for this test is that the two attributes are independent. Therefore, statistically significant results are those that indicate some sort of dependence. As usual, this puts the burden of proof on the alternative hypothesis of dependence. In the smoking–drinking example, we would continue to believe that smoking and drinking habits are unrelated—that is, independent—unless there is sufficient evidence from the data that they are dependent. Furthermore, even if we are able to conclude that they are dependent, the test itself does not indicate the *form* of dependence. It could be that heavy drinkers tend to be nonsmokers, and nondrinkers tend to be heavy smokers. Although this is probably unlikely, it is definitely a form of dependence. The only way we can decide which form of dependence we have is to look closely at the data.

    The data for this test consist of *counts* in various combinations of categories. We usually arrange these in a rectangular table called a **contingency table**, a **cross-tabs,** or, using

---

[9]Actually, all of the tests for normality suffer from this latter problem.

Excel terminology, a pivot table.[10] For example, if there are three smoking categories and three drinking categories, the table would have three rows and three columns, for a total of nine cells. The data entry in a cell is the number of observations in that particular combination of categories. We illustrate this data setup and the resulting analysis in the following example.

> ### Chi-Square Test for Independence
>
> The **chi-square test for independence** is based on the counts in a contingency (or cross-tabs) table. It tests whether the counts for the row categories are probabilistically independent of the counts for the column categories.

EXAMPLE

10.8 RELATIONSHIP BETWEEN DEMANDS FOR DESKTOPS AND LAPTOPS AT BIG OFFICE

Big Office, a chain of large office supply stores, sells an extensive line of desktop and laptop computers. Company executives want to know whether the demands for these two types of computers are related in any way. They might act as complementary products, where high demand for desktops accompanies high demand for laptops (computers in general are hot), they might act as substitute products (demand for one takes away demand for the other), or their demands might be unrelated. Because of limitations in its information system, Big Office does not have the exact demands for these products. However, it does have daily information on categories of demand, listed in aggregate (that is, over all stores). These data appear in Figure 10.29. (See the file **PC Demand.xlsx.**) Each day's demand for each type of computer is categorized as Low, Medium–Low, Medium–High, or High. The table is based on 250 days, so that the counts add to 250. The individual counts show, for example, that demand was high for both desktops *and* laptops on 11 of the 250 days. For convenience, we include row and column totals in the margins. Based on these data, can Big Office conclude that demands for these two products are independent?

Figure 10.29

Counts of Daily Demands for Desktops and Laptops

	A	B	C	D	E	F	G
1	Counts on 250 days of demands at Big Office						
2							
3			Desktops				
4			Low	MedLow	MedHigh	High	
5	Laptops	Low	4	17	17	5	43
6		MedLow	8	23	22	27	80
7		MedHigh	16	20	14	20	70
8		High	10	17	19	11	57
9			38	77	72	63	250

Objective   To use the chi-square test of independence to see whether demand for desktops is independent of demand for laptops.

Solution

The idea of the test is to compare the actual counts in the table with what we would *expect* them to be under independence. If the actual counts are sufficiently far from the expected

---

[10]Statisticians have long used the terms *contingency table* and *cross-tabs* (interchangeably) for the tables we are discussing here. Pivot tables are more general—they can contain summary measures such as averages and standard deviations, not just counts—but when they contain counts, they are equivalent to contingency tables and cross-tabs.

counts, we can then reject the null hypothesis of independence. The "distance" measure used to check how far apart they are, shown in equation (10.8), is essentially the same chi-square statistic used in the chi-square test for normality. Here, O_{ij} is the actual count in cell i, j (row i, column j), E_{ij} is the expected count for that cell assuming independence, and the sum is over all cells in the table. If this test statistic is sufficiently large, we reject the independence hypothesis. (We provide more details of the test shortly.)

Test Statistic for Chi-Square Test for Independence

$$\text{Chi-square test statistic} = \sum_{ij} (O_{ij} - E_{ij})^2 / E_{ij} \qquad \textbf{(10.8)}$$

What do we expect under independence? The totals in row 9 indicate that demand for desktops was low on 38 of the 250 days. Therefore, if we had to estimate the probability of low demand for desktops, this estimate would be $38/250 = 0.152$. Now, if demands for the two products were independent, we should arrive at this *same* estimate from the data in any of rows 5 through 8. That is, a prediction about desktops should be the same regardless of the demand for laptops. The probability estimate of low desktop from row 5, for example, is $4/43 = 0.093$. Similarly, for rows 6, 7, and 8, it is $8/80 = 0.100$, $16/70 = 0.229$, and $10/57 = 0.175$. These calculations provide some evidence that desktops and laptops act as *substitute* products—the probability of low desktop demand is larger when laptop demand is medium–high or high than when it is low or medium–low.

This reasoning is the basis for calculating the E_{ij}'s. Specifically, it can be shown that the relevant formula for E_{ij} is given by equation (10.9), where R_i is the row total in row i, C_j is the total in column j, and N is the number of observations. For example, E_{11} for these data is $43(38)/250 = 6.536$, which is slightly larger than the corresponding observed count, $O_{11} = 4$.

Expected Counts Assuming Row and Column Independence

$$E_{ij} = R_i C_j / N \qquad \textbf{(10.9)}$$

We can perform the calculations for the test easily with StatTools. This is one StatTools procedure that does *not* require a data set to be defined. We simply select Chi-square Independence Test from the StatTools Statistical Inference dropdown to obtain the dialog box shown in Figure 10.30. Here, we select the range of the contingency table. This range can include the row and column category labels (row 4 and column B), in which case we should check the top checkbox. The other two checkboxes, along with the titles, are used to provide labels the resulting output.

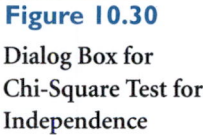

Figure 10.30

Dialog Box for Chi-Square Test for Independence

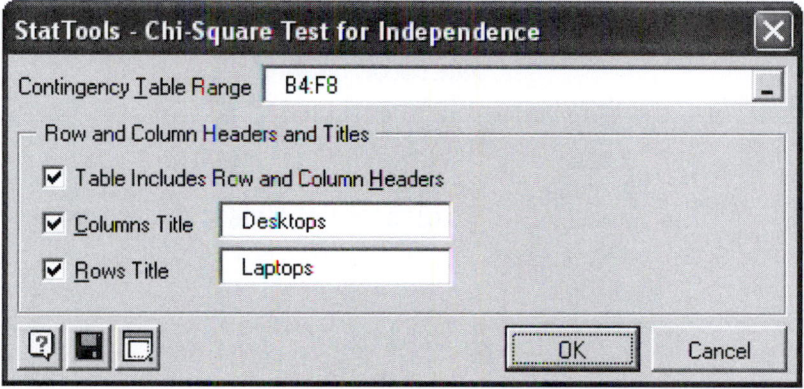

Tables of counts expressed as percentages of rows or of columns are useful for judging the form (and extent) of any possible dependence.

The output appears in Figure 10.31. The top table repeats the counts from the original table. The next two tables show these counts as percentages of rows and percentages of columns, respectively. The expected counts and distances from actual to expected are shown next. They lead to the chi-square statistic and corresponding *p*-value at the bottom.

We interpret the *p*-value of the test, 0.045, in the usual way. Specifically, we can reject the null hypothesis of independence at the 5% or 10% significance levels, but not at the 1% level. There is a good bit of evidence that the demands for the two products are not independent.

Figure 10.31 Output for Chi-square Test

	A	B	C	D	E	F
7			Rows: Laptops / Columns: Desktops			
8	Original Counts	Low	MedLow	MedHigh	High	Total
9	Low	4	17	17	5	43
10	MedLow	8	23	22	27	80
11	MedHigh	16	20	14	20	70
12	High	10	17	19	11	57
13	Total	38	77	72	63	250
14						
15			Rows: Laptops / Columns: Desktops			
16	Percentage of Rows	Low	MedLow	MedHigh	High	
17	Low	9.30%	39.53%	39.53%	11.63%	100.00%
18	MedLow	10.00%	28.75%	27.50%	33.75%	100.00%
19	MedHigh	22.86%	28.57%	20.00%	28.57%	100.00%
20	High	17.54%	29.82%	33.33%	19.30%	100.00%
21						
22			Rows: Laptops / Columns: Desktops			
23	Percentage of Columns	Low	MedLow	MedHigh	High	
24	Low	10.53%	22.08%	23.61%	7.94%	
25	MedLow	21.05%	29.87%	30.56%	42.86%	
26	MedHigh	42.11%	25.97%	19.44%	31.75%	
27	High	26.32%	22.08%	26.39%	17.46%	
28		100.00%	100.00%	100.00%	100.00%	
29						
30			Rows: Laptops / Columns: Desktops			
31	Expected Counts	Low	MedLow	MedHigh	High	
32	Low	6.5360	13.2440	12.3840	10.8360	
33	MedLow	12.1600	24.6400	23.0400	20.1600	
34	MedHigh	10.6400	21.5600	20.1600	17.6400	
35	High	8.6640	17.5560	16.4160	14.3640	
36						
37			Rows: Laptops / Columns: Desktops			
38	Distance from Expected	Low	MedLow	MedHigh	High	
39	Low	0.9840	1.0652	1.7206	3.1431	
40	MedLow	1.4232	0.1092	0.0469	2.3207	
41	MedHigh	2.7002	0.1129	1.8822	0.3157	
42	High	0.2060	0.0176	0.4067	0.7878	
43						
44						
45	Chi-Square Statistic					
46	Chi-Square	17.2420				
47	p-Value	0.0451				

If we accept that there is some sort of dependence, we can use the output in Figure 10.31 to examine its form. The two tables in rows 17 through 20 and rows 24 through 27 are especially helpful. If the demands *were* independent, the rows of this first table should be identical, and the columns of the second table should be identical. This is because each row in the first table shows the distribution of desktop demand for a given category of laptop demand, whereas each column in the second table shows the distribution of laptop demand for a given category of desktop demand. A close study of these percentages again provides some evidence that the two products act as substitutes, but the evidence is not overwhelming. ■

It is worth noting that the table of counts necessary for the chi-square test of independence can be a pivot table. For example, the pivot table in Figure 10.32 shows counts of the Married and OwnHome attributes. (For Married, 1 means married, 0 means unmarried, and for OwnHome, 1 means a home owner, 0 means not a home owner. This pivot table is based on the data in the **Catalog Marketing.xlsx** file we examined in Chapter 3.) To see whether these two attributes are independent, we would perform the chi-square test on the table in the range B5:C6. You might want to check that the *p*-value for the test is 0.000, so that Married and OwnHome are *definitely* not independent.

Figure 10.32

Using a Pivot Table for a Chi-Square Test

	A	B	C	D
3	Count	OwnHome ▼		
4	Married ▼	0	1	Grand Total
5	0	307	191	498
6	1	177	325	502
7	Grand Total	484	516	1000

PROBLEMS

Level A

47. The file **P09_49.xlsx** contains data on 400 orders placed to the ElecMart company over the period of several months. For each order, the file lists the time of day, the type of credit card used, the region of the country where the customer resides, and others. Use a chi-square test for independence to see whether the following variables are independent. If the variables appear to be related, discuss the form of dependence you see.
   a. Time and Region
   b. Region and BuyCategory
   c. Gender and CardType

48. The file **P09_17.xlsx** categorizes 250 randomly selected consumers on the basis of their gender, their age, and their preference for Pepsi or Coke. Use a chi-square test for independence to see whether the drink preference is independent of gender; whether it is independent of age. If you find any dependence, discuss its nature.

49. The file **P02_07.xlsx** contains data on 150 houses that were recently sold. Two variables in this data set are Price, the selling price of the house in $1000s, and Number_Bedrooms, the number of bedrooms in the house. We want to use a chi-square test for independence

to see whether these two variables are independent. However, this test requires *categorical* variables, and Price is essentially continuous. Therefore, to run the test, first divide the prices into several categories: less than 120, 120 to 130, 130 to 140, and greater than 140. Then run the test and report your results.

Level B

50. The file **P03_86.xlsx** contains salary data on almost 1800 NFL football players in the 2000 season. We want to use a chi-square test of independence to see whether Total (Salary plus Bonus) is related to other variables in the data set, such as the conference (NFC or AFC) or the player's position (quarterback, running back, and so on). Because the chi-square test requires *categorical* variables, you must first divide all salaries into several categories. Use these categories (in $1000s): less than 300, 300 to 600, 600 to 900, and greater than 900. Then test whether the following variables are independent. If they are not, discuss the type of dependence that appears to exist.
   a. Salary and Conference
   b. Salary and Off/Def
   c. Salary and Position
   d. Salary and Team

51. The file **P03_83.xlsx** contains data on 1000 Marvak customers. The data set includes demographic variables for each customer as well as their salaries and the amounts they have spent at Marvak during the past year.

    a. A lookup table in the file suggests a way to categorize the salaries. Use this categorization and chi-square tests of independence to see whether Salary is independent of (i) Age, (ii) Gender, (iii) Home, or (iv) Married. Discuss any types of dependence you find.

    b. Repeat part **a**, replacing Salary with AmtSpent. First you must categorize AmtSpent. Create four categories for AmtSpent based on the four quartiles. The first category is all values of AmtSpent below the first quartile of AmtSpent, the second category is between the first quartile and the median, and so on.

52. The file **Videos.xlsx** (the file that accompanies the case for Chapter 8) contains data on close to 10,000 videotape customers from several large cities in the United States. The variables include the customers' gender and their first choice among several types of movies. Perform chi-square tests of independence to see whether the following variables are related. If they are, discuss the form of dependence you are seeing.

    a. State and FirstChoice

    b. City and FirstChoice

    c. Gender and FirstChoice

10.7 ONE-WAY ANOVA

In Sections 9.7.1 and 10.4.2 we discussed the two-sample procedure for analyzing the difference between two population means. A natural extension is to *more* than two population means. The resulting procedure is commonly called *one-way analysis of variance,* or *one-way ANOVA.* There are two typical situations where one-way ANOVA is used. The first is when there are several distinct populations. For example, consider recent graduates with BS degrees in one of three disciplines: Business, Engineering, and Computer Science. We might sample randomly from each of these populations to discover whether there are any significant differences between them with respect to mean starting salary.

A second situation where one-way ANOVA is used is in randomized experiments. In this case a *single* population is treated in one of several ways. For example, a pharmaceutical company might select a group of people who suffer from allergies and randomly assign each person to a different type of allergy medicine currently being developed. Then the question is whether any of the treatments differ from one another with respect to the mean amount of symptom relief.

The data analysis in these two situations is identical; only the interpretation of the results differs. For the sake of clarity, we will phrase this discussion in terms of the first situation, where we randomly sample from each of several populations. Let I be the number of populations, and denote the means of these populations by μ_1 through μ_I. The null hypothesis is that the I means are all equal, whereas the alternative is that they are not all equal. Note that this alternative admits many possibilities. With $I = 4$, for example, we could have $\mu_1 = \mu_2 = \mu_3 = 5$ and $\mu_4 = 10$, or we could have $\mu_1 = \mu_2 = 5$ and $\mu_3 = \mu_4 = 10$, or we could have $\mu_1 = 5$, $\mu_2 = 7$, $\mu_3 = 9$, and $\mu_4 = 10$. The alternative hypothesis simply specifies that *the means are not all equal.*

> *Hypotheses for One-Way ANOVA*
> Null hypothesis: All means are equal
> Alternative hypothesis: At least one mean is different from others

The one-way ANOVA procedure is usually run in two stages. In the first stage we test the null hypothesis of equal means. If the resulting *p*-value is not sufficiently small, then there is not enough evidence to reject the equal-means hypothesis, and the analysis stops. However, if the *p*-value is sufficiently small, we can conclude with some assurance that the means are not all equal. Then the second stage attempts to discover which means are significantly different from which other means. This latter analysis is usually accomplished via confidence intervals.

One-way ANOVA is basically a test of differences between means, so why is it called analysis of *variance*? The answer to this question is the key to the procedure. Consider the box plot in Figure 10.33. It corresponds to observations from four populations with slightly different means and fairly large variances. (The large variances are indicated by the relatively wide boxes and long lines extending from them.) From these box plots, would you conclude that the population means differ across the four populations? Would your answer change if the data were instead as in Figure 10.34? We expect that it would.

The sample means in these two figures are virtually the same, but the variances *within* each population in Figure 10.33 are quite large relative to the variance *between* the sample means. In contrast, there is very little variance within each population in Figure 10.34. In the first case the large "within" variance makes it difficult to infer whether there are really any differences between population means, whereas the small "within" variance in the second case makes it easy to infer differences between population means.

Figure 10.33 Samples with Large Within Variation

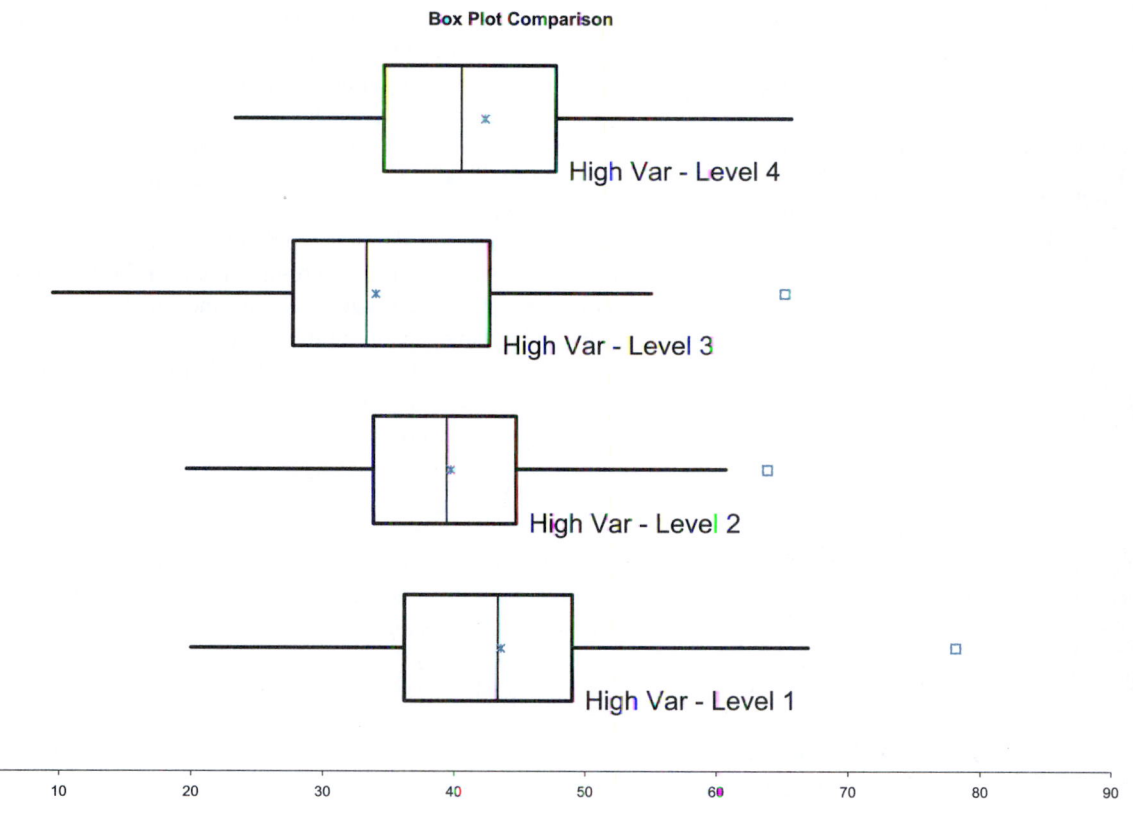

Figure 10.34 Samples with Small Within Variation

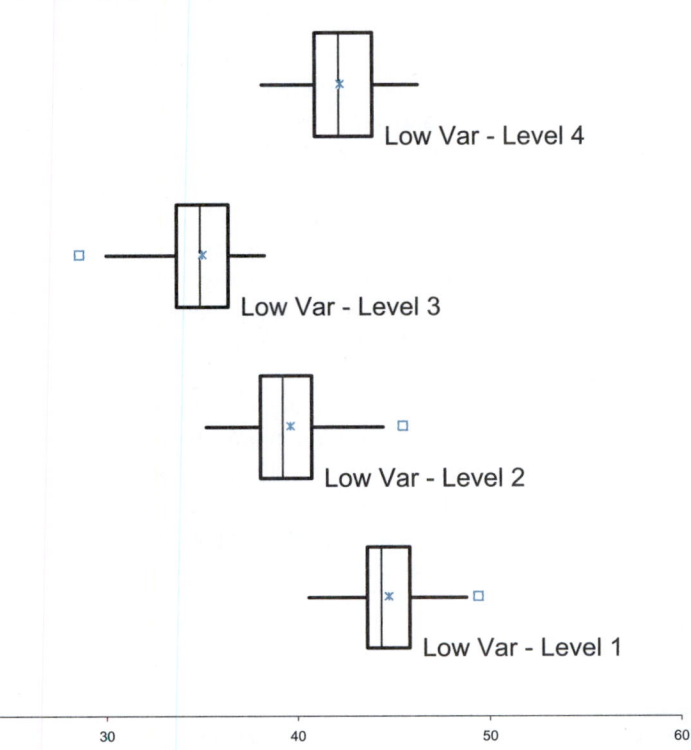

Box Plot Comparison

This is the essence of the ANOVA test. We compare variances *within* the individual samples to variance *between* the sample means. Only if the between variance is large relative to the within variance can we conclude with any assurance that there are differences between population means—and reject the equal-means hypothesis.

A test is robust if its results are valid even when the assumptions behind it are not exactly true.

The test itself is based on two assumptions: (1) the population variances are all equal to some common variance σ^2, and (2) the populations are normally distributed. These are analogous to the assumptions we made for the two-sample t test. Although these assumptions are never satisfied exactly in any application, we should keep them in mind and check for gross violations whenever possible. Fortunately, the test we present is fairly robust to violations of these assumptions, particularly when the sample sizes are large and roughly the same.

The between variation measures how much the sample means differ from one another.

To understand the test, let $\bar{Y}_i$, s_i^2, and n_i be the sample mean, sample variance, and sample size from sample i. Also, let n and $\bar{Y}$ be the combined number of observations and the sample mean of all n observations. (We call $\bar{\bar{Y}}$ the **grand mean.**) Then a measure of the between variation is *SSB* (sum of squares between):

$$SSB = \sum_{i=1}^{I} n_i \, (\bar{Y}_i - \bar{\bar{Y}})^2$$

The within variation measures how much the observations within each sample differ from one another.

Note that *SSB* is large if the individual sample means differ substantially from the grand mean $\bar{\bar{Y}}$, and this occurs only if they differ substantially from one another. A measure of the within variation is *SSW* (sum of squares within):

$$SSW = \sum_{i=1}^{I} (n_i - 1)s_i^2$$

This sum of squares is large if the individual sample variances are large. For example, *SSW* is much larger in Figure 10.33 than in Figure 10.34. However, *SSB* is the same in both figures.

Each of these sums of squares has an associated degrees of freedom, *dfB* and *dfW:*

$$dfB = I - 1$$

and

$$dfW = n - I$$

When we divide the sums of squares by their degrees of freedom, we obtain *mean squares,* *MSB* and *MSW:*

$$MSB = \frac{SSB}{dfB}$$

and

$$MSW = \frac{SSW}{dfW}$$

Actually, it can be shown that *MSW* is a weighted average of the individual sample variances, where the sample variance s_i^2 receives weight $(n_i - 1)/(n - I)$. In this sense *MSW* is a pooled estimate of the common variance σ^2, just as in the two-sample procedure.

Finally, the ratio of these means squares, shown in equation (10.10), is the test statistic we use. Under the null hypothesis of equal population means, this test statistic has an *F* distribution with *dfB* and *dfW* degrees of freedom. If the null hypothesis is *not* true, then we would expect *MSB* to be large relative to *MSW,* as in Figure 10.34. Therefore, the *p*-value for the test is found by finding the probability to the *right* of the *F*-ratio in the *F* distribution with *dfB* and *dfW* degrees of freedom.

Test Statistic for One-Way ANOVA Test of Equal Means

$$F\text{-ratio} = \frac{MSB}{MSW} \qquad\qquad (10.10)$$

The elements of this test are usually presented in an **ANOVA table,** as we see shortly. The "bottom line" in this table is the *p*-value. If it is sufficiently small, we can conclude that the population means are not all equal. Otherwise, we cannot reject the equal-means hypothesis.

If we do reject the equal-means hypothesis, then it is customary to examine confidence intervals for the differences between all pairs of population means. This can lead to quite a few confidence intervals. For example, if there are $I = 5$ samples, then there are 10 pairs of differences (the number of ways 2 means can be chosen from 5 means). As usual, the confidence interval for any difference $\mu_i - \mu_j$ is of the form

$$\overline{Y}_i - \overline{Y}_j \pm \text{multiplier} \times \text{SE}(\overline{Y}_i - \overline{Y}_j)$$

The appropriate standard error is

$$\text{SE}(\overline{Y}_i - \overline{Y}_j) = s_p \sqrt{1/n_i + 1/n_j}$$

If the confidence interval for a particular difference does not include 0, we can conclude that these two means are different.

where s_p is the pooled standard deviation, calculated as $\sqrt{MSW}$.

There are several forms of these confidence intervals, four of which are implemented in StatTools. In particular, the appropriate multiplier for the confidence intervals depends on which form is being used. We will not pursue the technical details here, except to say that the multiplier is sometimes chosen to be its "usual" value near 2 and is sometimes chosen to be considerably larger, say, around 3.5. The reason for the latter is that if we want to conclude with 95% confidence that *each* of these confidence intervals includes its corresponding mean difference, we must make the confidence intervals relatively wide.

For any of these confidence intervals that does *not* include the value 0, we infer that the corresponding means are not equal. But if a confidence interval does include 0, we cannot conclude that the corresponding means are unequal.

We have presented the formulas for one-way ANOVA to provide some insight into the procedure. However, StatTools's one-way ANOVA procedure takes care of all the calculations, as illustrated in the following example.

EXAMPLE | **10.9 EMPLOYEE EMPOWERMENT AT ARMCO COMPANY**

We discussed the ArmCo Company in Example 10.6. It initiated an employee empowerment program at its Midwest plant, and the reaction from employees was basically positive. Let's assume now that ArmCo has initiated this policy in all five of its plants—in the South, Midwest, Northeast, Southwest, and West—and several months later it wants to see whether the policy is being perceived equally by employees across the plants. Random samples of employees at the five plants have been asked to rate the success of the empowerment policy on a scale of 1 to 10, 10 being the most favorable rating. The data appear in Figure 10.35.[11] (See the file **Empowerment 2.xlsx**.) Is there any indication of mean differences across the plants? If so, which plants appear to differ from which others?

Figure 10.35

Data for Empowerment Example

	A South	B Midwest	C Northeast	D Southwest	E West
1	South	Midwest	Northeast	Southwest	West
2	7	7	7	6	6
3	1	6	5	4	6
4	8	10	5	7	6
5	7	3	5	10	6
6	2	9	4	7	3
7	9	10	3	6	4
8	3	8	4	6	8
9	8	4	5	7	6
40	7	2	3	3	4
41	4	7	3	7	5
42		7	3	8	6
43		5	5	9	4
44		10	5	10	7
45		10		4	4
46		6		10	3
47		3		4	5
48		5		6	4
49		2			7
50		6			6
51		4			4
52		5			
53		2			
54		7			
55		8			
56		7			

[11]StatTools's One-Way ANOVA procedure accepts the data in stacked or unstacked form. The data in this example are unstacked.

Objective   To use one-way ANOVA to test whether the empowerment initiatives are appreciated equally across Armco's five plants.

Solution

One-way ANOVA does not require equal sample sizes.

First, note that the sample sizes are not equal. This could be because some employees opted not to cooperate or it could be due to other reasons. Fortunately, equal sample sizes are not necessary for the ANOVA test. (Still, it is worth noting that when you create a StatTools data set as a first step in the ANOVA procedure, the data set range will extend to the longest of the data columns, in this case the Midwest column.)

To run one-way ANOVA with StatTools on these data, select One-Way ANOVA from the StatTools Statistical Inference dropdown, and fill out the resulting dialog box as shown in Figure 10.36. In particular, click on the Format button and make sure the Unstacked option is selected, and then select the five variables. This dialog box indicates that there are several "types" of confidence intervals available. Each of these uses a slightly different multiplier in the general confidence interval formula. Again, we will not pursue the differences between these confidence interval types, except to say that the default Tukey type is generally a good choice.

The main thing to remember from the ANOVA table is that a small p-value indicates that the population means are not all equal.

The resulting output in Figure 10.37 consists of three basic parts: summary measures and summary statistics, the ANOVA table, and confidence intervals. The summary statistics indicate that the Southwest has the largest mean rating, 6.745, and the Northeast has the smallest, 4.140, with the others in between. The sample standard deviations (or variances) vary somewhat across the plants, but not enough to invalidate the procedure. The side-by-side box plots in Figure 10.38 illustrate these summary measures graphically. However, there is too much overlap between the box plots to tell (graphically) whether the observed differences between plants are statistically significant.

Figure 10.36

One-Way ANOVA Dialog Box

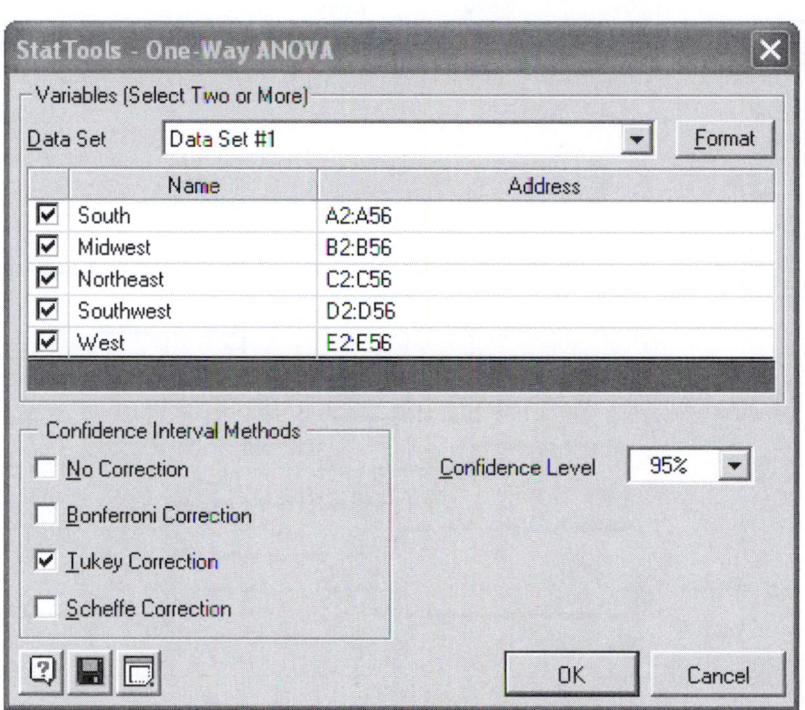

Figure 10.37   Analysis of Empowerment Data

	A	B	C	D	E	F
8	ANOVA Summary					
9	Total Sample Size	235				
10	Grand Mean	5.383				
11	Pooled Std Dev	1.976				
12	Pooled Variance	3.904				
13	Number of Samples	5				
14	Confidence Level	95.00%				
15						
16		South	Midwest	Northeast	Southwest	West
17	ANOVA Sample Stats	Data Set #1	Data Set #1	Data Set #1	Data Set #1	Data Set #1
18	Sample Size	40	55	43	47	50
19	Sample Mean	5.600	5.400	4.140	6.745	4.980
20	Sample Std Dev	2.073	2.469	1.820	1.687	1.635
21	Sample Variance	4.297	6.096	3.313	2.846	2.673
22	Pooling Weight	0.1696	0.2348	0.1826	0.2000	0.2130
23						
24		Sum of	Degrees of	Mean	F-Ratio	p-Value
25	OneWay ANOVA Table	Squares	Freedom	Squares		
26	Between Variation	163.653	4	40.913	10.480	< 0.0001
27	Within Variation	897.879	230	3.904		
28	Total Variation	1061.532	234			
29						
30		Difference		Tukey		
31	Confidence Interval Tests	of Means	Lower	Upper		
32	South-Midwest	0.200	-0.920	1.320		
33	South-Northeast	1.460	**0.276**	**2.644**		
34	South-Southwest	-1.145	-2.304	0.015		
35	South-West	0.620	-0.523	1.763		
36	Midwest-Northeast	1.260	**0.163**	**2.358**		
37	Midwest-Southwest	-1.345	**-2.415**	**-0.274**		
38	Midwest-West	0.420	-0.633	1.473		
39	Northeast-Southwest	-2.605	**-3.743**	**-1.468**		
40	Northeast-West	-0.840	-1.961	0.280		
41	Southwest-West	1.765	**0.670**	**2.860**		

Figure 10.38

Box Plots for
Empowerment Data

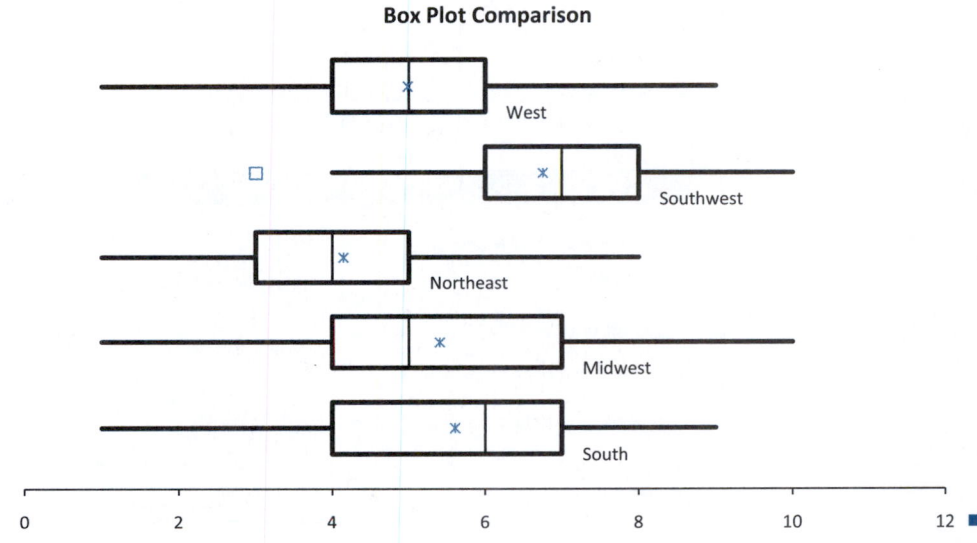

The ANOVA table in rows 26 through 28 of Figure 10.37 shows the elements for the *F* test of equal means. All of it is based on the theory we developed above. The only part we didn't discuss is the Total Variation in row 28. It is based on the total variation of all observations around the Grand Mean in cell B10, and is used mainly to check the calculations. Specifically, note that *SSB* and *SSW* in cells B26 and B27 add up to the total sum of squares in cell B28. Similarly, the degrees of freedom add up in column C. The *F*-ratio for the test is 10.480, in cell E26. Its corresponding *p*-value (to three decimal places) is 0.000. This leaves practically no doubt that the five population means are *not* all equal. Employees evidently do not perceive the empowerment policy equally across plants.

The 95% confidence intervals in rows 32 through 41 indicate which plants differ significantly from which others. For example, the mean for the Southwest plant is somewhere between 1.468 and 3.743 rating points above the mean for the Northeast plant. We see that the Southwest plant is rated significantly higher than the Northeast, West, and Midwest plants, and the South and Midwest plants are also rated significantly higher than the Northeast plant. (StatTools boldfaces the significant differences.) Now it is up to ArmCo management to decide whether the magnitudes of these differences are *practically* significant, and, if so, what they can do to increase employee perceptions at the lower-rated plants.

PROBLEMS

Level A

53. An automobile manufacturer employs sales representatives who make calls on dealers. The manufacturer wishes to compare the effectiveness of four different call-frequency plans for the sales representatives. Thirty-two representatives are chosen at random from the sales force and randomly assigned to the four call plans (eight per plan). The representatives follow their plans for 6 months, and their sales for the 6-month study period are recorded. These data are given in the file **P10_53.xlsx**.
   a. Do the sample data support the hypothesis that at least one of the call plans helps produce a higher average level of sales than some other call plan? Perform an appropriate statistical test and report a *p*-value.
   b. If the sample data indicate the existence of mean sales differences across the call plans, which plans appear to produce different average sales levels? Construct 95% confidence levels for the differences between all pairs of means to help answer this question.

54. Consider a large chain of supermarkets that sell their own brand of potato chips in addition to many other name brands. Management would like to know whether the type of display used for the store brand has any effect on sales. Because there are four types of displays being considered, management decides to choose 24 similar stores to serve as experimental units. A random six of these are instructed to use display type 1, another random six are instructed to use display type 2, a third random six are instructed to use display type 3, and the final

six stores are instructed to use display type 4. For a period of 1 month, each store keeps track of the *fraction* of total potato chips sales that are of the store brand. The data for the 24 stores are shown in the file **P10_54.xlsx**. Note that one of the stores using display 3 has a blank cell. This store did not follow instructions properly, so its observation is disregarded.
   a. Why do you think each store keeps track of the fraction of total potato chips sales that are of the store brand? Why do they not simply record the total amount of sales of the store brand potato chips?
   b. Do the data suggest different mean proportions of store brand sales at the 10% significance level? If so, construct 90% confidence intervals for the differences between all pairs of mean proportions to identify which of the display types are associated with higher fractions of sales.

55. National Airlines recently introduced a daily early-morning nonstop flight between Houston and Chicago. The vice president of marketing for National Airlines decided to perform a statistical test to see whether National's average passenger load on this new flight is different from that of each of its two major competitors (which we will call competitor 1 and competitor 2). Ten early-morning flights were selected at random from each of the three airlines and the percentage of *unfilled* seats on each flight was recorded. These data are stored in the file **P10_55.xlsx**.
   a. Is there evidence that National's average passenger load on the new flight is different from that of its two competitors? Report a *p*-value and interpret the results of the statistical test.

b. Select an appropriate significance level and construct confidence intervals for all pairs of differences between means. Which of these differences, if any, are statistically significant at the selected significance level?

56. Do graduates of undergraduate business programs with different majors tend to earn disparate average starting salaries? Consider the data given in the file **P10_56.xlsx**.

   a. Is there any reason to doubt the equal-variance assumption made in the one-way ANOVA model in

this particular case? Support your response to this question.

   b. Assuming that the variances of the four underlying populations are indeed equal, can you reject at the 10% significance level that the mean starting salary is the same for each of the given business majors? Explain why or why not.

   c. Generate 90% confidence intervals for all pairs of differences between means. Which of these differences, if any, are statistically significant at $\alpha = 0.10$?

10.8 CONCLUSION

The concepts and procedures we have discussed in this chapter occupy a cornerstone in both applied and theoretical statistics. Of particular importance is the interpretation of a p-value, especially because p-values are common outputs of all statistical software packages. A p-value summarizes the evidence in support of an alternative hypothesis, which is usually the hypothesis an analyst is trying to prove. Small p-values provide support for the alternative hypothesis, whereas large p-values provide little or no support for it.

Although hypothesis testing continues to be an important tool for analysts, it is important to note its limitations, particularly in business applications. First, given a choice between a confidence interval for some population parameter and a test of this parameter, we generally favor the confidence interval. A confidence interval not only tells us whether a mean difference is 0, but it also gives us a plausible range for this difference. Second, many business *decision* problems cannot be handled adequately with hypothesis-testing procedures. Either they ignore important cost information or they treat the consequences of incorrect decisions (type I and type II errors) in an inappropriate way. Finally, the *statistical* significance at the core of hypothesis testing is sometimes quite different from the *practical* significance that is of most interest to business managers.

Summary of Key Terms

Term	Explanation	Excel	Page	Equation Number
Null hypothesis	Hypothesis that represents the current thinking or status quo		499	
Alternative hypothesis	Typically, the hypothesis the analyst is trying to prove, also called the research hypothesis		499	
One-tailed test	Test where values in only one direction will lead to rejection of null hypothesis		501	
Two-tailed test	Test where values in both directions will lead to rejection of null hypothesis		501	
Type I error	Error committed when null hypothesis is true but is rejected		501	
Type II error	Error committed when null hypothesis is false but is not rejected		501	

(continued)

Term	Explanation	Excel	Page	Equation Number
Rejection region	Sample results that lead to rejection of null hypothesis		502	
Statistically significant results	Sample results that lead to rejection of null hypothesis		502	
p-value	Probability of observing a sample result at least as extreme as the one actually observed		503	
Power	Probability of correctly rejecting null hypothesis when it is false		504	
t test for a population mean	Test for a mean from a single population	StatTools/ Statistical Inference/ Hypothesis Test	506	10.1
Z test for a population proportion	Test for a proportion from a single population	Must be done manually.	514	10.2
t test for difference between means from paired samples	Test for the difference between two population means when samples are paired in a natural way	StatTools/ Statistical Inference/ Hypothesis Test	516	10.3
t test for difference between means from independent samples	Test for the difference between two population means when samples are independent of one another	StatTools/ Statistical Inference/ Hypothesis Test	517	10.4
F test for equality of two variances	Test to check whether two population variances are equal, used to check an assumption of two-sample *t* test for difference between means	StatTools/ Statistical Inference/ Hypothesis Test	527	
F distribution	Skewed distribution useful for testing equality of variances	= FDIST($value$, $df1$, $df2$) = FINV($prob$, $df1$, $df2$)	527	
Z test for difference between proportions	Test for difference between similarly defined proportions from two populations	Must be done manually	528	10.5, 10.6
Tests for normality	Tests to check whether a population is normally distributed; alternatives include chi-square test, Lilliefors test, and Q-Q plot	StatTools/ Normality Tests	535–540	10.7
Chi-square test for independence	Test to check whether two attributes are probabilistically independent	StatTools/ Statistical Inference/Chi-square Independence Test	543	10.8, 10.9
One-way ANOVA	Generalization of two-sample *t* test, used to test whether means from several populations are all equal, and if not, which are significantly different from which others	StatTools/ Statistical Inference/ One-Way ANOVA	549	10.10

PROBLEMS

Conceptual Exercises

C.1. Suppose that you wish to test a researcher's claim that the mean of a normally distributed population has increased from its commonly accepted value of 1.60. To carry out this test, you obtain a random sample of size 150 from this population. This sample yields a mean of 1.80 and a standard deviation of 1.30. What are the appropriate null and alternative hypotheses? Is this a one-tailed or two-tailed test?

C.2. Suppose that you wish to test a manager's claim that the proportion of defective items generated by a particular production process has decreased from its long-run historical value of 0.30. To carry out this test, you obtain a random sample of 300 items produced through this process. Computer-generated output indicates that the p-value for the sample is 0.01. Carefully interpret this p-value. At what levels of significance would you reject the null hypothesis?

C.3. A 99% confidence interval for the proportion (π) of all Lewisburg residents whose annual income exceeds $80,000 extends from 0.10 to 0.18. The confidence interval is based on a random sample of 150 Lewisburg residents. Using this information and a 1% level of significance, we wish to test the following hypotheses:

H_0: $\pi = 0.08$

H_a: $\pi \neq 0.08$

Based on the given information, what is the correct statistical decision in this case? Explain your recommendation.

C.4. Suppose that you are performing a one-tailed hypothesis test. "Assuming that everything else remains constant, a decrease in the test's level of significance (α) leads to a higher probability of rejecting the null hypothesis." Is this statement true or false? Explain your choice.

C.5. Can pleasant aromas help people work more efficiently? Researchers conducted an investigation to answer this question. Fifty students worked a paper-and-pencil maze ten times. On five attempts, the students wore a mask with floral scents. On the other five attempts, they wore a mask with no scent. The 10 trials were done in random order and each used a different maze. The researchers found that the subjects took less time to complete the maze when wearing the scented mask. Is this an example of an *observational study?* Explain why or why not.

Level A

57. The file **P10_57.xlsx** contains the number of days 44 mothers spent in the hospital giving birth (in the year 2005). Before health insurance rules were changed (the change was effective January 1, 2005), the average number of days spent in a hospital by a new mother was 2 days. For a 0.05 level of significance, do the data in the file indicate (the research hypothesis) that women are now spending less time in the hospital after giving birth than they were prior to 2005? Explain your answer in terms of the p-value for the test.

58. Eighteen readers took a speed-reading course. The file **P10_58.xlsx** contains the number of words that they could read before and after the course. Test the alternative hypothesis at the 5% significance level that reading speeds have increased, on average, as a result of the course. Explain your answer in terms of the p-value. Do you need to assume that reading speeds (before and after) are normally distributed? Exactly what assumption do you need?

59. Statistics show that a child 0 to 4 years of age has a 0.04 probability of getting cancer in any given year. Assume that during each of the last 7 years there have been 100 children ages 0 to 4 years whose parents work in the business school. Four of these children have gotten cancer. Use this evidence to test whether the incidence of childhood cancer among children age 0 to 4 years whose parents work at the business school exceeds the national average. Write down your hypotheses and determine the appropriate p-value.

60. African Americans in a St. Louis suburb sued the city claiming they were discriminated against in school-teacher hiring. Of the city's population, 5.7% were African American; of 405 teachers in the school system, 15 were African American. Set up appropriate hypotheses and determine whether African Americans are underrepresented. Does your answer depend on whether you use a one-tailed or two-tailed test? In discrimination cases, the Supreme Court always uses a two-tailed test with $\alpha = .05$. (Source: U.S. Supreme Court Case, *Hazlewood versus City of St. Louis*)

61. In the past, monthly sales for HOOPS, a small software firm, have averaged $20,000 with standard deviation $4000. During the last year sales averaged $22,000 per month. Does this indicate that monthly sales have changed (in a statistically significant sense)? Use $\alpha = 0.05$. Assume monthly sales are normally distributed.

62. Twenty people have rated a new beer on a taste scale of 0 to 100. Their ratings are in the file **P10_62.xlsx**.

Marketing has determined that the beer will be a success if the average taste rating exceeds 76. If we use α = 0.05, is there sufficient evidence to conclude that the beer will be a success? Discuss your result in terms of a *p*-value. Assume ratings are normally distributed.

63. We have asked 22 people to rate a competitive beer on a taste scale of 0 to 100. Another 22 people rated our beer on a taste scale of 0 to 100. The file **P10_63.xlsx** contains the results. Do these data provide sufficient evidence to conclude, at the α = 0.01 level, that people believe our beer tastes better than the competition? Assume ratings are normally distributed.

64. Callaway is thinking about entering the golf ball market. The company will make a profit if its market share is more than 20%. A market survey indicates that 140 of 624 golf ball purchasers will buy a Callaway golf ball.
   a. Is this enough evidence to persuade Callaway to enter the golf ball market?
   b. How would you make the decision if you were Callaway management?

65. Sales of a new product will be profitable if the average sales per store exceeds 100 per week. The product was test marketed for 1 week at 10 stores, with the results listed in the file **P10_65.xlsx**. Assume that sales at each store follow a normal distribution.
   a. Is this enough evidence to persuade the company to market the new product?
   b. How would you make the decision if you were deciding whether to market the new product?

66. We are interested in determining whether the position of Coca-Cola in a store affects sales. Specifically, does Coke sell better when it is placed in the front or middle of an aisle? The file **P10_66.xlsx** contains sales of Coke at 10 stores when Coke was placed in the front of an aisle and at another 10 stores when Coke was placed in the back of an aisle. What are reasonable null and alternative hypotheses to test? Use the data to test them. What can you conclude?

67. Target wants to know whether red or blue coats sell better. The sales of red and blue coats last winter were measured at several different stores. The file **P10_67.xlsx** contains the results. What are reasonable null and alternative hypotheses to test? Use the data to test them. What can you conclude?

68. Marsh Supermarket wants to know whether putting a color flyer in the local paper has a greater effect on sales than putting a black-and-white flyer in the paper. For the last 9 times a color flyer was put in the paper, Marsh compared sales (in thousands of dollars) to the last week (at the same store) for which a black-and-white flyer was put in the paper. The file **P10_68.xlsx** contains the data. Formulate reasonable hypotheses and test them. What do you conclude?

69. In the past, the Algood Company has produced an average of 12,000 good parts per day. Since the compensation system was changed 15 days ago, the average production has been 12,100 good parts per day. The sample standard deviation of the number of good parts produced during the last 15 days is 400. Is this sufficient evidence to conclude, at the α = 0.10 level, that the new compensation plan has improved productivity? Justify your answer with a *p*-value.

Level B

70. You are trying to determine whether male and female Central Bank employees having equal qualifications receive different salaries. The file **P10_70.xlsx** contains the salaries (in thousands of dollars) for 9 male and 9 female employees. Assume salaries are normally distributed.
   a. Assuming that each row of data represents paired observations, and using α = 0.05, can you conclude that members of different genders are paid equally? Be sure to write down your hypotheses.
   b. How would you collect data to ensure that the observations are actually paired?

71. You are trying to determine whether male and female Indiana University grads having equal qualifications receive different starting salaries for their first job. The file **P10_71.xlsx** contains the starting salaries for 10 male and 10 female IU grads.
   a. Assuming that each row of data represents paired observations, and using α = 0.05, can you conclude that equally qualified people of different genders have the same starting salaries on average? Be sure to write down your null and alternative hypotheses.
   b. How would you collect data to ensure that the observations are actually paired?

72. A recent study concluded that children born to mothers who take Prozac tend to have more birth defects than children born to mothers who do not take Prozac.
   a. What do you think the null and alternative hypotheses were for this study?
   b. If you were a spokesperson for Eli Lilly (the company that produces Prozac), how would you rebut the conclusions of this study?

73. Suppose you are the state superintendent of Tennessee public schools. You want to know whether decreasing the class size in grades 1 through 3 will improve student performance. Explain how you would set up a test to determine whether decreased class size will improve student performance. What hypotheses would you use in this experiment. (This was actually done and smaller class size did help, particularly with minority students.)

74. Do chief executive officers of large U.S. corporations in different industries typically earn disparate annual salaries? Consider the data in the file **P02_13.xlsx**, which came from a survey of CEOs of the largest U.S. public companies (*The Wall Street Journal*, May 2004). In particular, we seek to discover whether significant differences exist between the mean levels of the fiscal 2003 salaries earned by executives of *Technology* companies and those of each of the other company types. For instance, is the difference between the mean 2003 salaries of executives from *Technology* and *Basic Materials* companies significant?

   a. Before conducting these hypothesis tests, perform a test for equal population variances for each pair of company types. For each pair, report a p-value and interpret it.

   b. Based on your conclusions in part **a,** which test statistic should be used in performing a test for the existence of a difference between population means in each pair?

   c. Given your conclusions in part **b,** perform a test for the existence of a difference in mean annual CEO salaries. For each pair of company types, report a p-value and interpret its meaning.

75. Is the overall cost of living higher or lower for urban areas in particular geographical regions of the United States? Consider the random sample of urban areas provided in the file **P10_75.xlsx** (Source: *ACCRA Cost of Living Index*). In particular, determine whether the mean composite (cost of living) value in urban areas of the northeastern states is higher than the mean composite value in urban areas of each of the following: (a) southeastern states, (b) central states, (c) southwestern states, and (d) northwestern states. Note that you will need to assign each of the urban areas in the given sample to one of these five geographical regions before you can proceed further.

   a. Before conducting any hypothesis tests on the difference between various pairs of mean composite values, perform a test for equal population variances in each pair of geographical regions. For each pair, report a p-value and interpret its meaning.

   b. Based on your conclusions in part **a,** which test statistic should be used in performing a test for a difference between population means in each pair?

   c. Given your conclusions in part **b,** perform a test for the difference between composite cost of living values in each pair of geographical regions. For each pair, report a p-value and interpret its meaning.

76. Consider a random sample of 100 households from a middle-class neighborhood that was the recent focus of an economic development study conducted by the local government. Specifically, for each of the 100 households in the sample, information was gathered on the gross annual income earned by the first wage earner of the household and on each of several other variables. The data are given in the file **P09_26.xlsx**. Economic researchers would like to test for the existence of a significant difference between the mean annual income levels of the first household wage earners in the first (i.e., SW) and second (i.e., NW) sectors of this community. In fact, they intend to perform similar hypothesis tests for the differences between the mean annual income levels of the first household wage earners from all other pairs of locations (i.e., first and third, first and fourth, second and third, second and fourth, and third and fourth).

   a. Before conducting any hypothesis tests on the difference between various pairs of mean income levels, perform a test for equal population variances in each pair of locations. For each pair, report a p-value and interpret its meaning.

   b. Based on your conclusions in part **a,** which test statistic should be used in performing a test for the existence of a difference between population means?

   c. Given your conclusions in part **b,** perform a test for the existence of a difference in mean annual income levels in each pair of locations. For each pair, report a p-value and interpret its meaning.

77. A group of 25 husbands and wives were chosen randomly. Each person was asked to write the most he or she would be willing to pay for a new car (assuming they had decided to buy a new car). The results are shown in the file **P10_77.xlsx**. Can you accept the alternative hypothesis that the husbands are willing to spend more, on average, than the wives at the 5% significance level? What is the associated p-value?

78. A company is concerned with the high cholesterol levels of many of its employees. To help combat the problem, it opens an exercise facility and encourages its employees to use this facility. After a year, it chooses a random 100 employees who claim they use the facility regularly, and another 200 who claim they don't use it at all. The cholesterol levels of these 300 employees are checked, with the results shown in the file **P10_78.xlsx**.

   a. Is this sample evidence "proof" that the exercise facility, when used, tends to lower the mean cholesterol level? Phrase this as a hypothesis-testing problem and do the appropriate analysis. Do you feel comfortable that your analysis answers the question definitively (one way or the other)? Why or why not?

   b. Repeat part **a,** but replace "mean level" with "percentage with level over 215." (The company believes that any level over 215 is dangerous.)

79. Suppose that you are trying to compare two populations on some variable (GMAT scores of men versus women, for example). Specifically, you are testing the null hypothesis that the means of the two populations are equal versus a two-tailed hypothesis. Are the following statements correct? Why or why not?

a. A given difference (such as 5 points) between sample means from these populations will probably not be considered statistically significant if the sample sizes are small, but will probably be considered statistically significant if the sample sizes are large.

b. Virtually any difference between the population means will lead to statistically significant sample results if the sample sizes are sufficiently large.

80. Continuing the previous problem, analyze part **b** in Excel as follows. Start with hypothetical population mean GMAT scores for men and women, along with population standard deviations. Enter these at the top of a spreadsheet. You can make the two means as close as you like, but not identical. In column A simulate a sample of men's GMAT scores with your mean and standard deviation. Do the same for women in column B. The sample sizes do not have to be the same, but you can make them the same. Then run the test for the difference between two means. (The point of this problem is that if the population means are fairly close and you pick relatively small sample sizes, the sample mean differences probably won't be significant. If you find this, generate new samples of a larger sample size and redo the test. Now they might be significant. If not, try again with a still larger sample size. Eventually, you should get statistically significant differences.)

81. This problem concerns course scores (on a 0–100 scale) for a large undergraduate computer programming course. The class is composed of both underclassmen (freshmen and sophomores) and upperclassmen (juniors and seniors). Also, the students can be categorized according to their previous mathematical background from previous courses as "low" or "high" mathematical background. The data for these students are in the file **P10_81.xlsx**. The variables are:
- Score: score on a 0–100 scale
- UpperCl: 1 for an upperclassman, 0 otherwise
- HighMath: 1 for a high mathematical background, 0 otherwise

For the following questions, assume that the students in this course represent a random sample from all college students who might take the course. This latter group is the "population."

a. Find a 90% confidence interval for the population mean score for the course. Do the same for the mean of all upperclassmen. Do the same for the mean of all upperclassmen with a high mathematical background.

b. The professor believes he has enough evidence to prove the research hypothesis that upperclassmen score at least 5 points better, on average, than lowerclassmen. Do you agree?

c. If we consider a "good" grade to be one that is at least 80, is there enough evidence to reject the null hypothesis that the fraction of good grades is the same for students with low math backgrounds as those with high math backgrounds?

82. A cereal company wants to see which of two promotional strategies, supplying coupons in a local newspaper or including coupons in the cereal package itself, is more effective. (In the latter case, there is a sign on the package indicating the presence of the coupon inside.) The company randomly chooses 80 Kroger's stores around the country—all of approximately the same size and overall sales volume—and promotes its cereal one way at 40 of these sites, and the other way at the other 40 sites. (All are at different geographical locations, so local newspaper ads for one of the sites should not affect sales at any other site.) Unfortunately, as in many business "experiments," there is a factor beyond the company's control, namely, whether its main competitor at any particular site happens to be running a promotion of its own. The file **P10_82.xlsx** has 80 observations on three variables:
- Sales: number of boxes sold during the first week of the company's promotion
- PromType:1 if coupons are in local paper, 0 if coupons are inside box
- CompProm:1 if main competitor is running a promotion, 0 otherwise

a. Based on all 80 observations, find (1) the difference in sample mean sales between stores running the two different promotional types (and indicate which sample mean is larger), (2) the standard error of this difference, and (3) a 90% confidence interval for the population mean difference.

b. Test whether the population mean difference is 0 (the null hypothesis) versus a two-tailed alternative. State whether you should accept or reject the null hypothesis, and why.

c. Repeat part **b,** but now restrict the "population" to stores where the competitor is not running a promotion of its own.

d. Based on data from all 80 observations, can you accept the (alternative) hypothesis, at the 5% level, that the mean company sales drops by at least 30 boxes when the competitor runs its own promotion (as opposed to not running its own promotion)?

e. We often use the term "population" without really thinking what it means. If you talk about the population mean for the case, say, where coupons are put in boxes, explain in words exactly what this population mean refers to.

In Chapters 11 and 12 we study regression, a method for relating one variable to other explanatory variables. However, the term *regression* has sometimes been used in a slightly different way, meaning "regression toward the mean." The example often cited is of male heights. If a father is unusually tall, for example, his son will typically be taller than average but not as tall as the father. Similarly, if a father is unusually short, the son will typically be shorter than average but not as short as the father. We say that the son's height tends to regress toward the mean. This case illustrates how regression toward the mean can occur.

Suppose a company administers an aptitude test to all of its job applicants. If an applicant scores below some value, he or she cannot be hired immediately but is allowed to retake a similar exam at a later time. In the interim the applicant can presumably study to prepare for the second exam. If we focus on the applicants who fail the exam the first time and then take it a second time, we would probably expect them to score better on the second exam. One plausible reason is that they are more familiar with the exam the second time. However, we will rule this out by assuming that the two exams are sufficiently different from one another. A second plausible reason is that the applicants have studied between exams, which has a beneficial effect. However, we will argue that even if studying has *no beneficial effect whatsoever,* these applicants will tend to do better the second time around. The reason is regression toward the mean. All of these applicants scored unusually low on the first exam, so they will tend to regress toward the mean on the second exam—that is, they will tend to score higher.

You can employ simulation to demonstrate this phenomenon, using the following model. Assume that the scores of *all* potential applicants are normally distributed with mean μ and standard deviation σ. Because we are assuming that any studying between exams has no beneficial effect, this distribution of scores is the *same* on the second exam as on the first. An applicant fails the first exam if his or her score is below some cutoff value L. Now, we would certainly expect scores on the two exams to be positively correlated, with some correlation ρ. That is, if everyone took both exams, then applicants who scored high on the first would tend to score high on the second, and those who scored low on the first would tend to score low on the second. (This isn't regression to the mean, but simply that some applicants are better than others.)

Given this model, you can proceed by simulating many pairs of scores, one pair for each applicant. The scores for each exam should be normally distributed with parameters μ and σ, but the trick is to make them correlated. You can use our Binormal_ function to do this. (Binormal is short for bivariate normal.) This function is supplied in the file **Regression Toward Mean.xlsx**, included on the CD-ROM. (Binormal_ is *not* a built-in Excel function.) It takes a pair of means (both equal to μ), a pair of standard deviations (both equal to σ), and a correlation ρ as arguments, with the syntax =BINORMAL_(*means,stdevs,correlation*). To enter the formula, highlight two adjacent cells such as B5 and C5, type the formula, and press Ctrl-Shift-Enter. Then copy and paste to generate similar values for other applicants. (The Binormal_ Example sheet in this file illustrates the procedure. You should create another sheet in the same file to solve this case.)

Once you have generated pairs of scores for many applicants, you should ignore all pairs except for those where the score on the first exam is less than L. (Sorting is suggested here, but "freeze" the random numbers first.) For these pairs, test whether the mean score on the second exam is *higher* than on the first, using a paired-samples test. If it is, you have demonstrated regression toward the mean. As you'll probably discover, however, the results will depend on the parameters you choose: μ, σ, ρ, and L. You should experiment with these. Assuming that you are able to demonstrate regression toward the mean, can you explain intuitively why it occurs? ■

Baseball has long been the sport of statistics. Probably more statistics—both relevant and completely obscure—are kept on baseball games and players than for any other sport. During the early 1990s, the first author of this book was able to acquire an enormous set of baseball data.[12] It includes data on every at-bat for every player in every game for the 4-year period from 1987 to 1990. The majority of these data are on the CD-ROM that accompanies this book. (The bulk of the data are in eight large files with names such as **89AL.exe**—for the 1989 American League. See the **BB_Readme.txt** file for detailed information about the files.) The files include data for approximately 500 player-years during this period. Each text file contains data for a particular player during an entire year, such as Barry Bonds during 1989, provided that the player had at least 500 at-bats during that year. Each record (row) of such a file lists the information pertaining to a single at-bat, such as whether the player got a hit, how many runners were on base, the earned-run-average (ERA) of the pitcher, and more.

The author analyzed these data to see whether batters tend to hit in "streaks," a phenomenon that has been debated for years among avid fans. [The results of this study are described in Albright (1993).] However, the data set is sufficiently rich to enable testing of any number of hypotheses. We challenge you to develop your own hypotheses and test them with these data. ■

---

[12]The data were collected by volunteers of a group called Project Scoresheet. These volunteers attended each game and kept detailed records of virtually everything that occurred. Such detail is certainly not available in newspaper box scores—it is probably not even available on the Web!

10.3 THE WICHITA ANTI–DRUNK DRIVING ADVERTISING CAMPAIGN[13]

Each year drinking and driving behavior are estimated to be responsible for approximately 24,000 traffic fatalities in the United States. Data show that a preponderance of this problem is due to the behavior of young males. Indeed, a disproportionate number of traffic fatalities are young people between 15 and 24 years of age. Market research among young people has suggested that this perverse behavior of driving automobiles while under the influence of alcoholic beverages might be reduced by a mass media communications/advertising program based on an understanding of the "consumer psychology" of young male drinking and driving. There is some precedent for this belief. Reduction in cigarette smoking over the last 25 years is often attributed in part to mass antismoking advertising campaigns. There is also precedent for being less optimistic because past experimental campaigns against drunk driving have shown little success.

Between March and August of 1986, an anti–drinking and driving advertising campaign was conducted in the city of Wichita, Kansas. In this federally sponsored experiment, several carefully constructed messages were aired on television and radio and also appeared in newspapers and on billboards. Unlike earlier and largely ineffective campaigns that depended on donated talent and media time, this test was sufficiently funded to create impressive anti–drinking and driving messages, and to place them so that the targeted audience would be reached. The messages were pretested before the program and the final version won an OMNI advertising award.

To evaluate the effectiveness of this anti–drinking and driving campaign, researchers collected before and after data (preprogram and postprogram) of several types. In addition to data collection in Wichita, they also selected Omaha, Nebraska, as a "control" city. Omaha, another midwestern city on the Great Plains, was arguably similar to Wichita, but was not subjected to such an advertising campaign. The following tables contain some of the data gathered by researchers to evaluate the impact of the program.

Table 10.1 contains background demographics on the test and control cities. Table 10.2 contains

data obtained from telephone surveys of 18- to 24-year-old males in both cities. The surveys were done using a random telephone dialing technique. They had an 88% response rate during the preprogram survey and a 91% response rate during the postprogram survey. Respondents were asked whether they had driven under the influence of 4 or more alcoholic drinks, or 6 or more alcoholic drinks, at least once in the previous month. The pre-program data were collected in September 1985, and the postprogram data were collected in September 1986.

Table 10.1   Demographics for Wichita and Omaha

	Wichita	Omaha
Total population	411,313	483,053
Percentage 15–24 years	19.2	19.5
Race		
White	85	87
Black	8	9
Hispanic	4	2
Other	3	2
Percent high school graduates among those 18 years and older	75.4	79.9
Private car ownership	184,641	198,723

Table 10.2   Telephone Survey of 18- to 24-Year-Old Males

	Wichita		Omaha	
	Before Program	After Program	Before Program	After Program
Respondents	205	221	203	157
Drove after 4 drinks	71	61	77	69
Drove after 6 drinks	42	37	45	38

Table 10.3 contains counts of fatal or incapacitating accidents involving young people gathered from the Kansas and Nebraska Traffic Safety Departments during the spring and summer months

[13]This case was contributed by Peter Kolesar from Columbia University.

of 1985 (before program) and 1986 (during the program). The spring and summer months were defined to be the period from March to August. These data were taken by the research team as "indicators" of driving under the influence of alcohol. Researchers at first proposed to also gather data on the blood alcohol content of drivers involved in fatal accidents. However, traffic safety experts pointed out that such data are often inconsistent and incomplete because police at the scene of a fatal accident have more pressing duties to perform than to gather such data. On the other hand, it is well established that alcohol is implicated in a major proportion of nighttime traffic fatalities, and for that reason, the data also focus on accidents at night among two classes of young people: the group of accidents involving 18- to 24-year-old males as a driver, and the group of accidents involving 15- to 24-year-old males and/or females as a driver.

The categories of accidents recorded were as follows:

- Total: total count of all fatal and incapacitating accidents in the indicated driver group
- Single vehicle: single vehicle fatal and incapacitating accidents in the indicated driver group
- Nighttime: nighttime (8 P.M. to 8 A.M.) fatal and incapacitating accidents in the indicated driver group

It was estimated that if a similar 6-month advertising campaign were run nationally, it would cost about $25 million. The Commissioner of the U.S. National Highway Safety Commission had funded a substantial part of the study and needed to decide what, if anything, to do next.

Table 10.3 Average Monthly Number of Fatal and Incapacitating Accidents, March to August

Driver Group	Accident Type	Wichita 1985	Wichita 1986	Omaha 1985	Omaha 1986
18- to 24-year-old males	Total	68	55	41	40
	Single	13	13	13	14
	Night	36	35	25	26
15- to 24-year-old males and females	Total	117	97	59	57
	Single	22	17	16	20
	Night	56	52	34	38

10.4 DECIDING WHETHER TO SWITCH TO A NEW TOOTHPASTE DISPENSER

John Jacobs works for the Fresh Toothpaste Company and has recently been assigned to investigate a new type of toothpaste dispenser. The traditional tube of toothpaste uses a screw-off cap. The new dispenser uses the same type of tube, but there is now a flip-top cap on a hinge. John believes this new cap is easier to use, although it is a bit messier than the screw-off cap—toothpaste tends to accumulate around the new cap. So far, the positive aspects appear to outweigh the negatives. In informal tests, consumers reacted favorably to the new cap. The next step was to introduce the new cap in a regional test market. The company has just conducted this test market for a 6-month period in 85 stores in the Cincinnati region. The results, in units sold per store, appear in Figure 10.39. (See the file **Toothpaste.xlsx**.)

John has done his homework on the financial side. Figure 10.40 shows a break-even analysis for the new dispenser relative to the current dispenser. The analysis is over the entire U.S. market, which consists of 9530 stores (of roughly similar size) that stock the product. Based on several assumptions that we soon

discuss, John figures that to break even with the new dispenser, the sales volume per store per 6-month period must be 3622 units. The question is whether the test market data support a decision to abandon the current dispenser and market the new dispenser nationally.

We first discuss the break-even analysis in Figure 10.40. The assumptions are listed in rows 4 through 8 and relevant inputs are listed in rows 11 through 17. In particular, the new dispenser involves an up-front investment of \$1.5 million, and its unit cost is 2 cents higher than the unit cost for the current dispenser. However, the company doesn't plan to raise the selling price. Rows 22 through 26 calculate the net present value (NPV) for the next 4 years, assuming that the company does not switch to the new dispenser. Starting with *any* first-year sales volume in cell C30, rows 29 through 35 calculate the NPV for the next 4 years, assuming that the company does switch to the new dispenser. The goal of the break-even analysis is to find a value in cell C30 that makes the two NPVs (in cells B26 and B35) equal.

Figure 10.39

Toothpaste Dispenser Data from Cincinnati Region

	A	B	C	D	E	F
1	Sales volumes in Cincinnati regional test market for 6 months					
2						
3	Store	Units sold				
4	1	4106				
5	2	2786				
6	3	3858				
7	4	3015				
8	5	3900				
9	6	3572				
10	7	4633				
11	8	4128				
12	9	3044				
13	10	2585				
85	82	1889				
86	83	6436				
87	84	4179				
88	85	3539				

Figure 10.40

Break-even Analysis for Toothpaste Example

	A	B	C	D	E	F
1	Breakeven analysis for Stripe Toothpaste					
2						
3	Assumptions:					
4	The planning horizon is 4 years					
5	Sales volume is expected to remain constant over the 4 years					
6	Unit selling prices and unit costs will remain constant over the 4 years					
7	Straight-line depreciation is used to depreciate the initial investment for the new dispenser					
8	Breakeven analysis is based on NPV for the four-year period					
9						
10	Given data					
11	Current volume (millions of units) using current dispenser		65.317			
12	Initial investment ($ millions) for new dispenser		1.5			
13	Unit selling price (either dispenser)		$1.79			
14	Unit cost (current dispenser)		$1.25			
15	Unit cost (new dispenser)		$1.27			
16	Tax rate		35%			
17	Discount rate		16%			
18						
19	Note: From here on, all sales volumes are in millions of units, monetary values are in $ millions					
20						
21	Analysis of current dispenser		Year 1	Year 2	Year 3	Year 4
22	Sales volume					
23	Before-tax contribution					
24	After-tax profit					
25	Cash flow					
26	NPV					
27						
28	Analysis of new dispenser		Year 1	Year 2	Year 3	Year 4
29	Initial investment	$1.5				
30	Sales volume					
31	Before-tax contribution					
32	Depreciation					
33	After-tax profit					
34	Cash flow					
35	NPV					
36						
37	Number of stores nationally	9530				
38	Breakeven sales volume per store per 6 months					

The trickiest part of the analysis concerns the depreciation calculations for the new dispenser. We find the before-tax contribution from sales in row 31 and subtract the depreciation each year (one-quarter of the investment) to figure the after-tax profit. For example, the formula in cell C33 is

=(C31-C32)*(1-$C$16)

Then the depreciation is added back to obtain the cash flow, so that the formula in cell C34 is

=C33+C32

Finally, we calculate the NPV for the new dispenser in cell B35 with the formula

=B34+NPV(C17,C34:F34)

Note that the initial investment, which is assumed to occur at the *beginning* of year 1, is not part of the NPV function, which includes only *end-of-year* cash flows.

We then use Excel's Goal Seek tool to force the NPVs in cells B26 and B35 to be equal. Again, we begin by entering any value for first-year sales volume with the new dispenser in cell C30. Then we select Goal Seek from the What-If Analysis dropdown on the Data ribbon and fill out the dialog box as shown in Figure 10.41.

Figure 10.41

Goal Seek Dialog Box

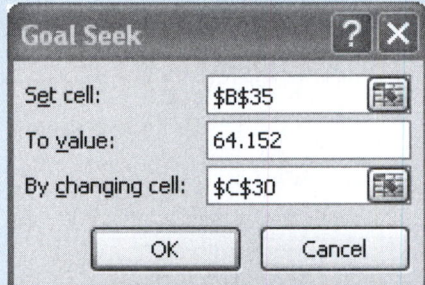

The file **Toothpaste.xlsx** does not yet contain the break-even calculations. Your first job is to enter the appropriate formulas, using any year 1 sales volume figure in cell C30. Next, you should use Excel's Goal Seek tool to find the break-even point. Finally, you should test the alternative hypothesis that the mean sales volume over all stores (for a 6-month period) will be large enough to warrant switching to the new dispenser. This hypothesis test should be based on the test market data from Cincinnati. Do you recommend that the company should switch to the new dispenser? Discuss whether this decision should be based on the results of a hypothesis test. ∎

For years, the drug Vioxx, developed and marketed by Merck, was one of the blockbuster drugs on the market. One of a number of so-called Cox-2 anti-inflammatory drugs, Vioxx was considered by many people a miracle drug for alleviating the pain from arthritis and other painful afflictions. Vioxx was marketed heavily on television, it was prescribed by most physicians, and it was used by an estimated 2 million Americans.

All of that changed in October 2004, when the results of a large study were released. The study, which followed approximately 2600 subjects over a period of about 18 months, concluded that Vioxx use over a long period of time caused a significant increase in the risk of developing serious heart problems. Merck almost immediately pulled Vioxx from the American market, and doctors stopped prescribing it. On the basis of the study, Merck faced not only public embarrassment but the prospect of huge financial losses.

More specifically, the study had 1287 patients use Vioxx for an 18-month period, and it had another 1299 patients use a placebo over the same period.

After 18 months, 45 of the Vioxx patients had developed serious heart problems, whereas only 25 patients on the placebo developed such problems.

Given these results, would you agree with the conclusion that Vioxx caused a *significant* increase in the risk of developing serious heart problems? First, answer this from a purely statistical point of view, where "significant" means statistically significant. What hypothesis should you test, and how should you test it? When you run the test, what is the corresponding p-value? Next, look at it from the point of view of patients. If you were a Vioxx user, would these results cause you "significant" worry? After all, some of the subjects who took placebos also developed heart problems, and 45 might not be considered that much larger than 25. Finally, look at it from Merck's point of view. Are the results practically "significant" to the company? What does it stand to lose? Develop an estimate, no matter how wild it might be, of the financial losses Merck might incur. Just think of all of those American Vioxx users and what they might do! ∎

Regression Analysis: Estimating Relationships

© Digital Vision/Photodisc/Getty Images

SITE LOCATION OF LA QUINTA MOTOR INNS

Regression analysis is an extremely flexible tool that can aid decision making in many areas. Kimes and Fitzsimmons (1990) describe how it has been used by La Quinta Motor Inns, a moderately priced hotel chain oriented toward serving the business traveler, to help make site location decisions. Location is one of the most important decisions for a lodging firm. All hotel chains search for ideal locations and often compete against each other for the same sites. A hotel chain that can select good sites more accurately and quickly than its competition has a distinct competitive advantage.

Kimes and Fitzsimmons, academics hired by La Quinta to model its site location decision process, used regression analysis. They collected data on 57 mature inns belonging to La Quinta during a 3-year business cycle. The data included profitability for each inn (defined as operating margin percentage—profit plus depreciation and interest expenses, divided by the total revenue), as well as a number of potential explanatory variables that could be used to predict profitability. These explanatory variables fell into five categories: competitive characteristics (such as number of hotel rooms in the vicinity and average room rates); demand generators (such as hospitals and office buildings within a 4-mile radius that might attract customers to the area); demographic characteristics (such as local population, unemployment rate, and median family income); market awareness (such as years the inn has been open and state population per inn); and physical considerations (such as accessibility, distance to downtown, and sign visibility).

The analysts then determined which of these potential explanatory variables were most highly correlated (positively or negatively) with profitability and entered these variables into a regression equation for profitability. The estimated regression equation was

$$\text{Predicted Profitability} = 39.05 - 5.41\text{StatePop} + 5.81\text{Price}$$
$$- 3.09\sqrt{\text{MedIncome}} + 1.75\text{ColStudents}$$

where *StatePop* is the state population (1000s) per inn, *Price* is the room rate for the inn, *MedIncome* is the median income ($1000s) of the area, *ColStudents* is the number of college students (1000s) within 4 miles, and all variables in this equation are standardized to have mean 0 and standard deviation 1. This equation predicts that profitability will increase when room rate and the number of college students *increase* and when state population and median income *decrease*. The R^2 value (to be discussed in this chapter) was a respectable 0.51, indicating a reasonable predictive ability. Using good statistical practice, the analysts validated this equation by feeding it explanatory variable data on a set of *different* inns, attempting to predict profitability for these new inns. The validation was a success—the regression equation predicted profitability fairly accurately for this new set of inns.

La Quinta management, however, was not as interested in predicting the exact profitability of inns as in predicting which would be profitable and which would be unprofitable. A cutoff value of 35% for operating margin was used to divide the profitable inns from the unprofitable inns. (Approximately 60% of the inns in the original sample were profitable by this definition.) The analysts were still able to use the regression equation they had developed. For any prospective site, they used the regression equation to predict profitability, and if the predicted value was sufficiently high, they predicted that this site would be profitable. They selected a decision rule—that is, how high was "sufficiently high"—from considerations of the two potential types of errors. One type of error, a false positive, was predicting that a site would be profitable when in fact it was headed for unprofitability. The opposite type of error, a false negative, was predicting that a site would be unprofitable (and rejecting the site) when in fact it would have been profitable. La Quinta management was more concerned about false positives, so it was willing to be conservative in its decision rule and miss a few potential opportunities for profitable sites.

Since the time of the study, La Quinta has implemented the regression model in spreadsheet form. For each potential site, it collects data on the relevant explanatory variables, uses the regression equation to predict the site's profitability, and applies the decision rule on whether to build. Of course, the model's recommendation is only that—a recommendation. Top management has the ultimate say on whether any site is used. As Sam Barshop, then chairman of the board and president of La Quinta Motor Inns stated, "We currently use the model to help us in our site-screening process and have found that it has raised the 'red flag' on several sites we had under consideration. We plan to continue using and updating the model in the future in our attempt to make La Quinta a leader in the business hotel market." ■

11.1 INTRODUCTION

Regression analysis is the study of relationships between variables. It is one of the most useful tools for a business analyst because it applies to so many situations. Some potential uses of regression analysis in business include the following:

- How do wages of employees depend on years of experience, years of education, and gender?

- How does the current price of a stock depend on its own past values, as well as the current and past values of a market index?

- How does a company's current sales level depend on its current and past advertising levels, the advertising levels of its competitors, the company's own past sales levels, and the general level of the market?

- How does the unit cost of producing an item depend on the total quantity of items that have been produced?

- How does the selling price of a house depend on such factors as the appraised value of the house, the square footage of the house, the number of bedrooms in the house, and perhaps others?

Each of these questions asks how a single variable, such as selling price or employee wages, depends on other relevant variables. If we can estimate this relationship, then we can not only better understand how the world operates, but we can also do a better job of predicting the variable in question. For example, we can not only understand how a company's sales are affected by its advertising, but we can also use the company's records of current and past advertising levels to predict future sales.

The branch of statistics that studies such relationships is called *regression analysis*, and it is the subject of this chapter and the next. Regression analysis is one of the most pervasive of all statistical methods in the business world. This is because of its generality and applicability.

There are several ways to categorize regression analysis. One categorization is based on the overall purpose of the analysis. As suggested previously, there are two potential objectives of regression analysis: to understand how the world operates and to make predictions. Either of these objectives could be paramount in any particular application. If the variable in question is employee wages and we are using variables such as years of experience, years of education, and gender to explain wage levels, then the purpose of the analysis is probably to understand how the world operates—that is, to explain how the variables combine in any given company to determine wages. More specifically, the purpose of the analysis might be to discover whether there is any gender discrimination in wages, after allowing for differences in work experience and education level.

Regression can be used to understand how the world operates, and it can be used for prediction.

On the other hand, the primary objective of the analysis might be prediction. A good example of this is when the variable in question is company sales, and variables such as advertising and past sales levels are used as explanatory variables. In this case it is certainly important for the company to know how the relevant variables impact its sales. But the company's primary objective is probably to predict *future* sales levels, given current and past values of the explanatory variables. A company might also use a regression model for a what-if analysis, where it predicts future sales for many conceivable patterns of advertising and then selects its advertising level on the basis of these predictions.

Fortunately, the same regression analysis enables us to solve both problems simultaneously. That is, it indicates how the world operates and it enables us to make predictions. So although the objectives of regression studies might differ, the same basic analysis always applies.

A second categorization of regression analysis is based on the type of data being analyzed. There are two basic types: *cross-sectional data* and *time series data*. **Cross-sectional data** are usually data gathered from approximately the same period of time from a cross section of a population. The housing and wage examples mentioned previously are typical cross-sectional studies. The first concerns a sample of houses, presumably sold during a short period of time, such as houses sold in Florida during the first couple of months of 2004. The second concerns a sample of employees observed at a particular point in time, such as a sample of automobile workers observed at the beginning of 2005.

In contrast, **time series data** involve one or more variables that are observed at several, usually equally spaced, points in time. The stock price example mentioned previously fits this description. We observe the price of a particular stock and possibly the price of a market index at the beginning of every week, say, and then try to explain the movement of the stock's price through time.

Regression can be used to analyze cross-sectional data or time series data.

Regression analysis can be applied equally well to cross-sectional and time series data. However, there are technical reasons for treating time series analysis somewhat differently. The primary reason is that time series variables are usually related to their own past values. This property of many time series variables is called **autocorrelation**, and it adds complications to the analysis that we will discuss briefly.

A third categorization of regression analysis involves the number of explanatory variables in the analysis. First, we need to introduce some terms. In every regression study there is a single variable that we are trying to explain or predict, called the **dependent** variable or the **response** variable. To help explain or predict the dependent variable, we use one or more **explanatory** variables. These explanatory variables are also called **independent** variables or **predictor** variables. If there is a single explanatory variable, the analysis is called **simple regression**. If there are several explanatory variables, it is called **multiple regression**.[1]

> The **dependent** (or **response**) variable is the single variable being explained by the regression. The **explanatory** (or **independent**) variables are used to explain the dependent variable.

There are important differences between simple and multiple regression. The primary difference, as the name implies, is that simple regression is simpler. The calculations are simpler, the interpretation of output is somewhat simpler, and fewer complications can occur. We begin with simple regression examples to introduce the ideas of regression. But we soon see that simple regression is no more than a special case of multiple regression, and there is little need to single it out for separate discussion—especially when computer software is available to perform the calculations in either case.

> A **simple** regression includes a single explanatory variable, whereas a **multiple** regression can include any number of explanatory variables.

"Linear" regression allows us to estimate linear relationships as well as some nonlinear relationships.

A final categorization of regression analysis concerns linear versus nonlinear models. The only type of regression analysis we study here is *linear* regression. Generally, this means that the relationships between variables are *straight-line* relationships, whereas the term *nonlinear* implies curved relationships. By focusing on linear regression, it might appear that we are ignoring the many nonlinear relationships that exist in the business world. Fortunately, linear regression can often be used to estimate nonlinear relationships. As we will see, the term *linear regression* is more general than it appears. Admittedly, many of the relationships we study can be explained adequately by straight lines. But it is also true that many nonlinear relationships can be "linearized" by suitable mathematical transformations. Therefore, the only relationships we are ignoring in this book are those— and there are some—that cannot be transformed to linear. Such relationships can be studied, but only by advanced methods beyond the level of this book.

In this chapter we focus on line-fitting and curve-fitting, that is, on estimating equations that describe relationships between variables. We also discuss the interpretation of these equations, and we provide numerical measures that indicate the goodness of fit of the equations we estimate. In the next chapter we extend the analysis to statistical inference of regression output.

---

[1]The traditional terms used in regression are *dependent* and *independent* variables. However, because these terms can cause confusion with probabilistic independence, a totally different concept, there has been an increasing use of the terms *response* and *explanatory* (or *predictor*) variables. We tend to prefer the terms *dependent* and *explanatory*, but this is largely a matter of taste.

11.2 SCATTERPLOTS: GRAPHING RELATIONSHIPS

A good way to begin any regression analysis is to draw one or more scatterplots. As discussed in Chapter 2, a scatterplot is a graphical plot of two variables, an X and a Y. If there is any relationship between the two variables, it is usually apparent from the scatterplot.

The following example, which we will continue through this chapter, illustrates the usefulness of scatterplots. It is a typical example of cross-sectional data.

| EXAMPLE | 11.1 SALES VERSUS PROMOTIONS AT PHARMEX |

Pharmex is a chain of drugstores that operate around the country. To see how effective its advertising and other promotional activities are, the company has collected data from 50 randomly selected metropolitan regions. In each region it has compared its own promotional expenditures and sales to those of the leading competitor in the region over the past year. There are two variables:

- Promote: Pharmex's promotional expenditures as a percentage of those of the leading competitor
- Sales: Pharmex's sales as a percentage of those of the leading competitor

Note that each of these variables is an "index," not a dollar amount. For example, if Promote equals 95 for some region, this tells us only that Pharmex's promotional expenditures in that region are 95% as large as those for the leading competitor in that region. The company expects that there is a positive relationship between these two variables, so that regions with relatively larger expenditures have relatively larger sales. However, it is not clear what the nature of this relationship is. The data are listed in the file **Drugstore Sales.xlsx**. (See Figure 11.1 for a partial listing of the data.) What type of relationship, if any, is apparent from a scatterplot?

Figure 11.1

Data for Drugstore Example

	A	B	C	D	E	F	G	H
1	Region	Promote	Sales					
2	1	77	85					
3	2	110	103					
4	3	110	102		Each value is a percentage of what			
5	4	93	109		the leading competitor did.			
6	5	90	85					
7	6	95	103					
8	7	100	110					
9	8	85	86					
10	9	96	92					
11	10	83	87					

Objective To use a scatterplot to examine the relationship between promotional expenses and sales at Pharmex.

Solution

First, recall from Chapter 2 that there are two ways to create a scatterplot in Excel. We can use Excel's Chart Wizard to create an X–Y chart, or we can use StatTools's Scatterplot procedure. The advantages of the latter are that it is slightly easier to implement and it provides automatic formatting of the chart.

Which variable should be on the horizontal axis? In regression we always put the explanatory variable on the horizontal axis and the dependent variable on the vertical axis. In this example the store believes large promotional expenditures tend to "cause" larger values of sales, so we put Sales on the vertical axis and Promote on the horizontal axis. The resulting scatterplot appears in Figure 11.2.

Figure 11.2

Scatterplot of Sales versus Promote

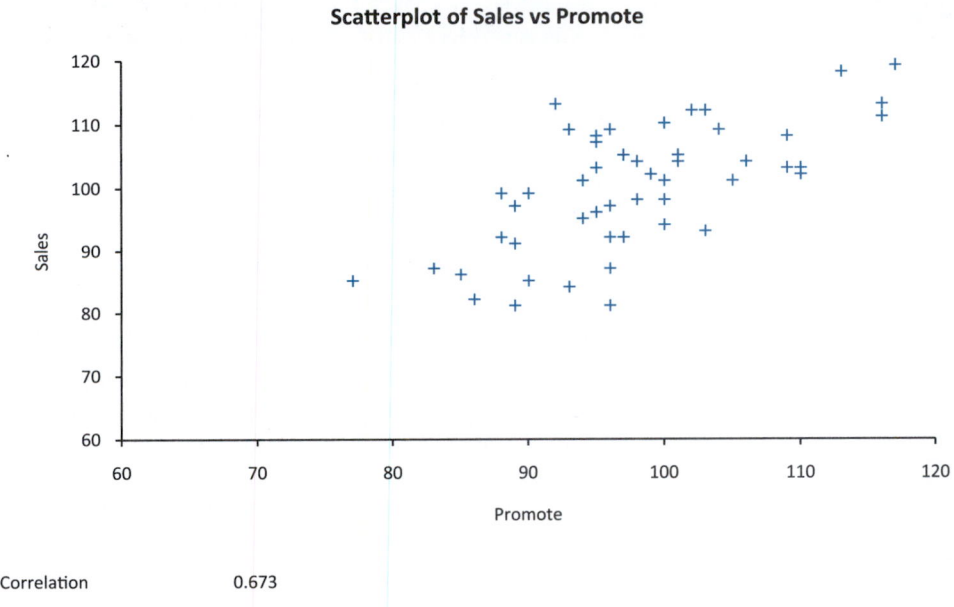

Remember that a StatTools chart is really just an Excel chart. So you can manipulate it using Excel tools. For this scatterplot, we changed the scales of the axes so that the scatter filled up more of the chart area.

This scatterplot indicates that there is indeed a positive relationship between Promote and Sales—the points tend to rise from bottom left to top right—but the relationship is not perfect. If it were perfect, a given value of Promote would prescribe the value of Sales exactly. Clearly, this is not the case. For example, there are five regions with promotional values of 96 but all of them have different sales values. So the scatterplot indicates that while the variable Promote is helpful for predicting Sales, it will not yield perfect predictions.

Note the correlation of 0.673 shown at the bottom of Figure 11.2. StatTools inserts this value automatically (if you request it) to indicate the strength of the linear relationship between the two variables. For now, just note that it is positive and its magnitude is moderately large. We say more about correlations in the next section.

Finally, we briefly discuss causation. There is a tendency for an analyst (such as a drugstore manager) to say that larger promotional expenses *cause* larger sales values. However, unless the data are obtained in a carefully controlled experiment—which is certainly not the case here—we can never make definitive statements about causation in regression analysis. The reason is that we can almost never rule out the possibility that some other variable is causing the variation in *both* of the observed variables. While this might be unlikely in this drugstore example, it is still a possibility. ■

The following example uses time series data to illustrate several other features of scatterplots. We will also follow this example throughout the chapter.

EXAMPLE   11.2 EXPLAINING OVERHEAD COSTS AT BENDRIX

The Bendrix Company manufactures various types of parts for automobiles. The manager of the factory wants to get a better understanding of overhead costs. These overhead costs include supervision, indirect labor, supplies, payroll taxes, overtime premiums, depreciation, and a number of miscellaneous items such as insurance, utilities, and janitorial and maintenance expenses. Some of these overhead costs are "fixed" in the sense that they do not vary appreciably with the volume of work being done, whereas others are "variable" and do vary directly with the volume of work. The fixed overhead costs tend to come from the supervision, depreciation, and miscellaneous categories, whereas the variable overhead costs tend to come from the indirect labor, supplies, payroll taxes, and overtime categories. However, it is not easy to draw a clear line between the fixed and variable overhead components.

The Bendrix manager has tracked total overhead costs for the past 36 months. To help "explain" these, he has also collected data on two variables that are related to the amount of work done at the factory. These variables are:

- MachHrs: number of machine hours used during the month
- ProdRuns: the number of separate production runs during the month

The first of these is a direct measure of the amount of work being done. To understand the second, we note that Bendrix manufactures parts in large batches. Each batch corresponds to a production run. Once a production run is completed, the factory must "set up" for the next production run. During this setup there is typically some downtime while the machinery is reconfigured for the part type scheduled for production in the next batch. Therefore, the manager believes that both of these variables could be responsible (in different ways) for variations in overhead costs. Do scatterplots support this belief?

Objective To use scatterplots to examine the relationships among overhead, machine hours, and production runs at Bendrix.

Solution

The data appear in Figure 11.3. (See the **Overhead Costs.xlsx** file.) Each observation (row) corresponds to a single month. We want to investigate any possible relationship between the Overhead variable and the MachHrs and ProdRuns variables, but because these are time series variables, we should also be on the lookout for any relationships between these variables and the Month variable. That is, we should also investigate any time series behavior in these variables.

Figure 11.3

Data for Bendrix
Overhead Example

	A	B	C	D
	Month	MachHrs	ProdRuns	Overhead
1				
2	1	1539	31	99798
3	2	1284	29	87804
4	3	1490	27	93681
5	4	1355	22	82262
6	5	1500	35	106968
7	6	1777	30	107925
8	7	1716	41	117287
9	8	1045	29	76868
10	9	1364	47	106001
11	10	1516	21	88738
35	34	1723	35	107828
36	35	1413	30	88032
37	36	1390	54	117943

This data set illustrates, even with a modest number of variables, how the number of potentially useful scatterplots can grow quickly. At the very least, we should examine the scatterplot between each potential explanatory variable (MachHrs and ProdRuns) and the dependent variable (Overhead). These appear in Figures 11.4 and 11.5. We see that Overhead tends to increase as either MachHrs increases or ProdRuns increases. However, both relationships are far from perfect.

Figure 11.4

Scatterplot of Overhead versus Machine Hours

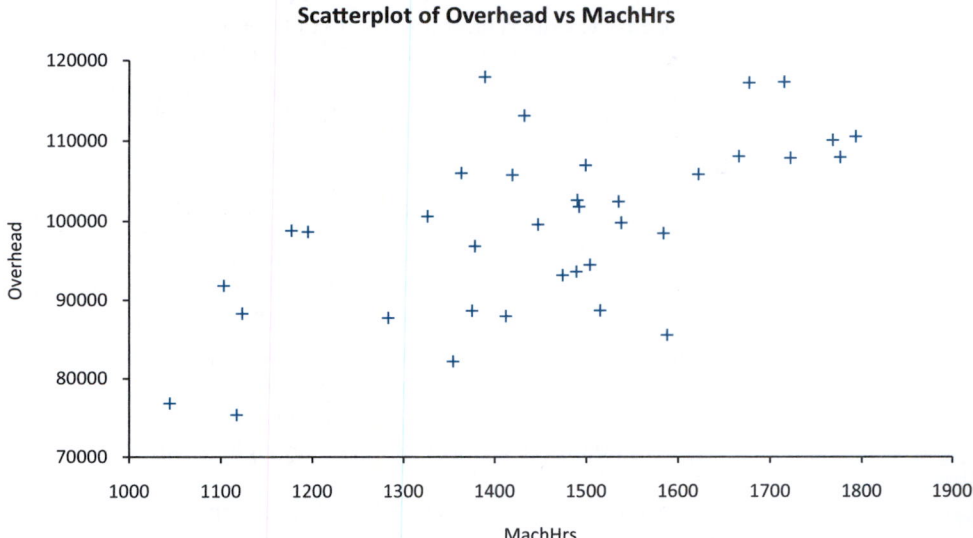

Figure 11.5

Scatterplot of Overhead versus Production Runs

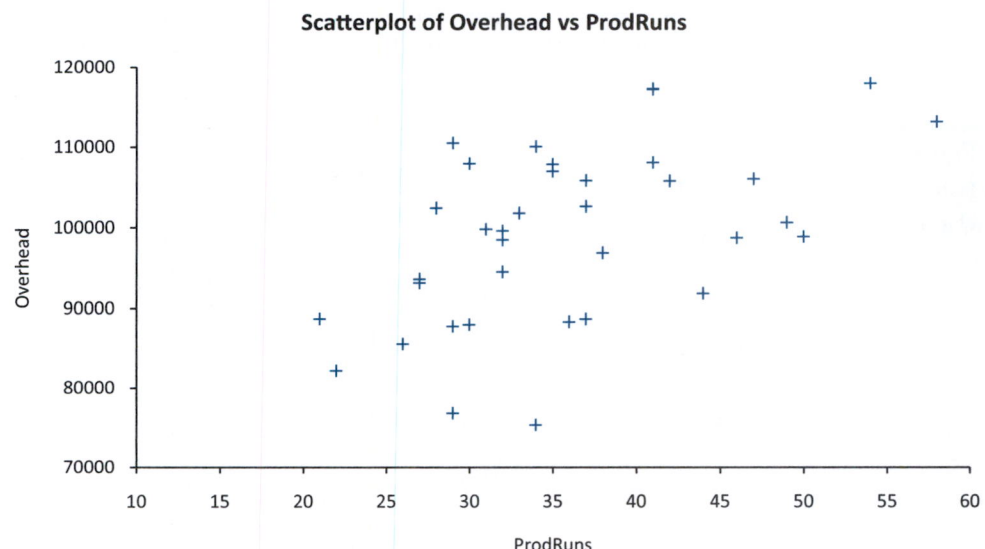

To check for possible time series patterns, we can also create a time series graph for any of the variables. One of these, the time series graph for Overhead, is shown in Figure 11.6. It indicates a fairly random pattern through time, with no apparent upward trend or other obvious time series pattern. You can check that time series graphs of the MachHrs and ProdRuns variables also indicate no obvious time series patterns.

Figure 11.6

Time Series Graph of Overhead versus Month

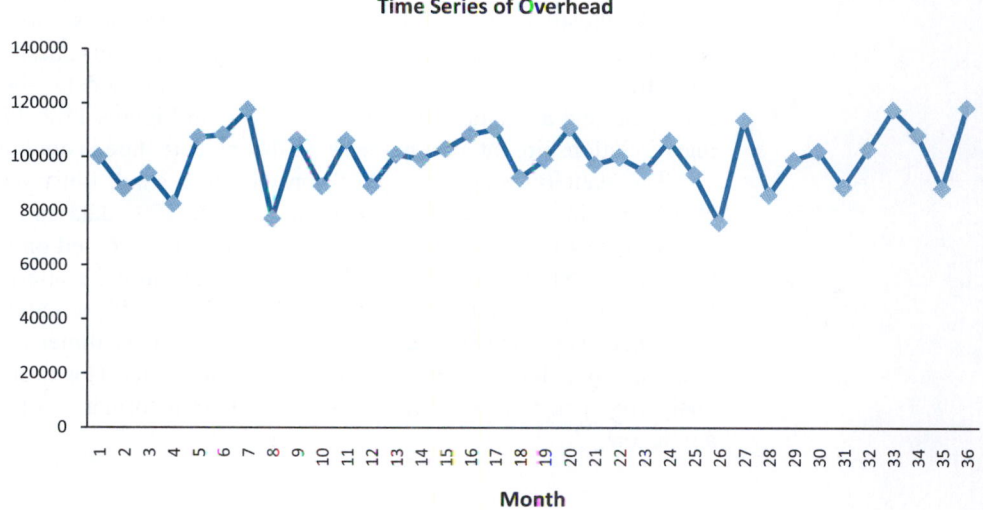

This is precisely the role of scatterplots: to give us a visual representation of relationships or the lack of relationships between variables.

Finally, when there are multiple explanatory variables, we can check for relationships among them. The scatterplot of MachHrs versus ProdRuns appears in Figure 11.7. (Either variable could be chosen for the vertical axis.) This "cloud" of points indicates no relationship worth pursuing.

Figure 11.7

Scatterplot of Machine Hours versus Production Runs

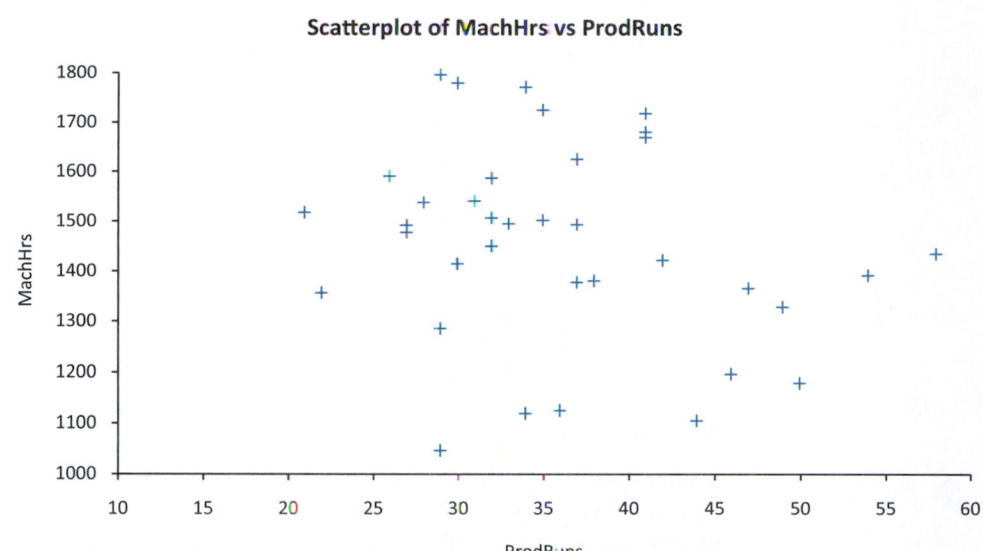

In summary, the Bendrix manager should continue to explore the positive relationship between Overhead and each of the MachHrs and ProdRuns variables. However, none of the variables appears to have any time series behavior, and the two potential explanatory variables do not appear to be related to each other. ■

11.2.1 Linear Versus Nonlinear Relationships

Scatterplots are extremely useful for detecting behavior that might not be obvious otherwise. We illustrate some of these in the next few subsections. First, the typical relationship we hope to see is a straight-line, or *linear*, relationship. This doesn't mean that all points lie on a straight line—this is too much to expect in business data—but that the points tend to cluster around a straight line. The scatterplots in Figures 11.2, 11.4, and 11.5 all exhibit linear relationships, at least in the sense that no curvature is obvious.

The scatterplot in Figure 11.8, on the other hand, illustrates a relationship that is clearly nonlinear. The data in this scatterplot are 1990 data on more than 100 countries. The variables listed are life expectancy (of newborns, based on current mortality conditions) and GNP per capita. The obvious curvature in the scatterplot can be explained as follows. For poor countries, a slight increase in GNP per capita has a large effect on life expectancy. However, this effect decreases for wealthier countries. A straight-line relationship is definitely not appropriate for these data. However, as we discussed previously, *linear* regression—after an appropriate transformation of the data—still might be applicable.

Figure 11.8

Scatterplot of Life
Expectancy versus
GNP per Capita

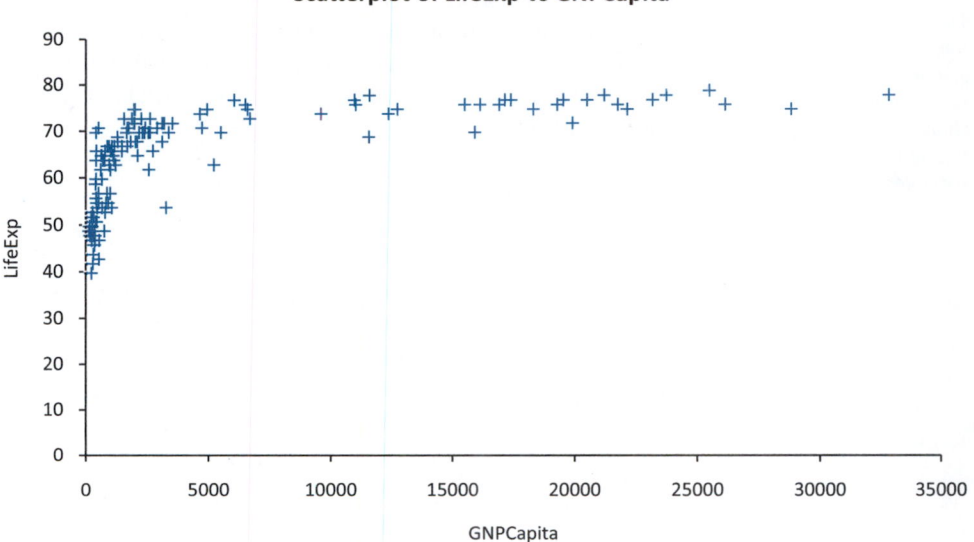

11.2.2 Outliers

Scatterplots are especially useful for identifying **outliers**, observations that lie outside the typical pattern of points. The scatterplot in Figure 11.9 shows annual salaries versus years of experience for a sample of employees at a particular company. There is a clear linear relationship between these two variables—for all employees except the point at the top right. Closer scrutiny of the data reveals that this one employee is the company president, whose salary is well above that of all the other employees!

> An **outlier** is an observation that falls outside of the general pattern of the rest of the observations.

Figure 11.9 Scatterplot of Salary versus Years of Experience

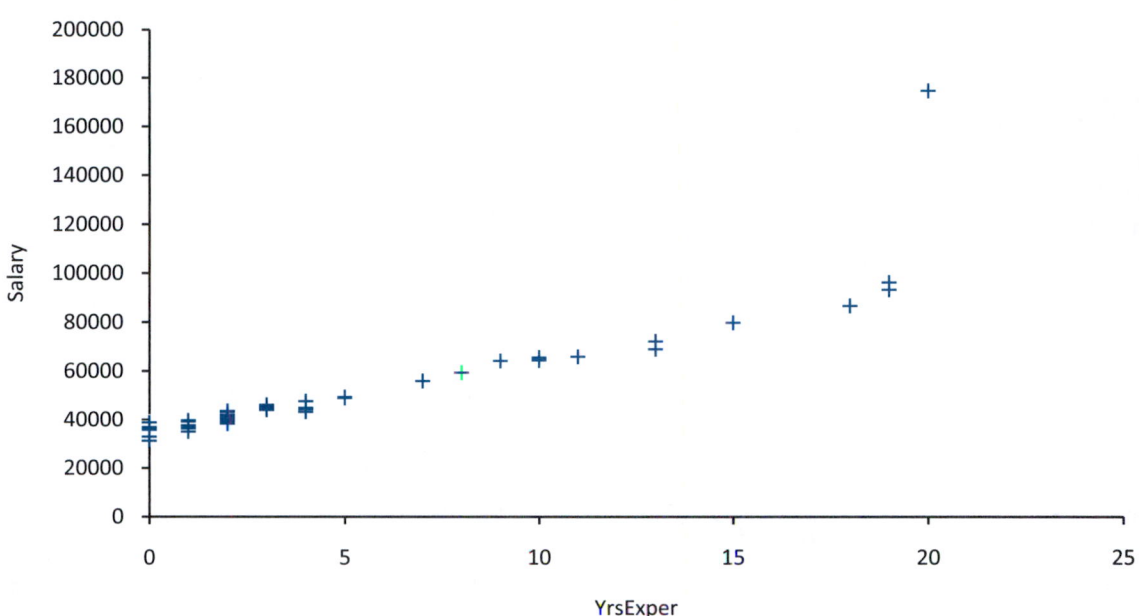

Although scatterplots are good for detecting outliers, they do not necessarily indicate what we ought to do about any outliers we find. This depends entirely on the particular situation. If we are attempting to investigate the salary structure for "typical" employees at a company, then we probably should not include the company president. First, the president's salary is not determined in the same way as the salaries for typical employees. Second, if we do include the president in the analysis, it can greatly distort the results for the mass of typical employees. In other situations, however, it might *not* be appropriate to eliminate outliers just to make the analysis come out more nicely.

It is difficult to generalize about the treatment of outliers, but the following points are worth noting.

- If an outlier is clearly not a member of the population of interest, then it is probably best to delete it from the analysis. This is the case for the company president in Figure 11.9.

- If it isn't clear whether outliers are members of the relevant population, we should run the regression analysis with them and without them. If the results are practically the same in both cases, then it is probably best to report the results with the outliers included. Otherwise, we should report both sets of results with a verbal explanation of the outliers.

11.2.3 Unequal Variance

Occasionally, there is a clear relationship between two variables, but the variance of the dependent variable depends on the value of the explanatory variable. We saw a good example of this in the catalog data in Example 3.11 of Chapter 3. Figure 11.10 reproduces one of the scatterplots from the data in that example. It shows AmountSpent versus Salary for the customers in the data set. There is a clear linear relationship, but the variability of AmountSpent increases as Salary increases. This is evident from the "fan" shape. As we see in the next chapter, this unequal variance violates one of the assumptions of linear regression analysis, and there are special techniques to deal with it.

Figure 11.10

Unequal Variance of Dependent Variable in a Scatterplot

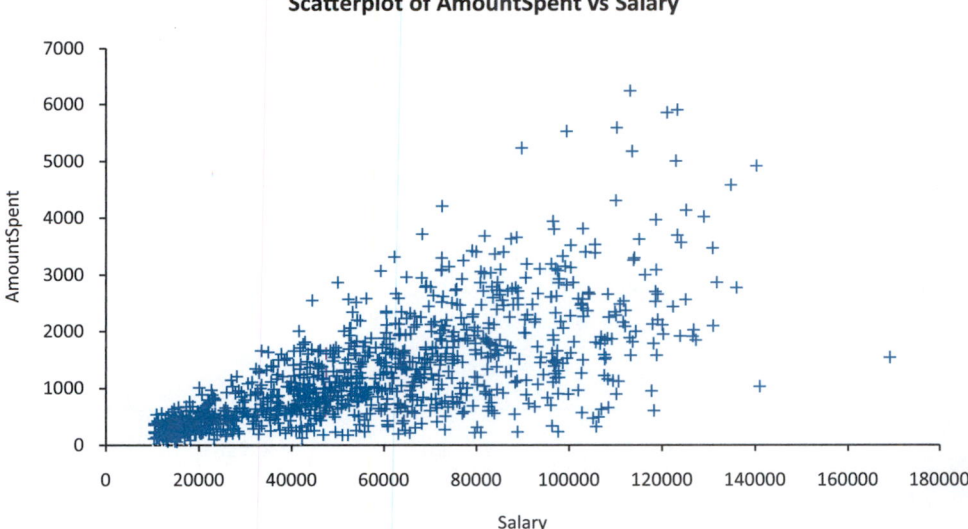

Scatterplot of AmountSpent vs Salary

11.2.4 No Relationship

A scatterplot can provide one other useful piece of information—it can indicate that there is *no* relationship between a pair of variables, at least none worth pursuing. This is usually the case when the scatterplot appears as a shapeless swarm of points, as illustrated in Figure 11.11. Here the variables are an employee performance score and the number of overtime hours worked in the previous month for a sample of employees. There is virtually no hint of a relationship between these two variables in this plot, and if these are the only two variables in the data set, the analysis could stop right here. Many people who use statistics evidently believe that a computer can perform magic on a set of numbers and find relationships that were completely hidden. Occasionally this is true, but when a scatterplot appears as in Figure 11.11, the variables are not related in any useful way, and that's all there is to it.

Figure 11.11   An Example of No Relationship

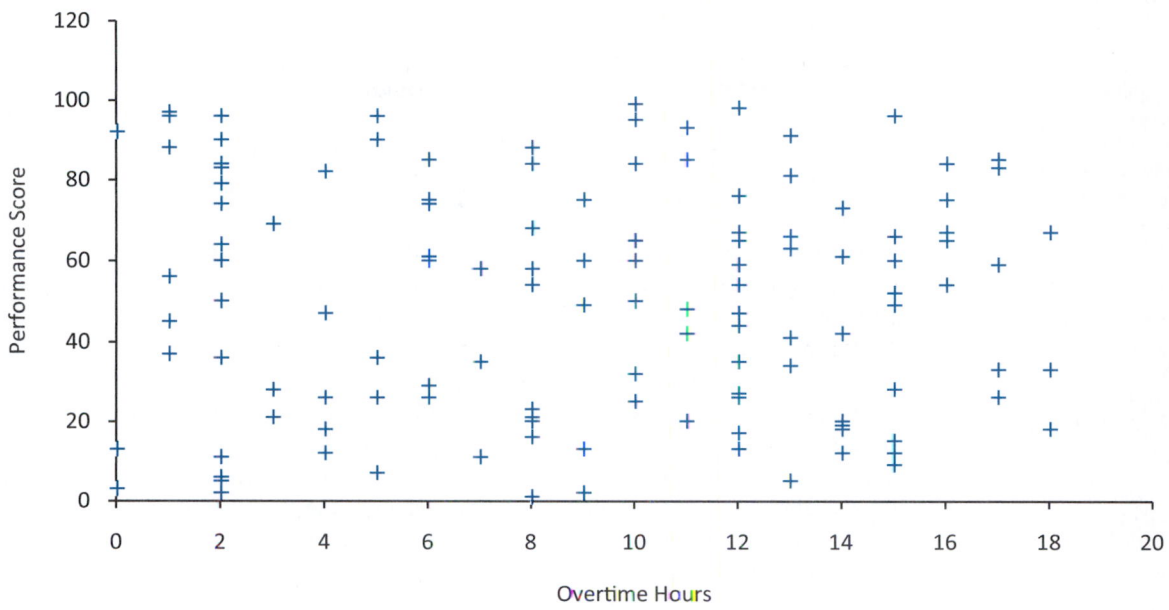

Scatterplot of Performance Score vs Overtime Hours

11.3 CORRELATIONS: INDICATORS OF LINEAR RELATIONSHIPS

Scatterplots provide graphical indications of relationships, whether they be linear, nonlinear, or essentially nonexistent. **Correlations** are numerical summary measures that indicate the strength of linear relationships between pairs of variables.[2] A correlation between a pair of variables is a single number that summarizes the information in a scatterplot. A correlation can be very useful, but it has an important limitation: It can only measure the strength of a *linear* relationship. If there is a nonlinear relationship, as suggested by a scatterplot, the correlation can be completely misleading. With this important limitation in mind, let's look a bit more closely at correlations.

The usual notation for a correlation between two variables X and Y is r_{XY}. (The subscripts can be omitted if the variables are clear from the context of the problem.) The formula for r_{XY} is given by equation (11.1). Note that it is a sum of products in the numerator, divided by the product $s_X s_Y$ of the sample standard deviations of X and Y. This requires a considerable amount of computation, so that correlations are almost always computed by software packages.

Formula for Correlation

$$r_{XY} = \frac{\Sigma(X_i - \overline{X})(Y_i - \overline{Y})/(n - 1)}{s_X s_Y}$$

(11.1)

---

[2]This section includes some material from Section 3.7, which we repeat here for convenience.

The numerator of equation (11.1) is also a measure of association between two variables X and Y, called the **covariance** between X and Y. Like a correlation, a covariance is a single number that measures the strength of the linear relationship between two variables. By looking at the sign of the covariance or correlation—plus or minus—we can tell whether the two variables are positively or negatively related. The drawback to a covariance, however, is that its magnitude depends on the units in which the variables are measured.

The magnitude of a covariance is difficult to interpret because it depends on the units of measurement.

To illustrate, the covariance between Overhead and MachHrs in the Bendrix manufacturing data set is 1,333,138. (It can be found with Excel's COVAR function or with StatTools.) However, if we divide each overhead value by 1000, so that overhead costs are expressed in thousands of dollars, and we divide each value of MachHrs by 100, so that machine hours are expressed in hundreds of hours, the covariance decreases by a factor of 100,000 to 13.33138. This is in spite of the fact that the basic relationship between these variables has not changed and the revised scatterplot has exactly the same shape. For this reason it is often difficult to interpret the magnitude of a covariance, and we concentrate instead on correlations.

Unlike covariances, correlations have the attractive property that they are completely unaffected by the units of measurement. The rescaling described in the previous paragraph has absolutely no effect on the correlation between Overhead and MachHrs. In either case the correlation is 0.632. Moreover, all correlations are between -1 and $+1$, inclusive. The sign of a correlation, plus or minus, determines whether the linear relationship between two variables is positive or negative. In this respect, a correlation is just like a covariance. However, the strength of the linear relationship between the variables is measured by the absolute value, or magnitude, of the correlation. The closer this magnitude is to 1, the stronger the linear relationship is.

A correlation close to -1 or $+1$ indicates a strong linear relationship. A correlation close to 0 indicates virtually no linear relationship.

A correlation equal to zero or near zero indicates practically no linear relationship. A correlation with magnitude close to 1, on the other hand, indicates a strong linear relationship. At the extreme, a correlation equal to -1 or $+1$ occurs only when the linear relationship is perfect—that is, when all points in the scatterplot lie on a single straight line. Although such extremes practically never occur in business applications, "large" correlations, say, greater than 0.9 in magnitude, are not at all uncommon.

Looking back at the scatterplots for the Pharmex drugstore data in Figure 11.2, we see that the correlation between Sales and Promote is positive—as we would guess from the upward-sloping scatter of points—and that it is equal to 0.673. This is a moderately large correlation. It indicates what we see in the scatterplot, namely, that the points vary considerably around any particular straight line.

Similarly, the scatterplots for the Bendrix manufacturing data in Figures 11.4 and 11.5 indicate moderately large positive correlations, 0.632 and 0.521, between Overhead and MachHrs and between Overhead and ProdRuns. However, the correlation indicated in Figure 11.7 between MachHrs and ProdRuns, -0.229, is quite small and indicates almost no relationship between these two variables.

Correlations can be misleading when variables are related nonlinearly.

We must be a bit more careful when interpreting the correlations in Figures 11.8 and 11.9. The scatterplot between life expectancy and GNP per capita in Figure 11.8 is obviously nonlinear, and correlations are relevant descriptors only for *linear* relationships. If anything, the correlation of 0.616 in this example tends to underestimate the true strength of the relationship—the nonlinear one—between life expectancy and GNP per capita. In contrast, the correlation between salary and years of experience in Figure 11.9 is large, 0.894, but it is not nearly as large as it would be if the outlier were omitted. (It is then 0.992.) This example illustrates the considerable effect a single outlier can have on a correlation.

An obvious question is whether a given correlation is "large." This is a difficult question to answer directly. Clearly, a correlation such as 0.992 is quite large—the points tend to cluster very closely around a straight line. Similarly, a correlation of 0.034 is quite small—the points tend to be a shapeless swarm. But there is a continuum of in-between values, as exhibited in Figures 11.2, 11.4, and 11.5. We give a more definite answer to this question when we examine the *square* of the correlation later in this chapter.

As for calculating correlations, there are two possibilities in Excel. To calculate a *single* correlation r_{XY} between variables X and Y, we can use Excel's CORREL function in the form

=CORREL(*X*-range,*Y*-range)

Alternatively, we can use StatTools to obtain a whole table of correlations between a set of variables.

Finally, we reiterate the important limitation of correlations (and covariances), namely, that they apply only to *linear* relationships. If a correlation is close to zero, we cannot automatically conclude that there is no relationship between the two variables. We should look at a scatterplot first. The chances are that the points are a shapeless swarm and that no relationship exists. But it is also possible that the points cluster around some curve. In this case the correlation is a misleading measure of the relationship.

11.4 SIMPLE LINEAR REGRESSION

Scatterplots and correlations are very useful for indicating linear relationships and the strengths of these relationships. But they do not actually *quantify* the relationships. For example, we know from the Pharmex drugstore data that sales are related to promotional expenditures. But from the knowledge presented so far, we do not know exactly what this relationship is. If the expenditure index for a given region is 95, what would we predict this region's sales index to be? Or if one region's expenditure index is 5 points higher than another region's, we would expect the former to have a larger sales index, but how much larger? To answer these questions, we need to quantify the relationship between the dependent variable Sales and the explanatory variable Promote.

Remember that "simple" linear regression does not mean "easy"; it means only that there is a single explanatory variable.

In this section we answer these types of questions for simple linear regression, where there is a *single* explanatory variable. We do so by fitting a straight line through the scatterplot of the dependent variable Y versus the explanatory variable X and then basing the answers to the questions on the fitted straight line. But which straight line? We address this issue next.

11.4.1 Least Squares Estimation

The scatterplot between Sales and Promote, repeated in Figure 11.12, hints at a linear relationship between these two variables. It would not be difficult to draw a straight line through these points to produce a reasonably good fit. In fact, a possible linear fit is indicated in the graph. But we proceed more systematically than simply drawing lines freehand. Specifically, we choose the line that makes the vertical distances from the points to the line as small as possible, as explained next.

Consider the magnified graph in Figure 11.13. Here we show several points in the scatterplot, along with a line drawn through them. Note that the vertical distance from the horizontal axis to any point, which is just the value of Sales for that point, can be decomposed into two parts: the vertical distance from the horizontal axis to the line, and the vertical distance from the line to the point. The first of these is called the **fitted value**, and the second is called the **residual**. The idea is very simple. By using a straight line to reflect the relationship between Sales and Promote, we expect a given Sales to be at the height of the line above any particular value of Promote. That is, we expect Sales to equal the fitted value. These terms are summarized in the box.

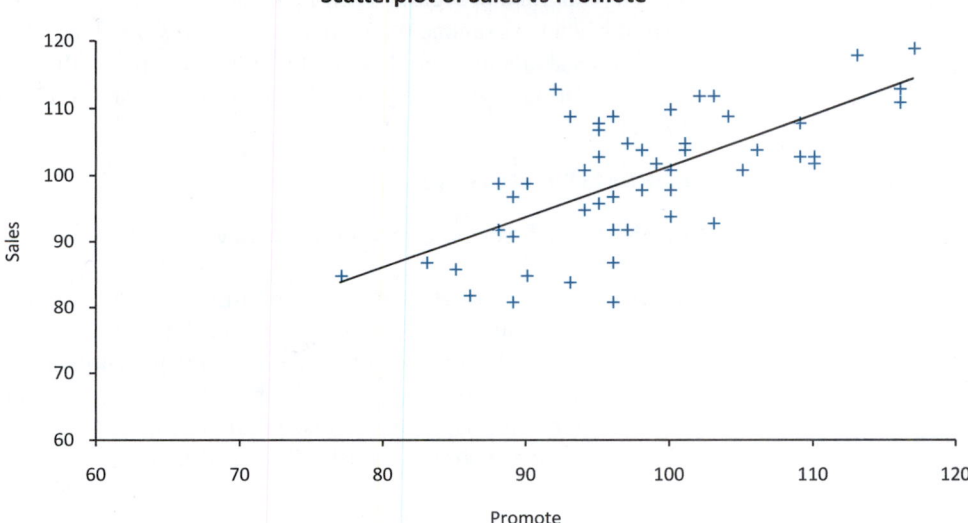

Figure 11.12

Scatterplot with
Possible Linear Fit
Superimposed

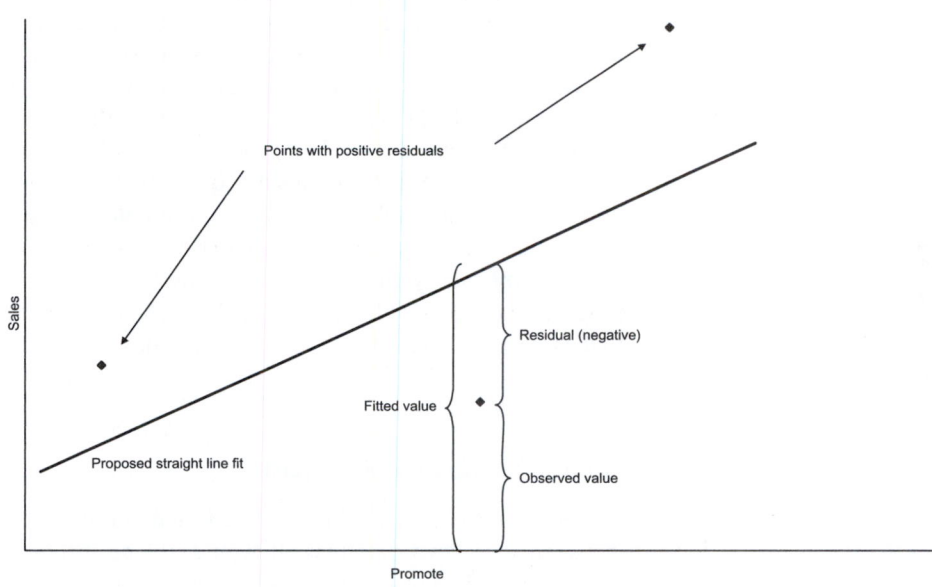

Figure 11.13

Fitted Values and
Residuals

> A **fitted value** is the predicted value of the dependent variable. Graphically, it is the
> height of the line above a given explanatory value. The corresponding **residual** is the
> difference between the actual and fitted values of the dependent variable.

But the relationship is not perfect. Not all (perhaps not any) of the points lie exactly on
the line. The differences are the residuals. They show how much the observed values differ
from the fitted values. If a particular residual is positive, the corresponding point is above

the line; if it is negative, the point is below the line. The only time a residual is zero is when the point lies directly on the line. The relationship between observed values, fitted values, and residuals is very general and is stated in equation (11.2).

Fundamental Equation for Regression

$$\text{Observed Value} = \text{Fitted Value} + \text{Residual} \qquad \textbf{(11.2)}$$

We can now explain how to choose the "best-fitting" line through the points in the scatterplot. We choose the one with the *smallest sum of squared residuals*. The resulting line is called the **least squares line**. Why do we use the sum of *squared* residuals? Why not minimize some other measure of the residuals? First, we do not simply minimize the sum of the residuals. This is because the positive residuals would cancel the negative residuals. In fact, the least squares line has the property that the sum of the residuals is always exactly zero. To adjust for this, we could minimize the sum of the *absolute values* of the residuals, and this is a perfectly reasonable procedure. However, for technical reasons it is not the procedure usually chosen. We settle on the sum of squared residuals because this method is deeply rooted in statistical tradition, and it works well.

The **least squares line** is the line that minimizes the sum of the squared residuals. It is the line quoted in regression outputs.

The minimization problem itself is a calculus problem that we do not discuss here. Virtually all statistical software packages perform this minimization automatically, so we need not be concerned with the technical details. However, we do provide the formulas for the least squares line.

Recall from basic algebra that the equation for any straight line can be written as

$$Y = a + bX$$

Here, a is the Y-intercept of the line, the value of Y when $X = 0$, and b is the slope of the line, the change in Y when X increases by 1 unit. Therefore, to specify the least squares line, all we need to specify is the slope and intercept. These are given by equations (11.3) and (11.4).

Equation for Slope in Simple Linear Regression

$$b = \frac{\Sigma(X_i - \overline{X})(Y_i - \overline{Y})}{\Sigma(X_i - \overline{X})^2} = r_{XY}\frac{s_Y}{s_X} \qquad \textbf{(11.3)}$$

Equation for Intercept in Simple Linear Regression

$$a = \overline{Y} - b\overline{X} \qquad \textbf{(11.4)}$$

We have presented these formulas primarily for conceptual purposes, not for hand calculations—the computer takes care of the calculations. From the right-hand formula for b, we see that it is closely related to the correlation between X and Y. Specifically, if we keep the standard deviations, s_X and s_Y, of X and Y constant, then the slope b of the least squares line varies directly with the correlation between the two variables. A relationship with a large correlation (negative or positive) has a steep slope, and a relationship with a small correlation has a shallow slope. At the extreme, a nonrelationship with a correlation of 0 has a slope of 0; that is, it results in a horizontal line. The effect of the formula for a is not quite as interesting. It simply forces the least squares line to go through the point of sample means, $(\overline{X}, \overline{Y})$.

It is easy to obtain the least squares line in Excel with StatTools's Regression procedure. We illustrate this in the following continuations of Examples 11.1 and 11.2.

EXAMPLE 11.1 SALES VERSUS PROMOTIONS AT PHARMEX (CONTINUED)

Find the least squares line for the Pharmex drugstore data, using Sales as the dependent variable and Promote as the explanatory variable.

Objective To use StatTools's Regression procedure to find the least squares line for sales as a function of promotional expenses at Pharmex.

Solution

We select Regression from the StatTools Regression and Classification dropdown. The resulting dialog box should be filled in as shown in Figure 11.14. Specifically, select Multiple as the Regression Type (this type is used for both single and multiple regression in StatTools), and select Promote as the single I variable and Sales as the single D variable, where I and D stand for independent and dependent. (There is always a *single D* variable, but in multiple regression there can be several I variables.) Note that there is an option to create several scatterplots involving the fitted values and residuals. We suggest checking the third option, as shown. Finally, there is an Include Prediction option. We explain it in a later section. You can leave it unchecked for now.

Figure 11.14

Regression
Dialog Box

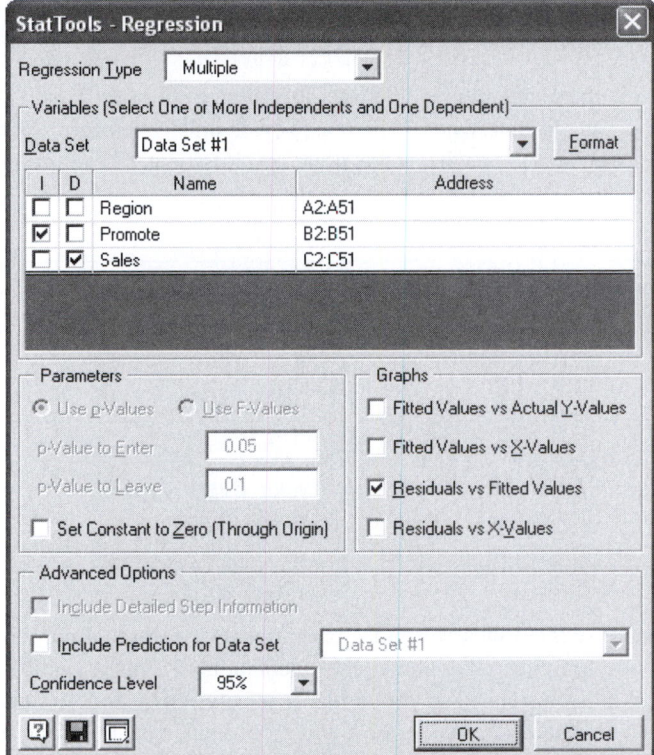

The regression output includes three parts. The first is the main regression output shown in Figure 11.15. The last two are a scatterplot of residuals and fitted values requested in the regression dialog box and a list of fitted values and residuals, a few of which are shown in Figure 11.16. (The list of fitted values and residuals is part of the output only if at least one of the optional scatterplots in the regression dialog box is selected.)

Figure 11.15

Regression Output for Drugstore Example

	A	B	C	D	E	F	G
7		Multiple R	R-Square	Adjusted R-Square	StErr of Estimate		
8	Summary						
9		0.6730	0.4529	0.4415	7.3947		
10							
11		Degrees of Freedom	Sum of Squares	Mean of Squares	F-Ratio	p-Value	
12	ANOVA Table						
13	Explained	1	2172.8804	2172.8804	39.7366	< 0.0001	
14	Unexplained	48	2624.7396	54.6821			
15							
16		Coefficient	Standard Error	t-Value	p-Value	Confidence Interval 95%	
17	Regression Table					Lower	Upper
18	Constant	25.1264	11.8826	2.1146	0.0397	1.2349	49.0180
19	Promote	0.7623	0.1209	6.3037	< 0.0001	0.5192	1.0054

Figure 11.16

Scatterplot and Partial List of Residuals versus Fitted Values

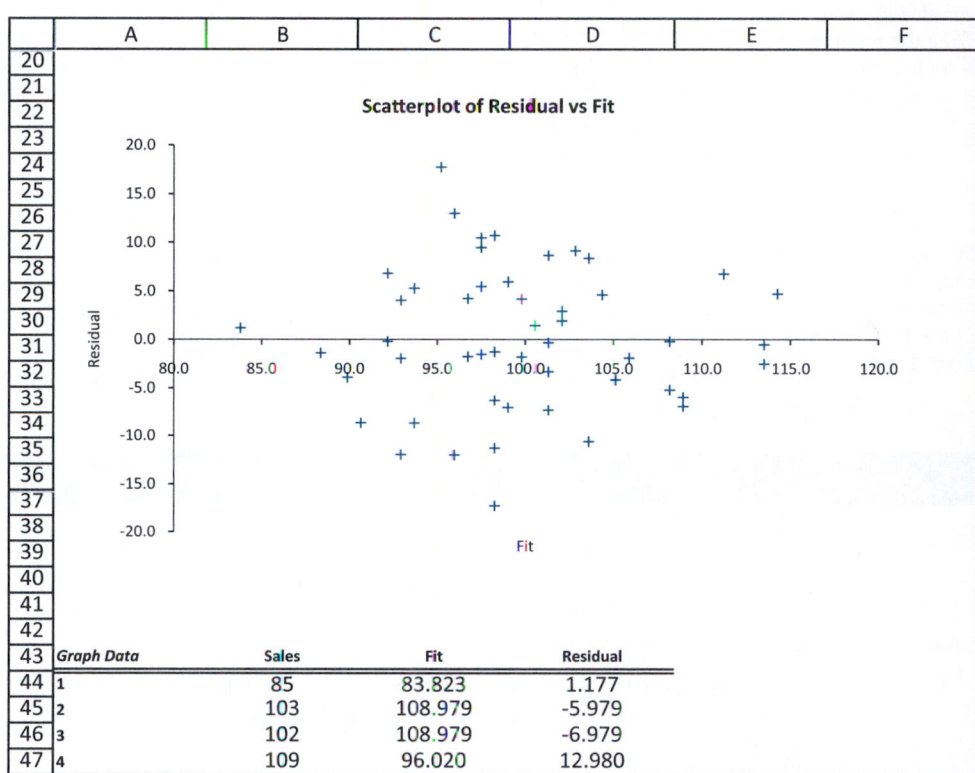

	A	B	C	D
43	Graph Data	Sales	Fit	Residual
44	1	85	83.823	1.177
45	2	103	108.979	-5.979
46	3	102	108.979	-6.979
47	4	109	96.020	12.980

We eventually learn what all of the output in Figure 11.15 means, but for now, we concentrate on only a small part of it. Specifically, we find the intercept and slope of the least squares line under the Coefficient label in cells B18 and B19. They imply that the equation for the least squares line is[3]

$$\text{Predicted Sales} = 25.1264 + 0.7623\text{Promote}$$

[3]We always report the left side of the estimated regression equation as the *predicted* value of the dependent variable. It is not the *actual* value of the dependent variable because the observations do not all lie on the estimated regression line.

Excel Tip *The Regression procedure for simple regression uses special StatTools functions to calculate all of the regression output. However, it can also be generated by taking advantage of several built-in statistical functions available in Excel. These include the CORREL, RSQ, STEYX, INTERCEPT, and SLOPE functions. For example, the slope and intercept of the least squares line can be calculated directly with the formulas*

=SLOPE(Y-range,X-range)

and

=INTERCEPT(Y-range,X-range)

*These formulas (with the appropriate X and Y ranges) can be entered anywhere in a spreadsheet to obtain the slope and intercept for a **simple** regression equation—no add-ins are necessary. You can look up the other functions in Excel's online help.*

In many applications it makes no sense to have the explanatory variable(s) equal to 0. Then the intercept term has no practical or economic meaning.

We can interpret the regression equation for this example as follows. The slope, 0.7623, indicates that the sales index tends to increase by about 0.76 for each 1-unit increase in the promotional expenses index. Alternatively, if we compare two regions, where region 2 spends 1 unit higher than region 1, we predict the sales index for region 2 to be 0.76 larger than the sales index for region 1. The interpretation of the intercept is less important. It is literally the predicted sales index for a region that does no promotions. However, no region in the sample has anywhere near a zero promotional value. Therefore, in a situation like this, where the range of observed explanatory variable values does not include 0, it is best to think of the intercept term as an "anchor" for the least squares line that allows us to predict *Y* values for the range of *observed X* values.

We typically like a shapeless "swarm" of points in a scatterplot of residuals versus fitted values.

A useful graph in almost any regression analysis is a scatterplot of residuals (on the vertical axis) versus fitted values. This scatterplot for the Pharmex data appears in Figure 11.16 (along with a few of the residuals and fitted values used to create the chart). We typically examine such a scatterplot for any striking patterns. A "good" fit not only has small residuals, but it has residuals scattered *randomly* around 0 with no apparent pattern. This appears to be the case for the Pharmex data. ∎

EXAMPLE | **11.2 EXPLAINING OVERHEAD COSTS AT BENDRIX (CONTINUED)**

The Bendrix manufacturing data set has two potential explanatory variables, MachHrs and ProdRuns. Eventually, we will estimate a regression equation with *both* of these variables included. However, if we include only one at a time, what do they tell us about overhead costs?

Objective To use StatTools's Regression procedure to regress overhead expenses at Bendrix against machine hours and then against production runs.

Solution

The regression output for Overhead with MachHrs as the single explanatory variable appears in Figure 11.17. The output when ProdRuns is the only explanatory variable appears in Figure 11.18. The two least squares lines are therefore

$$\text{Predicted Overhead} = 48{,}621 + 34.7\text{MachHrs} \tag{11.5}$$

and

$$\text{Predicted Overhead} = 75{,}606 + 655.1\text{ProdRuns} \tag{11.6}$$

Figure 11.17

Regression Output for Overhead versus MachHrs

	A	B	C	D	E	F	G
7		Multiple R	R-Square	Adjusted R-Square	StErr of Estimate		
8	Summary						
9		0.6319	0.3993	0.3816	8584.739		
10							
11		Degrees of Freedom	Sum of Squares	Mean of Squares	F-Ratio	p-Value	
12	ANOVA Table						
13	Explained	1	1665463368	1665463368	22.5986	< 0.0001	
14	Unexplained	34	2505723492	73697749.75			
15							
16		Coefficient	Standard Error	t-Value	p-Value	Confidence Interval 95% Lower	Upper
17	Regression Table						
18	Constant	48621.355	10725.333	4.5333	< 0.0001	26824.856	70417.853
19	MachHrs	34.702	7.300	4.7538	< 0.0001	19.867	49.537

Figure 11.18

Regression Output for Overhead versus ProdRuns

	A	B	C	D	E	F	G
7		Multiple R	R-Square	Adjusted R-Square	StErr of Estimate		
8	Summary						
9		0.5205	0.2710	0.2495	9457.239		
10							
11		Degrees of Freedom	Sum of Squares	Mean of Squares	F-Ratio	p-Value	
12	ANOVA Table						
13	Explained	1	1130247999	1130247999	12.6370	0.0011	
14	Unexplained	34	3040938861	89439378.26			
15							
16		Coefficient	Standard Error	t-Value	p-Value	Confidence Interval 95% Lower	Upper
17	Regression Table						
18	Constant	75605.516	6808.611	11.1044	< 0.0001	61768.754	89442.277
19	ProdRuns	655.071	184.275	3.5549	0.0011	280.579	1029.562

Clearly, these two equations are quite different, although each effectively breaks Overhead into a fixed component and a variable component. Equation (11.5) implies that the fixed component of overhead is about $48,621. Bendrix can expect to incur this amount even if zero machine hours are used. The variable component is the 34.7MachHrs term. It implies that the expected overhead increases by about $35 for each extra machine hour. Equation (11.6), on the other hand, breaks overhead down into a fixed component of $75,606 and a variable component of about $655 per each production run.

The difference between these two equations can be attributed to the fact that neither tells the whole story. If the manager's goal is to split overhead into a fixed component and a variable component, then the variable component should include *both* of the measures of work activity (and maybe even others) to give a more complete explanation of overhead. We see how to do this when we reanalyze this example with multiple regression. ∎

11.4.2 Standard Error of Estimate

We now reexamine fitted values and residuals to see how they lead to a useful summary measure for a regression equation. In a typical simple regression model, the expression $a + bX$ is the fitted value of Y. Graphically, it is the height of the estimated line above the value X. We often denote it by $\hat{Y}$ (pronounced Y-hat):[4]

$$\hat{Y} = a + bX$$

Then a typical residual, denoted by e, is the difference between the observed value Y and the fitted value $\hat{Y}$ [a restatement of equation (11.2)]:

$$e = Y - \hat{Y}$$

---

[4]We could write Predicted Y instead of $\hat{Y}$, but the latter notation is more common in statistics literature.

We show some of the fitted values and associated residuals for the Pharmex drugstore example in Figure 11.19. (Recall that these columns are inserted automatically by StatTools's Regression procedure when we request the optional scatterplot of residuals versus fitted values.)

Figure 11.19

Fitted Values and Residuals for Pharmex Example

	A	B	C	D
43	Graph Data	Sales	Fit	Residual
44	1	85	83.823	1.177
45	2	103	108.979	-5.979
46	3	102	108.979	-6.979
47	4	109	96.020	12.980
48	5	85	93.733	-8.733
49	6	103	97.545	5.455
50	7	110	101.356	8.644
51	8	86	89.922	-3.922
52	9	92	98.307	-6.307
53	10	87	88.397	-1.397

The magnitudes of the residuals provide a good indication of how useful the regression line is for predicting Y values from X values. However, because there are numerous residuals, it is useful to summarize them with a single numerical measure. This measure, called the **standard error of estimate** and denoted s_e, is essentially the standard deviation of the residuals. It is given by equation (11.7).

Formula for Standard Error of Estimate

$$s_e = \sqrt{\frac{\Sigma e_i^2}{n-2}}$$

(11.7)

Actually, because the average of the residuals from a least squares fit is always 0, this is identical to the standard deviation of the residuals except that we use the denominator $n - 2$ rather than the usual $n - 1$. As we see in more generality later on, the rule is to subtract the number of parameters being estimated from the sample size n to obtain the denominator. Here there are two parameters being estimated: the intercept a and the slope b.

About 2/3 of the fitted $\hat{Y}$ values are typically within 1 standard error of the actual Y values. About 95% are within 2 standard errors.

The usual empirical rules for standard deviations can be applied to the standard error of estimate. For example, we expect about 2/3 of the residuals to be within 1 standard error of their mean (which is 0). Stated another way, we expect about 2/3 of the observed Y values to be within 1 standard error of the corresponding fitted $\hat{Y}$ values. Similarly, we expect about 95% of the observed Y values to be within 2 standard errors of the corresponding fitted $\hat{Y}$ values.[5]

The standard error of estimate s_e is included in all StatTools regression outputs. Alternatively, it can be calculated directly with Excel's STEYX function in the form

=STEYX(Y-range,X-range)

---

[5]This requires that the residuals be at least approximately normally distributed, a requirement we discuss more fully in the next chapter.

In general, the standard error of estimate indicates the level of accuracy of predictions made from the regression equation. The smaller it is, the more accurate predictions tend to be.

The standard error for the Pharmex data appears in cell E9 of Figure 11.15. Its value, approximately 7.39, indicates the typical error we are likely to make when we use the fitted value (based on the regression line) to predict sales from promotional expenses. More specifically, if we use the regression equation to predict sales for many regions, based on the promotional expenses in each region, then about 2/3 of the predictions will be within 7.39 of the actual sales values, and about 95% of the predictions will be within 2 standard errors, or 14.78, of the actual sales values.

Is this level of accuracy good? One measure of comparison is the standard deviation of the sales variable, namely, 9.90. (This is obtained by the usual STDEV function applied to the observed sales values.) It can be interpreted as the standard deviation of the residuals around a *horizontal* line positioned at the mean value of Sales. This would be the relevant regression line if there were no explanatory variables—that is, if we ignored Promote. In other words, it is a measure of the prediction error we would make if we used the sample mean of Sales as the prediction for *every* region and ignored Promote. The fact that the standard error of estimate, 7.39, is not much less than 9.90 means that the Promote variable adds a relatively small amount to prediction accuracy. We can do nearly as well without it as with it. We would certainly prefer a standard error of estimate *well* below 9.90.

We can often use the standard error of estimate to judge which of several potential regression equations is the most useful. In the Bendrix manufacturing example we estimated two regression lines, one using MachHrs and one using ProdRuns. From Figures 11.17 and 11.18, their standard errors are approximately $8585 and $9457. These imply that MachHrs is a slightly better predictor of overhead. The predictions based on MachHrs will tend to be slightly more accurate than those based on ProdRuns. Of course, we might guess that predictions based on *both* predictors will yield even more accurate predictions, and this is definitely the case, as we see when we discuss multiple regression.

11.4.3 R^2: The Coefficient of Determination

We now discuss another important measure of the goodness of fit of the least squares line: the *coefficient of determination*, or simply R^2. Along with the standard error of estimate s_e, it is the most frequently quoted measure in applied regression analysis. With a value always between 0 and 1, the **coefficient of determination** can be interpreted as the *fraction of variation of the dependent variable explained by the regression line*. (It is often expressed as a percentage, so that we talk about the *percentage* of variation explained by the regression line.)

> The **coefficient of determination (R^2)** is the percentage of variation of the dependent variable explained by the regression.

To see more precisely what this means, we look briefly into the derivation of R^2. In the previous section we suggested that one way to measure the regression equation's ability to predict is to compare the standard error of estimate, s_e, to the standard deviation of the dependent variable, s_Y. The idea is that s_e is (essentially) the standard deviation of the residuals, whereas s_Y is the standard deviation of the residuals that we would obtain from a horizontal regression line at height $\overline{Y}$, the dependent variable's mean. Therefore, if s_e is small compared to s_Y (that is, if s_e/s_Y is small), the regression line has evidently done a good job in explaining the variation of the dependent variable.

The coefficient of determination is based on this idea. R^2 is defined by equation (11.8). (This value is obtained automatically with StatTools's regression procedure, or it can be calculated with Excel's RSQ function.) Equation (11.8) indicates that when the residuals are small, then R^2 will be close to 1, but when they are large, R^2 will be close to 0.

$$R^2 = 1 - \frac{\Sigma e_i^2}{\Sigma(Y_i - \overline{Y})^2} \qquad (11.8)$$

R^2 measures the goodness of a linear fit. The better the linear fit is, the closer R^2 is to 1.

We see from cell C9 of Figure 11.15 that the R^2 measure for the Pharmex drugstore data is 0.453. In words, the single explanatory variable Promote is able to explain only 45.3% of the variation in the Sales variable. This is not particularly good—the same conclusion we made when we based goodness of fit on s_e. There is still 54.7% of the variation left unexplained. Of course, we would like R^2 to be as close to 1 as possible. Usually, the only way to increase it is to use better and/or more explanatory variables.

Analysts often compare equations on the basis of their R^2 values. We see from Figures 11.17 and 11.18 that the R^2 values using MachHrs and ProdRuns as single explanatory variables for the Bendrix overhead data are 39.9% and 27.1%. These provide one more piece of evidence that MachHrs is a slightly better predictor of Overhead than ProdRuns. Of course, they also suggest that the percentage of variation of Overhead explained could be increased by including *both* variables in a single equation. This is true, as we see shortly.

In simple linear regression, R^2 is the square of the correlation between the dependent variable and the explanatory variable.

There is a good reason for the notation R^2. It turns out that R^2 is the square of the correlation between the observed Y values and the fitted $\hat{Y}$ values. This correlation appears in all regression outputs. For the Pharmex data it is 0.673, as seen in cell B9 of Figure 11.15. Aside from rounding, the square of 0.673 is 0.453, the R^2 value right next to it. In the case of simple linear regression, when there is only a single explanatory variable in the equation, the correlation between the Y variable and the fitted $\hat{Y}$ values is the same as the absolute value of the correlation between the Y variable and the explanatory X variable. For the Pharmex data we already saw that the correlation between Sales and Promote is indeed 0.673.

This interpretation of R^2 as the square of a correlation helps to clarify the issue of when a correlation is "large." For example, if the correlation between two variables Y and X is ± 0.8, we know that the regression of Y on X will produce an R^2 of 0.64; that is, the regression with X as the only explanatory variable will explain 64% of the variation in Y. If the correlation drops to ± 0.7, this percentage drops to 49%; if the correlation increases to ± 0.9, the percentage increases to 81%. The point is that before a single variable X can explain a large percentage of the variation in some other variable Y, the two variables must be highly correlated—in *either* a positive or negative direction.

PROBLEMS

Level A

1. Explore the relationship between the selling prices (Y) and the appraised values (X) of the 150 homes in the file **P02_07.xlsx** by estimating a simple linear regression model. Also, compute the standard error of estimate s_e and the coefficient of determination R^2 for the estimated least squares line. Interpret these measures and the least squares line for these data.

   a. Is there evidence of a *linear* relationship between the selling price and appraised value? If so, characterize the relationship (i.e., indicate whether the relationship is a positive or negative one, a strong or weak one, etc.).

   b. For which of the two remaining variables, the size of the home and the number of bedrooms in the home, is the relationship with the home's selling price *stronger*? Justify your choice with additional simple linear regression models.

2. What is the relationship between the number of short-term general hospitals (Y) and the number of general or family physicians (X) in U.S. metropolitan areas? Explore this question by estimating a simple linear regression model using the data in the file **P02_17.xlsx**. Interpret your estimated regression model as well as the coefficient of determination R^2.

3. Motorco produces electric motors for use in home appliances. One of the company's production managers is interested in examining the relationship between the dollars spent per month in inspecting finished motor products (X) and the number of motors produced during that month that were returned by dissatisfied customers (Y). He has collected the data in the file **P02_18.xlsx** to explore this relationship for the past 36 months. Generate a simple linear regression model using the given data and interpret it for this production manager. Also, compute and interpret s_e and R^2 for these data.

4. The owner of the Original Italian Pizza restaurant chain would like to understand which variable most strongly influences the sales of his specialty, deep-dish pizza. He has gathered data on the monthly sales of deep-dish pizzas at his restaurants and observations on other potentially relevant variables for each of his 15 outlets in central Pennsylvania. These data are provided in the file **P11_04.xlsx**. Estimate a simple linear regression model between the quantity sold (Y) and each of the following candidates for the best explanatory variable: average price of deep-dish pizzas, monthly advertising expenditures, and disposable income per household in the areas surrounding the outlets. Which variable is *most* strongly associated with the number of pizzas sold? Be sure to explain your choice.

5. The human resources manager of DataCom, Inc., wants to examine the relationship between annual salaries (Y) and the number of years employees have worked at DataCom (X). These data have been collected for a sample of employees and are given in the file **P11_05.xlsx**.
   a. Estimate the relationship between Y and X. Interpret the least squares line.
   b. How well does the estimated simple linear regression model fit the given data? Document your answer.

6. Consider the relationship between the size of the population (X) and the average household income level for residents of U.S. towns (Y). What do you expect the relationship between these two variables to be? Using the data in the file **P02_24.xlsx**, produce and interpret a simple linear regression model involving these two variables. How well does the estimated model fit the given data?

7. Examine the relationship between the average utility bills for homes of a particular size (Y) and the average monthly temperature (X). The data in the file **P11_07.xlsx** include the average monthly bill and temperature for each month of the past year.
   a. Use the given data to estimate a simple linear regression model. Interpret the least squares line.
   b. How well does the estimated regression model fit the given data? How might we do a better job of explaining the variation of the average utility bills for homes of a certain size?

8. The U.S. Bureau of Labor Statistics provides data on the year-to-year percentage changes in the wages and salaries of workers in private industries, including both "white-collar" and "blue-collar" occupations. Here we consider selected annual data in the file **P02_56.xlsx**. Is there evidence of a strong relationship between the yearly changes in the wages and salaries of white-collar and blue-collar workers in the United States over the given time period? Answer this question by estimating and interpreting a simple linear regression model.

9. Management of a home appliance store in Charlotte would like to understand the growth pattern of the monthly sales of VCR units over the past 2 years. The managers have recorded the relevant data in the file **P11_09.xlsx**. Have the sales of VCR units been growing linearly over the past 24 months? Using simple linear regression, explain why or why not.

10. Do the sales prices of houses in a given community vary systematically with their sizes (as measured in square feet)? Attempt to answer this question by estimating a simple regression model where the sales price of the house is the dependent variable and the size of the house is the explanatory variable. Use the sample data given in the file **P11_10.xlsx**. Interpret your estimated model and the associated coefficient of determination R^2.

11. The file **P11_11.xlsx** contains annual observations of the American minimum wage. Has the minimum wage been growing at roughly a *constant* rate over this period? Use simple linear regression analysis to address this question. Explain the results you obtain.

12. Based on the data in the file **P02_25.xlsx** from the U.S. Department of Agriculture, explore the relationship between the number of farms (X) and the average size of a farm (Y) in the United States. Specifically, generate a simple linear regression model and interpret it.

13. Estimate the relationship between monthly electrical power usage (Y) and home size (X) using the data in the file **P11_13.xlsx**. Interpret your results. How well does a simple linear regression model explain the variation in monthly electrical power usage?

14. The *ACCRA Cost of Living Index* provides a useful and reasonably accurate measure of cost of living differences among a large number of urban areas. Items on which the index is based have been carefully chosen to reflect the different categories of consumer expenditures. The data are in the file **P02_19.xlsx**. Use the given data to estimate simple linear regression models to explore the relationship between the composite index (i.e., dependent variable) and each of the

various expenditure components (i.e., explanatory variable).

a. Which expenditure component has the *strongest* linear relationship with the composite index?

b. Which expenditure component has the *weakest* linear relationship with the composite index?

15. The management of Beta Technologies, Inc., is trying to determine the variable that best explains the varia-

tion of employee salaries using a sample of 52 full-time employees in the file **P02_01.xlsx**. Estimate simple linear regression models to identify which of the following has the *strongest* linear relationship with annual salary: the employee's gender, age, number of years of relevant work experience prior to employment at Beta, number of years of employment at Beta, or number of years of postsecondary education. Provide support for your conclusion.

11.5 MULTIPLE REGRESSION

In general, there are two possible approaches to obtaining improved fits. The first is to examine a scatterplot of residuals for nonlinear patterns and then make appropriate modifications to the regression equation. We discuss this approach later in this chapter. The second approach is much more straightforward: We simply add more explanatory variables to the regression equation. In the Bendrix manufacturing example we deliberately included only a single explanatory variable in the equation at a time so that we could keep the equations simple. But because scatterplots indicate that both explanatory variables are also related to Overhead, we ought to try including both in the regression equation. With any luck, the linear fit should improve.

When we include several explanatory variables in the regression equation, we move into the realm of *multiple* regression. Some of the concepts from simple regression carry over naturally to multiple regression, but some change considerably. The following list provides a starting point that we expand on throughout this section.

Characteristics of Multiple Regression

■ Graphically, we are no longer fitting a *line* to a set of points. If there are exactly two explanatory variables, then we are fitting a *plane* to the data in three-dimensional space. There is one dimension for the dependent variable and one for each of the two explanatory variables. Although we can imagine a flat plane passing through a swarm of points, it is difficult to graph this on a two-dimensional screen. If there are more than two explanatory variables, then we can only imagine the regression plane; drawing in four or more dimensions is impossible.

■ The regression equation is still estimated by the least squares method—that is, by minimizing the sum of squared residuals. However, it is definitely not practical to implement this method by hand. A statistical software package such as StatTools is required.

■ Simple regression is actually a special case of multiple regression—that is, an equation with a single explanatory variable can be considered as a "multiple" regression equation. This explains why it is possible to use StatTools's Multiple Regression procedure for simple regression.

■ There is a "slope" term for each explanatory variable in the equation. The interpretation of these slope terms is somewhat more difficult than in simple regression, as we discuss in the following subsection.

■ The standard error of estimate and R^2 summary measures are almost exactly as in simple regression, as we discuss in Section 11.5.2.

■ Many *types* of explanatory variables can be included in the regression equation, as we discuss in Section 11.6. To a large part, these are responsible for the wide applicability of multiple regression in the business world.

11.5.1 Interpretation of Regression Coefficients

A typical slope term measures the expected change in Y when the corresponding X increases by 1 unit.

If Y is the dependent variable and X_1 through X_k are the explanatory variables, then a typical multiple regression equation has the form shown in equation (11.9), where a is again the Y-intercept, and b_1 through b_k are the slopes. Collectively, we refer to a and the b's in equation (11.9) as the **regression coefficients**. The intercept a is the expected value of Y when all of the X's equal 0. (Of course, this makes sense only if it is practical for all of the X's to equal 0, which is seldom the case.) Each slope coefficient is the expected change in Y when this particular X increases by one unit and the other X's in the equation remain constant. For example, b_1 is the expected change in Y when X_1 increases by one unit and the other X's in the equation, X_2 through X_k, remain constant.

General Multiple Regression Equation

$$Y = a + b_1X_1 + b_2X_2 + \cdots + b_kX_k \qquad \textbf{(11.9)}$$

This extra proviso, "when the other X's in the equation remain constant," is very important for the interpretation of the regression coefficients. In particular, it means that the estimates of the b's depend on which other X's are included in the regression equation. We illustrate these ideas in the following continuation of the Bendrix manufacturing example.

EXAMPLE | **11.2 EXPLAINING OVERHEAD COSTS AT BENDRIX (CONTINUED)**

Estimate and interpret the equation for Overhead when both explanatory variables, MachHrs and ProdRuns, are included in the regression equation.

Objective To use StatTools's Regression procedure to estimate the equation for overhead costs at Bendrix as a function of machine hours and production runs.

Solution

To obtain the regression output, we select Regression from the StatTools Regression and Classification dropdown and fill out the resulting dialog box as shown in Figure 11.20. As before, we choose the Multiple option, specify the single *D* variable and the two *I* variables, and check any optional graphs we would like to see. (This time we have selected the first and third options.)

The main regression output appears in Figure 11.21. The coefficients in the range B18:B20 indicates that the estimated regression equation is

$$\text{Predicted Overhead} = 3997 + 43.54\text{MachHrs} + 883.62\text{ProdRuns} \qquad \textbf{(11.10)}$$

The interpretation of equation (11.10) is that if the number of production runs is held constant, then the overhead cost is expected to increase by \$43.54 for each extra machine hour, and if the number of machine hours is held constant, the overhead cost is expected to increase by \$883.62 for each extra production run. The Bendrix manager can interpret the intercept, \$3997, as the fixed component of overhead. The slope terms involving MachHrs and ProdRuns are the variable components of overhead.

It is interesting to compare equation (11.10) with the separate equations for Overhead involving only a single variable each. From the previous section these are

$$\text{Predicted Overhead} = 48{,}621 + 34.7\text{MachHrs}$$

and

$$\text{Predicted Overhead} = 75{,}606 + 655.1\text{ProdRuns}$$

Figure 11.20

Multiple Regression Dialog Box

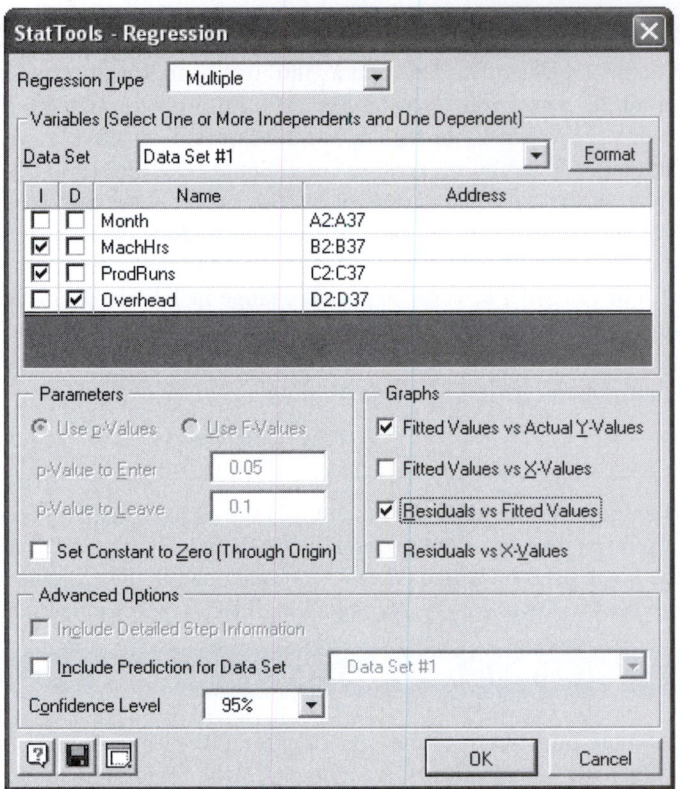

Figure 11.21

Multiple Regression Output for Bendrix Example

	A	B	C	D	E	F	G
7		Multiple R	R-Square	Adjusted R-Square	StErr of Estimate		
8	*Summary*						
9		0.9308	0.8664	0.8583	4108.993		
10							
11		Degrees of Freedom	Sum of Squares	Mean of Squares	F-Ratio	p-Value	
12	*ANOVA Table*						
13	Explained	2	3614020661	1807010330	107.0261	< 0.0001	
14	Unexplained	33	557166199.1	16883824.22			
15							
16			Standard Error	t-Value	p-Value	Confidence Interval 95%	
17	*Regression Table*	Coefficient				Lower	Upper
18	Constant	3996.678	6603.651	0.6052	0.5492	-9438.551	17431.907
19	MachHrs	43.536	3.589	12.1289	< 0.0001	36.234	50.839
20	ProdRuns	883.618	82.251	10.7429	< 0.0001	716.276	1050.960

Note that the coefficient of MachHrs has increased from 34.7 to 43.5 and the coefficient of ProdRuns has increased from 655.1 to 883.6. Also, the intercept is now lower than either intercept in the single-variable equations. In general, it is difficult to guess the changes that will occur when we introduce more explanatory variables into the equation, but it is likely that changes *will* occur.

The reasoning is that when MachHrs is the only variable in the equation, we are obviously *not* holding ProdRuns constant—we are ignoring it—so in effect the coefficient 34.7 of MachHrs indicates the effect of MachHrs *and* the omitted ProdRuns on Overhead. But when we include both variables, then the coefficient 43.5 of MachHrs indicates the effect of MachHrs only, holding ProdRuns constant. Because the coefficients of MachHrs in the two equations have different *meanings*, it is not surprising that we obtain different numerical estimates of them. ■

The estimated coefficient of any explanatory variable typically depends on which other explanatory variables are included in the equation.

11.5.2 Interpretation of Standard Error of Estimate and R-Square

The multiple regression output in Figure 11.21 is very similar to simple regression output.[6] In particular, cells C9 and E9 again show R^2 and the standard error of estimate s_e. Also, the square root of R^2 appears in cell B9. We interpret these quantities almost exactly as in simple regression. The standard error of estimate is essentially the standard deviation of residuals, but it is now given by equation (11.11), where n is the number of observations and k is the number of explanatory variables in the equation.

Formula for Standard Error of Estimate in Multiple Regression

$$s_e = \sqrt{\frac{\Sigma e_i^2}{n - k - 1}}$$

(11.11)

Fortunately, we interpret s_e exactly as before. It is a measure of the prediction error we are likely to make when we use the multiple regression equation to predict the dependent variable. In this example, about 2/3 of the predictions should be within 1 standard error, or \$4109, of the actual overhead cost. By comparing this with the standard errors from the single-variable equations for Overhead, \$8585 and \$9457, we see that the multiple regression equation is likely to provide predictions that are more than twice as accurate as the single-variable equations—quite an improvement!

The R^2 value is again the percentage of variation of the dependent variable explained by the combined set of explanatory variables. In fact, it even has the same formula as before [see equation (11.8)]. For the Bendrix data we see that MachHrs and ProdRuns combine to explain 86.6% of the variation in Overhead. This is a big improvement over the single-variable equations that were able to explain only 39.9% and 27.1% of the variation in Overhead. Remarkably, the combination of the two explanatory variables explains a larger percentage than the *sum* of their individual effects. This is not common, but as this example shows, it is possible.

R^2 is always the square of the correlation between the actual and fitted Y values—in both simple and multiple regression.

The square root of R^2 shown in cell B9 of Figure 11.21 is again the correlation between the fitted values and the observed values of the dependent variable. For the Bendrix data the correlation between them is 0.931, quite high. A graphical indication of this high correlation can be seen in one of the scatterplots we requested, the plot of fitted versus observed values of Overhead. This scatterplot appears in Figure 11.22. If the regression equation gave *perfect* predictions, then all of the points in this plot would lie on a 45° line—each fitted value would *equal* the corresponding observed value. Although a perfect fit virtually never occurs, the closer the points are to a 45° line, the better the fit is, as indicated by R^2 or its square root.

Although the R^2 value is one of the most frequently quoted values from a regression analysis, it does have one serious drawback: R^2 can only *increase* when extra explanatory variables are added to an equation. This can lead to "fishing expeditions," where an analyst keeps adding variables to an equation, some of which have no conceptual relationship to the dependent variable, just to inflate the R^2 value. To "penalize" the addition of extra variables that do not really belong, an **adjusted** R^2 value is typically listed in regression outputs. This adjusted value appears in cell D9 of Figure 11.21. Although it has no direct interpretation as "percentage of variation explained," it *can* decrease when extra explanatory variables that do not really belong are added to an equation. Therefore, it is a useful index that we can monitor. If we add variables and the adjusted R^2 *decreases*, then the extra variables are essentially not pulling their weight and should probably be omitted. We have much more to say about this issue in the next chapter.

[6]In particular, neither regression output is linked to the data by formulas. If the data change, you must rerun the regression procedure to update the output.

Figure 11.22

Scatterplot of Fitted Values versus Observed Values of Overhead

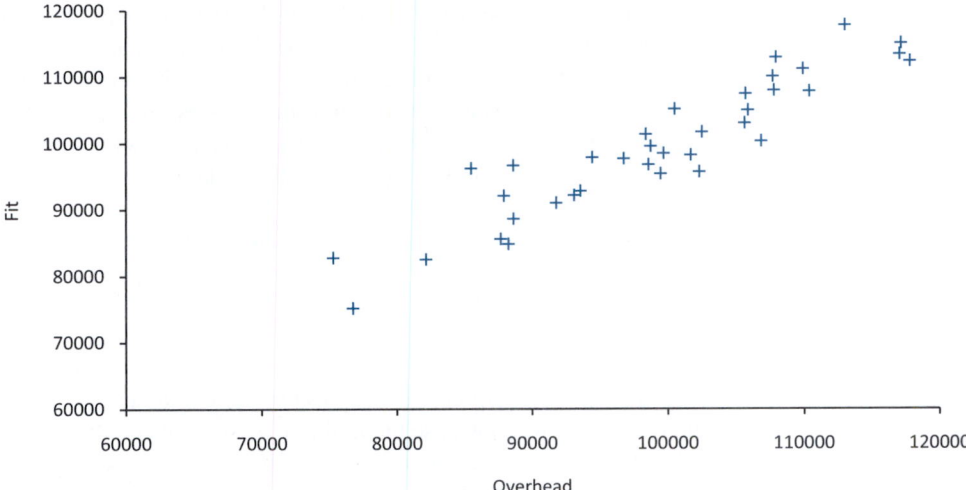

The **adjusted R^2** is a measure that adjusts R^2 for the number of explanatory variables in the equation. It is used primarily to monitor whether extra explanatory variables really belong in the equation.

PROBLEMS

Level A

16. A trucking company wants to predict the yearly maintenance expense (Y) for a truck using the number of miles driven during the year (X_1) and the age of the truck (X_2, in years) at the beginning of the year. The company has gathered the data given in the file **P11_16.xlsx**. Note that each observation corresponds to a particular truck.

   a. Formulate and estimate a multiple regression model using the given data. Interpret each of the estimated regression coefficients.

   b. Compute and interpret the standard error of estimate s_e and the coefficient of determination R^2 for these data.

17. DataPro is a small but rapidly growing firm that provides electronic data-processing services to commercial firms, hospitals, and other organizations. For each of the past 12 months, DataPro has tracked the number of

contracts sold, the average contract price, advertising expenditures, and personal selling expenditures. These data are provided in **P11_17.xlsx**. Assuming that the number of contracts sold is the dependent variable, estimate a multiple regression model with three explanatory variables. Interpret each of the estimated regression coefficients and the coefficient of determination R^2.

18. An antique collector believes that the price received for a particular item increases with its age and with the number of bidders. The file **P11_18.xlsx** contains data on these three variables for 32 recently auctioned comparable items.

   a. Formulate and estimate a multiple regression model using the given data. Interpret each of the estimated regression coefficients. Is the antique collector correct in believing that the price received for the item increases with its age and with the number of bidders?

b. Interpret the standard error of estimate s_e and the coefficient of determination R^2.

19. Stock market analysts are continually looking for reliable predictors of stock prices. Consider the problem of modeling the price per share of electric utility stocks (Y). Two variables thought to influence this stock price are return on average equity (X_1) and annual dividend rate (X_2). The stock price, returns on equity, and dividend rates on a randomly selected day for 16 electric utility stocks are provided in the file **P11_19.xlsx**.
   a. Formulate and estimate a multiple regression model using the given data. Interpret each of the estimated regression coefficients.
   b. Interpret the standard error of estimate s_e, the coefficient of determination R^2, and the adjusted R^2.

20. The manager of a commuter rail transportation system was recently asked by her governing board to determine which factors have a significant impact on the demand for rides in the large city served by the transportation network. The system manager has collected data on variables thought to be possibly related to the number of weekly riders on the city's rail system. The file **P11_20.xlsx** contain these data.
   a. What are the expected signs of the coefficients of the explanatory variables in this multiple regression model? Provide reasoning for each of your stated expectations. (Answer this *before* using regression.)
   b. Formulate and estimate a multiple regression model using the given data. Interpret each of the estimated regression coefficients. Are the signs of the estimated coefficients consistent with your expectations as stated in part **a**?
   c. What proportion of the total variation in the number of weekly riders is *not* explained by this estimated multiple regression model?

21. Consider the enrollment data for *Business Week*'s top U.S. graduate business programs in the file **P02_03.xlsx**. Use these data to estimate a multiple regression model to assess whether there is a systematic relationship between the total number of full-time students and the following explanatory variables: (a) the proportion of female students, (b) the proportion of minority students, and (c) the proportion of international students enrolled at these distinguished business schools.
   a. Interpret the coefficients of your estimated regression model. Do any of these results surprise you? Explain.
   b. How well does your estimated regression model fit the given data?

22. David Savageau and Geoffrey Loftus, the authors of *Places Rated Almanac*, have ranked metropolitan areas in the United States with consideration of the following aspects of life in each area: cost of living, transporta-

tion, jobs, education, climate, crime, arts, health, and recreation. The data are in the file **P02_55.xlsx**.
   a. Use multiple regression analysis to explore the relationship between the metropolitan area's overall score and the set of potential explanatory variables.
   b. Interpret each of the estimated coefficients in the regression model. Are the signs of the estimated coefficients consistent with your expectations? If not, can you explain any discrepancies between your findings and expectations?
   c. Does the given set of explanatory variables do a good job of explaining changes in the overall score? Explain why or why not.

Level B

23. The owner of a restaurant in Bloomington, Indiana, has recorded sales data for the past 19 years. He has also recorded data on potentially relevant variables. The entire data set appears in the file **P11_23.xlsx**.
   a. Estimate a simple linear regression model involving annual sales (the dependent variable) and the size of the population residing within 10 miles of the restaurant (the explanatory variable). Interpret R^2.
   b. Add another explanatory variable—annual advertising expenditures—to the regression model in part **a**. Estimate and interpret this expanded model. How does the R^2 value for this multiple regression model compare to that of the simple regression model estimated in part **a**? Explain any difference between the two R^2 values. Interpret the *adjusted* R^2 value for the revised model.
   c. Add one more explanatory variable to the multiple regression model estimated in part **b**. In particular, estimate and interpret the coefficients of a multiple regression model that includes the *previous* year's advertising expenditure. How does the inclusion of this third explanatory variable affect the R^2 and adjusted R^2 values, in comparison to the corresponding values for the model of part **b**? Explain any changes in these values.

24. A regional express delivery service company recently conducted a study to investigate the relationship between the cost of shipping a package (Y), the package weight (X_1), and the distance shipped (X_2). Twenty packages were randomly selected from among the large number received for shipment, and a detailed analysis of the shipping cost was conducted for each package. These sample observations are given in the file **P11_24.xlsx**.
   a. Estimate a simple linear regression model involving shipping cost and package weight. Interpret the slope coefficient of the least squares line as well as the computed value of R^2.

b. Add another explanatory variable—distance shipped—to the regression model in part **a**. Estimate and interpret this expanded model. How does the R^2 value for this multiple regression model compare to that of the simple regression model estimated in part **a**? Explain any difference between the two R^2 values. Interpret the *adjusted* R^2 value for the revised model.

25. Using the sample data given in the file **P11_10.xlsx**, formulate a multiple regression model to predict the sales price of houses in a given community.

a. Add one explanatory variable at a time and estimate each partial regression equation. Report and explain changes in the standard error of estimate s_e, the coefficient of determination R^2, and the adjusted R^2 as each explanatory variable is added to the model.

b. Interpret each of the estimated regression coefficients in the full model.

c. What proportion of the total variation in the sales price is explained by the multiple regression model that includes all four explanatory variables?

11.6 MODELING POSSIBILITIES

Once we move from simple to multiple regression, the floodgates open. All types of explanatory variables are potential candidates for inclusion in the regression equation. In this section we examine several new types of explanatory variables. These include "dummy" variables, interaction variables, and nonlinear transformations. The techniques in this section provide us with many alternative approaches to modeling the relationship between a dependent variable and potential explanatory variables. In many applications these techniques produce much better fits than we could obtain without them.

As the title of this section suggests, these techniques are modeling *possibilities*. They provide a wide variety of explanatory variables to choose from. However, this does not mean that it is wise to include all or even many of these new types of explanatory variables in any particular regression equation. The chances are that only a few, if any, will significantly improve the linear fit. Knowing which explanatory variables to include requires a great deal of practical experience with regression, as well as a thorough understanding of the particular problem to be solved. The material in this section should *not* be an excuse for a mindless fishing expedition.

11.6.1 Dummy Variables

Some potential explanatory variables are categorical and cannot be measured on a quantitative scale. However, these categorical variables are often related to the dependent variable, so we need a way to include them in a regression equation. The trick is to use **dummy** variables, also called **indicator** or **0–1** variables. Dummy variables are variables that indicate the category a given observation is in. If a dummy variable for a given category equals 1, the observation is in that category; if it equals 0, the observation is not in that category.

> A **dummy variable** is a variable with possible values 0 and 1. It equals 1 if the observation is in a particular category and 0 if it is not.

Categorical variables are used in two situations. The first and perhaps most common situation is when a categorical variable has only two categories. A good example of this is a gender variable that has the two categories "male" and "female." In this case we need only a *single* dummy variable, and we have the choice of assigning the 1's to either category. If we label the dummy variable Gender, then we can code Gender as 1 for males and 0 for females, or we can code Gender as 1 for females and 0 for males. We just need to be consistent and specify explicitly which coding scheme we are using.

The other situation is when there are more than two categories. A good example of this is when we have quarterly time series data and we want to treat the quarter of the year as a categorical variable with four categories, 1 through 4. Then we can create four dummy variables, Q1 through Q4. For example, Q2 equals 1 for all second-quarter observations and equals 0 for all other observations. Although we can create four dummy variables, we will see that only three of them—*any* three—should be used in a regression equation.

The following example illustrates how we form, use, and interpret dummy variables in regression analysis.

| EXAMPLE | 11.3 POSSIBLE GENDER DISCRIMINATION IN SALARY AT FIFTH NATIONAL BANK OF SPRINGFIELD |

The Fifth National Bank of Springfield is facing a gender discrimination suit.[7] The charge is that its female employees receive substantially smaller salaries than its male employees. The bank's employee database is listed in the file **Bank Salaries.xlsx**. For each of its 208 employees, the data set includes the following variables:

- EducLev: education level, a categorical variable with categories 1 (finished high school), 2 (finished some college courses), 3 (obtained a bachelor's degree), 4 (took some graduate courses), 5 (obtained a graduate degree)

- JobGrade: a categorical variable indicating the current job level, the possible levels being 1 through 6 (6 is highest)

- YrsExper: years of experience with this bank

- Age: employee's current age

- Gender: a categorical variable with values "Female" and "Male"

- YrsPrior: number of years of work experience at another bank prior to working at Fifth National

- PCJob: a categorical yes/no variable depending on whether the employee's current job is computer-related

- Salary: current annual salary

Figure 11.23 lists a few of the observations. Do these data provide evidence that females are discriminated against in terms of salary?

Figure 11.23

Selected Data for Bank Example

	A	B	C	D	E	F	G	H	I
1	Employee	EducLev	JobGrade	YrsExper	Age	Gender	YrsPrior	PCJob	Salary
2	1	3	1	3	26	Male	1	No	$32,000
3	2	1	1	14	38	Female	1	No	$39,100
4	3	1	1	12	35	Female	0	No	$33,200
5	4	2	1	8	40	Female	7	No	$30,600
6	5	3	1	3	28	Male	0	No	$29,000
7	6	3	1	3	24	Female	0	No	$30,500
8	7	3	1	4	27	Female	0	No	$30,000
9	8	3	1	8	33	Male	2	No	$27,000
10	9	1	1	4	62	Female	0	No	$34,000
11	10	3	1	9	31	Female	0	No	$29,500
12	11	3	1	9	34	Female	2	No	$26,800
13	12	2	1	8	37	Female	8	No	$31,300
14	13	2	1	9	37	Female	0	No	$31,200
15	14	2	1	10	58	Female	6	No	$34,700
16	15	3	1	4	33	Female	0	No	$30,000

[7]This example and the accompanying data set are based on a real case. Only the bank's name has been changed.

Objective To use StatTools's Regression procedure to analyze whether the bank discriminates against females in terms of salary.

Solution

A naive approach to this problem compares the average female salary to the average male salary. This can be done with a pivot table, as in Chapter 2, or with a more formal hypothesis test, as in Chapter 10. Using these methods, we find that the average of all salaries is $39,922, the female average is $37,210, the male average is $45,505, and the difference between the male and female averages is statistically significant at any reasonable level of significance. In short, the females definitely earn less. But perhaps there is a reason for this. They might have lower education levels, they might have been hired more recently, they might be working at lower job grades, and so on. The question is whether the difference between female and male salaries is still evident after taking these other attributes into account. This is a perfect task for regression.

We first need to create dummy variables for the various categorical variables. We can do this manually with IF functions or we can use StatTools's Dummy procedure. To do it manually, we can create a dummy variable Female based on Gender in column J by entering the formula

=IF(F45="Female",1,0)

in cell J4 and copying it down. Note that we are coding the females as 1's and the males as 0's. (The quotes are necessary when a text value is used in an IF function.)

StatTools's Dummy procedure is somewhat easier, especially when there are multiple categories. For example, to create five dummies, Ed_1 through Ed_5, for the education levels, we select Dummy from the StatTools Utilities dropdown, select the Create One Dummy Variable for Each Distinct Category option, and select the EducLev variable to base the dummies on. This creates five dummy columns with variable names EducLev=1 through EducLev=5. We can follow the same procedure to create six dummies, JobGrade=1 through JobGrade=6, for the job grade categories.

We can add dummies to effectively collapse categories.

Sometimes we might want to collapse several categories. For example, we might want to collapse the five education categories into three categories: 1, (2,3), and (4,5). The new second category includes employees who have taken undergraduate courses or have completed a bachelor's degree, and the new third category includes employees who have taken graduate courses or have completed a graduate degree. It is easy to do this. We simply add the EducLev=2 and EducLev=3 columns to get the dummy for the new second category, and we add the EducLev=4 and EducLev=5 columns for the new third category.

Once the dummies have been created, we can run a regression analysis with Salary as the dependent variable, using any combination of numerical and dummy explanatory variables. However, there are two rules we must follow:

- We shouldn't use any of the *original* categorical variables, such as EducLev, that the dummies are based on.

- We should always use *one less dummy* than the number of categories for any categorical variable.

Always include one less dummy than the number of categories. The omitted dummy corresponds to the reference category.

This second rule is a technical one. If we violate it, the statistical software will give us an error message. For example, if we want to use education level as an explanatory variable, we should enter only four of the five dummies EducLev=1 through EducLev=5. *Any* four of these can be used. The omitted dummy then corresponds to the **reference** category. As we will see, the interpretation of the dummy variable coefficients are all relative to this reference category. When there are only two categories, as with the gender variable, we typically name the variable with the category, such as Female, that corresponds to the 1's. If we create the dummy variables manually, we probably don't even bother to create a Male dummy. In this case "Male" automatically becomes the reference category.

To explain dummy variables in regression, we proceed in several stages in this example. We first estimate a regression equation with only one explanatory variable, Female. The output appears in Figure 11.24. The resulting equation is

$$\text{Predicted Salary} = 45505 - 8296\text{Female} \tag{11.12}$$

Figure 11.24

Output for Bank Example with a Single Explanatory Variable

	A	B	C	D	E	F	G
7		Multiple	R-Square	Adjusted	StErr of		
8	Summary	R		R-Square	Estimate		
9		0.3465	0.1201	0.1158	10584.3		
10							
11		Degrees of	Sum of	Mean of	F-Ratio	p-Value	
12	ANOVA Table	Freedom	Squares	Squares			
13	Explained	1	3149633845	3149633845	28.1151	< 0.0001	
14	Unexplained	206	23077473386	112026569.8			
15							
16		Coefficient	Standard	t-Value	p-Value	Confidence Interval 95%	
17	Regression Table		Error			Lower	Upper
18	Constant	45505.4	1283.5	35.4533	< 0.0001	42974.9	48036.0
19	Female	-8295.5	1564.5	-5.3024	< 0.0001	-11380.0	-5211.0

To interpret regression equations with dummy variables, it is useful to rewrite the equation for each category.

To interpret this equation, recall that Female has only two possible values, 0 and 1. If we substitute Female=1 into equation (11.12), we obtain

$$\text{Predicted Salary} = 45505 - 8296(1) = 37209$$

Because Female=1 corresponds to females, this equation simply indicates the average female salary. Similarly, if we substitute Female=0 into equation (11.12), we obtain

$$\text{Predicted Salary} = 45505 - 8296(0) = 45505$$

Because Female=0 corresponds to males, this equation indicates the average male salary. Therefore, the interpretation of the -8296 coefficient of the Female dummy variable is straightforward. It is the average female salary relative to the reference (male) category—females get paid $8296 less on average than males.

Obviously, equation (11.12) tells only part of the story. It ignores all information except for gender. We expand this equation by adding the experience variables YrsPrior and YrsExper. The output with the Female dummy variable and these two experience variables appears in Figure 11.25. The corresponding regression equation is

$$\text{Predicted Salary} = 35492 + 988\text{YrsExper} + 131\text{YrsPrior} - 8080\text{Female} \tag{11.13}$$

Figure 11.25

Regression Output with Two Numerical Explanatory Variables Included

	A	B	C	D	E	F	G
7		Multiple	R-Square	Adjusted	StErr of		
8	Summary	R		R-Square	Estimate		
9		0.7016	0.4923	0.4848	8079.4		
10							
11		Degrees of	Sum of	Mean of	F-Ratio	p-Value	
12	ANOVA Table	Freedom	Squares	Squares			
13	Explained	3	12910668018	4303556006	65.9279	< 0.0001	
14	Unexplained	204	13316439212	65276662.81			
15							
16		Coefficient	Standard	t-Value	p-Value	Confidence Interval 95%	
17	Regression Table		Error			Lower	Upper
18	Constant	35491.7	1341.0	26.4661	< 0.0001	32847.6	38135.7
19	YrsExper	988.0	80.9	12.2083	< 0.0001	828.4	1147.6
20	YrsPrior	131.3	180.9	0.7259	0.4687	-225.4	488.1
21	Female	-8080.2	1198.2	-6.7438	< 0.0001	-10442.6	-5717.8

It is again useful to write equation (11.13) in two forms: one for females (substituting Female=1) and one for males (substituting Female=0). After doing the arithmetic, they become

$$\text{Predicted Salary} = 27412 + 988\text{YrsExper} + 131\text{YrsPrior}$$

and

$$\text{Predicted Salary} = 35492 + 988\text{YrsExper} + 131\text{YrsPrior}$$

Except for the intercept term, these equations are identical. We can now interpret the coefficient -8080 of the Female dummy variable as the average salary disadvantage for females relative to males *after controlling for job experience*. Gender discrimination still appears to be a very plausible conclusion. However, note that the R^2 value is only 49.2%. Perhaps there is still more to the story.

We next add education level to the equation by including four of the five education level dummies. Although *any* four could be used, we use EducLev=2 through EducLev=5, so that the lowest level becomes the reference category. (We would expect this to lead to *positive* coefficients for these dummies, which are easier to interpret.) The resulting output appears in Figure 11.26. The estimated regression equation is now

$$\text{Predicted Salary} = 26613 + 1033\text{YrsExper} + 362\text{YrsPrior} - 4501\text{Female}$$

$$+ 160\text{EducLev=2} + 4765\text{EducLev=3} + 7320\text{EducLev=4} + 11770\text{EducLev=5} \quad \textbf{(11.14)}$$

Figure 11.26

Regression Output with Education Dummies Included

	A	B	C	D	E	F	G
7		Multiple R	R-Square	Adjusted R-Square	StErr of Estimate		
8	Summary						
9		0.8030	0.6449	0.6324	6824.4		
10							
11		Degrees of Freedom	Sum of Squares	Mean of Squares	F-Ratio	p-Value	
12	ANOVA Table						
13	Explained	7	16912692100	2416098871	51.8787	< 0.0001	
14	Unexplained	200	9314415131	46572075.65			
15							
16		Coefficient	Standard Error	t-Value	p-Value	Confidence Interval 95%	
17	Regression Table					Lower	Upper
18	Constant	26613.4	1794.1	14.8335	< 0.0001	23075.5	30151.2
19	YrsExper	1032.9	69.6	14.8404	< 0.0001	895.7	1170.2
20	YrsPrior	362.2	158.1	2.2908	0.0230	50.4	674.0
21	Female	-4501.3	1085.8	-4.1458	< 0.0001	-6642.3	-2360.3
22	EducLev = 2	160.2	1656.0	0.0968	0.9230	-3105.2	3425.7
23	EducLev = 3	4764.6	1473.4	3.2336	0.0014	1859.1	7670.0
24	EducLev = 4	7319.8	2694.2	2.7169	0.0072	2007.2	12632.5
25	EducLev = 5	11770.2	1510.2	7.7937	< 0.0001	8792.2	14748.2

Now there are two categorical variables involved, gender and education level. However, we can still write a separate equation *for any combination* of categories by setting the dummies to the appropriate values. For example, the equation for females at the fifth education level is found by setting Female and EducLev=5 equal to 1, and setting the other education dummies equal to 0. After terms are combined, this equation is

$$\text{Predicted Salary} = 33882 + 1033\text{YrsExper} + 362\text{YrsPrior}$$

The intercept 33882 is the intercept from equation (11.14), 26613, plus the coefficients of Female and EducLev=5.

We can interpret equation (11.14) as follows. For either gender and any education level, the expected increase in salary for one extra year of experience with Fifth National is $1033; the expected increase in salary for one extra year of prior experience with another bank is $362. The coefficients of the education dummies indicate the average increase in salary an employee can expect relative to the reference (lowest) education level. For example, an employee with education level 4 can expect to earn $7320 more than an employee with education level 1, all else being equal. Finally, the key coefficient, −$4501 for females, indicates the average salary disadvantage for females relative to males, given that they have the same experience levels *and* the same education levels. Note that the R^2 value is now 64.5%, quite a bit larger than when the education dummies were not included. We appear to be getting closer to the truth. In particular, we see that there appears to be gender discrimination in salaries, even after accounting for job experience and education level.

One further explanation for gender differences in salary might be job grade. Perhaps females tend to be in lower job grades, which would help explain why they get lower salaries on average. One way to check this is with a pivot table, as in Figure 11.27, where we put job grade in the row area, gender in the column area, and request counts, displayed as percentages of columns. Clearly, females tend to be concentrated at the lower job grades. For example, 28.85% of all employees are at the lowest job grade, but 34.29% of all females are at this grade and only 17.65% of males are at this grade. The opposite is true at the higher job grades. This certainly helps to explain why females get lower salaries on average.

Figure 11.27

Pivot Table of Job Grade Counts for Bank Data

	A	B	C	D
1				
2				
3	Count of Employee	Gender		
4	JobGrade	Female	Male	Grand Total
5	1	34.29%	17.65%	28.85%
6	2	20.71%	19.12%	20.19%
7	3	25.71%	10.29%	20.67%
8	4	12.14%	16.18%	13.46%
9	5	6.43%	17.65%	10.10%
10	6	0.71%	19.12%	6.73%
11	Grand Total	100.00%	100.00%	100.00%

We can go one step further to see the effect of job grade on salary by including the dummies for job grade in the equation, along with the other variables we have included so far. As with the education dummies, we use the lowest job grade as the reference category and include only the five dummies for the other categories. While we are at it, we include the other two potential explanatory variables to the equation: Age and HasPCJob, a dummy based on the PCJob categorical variable. The regression output for this equation appears in Figure 11.28.

Figure 11.28

Regression Output with Other Variables Added

	A	B	C	D	E	F	G
7		Multiple R	R-Square	Adjusted R-Square	StErr of Estimate		
8	Summary						
9		0.8748	0.7652	0.7482	5648.1		
10							
11		Degrees of Freedom	Sum of Squares	Mean of Squares	F-Ratio	p-Value	
12	ANOVA Table						
13	Explained	14	20070250768	1433589341	44.9390	< 0.0001	
14	Unexplained	193	6156856463	31900810.69			
15							
16		Coefficient	Standard Error	t-Value	p-Value	Confidence Interval 95%	
17	Regression Table					Lower	Upper
18	Constant	29689.9	2490.0	11.9236	< 0.0001	24778.8	34601.1
19	YrsExper	515.6	98.0	5.2621	< 0.0001	322.3	708.8
20	Age	-9.0	57.7	-0.1553	0.8767	-122.8	104.8
21	YrsPrior	157.7	140.4	1.1943	0.2338	-109.3	444.7
22	Female	-2554.5	1012.0	-2.5242	0.0124	-4550.4	-558.5
23	EducLev = 2	-485.6	1398.7	-0.3472	0.7289	-3244.2	2273.1
24	EducLev = 3	527.9	1357.5	0.3889	0.6978	-2149.6	3205.4
25	EducLev = 4	285.2	2404.7	0.1186	0.9057	-4457.7	5028.1
26	EducLev = 5	2690.8	1620.9	1.6601	0.0985	-506.1	5887.7
27	JobGrade = 2	1564.5	1185.8	1.3194	0.1886	-774.2	3903.2
28	JobGrade = 3	5219.4	1262.4	4.1345	< 0.0001	2729.5	7709.2
29	JobGrade = 4	8594.8	1496.0	5.7451	< 0.0001	5644.2	11545.5
30	JobGrade = 5	13659.4	1874.3	7.2879	< 0.0001	9962.7	17356.1
31	JobGrade = 6	23832.4	2799.9	8.5119	< 0.0001	18310.1	29354.7
32	HasPCJob	4922.8	1473.8	3.3402	0.0010	2016.0	7829.7

As expected, the coefficients of the job grade dummies are all positive, and they increase as the job grade increases—it pays to be in the higher job grades. The effect of age appears to be minimal, and there appears to be a "bonus" of close to $5000 for having a PC-related job. The R^2 value has now increased to 76.5%, and the penalty for being a female has decreased to $2555—still large but not as large as before.

However, even if this penalty, the coefficient of Female in this last equation, is considered "small," is it convincing evidence against the argument for gender discrimination? We believe the answer is "no." We have used variations in job grades to reduce the penalty for being female. But the remaining question is then, Why are females predominantly in the low job grades? Perhaps this is the real source of gender discrimination. Perhaps management is not advancing the females as quickly as it should, which naturally results in lower salaries for females.

We conclude this example for now, but we will say more about it in the next two subsections. ∎

The regression indicates that being in lower job grades implies lower salaries, but it doesn't explain why females are in the lower job grades in the first place.

11.6.2 Interaction Variables

Suppose that we regress a variable Y on a numerical variable X and a dummy variable D. If the estimated equation is of the form

$$\hat{Y} = a + b_1 X + b_2 D \tag{11.15}$$

then, as in the previous section, we can break this equation down into two separate equations:

$$\hat{Y} = (a + b_2) + b_1 X$$

and

$$\hat{Y} = a + b_1 X$$

The first corresponds to $D = 1$, and the second corresponds to $D = 0$. The only difference between these two equations is the intercept term; the slope for each is b_1. Geometrically, they correspond to two *parallel* lines that are a distance b_2 apart. For example, if D corresponds to gender, then there is a female line and a parallel male line. The effect of X on Y is the same for females and males. When X increases by 1 unit, we predict Y to change by b_1 units for both males or females.

In effect, when we include *only* a dummy variable in a regression equation, as in equation (11.15), we are allowing the intercepts of the two lines to differ (by an amount b_2), but we are *forcing* the lines to be parallel. Sometimes we want to allow them to have different slopes, in addition to possibly different intercepts. We can do this with an **interaction** variable. Algebraically, an interaction variable is the *product* of two variables. Its effect is to allow the effect of one of the variables on Y to depend on the value of the other variable.

> An **interaction** variable is the product of two explanatory variables. We include such a variable in a regression equation if we believe the effect of one explanatory variable on Y depends on the value of another explanatory variable.

Suppose we create the interaction variable XD (the product of X and D) and then estimate the equation

$$\hat{Y} = a + b_1 X + b_2 D + b_3 XD$$

As usual, we rewrite this equation as two separate equations, depending on whether $D = 0$ or $D = 1$. If $D = 1$, we combine terms to write

$$\hat{Y} = (a + b_2) + (b_1 + b_3)X$$

If $D = 0$, the dummy and interaction variables drop out and we obtain

$$\hat{Y} = a + b_1 X$$

The notation is not important. The important part is that the interaction term, $b_3 XD$, allows the slope of the regression line to differ between the two categories.

The following continuation of the bank discrimination example illustrates one possible use of interaction variables.

EXAMPLE

11.3 POSSIBLE GENDER DISCRIMINATION IN SALARY AT FIFTH NATIONAL BANK OF SPRINGFIELD (CONTINUED)

Earlier we estimated an equation for Salary using the numerical explanatory variables YrsExper and YrsPrior and the dummy variable Female. If we drop the YrsPrior variable from this equation (for simplicity) and rerun the regression, we obtain the equation

$$\text{Predicted Salary} = 35824 + 981\text{YrsExper} - 8012\text{Female} \qquad (11.16)$$

The R^2 value for this equation is 49.1%. If we decide to include an interaction variable between YrsExper and Female in this equation, what is its effect?

Objective To use multiple regression with an interaction variable to see whether the effect of years of experience on salary is different across the two genders.

Solution

We first need to form an interaction variable that is the product of YrsExper and Female. This can be done in two ways in Excel. We can do it manually by introducing a new variable that contains the product of the two variables involved, or we can use the Interaction item from the StatTools Utilities dropdown. For the latter, we select the Two Numeric Variables option in the Interaction Between dropdown, and we select Female and YrsExper as the variables to be used to create an interaction variable.[8]

Once the interaction variable has been created, we include it in the regression equation in addition to the other variables in equation (11.16). The multiple regression output appears in Figure 11.29. The estimated regression equation is

$$\text{Predicted Salary} = 30430 + 1528\text{YrsExper} + 4098\text{Female}$$

$$- 1248\text{Interaction}(\text{YrsExper,Female})$$

where Interaction(YrsExper,Female) is StatTools's default name for the interaction variable. As in the general discussion, it is useful to write this as two separate equations, one for females and one for males. The female equation (Female=1, so that Interaction(YrsExper,Female) = YrsExper) is

$$\text{Predicted Salary} = (30430 + 4098) + (1528 - 1248)\text{YrsExper}$$

$$= 34528 + 280\text{YrsExper}$$

and the male equation (Female=0, so that Interaction(YrsExper,Female) = 0) is

$$\text{Predicted Salary} = 30430 + 1528\text{YrsExper}$$

---

[8]See the StatTools online help for this data utility. It explains the various options for creating interaction variables.

Figure 11.29

Regression Output with an Interaction Variable

	A	B	C	D	E	F	G
7		Multiple R	R-Square	Adjusted R-Square	StErr of Estimate		
8	*Summary*						
9		0.7991	0.6386	0.6333	6816.3		
10							
11		Degrees of Freedom	Sum of Squares	Mean of Squares	F-Ratio	p-Value	
12	*ANOVA Table*						
13	Explained	3	16748875071	5582958357	120.1620	< 0.0001	
14	Unexplained	204	9478232160	46461922.35			
15							
16		Coefficient	Standard Error	t-Value	p-Value	Confidence Interval 95%	
17	*Regression Table*					Lower	Upper
18	Constant	30430.0	1216.6	25.0129	< 0.0001	28031.4	32828.7
19	YrsExper	1527.8	90.5	16.8887	< 0.0001	1349.4	1706.1
20	Female	4098.3	1665.8	2.4602	0.0147	813.8	7382.7
21	Interaction(YrsExper,Female)	-1247.8	136.7	-9.1296	< 0.0001	-1517.3	-978.3

Graphically, these equations appear as in Figure 11.30. The *Y*-intercept for the female line is slightly higher—females with no experience with Fifth National tend to start out slightly higher than males—but the slope of the female line is much lower. That is, males tend to move up the salary ladder much more quickly than females. Again, this provides another argument, although a somewhat different one, for gender discrimination against females. By the way, the R^2 value with the interaction variable has increased from 49.1% to 63.9%. The interaction variable has definitely added to the explanatory power of the equation.

Figure 11.30 Nonparallel Female and Male Salary Lines

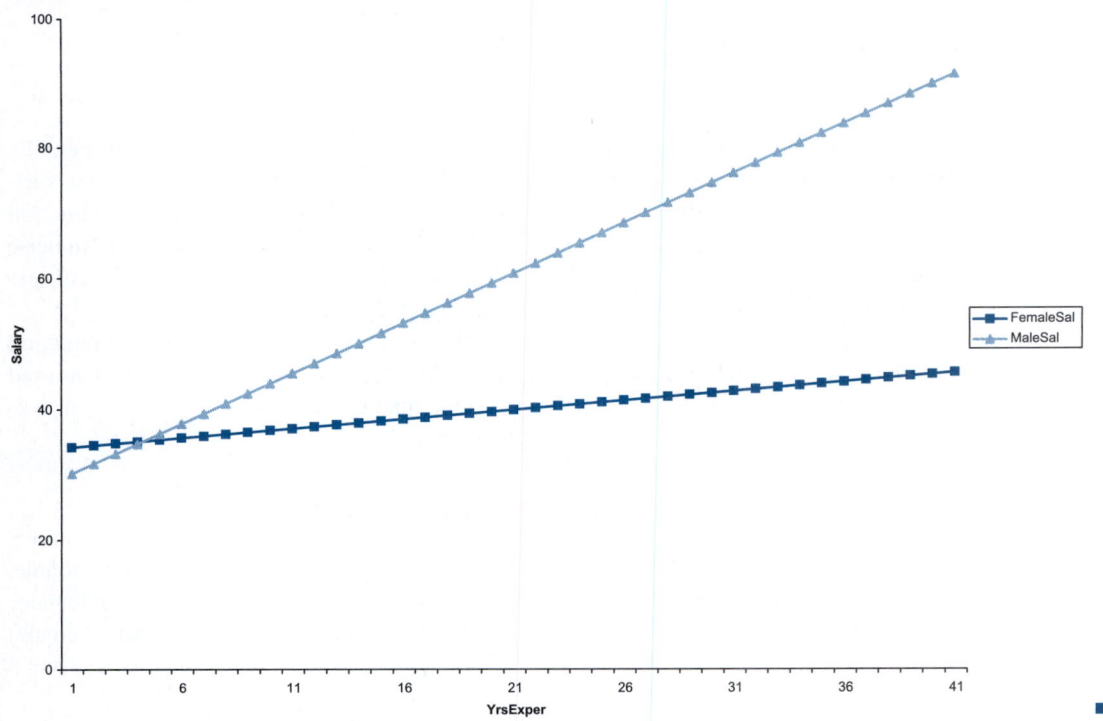

This example illustrates just one possible use of interaction variables. The product of *any* two variables, a numerical and a dummy variable, two dummy variables, or even two numerical variables, can be used. The trick is to interpret the results correctly, and the easiest way to do this is the way we've been doing it—by writing several separate equations and seeing how they differ. To illustrate one further possibility (among many), suppose we include the variables YrsExper, Female, and HighJob in the equation for Salary, along with interactions between Female and YrsExper and between Female and HighJob. Here,

HighJob is a new dummy variable that is 1 for job grades 4 to 6 and is 0 for job grades 1 to 3. (It can be calculated as the sum of the dummies JobGrade=4 through JobGrade=6.) The resulting equation is

$$\text{Predicted Salary} = 28168 + 1261\text{YrsExper} + 9242\text{HighJob} + 6601\text{Female}$$

$$- 1224\text{Interaction(YrsExper,Female)} + 1564\text{Interaction(Female,HighJob)} \quad \textbf{(11.17)}$$

and the R^2 value is now 76.6%.

The interpretation of equation (11.17) is quite a challenge because it is really composed of four separate equations, one for each combination of Female and HighJob. For females in the high job category, the equation becomes

$$\text{Predicted Salary} = (28168 + 9242 + 6601 + 1564) + (1261 - 1224)\text{YrsExper}$$

$$= 45575 + 37\text{YrsExper}$$

and for females in the low job category it is

$$\text{Predicted Salary} = (28168 + 6601) + (1261 - 1224)\text{YrsExper}$$

$$= 34769 + 37\text{YrsExper}$$

Similarly, for males in the high job category, the equation becomes

$$\text{Predicted Salary} = (28168 + 9242) + 1261\text{YrsExper}$$

$$= 37410 + 1261\text{YrsExper}$$

and for males in the low job category it is

$$\text{Predicted Salary} = 28168 + 1261\text{YrsExper}$$

Putting this into words, we can interpret the various coefficients as follows:

Interpretation of Regression Coefficients

- The intercept 28168 is the average *starting* salary (that is, with no experience at Fifth National) for males in the low job category.
- The coefficient 1261 of YrsExper is the expected increase in salary per extra year of experience for males (in either job category).
- The coefficient 9242 of HighJob is the expected salary "premium" for males starting in the high job category instead of the low job category.
- The coefficient 6601 of Female is the expected starting salary premium for females relative to males, given that they start in the low job category.
- The coefficient -1224 of Interaction(YrsExper,Female) is the penalty per extra year of experience for females relative to males—that is, male salaries increase this much more than female salaries each year.
- The coefficient 1564 of Interaction(Female,HighJob) is the extra premium (in addition to the male premium) for females starting in the high job category instead of the low job category.

As we see, there are pros and cons to adding interaction variables. On the plus side, they allow for more complex and interesting models, and they can provide significantly better fits. On the minus side, they can become extremely difficult to interpret correctly. Therefore, we recommend that they be added only when there is good economic and statistical justification for doing so.

11.6.3 Nonlinear Transformations

The general linear regression equation has the form

$$\hat{Y} = a + b_1 X_1 + b_2 X_2 + \cdots + b_k X_k$$

We typically include nonlinear transformations in a regression equation because of economic considerations or curvature detected in scatterplots.

It is *linear* in the sense that the right-hand side of the equation is a constant plus a sum of products of constants and variables. However, there is no requirement that the dependent variable Y or the explanatory variables X_1 through X_k be *original* variables in the data set. Most often they are, but they are also allowed to be transformations of original variables. We already saw one example of this in the previous section with interaction variables. They are not original variables but are instead products of original (or even transformed) variables. We enter them in the same way as original variables; only the interpretation differs. In this section we look at several nonlinear transformations of variables. These are often used because of curvature detected in scatterplots. They can also arise because of economic considerations. That is, economic theory often leads us to particular nonlinear transformations.

We can transform the dependent variable Y or we can transform any of the explanatory variables, the X's. We can also do both. In either case there are a few nonlinear transformations that are typically used. These include the natural logarithm, the square root, the reciprocal, and the square. The point of any of these is usually to "straighten out" the points in a scatterplot. If several different transformations straighten out the data equally well, then we prefer the one that is easiest to interpret.

We begin with a small example where only the X variable needs to be transformed.

EXAMPLE | **11.4 DEMAND AND COST FOR ELECTRICITY**

The Public Service Electric Company produces different quantities of electricity each month, depending on the demand. The file **Cost of Power.xlsx** lists the number of units of electricity produced (Units) and the total cost of producing these (Cost) for a 36-month period. The data appear in Figure 11.31. How can regression be used to analyze the relationship between Cost and Units?

Figure 11.31

Data for Electric Power Example

	A	B	C
1	Month	Cost	Units
2	1	45623	601
3	2	46507	738
4	3	43343	686
5	4	46495	736
6	5	47317	756
7	6	41172	498
8	7	43974	828
9	8	44290	671
10	9	29297	305
11	10	47244	637
12	11	43185	499
13	12	42658	578

Objective To see whether the cost of supplying electricity is a nonlinear function of demand, and if it is, what form the nonlinearity takes.

Solution

A good place to start is with a scatterplot of Cost versus Units. This appears in Figure 11.32. It indicates a definite positive relationship and one that is nearly linear. However, there is also some evidence of curvature in the plot. The points increase slightly less rapidly as Units increases from left to right. In economic terms, there might be economies of scale, so that the marginal cost of electricity decreases as more units of electricity are produced.

Figure 11.32

Scatterplot of Cost Versus Units for Electricity Example

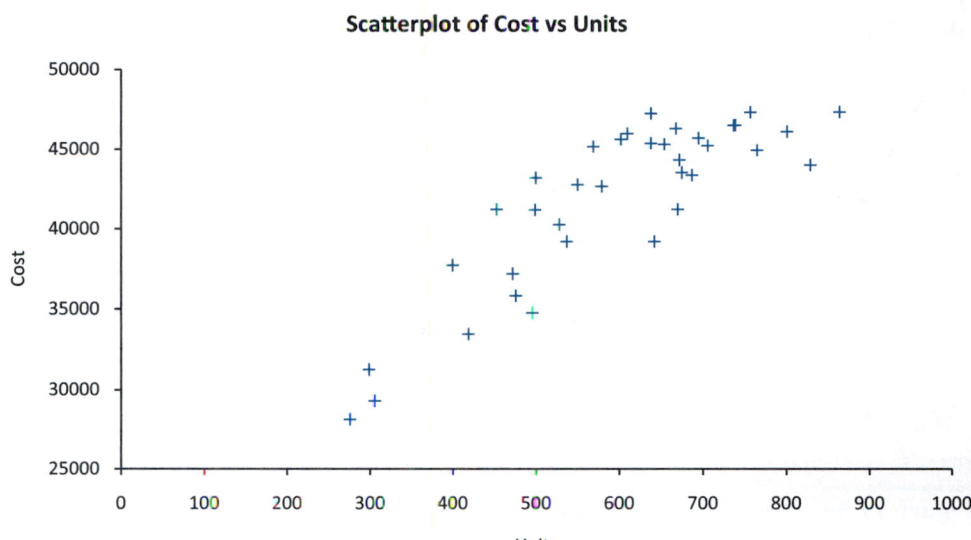

Nevertheless, we first use regression to estimate a *linear* relationship between Cost and Units. The resulting regression equation is

$$\text{Predicted Cost} = 23{,}651 + 30.53\text{Units}$$

The corresponding R^2 and s_e are 73.6% and $2734. We also requested a scatterplot of the residuals versus the fitted values, always a good idea when nonlinearity is suspected. This plot is shown in Figure 11.33. The sign of nonlinearity in this plot is that the residuals to the far left and the far right are all negative, whereas the majority of the residuals in the middle are positive. Admittedly, the pattern is far from perfect—there are several negative residuals in the middle—but the plot does hint at nonlinear behavior.

This negative–positive–negative behavior of residuals suggests a *parabola*—that is, a quadratic relationship with the *square* of Units included in the equation. We first create a new variable (Units)^2 in the data set. This can be done manually (with the formula =C4^2 in

A scatterplot of residuals versus fitted values often indicates the need for a nonlinear transformation.

cell D4, copied down) or with the Transform item in the StatTools Utilities dropdown.[9] This latter method has the advantage that it allows us to transform several variables simultaneously. Then we use multiple regression to estimate the equation for Cost with *both* explanatory variables, Units and (Units)^2, included. The resulting equation, as shown in Figure 11.34, is

$$\text{Predicted Cost} = 5793 + 98.35\text{Units} - 0.0600(\text{Units})^2 \qquad (11.18)$$

Note that R^2 has increased to 82.2% and s_e has decreased to \$2281.

Figure 11.33

Residuals from a Straight-Line Fit

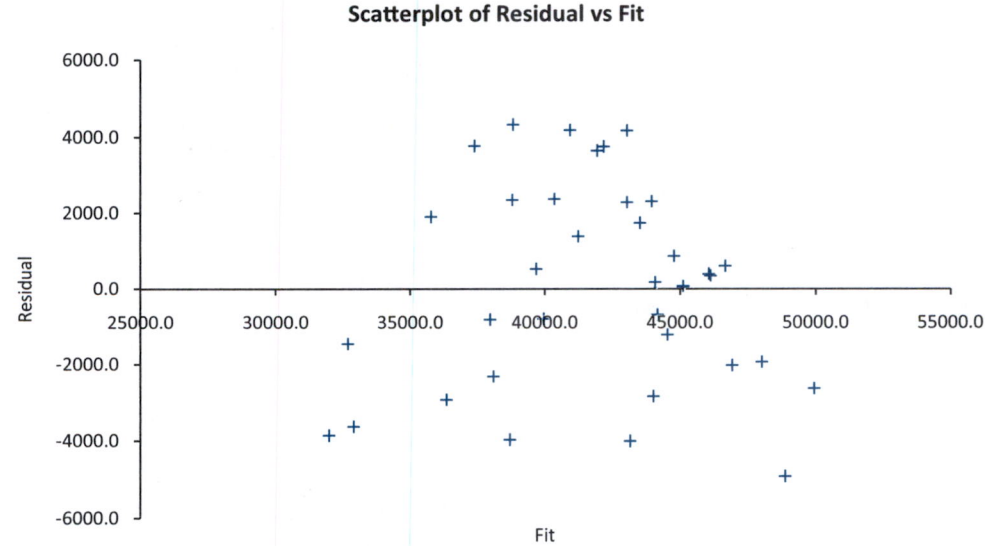

Figure 11.34   Regression Output with Squared Term Included

	A	B	C	D	E	F	G
7		Multiple	R-Square	Adjusted	StErr of		
8	Summary	R		R-Square	Estimate		
9		0.9064	0.8216	0.8108	2280.800		
10							
11		Degrees of	Sum of	Mean of	F-Ratio	p-Value	
12	ANOVA Table	Freedom	Squares	Squares			
13	Explained	2	790511518.3	395255759.1	75.9808	< 0.0001	
14	Unexplained	33	171667570.7	5202047.597			
15							
16			Standard			Confidence Interval 95%	
17	Regression Table	Coefficient	Error	t-Value	p-Value	Lower	Upper
18	Constant	5792.80	4763.06	1.2162	0.2325	-3897.72	15483.31
19	Units	98.350	17.237	5.7058	< 0.0001	63.282	133.419
20	(Units)^2	-0.0600	0.0151	-3.9806	0.0004	-0.0906	-0.0293

[9]StatTools provides four nonlinear transformations: natural logarithm, square, square root, and reciprocal.

One way to see how this regression equation fits the scatterplot of Cost versus Units (in Figure 11.32) is to use Excel's trendline option. To do so, activate the scatterplot, select More Trendline Options from the Trendline dropdown on the Chart Tools Layout ribbon, and select the Polynomial type or order 2, that is, a quadratic. A graph of equation (11.18) is superimposed on the scatterplot, as shown in Figure 11.35. It shows a reasonably good fit, plus an obvious curvature.

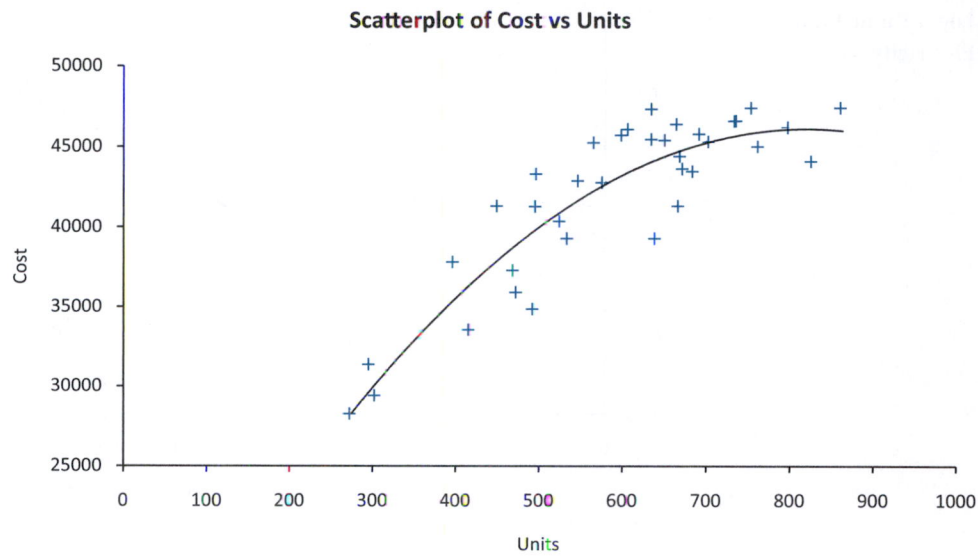

Scatterplot of Cost vs Units

The main downside to a quadratic regression equation, as in equation (11.18), is that there is no easy interpretation of the coefficients of Units and (Units)^2. For example, we can't conclude from the 98.35 coefficient of Units that Cost increases by 98.35 dollars when Units increases by 1. The reason is that when Units increases by 1, (Units)^2 doesn't stay constant; it *also* increases. All we can say is that the terms in equation (11.18) combine to explain the nonlinear relationship between units produced and total cost.

A final note about this equation concerns the coefficient of (Units)^2, −0.0600. First, the fact that it is negative makes the parabola bend "downward." This produces the decreasing marginal cost behavior, where every extra unit of electricity incurs a smaller cost. Actually, the curve described by equation (11.18) eventually goes *downhill* for large values of Units, but this part of the curve is irrelevant because the company evidently never produces such large quantities. Second, we should not be fooled by the small magnitude of this coefficient. Remember that it is the coefficient of Units *squared*, which is a large quantity. Therefore, the effect of the product −0.0600(Units)^2 is sizable.

There is at least one other possibility we can examine. Rather than a quadratic fit, we can try a logarithmic fit. In this case we create a new variable, Log(Units), the natural logarithm of Units, and then regress Cost against the *single* variable Log(Units). To create the new variable, we can proceed manually with Excel's LN function or we can use the Transform item from StatTools Utilities. Also, we can superimpose a logarithmic curve on the scatterplot of Cost versus Units by using Excel's trendline feature with the logarithmic option. This curve appears in Figure 11.36. To the naked eye, it appears to be similar, and about as good a fit, as the quadratic curve in Figure 11.35.

Figure 11.36

Logarithmic Fit to Electricity Data

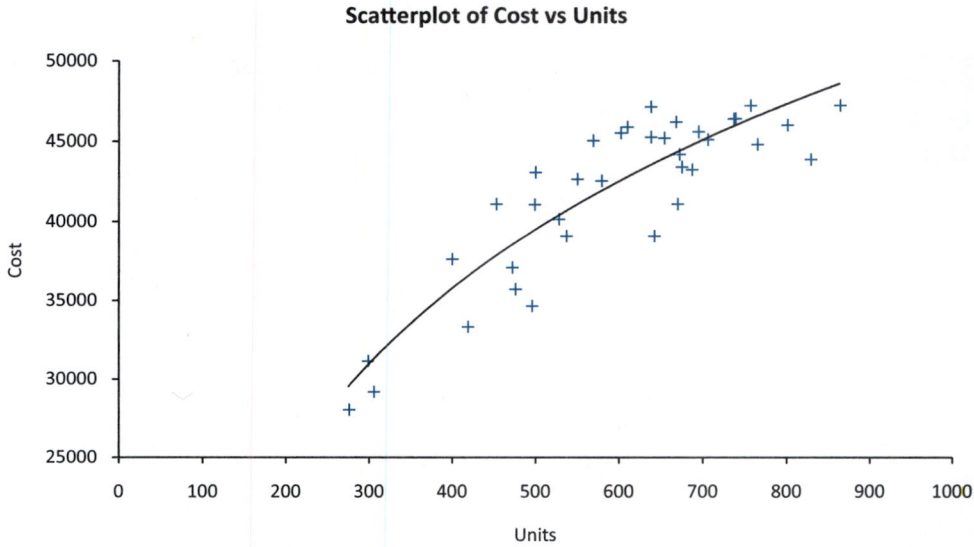

Scatterplot of Cost vs Units

The resulting regression equation is

$$\text{Predicted Cost} = -63{,}993 + 16{,}654 \text{Log(Units)} \qquad \textbf{(11.19)}$$

and the R^2 and s_e values are 79.8% and 2393. These latter values indicate that the logarithmic fit is not quite as good as the quadratic fit. However, the advantage of the logarithmic equation is that it is easier to interpret. In fact, one reason logarithmic transformations of variables are used as widely as they are in regression analysis is that they are fairly easy to interpret.

In general, if b is the coefficient of the log of X, then the expected change in Y when X increases by 1% is approximately 0.01 times b.

In the present case, where the log of an *explanatory* variable is used, we can interpret its coefficient as follows. Suppose that Units increases by 1%, for example, from 600 to 606. Then equation (11.19) implies that the expected Cost will increase by approximately

0.01(16,654) = 166.54 dollars. In words, every 1% increase in Units is accompanied by an expected $166.54 increase in Cost. Note that for larger values of Units, a 1% increase represents a larger absolute increase (from 700 to 707 instead of from 600 to 606, say). But each such 1% increase entails the *same* increase in Cost. This is another way of describing the decreasing marginal cost property. ∎

The electricity example has shown two possible nonlinear transformations of the *explanatory* variable (or variables) that we can use. All we need to do is create the transformed X's and run the regression. The interpretation of statistics such as R^2 and s_e is exactly the same as before; only the interpretation of the coefficients of the transformed X's changes. It is also possible to transform the dependent variable Y. Now, however, we must be careful when interpreting summary statistics such as R^2 and s_e, as we explain in the following examples.

A logarithmic transformation of Y *is often useful when the distribution of* Y *values is skewed to the right.*

Each of these examples transforms the dependent variable Y by taking its natural logarithm and then using the log of Y as the new dependent variable. This approach is taken in a wide variety of business applications. Essentially, it is often a good option when the distribution of Y is skewed to the right, with a few very large values and many small to medium values. The effect of the logarithm transformation is to spread the small values out and squeeze the large values together, making the distribution more symmetric. This is illustrated in Figures 11.37 and 11.38 for a hypothetical distribution of household incomes. The histogram of incomes in Figure 11.37 is clearly skewed to the right. However, the histogram of the natural log of income in Figure 11.38 is much more nearly symmetric—and, for technical reasons, more suitable for use as the dependent variable in regression.

Figure 11.37

Skewed Distribution of Income

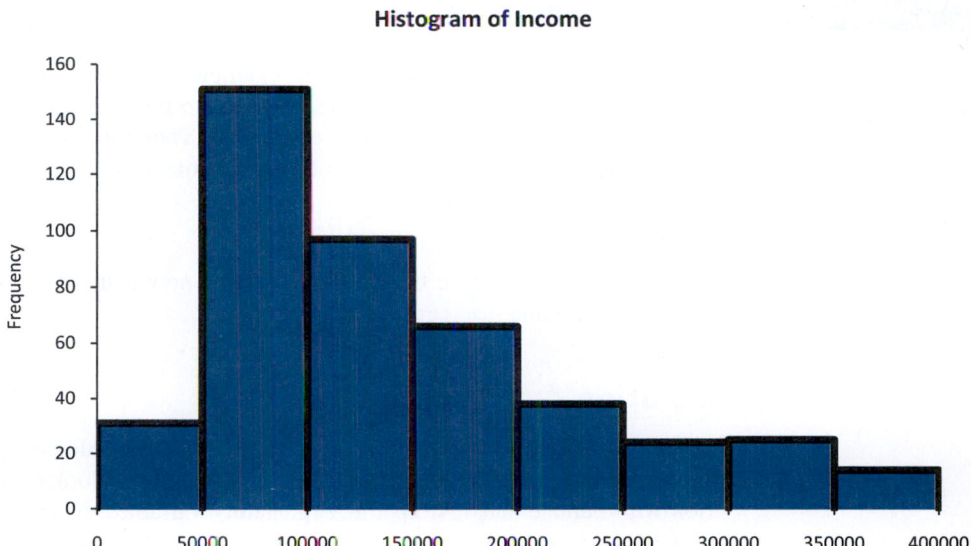

Figure 11.38

Symmetric
Distribution of
Log(Income)

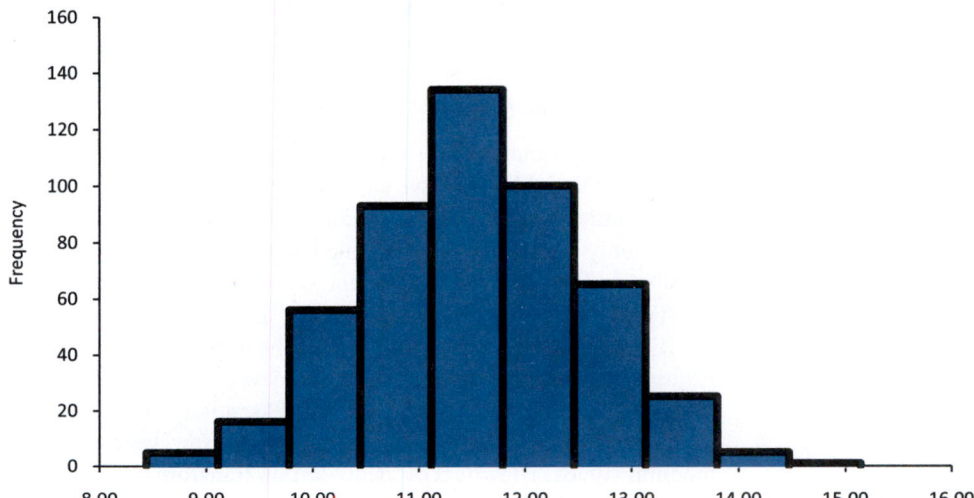

Histogram of Log income

EXAMPLE

11.3 POSSIBLE GENDER DISCRIMINATION IN SALARY AT FIFTH NATIONAL BANK OF SPRINGFIELD (CONTINUED)

Returning to the bank discrimination example, a glance at the distribution of salaries of the 208 employees shows some skewness to the right—a few employees make substantially more than the majority of employees. Therefore, it might make sense to use the natural logarithm of Salary instead of Salary as the dependent variable. If we do this, how do we interpret the results?

Objective   To reanalyze the bank salary data, now using the logarithm of salary as the dependent variable.

Solution

All of the analyses we did previously with this data set could be repeated with Log(Salary) as the dependent variable. For the sake of discussion, we look only at the regression equation with Female and YrsExper as explanatory variables. After we create the Log(Salary) variable and run the regression, we obtain the output in Figure 11.39. The estimated regression equation is

$$\text{Predicted Log(Salary)} = 10.4907 + 0.0188\text{YrsExper} - 0.1616\text{Female} \quad \textbf{(11.20)}$$

Figure 11.39

Regression Output
with Log of Salary as
Dependent Variable

	A	B	C	D	E	F	G
7		Multiple	R-Square	Adjusted	StErr of		
8	Summary	R		R-Square	Estimate		
9		0.6514	0.4243	0.4187	0.1794		
10							
11		Degrees of	Sum of	Mean of	F-Ratio	p-Value	
12	ANOVA Table	Freedom	Squares	Squares			
13	Explained	2	4.861326452	2.430663226	75.5556	< 0.0001	
14	Unexplained	205	6.59495595	0.032170517			
15							
16			Standard			Confidence Interval 95%	
17	Regression Table	Coefficient	Error	t-Value	p-Value	Lower	Upper
18	Constant	10.4907	0.0280	374.8768	< 0.0001	10.4355	10.5458
19	YrsExper	0.0188	0.0018	10.5556	< 0.0001	0.0153	0.0224
20	Female	-0.1616	0.0265	-6.0936	< 0.0001	-0.2139	-0.1093

The R^2 and s_e values are 42.4% and 0.1794. For comparison, when this same equation was estimated with Salary as the dependent variable, R^2 and s_e were 49.1% and 8.070.

We first interpret R^2 and s_e. Neither is directly comparable to the R^2 or s_e value with Salary as the dependent variable. Recall that R^2 in general is the percentage of the dependent variable explained by the regression equation. The problem here is that the two R^2 values are percentages explained of *different* dependent variables, Log(Salary) and Salary. The fact that one is smaller than the other (42.4% versus 49.1%) does not necessarily mean that it corresponds to a "worse" fit. They simply are not comparable.

When logarithm of Y is used in the regression equation, the interpretations of s_e and R^2 are different because the units of the dependent variable are completely different.

The situation is even worse with s_e. Each s_e is a measure of a typical residual, but the residuals in the Log(Salary) equation are in log dollars, whereas the residuals in the Salary equation are in dollars. These units are completely different. For example, the log of $1000 is only 6.91. Therefore, it is no surprise that s_e for the Log(Salary) equation is *much* smaller than s_e for the Salary equation. If we want comparable standard error measures for the two equations, we should take antilogs of fitted values from the Log(Salary) equation to convert them back to dollars, subtract these from the original Salary values, and take the standard deviation of these "residuals." (The EXP function in Excel can be used to take antilogs.) You can check that the resulting standard deviation is 7774.[10] This is somewhat smaller than s_e from the Salary equation, an indication of a slightly *better* fit.

Finally, we interpret equation (11.20) itself. Fortunately, this is fairly easy. When the dependent variable is Log(Y) and a term on the right-hand side of the equation is of the form bX, then whenever X increases by 1 unit, $\hat{Y}$ changes by a constant *percentage*, and this percentage is approximately equal to b (written as a percentage). For example, if $b = 0.035$, then when X increases by one unit, $\hat{Y}$ increases by approximately 3.5%. Applied to equation (11.20), this means that for each extra year of experience with Fifth National, an employee's salary can be expected to increase by about 1.88%. To interpret the Female coefficient, note that the only possible increase in Female is 1 unit (from 0 for male to 1 for female). When this occurs, the expected percentage *decrease* in salary is approximately 16.16%. In other words, equation (11.20) implies that females can expect to make about 16% less than men for comparable years of experience. ∎

The coefficient b can now be interpreted as the approximate percentage change in Y when X increases by 1 unit.

We are not necessarily claiming that the bank data are fit better with Log(Salary) as the dependent variable than with Salary—it appears to be a virtual toss-up. However, the lessons from this example are important in general. They are as follows.

1. The R^2 values with Y and Log(Y) as dependent variables are not directly comparable. They are percentages explained of *different* variables.

2. The s_e values with Y and Log(Y) as dependent variables are usually of totally different magnitudes. To make the s_e from the log equation comparable, we need to

---

[10]To make the two "standard deviations" comparable, we use the denominator $n - 3$ in each.

go through the procedure described in the example, so that the residuals are in *original* units.

3. To interpret any term of the form bX in the log equation, we first express b as a percentage. For example, $b = 0.035$ becomes 3.5%. Then when X increases by 1 unit, the expected *percentage* change in Y is approximately this percentage b.

Remember these points, especially the third, when using the logarithm of Y as the dependent variable.

The log transformation of a dependent variable Y is used frequently. This is partly because it induces nice statistical properties (such as making the distribution of Y more symmetric). But an important advantage of this transformation is its ease of interpretation in terms of percentage changes.

Constant Elasticity Relationships A particular type of nonlinear relationship that has firm grounding in economic theory is called a *constant elasticity* relationship. It is also called a *multiplicative* relationship. It has the form shown in equation (11.21).

Formula for Multiplicative Relationship

$$Y = aX_1^{b_1}X_2^{b_2} \cdots X_k^{b_k} \tag{11.21}$$

One property of this type of relationship is that the effect of a change of any explanatory variable X_i on Y depends on the levels of the other X's in the equation. This is not true for the *additive* relationships

$$Y = a + b_1X_1 + b_2X_2 + \cdots + b_kX_k$$

that we have been discussing. For additive relationships, when any X_i increases by one unit, Y changes by b_i units, regardless of the levels of the other X's. Multiplicative relationships are defined in the box.

> In a **multiplicative** (or **constant elasticity**) **relationship**, the dependent variable is expressed as a *product* of explanatory variables raised to powers. When any explanatory variable changes by 1%, the dependent variable changes by a constant *percentage*.

The term *constant elasticity* comes from economics. Economists define the elasticity of Y with respect to X as the percentage change in Y that accompanies a 1% increase in X. Often this is in reference to a demand–price relationship. Then the *price elasticity* is the percentage decrease in demand when price increases by 1%. Usually, the elasticity depends on the current value of X. For example, the price elasticity when the price is \$35 might be different than when the price is \$50. However, if the relationship is of the form

$$Y = aX^b$$

then the elasticity is *constant*, the same for any value of X. Moreover, it is approximately equal to the exponent b. For example, if $Y = 2X^{-1.5}$, then the constant elasticity is approximately -1.5, so that when X increases by 1%, Y decreases by approximately 1.5%.

The constant elasticity for any X is approximately equal to the exponent of that X.

The constant elasticity property carries over to the multiple-X relationship in equation (11.21). Then each exponent is the approximate elasticity for its X. For example, if $Y = 2X_1^{-1.5}X_2^{0.7}$, then we can make the following statements:

- When X_1 increases by 1%, Y decreases by approximately 1.5%, regardless of the current values of X_1 and X_2.

- When X_2 increases by 1%, Y increases by approximately 0.7%, regardless of the current values of X_1 and X_2.

We can use linear regression to estimate the nonlinear relationship in equation (11.21) by taking natural logarithms of *all* variables. Here we exploit two properties of logarithms: (1) the log of a product is the sum of the logs, and (2) the log of X^b is b times the log of X. Therefore, taking logs of both sides of equation (11.21) gives

$$\text{Log}(Y) = \text{Log}(a) + b_1\text{Log}(X_1) + \cdots + b_k\text{Log}(X_k)$$

This equation is *linear* in the log variables $\text{Log}(Y)$ and $\text{Log}(X_1)$ through $\text{Log}(X_k)$, so it can be estimated in the usual way with multiple regression. We can then interpret the coefficients of the explanatory variables directly as elasticities. The following example illustrates the method.

EXAMPLE **11.5 FACTORS RELATED TO SALES OF DOMESTIC AUTOMOBILES**

The file **Car Sales.xlsx** contains annual data (1970–1999) on domestic auto sales in the United States. The data are listed in Figure 11.40. The variables are defined as

- Sales: annual domestic auto sales (in number of units)
- PriceIndex: consumer price index of transportation
- Income: real disposable income
- Interest: prime rate of interest

Figure 11.40 Data for Automobile Demand Example

	A	B	C	D	E	F	G	H	I
1	Year	Sales	PriceIndex	Income	Interest				
2	1970	7,115,270	37.5	2630	7.91%				
3	1971	8,676,410	39.5	2745.3	5.72%	Sources: Automotive News, Market			
4	1972	9,321,310	39.9	2874.3	5.25%	Data Book (various issues) for column			
5	1973	9,618,510	41.2	3072.3	8.03%	B, from Economic Report of the			
6	1974	7,448,340	45.8	3051.9	10.81%	President, 2000, for columns C, D, E			
7	1975	7,049,840	50.1	3108.5	7.86%				
8	1976	8,606,860	55.1	3243.5	6.84%				
9	1977	9,104,930	59	3360.7	6.83%				
10	1978	9,304,250	61.7	3527.5	9.06%				
11	1979	8,316,020	70.5	3628.6	12.67%				
12	1980	6,578,360	83.1	3658	15.27%				
13	1981	6,206,690	93.2	3741.1	18.87%				
14	1982	5,756,610	97	3791.7	14.86%				
15	1983	6,795,230	99.3	3906.9	10.79%				
16	1984	7,951,790	103.7	4207.6	12.04%				
17	1985	8,204,690	106.4	4347.8	9.93%				
18	1986	8,222,480	102.3	4486.6	8.33%				
19	1987	7,080,890	105.4	4582.5	8.21%				
20	1988	7,526,334	108.7	4784.1	9.32%				
21	1989	7,014,850	114.1	4906.5	10.87%				
22	1990	6,842,733	120.5	5041.2	10.01%				
23	1991	6,072,255	123.8	5033	8.46%				
24	1992	6,216,488	126.5	5189.3	6.25%				
25	1993	6,674,458	130.4	5261.3	6.00%				
26	1994	7,181,975	134.3	5397.2	7.15%				
27	1995	7,023,843	139.1	5539.1	8.83%				
28	1996	7,139,884	143	5677.7	8.27%				
29	1997	6,907,992	144.3	5854.5	8.44%				
30	1998	6,756,804	141.6	6168.6	8.35%				
31	1999	6,987,208	144.4	6320	8.00%				

Estimate and interpret a multiplicative (constant elasticity) relationship between Sales and PriceIndex, Income, and Interest.

Objective To use logarithms of variables in a multiple regression to estimate a multiplicative relationship for automobile sales as a function of price, income, and interest rate.

Solution

We first take natural logs of all four variables. (This can be done in one step with the StatTools Transform utility or we can use Excel's LN function.) We then use multiple regression, with Log(Quantity) as the dependent variable and Log(PriceIndex), Log(Income), and Log(Interest) as the explanatory variables. The resulting output is shown in Figure 11.41. The corresponding equation for Log(Quantity) is

Predicted Log(Sales) = 14.126 − 0.384Log(PriceIndex) + 0.388Log(Income) − 0.070Log(Interest)

Figure 11.41

Regression Output for Multiplicative Relationship

	A	B	C	D	E	F	G
7		Multiple	R-Square	Adjusted	StErr of		
8	Summary	R		R-Square	Estimate		
9		0.6813	0.4642	0.4023	0.1053		
10							
11		Degrees of	Sum of	Mean of	F-Ratio	p-Value	
12	ANOVA Table	Freedom	Squares	Squares			
13	Explained	3	0.249567775	0.083189258	7.5073	0.0009	
14	Unexplained	26	0.288107728	0.011081066			
15							
16		Coefficient	Standard	t-Value	p-Value	Confidence Interval 95%	
17	Regression Table		Error			Lower	Upper
18	Constant	14.1260	1.9838	7.1206	< 0.0001	10.0482	18.2037
19	Log(PriceIndex)	-0.3837	0.2091	-1.8351	0.0780	-0.8135	0.0461
20	Log(Income)	0.3881	0.3621	1.0720	0.2936	-0.3561	1.1324
21	Log(Interest)	-0.0698	0.0893	-0.7821	0.4412	-0.2534	0.1137

If we like, we can convert this back to original variables, that is, back to multiplicative form, by taking antilogs. The result is

$$\text{Predicted Sales} = 1364048 \, \text{PriceIndex}^{-0.384} \, \text{Income}^{0.388} \, \text{Interest}^{-0.070}$$

where the constant 1364048 is the antilog of 14.126 (and be calculated in Excel with the EXP function).

In either form the equation implies that the elasticities are approximately equal to −0.384, 0.388, and −0.070. When PriceIndex increases by 1%, Sales tends to decrease by about 0.384%; when Income increases by 1%, Sales tends to increase by about 0.388%; and when Interest increases by 1%, Sales tends to decrease by about 0.070%.

Does this multiplicative equation provide a better fit to the automobile data than an additive relationship? Without doing considerably more work, it is difficult to answer this question with any certainty. As we discussed in the previous example, it is *not* sufficient to compare R^2 and s_e values for the two fits. Again, the reason is that one has Log(Sales) as the dependent variable, whereas the other has Sales, so the R^2 and s_e measures aren't comparable. We simply state that the multiplicative relationship provides a reasonably good fit (for example, a scatterplot of its fitted values versus residuals shows no unusual patterns), and it makes sense economically.

Before leaving this example, we note that the results for this data set are not quite as clear as they might appear. (This is often the case with real data.) First, the correlation between Sales and Income, or between Log(Sales) and Log(Income), is negative, not positive.

However, because of multicollinearity, a topic discussed in the next chapter, the regression coefficient of Log(Income) is positive. Second, most of the behavior appears to be driven by the early years. If you rerun the analysis from 1980 on, you will discover almost no relationship between Sales and the other variables. ∎

One final example of a multiplicative relationship is the *learning curve* model. A **learning curve** relates the unit production time (or cost) to the cumulative volume of output since that production process first began. Empirical studies indicate that production times tend to decrease by a relatively constant *percentage* every time cumulative output doubles. To model this phenomenon, let Y be the time required to produce a unit of output, and let X be the *cumulative* amount of output that has been produced. If we assume that the relationship between Y and X is of the form

$$Y = aX^b$$

then it can be shown that whenever X doubles, Y decreases to a *constant* percentage of its previous value. This constant is often called the **learning rate**. For example, if the learning rate is 80%, then each doubling of cumulative production yields a 20% reduction in unit production time. It can be shown that the learning rate satisfies the equation

$$b = \ln(\text{learning rate})/\ln(2) \qquad \textbf{(11.22)}$$

(where "ln" refers to the natural logarithm). So once we estimate b, we can use equation (11.22) to estimate the learning rate.

The following example illustrates a typical application of the learning curve model.

EXAMPLE

11.6 THE LEARNING CURVE FOR PRODUCTION OF A NEW PRODUCT AT PRESARIO

The Presario Company produces a variety of small industrial products. It has just finished producing 22 batches of a new product (new to Presario) for a customer. The file **Learning Curve.xlsx** contains the times (in hours) to produce each batch. These data are listed in Figure 11.42. Clearly, the times have tended to decrease as Presario has gained more experience in making the product. Does the multiplicative learning model apply to these data, and what does it imply about the learning rate?

Objective   To use a multiplicative regression equation to estimate the learning rate for production time.

Solution

One way to check whether the multiplicative learning model is reasonable is to create the log variables Log(Time) and Log(Batch) in the usual way and then see whether a scatterplot of Log(Time) versus Log(Batch) is approximately *linear*. The multiplicative model implies that it should be. Such a scatterplot appears in Figure 11.43, along with a superimposed linear trend line. The fit appears to be quite good.

To estimate the relationship, we regress Log(Time) on Log(Batch). The resulting equation is

$$\text{Predicted Log(Time)} = 4.834 - 0.155\text{Log(Batch)} \qquad \textbf{(11.23)}$$

Figure 11.42

Data for Learning
Curve Example

	A	B
1	Batch	Time
2	1	125.00
3	2	110.87
4	3	105.35
5	4	103.34
6	5	98.98
7	6	99.90
8	7	91.49
9	8	93.10
10	9	92.23
11	10	86.19
12	11	82.09
13	12	82.32
14	13	87.67
15	14	81.72
16	15	83.72
17	16	81.53
18	17	80.46
19	18	76.53
20	19	82.06
21	20	82.81
22	21	76.52
23	22	78.45

Figure 11.43

Scatterplot of Log
Variables with
Linear Trend
Superimposed

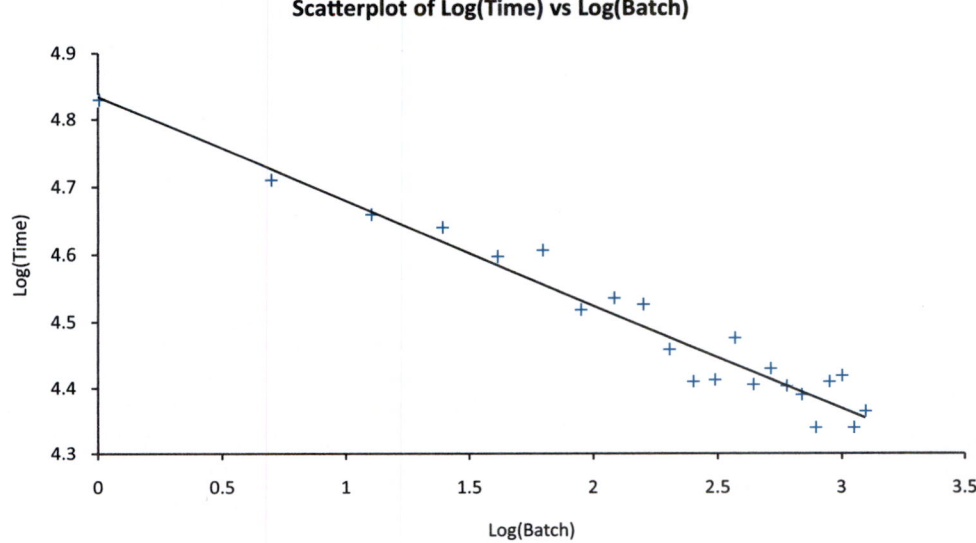

There are a couple of ways to interpret this equation. First, because it is based on a multiplicative relationship, we can interpret the coefficient -0.155 as an elasticity. That is, when Batch increases by 1%, Time tends to decrease by approximately 0.155%.

Although this interpretation is correct, it is not as useful as the "doubling" interpretation we discussed previously. We know from equation (11.22) that the estimated learning rate satisfies

$$-0.155 = \ln(\text{learning rate})/\ln(2)$$

Solving for the learning rate (multiply through by $\ln(2)$ and then take antilogs), we find that it is 0.898, or approximately 90%. In words, whenever cumulative production doubles, the time to produce a batch decreases by about 10%.

Presario could use this regression equation to predict future production times. For example, suppose the customer places an order for 15 more batches of the same product. Note that Presario is already partway up the learning curve, that is, these batches are numbers 23 through 37, and the company already has experience producing the product. We can use equation (11.23) to predict the log of production time for each batch, then take their antilogs and sum them to obtain the total production time. The calculations are shown in rows 24 through 39 of Figure 11.44. We enter the batch numbers and calculate their logs in columns A and C. Then we substitute the values of Log(Batch) in column C into equation (11.23) to obtain the predicted values of Log(Time) in column E. Finally, we use Excel's EXP function to calculate the antilogs of these predictions in column B, and we calculate their sum in cell B39. The total predicted time to finish the order is about 1115 hours.

Figure 11.44 Using the Learning Curve Model for Predictions

	A	B	C	D	E	F
21	20	82.81	2.995732274	4.416548827		
22	21	76.52	3.044522438	4.337552145		
23	22	78.45	3.091042453	4.362461479		
24	23	77.324	3.135494216	4.348009995		
25	24	76.816	3.17805383	4.341413654		
26	25	76.332	3.218875825	4.335086627		
27	26	75.869	3.258096538	4.329007785		
28	27	75.426	3.295836866	4.323158388		
29	28	75.003	3.33220451	4.317521744		
30	29	74.596	3.36729583	4.312082919		
31	30	74.205	3.401197382	4.306828497		
32	31	73.829	3.433987204	4.301746382		
33	32	73.466	3.465735903	4.296825631		
34	33	73.117	3.496507561	4.292056313		
35	34	72.779	3.526360525	4.287429384		
36	35	72.453	3.555348061	4.282936587		
37	36	72.137	3.583518938	4.278570366		
38	37	71.832	3.610917913	4.274323782		
39		1115.183	←———	Predicted time for next 15 batches		

PROBLEMS

Level A

26. In a study of housing demand, a county assessor is interested in developing a regression model to estimate the selling price of residential properties within her jurisdiction. She randomly selects 15 houses and records the selling price in addition to the following values: the size of the house (in hundreds of square feet), the total number of rooms in the house, the age of the house, and an indication of whether the house has an attached garage. These data are stored in the file **P11_26.xlsx**.
  a. Estimate and thoroughly interpret a multiple regression model that includes the four potential explanatory variables.
  b. Evaluate the estimated regression model's goodness of fit.
  c. Use the estimated model to predict the sales price of a 3000-square-foot, 20-year-old home that has 7 rooms but no attached garage.

27. A manager of boiler drums wants to use regression analysis to predict the number of worker-hours needed to erect the drums in future projects. Consequently, data for 36 randomly selected boilers were collected. In addition to worker-hours (Y), the variables measured include boiler capacity, boiler design pressure, boiler type, and drum type. All of these measurements can be found in the file **P11_27.xlsx**.
  a. Formulate an appropriate multiple regression model to predict the number of worker-hours needed to erect boiler drums.
  b. Estimate the formulated model using the given sample data, and interpret the estimated regression coefficients.
  c. According to the estimated regression model, what is the difference between the mean number of worker-hours required for erecting industrial and utility field boilers?
  d. According to the estimated regression model, what is the difference between the mean number of worker-hours required for erecting boilers with steam drums and those with mud drums?
  e. Given the estimated regression model, predict the number of worker-hours needed to erect a utility-field, steam-drum boiler with a capacity of 550,000 pounds per hour and a design pressure of 1400 pounds per square inch.
  f. Given the estimated regression model, predict the number of worker-hours needed to erect an industrial-field, mud-drum boiler with a capacity of 100,000 pounds per hour and a design pressure of 1000 pounds per square inch.

28. Suppose that a regional express delivery service company wants to estimate the cost of shipping a package (Y) as a function of cargo type, where cargo type includes the following possibilities: fragile, semifragile, and durable. Costs for 15 randomly chosen packages of approximately the same weight and same distance shipped, but of different cargo types, are provided in the file **P11_28.xlsx**.
  a. Formulate an appropriate multiple regression model to predict the cost of shipping a given package.
  b. Estimate the formulated model using the given sample data, and interpret the estimated regression coefficients.
  c. According to the estimated regression model, which cargo type is the *most* costly to ship? Which cargo type is the *least* costly to ship?
  d. How well does the estimated model fit the given sample data? How can the model's goodness of fit be improved?
  e. Given the estimated regression model, predict the cost of shipping a package with semifragile cargo.

29. The file **P11_11.xlsx** contains annual observations of the American minimum wage. Has the minimum wage been growing at roughly a *constant* rate over this period?
  a. Generate a scatterplot for these data. Comment on the observed behavior of the minimum wage over time.
  b. Formulate and estimate an appropriate regression model to explain the variation of the American minimum age over the given time period. Interpret the estimated regression coefficients.
  c. Analyze the estimated model's residuals. Is your estimated regression model adequate? If not, return to part **b** and revise your model. Continue to revise the model until your results are satisfactory.

30. Formulate a regression model that adequately estimates the relationship between monthly electrical power usage (Y) and home size (X) using the data in the file **P11_13.xlsx**. Interpret your results. How well does your model explain the variation in monthly electrical power usage?

31. An insurance company wants to determine how its annual operating costs depend on the number of home insurance (X_1) and automobile insurance (X_2) policies that have been written. The file **P11_31.xlsx** contains relevant information for 10 branches of the insurance company. The company believes that a multiplicative model might be appropriate because operating costs typically increase by a constant percentage as the number of either type of policy increases by a given percentage. Use the given data to estimate a multiplicative model for this insurance company. Interpret your results. Does a multiplicative model provide a good fit with these data?

32. Suppose that an operations manager is trying to determine the number of labor hours required to produce the ith unit of a certain product. Consider the data provided in the file **P11_32.xlsx**. For example, the second unit produced required 517 labor hours, and the 600th unit required 34 labor hours.

   a. Use the given data to estimate a relationship between the total number of units produced and the labor hours required to produce the last unit in the total set. Interpret your findings.

   b. Use your estimated relationship to predict the number of labor hours that will be needed to produce the 800th unit.

Level B

33. The human resources manager of DataCom, Inc., wants to predict the annual salaries of given employees using the following explanatory variables: the number of years of prior relevant work experience, the number of years of employment at DataCom, the number of years of education beyond high school, the employee's gender, the employee's department, and the number of individuals supervised by the given employee. These data have been collected for a sample of employees and are given in the file **P11_05.xlsx**.

   a. Formulate an appropriate multiple regression model to predict the annual salary of a given DataCom employee.

   b. Estimate the formulated model using the given sample data, and interpret the estimated regression coefficients.

   c. According to the estimated regression model, is there a difference between the mean salaries earned by male and female employees at DataCom? If so, how large is the difference?

   d. According to the estimated regression model, is there a difference between the mean salaries earned by employees in the sales department and those in the advertising department at DataCom? If so, how large is the difference?

   e. According to the estimated regression model, in which department are DataCom employees paid the *highest* mean salary? In which department are DataCom employees paid the *lowest* mean salary?

   f. Given the estimated regression model, predict the annual salary of a female employee who served in a similar department at another company for 10 years prior to coming to work at DataCom. This woman, a graduate of a 4-year collegiate business program, has been supervising 12 subordinates in the purchasing department since joining the organization 5 years ago.

34. Does the rate of violent crime acts vary across different regions of the United States?

   a. Using the data in the file **P11_34.xlsx**, develop and estimate an appropriate regression model to explain the variation in acts of violent crime across the four established regions of the United States. Thoroughly interpret the estimated model. Rank the four regions from highest to lowest according to their mean violent crime rate.

   b. How would you modify the regression model in part **a** to account for possible differences in the violent crime rate across the various subdivisions of the given regions? Estimate your revised model and interpret your findings. Rank the nine subdivisions from highest to lowest according to their mean violent crime rate.

35. Suppose that you are interested in predicting the price of a laptop computer based on its various features. The file **P11_35.xlsx** contains observations on the sales price and a number of potentially relevant variables for a randomly chosen sample of laptop computers.

   a. Formulate a multiple regression model that includes all potential explanatory variables and estimate it with the given sample data.

   b. Interpret the estimated regression equation. Be sure to indicate the impact of each attribute on the computer's sales price. For example, what impact does the monitor type have on the average sales price of a laptop computer?

   c. How well does the estimated regression model fit the data given in the file?

   d. Use the estimated regression equation to predict the price of a laptop computer with the following features: a 60-megahertz processor, a battery that holds its charge for 240 minutes, 32 megabytes of RAM, a DX chip, a color monitor, a mouse pointing device, and a 24-hour, toll-free customer service hotline.

36. Continuing Problem 18, suppose that the antique collector believes that the *rate of increase* of the auction price with the age of the item will be driven upward by a large number of bidders. How would you revise the multiple regression model developed previously to model this feature of the problem?

   a. Estimate your revised model using the data in the file **P11_18.xlsx**.

   b. Interpret each of the estimated coefficients in your revised model.

   c. Does this revised model fit the given data better than the original multiple regression model? Explain why or why not.

37. Continuing Problem 19, revise the multiple regression model developed previously to include an interaction term between the return on average equity (X_1) and annual dividend rate (X_2).

   a. Estimate your revised model using the data provided in the file **P11_19.xlsx**.

   b. Interpret each of the estimated coefficients in your revised model. In particular, how do you interpret the coefficient for the interaction term in the revised model?

c. Does this revised model fit the given data better than does the original multiple regression model? Explain why or why not.

38. Continuing Problem 24, suppose that one of the managers of this regional express delivery service company is trying to decide whether to add an interaction term involving the package weight (X_1) and the distance shipped (X_2) in the multiple regression model developed previously.

a. Why would the manager want to add such a term to the regression equation?

b. Estimate the revised model using the data given in the file **P11_24.xlsx**.

c. Interpret each of the estimated coefficients in your revised model. In particular, how do you interpret the coefficient for the interaction term in the revised model?

d. Does this revised model fit the given data better than the original multiple regression model? Explain why or why not.

11.7 VALIDATION OF THE FIT

The fit from a regression analysis is often overly optimistic. When we use the least squares procedure on a given set of data, we exploit all of the idiosyncrasies of the particular data set to obtain the best possible fit. There is no guarantee that the fit will be as good when the estimated regression equation is applied to *new* data. In fact, it usually isn't. This is particularly important when our goal is to use the regression equation to predict new values of the dependent variable. The usual situation is that we use a given data set to estimate a regression equation. Then we gather new data on the *explanatory* variables and use these, along with the already-estimated regression equation, to predict the new (but unknown) values of the dependent variable.

One way to see whether this procedure will be successful is to split the original data set into two subsets: one subset for estimation and one subset for validation. We estimate the regression equation from the first subset. Then we substitute the values of explanatory variables from the second subset into this equation to obtain predicted values for the dependent variable. Finally, we compare these predicted values with the known values of the dependent variable in the second subset. If the agreement is good, there is reason to believe that the regression equation will predict well for new data.

This validation procedure is fairly simple to perform in Excel. We illustrate it for the Bendrix manufacturing data in Example 11.2. (See the file **Overhead Costs Validation.xlsx**.) There we used 36 monthly observations to regress Overhead on MachHrs and ProdRuns. For convenience, we repeat the regression output in Figure 11.45. In particular, it shows an R^2 value of 86.6% and an s_e value of $4109.

Figure 11.45

Multiple Regression Output for Bendrix Example

	A	B	C	D	E	F	G
7		Multiple R	R-Square	Adjusted R-Square	StErr of Estimate		
8	*Summary*						
9		0.9308	0.8664	0.8583	4108.993		
10							
11		Degrees of Freedom	Sum of Squares	Mean of Squares	F-Ratio	p-Value	
12	*ANOVA Table*						
13	Explained	2	3614020661	1807010330	107.0261	< 0.0001	
14	Unexplained	33	557166199.1	16883824.22			
15							
16		Coefficient	Standard Error	t-Value	p-Value	Confidence Interval 95%	
17	*Regression Table*					Lower	Upper
18	Constant	3996.678	6603.651	0.6052	0.5492	-9438.551	17431.907
19	MachHrs	43.536	3.589	12.1289	< 0.0001	36.234	50.839
20	ProdRuns	883.618	82.251	10.7429	< 0.0001	716.276	1050.960

Now suppose that this data set is from one of Bendrix's two plants. The company would like to predict overhead costs for the other plant by using data on machine hours and production runs at the other plant. The first step is to see how well the regression from Figure 11.45 fits data from the other plant. We perform this validation on the 36 months of data shown in Figure 11.46. The validation results also appear in this figure.

Figure 11.46

Validation of
Bendrix Regression
Results

	A	B	C	D	E	F
1	Validation data					
2						
3	Coefficients from regression equation (based on original data)					
4		Constant	MachHrs	ProdRuns		
5		3996.6782	43.5364	883.6179		
6						
7	Comparison of summary measures					
8		Original	Validation			
9	R-square	0.8664	0.7733			
10	StErr of Est	4108.99	5256.50			
11						
12	Month	MachHrs	ProdRuns	Overhead	Fitted	Residual
13	1	1374	24	92414	85023	7391
14	2	1510	35	92433	100663	-8230
15	3	1213	21	81907	75362	6545
16	4	1629	27	93451	98775	-5324
17	5	1858	28	112203	109629	2574
18	6	1763	40	112673	116096	-3423
19	7	1449	44	104091	105960	-1869
20	8	1422	46	104354	106552	-2198
45	33	1534	38	104946	104359	587
46	34	1529	29	94325	96189	-1864
47	35	1389	47	98474	105999	-7525
48	36	1350	34	90857	92814	-1957

To obtain the results in this figure, we proceed as follows.

PROCEDURE FOR VALIDATING REGRESSION RESULTS

1 Copy old results. Copy the results from the original regression to the ranges B5:D5 and B9:B10.

2 Calculate fitted values and residuals. The fitted values are now the predicted values of overhead for the other plant, based on the original regression equation. We find these by substituting the new values of MachHrs and ProdRuns into the original equation. To do so, enter the formula

=$B$5+SUMPRODUCT($C$5:$D$5,B13:C13)

in cell E13 and copy it down. Then calculate the residuals (prediction errors for the other plant) by entering the formula

=D13-E13

in cell F13 and copying it down.

3 Calculate summary measures. We see how well the original equation fits the new data by calculating R^2 and s_e values. Recall that R^2 in general is the square of the correlation between observed and fitted values. Therefore, enter the formula

=CORREL(E13:E48,D13:D48)^2

in cell C9. The s_e value is essentially the average of the squared residuals, but it uses the denominator $n - 3$ (when there are two explanatory variables) rather than $n - 1$. Therefore, enter the formula

=SQRT(SUMSQ((F13:F48)/33)

in cell C10.

*Excel's SUMSQ func-
tion is often handy. It
sums the squares of
values in a range.*

The results in Figure 11.46 are typical. The validation results are usually not as good as the original results. The value of R^2 has decreased from 86.6% to 77.3%, and the value of s_e has increased from \$4109 to \$5257. Nevertheless, Bendrix might conclude that the original regression equation is adequate for making future predictions at either plant.

11.8 CONCLUSION

The material in this chapter has illustrated how to fit an equation to a set of points and how to interpret the resulting equation. We have also discussed two measures, R^2 and s_e, that indicate the goodness of fit of the regression equation. Although the general technique is called *linear* regression, we have seen how it can be used to estimate nonlinear relationships through suitable transformations of variables. We are not finished with our study of regression, however. In the next chapter we make some statistical assumptions about the regression model and then discuss the types of inferences that can be made from regression output. In particular, we discuss the accuracy of the estimated regression coefficients, the accuracy of predictions made from the regression equation, and the general topic of which explanatory variables "belong" in the regression equation.

Summary of Key Terms

Term	Symbol	Explanation	Excel	Page	Equation Number
Regression analysis		A general method for estimating the relationship between a dependent variable and one or more explanatory variables		572	
Dependent (or response) variable	Y	The variable being estimated or predicted in a regression analysis		574	
Explanatory (or independent) variables	$X_1, X_2,$ and so on	The variables used to explain or predict the dependent variable		574	
Simple regression		A regression model with a single explanatory variable	StatTools/ Regression & Classification/ Regression	574	
Multiple regression		A regression model with any number of explanatory variables	StatTools/ Regression & Classification/ Regression	574	
Correlation	r_{XY}	A measure of strength of the linear relationship between two variables X and Y	=CORREL(range1, range2), or StatTools/ Summary Statistics/ Correlation and Covariance	583	11.1

(continued)

Term	Symbol	Explanation	Excel	Page	Equation Number
Fitted value		The predicted value of dependent variable found by substituting explanatory values into the regression equation		585–587	11.2
Residual		The difference between actual and fitted values of dependent variable		585–587	11.2
Least squares line		The regression equation that minimizes the sum of squared residuals	StatTools/ Regression & Classification/ Regression	587	11.3, 11.4
Standard error of estimate	s_e	Essentially, the standard deviation of the residuals; indicates the magnitude of the prediction errors	StatTools/ Regression & Classification/ Regression	591, 592	11.7, 11.11
Coefficient of determination	R^2	The percentage of variation in the response variable explained by the regression model	StatTools/ Regression & Classification/ Regression	593, 594	11.8
Adjusted R^2		A measure similar to R^2, but adjusted for the number of explanatory variables in the equation		600	
Regression coefficients	$b_1, b_2,$ and so on	The coefficients of the explanatory variables in a regression equation	StatTools/ Regression & Classification/ Regression	597	11.9
Dummy variables		Variables coded as 0 or 1, used to capture categorical variables in a regression analysis	StatTools/Data Utilities/ Dummy	602	
Interaction variables		Products of explanatory variables, used when the effect of one on the dependent variable depends on the value of the other	StatTools/Data Utilities/ Interaction	608	
Nonlinear transformations		Variables created to capture nonlinear relationships in a regression model	StatTools/Data Utilities/ Transform	612	
Quadratic model		A regression model with linear and squared explanatory variables	StatTools/ Regression & Classification/ Regression	615	
Model with logarithmic transformations		A regression model using logarithms of Y and/or X's	StatTools/ Regression & Classification/ Regression	616	
Constant elasticity (or multiplicative relationship)		A relationship where Y changes by a constant percentage when any X changes by 1%; requires logarithmic transformations	StatTools/ Regression & Classification/ Regression	620	11.21

(continued)

Term	Symbol	Explanation	Excel	Page	Equation Number
Learning curve		A particular multiplicative relationship used to indicate how cost or time in production decreases through time	StatTools/ Regression & Classification/ Regression	623	11.22
Validation of fit		Checks how well a regression model based on one sample predicts a related sample	StatTools/ Regression & Classification/ Regression	628	

PROBLEMS

Conceptual Exercises

C.1. Consider the relationship between yearly wine consumption (liters of alcohol from drinking wine, per person) and yearly deaths from heart disease (deaths per 100,000 people) in 19 developed countries. Suppose that you read a newspaper article in which the reporter states the following:

Researchers find that the correlation between yearly wine consumption and yearly deaths from heart disease is −0.84. Thus, it is reasonable to conclude that increased consumption of alcohol from wine causes fewer deaths from heart disease in industrialized societies.

Comment on the reporter's interpretation of the correlation measure in this case.

C.2. "It is generally appropriate to delete all outliers in the given data set when producing a scatterplot." Is this statement true or false? Explain your choice.

C.3. How does one interpret the relationship between two numeric variables when the estimated least squares regression line for them is essentially *horizontal* (i.e., flat)?

C.4. Suppose that you generate a scatterplot of residuals versus fitted values of the dependent variable for a given estimated regression model. Furthermore, you find the correlation between the residuals and fitted values to be 0.829. Does this provide a good indication that the estimated regression model is satisfactory? Explain why or why not.

C.5. Suppose that you have generated three alternative multiple regression models to explain the variation in a particular dependent variable. The regression output for each model can be summarized as follows:

	Model 1	Model 2	Model 3
No. of indep. vars.	4	6	9
R^2	0.76	0.77	0.79
Adj. R^2	0.75	0.74	0.73

Which of these models would you select as "best"? Explain your choice.

Level A

39. Many companies manufacture products that are at least partially produced using chemicals (e.g., paint, gasoline, and steel). In many cases, the quality of the finished product is a function of the temperature and pressure at which the chemical reactions take place. Suppose that a particular manufacturer wants to model the quality (Y) of a product as a function of the temperature (X_1) and the pressure (X_2) at which it is produced. The file **P11_39.xlsx** contains data obtained from a carefully designed experiment involving these variables. Note that the assigned quality score can range from a maximum of 100 to a minimum of 0 for each manufactured product.
  a. Formulate a multiple regression model that includes the two given explanatory variables. Estimate the model using the given sample data. Does the estimated model fit the data well?
  b. Interpret each of the estimated coefficients in the multiple regression model.
  c. Consider adding a term to model a possible interaction between the two explanatory models. Reformulate the model and estimate it again using the given data. Does the inclusion of the interaction term improve the model's goodness of fit?
  d. Interpret each of the estimated coefficients in the revised model. In particular, how do you interpret the coefficient for the interaction term in the revised model?

40. Suppose that a power company located in southern Alabama wants to predict the peak power load (i.e., the maximum amount of power that must be generated each day to meet demand) as a function of the daily high temperature (X). A random sample of 25 summer days is chosen, and the peak power load and the high temperature are recorded on each day. The file **P11_40.xlsx** contains these observations.

a. Generate a scatterplot for these data. Comment on the observed relationship between the dependent variable and explanatory variable.

b. Formulate and estimate an appropriate regression model to predict the peak power load for this power company. Interpret the estimated regression coefficients.

c. Analyze the estimated model's residuals. Is your estimated regression model adequate? If not, return to part **b** and revise your model. Continue to revise the model until your results are satisfactory.

d. Use the final version of your model to predict the peak power load on a summer day with a high temperature of 100 degrees.

41. Management of a home appliance store in Charlotte would like to understand the growth pattern of the monthly sales of VCR units over the past 2 years. Managers have recorded the relevant data in an Excel spreadsheet, which can be found in the file **P11_09.xlsx**. Have the sales of VCR units been growing *linearly* over the past 24 months?

a. Generate a scatterplot for these data. Comment on the observed behavior of monthly VCR sales at this store over time.

b. Formulate and estimate an appropriate regression model to explain the variation of monthly VCR sales over the given time period. Interpret the estimated regression coefficients.

c. Analyze the estimated model's residuals. Is your estimated regression model adequate? If not, return to part **b** and revise your model. Continue to revise the model until your results are satisfactory.

42. Chipco, a small computer chip manufacturer, wants to be able to forecast monthly operating costs as a function of the number of units produced during a month. They have collected the 16 months of data in the file **P11_42.xlsx**.

a. Determine an equation that can be used to predict monthly production costs from units produced. Are there any outliers?

b. How could the regression line obtained in part **a** be used to determine whether the company was efficient or inefficient during any particular month?

43. The file **P11_43.xlsx** contains data on the following variables for several underdeveloped countries:

- Infant mortality rate
- Per capita GNP
- Percentage of people completing primary school
- Percentage of adults who can read (adult literacy)

Use these data to determine which of the given variables (by itself) best predicts infant mortality. Can you give an explanation for your answer?

44. The file **P11_44.xlsx** contains data that relate the unit cost of producing a fuel pressure regulator to the cumulative number of fuel pressure regulators produced at the Ford plant in Bedford. For example, the 4000th unit cost $13.70 to produce.

a. Fit a learning curve to these data.

b. We would predict that doubling cumulative production reduces the cost of producing a regulator by what amount?

45. The "beta" of a stock is found by running a regression with the explanatory variable being the monthly return on a market index and the dependent variable being the monthly return on the stock. The beta of the stock is then the slope of this regression.

a. Explain why most stocks have a positive beta.

b. Explain why a stock with a beta with absolute value greater than 1 is more volatile than the market and a stock with a beta less than 1 (in absolute value) is less volatile than the market.

c. Use the data in the file **P11_45.xlsx** to estimate the beta for Ford Motor Company.

d. What percentage of the variation in Ford's return is explained by market variation? What percentage is unexplained by market variation?

e. Verify (using Excel's COVAR and VARP functions) that the beta for Ford is given by

$$\frac{\text{Covariance between Ford and Market}}{\text{Variance of Market}}$$

Also, verify that the correlation between Ford return and Market return is the square root of R^2.

46. The file **P11_46.xlsx** contains monthly returns on Anheuser-Busch (AB) and a market index. Use these data to answer the following questions:

a. What percentage of the variation in the return in AB is explained by variation in the market? What percentage is unexplained by variation in the market?

b. Predict the change in AB during a month in which the market goes up by 2%.

c. Use Excel's CORREL functions to determine the correlation between the return on AB and the market. Verify that this correlation between AB and the market is equal to the square root of R^2 from the regression output.

d. Estimate the beta (refer to the previous problem) for AB by using regression. Then verify that it can also be found (using Excel's COVAR and VARP functions) from

$$\frac{\text{Covariance between AB and Market}}{\text{Variance of Market}}$$

47. Investors are interested in knowing whether estimates of stock betas based on past history are good predictors of future betas (refer to Problem 45). How could you use a data set that gives monthly returns on several stocks over a 5-year period to see whether this is true?

48. The file **P11_48.xlsx** contains monthly sales (in thousands) and price of a popular candy bar.

a. Describe the type of relationship between price and sales (linear, nonlinear, strong, weak).

b. What percentage of variation in monthly sales is explained by variation in price? What percentage is unexplained?

c. If the price of the candy bar is 55 cents, predict monthly candy bar sales.

d. Use the regression output to determine the correlation between price and candy bar sales.

e. Are there any outliers?

49. The file **P11_49.xlsx** contains the amount of money spent advertising a product (in thousands of dollars) and the number of units sold (in millions) for 8 months.

a. Assume that the only factor influencing monthly sales is advertising. Fit the following three curves to these data: linear ($Y = a + bX$), exponential ($Y = ab^X$), and multiplicative ($Y = aX^b$). Which equation best fits the data?

b. Interpret the best-fitting equation.

c. Using the best-fitting equation, predict sales during a month in which $60,000 is spent on advertising.

50. Callaway Golf is trying to determine how the price of a set of clubs affects the demand for clubs. The file **P11_50.xlsx** contains the price of a set of clubs (in dollars) and the monthly sales (in millions of sets sold).

a. Assume the only factor influencing monthly sales is price. Fit the following three curves to these data: linear ($Y = a + bX$), exponential ($Y = ab^X$), and multiplicative ($Y = aX^b$). Which equation best fits the data?

b. Interpret your best-fitting equation.

c. Using the best-fitting equation, predict sales during a month in which the price is $470.

51. The number of cars per 1000 people is known for virtually every country in the world. For many countries, however, per capita income is not known. Can you think of a way to estimate per capita income for countries where it is unknown?

52. The file **P11_52.xlsx** contains the cost (in 1990 dollars) of making a 3-minute phone call from London to New York. Use regression to estimate how (or whether) the cost of a London to New York call has declined over time. Based on these data, predict the cost of a 3-minute phone call in the year 2000. (Source: *The Economist*, September 28, 1996)

53. The file **P11_53.xlsx** contains the databit power per chip for computers. Use regression to estimate how databit power per chip has changed over time. (This result is called Moore's law.) Also predict the databit power per chip in the year 2000. Do you think Moore's law can continue indefinitely? (Source: *One World Ready or Not*, by William Greider, 1996)

54. The file **P11_54.xlsx** contains the cost of building (in hundreds of millions of dollars) a plant to produce RAM chips for PCs. Use regression to estimate how (or whether) the cost of building a RAM plant has increased over time. Predict the cost of building a

RAM plant in the year 2000. (Source: *One World Ready or Not*, by William Greider, 1996)

55. The file **P11_55.xlsx** contains the unit cost of producing a unit of computer memory, as a function of the number of units of computer memory that have been produced to date. Use regression to analyze how (or whether) the price of a bit of memory has changed as more memory has been produced (Source: *Every Investor's Guide to High-Tech Stocks*, by Michael Murphy, 1998)

56. The Baker Company wants to develop a budget to predict how overhead costs vary with activity levels. Management is trying to decide whether direct labor hours (DLH) or units produced is the better measure of activity for the firm. Monthly data for the preceding 24 months appear in the file **P11_56.xlsx**. Use regression analysis to determine which measure, DLH or Units (or both), should be used for the budget. How would the regression equation be used to obtain the budget for the firm's overhead costs?

57. The auditor of Kiely Manufacturing is concerned about the number and magnitude of year-end adjustments that are made annually when the financial statements of Kiely Manufacturing are prepared. Specifically, the auditor suspects that the management of Kiely Manufacturing is using discretionary write-offs to manipulate the reported net income. To check this, the auditor has collected data from 25 firms that are similar to Kiely Manufacturing in terms of manufacturing facilities and product lines. The cumulative reported third quarter income and the final net income reported are listed in the file **P11_57.xlsx** for each of these 25 firms. If Kiely Manufacturing reported a cumulative third quarter income of $2,500,000 and a preliminary net income of $4,900,000, should the auditor conclude that the relationship between cumulative third quarter income and the annual income for Kiely Manufacturing differs from that of the 25 firms in this sample? Explain why or why not.

Level B

58. An economic development researcher wants to understand the relationship between the size of the monthly home mortgage or rent payment for households in a particular middle-class neighborhood and the following set of household variables: family size, approximate location of the household within the neighborhood, an indication of whether those surveyed own or rent their home, gross annual income of the first household wage earner, gross annual income of the second household wage earner (if applicable), average monthly expenditure on utilities, and the total indebtedness (excluding the value of a home mortgage) of the household. Observations on each of these variables for a large sample of households are recorded in the file **P02_06.xlsx**.

a. Beginning with *family size*, iteratively add one explanatory variable and estimate the resulting regression equation to explain the variation in the monthly home mortgage or rent payment. If adding any explanatory variable causes the *adjusted* R^2 measure to fall, do not include that variable in subsequent versions of the regression model. Otherwise, include the variable and consider adding the next variable in the set. Which variables are included in the final version of your regression model?

b. Interpret the final estimated regression equation you obtained through the process outlined in part **a**. Also, report and interpret the standard error of estimate s_e, the coefficient of determination R^2, and the adjusted R^2 for the final estimated model.

59. (This problem is based on an actual court case in Philadelphia.) In the 1994 congressional election, the Republican candidate outpolled the Democratic candidate by 400 votes (excluding absentee ballots). The Democratic candidate outpolled the Republican candidate by 500 absentee votes. The Republican candidate sued (and won), claiming that vote fraud must have played a role in the absentee ballot count. The Republican's lawyer ran a regression to predict (based on past elections) how the absentee ballot margin could be predicted from the votes tabulated on voting machines. Selected results are given in the file **P11_59.xlsx**. Show how this regression could be used by the Republican to prove his claim of vote fraud. (*Hint*: Is the 1994 result an outlier?)

60. The file **P11_60.xlsx** contains data on the price of new and used Taurus sedans. All prices for used cars are from 1995. For example, a new Taurus bought in 1985 cost $11,790 and the wholesale used price of that car in 1995 was $1700. A new Taurus bought in 1994 cost $18,680 and it could be sold used in 1995 for $12,600.

a. You want to predict the resale value (as a percentage of the original price of the vehicle) as a function of the vehicle's age. Find an equation to do this. (You should try at least two different equations and choose the one with the best fit.)

b. Suppose all police cars are Ford Tauruses. If you were the business manager for the New York Police Department, what use would you make of your findings from part **a**?

61. The data for this problem are fictitious, but they are not far off.) For each of the top 25 business schools, the file **P11_61.xlsx** contains the average salary of a professor at Indiana University (number 15 in the rankings), the average salary is $46,000. Use this information and regression to show that IU is doing a great job with its available resources.

62. Suppose the correlation between the average height of parents and the height of their firstborn male child is 0.5.

You are also told that:

- The average height of all parents is 66 inches.
- The standard deviation of the average height of parents is 4 inches.
- The average height of all male children is 70 inches.
- The standard deviation of the height of all male children is 4 inches.

If a mother and father are 73 and 80 inches tall, respectively, how tall do you predict their son to be? Explain why this is called "regression toward the mean."

63. Do increased taxes increase or decrease economic growth? Table 11.1 gives tax revenues as a percentage of Gross Domestic Product (GDP) and the average annual percentage growth in GDP per capita for nine countries during the years 1970 through 1994. Do these data support or contradict the dictum of supply-side economics? (Source: *The Economist*, August 24, 1996)

Table 11.1 Economic Data from Nine Countries

Country	Tax revenues as % of GDP	Average annual growth in GDP per capita
Japan	26%	3.1%
United States	27%	1.6%
Italy	33%	2.5%
Canada	34%	2.0%
Switzerland	30%	1.0%
Britain	36%	1.9%
Germany	38%	2.2%
France	42%	1.9%
Sweden	49%	1.1%

64. For each of the four data sets in the file **P11_64.xlsx**, calculate the least squares line. For which of these data sets would you feel comfortable in using the least squares line to predict Y? (Source: Frederic Anscombe, *The American Statistician*)

65. Suppose we run a regression on a data set of X's and Y's and obtain a least squares line of $Y = 12 - 3X$.

a. If we double each value of X, what is the new least squares line?

b. If we triple each value of Y, what is the new least squares line?

c. If we add 6 to each value of X, what is the new least squares line?

d. If we subtract 4 from each value of Y, what is the new least squares line?

66. The file **P11_66.xlsx** contains monthly cost accounting data on overhead costs, machine hours, and direct material costs. This problem will help you explore the meaning of R^2 and the relationship between R^2 and correlations.

a. Create a table of correlations between the individual variables.

b. If you ignored the two explanatory variables MachHrs and DirMatCost and predicted each OHCost as the *mean* of all OHCosts, then a typical "error" would be OHCost minus the mean of all OHCosts. Find the sum of squared errors using this form of prediction, where the sum is over all observations.

c. Now run three regressions: (1) OHCost versus MachHrs, (2) OHCost versus DirMatCost, and (3) OHCost versus both MachHrs and DirMatCost. (The first two are simple regressions, the third is a multiple regression.) For each, find the sum of squared residuals, and divide this by the sum of squared errors from part **b**. What is the relationship between this ratio and the associated R^2 for that equation? (Now do you see why R^2 is referred to as the percentage of variation explained?)

d. For the first two regressions in part **c**, what is the relationship between R^2 and the corresponding correlation between the dependent and explanatory variable? For the third regression it turns out that the R^2 can be expressed as a complicated function of all three correlations in part **a**, that is, not just the correlations between the dependent variable and each explanatory variable, but also the correlation between the explanatory variables. Note that this R^2 is not just the sum of the R^2 values from the first two regressions in part **c**. Why do you think this is true, intuitively? However, R^2 for the multiple regression is still the square of a correlation—namely, the correlation between the observed and predicted values of OHCost. Verify that this is the case for these data.

67. The file **P11_67.xlsx** contains hypothetical starting salaries (in $1000's) for MBA students directly after graduation. The file also lists their years of experience prior to the MBA program and their class standing in the MBA program (on a 0–100 scale).

a. Estimate the regression equation with Salary as the dependent variable and Exper and Class as the explanatory variables. What does this equation imply? What does the standard error of estimate s_e tell you? What about R^2?

b. Repeat part **a**, but now include the interaction term Exper*Class (the product) in the equation as well as Exper and Class individually. Answer the same questions as in part **a**. What evidence is there that this extra variable (the interaction variable) is worth including? How do you interpret this regression equation?

68. In a study published in 1985 in *Business Horizons*, Platt and McCarthy employed multiple regression analysis to explain variations in compensations among the CEOs of large companies. Their primary objective

was to discover whether levels of compensations are affected more by short-run considerations—"I'll earn more now if my company does well in the short run"—or long-run considerations—"My best method for obtaining high compensation is to stay with my company for a long time." The study used as its dependent variable the total compensation for each of the 100 highest paid CEOs in 1981. This variable was defined as the sum of salary, bonuses, and other benefits (measured in $1000s).

The following potential explanatory variables were considered. To capture short-run effects, the average of the company's previous 5 years' percentage changes in earnings per share (EPS) and the projected percentage change in next year's EPS were used. To capture the long-run effect, age and years as CEO, two admittedly correlated variables, were used. Dummy variables for the CEO's background (finance, marketing, and so on) were also considered. Finally, the researchers considered several nonlinear and interaction terms based on these variables. The best-fitting equation was the following:

$$\text{TotComp} = -3493 + 898.7(\text{Years as CEO})$$
$$+ 9.28(\text{Years as CEO})^2 - 17.19(\text{Years as CEO})(\text{Age})$$
$$+ 88.27\text{Age} + 867.4\text{Finance}$$

(The last variable represents a dummy variable, equal to 1 if the CEO had a finance background, 0 otherwise.) The corresponding R^2 was 19.4%.

a. Explain what this equation implies about CEO compensations.

b. The researchers drew the following conclusions. First, it appears that CEOs should indeed concentrate on long-run considerations—namely, those that keep them on their jobs the longest. Second, the absence of the short-run company-related variables from the equations helps to confirm the conjecture that CEOs who concentrate on earning the quick buck for their companies may not be acting in their best self-interest. Finally, the positive coefficient of the dummy variable may imply that financial people possess skills that are vitally important, and firms therefore outbid one another for the best financial talent. Based on the data given, do you agree with these conclusions?

c. Consider a CEO (other than those in the study) who has been in his position for 10 years and has a financial background. Predict his total yearly compensation (in $1000s) if he is 50 years old; if he is 55 years old. Explain why the difference between these two predictions is not 5(88.27), where 88.27 is the coefficient of the Age variable.

69. The Wilhoit Company has observed that there is a linear relationship between indirect labor expense (ILE) and direct labor hours (DLH). Data for direct labor hours and indirect labor expense for 18 months are given in the file **P11_69.xlsx**. At the start of month 7, all cost categories in the Wilhoit Company increased by 10%, and they stayed at this level for months 7 through 12. Then at the start of month 13, another 10% across-the-board increase in all costs occurred, and the company operated at this price level for months 13 through 18.

a. Plot the data. Verify that the relationship between ILE and DLH is approximately linear within each 6-month period. Use regression (three times) to estimate the slope and intercept during months 1 through 6; during months 7 through 12; during months 13 through 18.

b. Use regression to fit a straight line to all 18 data points simultaneously. What values of the slope and intercept do you obtain?

c. Perform a price level adjustment to the data and re-estimate the slope and intercept using all 18 data points. Assuming no cost increases for month 19, what is your prediction for indirect labor expense if there are 35,000 direct labor-hours in month 19?

d. Interpret your results. What causes the difference in the linear relationship estimated in parts **b** and **c**?

70. The Bohring Company manufactures a sophisticated radar unit that is used in a fighter aircraft built by Seaways Aircraft. The first 50 units of the radar unit have been completed, and Bohring is preparing to submit a proposal to Seaways Aircraft to manufacture the next 50 units. Bohring wants to submit a competitive bid, but at the same time, it wants to ensure that all the costs of manufacturing the radar unit are fully covered. As part of this process, Bohring is attempting to develop a standard for the number of labor hours required to manufacture each radar unit. Developing a labor standard has been a continuing problem in the past. The file **P11_70.xlsx** lists the number of labor hours required for each of the first 50 units of production. Bohring accountants want to see whether regression analysis, together with the concept of learning curves, can help solve the company's problem.

The Firm Chair Company manufactures customized wood furniture and sells the furniture in large quantities to major furniture retailers. Jim Bolling has recently been assigned to analyze the company's pricing policy. He has been told that quantity discounts were usually given. For example, for one type of chair, the pricing changed at quantities of 200 and 400—that is, these were the quantity "breaks," where the marginal cost of the next chair changed. For this type of chair, the file **Firm Chair.xlsx** contains the quantity and total price to the customer for 81 orders. Use regression to help Jim discover the pricing structure that Firm Chair evidently used. (*Note*: A linear regression of TotPrice versus Quantity will give you a "decent" fit, but you can do much better by introducing appropriate variables into the regression.) ■

Sales of single-family houses have been brisk in Mid City this year. This has especially been true in older, more established neighborhoods, where housing is relatively inexpensive compared to the new homes being built in the newer neighborhoods. Nevertheless, there are also many families who are willing to pay a higher price for the prestige of living in one of the newer neighborhoods. The file **Mid City.xlsx** contains data on 128 recent sales in Mid City. For each sale, the file shows the neighborhood (1, 2, or 3) in which the house is located, the number of offers made on the house, the square footage, whether the house is made primarily of brick, the number of bathrooms, the number of bedrooms, and the selling price. Neighborhoods 1 and 2 are more traditional neighborhoods, whereas neighborhood 3 is a newer, more prestigious, neighborhood.

Use regression to estimate and interpret the pricing structure of houses in Mid City. Here are some considerations.

1. Is there a "premium" for a brick house, everything else being equal?

2. Is there a premium for a house in neighborhood 3, everything else being equal?

3. Is there an *extra* premium for a brick house in neighborhood 3, in addition to the usual premium for a brick house?

4. For purposes of estimation and prediction, could neighborhoods 1 and 2 be collapsed into a single "older" neighborhood? ∎

Howie's Bakery is one of the most popular bakeries in town, and the favorite at Howie's is French bread. Each day of the week, Howie's bakes a number of loaves of French bread, more or less according to a daily schedule. To maintain its fine reputation, Howie's gives away to charity any loaves not sold on the day they are baked. Although this occurs frequently, it is also common for Howie's to run out of French bread on any given day—more demand than supply. In this case, no extra loaves are baked that day; the customers have to go elsewhere (or come back to Howie's the next day) for their French bread. Although French bread at Howie's is always popular, Howie's stimulates demand by running occasional 10% off sales.

Howie's has collected data for 20 consecutive weeks, 140 days in all. These data are listed in the file **Howies Bakery.xlsx**. The variables are Day (Monday–Sunday), Supply (number of loaves baked that day), OnSale (whether French bread is on sale that day), and Demand (loaves actually sold that day). Howie's would like you to see whether regression can be used successfully to estimate Demand from the other data in the file. Howie reasons that if these other variables can be used to predict Demand, then he might be able to determine his daily supply (number of loaves to bake) in a more cost-effective way.

How successful is regression with these data? Is Howie correct that regression can help him determine his daily supply? Is any information "missing" that would be useful? How would you obtain it? How would you use it? Is this extra information *really* necessary? ■

11.4 INVESTING FOR RETIREMENT

Financial advisors offer many types of advice to customers, but they generally agree that one of the best things people can do is invest as much as possible in tax-deferred retirement plans. Not only are the earnings from these investments exempt from income tax (until retirement), but the investment itself is tax-exempt. This means that if a person invests, say, $10,000 income of his $100,000 income in a tax-deferred retirement plan, he pays income tax that year on only $90,000 of his income. This is probably the best method available to most people for avoiding tax payments. However, which group takes advantage of this attractive investment opportunity: everyone, people with low salaries, people with high salaries, or who?

The file **Retirement Plan.xlsx** lets you investigate this question. It contains data on 194 couples: number of dependent children, combined annual salary of husband and wife, current mortgage on home, average amount of other (nonmortgage) debt, and percentage of combined income invested in tax-deferred retirement plans (assumed to be limited to 15%, which is realistic). Using correlations, scatterplots, and regression analysis, what can you conclude about the tendency to invest in tax-deferred retirement plans in this group of people? ∎

PREDICTING MOVIE REVENUES

In the opener for Chapter 3, we discussed the article by Simonoff and Sparrow (2000) that examined movie revenues for 311 movies released in 1998 and late 1997. We saw that movie revenues were related to several variables, including genre, Motion Picture Association of America (MPAA) rating, country of origin, number of stars in the cast, whether the movie was a sequel, and whether the movie was released during a few "choice" times. In Chapter 3, we were limited to looking at summary measures and charts of the data. Now that we are studying regression, we can look further into the analysis performed by Simonoff and Sparrow. Specifically, they examined whether these variables, plus others, are effective in predicting movie revenues.

The authors actually report the results from three multiple regression models. All of these used the logarithm of the total U.S. gross revenue from the film as the dependent variable. (They used the *logarithm* because the distribution of gross revenues is very positively skewed.) The first model used only the "prerelease" variables listed in the previous paragraph. The values of these variables were all known prior to the movie's release. Therefore, the purpose of this model was to see how well revenues could be predicted *before* the movie was released.

The second model used the variables from model 1, along with two variables that could be observed after the first week of the movie's release: the first weekend gross, and the number of screens the movie opened on. (Actually, the logarithms of these latter two variables were used, again because of positive skewness. Also, the authors found it necessary to run two separate regressions at this stage—one for movies that opened on 10 or fewer screens, and another for movies that opened on more than 10 screens.) The idea here was that the success or failure of many movies depends to a large extent on how they do right after they are released. Therefore, it was expected that this information would add significantly to the predictive power of the regression model.

The third model built on the second by adding an additional explanatory variable: the number of Oscar nominations the movie received for key awards (Best Picture, Best Director, Best Actor, Best Actress, Best Supporting Actor, and Best Supporting Actress). This information is often not known until well after a movie's release, but it was hypothesized that Oscar nominations would lead to a significant increase in a movie's revenues, and that a regression model with this information could lead to very different predictions of revenue.

Simonoff and Sparrow found that the coefficients of the first regression model were in line with the box plots we saw in Figure 3.1 of Chapter 3. For example, the variables that measured the number of "best" actors and actresses were both positive and significant, indicating that star power tends to lead to larger revenues. However, the predictive power of this model was poor. Given its standard error of prediction (and taking into account that the *logarithm* of revenue was the dependent variable), the authors stated that "the predictions of total grosses for an individual movie can be expected to be off by as much as a multiplicative factor of 100 high or low." It appears that there is no way to predict which movies will succeed and which will fail based on prerelease data only.

The second model added considerable predictive power. The regression equations indicated that gross revenue is positively related to first weekend gross and negatively related to the number of opening screens, both of these variables being significant. As for prediction, the factor of 100 mentioned in the previous paragraph decreased to a factor of 10 (for movies with 10 or fewer opening screens) or 2 (for movies with more than 10 opening screens). This is still not perfect—predictions of total revenue made after the movie's first weekend can still be pretty far off—but this additional information about initial success certainly helps.

The third model added only slightly to the predictive power, primarily because so few of the movies (10 out of 311) received Oscar nominations for key awards. However, the predictions for those that did receive nominations increased considerably. For example, the prediction for the multiple Oscar nominee *Saving Private Ryan,* based on the second model, was 194.622 (millions of dollars). Its prediction based on the third model increased to a whopping 358.237. (Interestingly, the prediction for this movie from the first model was only 14.791, and its actual gross revenue was 216.119. Perhaps the reason *Saving Private Ryan* did not make as much as the third model predicted was that the Oscar nominations were announced about 9 months after its release—too long to do much good.)

Simonoff and Sparrow then used their third model to predict gross revenues for 24 movies released in 1999—movies that were not in the data set used to estimate the regression model. They found that 21 out of 24 of the resulting 95% prediction intervals captured the actual gross revenues, which is about what we would expect. However, many of these prediction intervals were extremely wide, and several of the predictions were well above or below the actual revenues. The authors conclude by quoting Tim Noonan, a former movie executive: "Since predicting gross is extremely difficult, you have to serve up a [yearly] slate of movies and know that over time you'll have 3 or 4 to the left and 2 or 3 to the right. You must make sure you are doing things that mitigate your downside risk." ■

12.1 INTRODUCTION

In the previous chapter we learned how to fit a regression equation to a set of points by using the least squares method. The purpose of this regression equation is to provide a good fit to the points in the sample so that we can understand the relationship between a dependent variable and one or more explanatory variables. The entire emphasis of the discussion in the previous chapter was on finding a regression model that fits the observations in the sample. In this chapter we take a slightly different point of view: We assume that the observations in the sample are taken from some larger population. For example, the sample of 50 regions from the Pharmex drugstore example could represent a sample of all the regions where Pharmex does business. If that is the case, then we might be interested in the relationship between variables in the entire population, not just in the sample.

There are two basic problems we discuss in this chapter. The first has to do with a *population regression model*. We want to infer its characteristics—that is, its intercept and slope term(s)—from the corresponding terms estimated by least squares. We also want to know which explanatory variables "belong" in the equation. We have seen that there are typically a large number of *potential* explanatory variables, and it is often not clear which of these do the best job of explaining variation in the dependent variable. In addition, we would like to infer whether there is any population regression equation worth pursuing. It might be that the potential explanatory variables provide very little explanation of the dependent variable, based on the sample data.

The second problem we discuss in this chapter is prediction. We touched on the prediction problem in the previous chapter, primarily in the context of predicting the dependent variable for part of the sample held out for validation purposes. In reality, we had the values of the dependent variable for that part of the sample, so prediction was not really necessary. Now we go beyond the sample and predict values of the dependent variable for *new* observations. There is no way to check the accuracy of these predictions, at least not right away, because the true values of the dependent variable are not yet known. However, we provide prediction intervals to measure the accuracy of the predictions.

12.2 THE STATISTICAL MODEL

To perform statistical inference in a regression context, we must first make several assumptions about the population. Throughout the analysis these assumptions remain exactly that—they are only assumptions, not facts. These assumptions represent an idealization of reality, and as such, they are never likely to be entirely satisfied for the population in any real study. From a practical point of view, all we can ask is that they represent a close approximation to reality. If this is the case, then the analysis in this chapter is valid. But if the assumptions are grossly violated, we should be very suspicious of the statistical inferences that are based on these assumptions. Although we can never be entirely certain of the validity of the assumptions, there are ways to check for gross violations, and we discuss some of these.

Regression Assumptions

1. There is a population regression line. It joins the *means* of the dependent variable for all values of the explanatory variables. For any fixed values of the explanatory variables, the mean of the errors is 0.

2. For any values of the explanatory variables, the standard deviation of the dependent variable is a constant, the same for all such values.

3. For any values of the explanatory variables, the dependent variable is normally distributed.

4. The errors are probabilistically independent.

Because these assumptions are so crucial to the regression analysis that follows, it is important to understand exactly what they mean. Assumption 1 is probably the most important. It implies that for some set of explanatory variables, there is an exact linear relationship in the population between the *means* of the dependent variable and the values of the explanatory variables.

These explanatory variables could be original variables or variables we create, such as dummies, interactions, or nonlinear transformations.

Because of its importance, we discuss assumption 1 in more detail. Let Y be the dependent variable, and assume that there are k explanatory variables, X_1 through X_k. Let $\mu_{Y|X_1,\ldots,X_k}$ be the mean of all Y's for any fixed values of the X's. Then assumption 1 implies that there is an exact linear relationship between the mean $\mu_{Y|X_1,\ldots,X_k}$ and the X's. Specifically, it implies that there are coefficients α and β_1 through β_k such that the following equation holds for all values of the X's:

Population Regression Line Joining Means

$$\mu_{Y|X_1,\ldots,X_k} = \alpha + \beta_1 X_1 + \cdots + \beta_k X_k \qquad (12.1)$$

We commonly use Greek letters to denote population parameters and regular letters for their sample estimates.

In the terminology of the previous chapter, α is the intercept term, and β_1 through β_k are the slope terms. We use Greek letters for these coefficients to denote that they are *unobservable* population parameters. Assumption 1 implies the existence of a population regression equation and the corresponding α and β's. However, it tells us nothing about the values of these parameters. We still need to estimate them from sample data, and we continue to use the least squares method to do so.

Equation (12.1) says that the *means* of the Y's lie on the population regression line. However, we know from a scatterplot that most *individual* Y's do not lie on this line. The vertical distance from any point to the line is called an **error term**. The error for any point, labeled ϵ, is the difference between Y and $\mu_{Y|X_1,\ldots,X_k}$, that is,

$$Y = \mu_{Y|X_1,\ldots,X_k} + \epsilon$$

By substituting the assumed linear form for $\mu_{Y|X_1,\ldots,X_k}$, we obtain equation (12.2). This equation states that each value of Y is equal to a fitted part plus an error term. The fitted part is the linear expression $\alpha + \beta_1 X_1 + \cdots + \beta_k X_k$. The error term ϵ is sometimes positive, in which case the point is above the regression line, and sometimes negative, in which case the point is below the regression line. The last part of assumption 1 states that these errors average to 0 in the population, so that the positive errors cancel the negative errors.

Population Regression Line with Error Term

$$Y = \alpha + \beta_1 X_1 + \cdots + \beta_k X_k + \epsilon \qquad (12.2)$$

Note that an error term ϵ is similar to, but not the same as, a residual e. An error term is the vertical distance from a point to the (unobservable) population regression line. A residual is the vertical distance from a point to the estimated regression line. Residuals can be calculated from observed data; error terms cannot.

Assumption 2 concerns variation around the population regression line. Specifically, it states that the variation of the Y's about the regression line is the *same*, regardless of the values of the X's. A technical term for this property is **homoscedasticity**. A simpler term is **constant error variance**. In the Pharmex example (Example 11.1), constant error variance implies that the variation in Sales values is the same regardless of the value of Promote. As another example, recall the Bendrix manufacturing example (Example 11.2). There we related overhead costs (Overhead) to the number of machine hours (MachHrs) and the number of production runs (ProdRuns). Constant error variance implies that overhead costs vary just as much for small values of MachHrs and ProdRuns as for large values—or any values in between.

There are many applications in which assumption 2 is questionable. The variation in Y often increases as X increases—a violation of assumption 2. We saw an example of this in Figure 11.10 (repeated here in Figure 12.1), which is based on the HyTex mail-order data in Example 3.11 from Chapter 3. This scatterplot shows AmountSpent versus Salary for a sample of HyTex's customers. Clearly, the variation in AmountSpent increases as Salary increases, which makes intuitive sense. Customers with small salaries have little disposable income, so they all tend to spend small amounts for mail-order items. Customers with large salaries have more disposable income. Some of them spend a lot of it on mail-order items and some spend only a little of it—hence, a larger variation. Scatterplots with this "fan" shape are not at all uncommon in real studies, and they exhibit a clear violation of assumption 2.[1] We say that the data in this graph exhibit **heteroscedasticity**, or more simply, **nonconstant error variance**. These terms are summarized in the following box.

Homoscedasticity means that the variability of Y values is the same for all X values. **Heteroscedasticity** means that the variability of Y values is larger for some X values than for others.

Figure 12.1

Illustration of Nonconstant Error Variance

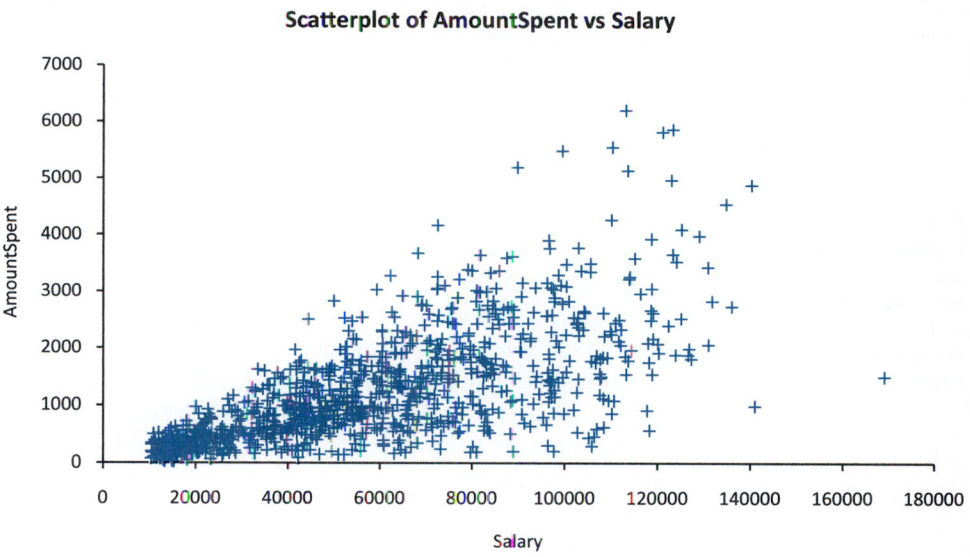

Scatterplot of AmountSpent vs Salary

---

[1]The fan shape in Figure 12.1 is probably the most common form of nonconstant error variance, but it is not the only possible form.

The easiest way to detect nonconstant error variance is through a visual inspection of a scatterplot. We draw a scatterplot of the dependent variable versus an explanatory variable X and see whether the points vary more for some values of X than for others. We can also examine the residuals with a residual plot, where residual values are on the vertical axis and some other variable (Y or one of the X's) is on the horizontal axis. If the residual plot exhibits a fan shape or other evidence of nonconstant error variance, this also indicates a violation of assumption 2.

Assumption 3 states that the errors are normally distributed. We can check this by forming a histogram or a Q-Q plot of the residuals. If assumption 3 holds, then the histogram should be approximately symmetric and bell shaped, and the points in the Q-Q plot should be close to a 45° line. But if there is an obvious skewness, too many residuals more than, say, 2 standard deviations from the mean, or some other nonnormal property, then this indicates a violation of assumption 3.

Finally, assumption 4 requires probabilistic independence of the errors. Intuitively, this assumption means that information on some of the errors provides no information on other errors. For example, if we are told that the overhead costs for months 1 through 4 are all above the regression line (positive residuals), we cannot infer anything about the residual for month 5 if assumption 4 holds.

Assumption 4 (independence of residuals) is usually suspect only for time series data.

For cross-sectional data there is generally little reason to doubt the validity of assumption 4 unless the observations are ordered in some particular way. For cross-sectional data we generally take assumption 4 for granted. However, for time series data, assumption 4 is often violated. This is because of a property called *autocorrelation*. For now, we simply mention that one output given automatically in many regression packages is the *Durbin–Watson statistic*. The Durbin–Watson statistic is one measure of autocorrelation and thus it measures the extent to which assumption 4 is violated. We can usually ignore it in cross-sectional studies, but it is important for time series data. We briefly discuss this Durbin–Watson statistic toward the end of this chapter and in Chapter 13.

One other assumption is important for numerical calculations. We must assume that no explanatory variable is an *exact* linear combination of any other explanatory variables. Another way of stating this is that there is no exact linear relationship between any set of explanatory variables. This would occur, for example, if one variable were an exact multiple of another, or if one variable were equal to the sum of several other variables. More generally, it occurs if one of the explanatory variables can be written as a weighted sum of several of the others.

Exact multicollinearity means that at least one of the explanatory variables is redundant and is not needed in the regression equation.

If such a relationship holds, it means that there is *redundancy* in the data. One of the X's could be eliminated without any loss of information. Here is a simple example. Suppose that MachHrs1 is machine hours measured in hours, and MachHrs2 is machine hours measured in *hundreds* of hours. Then it is clear that these two variables contain exactly the same information, and either of them could (and should) be eliminated.

As another example, suppose that Ad1, Ad2, and Ad3 are the amounts spent on radio ads, television ads, and newspaper ads. Also, suppose that TotAd is the amount spent on radio, television, and newspaper ads combined. Then there is an exact linear relationship among these variables:

$$\text{TotAd} = \text{Ad1} + \text{Ad2} + \text{Ad3}$$

In this case there is no need to include TotAd in the analysis because it contains no information that is not already contained in the variables Ad1, Ad2, and Ad3.

Excel Tip *StatTools issues a warning if it detects an exact linear relationship between explanatory variables in a regression model.*

Generally, it is fairly simple to spot an exact linear relationship such as these, and then to eliminate it by excluding the redundant variable from the analysis. However, if we do *not* spot the relationship and try to run the regression analysis with the redundant variable included, regression packages will typically respond with an error message. If the package interrupts the analysis with an error message containing the words "exact multicollinearity" or "linear dependence," then you should look for a redundant explanatory variable. As an example, the message from StatTools in this case is shown in Figure 12.2. We got it by deliberately entering dummy variables from *each* category of a categorical variable— something we have warned *not* to do.

Figure 12.2

Error Message
from StatTools
Indicating Exact
Multicollinearity

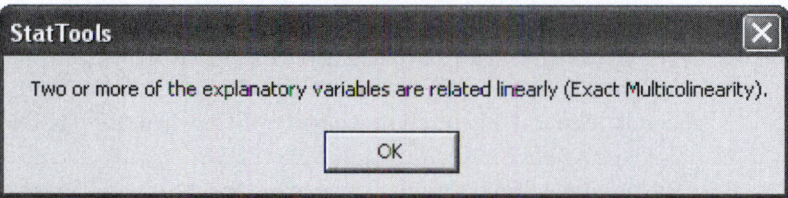

Although this problem can be a nuisance, it is usually caused by an oversight and can be fixed easily by eliminating a redundant variable. A more common and serious problem is **multicollinearity**, where explanatory variables are highly, but not exactly, correlated. A typical example is an employee's years of experience and age. Although these two variables are not equal for all employees, they are likely to be highly correlated. If they are both included as explanatory variables in a regression analysis, the software will not issue any error messages, but the estimates it produces can be unreliable. We discuss multicollinearity in more detail later in this chapter.

12.3 INFERENCES ABOUT THE REGRESSION COEFFICIENTS

In this section we show how to make inferences about the population regression coefficients from sample data. We begin by making the assumptions discussed in the previous section. In particular, the first assumption states that there is a population regression line. Equation (12.2) for this line is repeated here:

$$Y = \alpha + \beta_1 X_1 + \cdots + \beta_k X_k + \epsilon$$

We refer to α and the β's collectively as the **regression coefficients**. Again, Greek letters are used to indicate that these quantities are unknown and unobservable. Actually, there is one other unknown constant in the model: the variance of the error terms. Regression assumption 2 states that these errors have a constant variance, the same for all values of the X's. We label this constant variance σ^2. Equivalently, the common standard deviation of the errors is σ.

This is how it looks in theory. There is a fixed set of explanatory variables, and given these variables, the problem is to estimate α, the β's, and σ. In practice, however, it is not usually this straightforward. In real regression applications the choice of relevant explanatory variables is almost never obvious. There are at least two guiding principles: relevance and data availability. We certainly want variables that are related to the dependent variable. The best situation is when there is an established economic or physical theory to guide us. For example, economic theory suggests that the demand for a product (dependent variable) is related to its price (possible explanatory variable). But there are not enough established theories to cover every situation. We often have to use the available data, plus some trial and error, to determine a *useful* set of explanatory variables. In this sense, it is usually pointless to search for one single "true" population regression equation. Instead, we typically estimate several competing models, each with a different set of explanatory variables, and ultimately select one of them as being the most useful.

Typically, the most challenging part of a regression analysis is deciding which explanatory variables to include in the regression equation.

Deciding which explanatory variables to include in a regression equation is probably the most difficult part of any applied regression analysis. Available data sets frequently offer an overabundance of potential explanatory variables. In addition, it is possible and often useful to create new variables from original variables, such as their logarithms. So where do we stop? Is it best to include every conceivable explanatory variable that might be related to the dependent variable? One overriding principle is **parsimony**—explaining the most with the least. For example, if we can explain a dependent variable just as well (or nearly as well) with two explanatory variables as with 10 explanatory variables, then the principle of parsimony says to use only two. Models with fewer explanatory variables are generally easier to interpret, so we prefer them whenever possible.

> The principle of **parsimony** is to explain the most with the least. It favors a model with fewer explanatory variables, assuming that this model explains the dependent variable almost as well as a model with additional explanatory variables.

Before we can determine which equation has the "best" set of explanatory variables, however, we must be able to estimate the unknown parameters for a given equation. That is, for a given set of explanatory variables X_1 through X_k, we must be able to estimate α, the β's, and σ. We learned how to find point estimates of these parameters in the previous chapter. The estimates of α and the β's are the least squares estimates of the intercept and slope terms. For example, we used the 36 months of overhead data in the Bendrix example to estimate the equation

$$\text{Predicted Overhead} = 3997 + 43.54\text{MachHrs} + 883.62\text{ProdRuns}$$

This implies that the least squares estimates of α, β_1, and β_2 are 3997, 43.54, and 883.62. Furthermore, because the residuals are really estimates of the error terms, the standard error of estimate s_e is an estimate of σ. For the same overhead equation this estimate is $s_e = \$4109$.

However, we know from Chapters 8 and 9 that there is more to statistical estimation than finding point estimates of population parameters. Each potential sample from the population would typically lead to *different* point estimates. For example, if Bendrix estimated the equation for overhead from a different 36-month period, the results would almost certainly be different. Therefore, we now discuss how these point estimates vary from sample to sample.

12.3.1 Sampling Distribution of the Regression Coefficients

The key idea is again sampling distributions. Recall that the sampling distribution of any estimate derived from sample data is the distribution of this estimate over all possible samples. This idea can be applied to the least squares estimate of a regression coefficient. For example, the sampling distribution of b_1, the least squares estimate of β_1, is the distribution of b_1's we would see if we observed many samples and ran a least squares regression on each of them.

Fortunately, mathematicians have used theoretical arguments to find the required sampling distributions. We state the main result as follows. Let β be any of the β's, and let b be the least squares estimate of β. Then if the regression assumptions hold, the standardized value $(b - \beta)/s_b$ has a t distribution with $n - k - 1$ degrees of freedom, as given in the box. Here, k is the number of explanatory variables included in the equation, and s_b is the estimated standard deviation of the sampling distribution of b.

Sampling Distribution of a Regression Coefficient

If the regression assumptions are valid, the standardized value

$$t = \frac{b - \beta}{s_b}$$

has a t distribution with $n - k - 1$ degrees of freedom.

This important result can be interpreted as follows. First, the estimate b is *unbiased* in the sense that its mean is β, the true but unknown value of the slope. If we calculated b's from repeated samples, some would underestimate β and others would overestimate β, but on average they would be on target.

Second, the estimated standard deviation of b is labeled s_b. It is usually called the **standard error of b**. This standard error is related to the standard error of estimate s_e, but it is not the same. Generally, the formula for s_b is quite complicated, and it is not shown here, but its value is printed in all standard regression outputs. It measures how much the b's would vary from sample to sample. A small value of s_b is preferred—it means that b is a more accurate estimate of the true coefficient β.

Finally, the shape of the distribution of b is symmetric and bell shaped. The relevant distribution is the t distribution with $n - k - 1$ degrees of freedom.

We have stated this result for a typical coefficient of one of the X's. These are usually the coefficients of most interest. However, exactly the same result holds for the intercept term α. Now we see how to use this result.

EXAMPLE | 12.1 EXPLAINING OVERHEAD COSTS AT BENDRIX

This example is a continuation of the Bendrix manufacturing example from the previous chapter. As before, the dependent variable is Overhead and the explanatory variables are MachHrs and ProdRuns. What inferences can we make about the regression coefficients?

Objective   To use standard regression output to make inferences about the regression coefficients of machine hours and production runs in the equation for overhead costs.

Solution

When we use StatTools's Regression procedure, we obtain the output shown in Figure 12.3. (See the file **Overhead Costs.xlsx**.) This output is practically identical to regression outputs from all other statistical software packages. We have already seen that the estimates of the regression coefficients appear under the label Coefficient in the range B18:B20. These values estimate the true, but unobservable, population coefficients. The next column, labeled Standard Error, shows the s_b's. Specifically, 3.589 is the standard error of the coefficient of MachHrs, and 82.251 is the standard error of the coefficient of ProdRuns.

Figure 12.3 Regression Output for Bendrix Example

	A	B	C	D	E	F	G
7		Multiple	R-Square	Adjusted	StErr of		
8	*Summary*	R		R-Square	Estimate		
9		0.9308	0.8664	0.8583	4108.993		
10							
11		Degrees of	Sum of	Mean of	F-Ratio	p-Value	
12	*ANOVA Table*	Freedom	Squares	Squares			
13	Explained	2	3614020661	1807010330	107.0261	< 0.0001	
14	Unexplained	33	557166199.1	16883824.22			
15							
16			Standard			Confidence Interval 95%	
17	*Regression Table*	Coefficient	Error	t-Value	p-Value	Lower	Upper
18	Constant	3996.678	6603.651	0.6052	0.5492	-9438.551	17431.907
19	MachHrs	43.536	3.589	12.1289	< 0.0001	36.234	50.839
20	ProdRuns	883.618	82.251	10.7429	< 0.0001	716.276	1050.960

The b's represent point estimates of the β's, based on this particular sample. The s_b's indicate the accuracy of these point estimates. For example, the point estimate of β_1, the effect on Overhead of a 1-unit increase in MachHrs, is 43.536. We are about 95% confident that the true β_1 is within 2 standard errors of this point estimate, that is, from approximately 36.357 to 50.715. Similar statements can be made for the coefficient of ProdRuns and the intercept (Constant) term. ∎

12.3.2 Confidence Intervals for the Regression Coefficients

As with any population parameters, we can use the sample data to obtain confidence intervals for the regression coefficients. For example, the preceding paragraph implies that an approximate 95% confidence interval for the coefficient of MachHrs extends from approximately 36.357 to 50.715. More precisely, a confidence interval for any β is of the form

$$b \pm t\text{-multiple} \times s_b$$

where the t-multiple depends on the confidence level and the degrees of freedom (here $n - k - 1$). For example, the relevant t-multiple for the Bendrix data, assuming we want a 95% confidence interval, is the value that cuts off probability 0.025 of the t distribution with $36 - 2 - 1 = 33$ degrees of freedom. [It is 2.035 and can be found in Excel with the function TINV(0.05,33).][2] Using this multiple gives a 95% confidence interval from 36.234 to 50.839, as shown in Figure 12.3. StatTools always provides 95% confidence intervals for the regression coefficients automatically.

12.3.3 Hypothesis Tests for the Regression Coefficients

There is another important piece of information in regression outputs: the t-values for the individual regression coefficients. These are shown in the "t-value" column of the regression output in Figure 12.3. The formula for a t-value is simple. It is the ratio of the estimated coefficient to its standard error, as shown in equation (12.3). Therefore, it indicates how many standard errors the regression coefficient is from 0. For example, the t-value for MachHrs is about 12.13, so we know that the regression coefficient of MachHrs, 43.536, is over 12 of its standard errors to the right of 0. Similarly, the coefficient of ProdRuns is more than 10 of its standard errors to the right of 0.

[2]StatTools uses its own built-in function to calculate this value, but it is equivalent to TINV.

> **t-*value for Test of Regression Coefficient***
>
> $$t\text{-value} = b/s_b \qquad\qquad (12.3)$$

A t-value can be used in an important hypothesis test for the corresponding regression coefficient. To motivate this test, suppose that we want to decide whether a particular explanatory variable belongs in the regression equation. A sensible criterion for making this decision is to check whether the corresponding regression coefficient is 0. If a variable's coefficient is 0, there is no point in including this variable in the equation; the 0 coefficient will cancel its effect on the dependent variable.

Therefore, it is reasonable to test whether a variable's coefficient is 0. This is usually tested versus a *two-tailed* alternative. The null and alternative hypotheses are of the form $H_0\colon\beta = 0$ versus $H_a\colon\beta \neq 0$. If we can reject the null hypothesis and conclude that this coefficient is *not* 0, then we have an argument for including the variable in the regression equation. Conversely, if we cannot reject the null hypothesis, we might decide to eliminate this variable from the equation.

The t-value for a variable allows us to run this test easily. We simply compare the t-value in the regression output with a tabulated t-value and reject the null hypothesis only if the t-value from the computer output is greater in magnitude than the tabulated t-value. If the test is run at the 5% significance level, for example, then the appropriate tabulated t-value can be found in Excel with TINV$(0.05, n - k - 1)$, the same t-value used previously for confidence intervals.

Most computer packages, including StatTools, make this test even easier to run by reporting the corresponding p-value for the test. This eliminates the need for finding the tabulated t-value (or using the TINV function). The p-value is interpreted exactly as in Chapter 10. It is the probability (in both tails) of the relevant t distribution beyond the listed t-value. For example, referring again to Figure 12.3, the t-value for MachHrs is 12.13, and the associated p-value is less than 0.0001. This means that there is virtually no probability beyond the observed t-value. In words, we are still not exactly sure of the true coefficient of MachHrs, but we are virtually sure it is not 0. The same can be said for the coefficient of ProdRuns.

We soon say even more about these t-values and how they can help to decide which variables to include or exclude in a regression equation. But we first make the following points about hypothesis tests for regression coefficients.

The test for whether a regression coefficient is 0 can be run by looking at the corresponding p-value: Reject the "equals 0" hypothesis if the p-value is small, say, less than 0.05. It can also be run by looking at the confidence interval for the coefficient: Reject the "equals 0" hypothesis if the confidence interval does not contain the value 0.

Hypothesis Tests and Regression Coefficients

1. A t-value is usually reported for the intercept (constant) term in the equation, as well as for the other coefficients. However, this information is usually of little relevance. The reason is that there is usually no practical reason for testing whether the intercept is 0. There are rare situations where an intercept equal to 0 has a meaningful interpretation, and in such situations the hypothesis test is relevant.

2. The test of $\beta = 0$ versus a two-tailed alternative at the 5% level, say, can also be run by calculating a 95% confidence interval for β and rejecting the null hypothesis if 0 is not within the confidence interval. That is, if a 95% confidence interval for β extends from a negative number to a positive number, we cannot reject the null hypothesis that $\beta = 0$.

3. The previous test, a two-tailed test of whether a particular β is 0, is only one of many hypothesis tests that can be run. For example, consider a sample of houses that have been sold recently. We would like to regress the selling prices of the houses on their appraised values, as obtained by a professional appraiser. Now, it is pretty clear, even

before the data are observed, that selling prices will be *positively* related to appraised values. Therefore, there isn't much point in testing whether the coefficient of AppraisedValue is 0.

A more interesting test in this example is whether the coefficient of AppraisedValue is less than or greater than 1. If it is less than 1, say, then every extra dollar of appraised value contributes *less than* an extra dollar to the selling price. Therefore, we might run the one-tailed test of $H_0: \beta \geq 1$ versus $H_a: \beta < 1$. (We could also run a two-tailed test. It just depends on what we're trying to prove.) In this case we would base the test on the test statistic

$$t\text{-value} = \frac{b - 1}{s_b}$$

where b and s_b are the coefficient and standard error of AppraisedValue in the regression output. Its p-value could be calculated in Excel with the function TDIST(ABS(t-value),$n-2$,1). This t-value and the corresponding p-value are *not* reported in computer outputs, but they are easy to obtain.

The point here is that most computer outputs provide the ingredients for a very natural test—whether a given regression coefficient is 0. Virtually no work is needed to perform this test because the t-value and p-value are given in the regression output. But other hypothesis tests on the coefficients are sometimes relevant, and they can be performed easily with Excel functions.

12.3.4 A Test for the Overall Fit: The ANOVA Table

The t-values for the regression coefficients allow us to see which of the potential explanatory variables are useful in explaining the dependent variable. But it is conceivable that *none* of these variables does a very good job. That is, it is conceivable that the entire group of explanatory variables explains only an insignificant portion of the variability of the dependent variable. Although this is the exception rather than the rule in most real applications, it can certainly happen. An indication of this is that we obtain a very small R^2 value. Because R^2 is the square of the correlation between the observed values of the dependent variable and the fitted values from the regression equation, another indication of a lack of fit is that this correlation (the "multiple R") is small. In this section we state a formal procedure for testing the overall fit, or explanatory power, of a regression equation.

Suppose that the dependent variable is Y and the explanatory variables are X_1 through X_k. Then the proposed population regression equation is

$$Y = \alpha + \beta_1 X_1 + \cdots + \beta_k X_k + \epsilon$$

To say that this equation has absolutely no explanatory power means that the same value of Y will be predicted regardless of the values of the X's. In this case it makes no difference which values of the X's we use because they all lead to the same predicted value of Y. But the only way this can occur is if all of the β's are 0. So the formal hypothesis we test in this section is $H_0: \beta_1 = \cdots = \beta_k = 0$ versus the alternative that at least one of the β's is not 0. In words, the null hypothesis is that this set of explanatory variables has no power to explain the variation in the dependent variable Y. If we can reject the null hypothesis, as we can in the majority of applications, this means that the explanatory variables *as a group* provide at least some explanatory power. These hypotheses are summarized in the box.

Hypotheses for ANOVA Test

The null hypothesis is that all coefficients of the explanatory variables are 0. The alternative is that at least one of these coefficients is not 0.

At first glance it might appear that we can test this null hypothesis by looking at the individual t-values. If they are all small (statistically insignificant), then we can accept the null hypothesis of no fit; otherwise, we can reject it. However, as we see in the next section, it is possible, because of multicollinearity, to have small t-values even though the variables as a whole have *significant* explanatory power.

The alternative is to use an F test. This is sometimes referred to as the ANOVA (analysis of variance) test because the elements for calculating the required F-value are shown in an ANOVA table.[3] In general, an ANOVA table analyzes different sources of variation. In the case of regression, the variation in question is the variation of the dependent variable Y. The "total variation" of this variable is the sum of squared deviations about the mean and is labeled SST (sum of squares total).

$$SST = \sum (Y_i - \overline{Y})^2$$

The ANOVA table splits this total variation into two parts, the part *explained* by the regression equation, and the part left *unexplained*. The unexplained part is the sum of squared residuals, usually labeled SSE (sum of squared errors):

$$SSE = \sum e_i^2 = \sum (Y_i - \hat{Y}_i)^2$$

The explained part is then the difference between the total and unexplained variation. It is usually labeled SSR (sum of squares due to regression):

$$SSR = SST - SSE$$

The F test is a formal procedure for testing whether the explained variation is "large" compared to the unexplained variation. Specifically, each of these sources of variation has an associated degrees of freedom (df). For the explained variation, $df = k$, the number of explanatory variables. For the unexplained variation, $df = n - k - 1$, the sample size minus the total number of coefficients (including the intercept term). When we divide the explained or unexplained variation by its degrees of freedom, the result is called a mean square, or MS. The two mean squares we need are MSR and MSE, given by

$$MSR = \frac{SSR}{k}$$

and

$$MSE = \frac{SSE}{n - k - 1}$$

Note that MSE is the square of the standard error of estimate, that is,

$$MSE = s_e^2$$

Finally, the ratio of these mean squares is the required F-ratio for the test:

$$F\text{-ratio} = \frac{MSR}{MSE}$$

When the null hypothesis of no explanatory power is true, this F-ratio has an F distribution with k and $n - k - 1$ degrees of freedom. If the F-ratio is small, then the explained variation is small relative to the unexplained variation, and there is evidence that the regression

---

[3]This ANOVA table is similar to the ANOVA table we discussed in the Chapter 10. However, we repeat the necessary material here for those who didn't cover the ANOVA section in Chapter 10.

equation provides little explanatory power. But if the F-ratio is large, then the explained variation is large relative to the unexplained variation, and we can conclude that the equation does have some explanatory power.

As usual, the F-ratio has an associated p-value that allows us to run the test easily. In this case the p-value is the probability to the *right* of the observed F-ratio in the appropriate F distribution. This p-value is reported in most regression outputs, along with the elements that lead up to it. If it is sufficiently small, less than 0.05, say, then we can conclude that the explanatory variables as a whole have at least some explanatory power.

Although this test is run routinely in most applications, there is often little doubt that the equation has some explanatory power; the only questions are how much, and which explanatory variables provide the best combination. In such cases the F-ratio from the ANOVA table is typically "off the charts" and the corresponding p-value is practically 0. On the other hand, F-ratios, particularly large ones, should not necessarily be used to choose between equations with different explanatory variables included.

For example, suppose that one equation with three explanatory variables has an F-ratio of 54 with an extremely small p-value—obviously very significant. Also, suppose that another equation that includes these three variables plus a few more has an F-ratio of 37 and also has a very small p-value. (When we say small, we mean *small*. These p-values are probably listed as <0.001.) Is the first equation better because its F-ratio is higher? Not necessarily. The two F-ratios imply only that both of these equations have a good deal of explanatory power. It is better to look at their s_e values (or adjusted R^2 values) and their t-values to choose between them.

The ANOVA table is part of the StatTools output for any regression run. It appeared for the Bendrix example in Figure 12.3, which is repeated for convenience in Figure 12.4. The ANOVA table is in rows 12 through 14. We see the degrees of freedom in column B, the sums of squares in column C, the mean squares in column D, the F-ratio in cell E13, and its associated p-value in cell F13. As predicted, this F-ratio is "off the charts," and the p-value is practically 0.

Reject the null hypothesis—and conclude that these X variables have at least some explanatory power—if the F-value in the ANOVA table is large and the corresponding p-value is small.

Figure 12.4 **Regression Output for Bendrix Example**

	A	B	C	D	E	F	G
7		Multiple	R-Square	Adjusted	StErr of		
8	Summary	R		R-Square	Estimate		
9		0.9308	0.8664	0.8583	4108.993		
10							
11		Degrees of	Sum of	Mean of	F-Ratio	p-Value	
12	ANOVA Table	Freedom	Squares	Squares			
13	Explained	2	3614020661	1807010330	107.0261	< 0.0001	
14	Unexplained	33	557166199.1	16883824.22			
15							
16		Coefficient	Standard	t-Value	p-Value	Confidence Interval 95%	
17	Regression Table		Error			Lower	Upper
18	Constant	3996.678	6603.651	0.6052	0.5492	-9438.551	17431.907
19	MachHrs	43.536	3.589	12.1289	< 0.0001	36.234	50.839
20	ProdRuns	883.618	82.251	10.7429	< 0.0001	716.276	1050.960

This information wouldn't be much comfort for the Bendrix manager who is trying to understand the causes of variation in overhead costs. This manager already *knows* that machine hours and production runs are related positively to overhead costs—everyone in the company knows that! What he really wants is a set of explanatory variables that yields a high R^2 and a low s_e. The low p-value in the ANOVA tables does not guarantee these. All it guarantees is that MachHrs and ProdRuns are of "some help" in explaining variations in Overhead.

As this example indicates, the ANOVA table can be used as a screening device. If the explanatory variables do not explain a significant percentage of the variation in the dependent variable, then we can either discontinue the analysis or search for an entirely new set of explanatory variables. But even if the F-ratio in the ANOVA table is extremely significant, there is no guarantee that the regression equation provides a good enough fit for practical uses. This depends on other measures such as s_e and R^2.

PROBLEMS

Level A

1. Explore the relationship between the selling prices (Y) and the appraised values (X) of the 150 homes in the file **P02_07.xlsx** by estimating a simple linear regression model. Construct a 95% confidence interval for the model's slope (i.e., β_1) parameter. What does this confidence interval tell you about the relationship between Y and X for these data?

2. The owner of the Original Italian Pizza restaurant chain would like to predict the sales of his specialty, deep-dish pizza. He has gathered data on the monthly sales of deep-dish pizzas at his restaurants and observations on other potentially relevant variables for each of his 15 outlets in central Pennsylvania. These data are provided in the file **P11_04.xlsx**.
   a. Estimate a multiple regression model between the quantity sold (Y) and the following explanatory variables: average price of deep-dish pizzas, monthly advertising expenditures, and disposable income per household in the areas surrounding the outlets.
   b. Is there evidence of any violations of the key assumptions of regression analysis in this case?
   c. Which of the variables in this model have regression coefficients that are statistically different from 0 at the 5% significance level?
   d. Given your findings in part **c**, which variables, if any, would you choose to remove from the model estimated in part **a**? Explain your decision.

3. The *ACCRA Cost of Living Index* provides a useful and reasonably accurate measure of cost of living differences among a large number of urban areas. Items on which the index is based have been carefully chosen to reflect the different categories of consumer expenditures. The data are in the file **P02_19.xlsx**.
   a. Use multiple regression to explore the relationship between the composite index (dependent variable) and the various expenditure components (explanatory variables).
   b. Is there evidence of any violations of the key assumptions of regression analysis?

   c. Which of the variables in this model have regression coefficients that are statistically different from 0 at the 5% significance level?
   d. Given your findings in part **c**, which variables, if any, would you choose to remove from the model estimated in part **a**? Explain your decision.

4. A trucking company wants to predict the yearly maintenance expense (Y) for a truck using the number of miles driven during the year (X_1) and the age of the truck (X_2, in years) at the beginning of the year. The company has gathered the information given in the file **P11_16.xlsx**. Note that each observation corresponds to a particular truck.
   a. Formulate and estimate a multiple regression model using the given data.
   b. Does autocorrelation, multicollinearity, or heteroscedasticity appear to be a problem?
   c. Construct 95% confidence intervals for the regression coefficients of X_1 and X_2. Based on these interval estimates, which variables, if any, would you choose to remove from the model estimated in part **a**? Explain your decision.

5. Based on the data in the file **P02_25.xlsx** from the U.S. Department of Agriculture, explore the relationship between the number of farms (X) and the average size of a farm (Y) in the United States.
   a. Use the given data to estimate a simple linear regression model.
   b. Test whether there is sufficient evidence to conclude that the slope parameter (i.e., β_1) is *less than* 0. Use a 5% significance level.
   c. Based on your finding in part **b**, is it possible to conclude that a linear relationship exists between the number of farms and the average farm size between 1950 and 2003? Explain.

6. An antique collector believes that the price received for a particular item increases with its age and the number of bidders. The file **P11_18.xlsx** contains data on these three variables for 32 recently auctioned comparable items.
   a. Estimate an appropriate multiple regression model using the given data.

b. Interpret the ANOVA table for this model. In particular, does this set of explanatory variables provide at least some power in explaining the variation in price? Report a p-value for this hypothesis test.

7. Consider the enrollment data for *Business Week*'s top U.S. graduate business programs in the file **P02_03.xlsx**. Use these data to estimate a multiple regression model to assess whether there is a systematic relationship between the total number of full-time students and the following explanatory variables: (a) the proportion of female students, (b) the proportion of minority students, and (c) the proportion of international students enrolled at these distinguished business schools. Next, interpret the ANOVA table for this model. In particular, does this set of explanatory variables provide at least some power in explaining the variation in total full-time enrollment at the top graduate business programs? Report a p-value for this hypothesis test.

8. The U.S. Bureau of Labor Statistics provides data on the year-to-year percentage changes in the wages and salaries of workers in private industries, including both "white-collar" and "blue-collar" occupations. Here we consider these data in the file **P02_56.xlsx**. Is there evidence of a linear relationship between the yearly changes in the wages and salaries of "white-collar" (Y) and "blue-collar" (X) workers in the United States over the given time period? Begin to answer this question by estimating a simple linear regression model.
   a. Construct a 95% confidence interval for the model's slope (i.e., β_1) parameter. Interpret this interval estimate to answer the question posed above.
   b. Interpret the ANOVA table for this model. In particular, does the explanatory variable included in this simple regression model provide at least some power in explaining the variation in the dependent variable? Report a p-value for this hypothesis test.
   c. What is the relationship between the t-ratio for the estimated coefficient of the explanatory variable and the F-ratio found in the ANOVA section of the output? Do these two test statistic values provide the same indication regarding a possible relationship between yearly changes in the wages and salaries of white-collar and blue-collar workers? Explain why or why not.

9. Suppose that a regional express delivery service company wants to estimate the cost of shipping a package (Y) as a function of cargo type, where cargo type includes the following possibilities: fragile, semi-fragile, and durable. Costs for 15 randomly chosen packages of approximately the same weight and same distance shipped, but of different cargo types, are provided in the file **P11_28.xlsx**.

a. Estimate an appropriate multiple regression model to predict the cost of shipping a given package.
b. Interpret the ANOVA table for this model. In particular, do the explanatory variables included in your model formulated in part **a** provide at least some power in explaining the variation in the cost of shipping a package? Report a p-value for this hypothesis test.

10. A simple linear regression with 11 observations yielded the ANOVA table in Table 12.1.
   a. Complete this ANOVA table.
   b. Using $\alpha = 0.05$, test the hypothesis of no linear regression.

Table 12.1   ANOVA Table

Degrees of Freedom	Sum of Squares
Regression	1000
Error	
Total	2500

Level B

11. Consider the relationship between the size of the population (X) and the average household income level (Y) for residents of U.S. towns.
   a. Using the data in the file **P02_24.xlsx**, estimate a regression model involving these two variables.
   b. Does autocorrelation, multicollinearity, or heteroscedasticity appear to be a problem?
   c. Test whether there is sufficient evidence to conclude that the slope parameter (i.e., β_1) is *greater than* 0.0035. Use a 5% significance level.
   d. Based on your finding in part **c**, is it possible to conclude that a linear relationship exists between the size of the population and the average household income level for residents of U.S. towns? Explain.

12. Suppose you find the ANOVA table shown in Table 12.2 for a simple linear regression.
   a. Find the correlation between X and Y. Assume the slope of the least squares line is negative.
   b. Find the p-value for the test of the hypothesis of no linear regression.

Table 12.2   ANOVA Table

Degrees of Freedom	Sum of Squares
SSR	20
SSE	4
SST	100

12.4 MULTICOLLINEARITY

Recall that the coefficient of any variable in a regression equation indicates the effect of this variable on the dependent variable, provided that the other variables in the equation remain constant. Another way of stating this is that the coefficient represents the effect of this variable on the dependent variable *in addition to* the effects of the other variables in the equation. For example, if MachHrs and ProdRuns are included in the equation for Overhead, then the coefficient of MachHrs indicates the *extra* amount MachHrs explains about variation in Overhead, in addition to the amount already explained by ProdRuns. Similarly, the coefficient of ProdRuns indicates the extra amount ProdRuns explains about variation in Overhead, in addition to the amount already explained by MachHrs. Therefore, the relationship between an explanatory variable *X* and the dependent variable *Y* is not always accurately reflected in the coefficient of *X*; it depends on which *other X*'s are included or not included in the equation.

This is especially true when there is a linear relationship between two or more *explanatory* variables, in which case we have *multicollinearity*. By definition, **multicollinearity** is the presence of a fairly strong linear relationship between two or more explanatory variables, and it can make estimation difficult.

> **Multicollinearity** occurs when there is a fairly strong linear relationship among a set of explanatory variables.

Consider the following example. It is a rather trivial example, but it is useful for illustrating the potential effects of multicollinearity.

EXAMPLE 12.2 HEIGHT AS A FUNCTION OF FOOT LENGTH

We want to explain a person's height by means of foot length. The dependent variable is Height, and the explanatory variables are Right and Left, the length of the right foot and the left foot, respectively. What can occur when we regress Height on *both* Right and Left?

Objective   To illustrate the problem of multicollinearity when both foot length variables are used in a regression for height.

Solution

Admittedly, there is no need to include both Right and Left in an equation for Height—either one of them would do—but we include them both to make a point. Now, it is likely that there is a large correlation between height and foot size, so we would expect this regression equation to do a good job. For example, the R^2 value will probably be large. But what about the coefficients of Right and Left? Here we have a problem. The coefficient of Right indicates the right foot's effect on Height in addition to the effect of the left foot. This additional effect is probably minimal. That is, after the effect of Left on Height has already been taken into account, the extra information provided by Right is probably minimal. But it goes the other way also. The extra effect of Left, in addition to that provided by Right, is probably also minimal.

To show what can happen numerically, we generated a hypothetical data set of heights and left and right foot lengths. (See the file **Heights.xlsx**.) We did this so that, except for random error, height is approximately 32 plus 3.2 times foot length (all expressed in inches). As shown in Figure 12.5, the correlation between Height and either Right or Left in our data set is quite large, and the correlation between Right and Left is very close to 1.

Figure 12.5

Correlations in Example of Height versus Foot Length

	A	B	C	D
7		Height	Right	Left
8	Correlation Table	Data Set #1	Data Set #1	Data Set #1
9	Height	1.000		
10	Right	0.903	1.000	
11	Left	0.900	0.999	1.000

The regression output when both Right and Left are entered in the equation for Height appears in Figure 12.6. This tells a somewhat confusing story. The multiple R and the corresponding R^2 are about what we would expect, given the correlations between Height and either Right or Left in Figure 12.5. In particular, the multiple R is close to the correlation between Height and either Right or Left. Also, the s_e value is quite good. It implies that predictions of height from this regression equation will typically be off by only about 2 inches.

Figure 12.6 Regression Output for Height versus Foot Length Example

	A	B	C	D	E	F	G
7		Multiple	R-Square	Adjusted	StErr of		
8	Summary	R		R-Square	Estimate		
9		0.9042	0.8176	0.8140	2.004		
10							
11		Degrees of	Sum of	Mean of	F-Ratio	p-Value	
12	ANOVA Table	Freedom	Squares	Squares			
13	Explained	2	1836.384497	918.1922484	228.6003	< 0.0001	
14	Unexplained	102	409.6916079	4.016584391			
15							
16		Coefficient	Standard	t-Value	p-Value	Confidence Interval 95%	
17	Regression Table		Error			Lower	Upper
18	Constant	31.760	1.959	16.2087	< 0.0001	27.874	35.647
19	Right	6.823	3.428	1.9901	0.0493	0.023	13.623
20	Left	-3.645	3.441	-1.0592	0.2920	-10.470	3.181

Multicollinearity often causes regression coefficients to have the "wrong" sign, t-values to be too small, and p-values to be too large.

However, the coefficients of Right and Left are not at all what we might expect, given that we generated heights as approximately 32 plus 3.2 times foot length. In fact, the coefficient of Left is the wrong sign—it is *negative*! Besides this "wrong" sign, the tip-off that there is a problem is that the *t*-value of Left is quite small and the corresponding *p*-value is quite large. Judging by this, we might conclude that Height and Left are either not related or are related negatively. But we know from Figure 12.5 that both of these conclusions are wrong. In contrast, the coefficient of Right has the "correct" sign, and its *t*-value and associated *p*-value do imply statistical significance, at least at the 5% level. However, this happened mostly by chance. Slight changes in the data could change the results completely—the coefficient of Right could become negative and insignificant, or both coefficients could become insignificant.

The problem is that although both Right and Left are clearly related to Height, it is impossible for the least squares method to distinguish their *separate* effects. Note that the regression equation does estimate the combined effect fairly well—the sum of the coefficients of Right and Left is $6.823 + (-3.645) = 3.178$. This is close to the coefficient 3.2 we used to

Multicollinearity typically causes unreliable estimates of regression coefficients, but it does not generally cause poor predictions.

generate the data. Also, the estimated intercept 31.760 is close to the intercept 32 we used to generate the data. Therefore, the estimated equation will work well for predicting heights. It just does not have reliable estimates of the individual coefficients of Right and Left.

To see what happens when either Right or Left is excluded from the regression equation, we show the results of *simple* regression. When Right is the only variable in the equation, it becomes

$$\text{Predicted Height} = 31.546 + 3.195\text{Right}$$

The R^2 and s_e values are 81.6% and 2.005, and the t-value and p-value for the coefficient of Right are now 21.34 and <0.0001—very significant. Similarly, when Left is the only variable in the equation, it becomes

$$\text{Predicted Height} = 31.526 + 3.197\text{Left}$$

The R^2 and s_e values are 81.1% and 2.033, and the t-value and p-value for the coefficient of Left are 20.99 and and <0.0001—again very significant. Clearly, both of these equations tell almost identical stories, and they are much easier to interpret than the equation with both Right and Left included. The message, therefore, is that when two variables are very highly correlated, only one of them should be included in the regression equation. ■

This example illustrates an extreme form of multicollinearity, where two explanatory variables are very highly correlated. In general, there are various degrees of multicollinearity. In each of them, there is a linear relationship between two or more explanatory variables, and this relationship makes it difficult to estimate the individual effects of the X's on the dependent variable. The symptoms of multicollinearity can be "wrong" signs of the coefficients, smaller-than-expected t-values, and larger-than-expected (insignificant) p-values. In other words, variables that are really related to the dependent variable can look like they aren't related, based on their p-values. The reason is that their effects on Y are already explained by other X's in the equation.

Sometimes multicollinearity is easy to spot and treat. For example, it would be silly to include both Right and Left foot length in the equation for Height. They are obviously very highly correlated and only one is needed in the equation for Height. We should exclude one of them—either one—and reestimate the equation. However, multicollinearity is not usually this easy to treat or even diagnose.

Moderate to extreme multicollinearity poses a problem in many regression applications. Unfortunately, there are usually no easy solutions.

Suppose, for example, that we want to use regression to explain variations in salary. Three potentially useful explanatory variables are age, years of experience in the company, and years of experience in the industry. It is very likely that each of these is positively related to salary, and it is also very likely that they are very closely related to each other. However, it isn't clear which, if any, we should exclude from the regression equation. If we include all three, we are likely to find that at least one of them is insignificant (high p-value), in which case we might consider excluding it from the equation. If we do so, the s_e and R^2 values will probably not change very much—the equation will provide equally good predicted values—but the coefficients of the variables that remain in the equation could change considerably.

PROBLEMS

Level A

13. Using the data given in **P11_10.xlsx**, estimate a multiple regression equation to predict the sales price of houses in a given community. Employ all available explanatory variables. Is there evidence of multicollinearity in this model? Explain why or why not.

14. Consider the enrollment data for *Business Week*'s top U.S. graduate business programs in the file **P02_03.xlsx**. Use these data to estimate a multiple regression model to assess whether there is a systematic relationship between the total number of full-time students and the following explanatory variables: (a) the proportion of female students, (b) the proportion of minority students, and (c) the proportion of international students enrolled at these distinguished business schools.

   a. Determine whether each of the regression coefficients for the explanatory variables in this model is statistically different from 0 at the 5% significance level. Summarize your findings.

   b. Is there evidence of multicollinearity in this model? Explain why or why not.

15. The manager of a commuter rail transportation system was recently asked by her governing board to determine the factors that have a significant impact on the demand for rides in the large city served by the transportation network. The system manager has collected data on variables that might be related to the number of weekly riders on the city's rail system. The file **P11_20.xlsx** contains these data.

   a. Estimate a multiple regression model using all of the available explanatory variables. Perform a test of significance for each of the model's regression coefficients. Are the signs of the estimated coefficients consistent with your expectations?

   b. Is there evidence of multicollinearity in this model? Explain why or why not. If multicollinearity appears to be present, explain what you would do to eliminate this problem.

Level B

16. The human resources manager of DataCom, Inc., wants to examine the relationship between annual salaries (Y) and the number of years employees have worked at DataCom (X). These data have been collected for a sample of employees and are given in the file **P11_05.xlsx**.

   a. Estimate the relationship between Y and X using simple linear regression analysis. Is there evidence to support the hypothesis that the coefficient for the number of years employed is statistically different from 0 at the $\alpha = 0.05$ level?

   b. Next, formulate a multiple regression model to explain annual salaries of DataCom employees with X and X^2 as explanatory variables. Estimate this model using the given data. Perform relevant hypothesis tests to determine the significance of the regression coefficients of these two variables. Let $\alpha = 0.05$. Summarize your findings.

   c. How do you explain your findings in part **b** in light of the results found in part **a**?

17. The owner of a restaurant in Bloomington, Indiana, has recorded sales data for the past 19 years. He has also recorded data on potentially relevant variables. The data appear in the file **P11_23.xlsx**.

   a. Estimate a multiple regression equation that includes annual sales as the dependent variable and the following explanatory variables: year, size of the population residing within 10 miles of the restaurant, annual advertising expenditures, and advertising expenditures in the *previous* year.

   b. Which of the explanatory variables have significant effects on sales at the 10% significance level? Do any of these results surprise you? Explain why or why not.

   c. Exclude all insignificant explanatory variables from the full model and estimate the reduced model. Comment on the significance of each remaining explanatory variable. Again, use a 10% significance level.

   d. Based on your analysis of this problem, does multicollinearity appear to be present in the original or revised versions of the model? Provide the reasoning behind your response.

12.5 INCLUDE/EXCLUDE DECISIONS

In this section we make further use of the *t*-values of regression coefficients. In particular, we see how they can be used to make include/exclude decisions for explanatory variables in a regression equation. From Section 12.3 we know that a *t*-value can be used to test whether a population regression coefficient is 0. But does this mean that we should automatically include a variable if its *t*-value is significant and automatically exclude it if its *t*-value is insignificant? The decision is not always this simple.

The bottom line is that we are always trying to get the best fit possible, and because of the principle of parsimony, we want to use the fewest number of variables. This presents a trade-off, where there are often no easy answers. On the one hand, more variables certainly increase R^2 and they usually reduce the standard error of estimate s_e. On the other hand, fewer variables are better for parsimony. Therefore, we present several guidelines. These guidelines are not hard and fast rules, and they are sometimes contradictory. In real applications there are often several equations that are equally good for all practical purposes, and it is rather pointless to search for a single "true" equation.

Guidelines for Including/Excluding Variables in a Regression Equation

1. Look at a variable's t-value and its associated p-value. If the p-value is above some accepted significance level, such as 0.05, then this variable is a candidate for exclusion.

2. Check whether a variable's t-value is less than 1 or greater than 1 in magnitude. If it is less than 1, then s_e will decrease (and adjusted R^2 will increase) if this variable is excluded from the equation. If it is greater than 1, the opposite will occur. These are mathematical facts. Because of them, some statisticians advocate excluding variables with t-values less than 1 and including variables with t-values greater than 1.

3. Look at t-values and p-values, rather than correlations, when making include/exclude decisions. An explanatory variable can have a fairly high correlation with the dependent variable, but because of *other* variables included in the equation, it might not be needed. This would be reflected in a low t-value and a high p-value, and this variable could possibly be excluded for reasons of parsimony. This often occurs in the presence of multicollinearity.

4. When there is a group of variables that are in some sense logically related, it is sometimes a good idea to include all of them or exclude all of them. In this case, their individual t-values are less relevant. Instead, the "partial F test" discussed in Section 12.7 should be used.

5. Use economic and/or physical theory to decide whether to include or exclude variables, and put less reliance on t-values and/or p-values. The idea is that some variables might really *belong* in an equation because of their theoretical relationship with the dependent variable, and their low t-values, possibly the result of an unlucky sample, should not disqualify them from being in the equation. Similarly, a variable that has no economic or physical relationship with the dependent variable might have a significant t-value just by chance. This does not necessarily mean that it should be included in the equation. We should not use a computer package blindly to hunt for "good" explanatory variables. We should have some idea, before running the package, which variables belong and which do not.

Again, these guidelines can give contradictory signals. Specifically, guideline 2 bases the include/exclude decision on whether the magnitude of the t-value is greater or less than 1. However, analysts who base the decision on statistical significance at the usual 5% level, as in guideline 1, typically exclude a variable from the equation unless its t-value is at least 2 (approximately). This latter approach is more stringent—fewer variables will be retained—but it is probably the more popular approach. However, either approach is likely to result in "similar" equations for all practical purposes.

We illustrate how these guidelines can be used in the following example. It uses a slightly modified version of the data set on HyTex's mail-order customers from Chapter 3.

EXAMPLE | **12.3 EXPLAINING SPENDING AMOUNTS AT HYTEX**

The file **Catalog Marketing.xlsx** contains data on 1000 customers who purchased mail-order products from the HyTex Company in the current year. Recall from Example 3.11 in Chapter 3 that HyTex is a direct marketer of stereo equipment, personal computers, and other electronic products. HyTex advertises entirely by mailing catalogs to its customers, and all of its orders are taken over the telephone. The company spends a great deal of money on its catalog mailings, and it wants to be sure that this is paying off in sales. For each customer there are data on the following variables:

- Age: age of the customer at the end of the current year
- Gender: coded as 1 for males, 0 for females

- OwnHome: coded as 1 if customer owns a home, 0 otherwise
- Married: coded as 1 if customer is currently married, 0 otherwise
- Close: coded as 1 if customer lives reasonably close to a shopping area that sells similar merchandise, 0 otherwise
- Salary: combined annual salary of customer and spouse (if any)
- Children: number of children living with customer
- PrevCust: coded as 1 if customer purchased from HyTex during the previous year, 0 otherwise
- PrevSpent: total amount of purchases made from HyTex during the previous year
- Catalogs: number of catalogs sent to the customer this year
- AmountSpent: total amount of purchases made from HyTex this year

Estimate and interpret a regression equation for AmountSpent based on all of these variables.

Objective   To see which potential explanatory variables are useful for explaining current year spending amounts at HyTex with multiple regression.

Solution

First, if you compare this data set to the data set in Chapter 3, you will see that we made the following modifications to simplify the regression analysis.

- Age is now a continuous variable, not a categorical variable with three categories.
- Before, we had a History variable with four categories, depending on how much, if any, the customer purchased from HyTex in the previous year. Now we use the dummy variable PrevCust to indicate whether the customer purchased anything from HyTex in the previous year. We also use the continuous variable PrevSpent for the amount purchased the previous year. Of course, if PrevCust equals 0, so does PrevSpent.

With this much data, 1000 observations, we can certainly afford to set aside part of the data set for validation, as discussed in Section 11.7. Although any split can be used, we decided to base the regression on the first 250 observations and use the other 750 for validation. Therefore, you should select only the range through row 253 when defining the StatTools data set.

We begin by entering all of the potential explanatory variables. Our goal is then to exclude variables that aren't necessary, based on their t-values and p-values. The multiple regression output with all explanatory variables appears in Figure 12.7. It indicates a fairly good fit. The R^2 value is 79.1% and s_e is about $424. When we consider that the actual amounts spent in the current year vary from a low of under $50 to a high of over $5500, with a median of about $950, a typical prediction error of around $424 is decent but not great.

From the p-value column, we see that there are three variables, Age, OwnHome, and Married, that have p-values well above 0.05. These are the obvious candidates for exclusion from the equation. We could rerun the equation with all three of these variables excluded, but it is a better practice to exclude one variable at a time. It is possible that when one of these variables is excluded, another one of them will become significant (the Right–Left foot phenomenon).

Actually, this did not happen. We first excluded the variable with the largest p-value, Age, and reran the regression. At this point, OwnHome and Married still had large p-values, and all other variables had small p-values. Next, we excluded Married, the variable with the largest remaining *p*-value, and reran the regression. Now, only OwnHome had a large *p*-value, so we ran one more regression with this variable excluded. The resulting output appears in Figure 12.8. As we see, the R^2 and s_e values of 79.0% and $423 are practically as good as they were with all variables included, and all of the *t*-values are now large (well above 2 in absolute value) and the *p*-values are all small (well below 0.05).

Figure 12.7 Regression Output with All Explanatory Variables Included

	A	B	C	D	E	F	G
7		Multiple	R-Square	Adjusted	StErr of		
8	**Summary**	R		R-Square	Estimate		
9		0.8893	0.7908	0.7820	423.8584		
10							
11		Degrees of	Sum of	Mean of	F-Ratio	p-Value	
12	**ANOVA Table**	Freedom	Squares	Squares			
13	Explained	10	162299315.6	16229931.56	90.3390	< 0.0001	
14	Unexplained	239	42937764.53	179655.9186			
15							
16		Coefficient	Standard	t-Value	p-Value	Confidence Interval 95%	
17	**Regression Table**		Error			Lower	Upper
18	Constant	257.3477	132.9876	1.9351	0.0542	-4.6299	519.3253
19	Age	0.1884	1.7626	0.1069	0.9150	-3.2839	3.6607
20	Gender	-124.0805	55.7627	-2.2252	0.0270	-233.9296	-14.2315
21	OwnHome	62.2752	60.7581	1.0250	0.3064	-57.4145	181.9649
22	Married	49.8426	70.1742	0.7103	0.4782	-88.3964	188.0816
23	Close	-282.7266	71.7762	-3.9390	0.0001	-424.1214	-141.3319
24	Salary	0.0143	0.0017	8.4930	< 0.0001	0.0110	0.0177
25	Children	-155.2858	31.5902	-4.9156	< 0.0001	-217.5166	-93.0550
26	PrevCust	-729.7212	92.3670	-7.9002	< 0.0001	-911.6787	-547.7638
27	PrevSpent	0.4725	0.0782	6.0447	< 0.0001	0.3185	0.6264
28	Catalogs	42.5806	4.3503	9.7880	< 0.0001	34.0108	51.1504

Figure 12.8 Regression Output with Insignificant Variables Excluded

	A	B	C	D	E	F	G
7		Multiple	R-Square	Adjusted	StErr of		
8	**Summary**	R		R-Square	Estimate		
9		0.8885	0.7895	0.7834	422.5169		
10							
11		Degrees of	Sum of	Mean of	F-Ratio	p-Value	
12	**ANOVA Table**	Freedom	Squares	Squares			
13	Explained	7	162035109	23147872.71	129.6650	< 0.0001	
14	Unexplained	242	43201971.22	178520.5422			
15							
16		Coefficient	Standard	t-Value	p-Value	Confidence Interval 95%	
17	**Regression Table**		Error			Lower	Upper
18	Constant	269.8642	108.5596	2.4859	0.0136	56.0219	483.7066
19	Gender	-130.3226	55.2112	-2.3604	0.0190	-239.0784	-21.5668
20	Close	-287.5537	70.8671	-4.0576	< 0.0001	-427.1488	-147.9586
21	Salary	0.0154	0.0014	11.1924	< 0.0001	0.0127	0.0181
22	Children	-158.4511	31.3378	-5.0562	< 0.0001	-220.1809	-96.7214
23	PrevCust	-724.0651	91.5870	-7.9058	< 0.0001	-904.4746	-543.6557
24	PrevSpent	0.4699	0.0777	6.0452	< 0.0001	0.3168	0.6230
25	Catalogs	42.6638	4.3204	9.8751	< 0.0001	34.1535	51.1741

We can interpret this final regression equation as follows:

Interpretation of Regression Equation

- The coefficient of Gender implies that an average male customer spent about $130 less than an average female customer, all other variables being equal. Similarly, an average customer living close to stores with this type of merchandise spent about $288 less than an average customer living far from such stores.

- The coefficient of Salary implies that, on average, about 1.5 cents of every extra salary dollar was spent on HyTex merchandise.

- The coefficient of Children implies that about $158 *less* was spent for every extra child living at home.

- The PrevCust and PrevSpent terms are somewhat more difficult to interpret. First, both of these terms are 0 for customers who didn't purchase from HyTex in the previous year. For those who did, the terms become $-724 + 0.47$PrevSpent. The coefficient 0.47 implies that each extra dollar spent the previous year can be expected to contribute an extra 47 cents in the current year. The -724 literally means that if we compare a customer who didn't purchase from HyTex last year to another customer who purchased only a tiny amount, the latter would be expected to spend about $724 less than the former this year. However, none of the latter customers were in the data set. A look at the data shows that of all customers who purchased from HyTex last year, almost all spent at least $100 and most spent considerably more. In fact, the median amount spent by these customers last year was about $900 (the median of all positive values for the PrevSpent variable). If we substitute this median value into the expression $-724 + 0.47$PrevSpent, we obtain -301. Therefore, this "median" spender from last year can be expected to spend about $301 less this year than the previous year nonspender.

- The coefficient of Catalogs implies that each extra catalog can be expected to generate about $43 in extra spending.

We conclude this example with a couple of cautionary notes. First, when we validate this final regression equation on the other 750 customers, using the procedure from Section 11.7, we find R^2 and s_e values of 71.8% and $522. Actually, these aren't bad. They show only a little deterioration from the values based on the original 250 customers. Second, we haven't tried all possibilities yet. We haven't tried nonlinear or interaction variables, nor have we looked at different coding schemes (such as treating Catalogs as a categorical variable and using dummy variables to represent it); we haven't checked for nonconstant error variance (remember that Figure 12.1 is based on this data set) or looked at the potential effects of outliers. ■

PROBLEMS

Level A

18. David Savageau and Geoffrey Loftus, the authors of *Places Rated Almanac*, have ranked metropolitan areas in the United States with consideration of the following aspects of life in each area: cost of living, transportation, jobs, education, climate, crime, arts, health, and recreation. The data are in the file **P02_55.xlsx**. Use multiple regression analysis to explore the relationship between the metropolitan areas' overall score and the set of potential explanatory variables. Which explanatory variables should be included in a final version of this regression model? Justify your choices.

19. A manager of boiler drums wants to use regression analysis to predict the number of worker-hours needed to erect the drums in future projects. Consequently, data for 36 randomly selected boilers were collected.

In addition to worker-hours (Y), the variables measured include boiler capacity, boiler design pressure, boiler type, and drum type. All of these measurements are listed in the file **P11_27.xlsx**. Estimate an appropriate multiple regression model to predict the number of worker-hours needed to erect given boiler drums using all available explanatory variables. Which explanatory variables should be included in a final version of this regression model? Justify your choices.

20. An economic development researcher wants to understand the relationship between the size of the monthly home mortgage or rent payment for households in a particular middle-class neighborhood and the following set of household variables: family size, approximate location of the household within the neighborhood, an indication of whether those surveyed own or rent their home, gross annual income of the first household wage earner, gross annual income of the second household wage earner (if applicable), average monthly expenditure on utilities, and the total indebtedness (excluding the value of a home mortgage) of the household. Observations on each of these variables for a large sample of households are recorded in the file **P02_06.xlsx**.
   a. In an effort to explain the variation in the size of the monthly home mortgage or rent payment, estimate a multiple regression model that includes all of the potential household explanatory variables.
   b. Using your regression output, determine which of the explanatory variables should be *excluded* from the regression equation. Explain why you decide to remove each such variable.

21. Managers at Beta Technologies, Inc., have collected current annual salary figures and potentially related

data for a random sample of 52 of the company's full-time employees. The data are in the file **P02_01.xlsx**. These data include each selected employee's gender, age, number of years of relevant work experience prior to employment at Beta, the number of years of employment at Beta, and the number of years of post-secondary education.
   a. Estimate a multiple regression model to explain the variation in employee salaries at Beta Technologies using all of the potential explanatory variables.
   b. Using your regression output, determine which of the explanatory variables should be *excluded* from the regression equation. Provide reasoning for your decision to remove each such variable.

22. Stock market analysts are continually looking for reliable predictors of stock prices. Consider the problem of modeling the price per share of electric utility stocks (Y). Two variables thought to influence such a stock price are return on average equity (X_1) and annual dividend rate (X_2). The stock price, returns on equity, and dividend rates on a randomly selected day for 16 electric utility stocks are provided in the file **P11_19.xlsx**.
   a. Estimate a multiple regression model using the given data. Include linear terms as well as an interaction term involving the return on average equity (X_1) and annual dividend rate (X_2).
   b. Which of the three explanatory variables (X_1, X_2, and X_1X_2) should be included in a final version of this regression model? Explain. Does your conclusion make sense in light of your knowledge of corporate finance?

12.6 STEPWISE REGRESSION[4]

Multiple regression represents an improvement over simple regression because it allows any number of explanatory variables to be included in the analysis. Sometimes, however, the large number of potential explanatory variables makes it difficult to know which variables to include. Many statistical packages provide some assistance by including automatic equation-building options. These options estimate a series of regression equations by successively adding (or deleting) variables according to prescribed rules. Generically, the methods are referred to as **stepwise regression**.

Before discussing how stepwise procedures work, consider a naive approach to the problem. We have already looked at correlation tables for indications of linear relationships. Why not simply include all explanatory variables that have large correlations with the dependent variable? There are two reasons for not doing this. First, although a variable is highly correlated with the dependent variable, it might also be highly correlated with other explanatory variables. Therefore, this variable might not be needed in the equation once the other explanatory variables have been included.

Second, even if a variable's correlation with the dependent variable is small, its contribution when it is included with a number of other explanatory variables can be greater

[4]This section can be omitted without any loss of continuity.

than anticipated. Essentially, this variable can have something unique to say about the dependent variable that none of the other variables provides, and this fact might not be apparent from the correlation table.

For these reasons it is sometimes useful to let the computer discover the best combination of variables by means of a stepwise procedure. There are a number of procedures for building equations in a stepwise manner, but they all share a basic idea. Suppose that we have an existing regression equation and we want to add another variable to this equation from a set of variables not yet included. At this point, the variables already in the equation have explained a certain percentage of the variation of the dependent variable. The residuals represent the part still unexplained. Therefore, in choosing the next variable to enter the equation, we pick the one that is most highly correlated with the current residuals. If none of the remaining variables is highly correlated with the residuals, we might decide to quit. This is the essence of stepwise regression. However, besides adding variables to the equation, a stepwise procedure might delete a variable. This is sometimes reasonable because a variable entered early in the procedure might no longer be needed, given the presence of other variables that have entered since.

Stepwise regression (and its variations) can be helpful in discovering a useful regression model, but it should not be used mindlessly.

Many statistical packages have three types of equation-building procedures: *forward, backward,* and *stepwise.* A **forward** procedure begins with no explanatory variables in the equation and successively adds one at a time until no remaining variables make a significant contribution. A **backward** procedure begins with all potential explanatory variables in the equation and deletes them one at a time until further deletion would do more harm than good. Finally, a true **stepwise** procedure is much like a forward procedure, except that it also considers possible deletions along the way. All of these procedures have the same basic objective—namely, to find an equation with a small s_e and a large R^2 (or adjusted R^2). There is no guarantee that they will all produce exactly the same final equation, but in most cases their final results are very similar. The important thing to realize is that the equations estimated along the way, including the final equation, are estimated exactly as before—by least squares. Therefore, none of these procedures produces any new results. They merely take the burden off the user of having to decide ahead of time which variables to include in the equation.

The StatTools add-in implements each of the forward, backward, and stepwise procedures. To use them, we select the dependent variable and a set of *potential* explanatory variables. Then we specify the criterion for adding and/or deleting variables from the equation. This can be done in two ways, with an F-value or a p-value. We suggest using p-values because they are easier to understand, but either method is easy to use. In the p-value method, we select a p-value such as 0.05. If the regression coefficient for a potential entering variable would have a p-value less than 0.05 (if it were entered), then it is a candidate for entering (if the forward or stepwise procedure is used). The procedure selects the variable with the *smallest* p-value as the next entering variable. Similarly, if any currently included variable has a p-value greater than some value such as 0.05, then (with the stepwise and backward procedures) it is a candidate for leaving the equation. The methods stop when there are no candidates (according to their p-values) for entering or leaving the current equation.

The following continuation of the HyTex mail-order example illustrates these stepwise procedures.

EXAMPLE **12.3 EXPLAINING SPENDING AMOUNTS AT HYTEX (CONTINUED)**

The analysis of the HyTex mail-order data (for the first 250 customers in the data set) resulted in a regression equation that included all potential explanatory variables except for Age, OwnHome, and Married. We excluded these because their t-values were large and their *p*-values were small (less than 0.05). Do forward, backward, and stepwise procedures produce the same regression equation for the amount spent in the current year?

Objective To use StatTools's Stepwise Regression procedure to analyze the HyTex data.

Solution

Each of these options is found in the StatTools Regression dialog box. It is just a matter of choosing the appropriate option from the Regression Type dropdown list. (See Figure 12.9.) In each, we specify AmountSpent as the dependent variable and select all of the other variables (besides Customer) as *potential* explanatory variables. Once you choose one of the stepwise types, the dialog box changes, as shown in Figure 12.10, to include a Parameters section and enables the Include Detailed Step Information option. We suggest the choices in Figure 12.10 for stepwise regression.

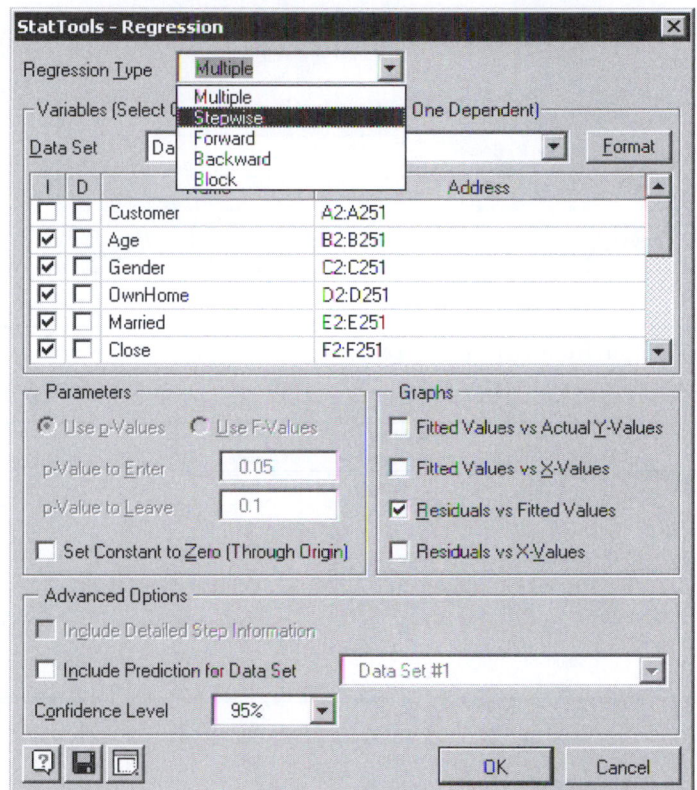

It turns out that each procedure produces a *final* equation that is exactly the same as we obtained previously, with all variables except Age, OwnHome, and Married included. This often happens, but not always. The stepwise and forward procedures add the variables in the order Salary, Catalogs, Children, Close, PrevCust, PrevSpent, and Gender. The backward procedure, which starts with *all* variables in the equation, eliminates variables in the order Age, Married, and OwnHome. A sample of the stepwise output appears in Figure 12.11. At the bottom of the output, we see which variable enters or exits the equation. We also see the usual regression output for the final equation. Again, however, this final equation's output is *exactly* the same as if we used multiple regression with these particular variables.

Figure 12.10

Dialog Box for
Stepwise Regression

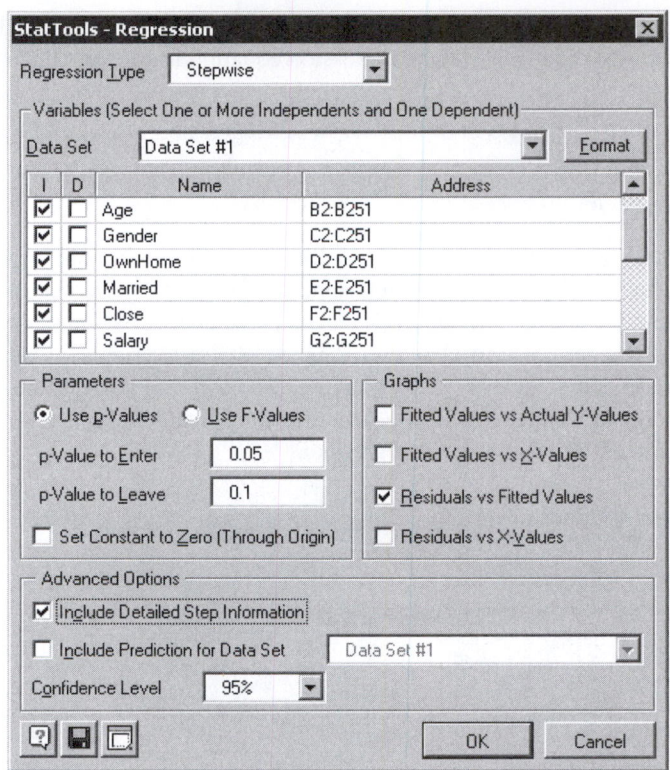

Figure 12.11   Regression Output from Stepwise Procedure

	A	B	C	D	E	F	G
7		Multiple	R-Square	Adjusted	StErr of		
8	*Summary*	R		R-Square	Estimate		
9		0.8885	0.7895	0.7834	422.5169		
10							
11		Degrees of	Sum of	Mean of	F-Ratio	p-Value	
12	*ANOVA Table*	Freedom	Squares	Squares			
13	Explained	7	162035109	23147872.71	129.6650	< 0.0001	
14	Unexplained	242	43201971.22	178520.5422			
15							
16		Coefficient	Standard	t-Value	p-Value	Confidence Interval 95%	
17	*Regression Table*		Error			Lower	Upper
18	Constant	269.8642	108.5596	2.4859	0.0136	56.0219	483.7066
19	Salary	0.0154	0.0014	11.1924	< 0.0001	0.0127	0.0181
20	Catalogs	42.6638	4.3204	9.8751	< 0.0001	34.1535	51.1741
21	Children	-158.4511	31.3378	-5.0562	< 0.0001	-220.1809	-96.7214
22	Close	-287.5537	70.8671	-4.0576	< 0.0001	-427.1488	-147.9586
23	PrevCust	-724.0651	91.5870	-7.9058	< 0.0001	-904.4746	-543.6557
24	PrevSpent	0.4699	0.0777	6.0452	< 0.0001	0.3168	0.6230
25	Gender	-130.3226	55.2112	-2.3604	0.0190	-239.0784	-21.5668
26							
27		Multiple	R-Square	Adjusted	StErr of	Enter or	
28	*Step Information*	R		R-Square	Estimate	Exit	
29	Salary	0.6624	0.4387	0.4365	681.5285	Enter	
30	Catalogs	0.7718	0.5957	0.5924	579.6088	Enter	
31	Children	0.8256	0.6815	0.6777	515.4461	Enter	
32	Close	0.8540	0.7293	0.7249	476.2003	Enter	
33	PrevCust	0.8670	0.7516	0.7465	457.0666	Enter	
34	PrevSpent	0.8858	0.7847	0.7793	426.4729	Enter	
35	Gender	0.8885	0.7895	0.7834	422.5169	Enter	

Stepwise regression or any of its variations can be very useful for narrowing down the set of all possible explanatory variables to a set that is useful for explaining a dependent variable. However, these procedures should not be used as a substitute for thoughtful analysis. With the availability of such procedures in statistical software packages, there is sometimes a tendency to turn the analysis over to the computer and accept its output. A good analyst does not just collect as much data as possible, throw it into a computer package, and blindly report the results. There should always be some rationale, whether it be based on economic theory, business experience, or common sense, for the variables that we use to explain a given dependent variable. A thoughtless use of stepwise regression can sometimes capitalize on chance to obtain an equation with a reasonably large R^2 but no useful or practical interpretation.

PROBLEMS

Level A

23. Suppose that you are interested in predicting the price of a laptop computer based on its various features. The file **P11_35.xlsx** contains observations on the sales price and a number of potentially relevant variables for a randomly chosen sample of laptop computers. Employ stepwise regression to decide which explanatory variables to include in a regression equation. Use the p-value method with a cutoff value of 0.05 for entering and leaving. Summarize your findings.

24. Does the rate of violent crime acts vary across different regions of the United States? Using the data in **P11_34.xlsx** and a stepwise regression procedure, develop an appropriate regression model to explain the variation in acts of violent crime across the United States. Use the p-value method with a cutoff value of 0.05 for entering and leaving. Summarize your results.

25. In a study of housing demand, a county assessor is interested in developing a regression model to estimate the selling price of residential properties within her jurisdiction. She randomly selects 15 houses and records the selling price in addition to the following values: the size of the house (in hundreds of square feet), the total number of rooms in the house, the age of the house, and an indication of whether the house has an attached garage. These data are stored in the file **P11_26.xlsx**.
   a. Use stepwise regression to decide which explanatory variables should be included in the assessor's statistical model. Use the p-value method with a cutoff value of 0.05 for entering and leaving. Summarize your findings.
   b. How do your results in part **a** change when the critical p-value for entering and leaving is increased to 0.10? Explain any differences between the

regression equation obtained here and the one found in part **a**.

26. Continuing Problem 2, employ stepwise regression to evaluate your conclusions regarding the specification of a regression model to predict the sales of deep-dish pizza by the Original Italian Pizza restaurant chain. Sample observations on all potentially relevant variables are provided in **P11_04.xlsx**. Use the p-value method with a cutoff value of 0.05 for entering and leaving. Compare your conclusions in Problem 2 with those derived from a stepwise regression procedure in completing this problem.

27. Continuing Problem 3, employ stepwise regression to evaluate your conclusions regarding the specification of a regression model to explain the variation in values of the *ACCRA Cost of Living Index*. Data on potentially relevant expenditure components (i.e., explanatory variables) are provided in the file **P02_19.xlsx**. Use the p-value method with a cutoff value of 0.05 for entering and leaving. Compare your conclusions in Problem 3 with those derived from a stepwise regression procedure in completing this problem.

Level B

28. What factors are truly useful in predicting a chief executive officer's annual base salary? Explore this question by employing a stepwise regression procedure on potentially relevant variables for which survey data have been collected and recorded in the file **P02_13.xlsx**. Assess only those variables that make economic sense in predicting CEO base salaries. Also, consider incorporating a set of categorical variables to account for any potential variation in the base salaries that is explained by the CEO's company type. Use the p-value method with a cutoff value of 0.10 for entering and leaving. Summarize your findings.

12.7 THE PARTIAL F TEST[5]

There are many situations where a set of explanatory variables form a logical group. It is then common to include all of the variables in the equation or exclude all of them. An example of this is when one of the explanatory variables is categorical with more than two categories. In this case we model it by including dummy variables—one less than the number of categories. If we decide that the categorical variable is worth including, we might want to keep all of the dummies. Otherwise, we might exclude all of them. We look at an example of this type subsequently.

For now, consider the following general situation. We have already estimated an equation that includes the variables X_1 through X_j, and we are proposing to estimate a larger equation that includes X_{j+1} through X_k in addition to the variables X_1 through X_j. That is, the larger equation includes all of the variables from the smaller equation, but it also includes $k - j$ extra variables. These extra variables are the ones that form a group. We assume that it makes logical sense to include all of them or none of them.

The complete equation always contains all of the explanatory variables in the reduced equation, plus some more. In other words, the reduced equation is a subset of the complete equation.

In this section we describe a test to determine whether the extra variables provide enough *extra* explanatory power as a group to warrant their inclusion in the equation. The test is called the partial F test. The original equation is called the **reduced** equation, and the larger equation is called the **complete** equation. In simple terms, the partial F test tests whether the complete equation is significantly better than the reduced equation.[6]

The test itself is intuitive. We use the output from the ANOVA tables of the reduced and complete equations to form an F-ratio. This ratio measures how much the sum of squared residuals, *SSE, decreases* by including the extra variables in the equation. It *must* decrease by some amount because the sum of squared residuals cannot increase when extra variables are added to an equation. But if it does not decrease sufficiently, then the extra variables might not explain enough to warrant their inclusion in the equation, and we should probably exclude them. The F-ratio measures this. If it is sufficiently large, then we can conclude that the extra variables are worth including; otherwise, we can safely exclude them.

To state the test formally, we first state the relevant hypotheses. Let β_{j+1} through β_k be the coefficients of the extra variables in the complete equation. Then the null hypothesis is that these extra variables have no effect on the dependent variable, that is, $H_0 : \beta_{j+1} = \cdots = \beta_k = 0$. The alternative is that at least one of the extra variables has an effect on the dependent variable, so that at least one of these β's is not 0. The hypotheses are summarized in the box.

Hypotheses for the Partial F Test

The null hypothesis is that the coefficients of all the extra explanatory variables in the complete equation are 0. The alternative is that at least one of these coefficients is not 0.

To run the test, we estimate both the reduced and complete equations and look at the associated ANOVA tables. Let SSE_R and SSE_C be the sums of squared errors from the reduced and complete equations, respectively. Also, let MSE_C be the mean square error for the complete equation. All of these quantities appear in the ANOVA tables. Next, we form the F-ratio in equation (12.4).

Test Statistic for Partial F Test

$$F\text{-ratio} = \frac{(SSE_R - SSE_C)/(k - j)}{MSE_C} \qquad (12.4)$$

---

[5]This section is somewhat more advanced and can be omitted without any loss of continuity.
[6]StatTools does not run the partial F test, but it provides all of the ingredients.

Note that the numerator includes the reduction in sum of squared errors discussed previously. If the null hypothesis is true, then this F-ratio has an F distribution with $k - j$ and $n - k - 1$ degrees of freedom. If it is sufficiently large, we reject H_0. As usual, the best way to run the test is to find the p-value corresponding to this F-ratio. This is the probability beyond the calculated F-ratio in the F distribution with $k - j$ and $n - k - 1$ degrees of freedom. In words, we reject the hypothesis that the extra variables have no explanatory power if this p-value is sufficiently small, less than 0.05, say.

This F-ratio and corresponding p-value are *not* part of the StatTools regression output. However, they are fairly easy to obtain. We run two regressions, one for the reduced equation and one for the complete equation, and we use the appropriate values from their ANOVA tables to calculate the F-ratio in equation (12.4). Then we use Excel's FDIST function in the form FDIST(F-ratio,$k - j$,$n - k - 1$) to calculate the corresponding p-value. The procedure is illustrated in the following example. It uses the bank discrimination data from Example 11.3 of the previous chapter.

EXAMPLE	12.4 POSSIBLE GENDER DISCRIMINATION IN SALARY AT FIFTH NATIONAL BANK OF SPRINGFIELD

Recall from Example 11.3 that Fifth National Bank has 208 employees. The data for these employees are stored in the file **Bank Salaries.xlsx**. In the previous chapter we ran several regressions for Salary to see whether there is convincing evidence of salary discrimination against females. We will continue this analysis here. First, we regress Salary versus the Female dummy, YrsExper, and the interaction between Female and YrsExper, Interaction(YrsExper,Female). This is the reduced equation. Then we'll see whether the JobGrade dummies JobGrade=2 to JobGrade=6 add anything significant to the reduced equation. If so, we then see whether the interactions between the Female dummy and the JobGrade dummies, Interaction(Female,JobGrade=2) to Interaction(Female,JobGrade=6), add anything significant to what we already have. If so, we finally see whether the education dummies EducLev=2 to EducLev=5 add anything significant to what we already have.

Objective   To use several partial F tests to see whether various groups of explanatory variables should be included in a regression equation for salary, given that other variables are already in the equation.

Solution

First, note that we created all of the dummies and interaction variables with StatTools's Data Utilities procedures. These could be entered directly with Excel functions, but StatTools makes the process much quicker and easier. Also, note that we have used three sets of dummies, for gender, job grade, and education level. When we use these in a regression equation, the dummy for one category of each should always be excluded; it is the reference category. The reference categories we have used are "male," job grade 1, and education level 1.

The output for the "smallest" equation, using Female, YrsExper, and Interaction(YrsExper,Female) as explanatory variables, appears in Figure 12.12. (We put this output in a sheet called Regression1.) We're off to a good start. These three variables already explain 63.9% of the variation in Salary.

Figure 12.12   Reduced Equation for Bank Example

	A	B	C	D	E	F	G
7		Multiple	R-Square	Adjusted	StErr of		
8	*Summary*	R		R-Square	Estimate		
9		0.7991	0.6386	0.6333	6816.298		
10							
11		Degrees of	Sum of	Mean of	F-Ratio	p-Value	
12	*ANOVA Table*	Freedom	Squares	Squares			
13	Explained	3	16748875071	5582958357	120.1620	< 0.0001	
14	Unexplained	204	9478232160	46461922.35			
15							
16		Coefficient	Standard	t-Value	p-Value	Confidence Interval 95%	
17	*Regression Table*		Error			Lower	Upper
18	Constant	30430.028	1216.574	25.0129	< 0.0001	28031.356	32828.700
19	YrsExper	1527.762	90.460	16.8887	< 0.0001	1349.405	1706.119
20	Female	4098.252	1665.842	2.4602	0.0147	813.776	7382.727
21	Interaction(YrsExper,Female)	-1247.798	136.676	-9.1296	< 0.0001	-1517.277	-978.320

The output for the next equation, which adds the explanatory variables JobGrade=2 to JobGrade=6, appears in Figure 12.13. (We put this output in a sheet called Regression2.) This equation appears to be much better. For example, R^2 has increased to 81.1%. We check whether it is *significantly* better with the partial F test in rows 28 through 32. (This part of the output is not given by StatTools; we have to enter it manually.) The degrees of freedom in cell B29 is 5, the number of *extra* variables. The degrees of freedom in cell B30 is the same as the value in cell B14, the degrees of freedom for *SSE*. Then we calculate the F-ratio in cell B31 with the formula

=((Regression1!C14-Regression2!C14)/Regression2!B29)/Regression2!D14

Figure 12.13   Equation with Job Dummies Added

	A	B	C	D	E	F	G
7		Multiple	R-Square	Adjusted	StErr of		
8	*Summary*	R		R-Square	Estimate		
9		0.9005	0.8109	0.8033	4991.64		
10							
11		Degrees of	Sum of	Mean of	F-Ratio	p-Value	
12	*ANOVA Table*	Freedom	Squares	Squares			
13	Explained	8	21268738998	2658592375	106.7004	< 0.0001	
14	Unexplained	199	4958368233	24916423.28			
15							
16		Coefficient	Standard	t-Value	p-Value	Confidence Interval 95%	
17	*Regression Table*		Error			Lower	Upper
18	Constant	26104.22	1105.44	23.6143	< 0.0001	23924.34	28284.11
19	YrsExper	1070.88	102.01	10.4975	< 0.0001	869.72	1272.05
20	Female	6063.33	1266.32	4.7881	< 0.0001	3566.20	8560.46
21	JobGrade = 2	2596.49	1010.12	2.5705	0.0109	604.58	4588.41
22	JobGrade = 3	6221.39	998.18	6.2328	< 0.0001	4253.03	8189.76
23	JobGrade = 4	11071.95	1172.59	9.4423	< 0.0001	8759.66	13384.25
24	JobGrade = 5	14946.58	1340.25	11.1521	< 0.0001	12303.66	17589.49
25	JobGrade = 6	17097.37	2390.67	7.1517	< 0.0001	12383.07	21811.67
26	Interaction(YrsExper,Female)	-1021.05	118.73	-8.6001	< 0.0001	-1255.17	-786.93
27							
28	Partial F test for including JobGrade dummies						
29	df numerator	5					
30	df denominator	199					
31	F ratio	36.2802					
32	p-value	0.0000					

where Regression1!C14 refers to *SSE* for the reduced equation from the Regression1 sheet. Finally, we calculate the corresponding *p*-value in cell B32 with the formula

=FDIST(B31,B29,B30)

It is practically 0, so there is no doubt that the job grade dummies add significantly to the explanatory power of the equation.

Do the interactions between the Female dummy and the job dummies add anything more? We again use the partial *F* test, but now the previous *complete* equation becomes the new *reduced* equation, and the equation that includes the new interaction terms becomes the new complete equation. The output for this new complete equation appears in Figure 12.14. (We put this output in a sheet called Regression3.) We perform the partial *F* test in rows 34 through 37 exactly as before. For example, the formula for the *F*-ratio in cell B36 is

=((Regression2!C14-Regression3!C14)/Regression3!B34)/Regression3!D14

Figure 12.14 Regression Output with Interaction Terms Added

	A	B	C	D	E	F	G
7		Multiple	R-Square	Adjusted	StErr of		
8	Summary	R		R-Square	Estimate		
9		0.9163	0.8396	0.8289	4656.41		
10							
11		Degrees of	Sum of	Mean of	F-Ratio	p-Value	
12	ANOVA Table	Freedom	Squares	Squares			
13	Explained	13	22020761739	1693904749	78.1242	< 0.0001	
14	Unexplained	194	4206345492	21682193.26			
15							
16			Standard			Confidence Interval 95%	
17	Regression Table	Coefficient	Error	t-Value	p-Value	Lower	Upper
18	Constant	26515.48	1432.40	18.5112	< 0.0001	23690.40	29340.56
19	YrsExper	960.78	104.19	9.2214	< 0.0001	755.28	1166.27
20	Female	4724.46	1735.36	2.7225	0.0071	1301.88	8147.05
21	JobGrade = 2	3341.00	1864.19	1.7922	0.0747	-335.68	7017.67
22	JobGrade = 3	7871.96	2214.94	3.5540	0.0005	3503.49	12240.42
23	JobGrade = 4	10691.89	1956.67	5.4643	< 0.0001	6832.81	14550.97
24	JobGrade = 5	13146.37	1993.14	6.5958	< 0.0001	9215.36	17077.38
25	JobGrade = 6	20979.45	2767.63	7.5803	< 0.0001	15520.95	26437.94
26	Interaction(YrsExper,Female)	-805.99	130.32	-6.1845	< 0.0001	-1063.02	-548.95
27	Interaction(Female,JobGrade = 2)	-943.40	2164.03	-0.4359	0.6634	-5211.44	3324.63
28	Interaction(Female,JobGrade = 3)	-1935.05	2441.44	-0.7926	0.4290	-6750.22	2880.13
29	Interaction(Female,JobGrade = 4)	433.82	2374.97	0.1827	0.8553	-4250.25	5117.90
30	Interaction(Female,JobGrade = 5)	4873.42	2623.16	1.8578	0.0647	-300.16	10047.00
31	Interaction(Female,JobGrade = 6)	-27327.42	5770.02	-4.7361	< 0.0001	-38707.44	-15947.40
32							
33	Partial F test for including Female, JobGrade interactions						
34	df numerator	5					
35	df denominator	194					
36	F ratio	6.9368					
37	p-value	0.0000					

Note how the SSE_R term in equation (12.4) now comes from the Regression2 sheet because this sheet contains the current *reduced* equation. As we see, the terms "reduced" and "complete" are relative. What is complete in one stage becomes reduced in the next stage. In any case, the *p*-value in cell B37 is again extremely small, so there is no doubt that the interaction terms add significantly to what we already had (even though R^2 has increased from 81.1% to only 84.0%).

Finally, we add the education dummies. The resulting output is shown in Figure 12.15. (We put this output in a sheet called Regression4.) Again, we see how the terms reduced and complete are relative. This output now corresponds to the complete equation, and the previous output corresponds to the reduced equation. The formula in cell B40 for the F-ratio is now

=((Regression3!C14-Regression4!C14)/Regression4!B38)/Regression4!D14

Figure 12.15 Regression Output with Education Dummies Added

	A	B	C	D	E	F	G
7		Multiple		Adjusted	StErr of		
8	*Summary*	R	R-Square	R-Square	Estimate		
9		0.9205	0.8473	0.8336	4591.42		
10							
11		Degrees of	Sum of	Mean of			
12	*ANOVA Table*	Freedom	Squares	Squares	F-Ratio	p-Value	
13	Explained	17	22221688817	1307158166	62.0060	< 0.0001	
14	Unexplained	190	4005418414	21081149.55			
15							
16			Standard			Confidence Interval 95%	
17	*Regression Table*	Coefficient	Error	t-Value	p-Value	Lower	Upper
18	Constant	26020.52	1678.45	15.5027	< 0.0001	22709.73	29331.31
19	YrsExper	1002.35	104.54	9.5878	< 0.0001	796.14	1208.57
20	Female	4373.78	1724.69	2.5360	0.0120	971.78	7775.78
21	EducLev = 2	-664.78	1120.42	-0.5933	0.5537	-2874.84	1545.29
22	EducLev = 3	612.39	1082.33	0.5658	0.5722	-1522.54	2747.32
23	EducLev = 4	49.13	1961.56	0.0250	0.9800	-3820.11	3918.37
24	EducLev = 5	2808.15	1303.50	2.1543	0.0325	236.97	5379.34
25	JobGrade = 2	2697.31	1875.67	1.4380	0.1521	-1002.51	6397.12
26	JobGrade = 3	6862.57	2249.25	3.0511	0.0026	2425.87	11299.27
27	JobGrade = 4	8745.94	2054.71	4.2565	< 0.0001	4692.97	12798.91
28	JobGrade = 5	10579.59	2180.01	4.8530	< 0.0001	6279.45	14879.72
29	JobGrade = 6	18202.42	2940.22	6.1908	< 0.0001	12402.75	24002.09
30	Interaction(YrsExper,Female)	-760.83	129.87	-5.8584	< 0.0001	-1017.00	-504.66
31	Interaction(Female,JobGrade = 2)	-713.83	2148.35	-0.3323	0.7401	-4951.52	3523.86
32	Interaction(Female,JobGrade = 3)	-1752.87	2430.55	-0.7212	0.4717	-6547.19	3041.46
33	Interaction(Female,JobGrade = 4)	1023.20	2383.88	0.4292	0.6683	-3679.07	5725.47
34	Interaction(Female,JobGrade = 5)	5241.00	2623.06	1.9980	0.0471	66.93	10415.06
35	Interaction(Female,JobGrade = 6)	-29375.22	5753.89	-5.1053	< 0.0001	-40724.94	-18025.50
36							
37	Partial F test for including EducLev dummies						
38	df numerator	4					
39	df denominator	190					
40	F ratio	2.3828					
41	p-value	0.0530					

Its SSE_R value comes from the Regression3 sheet. Note that the increase in R^2 is from 84.0% to only 84.7%. Also, the p-value in cell B41 is not extremely small. According to the partial F test, it is not quite enough to qualify for statistical significance at the 5% level. Based on this evidence, there is not much to gain from including the education dummies in the equation, so we would probably elect to exclude them.

Note that the results could be very different if we had entered groups in a different order. For example, you might try entering the education dummies, and then interactions between these dummies and Female, *before* entering the job grade dummies. The results will be quite different. Again, remember that because of potential multicollinearity, what is significant can depend on what *other* variables are already in the equation.

Before leaving this example, we make several comments. First, the partial test is *the* formal test of significance for an extra set of variables. Many users look only at the R^2 and/or s_e values to check whether extra variables are doing a "good job." For example, they might cite that R^2 went from 81.1% to 84.0% or that s_e went from 4.992 to 4.656 as evidence that extra variables provide a "significantly" better fit. Although these are important indicators, they are not the basis for a *formal* hypothesis test.

Second, if the partial F test shows that a block of variables is significant, it does not imply that each variable in this block is significant. Some of these variables can have low t-values. Consider Figure 12.14, for example. We are able to conclude that the Female/Job interactions as a whole are significant. But three of these interactions, Interaction(Female, JobGrade=2) to Interaction(Female,JobGrade=4), are clearly not significant, and Interaction(Female,JobGrade=5) is borderline. In fact, Interaction(Female,JobGrade=6) is the only one that is clearly significant. Some analysts favor excluding the *individual* variables that aren't significant, whereas others favor keeping the whole block or excluding the whole block. We lean toward the latter but recognize that either approach is valid—and the results are nearly the same either way.

Third, producing all of these outputs and doing the partial F tests is a lot of work. Therefore, a "Block" option is included in StatTools to simplify the analysis. To run the analysis in this example in one step, select the Block option from the Regression Type dropdown list. The dialog box then changes, as shown in Figure 12.16. We select 4 blocks and then check which variables are in which blocks (B1 to B4). Block 1 has Female, YrsExper, and Interaction(YrsExper,Female), block 2 has the job grade dummies, block 3 has the interactions between Female and the job grade dummies, and block 4 has the education dummies. Finally, we specify 0.05 as the p-value to enter, which in this case indicates how significant the block *as a whole* must be to enter (for the partial F test).

Figure 12.16

Dialog Box for Block Regression Option

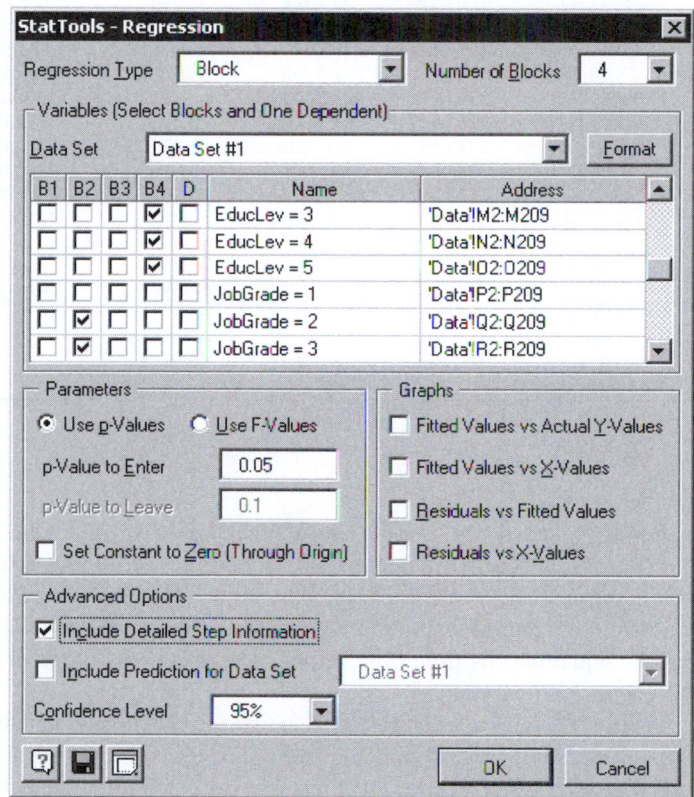

Once we have specified all of this, the regression calculations are done in stages. At each stage, the partial F test checks whether a block is significant. If so, the variables in this block enter and we progress to the next stage. If not, the process ends; neither this block nor any later blocks are entered.

The output from this procedure appears in Figure 12.17. The middle part of the output shows the final regression equation. The output in rows 35 through 38 indicates summary measures after successive blocks have entered. Note that the final block, the education dummies, is not in the final equation. This block did not pass the partial F test at the 5% level.

Figure 12.17 Block Regression Output

	A	B	C	D	E	F	G
7		Multiple	R-Square	Adjusted	StErr of		
8	Summary	R		R-Square	Estimate		
9		0.9163	0.8396	0.8289	4656.41		
10							
11		Degrees of	Sum of	Mean of	F-Ratio	p-Value	
12	ANOVA Table	Freedom	Squares	Squares			
13	Explained	13	22020761739	1693904749	76.5134	< 0.0001	
14	Unexplained	190	4206345492	22138660.48			
15							
16		Coefficient	Standard	t-Value	p-Value	Confidence Interval 95%	
17	Regression Table		Error			Lower	Upper
18	Constant	26515.48	1432.40	18.5112	< 0.0001	23690.03	29340.94
19	YrsExper	960.78	104.19	9.2214	< 0.0001	755.26	1166.29
20	Female	4724.46	1735.36	2.7225	0.0071	1301.42	8147.50
21	Interaction(YrsExper,Female)	-805.99	130.32	-6.1845	< 0.0001	-1063.05	-548.92
22	JobGrade = 2	3341.00	1864.19	1.7922	0.0747	-336.17	7018.16
23	JobGrade = 3	7871.96	2214.94	3.5540	0.0005	3502.92	12241.00
24	JobGrade = 4	10691.89	1956.67	5.4643	< 0.0001	6832.30	14551.48
25	JobGrade = 5	13146.37	1993.14	6.5958	< 0.0001	9214.84	17077.90
26	JobGrade = 6	20979.45	2767.63	7.5803	< 0.0001	15520.23	26438.67
27	Interaction(Female,JobGrade = 2)	-943.40	2164.03	-0.4359	0.6634	-5212.00	3325.20
28	Interaction(Female,JobGrade = 3)	-1935.05	2441.44	-0.7926	0.4290	-6750.86	2880.76
29	Interaction(Female,JobGrade = 4)	433.82	2374.97	0.1827	0.8553	-4250.87	5118.51
30	Interaction(Female,JobGrade = 5)	4873.42	2623.16	1.8578	0.0647	-300.85	10047.68
31	Interaction(Female,JobGrade = 6)	-27327.42	5770.02	-4.7361	< 0.0001	-38708.94	-15945.90
32							
33		Multiple	R-Square	Adjusted	StErr of	Entry	
34	Step Information	R		R-Square	Estimate	Number	
35	Block 1	0.7991	0.6386	0.6333	6816.298	1	
36	Block 2	0.9005	0.8109	0.8033	4991.635	2	
37	Block 3	0.9163	0.8396	0.8289	4656.414	3	
38	Block 4	Did Not Enter					

For comparison, we ran the block procedure a second time, changing the order of the blocks. Now block 2 includes the education level dummies, block 3 includes the job grade dummies, and block 4 includes the interactions between Female and the job grade dummies. The regression output appears in Figure 12.18. Note that *all* four blocks enter the equation this time. The implication is that the order of the blocks can make a difference.

Finally, we have concentrated on the partial F test and statistical significance in this example. We don't want you to lose sight, however, of the bigger picture. Once we have decided on a "final" regression equation, say, the one in Figure 12.14, we need to analyze its implications for the problem at hand. In this case the bank is interested in possible salary discrimination against females, so we should interpret this final equation in these terms. We do not go through this exercise again here—we did similar interpretations in the previous chapter. Our point is simply that you shouldn't get so immersed in the details of statistical significance that you lose sight of the original purpose of the analysis!

Figure 12.18 Block Regression Output with Order of Blocks Changed

	A	B	C	D	E	F	G
7		Multiple	R-Square	Adjusted	StErr of		
8	*Summary*	R		R-Square	Estimate		
9		0.9205	0.8473	0.8336	4591.42		
10							
11		Degrees of	Sum of	Mean of	F-Ratio	p-Value	
12	*ANOVA Table*	Freedom	Squares	Squares			
13	Explained	17	22221688817	1307158166	62.0060	< 0.0001	
14	Unexplained	190	4005418414	21081149.55			
15							
16		Coefficient	Standard	t-Value	p-Value	Confidence Interval 95%	
17	*Regression Table*		Error			Lower	Upper
18	Constant	26020.52	1678.45	15.503	< 0.0001	22709.73	29331.31
19	YrsExper	1002.35	104.54	9.588	< 0.0001	796.14	1208.57
20	Female	4373.78	1724.69	2.536	0.0120	971.78	7775.78
21	Interaction(YrsExper,Female)	-760.83	129.87	-5.858	< 0.0001	-1017.00	-504.66
22	EducLev = 2	-664.78	1120.42	-0.593	0.5537	-2874.84	1545.29
23	EducLev = 3	612.39	1082.33	0.566	0.5722	-1522.54	2747.32
24	EducLev = 4	49.13	1961.56	0.025	0.9800	-3820.11	3918.37
25	EducLev = 5	2808.15	1303.50	2.154	0.0325	236.97	5379.34
26	JobGrade = 2	2697.31	1875.67	1.438	0.1521	-1002.51	6397.12
27	JobGrade = 3	6862.57	2249.25	3.051	0.0026	2425.87	11299.27
28	JobGrade = 4	8745.94	2054.71	4.257	< 0.0001	4692.97	12798.91
29	JobGrade = 5	10579.59	2180.01	4.853	< 0.0001	6279.45	14879.72
30	JobGrade = 6	18202.42	2940.22	6.191	< 0.0001	12402.75	24002.09
31	Interaction(Female,JobGrade = 2)	-713.83	2148.35	-0.332	0.7401	-4951.52	3523.86
32	Interaction(Female,JobGrade = 3)	-1752.87	2430.55	-0.721	0.4717	-6547.19	3041.46
33	Interaction(Female,JobGrade = 4)	1023.20	2383.88	0.429	0.6683	-3679.07	5725.47
34	Interaction(Female,JobGrade = 5)	5241.00	2623.06	1.998	0.0471	66.93	10415.06
35	Interaction(Female,JobGrade = 6)	-29375.22	5753.89	-5.105	< 0.0001	-40724.94	-18025.50
36							
37		Multiple	R-Square	Adjusted	StErr of	Entry	
38	*Step Information*	R		R-Square	Estimate	Number	
39	Block 1	0.7991	0.6386	0.6333	6816.30	1	
40	Block 2	0.8552	0.7314	0.7220	5935.25	2	
41	Block 3	0.9028	0.8150	0.8036	4988.13	3	
42	Block 4	0.9205	0.8473	0.8336	4591.42	4	

PROBLEMS

Level A

29. A regional express delivery service company recently conducted a study to investigate the relationship between the cost of shipping a package (Y), the package weight (X_1), and the distance shipped (X_2). Twenty packages were randomly selected from among the large number received for shipment and a detailed analysis of the shipping cost was conducted for each package. These sample observations are given in the file **P11_24.xlsx**.

  a. Estimate a multiple regression model involving the two given explanatory variables. Using the ANOVA table, perform and interpret the result of an F test. Use a 5% significance level in making the statistical decision in this case.

  b. Is it worthwhile to add the terms X_1^2 and X_2^2 to the regression equation of part **a**? Base your decision here on a partial F test. Once again, employ a 5% significance level in performing this test.

  c. Is it worthwhile to add the term $X_1 X_2$ to the most appropriate reduced equation as determined in part **b**? Again, perform a partial F test with a 5% significance level.

  d. Based on the previous findings, what regression equation should this company use in predicting the cost of shipping a package? Defend your recommendation.

30. Suppose you are interested in predicting the price of a laptop computer based on its features. The file **P11_35.xlsx** contains observations on the sales price and a number of potentially relevant variables for a randomly chosen sample of laptop computers.

  a. Estimate a multiple regression model that predicts the price of a laptop computer using the following quantitative variables: the speed of the computer's CPU, the length of time the computer's battery maintains its charge, and the size of the computer's RAM. Assess this set of explanatory variables with an F test, and report a p-value.

b. Do explanatory variables that model the computer's chip type and monitor type contribute significantly to the prediction of the laptop's sales price? Let the equation estimated in part **a** serve as the reduced equation in a partial F test. Employ a 5% significance level in conducting the appropriate hypothesis test in this case.

c. Do explanatory variables that model the computer's pointing device and the availability of a help line for buyers contribute significantly to the prediction of the laptop's sales price? Let the most appropriate equation found from the analysis in part **b** serve as the reduced equation in a partial F test. Again, employ a 5% significance level in conducting the appropriate hypothesis test in this case.

31. Many companies manufacture products that are at least partially produced using chemicals (for example, paint, gasoline, and steel). In many cases, the quality of the finished product is a function of the temperature and pressure at which the chemical reactions take place. Suppose that a particular manufacturer wants to model the quality (Y) of a product as a function of the temperature (X_1) and the pressure (X_2) at which it is produced. The file **P11_39.xlsx** contains data obtained from a designed experiment involving these variables. Note that the assigned quality score can range from a minimum of 0 to a maximum of 100 for each manufactured product.

a. Estimate a multiple regression model that includes the two given explanatory variables. Assess this set of explanatory variables with an F test, and report a p-value.

b. Conduct a partial F test to decide whether it is worthwhile to add second-order terms (X_1^2, X_2^2, and X_1X_2) to the multiple regression equation estimated in part **a**. Employ a 5% significance level in conducting this hypothesis test.

c. Which regression equation is the most appropriate one for modeling the quality of the given product? Bear in mind that a good statistical model is usually parsimonious.

Level B

32. Continuing Problem 6, we'll refer to the original multiple regression model (i.e., the one that includes the age

of the auctioned item and the number of bidders as explanatory variables) as the *reduced* equation. Suppose now that the antique collector believes that the *rate of increase* of the auction price with the age of the item will be driven upward by a large number of bidders.

a. Revise the multiple regression model developed previously to model this additional feature of the problem. Estimate this larger regression equation, which we call the *complete* equation, using the sample data in the file **P11_18.xlsx**.

b. Perform a partial F test to check whether the complete equation is significantly better than the reduced equation. Use a 5% level of significance.

33. An economic development researcher wants to understand the relationship between the size of the monthly home mortgage or rent payment for households in a particular middle-class neighborhood and the following set of household variables: family size, approximate location of the household within the neighborhood, an indication of whether those surveyed owned or rented their home, gross annual income of the first household wage earner, gross annual income of the second household wage earner (if applicable), average monthly expenditure on utilities, and the total indebtedness (excluding the value of a home mortgage) of the household. Observations on these variables for a large sample of households are recorded in the file **P02_06.xlsx**.

a. To explain the variation in the size of the monthly home mortgage or rent payment, formulate a multiple regression model that includes all of the *quantitative* household variables in the aforementioned set. Estimate this model using the given sample data. Perform an F test of the model's overall significance, and report a p-value.

b. Determine whether the *qualitative* (i.e., categorical) variable that models the location of the household within the neighborhood adds significantly to explaining the variation in the size of the monthly home mortgage or rent payment. Use a 5% significance level in conducting this hypothesis test.

c. Determine whether it is worthwhile to add a variable that models whether the home is owned or rented to the most appropriate regression equation from part **b**. Again, use a 5% significance level in conducting this hypothesis test.

12.8 OUTLIERS

In all of the regression examples we have analyzed to this point, we have ignored the possibility of outliers. Unfortunately, in many real applications we cannot afford to ignore outliers. They are often present, and they can often have a substantial effect on the results. In this section we briefly discuss outliers in the context of regression—how to detect them and what to do about them.

We tend to think of an outlier as an observation that has an extreme value for at least one variable. For example, if salaries in a data set are mostly in the $40,000 to $80,000 range, but one salary is $350,000, then this observation is a clear outlier with respect to salary. However, in a regression context outliers are not always this obvious. In fact, an observation can be considered an outlier for several reasons, and some types of outliers can be difficult to detect. An observation can be an outlier for one or more of the following reasons.

Characteristics of an Outlier

Outliers can come in several forms, as indicated in this list.

1. It has an extreme value for one or more variables.

2. Its value of the dependent variable is much larger or smaller than predicted by the regression line, and its residual is abnormally large in magnitude. An example appears in Figure 12.19. The line in this scatterplot fits most of the points, but it misses badly on the one obvious outlier. This outlier has a large positive residual, but its Y value is not abnormally large. Its Y value is only large relative to points with the same X value that it has.

Figure 12.19   Outlier with a Large Residual

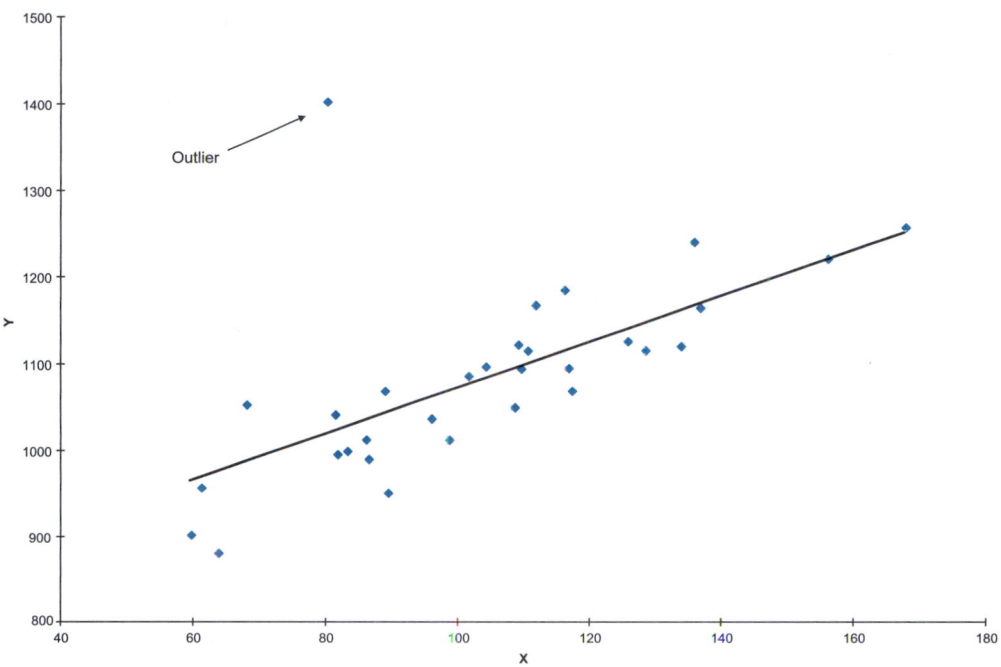

3. Its residual is not only large in magnitude, but this point "tilts" the regression line toward it. An example appears in Figure 12.20. The two lines shown are the regression lines with the outlier and without it. If we keep the outlier, it makes a big difference for the slope and intercept of the regression line. This type of outlier is called an **influential** point, for the obvious reason.

4. Its values of individual explanatory variables are not extreme, but they fall outside the general pattern of the other observations. An example appears in Figure 12.21. Here, we assume that the two variables shown, YrsExper (years of experience) and Rating (an employee's performance rating) are both explanatory variables for some other dependent variable (Salary) that isn't shown in the plot. The obvious outlier does not have an abnormal value of either YrsExper or Rating, but it falls well outside the pattern of most employees.

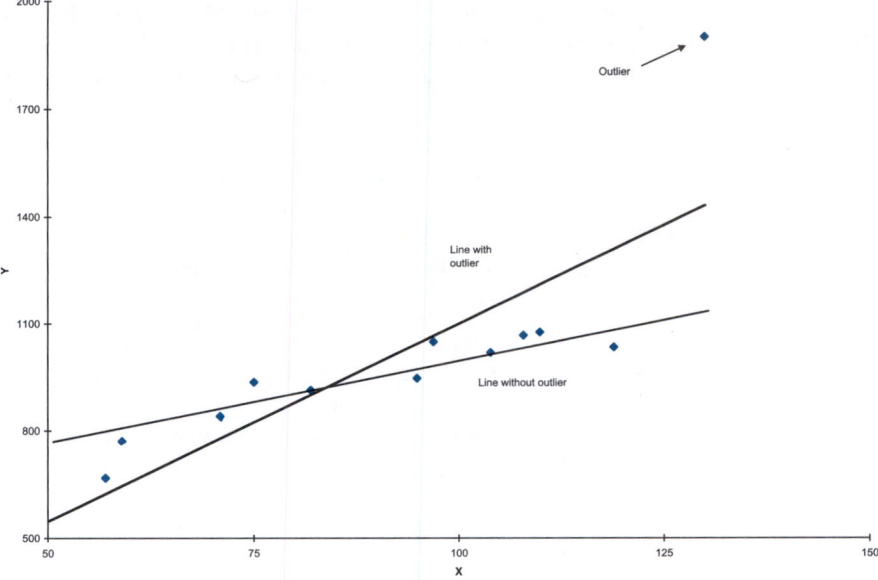

Figure 12.20

Outlier That Tilts
the Regression Line

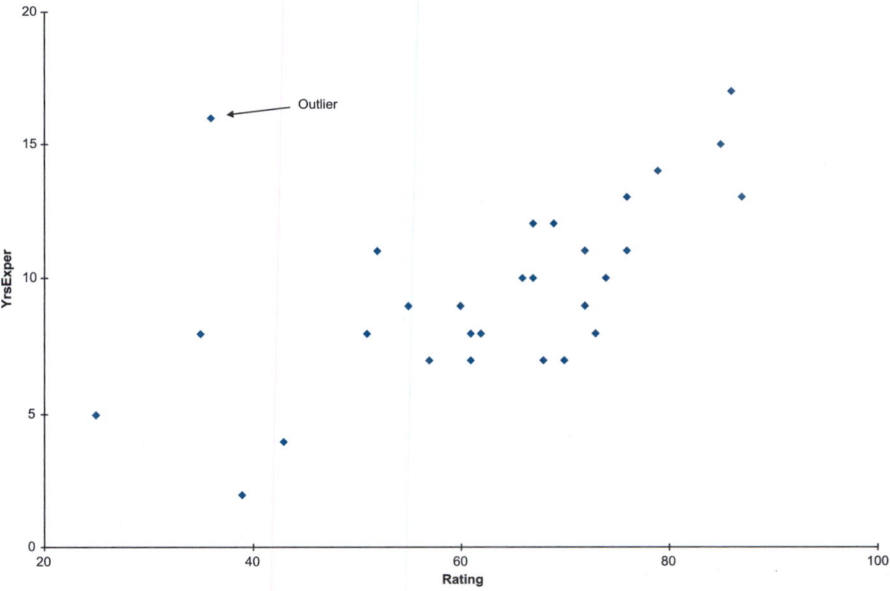

Figure 12.21

Outlier Outside
Pattern of
Explanatory
Variables

Once we have identified outliers, there is still the thorny problem of what to do with them. In most cases the regression output will look "nicer" if we delete outliers, but this is not necessarily appropriate. If we can argue that the outlier isn't really a member of the relevant population, then it is appropriate and probably best to delete it. But if no such argument can be made, then it is not really appropriate to delete the outlier just to make the analysis come out better. Perhaps the best advice in this case is the advice we gave in the previous chapter. Run the analysis with the outliers and run it again without them. If the key outputs do not change much, then it does not really matter whether the outliers are included or not. If the key outputs do change substantially, then report the results both with and without the outliers, along with a verbal explanation.

We illustrate this procedure in the following continuation of the bank discrimination example.

12.4 POSSIBLE GENDER DISCRIMINATION IN SALARY AT FIFTH NATIONAL BANK OF SPRINGFIELD (CONTINUED)

Of the 208 employees at Fifth National Bank, are there any obvious outliers? In what sense are they outliers? Does it matter to the regression results, particularly those concerning gender discrimination, whether the outliers are removed?

Objective   To locate possible outliers in the bank salary data, and to see to what extent they affect the regression model.

Solution

There are several places we could look for outliers. An obvious place is the Salary variable. The box plot in Figure 12.22 shows that there are several employees making substantially more in salary than most of the employees. We could consider these outliers and remove them, arguing perhaps that these are senior managers who shouldn't be included in the discrimination analysis. We leave it to you to check whether the regression results are any different with these high-salary employees than without them.

Figure 12.22

Box Plot of Salaries for Bank Data

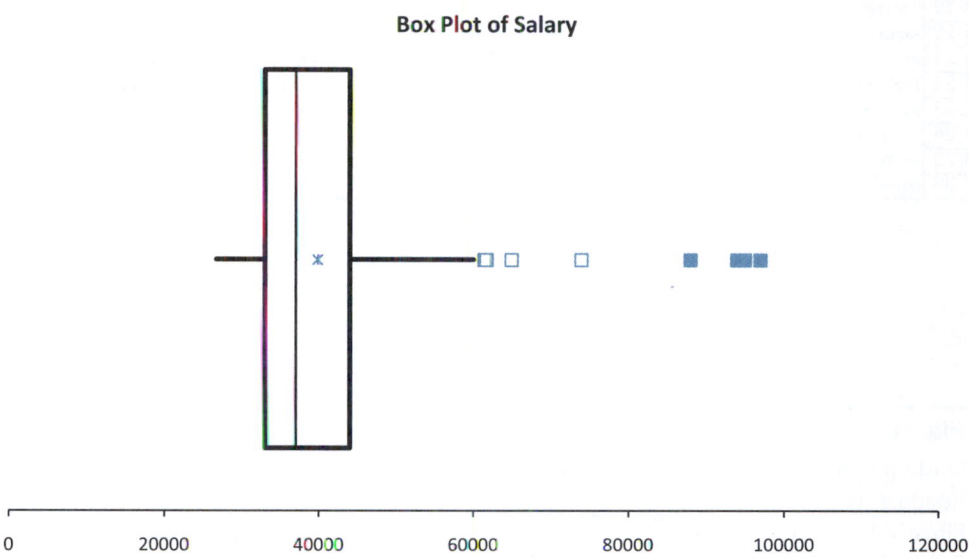

Another place to look is at a scatterplot of the residuals versus the fitted values. This type of plot (offered as an option by StatTools) shows points with abnormally large residuals. For example, we ran the regression with Female, YrsExper, Interaction(YrsExper,Female), and the five job grade dummies, and we obtained the output and scatterplot in Figures 12.23 and 12.24. This scatterplot has several points that could be considered outliers, but we focus on the point identified in the figure. The residual for this point is approximately -21. Given that s_e for this regression is approximately 5, this residual is over four standard errors below 0—quite a lot. When we examine this point more closely, we see that it corresponds to employee 208, who is a 62-year-old female employee in the highest job grade. She has 33 years of experience with Fifth National, she has a graduate degree, and she earns only $30,000. She is clearly an unusual employee, and there are probably special circumstances that can explain her small salary, although we can only guess at what they are.

Figure 12.23   **Regression Output with Outlier Included**

	A	B	C	D	E	F	G
7		Multiple R	R-Square	Adjusted R-Square	StErr of Estimate		
8	Summary						
9		0.9005	0.8109	0.8033	4991.64		
10							
11		Degrees of Freedom	Sum of Squares	Mean of Squares	F-Ratio	p-Value	
12	ANOVA Table						
13	Explained	8	21268738998	2658592375	106.7004	< 0.0001	
14	Unexplained	199	4958368233	24916423.28			
15							
16		Coefficient	Standard Error	t-Value	p-Value	Confidence Interval 95%	
17	Regression Table					Lower	Upper
18	Constant	26104.22	1105.44	23.6143	< 0.0001	23924.34	28284.11
19	YrsExper	1070.88	102.01	10.4975	< 0.0001	869.72	1272.05
20	Female	6063.33	1266.32	4.7881	< 0.0001	3566.20	8560.46
21	JobGrade = 2	2596.49	1010.12	2.5705	0.0109	604.58	4588.41
22	JobGrade = 3	6221.39	998.18	6.2328	< 0.0001	4253.03	8189.76
23	JobGrade = 4	11071.95	1172.59	9.4423	< 0.0001	8759.66	13384.25
24	JobGrade = 5	14946.58	1340.25	11.1521	< 0.0001	12303.66	17589.49
25	JobGrade = 6	17097.37	2390.67	7.1517	< 0.0001	12383.07	21811.67
26	Interaction(YrsExper,Female)	-1021.05	118.73	-8.6001	< 0.0001	-1255.17	-786.93

Figure 12.24

Scatterplot of Residuals versus Fitted Values with Outlier Identified

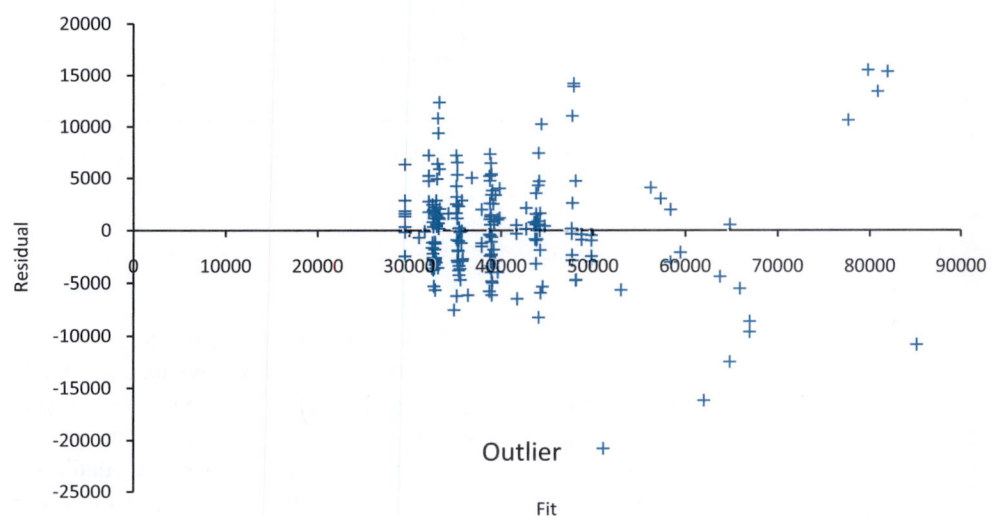

In any case, if we delete this employee and rerun the regression with the same variables, we obtain the output in Figure 12.25.[7] Now, recalling that gender discrimination is the key issue in this example, we compare the coefficients of Female and Interaction(YrsExper,Female) in the two outputs. The coefficient of Female has dropped from 6.063 to 4.353. In words, the Y-intercept for the female regression line used to be about $6000 higher than for the male line; now it is only about $4350 higher. More importantly, the coefficient of Interaction(YrsExper,Female) has changed from -1.021 to -0.721. This coefficient indicates how much less steep the female line for Salary versus YrsExper is than the male line. So a change from -1.021 to -0.721 indicates *less* discrimination against females now than before. In other words, this unusual female employee accounts for a good bit of the discrimination argument—although a strong argument still exists even without her.

Figure 12.25 Regression Output with Outlier Excluded

	A	B	C	D	E	F	G
7		Multiple	R-Square	Adjusted	StErr of		
8	Summary	R		R-Square	Estimate		
9		0.9130	0.8336	0.8269	4685.67		
10							
11		Degrees of	Sum of	Mean of	F-Ratio	p-Value	
12	ANOVA Table	Freedom	Squares	Squares			
13	Explained	8	21780996415	2722624552	124.0064	< 0.0001	
14	Unexplained	198	4347190681	21955508.49			
15							
16		Coefficient	Standard	t-Value	p-Value	Confidence Interval 95%	
17	Regression Table		Error			Lower	Upper
18	Constant	26710.31	1044.02	25.5840	< 0.0001	24651.48	28769.14
19	YrsExper	897.67	101.23	8.8675	< 0.0001	698.04	1097.30
20	Female	4353.11	1232.10	3.5331	0.0005	1923.37	6782.84
21	JobGrade = 2	2717.87	948.49	2.8655	0.0046	847.44	4588.30
22	JobGrade = 3	6257.16	937.02	6.6777	< 0.0001	4409.34	8104.98
23	JobGrade = 4	10983.81	1100.84	9.9777	< 0.0001	8812.93	13154.68
24	JobGrade = 5	15464.47	1261.92	12.2547	< 0.0001	12975.94	17953.00
25	JobGrade = 6	22323.45	2453.01	9.1004	< 0.0001	17486.06	27160.83
26	Interaction(YrsExper,Female)	-720.61	125.15	-5.7578	< 0.0001	-967.41	-473.81

PROBLEMS

Level A

34. The file **P12_34.xlsx** contains the sales, Y, in thousands of dollars per week, for randomly selected fast-food outlets in each of four cities. Furthermore, this data set includes the traffic flow, in thousands of cars, through each of the selected fast-food outlets.

a. Use the given data to estimate a model for predicting sales as a function of traffic flow. This regression model should account for city-to-city variations that might be due to size or other market conditions. Assume that the level of mean sales will differ from city to city, but that the change in

mean sales per unit increase in traffic flow will remain the same for all cities (i.e., traffic flow and city factors do not interact).

b. Perform an F test of the overall significance of the multiple regression model estimated in part **a**, and report a p-value.

c. How do you explain the result of your statistical hypothesis test in part **b**? What, if anything, would you do to obtain more satisfactory results?

35. A manufacturing firm wants to determine whether a relationship exists between the number of work-hours an employee misses per year (Y) and the employee's annual wages (X). The data provided in the file

---

[7]As it turns out, this employee is the last observation in the data set. An easy way to run the regression (with StatTools) without this employee is to redefine the StatTools data set so that it doesn't include this last row.

P12_35.xlsx are based on a random sample of 15 employees from this organization.

  a. Estimate a simple linear regression model using the sample data. How well does the estimated model fit the sample data?
  b. Perform an *F* test for the existence of a linear relationship between *Y* and *X*. Use a 5% level of significance.
  c. How do you explain the results you have found in parts **a** and **b**?
  d. Suppose you learn that the 10th worker in the sample has been fired for missing an excessive number of work-hours during the past year. In light of this information, how would you proceed to estimate the relationship between the number of work-hours an employee misses per year and the employee's annual wages, using the available information? If you decide to revise your estimate of this regression equation, repeat parts **a** and **b**.

Level B

36. Statistician Frank J. Anscombe created a data set to illustrate the importance of doing more than just examining the standard regression output. These data are provided in the file **P12_36.xlsx**.

  a. Regress Y_1 on X. How well does the estimated model fit the data? Is there evidence of a linear relationship between Y_1 and X at the 5% significance level?
  b. Regress Y_2 on X. How well does the estimated model fit the data? Is there evidence of a linear relationship between Y_2 and X at the 5% significance level?
  c. Regress Y_3 on X. How well does the estimated model fit the data? Is there evidence of a linear relationship between Y_3 and X at the 5% significance level?
  d. Regress Y_4 on X_4. How well does the estimated model fit the data? Is there evidence of a linear relationship between Y_4 and X_4 at the 5% significance level?
  e. Compare these four simple linear regression models (i) in terms of goodness of fit and (ii) in terms of overall statistical significance.
  f. How do you explain these findings, considering that each of the regression equations is based on a *different* set of variables?
  g. What role, if any, do outliers have on each of these estimated regression models?

12.9 VIOLATIONS OF REGRESSION ASSUMPTIONS

Much of the theoretical research in the area of regression has dealt with violations of the regression assumptions in Section 12.2. There are three issues: how to detect violations of the assumptions, what goes wrong if we ignore violations, and what to do about them if they are detected. Detection is usually relatively easy. We can look at scatterplots, histograms, and time series graphs for visual signs of violations, and there are a number of numerical measures (many not covered here) that have been developed for diagnostic purposes. The second issue, what goes wrong if we ignore violations, depends on the type of violation and its severity. The third issue is the most difficult. There are some relatively easy fixes and some that are well beyond the level of this book. In this section we briefly discuss some of the most common violations and a few possible remedies for them.

12.9.1 Nonconstant Error Variance

The second regression assumption states that the variance of the errors should be *constant* for all values of the explanatory variables. This is a lot to ask, and it is almost always violated to some extent. Fortunately, mild violations do not have much effect on the validity of the regression output, so we can usually ignore them.

A fan shape can cause an incorrect value for the standard error of estimate, so that confidence intervals and hypothesis tests for the regression coefficients are not valid.

However, one particular form of nonconstant error variance occurs fairly often and should be dealt with. This is the "fan shape" we saw in the scatterplot of AmountSpent versus Salary in Figure 12.1. As salaries increase, the variability of amounts spent also increases. Although this fan shape appears in the scatterplot of the dependent variable AmountSpent versus the explanatory variable Salary, it also appears in the scatterplot of residuals versus fitted values when we regress AmountSpent versus Salary. If we ignore this nonconstant error variance, then the standard error of the regression coefficient of Salary is inaccurate, so that a confidence interval for this coefficient or a hypothesis test concerning it can be misleading.

There are at least two ways to deal with this fan-shape phenomenon. The first is to use a different estimation method than least squares. It is called *weighted least squares,* and it is an option available in many statistical software packages. However, it is fairly advanced and it is not available with Excel (or StatTools), so we won't discuss it here.

A logarithmic transfor-mation of Y can sometimes cure the fan-shape problem.

The second method is simpler. When we see a fan shape, where the variability increases from left to right in a scatterplot, we can try a logarithmic transformation of the dependent variable. The reason this often works is that the logarithmic transformation squeezes the large values closer together and pulls the small values farther apart. The scatterplot of the log of AmountSpent versus Salary is in Figure 12.26. Clearly, the fan shape evident in Figure 12.1 is gone.

Figure 12.26

Scatterplot without Fan Shape

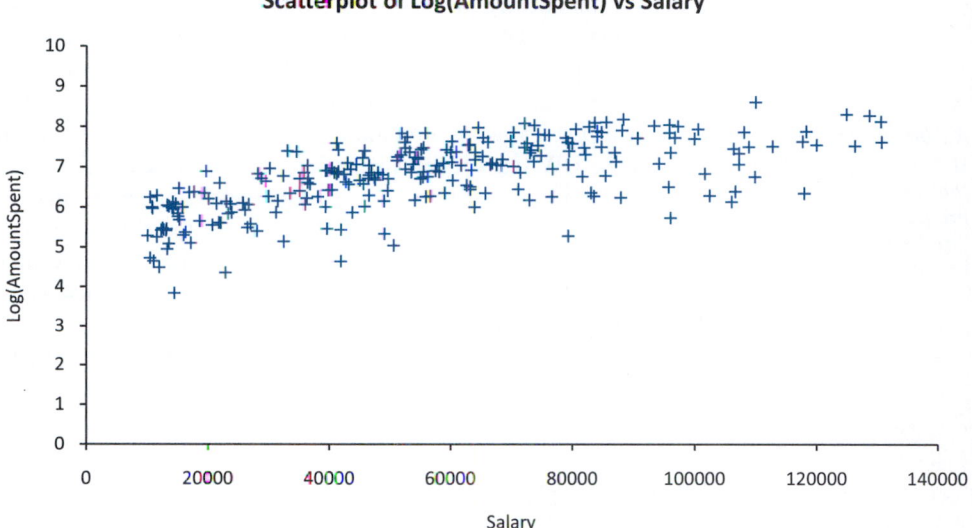

This logarithmic transformation is not a magical cure for all instances of nonconstant error variance. For example, it appears to have introduced some curvature into the plot in Figure 12.26. However, as we discussed in the previous chapter, whenever the distribution of the dependent variable is heavily skewed to the right, as it often is, the logarithmic trans-formation is worth exploring.

12.9.2 Nonnormality of Residuals

The third regression assumption states that the error terms are normally distributed. We can check this assumption fairly easily by forming a histogram of the residuals. We can even perform a formal test of normality of the residuals by using the procedures discussed in

Section 10.5 of Chapter 10. However, unless the distribution of the residuals is severely nonnormal, the inferences we make from the regression output are still approximately valid. In addition, a form of nonnormality often encountered is skewness to the right, and this can often be remedied by the same logarithmic transformation of the dependent variable that remedies nonconstant error variance.

12.9.3 Autocorrelated Residuals

The fourth regression assumption states that the error terms are probabilistically independent. This assumption is usually valid for cross-sectional data, but it is often violated for time series data. The problem with time series data is that the residuals are often correlated with nearby residuals, a property called **autocorrelation**. The most frequent type of autocorrelation is positive autocorrelation. For example, if residuals separated by 1 month are autocorrelated—called **lag 1 autocorrelation**—in a positive direction, then an overprediction in January, say, will likely lead to an overprediction in February, and an underprediction in January will likely lead to an underprediction in February. If this autocorrelation is large, then serious prediction errors can occur if it isn't dealt with appropriately.

A numerical measure has been developed to check for lag 1 autocorrelation. It is called the **Durbin–Watson statistic** (after the two statisticians who developed it), and it is quoted automatically in the regression output of many statistical software packages. The Durbin–Watson (DW) statistic is scaled to be between 0 and 4. Values close to 2 indicate very little lag 1 autocorrelation, values below 2 indicate positive autocorrelation, and values above 2 indicate negative autocorrelation.

A Durbin–Watson statistic below 2 signals that nearby residuals are positively correlated with one another.

Since *positive* autocorrelation is the usual culprit, the question becomes how much below 2 the DW statistic must be before we should react. There is a formal hypothesis test for answering this question, and a set of tables appears in many statistics texts. Without going into the details, we simply state that when the number of time series observations, n, is about 30 and the number of explanatory variables is fairly small, say, 1 to 5, then any DW statistic less than 1.2 should get our attention. If n increases to around 100, then we shouldn't be concerned unless the DW statistic is below 1.5.

If e_i is the ith residual, then the formula for the DW statistic is

$$DW = \frac{\sum_{i=2}^{n}(e_i - e_{i-1})^2}{\sum_{i=1}^{n}e_i^2}$$

This is obviously not very attractive for hand calculation, so the StatDurbinWatson function is included in the StatTools add-in. To use it, run any regression and check the option to create a graph of residuals versus fitted values. This automatically creates columns of fitted values and residuals. Then enter the formula

=**StatDurbinWatson**(*ResidRange*)

in any cell, substituting the actual range of residuals for "ResidRange."

The following continuation of Example 12.1 with the Bendrix manufacturing data—the only time series data set we have analyzed with regression—checks for possible lag 1 autocorrelation.

EXAMPLE | **12.5 Explaining Overhead Costs at Bendrix (continued)**

Is there any evidence of lag 1 autocorrelation in the Bendrix data when Overhead is regressed on MachHrs and ProdRuns?

Objective To use the Durbin–Watson statistic to check whether there is any serious autocorrelation in the residuals from the Bendrix regression model for overhead costs.

Solution

We run the usual multiple regression and check that we want a graph of residuals versus fitted values. The results are shown in Figure 12.27. The residuals are listed in column D. Each represents how much the regression overpredicts (if negative) or underpredicts (if positive) the overhead cost for that month. We can check for lag 1 autocorrelation in two ways, with the DW statistic and by examining the time series graph of the residuals in Figure 12.28.

Figure 12.27 Regression Output with Residuals and DW Statistic

	A	B	C	D	E	F
44	*Graph Data*	Overhead	Fit	Residual		**Durbin-Watson for residuals**
45	1	99798	98391.35059	1406.649409		1.313
46	2	87804	85522.33322	2281.666779		
47	3	93681	92723.59538	957.4046174		
48	4	82262	82428.09201	-166.0920107		
49	5	106968	100227.9028	6740.097234		

Figure 12.28

Time Series Graph of Residuals

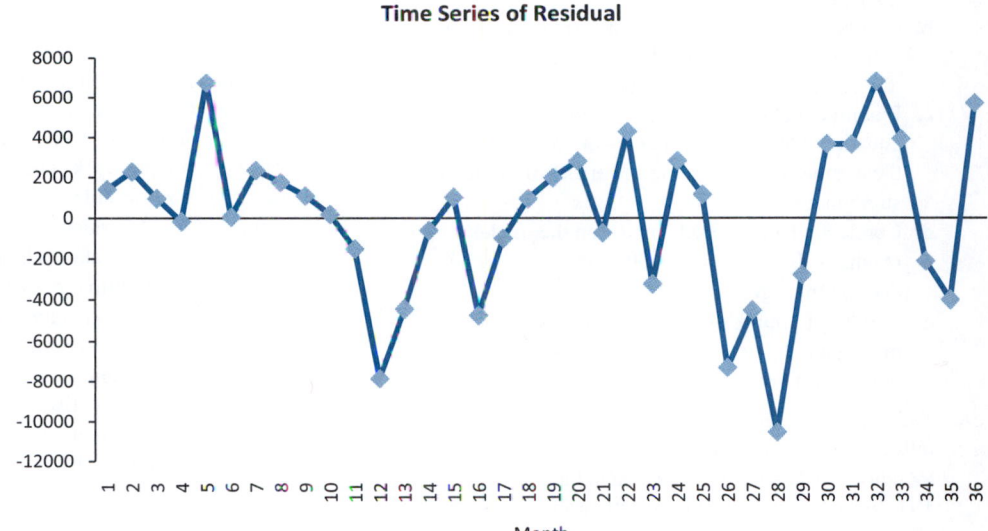

We calculate the DW statistic in cell F45 of Figure 12.27 with the formula

=StatDurbinWatson(D45:D80)

(Remember that StatDurbinWatson is *not* a built-in Excel function. It is available only if StatTools is loaded.) Based on our guidelines for DW values, 1.3131 suggests positive autocorrelation—it is less than 2—but not enough to cause concern.[8] This general conclusion is supported by the time series graph. Serious autocorrelation of lag 1 would tend to show long runs of residuals alternating above and below the horizontal axis—positives would tend to follow positives, and negatives would tend to follow negatives. There is some indication of this behavior in the graph but not an excessive amount. ■

What should we do if the DW statistic signals significant autocorrelation? Unfortunately, the answer to this question would take us much deeper into time series analysis than we can go in this book. Suffice it to say that time series analysis in the context of regression can become very complex, and there are no easy fixes for the autocorrelation that often occurs.

PROBLEMS

Level A

37. Motorco produces electric motors for use in home appliances. One of the company's production managers is interested in examining the relationship between the dollars spent per month in inspecting finished motor products (X) and the number of motors produced during that month that were returned by dissatisfied customers (Y). He has collected the data in the file **P02_18.xlsx** to explore this relationship for the past 36 months.

  a. Generate a simple linear regression model using the given data and interpret it for this production manager.

  b. Conduct an appropriate hypothesis test for the existence of a linear relationship between Y and X in this case, and report a p-value.

  c. Examine the residuals of the estimated regression equation. Do you see evidence of any violations of the assumptions regarding the errors of the regression model?

  d. Conduct a Durbin–Watson test on the model's residuals. Interpret the result of this test for the production manager.

  e. In light of your result in part **d**, do you recommend modifying the original regression model? If so, how would you revise it?

38. Examine the relationship between the average utility bills for homes of a particular size (Y) and the average monthly temperature (X). The data in the file **P11_07.xlsx** include the average monthly bill and temperature for each month of the past year.

  a. Use the given data to estimate a simple linear regression model. How well does the estimated regression model fit the given data?

  b. Conduct an appropriate hypothesis test for the existence of a linear relationship between Y and X, and report a p-value.

  c. Examine the residuals of the estimated regression equation. Do you see evidence of any violations of the assumptions regarding the errors of the regression model?

  d. Conduct a Durbin–Watson test on the model's residuals. Interpret the result of this test.

  e. In light of your result in part **d**, do you recommend modifying the original regression model? If so, how would you revise it?

39. The manager of a commuter rail transportation system was recently asked by her governing board to predict the demand for rides in the large city served by the transportation network. The system manager has collected data on variables thought to be related to the number of weekly riders on the city's rail system. The file **P11_20.xlsx** contains these data.

  a. Estimate a multiple regression model using all of the available explanatory variables.

  b. Conduct and interpret the result of an F test on the given model. Employ a 5% level of significance in conducting this statistical hypothesis test.

  c. Is there evidence of autocorrelated residuals in this model? Explain why or why not.

[8]A more formal test, using Durbin–Watson tables, supports this conclusion.

12.10 PREDICTION

Once we have estimated a regression equation from a set of data, we might want to use this equation to predict the value of the dependent variable for *new* observations. As an example, suppose that a retail chain is considering opening a new store in one of several proposed locations. It naturally wants to choose the location that will result in the largest revenues. The problem is that the revenues for the new locations are not yet known. They can be observed only after stores are opened in these locations, and the chain cannot afford to open more than one store at the current time. An alternative is to use regression analysis. Using data from *existing* stores, the chain can run a regression of the dependent variable revenue on several explanatory variables such as population density, level of wealth in the vicinity, number of competitors nearby, ease of access given the existing roads, and so on.

Assuming that the regression equation has a reasonably large R^2 and, even more important, a reasonably small s_e, the chain can then use this equation to predict revenues for the proposed locations. Specifically, it will gather values of the explanatory variables for each of the proposed locations, substitute these into the regression equation, and look at the predicted revenue for each proposed location. All else being equal, the chain will probably choose the location with the highest predicted revenue.

As another example, suppose that we are trying to explain the starting salaries for undergraduate college students. We want to predict the *mean* salary of all graduates with certain characteristics, such as all male marketing majors from state-supported universities. To do this, we first gather salary data from a sample of graduates from various universities. Included in this data set are relevant explanatory variables for each graduate in the sample, such as the type of university, the student's major, GPA, years of work experience, and so on. We then use these data to estimate a regression equation for starting salary and substitute the relevant values of the explanatory variables into the regression equation to obtain the required prediction.

Regression can be used to predict Y for a single observation, or it can be used to predict the mean Y for many observations, all with the same X values.

These two examples illustrate two types of prediction problems in regression. The first problem, illustrated by the retail chain example, is probably the more common of the two. Here we are trying to predict the value of the dependent variable for one or more *individual* members of the population. In this specific example we are trying to predict the future revenue for several potential locations of the new store. In the second problem, illustrated by the salary example, we are trying to predict the *mean* of the dependent variable for all members of the population with certain values of the explanatory variables. In the first problem we are predicting an individual value; in the second problem we are predicting a mean.

The second problem is inherently easier than the first in the sense that the resulting prediction is bound to be more accurate. The reason should be intuitive. Recall that the mean of the dependent variable for any fixed values of the explanatory variables lies on the population regression line. Therefore, if we can accurately estimate this line—that is, if we can accurately estimate the regression coefficients—we can accurately predict the required mean. In contrast, most individual points do *not* lie on the population regression line. Therefore, even if our estimate of the population regression line is perfectly accurate, we still cannot predict exactly where an individual point will fall.

Stated another way, when we predict a mean, there is a single source of error: the possibly inaccurate estimates of the regression coefficients. But when we predict an individual value, there are two sources of error: the inaccurate estimates of the regression coefficients and the inherent variation of individual points around the regression line. This second source of error often dominates the first.

We illustrate these comments in Figure 12.29. For the sake of illustration, the dependent variable is salary and the single explanatory variable is years of experience with the company. Let's suppose that we want to predict either the salary for a particular employee with 10 years of experience or the mean salary of all employees with 10 years of experience. The two lines in this graph represent the population regression line (which in reality is unobservable) and the estimated regression line. For each prediction problem the point prediction—the best guess—is the value above 10 on the estimated regression line. The error in predicting the mean occurs because the two lines in the graph are not the same, that is, the estimated line is not quite correct. The error in predicting the individual value (the point shown in the graph) occurs because the two lines are not the same and also because this point does not lie on the population regression line.

Figure 12.29

Prediction Errors for an Individual Value and a Mean

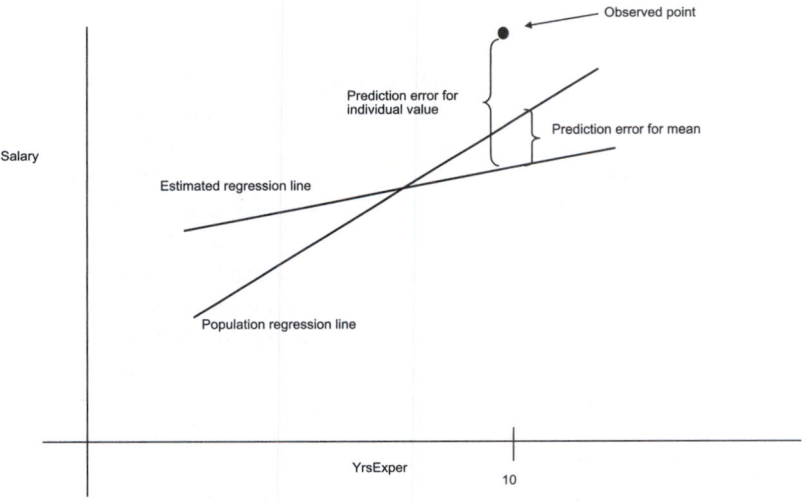

One general aspect of prediction becomes apparent by looking at this graph. If we let X's denote the explanatory variables, predictions for values of the X's close to their means are likely to be more accurate than predictions for X's far from their means. In the graph, the mean years of experience is about 7. (This is approximately where the two lines cross.) Because the slopes of the two lines are different, they get farther apart as YrsExper gets farther away from 7 (on either side). As a result, predictions tend to become less accurate.

This phenomenon shows up as higher standard errors of prediction as the X's get farther away from their means. However, for extreme values of the X's, there is another problem. Suppose, for example, that all values of YrsExper in the data set are between 1 and 15, and we attempt to predict the salary for an employee with 25 years of experience. This is called **extrapolation**; we are attempting to predict beyond the limits of the sample.

It is more difficult to predict for extreme X's than for X's close to the mean. Trying to predict for X's beyond the range of the data set (extrapolation) is quite risky.

The problem here is that there is no guarantee, and sometimes no reason to believe, that the relationship within the range of the sample is valid outside of this range. It is perfectly possible that the effect of years of experience on salary is considerably different in the 25-year range than in the range of the sample. If it is, then extrapolation is bound to yield inaccurate predictions. In general, we should try to avoid extrapolation whenever possible. If we really want to predict the salaries of employees with 25-plus years of experience, then we should include some employees of this type in the original sample.

We now discuss how to make predictions and how to estimate their accuracy, both for individual values and for means. To keep it simple, we first assume that there is a single explanatory variable X. We choose a fixed "trial" value of X, labeled X_0, and predict the value of a single Y or the mean of all Y's when $X = X_0$. For both prediction problems the **point prediction**, or best guess, is found by substituting into the right-hand side of the estimated regression equation. Graphically, this is the height of the estimated regression line above X_0.

> To calculate the **point prediction**, substitute the given values of the X's into the estimated regression equation.

The standard error of prediction for a single Y is approximately equal to the standard error of estimate.

To measure the accuracy of these point predictions, we calculate a standard error for each prediction. These standard errors can be interpreted in the usual way. For example, we are about 68% certain that the actual values will be within 1 standard error of the point predictions, and we are about 95% certain that the actual values will be within 2 standard errors of the point predictions. For the individual prediction problem, the standard error is labeled s_{ind} and is given by equation (12.5). As indicated by the approximate equality on the right, when the sample size n is large and X_0 is fairly close to $\overline{X}$, the last two terms inside the square root are relatively small, and this standard error of prediction can be approximated by s_e, the standard error of estimate.

Standard Error of Prediction for a Single Y

$$s_{\text{ind}} = s_e \sqrt{1 + \frac{1}{n} + \frac{(X_0 - \overline{X})^2}{\sum_{i=1}^{n}(X_i - \overline{X})^2}} \simeq s_e \qquad (12.5)$$

For the prediction of the mean, the standard error is labeled s_{mean} and is given by equation (12.6). Here, if X_0 is fairly close to $\overline{X}$, then the last term inside the square root is relatively small, and this standard error of prediction is approximately the expression on the right.

Standard Error of Prediction for the Mean Y

$$s_{\text{mean}} = s_e \sqrt{\frac{1}{n} + \frac{(X_0 - \overline{X})^2}{\sum_{i=1}^{n}(X_i - \overline{X})^2}} \simeq s_e / \sqrt{n} \qquad (12.6)$$

The standard error of prediction for a mean of Y's is approximately equal to the standard error of estimate divided by the square root of the sample size.

These standard errors can be used to calculate a 95% prediction interval for an individual value and a 95% confidence interval for a mean value. Exactly as in Chapter 9, we go out a t-multiple of the relevant standard error on either side of the point prediction. The t-multiple is the value that cuts off 0.025 probability in the right-hand tail of a t distribution with $n - 2$ degrees of freedom.

The term *prediction* interval (rather than confidence interval) is used for an individual value because an individual value of Y is not a population *parameter*. However, the interpretation is basically the same. If we calculate a 95% prediction interval for many members of the population, we expect their actual Y values to fall within the corresponding prediction intervals about 95% of the time.

To see how all of this can be implemented in Excel, we revisit the Bendrix example of predicting overhead expenses.

EXAMPLE | **12.6 PREDICTING OVERHEAD AT BENDRIX**

We have already used regression to analyze overhead expenses at Bendrix, based on 36 months of data. Suppose Bendrix expects the values of MachHrs and ProdRuns for the next three months to be 1430, 1560, 1520, and 35, 45, 40, respectively. What are their point predictions and 95% prediction intervals for Overhead for these three months?

Objective To predict Overhead at Bendrix for the next three months, given anticipated values of MachHrs and ProdRuns.

Solution

StatTools provides the capability to provide predictions and 95% prediction intervals, but you must set up a second data set to capture the results. This second data set can be placed next to (or below) the original data set. It should have the same variable name headings, plus LowerLimit95 and UpperLimit95 headings, and it should include values of the explanatory variable to be used for prediction. For this example we called the original data set Original Data and the new data set Data for Prediction. The regression dialog box and results in Data for Prediction appear in Figures 12.30 and 12.31. In the dialog box, note that the Prediction option is checked, and the second data set is specified in the corresponding dropdown list.

Figure 12.30

Regression Dialog
Box with Predictions
Checked

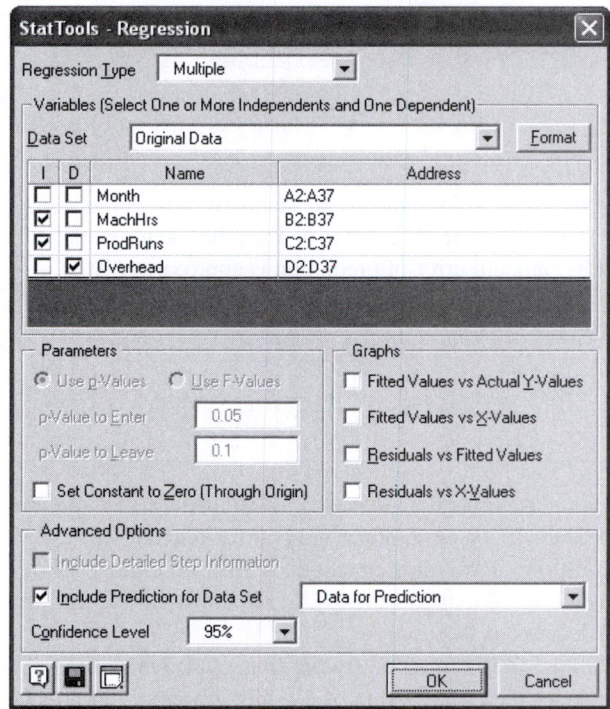

The text box in Figure 12.31 explains how the second data set range should be set up. Initially, you should enter the given values in the Month, MachHrs, and ProdRuns columns. Then when the regression is run (with the Prediction option checked), the values in the Overhead, LowerLimit95, and UpperLimit95 columns will be filled. (If you forget to create LowerLimit95 and UpperLimit95 columns as part of the second data set, StatTools will do it for you.)

The Overhead values in column I are the point predictions for the next three months, and the LowerLimit95 and UpperLimit95 values in column J and K indicate the 95% prediction intervals. We see from the wide prediction intervals how much uncertainty remains. The reason is the relatively large standard error of estimate, s_e. If we could halve the value of s_e, the length of the prediction interval would be only half as large. Contrary to what you might expect, this is not a sample size problem. That is, a larger sample size would almost surely *not* produce a smaller value of s_e. The whole problem is that MachHrs and ProdRuns are not perfectly correlated with Overhead. The only way to decrease s_e and get more accurate predictions is to find other explanatory variables that are more closely related to Overhead.

Figure 12.31 Prediction of Overhead

	F	G	H	I	J	K	L
1	Month	MachHrs	ProdRuns	Overhead	LowerLimit95	UpperLimit95	
2	37	1430	35	97180.35	88700.80	105659.91	
3	38	1560	45	111676.27	103002.95	120349.58	
4	39	1520	40	105516.72	96993.16	114040.28	
5							
6							
7		Above is the data set for prediction. It is best to set this up ahead of time, entering all of the column headings, entering the values of the explanatory variables you want to test, and defining this entire range as a new StatTools data set. The values in the last three columns can be blank or have values, but when regression is run with the prediction options, they will be filled in or overwritten.					
8							
9							
10							
11							
12							

StatTools provides prediction intervals for individual values, as we have just seen, but it does not provide confidence intervals for the mean of Y, given a set of X's. To obtain such a confidence interval, you can use equation (12.6) to get the required standard error of prediction (for simple regression only), or you can approximate it by $s_e/\sqrt{n}$.

PROBLEMS

Level A

40. The human resources manager of DataCom, Inc., wants to predict the annual salaries of given employees using the following explanatory variables: (a) the number of years of prior relevant work experience, (b) the number of years of employment at DataCom, (c) the number of years of education beyond high school, (d) the employee's gender, (e) the employee's department, and (f) the number of individuals supervised by the given employee. These data have been collected for a sample of employees and are given in the file **P11_05.xlsx**.

   a. Estimate an appropriate multiple regression model to predict the annual salary of a given DataCom employee.

   b. Conduct and interpret the result of an F test from the ANOVA table on the given model. Employ a 5% level of significance in this test.

   c. Given the estimated regression model, predict the annual salary of a male employee who served in a similar department at another company for 5 years prior to coming to work at DataCom. This man, a graduate of a 4-year collegiate business program, has been supervising 6 subordinates in the sales department since joining the organization 7 years ago.

   d. Find a 95% prediction interval for the salary earned by a DataCom employee as characterized in part **c**.

   e. Find a 95% confidence interval for the mean salary earned by all DataCom employees sharing the characteristics provided in part **c**.

   f. How do you explain the difference between the widths of the intervals in parts **d** and **e**?

41. Suppose you are interested in predicting the price of a laptop computer based on its various features. The file **P11_35.xlsx** contains observations on the sales price and on a number of potentially relevant variables for a randomly chosen sample of laptop computers.

   a. Estimate a multiple regression model that includes all available explanatory variables.

   b. Conduct and interpret the result of an F test from the ANOVA table on the given model. Employ a 5% level of significance in this test.

   c. Use the estimated regression equation to predict the price of a laptop computer with the following features: a 50-megahertz processor, a battery that holds its charge for 180 minutes, 20 megabytes of RAM, a DX chip, a color monitor, a trackball pointing device, and a 24-hour, toll-free customer service hotline.

   d. Find a 99% prediction interval for the price of a laptop computer as characterized in part **c**.

e. Find a 99% confidence interval for the average price of all laptop computers sharing the characteristics provided in part **c**.

f. How do you explain the difference between the widths of the intervals in parts **d** and **e**?

42. Suppose that a power company located in southern Alabama wants to predict the peak power load (i.e., Y, the maximum amount of power that must be generated each day to meet demand) as a function of the daily high temperature (X). A random sample of 25 summer days is chosen, and the peak power load and the high temperature are recorded on each day. The file **P11_40.xlsx** contain these observations.

a. Use the given data to estimate a simple linear regression model. How well does the estimated regression model fit the given data?

b. Conduct an appropriate hypothesis test for the existence of a linear relationship between Y and X, and report a p-value.

c. Examine the residuals of the estimated regression equation. Do you see evidence of any violations of the assumptions regarding the errors of the regression model?

d. Conduct a Durbin–Watson test on the model's residuals. Interpret the result of this test.

e. Given your result in part **d**, do you recommend modifying the original regression model in this case? If so, how would you revise it?

f. Use the final version of your regression model to predict the peak power load on a summer day with a high temperature of 90 degrees.

g. Find a 95% prediction interval for the peak power load on a summer day with a high temperature of 90 degrees.

h. Find a 99% confidence interval for the average peak power load on all summer days with a high temperature of 90 degrees.

12.11 CONCLUSION

In these two chapters on regression, we have seen how useful regression analysis can be for a variety of business applications and how statistical software such as the StatTools add-in in Excel enables us to obtain relevant output—both graphical and numerical—with very little effort. However, we have also seen that there are many concepts that need to be understood well before regression analysis can be used appropriately. Given the user-friendly software currently available, it is all too easy to generate enormous amounts of regression output and then misinterpret or misuse much of it.

At the very least, you should (1) be able to interpret the standard regression output, including statistics on the regression coefficients, summary measures such as R^2 and s_e, and the ANOVA table, (2) know what to look for in the many scatterplots available, (3) know how to use dummy variables, interaction terms, and nonlinear transformations to improve a fit, and (4) be able to spot clear violations of the regression assumptions. However, we haven't covered everything. Indeed, many entire books are devoted exclusively to regression analysis. Therefore, you should recognize when you *don't* know enough to handle a regression problem such as nonconstant error variance or autocorrelation appropriately. In this case you should consult a statistical expert.

Summary of Key Terms

Term	Symbol	Explanation	Excel	Page	Equation Number
Statistical model for regression		A theoretical model, including several assumptions, that must be satisfied, at least approximately, for inferences from regression output to be valid		646	12.1

(continued)

Term	Symbol	Explanation	Excel	Page	Equation Number
Homoscedasticity (and heteroscedasticity)		Equal (and unequal) variance of the dependent variable for different values of the explanatory variables		647	
Autocorrelation of residuals		Lack of independence in the series of residuals, especially relevant for time series data		648	
Parsimony		The concept of explaining the most with the least		650	
Standard error of regression coefficient	s_b	Measures how much the estimates of a regression coefficient vary from sample to sample	StatTools/ Regression & Classification/ Regression	651	
Confidence interval for regression coefficient		An interval likely to contain the population regression coefficient	StatTools/ Regression & Classification/ Regression	652	
t-value for regression coefficient	t	The ratio of the estimate of a regression coefficient to its standard error, used to test whether the coefficient is 0	StatTools/ Regression & Classification/ Regression	653	12.3
Hypothesis test for regression coefficient		Typically, a two-tailed test, where the null hypothesis is that the regression coefficient is 0	StatTools/ Regression & Classification/ Regression	653	
ANOVA table for regression		Used to test whether the explanatory variables, as a whole, have any significant explanatory power	StatTools/ Regression & Classification/ Regression	654	
Multicollinearity		Occurs when there is a fairly strong linear relationship between explanatory variables		659	
Include/exclude decisions		Guidelines for deciding whether to include or exclude potential explanatory variables		662	
Stepwise regression		A class of "automatic" equation-building methods, where variables are added (or deleted) in order of their importance	StatTools/ Regression & Classification/ Regression	667	
Partial F test		Tests whether a set of extra explanatory variables adds any explanatory power to an existing regression equation	Must be done manually	672	12.4
Outliers		Observations that lie outside the general pattern of points and can have a substantial effect on the regression model		680	
Influential point		A point that can "tilt" the regression line		681	

(*continued*)

Term	Symbol	Explanation	Excel	Page	Equation Number
Durbin–Watson statistic		A measure of the autocorrelation between residuals, especially useful for time series data	=StatDurbin Watson(*range*), a StatTools function	688	
Standard errors of prediction	s_{ind}, s_{mean}	Measures of the accuracy of prediction when predicting Y for an individual observation, or predicting the mean of all Y's, for fixed values of the explanatory variables	StatTools/ Regression & Classification/ Regression	693	12.5, 12.6

PROBLEMS

Conceptual Exercises

C.1. Suppose a regression output produces the following 99% confidence interval for one of the regression coefficients:

$$[-32.47, -16.88]$$

Given this information, should an analyst reject the null hypothesis that this population regression coefficient is equal to 0? Explain your answer.

C.2. Explain why it is not possible to estimate a linear regression model that contains *all* dummy variables associated with a particular categorical explanatory variable.

C.3. Suppose that you are serving as the mentor for a summer intern in your organization. As a first assignment, you direct this undergraduate student to generate a multiple regression model that does a good job of explaining the variation in the monthly sales of one of the products your company manufactures. Shortly thereafter, the intern submits a report that recommends a particular estimated equation. The student tells you that she found the "best" model by enumerating all possible explanatory variables, gathering a random sample for each possible variable, and using a statistical software package that automatically finds a model containing only those variables with statistically significant regression coefficients. What feedback would you give to the intern based on the overall approach she has taken in completing this statistical assignment?

C.4. Distinguish between the test of significance of an individual regression coefficient and the ANOVA test. When, if ever, are these two statistical tests essentially equivalent?

C.5. Which of these intervals based on the same estimated regression equation with fixed values of the explanatory variables would be *wider*: (i) a 95% prediction interval for an individual value of Y or (ii) a 95% confidence interval for the mean value of Y? Explain your answer. How would you interpret the wider of these two intervals in words?

Level A

43. For 12 straight weeks you have observed the sales (in number of cases) of canned tomatoes at Mr. D's. Each week you kept track of the following:
- Was a promotional notice placed in all shopping carts for canned tomatoes?
- Was a coupon given for canned tomatoes?
- Was a price reduction (none, 1, or 2 cents off) given?

The file **P12_43.xlsx** contains these data.
a. Use multiple regression to determine how these factors influence sales.
b. Discuss whether your final equation has any problems with autocorrelation, heteroscedasticity, or multicollinearity.
c. Predict sales of canned tomatoes during a week in which Mr. D's uses a shopping cart notice, a coupon, and a 1-cent price reduction.

44. The file **P12_44.xlsx** contains data on pork sales. Price is in dollars per hundred pounds, quantity sold is in billions of pounds, per capita income is in dollars, U.S. population is in millions, and GNP is in billions of dollars.
a. Use the data to develop a regression equation that could be used to predict the quantity of pork sold during future periods. Does heteroscedasticity, autocorrelation, or multicollinearity appear to be a problem?

b. Suppose that during each of the next two quarters, price is 45, U.S. population is 240, GNP is 2620, and per capita income is 10,000. (These are in the units described previously.) Predict the quantity of pork sold during each of the next two quarters.

45. The file **P12_45.xlsx** contains monthly sales (in thousands of dollars) for a photography studio and the price charged per portrait during each month. Suppose we try to predict the current month's sales from last month's sales and the current month's price.
  a. If the price of a portrait during month 21 is $10, predict month 21 sales.
  b. Does autocorrelation, multicollinearity, or heteroscedasticity appear to be a problem?

46. The file **P12_46.xlsx** contains data on a motel chain's revenue and advertising.
  a. Use the data and multiple regression to make predictions for the motel chain's revenues during the next four quarters. Assume that advertising during each of the next four quarters is $50,000.
  b. Does autocorrelation appear to be a problem?

47. The file **P12_47.xlsx** contains the quarterly revenues (in millions of dollars) of Washington Gas and Light for the years 1992 through 1998. We want to use these data to build a multiple regression model that can be used to forecast future revenues.
  a. Which variables should be included in the regression? Explain your rationale for including or excluding variables.
  b. Interpret the coefficients of your final equation.
  c. Make a forecast for revenues during the first quarter of 1999. Also, estimate the probability that 1999 Quarter 1 revenues will be at least $150 million. (*Hint*: Use the standard error of prediction and the fact that the errors are approximately normally distributed.)

48. The file **P11_43.xlsx** contains the following data for several underdeveloped countries:
  ■ Infant mortality rate
  ■ Adult literacy rate
  ■ Percentage of students finishing primary school
  ■ Per capita GNP
  a. Use these data to develop an equation that can be used to predict the infant mortality rate. Justify your equation.
  b. Are there any outliers? If so, what happens if you omit them? *Should* they be omitted?
  c. Interpret the coefficients in your equation.
  d. Does heteroscedasticity or multicollinearity appear to be a problem?
  e. Why is autocorrelation not important in this problem?
  f. Within what amount should 95% of our predictions for the infant mortality rate be accurate?
  g. For a country with a $2000 GNP, 90% adult literacy, and 80% finishing primary school, the regression implies that there is a 1% chance of infant mortality exceeding what value? (*Hint*: Use the standard error of prediction and the fact that the errors are approximately normally distributed.)

49. The file **P12_49.xlsx** contains data on 128 recent home sales in MidCity. For each sale, the file shows the neighborhood (1, 2, or 3) in which the house is located, the number of offers made on the house, the square footage, whether the house is made primarily of brick, the number of bathrooms, the number of bedrooms, and the selling price. Neighborhoods 1 and 2 are more traditional neighborhoods, whereas neighborhood 3 is a newer, more prestigious, neighborhood. For each part below, use StatTools to estimate the relevant regression equation for selling price.
  a. Base this first equation on all variables (other than Home in column A), treating information on brick and neighborhood as categorical and treating all other variables as regular quantitative variables. From this equation, explain what the "premium" is for a house being made of brick, all else being equal. What is the premium for a house being in neighborhood 3, all else being equal? Also, explain the effect of the other variables (besides brick and neighborhood) on price. Are they all significant? (For now, don't eliminate any variables, even if they are insignificant.)
  b. Is there an *extra* premium for a brick house in neighborhood 3, in addition to the usual premium for being brick? Answer by allowing an interaction effect between brick and neighborhood. (This equation should have two extra variables in addition to those in the equation part **a**.)
  c. Starting with the equation in part **b**, remove any variables with p-values greater than 0.1. Explain exactly what this latter equation says about the effect of neighborhood on price. Does it provide much different information than the equation in part **b**?

50. Recall the movie star data from Chapter 2 (in the file **Movie Stars.xlsx**).
  a. Determine an equation to predict salary on the basis of gender, domestic gross, and foreign gross. Make sure all variables in your equation are significant at the 0.15 level.
  b. Interpret the coefficients in your equation.
  c. Does your equation exhibit any autocorrelation, heteroscedasticity, or multicollinearity?
  d. Identify and interpret any outliers.

51. You are trying to determine how the marketing mix influences the sale of Cornpone cereal. The file **P12_51.xlsx** contains the following information for 17 consecutive weeks. (*Note*: Weekly sales are in millions of boxes.)
  ■ Was price cut during the week?
  ■ Was there a prize in the package?
  ■ Was there a coupon in the package?

a. Use these data to determine an equation that can be used to predict weekly Cornpone sales. (Ignore any possible effect of trend.) Make sure all variables in your equation are significant at the 0.15 level.

b. Interpret the coefficients in your equation.

c. Are there any outliers?

d. Is either multicollinearity or autocorrelation a problem?

e. During a week in which there is a price cut and both a prize and a coupon are in the package, what is the probability that sales will be less than 50 million boxes? You may assume that heteroscedasticity and autocorrelation are not problems. (*Hint:* Use the standard error of prediction and the fact that the errors are approximately normally distributed.)

52. The belief that larger majorities for a president in a presidential election help the president's party increase its representation in the House and Senate is called the "coat-tail" effect. The file **P12_52.xlsx** gives the percentage by which each president since 1948 won the election and the number of seats in the House and Senate gained (or lost) during each election. Are these data consistent with the idea of presidential coat-tails? (Source: *Wall Street Journal,* September 10, 1996)

53. The file **P12_53.xlsx** lists the U.S. unemployment rate, the percentage growth in the U.S. economy (in real terms), and the percentage growth in prices for years 1960 through 2001. Determine how changes in unemployment, economic growth, and price changes are related. (Source: *Wall Street Journal Almanac*)

54. The file **P12_54.xlsx** contains the golf handicap and an index of their company's stock performance over the last 3 years for 50 CEOs. A higher index indicates a better stock performance, whereas a lower handicap indicates better golfing ability. For example, Jerry Choate, the CEO of Allstate, has a 10.1 golf handicap, and his company's stock performance index is 83. (The maximum possible stock performance index is 100.) The May 31, 1998, *New York Times* reported that these data indicate that better golfers make better CEOs. What do you think?

55. When potential workers apply for a job that requires extensive manual assembly of small intricate parts, they are initially given three different tests to measure their manual dexterity. The ones who are hired are then periodically given a performance rating on a 0 to 100 scale that combines their speed and accuracy in performing the required assembly operations. The file **P12_55.xlsx** lists the test scores and performance ratings for a randomly selected group of employees. It also lists their seniority (months with the company) at the time of the performance rating.

a. Look at a matrix of correlations. Can you say with certainty (based only on these correlations) that the

R^2 value for the regression will be at least 35%? Why or why not?

b. Is there any evidence (from the correlation matrix) that multicollinearity will be a problem? Why or why not?

c. Run the regression of JobPerf versus all four independent variables. List the equation, the value of R^2, and the value of s_e. Do all of the coefficients have the signs you would expect? Briefly explain.

d. Referring to the equation in part **c**, if a worker (outside of the 80 in the sample) has 15 months of seniority and test scores of 57, 71, and 63, give a prediction and an approximate 95% prediction interval for this worker's JobPerf score.

e. One of the t-values for the coefficients in part **c** is less than 1. Explain briefly why this occurred. Does it mean that this variable is not related to JobPerf?

f. Arguably, the three test measures provide overlapping (or redundant) information. For the sake of parsimony (explaining "the most with the least"), it might be sensible to regress JobPerf versus only two explanatory variables, Sen and AvgTest, where AvgTest is the average of the three test scores— that is, AvgTest = (Test1 + Test2 + Test3)/3. Run this regression and report the same measures as in part **c**: the equation itself, R^2, and s_e. Would you argue that this equation is "just as good as" the equation in part **c**? Explain briefly.

56. Nicklaus Electronics manufactures electronic components used in the computer and space industries. The annual rate of return on the market portfolio and the annual rate of return on Nicklaus Electronics stock for the last 36 months are shown in the file **P12_56.xlsx**. The company wants to calculate the "systematic risk" of its common stock. (It is systematic in the sense that it represents the part of the risk that Nicklaus shares with the market as a whole.) The rate of return Y_t in period t on a security is hypothesized to be related to the rate of return m_t on a market portfolio by the equation

$$Y_t = a + bm_t + e_t$$

Here, a is the risk-free rate of return, b is the security's systematic risk, and e_t is an error term. Using the data available, estimate the systematic risk of the common stock of Nicklaus Electronics. Would you say that Nicklaus stock is a "risky" investment? Why or why not?

57. The auditor of Kaefer Manufacturing uses regression analysis during the analytical review stage of the firm's annual audit. The regression analysis attempts to uncover relationships that exist between various account balances. Any such relationship is subsequently used as a preliminary test of the reasonableness of the reported account balances. The auditor wants to determine whether a relationship exists between the balance of accounts receivable at the end of the month and that month's sales. The file **P12_57.xlsx** contains data on these two accounts for the last 36 months. It also shows the sales levels 2 months before month 1.

a. Is there any statistical evidence to suggest a relationship between the monthly sales level and accounts receivable?

b. Referring to part **a**, would the relationship be described any better by including this month's sales and the previous month's sales (called lagged sales) in the equation for accounts receivable? What about adding the sales from more than a month ago to the equation? For this problem, why might it make accounting sense to include lagged sales variables in the equation? How do you interpret their coefficients?

c. During month 37, which is a fiscal year-end month, the sales were $1,800,000. The reported accounts receivable balance was $3,000,000. Does this reported amount seem consistent with past experience? Explain.

58. A company gives prospective managers four separate tests for judging their potential. For a sample of 30 managers, the test scores and the subsequent job effectiveness ratings (JobEff) given 1 year later are listed in the file **P12_58.xlsx**.

a. Look at scatterplots and the table of correlations for these five variables. Does it appear that a multiple regression equation for JobEff, with the test scores as explanatory variables, will be successful? Can you foresee any problems in obtaining accurate estimates of the individual regression coefficients?

b. Estimate the regression equation that includes all four test scores, and find 95% confidence intervals for the coefficients of the explanatory variables. How can you explain the negative coefficient of Test3, given that the correlation between JobEff and Test3 is positive?

c. Can you reject the null hypothesis that these test scores, as a whole, have no predictive ability for job effectiveness at the 1% level? Why or why not?

d. If a new prospective manager has test scores of 83, 74, 65, and 77, what do you predict his job effectiveness rating will be in 1 year? What is the standard error of this prediction?

Level B

59. Confederate Express is attempting to determine how its monthly shipping costs depend on the number of units shipped during a month. The file **P12_59.xlsx** contains the number of units shipped and total shipping costs for the last 15 months.

a. Use regression to determine a relationship between units shipped and monthly shipping costs.

b. Plot the errors for the predictions in order of time sequence. Is there any unusual pattern?

c. We have been told that there was a trucking strike during months 11 through 15, and we believe that this might have influenced shipping costs. How could the answer to part **a** be modified to account for the effects of the strike? After accounting for the effects of the strike, does the unusual pattern in part **b** disappear?

60. You are trying to determine the effects of three packaging displays (A, B, and C) on sales of toothpaste. The file **P12_60.xlsx** contains the number of cases of toothpaste sold for 9 consecutive weeks. The type of store (GR = grocery, DI = discount, and DE = department store) and the store location (U = urban, S = suburban, and R = rural) are also listed.

a. Run a multiple regression to determine how the type of store, display, and store location influence sales. Which potential explanatory variables should be included in the equation? Explain your rationale for including or excluding variables.

b. What type of store, store location, and display appears to maximize sales?

c. For the type of store in your part **b** answer, estimate the probability that 80 or more cases of toothpaste will be sold during a week. (*Hint*: Use the standard error of prediction and the fact that the errors are approximately normally distributed.)

d. Does multicollinearity or autocorrelation seem to be a problem?

61. You want to determine the variables that influence bus usage in major American cities. For 24 cities, the following data are listed in the file **P12_61.xlsx**:

■ Bus travel (annual, in thousands of hours)
■ Income (average per capita income)
■ Population (in thousands)
■ Land area (in square miles)

a. Use these data to fit the multiplicative equation

$$BusTravel = \alpha Income^{\beta_1} Population^{\beta_2} LandArea^{\beta_3}$$

b. Are all variables significant at the 0.05 level?

c. Interpret the values of β_1, β_2, and β_3.

62. The file **P12_62.xlsx** contains data on 80 managers at a large (fictitious) corporation. The variables are Salary (current annual salary), YrsExper (years of experience in the industry), YrsHere (years of experience with this company), and MglLevel (current level in the company, coded 1 to 4). You want to regress Salary on the potential explanatory variables. What is the "best" ways to do so? Specifically, how should you handle MglLevel? Also, should you include both YrsExper and YrsHere or only one of these, and if only one, which one? Present your results, and explain them and your reasoning behind them.

63. Mattel has assigned you to analyze the factors influencing Barbie sales. The number of Barbie dolls sold (in millions) during the last 23 years is given in the file **P12_63.xlsx**. Year 23 is last year, year 22 is the year before that, and so on. The following factors are thought to influence Barbie sales:

- Was there a recession?
- Were Barbies on sale at Christmas?
- Was there an upward trend over time?

a. Determine an equation that can be used to predict annual Barbie sales. Make sure that all variables in your equation are significant at the 0.15 level.
b. Interpret the coefficients in your equation.
c. Are there any outliers?
d. Is heteroscedasticity or autocorrelation a problem?
e. During the current year (year 24), a recession is predicted and Barbies will be put on sale at Christmas. There is a 1% chance that sales of Barbies will exceed what value? You may assume here that heteroscedasticity and autocorrelation are not a problem. (*Hint:* Use the standard error of prediction and the fact that the errors are approximately normally distributed.)

64. The capital asset pricing model (CAPM) is a cornerstone of finance. To apply the CAPM, we assume that each stock has a risk measure (called the beta of the stock) associated with it. Then the CAPM asserts that

- The expected return on $1 invested in a stock is a linear function of the stock's beta.
- $1 invested in a stock with a 0 beta will earn an annual return equal to the risk-free interest rate (r_f) on 90-day treasury bills.
- $1 invested in a stock with a beta of 1 will yield an annual return equal to the annual return (r_m) on the market portfolio.

a. Formulate a population regression model incorporating these features of the CAPM. The explanatory variable is the stock's beta and the dependent variable is the annual return on $1 invested in the stock.
b. Given the data in Table 12.3, test the adequacy of the model developed in part **a**. Assume $r_f = 0.09$ and $r_m = 0.18$.

Table 12.3 Stock Returns and Betas

Company	Beta	Annual Return
AT&T	0.56	0.14
IBM	1.07	0.19
GM	0.76	0.16
Polaroid	2.17	0.28
Chrysler	1.04	0.18

65. How does inflation in a country affect changes in exchange rates? The file **P12_65.xlsx** contains the following information for 11 countries.

- Ratio of percentage increase in prices in local country to percentage increase in U.S. prices from 1973 to 1995.
- Ratio of 1995 units of local currency per dollar to 1973 units of local currency per dollar.

Use these data to explain how inflation affects exchange rates. Do you have an explanation for these results? (Source: *The Economist*, January 20, 1996)

66. The file **P12_66.xlsx** shows the "yield curve" (at monthly intervals). For example, in January 1985 the annual rate on a 3-month T-bill was 7.76% and the annual rate on a 30-year government bond was 11.45%. Use regression to determine which interest rates tend to move together most closely. (Source: International Investment and Exchange Database Developed by Craig Holden, Indiana University School of Business)

67. The Keynesian school of macroeconomics believes that increased government spending leads to increased growth. The file **P12_67.xlsx** contains the following annual data:

- Government spending as percentage of GDP (gross domestic product)
- Percentage annual growth in annual GDP

Are these data consistent with the Keynesian school of economics? (Source: *Wall Street Journal*)

68. The June 1997 issue of *Management Accounting* gave the following rule for predicting your current salary if you are a managerial accountant. Take $31,865. Next, add $20,811 if you are top management, add $3604 if you are senior management, or subtract $11,419 if you are entry management. Then add $1105 for every year you have been a managerial accountant. Add $7600 if you have a master's degree or subtract $12,467 if you have no college degree. Add $11,257 if you have a professional certification. Finally, add $8667 if you are male.

a. How do you think the journal derived this method of estimating an accountant's current salary? Be specific.
b. How could a managerial accountant use this information to determine whether he or she is significantly underpaid?

69. Suppose you are trying to use regression to predict the current salary of a major league baseball player. What variables might you use?

70. The file **P12_70.xlsx** contains sample data on annual sales for Prozac, a drug produced by Eli Lilly. For each year, the file lists the price per day of therapy (DOT) charged for Prozac and total Prozac sales (in millions of DOT) for the year. Assuming that price is the only factor influencing Prozac sales, determine the number of DOT of Prozac that Lilly should produce for the year to ensure that there is only a 1% chance that Lilly runs out of Prozac. Assume the current price of Prozac is $1.75. (*Hint:* Use the standard error of prediction and the fact that the errors are approximately normally distributed.)

71. A business school committee was charged with studying admissions criteria to the school. Until that time, only juniors were admitted. Part of the committee's task was to see whether freshman courses would be equally good predictors of success as freshman and sophomore courses combined. Here, we take "success" to mean doing well in A-core (a combination of the junior level finance, marketing, and production courses, F301, M301, and P301). The file **P12_71.xlsx** contains data on 250 students who had just completed A-core. For each student, the file lists their grades in the following courses:

- M118 (freshman)—finite math
- M119 (freshman)—calculus
- K201 (freshman)—computers
- W131 (freshman)—writing
- E201, E202 (sophomore)—micro- and macroeconomics
- L201 (sophomore)—business law
- A201, A202 (sophomore)—accounting
- E270 (sophomore)—statistics
- A-core (junior)—finance, marketing, and production

Except for A-core, each value is a grade point for a specific course (such as 3.7 for an A−). For A-core, each value is the average grade point for the three courses comprising A-core.

a. The A-core grade point is the eventual dependent variable in a regression analysis. Look at the correlations between all variables. Is multicollinearity likely to be a problem? Why or why not?

b. Run a multiple regression using all of the potential explanatory variables. Now, eliminate the variables as follows. (This is a reasonable variation of the procedures discussed in the chapter.) Look at 95% confidence intervals for their coefficients (as usual, not counting the intercept term). Any variable whose confidence interval contains the value 0 is a candidate for exclusion. For all such candidates, eliminate the variable with the *t*-value lowest in magnitude. Then rerun the regression, and use the same procedure to possibly exclude another variable. Keep doing this until 95% confidence intervals of the coefficients of all remaining variables do *not* include 0. Report this final equation, its R^2 value, and its standard error of estimate s_e.

c. Give a quick summary of the properties of the equation in part **b**. Specifically, (i) do the variables have the "correct" signs, (ii) which courses tend to be the best predictors, (iii) are the predictions from

this equation likely to be much good, and (iv) are there any obvious violations of the regression assumptions?

d. Redo part **b**, but now use as your potential explanatory variables only courses taken in the freshman year. As in part **b**, report the final equation, its R^2, and its standard error of estimate s_e.

e. Briefly, do you think there is enough predictive power in the freshman courses, relative to the freshman and sophomore courses combined, to change to a sophomore admit policy? (Answer only on the basis of the regression results; don't get into other merits of the argument.)

72. The file **P12_72.xlsx** has data on several countries. The variables are listed here.

- Country: name of country
- GNPCapita: GNP per capita
- PopGrowth: average annual percentage change in population, 1980–1990
- Calorie: daily per capita calorie content of food used for domestic consumption
- LifeExp: average life expectancy of newborn given current mortality conditions
- Fertility: births per woman given current fertility rates

With data such as these, cause and effect are difficult to determine. For example, does low LifeExp cause GNPCapita to be low, or vice versa? Therefore, the purpose of this problem is to experiment with the following sets of dependent and explanatory variables. In each case, look at scatterplots (and use economic reasoning) to find and estimate the best form of the equation, using only linear and logarithmic variables. Then interpret precisely what each equation is saying.

a. Dependent: LifeExp; Explanatories: Calorie, Fertility

b. Dependent: LifeExp; Explanatories: GNPCapita, PopGrowth

c. Dependent: GNPCapita; Explanatories: PopGrowth, Calorie, Fertility

73. Suppose that an economist has been able to gather data on the relationship between demand and price for a particular product. After analyzing scatterplots and using economic theory, the economist decides to estimate an equation of the form $Q = aP^b$, where Q is quantity demanded and P is price. An appropriate regression analysis is then performed, and the estimated parameters turn out to be $a = 1000$ and $b = -1.3$. Now consider two scenarios: (1) the price increases from $10 to $12.50; (2) the price increases from $20 to $25.

a. Do you expect the percentage decrease in demand to be the same in scenario (1) as in scenario (2)? Why or why not?

b. What is the expected percentage decrease in demand in scenario (1); in scenario (2)? Be as exact as possible. (*Hint*: Remember from economics that an elasticity shows directly what happens for a "small" percentage change in price. These changes aren't that small, so you'll have to do some calculating.)

74. A human resources analyst believes that in a particular industry, the wage rate ($/hr) is related to seniority by an equation of the form $W = ae^{bS}$, where W equals wage rate and S equals seniority (in years). However, the analyst suspects that both parameters, a and b, might depend on whether the workers belong to a union. Therefore, the analyst gathers data on a number of workers, both union and nonunion, and estimates the following equation with regression:

$$\ln(W) = 2.14 + 0.027S + 0.12U + 0.006SU$$

Here $\ln(W)$ is the natural log of W, U is 1 for union workers and 0 for nonunion workers, and SU is the product of S and U.

a. According to this model, what is the predicted wage rate for a nonunion worker with 0 years of seniority? What is it for a union worker with 0 years of seniority?

b. Explain exactly what this equation implies about the predicted effect of seniority on wage rate for a nonunion worker; for a union worker.

75. A company has recorded its overhead costs, machine hours, and labor hours for the past 60 months. The data are in the file **P12_75.xlsx**. The company decides to use regression to explain its overhead hours linearly as a function of machine hours and labor hours. However, recognizing good statistical practice, it decides to estimate a regression equation for the first 36 months, then validate this regression with the data from the last 24 months. That is, it will substitute the values of machine and labor hours from the last 24 months into the regression equation that is based on the first 36 months and see how well it does.

a. Run the regression for the first 36 months. Explain briefly why the coefficient of labor hours is not significant.

b. For this part, use the regression equation from part **a** with both variables still in the equation (even though one was insignificant). Fill in the fitted and residual columns for months 37 through 60. Then do relevant calculations to see whether the R^2 (or multiple R) and the standard error of estimate s_e are as good for these 24 months as they are for the first 36 months. Explain your results briefly. (*Hint*: Remember the meaning of the multiple R and the standard error of estimate.)

76. Pernavik Dairy produces and sells a wide range of dairy products. Because most of the dairy's costs and prices are set by a government regulatory board, most

of the competition between the dairy and its competitors takes place through advertising. The controller of Pernavik has developed the sales and advertising levels for the last 52 weeks. These appear in the file **P12_76.xlsx**. Note that the advertising levels for the 3 weeks prior to week 1 are also listed. The controller wonders whether Pernavik is spending too much money on advertising. He argues that the company's contribution-margin ratio is about 10%. That is, 10% of each sales dollar goes toward covering fixed costs. This means that each advertising dollar has to generate at least $10 of sales or the advertising is not cost-effective. Use regression to determine whether advertising dollars are generating this type of sales response. (*Hint*: It is very possible that the sales value in any week is affected not only by advertising this week, but also by advertising levels in the past 1, 2, or 3 weeks. These are called "lagged" values of advertising. Try regression models with lagged values of advertising included, and see whether you get better results.)

77. The Pierce Company manufactures drill bits. The production of the drill bits occurs in lots of 1000 units. Due to the intense competition in the industry and the correspondingly low prices, Pierce has undertaken a study of the manufacturing costs of each of the products it manufactures. One part of this study concerns the overhead costs associated with producing the drill bits. Senior production personnel have determined that the number of lots produced, the direct labor hours used, and the number of production runs per month might help to explain the behavior of overhead costs. The file **P12_77.xlsx** contains the data on these variables for the past 36 months.

a. See how well you can predict overhead costs on the basis of these variables with a linear regression equation. Why might you be disappointed with the results?

b. A production supervisor believes that labor hours and the number of production run setups affect overhead because Pierce uses a lot of supplies when it is working on the machines and because the machine setup time for each run is charged to overhead. As he says, "When the rate of production increases, we use overtime until we can train the additional people that we require for the machines. When the rate of production falls, we incur idle time until the surplus workers are transferred to other parts of the plant. So it would seem to me that there will be an additional overhead cost whenever the level of production changes. I would also say that because of the nature of this rescheduling process, the bigger the change in production, the greater the effect of the change in production on the increase in overhead." How might you use this information to find a better regression equation than in part **a**? (*Hint*: Develop a new explanatory variable, and use the fact that the number of lots produced in the month preceding month 1 was 5964.)

78. Danielson Electronics manufactures color television sets for sale in a highly competitive marketplace. Recently Ron Thomas, the marketing manager of Danielson Electronics, has been complaining that the company is losing market share because of a poor-quality image, and he has asked that the company's major product, the 25-inch console model, be redesigned to incorporate a higher quality level. The company general manager, Steve Hatting, is considering the request to improve the product quality but is not convinced that consumers will be willing to pay the additional expense for improved quality.

   As the company controller, you are in charge of determining the cost effectiveness of improving the quality of the television sets. With the help of the marketing staff, you have obtained a summary of the average retail price of the company's television set and the prices of 29 competitive sets. In addition, you have obtained from *The Shoppers' Guide,* a magazine that evaluates and reports on various consumer products, a quality rating of the television sets produced by Danielson Electronics and its competitors. The file **P12_78.xlsx** summarizes these data. According to *The Shoppers' Guide,* the quality rating, which varies from 0 to 10 (10 being the highest level of quality), considers such factors as the quality of the picture, the frequency of repair, and the cost of repairs. Discussions with the product design group suggest that the cost of manufacturing this type of television set is $125 + Q^2$, where Q is the quality rating.
   a. Regress AvgPrice versus QualityRating. Does the regression equation imply that customers are willing to pay a premium for quality? Explain.
   b. Given the results from part **a**, is there a preferred level of quality for this product? Assume that the quality level will affect only the price charged and not the level of sales of the product.
   c. How might you answer part **b** if the level of sales is also affected by the quality level (or alternatively, if the level of sales is affected by price)?

79. The file **P12_79.xlsx** contains data on gasoline consumption and several economic variables. The variables are gasoline consumption for passenger cars (GasUsed), service station price excluding taxes (SSPrice), retail price of gasoline including state and federal taxes (RPrice), Consumer Price Index for all items (CPI), Consumer Price Index for public transportation (CPIT), number of registered passenger cars (Cars), average miles traveled per gallon (MPG), and real per capita disposable income (DispInc). (Sources: *Basic Petroleum Data Book,* published by the American Petroleum Institute, 2001, and *Economic Report of the President,* 2002)

   a. Regress GasUsed linearly versus CPIT, Cars, MPG, DispInc, and DefRPrice, where DefRPrice is the deflated retail price of gasoline (RPrice divided by CPI). What signs would you expect the coefficients to have? Do they have these signs? Which of the coefficients are statistically significant at the 0.05 level?
   b. Suppose the government makes the claim that for every 1 cent of tax on gasoline, there will be a $1 billion increase in tax revenue. Use the estimated equation in part **a** to support or refute the government's claim.

80. On October 30, 1995, the citizens of Quebec went to the polls to decide the future of their province. They were asked to vote "Yes" or "No" to whether Quebec, a predominantly French-speaking province, should secede from Canada and become a sovereign country. The "No" side was declared the winner, but only by a thin margin. Immediately following the vote, however, allegations began to surface that the result was closer than it should have been. [Source: Cawley and Sommers (1996)]. In particular, the ruling separatist Parti Québécois, whose job was to decide which ballots were rejected, was accused by the "No" voters of systematic electoral fraud by voiding thousands of "No" votes in the predominantly allophone and anglophone electoral divisions of Montreal. (An allophone refers to someone whose first language is neither English nor French. An anglophone refers to someone whose first language is English.)

   Cawley and Sommers examined whether electoral fraud had been committed by running a regression, using data from the 125 electoral divisions in the October 1995 referendum. The dependent variable was REJECT, the percentage of rejected ballots in the electoral division. The explanatory variables were as follows:
   - ALLOPHONE: percentage of allophones in the electoral division
   - ANGLOPHONE: percentage of anglophones in the electoral division
   - REJECT94: percentage of rejected votes from that electoral division during a similar referendum in 1994
   - LAVAL: dummy variable equal to 1 for electoral divisions in the Laval region, 0 otherwise
   - LAV_ALL: interaction (i.e., product) of LAVAL and ALLOPHONE

   The estimated regression equation (with *t*-values in parentheses) is

$$\text{Prediced REJECT} = \underset{(5.68)}{1.112} + \underset{(4.34)}{0.020} \text{ ALLOPHONE}$$

$$+ \underset{(0.12)}{0.001} \text{ ANGLOPHONE} + \underset{(2.64)}{0.223} \text{ REJECT94}$$

$$- \underset{(-8.61)}{3.773} \text{ LAVAL} + \underset{(15.62)}{0.387} \text{ LAV\_ALL}$$

The R^2 value was 0.759. Based on this analysis, Cawley and Sommers state that, "The evidence presented here suggests that there were voting irregularities in the October 1995 Quebec referendum, especially in Laval." Discuss how they came to this conclusion.

81. Suppose we are trying to explain variations in salaries for technicians in a particular field of work. The file **P12_81.xlsx** contains annual salaries for 200 technicians. It also shows how many years of experience each technician has, as well as his or her education level. There are four education levels, as explained in the comment in cell D3. Three suggestions are put forth for the relationship between Salary and these two explanatory variables:

- We should regress Salary linearly versus the two given variables, YrsExper and EducLev.
- All that really matters in terms of education is whether the person got a college degree or not. Therefore, we should regress Salary linearly versus YrsExper and a dummy variable indicating whether he or she got a college degree.
- Each level of education might result in different jumps in salary. Therefore, we should regress

Salary linearly versus YrsExper and dummy variables for the different education levels.

a. Run the indicated regressions for each of these three suggestions. Then (i) explain what each equation is saying and how the three are different (focus here on the coefficients), (ii) which you prefer, and (iii) whether (or how) the regression results in your preferred equation contradict the average salary results shown in the PivTab sheet of the file.

b. Consider the four workers shown on the Predict sheet of the file. (These are four new workers, not among the original 200.) Using your preferred equation, calculate a predicted salary and a 95% prediction interval for each of these four workers.

c. It turns out (you don't have to check this) that the interaction between years of experience and education level is *not* significant for this data set. In general, however, argue why we might expect an interaction between them for salary data of technical workers. What form of interaction would you suspect? (There is not necessarily one right answer, but argue convincingly one way or the other, that is, for a positive or a negative interaction.)

The Artsy Corporation has been sued in the U.S. Federal Court on charges of sex discrimination in employment under Title VII of the Civil Rights Act of 1964.[10] The litigation at contention here is a class-action lawsuit brought on behalf of all females who were employed by the company, or who had applied for work with the company, between 1979 and 1987. Artsy operates in several states, runs four quite distinct businesses, and has many different types of employees. The allegations of the plaintiffs deal with issues of hiring, pay, promotions, and other "conditions of employment."

In such large class-action employment discrimination lawsuits, it has become common for statistical evidence to play a central role in the determination of guilt or damages. In an interesting twist on typical legal procedures, a precedent has developed in these cases that plaintiffs may make a prima facie case purely in terms of circumstantial statistical evidence. If that statistical evidence is reasonably strong, the burden of proof shifts to the defendants to rebut the plaintffs' statistics with other data, other analyses of the same data, or nonstatistical testimony. In practice, statistical arguments often dominate the proceedings of such Equal Employment Opportunity (EEO) cases. Indeed, in this case the statistical data used as evidence filled numerous computer tapes, and the supporting statistical analysis comprised thousands of pages of printouts and reports. We work here with a typical subset that pertains to one contested issue at one of the company's locations.

The data in the file **Artsy Lawsuit.xlsx** relate to the pay of 256 employees on the hourly payroll at one of the company's production facilities. The data include an identification number (ID) that would permit us to identify the person by name or social security number; the person's gender (Gender), where 0 denotes female and 1 denotes male; the person's job grade in 1986 (Grade); the length of time (in years) the person had been in that job grade as of December 31, 1986 (TInGrade); and the person's weekly pay rate as of December 31, 1986 (Rate). These data permit a statistical examination of one of the issues in the case—fair pay for female employees. We deal with one of three pay classes of employees—those on the biweekly payroll, and at one of the company's locations at Pocahantus, Maine.

The plaintiffs' attorneys have proposed settling the pay issues in the case for this group of female employees for a "back pay" lump payment to female employees of 25% of their pay during the period 1979 to 1987. It is our task to examine the data statistically for evidence in favor of, or against, the charges. We are to advise the lawyers for the company on how to proceed. Consider the following issues as they have been laid out to us by the attorneys representing the firm:

1. Overall, how different is pay by gender? Are the differences in pay statistically significant? Does a statistical significance test have meaning in a case like this? If so, how should it be performed? Lay out as succinctly as possible the arguments that you anticipate the plaintiffs will make with this data set.

2. The company wishes to argue that a legitimate explanation of the pay rate differences may be the difference in job grades. (In this analysis, we will tacitly assume that each person's job grade is, in fact, appropriate for him or her, even though the plaintiffs' attorneys have charged that females have been unfairly kept in the lower grades. Other statistical data, not available here, are used in that analysis.) The lawyers ask, "Is there a relatively easy way to understand, analyze, and display the pay differences by job grade? Is it easy enough that it could be presented to an average jury without confusing them?" Again, use the data to anticipate the possible arguments of the plaintiffs. To what extent does job grade appear to explain the pay rate differences between the genders? Propose and carry out appropriate hypothesis tests or confidence intervals to check whether the difference in pay between genders is statistically significant within each of the grades.

[9]This case was contributed by Peter Kolesar from Columbia University.
[10]Artsy is an actual corporation, and the data given in this case are real, but the name has been changed to protect the firm's true identity.

3. In the actual case, the previous analysis suggested to the attorneys that differences in pay rates are due, at least in part, to differences in job grades. They had heard that in another EEO case, the dependence of pay rate on job grade had been investigated with regression analysis. Perform a simple linear regression of pay rate on job grade for them. Interpret the results fully. Is the regression significant? How much of the variability in pay does job grade account for? Carry out a full check of the quality of your regression. What light does this shed on the pay fairness issue? Does it help or hurt the company? Is it fair to the female employees?

4. It is argued that seniority within a job grade should be taken into account because the company's written pay policy explicitly calls for the consideration of this factor. How different are times in grade by gender? Are they enough to matter?

5. The Artsy legal team wants an analysis of the simultaneous influence of grade and time in grade on pay. Perform a multiple regression of pay rate versus grade and time in grade. Is the regression significant? How much of the variability in pay rates is explained by this model? Will this analysis help your clients? Could the plaintiffs effectively attack it? Consider residuals in your analysis of these issues.

6. Organize your analyses and conclusions in a brief report summarizing your findings for your client, the Artsy Corporation. Be complete but succinct. Be sure to advise them on the settlement issue. Be as forceful as you can be in arguing "the Artsy Case" without misusing the data or statistical theory. Apprise your client of the risks they face by developing the forceful and legitimate counterargument the female plaintiffs could make. ■

Dupree Fuels Company is facing a difficult problem. Dupree sells heating oil to residential customers. Given the amount of competition in the industry, both from other home heating oil suppliers and from electric and natural gas utilities, the price of the oil supplied and the level of service are critical in determining a company's success. Unlike electric and natural gas customers, oil customers are exposed to the risk of running out of fuel. Home heating oil suppliers therefore have to guarantee that the customer's oil tank will not be allowed to run dry. In fact, Dupree's service pledge is, "50 free gallons on us if we let you run dry." Beyond the cost of the oil, however, Dupree is concerned about the perceived reliability of his service if a customer is allowed to run out of oil.

To estimate customer oil use, the home heating oil industry uses the concept of "degree days." A degree day is equal to the difference between the average daily temperature and 68 degrees Fahrenheit. So if the average temperature on a given day is 50, the degree days for that day will be 18. (If the degree day calculation results in a negative number, the degree days number is recorded as 0.) By keeping track of the number of degree days since the customer's last oil fill, by knowing the size of the customer's oil tank, and by estimating the customer's oil consumption as a function of the number of degree days, the oil supplier can estimate when the customer is getting low on fuel and then resupply the customer.

Dupree has used this scheme in the past but is disappointed with the results and the computational burdens it places on the company. First, the system requires that a consumption-per-degree-day figure be estimated for each customer to reflect that customer's consumption habits, size of home, quality of home insulation, and family size. Because Dupree has more than 1500 customers, the computational burden of keeping track of all of these customers is enormous. Second, the system is crude and unreliable. The consumption per degree day for each customer is computed by dividing the oil consumption during the preceding year by the degree days during

the preceding year. Customers have tended to use less fuel than estimated during the colder months and more fuel than estimated during the warmer months. This means that Dupree is making more deliveries than necessary during the colder months and customers are running out of oil during the warmer months.

Dupree wants to develop a consumption estimation model that is practical and more reliable. The following data are available in the file **Dupree Fuels.xlsx**:

- The number of degree days since the last oil fill and the consumption amounts for 40 customers.

- The number of people residing in the homes of each of the 40 customers. Dupree thinks that this might be important in predicting the oil consumption of customers using oil-fired hot water heaters because it provides an estimate of the hot-water requirements of each customer. Each of the customers in this sample uses an oil-fired hot water heater.

- An assessment, provided by Dupree sales staff, of the home type of each of these 40 customers. The home type classification, which is a number between 1 and 5, is a composite index of the home size, age, exposure to wind, level of insulation, and furnace type. A low index implies a lower oil consumption per degree day, and a high index implies a higher consumption of oil per degree day. Dupree thinks that the use of such an index will allow them to estimate a consumption model based on a sample data set and then to apply the same model to predict the oil demand of each of his customers.

Use regression to see whether a statistically reliable oil consumption model can be estimated from the data. ■

[11]Case Studies 12.2 through 12.4 are based on problems from *Advanced Management Accounting,* 2nd edition, by Robert S. Kaplan and Anthony A. Atkinson, Prentice Hall, 1989. We thank them for allowing us to adopt their problems.

12.3 DEVELOPING A FLEXIBLE BUDGET AT THE GUNDERSON PLANT

The Gunderson Plant manufactures the industrial product line of FGT Industries. Plant management wants to be able to get a good, yet quick, estimate of the manufacturing overhead costs that can be expected each month. The easiest and simplest method to accomplish this task is to develop a flexible budget formula for the manufacturing overhead costs. The plant's accounting staff has suggested that simple linear regression be used to determine the behavior pattern of the overhead costs. The regression data can provide the basis for the flexible budget formula. Sufficient evidence is available to conclude that manufacturing overhead costs vary with direct labor hours. The actual direct labor hours and the corresponding manufacturing overhead costs for each month of the last 3 years have been used in the linear regression analysis.

The 3-year period contained various occurrences not uncommon to many businesses. During the first year, production was severely curtailed during 2 months due to wildcat strikes. In the second year, production was reduced in 1 month because of material shortages, and increased significantly (scheduled overtime) during 2 months to meet the units required for a one-time sales order. At the end of the second year, employee benefits were raised significantly as the result of a labor agreement. Production during the third year was not affected by any special circumstances. Various members of Gunderson's accounting staff raised some issues regarding the historical data collected for the regression analysis. These issues were as follows.

■ Some members of the accounting staff believed that the use of data from all 36 months would provide a more accurate portrayal of the cost behavior. While they recognized that any of the monthly data could include efficiencies and inefficiencies, they believed these efficiencies and inefficiencies would tend to balance out over a longer period of time.

■ Other members of the accounting staff suggested that only those months that were considered normal should be used so that the regression would not be distorted.

■ Still other members felt that only the most recent 12 months should be used because they were the most current.

■ Some members questioned whether historical data should be used at all to form the basis for a flexible budget formula.

The accounting department ran two regression analyses of the data—one using the data from all 36 months and the other using only the data from the last 12 months. The information derived from the two linear regressions is shown below (t-values shown in parentheses). The 36-month regression is

$$OH_t = 123,810 + 1.60 \ DLH_t, \quad R^2 = 0.32$$
$$(1.64)$$

The 12-month regression is

$$OH_t = 109,020 + 3.00 \ DLH_t, \quad R^2 = 0.48$$
$$(3.01)$$

Questions

1. Which of the two results (12 months versus 36 months) would you use as a basis for the flexible budget formula?

2. How would the four specific issues raised by the members of Gunderson's accounting staff influence your willingness to use the results of the statistical analyses as the basis for the flexible budget formula? Explain your answer. ■

Wagner Printers performs all types of printing including custom work, such as advertising displays, and standard work, such as business cards. Market prices exist for standard work, and Wagner Printers must match or better these prices to get the business. The key issue is whether the existing market price covers the cost associated with doing the work. On the other hand, most of the custom work must be priced individually. Because all custom work is done on a job-order basis, Wagner routinely keeps track of all the direct labor and direct materials costs associated with each job. However, the overhead for each job must be estimated. The overhead is applied to each job using a predetermined (normalized) rate based on estimated overhead and labor hours. Once the cost of the prospective job is determined, the sales manager develops a bid that reflects both the existing market conditions and the estimated price of completing the job.

In the past, the normalized rate for overhead has been computed by using the historical average of overhead per direct labor hour. Wagner has become increasingly concerned about this practice for two reasons. First, it hasn't produced accurate forecasts of overhead in the past. Second, technology has changed the printing process, so that the labor content of jobs has been decreasing, and the normalized rate of overhead per direct labor hour has steadily been increasing. The file **Wagner Printers.xlsx** shows the overhead data that Wagner has collected for its shop for the past 52 weeks. The average weekly overhead for the last 52 weeks is $54,208, and the average weekly number of labor hours worked is 716. Therefore, the normalized rate for overhead that will be used in the upcoming week is about $76 (= 54,208/716) per direct labor hour.

Questions

1. Determine whether you can develop a more accurate estimate of overhead costs.

2. Wagner is now preparing a bid for an important order that may involve a considerable amount of repeat business. The estimated requirements for this project are 15 labor hours, 8 machine hours, $150 direct labor cost, and $750 direct material cost. Using the existing approach to cost estimation, Wagner has estimated the cost for this job as $2040 (= 150 + 750 + (76 × 15)). Given the existing data, what cost would you estimate for this job? ∎

Time Series Analysis and Forecasting

©Mark Richards/Photo Edit, Inc.

FORECASTING LABOR REQUIREMENTS AT TACO BELL

How much quantitative analysis occurs at fast-food restaurants? At Taco Bell, a lot! An article by Huerter and Swart (1998) explains the approach to labor management that has occurred at Taco Bell restaurants over the past decade. Labor is a large component of costs at Taco Bell. Approximately 30% of every sales dollar goes to labor. However, the unique characteristics of fast-food restaurants make it difficult to plan labor utilization efficiently. In particular, the Taco Bell product—food—cannot be inventoried; it must be made fresh at the time the customer orders it. Because of shifting demand throughout any given day, where the lunch period accounts for approximately 52% of a day's sales and as much as 25% of a day's sales can occur during the busiest hour, labor requirements vary greatly throughout the day. If too many workers are on hand during slack times, they are paid for doing practically nothing. Worse than that, however, are the lost sales (and unhappy customers) that occur if too few workers are on hand during peak times. Before 1988, Taco Bell made very little effort to manage the labor problem in an efficient, centralized manner. The company simply allocated about 30% of each store's sales to the store managers and let them allocate it as best they could—not always with good results.

In 1988 Taco Bell initiated its "value meal" deals, where certain meals were priced as low as 59 cents. This increased demand to the point where management could no longer ignore the labor allocation problem. Therefore, in-store computers were installed, data from all stores were collected, and a team of analysts was assigned the task of developing a cost-efficient labor allocation system. This system, which has now been fully integrated into all Taco Bell stores since 1993, is composed of three subsystems: (1) a forecasting subsystem that, for each store, forecasts the arrival rate of customers by 15-minute interval by day of week; (2) a simulation subsystem that, for each store, simulates the congestion and number of lost customers that will occur for any customer arrival rate, given a specific number (and deployment) of workers; and (3) an optimization subsystem that, for each store, indicates the minimum cost allocation of workers, subject to various constraints, such as a minimum service level and a minimum shift length for workers. Although all three of these subsystems are important, the forecasting subsystem is where it all starts. Each store must have a reasonably accurate forecast of future customer arrival rates, broken down by small time intervals (such as 11:15 A.M. to 11:30 A.M. on Friday), before labor requirements can be predicted and labor allocations can be made in an intelligent manner. Like many real-world forecasting systems, Taco Bell's has two important characteristics: (1) it requires extensive data, which have been made available by the in-store computer systems, and (2) the eventual forecasting method used is mathematically a fairly simple one, namely, 6-week moving averages, which we study in this chapter.

Simple or not, the forecasts, as well as the other system components, have enabled Taco Bell to cut costs and increase profits considerably. In its first 4 years, 1993 to 1996, the labor management system is estimated to have saved Taco Bell approximately $40.34 million in labor costs. Because the number of Taco Bell stores is constantly increasing, the annual company-wide savings from the system will certainly grow in the future. In addition, the focus on quantitative analysis has produced other side benefits for Taco Bell. Its service is now better and more consistent across stores, with many fewer customers leaving because of slow service. Also, the quantitative models developed have enabled Taco Bell to evaluate the effectiveness of various potential productivity enhancements, including self-service drink islands, customer-activated touch screens for ordering, and smaller kitchen areas. So the next time you order food from Taco Bell, you can be assured that there is definitely a method to the madness! ■

13.1 INTRODUCTION

Many decision-making applications depend on a forecast of some quantity. Here are several examples.

Examples of Forecasting Applications

- When a service organization, such as a fast-food restaurant, plans its staffing over some time period, it must forecast the customer demand as a function of time. This might be done at a very detailed level, such as the demand in successive 15-minute periods, or at a more aggregate level, such as the demand in successive weeks.

- When a company plans its ordering or production schedule for a product it sells to the public, it must forecast the customer demand for this product so that it can stock appropriate quantities—neither too much nor too little.

- When an organization plans to invest in stocks, bonds, or other financial instruments, it typically attempts to forecast movements in stock prices and interest rates.

- When government representatives plan policy, they attempt to forecast movements in macroeconomic variables such as inflation, interest rates, and unemployment.

Unfortunately, forecasting is a very difficult task, both in the short run and in the long run. Typically, we base forecasts on historical data. We search for patterns or relationships in the historical data, and then we make forecasts. There are two problems with this approach. The first is that it is not always easy to uncover historical patterns or relationships. In particular, it is often difficult to separate the noise, or random behavior, from the underlying patterns. Some forecasts can even overdo it, by attributing importance to patterns that are in fact random variations and are unlikely to repeat themselves.

The second problem is that there are no guarantees that past patterns will continue in the future. A new war could break out somewhere in the world, a company's competitor could introduce a new product into the market, the bottom could fall out of the stock market, and so on. Each of these shocks to the system being studied could drastically alter the future in a highly unpredictable way. This partly explains why forecasts are almost always wrong. Unless they have inside information to the contrary, forecasters must assume that history will repeat itself. But we all know that history does *not* always repeat itself. Therefore, there are many famous forecasts that turned out to be way off the mark, even though the forecasters made reasonable assumptions and used standard forecasting techniques. Nevertheless, forecasts are required constantly, so fear of failure is no excuse for not giving it our best effort.

13.2 FORECASTING METHODS: AN OVERVIEW

There are many forecasting methods available, and all practitioners have their favorites. To say the least, there is little agreement among practitioners or theoreticians as to the best forecasting method. The methods can generally be divided into three groups: (1) *judgmental* methods, (2) *extrapolation* (or *time series*) methods, and (3) *econometric* (or *causal*) methods. The first of these is basically nonquantitative and will not be discussed here; the last two are quantitative. In this section we describe extrapolation and econometric methods in some generality. In the rest of the chapter, we go into more detail, particularly about the extrapolation methods.

13.2.1 Extrapolation Methods

Extrapolation methods are quantitative methods that use past data of a time series variable—and nothing else, except possibly time itself—to forecast future values of the variable. The idea is that we can use past movements of a variable, such as company sales or U.S. exports to Japan, to forecast its future values. Many extrapolation methods are available, including trend-based regression, exponential smoothing, moving averages, and autoregression. Some of these methods are relatively simple, both conceptually and in terms of the calculations required, whereas others are quite complex. Also, as the names imply, some of these methods use the same regression methods we discussed in the previous two chapters, whereas others do not.

All of these extrapolation methods search for *patterns* in the historical series and then extrapolate these patterns into the future. Some try to track long-term upward or downward trends and then project these. Some try to track the seasonal patterns (sales up in November and December, down in other months, for example) and then project these. Basically, the more complex the method, the more closely it tries to track historical patterns. Researchers have long believed that good forecasting methods should be able to track the ups and downs—the zigzags on a graph—of a time series. This has led to voluminous research and increasingly complex methods. But is complexity always better?

Surprisingly, empirical evidence shows that it is sometimes worse. This is documented in the quarter-century review article by Armstrong (1986) and the article by Schnarrs and Bavuso (1986). They document a number of empirical studies on literally thousands of time series forecasts where complex methods fared no better, and often worse, than simple methods. In fact, the Schnarrs and Bavuso article presents evidence that a naive forecast from a "random walk" model often outperforms all of the more sophisticated extrapolation methods. With this naive model we forecast that next period's value will be the same as this period's value. So if today's closing stock price is 51.375, we forecast that tomorrow's closing stock price will be 51.375. This method is certainly simple, and it sometimes works quite well. We discuss random walks in more detail in Section 13.5.

The evidence in favor of simpler models is not accepted by everyone, particularly not those who have spent years investigating complex models, and complex models continue to be studied and used. However, there is a very plausible reason why simple models might provide better forecasts. The whole idea behind extrapolation methods is to extrapolate historical patterns into the future. But it is often difficult to determine which patterns are real and which represent noise—random ups and downs that are not likely to repeat themselves. Also, if something important changes (a competitor introduces a new product or interest rates increase, for example), it is certainly possible that the historical patterns will change. A potential problem with complex methods is that they often track a historical series *too* closely. That is, they often track patterns that are really noise. Simpler methods, on the other hand, track only the most basic underlying patterns and therefore can be more flexible and accurate in forecasting the future.

13.2.2 Econometric Models

Econometric models, also called **causal** models, use regression to forecast a time series variable by using other explanatory time series variables. For example, a company might use a causal model to regress future sales on its advertising level, the population income level, the interest rate, and possibly others. In one sense, regression analysis involving time series variables is similar to the regression analysis discussed in the previous two chapters. We can still use the same least squares approach and the same multiple regression software in many time series regression models. In fact, several examples and problems in the previous two chapters used time series data.

However, causal regression models for time series data present new mathematical challenges that go well beyond the level of this book. To get a glimpse of the potential difficulties, suppose a company wants to use a causal regression model to forecast its monthly sales for some product, based on two other time series variables: its monthly advertising levels for the product and its main competitor's monthly advertising levels for a competing product. We could simply estimate a regression equation of the form

$$Y_t = \alpha + \beta_1 X_{1t} + \beta_2 X_{2t} \tag{13.1}$$

Here, Y_t is the company's sales in month t, and X_{1t} and X_{2t} are the company's and the competitor's advertising levels in month t. We might learn something useful from this regression model, but we should be aware of the following problems.

One problem is that we must decide on the appropriate "lags" for the regression equation. Do sales this month depend only on advertising levels *this* month, as specified in equation (13.1), or also on advertising levels in the previous month, the previous two months, and so on? A second problem is whether to include lags of the *sales* variable in the regression equation as explanatory variables. Presumably, sales in one month might depend on the level of sales in previous months (as well as on advertising levels). A third problem is that the two advertising variables can be *autocorrelated* and *cross-correlated*. Autocorrelation means, for example, that the company's advertising level in one month can depend on its advertising levels in previous months. Cross-correlation means, for example, that the company's advertising level in one month can be related to the competitor's advertising levels in previous months, or that the competitor's advertising in one month can be related to the company's advertising levels in previous months.

These are difficult issues, and the way in which they are addressed can make a big difference in the usefulness of the resulting regression model. We examine several regression-based models in this chapter, but we avoid situations such as the one just described, where one time series variable Y is regressed on one or more time series X's. [Pankratz (1991) is a good reference for these latter types of models.]

13.2.3 Combining Forecasts

There is one other general forecasting method that is worth mentioning. In fact, it has attracted a lot of attention in recent years, and many researchers believe that it has great potential for increasing forecast accuracy. The method is simple—we combine two or more forecasts to obtain the final forecast. The reasoning behind this method is also simple—the forecast errors from different forecasting methods might cancel one another. The forecasts that are combined can be of the same general type—extrapolation forecasts, for example—or they can be of different types, such as judgmental and extrapolation. The *number* of forecasts to combine and the *weights* to use in combining them have been the subject of several research studies.

Although the findings are not entirely consistent, it appears that the marginal benefit from each individual forecast after the first two or three is minor. Also, there is not much evidence to suggest that the simplest weighting scheme—weight each forecast equally, that is, average them—is any less accurate than more complex weighting schemes.

13.2.4 Components of Time Series Data

In Chapter 2 we discussed time series graphs, a useful graphical means of depicting time series data. We now use these time series graphs to help explain and identify four important components of a time series. These components are called the *trend* component, the *seasonal* component, the *cyclic* component, and the *random* (or *noise*) component.

Let's start by looking at a very simple time series. This is a time series where every observation is the same. Such a series is shown in Figure 13.1. The graph in this figure shows time (t) on the horizontal axis and the observation values (Y) on the vertical axis. We assume that Y is measured at regularly spaced intervals, usually days, weeks, months, quarters, or years, with Y_t being the value of the observation at time period t. As indicated in Figure 13.1, the individual observation points are usually joined by straight lines to make any patterns in the time series more apparent. Because all observations in this time series are equal, the resulting time series graph is a horizontal line. We refer to this time series as the *base* series. We will now illustrate more interesting time series built from this base series.

Figure 13.1

The Base Series

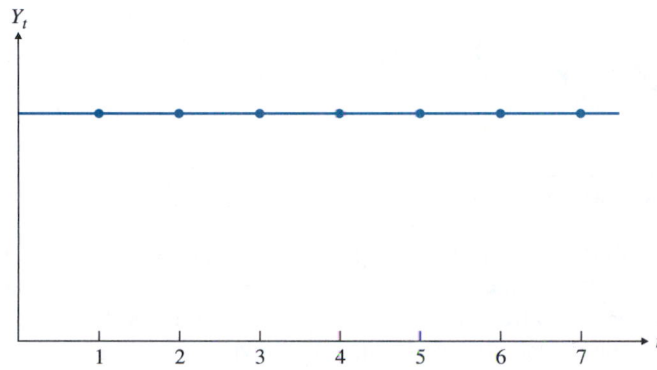

If the observations increase or decrease regularly through time, we say that the time series has a **trend**. The graphs in Figure 13.2 illustrate several possible trends. The *linear* trend in Figure 13.2a occurs if a company's sales, for example, increase by the same amount from period to period. This constant per period change is then the slope of the linear trend line. The curve in Figure 13.2b is an *exponential* trend curve. It occurs in a business such as the personal computer business, where sales have increased at a tremendous rate (at least in the 1990s, the boom years). For this type of curve, the *percentage* increase in Y_t from period to period remains constant. The curve in Figure 13.2c is an *S-shaped* trend curve. For example, this type of trend curve is appropriate for a new product that takes a while to catch on, then exhibits a rapid increase in sales as the public becomes aware of it, and finally tapers off to a fairly constant level. The curves in Figure 13.2 all represent *upward* trends. Of course, we could just as well have *downward* trends of the same types.

Figure 13.2 Series with Trends

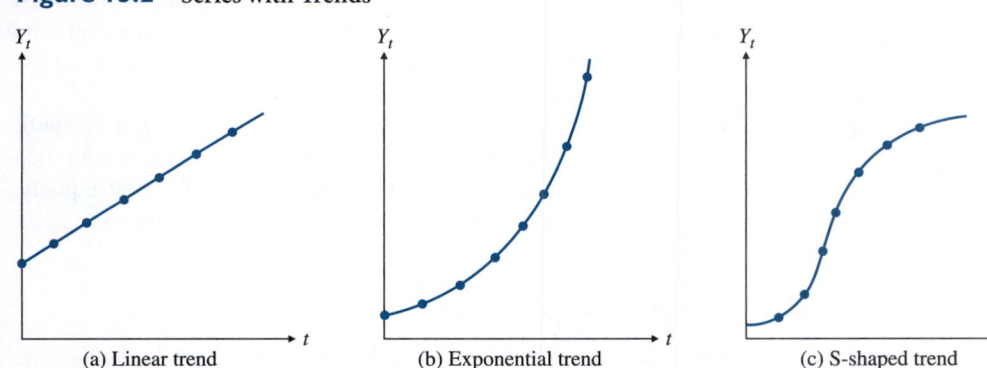

(a) Linear trend (b) Exponential trend (c) S-shaped trend

Many time series have a **seasonal** component. For example, a company's sales of swimming pool equipment increase every spring, then stay relatively high during the summer, and then drop off until next spring, at which time the yearly pattern repeats itself. An important aspect of the seasonal component is that it tends to be predictable from one year to the next. That is, the *same* seasonal pattern tends to repeat itself every year.

In Figure 13.3 we show two possible seasonal patterns. In Figure 13.3a there is nothing but the seasonal component. That is, if there were no seasonal variation, we would have the base series in Figure 13.1. In Figure 13.3b we show a seasonal pattern superimposed on a linear trend line.

Figure 13.3

Series with Seasonality

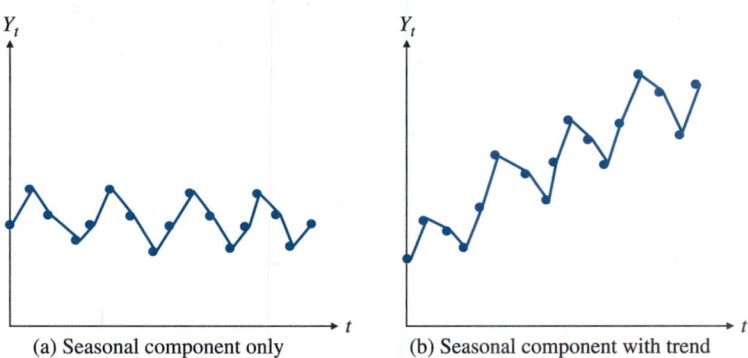

(a) Seasonal component only (b) Seasonal component with trend

The third component of a time series is the **cyclic** component. By studying past movements of many business and economic variables, it becomes apparent that there are business cycles that affect many variables in similar ways. For example, during a recession housing starts generally go down, unemployment goes up, stock prices go down, and so on. But when the recession is over, all of these variables tend to move in the opposite direction. Unfortunately, the cyclic component is harder to predict than the seasonal component. The reason is that seasonal variation is much more regular. For example, swimming pool supplies sales *always* start to increase during the spring. Cyclic variation, on the other hand, is more irregular for the simple reason that the "business cycle" does not always have the same length. A further distinction is that the length of a seasonal cycle is generally one year; the length of a business cycle is generally much longer than one year.

The graphs in Figure 13.4 illustrate the cyclic component of a time series. In Figure 13.4a cyclic variation is superimposed on the base series in Figure 13.1. In Figure 13.4b this same cyclic variation is superimposed on the series in Figure 13.3b. The resulting graph has trend, seasonal variation, and cyclic variation.

Figure 13.4

Series with Cyclic Component

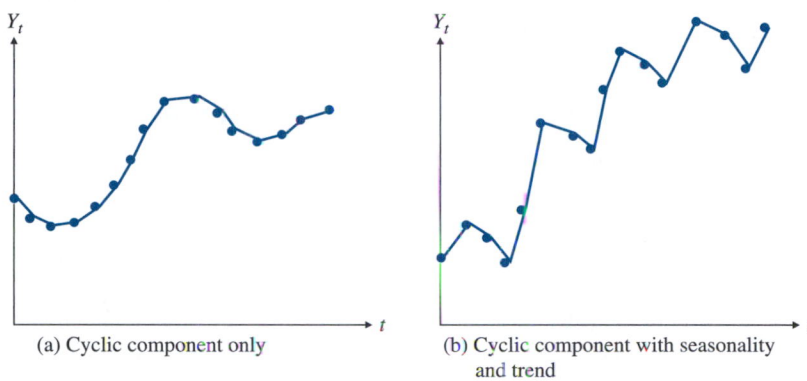

(a) Cyclic component only

(b) Cyclic component with seasonality and trend

The final component in a time series is called the **random** component, or simply **noise**. This unpredictable component gives most time series graphs their irregular, jagged-edge appearances. Usually, a time series can be determined only to a certain extent by its trend, seasonal, and cyclic components. Then other factors determine the rest. These other factors may be inherent randomness, unpredictable "shocks" to the system, the unpredictable behavior of human beings who interact with the system, and possibly others. These factors combine to create a certain amount of unpredictability in almost all time series.

Figures 13.5 and 13.6 show the effect that noise can have on a time series graph. The graph on the left of each figure shows the random component only, superimposed on the base series. Then on the right of each figure, the random component is superimposed on the trend-with-seasonal-component graph from Figure 13.3b. The difference between Figures 13.5 and 13.6 is the relative magnitude of the noise. When it is small, as in Figure 13.5, the other components emerge fairly clearly; they are not disguised by the noise. But if the noise is large in magnitude, as in Figure 13.6, the noise makes it very difficult to distinguish the other components.

Figure 13.5

Series with Noise

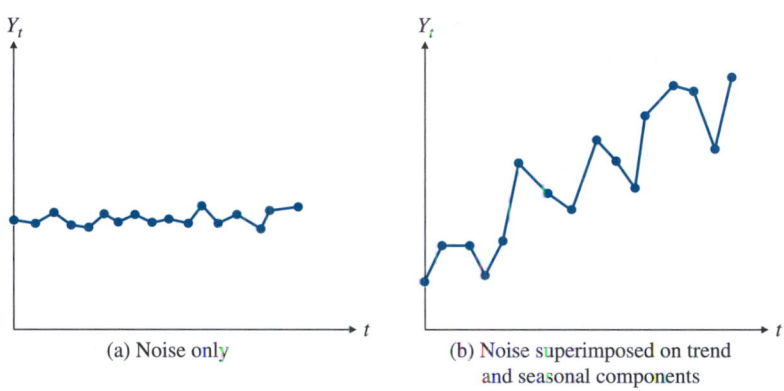

(a) Noise only

(b) Noise superimposed on trend and seasonal components

Figure 13.6

Series with
More Noise

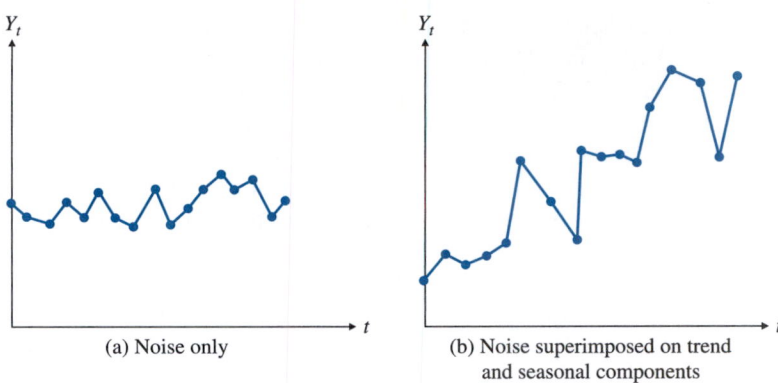

(a) Noise only

(b) Noise superimposed on trend
and seasonal components

13.2.5 General Notation and Formulas

We now introduce a bit of notation and discuss some aspects common to most forecasting methods. In general, we let Y denote the variable we want to forecast. Then Y_t denotes the observed value of Y at time t. Typically, the first observation (the most distant one) corresponds to period $t = 1$, and the last observation (the most recent one) corresponds to period $t = T$, so that T denotes the number of historical observations of Y. The periods themselves might be weeks, months, quarters, years, or any other convenient unit of time.

Suppose we have just observed Y_{t-k} and want to make a "k-period-ahead" forecast; that is, we want to use the information through time $t - k$ to forecast Y_t. Then we denote the resulting forecast by $F_{t-k,t}$. The first subscript denotes the period in which the forecast is made, and the second subscript denotes the period being forecasted. As an example, if the data are monthly and September 2004 corresponds to $t = 67$, then a forecast of Y_{69}, the value in November 2004, would be labeled $F_{67,69}$. The **forecast error** is the difference between the actual value and the forecast. It is denoted by E with appropriate subscripts. Specifically, the forecast error associated with $F_{t-k,t}$ is

$$E_{t-k,t} = Y_t - F_{t-k,t}$$

This double-subscript notation is necessary to specify when the forecast is being made and which period is being forecasted. However, the former is often clear from context. Therefore, to simplify the notation, we usually drop the first subscript and write F_t and E_t to denote the forecast of Y_t and the error in this forecast.

We first develop a model to fit the histori-cal data. Then we use this model to forecast the future.

There are actually two steps in any forecasting procedure. The first step is to build a model that fits the historical data well. The second step is to use this model to forecast the future. Most of the work goes into the first step. For any trial model we see how well it "tracks" the known values of the time series. Specifically, we calculate the one-period-ahead forecasts, F_t (or more precisely, $F_{t-1,t}$), from the model and compare these to the known values, Y_t, for each t in the historical time period. We attempt to find a model that produces small forecast errors, E_t. We expect that if the model forecasts the *historical* data well, it will also forecast *future* data well.

Forecasting software packages typically report several summary measures of the forecast errors. The most important of these are MAE (mean absolute error), RMSE (root mean square error), and MAPE (mean absolute percentage error). These are defined in equations (13.2), (13.3), and (13.4). Fortunately, models that make any one of these measures small tend to make the others small, so that we can choose whichever measure we want to minimize. In the following formulas, N denotes the number of terms in each sum. This value is typically slightly less than T, the number of historical observations, because it is usually not possible to provide a forecast for each historical period.

A model that makes any one of these error measures small tends to make the other two small as well.

RMSE is similar to a standard deviation in that the errors are squared; because of the square root, its units are the same as those of the forecasted variable. The MAE is similar to the RMSE, except that absolute values of errors are used instead of squared errors. The MAPE is probably the most easily understood measure because it does not depend on the units of the forecasted variable; it is always stated as a percentage. For example, the statement that the forecasts are off on average by 2% has a clear meaning, even if you do not know the units of the variable being forecasted.

Some forecasting software packages choose the best model from a given class (such as the best exponential smoothing model) by minimizing MAE, RMSE, or MAPE. However, small values of these measures guarantee only that the model forecasts the *historical* observations well. There is still no guarantee that the model will forecast *future* values accurately.

We now examine a number of useful forecasting models. You should be aware that more than one of these models can be appropriate for any particular time series data. For example, a random walk model and an autoregression model could be equally effective for forecasting stock price data. (Remember also that we can combine forecasts from more than one model to obtain a possibly better forecast.) We try to give some insights into choosing the best type of model for various types of time series data, but ultimately the choice depends on the experience of the forecaster.

13.3 TESTING FOR RANDOMNESS

All forecasting models we build have the general form shown in equation (13.5). The fitted value in this equation is the part we calculate from past data and any other available information (such as the season of the year), and it is used as a forecast for Y. The residual is the forecast error, the difference between the observed value of Y and its forecast:

$$Y_t = \text{Fitted Value} + \text{Residual} \qquad (13.5)$$

In a time series context the terms residual *and* forecast error *are used interchangeably.*

For time series data, there is a residual for each historical period, that is, for each value of t. We want this time series of residuals to be random "noise," as discussed in Section 13.2.4. The reason is that if this series of residuals is not noise, then it can be modeled further. For example, if the residuals trend upwardly, then we can refine our model to include this trend component in the *fitted* value. The point is that we want the fitted value to include all components of the original series that can possibly be forecasted, and we want the leftover residuals to be noise.

We now discuss ways to determine whether a time series of residuals is random noise (which we usually abbreviate to "random"). The simplest method, but not always a reliable one, is to examine time series graphs of residuals visually. This often enables us to detect nonrandom patterns. For example, the time series graphs in Figures 13.7 through 13.11 illustrate some common nonrandom patterns. In Figure 13.7, there is an upward trend. In Figure 13.8, the variance increases through time (larger zigzags to the right). Figure 13.9 exhibits seasonality, where observations in certain months are consistently larger than those in other months. There is a "meandering" pattern in Figure 13.10, where large observations tend to be followed by other large observations, and small observations tend to be followed by other small observations. Finally, the opposite behavior of Figure 13.10 is illustrated in Figure 13.11. Here, there are *too many* zigzags—large observations tend to follow small observations and vice versa. None of the time series in these figures can be considered random.

Figure 13.7

A Series with Trend

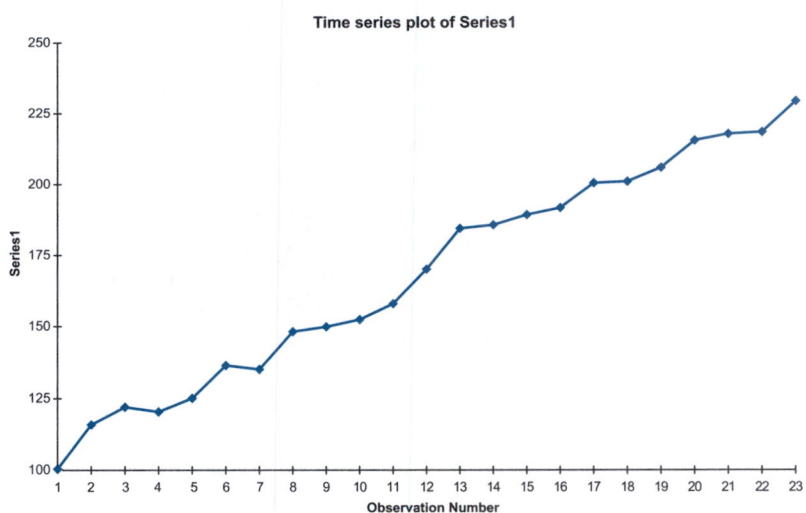

Figure 13.8

A Series with Increasing Variance Through Time

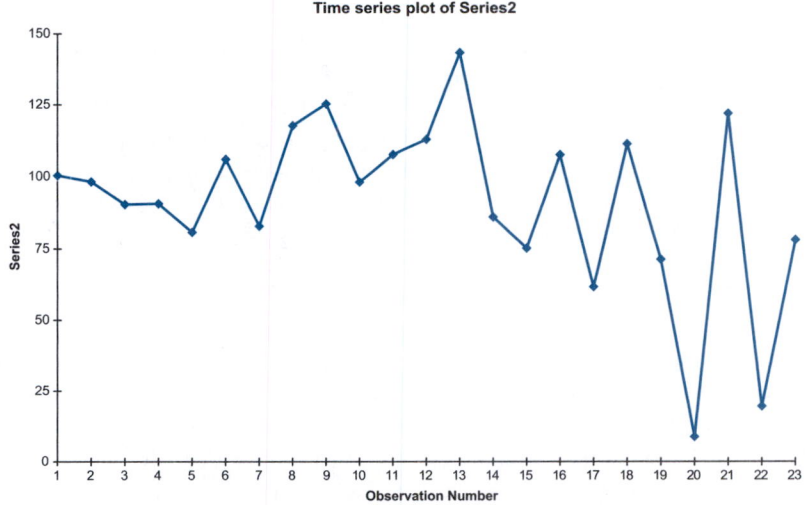

Figure 13.9
A Series with
Seasonality

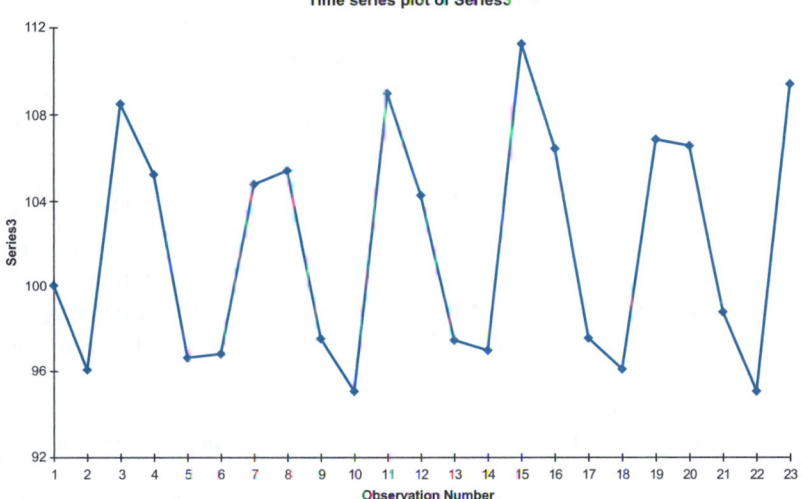

Figure 13.10
A Series That
Meanders

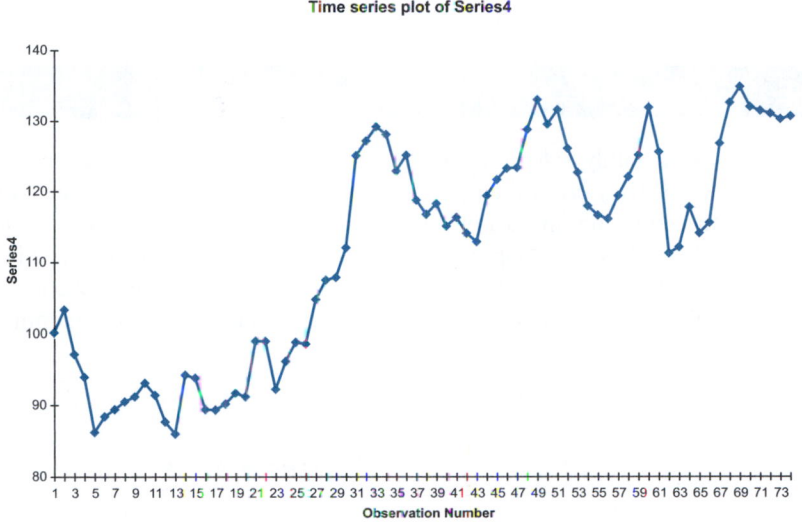

Figure 13.11
A Series That
Oscillates Frequently

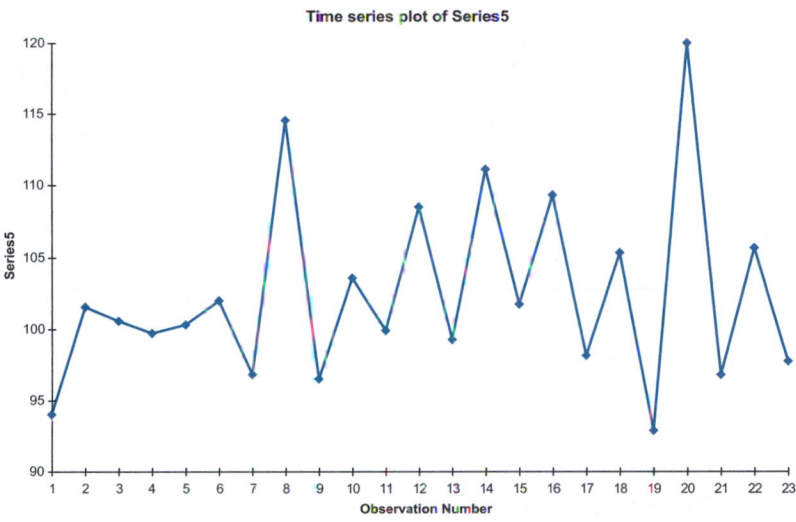

13.3.1 The Runs Test

It is not always easy to detect randomness or the lack of it from the visual inspection of a graph. Therefore, we discuss two quantitative methods of that test for randomness. The first is called the *runs test*. We first choose a base value, which could be the average value of the series, the median value, or even some other value. Then we define a **run** as a consecutive series of observations that remain on one side of this base level. For example, if the base level is 0 and we observe the series 1, 5, 3, −3, −2, −4, −1, 3, 2, then there are three runs: 1, 5, 3; −3, −2, −4, −1; and 3, 2. The idea behind the runs test is that a random series should have a number of runs that is neither too large nor too small. If the series has too few runs, then it could be trending (as in Figure 13.7) or it could be meandering (as in Figure 13.10). If the series has too many runs, then it is zigzagging too often (as in Figure 13.11).

This runs test can be used on any time series, not just a series of residuals.

> The **runs test** is a formal test of the null hypothesis of randomness. If there are too many or too few runs in the series, then we conclude that the series is not random.

We do not provide the mathematical details of the runs test, but we illustrate how it is implemented in StatTools in the following example.

EXAMPLE   **13.1 FORECASTING MONTHLY STEREO SALES**

Monthly sales for a chain of stereo retailers are listed in the file **Stereo Sales.xlsx**. They cover the period from the beginning of 2004 to the end of 2007, during which there was no upward or downward trend in sales and no clear seasonal peaks or valleys. This behavior is apparent in the time series graph of sales in Figure 13.12. Therefore, a simple forecast model of sales is to use the *average* of the series, 182.67, as a forecast of sales for each month. Do the resulting residuals represent random noise?

Figure 13.12

Time Series Graph of Stereo Sales

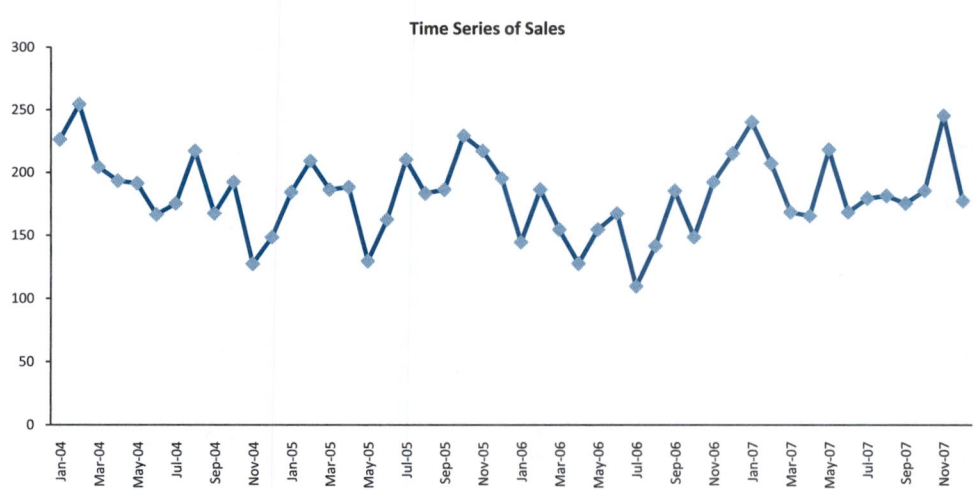

Objective   To use StatTools's Runs Test procedure to check whether the residuals from this simple forecasting model represent random noise.

Solution

To obtain the residuals for this forecasting model, we subtract the average, 182.67, from each observation. Therefore, the plot of the residuals, shown in Figure 13.13, has exactly the same shape as the plot of sales. The only difference is that it is shifted down by 182.67 and has mean 0. We now use the runs test to check whether there are too many or too few runs around the base value of 0 in this residual plot. To do so, we select Runs Test for Randomness from the StatTools Time Series and Forecasting dropdown, choose Residual as the variable to analyze, and choose Mean of Series as the cutoff value. (This corresponds to the horizontal line at 0 in Figure 13.13.) This produces the output in shown in Figure 13.14.

Figure 13.13

Time Series Graph of Residuals

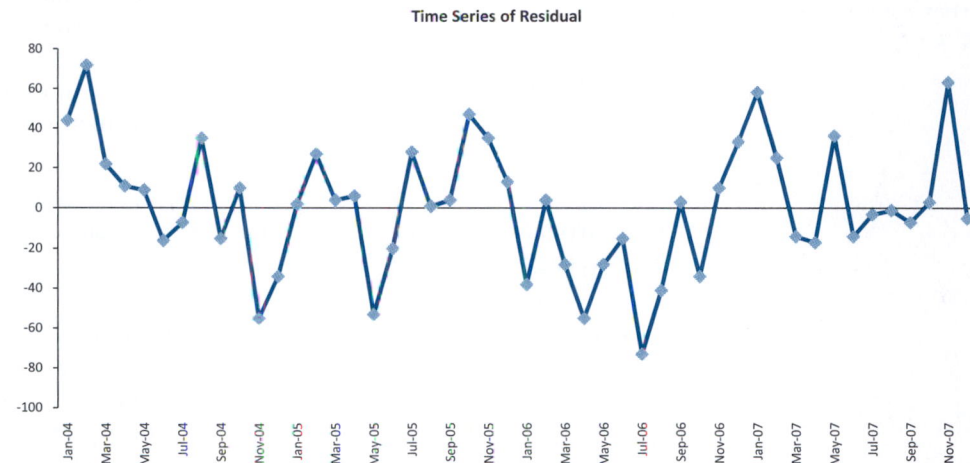

Figure 13.14

Runs Test for Randomness

	I	J
7		Residual
8	**Runs Test for Randomness**	Data Set #1
9	Observations	48
10	Below Mean	22
11	Above Mean	26
12	Number of Runs	20
13	Mean	0.00
14	E(R)	24.8333
15	StdDev(R)	3.4027
16	Z-Value	-1.4204
17	P-Value (two-tailed)	0.1555

The important elements of this output are the following:

- The number of observed runs is 20, in cell J12.
- The number of runs *expected* under an assumption of randomness is 24.833, in cell J14. Therefore, the series of residuals has too *few* runs. Positive values tend to follow positive values, and negative values tend to follow negative values.

A small p-value in the runs test provides evidence of nonrandomness.

- The z-value in cell J16, -1.42, indicates how many standard errors the observed number of runs is below the expected number of runs. The corresponding p-value indicates how extreme this z-value is. It can be interpreted just like other p-values for hypothesis tests. If it is small, say, less than 0.05, then we can reject the null hypothesis of randomness and conclude that the series of residuals is *not* random noise. However, the p-value for this example is only 0.1555. Therefore, there is not convincing evidence of nonrandomness in the residuals, and we can conclude that the residuals represent noise. ■

13.3.2 Autocorrelation

Like the runs test, autocorrelations can be calculated for any time series, not just a series of residuals.

In this section we discuss another way to check for randomness of a time series of residuals—we examine its *autocorrelations*. The "auto" means that successive observations are correlated with one another. For example, in the most common form of autocorrelation, *positive* autocorrelation, large observations tend to follow large observations, and small observations tend to follow small observations. In this case the runs test is likely to pick it up because there will be fewer runs than expected. Another way to check for the same nonrandomness property is to calculate the autocorrelations of the time series.

An **autocorrelation** is a type of correlation used to measure whether values of a time series are related to their own past values.

To understand autocorrelations it is first necessary to understand what it means to *lag* a time series. This concept is easy to illustrate in a spreadsheet. We again use the monthly stereo sales data in the **Stereo Sales.xlsx** file. To lag by 1 month, we simply "push down" the series by one row. See column D of Figure 13.15. Note that there is a blank cell at the top of the lagged series (in cell D2). We can continue to push the series down one row at a time to obtain other lags. For example, the lag 3 version of the series appears in column F. Now there are three missing observations at the top. Note that in December 2004, say, the first, second, and third lags correspond to the observations in November 2004, October 2004, and September 2004, respectively. That is, lags are simply previous observations, removed by a certain number of periods from the present time. These lagged columns can be obtained by copying and pasting the original series or by using Lag from the StatTools Utilities dropdown.

Figure 13.15

Lags for Stereo Sales

	A	B	C	D	E	F
1	Month	Sales	Residual	Lag1(Residual)	Lag2(Residual)	Lag3(Residual)
2	Jan-04	226	43.333			
3	Feb-04	254	71.333	43.333		
4	Mar-04	204	21.333	71.333	43.333	
5	Apr-04	193	10.333	21.333	71.333	43.333
6	May-04	191	8.333	10.333	21.333	71.333
7	Jun-04	166	-16.667	8.333	10.333	21.333
8	Jul-04	175	-7.667	-16.667	8.333	10.333
9	Aug-04	217	34.333	-7.667	-16.667	8.333
10	Sep-04	167	-15.667	34.333	-7.667	-16.667
11	Oct-04	192	9.333	-15.667	34.333	-7.667
12	Nov-04	127	-55.667	9.333	-15.667	34.333
13	Dec-04	148	-34.667	-55.667	9.333	-15.667
14	Jan-05	184	1.333	-34.667	-55.667	9.333
15	Feb-05	209	26.333	1.333	-34.667	-55.667
16	Mar-05	186	3.333	26.333	1.333	-34.667

Then the autocorrelation of lag k, for any integer k, is essentially the correlation between the original series and the lag k version of the series. For example, in Figure 13.15 the lag 1 autocorrelation is the correlation between the observations in columns C and D. Similarly, the lag 2 autocorrelation is the correlation between the observations in columns C and E.[1]

We have shown the lagged versions of Sales in Figure 13.15, and we have explained autocorrelations in terms of these lagged variables, to help motivate the concept of auto-correlation. However, we can use StatTools's Autocorrelation procedure directly, *without* forming the lagged variables, to calculate autocorrelations. This is illustrated in the following continuation of Example 13.1.

| EXAMPLE | 13.1 FORECASTING MONTHLY STEREO SALES (CONTINUED) |

The runs test on the stereo sales data suggests that the pattern of sales is not random. Large values tend to follow large values, and small values tend to follow small values. Do autocorrelations support this conclusion?

Objective   To examine the autocorrelations of the residuals from the forecasting model for evidence of nonrandomness.

Solution

We use StatTools's Autocorrelation procedure, found under the StatTools Time Series and Forecasting dropdown. It requires us to specify the time series variable (Residual), the number of lags we want (we chose the StatTools default value), and whether we want a chart of the autocorrelations. This chart is called a **correlogram**. The resulting autocorrelations and correlogram appear in Figure 13.16. A typical autocorrelation of lag k indicates the relationship between observations k periods apart. For example, the autocorrelation of lag 3, 0.0814, indicates that there is very little relationship between residuals separated by 3 months.

How large is a "large" autocorrelation? Under the assumption of randomness, it can be shown that the standard error of any autocorrelation is approximately $1/\sqrt{T}$, in this case $1/\sqrt{48} = 0.1443$. (Recall that T denotes the number of observations in the series.) If the series is truly random, then only an occasional autocorrelation will be larger than 2 standard errors in magnitude. Therefore, any autocorrelation that *is* larger than 2 standard errors in magnitude is worth our attention. These significantly nonzero autocorrelations are boldfaced in the StatTools output. The only "large" autocorrelation for the residuals is the first, or lag 1, autocorrelation of 0.3492. The fact that it is *positive* indicates once again that there is some tendency for large residuals to follow large residuals and for small to follow small. The autocorrelations for other lags are less than two standard errors in magnitude and can be ignored.

---

[1] We ignore the exact details of the calculations here. Just be aware that the formula for autocorrelations that is usually used differs slightly from the correlation formula in Chapter 3. However, the difference is very slight and of little practical importance.

Figure 13.16

Correlogram and
Autocorrelations of
Residuals

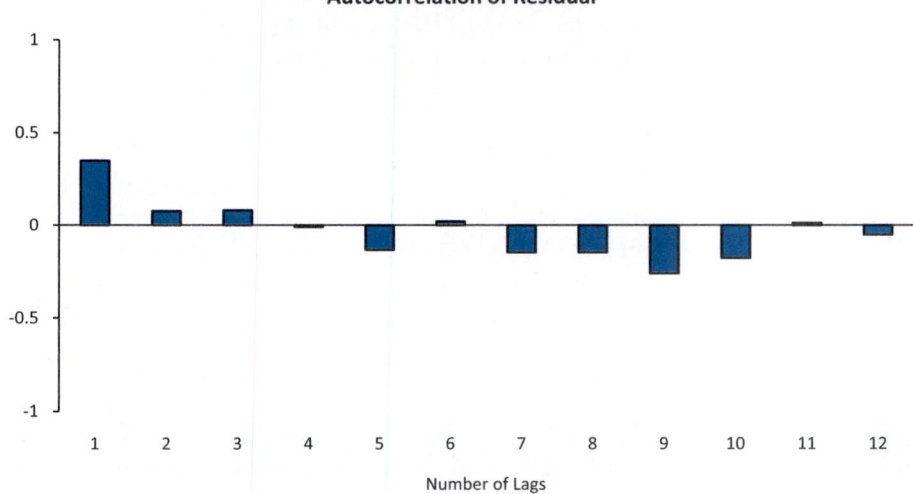

Autocorrelation of Residual

Autocorrelation Table	Residual Data Set #1
Number of Values	48
Standard Error	0.1443
Lag #1	**0.3492**
Lag #2	0.0772
Lag #3	0.0814
Lag #4	-0.0095
Lag #5	-0.1353
Lag #6	0.0206
Lag #7	-0.1494
Lag #8	-0.1492
Lag #9	-0.2626
Lag #10	-0.1792
Lag #11	0.0121
Lag #12	-0.0516

Typically, we can ask for autocorrelations up to as many lags as we like. However, there are several practical considerations to keep in mind. First, it is common practice to ask for no more lags than 25% of the number of observations. For example, if there are 48 observations, we should ask for no more than 12 autocorrelations (lags 1–12). (StatTools chooses this number of lags if you accept its "auto" setting.)

Second, the first few lags are typically the most important. Intuitively, if there is any relationship between successive observations, it is likely to be between nearby observations. The June 2007 observation is more likely to be related to the May 2007 observation than to the October 2006 observation. Sometimes there is a fairly large spike in the correlogram at some large lag, such as lag 9. However, this can often be ignored as a random "blip" unless there is some obvious reason for its occurrence. A similarly large autocorrelation at lag 1 or 2 is usually taken more seriously. The one exception to this is a *seasonal* lag. For example, for monthly data an autocorrelation at lag 12 corresponds to a relationship between observations a year apart, such as May 2007 and May 2006. If this autocorrelation is significantly large, it probably should not be ignored.

Autocorrelation analysis is somewhat advanced. However, it is the basis for many important forecasting methods.

We do not examine autocorrelations much further in this book. However, many advanced forecasting techniques are based largely on the examination of the autocorrelation structure of time series. This autocorrelation structure tells us how a series is related to its own past values through time, which can be very valuable information for forecasting *future* values.

PROBLEMS

Level A

1. The file **P13_01.xlsx** contains the monthly number of airline tickets sold by the CareFree Travel Agency. Is this time series *random*? Perform a runs test and compute a few autocorrelations to support your answer.

2. The file **P13_02.xlsx** contains the weekly sales at a local bookstore for each of the past 25 weeks. Is this time series *random*? Perform a runs test and compute a few autocorrelations to support your answer.

3. The number of employees on the payroll at a food-processing plant is recorded at the start of each month. These data are provided in the file **P13_03.xlsx**. Perform a runs test and compute a few autocorrelations to determine whether this time series is random.

4. The quarterly numbers of applications for home mortgage loans at a branch office of Northern Central Bank are recorded in the file **P13_04.xlsx**. Perform a runs test and compute a few autocorrelations to determine whether this time series is random.

5. The number of reported accidents at a manufacturing plant located in Flint, Michigan, was recorded at the start of each month. These data are provided in the file **P13_05.xlsx**. Is this time series *random*? Perform a runs test and compute a few autocorrelations to support your answer.

6. The file **P13_06.xlsx** contains the weekly sales at the local outlet of WestCoast Video Rentals for each of the past 36 weeks. Perform a runs test and compute a few autocorrelations to determine whether this time series is random.

Level B

7. Determine whether the RAND() function in Excel actually generates a random stream of numbers. Generate at least 100 random numbers to test their randomness with a runs test and with autocorrelations. Summarize your findings.

8. Use a runs test and calculate autorrelations to decide whether the random series explained in each part (**a–c**) are random. For each part, generate at least 100 random numbers in the series.
   a. A series of independent normally distributed values, each with mean 70 and standard deviation 5.
   b. A series where the first value is normally distributed with mean 70 and standard deviation 5, and each succeeding value is normally distributed with mean equal to the *previous* value and standard deviation 5. (For example, if the fourth value is 67.32, then the fifth value will be normally distributed with mean 67.32.)
   c. A series where the first value, Y_1, is normally distributed with mean 70 and standard deviation 5, and each succeeding value, Y_t, is normally distributed with mean $(1 + a_t)Y_{t-1}$ and standard deviation $5(1 + a_t)$, where the a_t's are independent, normally distributed values with mean 0 and standard deviation 0.2. (For example, if $Y_{t-1} = 67.32$ and $a_t = -0.2$, then Y_t will be normally distributed with mean $0.8(67.32) = 53.856$ and standard deviation $0.8(5) = 4$.)

13.4 REGRESSION-BASED TREND MODELS

Many time series follow a long-term trend except for random variation. This trend can be upward or downward. A straightforward way to model this trend is to estimate a regression equation for Y_t, using time t as the *single* explanatory variable. In this section we discuss the two most frequently used trend models, *linear* trend and *exponential* trend.

13.4.1 Linear Trend

A linear trend means that the time series variable changes by a constant *amount* each time period. The relevant equation is equation (13.6), where, as in previous regression equations, a is the intercept, b is the slope, and ϵ_t is an error term.

Linear Trend Model

$$Y_t = a + bt + \epsilon_t \tag{13.6}$$

The interpretation of b is that it represents the expected change in the series from one period to the next. If b is positive, the trend is upward; if b is negative, the trend is downward. The intercept term a is less important. It literally represents the expected value of the series at time $t = 0$. If time t is coded so that the first observation corresponds to $t = 1$, then a is where we expect the series to have been one period before we started observing. However, it is possible that time is coded in another way. For example, we might have annual data that start in 1997. Then the first value of t might be entered as 1997, which means that the intercept a corresponds to a period 1997 years earlier! Clearly, we would not take its value literally in this case.

As always, a graph of the time series is a good place to start. It indicates whether a linear trend model is likely to provide a good fit. Generally, the graph should rise or fall at approximately a constant rate through time, without too much random variation. But even if there is a lot of random variation—a lot of zigzags—a linear trend to the data might be a good starting point. Then the *residuals* from this trend line, which should have no remaining trend, could possibly be modeled by some other method in this chapter.

EXAMPLE   **13.2 QUARTERLY PHARMACEUTICAL SALES**

The file **Pharmaceutical Sales.xlsx** contains quarterly sales data for a large pharmaceutical company from first quarter 1998 through fourth quarter 2007 (in millions of dollars). The time series graph of these data appears in Figure 13.17. Sales increase from \$3062 million in the initial quarter to \$8307 million in the final quarter. How well does a linear trend fit these data? Are the residuals from this fit random?

Figure 13.17

Time Series Graph of Pharmaceutical Sales

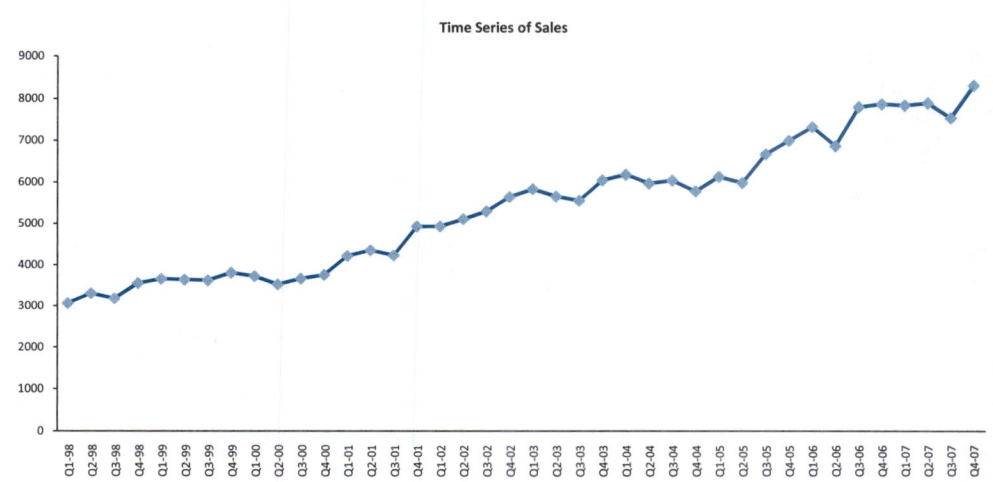

Objective   To fit a linear trend line to quarterly sales and examine its residuals for randomness.

Solution

The graph in Figure 13.17 indicates a clear upward trend with little or no curvature. Therefore, a linear trend is certainly plausible. To estimate it with regression, we first need a *numeric* time variable—labels such as Q1-98 will not do. We construct this time variable in column C of the data set, using the consecutive values 1 through 40. We then run a simple regression of Sales versus Time, with the results shown in Figure 13.18. The estimated linear trend line is

$$\text{Forecasted Sales} = 2686.7 + 131.991\text{Time}$$

Figure 13.18

Regression Output for Linear Trend

Summary	Multiple R	R-Square	Adjusted R-Square	StErr of Estimate
	0.9806	0.9615	0.9605	312.87

ANOVA Table	Degrees of Freedom	Sum of Squares	Mean of Squares	F-Ratio	p-Value
Explained	1	92856588.48	92856588.48	948.5801	< 0.0001
Unexplained	38	3719823.497	97890.09201		

Regression Table	Coefficient	Standard Error	t-Value	p-Value	Confidence Interval 95% Lower	Upper
Constant	2686.72	100.82	26.6476	< 0.0001	2482.61	2890.83
Time	131.991	4.29	30.7990	< 0.0001	123.31	140.67

This equation implies that we expect sales to increase by \$131.991 million per quarter. (The 2686.7 value in this equation is what we would predict sales to be at time 0— quarter 4 of 1997.) To use this equation to forecast future sales, we substitute later values of Time into the regression equation, so that each future prediction is \$131.991 larger than the previous prediction. For example, the forecast for Q4 of 2008 is

$$\text{Forecasted Sales Q4-08} = 2686.7 + 131.991(44) = 8494.3$$

Excel provides an easier way to obtain this trend line. Once the graph in Figure 13.17 is constructed, we can use Excel's Trendline tool. (Select the chart and then select More Trendline Options from the Trendline dropdown on the Chart Tools Layout ribbon.) This gives us several types of trend lines to choose from, and we select the linear option for this example. We can also check the options to show the regression equation and its R^2 value on the chart, as we have done in Figure 13.19. This superimposed trend line indicates a reasonably good fit.

Figure 13.19

Time Series Graph with Linear Trend Superimposed

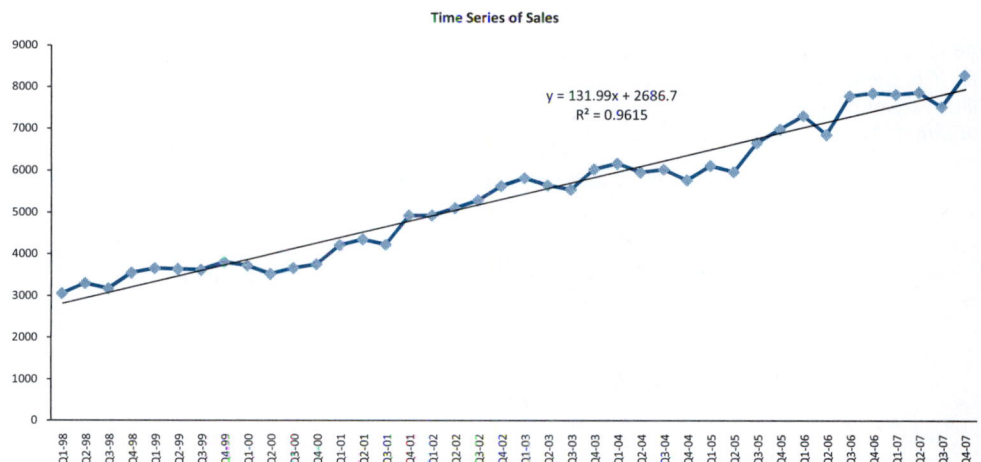

However, the fit is not perfect, as the plot of the residuals in Figure 13.20 indicates. These residuals tend to "meander," staying positive for a while, then negative, then positive, and so on. You can check that the runs test for these residuals produces a z-value of -3.074, with a corresponding p-value of 0.002, and that its first two autocorrelations are significantly positive. In short, these residuals are *not* random noise, and they could be modeled further. However, we do not pursue this analysis here.

Figure 13.20

Time Series Graph
of Residuals

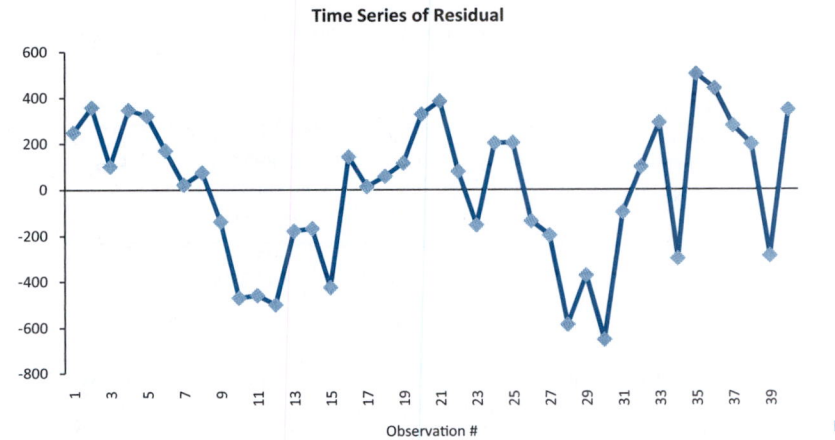

13.4.2 Exponential Trend

In contrast to a linear trend, an exponential trend is appropriate when the time series changes by a constant *percentage* (as opposed to a constant dollar amount) each period. Then the appropriate regression equation is equation (13.7), where c and b are constants, and u_t represents a *multiplicative* error term.

Exponential Trend Model

$$Y_t = ce^{bt}u_t \qquad \text{(13.7)}$$

An exponential trend for Y is equivalent to a linear trend for the logarithm of Y.

Equation (13.7) is useful for understanding how an exponential trend works, as we will discuss, but it is not useful for estimation. For that, we require a *linear* equation. Fortunately, we can achieve linearity by taking natural logarithms of both sides of equation (13.7). (The key, as usual, is that the logarithm of a product is the sum of the logarithms.) The result appears in equation (13.8), where $a = \ln(c)$ and $\epsilon_t = \ln(u_t)$. This equation represents a *linear* trend, but the dependent variable is now the logarithm of the original Y_t. This implies the following important fact: If a time series exhibits an exponential trend, then a plot of its logarithm should be approximately linear.

***Equivalent Linear Trend for Logarithm of* Y**

$$\ln(Y_t) = a + bt + \epsilon_t \qquad \text{(13.8)}$$

Because the computer does the calculations, our main responsibility is to interpret the final result. This is not too difficult. It can be shown that the coefficient b (expressed as a percentage) is approximately the percentage change per period. For example, if $b = 0.05$, then the series is increasing by approximately 5% per period.[2] On the other hand, if $b = -0.05$, then the series is decreasing by approximately 5% per period.

An exponential trend can be estimated with StatTools's Regression procedure, but only after the log transformation has been made on Y_t. We illustrate this in the following example.

EXAMPLE | **13.3 QUARTERLY PC DEVICE SALES**

The file **PC Device Sales.xlsx** contains quarterly sales data (in millions of dollars) for a large PC device manufacturer from the first quarter of 1993 through the fourth quarter of 2007. Are the company's sales growing exponentially through this entire period?

Objective   To estimate the company's exponential growth and to see whether it has been maintained during the entire period from 1993 until the end of 2007.

Solution

We first estimate and interpret an exponential trend for the years 1993 through 2003. Then we see how well the projection of this trend into the future fits the data after 2003. The time series graph through 2003 appears in Figure 13.21. We have used Excel's Trendline tool, with the Exponential option, to superimpose an exponential trend line and the corresponding equation on this plot. The fit is evidently quite good. Equivalently, Figure 13.22 illustrates the time series of log sales for this same period, with a *linear* trend line superimposed. Its fit is equally good.

Figure 13.21

Time Series Graph of Sales with Exponential Trend Superimposed

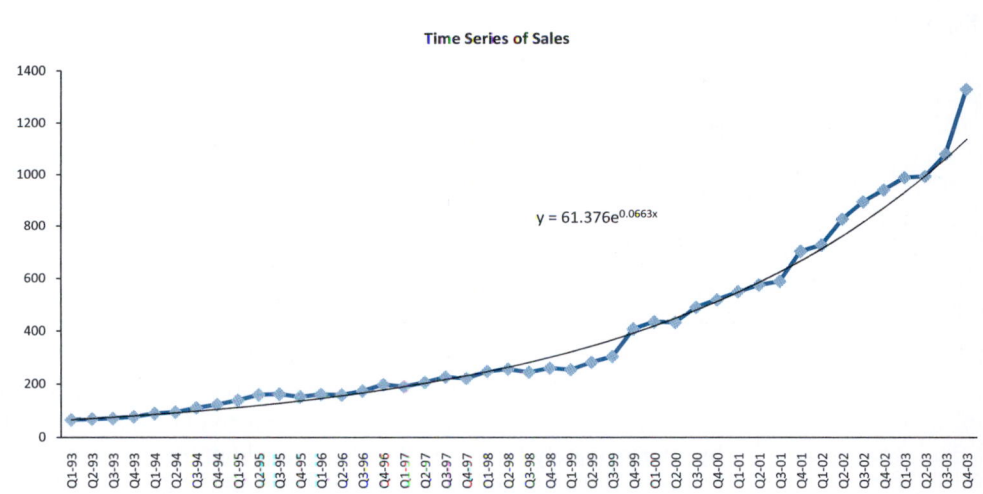

---

[2]More precisely, this percentage change is $e^b - 1$. For example, when $b = 0.05$, this is $e^b - 1 = 5.13\%$.

Figure 13.22

Time Series Graph of Log Sales with Linear Trend Superimposed

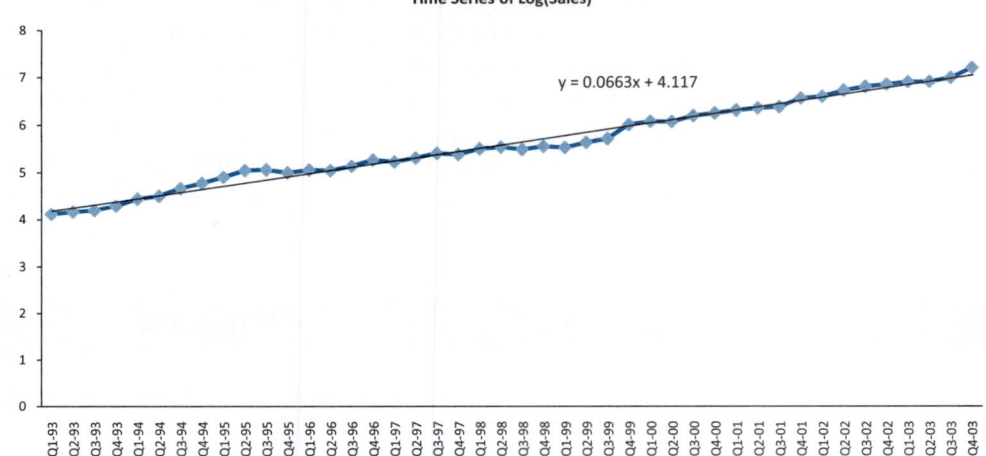

Time Series of Log(Sales)

$y = 0.0663x + 4.117$

We can also use StatTools's Regression procedure to estimate this exponential trend, as shown in Figure 13.23. To produce this output, we must first add a time variable in column C (with values 1 through 44) and make a logarithmic transformation of Sales in column D. Then we regress Log(Sales) on Time (using the data through 2003 only) to obtain the regression output. Note that its two coefficients in cells B18 and B19 are the same as those shown for the linear trend in Figure 13.22. If we take the antilog of the constant 4.117 (with the formula $= EXP(B18)$), we obtain the constant *multiple* shown in Figure 13.21. It corresponds to the constant c in equation (13.7).

Figure 13.23

Regression Output for Estimating Exponential Trend

	A	B	C	D	E	F	G
7		Multiple		Adjusted	StErr of		
8	Summary	R	R-Square	R-Square	Estimate		
9		0.9922	0.9844	0.9840	0.1086		
10							
11		Degrees of	Sum of	Mean of			
12	ANOVA Table	Freedom	Squares	Squares	F-Ratio	p-Value	
13	Explained	1	31.21992793	31.21992793	2645.6403	< 0.0001	
14	Unexplained	42	0.495621782	0.011800519			
15							
16			Standard			Confidence Interval 95%	
17	Regression Table	Coefficient	Error	t-Value	p-Value	Lower	Upper
18	Constant	4.1170	0.0333	123.5616	< 0.0001	4.0498	4.1843
19	Time	0.0663	0.0013	51.4358	< 0.0001	0.0637	0.0689

What does it all mean? The estimated equation (13.7) is

$$\text{Forecasted Sales} = 61.376e^{0.0663t}$$

The most important constant in this equation is the coefficient of Time, $b = 0.0663$. Expressed as a percentage, this coefficient implies that the company's sales increased by approximately 6.63% per quarter throughout this 11-year period. (The constant multiple, $c = 61.376$, is our forecast of sales at time 0—in quarter 4 of 1992.) To use this equation for forecasting the future, we substitute later values of Time into the regression equation, so that each future forecast is about 6.63% larger than the previous forecast. For example, the forecast of the second quarter of 2004 is

$$\text{Forecasted Sales in Q2-04} = 61.376e^{0.0663(46)} = 1295.72$$

Has this exponential growth continued beyond 2003? It has *not*, due possibly to slumping sales in the computer industry or increased competition from other manufacturers. We checked this by creating the Forecast column in Figure 13.24 (by substituting into the regression equation for the entire period though Q4–07). We then used StatTools to create a time series graph of the two series Sales and Forecast, shown in Figure 13.25. It is clear that sales in the forecast period did not exhibit nearly the 6.63% growth observed in the estimation period. As the company clearly realizes, nothing that good lasts forever.

Figure 13.24

Creating Forecasts of Sales

	A	B	C	D	E
1	Quarter	Sales	Time	Log(Sales)	Forecast
2	Q1-93	61.14	1	4.1131663	65.58583
3	Q2-93	64.07	2	4.1599762	70.08398
4	Q3-93	66.18	3	4.1923783	74.89063
5	Q4-93	72.76	4	4.2871664	80.02694
6	Q1-94	84.70	5	4.4391156	85.51552
7	Q2-94	90.05	6	4.5003651	91.38053
8	Q3-94	106.06	7	4.664005	97.64778
9	Q4-94	118.21	8	4.7724627	104.3449
10	Q1-95	134.38	9	4.9006716	111.5013
11	Q2-95	154.67	10	5.0412938	119.1485
12	Q3-95	157.41	11	5.0588539	127.3202
13	Q4-95	147.16	12	4.9915204	136.0523

Figure 13.25   Time Series Graph of Forecasts Superimposed on Sales for the Entire Period

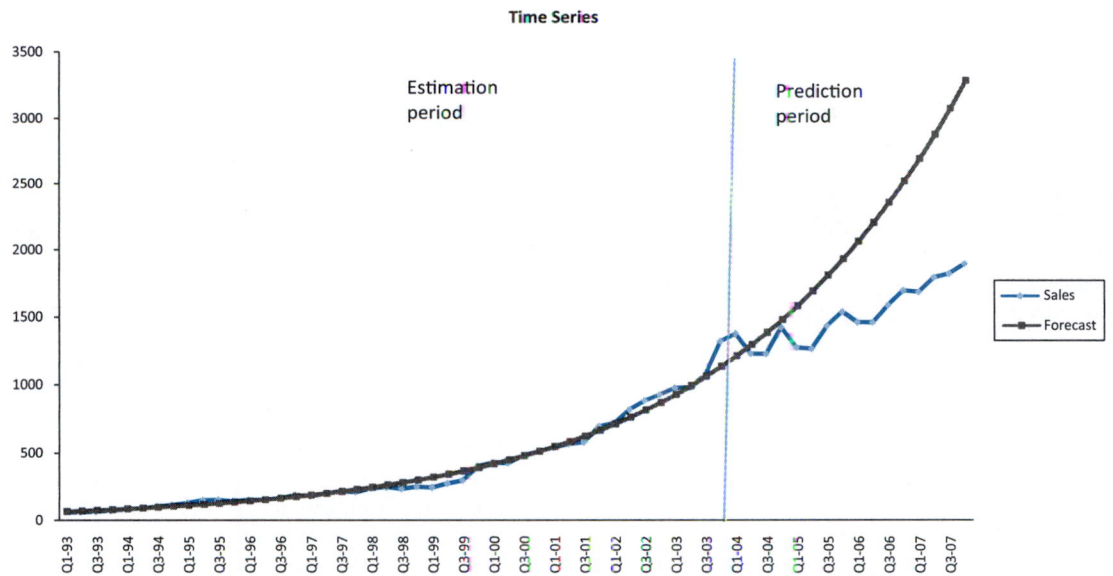

Before leaving this example, we comment briefly on the standard error of estimate shown in cell E9 of Figure 13.23. This value, 0.1086, is in *log* units, not original dollar units. Therefore, it is a totally misleading indicator of the forecast errors we might make from the exponential trend equation. To obtain more meaningful measures, we first obtain the forecasts of sales, as explained previously. Then we can easily obtain any of the three forecast error measures discussed previously in equations (13.2), (13.3), and (13.4). The results appear in Figure 13.26. The squared errors, absolute errors, and absolute percentage errors are first calculated with the formulas $=(B2-E2)^{\wedge}2$, $=ABS(B2-E2)$, and $=G2/B2$ in cells F2, G2, and H2, which are then copied down. The error measures (for the data through 2003 only) then appear in cells K2, K3, and K4. The corresponding formulas for RMSE, MAE, and MAPE are straightforward. RMSE is the square root of the average of the squared errors in column F, and MAE and MAPE are the averages of the values in columns G and H, respectively. The latter is particularly simple to interpret. Forecasts for the 11-year estimate period were off, on average, by 7.86%. (Of course, as you can check, forecasts for the quarters *after* 2003 were off by much more!)

Figure 13.26

Measures of Forecast Errors

	A	B	C	D	E	F	G	H	I	J	K	L
1	Quarter	Sales	Time	Log(Sales)	Forecast	SqError	AbsError	AbsPctError		Measures of forecast error		
2	Q1-93	61.14	1	4.1131663	65.58583	19.76541	4.445831	0.07271559		RMSE	41.86	
3	Q2-93	64.07	2	4.1599762	70.08398	36.16795	6.013979	0.09386576		MAE	25.44	
4	Q3-93	66.18	3	4.1923783	74.89063	75.87506	8.710629	0.13162027		MAPE	7.86%	
5	Q4-93	72.76	4	4.2871664	80.02694	52.8084	7.266939	0.09987547				
6	Q1-94	84.70	5	4.4391156	85.51552	0.66507	0.815518	0.00962831				
7	Q2-94	90.05	6	4.5003651	91.38053	1.770302	1.330527	0.01477542				
8	Q3-94	106.06	7	4.664005	97.64778	70.7654	8.412218	0.07931565				

Whenever we observe a time series that is increasing at an increasing rate (or decreasing at a decreasing rate), an exponential trend model is worth trying. The key to the analysis is to regress the *logarithm* of the time series variable versus time (or use Excel's Trendline tool). The coefficient of time, written as a percentage, is then the approximate percentage increase (if positive) or decrease (if negative) per period.

PROBLEMS

Level A

9. The file **P13_01.xlsx** contains the monthly number of airline tickets sold by the CareFree Travel Agency.
   a. Does a linear trend appear to fit these data well? If so, estimate and interpret the linear-trend model for this time series. Also, interpret the R^2 and s_e values.
   b. Provide an indication of the typical forecast error generated by the estimated model in part **a**.
   c. Is there evidence of some seasonal pattern in these sales data? If so, characterize the seasonal pattern.

10. The file **P13_10.xlsx** contains the daily closing prices of Wal-Mart stock for a 1-year period. Does a linear or exponential trend fit these data well? If so, estimate and interpret the best trend model for this time series. Also, interpret the R^2 and s_e values.

11. The file **P13_11.xlsx** contains annual data on the amount of life insurance in force in the United States.

Fit an exponential growth curve to these data. Write a short report to summarize your findings.

12. The file **P13_12.xlsx** contains 5 years of monthly data on sales (number of units sold) for a particular company. The company suspects that except for random noise, its sales are growing by a constant *percentage* each month and that they will continue to do so for at least the near future.
   a. Explain briefly whether the plot of the series visually supports the company's suspicion.
   b. Fit the appropriate regression model to the data. Report the resulting equation and state explicitly what it says about the percentage growth per month.
   c. What are the RMSE and MAPE for the forecast model in part **b**? In words, what do they measure? Considering their magnitudes, does the model seem to be doing a good job?
   d. In words, how does the model make forecasts for future months? Specifically, given the forecast

value for the last month in the data set, what simple arithmetic could you use to obtain forecasts for the next few months?

13. The file **P13_13.xlsx** contains quarterly data on GDP. (The data are expressed in billions of current dollars, they are seasonally adjusted, and they represent annualized rates.)
   a. Look at a time series plot of GDP. Does it suggest a linear relationship; an exponential relationship?
   b. Use regression to estimate a linear relationship between GDP and Time. Interpret the associated "constant" term and the "slope" term. Would you say that the fit is good?

Level B

14. The file **P13_14.xlsx** gives monthly exchange rates (dollars per unit of local currency) for 25 countries. Technical analysts believe that by charting past changes in exchange rates, it is possible to predict future changes of exchange rates. After analyzing the autocorrelations for these data, do you believe that technical analysis has potential?

15. The unit sales of a new drug for the first 25 months after its introduction to the marketplace are recorded in the file **P13_15.xlsx**.
   a. Estimate a linear trend equation using the given data. How well does the linear trend fit these data? Are the residuals from this linear trend model *random*?
   b. If the residuals from this linear trend model are *not* random, propose another regression-based trend model that more adequately explains the long-term trend in this time series. Estimate the alternative model(s) using the given data. Check the residuals from the model(s) for randomness. Summarize your findings.
   c. Given the best estimated model of the trend in this time series, interpret R^2 and s_e.

13.5 THE RANDOM WALK MODEL

Random series are sometimes building blocks for other time series models. The model we now discuss, the **random walk** model, is an example of this. In a random walk model the series itself is not random. However, its *differences*—that is, the changes from one period to the next—are random. This type of behavior is typical of stock price data (as well as various other time series data). For example, the graph in Figure 13.27 shows monthly closing prices for a tractor manufactor's stock from January 2001 through April 2007. (See the file **Tractor Closing Prices.xlsx**.) This series is not random, as can be seen from its gradual upward trend at the beginning and the general meandering behavior throughout. (Although the runs test and autocorrelations are not shown for the series itself, they confirm that the series is not random. There are significantly *fewer* runs than expected, and the autocorrelations are significantly *positive* for many lags.)

Figure 13.27

Time Series Graph of Tractor Stock Prices

If we were standing in April 2007 and were asked to forecast the company's prices for the next few months, it is intuitive that we would not use the average of the historical values as our forecast. This forecast would tend to be too low because of the upward trend. Instead, we might base our forecast on the most recent observation. This is exactly what the random walk model does.

Equation (13.9) for the random walk model is given in the box, where μ is a constant and ϵ_t is a random series (noise) with mean 0 and some standard deviation σ that remains *constant* through time.

Random Walk Model

$$Y_t = Y_{t-1} + \mu + \epsilon_t \qquad \text{(13.9)}$$

If we let $DY_t = Y_t - Y_{t-1}$, the change in the series from time t to time $t-1$ (where D stands for difference), then we can write the random walk model as in equation (13.10). This implies that the differences form a random series with mean μ and standard deviation σ. An estimate of μ is the average of the differences, labeled $\overline{Y}_D$, and an estimate of σ is the sample standard deviation of the differences, labeled s_D.

Difference Form of Random Walk Model

$$DY_t = \mu + \epsilon_t \qquad \text{(13.10)}$$

In words, a series that behaves according to this random walk model has random differences, and the series tends to trend upward (if $\mu > 0$) or downward (if $\mu < 0$) by an amount μ each period. If we are standing in period t and want to forecast Y_{t+1}, then a reasonable forecast is given by equation (13.11). That is, we add the estimated trend to the current observation to forecast the next observation.

One-Step-Ahead Forecast for Random Walk Model

$$F_{t+1} = Y_t + \overline{Y}_D \qquad \text{(13.11)}$$

We illustrate this method in the following example.

EXAMPLE | **13.4 RANDOM WALK MODEL OF STOCK PRICES**

The monthly closing prices of the tractor company's stock from January 2001 through April 2007, shown in Figure 13.27, indicate some upward trend. Does this series follow a random walk model with an upward trend? If so, how should future values of these stock prices be forecasted?

Objective To check whether the company's monthly closing prices follow a random walk model with an upward trend, and to see how future prices can be forecasted.

Solution

We have already seen that the closing price series itself is not random, due to the upward trend. To check for the adequacy of a random walk model, we need the *differenced* series. Each value in the differenced series is that month's closing price minus the previous month's closing price. This series can be calculated easily with an Excel formula, or it can be generated automatically with the Difference item on the StatTools Utilities dropdown. (When asked for the *number* of difference variables, we accept the default value of 1.) This differenced series appears in column C of Figure 13.28. This figure also shows the mean and standard deviation of the differences, 0.418 and 4.245, which are used in forecasting. Finally, Figure 13.28 shows several autocorrelations of the differences, only one of which is (barely) significant. A runs test for the differences, not shown here, has a large *p*-value, which supports the conclusion that the differences are random.

Figure 13.28

Differences of Closing Prices

	A	B	C	D	E	F
1	Month	Closing Price	Diff1(Closing Price)			Diff1(Closing Price)
2	Jan-01	22.595			One Variable Summary	Data Set #1
3	Feb-01	22.134	-0.461		Mean	0.418
4	Mar-01	24.655	2.521		Std. Dev.	4.245
5	Apr-01	26.649	1.994		Count	75
6	May-01	26.303	-0.346			
7	Jun-01	27.787	1.484			Diff1(Closing Price)
8	Jul-01	32.705	4.918		Autocorrelation Table	Data Set #1
9	Aug-01	29.745	-2.96		Number of Values	75
10	Sep-01	26.741	-3.004		Standard Error	0.1155
11	Oct-01	24.852	-1.889		Lag #1	**-0.2435**
12	Nov-01	28.050	3.198		Lag #2	0.1348
13	Dec-01	27.847	-0.203		Lag #3	-0.0049
14	Jan-02	30.040	2.193		Lag #4	-0.0507
15	Feb-02	29.680	-0.36		Lag #5	0.0696
16	Mar-02	30.139	0.459		Lag #6	0.0009
17	Apr-02	29.276	-0.863		Lag #7	-0.0630
18	May-02	29.703	0.427		Lag #8	-0.0295
19	Jun-02	30.017	0.314		Lag #9	0.0496
20	Jul-02	29.687	-0.33		Lag #10	-0.1728
21	Aug-02	31.765	2.078		Lag #11	-0.0334
22	Sep-02	33.788	2.023		Lag #12	-0.0554
23	Oct-02	30.942	-2.846			
24	Nov-02	38.526	7.584			
25	Dec-02	34.099	-4.427			

The plot of the differences appears in Figure 13.29. A visual inspection of the plot also supports the conclusion of random differences, although these differences do not vary around a mean of 0. Rather, they vary around a mean of 0.418. This positive value measures the upward trend—the closing prices increase, on average, by 0.418 per month. Finally, the variability in this figure is fairly constant (except for the two wide swings in 2005). Specifically, the zigzags do not tend to get appreciably wider through time. Therefore, we can conclude that the random walk model with an upward drift fits these data quite well.

To forecast future closing prices, we add the number of months ahead being forecasted times the mean difference to the final closing price (53.947 in April 2007). For example, a forecast of the closing price for September 2007 is as follows:

Forecasted Closing Price for 9/07 = 53.947 + 0.418(5) = 56.037

As a rough measure of the accuracy of this forecast, we can use the standard deviation of the differences, 4.245. Specifically, it can be shown that the standard error for forecasting *k* periods ahead is the standard deviation of the differences multiplied by the square root of *k*. In this case, the standard error is 9.492. As usual, we can be 95% confident that the actual closing price in September will be no more than 2 standard errors from the forecast. Unfortunately, this results in a wide interval—from about 37 to 75. This reflects the fact that it is very difficult to make accurate forecasts for a series with this much variability.

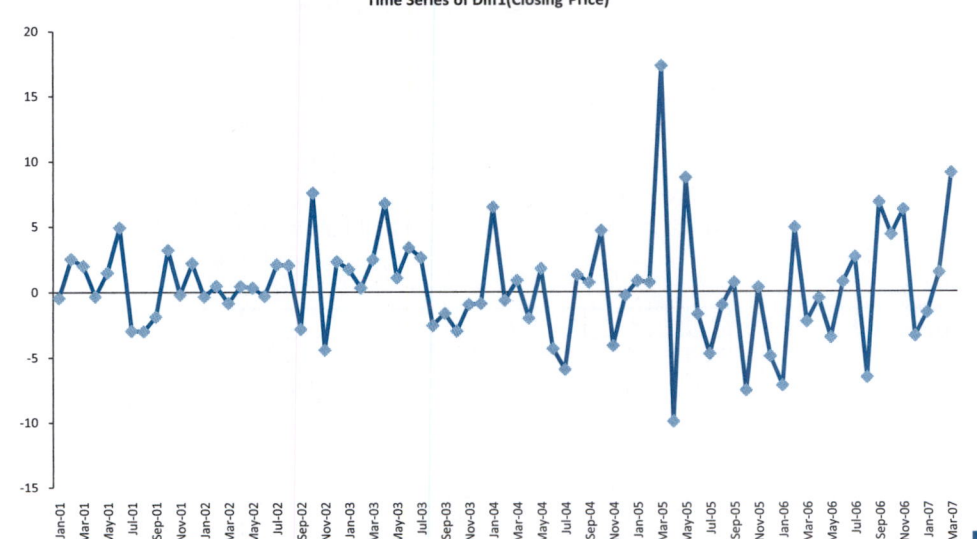

Figure 13.29

Time Series Graph of Differences

Time Series of Diff1(Closing Price)

PROBLEMS

Level A

16. The file **P13_16.xlsx** contains the daily closing prices of American Express stock for a 1-year period.
   a. Use the random walk model to forecast the closing price of this stock on the next trading day.
   b. We can be about 95% certain that the forecast made in part **a** is off by no more than how many dollars?

17. The closing value of the AMEX Airline Index for each trading day during a 1-year period, is given in the file **P13_17.xlsx**.
   a. Use the random walk model to forecast the closing price of this stock on the next trading day.
   b. We can be about 68% certain that the forecast made in part **a** is off by no more than how many dollars?

18. The file **P13_18.xlsx** contains the daily closing prices of ChevronTexaco stock for a 1-year period.
   a. Use the random walk model to forecast the closing price of this stock on the next trading day.
   b. We can be about 99.7% certain that the forecast made in part **a** is off by no more than how many dollars?

19. The closing value of the Dow Jones Industrial Average for each trading day for a 1-year period is provided in the file **P13_19.xlsx**.
   a. Use the random walk model to forecast the closing price of this index on the next trading day.
   b. Would it be wise to use the random walk model to forecast the closing price of this index for a trading day approximately *one month* after the next trading day? Explain why or why not.

20. Continuing the previous problem, consider the differences between consecutive closing values of the Dow Jones Industrial Average for the given set of trading days. Do these differences form a random series? Demonstrate why or why not.

21. The closing price of a share of JPMorgan's stock for each trading day during a 1-year period is recorded in the file **P13_21.xlsx**.
   a. Use the random walk model to forecast the closing price of this stock on the next trading day.
   b. We can be about 68% certain that the forecast made in part **a** is off by no more than how many dollars?

22. The purpose of this problem is to get you used to the concept of autocorrelation in a time series. You could do it with any time series, but here you should use the series of Wal-Mart daily stock prices in the file **P13_10.xlsx**.
   a. First, do it the "easy" way. Use the Autocorrelation procedure in StatTools to get a list of autocorrelations and a corresponding correlogram of the closing prices. You can choose the number of lags.
   b. Now do it the "hard" way. Create columns of lagged versions of the Close variable—3 or 4 lags will suffice. Next, look at scatterplots of Close versus its first few lags. If the autocorrelations are large, you should see fairly tight scatters—that's

what autocorrelation is all about. Also, generate a correlation matrix to see the correlations between Close and its first few lags. These should be approximately the same as the autocorrelations from part **a**. (Autocorrelations are calculated slightly differently than regular correlations, which accounts for any slight discrepancies you might notice, but these discrepancies should be minor.)

c. Create the first differences of Close in a new column. (You can do this manually with formulas, or you can use StatTools's Difference procedure under Data Utilities.) Now repeat parts **a** and **b** with the differences instead of the original closing prices—that is, examine the autocorrelations of the differences. They should be small, and the scatterplots of the differences versus lags of the differences should be "swarms." This illustrates what happens when the differences of a time series variable have "insignificant" autocorrelations.

d. Write a short report of your findings.

23. Consider a random walk model with the following equation: $Y_t = Y_{t-1} + 500 + \epsilon_t$, where ϵ_t is a normally distributed random series with mean 0 and standard deviation 10.
   a. Use Excel to simulate a time series that behaves according to this random walk model.
   b. Use the time series you constructed in part **a** to forecast the next observation.

24. The file **P13_24.xlsx** contains the daily closing prices of Procter & Gamble stock for a one-year period. Use only the data from 2003 to estimate the trend component of the random walk model. Next, use the estimated random walk model to forecast the behavior of the time series for the 2004 dates in the series. Comment on the accuracy of the generated forecasts over this period. How could you improve the forecasts as you progress through the 2004 trading days?

13.6 AUTOREGRESSION MODELS[3]

We now discuss a regression-based extrapolation method that regresses the current value of the time series on past (lagged) values. This is called **autoregression**, where the "auto" means that the explanatory variables in the equation are lagged values of the dependent variable, so that we are regressing the dependent variable on lagged versions of itself. This procedure is fairly straightforward on a spreadsheet. We first create lags of the dependent variable and then use a regression procedure to regress the original column on the lagged columns. Some trial and error is generally required to see how many lags are useful in the regression equation. The following example illustrates the procedure.

| EXAMPLE | 13.5 FORECASTING HAMMER SALES |

A retailer has recorded its weekly sales of hammers (units purchased) for the past 42 weeks. (See the file **Hammer Sales.xlsx**.) A graph of this time series appears in Figure 13.30. It reveals a "meandering" behavior. The values begin high and stay high awhile, then get lower and stay lower awhile, then get higher again. (This behavior could be caused by any number of things, including the weather, increases and decreases in building projects, and possibly others.) How useful is autoregression for modeling these data and how can it be used for forecasting?

[3]This section can be omitted without any loss of continuity.

Objective To use autoregression, with an appropriate number of lagged terms, to forecast hammer sales.

Solution

A good place to start is with the autocorrelations of the series. These indicate whether the Sales variable is linearly related to any of its lags. The first six autocorrelations are shown in Figure 13.31. The first three of them are significantly positive, and then they decrease. Based on this information, we create three lags of Sales and run a regression of Sales versus these three lags. The output from this regression appears in Figure 13.32. We see that R^2 is fairly high, about 57%, and that s_e is about 15.7. However, the p-values for lags 2 and 3 are both quite large. It appears that once the first lag is included in the regression equation, the other two are not really needed.

It is generally best to begin with plenty of lags and then delete the higher numbered lags that aren't necessary.

Figure 13.30 Time Series Graph of Sales of Hammers

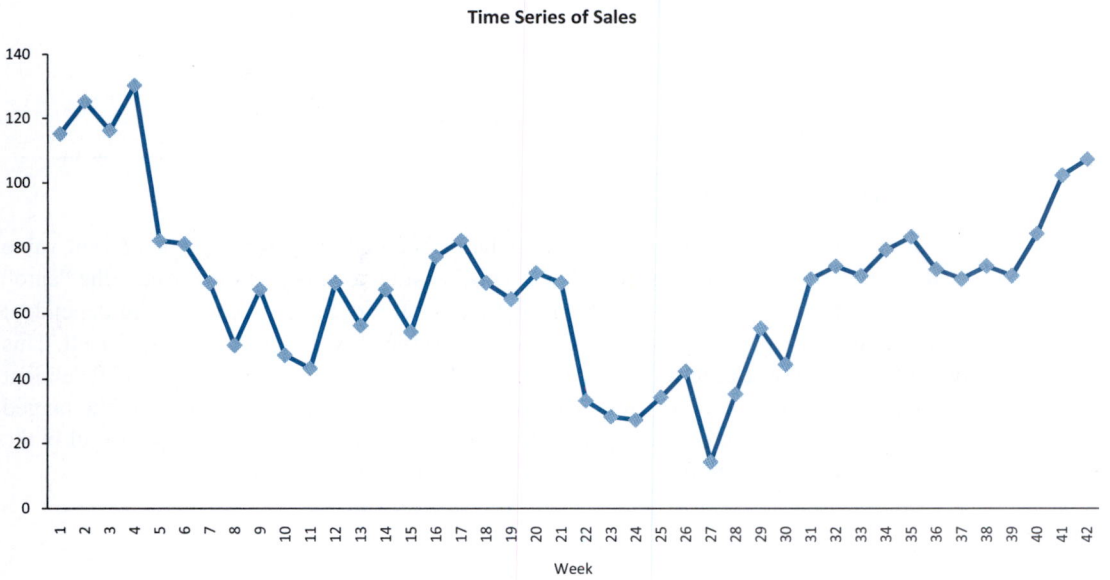

Figure 13.31

Autocorrelations for Hammer Sales Data

	A	B
27		Sales
28	*Autocorrelation Table*	Data Set #1
29	Number of Values	42
30	Standard Error	0.1543
31	Lag #1	**0.7523**
32	Lag #2	**0.5780**
33	Lag #3	**0.4328**
34	Lag #4	0.2042
35	Lag #5	0.1093
36	Lag #6	-0.0502

Figure 13.32 Autoregression Output with Three Lagged Variables

	A	B	C	D	E	F	G
7		Multiple	R-Square	Adjusted	StErr of		
8	*Summary*	R		R-Square	Estimate		
9		0.7573	0.5736	0.5370	15.7202		
10							
11		Degrees of	Sum of	Mean of	F-Ratio	p-Value	
12	*ANOVA Table*	Freedom	Squares	Squares			
13	Explained	3	11634.19978	3878.066594	15.6927	< 0.0001	
14	Unexplained	35	8649.38996	247.1254274			
15							
16		Coefficient	Standard	t-Value	p-Value	Confidence Interval 95%	
17	*Regression Table*		Error			Lower	Upper
18	Constant	15.4986	7.8820	1.9663	0.0572	-0.5027	31.5000
19	Lag1(Sales)	0.6398	0.1712	3.7364	0.0007	0.2922	0.9874
20	Lag2(Sales)	0.1523	0.1987	0.7665	0.4485	-0.2510	0.5556
21	Lag3(Sales)	-0.0354	0.1641	-0.2159	0.8303	-0.3686	0.2977

The two curves in this figure look pretty close to one another. However, a comparison of the vertical distances between pairs of points indicates that they are not so close after all.

Therefore, we reran the regression with only the first lag included. (Actually, we first omitted only the third lag. But the resulting output showed that the second lag was still insignificant.) The regression output with only the first lag included appears in Figure 13.33. In addition, a graph of the dependent and fitted variables, that is, the original Sales variable and its forecasts, appears in Figure 13.34. (This latter graph was formed from the Week, Sales, and Fitted columns.) The estimated regression equation is

$$\text{Forecasted Sales}_t = 13.763 + 0.793 \text{Sales}_{t-1}$$

The associated R^2 and s_e values are approximately 65% and 15.4. The R^2 value is a measure of the reasonably good fit we see in Figure 13.34, whereas s_e is a measure of the likely forecast error for short-term forecasts. It implies that a short-term forecast could easily be off by as much as 2 standard errors, or about 31 hammers.

Figure 13.33 Autoregression Output with a Single Lagged Variable

	A	B	C	D	E	F	G
7		Multiple	R-Square	Adjusted	StErr of		
8	*Summary*	R		R-Square	Estimate		
9		0.8036	0.6458	0.6367	15.4476		
10							
11		Degrees of	Sum of	Mean of	F-Ratio	p-Value	
12	*ANOVA Table*	Freedom	Squares	Squares			
13	Explained	1	16969.97657	16969.97657	71.1146	< 0.0001	
14	Unexplained	39	9306.511237	238.6284932			
15							
16		Coefficient	Standard	t-Value	p-Value	Confidence Interval 95%	
17	*Regression Table*		Error			Lower	Upper
18	Constant	13.7634	6.7906	2.0268	0.0496	0.0281	27.4988
19	Lag1(Sales)	0.7932	0.0941	8.4329	< 0.0001	0.6029	0.9834

Figure 13.34   Forecasts from Autoregression

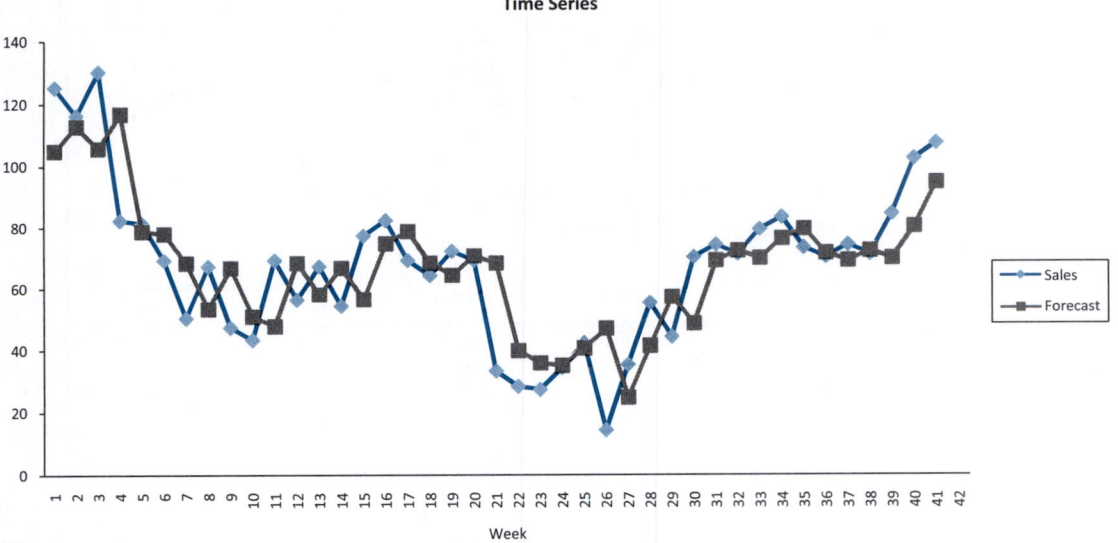

To forecast, substitute
known values of Y
into the regression
equation if they are
available. Otherwise,
substitute forecasted
values.

To use the regression equation for forecasting *future* sales values, we substitute known or forecasted sales values in the right-hand side of the equation. Specifically, the forecast for week 43, the first week after the data period, is

$$\text{Forecasted Sales}_{43} = 13.763 + 0.793\text{Sales}_{42} = 13.763 + 0.793(107) \approx 98.6$$

Here we use the *known* value of sales in week 42. However, the forecast for week 44 requires the *forecasted* value of sales in week 43:

$$\text{Forecasted Sales}_{44} = 13.763 + 0.793\text{Forecasted Sales}_{43}$$

$$\text{Forecasted Sales}_{44} = 13.763 + 0.793(98.6) \approx 92.0$$

Perhaps these two forecasts of future sales values are on the mark, and perhaps they are not. The only way we will know for certain is by observing future sales values. However, it is interesting that in spite of the *upward* movement in the series in the last 3 weeks, the forecasts for weeks 43 and 44 are for *downward* movements. This is a combination of two properties of the regression equation. First, the coefficient of Sales_{t-1}, 0.793, is positive. Therefore, the equation forecasts that large sales will be followed by large sales, that is, positive autocorrelation. Second, however, this coefficient is less than 1, and this provides a dampening effect. The equation forecasts that a large will follow a large, but not *that* large. ■

Sometimes an autoregression model can be virtually equivalent to another forecasting model. As an example, suppose we find that the following equation adequately models a time series variable *Y*:

$$Y_t = 75.65 + 0.976Y_{t-1}$$

The coefficient of the lagged term, 0.976, is nearly equal to 1. If this coefficient were 1, we could subtract the lagged term from both sides of the equation and write that the *difference* series is a constant—that is, we would have a random walk model. As you can see, a random walk model is a special case of an autoregression model. However, autoregression models are much more general. Unfortunately, a more thorough study of them would take us into the realm of econometrics, which is well beyond the level of this book.

PROBLEMS

Level A

25. Consider the Consumer Price Index (CPI), which provides the annual percentage change in consumer prices. The data are in the file **P02_26.xlsx**.
   a. Compute the first six autocorrelations of this time series.
   b. Use the results of part **a** to specify one or more "promising" autoregression models. Estimate each model with the available data. Which model provides the best fit to the given data?
   c. Use the best autoregression model from part **b** to produce a forecast of the CPI in the next year. Also, provide a measure of the likely forecast error.

26. The Consumer Confidence Index (CCI) attempts to measure people's feelings about general business conditions, employment opportunities, and their own income prospects. The file **P02_28.xlsx** contains the annual average values of the CCI.
   a. Compute the first six autocorrelations of this time series.
   b. Use the results of part **a** to specify one or more "promising" autoregression models. Estimate each model with the available data. Which model provides the best fit to the given data?
   c. Use the best autoregression model from part **b** to produce a forecast of the CCI in the next year. Also, provide a measure of the likely forecast error.

27. Consider the proportion of Americans under the age of 18 living below the poverty level. The data are in the file **P02_29.xlsx**.
   a. Compute the first six autocorrelations of this time series.
   b. Use the results of part **a** to specify one or more "promising" autoregression models. Estimate each model with the available data. Which model provides the best fit to the given data?
   c. Use the best autoregression model from part **b** to produce a forecast of the proportion of American children living below the poverty level in the next year. Also, provide a measure of the likely forecast error.

28. Examine the trend in the annual average values of the discount rate. The data are in the file **P02_30.xlsx**.
   a. Specify one or more "promising" autoregression models based on autocorrelations of this time series. Estimate each model with the available data. Which model provides the best fit to given data?
   b. Use the best autoregression model from part **a** to produce forecasts of the discount rate in the next 2 years.

29. The file **P02_34.xlsx** contains time series data on the percentage of the resident population in the United States who completed four or more years of college.
   a. Specify one or more "promising" autoregression models based on autocorrelations of this time series. Estimate each model with the available data. Which model provides the best fit to the given data?
   b. Use the best autoregression model from part **a** to produce forecasts of higher education attainment (i.e., completion of four or more years of college) in the United States in the next 3 years.

30. Consider the average annual interest rates on 30-year fixed mortgages in the United States. The data are recorded in the file **P02_35.xlsx**.
   a. Specify one or more "promising" autoregression models based on autocorrelations of this time series. Estimate each model with the available data. Which model provides the best fit to the given data?
   b. Use the best autoregression model from part **a** to produce forecasts of the average annual interest rates on 30-year fixed mortgages in the next 3 years.

31. The file **P13_31.xlsx** lists the monthly unemployment rates for several years. A common way to forecast time series is by using regression with lagged variables.

a. Predict future monthly unemployment rates using some combination of the unemployment rates for the last 4 months. For example, you might use last month's unemployment rate and the unemployment rate from 3 months ago as explanatory variables. Make sure all variables that you finally decide to keep in your equation are significant at the 0.15 level.

b. Do the residuals in your equation exhibit any autocorrelation?

c. Predict the next month's unemployment rate.

d. There is a 5% chance that the next month's unemployment rate will be less than what value?

e. What is the probability the next month's unemployment rate will be less than 6%?

Level B

32. The unit sales of a new drug for the first 25 months after its introduction to the marketplace are recorded in the file **P13_15.xlsx**. Specify one or more "promising" autoregression models based on autocorrelations of this time series. Estimate each model with the available data. Which model provides the best fit to the given data? Use the best autoregression model you found to forecast the sales of this new drug in the 26th month.

33. The file **P13_02.xlsx** contains the weekly sales at a local bookstore for each of the past 25 weeks.
   a. Specify one or more "promising" autoregression models based on autocorrelations of this time series. Estimate each model with the available data. Which model provides the best fit to the given data?
   b. What general result emerges from your analysis in part **a**? In other words, what is the most appropriate autoregression model for any given *random* time series?
   c. Use the best autoregression model from part **a** to produce forecasts of the weekly sales at this bookstore for the next 3 weeks.

34. The file **P13_24.xlsx** contains the daily closing prices of Procter & Gamble stock for a one-year period.
   a. Use only the data from 2003 to estimate an appropriate autoregression model.
   b. Next, use the estimated autoregression model from part **a** to forecast the behavior of this time series for the 2004 dates of the series. Comment on the accuracy of the generated forecasts over this period.
   c. How well does the autoregression model perform in comparison to the random walk model with respect to the accuracy of these forecasts? Explain any significant differences between the forecasting abilities of the two models.

13.7 MOVING AVERAGES

Perhaps the simplest and one of the most frequently used extrapolation methods is the method of **moving averages**. To implement the moving averages method, we first choose a **span**, the number of terms in each moving average. Let's say the data are monthly and we choose a span of 6 months. Then the forecast of next month's value is the average of the values of the last 6 months. For example, we average January to June to forecast July, we average February to July to forecast August, and so on. This procedure is the reason for the term *moving* averages.

> A **moving average** is the average of the observations in the past few periods, where the number of terms in the average is the **span**.

A moving averages model with a span of 1 is a random walk model with a mean trend of 0.

The role of the span is important. If the span is large—say, 12 months—then many observations go into each average, and extreme values have relatively little effect on the forecasts. The resulting series of forecasts will be much smoother than the original series. (For this reason, the moving average method is called a *smoothing* method.) In contrast, if the span is small—say, 3 months—then extreme observations have a larger effect on the forecasts, and the forecast series will be much less smooth. In the extreme, if the span is 1, there is no smoothing effect at all. The method simply forecasts next month's value to be the same as the current month's value. This is often called the **naive** forecasting model. It is a special case of the random walk model we discussed previously, with the mean difference equal to 0.

What span should we use? This requires some judgment. If we believe the ups and downs in the series are random noise, then we don't want future forecasts to react too quickly to these ups and downs, and we should use a relatively large span. But if we want to track every little zigzag—under the belief that each up or down is predictable—then we should use a smaller span. We shouldn't be fooled, however, by a plot of the (smoothed) forecast series superimposed on the original series. This graph will almost always look better when a small span is used, because the forecast series will appear to track the original series better. Does this mean it will always provide better future forecasts? Not necessarily. There is little point in tracking random ups and downs closely if they represent unpredictable noise.

The following example illustrates the use of moving averages.

EXAMPLE | **13.6 HOUSES SOLD IN THE MIDWEST**

The file **House Sales.xlsx** contains monthly data on the number of houses sold in the Midwest (in thousands) from January 1994 through May 2001. (These data are seasonally adjusted.)[4] A time series graph of the data appears in Figure 13.35. Does a moving averages model fit this data set well? What span should be used?

Figure 13.35   Time Series Plot of Monthly House Sales

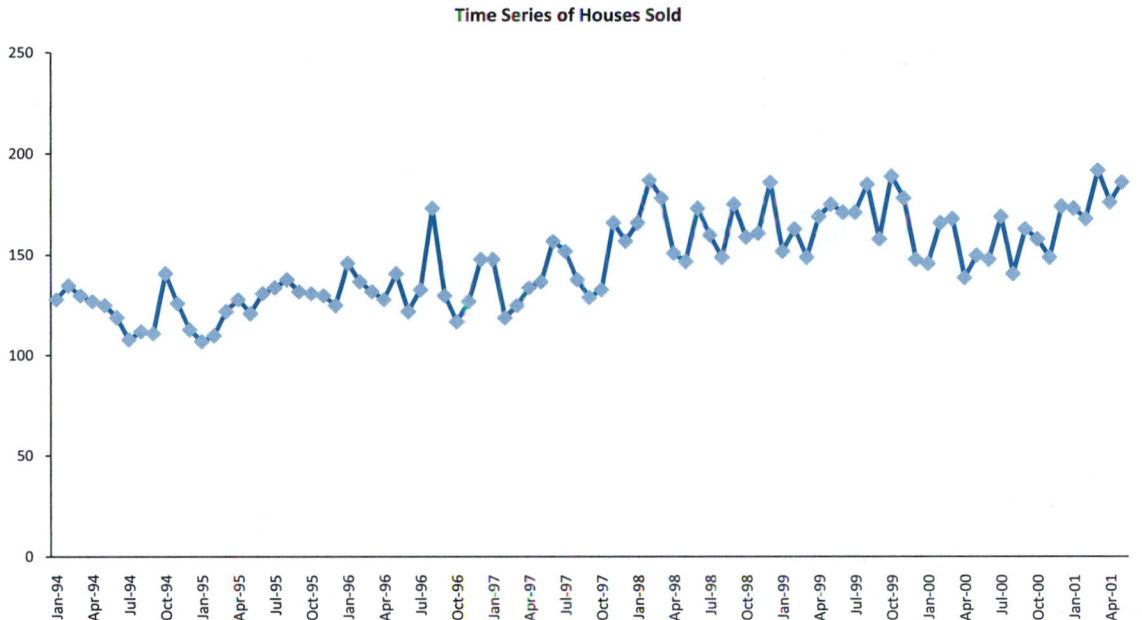

Objective   To see whether a moving averages model with an appropriate span fits the housing sales data, and to see how StatTools implements this method.

---

[4]We discuss seasonal adjustment in Section 13.9. Government data are often reported in seasonally adjusted form, with the seasonality removed, to make any trends more apparent.

Solution

Although the moving averages method is quite easy to implement in Excel—we just form an average of the appropriate span and copy it down—it can be tedious. Therefore, we call on the forecasting procedure of StatTools. Actually, this procedure is fairly general in that it allows us to forecast with several methods, either with or without taking seasonality into account. Because this is our first exposure to this procedure, we go through it in some detail in this example. In later examples, we mention some of its other capabilities.

To use the StatTools Forecasting procedure, select Forecast from the StatTools Time Series and Forecasting dropdown. This brings up the dialog box in Figure 13.36, which has three tabs in its bottom section. The Time Scale tab, shown in Figure 13.36, allows us to select the time period. The Forecast Settings tab, shown in Figure 13.37, allows us to select a forecasting method. Finally, the Graphs to Display tab, not shown here, allows us to select several optional time series graphs. For now, fill out the dialog box sections as shown and select the Forecast Overlay option in the Graphs to Display tab. In particular, note from Figure 13.37 that we are using the moving averages method with a span of 3, and we are asking for forecasts of the next 12 months.

Figure 13.36

Forecast Dialog Box with Time Scale Tab Visible

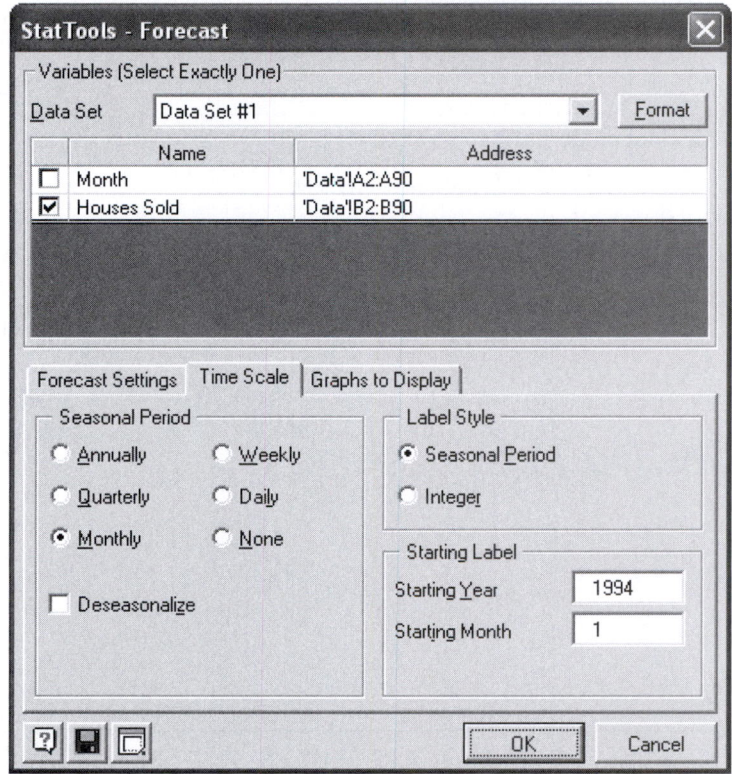

Another option in Figure 13.37 is that we can elect to "hold out" a subset of the data for validation purposes. If we hold out several periods at the end of the data set for validation, then any model that is built is estimated only for the nonholdout observations, and summary measures are reported for the nonholdout and holdout subsets separately. For now, we are not using a holdout period.

Figure 13.37

Forecast Dialog Box with Forecast Settings Tab Visible

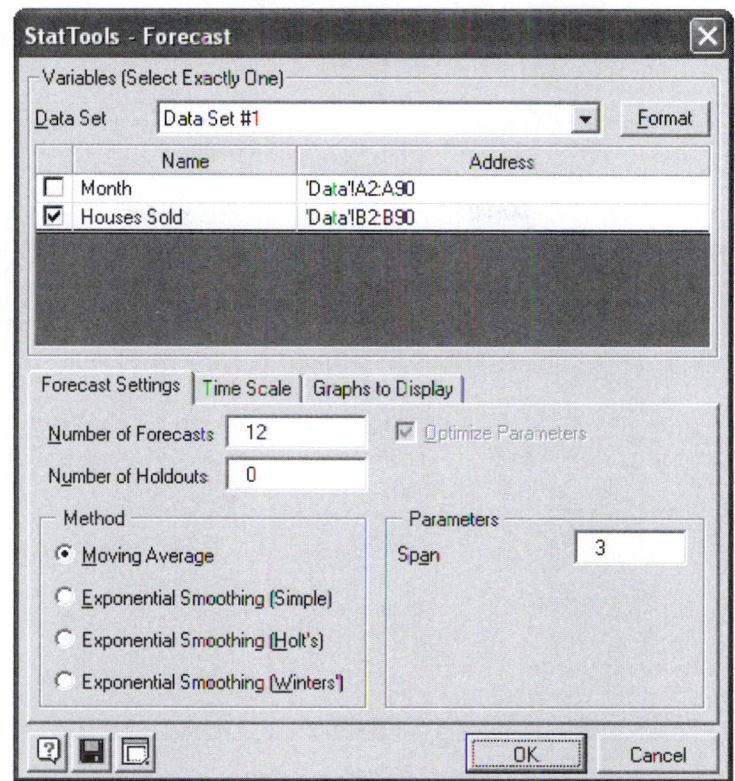

The output consists of several parts, as shown in Figures 13.38 through 13.41. We actually ran the analysis twice, once for a span of 3 and once for a span of 12. These figures show the comparison. (We also obtained output for a span of 6, with results similar to those for a span of 12.) First, the summary measures MAE, RMSE, and MAPE of the forecast errors are shown in Figure 13.38. As we see, both spans produce similar magnitudes of forecast errors. For example, they are both off, on average, by slightly more than 8%.

Figure 13.38   Moving Averages Summary Output

	A	B	C	D	E	F	G	H
8	*Forecasting Constant*						*Forecasting Constant*	
9	Span	3					Span	12
10								
11				Moving averages method				
12	*Moving Averages*			with spans 3 and 12			*Moving Averages*	
13	Mean Abs Err	12.26					Mean Abs Err	12.43
14	Root Mean Sq Err	14.96					Root Mean Sq Err	15.62
15	Mean Abs Per% Err	8.37%					Mean Abs Per% Err	8.07%

Figure 13.39 Moving Averages Detailed Output

	A	B	C	D	E	F	G	H	I	J
40	*Forecasting Data*	**Houses Sold**	Forecast	Error			*Forecasting Data*	**Houses Sold**	Forecast	Error
41	Jan-1994	128.0000					Jan-1994	128.0000		
42	Feb-1994	135.0000					Feb-1994	135.0000		
43	Mar-1994	130.0000					Mar-1994	130.0000		
44	Apr-1994	127.0000	131.00	-4.00			Apr-1994	127.0000		
45	May-1994	125.0000	130.67	-5.67			May-1994	125.0000		
46	Jun-1994	119.0000	127.33	-8.33			Jun-1994	119.0000		
47	Jul-1994	108.0000	123.67	-15.67			Jul-1994	108.0000		
48	Aug-1994	112.0000	117.33	-5.33			Aug-1994	112.0000		
49	Sep-1994	111.0000	113.00	-2.00			Sep-1994	111.0000		
50	Oct-1994	141.0000	110.33	30.67			Oct-1994	141.0000		
51	Nov-1994	126.0000	121.33	4.67			Nov-1994	126.0000		
52	Dec-1994	113.0000	126.00	-13.00			Dec-1994	113.0000		
53	Jan-1995	107.0000	126.67	-19.67			Jan-1995	107.0000	122.92	-15.92
54	Feb-1995	110.0000	115.33	-5.33			Feb-1995	110.0000	121.17	-11.17
55	Mar-1995	122.0000	110.00	12.00			Mar-1995	122.0000	119.08	2.92
56	Apr-1995	128.0000	113.00	15.00			Apr-1995	128.0000	118.42	9.58
126	Feb-2001	168.0000	165.33	2.67			Feb-2001	168.0000	158.17	9.83
127	Mar-2001	192.0000	171.67	20.33			Mar-2001	192.0000	158.33	33.67
128	Apr-2001	176.0000	177.67	-1.67			Apr-2001	176.0000	160.33	15.67
129	May-2001	186.0000	178.67	7.33			May-2001	186.0000	163.42	22.58
130	Jun-2001		184.67				Jun-2001		166.42	
131	Jul-2001		182.22				Jul-2001		167.95	
132	Aug-2001		184.30				Aug-2001		167.86	
133	Sep-2001		183.73				Sep-2001		170.10	
134	Oct-2001		183.42				Oct-2001		170.69	
135	Nov-2001		183.81				Nov-2001		171.75	
136	Dec-2001		183.65				Dec-2001		173.65	
137	Jan-2002		183.63				Jan-2002		173.62	
138	Feb-2002		183.70				Feb-2002		173.67	
139	Mar-2002		183.66				Mar-2002		174.14	
140	Apr-2002		183.66				Apr-2002		172.66	
141	May-2002		183.67				May-2002		172.38	

Figure 13.40

Moving Averages Forecasts with Span 3

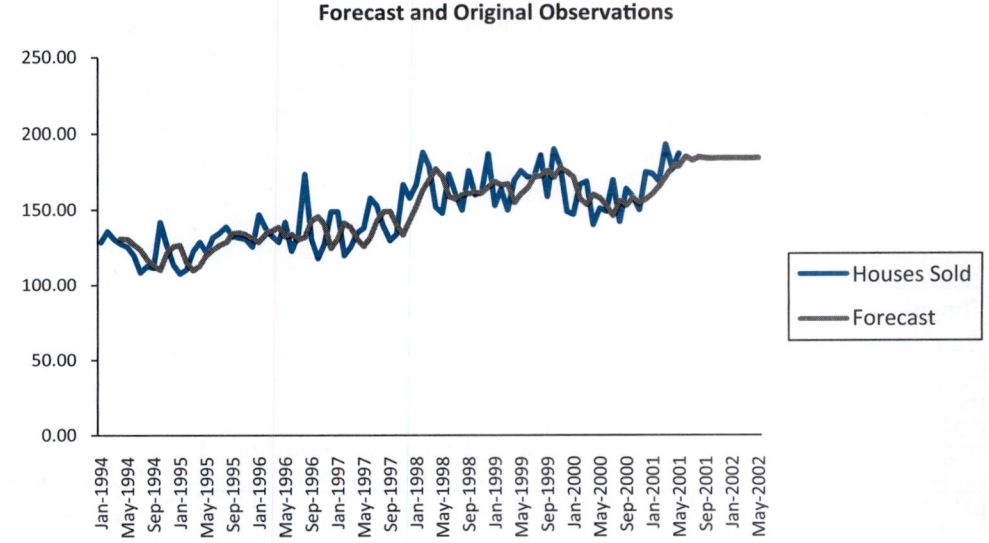

Forecast and Original Observations

Figure 13.41

Moving Averages
Forecasts with
Span 12

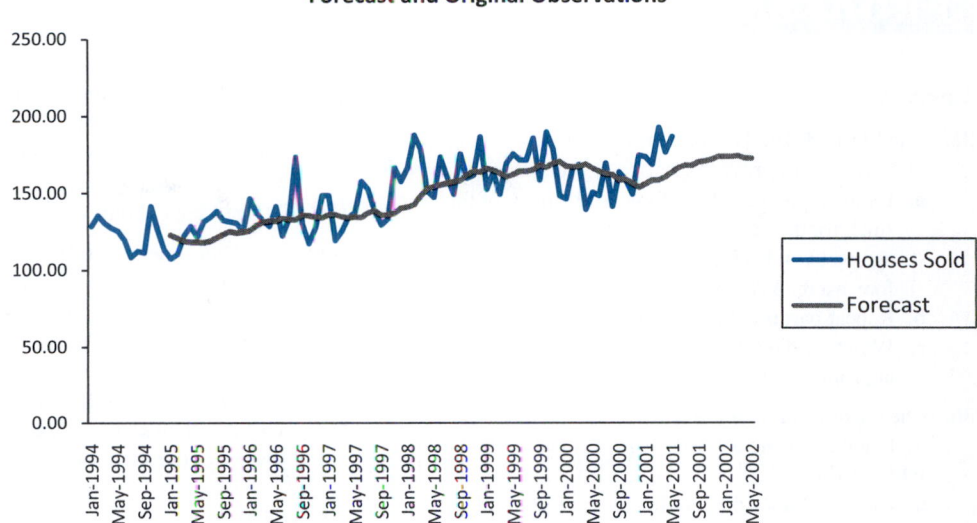

Forecast and Original Observations

The essence of the forecasting method is very simple and is captured in column C of Figure 13.39 (for a span of 3). Each value in the historical period in this column is an average of the three preceding values in column B. The forecast errors are then just the differences between columns B and C. For the future periods, the forecast formulas in column C use observations when they are available. If they are not available, previous forecasts are used. For example, the value in cell C131, the forecast for July 2001, is the average of the *observed* values in April and May and the *forecasted* value in June.

The graphs in Figures 13.40 and 13.41 show the behavior of the forecasts. The forecasted series with span 3 follows the ups and downs of the actual series fairly closely, whereas the forecasted series with span 12 is much smoother and doesn't react nearly as much to these ups and downs. Which of these is better? The error summary measures indicate that it is a virtual toss-up. The MAPE with span 12 is slightly lower, but the RMSE with span 3 is slightly lower. Note that the *future* forecasts are considerably lower with span 12 than with span 3.

At this point, how to proceed is up to the judgment of the forecaster, who presumably has some knowledge of the housing sales market in the Midwest. If she believes that the ups and downs in the original series are largely unpredictable noise, then she will probably trust the smooth forecasts from a span of 12. Otherwise, she might use a span of 3 (or some other intermediate span, such as 6). ■

The moving average method we have presented is the simplest of a group of moving average methods used by professional forecasters. We *smoothed* exactly once; that is, we took moving averages of several observations at a time and used these as forecasts. More complex methods smooth more than once, basically to get rid of random noise. They take moving averages, then moving averages of these moving averages, and so on for several stages. This can become quite complex, but the objective is quite simple—to smooth the data so that we can see underlying patterns.

Level A

35. The file **P13_16.xlsx** contains the daily closing prices of American Express stock for a 1-year period.
  a. Using a span of 3 days, forecast the price of this stock for the next trading day with the moving average method. How well does this method with span 3 forecast the known observations in this data set?
  b. Repeat part **a** with a span of 10.
  c. Which of these two spans appears to be more appropriate? Explain your choice.

36. The closing value of the AMEX Airline Index for each trading day during a 1-year period is given in the file **P13_17.xlsx**.
  a. How well does the moving average method track this series when the span is 4 days; when the span is 12 days?
  b. Using the more appropriate span, forecast the closing value of this index on the next trading day with the moving average method.

37. The closing value of the Dow Jones Industrial Average for each trading day during a 1-year period is provided in the file **P13_19.xlsx**.
  a. Using a span of 2 days, forecast the price of this index on the next trading day with the moving average method. How well does the moving average method with span 2 forecast the known observations in this data set?
  b. Repeat part **a** with a span of 5 days; with a span of 15 days.
  c. Which of these three spans appears to be most appropriate? Explain your choice.

38. The file **P13_10.xlsx** contains the daily closing prices of Wal-Mart stock during a 1-year period. Use the moving average method with a carefully chosen span to forecast this time series for the next 3 trading days. Defend your choice of the span used.

39. The Consumer Confidence Index (CCI) attempts to measure people's feelings about general business conditions, employment opportunities, and their own income prospects. The file **P02_28.xlsx** contains the annual average values of the CCI. Use the moving average method with a carefully chosen span to forecast this time series in the next 2 years. Defend your choice of the span used here.

Level B

40. Consider the file **P02_37.xlsx**, which contains total monthly U.S. retail sales data. While retaining the final 6 months of observations for validation purposes, use the method of moving averages with a carefully chosen span to forecast U.S. retail sales in the next year. Comment on the performance of your model. What makes this time series more challenging to forecast?

41. Consider a random walk model with the following equation: $Y_t = Y_{t-1} + \epsilon_t$, where ϵ_t is a random series with mean 0 and standard deviation 1. Specify a moving average model that is equivalent to this random walk model. In particular, what is the appropriate size of the span in the equivalent moving average model? Describe the smoothing effect of this span choice.

13.8 EXPONENTIAL SMOOTHING

There are two possible criticisms of the moving averages method. First, it puts equal weight on each value in a typical moving average when making a forecast. Many people would argue that if next month's forecast is to be based on the previous 12 months' observations, then more weight ought to be placed on the more recent observations. The second criticism is that the moving averages method requires a lot of data storage. This is particularly true for companies that routinely make forecasts of hundreds or even thousands of items. If 12-month moving averages are used for 1000 items, then 12,000 values are needed for next month's forecasts. This may or may not be a concern considering today's inexpensive computer storage capabilities.

Exponential smoothing is a method that addresses both of these criticisms. It bases its forecasts on a weighted average of past observations, with more weight put on the more recent observations, and it requires very little data storage. In addition, it is not difficult for most business people to understand, at least conceptually. Therefore, this method finds widespread use in the business world, particularly when frequent and automatic forecasts of many items are required.

There are many versions of exponential smoothing. The simplest is appropriately called *simple* exponential smoothing. It is relevant when there is no pronounced trend or seasonality in the series. If there is a trend but no seasonality, then *Holt's* method is applicable. If, in addition, there is seasonality, then *Winters'* method can be used. This does not exhaust the list of exponential smoothing models—researchers have invented many other variations—but these three models will suffice for us.

Exponential Smoothing Models

Simple exponential smoothing is appropriate for a series with no pronounced trend or seasonality. **Holt's** method is appropriate for a series with trend but no seasonality. **Winters'** method is appropriate for a series with seasonality (and possibly trend).

In this section we examine simple exponential smoothing and Holt's model for trend. Then in the next section we examine Winters' model when we focus on seasonal models in general.

13.8.1 Simple Exponential Smoothing

The level is where we think the series would be if it were not for random noise.

We now examine simple exponential smoothing in some detail. We first introduce two new terms. Every exponential model has at least one **smoothing constant**, which is always between 0 and 1. Simple exponential smoothing has a single smoothing constant denoted by α. (Its role is discussed shortly.) The second new term is L_t, called the **level** of the series at time t. This value is not observable but can only be estimated. Essentially, it is where we think the series would be at time t if there were no random noise. Then the simple exponential smoothing method is defined by the following two equations, where F_{t+k} is the forecast of Y_{t+k} made at time t:

Simple Exponential Smoothing Formulas

$$L_t = \alpha Y_t + (1 - \alpha)L_{t-1} \qquad \textbf{(13.12)}$$
$$F_{t+k} = L_t \qquad \textbf{(13.13)}$$

Even though you usually won't have to substitute into these equations manually, you should understand what they say. Equation (13.12) shows how to update the estimate of the level. It is a weighted average of the current observation, Y_t, and the previous level, L_{t-1}, with respective weights α and $1 - \alpha$. Equation (13.13) shows how forecasts are made. It says that the k-period-ahead forecast, F_{t+k}, made of Y_{t+k} in period t is the most recently estimated level, L_t. This is the *same* for any value of $k \geq 1$. The idea is that in simple exponential smoothing, we believe that the series is not really going anywhere. So as soon as we estimate where the series ought to be in period t (if it weren't for random noise), we forecast that this is where it will also be in any future period.

The smoothing constant α is analogous to the span in moving averages. There are two ways to see this. The first way is to rewrite equation (13.12), using the fact that the forecast error, E_t, made in forecasting Y_t at time $t - 1$ is $Y_t - F_t = Y_t - L_{t-1}$. A bit of algebra then gives equation (13.14).

Equivalent Formula for Simple Exponential Smoothing

$$L_t = L_{t-1} + \alpha E_t \qquad \textbf{(13.14)}$$

This equation says that the next estimate of the level is adjusted from the previous estimate by adding a multiple of the most recent forecast error. This makes sense. If our previous forecast was too high, then E_t is negative, and we adjust the estimate of the level downward. The opposite is true if our previous forecast was too low. However, equation (13.14) says that we do not adjust by the entire magnitude of E_t, but only by a fraction of it. If α is small, say, $\alpha = 0.1$, then the adjustment is minor; if α is close to 1, the adjustment is large. So if we want to react quickly to movements in the series, we choose a large α; otherwise, we choose a small α.

Another way to see the effect of α is to substitute recursively into the equation for L_t. If you are willing to go through some algebra, you can verify that L_t satisfies equation (13.15), where the sum extends back to the first observation at time $t = 1$.

> **Another Equivalent Formula for Simple Exponential Smoothing**
> $$L_t = \alpha Y_t + \alpha(1 - \alpha)Y_{t-1} + \alpha(1 - \alpha)^2 Y_{t-2} + \alpha(1 - \alpha)^3 Y_{t-3} + \cdots \quad (13.15)$$

Equation (13.15) shows how the exponentially smoothed forecast is a weighted average of previous observations. Furthermore, because $1 - \alpha$ is less than 1, the weights on the Y's decrease from time t backward. Therefore, if α is close to 0, then $1 - \alpha$ is close to 1 and the weights decrease very slowly. In other words, observations from the distant past continue to have a large influence on the next forecast. This means that the graph of the forecasts will be relatively smooth, just as with a large span in the moving averages method. But when α is close to 1, the weights decrease rapidly, and only very recent observations have much influence on the next forecast. In this case forecasts react quickly to sudden changes in the series.

Small smoothing constants provide forecasts that respond slowly to changes in the data. Large smoothing constants do the opposite.

What value of α should we use? There is no universally accepted answer to this question. Some practitioners recommend always using a value around 0.1 or 0.2. Others recommend experimenting with different values of α until a measure such as RMSE or MAPE is minimized. Some packages even have an optimization feature to find this optimal value of α. (This is the case with StatTools.) But just as we discussed in the moving averages section, the value of α that tracks the historical series most closely does not necessarily guarantee the most accurate *future* forecasts.

EXAMPLE | **13.6 HOUSES SOLD IN THE MIDWEST (CONTINUED)**

Previously, we used the moving averages method to forecast monthly housing sales in the Midwest. (See the **House Sales.xlsx** file.) How well does simple exponential smoothing work with this data set? What smoothing constant should we use?

Objective   To see how well a simple exponential smoothing model, with an appropriate smoothing constant, fits the housing sales data, and to see how StatTools implements this method.

Solution

We use StatTools to implement the simple exponential smoothing model, specifically equations (13.12) and (13.13). We do this again with the Forecast item from StatTools Time Series and Forecasting dropdown. We then fill in the forecast dialog box essentially like we did with moving averages, except that we select the exponential smoothing options in the Forecast Settings tab (see Figure 13.42). That is, we select the simple exponential smoothing option, choose a smoothing constant (0.1 was chosen here, but any other value could be chosen), and elect not to optimize.

Figure 13.42

Forecast Settings for Exponential Smoothing

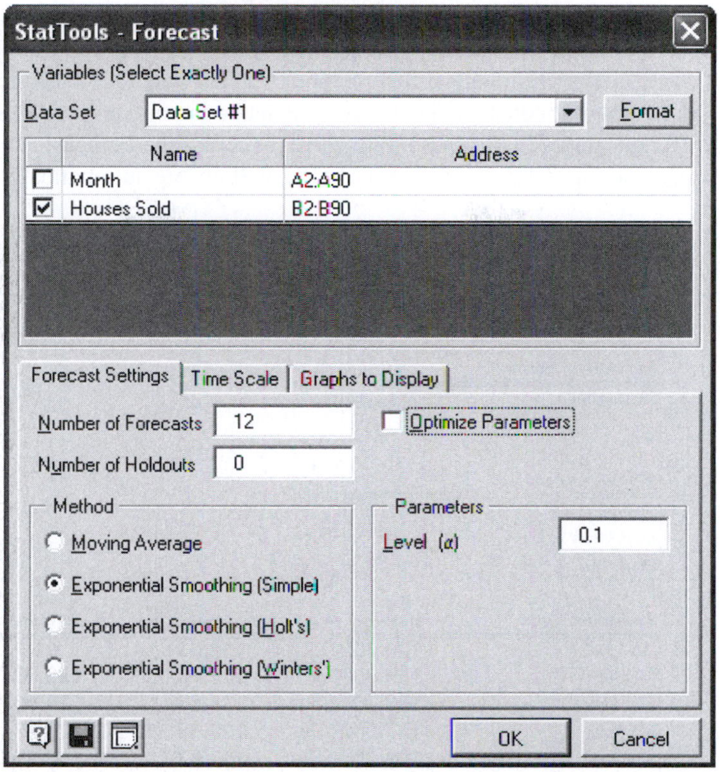

The results appear in Figures 13.43 and 13.44. The heart of the method takes place in columns C, D, and E of Figure 13.43. Column C calculates the smoothed levels (L_t) from equation (13.12), column D calculates the forecasts (F_t) from equation (13.13), and column E calculates the forecast errors (E_t) as the observed values minus the forecasts. Although we do not list the Excel formulas here, you can examine them in the StatTools output.

Every exponential smoothing method requires *initial* values, in this case the initial smoothed level in cell C41. There is no way to calculate this value, L_1, from equation (13.12) because the *previous* value, L_0, is unknown. Different implementations of exponential smoothing initialize in different ways. We have simply set L_1 equal to Y_1 (in cell B41). The effect of initializing in different ways is usually minimal because any effect of early data is usually washed out as we forecast into the future. In the present example, data from 1994 have little effect on forecasts of 2001 and beyond.

Note that the 12 future forecasts (rows 130 down) are all equal to the last calculated smoothed level, the one for May 2001 in cell C129. The fact that these remain constant is a consequence of the assumption behind *simple* exponential smoothing, namely, that the series is not really going anywhere. Therefore, the last smoothed level is the best indication of future values of the series we have.

Figure 13.44 shows the forecast series superimposed on the original series. We see the obvious smoothing effect of a relatively small α level. The forecasts don't track the series very well, but if the various zigzags in the original series are really random noise, then perhaps we don't want the forecasts to track these random ups and downs too closely. Perhaps we instead prefer a forecast series that emphasizes the basic underlying pattern.

In the next subsection we use Holt's method on this series to see whether it captures the trend better than simple exponential smoothing.

We see several summary measures of the forecast errors in Figure 13.43. The RMSE and MAE indicate that the forecasts from this model are typically off by a magnitude of about 12 to 15 thousand, and the MAPE indicates that they are off by about 7.9%. (These are similar to the errors we obtained with moving averages.) These imply fairly sizable errors. One way to reduce the errors is to use a different smoothing method. We try this in the next subsection with Holt's method. Another way to reduce the errors is to use a different smoothing constant. There are two methods you can use. First, you can simply enter different values in the smoothing constant cell in the Forecast sheet. All formulas, including those for MAE, RMSE, and MAPE, will update automatically.

Figure 13.43

Simple Exponential Smoothing Output

	A	B	C	D	E
7					
8	*Forecasting Constant*				
9	Level (Alpha)	0.100			
10					
11					
12	*Simple Exponential*				
13	Mean Abs Err	11.93			
14	Root Mean Sq Err	15.08			
15	Mean Abs Per% Err	7.91%			
39					
40	*Forecasting Data*	Houses Sold	Level	Forecast	Error
41	Jan-1994	128.0000	128.00		
42	Feb-1994	135.0000	128.70	128.00	7.00
43	Mar-1994	130.0000	128.83	128.70	1.30
44	Apr-1994	127.0000	128.65	128.83	-1.83
123	Nov-2000	149.0000	157.82	158.80	-9.80
124	Dec-2000	174.0000	159.44	157.82	16.18
125	Jan-2001	173.0000	160.80	159.44	13.56
126	Feb-2001	168.0000	161.52	160.80	7.20
127	Mar-2001	192.0000	164.56	161.52	30.48
128	Apr-2001	176.0000	165.71	164.56	11.44
129	May-2001	186.0000	167.74	165.71	20.29
130	Jun-2001			167.74	
131	Jul-2001			167.74	
132	Aug-2001			167.74	
133	Sep-2001			167.74	
134	Oct-2001			167.74	
135	Nov-2001			167.74	
136	Dec-2001			167.74	
137	Jan-2002			167.74	
138	Feb-2002			167.74	
139	Mar-2002			167.74	
140	Apr-2002			167.74	
141	May-2002			167.74	

Second, you can check the Optimize Parameters option in Figure 13.42. This automatically runs an optimization algorithm (not Solver, by the way) to find the smoothing constant that minimizes RMSE. (StatTools is programmed to minimize RMSE. However, you could try minimizing MAPE, say, by using Excel's Solver add-in.) We did this for the housing data and obtained the forecasts in Figure 13.45 (from a smoothing constant of 0.295). The corresponding MAE, RMSE, and MAPE are 11.4, 14.1, and 7.7%, respectively—slightly better than before. This larger smoothing constant produces a less smooth forecast curve and slightly better error measures. However, there is no guarantee that *future* forecasts made with this optimal smoothing constant will be any better than with a smoothing constant of 0.1.

Figure 13.44

Graph of Forecasts
from Simple
Exponential
Smoothing

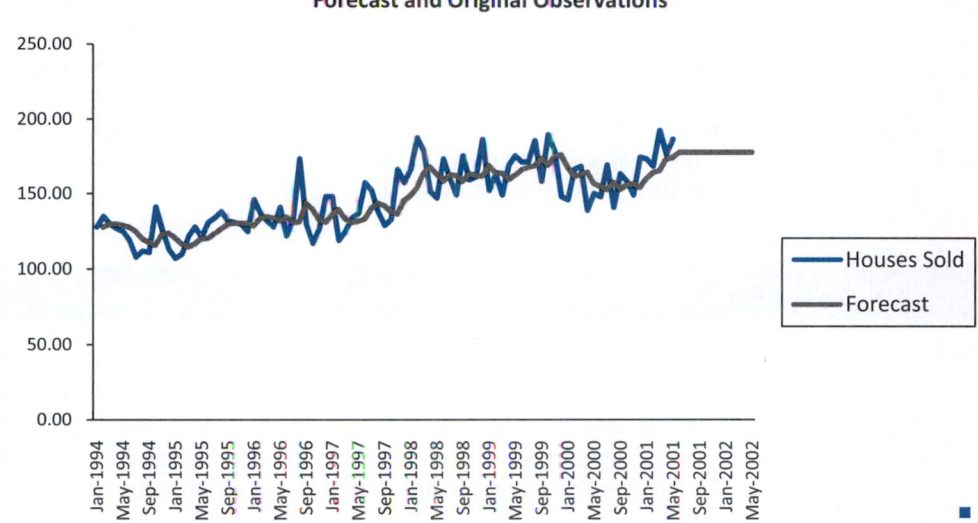

Forecast and Original Observations

Figure 13.45

Graph of Forecasts
with an Optimal
Smoothing Constant

Forecast and Original Observations

13.8.2 Holt's Model for Trend

The trend term in Holt's method estimates the change from one period to the next.

The simple exponential smoothing model generally works well if there is no obvious trend in the series. But if there is a trend, then this method consistently lags behind it. For example, if the series is constantly increasing, simple exponential smoothing forecasts will be consistently low. Holt's method rectifies this by dealing with trend explicitly. In addition to the level of the series, L_t, Holt's method includes a trend term, T_t, and a corresponding smoothing constant β. The interpretation of L_t is exactly as before. The interpretation of T_t is that it represents an estimate of the change in the series from one period to the next. The equations for Holt's model are as follows.

Formula's for Holt's Exponential Smoothing Method

$$L_t = \alpha Y_t + (1 - \alpha)(L_{t-1} + T_{t-1}) \tag{13.16}$$
$$T_t = \beta(L_t - L_{t-1}) + (1 - \beta)T_{t-1} \tag{13.17}$$
$$F_{t+k} = L_t + kT_t \tag{13.18}$$

These equations are not as bad as they look. (And don't forget that the computer typically does all of the calculations for you.) Equation (13.16) says that the updated level is a weighted average of the current observation and the previous level plus the estimated change. Equation (13.17) says that the updated trend term is a weighted average of the difference between two consecutive levels and the previous trend term. Finally, equation (13.18) says that the k-period-ahead forecast made in period t is the estimated level plus k times the estimated change per period.

Everything we said about α for simple exponential smoothing applies to both α and β in Holt's model. The new smoothing constant β controls how quickly the method reacts to perceived changes in the trend. If β is small, the method reacts slowly. If it is large, the method reacts more quickly. Of course, there are now two smoothing constants to select. Some practitioners suggest using a small value of α (0.1 to 0.2, say) and setting β equal to α. Others suggest using an optimization option (available in StatTools) to select the "best" smoothing constants. We illustrate the possibilities in the following continuation of the housing sales example.

EXAMPLE **13.6 HOUSES SOLD IN THE MIDWEST (CONTINUED)**

We again examine the monthly data on housing sales in the Midwest. In the previous subsection, we saw that simple exponential smoothing, even with an optimal smoothing constant, does only a "fair" job of forecasting housing sales. Given that there is an upward trend in housing sales over this period, we might expect Holt's method to perform better. Does it? What smoothing constants are appropriate?

Objective   To see whether Holt's method, with appropriate smoothing constants, captures the trend in the housing sales data better than simple exponential smoothing (or moving averages).

Solution

We implement Holt's method in StatTools almost exactly like we did for simple exponential smoothing. The only difference is that we can now choose *two* smoothing constants, as shown in Figure 13.46. They can have different values, although we have chosen them to be their default values of 0.1.

Figure 13.46

Dialog Box for Holt's Method

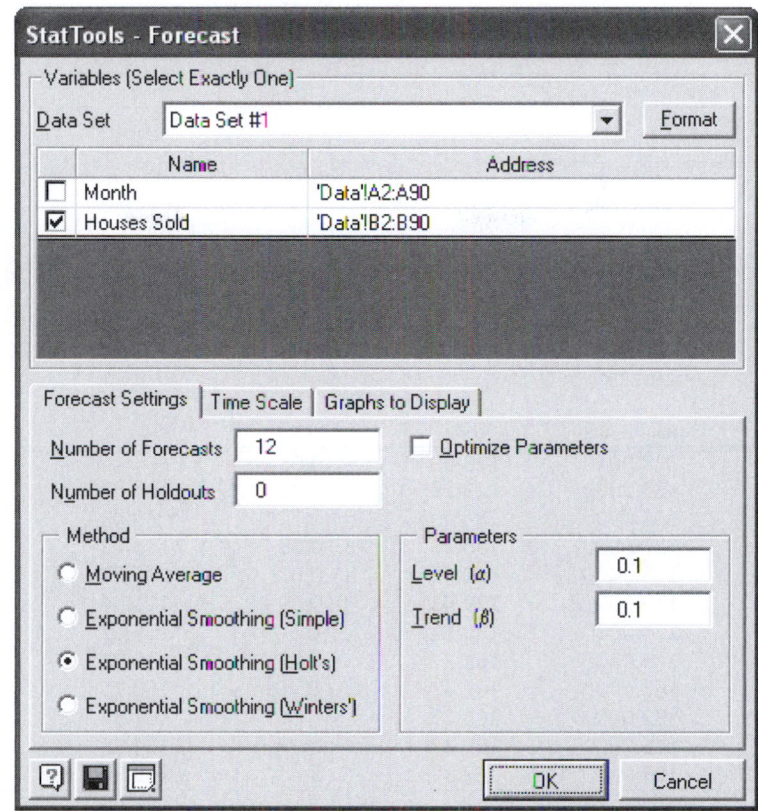

The StatTools outputs in Figures 13.47 and 13.48 are also very similar to the simple exponential smoothing outputs. The only difference is that there is now a trend column, column D, in the numerical output. You can check that the formulas in columns C, D, and E implement equations (13.16), (13.17), and (13.18). As before, there is an initialization problem in row 42. These require values of L_1 and T_1 to get the method started. Different implementations of Holt's method obtain these initial values in slightly different ways, but the effect is fairly minimal in most cases. (You can check cells C42 and D42 to see how StatTools does it.)

Somewhat surprisingly, the error measures for this implementation of Holt's method are no better than for simple exponential smoothing, even though this series exhibits a gradual upward trend. Perhaps this is because 0.1 and 0.1 are not the *optimal* smoothing constants. Therefore, we ran Holt's method a second time, checking the Optimize Parameters option. This resulted in somewhat better results and the forecasts shown in Figure 13.49. The optimal smoothing constants are $\alpha = 0.251$ and $\beta = 0.000$, and the MAE, RMSE, and MAPE values were 11.2, 13.9, and 7.7%—almost identical to simple exponential smoothing with an optimal smoothing constant.[5]

---

[5]The fact that β is 0 does not mean there is no trend. It simply means that we never update our initial estimate of trend, which is positive.

Figure 13.47 Output from Holt's Method

	A	B	C	D	E	F
7						
8	*Forecasting Constants*					
9	Level (Alpha)	0.100				
10	Trend (Beta)	0.100				
11						
12						
13	*Holt's Exponential*					
14	Mean Abs Err	12.05				
15	Root Mean Sq Err	15.08				
16	Mean Abs Per% Err	8.23%				
17						
41	Forecasting Data	Houses Sold	Level	Trend	Forecast	Error
42	Jan-1994	128.0000	128.00	0.65		
43	Feb-1994	135.0000	129.29	0.72	128.65	6.35
44	Mar-1994	130.0000	130.00	0.72	130.00	0.00
45	Apr-1994	127.0000	130.35	0.68	130.72	-3.72
46	May-1994	125.0000	130.42	0.62	131.02	-6.02
47	Jun-1994	119.0000	129.83	0.50	131.04	-12.04
125	Dec-2000	174.0000	160.52	-0.60	159.02	14.98
126	Jan-2001	173.0000	161.22	-0.47	159.91	13.09
127	Feb-2001	168.0000	161.47	-0.40	160.75	7.25
128	Mar-2001	192.0000	164.17	-0.09	161.07	30.93
129	Apr-2001	176.0000	165.27	0.03	164.08	11.92
130	May-2001	186.0000	167.37	0.23	165.30	20.70
131	Jun-2001				167.60	
132	Jul-2001				167.84	
133	Aug-2001				168.07	
134	Sep-2001				168.31	
135	Oct-2001				168.54	
136	Nov-2001				168.78	
137	Dec-2001				169.01	
138	Jan-2002				169.25	
139	Feb-2002				169.48	
140	Mar-2002				169.72	
141	Apr-2002				169.95	
142	May-2002				170.19	

You should not conclude from this example that Holt's method is never superior to simple exponential smoothing. Holt's method is often able to react quickly to a sudden upswing or downswing in the data, whereas simple exponential smoothing typically has a delayed reaction to such a change. It just happened in this example that the trend was gradual, so that both methods were able to react to it in equivalent ways.

Figure 13.48

Forecasts from
Holt's Method
with Nonoptimal
Smoothing
Constants

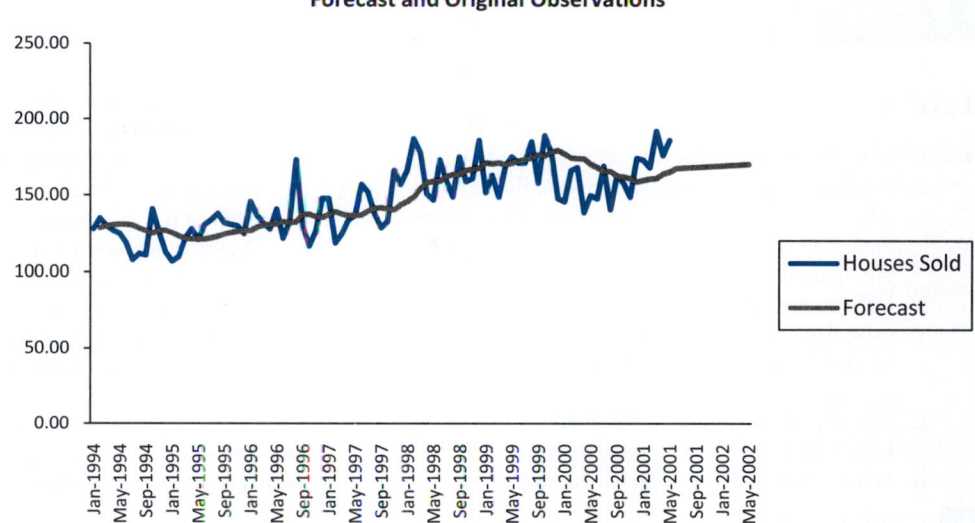

Forecast and Original Observations

Figure 13.49

Forecasts from
Holt's Method with
Optimal Smoothing
Constants

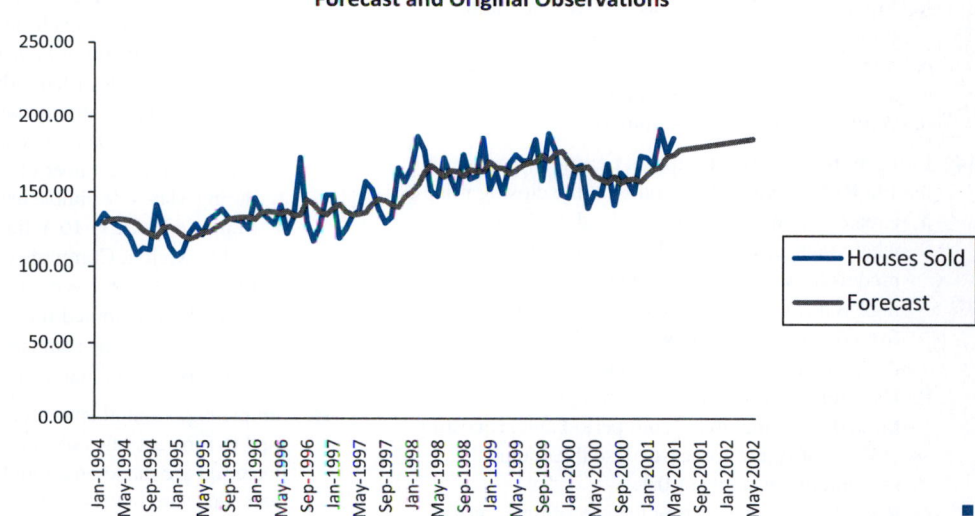

Forecast and Original Observations

PROBLEMS

Level A

42. Consider the airline ticket data in the file **P13_01.xlsx**.
    a. Create a time series chart of the data. Based on what you see, which of the exponential smoothing models do you think should be used for forecasting? Why?
    b. Use simple exponential smoothing to forecast these data, using no holdout period and requesting 12 months of future forecasts. Use the default smoothing constant of 0.1.
    c. Repeat part **b**, optimizing the smoothing constant. Does it make much of an improvement?
    d. Write a short report to summarize your results.

43. Consider the applications for home mortgages data in the file **P13_04.xlsx**.
    a. Create a time series chart of the data. Based on what you see, which of the exponential smoothing models do you think should be used for forecasting? Why?
    b. Use simple exponential smoothing to forecast these data, using no holdout period and requesting 4 quarters of future forecasts. Use the default smoothing constant of 0.1.
    c. Repeat part **b**, optimizing the smoothing constant. Does it make much of an improvement?
    d. Write a short report to summarize your results.

44. Consider the American Express closing price data in the file **P13_16.xlsx**. Focus only on the closing prices.
    a. Create a time series chart of the data. Based on what you see, which of the exponential smoothing models do you think should be used for forecasting? Why? (*Note*: The data are currently sorted from most recent to most distant in the past. Sort them in the opposite order first.)
    b. Use Holt's exponential smoothing to forecast these data, using no holdout period and requesting 20 days of future forecasts. Use the default smoothing constants of 0.1.
    c. Repeat part **b**, optimizing the smoothing constant. Does it make much of an improvement?
    d. Repeat parts **a** and **b**, this time using a holdout period of 50 days.
    e. Write a short report to summarize your results.

45. Consider the poverty level data in the file **P02_29.xlsx**. Focus only on the Percent variable.
    a. Create a time series chart of the data. Based on what you see, which of the exponential smoothing models do you think should be used for forecasting? Why?

    b. Use simple exponential smoothing to forecast these data, using no holdout period and requesting 3 years of future forecasts. Use the default smoothing constants of 0.1.
    c. Repeat part **b**, optimizing the smoothing constant. Make sure you request a chart of the series with the forecasts superimposed. Does the optimal smoothing constant make much of an improvement?
    d. Write a short report to summarize your results. Considering the chart in part **c**, would you say the forecasts are "good"?

Problems 46 through 48 ask you to apply the exponential smoothing formulas. These do not require StatTools. In fact, they do not even require Excel. You can do them with a hand calculator (or with Excel).

46. TOD Chevy is using Holt's method to forecast weekly car sales. Currently, the level is estimated to be 50 cars per week, and the trend is estimated to be 6 cars per week. During the current week, 30 cars are sold. After observing the current week's sales, forecast the number of cars 3 weeks from now. Use $\alpha = \beta = 0.3$.

47. You have been assigned to forecast the number of aircraft engines ordered each month by Commins Engine Company. At the end of February, the forecast is that 100 engines will be ordered during April. Then during March, 120 engines are actually ordered.
    a. Using $\alpha = 0.3$, determine a forecast (at the end of March) for the number of orders placed during April; during May. Use simple exponential smoothing.
    b. Suppose MAE = 16 at the end of March. At the end of March, Commins can be 68% sure that April orders will be between what two values, assuming normally distributed forecast errors? (*Hint*: It can be shown that the standard deviation of forecast errors is approximately 1.25 times MAE.)

48. Simple exponential smoothing with $\alpha = 0.3$ is being used to forecast sales of radios at Lowland Appliance. Forecasts are made on a monthly basis. After August radio sales are observed, the forecast for September is 100 radios.
    a. During September, 120 radios are sold. After observing September sales, what do we forecast for October radio sales? For November radio sales?
    b. It turns out that June sales were recorded as 10 radios. Actually, however, 100 radios were sold in June. After correcting for this error, develop a forecast for October radio sales.

Level B

49. Holt's method assumes an additive trend. For example, a trend of 5 means that the level will increase by 5 units per period. Suppose there is actually a **multiplicative trend**. For example, if the current estimate of the level is 50 and the current estimate of the trend is 1.2, we would predict demand to increase by 20% per period. So we would forecast the next period's demand to be 50(1.2) and forecast the demand 2 periods in the future to be $50(1.2)^2$. If we want to use a multiplicative trend in Holt's method, we should use the following equations:

$$L_t = \alpha Y_t + (1 - \alpha)(I)$$
$$T_t = \beta(II) + (1 - \beta)T_{t-1}$$

  a. What should (*I*) and (*II*) be?
  b. Suppose we are working with monthly data and month 12 is December, month 13 is January, and so on. Also suppose that $L_{12} = 100$ and $T_{12} = 1.2$. Suppose $Y_{13} = 200$. At the end of month 13, what is the prediction for Y_{15}? Assume $\alpha = \beta = 0.5$ and a multiplicative trend.

50. A version of simple exponential smoothing can be used to predict the outcome of sporting events. To illustrate, consider pro football. We first assume that all games are played on a neutral field. Before each day of play, we assume that each team has a rating. For example, if the rating for the Bears is +10 and the rating for the Bengals is +6, we predict the Bears to beat the Bengals by $10 - 6 = 4$ points. Suppose that the Bears play the Bengals and win by 20 points. For this game, we "underpredicted" the Bears' performance by $20 - 4 = 16$ points. Assuming that the best α for pro football is $\alpha = 0.10$, we would increase the Bears' rating by $16(0.1) = 1.6$ and decrease the Bengals' rating by 1.6 points. In a rematch, the Bears would then be favored by $(10 + 1.6) - (6 - 1.6) = 7.2$ points.

  a. How does this approach relate to the equation $L_t = L_{t-1} + \alpha e_t$?
  b. Suppose that the home field advantage in pro football is 3 points; that is, home teams tend to outscore visiting teams by an average of 3 points a game. How could the home field advantage be incorporated into this system?
  c. How might we determine the *best* α for pro football?
  d. How might we determine ratings for each team at the beginning of the season?
  e. Suppose we apply this method to predict pro football (16-game schedule), college football (11-game schedule), college basketball (30-game schedule), and pro basketball (82-game schedule). Which sport do you think would have the smallest optimal α; the largest optimal α? Why?
  f. Why might this approach yield poor forecasts for major league baseball?

13.9 SEASONAL MODELS

So far we have said practically nothing about seasonality. Seasonality is the consistent month-to-month (or quarter-to-quarter) differences that occur each year. For example, there is seasonality in beer sales—high in the summer months, lower in other months. Toy sales are also seasonal, with a huge peak in the months preceding Christmas. In fact, if you start thinking about time series variables that you are familiar with, the majority of them probably have some degree of seasonality.

Some time series software packages have special types of graphs for spotting seasonality, but we don't discuss these here.

How do we know whether there is seasonality in a time series? The easiest way is to check whether a graph of the time series has a *regular* pattern of ups and/or downs in particular months or quarters. Although random noise can sometimes obscure such a pattern, the seasonal pattern is usually fairly obvious.

There are basically three methods for dealing with seasonality. First, we can use Winters' exponential smoothing model. It is similar to simple exponential smoothing and Holt's method, except that it includes another component (and smoothing constant) to capture seasonality. Second, we can *deseasonalize* the data, then use any of our forecasting methods to model the deseasonalized data, and finally "reseasonalize" these forecasts. Finally, we can use multiple regression with dummy variables for the seasons. We discuss all three of these methods in this section.

As we saw with the housing sales data, government agencies often perform part of the second method for us—that is, they deseasonalize the data.

Seasonal models are usually classified as *additive* or *multiplicative*. Suppose that we have monthly data, and that the average of the 12 monthly values for a typical year is 150. An **additive** model finds seasonal indexes, one for each month, that we *add* to the monthly average, 150, to get a particular month's value. For example, if the index for March is 22, then we expect a typical March value to be $150 + 22 = 172$. If the seasonal index for September is -12, then we expect a typical September value to be $150 - 12 = 138$. A **multiplicative** model also finds seasonal indexes, but we *multiply* the monthly average by these indexes to get a particular month's value. Now if the index for March is 1.3, we expect a typical March value to be $150(1.3) = 195$. If the index for September is 0.9, then we expect a typical September value to be $150(0.9) = 135$. These models are summarized here.

In an **additive** seasonal model, we add an appropriate seasonal index to a "base" forecast. These indexes, one for each season, typically average to 0.

In a **multiplicative** seasonal model, we multiply a "base" forecast by an appropriate seasonal index. These indexes, one for each season, typically average to 1.

Either an additive or a multiplicative model can be used to forecast seasonal data. However, because multiplicative models are somewhat easier to interpret (and have worked well in applications), we focus on them. Note that the seasonal index in a multiplicative model can be interpreted as a percentage. Using the figures in the previous paragraph as an example, March tends to be 30% above the monthly average, whereas September tends to be 10% below it. Also, the seasonal indexes in a multiplicative model should average to 1. Computer packages typically ensure that this happens.

13.9.1 Winters' Exponential Smoothing Model

We now turn to Winters' exponential smoothing model. It is very similar to Holt's model—it again has level and trend terms and corresponding smoothing constants α and β—but it also has seasonal indexes and a corresponding smoothing constant γ (gamma). This new smoothing constant γ controls how quickly the method reacts to perceived changes in the pattern of seasonality. If γ is small, the method reacts slowly. If it is large, the method reacts more quickly. As with Holt's model, there are equations for updating the level and trend terms, and there is one extra equation for updating the seasonal indexes. For completeness, we list these equations in the accompanying box, but they are clearly too complex for hand calculation and are best left to the computer. In equation (13.21), S_t refers to the multiplicative seasonal index for period t. In equations (13.19), (13.21), and (13.22), M refers to the number of seasons ($M = 4$ for quarterly data, $M = 12$ for monthly data).

Formulas for Winters' Exponential Smoothing Model

$$L_t = \alpha \frac{Y_t}{S_{t-M}} + (1 - \alpha)(L_{t-1} + T_{t-1}) \qquad (13.19)$$

$$T_t = \beta(L_t - L_{t-1}) + (1 - \beta)T_{t-1} \qquad (13.20)$$

$$S_t = \gamma \frac{Y_t}{L_t} + (1 - \gamma)S_{t-M} \qquad (13.21)$$

$$F_{t+k} = (L_t + kT_t)S_{t+k-M} \qquad (13.22)$$

To see how the forecasting in equation (13.22) works, suppose we have observed data through June and want a forecast for the coming September, that is, a 3-month-ahead forecast. (In this case t refers to June and $t + k = t + 3$ refers to September.) Then we first add 3 times the current trend term to the current level. This gives a forecast for September that would be appropriate if there were no seasonality. Next, we multiply this forecast by the most recent estimate of September's seasonal index (the one from the previous September) to get the forecast for September. Of course, the computer does all of the arithmetic, but this is basically what it is doing. We illustrate the method in the following example.

| EXAMPLE | 13.7 QUARTERLY SOFT DRINK SALES |

The data in the **Soft Drink Sales.xlsx** file represent quarterly sales (in millions of dollars) for a large soft drink company from quarter 1 of 1992 through quarter 1 of 2007. As we might expect, there has been an upward trend in sales during this period, and there is also a fairly regular seasonal pattern, as shown in Figure 13.50. Sales in the warmer quarters, 2 and 3, are consistently higher than in the colder quarters, 1 and 4. How well can Winters' method track this upward trend and seasonal pattern?

Figure 13.50   Time Series Graph of Soft Drink Sales

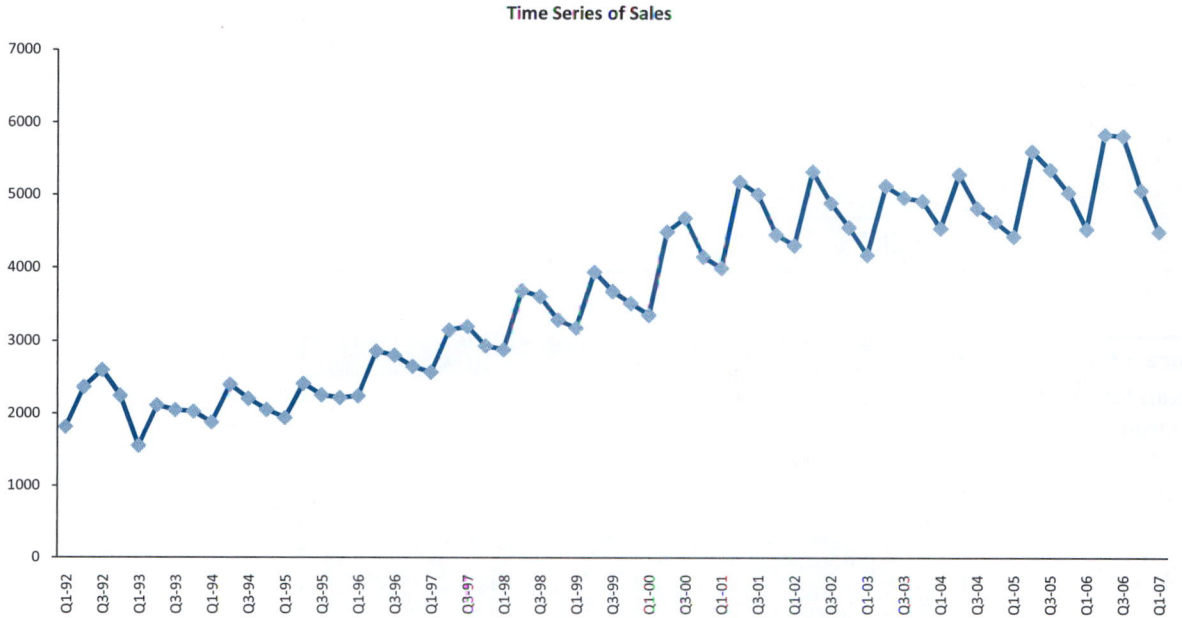

Objective   To see how well Winters' method, with appropriate smoothing constants, can forecast the company's seasonal soft drink sales.

Solution

To use Winters' method with StatTools, we proceed exactly as with any of the other exponential smoothing methods. However, for a change (and because we have so many years of data), we use StatTools's option of holding out some of the data for validation. Specifically, we fill out the Time Scale tab in the Forecast dialog box as shown in Figure 13.51. Then we fill in the Forecast Settings tab of this dialog box as shown in Figure 13.52, selecting Winters' method, basing the model on the data through quarter 1, 2003, holding out 8 quarters of data (quarter 2,

2003, through quarter 1, 2005), and forecasting 4 quarters into the future. Note that when we choose Winters' method in Figure 13.52, the Deseasonalize option in Figure 13.51 is automatically disabled. It wouldn't make sense to deseasonalize *and* use Winters' method; we do one or the other. Also, we have elected to optimize the smoothing constants, but this is optional.

Figure 13.51
Time Scale Settings for Soft Drink Sales

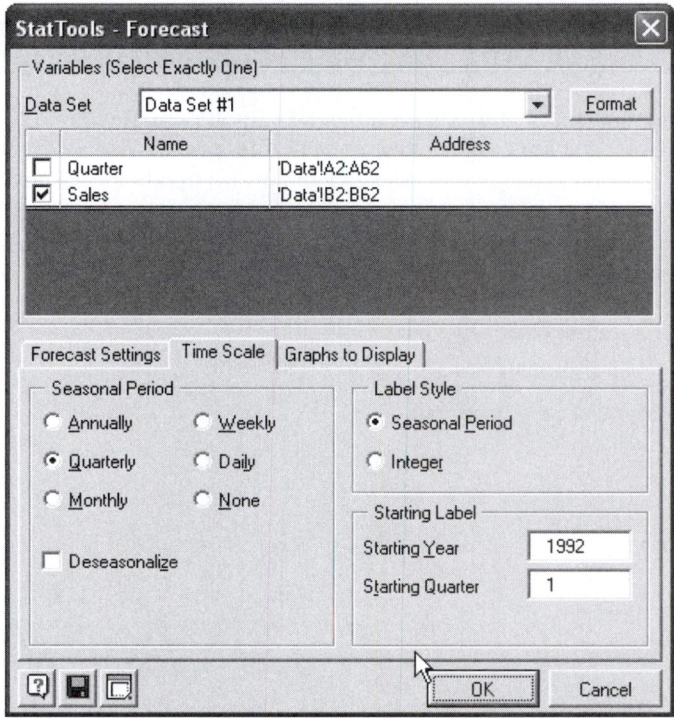

Figure 13.52
Forecast Settings for Soft Drink Sales

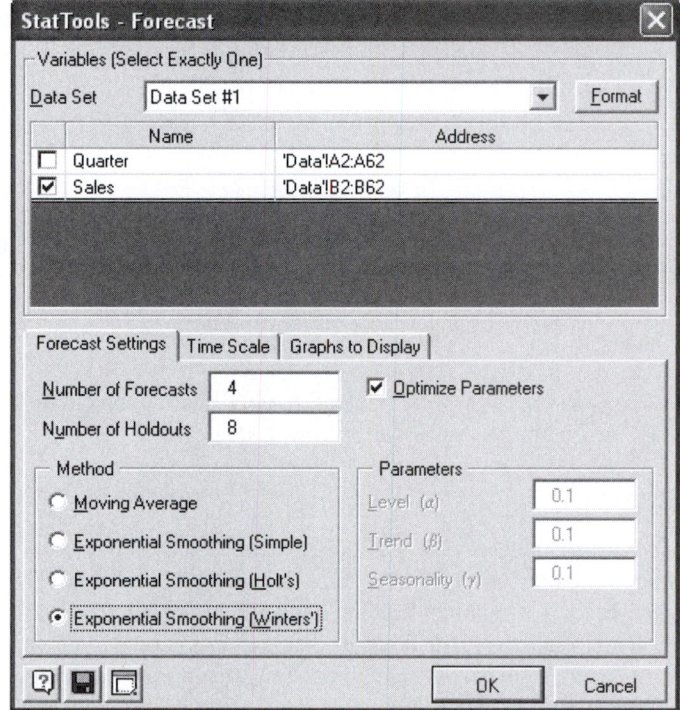

Parts of the output are shown in Figure 13.53. The following points are worth noting: (1) The optimal smoothing constants (those that minimize RMSE) are $\alpha = 1.0$, $\beta = 0.0$, and $\gamma = 0.0$. Intuitively, these mean that we react right away to changes in level, but we never react to changes in trend or the seasonal pattern. (2) If we ignore seasonality, the series is trending upward at a rate of 56.05 per quarter (see column D). This is our initial estimate of trend and, because $\beta = 0$, it never changes. (3) The seasonal pattern stays constant throughout this 10-year period. The seasonal indexes, shown in column E, are 0.88, 1.10, 1.05, and 0.96. For example, quarter 1 is 12% below the yearly average, and quarter 2 is 10% above the yearly average. (4) The forecast series tracks the actual series quite well during the nonholdout period. For example, MAPE is 3.98%, meaning that on average our forecasts are off by about 4% on average. Surprisingly, MAPE for the holdout period is even lower, at 2.20%.

Figure 13.53 Output from Winters' Method for Soft Drink Sales

	A	B	C	D	E	F	G
7							
8	Forecasting Constants (Optimized)						
9	Level (Alpha)	1.000					
10	Trend (Beta)	0.000					
11	Season (Gamma)	0.000					
12							
13		Estimation	Holdouts				
14	Winters' Exponential	Period	Period				
15	Mean Abs Err	125.59	108.31				
16	Root Mean Sq Err	168.81	148.94				
17	Mean Abs Per% Err	3.98%	2.20%				
18							
41							
42	Forecasting Data	Sales	Level	Trend	Season	Forecast	Error
43	Q1-1992	1807.3700	2046.27	56.05	0.88		
44	Q2-1992	2355.3200	2140.57	56.05	1.10	2313.24	42.08
45	Q3-1992	2591.8300	2463.29	56.05	1.05	2311.24	280.59
46	Q4-1992	2236.3900	2319.32	56.05	0.96	2429.27	-192.88
47	Q1-1993	1549.1400	1753.91	56.05	0.88	2098.05	-548.91
48	Q2-1993	2105.7900	1913.79	56.05	1.10	1991.54	114.25
49	Q3-1993	2041.3200	1940.09	56.05	1.05	2072.63	-31.31
50	Q4-1993	2021.0100	2095.95	56.05	0.96	1924.76	96.25
92	Q2-2004	5284.7100	4802.87	56.05	1.10	5720.69	-435.98
93	Q3-2004	4817.4300	4578.52	56.05	1.05	5112.46	-295.03
94	Q4-2004	4634.5000	4806.36	56.05	0.96	4468.86	165.64
95	Q1-2005	4431.3600	5017.10	56.05	0.88	4294.73	136.63
96	Q2-2005	5602.2100				5582.11	20.10
97	Q3-2005	5349.8500				5396.85	-47.00
98	Q4-2005	5036.0000				4999.85	36.15
99	Q1-2006	4534.6100				4629.40	-94.79
100	Q2-2006	5836.1700				5828.82	7.35
101	Q3-2006	5818.2800				5632.76	185.52
102	Q4-2006	5070.4200				5216.05	-145.63
103	Q1-2007	4497.4700				4827.43	-329.96
104	Q2-2007					6075.52	
105	Q3-2007					5868.67	
106	Q4-2007					5432.24	
107	Q1-2008					5025.47	

The plot of the forecasts superimposed on the original series, shown in Figure 13.54, indicates that Winters' method clearly picks up the seasonal pattern and the upward trend and projects both of these into the future. In later examples, we investigate whether other seasonal forecasting methods can do this well.

Figure 13.54

Graph of Forecasts from Winters' Method

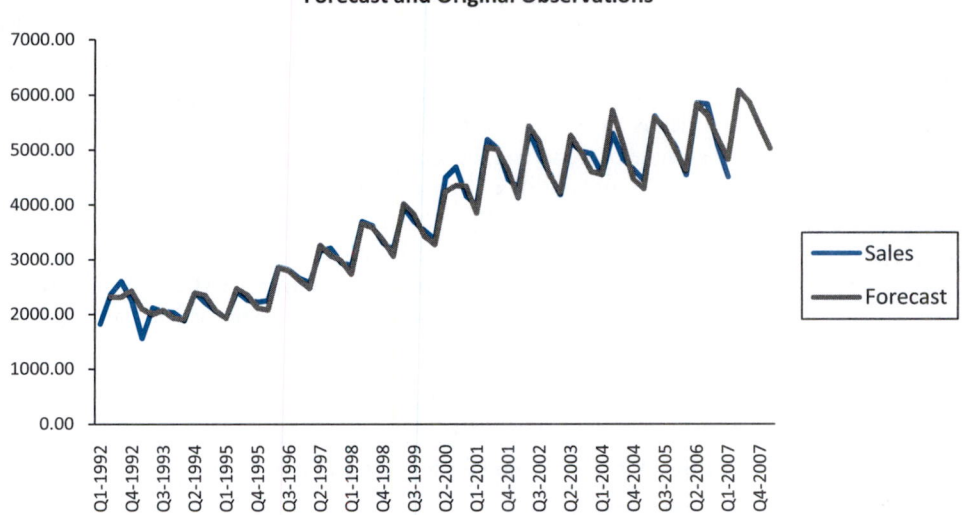

Forecast and Original Observations

One final comment is that we are not obligated to find the *optimal* smoothing constants. Some analysts might suggest using more "typical" values such as $\alpha = \beta = 0.2$ and $\gamma = 0.5$. (We often choose γ larger than α and β because each season's seasonal index gets updated only once per year.) To see how these smoothing constants affect the results, we can simply substitute their values in the range B9:B11 of Figure 13.53. As we would expect, MAE, RMSE, and MAPE all get somewhat worse (they increase to 184, 237, and 5.89%, respectively, for the estimation period), but a plot of the forecasts superimposed on the original sales data still indicates a very good fit. ■

The three exponential smoothing methods we have examined are not the only ones available. For example, there are linear and quadratic models available in some software packages. These are somewhat similar to Holt's model except that they use only a single smoothing constant. There are also adaptive exponential smoothing models, where the smoothing constants themselves are allowed to change through time. Although these more complex models have been studied thoroughly in the academic literature and are used by some practitioners, they typically offer only marginal gains in forecast accuracy over the models we have examined.

13.9.2 Deseasonalizing: The Ratio-to-Moving-Averages Method

You have probably seen references to time series data that have been *deseasonalized*. In this section we discuss why this is done and how it is done. We also see how it can be used to forecast seasonal time series. First, data are often published in deseasonalized form so that readers can spot trends more easily. For example, if we see a time series of sales that has not been deseasonalized, and it shows a large increase from November to December, we might not be sure whether this represents a real increase in sales or a seasonal phenomenon (Christmas sales). However, if this increase is really just a seasonal effect, then the deseasonalized version of the series will show no such increase in sales.

Government economists and statisticians have a variety of sophisticated methods for deseasonalizing time series data, but they are typically variations of the **ratio-to-moving-averages** method described here. This method is applicable when we believe that seasonality is multiplicative, as described in the previous section. Our job is to find the seasonal indexes, which can then be used to deseasonalize the data. For example, if we estimate the index for June to be 1.3, this means that June's values are typically about 30% larger than the average for all months. Therefore, to deseasonalize a June value, we *divide* it by 1.3 (to make it smaller). Similarly, if February's index is 0.85, then February's values are 15% below the average for all months. So to deseasonalize a February value, we divide it by 0.85 (to make it larger).

> To **deseasonalize** an observation (assuming a multiplicative model of seasonality), *divide* it by the appropriate seasonal index.

To find the seasonal index for June 2005 (or any other month) in the first place, we essentially divide June's observation by the average of the 12 observations surrounding June. (This is the reason for the term "ratio" in the name of the method.) There is one minor problem with this approach. June 2005 is not exactly in the middle of any 12-month sequence. If we use the 12 months from January 2005 to December 2005, June 2005 is in the *first* half of the sequence; if we use the 12 months from December 2004 to November 2005, June 2005 is in the *last* half of the sequence. Therefore, we compromise by averaging the January-to-December and December-to-November averages. This is called a **centered** average. Then the seasonal index for June is June's observation divided by this centered average. The following equation shows more specifically how it works.

$$\text{Jun2005 index} = \frac{\text{Jun2005}}{\left(\frac{\text{Dec2004} + \cdots + \text{Nov2005}}{12} + \frac{\text{Jan2005} + \cdots + \text{Dec2005}}{12}\right)/2}$$

The only remaining question is how to combine all of the indexes for any specific month such as June. After all, if we have data for several years, the above procedure produces several June indexes, one for each year. The usual way to combine them is simply to average them. This single average index for June is then used to deseasonalize *all* of the June observations.

Once the seasonal indexes are obtained, we divide each observation by its seasonal index to deseasonalize the data. The deseasonalized data can then be forecasted by *any* of the methods we have described (other than Winters' method, which wouldn't make much sense). For example, we could use Holt's method or the moving averages method to forecast the deseasonalized data. Finally, we "reseasonalize" the forecasts by *multiplying* them by the seasonal indexes.

As this description suggests, the method is not meant for hand calculations! However, it is straightforward to implement in StatTools, as we illustrate in the following example.

EXAMPLE | **13.7 QUARTERLY SOFT DRINK SALES (CONTINUED)**

We return to the soft drink sales data. (See the file **Soft Drink Sales.xlsx**.) Is it possible to obtain the same forecast accuracy with the ratio-to-moving-averages method as we obtained with Winters' method?

Objective   To use the ratio-to-moving-averages method to deseasonalize the soft drink data and then forecast the deseasonalized data.

Solution

The answer to this question depends on which forecasting method we use to forecast the *deseasonalized* data. The ratio-to-moving-averages method only provides a means for deseasonalizing the data and providing seasonal indexes. Beyond this, any method can be used to forecast the deseasonalized data, and some methods obviously work better than others. For this example, we compared two possibilities: the moving averages method with a span of 4 quarters, and Holt's exponential smoothing method optimized. However, we show the results only for the latter. Because the deseasonalized series still has a clear upward trend, we would expect Holt's method to do well, and we would expect the moving averages forecasts to lag behind the trend. This is exactly what occurred. For example, the values of MAPE for the two methods are 8.33% (moving averages) and 3.98% (Holt's). (To make a fair comparison with the Winters' method output for these data, we again held out 8 quarters. The MAPE values reported are for the nonholdout period.)

To implement this latter method in StatTools, we proceed exactly as before, but this time we check the Deseasonalize option in the Time Scale tab of the Forecast dialog box. (See Figure 13.55.) Note that when the Holt's option is checked, this Deseasonalize option is enabled. When we check this option, we get a larger selection of optional charts in the Graphs to Display tab. We can see charts of the deseasonalized data and/or the original "reseasonalized" data.

Figure 13.55

Checking the Deseasonalizing Option

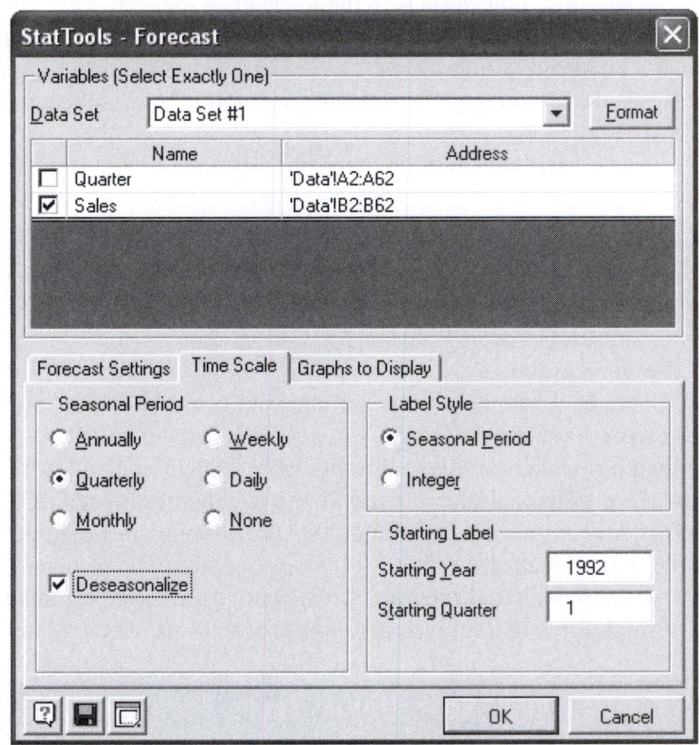

Selected outputs are shown in Figures 13.56 through 13.59. Figures 13.56 and 13.57 show the numerical output. In particular, Figure 13.57 shows the seasonal indexes from the ratio-to-moving averages method in column C. These are virtually identical to the seasonal indexes we found using Winters' method, although the methods are mathematically different. Column D contains the deseasonalized sales (column B divided by column C), columns E through H implement Holt's method on the deseasonalized data, and columns I and J are the "reseasonalized" forecasts and errors.

Figure 13.56

Summary Measures for Forecast Errors

	A	B	C	D	E
8	**Forecasting Constants (Optimized)**				
9	Level (Alpha)	1.000			
10	Trend (Beta)	0.000			
11					
12		Estimation	Holdouts	Deseason	Deseason
13	*Holt's Exponential*	Period	Period	Estimate	Holdouts
14	Mean Abs Err	125.59	108.31	126.66	114.42
15	Root Mean Sq Err	168.81	148.94	171.57	161.54
16	Mean Abs Per% Err	3.98%	2.20%	3.98%	2.20%

Figure 13.57 Ratio-to-Moving-Averages Output

	A	B	C	D	E	F	G	H	I	J
61			Season	Deseason	Deseason	Deseason	Deseason	Deseason	Season	Season
62	*Forecasting Data*	Sales	Index	Sales	Level	Trend	Forecast	Errors	Forecast	Errors
63	Q1-1992	1807.3700	0.88	2046.27	2046.27	56.05				
64	Q2-1992	2355.3200	1.10	2140.57	2140.57	56.05	2102.32	38.25	2313.24	42.08
65	Q3-1992	2591.8300	1.05	2463.29	2463.29	56.05	2196.62	266.67	2311.24	280.59
66	Q4-1992	2236.3900	0.96	2319.32	2319.32	56.05	2519.35	-200.03	2429.27	-192.88
67	Q1-1993	1549.1400	0.88	1753.91	1753.91	56.05	2375.37	-621.47	2098.05	-548.91
68	Q2-1993	2105.7900	1.10	1913.79	1913.79	56.05	1809.96	103.83	1991.54	114.25
69	Q3-1993	2041.3200	1.05	1940.09	1940.09	56.05	1969.84	-29.76	2072.63	-31.31
70	Q4-1993	2021.0100	0.96	2095.95	2095.95	56.05	1996.14	99.81	1924.76	96.25
112	Q2-2004	5284.7100	1.10	4802.87	4802.87	56.05	5199.09	-396.23	5720.69	-435.98
113	Q3-2004	4817.4300	1.05	4578.52	4578.52	56.05	4858.92	-280.40	5112.46	-295.03
114	Q4-2004	4634.5000	0.96	4806.36	4806.36	56.05	4634.58	171.78	4468.86	165.64
115	Q1-2005	4431.3600	0.88	5017.10	5017.10	56.05	4862.41	154.69	4294.73	136.63
116	Q2-2005	5602.2100	1.10	5091.42			5073.15	18.27	5582.11	20.10
117	Q3-2005	5349.8500	1.05	5084.54			5129.20	-44.67	5396.85	-47.00
118	Q4-2005	5036.0000	0.96	5222.75			5185.26	37.49	4999.85	36.15
119	Q1-2006	4534.6100	0.88	5133.99			5241.31	-107.32	4629.40	-94.79
120	Q2-2006	5836.1700	1.10	5304.05			5297.36	6.68	5828.82	7.35
121	Q3-2006	5818.2800	1.05	5529.74			5353.42	176.32	5632.76	185.52
122	Q4-2006	5070.4200	0.96	5258.44			5409.47	-151.03	5216.05	-145.63
123	Q1-2007	4497.4700	0.88	5091.95			5465.52	-373.58	4827.43	-329.96
124	Q2-2007		1.10				5521.58		6075.52	
125	Q3-2007		1.05				5577.63		5868.67	
126	Q4-2007		0.96				5633.68		5432.24	
127	Q1-2008		0.88				5689.74		5025.47	

Figure 13.58

Forecast Graph of Deseasonalized Series

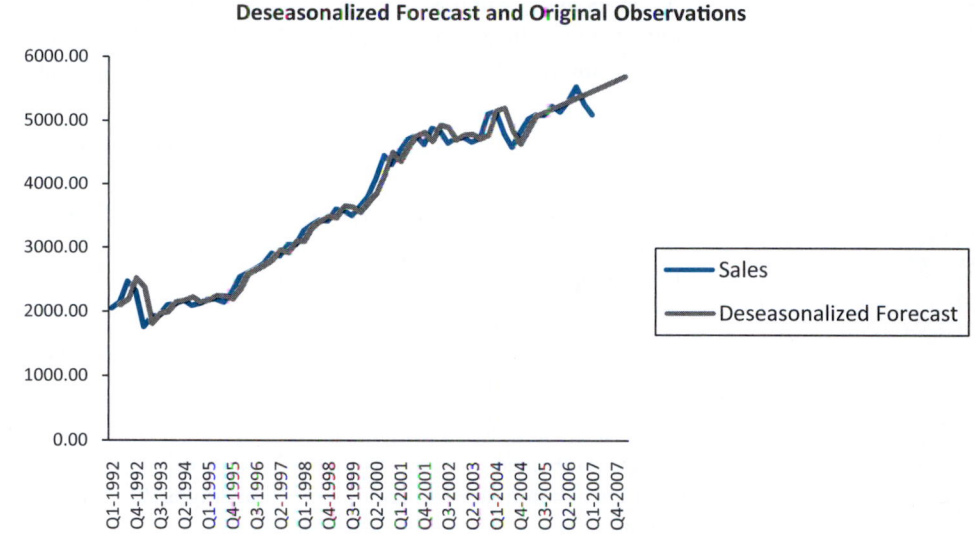

Deseasonalized Forecast and Original Observations

— Sales
— Deseasonalized Forecast

Figure 13.59

Forecast Graph of
Reseasonalized
(Original) Series

Forecast and Original Observations

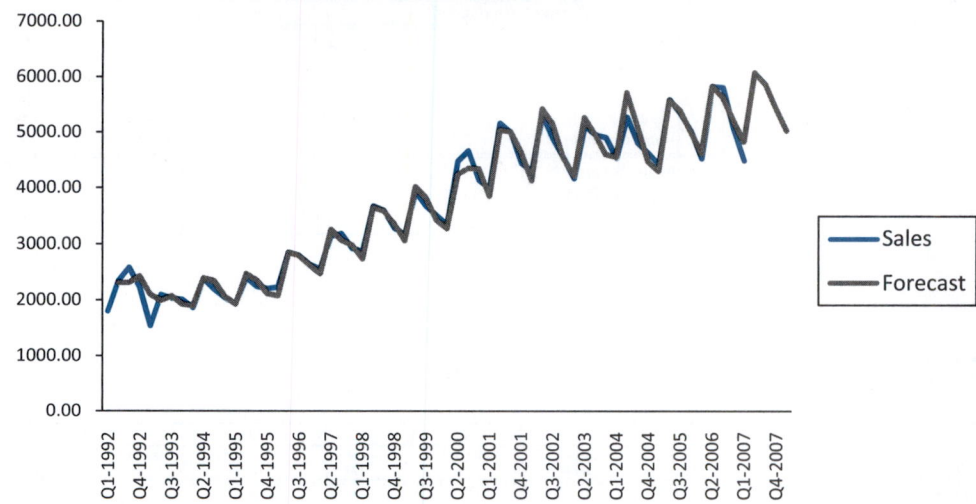

The deseasonalized data, with forecasts superimposed, appear in Figure 13.58. Here we see only the smooth upward trend with no seasonality, which Holt's method is able to track very well. Then Figure 13.59 shows the results of reseasonalizing. Again, the forecasts track the actual sales data very well. In fact, we see that the summary measures of forecast errors (in Figure 13.56, range B14:B16) are quite comparable to those from Winters' method. The reason is that both arrive at virtually the same seasonal pattern. ∎

13.9.3 Estimating Seasonality with Regression

We now examine a regression approach to forecasting seasonal data that uses dummy variables for the seasons. Depending on how we write the regression equation, we can create either an additive or a multiplicative seasonal model.

As an example, suppose that the data are quarterly data with a possible linear trend. Then we can introduce dummy variables Q_1, Q_2, and Q_3 for the first three quarters (using quarter 4 as the reference quarter) and estimate the additive equation

$$\hat{Y}_t = a + bt + b_1Q_1 + b_2Q_2 + b_3Q_3$$

Then the coefficients of the dummy variables, b_1, b_2 and b_3, indicate how much each quarter differs from the reference quarter, quarter 4, and the coefficient b represent the trend.

For example, if the estimated equation is

$$\hat{Y}_t = 130 + 25t + 15Q_1 + 5Q_2 - 20Q_3$$

then the average increase from one quarter to the next is 25 (the coefficient of t). This is the trend effect. However, quarter 1 averages 15 units higher than quarter 4, quarter 2 averages 5 units higher than quarter 4, and quarter 3 averages 20 units lower than quarter 4. These coefficients indicate the seasonality effect.

As discussed in Chapter 11, it is also possible to estimate a *multiplicative* model using dummy variables for seasonality (and possibly time for trend). Then we would estimate the equation

$$\hat{Y}_t = ae^{bt}e^{b_1 Q_1}e^{b_2 Q_2}e^{b_3 Q_3}$$

or, after taking logs,

$$\ln \hat{Y}_t = \ln a + bt + b_1 Q_1 + b_2 Q_2 + b_3 Q_3$$

One advantage of this approach is that it provides a model with *multiplicative* seasonal factors. It is also fairly easy to interpret the regression output, as illustrated in the following continuation of the soft drink sales example.

EXAMPLE | **13.7 QUARTERLY SOFT DRINK SALES (CONTINUED)**

Returning to the soft drink sales data (see the file **Soft Drink Sales.xlsx**), does a regression approach provide forecasts that are as accurate as those provided by the other seasonal methods in this chapter?

Objective To use a multiplicative regression equation, with dummy variables for seasons and a time variable for trend, to model soft drink sales.

Solution

We illustrate the multiplicative approach, although an additive approach is also possible. Figure 13.60 illustrates the data setup. Besides the Sales and Time variables, we need dummy variables for three of the four quarters (we created these manually), and a Log(Sales) variable. We then use multiple regression, with Log(Sales) as the dependent variable, and Time, Q1, Q2, and Q3 as the explanatory variables.

Figure 13.60

Data Setup for Multiplicative Model with Dummies

	A	B	C	D	E	F	G
1	Quarter	Sales	Time	Q1	Q2	Q3	Log(Sales)
2	Q1-92	1807.37	1	1	0	0	7.499628
3	Q2-92	2355.32	2	0	1	0	7.7644319
4	Q3-92	2591.83	3	0	0	1	7.8601195
5	Q4-92	2236.39	4	0	0	0	7.7126182
6	Q1-93	1549.14	5	1	0	0	7.3454552
7	Q2-93	2105.79	6	0	1	0	7.652446
8	Q3-93	2041.32	7	0	0	1	7.6213519
9	Q4-93	2021.01	8	0	0	0	7.6113527
10	Q1-94	1870.46	9	1	0	0	7.5339397
11	Q2-94	2390.56	10	0	1	0	7.7792829
12	Q3-94	2198.03	11	0	0	1	7.6953168
13	Q4-94	2046.83	12	0	0	0	7.6240475
14	Q1-95	1934.19	13	1	0	0	7.5674439
15	Q2-95	2406.41	14	0	1	0	7.7858913

The regression output appears in Figure 13.61. (Again, to make a fair comparison with previous methods, we base the regression only on the data through quarter 1 of 2005. That is, we again hold out the last 8 quarters. This means that the StatTools data set should be redefined so that it extends only through row 54.) Of particular interest are the coefficients of the explanatory variables. Recall that for a log dependent variable, these coefficients can be interpreted as *percentage* changes in the original sales variable. Specifically, the coefficient of Time means that deseasonalized sales increase by about 2.1% per quarter. Also, the coefficients of Q1, Q2, and Q3 mean that sales in quarters 1, 2, and 3 are, respectively, about 8.4% below, 14.0% above, and 8.9% above sales in the reference quarter, quarter 4. This pattern is quite comparable to the pattern of seasonal indexes we saw in previous models for these data.

Figure 13.61   Regression Output for Multiplicative Model

	A	B	C	D	E	F	G
7		Multiple	R-Square	Adjusted	StErr of		
8	Summary	R		R-Square	Estimate		
9		0.9660	0.9332	0.9276	0.0945		
10							
11		Degrees of	Sum of	Mean of	F-Ratio	p-Value	
12	ANOVA Table	Freedom	Squares	Squares			
13	Explained	4	5.9813	1.4953	167.6184	< 0.0001	
14	Unexplained	48	0.4282	0.0089			
15							
16		Coefficient	Standard	t-Value	p-Value	Confidence Interval 95%	
17	Regression Table		Error			Lower	Upper
18	Constant	7.4689	0.0354	211.1359	< 0.0001	7.3977	7.5400
19	Time	0.0214	0.0008	25.1710	< 0.0001	0.0197	0.0231
20	Q1	-0.0836	0.0364	-2.2973	0.0260	-0.1568	-0.0104
21	Q2	0.1402	0.0371	3.7806	0.0004	0.0656	0.2148
22	Q3	0.0894	0.0371	2.4122	0.0197	0.0149	0.1639

To compare the forecast accuracy of this method with earlier models, we must go through several steps manually. (See Figure 13.62 for reference.) We first calculate the forecasts in column H by entering the formula

=EXP(Regression!$B$18+MMULT(Data!C2:F2,Regression!$B$19:$B$22))

in cell H2 and copying it down. (This formula assumes the regression output is in a sheet named Regression. It uses Excel's MMULT function to sum the products of explanatory values and regression coefficients. You can replace this by "writing out" the sum of products if you like. The formula then takes EXP of the resulting sum to convert the log sales value back to the original sales units.) Next, we calculate the absolute errors, squared errors, and absolute percentage errors in columns I, J, and K, and we summarize them in the usual way, both for the estimation period and the holdout period, in columns N and O.

Note that these summary measures are considerably larger for this regression model than for the previous seasonality models, especially in the holdout period. We can get some idea why the holdout period does so poorly by looking at the plot of observations versus forecasts in Figure 13.63. The multiplicative regression model with Time included really implies *exponential* growth (as in Section 13.4.2), with seasonality superimposed. However, this company's sales growth tapered off in the last couple of years and did not keep up with the exponential growth curve. In short, the dummy variables do a good job of tracking seasonality, but the underlying exponential trend curve outpaces actual sales. We conclude that this regression model is *not* as good for forecasting this company's sales as Winters' method or Holt's method on the deseasonalized data.

Figure 13.62 Forecast Errors and Summary Measures

	A	B	C	D	E	F	G	H	I	J	K	L	M	N	O
1	Quarter	Sales	Time	Q1	Q2	Q3	Log(Sales)	Forecast	SqError	AbsError	PctAbsError		Error measures		
2	Q1-92	1807.37	1	1	0	0	7.499628	1646.363	25762.59	160.5073	0.0888071			Estimation	Holdout
3	Q2-92	2355.32	2	0	1	0	7.7644319	2104.437	62942.35	250.8831	0.10651764		RMSE	319.38	1035.32
4	Q3-92	2591.83	3	0	0	1	7.8601195	2043.366	300812.4	548.4637	0.21161252		MAE	244.81	1010.96
5	Q4-92	2236.39	4	0	0	0	7.7126182	1909.004	107181.4	327.3857	0.14639024		MAPE	7.28%	19.71%
6	Q1-93	1549.14	5	1	0	0	7.3454552	1793.833	59874.7	244.6931	0.15795414				
7	Q2-93	2105.79	6	0	1	0	7.652446	2292.242	34764.48	186.4524	0.08854271				
8	Q3-93	2041.32	7	0	0	1	7.6213519	2225.722	34004	184.4017	0.09033455				
9	Q4-93	2021.01	8	0	0	0	7.6113527	2079.369	3405.764	58.35892	0.02887612				
10	Q1-94	1870.46	9	1	0	0	7.5339397	1953.919	6965.484	83.45947	0.04461976				
11	Q2-94	2390.56	10	0	1	0	7.7792829	2496.808	11288.66	106.2481	0.04444486				
12	Q3-94	2198.03	11	0	0	1	7.6953168	2424.351	51221.2	226.321	0.10296538				
13	Q4-94	2046.83	12	0	0	0	7.6240475	2264.937	47570.79	218.1073	0.10655858				
14	Q1-95	1934.19	13	1	0	0	7.5674439	2128.292	37675.74	194.1024	0.10035333				

Figure 13.63 Graph of Forecasts for Multiplicative Model

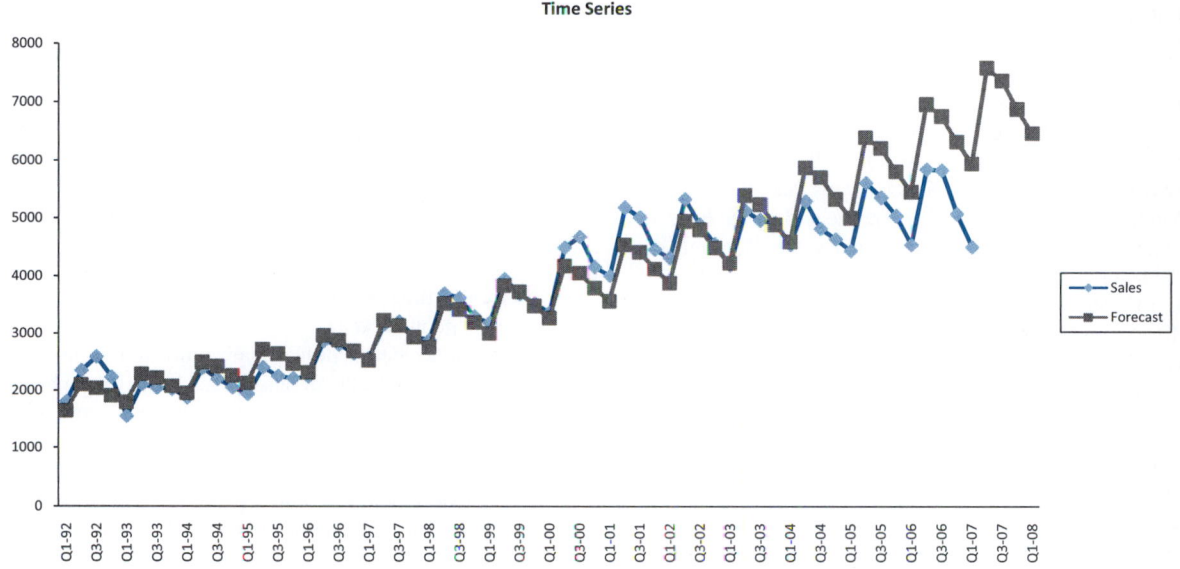

This method of detecting seasonality by using dummy variables in a regression equation is always an option. The other variables included in the regression equation could be time t, lagged versions of Y_t, and/or current or lagged versions of other independent variables. These variables would capture any time series behavior other than seasonality. Just remember that there is always one less dummy variable than the number of seasons. If the data are quarterly, then three dummies are needed; if the data are monthly, then 11 dummies are needed. If the coefficients of any of these dummies turn out to be statistically insignificant, they can be omitted from the equation. Then the omitted terms are effectively combined with the reference season. For example, if the Q_1 term were omitted, then quarters 1 and 4 would essentially be combined and treated as the reference season, and the other two seasons would be compared to them through their dummy variable coefficients. ■

PROBLEMS

Level A

51. The University Credit Union is open Monday through Saturday. Winters' method is being used (with $\alpha = \beta = \gamma = 0.5$) to predict the number of customers entering the bank each day. After incorporating the arrivals of 16 October, $L_t = 200$, $T_t = 1$, and the "seasonalities" are as follows: Monday, 0.90; Tuesday, 0.70; Wednesday, 0.80; Thursday, 1.1; Friday, 1.2; Saturday, 1.3. For example, the number of customers entering the bank on a typical Monday is 90% of the number of customers entering the bank on an average day. On Tuesday, 17 October, 182 customers enter the bank. At the close of business on 17 October, forecast the number of customers who will enter the bank on 25 October.

52. Last National Bank is using Winters' method (with $\alpha = 0.2$, $\beta = 0.1$, and $\gamma = 0.5$) to forecast the number of customers served each day. The bank is open Monday through Friday. At present, the following "seasonalities" have been estimated: Monday, 0.80; Tuesday, 0.90; Wednesday, 0.95; Thursday, 1.10; Friday, 1.25. A seasonality of 0.80 for Monday means that on a Monday, the number of customers served by the bank tends to be 80% of the average daily value. Currently, the level is estimated to be 20 customers, and the trend is estimated to equal 1 customer. After observing that 30 customers are served by the bank on Monday, forecast the number of customers who will be served by the bank on Wednesday.

53. Suppose that Winters' method is used to forecast quarterly U.S. retail sales (in billions of dollars). At the end of the first quarter of 2006, $L_t = 300$, $T_t = 30$, and the seasonal indexes are as follows: quarter 1, 0.90; quarter 2, 0.95; quarter 3, 0.95; quarter 4, 1.20. During the second quarter of 2006, retail sales are $360 billion. Assume $\alpha = 0.2$, $\beta = 0.4$, and $\gamma = 0.5$.
   a. At the end of the second quarter of 2006, develop a forecast for retail sales during the fourth quarter of 2006.
   b. At the end of the second quarter of 2006, develop a forecast for the second quarter of 2007.

54. The file **P02_38.xlsx** contains monthly retail sales of U.S. liquor stores.

   a. Is seasonality present in these data? If so, characterize the seasonality pattern and then deseasonalize this time series using the ratio-to-moving-average method.
   b. If you decided to deseasonalize this time series in part **a**, forecast the deseasonalized data for each month of the next year using the moving average method with an appropriate span.
   c. Does Holt's exponential smoothing method, with optimal smoothing constants, outperform the moving average method employed in part **b**? Demonstrate why or why not.

55. Continuing the previous problem, how do your responses to the questions change when you employ Winters' method to handle seasonality in this time series? Explain. Which forecasting method do you prefer, Winters' method or a method used in the previous problem? Defend your choice.

56. The file **P02_39.xlsx** contains monthly time series data for total U.S. retail sales of building materials (which includes retail sales of building materials, hardware and garden supply stores, and mobile home dealers).
   a. Is seasonality present in these data? If so, characterize the seasonality pattern and then deseasonalize this time series using the ratio-to-moving-average method.
   b. If you decided to deseasonalize this time series in part **a**, forecast the deseasonalized data for each month of the next year using the moving average method with an appropriate span.
   c. Does Holt's exponential smoothing method, with optimal smoothing constants, outperform the moving average method employed in part **b**? Demonstrate why or why not.

57. The file **P02_40.xlsx** consists of the monthly retail sales levels of U.S. gasoline service stations.
   a. Is there a seasonal pattern in these data? If so, how do you explain this seasonal pattern? Also, if necessary, deseasonalize these data using the ratio-to-moving-average method.
   b. Forecast this time series for the first 4 months of the next year using the most appropriate method for these data. Defend your choice of forecasting method.

58. The number of employees on the payroll at a food processing plant is recorded at the start of each month. These data are provided in the file **P13_03.xlsx**.

    a. Is there a seasonal pattern in these data? If so, how do you explain this seasonal pattern? Also, if necessary, deseasonalize these data using the ratio-to-moving-average method.

    b. Forecast this time series for the first 4 months of the next year using the most appropriate method. Defend your choice of forecasting method.

59. Consider the file **P02_37.xlsx**, which contains total monthly U.S. retail sales data. Compare the effectiveness of Winters' method with that of the ratio-to-moving-average method in deseasonalizing this time series. Using the deseasonalized time series generated by each of these two methods, forecast U.S. retail sales with the most appropriate method. Defend your choice of forecasting method.

60. Suppose that a time series consisting of 6 years (2000–2005) of quarterly data exhibits definite seasonality. In fact, assume that the seasonal indexes turn out to be 0.75, 1.45, 1.25, and 0.55.

    a. If the last four observations of the series (the four quarters of 2005) are 2502, 4872, 4269, and 1924, calculate the deseasonalized values for the four quarters of 2005.

    b. Suppose that a plot of the deseasonalized series shows an upward linear trend, except for some random noise. Therefore, a linear regression of this series versus time is estimated, and it produces the equation

Predicted deseasonalized value
= 2250 + 51Quarter

    Here the time variable "Quarter" is coded so that Quarter = 1 corresponds to first quarter 2000, Quarter = 24 corresponds to fourth quarter 2005, and the others fall in between. Forecast the actual (not deseasonalized) values for the four quarters of 2006.

61. The file **P13_61.xlsx** contains monthly data on federal receipts of taxes. There are two variables: IndTax (taxes from individuals) and CorpTax (corporate taxes). For this problem, work only with IndTax.

    a. What evidence is there that seasonality is important in this series? Find seasonal indexes (by any method you like) and state briefly what they mean.

    b. Forecast the next 12 months by using a linear trend on the seasonally adjusted data. State briefly the steps you use to get this type of forecast, give the final RMSE, MAPE, and forecast for the next month. Then show numerically how you could replicate this forecast (i.e., show on paper how the package uses its estimated model to get the next month forecast). (Substitute in specific numbers, and do the arithmetic.)

62. Quarterly sales for a department store over a 6-year period are given in the file **P13_62.xlsx**.

    a. Use multiple regression to develop a model that can be used to predict future quarterly sales. (*Hint*: Use dummy variables and an explanatory variable for the quarter number, 1–24.)

    b. Letting Y_t be the sales during quarter number t, discuss how to fit the following model to these data.

$$Y_t = \alpha\beta^t{}_1\beta_2{}^{X_1}\beta_3{}^{X_2}\beta_4{}^{X_3}$$

    Here $X_1 = 1$ if t is a first quarter, 0 otherwise; $X_2 = 1$ if t is a second quarter, 0 otherwise; and $X_3 = 1$ if t is a third quarter, 0 otherwise.

    a. Interpret the answer to part **b**.

    b. Which model appears to yield better predictions for sales, the one in part **a** or the one in part **b**?

63. Confederate Express Service is attempting to determine how its shipping costs for a month depend on the number of units shipped during a month. The number of units shipped and total shipping cost for the last 15 months are given in the file **P13_63.xlsx**.

    a. Determine a relationship between units shipped and monthly shipping cost.

    b. Plot the errors for the predictions in order of time sequence. Is there any unusual pattern?

    c. We have been told that there was a trucking strike during months 11 through 15, and we believe that this might have influenced shipping costs. How could the answer to part **a** be modified to account for the effect of the strike? After accounting for this effect, does the unusual pattern in part **b** disappear?

Level B

64. In our discussion of Winters' method, a monthly seasonality of 0.80 for January, say, means that during January, air conditioner (AC) sales are expected to be 80% of the sales during an average month. An alternative approach to modeling seasonality, called an **additive model**, is to let the seasonality factor for each month represent how far above average AC sales will be during the current month. For instance, if $S_{\text{Jan}} = -50$, then AC sales during January are expected to be 50 fewer than AC sales during an average month. (This is 50 ACs, not 50%.) If $S_{\text{July}} = 90$, then AC sales during July are expected to be 90 more than AC sales during an average month. Let

S_t = Seasonality for month t after observing month t demand

L_t = Estimate of level after observing month t demand

T_t = Estimate of trend after observing month t demand

Then the Winters' method equations given in the text should be modified as follows:

$$L_t = \alpha(I) + (1 - \alpha)(L_{t-1} + T_{t-1})$$

$T_t = \beta(L_t - L_{t-1}) + (1 - \beta)T_{t-1}$

$S_t = \gamma(II) + (1 - \gamma)S_{t-12}$

a. What should (*I*) and (*II*) be?

b. Suppose that month 13 is January, $L_{12} = 30$, $T_{12} = -3$, $S_1 = -50$, and $S_2 = -20$. Let $\alpha = \gamma = \beta = 0.5$. Suppose 12 ACs are sold during month 13. At the end of month 13, what is the prediction for AC sales during month 14 using this additive model?

65. Winters' method assumes a multiplicative seasonality but an additive trend. For example, a trend of 5 means that the level will increase by 5 units per period. Suppose that there is actually a *multiplicative* trend. Then (ignoring seasonality) if the current estimate of the level is 50 and the current estimate of the trend is 1.2, we would predict demand to increase by 20% per period. So we would forecast the next period's demand to be 50(1.2) and forecast the demand 2 periods in the future to be $50(1.2)^2$. If we want to use a multiplicative trend in Winters' method, we should use the following equations (assuming a period is a month):

$$L_t = \alpha\left(\frac{Y_t}{S_{t-12}}\right) + (1 - \alpha)(I)$$

$$T_t = \beta(II) + (1 - \beta)T_{t-1}$$

$$S_t = \gamma\left(\frac{Y_t}{L_t}\right) + (1 - \gamma)S_{t-12}$$

a. What should (*I*) and (*II*) be?

b. Suppose that we are working with monthly data and month 12 is December, month 13 is January, and so on. Also suppose that $L_{12} = 100$, $T_{12} = 1.2$, $S_1 = 0.90$, $S_2 = 0.70$, and $S_3 = 0.95$. Also, suppose $Y_{13} = 200$. At the end of month 13, what is the prediction for Y_{15} using $\alpha = \beta = \gamma = 0.5$ and a multiplicative trend?

66. Consider the file **P02_37.xlsx**, which contains total monthly U.S. retail sales data. Does a regression approach for estimating seasonality provide forecasts that are as accurate as those provided by (a) Winters' method and (b) the ratio-to-moving-average method? Compare the summary measures of forecast errors associated with each method for deseasonalizing the given time series. Summarize your findings after performing these comparisons.

67. The file **P02_39.xlsx** contains monthly time series data for total U.S. retail sales of building materials (which includes retail sales of building materials, hardware and garden supply stores, and mobile home dealers). Does a regression approach for estimating seasonality provide forecasts that are as accurate as those provided by (a) Winters' method and (b) the ratio-to-moving-average method? Compare the summary measures of forecast errors associated with each method for deseasonalizing the given time series. Summarize your findings after performing these comparisons.

13.10 CONCLUSION

We have covered a lot of ground in this chapter. Because forecasting is such an important activity in business, it has received a tremendous amount of attention by both academicians and practitioners. All of the methods discussed in this chapter—and more—are actually used, often on a day-to-day basis. There is really no point in arguing which of these methods is best. All of them have their strengths and weaknesses. The most important point is that when they are applied properly, they have all been found to be useful in real business situations.

Summary of Key Terms

Term	Explanation	Excel	Page	Equation Number
Extrapolation methods	Forecasting methods where only past values of a variable (and possibly time itself) are used to forecast future values		715	
Causal (or econometric) methods	Forecasting methods based on regression, where other time series variables are used as explanatory variables		716	
Trend	A systematic increase or decrease of a time series variable through time		718	

(continued)

Term	Explanation	Excel	Page	Equation Number
Seasonality	A regular pattern of ups and downs based on the season of the year, typically months or quarters		718	
Cyclic variation	An irregular pattern of ups and downs caused by business cycles		718	
Noise (or random variation)	The unpredictable ups and downs of a time series variable		719	
Mean absolute error (MAE)	The average of the absolute forecast errors	StatTools/ Time Series & Forecasting/Forecast	721	13.2
Root mean square error (RMSE)	The square root of the average of the squared forecast errors	StatTools/ Time Series & Forecasting/Forecast	721	13.3
Mean absolute percentage error (MAPE)	The average of the absolute percentage forecast errors	StatTools/ Time Series & Forecasting/Forecast	721	13.4
Runs test	A test of whether the forecast errors are random noise	StatTools/ Time Series & Forecasting/ Runs Test for Randomness	724	
Autocorrelations of residuals	Correlations of forecast errors with themselves, used to check whether they are random noise	StatTools/ Time Series & Forecasting/ Autocorrelation	726	
Correlogram	A bar chart of autocorrelations at different lags	StatTools/ Time Series & Forecasting/ Autocorrelation	727	
Linear trend model	A regression model where a time series variable changes by a constant amount each time period	StatTools/ Regression & Classification/ Regression	729	13.6
Exponential trend model	A regression model where a time series variable changes by a constant percentage each time period	StatTools/ Regression & Classification/ Regression	732	13.7
Random walk model	A model indicating that the differences between adjacent observations of a time series variable are constant except for random noise		738	13.9–13.11
Autoregression model	A regression model where the only explanatory variables are lagged values of the dependent variable	StatTools/ Regression & Classification/ Regression	741	
Moving averages model	A forecasting model where the average of several past observations is used to forecast the next observation	StatTools/ Time Series & Forecasting/ Forecast	746	

(continued)

Term	Explanation	Excel	Page	Equation Number
Span	The number of observations in each average of a moving averages model	StatTools/ Time Series & Forecasting/ Forecast	746	
Exponential smoothing models	A class of forecasting models where forecasts are based on weighted averages of previous observations, giving more weight to more recent observations	StatTools/ Time Series & Forecasting/ Forecast	753	
Smoothing constants	Constants between 0 and 1 that prescribe the weight attached to previous observations and hence the smoothness of the series of forecasts	StatTools/ Time Series & Forecasting/ Forecast	753	
Simple exponential smoothing	An exponential smoothing model useful for time series with no prominent trend or seasonality	StatTools/ Time Series & Forecasting/ Forecast	753	13.12–13.15
Holt's method	An exponential smoothing model useful for time series with trend but no seasonality	StatTools/ Time Series & Forecasting/ Forecast	753	13.16–13.18
Winters' method	An exponential smoothing model useful for time series with seasonality (and possibly trend)	StatTools/ Time Series & Forecasting/ Forecast	753	13.19–13.22
Deseasonalizing	A method for removing the seasonal component from time series data	StatTools/ Time Series & Forecasting/ Forecast	768	
Ratio-to-moving-averages method	A method for deseasonalizing a time series, so that some other method can then be used to forecast the deseasonalized series	StatTools/ Time Series & Forecasting/ Forecast	768	
Dummy variables for seasonality	A regression-based method for forecasting seasonality, where dummy variables are used for the seasons	StatTools/ Regression & Classification/ Regression	772	

PROBLEMS

Conceptual Exercises

C.1. "A truly random series will likely have a very small number of runs." Is this statement true or false? Explain your choice.

C.2. Distinguish between a *correlation* and an *autocorrelation.* How are these measures similar? How are these measures different?

C.3. What is the relationship between the random walk model and the autoregression model?

C.4. Under what conditions would you prefer a simple exponential smoothing model to the moving averages method for forecasting a time series?

C.5. Is it more appropriate to use an *additive* or a *multiplicative* model to forecast seasonal data? Summarize the difference(s) between these two types of seasonal models.

Level A

68. The file **P13_68.xlsx** contains quarterly revenues of Toys "R" Us. Discuss the seasonal and trend components of the growth of Toys "R" Us revenues. Also, use any reasonable forecasting method to forecast quarterly revenues for the next year. Explain your choice of forecasting method.

69. The file **P13_69.xlsx** contains quarterly revenues and earnings per share (EPS) for the following companies: Mattel, McDonald's, Eli Lilly, General Motors, Microsoft, AT&T, Nike, GE, Coca-Cola, and Ford.
  a. For each company, use a regression model with trend and seasonal components to forecast revenues and EPS.
  b. For each company, use Winters' method to forecast revenues and EPS.
  c. For each company, which method appears to be more accurate?

70. The file **P13_70.xlsx** contains the sales in (millions of dollars) for Sun Microsystems.
  a. Use these data to predict the company's sales for the next 2 years. You need consider only a linear and exponential trend, but you should justify the equation you choose.
  b. In words, how do your predictions of sales increase from year to year?
  c. Are there any outliers?

71. The file **P13_71.xlsx** contains the sales in (millions of dollars) for Procter & Gamble.
  a. Use these data to predict Procter & Gamble sales for the next 2 years. You need consider only a linear and exponential trend, but you should justify the equation you choose.
  b. Use your answer from part **a** to explain how your predictions of Procter & Gamble sales increase from year to year.
  c. Are there any outliers?
  d. We can be approximately 95% sure that Procter & Gamble sales in the year following next year will be between what two values?

72. The file **P13_72.xlsx** lists the sales of Nike. Forecast sales in the next 2 years with a linear or exponential trend. Are there any outliers in your predictions for the observed period?

73. The file **P12_44.xlsx** contains data on pork sales. Price is in dollars per hundred pounds sold, quantity sold is in billions of pounds, per capita income is in dollars, U.S. population is in millions, and GNP is in billions of dollars.
  a. Use these data to develop a regression equation that could be used to predict the quantity of pork sold during future periods. Is autocorrelation, heteroscedasticity, or multicollinearity a problem?

  b. Suppose that during each of the next two quarters, price is $45, U.S. population is 240, GNP is 2620, and per capita income is $10,000. (All of these are expressed in the units described above.) Predict the quantity of pork sold during each of the next 2 quarters.
  c. We expect our prediction of pork sales to be accurate within what value 68% of the time?
  d. Use Winters' method to develop a forecast of pork sales during the next 2 quarters.

74. The file **P13_74.xlsx** contains data on a motel chain's revenue and advertising.
  a. Use these data and multiple regression to make predictions of the motel chain's revenues during the next 4 quarters. Assume that advertising during each of the next 4 quarters is $50,000. (*Hint*: Try using advertising, lagged by 1 quarter, as an explanatory variable.)
  b. Use simple exponential smoothing to make predictions for the motel chain's revenues during the next 4 quarters.
  c. Use Holt's method to make forecasts for the motel chain's revenues during the next 4 quarters.
  d. Use Winters' method to determine predictions for the motel chain's revenues during the next 4 quarters.
  e. Which of these forecasting methods would you expect to be the most reliable for these data?

75. The file **P13_75.xlsx** contains data on monthly U.S. housing sales (in thousands of houses).
  a. Using Winters' method, find values of α, β, and γ that yield an RMSE as small as possible.
  b. Although we have not discussed autocorrelation for smoothing methods, good forecasts derived from smoothing methods should exhibit no autocorrelation. Do the forecast errors for this problem exhibit autocorrelation?
  c. At the end of the observed period, what is the forecast of housing sales during the next few months?

76. Let Y_t be the sales during month t (in thousands of dollars) for a photography studio, and let P_t be the price charged for portraits during month t. The data are in the file **P12_45.xlsx**. Use regression to fit the following model to these data:

$$Y_t = \alpha + \beta_1 Y_{t-1} + \beta_2 P_t + \epsilon_t$$

This equation indicates that last month's sales and the current month's price are explanatory variables. The last term, ϵ_t, is an error term.
  a. If the price of a portrait during month 21 is $10, what would we predict for sales in month 21?
  b. Does there appear to be a problem with autocorrelation, heteroscedasticity, or multicollinearity?

77. The file **P13_77.xlsx** gives quarterly auto sales, GNP, interest rates and unemployment rates.

a. With all but the most recent 2 years of data, use regression to forecast auto sales. Interpret the coefficients in your final equation.

b. Use all but the most recent 2 years of data to develop an exponential smoothing model to forecast future auto sales.

c. To *validate* your model, determine which model does the best job of forecasting for the most recent 2 years of data. It is usually recommended to hold out some of your data to validate any forecast model. This helps avoid "overfitting."

Level B

78. The file **P13_78.xlsx** contains monthly time series data on corporate bond yields. These are averages of daily figures, and each is expressed as an annual rate. The variables are:

- YieldAAA: average yield on AAA bonds
- YieldBAA: average yield on BAA bonds

If you examine either Yield variable, you will notice that the autocorrelations of the series are not only large for many lags, but that the lag 1 autocorrelation of the *differences* is significant. This is very common. It means that the series is not a random walk and that it is probably possible to provide a better forecast than the "naive" forecast from the random walk model. Here is the idea. The large lag 1 autocorrelation of the differences means that the differences are related to the first lag of the differences. This relationship can be estimated by creating the difference variable and a lag of it, then regressing the former on the latter, and finally using this information to forecast the original Yield variable.

a. Verify that the autocorrelations are as described, and form the difference variable and the first lag of it. Call these DYield and L1DYield (where D is for difference, L1 is for first lag).

b. Run a regression with DYield as the dependent variable and L1DYield as the single explanatory variable. In terms of the original variable Yield, this equation can be written as

$$\text{Yield}_t - \text{Yield}_{t-1} = a + b(\text{Yield}_{t-1} - \text{Yield}_{t-2})$$

Solving for Yield_t is equivalent to the following equation that can be used for forecasting:

$$\text{Yield}_t = a + (1 + b)\text{Yield}_{t-1} - b\text{Yield}_{t-2}$$

Try it—that is, try forecasting the next month from the known last 2 months' values. How might you forecast values 2 or 3 months from the last observed month? (*Hint*: If you do not have an *observed* value to use in the right side of the equation, use a forecasted value.)

c. The autocorrelation structure led us to the equation in part **b**. That is, the autocorrelations of the original series took a long time to die down, so we

looked at the autocorrelations of the differences, and the large spike at lag 1 led to regressing DYield on L1DYield. In turn, this led ultimately to an equation for Yield_t in terms of its first two lags. Now see what you would have obtained if you had tried regressing Yield_t on its first two lags in the first place—that is, if you had used regression to estimate the equation

$$\text{Yield}_t = a + b_1\text{Yield}_{t-1} + b_2\text{Yield}_{t-2}$$

When you use multiple regression to estimate this equation, do you get the same equation as in part **b**?

79. The file **P13_79.xlsx** contains 5 years of monthly data for a particular company. The first variable is Time (1–60). The second variable, Sales1, has data on sales of a product. Note that Sales1 increases linearly throughout the period, with only a minor amount of "noise." (The third variable, Sales2, is discussed and used in the next problem.) For this problem use the Sales1 variable to see how the following forecasting methods are able to track a linear trend.

a. Forecast this series with the moving average method with various spans such as 3, 6, and 12. What can you conclude?

b. Forecast this series with simple exponential smoothing with various smoothing constants such as 0.1, 0.3, 0.5, and 0.7. What can you conclude?

c. Now repeat part **b** with Holt's exponential smoothing method, again for various smoothing constants. Can you do significantly better than in parts **a** and **b**?

d. What can you conclude from your findings in parts **a**, **b**, and **c** about forecasting this type of series?

80. The Sales2 variable in the file from the previous problem was created from the Sales1 variable by multiplying by monthly seasonal factors. Basically, the summer months are high and the winter months are low. This might represent the sales of a product that has a linear trend and seasonality.

a. Repeat parts **a**, **b**, and **c** from the previous problem to see how well these forecasting methods can deal with trend *and* seasonality.

b. Now use Winters' method, with various values of the three smoothing constants, to forecast the series. Can you do much better? Which smoothing constants work well?

c. Use the ratio-to-moving-average method, where you first do the seasonal decomposition and then forecast (by any appropriate method) the deseasonalized series. Does this do as well as, or better than, Winters' method?

d. What can you conclude from your findings in parts **a**, **b**, and **c** about forecasting this type of series?

81. The file **P13_81.xlsx** contains monthly time series data on federal expenditures in various categories. All values are in billions of current dollars. The variables are:

- Defense: expenditures on national defense
- Science: expenditures on science, space, and technology
- Energy: expenditures on energy
- Environ: expenditures on natural resources and environment
- Trans: expenditures on transportation

Analyze the Science variable by (a) simple exponential smoothing, (b) Holt's method, (c) simple exponential smoothing on the trend-adjusted data (the residuals from regressing linearly versus time), and (d) moving averages on the adjusted or unadjusted data. Experiment with the smoothing constants [or span in (d)], or use the optimize feature. Do any of these methods produce significantly better fits than the others as measured by RMSE or MAPE?

82. The data in the file **P13_82.xlsx** represent annual changes in the average surface air temperature of the earth. (The source doesn't say exactly how this was measured.) A look at the time series shows a gradual upward trend, starting with negative values and ending with (mostly) positive values. This might be used to support the theory of global warming.

a. Is this series a random walk? Explain.

b. Regardless of your answer in part **a**, use a random walk model to forecast the next value of the series. What is your forecast, and what is an approximate 95% forecast interval?

c. Forecast the series in three ways: (i) simple exponential smoothing ($\alpha = 0.35$), (ii) Holt's method ($\alpha = 0.5$, $\beta = 0.1$), and (iii) simple exponential smoothing ($\alpha = 0.3$) on trend-adjusted data, that is, the residuals from regressing linearly versus time. (These smoothing constants are close to "optimal.") For each of these, list the MAPE, the RMSE, and the forecast for next year. Also, comment on any "problems" with forecast errors from any of these three approaches. Finally, compare the "qualitative" features of the three forecasts (for example, how do their short-run or longer-run forecasts differ?). Is any one of the methods clearly superior to the others?

d. Does your analysis predict convincingly that global warming would occur during the observed years? Explain.

The Indiana University Credit Union Eastland Plaza Branch was having trouble getting the correct staffing levels to match customer arrival patterns. On some days, the number of tellers was too high relative to the customer traffic, so that tellers were often idle. On other days, the opposite occurred. Long customer waiting lines formed because the relatively few tellers could not keep up with the number of customers. The credit union manager, James Chilton, knew that there was a problem, but he had little of the quantitative training he believed would be necessary to find a better staffing solution. James figured that the problem could be broken down into three parts. First, he needed a reliable forecast of each day's number of customer arrivals. Second, he needed to translate these forecasts into staffing levels that would make an adequate trade-off between teller idleness and customer waiting. Third, he needed to translate these staffing levels into individual teller work assignments—who should come to work when.

The last two parts of the problem require analysis tools (queueing and scheduling) that we have not covered. However, you can help James with the first part—forecasting. The file **Credit Union Arrivals.xlsx** lists the number of customers entering this credit union branch each day of the past year. It also lists other information: the day of the week, whether the day was a staff or faculty payday, and whether the day was the day before or after a holiday. Use this data set to develop one or more forecasting models that James could use to help solve his problem. Based on your model(s), make any recommendations about staffing that appear reasonable. ∎

Amanta Appliances sells two styles of refrigerators at more than 50 locations in the Midwest. The first style is a relatively expensive model, whereas the second is a standard, less expensive model. Although weekly demand for these two products is fairly stable from week to week, there is enough variation to concern management at Amanta. There have been relatively unsophisticated attempts to forecast weekly demand, but they haven't been very successful. Sometimes demand (and the corresponding sales) are lower than forecasted, so that inventory costs are high. Other times the forecasts are too low. When this happens and on-hand inventory is not sufficient to meet customer demand, Amanta requires expedited shipments to keep customers happy—and this nearly wipes out Amanta's profit margin on the expedited units.[6] Profits at Amanta would almost certainly increase if demand could be forecasted more accurately.

Data on weekly sales of both products appear in the file **Amanta Sales.xlsx**. A time series chart of the two sales variables indicates what Amanta management expected—namely, there is no evidence of any upward or downward trends or of any seasonality. In fact, it might appear that each series is an unpredictable sequence of random ups and downs. But is this really true? Is it possible to forecast either series, with some degree of accuracy, with an extrapolation method (where only past values of *that* series are used to forecast current and future values)? What method appears to be best? How accurate is it? Also, is it possible, when trying to forecast sales of one product, to somehow incorporate current or past sales of the *other* product in the forecast model? After all, these products might be "substitute" products, where high sales of one go with low sales of the other, or they might be complementary products, where sales of the two products tend to move in the *same* direction. ■

[6]Because Amanta uses expediting when necessary, its sales each week are equal to its customer demands. Therefore, we use the terms *demand* and *sales* interchangeably.

PART

5

Decision Modeling

DIET MODELS

One of the many classic applications of linear programming is the "diet problem." This problem appears as a prototype linear programming example in almost all management science (MS) textbooks. Basically, it involves finding a group of foods—a diet—that meets all daily nutritional requirements at minimum cost. The problem is important in many real settings, as outlined by Lancaster (1992). A number of versions of this model have actually been used by institutions such as hospitals, nursing homes, schools, prisons, and other food-systems operations. In many of these applications, the computer-generated menus have provided a 10% to 30% cost savings, the nutritional requirements are guaranteed (in contrast to menus generated by traditional, non-MS methods), and, surprisingly, the acceptance of the menus by consumers has been very high.

This problem provides a good example of how to distinguish between good models and poor models. In the simplified diet problems in most textbooks, it is easy to develop a model that satisfies the conditions of low-cost and minimal daily nutritional requirements, but the resulting diet is so bland (or weird) that no one would eat it. The trick is to incorporate suitable "constraints" (mathematical equations or inequalities) that rule out unappetizing menus. For example, the applications cited in Lancaster (1992) obtained more acceptable diets in one of two ways. Either they included a separation constraint (such as requiring at least three days between successive servings of mashed potatoes) or a frequency constraint (such as requiring that mashed potatoes be served at most three times per week). By adding enough of these types of constraints, they obtained menus that people were quite willing to eat.

A related article by Dantzig (1990) illustrates the humorous side of the problem. When Dantzig (one of the founders of linear programming) was developing his famous solution technique for linear programming in the late 1940s, he decided to use it to solve his own diet problem, one that would prescribe what he would actually eat each day. Even he was surprised by the outcome. His first solution called for various amounts of "normal" foods, plus 500 gallons of vinegar—he had forgotten a constraint! So he reformulated the problem, and his next solution called for 200 bouillon cubes per day. Still not (too) discouraged, he reformulated the problem with an upper limit on bouillon cubes, and his resulting solution called for two pounds of bran per day. After an upper limit on bran was imposed, his next diet called for two pounds of blackstrap molasses. By this time, he started to get the point: It is possible to generate a low-cost, nutritional, and tasty diet using management science techniques, but it is not as easy as it appears! ■

14.1 INTRODUCTION

In this chapter we introduce spreadsheet optimization, one of the most powerful and flexible methods of quantitative analysis. The specific type of optimization we will discuss here is **linear programming** (LP). LP is used in all types of organizations, often on a daily basis, to solve a wide variety of problems. These include problems in labor scheduling, inventory management, selection of advertising media, bond trading, management of cash flows, operation of an electrical utility's hydroelectric system, routing of delivery vehicles, blending in oil refineries, hospital staffing, and many others. The goal of this chapter is to introduce the basic elements of LP: the types of problems it can solve, how LP problems can be modeled in Excel, and how Excel's powerful Solver add-in can be used to find optimal solutions. Then in the next chapter we examine a variety of LP applications, and we also look at applications of integer and nonlinear programming, two important extensions of LP.

14.2 INTRODUCTION TO OPTIMIZATION

Before we discuss the details of LP modeling, it is useful to discuss optimization in general. All optimization problems have several elements in common. They all have **decision variables**, the variables whose values the decision maker is allowed to choose. Either directly or indirectly, the values of these variables determine such outputs as total cost, revenue, and profit. Essentially, they are the variables a company or organization must know to function properly; they determine everything else. All optimization problems have an **objective function** (**objective**, for short) whose value is to be optimized—maximized or minimized.[1] Finally, most optimization problems have **constraints** that must be satisfied. These are usually physical, logical, or economic restrictions that are due to the nature of the problem. In searching for the values of the decision variables that optimize the objective, we are allowed to choose only those values that satisfy all of the constraints.

[1]Actually, some optimization models are "multicriteria" models, where we try to optimize several objectives simultaneously. However, we do not discuss multicriteria models in this book.

Excel uses its own terminology for optimization, and we use it throughout the book. Excel refers to the decision variables as the **changing cells**. As we see, these cells must contain numbers that are allowed to change freely; they are *not* allowed to contain formulas. Excel refers to the objective as the **target cell**. There can be only one target cell, which could contain profit, total cost, total distance traveled, or others, and it must be related through formulas to the changing cells. When the changing cells change, the target cell should change accordingly.

The **changing cells** contain the values of the decision variables.

The **target cell** contains the objective to be minimized or maximized.

The **constraints** impose restrictions on the values in the changing cells.

Finally, there must be appropriate cells and cell formulas that allow us to operationalize the constraints. For example, there might be a constraint that says the amount of labor used is no more than the amount of labor available. In this case there must be cells for each of these two quantities, and typically at least one of them (probably the amount of labor used) will be related through formulas to the changing cells. Constraints can come in a variety of forms. One very common form is **nonnegativity**. This type of constraint states that changing cells must have nonnegative (zero or positive) values. We usually include nonnegativity constraints for physical reasons. For example, it is impossible to produce a negative number of automobiles.

Nonnegativity constraints imply that changing cells must contain nonnegative values.

Typically, most of our effort goes into the model development step.

There are basically two steps in solving an optimization problem. The first step is the **model development** step. Here we decide what the decision variables are, what the objective is, which constraints are required, and how everything fits together. If we are developing an algebraic model, we must derive the correct algebraic expressions. If we are developing a spreadsheet model, the main focus of this book, we must relate all variables with appropriate cell formulas. In particular, we must ensure that our model contains formulas for relating the changing cells to the target cell and that it contains formulas for operationalizing the constraints. This model development step, as we see, is where most of our effort goes.

The second step in any optimization model is to **optimize**. This means that we must systematically choose the values of the decision variables that make the objective as large (for maximization) or small (for minimization) as possible and cause all of the constraints to be satisfied. A bit of terminology is useful here. Any set of values of the decision variables that satisfies all of the constraints is called a **feasible solution**. The set of all feasible solutions is called the **feasible region**. In contrast, an **infeasible solution** is a solution where at least one constraint is not satisfied. We must rule out infeasible solutions. We want the feasible solution that provides the best value—minimum for a minimization problem, maximum for a maximization problem—of the objective. This solution is called the **optimal solution**.

A **feasible solution** is a solution that satisfies all of the constraints.

The **feasible region** is the set of all feasible solutions.

An **infeasible solution** violates at least one of the constraints.

The **optimal solution** is the feasible solution that optimizes the objective.

Although most of our effort typically goes into the model development step, much of the published research in optimization has gone into the optimization step. Algorithms have been devised for searching through the feasible region to find the optimal solution. One such algorithm is called the **simplex method**. It is suitable for linear models. There are other more complex algorithms suitable for other types of models (those with integer decision variables and/or nonlinearities).

Fortunately, in this book we do not need to discuss the details of these algorithms. They have been programmed into the Solver add-in that is part of Excel. All we need to do is develop the model and then tell Solver what the target cell is, what the changing cells are, what the constraints are, and what type of model (linear, integer, or nonlinear) we have. Solver then goes to work, finding the best feasible solution with the most suitable algorithm. You should appreciate that if we used a trial-and-error procedure, even a clever and fast one, it could take us hours, weeks, or even years to complete. However, by using the appropriate algorithm, Solver typically finds the optimal solution in a matter of seconds.

Before concluding this discussion, we mention that there is really a *third* step in the optimization process: **sensitivity analysis**. We typically choose the most likely values of input variables, such as unit costs, forecasted demands, and resource availabilities, and then find the optimal solution for these particular input values. This provides a single "answer." However, in any realistic setting, it is wishful thinking to believe that all of the input values we use are exactly correct. Therefore, it is useful—indeed, mandatory in most applied studies—to follow up the optimization step with a lot of "what-if" questions. What if the unit costs increased by 5%? What if forecasted demands were 10% lower? What if resource availabilities could be increased by 20%? What effects would such changes have on the optimal solution? This type of sensitivity analysis can be done in an informal manner or it can be highly structured. We say a lot about sensitivity analysis in later examples. Fortunately, as with the optimization step itself, good software allows us to obtain answers to a lot of what-if questions quickly and easily.

14.3 A TWO-VARIABLE MODEL

We begin with a very simple two-variable problem that is essentially a version of the diet problem discussed at the beginning of this chapter. We see how to model this problem algebraically and then how to model it in Excel. We also see how to find its optimal solution with Excel's Solver add-in. Next, because it contains only two decision variables, we see how it can be solved graphically. Although this graphical solution is not practical for most realistic problems, it provides useful insights into general optimization models. Finally, we ask a number of what-if questions about the completed model.

EXAMPLE | **14.1 PLANNING DESSERTS**

Maggie Stewart loves desserts, but due to weight and cholesterol concerns, she has decided that she must plan her desserts carefully. There are two possible desserts she is considering: snack bars and ice cream. After reading the nutrition labels on the snack bar and ice cream packages, she learns that each "serving" of a snack bar weighs 37 grams and contains 120 calories and 5 grams of fat. Each serving of ice cream weighs 65 grams and contains 160 calories and 10 grams of fat. Maggie will allow herself no more than 450 calories and 25 grams of fat in her daily desserts, but because she loves desserts so much, she requires at least 120 grams of dessert per day. Also, she assigns a "taste index" to each gram of each dessert, where 0 is the lowest and 100 is the highest. She assigns a taste index of 95 to ice cream and 85 to snack bars (because she prefers ice cream to snack bars). What should her daily dessert plan be to stay within her constraints and maximize the total taste index of her dessert?

Objective   To use linear programming to find the tastiest combination of desserts that stays within Maggie's constraints.

Solution

Tables such as this serve as a bridge between the problem statement and the ultimate spreadsheet (or algebraic) model.

In all optimization models we are given a variety of numbers—the inputs—and we are asked to make some decisions that optimize an objective, while satisfying some constraints. We summarize this information in a table, as shown in Table 14.1. We believe it is a good idea to create such a table before diving into the modeling details. In particular, you always need to identify the appropriate decision variables, the appropriate objective, and the constraints, and you should always think about the relationships between them. Without a clear idea of these elements, it is almost impossible to develop a correct algebraic or spreadsheet model.

Table 14.1   **Variables and Constraints for Dessert Model**

Input variables	Ingredients (calories, fat) per serving, serving sizes, taste indexes, maximum allowed daily ingredients, minimum required daily grams
Decision variables (changing cells)	Daily servings of each dessert consumed
Objective (target cell)	Total taste index
Other calculated variables	Daily ingredients consumed, daily grams consumed
Daily constraints	Daily ingredients consumed ≤ Maximum allowed grams consumed ≥ Minimum required

It is important to decide on a convenient unit of measurement and then be consistent in its use.

We make two comments about these variables. First, it is probably clear that the decision variables must be the daily amounts of the desserts consumed, but why do we choose *servings* rather than *grams*? The answer is that it doesn't really matter. Because we know the number of grams per serving of each dessert, it is simple to convert from servings to grams or vice versa. Choosing the unit of measurement is a common problem in modeling. It doesn't usually matter which unit of measurement we select, so long as we are consistent. Second, note that Maggie assigns a taste index of 85 to each gram of snack bar and 95 to each gram of ice cream. If she consumes, say, 50 grams of snack bar and 100 grams of ice cream, it seems reasonable that a measure of her total "taste satisfaction" is 50(85) + 100(95). This is how we define the total taste index, and it is the objective we attempt to maximize.

An Algebraic Model

In the traditional algebraic solution method, we first identify the decision variables.[2] In this small problem they are the numbers of servings of each dessert to consume daily. We label these x_1 and x_2, although any other labels would do. Next, we write expressions for the total taste index and the constraints in terms of the x's. Finally, because only nonnegative amounts can be consumed, we add explicit constraints to ensure that the x's are nonnegative. The resulting algebraic model is

$$\text{Maximize } 37(85)x_1 + 65(95)x_2$$

---

[2]This is not a book about algebraic models; our main focus is on *spreadsheet* modeling. However, we present algebraic models of the examples in this chapter, just for comparison with the spreadsheet models.

subject to:

$$120x_1 + 160x_2 \leq 450$$

$$5x_1 + 10x_2 \leq 25$$

$$37x_1 + 65x_2 \geq 120$$

$$x_1, x_2 \geq 0$$

To understand this model, consider the objective first. Each serving of snack bar weighs 37 grams, and each of these grams contributes 85 "points" to the total taste index. If x_1 servings of snack bar are consumed, they will contribute $37(85)x_1$ points to the total taste index. A similar calculation holds for ice cream. We then sum the contributions from snack bars and ice cream to obtain the total taste index.

The constraints are similar. For example, each serving of snack bar contains 120 calories and 5 grams of fat. These explain the $120x_1$ and $5x_1$ terms in the top two constraints (the calorie and fat constraints). We add these to the similar terms for ice cream to the left-hand sides of these constraints. Then the right-hand sides of these constraints are the given maximum daily allowances. The third constraint (minimal daily requirement of calories) follows similarly. Finally, we can't consume negative amounts of either dessert, so we include nonnegativity constraints on x_1 and x_2.

Many commercial optimization packages require, as input, an algebraic model of a problem. If you ever use one of these packages, you will be required to think algebraically.

For many years all LP problems were modeled this way in textbooks. This was because many commercial LP computer packages are written to accept LP problems in essentially this format. Since around 1990, however, a more intuitive method of expressing LP problems has emerged. This method takes advantage of the power and flexibility of spreadsheets. Actually, LP problems could always be *modeled* on spreadsheets, but now with the addition of Solver add-ins, spreadsheets have the ability to *solve*—that is, optimize—LP problems as well. Excel contains an add-in called Solver that can be used to solve many types of optimization problems. We use Excel's Solver for all examples in this book.[3]

A Graphical Solution

This graphical approach works only for problems with two decision variables.

When there are only two decision variables in an LP model, as there are in the dessert model, we can solve the problem graphically. Although this solution approach is not practical in most realistic optimization models—where there are many more than two decision variables—the graphical procedure we illustrate here still yields important insights.

In general, if the two decision variables are labeled x_1 and x_2, then we express the constraints and the objective in terms of x_1 and x_2, we graph the constraints to find the feasible region [the set of all pairs (x_1, x_2) satisfying the constraints, where x_1 is on the horizontal axis and x_2 is on the vertical axis], and we then move the objective through the feasible region until it is optimized.

Recall from algebra that any line of the form $ax_1 + bx_2 = c$ has slope $-a/b$. This is because it can be put into the slope–intercept form $x_2 = c/b - (a/b)x_1$.

To do this for the dessert problem, note that the constraint on calories can be expressed as $120x_1 + 160x_2 \leq 450$. To graph this, we consider the associated equality (replacing $\leq$ with $=$) and find where the associated line crosses the axes. Specifically, when $x_1 = 0$, then $x_2 = 450/160 = 2.81$, and when $x_2 = 0$, then $x_1 = 450/120 = 3.75$. This provides the line labeled "calories constraint" in Figure 14.1. It has slope $-120/160 = -0.75$. The set of all points that satisfy the calories constraint includes the points on this line plus the points *below* it, as indicated by the arrow drawn from the line. (We know that the feasible points are below the line because the point $(0, 0)$ is obviously below the line, and $(0, 0)$

---

[3]This Solver add-in is built into Microsoft Excel, but it has been developed by a third-party software company, Frontline Systems. We provide more information about Solver software offered by Frontline in the appendix to this chapter.

clearly satisfies the calories constraint.) Similarly, we can graph the fat constraint and the grams constraint, as shown in the figure. The points that satisfy all three of these constraints and are nonnegative comprise the feasible region, which is shaded in the figure.

Figure 14.1

Graphical Solution for Dessert Problem

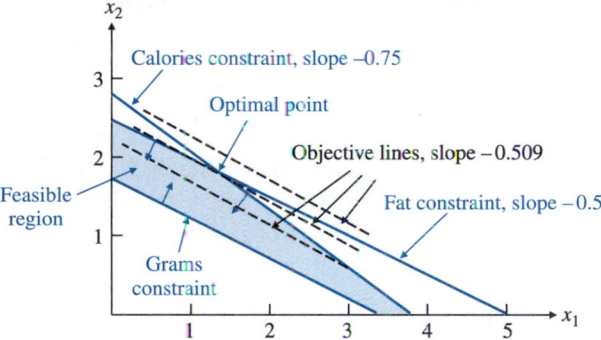

To see which feasible point maximizes the objective, we draw a sequence of lines where, for each, the objective is a constant. One such typical line is of the form $37(85)x_1 + 67(95)x_2 = c$, where c is a constant. Any such line has slope $-[37(85)]/[65(95)] = -0.509$, regardless of the value of c. This line is slightly steeper than the constraint line for fat, and it is not as steep as the constraint line for calories. We want to move a line with this slope up and to the right, making c larger, until it just barely touches the feasible region. The last feasible point that it touches is the optimal point.

Several lines with slope -0.509 are shown in Figure 14.1. The middle dotted line is the one with the largest total taste index that still touches the feasible region. The associated optimal point is clearly the point where the calories and fat lines intersect. We eventually find (from Solver) that this point is (1.25, 1.875), but even if we didn't have the Solver add-in, we could find the coordinates of this point by solving two equations (the ones for calories and fat) in two unknowns.

Again, the graphical procedure illustrated here can be used only for the simplest of LP models, those with two decision variables. However, the type of behavior pictured in Figure 14.1 generalizes to *all* LP problems. In general, all feasible regions are (the multidimensional versions of) solid polygons. That is, they are bounded by straight lines (actually, "hyperplanes") that intersect at several "corner points." (There are 5 corner points in Figure 14.1, 4 of which are on the axes.) When we push the objective line (again, really a hyperplane) as far as possible toward better values, the last feasible point it touches is one of the corner points. The actual corner point it last touches is determined by the slopes of the objective and constraint lines. Because there are only a finite number of corner points, we must search only among this finite set, not the infinite number of points in the entire feasible region.[4] This insight is largely responsible for the efficiency of the simplex method for solving LP problems.

Although limited in use, the graphical approach yields the important insight that the optimal solution to any LP model is a corner point of a polygon. This limits the search for the optimal solution and makes the simplex method possible.

A Spreadsheet Model

We now turn our focus to spreadsheet modeling. There are many ways to develop an LP spreadsheet model. Everyone has his or her own preferences for arranging the data in the various cells. We do not give any exact prescriptions, but we do present enough examples

---

[4]This is not entirely true. If the objective line is exactly parallel to one of the constraint lines, there can be **multiple optimal solutions**—a whole line segment of optimal solutions. Even in this case, however, at least one of the optimal solutions is a corner point.

to help you develop good habits. The common elements in all LP spreadsheet models are the inputs, changing cells, target cell, and constraints.

Inputs. All numerical **inputs**—that is, all numeric data given in the statement of the problem—must appear somewhere in the spreadsheet. Our convention is to color all of the input cells blue. We also try to put most of the inputs in the upper left section of the spreadsheet. However, we sometimes violate this latter convention when certain inputs fit more naturally somewhere else.

Changing cells. Instead of using variable names, such as x's, spreadsheet models use a set of designated cells for the decision variables. The values in these cells can be changed to optimize the objective. Excel calls these cells the **changing cells**. To designate them clearly, our convention is to color all of the changing cells red.

Target (objective) cell. One cell, called the **target cell**, contains the value of the objective. Solver systematically varies the values in the changing cells to optimize the value in the target cell. Our convention is to color the target cell gray.[5]

Our coloring conventions

Color all input cells blue (appears light blue on printed page)

Color all of the changing cells red (appears deep blue on printed page)

Color the target cell gray

Constraints. Excel does not show the constraints directly on the spreadsheet. Instead, we specify constraints in a Solver dialog box, to be discussed shortly. For example, we might designate a set of related constraints by

B15:D15<=B16:D16

This implies three separate constraints. The value in B15 must be less than or equal to the value in B16, the value in C15 must be less than or equal to the value in C16, and the value in D15 must be less than or equal to the value in D16. We will always assign range names to the ranges that appear in the constraints. Then a typical constraint might be specified as

Ingredients_consumed<=Ingredients_allowed

This is much easier to read and understand.

Nonnegativity. Normally, we want the decision variables—that is, the values in the changing cells—to be nonnegative. These constraints do not need to be written explicitly; we simply check an option in a Solver dialog box to indicate that we want nonnegative changing cells. Note, however, that if we want to constrain any *other* cells to be nonnegative, we need to specify these constraints explicitly.

Overview of the Solution Process

As we discussed previously, the complete solution of a problem involves three stages. In the model development stage we enter all of the inputs, trial values for the changing cells,

---

[5]Our blue/red/gray color scheme shows up very effectively on a color monitor. For users of previous editions who are used to colored *borders*, we find in Excel 2007 that it is easier to color the cells rather than put borders around them. (Our previous custom of inserting our own toolbar with our favorite macros is possible, but not easy, in Excel 2007.)

and formulas relating these in a spreadsheet. This stage is the most crucial because it is here that all of the "ingredients" of the model are included and related appropriately. In particular, the spreadsheet *must* include a formula that relates the objective to the changing cells, either directly or indirectly, so that if the values in the changing cells vary, the objective value varies accordingly. Similarly, the spreadsheet must include formulas for the various constraints (usually their left-hand sides) that are related directly or indirectly to the changing cells.

After the model is developed, we can proceed to the second stage—invoking Solver. At this point, we formally designate the objective cell, the changing cells, the constraints, and selected options, and we tell Solver to find the *optimal* solution. If the first stage has been done correctly, the second stage is usually very straightforward.

The third stage is sensitivity analysis. Here we see how the optimal solution changes (if at all) as we vary selected inputs. This often gives us important insights about how the model works.

We now carry out this procedure for the dessert problem in Example 14.1.

DEVELOPING THE SPREADSHEET MODEL

The spreadsheet model appears in Figure 14.2. (See the file **Dessert Planning.xlsx**.) To develop this model, use the following steps.

Figure 14.2

Spreadsheet Model for Dessert Problem

	A	B	C	D	E	F	G	H
1	Planning desserts					Range names used		
2						Grams_consumed	=Model!$B$25	
3	Ingredients (per serving) of each dessert					Grams_required	=Model!$D$25	
4		Snack bar	Ice cream			Ingredients_allowed	=Model!$D$20:$D$21	
5	Calories	120	160			Ingredients_consumed	=Model!$B$20:$B$21	
6	Fat (grams)	5	10			Servings_per_day	=Model!$B$16:$C$16	
7						Total_taste_index	=Model!$B$27	
8	Grams per serving	37	65					
9								
10	Taste index of each dessert (on a 100-point scale, per gram)							
11		Snack bar	Ice cream					
12		85	95					
13								
14	Dessert plan							
15		Snack bar	Ice cream					
16	Servings per day	1.5	2.0					
17								
18	Constraints on calories and fat (per day)							
19		Ingredients consumed		Ingredients allowed				
20	Calories	500	<=	450				
21	Fat (grams)	27.5	<=	25				
22								
23	Constraint on total grams of dessert per day							
24		Grams consumed		Grams required				
25		185.5	>=	120				
26								
27	Total taste index	17067.5						

① **Inputs.** Enter all of the inputs from the statement of the problem in the shaded cells as shown. Note that in later examples we often include a brief discussion on "Where Do the Numbers Come From?" For this problem it is easy to get the numbers. The inputs in rows 5, 6, and 8 are printed on the packages of most foods, and the other inputs are Maggie's preferences.

② **Range names.** Create the range names shown in columns F and G. Our convention is to enter "enough" range names but not to go overboard. Specifically, we enter enough range names so that the setup in the Solver dialog box, to be explained shortly, is entirely in terms of range names. Of course, you can add more range names if you like.

Excel Tip: *Here is a Shortcut for Creating Range Names*
Select a range such as A20:B21 that includes nice labels in column A and the cells you want to name in column B. Then from the Formulas ribbon, select Create from Selection and accept the default. You automatically get the labels in cells A20 and A21 as the range names for cells B20 and B21. This shortcut illustrates the usefulness of adding concise but informative labels next to ranges you want to name.

3 **Changing cells.** Enter any two values for the changing cells in the Dessert_plan range. *Any* trial values can be used initially; Solver eventually finds the *optimal* values. Note that the two values shown in Figure 14.2 cannot be optimal because they are not feasible—they contain more calories and fat than are allowed. However, we do not need to worry about satisfying constraints at this point; Solver takes care of this later on.

At this stage it is pointless to try to "outguess" the optimal solution. Any values in the changing cells will suffice.

4 **Ingredients consumed.** To operationalize the calorie and fat constraints, we must calculate the amounts consumed by the dessert plan. To do this, enter the formula

=SUMPRODUCT(B5:C5,Servings_per_day)

in cell B20 for calories and copy it to cell B21 for fat. This formula is a shortcut for the "written out" formula

=B5*B16+C5*C16

The "linear" in linear programming is all about sums of products. Therefore, the SUMPRODUCT function is natural and should be used whenever possible.

The SUMPRODUCT function is very useful in spreadsheet models, especially LP models, and we see it often. Here, it multiplies the amount of calories per serving by the number of servings for each dessert and then sums such products over the two desserts. When there are only two products in the sum, as in this example, the SUMPRODUCT formula is not really simpler to enter than the "written out" formula. However, imagine that there are 50 desserts. Then the SUMPRODUCT formula becomes *much* simpler to enter (and read). For this reason, we use it whenever possible. Note that each range in this function, B5:C5 and Servings_per_day, is a one-row, two-column range. It is important in the SUMPRODUCT function that the two ranges be exactly the same size and shape.

5 **Grams consumed.** Similarly, we must calculate the total number of grams of dessert consumed daily. To do this, enter the formula

=SUMPRODUCT(B8:C8,Servings_per_day)

in cell B25. Each product in this SUMPRODUCT is grams per serving times number of servings; hence, its units are grams.

6 **Total taste index.** To calculate the total taste index, enter the formula

=SUMPRODUCT(B12:C12,B8:C8,Servings_per_day)

Although the SUMPRODUCT function usually takes two range arguments, it can take three or more, provided they all have the same size and shape.

in cell B27. This formula shows that the SUMPRODUCT function can use three ranges (or more), provided that they are all exactly the same size and shape. Three are required here because we need to multiply taste points per gram times grams per serving times number of servings. Again, this formula is equivalent to the "written out" formula

=B12*B8*B16+C12*C8*C16

Experimenting with Possible Solutions

The next step is to specify the changing cells, the target cell, and the constraints in a Solver dialog box and then instruct Solver to find the optimal solution. However, before we do this, it is instructive to try a few guesses in the changing cells. There are two reasons for doing so. First, by entering different sets of values in the changing cells, you can confirm that the formulas in the other cells are working correctly. Second, this experimentation can help you to develop a better understanding of the model.

For example, Maggie prefers the taste of ice cream to snack bars, so you might guess that her dessert plan will consist of ice cream only. If so, she should consume as much ice cream as will fit into her constraints on calories and fat. You can check that this is 2.5 servings per day, as shown in Figure 14.3. With this plan, she could eat more calories, but she can't eat any more fat. Is this plan optimal? It turns out that it isn't, as we see shortly, but this fact is not obvious. By the way, if Maggie decided to go entirely with snack bars and no ice cream, you can check that she could then consume 3.75 servings, which would exhaust her calorie allowance, but not her fat allowance, and would provide a total taste index of 11,793.75. Because this is well less than the total taste index for the plan with ice cream only, it certainly cannot be optimal.

Figure 14.3

Best Plan with Ice Cream Only

	A	B	C	D	E	F	G	H
1	Planning desserts					Range names used		
2						Grams_consumed	=Model!$B$25	
3	Ingredients (per serving) of each dessert					Grams_required	=Model!$D$25	
4		Snack bar	Ice cream			Ingredients_allowed	=Model!$D$20:$D$21	
5	Calories	120	160			Ingredients_consumed	=Model!$B$20:$B$21	
6	Fat (grams)	5	10			Servings_per_day	=Model!$B$16:$C$16	
7						Total_taste_index	=Model!$B$27	
8	Grams per serving	37	65					
9								
10	Taste index of each dessert (on a 100-point scale, per gram)							
11		Snack bar	Ice cream					
12		85	95					
13								
14	Dessert plan							
15		Snack bar	Ice cream					
16	Servings per day	0	2.5					
17								
18	Constraints on calories and fat (per day)							
19		Ingredients consumed		Ingredients allowed				
20	Calories	400	<=	450				
21	Fat (grams)	25	<=	25				
22								
23	Constraint on total grams of dessert per day							
24		Grams consumed		Grams required				
25		162.5	>=	120				
26								
27	Total taste index	15437.5						

You can continue to try different values in the changing cells, attempting to get as large a total taste index as possible while staying within the constraints. Even for this small model with only two changing cells, it is not easy! You can only imagine how much more difficult it is when there are hundreds or even thousands of changing cells and many constraints. This is why we need software such as Excel's Solver. It uses a quick and efficient algorithm to search through all feasible solutions and eventually find the optimal solution. Fortunately, it is quite easy to use, as we now explain.

USING SOLVER

To invoke Excel's Solver, select Solver from the Data ribbon. (If there is no such item on your PC, see the appendix to this chapter.) The dialog box in Figure 14.4 appears. It has three important sections that you must fill in: the target cell, the changing cells, and the constraints. For the dessert problem, we can fill these in by typing cell references or we can point, click, and drag the appropriate ranges in the usual way. Better yet, if there are any named ranges, we can use these range names instead of cell addresses. In fact, for reasons of readability, our convention is to use only range names, not cell addresses, in this dialog box.

Figure 14.4

Solver Dialog Box
for Dessert Model

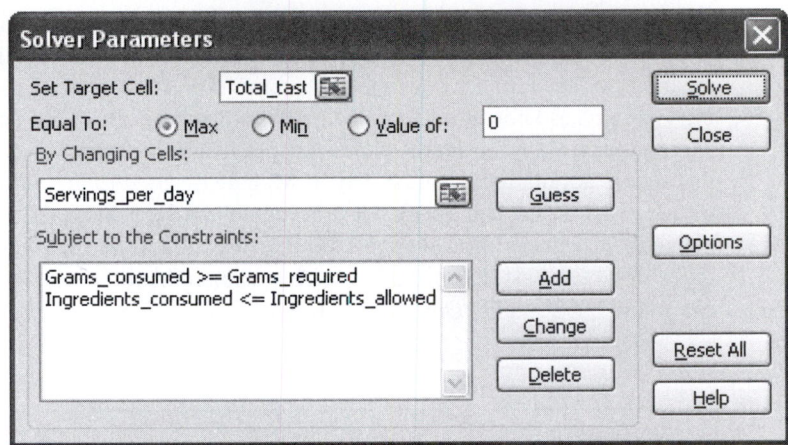

Excel Tip: *Range Names in Solver Dialog Box*
Our usual procedure is to use the mouse to select the relevant ranges for the Solver dialog box. Fortunately, if these ranges have already been named, then the range names will automatically replace the cell addresses.

1 **Objective.** Select the Total_taste_index cell as the target cell, and click on the Max option. (Actually, the default option is Max.)

2 **Changing cells.** Select the Servings_per_day range as the changing cells.

3 **Constraints.** Click on the Add button to bring up the dialog box in Figure 14.5. Here you specify a typical constraint by entering a cell reference or range name on the left, the type of constraint from the dropdown list in the middle, and a cell reference, range name, or numeric value on the right. Use this dialog box to enter the constraint

Ingredients_consumed<=Ingredients_allowed

Figure 14.5

Add Constraint
Dialog Box

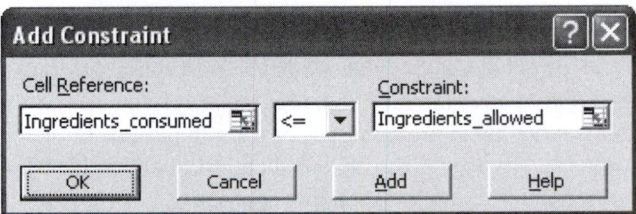

(*Note:* You can type these range names into the dialog box, or you can drag them in the usual way. If you drag them, the cell addresses eventually change into range names if range names exist.) Then click on the Add button and enter the constraint

Grams_consumed>=Grams_required

Then click on OK to get back to the Solver dialog box. The first constraint says to consume no more calories and fat than are allowed. The second constraint says to consume at least as many grams as are required.

Excel Tip: *Inequality and Equality Labels in Spreadsheet Models*

The <= signs in cells C20:C21 and the >= sign in cell C25 (see Figure 14.2 or Figure 14.3) are not a necessary part of the Excel model. They are entered simply as labels in the spreadsheet and do not substitute for entering the constraints in the Add Constraint dialog box. However, they help to document the model, so we include them in all of the examples. In fact, we try to plan our spreadsheet models so that the two sides of a constraint are in nearby cells, with "gutter" cells in between where we can attach a label like <=, >=, or =. This convention tends to make the resulting spreadsheet models much more readable.

4 **Nonnegativity.** Because negative quantities of dessert make no sense, we must tell Solver *explicitly* to make the changing cells nonnegative. To do this, click on the Options button in Figure 14.4 and check the Assume Non-Negative box in the resulting dialog box. (See Figure 14.6.) This automatically ensures that *all* changing cells are nonnegative.

Checking the Assume Non-Negative box ensures only that the changing cells, not any other cells, will be nonnegative.

Figure 14.6

Solver Options Dialog Box

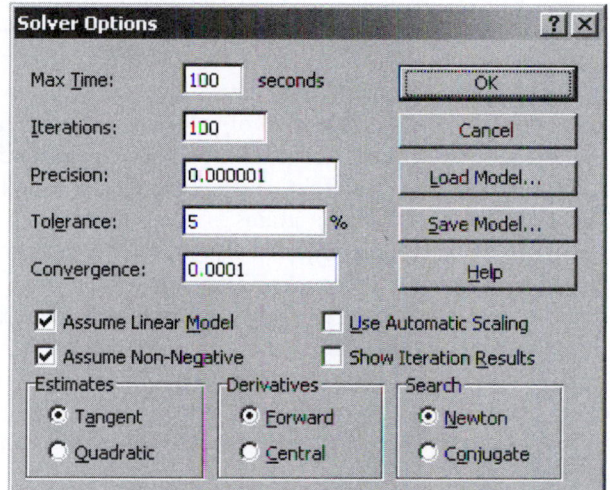

5 **Linear model.** There is one last step before clicking on the Solve button. As we stated previously, Solver uses one of several numerical algorithms to solve various types of models. The models discussed in this chapter are all *linear* models. (We discuss the properties of linear models shortly.) Linear models can be solved most efficiently by the simplex method. To instruct Solver to use this method, you must check the Assume Linear Model option in the Solver options dialog box shown in Figure 14.6.

6 **Optimize.** Click on the Solve button in the dialog box in Figure 14.4. At this point, Solver does its work. It searches through a number of possible solutions until it finds the optimal solution. (You can watch the progress on the lower left of the screen, although for small models the process is virtually instantaneous.) When it finishes, it displays the message shown in Figure 14.7. You can then instruct it to return the values in the changing cells to their original (probably nonoptimal) values or retain the optimal values found by Solver. In most cases you should choose the latter. For now, click on the OK button to keep the Solver solution. You should see the solution shown in Figure 14.8.

Solver Tip: *Messages from Solver*

Actually, the message in Figure 14.7 is the one we hope for. However, in some cases Solver is not able to find an optimal solution, in which case one of several other messages appears. We discuss some of these later in the chapter.

Figure 14.7

Solver Message That Optimal Solution Has Been Found

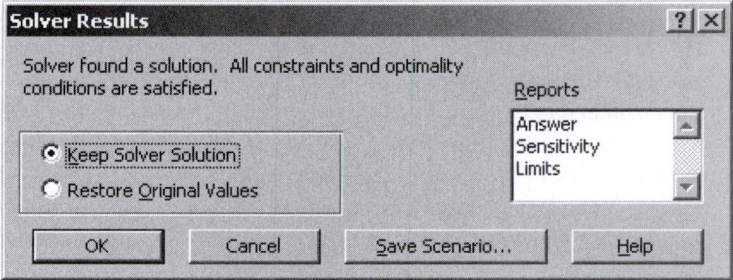

Discussion of the Solution

In reality, Maggie would probably vary this so that she averages these quantities over time.

This solution says that Maggie should consume 1.25 servings of snack bars and 1.875 servings of ice cream per day. This plan leaves no room for any more calories or fat, and it more than satisfies her requirement of 120 dessert grams per day. It provides a total taste index that is slightly more than the plan with ice cream only in Figure 14.3. In fact, we now know that no plan can provide a total taste index larger than this one—that is, without violating at least one of the constraints.

The solution in Figure 14.8 is typical of solutions to optimization models in the following sense. Of all the inequality constraints, some are satisfied exactly and others are not. In this solution the calorie and fat constraints are met exactly. We say that they are **binding**. However, the constraint on grams is **nonbinding**. The number of grams consumed is *greater than* the number required. The difference is called **slack**.[6] You can think of the binding constraints as "bottlenecks." They are the constraints that prevent the objective from being improved. If it were not for constraints on calories and fat, Maggie could obtain an even higher total taste index.

> An inequality constraint is **binding** if the solution makes it an equality. Otherwise, it is **nonbinding**, and the positive difference between the two sides of the constraint is called the **slack**.

Figure 14.8

Optimal Solution for Dessert Model

	A	B	C	D	E	F	G	H
1	Planning desserts					Range names used		
2						Grams_consumed	=Model!$B$25	
3	Ingredients (per serving) of each dessert					Grams_required	=Model!$D$25	
4		Snack bar	Ice cream			Ingredients_allowed	=Model!$D$20:$D$21	
5	Calories	120	160			Ingredients_consumed	=Model!$B$20:$B$21	
6	Fat (grams)	5	10			Servings_per_day	=Model!$B$16:$C$16	
7						Total_taste_index	=Model!$B$27	
8	Grams per serving	37	65					
9								
10	Taste index of each dessert (on a 100-point scale, per gram)							
11		Snack bar	Ice cream					
12		85	95					
13								
14	Dessert plan							
15		Snack bar	Ice cream					
16	Servings per day	1.25	1.875					
17								
18	Constraints on calories and fat (per day)							
19		Ingredients consumed		Ingredients allowed				
20	Calories	450	<=	450				
21	Fat (grams)	25	<=	25				
22								
23	Constraint on total grams of dessert per day							
24		Grams consumed		Grams required				
25		168.125	>=	120				
26								
27	Total taste index	15509.375						

[6]Some analysts use the term *slack* only for ≤ constraints and use the term **surplus** for ≥ constraints. We refer to each of these as *slack*—the absolute difference between the two sides of the constraint.

14.4 SENSITIVITY ANALYSIS

Indeed, many analysts view the "finished" model as a starting point for all sorts of what-if questions. We agree!

Now that we have solved Maggie's dessert problem, it might appear that we are finished. But in real LP applications the solution to a *single* model is hardly ever the end of the analysis. It is almost always useful to perform a sensitivity analysis to see how (or if) the optimal solution changes as we change one or more inputs. We illustrate systematic ways of doing so in this section. Actually, we discuss two approaches. The first uses an optional sensitivity report that Solver offers. The second uses an add-in called SolverTable that we have developed.

Solver's Sensitivity Report

When you run Solver, the dialog box in Figure 14.7 offers you the option to obtain a sensitivity report.[7] This report is based on a well-established theory of sensitivity analysis in optimization models, especially LP models. This theory was developed around algebraic models that are arranged in a "standardized" format. Essentially, all such algebraic models look alike, so the same type of sensitivity report applies to all of them. Specifically, they have an objective function of the form $c_1x_1 + \cdots + c_nx_n$, where n is the number of decision variables, the c's are constants, and the x's are the decision variables, and each constraint can be put in the form $a_1x_1 + \cdots + a_nx_n \leq b$, $a_1x_1 + \cdots + a_nx_n \geq b$, or $a_1x_1 + \cdots + a_nx_n = b$, where the a's and b's are constants. Solver's sensitivity report performs two types of sensitivity analysis: (1) on the coefficients of the objective, the c's, and (2) on the right-hand sides of the constraints, the b's.

We illustrate the typical analysis by looking at the sensitivity report for Maggie's dessert planning model in Example 14.1. For convenience, we repeat the algebraic model here, and we repeat the spreadsheet model in Figure 14.9.

$$\text{Maximize } 37(85)x_1 + 65(95)x_2$$

subject to:

$$120x_1 + 160x_2 \leq 450$$

$$5x_1 + 10x_2 \leq 25$$

$$37x_1 + 65x_2 \geq 120$$

$$x_1, x_2 \geq 0$$

This time, when we run Solver, we ask for a sensitivity report in Solver's final dialog box. (See Figure 14.7.) This creates the sensitivity report on a new worksheet, as shown in Figure 14.10.[8] It contains two sections. The top section is for sensitivity to changes in the two coefficients, $37(85) = 3145$ and $65(95) = 6175$, of the decision variables in the objective function. Each row in this section indicates how the optimal solution changes if we change one of these coefficients. The bottom section is for the sensitivity to changes in the right-hand sides, 450, 25, and 120, of the constraints. Each row of this section indicates how the optimal solution changes if we change one of these right-hand sides.

---

[7]It also offers Answer and Limits reports. We don't find these particularly useful, and we do not discuss them here.

[8]If your table looks different from ours, make sure you have checked Assume Linear Model. Otherwise, Solver uses a nonlinear algorithm and produces a different type of sensitivity report. Also, we should mention that we have gotten error messages when we have tried to create these sensitivity reports in Excel 2007. Frontline Systems confirms that Microsoft "broke" these reports with Excel 2007 and that a fix is being sought.

Figure 14.9

Dessert Model with Optimal Solution

	A	B	C	D	E	F	G	H
1	Planning desserts					Range names used		
2						Grams_consumed	=Model!$B$25	
3	Ingredients (per serving) of each dessert					Grams_required	=Model!$D$25	
4		Snack bar	Ice cream			Ingredients_allowed	=Model!$D$20:$D$21	
5	Calories	120	160			Ingredients_consumed	=Model!$B$20:$B$21	
6	Fat (grams)	5	10			Servings_per_day	=Model!$B$16:$C$16	
7						Total_taste_index	=Model!$B$27	
8	Grams per serving	37	65					
9								
10	Taste index of each dessert (on a 100-point scale, per gram)							
11		Snack bar	Ice cream					
12		85	95					
13								
14	Dessert plan							
15		Snack bar	Ice cream					
16	Servings per day	1.25	1.875					
17								
18	Constraints on calories and fat (per day)							
19		Ingredients consumed		Ingredients allowed				
20	Calories	450	<=	450				
21	Fat (grams)	25	<=	25				
22								
23	Constraint on total grams of dessert per day							
24		Grams consumed		Grams required				
25		168.125	>=	120				
26								
27	Total taste index	15509.375						

Figure 14.10

Solver's Sensitivity Report for Dessert Model

	A B	C	D	E	F	G	H
6	Adjustable Cells						
7			Final	Reduced	Objective	Allowable	Allowable
8	Cell	Name	Value	Cost	Coefficient	Increase	Decrease
9	$B$16	Servings per day Snack bar	1.25	0	3145	1486.25	57.50
10	$C$16	Servings per day Ice cream	1.875	0.000	6175	115	1981.67
11							
12	Constraints						
13			Final	Shadow	Constraint	Allowable	Allowable
14	Cell	Name	Value	Price	R.H. Side	Increase	Decrease
15	$B$20	Calories Ingredients consumed	450	1.4375	450	150	50
16	$B$21	Fat (grams) Ingredients consumed	25	594.5	25	3.125	6.25
17	$B$25	Grams_consumed	168.125	0	120	48.125	1E+30

Now let's look at the specific numbers and their interpretation. In the first row of the top section, the *allowable decrease* and *allowable increase* indicate how much the coefficient of snack bars in the objective, currently 3145, could change before the optimal dessert plan would change. If the coefficient of snack bars stays within this allowable range, the optimal dessert plan—the values in the changing cells—does not change at all. However, outside of these limits the optimal mix between snack bars and ice cream might change.

To see what this implies, change the value in cell B12 from 85 to 84. Then the coefficient of snack bars decreases by 37, from 37(85) to 37(84). This change is within the allowable decrease of 57.5. If you rerun Solver, you will obtain the *same* values in the changing cells, although the objective value will decrease. Next, change the value in cell B12 to 83. This time, the coefficient of snack bars decreases by 74 from its original value, from 37(85) to 37(83). This change is outside the allowable decrease, so the solution might change. If you rerun Solver, you will indeed see a change—*no* snack bars are now in the optimal solution.

The *reduced costs* in the second column indicate, in general, how much the objective coefficient of a decision variable that is currently 0—that is, not in the optimal solution—must change before that variable becomes positive. These reduced costs are always 0 if the corresponding decision variables are already positive, as they are in the original example. However, when we change the value in cell B12 to 83, as above, and rerun Solver, snack bars drop out of the optimal solution, and the new sensitivity report appears as in Figure 14.11. Now the reduced cost is −16.5. This implies that the coefficient of snack bars must be increased by 16.5 before snack bars enter the optimal mix.

Figure 14.11

Sensitivity Table for
Revised Model

	A	B	C	D	E	F	G	H
6		Adjustable Cells						
7				Final	Reduced	Objective	Allowable	Allowable
8		Cell	Name	Value	Cost	Coefficient	Increase	Decrease
9		$B$16	Servings per day Snack bar	0	-16.5	3071	16.5	1E+30
10		$C$16	Servings per day Ice cream	2.500	0.000	6175	1E+30	33.00
11								
12		Constraints						
13				Final	Shadow	Constraint	Allowable	Allowable
14		Cell	Name	Value	Price	R.H. Side	Increase	Decrease
15		$B$20	Calories Ingredients consumed	400	0	450	1E+30	50
16		$B$21	Fat (grams) Ingredients consumed	25	617.5	25	3.125	6.54
17		$B$25	Grams_consumed	162.5	0	120	42.5	1E+30

The **reduced cost** for any decision variable not currently in the optimal solution indicates how much better that coefficient must be before that variable enters at a positive level. The reduced cost for any variable already in the optimal solution is automatically 0.[9]

We now turn to the bottom section of the report in Figure 14.10. Each row in this section corresponds to a constraint. To have this part of the report make economic sense, the model should be developed as we have done here, where the right-hand side of each constraint is a numeric constant (not a formula). For example, the right-hand side of the calories constraint is 450, the maximum allowable calories. Then the report indicates how much these right-hand side constants can change before the optimal solution changes. To understand this more fully, we need the concept of shadow prices. A **shadow price** indicates the amount of change in the objective when a right-hand-side constant changes.

The term **shadow price** is an economic term. It indicates the change in the optimal value of the objective when the right-hand side of some constraint changes by a unit amount.

The shadow prices are reported for each constraint. For example, the shadow price for the calorie constraint is 1.4375. This means that if the right-hand side of the calorie constraint increases by 1 calorie, from 450 to 451, the optimal value of the objective increases by 1.4375 units. It works in the other direction as well. If the right-hand side of the calorie constraint *decreases* by 1 calorie, from 450 to 449, the optimal value of the objective decreases by 1.4375 units. However, as we continue to increase or decrease the right-hand side, this 1.4375 change in the objective might not continue. This is where the reported allowable decrease and allowable increase are relevant. As long as the right-hand side increases or decreases within its allowable limits, the same shadow price of 1.4375 still applies. Beyond these limits, however, a different shadow price probably applies.

You can prove this for yourself. First, increase the right-hand side of the calorie constraint by 150, from 450 to 600, and rerun Solver. You will see that the objective indeed increases by 1.4375(150), from 15,509.375 to 15,725. Now increase this right-hand side from 600 to 601 and rerun Solver. You will observe that the objective doesn't increase at all. This means that the shadow price beyond 600 is *less than* 1.4375; in fact, it is 0. This is

[9]As we see in Example 14.2, this is not quite true. If there are upper-bound constraints on certain decision variables, the reduced costs for these variables have a slightly different interpretation.

typical. When a right-hand side is increases beyond its allowable increase, the new shadow price is typically less than the original shadow price (although it doesn't always fall to 0, as in this example).

The idea is that a constraint "costs us" by keeping the objective from being better than we would like. A shadow price indicates how much we would be willing to pay (in units of the objective function) to "relax" a constraint. In this example, we would be willing to pay 1.4375 taste index units to increase the right-hand side of the calorie constraint by 1 calorie. This is because such a change would increase the objective by 1.4375 units. But beyond a certain point—150 calories, in this example—further relaxation of the calorie constraint does us no good, and we are not willing to pay for any further increases.

The constraint on grams consumed is slightly different. It has a shadow price of 0. This always occurs in a nonbinding constraint, which makes sense. If we change the right-hand side of this constraint from 120 to 121, nothing at all happens to the optimal dessert plan and its objective value; there is just 1 gram less slack in this constraint. However, the allowable increase of 48.125 indicates that something *does* change when the right-hand side reaches 168.125. At this point, the constraint becomes binding—the grams consumed equals the grams required—and beyond this, the optimal dessert plan starts to change. By the way, the allowable decrease for this constraint, shown as $1 + E30$, means that it is essentially infinite. We can decrease the right-hand side of this constraint below 120 as much as we like, and absolutely nothing changes in the optimal solution.

The SolverTable Add-In

Solver's sensitivity report is almost impossible to unravel for some models. In these cases SolverTable is preferable because of its easily interpreted results.

The reason we can interpret Solver's sensitivity report for the dessert model in a fairly natural way is that our spreadsheet model is almost a direct translation of a standard algebraic model. Unfortunately, given the flexibility of spreadsheets, this is not always the case. We have seen many perfectly good spreadsheet models—and have developed many ourselves—that are structured quite differently from their standard algebraic-model counterparts. In these cases, we have found Solver's sensitivity report to be more confusing than useful. Therefore, we developed an Excel add-in called SolverTable. SolverTable allows us to ask sensitivity questions about any of the input variables, not just coefficients of the objective and right-hand sides, and it provides straightforward answers.

The SolverTable add-in is contained on the CD that comes with this book.[10] To install it, simply run the Setup program on this CD-ROM and make sure the SolverTable option is selected. You can then check that it is installed by clicking on the Office button, selecting Excel Options, selecting Add-Ins, and clicking on Go. There should be a SolverTable item in the resulting list of add-ins. To actually add SolverTable—that is, to load it into memory—just check the SolverTable box in this list. To unload it from memory, just uncheck the box.

The SolverTable add-in was developed to mimic Excel's built-in Data Table feature. Recall that data tables allow you to vary one or two inputs in a spreadsheet model and see instantaneously how selected outputs change. SolverTable is similar except that it runs Solver for every new input (or pair of inputs). There are two ways it can be used.

1. **One-way table.** A one-way table means that there is a *single* input cell and *any number* of output cells. That is, there can be a single output cell or multiple output cells.

2. **Two-way table.** A two-way table means that there are *two* input cells and one or more outputs. (You might recall that an Excel two-way data table allows only *one* output. The SolverTable add-in allows more than one. It creates a separate table for each output as a function of the two inputs.)

[10]It is also on the authors' Web site at http://www.kelley.iu.edu/albrightbooks under Free Downloads. This Web site will contain any possible updates to SolverTable.

We illustrate some of the possibilities for the dessert example. Specifically, we check how sensitive the optimal dessert plan and total taste index are to (1) changes in the number of calories per serving of snack bars and (2) the number of daily dessert calories allowed. Then we check how sensitive the optimal objective value is to simultaneous changes in the taste indexes of snack bars and ice cream.

We assume that the dessert model has been formulated and optimized, as shown in Figure 14.8, and that the SolverTable add-in has been loaded. Then the solution to question 1 is shown in Figure 14.12. To obtain this output (the part in the range A30:D39), we select Run SolverTable from the SolverTable dropdown on the Add-Ins ribbon, select a one-way table in the first dialog box, and fill in the second dialog box as shown in Figure 14.13. (Note that ranges can be entered as cell addresses or range names. Also, multiple ranges in the Outputs box should be separated by commas.)

We chose the input range from 60 to 140 in increments of 10 fairly arbitrarily. You can choose any desired range of input values.

Figure 14.12

Sensitivity to Calories per Serving of Snack Bars

	A	B	C	D
29	Sensitivity to calories per serving of snack bars			
30		$B$16	$C$16	$B$27
31	60	5	0.000	15725
32	70	5	0.000	15725
33	80	5	0.000	15725
34	90	5	0.000	15725
35	100	2.5	1.250	15581.25
36	110	1.667	1.667	15533.333
37	120	1.25	1.875	15509.375
38	130	1	2.000	15495
39	140	0.833	2.083	15485.417

Figure 14.13

SolverTable Dialog Box for One-Way Table

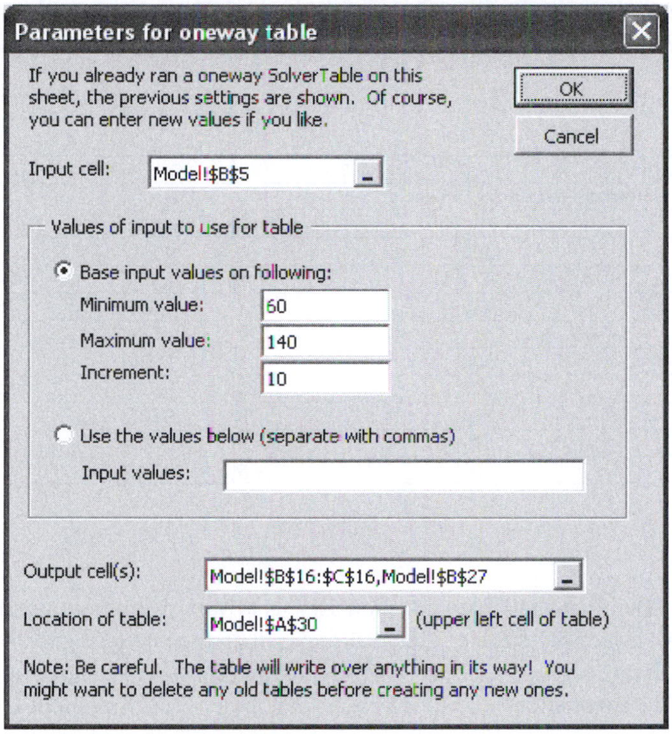

Parameters for oneway table

If you already ran a oneway SolverTable on this sheet, the previous settings are shown. Of course, you can enter new values if you like.

Input cell: Model!$B$5

Values of input to use for table

⦿ Base input values on following:
Minimum value: 60
Maximum value: 140
Increment: 10

◯ Use the values below (separate with commas)
Input values:

Output cell(s): Model!$B$16:$C$16,Model!$B$27

Location of table: Model!$A$30 (upper left cell of table)

Note: Be careful. The table will write over anything in its way! You might want to delete any old tables before creating any new ones.

OK   Cancel

Excel Tip: *Selecting Multiple Ranges*

If you need to select multiple output ranges, the trick is to keep your finger on the Ctrl key as you drag the ranges. This automatically enters the separating comma(s) for you. The same trick works for selecting multiple changing cell ranges in Solver's dialog box.

When you click on OK, Solver solves a separate optimization problem for each of the 9 rows of the table and then reports the requested outputs (servings consumed and total taste index) in the table. It can take a while, depending on the speed of your computer, but everything is automatic. However, if you want to update this table—by using new calorie values in column A, for example—you must repeat the procedure. SolverTable enters comments (indicated by the small red triangles) in several cells to help you interpret the output.

The outputs in this table show that as the calories per serving of snack bars increase, the optimal dessert plan is initially to eat snack bars only, and it stays this way for a while. But beyond 90 calories per serving, the optimal plan gradually uses fewer snack bars and starts using ice cream. Beyond some point—somewhere above 140 calories per serving—the optimal plan probably uses no snack bars at all. (This point could be found with another SolverTable run, using a different input range.) Also, note that as calories per serving increase beyond 90, the optimal total taste index in column D continually decreases. This makes sense. As one ingredient increases in calories, the total calorie limit dictates that not as much dessert can be eaten, so the total taste index decreases.

The answer to question 2 appears in Figure 14.14. It is formed through the same dialog box as in Figure 14.13, except that the input variable is now in cell D20, which we allow to vary from 400 to 600 calories in increments of 25 calories. Now we see that as the total calorie allowance increases, the optimal dessert plan uses more snack bars and less ice cream, and the total taste index increases. In fact, we calculate this latter increase in column E. (We do this manually, not with SolverTable. For example, the formula in cell E44 is =D44−D43.) We see that, at least for this input range, the objective increases by the *same* amount, 35.9375, for each 25-calorie increase in the daily calorie allowance. Alternatively, the *per unit* change, 1.4375 (=35.9375/25), is the same shadow price we saw previously. In this sense, SolverTable outputs often reinforce outputs from Solver's sensitivity report.

Figure 14.14

Sensitivity to Daily Calorie Allowance

	A	B	C	D	E
41	Sensitivity to calories allowed				
42			$B$16	$C$16	$B$27	Increase
43	400		0	2.500	15437.5	
44	425		0.625	2.187	15473.4375	35.9375
45	450		1.25	1.875	15509.375	35.9375
46	475		1.875	1.563	15545.3125	35.9375
47	500		2.5	1.250	15581.25	35.9375
48	525		3.125	0.938	15617.1875	35.9375
49	550		3.75	0.625	15653.125	35.9375
50	575		4.375	0.312	15689.0625	35.9375
51	600		5	0.000	15725	35.9375

The final sensitivity question asks us to vary two inputs simultaneously. This requires a two-way SolverTable. The resulting output appears in Figure 14.15 and is produced by the dialog settings in Figure 14.16. Here we specify two inputs and two input ranges, and we are again allowed to specify multiple output cells. An output table is generated for *each* of the output cells. For example, the top table in Figure 14.15 shows how the optimal servings of snack bars vary as the two taste index inputs vary. The results, especially in the two top tables, are probably not very surprising. When the taste index of either dessert increases, we tend to use more of it in the optimal dessert plan.

Figure 14.15

Sensitivity to Taste Indexes of Both Desserts

	G	H	I	J	K	L	M
29	Sensitivity to taste indexes of snack bars (along side) and ice cream (along top)						
30	$B$16	70	75	80	85	90	95
31	60	0	0	0	0	0	0
32	65	1.25	0	0	0	0	0
33	70	1.25	1.25	0	0	0	0
34	75	1.25	1.25	1.25	1.25	0	0
35	80	1.25	1.25	1.25	1.25	1.25	0
36	85	1.25	1.25	1.25	1.25	1.25	1.25
37	90	1.25	1.25	1.25	1.25	1.25	1.25
38	95	3.75	1.25	1.25	1.25	1.25	1.25
39							
40	$C$16	70	75	80	85	90	95
41	60	2.500	2.500	2.500	2.500	2.500	2.500
42	65	1.875	2.500	2.500	2.500	2.500	2.500
43	70	1.875	1.875	2.500	2.500	2.500	2.500
44	75	1.875	1.875	1.875	1.875	2.500	2.500
45	80	1.875	1.875	1.875	1.875	1.875	2.500
46	85	1.875	1.875	1.875	1.875	1.875	1.875
47	90	1.875	1.875	1.875	1.875	1.875	1.875
48	95	0.000	1.875	1.875	1.875	1.875	1.875
49							
50	$B$27	70	75	80	85	90	95
51	60	11375	12187.5	13000	13812.5	14625	15437.5
52	65	11537.5	12187.5	13000	13812.5	14625	15437.5
53	70	11768.75	12378.12	13000	13812.5	14625	15437.5
54	75	12000	12609.38	13218.75	13828.12	14625	15437.5
55	80	12231.25	12840.63	13450	14059.38	14668.75	15437.5
56	85	12462.5	13071.88	13681.25	14290.63	14900	15509.37
57	90	12693.75	13303.13	13912.5	14521.88	15131.25	15740.63
58	95	13181.25	13534.38	14143.75	14753.13	15362.5	15971.88

Figure 14.16   SolverTable Dialog Box for Two-Way Table

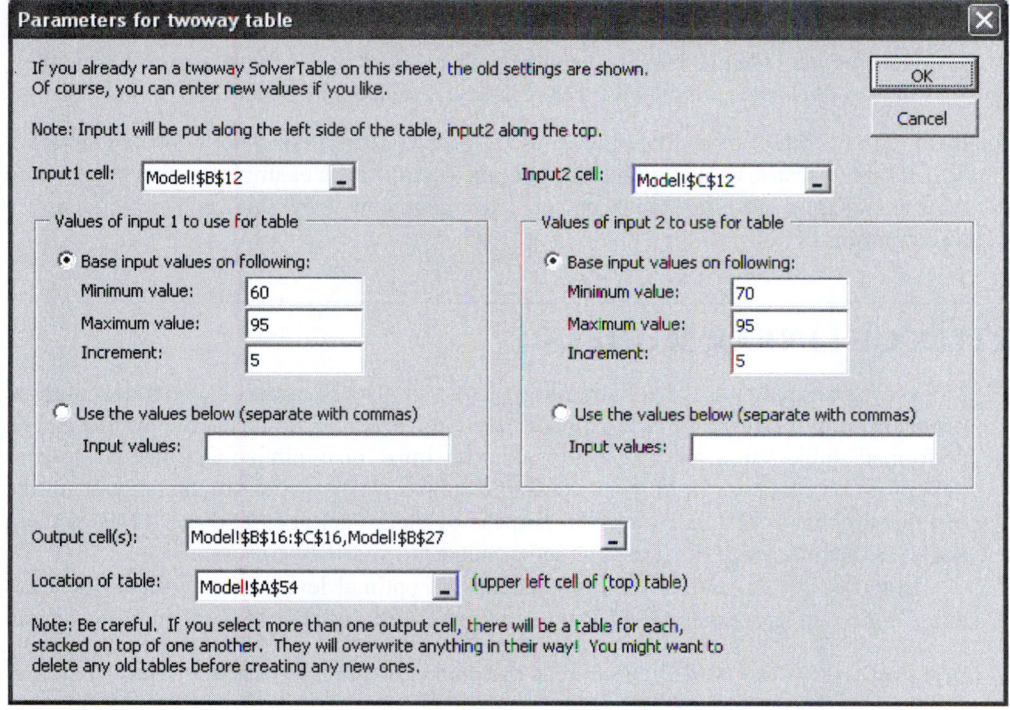

It is always possible to run a sensitivity analysis by changing inputs manually in the spreadsheet model and rerunning Solver. The advantages of the SolverTable add-in, however, are that it enables you to perform a *systematic* sensitivity analysis for any selected inputs and outputs, and it keeps track of the results in a table. We see other applications of this useful add-in later in this chapter and in the next chapter.

Comparison of Solver's Sensitivity Report and SolverTable

Sensitivity analysis in optimization models is extremely important, so it is important that you understand the pros and cons of the two tools we have discussed in this section. Here are some points to keep in mind.

- Solver's sensitivity report focuses only on the coefficients of the objective and the right-hand sides of the constraints. SolverTable allows you to vary *any* of the inputs.

- Solver's sensitivity report provides very useful information through its reduced costs, shadow prices, and allowable increases and decreases. This same information can be obtained with SolverTable, but it requires a bit more work and some experimentation with the appropriate input ranges.

- Solver's sensitivity report is based on changing only one objective coefficient or one right-hand side at a time. This one-at-a-time restriction prevents us from answering certain questions directly. SolverTable is much more flexible in this respect.

- Solver's sensitivity report is based on a well-established mathematical theory of sensitivity analysis in linear programming. If you lack this mathematical background—as many users do—the outputs can be difficult to understand, especially for somewhat "nonstandard" spreadsheet formulations. In contrast, SolverTable's outputs are straightforward. You vary one or two inputs and see directly how the optimal solution changes.

- Solver's sensitivity report is not even available for integer-constrained models, and its interpretation for nonlinear models is more difficult than for linear models. SolverTable's outputs have the same interpretation for any type of optimization model.

- Solver's sensitivity report comes with Excel. SolverTable is a separate add-in that is not included with Excel—but it is included with this book and is freely available from the authors' Web site at http://www.kelley.iu.edu/albrightbooks under Free Downloads.

In summary, each of these tools can be used to answer certain questions. We tend to favor SolverTable because of its flexibility, but in the optimization examples in this chapter and the next chapter we illustrate both tools to show how they can each provide useful information.

14.5 PROPERTIES OF LINEAR MODELS

Linear programming is an important subset of a larger class of models called **mathematical programming models**.[11] All such models select the levels of various activities that can be performed, subject to a set of constraints, to maximize or minimize an objective such as total profit or total cost. In Maggie's dessert example, the activities are the amounts of the two desserts consumed daily, and the purpose of the model is to find the levels of these activities that maximize the total taste index subject to specified constraints.

In terms of this general setup—selecting the optimal levels of activities—there are three important properties that LP models possess that distinguish them from general

---

[11]The word *programming* in linear programming or mathematical programming has nothing to do with computer programming. It originated with the British term *programme*, which is essentially a plan or a schedule of operations.

mathematical programming models: **proportionality**, **additivity**, and **divisibility**. We discuss these properties briefly in this section.

Proportionality

Proportionality means that if the level of any activity is multiplied by a constant factor, then the contribution of this activity to the objective, or to any of the constraints in which the activity is involved, is multiplied by the same factor. For example, suppose that the consumption of snack bars is cut from its optimal value of 1.25 (see Figure 14.8) to 0.625—that is, it is multiplied by 0.5. Then the amounts of calories, fat, and grams contributed to the dessert plan by snack bars are all cut in half, and the total taste index contributed by snack bars is also cut in half.

Proportionality is probably a perfectly valid assumption in the dessert model, but it is often violated in certain types of models. For example, in various *blending* models used by petroleum companies, chemical outputs vary in a nonlinear manner as chemical inputs are varied. If a chemical input is doubled, say, the resulting chemical output is not necessarily doubled. This type of behavior violates the proportionality property, and it takes us into the realm of *nonlinear* optimization, which we discuss briefly in the next chapter.

Additivity

The additivity property implies that the sum of the contributions from the various activities to a particular constraint equals the total contribution to that constraint. For example, if the two types of dessert contribute, respectively, 180 and 320 calories (as in Figure 14.2), then the total number of calories in the plan is the *sum* of these amounts, 500 calories. Similarly, the additivity property applies to the objective. That is, the value of the objective is the *sum* of the contributions from the various activities. The additivity property implies that the contribution of any decision variable to the objective or to any constraint is *independent* of the levels of the other decision variables.

Divisibility

The divisibility property simply means that we allow both integer and noninteger levels of the activities. In the dessert example, it turned out that the optimal values in the changing cells are nonintegers: 1.25 and 1.875. Because of the divisibility property, we allow such values in LP models. In some problems, however, they do not make physical sense. For example, if we are deciding how many refrigerators to produce, it makes no sense to make 47.53 refrigerators. If we want the levels of some activities to be integer values, there are two possible approaches: (1) We can solve the LP model without integer constraints, and if the solution turns out to have noninteger values, we can attempt to round them to integer values; or (2) we can explicitly constrain certain changing cells to contain integer values. The latter approach, however, takes us into the realm of *integer programming*, which we study briefly in the next chapter.

Discussion of Linear Properties

The previous discussion of these three properties, especially proportionality and additivity, is a bit abstract. How can you recognize whether a model satisfies proportionality and additivity? This is easy if the model is described algebraically. In this case the objective must be of the form

$$a_1 x_1 + a_2 x_2 + \cdots + a_n x_n$$

where n is the number of decision variables, the a's are constants, and the x's are decision variables. This expression is called a *linear combination* of the x's. Also, each constraint must be equivalent to a form where the left-hand side is a linear combination of the x's and the right-hand side is a constant. For example, the following is a typical linear constraint:

$$3x_1 + 7x_2 - 2x_3 \leq 50$$

It is not quite so easy to recognize proportionality and additivity—or the lack of them—in a spreadsheet model because the logic of the model can be embedded in a series of cell formulas. However, the ideas are the same. First, the target cell must ultimately (possibly through a series of formulas in intervening cells) be a sum of products of constants and changing cells, where a "constant" is defined by the fact that it does not depend on changing cells. Second, each side of each constraint must ultimately be either a constant or a sum of products of constants and changing cells. Sometimes it is easier to recognize when a model is *not* linear. Two particular situations that lead to nonlinear models are when (1) there are products or quotients of expressions involving changing cells and (2) there are nonlinear functions, such as squares, square roots, or logarithms, of changing cells. These are typically easy to spot, and they guarantee that the model is nonlinear.

Real-life problems are almost never exactly linear. However, linear approximations often yield very useful results.

Whenever we model a real problem, we usually make some simplifying assumptions. This is certainly the case with LP models. The world is frequently *not* linear, which means that an entirely realistic model typically violates some or all of the three properties we just discussed. However, numerous successful applications of LP have demonstrated the usefulness of linear models, even if they are only *approximations* of reality. If we suspect that the violations are serious enough to invalidate a linear model, then we should use an integer or nonlinear model, as we illustrate in the next chapter.

In terms of Excel's Solver, if the model is linear—that is, if it satisfies the proportionality, additivity, and divisibility properties—then we should check the Assume Linear Model box that appears in the Solver Options dialog box. Then Solver uses the simplex method, a very efficient method for a linear model, to solve the problem. Actually, we can check the Assume Linear Model box even if the divisibility property is violated—that is, for linear models with integer-constrained variables—but Solver then uses a method other than the simplex method in its solution procedure.

Linear Models and Scaling[12]

In some cases you might be sure that a model is linear, but when you check the Assume Linear Model box and then solve, you get a Solver message that "the conditions for Assume Linear Model are not satisfied." This can indicate a logical error in your formulation, so that at least one of the proportionality, additivity, and divisibility conditions is indeed not satisfied. However, it can also indicate that Solver erroneously *thinks* the linearity conditions are not satisfied, which is typically due to roundoff error in its calculations—not any error on your part. If the latter occurs and you are convinced that the model is correct, you can try *not* checking the Assume Linear Model box to see whether that works. If it does not, you should consult your instructor. It is possible that the nonlinear algorithm employed by Solver when this box is not checked simply cannot find the solution to your problem.

In any case, it always helps to have a *well-scaled* model. In a well-scaled model, all of the numbers are roughly the same magnitude. If the model contains some very large numbers—100,000 or more, say—and some very small numbers—0.001 or less, say—it is *poorly scaled*

---

[12]This section might seem overly technical. However, when you develop a model that you are sure is linear, and Solver then tells you it doesn't satisfy the linear conditions, you will appreciate this section.

for the methods used by Solver, and roundoff error is far more likely to be an issue, not only in Solver's test for linearity conditions but in all of its algorithms.

You can lessen the chance of getting an incorrect "Conditions for Assume Linear Model are not satisfied" message by changing Solver's Precision setting.

If you believe your model is poorly scaled, there are three possible remedies. The first is to check the Use Automatic Scaling box in the Solver Options dialog box (see Figure 14.6). This might help and it might not; we have had mixed success. (Frontline Systems, the company that developed Solver, has told us that the only drawback to checking this box is that the solution procedure can take more time.) The second option is to redefine the units in which the various quantities are defined. For example, if we had originally defined our changing cells in the dessert model as the number of *grams* consumed, we might decide later to rescale to the number of *servings* consumed. (In fact, this is partly why we chose number of *servings* in the first place, although scaling doesn't really cause any difficulties in this small problem.) Finally, you can change the Precision setting in Solver's Options dialog box (see Figure 14.6) to a larger number, such 0.00001 or 0.0001.

14.6 INFEASIBILITY AND UNBOUNDEDNESS

In this section we discuss two of the things that can go wrong when we invoke Solver. Both of these might indicate that there is a mistake in the model. Therefore, because mistakes are common in LP models, you should be aware of the error messages you might encounter.

Infeasibility

The first problem is infeasibility. Recall that a solution is *feasible* if it satisfies all of the constraints. Among all of the feasible solutions, we are looking for the one that optimizes the objective. However, it is possible that there are no feasible solutions to the model. There are generally two reasons for this: (1) There is a mistake in the model (an input was entered incorrectly, such as a $\geq$ instead of a $\leq$) or (2) the problem has been so constrained that there are no solutions left! In the former case, a careful check of the model should find the error. In the latter case, the analyst might need to change, or even eliminate, some of the constraints.

A perfectly reasonable model can have no feasible solutions because of too many constraints.

To show how an infeasible problem could occur, suppose in Maggie's dessert problem that we change the required daily grams of dessert from 120 to 200 (and leave everything else unchanged). If Solver is then used, the message in Figure 14.17 appears, indicating that Solver cannot find a feasible solution. The reason is clear: There is no way, given the constraints on daily allowances of calories and fat, that Maggie can find a dessert plan with at least 200 grams. Her only choice is to relax at least one of the constraints: increase the daily allowances of calories and/or fat, or decrease the required daily grams of dessert. In general, there is no foolproof way to find the problem when a "no feasible solution" message appears. Careful checking and rethinking are required.

Figure 14.17

Solver Dialog Box Indicating No Feasible Solution

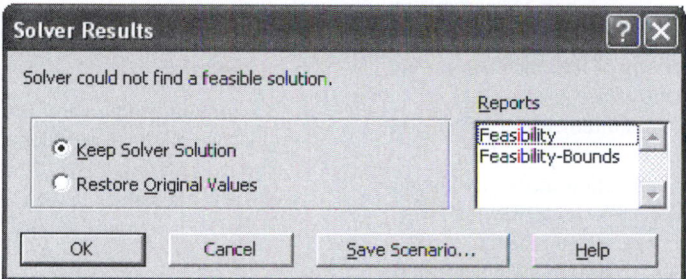

Unboundedness

A second type of problem is **unboundedness**. In this case, the model has been formulated in such a way that the objective is unbounded—that is, it can be made as large (or as small, for minimization problems) as we like. If this occurs, we have probably entered a wrong input or forgotten some constraints. To see how this could occur in the dessert problem, suppose that we enter daily allowance constraints on calories and fat with ≥ instead of ≤. Now there is no upper bound on how much of each dessert Maggie can consume (at least not in the model!). If we make this change in the model and then use Solver, the message in Figure 14.18 appears, stating that the target cell does not converge. In other words, the total taste index can grow without bound.

Figure 14.18

Solver Dialog Box Indicating an Unbounded Solution

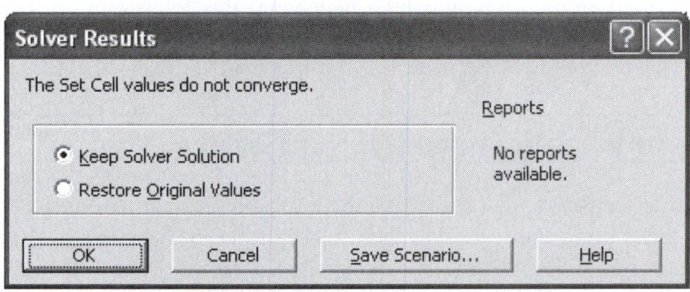

Comparison of Infeasibility and Unboundedness

Except in very rare situations, if Solver informs you that your model is unbounded you have made an error.

Infeasibility and unboundedness are quite different in a practical sense. It is quite possible for a reasonable model to have no feasible solutions. For example, the marketing department might impose several constraints, the production department might add some more, the engineering department might add even more, and so on. Together, they might constrain the problem so much that there are no feasible solutions left. The only way out is to change or eliminate some of the constraints. An unboundedness problem is quite different. There is no way a realistic model can have an unbounded solution. If you get the message shown in Figure 14.18, then you must have made a mistake: You entered an input incorrectly, you omitted one or more constraints, or there is a logical error in your model.

PROBLEMS

Level A

1. Other sensitivity analyses besides those discussed could be performed on Maggie's dessert model. Use SolverTable to perform each of the following. In each case keep track of the values in the changing cells and the target cell, and discuss your findings.
   a. Let the fat per serving of snack bars vary from 1 to 7 grams in increments of 1 gram.
   b. Let the calories per serving of ice cream vary from 140 to 200 in increments of 5.
   c. Let the total daily gram requirement vary from 100 to 200 in increments of 10.
   d. Let the calorie and fat daily allowances vary simultaneously, with the calorie allowance varying from 300 to 500 in increments of 50, and the fat allowance varying from 20 to 40 in increments of 5.

2. In Maggie's dessert problem, assume there is another possible dessert, in addition to snack bars and ice cream, that Maggie can consider: oatmeal raisin cookies. Each cookie, which is considered a "serving," weighs 43 grams and contains 140 calories and 6 grams of fat. Maggie likes these cookies almost as much as ice cream, and she gives each gram a taste index of 90. Modify the spreadsheet model to include this new dessert, and use Solver to find the optimal dessert plan.

3. Continuing the previous problem, perform a sensitivity analysis on the taste index of the cookies. Let this index vary from 60 to 100 in increments of 5, and keep track of the values in the changing cells and the target cell. Discuss your findings.

4. We stated that changing cells in the dessert model could be measured in servings or in grams. Modify the spreadsheet model so that they are measured in grams, and use Solver to find the optimal solution. Discuss how the solution to this modified model is different from the solution we found; discuss how they are the same.

5. Use the graphical solution of Maggie's dessert problem to determine all values of the right-hand side of the total daily gram requirement that make the model infeasible—that is, it has no feasible solutions.

6. There are 5 corner points in the feasible region for the dessert problem. We identified the coordinates of one of them: (1.25, 1.875). Identify the coordinates of the others. If we vary the taste index values in row 12 of the spreadsheet model, is it possible for each of these corner points to become an optimal solution? Why or why not?

Level B

7. The graphical solution to the dessert problem indicates why the optimal solution contains both snack bars and ice cream: It is because the slope of the total taste index line is *between* the slopes of the two constraint lines for calories and fat. With this in mind, consider changes in the taste index of snack bars, which is currently 85. How large would this have to be for Maggie to consume all snack bars and no ice cream? How small would it have to be for Maggie to consume all ice cream and no snack bars? Answer in terms of slopes and which corner points would become optimal.

8. The SolverTable add-in can be used for "less obvious" sensitivity analyses. Suppose in the dessert model that we want to vary both of the calories per serving values in row 5, but we want them to stay in the same ratio, 4 to 3. We want calories per serving of snack bars to vary from 100 to 140 in increments of 5, and we want to keep track of the values in the changing cells and the target cell. Modify the model slightly so that this analysis can be performed with a *one-way* SolverTable.

9. Consider the graphical solution to the dessert problem. Now imagine that another constraint—*any* constraint—is added. Which of the following three things are possible: (1) feasible region shrinks; (2) feasible region stays the same; (3) feasible region expands? Which of the following three things are possible: (1) optimal value in target cell decreases; (2) optimal value in target cell stays the same; (3) optimal value in target cell increases? Explain your answers. Do they hold just for this particular model, or do they hold in general?

14.7 A PRODUCT MIX MODEL

The problem we examine in this section is often considered the prototype LP problem. The basic problem is to select the optimal mix of products to produce to maximize profit. We refer to it as a *product mix* problem.

EXAMPLE | 14.2 PRODUCING FRAMES AT MONET

The Monet Company produces four types of picture frames, which we label 1, 2, 3, and 4. The four types of frames differ with respect to size, shape, and materials used. Each type requires a certain amount of skilled labor, metal, and glass, as shown in Table 14.2. This table also lists the unit selling price Monet charges for each type of frame. During the coming week, Monet can purchase up to 4000 hours of skilled labor, 6000 ounces of metal, and 10,000 ounces of glass. The unit costs are $8.00 per labor hour, $0.50 per ounce of metal, and $0.75 per ounce of glass. Also, market constraints are such that it is impossible to sell more than 1000 type 1 frames, 2000 type 2 frames, 500 type 3 frames, and 1000 type 4 frames, and Monet does not want to keep any frames in inventory at the end of the week. What should the company do to maximize its profit for this week?

Objective   To use LP to find the mix of frames to produce that maximizes profit and stays within the resource availability and maximum sales constraints.

Table 14.2 Data for Monet Picture Frame Example

	Frame 1	Frame 2	Frame 3	Frame 4
Skilled labor	2	1	3	2
Metal	4	2	1	2
Glass	6	2	1	2
Selling price	$28.50	$12.50	$29.25	$21.50

WHERE DO THE NUMBERS COME FROM?

Textbooks typically state a problem, including a number of input values, and proceed directly to a solution—without saying where these input values might come from. However, finding the correct input values can sometimes be the most difficult step in a real-world situation. (Recall that finding the necessary data was step 2 of the overall modeling process, as discussed in Chapter 1.) There are a variety of inputs in Monet's problem, some easy to find and others more difficult. Here are some ideas on how they might be obtained.

- The unit costs in cells B4:B6 should be easy to obtain. (See Figure 14.19.) These are the going rates for these resources. We might mention, however, that the $8 per hour labor rate is probably a regular-time rate. If Monet wants to consider overtime hours, then the overtime rate (and labor hour availability during overtime) would be necessary, and the model would need to be modified.
- The resource usages in the range B9:E11, often called *technological coefficients*, should be available from the production department. These people know how much of each resource it takes to make the various types of frames.
- The unit selling prices in row 12 have actually been *chosen* by Monet's management, probably in response to market pressures and the company's own costs. In reality, they would be chosen based on production costs and market pressures.
- The maximum sales values in row 18 are probably forecasts from the marketing department. These people have some sense of how much they can sell, based on current outstanding orders, historical data, and the unit prices they plan to charge.
- The labor hour availability in cell D21 is probably based on the current workforce size and possibly on new workers who could be hired in the short run. It is likely that the other resource availabilities in cells D22 and D23 are the amounts available from the regular suppliers, whereas any additional quantities would require prohibitively expensive expediting costs.

Solution

Table 14.3 lists the variables and constraints for this model. We must choose the number of frames of each type to produce, which cannot be larger than the maximum we can sell. This choice determines the amounts of resources used and all revenues and costs. We must also ensure that no more resources are used than are available.

Table 14.3 Variables and Constraints for Product Mix Model

Input variables	Unit costs of resources (labor, glass, metal), resources used per frame of each type, unit selling prices of frames, maximum sales of frames, availabilities of resources
Decision variables (changing cells)	Numbers of frames of various types to produce
Objective (target cell)	Profit
Other calculated variables	Amounts of resources used, revenues, costs
Constraints	Frames produced ≤ Maximum sales
	Amounts of resources used ≤ Amounts available

An Algebraic Model

To model this problem algebraically, we let x_1, x_2, x_3, and x_4 represent the numbers of frames of types 1, 2, 3, and 4 to produce. Next, we write total profit and the constraints in terms of the x's. Finally, because only nonnegative amounts can be produced, we add explicit constraints to ensure that the x's are nonnegative. The resulting algebraic model is as follows:

$$\text{Maximize } 6x_1 + 2x_2 + 4x_3 + 3x_4 \text{ (profit objective)}$$

subject to:

$$2x_1 + x_2 + 3x_3 + 2x_4 \le 4000 \text{ (labor constraint)}$$

$$4x_1 + 2x_2 + x_3 + 2x_4 \le 6000 \text{ (metal constraint)}$$

$$6x_1 + 2x_2 + x_3 + 2x_4 \le 10{,}000 \text{ (glass constraint)}$$

$$x_1 \le 1000 \text{ (frame 1 sales constraint)}$$

$$x_2 \le 2000 \text{ (frame 2 sales constraint)}$$

$$x_3 \le 500 \text{ (frame 3 sales constraint)}$$

$$x_4 \le 1000 \text{ (frame 4 sales constraint)}$$

$$x_1, x_2, x_3, x_4 \ge 0 \text{ (nonnegativity constraints)}$$

To understand this model, consider the profit objective first. The profit from x_1 frames of type 1 is $6x_1$ because each frame contributes \$6 to profit. This \$6 is calculated as the unit selling price minus the cost of the inputs that go into a single type 1 frame:

$$\text{Unit profit for type 1 frame} = 28.50 - [2(8.00) + 4(0.50) + 6(0.75)] = \$6$$

Profits for the other three types of frames are obtained similarly. Their unit profits are \$2.00, \$4.00, and \$3.00, respectively. Then the total profit is the sum of the profits from the four products.

Next, consider the skilled labor constraint. The right-hand side, 4000, is the number of hours available. On the left-hand side, each type 1 frame uses 2 hours of labor, so x_1 units require $2x_1$ hours of labor. Similar statements hold for the other three products, and the total number of labor hours used is the sum over the four products. Then the constraint states that the number of hours used cannot exceed the number of hours available. The constraints for metal and glass are similar. Finally, the maximum sales constraints and the nonnegativity constraints put upper and lower limits on the quantities that can be produced.

Again, many LP software packages accept this algebraic model exactly as we have stated it. However, because we are focusing on spreadsheet models, we now turn to a spreadsheet model of Monet's problem.

Note how the expressions in the model are sums of terms like $2x_1$. This makes the model linear. It also accounts for the widespread use of the SUMPRODUCT function in spreadsheet LP models.

DEVELOPING THE SPREADSHEET MODEL

The spreadsheet in Figure 14.19 illustrates the solution procedure for Monet's product mix problem. (See the file **Product Mix.xlsx**.) The first stage is to develop the spreadsheet model step by step.

Figure 14.19

An Initial Solution
for Product Mix
Model

	A	B	C	D	E	F	G	H	I
1	Product mix model						Range names used		
2							Frames_produced	=Model!$B$16:$E$16	
3	Input data						Maximum_sales	=Model!$B$18:$E$18	
4	Hourly wage rate	$8.00					Profit	=Model!$F$32	
5	Cost per oz of metal	$0.50					Resources_available	=Model!$D$21:$D$23	
6	Cost per oz of glass	$0.75					Resources_used	=Model!$B$21:$B$23	
7									
8	Frame type	1	2	3	4				
9	Labor hours per frame	2	1	3	2				
10	Metal (oz.) per frame	4	2	1	2				
11	Glass (oz.) per frame	6	2	1	2				
12	Unit selling price	$28.50	$12.50	$29.25	$21.50				
13									
14	Production plan								
15	Frame type	1	2	3	4				
16	Frames produced	500	800	400	1500				
17		<=	<=	<=	<=				
18	Maximum sales	1000	2000	500	1000				
19									
20	Resource constraints	Resources used		Resources available					
21	Labor hours	6000	<=	4000					
22	Metal (oz.)	7000	<=	6000					
23	Glass (oz.)	8000	<=	10000					
24									
25	Revenue, cost summary								
26	Frame type	1	2	3	4	Totals			
27	Revenue	$14,250	$10,000	$11,700	$32,250	$68,200			
28	Costs of inputs								
29	Labor	$8,000	$6,400	$9,600	$24,000	$48,000			
30	Metal	$1,000	$800	$200	$1,500	$3,500			
31	Glass	$2,250	$1,200	$300	$2,250	$6,000			
32	Profit	$3,000	$1,600	$1,600	$4,500	$10,700			

1 **Inputs.** Enter the various inputs in the blue ranges. Again, remember that our convention is to color all input cells blue. Enter only *numbers*, not formulas, in input cells. They should always be numbers directly from the problem statement.

2 **Range names.** Name the ranges we have indicated. According to our convention, we have again named enough ranges so that the Solver dialog box contains only range names, no cell addresses. Of course, you can name additional ranges if you like. (Note that we have again used the range-naming shortcut from the previous example. That is, we have taken advantage of labels in adjacent cells, except for the Profit cell.)

3 **Changing cells.** Enter *any* four values in the Frames_produced range and color these cells red. This range contains the changing cells. You do *not* have to enter the values shown in Figure 14.19. Any trial values can be used initially; Solver eventually finds the *optimal* values. Note that the four values shown in Figure 14.19 cannot be optimal because they do not satisfy all of the constraints. Specifically, this plan uses more labor hours and metal than are available, and it produces more type 4 frames than can be sold. However, we do not need to worry about satisfying constraints at this point; Solver takes care of this later.

4 **Resources used.** Enter the formula

=SUMPRODUCT(B9:E9,Frames_produced)

in cell B21 and copy it to the rest of the Resources_used range. These formulas calculate the amounts of labor, metal, and glass used by the current product mix. We see again how useful the SUMPRODUCT function is in LP models. Here it says to multiply each value in the range B9:E9 by the corresponding value in the Frames_produced range and then sum these products.

Excel Tip: *Copying formulas with range names*
When you enter a range name in an Excel formula and then copy it, the range name reference acts like an absolute reference.

⑤ Revenues, costs, and profits. The area from row 25 down shows the summary of monetary values. Actually, all we need is the total profit in cell F32, but it is useful to calculate the revenues and costs associated with each product. To obtain the revenues, enter the formula

=B12*B16

in cell B27 and copy this to the range C27:E27. For the costs, enter the formula

=$B4*B$16*B9

in cell B29 and copy this to the range B29:E31. (Note how the mixed absolute and relative references enable copying to the entire range.) Then calculate the profit for each product by entering the formula

=B27-SUM(B29:B31)

in cell B32 and copy this to the range C32:E32. Finally, calculate the totals in column F by summing across each row with the SUM function. (The cost sums in column F are easy to understand. For example, the $32,000 labor cost in cell F29 is the 4000 labor hours used multiplied by the unit $8 cost per labor hour.)

Experimenting with Other Solutions

Before going any further, you might want to experiment with other values in the changing cells. For example, here is one reasonable strategy. Because frame 1 has the highest profit margin ($6) and its market constraint permits at most 1000 frames, enter 1000 in cell B16. Note that none of the resources are yet used up completely. Therefore, we can make some type 3 frames, the type with the next highest profit margin. Because the type 3 market constraint permits at most 500 frames, enter 500 in cell D16. There is still some availability of each resource. This allows us to make some type 4 frames, the type with the next largest profit margin. However, the most we can make is 250 type 4 frames, because at this point we completely exhaust the available labor hours. The resulting solution appears in Figure 14.20. Its corresponding profit is $8750.

We have now produced as much as possible of the three frame types with the three highest profit margins. Does this guarantee that this solution is the best possible product mix? Unfortunately, it does not! The solution in Figure 14.20 is *not* optimal. In this small model it is difficult to guess the optimal solution, even when we use a relatively intelligent trial-and-error procedure. The problem is that a frame type with a high profit margin can use up a lot of the resources and preclude other profitable frames from being produced. Therefore, we turn to Solver to eliminate the guesswork and find the *real* optimal solution.

USING SOLVER

To use Solver, select the Tools/Solver menu item, and fill it in as shown in Figure 14.21. (Again, note that we have named enough ranges so that only range names appear in this dialog box.) Also, click on the Options button, and check the Assume Linear Model and Assume Non-Negative boxes, as in Figure 14.6. This is because the model is indeed linear, and we do not want to allow negative numbers of frames to be produced.

Figure 14.20

Another Possible Solution for Product Mix Model

	A	B	C	D	E	F	G	H	I
1	Product mix model						Range names used		
2							Frames_produced	=Model!$B$16:$E$16	
3	Input data						Maximum_sales	=Model!$B$18:$E$18	
4	Hourly wage rate	$8.00					Profit	=Model!$F$32	
5	Cost per oz of metal	$0.50					Resources_available	=Model!$D$21:$D$23	
6	Cost per oz of glass	$0.75					Resources_used	=Model!$B$21:$B$23	
7									
8	Frame type	1	2	3	4				
9	Labor hours per frame	2	1	3	2				
10	Metal (oz.) per frame	4	2	1	2				
11	Glass (oz.) per frame	6	2	1	2				
12	Unit selling price	$28.50	$12.50	$29.25	$21.50				
13									
14	Production plan								
15	Frame type	1	2	3	4				
16	Frames produced	1000	0	500	250				
17		<=	<=	<=	<=				
18	Maximum sales	1000	2000	500	1000				
19									
20	Resource constraints	Resources used		Resources available					
21	Labor hours	4000	<=	4000					
22	Metal (oz.)	5000	<=	6000					
23	Glass (oz.)	7000	<=	10000					
24									
25	Revenue, cost summary								
26	Frame type	1	2	3	4	Totals			
27	Revenue	$28,500	$0	$14,625	$5,375	$48,500			
28	Costs of inputs								
29	Labor	$16,000	$0	$12,000	$4,000	$32,000			
30	Metal	$2,000	$0	$250	$250	$2,500			
31	Glass	$4,500	$0	$375	$375	$5,250			
32	Profit	$6,000	$0	$2,000	$750	$8,750			

Figure 14.21

Solver Dialog Box for Product Mix Model

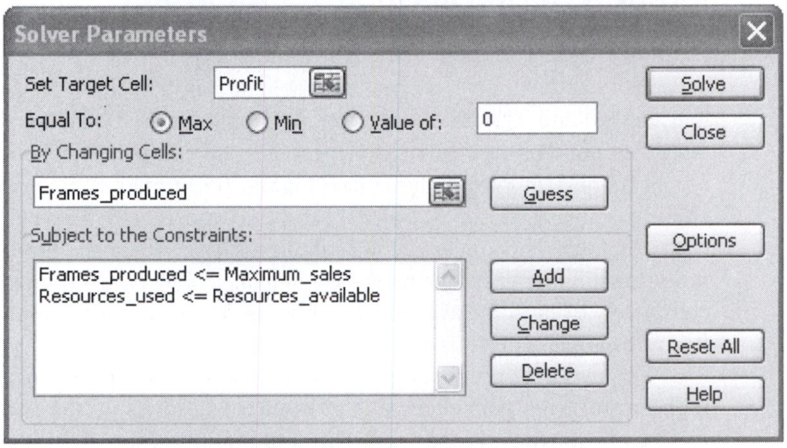

Discussion of the Solution

You typically gain insights into a solution by checking which constraints are binding and which contain slack.

When you click on Solve, you obtain the optimal solution shown in Figure 14.22. The optimal plan is to produce 1000 type 1 frames, 800 type 2 frames, 400 type 3 frames, and no type 4 frames. This is close to the production plan from Figure 14.20, but the current plan earns $450 more profit. Also, it uses all of the available labor hours and metal, but only 8000 of the 10,000 available ounces of glass. Finally, in terms of maximum sales, the optimal plan could produce more of frame types 2, 3, and 4 (if there were more skilled labor and/or metal available). This is typical of an LP solution. Some of the constraints are met exactly—they are binding—whereas others contain a certain amount of slack. The binding constraints are the ones that prevent Monet from earning an even higher profit.

Figure 14.22
Optimal Solution for Product Mix Model

	A	B	C	D	E	F	G	H
1	Product mix model						Range names used	
2							Frames_produced	=Model!$B$16:$E$16
3	Input data						Maximum_sales	=Model!$B$18:$E$18
4	Hourly wage rate	$8.00					Profit	=Model!$F$32
5	Cost per oz of metal	$0.50					Resources_available	=Model!$D$21:$D$23
6	Cost per oz of glass	$0.75					Resources_used	=Model!$B$21:$B$23
7								
8	Frame type	1	2	3	4			
9	Labor hours per frame	2	1	3	2			
10	Metal (oz.) per frame	4	2	1	2			
11	Glass (oz.) per frame	6	2	1	2			
12	Unit selling price	$28.50	$12.50	$29.25	$21.50			
13								
14	Production plan							
15	Frame type	1	2	3	4			
16	Frames produced	1000	800	400	0			
17		<=	<=	<=	<=			
18	Maximum sales	1000	2000	500	1000			
19								
20	Resource constraints	Resources used		Resources available				
21	Labor hours	4000	<=	4000				
22	Metal (oz.)	6000	<=	6000				
23	Glass (oz.)	8000	<=	10000				
24								
25	Revenue, cost summary							
26	Frame type	1	2	3	4	Totals		
27	Revenue	$28,500	$10,000	$11,700	$0	$50,200		
28	Costs of inputs							
29	Labor	$16,000	$6,400	$9,600	$0	$32,000		
30	Metal	$2,000	$800	$200	$0	$3,000		
31	Glass	$4,500	$1,200	$300	$0	$6,000		
32	Profit	$6,000	$1,600	$1,600	$0	$9,200		

Sensitivity Analysis

If we want to experiment with different inputs to this problem—the unit revenues or resource availabilities, for example—we can simply change the inputs and then rerun Solver. The second time we use Solver, we do not have to specify the target and changing cells or the constraints. Excel remembers all of these settings, and it saves them when we save the file.

As a simple what-if example, consider the modified model in Figure 14.23. Here the unit selling price for frame type 4 has increased from $21.50 to $26.50, and all other inputs are as before. By making type 4 frames more profitable, we might expect them to enter the optimal mix. This is exactly what happens. The new optimal plan (the one shown in the figure) discontinues production of frame types 2 and 3 and instead calls for production of 1000 type 4 frames. This solution increases the total profit to $14,000.

Excel Tip: *Roundoff Error*
Because of the way numbers are stored and calculated on a computer, the optimal values in the changing cells and elsewhere can contain small roundoff errors. For example, the value that really appeared in cell D16 (in Figure 14.23) on our PC was 8.731E-09, a very small number (0.000000008731). For all practical purposes, this number can be treated as 0, and we have formatted it as such in the spreadsheet.

We can also use SolverTable to perform a more systematic sensitivity analysis on one or more input variables. One possibility appears in Figure 14.24, where we allow the number of available labor hours to vary from 2500 to 5000 in increments of 250, and we keep track of the optimal product mix and profit. There are several ways to interpret the output from this sensitivity analysis. First, we can look at columns B through E to see how the product mix changes as more labor hours become available. For example, frames of type 4 are finally produced when 4500 labor hours are available, and frames of type 2 are discontinued in the final row. Second, we can see how extra labor hours add to the total profit. We show this numerically in column G, where each value is the increase in profit from the previous row. (We created column G manually; it is not part of the SolverTable output.) Note exactly what this increased profit means. For example, when labor hours increase from 2500 to 2750, the model requires that we *pay* $8 apiece for these extra hours (if we use them). But the *net* effect is that profit increases by $500. In other words, the labor cost increases by $2000 [=$8(250)], but this is more than offset by the increase in revenue that comes from having the extra labor hours.

Figure 14.23

Optimal Solution for Product Mix Model with a New Input Value

	A	B	C	D	E	F	G	H	I
1	Product mix model						Range names used		
2							Frames_produced	=Model!$B$16:$E$16	
3	Input data						Maximum_sales	=Model!$B$18:$E$18	
4	Hourly wage rate	$8.00					Profit	=Model!$F$32	
5	Cost per oz of metal	$0.50					Resources_available	=Model!$D$21:$D$23	
6	Cost per oz of glass	$0.75					Resources_used	=Model!$B$21:$B$23	
7									
8	Frame type	1	2	3	4				
9	Labor hours per frame	2	1	3	2				
10	Metal (oz.) per frame	4	2	1	2				
11	Glass (oz.) per frame	6	2	1	2				
12	Unit selling price	$28.50	$12.50	$29.25	$26.50				
13									
14	Production plan								
15	Frame type	1	2	3	4				
16	Frames produced	1000	0	0	1000				
17		<=	<=	<=	<=				
18	Maximum sales	1000	2000	500	1000				
19									
20	Resource constraints	Resources used		Resources available					
21	Labor hours	4000	<=	4000					
22	Metal (oz.)	6000	<=	6000					
23	Glass (oz.)	8000	<=	10000					
24									
25	Revenue, cost summary								
26	Frame type	1	2	3	4	Totals			
27	Revenue	$28,500	$0	$0	$26,500	$55,000			
28	Costs of inputs								
29	Labor	$16,000	$0	$0	$16,000	$32,000			
30	Metal	$2,000	$0	$0	$1,000	$3,000			
31	Glass	$4,500	$0	$0	$1,500	$6,000			
32	Profit	$6,000	$0	$0	$8,000	$14,000			

Figure 14.24

Sensitivity of Optimal Solution to Labor Hours

	A	B	C	D	E	F	G
34	Sensitivity of optimal solution to number of labor hours						
35		$B$16	$C$16	$D$16	$E$16	$F$32	Increase
36	2500	1000	500	0	0	$7,000	
37	2750	1000	750	0	0	$7,500	$500
38	3000	1000	1000	0	0	$8,000	$500
39	3250	1000	950	100	0	$8,300	$300
40	3500	1000	900	200	0	$8,600	$300
41	3750	1000	850	300	0	$8,900	$300
42	4000	1000	800	400	0	$9,200	$300
43	4250	1000	750	500	0	$9,500	$300
44	4500	1000	500	500	250	$9,750	$250
45	4750	1000	250	500	500	$10,000	$250
46	5000	1000	0	500	750	$10,250	$250

As column G illustrates, it is worthwhile to obtain extra labor hours, even though we have to pay for them, because profit increases. However, the increase in profit per extra labor hour—the *shadow price* of labor hours—is not constant. We see that it decreases as more labor hours are already owned. An extra 250 labor hours first results in $500 more profit, then $300, and then only $250. This is typical of shadow prices for scarce resources in LP models, where each extra unit of a resource is worth *at most* as much as the previous unit.

We can also chart the optimal profit values in column F (or any other quantities from a SolverTable output). The line chart in Figure 14.25 illustrates how the shadow price (slope of the line) decreases as more labor hours are already owned. (The first decrease in slope is perceptible; the second is hard to see in the chart, but it *is* there.)

Figure 14.25

Sensitivity of Optimal Profit to Labor Hours

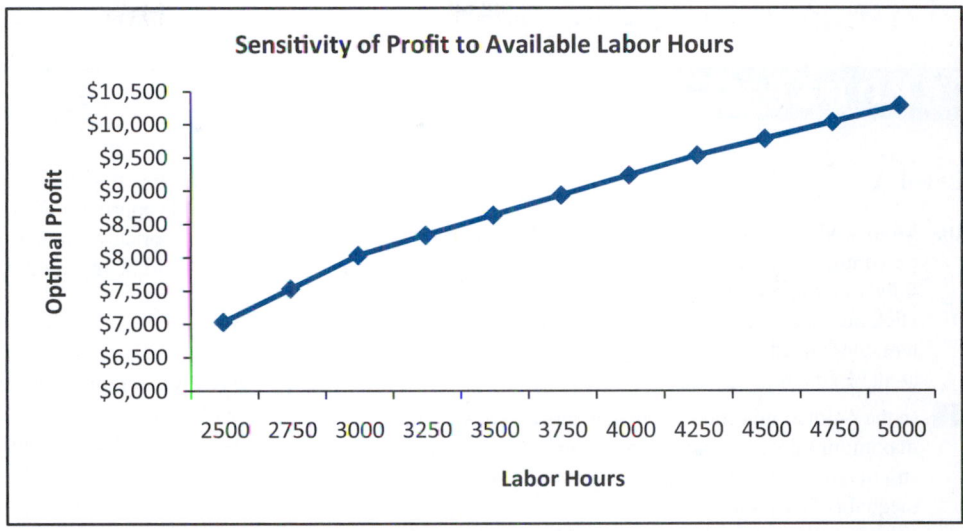

Finally, we can gain additional insight from Solver's sensitivity report, shown in Figure 14.26. This report contains a twist we did not see in the diet example. Now there are two types of constraints: upper bounds on the changing cells (the maximum sales constraints) and resource availability constraints. Solver treats the upper bound constraints differently from "normal" constraints in this report. First, it doesn't include rows for the upper bound constraints in the bottom section of the report. Second, in the top part of the report, a reduced cost can be nonzero even for a variable that is in the solution, provided that this variable is at its upper bound. Specifically, Monet is producing as many type 1 frames, 1000, as it is allowed to produce. The reduced cost of 2 means that the profit margin on type 1 frames must *decrease* by at least $2 before the company will produce less than 1000 of these frames.

The reduced cost for a variable with an upper constraint can be nonzero if that variable is currently at its upper bound.

Figure 14.26

Solver's Sensitivity Report

A	B	C	D	E	F	G	H
6	Adjustable Cells						
7			**Final**	**Reduced**	**Objective**	**Allowable**	**Allowable**
8	**Cell**	**Name**	**Value**	**Cost**	**Coefficient**	**Increase**	**Decrease**
9	$B$16	Frames produced	1000	2	6	1E+30	2
10	$C$16	Frames produced	800	0	2	1	0.25
11	$D$16	Frames produced	400	0	4	2	0.5
12	$E$16	Frames produced	0	-0.20	3	0.2	1E+30
13							
14	Constraints						
15			**Final**	**Shadow**	**Constraint**	**Allowable**	**Allowable**
16	**Cell**	**Name**	**Value**	**Price**	**R.H. Side**	**Increase**	**Decrease**
17	$B$21	Labor hours Resources used	4000	1.20	4000	250	1000
18	$B$22	Metal (oz.) Resources used	6000	0.40	6000	2000	500
19	$B$23	Glass (oz.) Resources used	8000	0	10000	1E+30	2000

In contrast, the reduced cost of -0.2 for type 4 frames implies that the profit margin on these frames would have to increase by at least $0.20 before the company would include them in its optimal mix (because they are currently *not* included).[13]

Finally, there are positive shadow prices on labor hours and metal, the two resources that are being used to capacity. The company's profit would increase by $1.20 for every extra labor hour and by $0.40 for every extra ounce of metal—but only up to the allowable increases shown in the report. ■

PROBLEMS

Level A

10. Modify Monet's product mix model so that there is no maximum sales constraint. (This is easy to do in the Solver dialog box. Just highlight the constraint and click on the Delete button.) Does this make the problem unbounded? Does it change the optimal solution at all? Explain its effect.

11. In the product mix model it makes sense to change the maximum sales constraint to a "minimum sales" constraint, simply by changing the direction of the inequality. Then the input values in row 18 can be considered customer demands that must be met. Make this change and rerun Solver. What do you find? What do you find if you run Solver again, this time making the values in row 18 half their current values?

12. Use SolverTable to run a sensitivity analysis on the cost per ounce of metal in the product mix model. Let this unit cost vary from $0.30 to $1.30 in increments of $0.20, and keep track of the values in the changing cells and the target cell. Discuss what happens to the optimal product mix. Also, does each 20-cent increase in the cost of metal result in the same decrease in profit?

13. Create a two-way SolverTable for the product mix model, where Profit is the only output and the two inputs are the hourly cost of labor and the total labor hours available. Let the former vary from $6 to $10 in increments of $1, and let the latter vary from 3000 to 7000 in increments of 500. Discuss the changes in profit you see as you look across the various rows of the table. Discuss the changes in profit you see as you look down the various columns of the table.

14. In the current solution to the product mix model, type 4 frames are not produced at all. This is due, at least in part, to the low unit selling price of type 4 frames. Use SolverTable appropriately to determine how large this unit selling price would have to be before type 4 frames would be included in the optimal product mix.

Level B

15. Suppose we want to increase *all three* of the resource availabilities in the product mix model simultaneously by the same factor. We want this factor to vary from 0.8 to 2.0 in increments of 0.1. For example, if this factor is 1.0, we get the current model, whereas if the factor is 2.0, the resource availabilities become 8000, 12,000, and 20,000. Modify the spreadsheet model slightly so that this sensitivity analysis can be performed with a *one-way* SolverTable, using the factor as the single input. Keep track of the values in the changing cells and the target cell. Discuss the results.

16. Some analysts complain that spreadsheet models are difficult to resize. We'll let you be the judge of this. Suppose the current product mix problem is changed so that there is an extra resource, plastic, and two additional frame types, 5 and 6. What additional data are required? What modifications are necessary in the spreadsheet model (including range name changes)? Make up values for any extra required data and incorporate these into a modified spreadsheet model. (You might want to try inserting new columns in the *middle* of your range, rather than inserting them at the end. See if you can discover why the former is more efficient.) Then optimize with Solver. Do you conclude that it is easy to resize a spreadsheet model? (By the way, it turns out that algebraic models are typically *much* easier to resize.)

14.8 A MULTIPERIOD PRODUCTION MODEL

The dessert and product mix examples illustrate typical LP models. However, LP models come in many forms. For variety, we now illustrate a quite different type of problem that can also be solved with LP. (In the next chapter we illustrate other examples, linear and

[13]Solver formats the numbers in its sensitivity reports in a strange way. Some numbers have a lot of decimals and some have none, so you have to be careful and possibly reformat. For example, the -0.2 in cell E12 was formatted as 0 in our report.

otherwise.) The distinguishing feature of the following problem is that it relates decisions made during several time periods. This type of problem occurs when a company must make a decision now that will have ramifications in the future. The company does not want to focus completely on the near future and forget about the long run.

EXAMPLE	14.3 PRODUCING FOOTBALLS AT PIGSKIN

The Pigskin Company produces footballs. Pigskin must decide how many footballs to produce each month. The company has decided to use a 6-month planning horizon. The forecasted demands for the next 6 months are 10,000, 15,000, 30,000, 35,000, 25,000, and 10,000. Pigskin wants to meet these demands on time, knowing that it currently has 5000 footballs in inventory and that it can use a given month's production to help meet the demand for that month. (For simplicity, we assume that production occurs during the month, and demand occurs at the end of the month.) During each month there is enough production capacity to produce up to 30,000 footballs, and there is enough storage capacity to store up to 10,000 footballs at the end of the month, after demand has occurred. The forecasted production costs per football for the next 6 months are $12.50, $12.55, $12.70, $12.80, $12.85, and $12.95, respectively. The holding cost per football held in inventory at the end of any month is figured at 5% of the production cost for that month. (This cost includes the cost of storage and also the cost of money tied up in inventory.) The selling price for footballs is not considered relevant to the production decision because Pigskin will satisfy all customer demand exactly when it occurs—at whatever the selling price is. Therefore, Pigskin wants to determine the production schedule that minimizes the total production and holding costs.

Objective To use LP to find the production schedule that meets demand on time and minimizes total production and inventory holding costs.

WHERE DO THE NUMBERS COME FROM?

The input values for this problem are not all easy to find. Here are some thoughts on where they might be obtained. (See Figure 14.27.)

- The initial inventory in cell B4 should be available from the company's database system or from a physical count.

- The unit production costs in row 8 would probably be estimated in two steps. First, the company might ask its cost accountants to estimate the current unit production cost. Then it could examine historical trends in costs to estimate inflation factors for future months.

- The holding cost percentage in cell B5 is typically difficult to determine. Depending on the type of inventory being held, this cost can include storage and handling, rent, property taxes, insurance, spoilage, and obsolescence. It can also include capital costs—the cost of money that could be used for other investments.

- The demands in row 18 are probably forecasts made by the marketing department. They might be "seat-of-the-pants" forecasts, or they might be the result of a formal quantitative forecasting procedure as discussed in Chapter 13. Of course, if there are already some orders on the books for future months, these are included in the demand figures.

- The production and storage capacities in rows 14 and 22 are probably supplied by the production department. They are based on the size of the workforce, the available machinery, availability of raw materials, and physical space.

Solution

The variables and constraints for this model are listed in Table 14.4. As we see when we develop the spreadsheet model, there are two keys to relating these variables. First, the months cannot be treated independently. This is because the ending inventory in one month is the beginning inventory for the next month. Second, to ensure that demand is satisfied on time, we must ensure that the amount on hand after production in each month is at least as large as the demand for that month.

Table 14.4   Variables and Constraints for Production/Inventory Planning Model

Input variables	Initial inventory, unit holding cost percentage, unit production costs, forecasted demands, production and storage capacities
Decision variables (changing cells)	Monthly production quantities
Objective (target cell)	Total cost
Other calculated variables	Units on hand after production, ending inventories, monthly production and inventory holding costs
Constraints	Units on hand after production $\geq$ Demand (each month)
	Units produced $\leq$ Production capacity (each month)
	Ending inventory $\leq$ Storage capacity (each month)

When we model this type of problem, we must be very specific about the *timing* of events. In fact, depending on the assumptions we make, there can be a variety of potential models. For example, when does the demand for footballs in a given month occur: at the beginning of the month, at the end of the month, or continually throughout the month? The same question can be asked about production in a given month. The answers to these two questions indicate how much of the production in a given month can be used to help satisfy the demand in that month. Also, are the maximum storage constraint and the holding cost based on the *ending* inventory in a month, the *average* amount of inventory in a month, or the *maximum* inventory in a month? Each of these possibilities is reasonable and could be implemented.

To simplify the model, we assume that (1) all production occurs at the beginning of the month, (2) all demand occurs *after* production, so that all units produced in a month can be used to satisfy that month's demand, and (3) the storage constraint and the holding cost are based on *ending* inventory for a given month. (You are asked in the problems to modify these assumptions.)

By modifying the timing assumptions in this type of model, we can get alternative—and equally realistic— models with very different solutions.

An Algebraic Model

In the traditional algebraic model, the decision variables are the production quantities for the 6 months, labeled P_1 through P_6. It is also convenient to let I_1 through I_6 be the corresponding end-of-month inventories (after demand has occurred).[14] For example, I_3 is the number of footballs left over at the end of month 3. Therefore, the obvious constraints are on production and inventory storage capacities: $P_j \leq 300$ and $I_j \leq 100$ for each month j, $1 \leq j \leq 6$. (From here on, to minimize the number of zeros shown, we express all quantities in *hundreds* of footballs.)

[14]This example illustrates a subtle difference between algebraic and spreadsheet models. It is often convenient in algebraic models to define "decision variables," in this case the I's, that are really determined by other decision variables, in this case the P's. In spreadsheet models, however, we typically define the changing cells as the smallest set of variables that really must be chosen—in this case the production quantities. Then we calculate values that are determined by these changing cells, such as the ending inventory levels, with spreadsheet formulas.

In addition to these constraints, we need "balance" constraints that relate the P's and I's. In any month the inventory from the previous month plus the current production equals the current demand plus leftover inventory. If D_j is the forecasted demand for month j, then the balance equation for month j is

$$I_{j-1} + P_j = D_j + I_j$$

The balance equation for month 1 uses the known beginning inventory, 50, for the previous inventory (the I_{j-1} term). By putting all variables (P's and I's) on the left and all known values on the right (a standard LP convention), we can write these balance constraints as

$$P_1 - I_1 = 100 - 50$$

$$I_1 + P_2 - I_2 = 150$$

$$I_2 + P_3 - I_3 = 300$$

$$I_3 + P_4 - I_4 = 350$$

$$I_4 + P_5 - I_5 = 250$$

$$I_5 + P_6 - I_6 = 100 \qquad \text{(14.1)}$$

As usual, we also impose nonnegativity constraints: all P's and I's must be nonnegative.

What about meeting demand on time? This requires that, in each month, the inventory from the preceding month plus the current production must be at least as large as the current demand. But take a look, for example, at the balance equation for month 3. By rearranging it slightly, we can write it as

$$I_3 = I_2 + P_3 - 300$$

Now, the nonnegativity constraint on I_3 implies that the right side of this equation, $I_2 + P_3 - 300$, is also nonnegative. But this implies that demand in month 3 is covered—the beginning inventory in month 3 plus month 3 production is at least 300. Therefore, the nonnegativity constraints on the I's *automatically* guarantee that all demands will be met on time, and no other constraints are needed. Alternatively, we could write directly that $I_2 + P_3 \geq 300$. In words, the amount on hand after production in month 3 must be at least as large as the demand in month 3. We take advantage of this interpretation in the spreadsheet model.

Finally, the objective we want to minimize is the sum of production and holding costs. It is the sum of unit production costs multiplied by P's, plus unit holding costs multiplied by I's.

DEVELOPING THE SPREADSHEET MODEL

The spreadsheet model of Pigskin's production problem is shown in Figure 14.27. (See the file **Production Scheduling.xlsx**.) The main feature that distinguishes this model from the product mix model is that some of the constraints, namely, the balance equations (14.1), are built into the spreadsheet itself by means of formulas. This means that the only changing cells are the production quantities. The ending inventories shown in row 20 are *determined* by the production quantities and equations (14.1). As we see, the decision variables in an algebraic model (the P's and I's) are not *necessarily* the same as the changing cells in an equivalent spreadsheet model. (The only changing cells in our spreadsheet model correspond to the P's.)

To develop the spreadsheet model in Figure 14.27, proceed as follows.

Figure 14.27   Nonoptimal Solution to Pigskin's Production Model

	A	B	C	D	E	F	G	H	I	J	K
1	Multiperiod production model								Range names used		
2									Demand	=Model!$B$18:$G$18	
3	Input data								Ending_inventory	=Model!$B$20:$G$20	
4	Initial inventory (100s)	50							On_hand_after_production	=Model!$B$16:$G$16	
5	Holding cost as % of prod cost	5%							Production_capacity	=Model!$B$14:$G$14	
6									Storage_capacity	=Model!$B$22:$G$22	
7	Month	1	2	3	4	5	6		Total_Cost	=Model!$H$28	
8	Production cost/unit	$12.50	$12.55	$12.70	$12.80	$12.85	$12.95		Units_produced	=Model!$B$12:$G$12	
9											
10	Production plan (all quantities are in 100s of footballs)										
11	Month	1	2	3	4	5	6				
12	Units produced	150	150	300	300	250	100				
13		<=	<=	<=	<=	<=	<=				
14	Production capacity	300	300	300	300	300	300				
15											
16	On hand after production	200	250	400	400	300	150				
17		>=	>=	>=	>=	>=	>=				
18	Demand	100	150	300	350	250	100				
19											
20	Ending inventory	100	100	100	50	50	50				
21		<=	<=	<=	<=	<=	<=				
22	Storage capacity	100	100	100	100	100	100				
23											
24	Summary of costs (all costs are in hundreds of dollars)										
25	Month	1	2	3	4	5	6	Totals			
26	Production costs	$1,875.00	$1,882.50	$3,810.00	$3,840.00	$3,212.50	$1,295.00	$15,915.00			
27	Holding costs	$62.50	$62.75	$63.50	$32.00	$32.13	$32.38	$285.25			
28	Totals	$1,937.50	$1,945.25	$3,873.50	$3,872.00	$3,244.63	$1,327.38	$16,200.25			

1 **Inputs.** Enter the inputs in the blue cells. Again, these are all entered as *numbers* straight from the problem statement. (Unlike some spreadsheet modelers who prefer to put all inputs in the upper left corner of the spreadsheet, we have entered the inputs wherever they fit most naturally. Of course, this takes some planning before diving in.)

2 **Name ranges.** Name the ranges indicated. Note that all but one of these (Total_cost) can be named easily with the range-naming shortcut, using the labels in column A.

3 **Production quantities.** Enter *any* values in the range Units_produced as production quantities. As always, you can enter values that you believe are good, maybe even optimal. This is not crucial, however, because Solver eventually finds the *optimal* production quantities.

4 **On-hand inventory.** Enter the formula

=B4+B12

in cell B16. This calculates the first month's on-hand inventory after production (but before demand). Then enter the "typical" formula

=B20+C12

for on-hand inventory after production in month 2 in cell C16 and copy it across row 16.

5 **Ending inventories.** Enter the formula

=B16-B18

In multiperiod problems, we often need one formula for the first period and a slightly different formula for all other periods.

for ending inventory in cell B20 and copy it across row 20. This formula calculates ending inventory in the current month as on-hand inventory before demand minus the demand in that month.

6 **Production and holding costs.** Enter the formula

=B8*B12

in cell B26 and copy it across to cell G26 to calculate the monthly production costs. Then enter the formula

=$B$5*B8*B20

in cell B27 and copy it across to cell G27 to calculate the monthly holding costs. Note that these are based on monthly ending inventories. Finally, calculate the cost totals in column H by using the SUM function.

USING SOLVER

To use Solver, fill out the main dialog box as shown in Figure 14.28. The logic behind the constraints is straightforward. All we have to guarantee is that (1) the production quantities do not exceed the production capacities, (2) the on-hand inventories after production are at least as large as demands, and (3) ending inventories do not exceed storage capacities. We also need to check the Assume Linear Model and Assume Non-Negative options, and then click on Solve.

Figure 14.28

Solver Dialog Box for Production Model

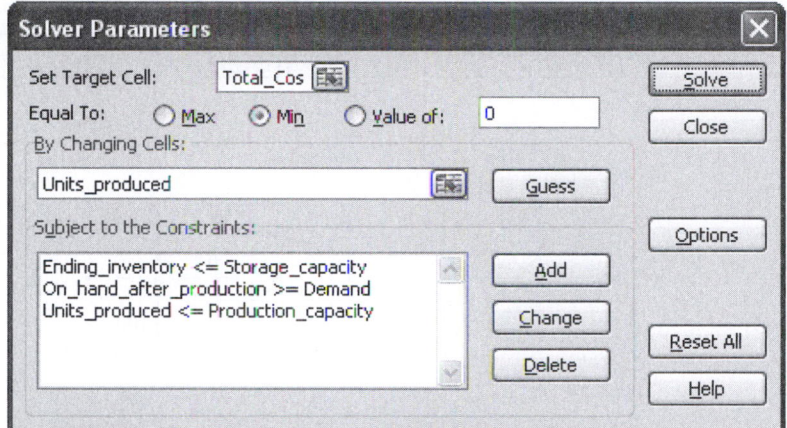

Discussion of the Solution

The optimal solution from Solver appears in Figure 14.29. This solution is also represented graphically in Figure 14.30. We can interpret the solution by comparing production quantities with demands. (Remember that all spreadsheet quantities are in units of 100 footballs.) In month 1 Pigskin should produce just enough to meet month 1 demand (taking into account the initial inventory of 5000). In month 2 it should produce 5000 more footballs than month 2 demand, and then in month 3 it should produce just enough to meet month 3 demand, while still carrying the extra 5000 footballs in inventory from month 2 production. In month 4 Pigskin should finally use these 5000 footballs, along with the maximum production amount, 30,000, to meet month 4 demand. Then in months 5 and 6 it should produce exactly enough to meet these months' demands. The total cost is $1,535,563, most of which is production cost. (This total cost is expressed in actual dollars. The value in the spreadsheet is in hundreds of dollars.)

Figure 14.29 Optimal Solution for the Production Model

	A	B	C	D	E	F	G	H	I	J	K
1	Multiperiod production model								Range names used		
2									Demand	=Model!$B$18:$G$18	
3	Input data								Ending_inventory	=Model!$B$20:$G$20	
4	Initial inventory (100s)	50							On_hand_after_production	=Model!$B$16:$G$16	
5	Holding cost as % of prod cost	5%							Production_capacity	=Model!$B$14:$G$14	
6									Storage_capacity	=Model!$B$22:$G$22	
7	Month	1	2	3	4	5	6		Total_Cost	=Model!$H$28	
8	Production cost/unit	$12.50	$12.55	$12.70	$12.80	$12.85	$12.95		Units_produced	=Model!$B$12:$G$12	
9											
10	Production plan (all quantities are in 100s of footballs)										
11	Month	1	2	3	4	5	6				
12	Units produced	50	200	300	300	250	100				
13		<=	<=	<=	<=	<=	<=				
14	Production capacity	300	300	300	300	300	300				
15											
16	On hand after production	100	200	350	350	250	100				
17		>=	>=	>=	>=	>=	>=				
18	Demand	100	150	300	350	250	100				
19											
20	Ending inventory	0	50	50	0	0	0				
21		<=	<=	<=	<=	<=	<=				
22	Storage capacity	100	100	100	100	100	100				
23											
24	Summary of costs (all costs are in hundreds of dollars)										
25	Month	1	2	3	4	5	6	Totals			
26	Production costs	$625.00	$2,510.00	$3,810.00	$3,840.00	$3,212.50	$1,295.00	$15,292.50			
27	Holding costs	$0.00	$31.38	$31.75	$0.00	$0.00	$0.00	$63.13			
28	Totals	$625.00	$2,541.38	$3,841.75	$3,840.00	$3,212.50	$1,295.00	$15,355.63			

Figure 14.30

Graphical Representation of Optimal Production Schedule

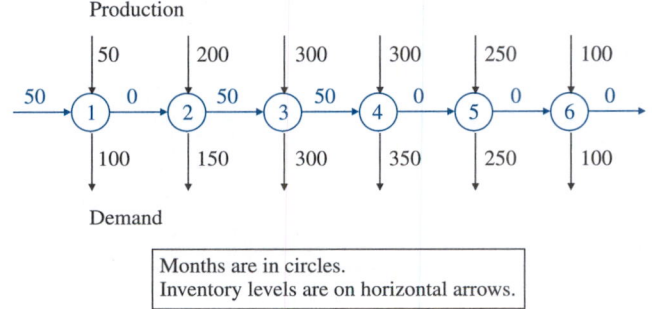

Months are in circles.
Inventory levels are on horizontal arrows.

You can often improve your intuition by trying to reason why Solver's solution is indeed optimal.

Could you have guessed this optimal solution? Upon reflection, it makes perfect sense. Because the monthly holding costs are large relative to the differences in monthly production costs, there is little incentive to produce footballs before they are needed to take advantage of a "cheap" production month. Therefore, the Pigskin Company produces footballs in the month when they are needed—when this is possible. The only exception to this rule is the 20,000 footballs produced during month 2 when only 15,000 are needed. The extra 5000 footballs produced in month 2 are needed, however, to meet month 4 demand of 35,000, because month 3 production capacity is used entirely to meet month 3 demand. Thus month 3 capacity is not available to meet month 4 demand, and 5000 units of month 2 capacity are used to meet month 4 demand.

Sensitivity Analysis

If you want SolverTable to keep track of a quantity that is not in your model, you need to create it with an appropriate formula in a new cell.

We can use SolverTable to perform a number of interesting sensitivity analyses. We illustrate two possibilities. First, note that the most inventory ever carried at the end of a month is 50 (5000 footballs), although the storage capacity each month is 100. Perhaps this is because the holding cost percentage, 5%, is fairly large. Would more ending inventory be carried if this holding cost percentage were lower? Or would even less be carried if it were higher? We can check this with the SolverTable output shown in Figure 14.31. Now the single input cell is cell B5, and the *single* output we keep track of is the maximum ending inventory ever held, which we calculate in cell B31 with the formula

=MAX(Ending_inventory)

As we see, only when the holding cost percentage decreases to 1% do we hit the storage capacity limit. (From this output we cannot tell which month or how many months the ending inventory will be at this upper limit.) On the other side, even when the holding cost percentage reaches 10%, we still continue to hold a maximum ending inventory of 50.

Figure 14.31

Sensitivity of Maximum Ending Inventory to Holding Cost Percentage

	A	B	C	D
30	Sensitivity of maximum ending inventory to holding cost percentage			
31	Output formula	50		
32				
33		$B$31		
34	1%	100		
35	2%	50		
36	3%	50		
37	4%	50		
38	5%	50		
39	6%	50		
40	7%	50		
41	8%	50		
42	9%	50		
43	10%	50		

A second possible sensitivity analysis is suggested by the way the optimal production schedule would probably be implemented. The optimal solution to Pigskin's model specifies the production level for each of the next 6 months. In reality, however, the company would probably implement the model's recommendation only for the *first* month. Then at the beginning of the second month, it would gather new forecasts for the *next* 6 months, months 2 through 7, solve a new 6-month model, and again implement the model's recommendation for the first of these months, month 2. If the company continues in this manner, we say that it is following a 6-month **rolling planning horizon**.

The question, then, is whether the assumed demands (really, forecasts) toward the end of the planning horizon have much effect on the optimal production quantity in month 1. We would hope not because these forecasts could be quite inaccurate. The two-way Solver table in Figure 14.32 shows how the optimal month 1 production quantity varies with the forecasted demands in months 5 and 6. As we see, if the forecasted demands for months 5 and 6 remain fairly small, the optimal month 1 production quantity remains at 50. This is good news. It means that the optimal production quantity in month 1 is fairly insensitive to the possibly inaccurate forecasts for months 5 and 6.

Solver's sensitivity report for this model appears in Figure 14.33. The bottom part of this report is fairly straightforward to interpret. The first 6 rows are for sensitivity to changes in the storage capacity, whereas the last 6 are for sensitivity to changes in the demands. (There are no rows for the production capacity constraints because these are simple upper-bound constraints on the decision variables. Recall that Solver's sensitivity report handles this type of constraint differently from "normal" constraints.) In contrast, the top part of the report is very difficult to unravel. This is because the objective coefficients of the decision variables are each based on *multiple* inputs. (Each is a combination of unit production costs and the holding cost percentage.) Therefore, if we want to know how the solution will change if we change a single unit production cost or the holding cost percentage, this report does not answer our question, at least not easily. This is one case where we believe sensitivity analysis with SolverTable is much more straightforward and intuitive. It allows us to change *any* of the model's inputs and directly see the effects on the solution.

Figure 14.32

Sensitivity of Month 1 Production to Demands in Months 5 and 6

	A	B	C	D	E	F
45	Sensitivity of month 1 production to demands in months 5 (along side) and 6 (along top)					
46	$B$12	100	200	300		
47	100	50	50	50		
48	200	50	50	50		
49	300	50	50	50		

Figure 14.33

Solver's Sensitivity Report for Production Model

	A B	C	D	E	F	G	H
6	Adjustable Cells						
7			Final	Reduced	Objective	Allowable	Allowable
8	Cell	Name	Value	Cost	Coefficient	Increase	Decrease
9	$B$12	Units produced	50	0	16.3175	1E+30	0.5750
10	$C$12	Units produced	200	0	15.7425	0.5750	0.4775
11	$D$12	Units produced	300	-0.4775	15.2650	0.4775	1E+30
12	$E$12	Units produced	300	-1.0125	14.7300	1.0125	1E+30
13	$F$12	Units produced	250	0	14.1400	1.6025	0.5425
14	$G$12	Units produced	100	0	13.5975	0.5425	13.5975
15							
16	Constraints						
17			Final	Shadow	Constraint	Allowable	Allowable
18	Cell	Name	Value	Price	R.H. Side	Increase	Decrease
19	$B$16	On hand after production <=	100	0.575	100	100	50
20	$C$16	On hand after production <=	200	0	150	50	1E+30
21	$D$16	On hand after production <=	350	0	300	50	1E+30
22	$E$16	On hand after production <=	350	1.6	350	50	50
23	$F$16	On hand after production <=	250	0.5	250	50	200
24	$G$16	On hand after production <=	100	13.6	100	100	100
25	$B$20	Ending inventory >=	0	0	100	1E+30	100
26	$C$20	Ending inventory >=	50	0	100	1E+30	50
27	$D$20	Ending inventory >=	50	0	100	1E+30	50
28	$E$20	Ending inventory >=	0	0	100	1E+30	100
29	$F$20	Ending inventory >=	0	0	100	1E+30	100
30	$G$20	Ending inventory >=	0	0	100	1E+30	100

MODELING ISSUES

We assume that Pigskin uses a 6-month planning horizon. Why 6 months? In multiperiod models such as this, the company has to make forecasts about the future, such as the level of customer demand. Therefore, the length of the planning horizon is usually the length of time for which the company can make reasonably accurate forecasts. Here, Pigskin evidently believes that it can forecast up to 6 months from now, so it uses a 6-month planning horizon. ∎

Level A

17. Can you guess the results of a sensitivity analysis on the initial inventory in the Pigskin model? See if your guess is correct by using SolverTable and allowing the initial inventory to vary from 0 to 100 in increments of 10. (These are in 100s of footballs.) Keep track of the values in the changing cells and the target cell.

18. Modify the Pigskin model so that there are 8 months in the planning horizon. You can make up reasonable values for any extra required data. Don't forget to modify range names. Then modify the model again so that there are only 4 months in the planning horizon. Do either of these modifications change the optimal production quantity in month 1?

19. As indicated by the algebraic formulation of the Pigskin model, there is no real need to calculate inventory on hand after production and constrain it to be greater than or equal to demand. An alternative is to calculate ending inventory directly and constrain it to be nonnegative. Modify the current spreadsheet model to do this. (Delete rows 16 and 17, and calculate ending inventory appropriately. Then add an *explicit* nonnegativity constraint on ending inventory.)

20. In one modification of the Pigskin problem, the maximum storage constraint and the holding cost are based on the *average* inventory (not ending inventory) for a given month, where the average inventory is defined as the sum of beginning inventory and ending inventory, divided by 2, and beginning inventory is before production or demand. Modify the Pigskin model with this new assumption, and use Solver to find the optimal solution. How does this change the optimal production schedule? How does it change the optimal total cost?

Level B

21. Modify the Pigskin spreadsheet model so that except for month 6, demand need not be met on time. The only requirement is that all demand be met eventually by the end of month 6. How does this change the optimal production schedule? How does it change the optimal total cost?

22. Modify the Pigskin spreadsheet model so that demand in any of the first 5 months must be met no later than a month late, whereas demand in month 6 must be met on time. For example, the demand in month 3 can be met partly in month 3 and partly in month 4. How does this change the optimal production schedule? How does it change the optimal total cost?

23. Modify the Pigskin spreadsheet model in the following way. Assume that the timing of demand and production are such that only 70% of the production in a given month can be used to satisfy the demand in that month. The other 30% occurs too late in that month and must be carried as inventory to help satisfy demand in later months. How does this change the optimal production schedule? How does it change the optimal total cost? Then use SolverTable to see how the optimal production schedule and optimal cost vary as the percentage of production usable for this month's demand (now 70%) is allowed to vary from 20% to 100% in increments of 10%.

14.9 A COMPARISON OF ALGEBRAIC AND SPREADSHEET MODELS

To this point we have seen three algebraic optimization models and three corresponding spreadsheet models. How do they differ? If you review the first two examples in this chapter, the diet and product mix examples, we believe you will agree that (1) the algebraic models are quite straightforward and (2) the spreadsheet models are almost direct translations into Excel of the algebraic models. In particular, each algebraic model has a set of x's that corresponds to the changing cell range in the spreadsheet model. In addition, each objective and each left-hand side of each constraint in the spreadsheet model corresponds to a linear expression involving x's in the algebraic model.

However, the Pigskin production planning model is quite different. The spreadsheet model includes one set of changing cells, the production quantities, and everything else is related to these through spreadsheet formulas. In contrast, the algebraic model has *two* sets of variables, the P's for the production quantities and the I's for the ending inventories, and together these comprise the "decision variables." These two sets of variables must then be related algebraically, and this is done through a series of "balance equations."

This is a typical situation in algebraic models, where one set of variables (the production quantities) corresponds to the *real* decision variables, whereas other sets of variables, along with extra equations or inequalities, must be introduced to capture the logic. We believe—and this belief is reinforced by many years of teaching experience—that this extra level of abstraction makes algebraic models much more difficult for typical users to develop and comprehend. It is the primary reason we have decided to focus almost exclusively on spreadsheet models in this book.

14.10 A DECISION SUPPORT SYSTEM

If your job is to develop an LP spreadsheet model to solve a problem such as Pigskin's production problem, then you will be considered the "expert" in LP. Many people who need to use such models, however, are *not* experts. They might understand the basic ideas behind LP and the types of problems it is intended to solve, but they will not know the details. In this case it is useful to provide these users with a **decision support system** (DSS) that can help them solve problems without having to worry about technical details.

We do not teach you in this book how to build a full-scale DSS, but we do show you what a typical DSS looks like and what it can do.[15] (We consider only DSSs built around spreadsheets. There are many other platforms for developing DSSs that we do not consider.) Basically, a spreadsheet-based DSS contains a spreadsheet model of a problem, such as the one in Figure 14.27. However, users will probably never even see this model. Instead, they see a "front end" and a "back end." The front end allows them to select input values for their particular problem. The user interface for this front end can include several features, such as buttons, dialog boxes, toolbars, and menus—the things they are used to seeing in Windows applications. The back end then produces a report that explains the solution in nontechnical terms.

We illustrate a DSS for a slight variation of the Pigskin problem in the file **Decision Support.xlsm**. This file has three sheets. When you open the file, you see the Explanation sheet. (See Figure 14.34.) It contains two buttons, one for setting up the problem (getting the user's inputs) and one for solving the problem (running Solver). When you click on the Set Up Problem button, you are asked for the inputs: the initial inventory, the forecasted demands for each month, and others. An example appears in Figure 14.35. These input boxes should be self-explanatory, so that all you need to do is enter the values you want to try. (To speed up the process, the inputs from the previous run are shown by default.) After you have entered all of these inputs, you can take a look at the Model sheet. This sheet contains a spreadsheet model similar to the one we saw previously in Figure 14.29, but with the inputs you just entered.

Now go back to the Explanation sheet and click on the Find Optimal Solution button. This automatically sets up the Solver dialog box and runs Solver. There are two possibilities. First, it is possible that there is no feasible solution to the problem with the inputs you entered. In this case you see a message to this effect, as in Figure 14.36. In most cases, however, the problem has a feasible solution. In this case you see the Report sheet, which summarizes the optimal solution in nontechnical terms. Part of one sample output appears in Figure 14.37.

---

[15]For readers interested in learning more about this DSS, the accompanying CD-ROM includes notes about its development in the file Developing the Decision Support Application.docx under the Chapter 14 Example Files folder. If you are interested in learning more about spreadsheet DSSs in general, Albright has written the book *VBA for Modelers*, now in its second edition. It contains a primer on the VBA language, and then it presents many applications and instructions for creating DSSs with VBA.

Figure 14.34

Explanation Sheet for DSS

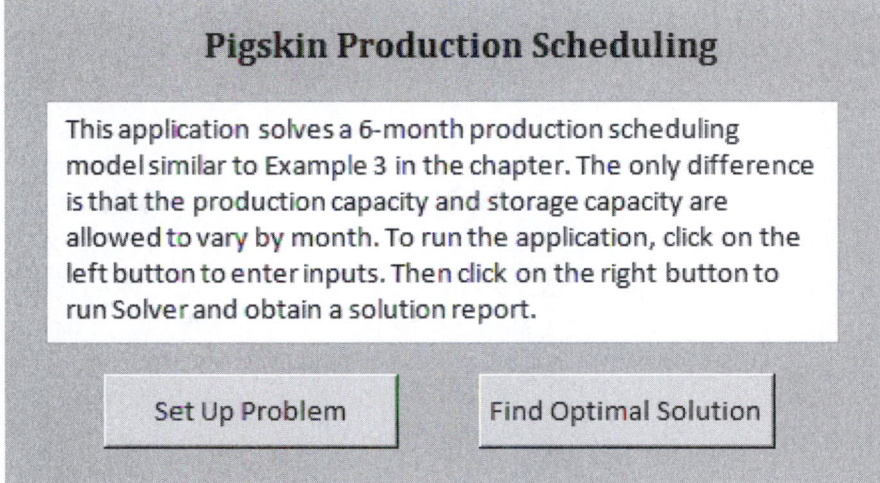

Pigskin Production Scheduling

This application solves a 6-month production scheduling model similar to Example 3 in the chapter. The only difference is that the production capacity and storage capacity are allowed to vary by month. To run the application, click on the left button to enter inputs. Then click on the right button to run Solver and obtain a solution report.

| Set Up Problem | Find Optimal Solution |

Figure 14.35

Model Dialog Box for Inputs

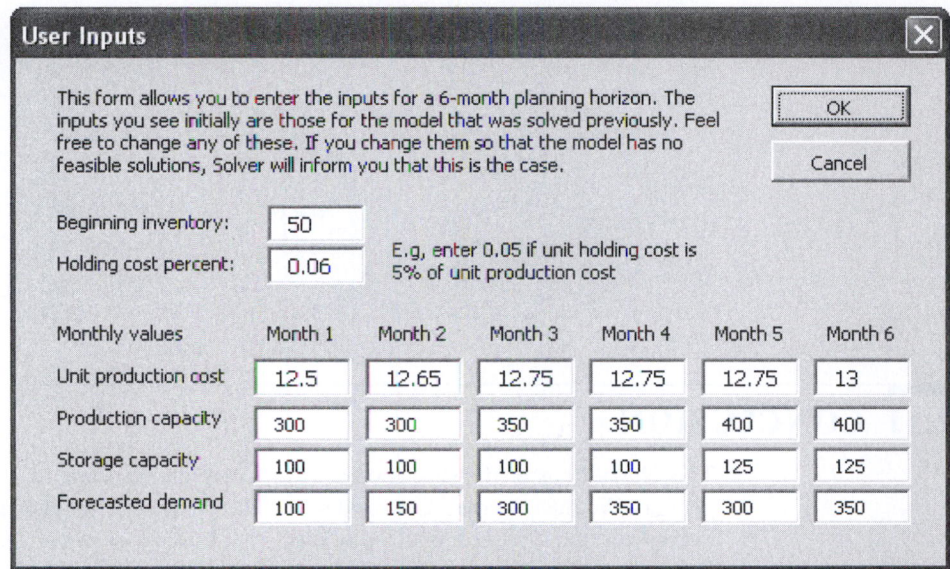

User Inputs

This form allows you to enter the inputs for a 6-month planning horizon. The inputs you see initially are those for the model that was solved previously. Feel free to change any of these. If you change them so that the model has no feasible solutions, Solver will inform you that this is the case.

OK

Cancel

Beginning inventory: 50

Holding cost percent: 0.06

E.g, enter 0.05 if unit holding cost is 5% of unit production cost

Monthly values	Month 1	Month 2	Month 3	Month 4	Month 5	Month 6
Unit production cost	12.5	12.65	12.75	12.75	12.75	13
Production capacity	300	300	350	350	400	400
Storage capacity	100	100	100	100	125	125
Forecasted demand	100	150	300	350	300	350

Figure 14.36

No Solution Message

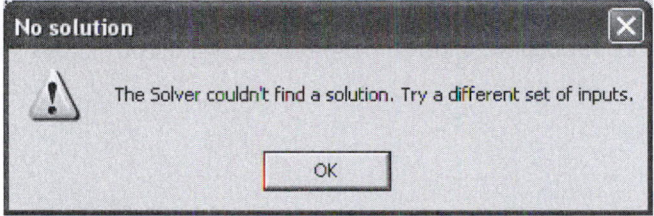

No solution

⚠ The Solver couldn't find a solution. Try a different set of inputs.

OK

After studying this report, you can then click on the Solve Another Problem button, which takes you back to the Explanation sheet so that you can solve a new problem. All of this is done automatically with Excel macros. These macros use Microsoft's Visual Basic for Applications (VBA) programming language to automate various tasks. In most professional applications, nontechnical people need only to enter inputs and look at reports. Therefore, the Model sheet and VBA code would most likely be hidden and protected from end users.

Figure 14.37
Report Sheet
for DSS

Monthly schedule

Month 1

Units		Dollars	
Start with	50		
Produce	50	Production cost	$625.00
Demand is	100		
End with	0	Holding cost	$0.00

Month 2

Units		Dollars	
Start with	0		
Produce	150	Production cost	$1,897.50
Demand is	150		
End with	0	Holding cost	$0.00

Month 3

Units		Dollars	
Start with	0		
Produce	300	Production cost	$3,825.00
Demand is	300		
End with	0	Holding cost	$0.00

14.11 CONCLUSION

This chapter has provided a good start to LP modeling—and to optimization modeling in general. We have learned how to develop three basic LP spreadsheet models, how to use Solver to find their optimal solutions, and how to perform sensitivity analyses with Solver's sensitivity reports or with the SolverTable add-in. We have also learned how to recognize whether a mathematical programming model satisfies the linear assumptions. In the next chapter we discuss a variety of other optimization models, but the three basic steps of model development, Solver optimization, and sensitivity analysis remain the same.

Summary of Key Terms

Term	Explanation	Excel	Page	Equation Number
Linear programming model	An optimization model with a linear objective and linear constraints		790	
Objective	The value, such as profit, to be optimized in an optimization model		790	
Constraints	Conditions that must be satisfied in an optimization model		790	

(*continued*)

Term	Explanation	Excel	Page	Equation Number
Nonnegativity constraints	Constraints that require the decision variables to be nonnegative, usually for physical reasons		791	
Feasible solution	A solution that satisfies all of the constraints		791	
Feasible region	The set of all feasible solutions		791	
Changing cells	Cells that contain the values of the decision variables	Specify in Solver dialog box	791	
Optimal solution	The feasible solution that has the best value of the objective		791	
Target cell	Cell that contains the value of the objective	Specify in Solver dialog box	791	
Solver	Add-in that ships with Excel for performing optimization	Solver from Data ribbon	792	
Simplex method	An efficient algorithm for finding the optimal solution in a linear programming model		792	
Sensitivity analysis	Seeing how the optimal solution changes as various input values change		792	
Algebraic model	A model that expresses the constraints and the objective algebraically		793	
Graphical solution	Shows the constraints and objective graphically so that the optimal solution can be identified; useful only when there are 2 decision variables		794	
Spreadsheet model	A model that uses spreadsheet formulas to express the logic of the model		795	
Binding constraint	A constraint that holds as an equality		802	
Nonbinding constraint, slack	A constraint where there is a difference, the slack, between the two sides of the inequality		802	
Solver's sensitivity report	Report available from Solver that shows sensitivity to objective coefficients and right-hand sides of constraints	Available in Solver dialog box right after Solver runs	803	
Reduced cost	Amount the objective coefficient of a variable currently equal to 0 must change before it is optimal for that variable to be positive		805	
Shadow price	The change in the objective for a change in the right-hand side of a constraint; indicates amount we'd pay for more of a scarce resource		805	
SolverTable add-in	Add-in that performs sensitivity analysis to any inputs and reports results similar to an Excel data table	SolverTable from Add-Ins ribbon	806	
Selecting multiple ranges	Useful when changing cells, e.g., are in noncontiguous ranges	Pressing Ctrl key, drag ranges, one after the other	807	
Mathematical programming model	Any optimization model, whether linear, integer, or nonlinear		810	
Proportionality, additivity, divisibility	Properties of optimization model that result in a linear programming model		811	

(continued)

Term	Explanation	Excel	Page	Equation Number
Infeasibility	Condition where a model has no feasible solutions		813	
Unboundedness	Condition where there is no limit to the objective; almost always a sign of an error in the model		814	
Decision support system	User-friendly system where an end user can enter inputs to a model and see outputs, but need not be concerned with technical details		834	

PROBLEMS

Level A

24. Leary Chemical manufactures three chemicals: A, B, and C. These chemicals are produced via two production processes: 1 and 2. Running process 1 for an hour costs $4 and yields 3 units of A, 1 unit of B, and 1 unit of C. Running process 2 for an hour costs $1 and yields 1 unit of A and 1 unit of B. To meet customer demands, at least 10 units of A, 5 units of B, and 3 units of C must be produced daily.
   a. Use Solver to determine a daily production plan that minimizes the cost of meeting Leary's daily demands.
   b. Confirm graphically that the daily production plan from part **a** minimizes the cost of meeting Leary's daily demands.

25. Starting with the optimal solution to the previous problem, use SolverTable to see what happens to the decision variables and the total cost when the hourly processing cost for process 2 increases in increments of $0.50. How large must this cost increase be before the decision variables change? What happens when it continues to increase beyond this point?

26. Furnco manufactures desks and chairs. Each desk uses 4 units of wood, and each chair uses 3 units of wood. A desk contributes $40 to profit, and a chair contributes $25. Marketing restrictions require that the number of chairs produced be at least twice the number of desks produced. There are 20 units of wood available.
   a. Use Solver to maximize Furnco's profit.
   b. Confirm graphically that the solution in part **a** maximizes Furnco's profit.

27. Starting with the optimal solution to the previous problem, use SolverTable to see what happens to the decision variables and the total profit when the availability of wood varies from 10 to 30 in 1-unit increments. Based on your findings, how much would Furnco be willing to pay for each extra unit of wood over its current 20 units? How much profit would Furnco lose if it lost any of its current 20 units?

28. A farmer in Iowa owns 45 acres of land. He is going to plant each acre with wheat or corn. Each acre planted with wheat yields $200 profit, requires 3 workers, and requires 2 tons of fertilizer; each with corn yields $300 profit, requires 2 workers, and requires 4 tons of fertilizer. One hundred workers and 120 tons of fertilizer are available.
   a. Use Solver to help the farmer maximize the profit from his land.
   b. Confirm graphically that the solution from part **a** maximizes the farmer's profit from his land.

29. Starting with the optimal solution to the previous problem, use SolverTable to see what happens to the decision variables and the total profit when the availability of fertilizer varies from 20 tons to 220 tons in 10-ton increments.
   a. When does the farmer discontinue producing wheat? When does he discontinue producing corn?
   b. How does the profit change for each 10-ton increment? Make this more obvious by creating a line chart of profit (vertical axis) versus fertilizer availability.

30. A customer requires during the next 4 months, respectively, 50, 65, 100, and 70 units of a commodity, and no backlogging is allowed (that is, the customer's requirements must be met on time). Production costs are $5, $8, $4, and $7 per unit during these months. The storage cost from one month to the next is $2 per unit (assessed on ending inventory). It is estimated that each unit on hand at the end of month 4 can be sold for $6. Determine how to minimize the net cost incurred in meeting the demands for the next 4 months.

31. Starting with the optimal solution to the previous problem, use SolverTable to see what happens to the decision variables and the total cost when the initial inventory varies from 0 (the implied value in the previous problem) to 100 in 10-unit increments. How much lower would the total cost be if the company started with 10 units in inventory, rather than none? Would this same cost decrease occur for every 10-unit increase in initial inventory?

32. A company faces the following demands during the next 3 weeks: week 1, 20 units; week 2, 10 units;

week 3, 15 units. The unit production costs during each week are as follows: week 1, $13; week 2, $14; week 3, $15. A holding cost of $2 per unit is assessed against each week's ending inventory. At the beginning of week 1, the company has 5 units on hand. In reality, not all goods produced during a month can be used to meet the current month's demand. To model this fact, we assume that only half of the goods produced during a week can be used to meet the current week's demands. Determine how to minimize the cost of meeting the demand for the next 3 weeks.

33. Revise the model for the previous problem so that the demands are of the form $D_t + k\Delta_t$, where D_t is the original demand (from the previous problem) in month t, k is a factor, and Δ_t is an amount of change in month t demand. (The Greek symbol Δ is typically used to indicate change.) Formulate the model in such a way that you can use SolverTable to analyze changes in the amounts produced and the total cost when k varies from 0 to 10 in 1-unit increments, for any fixed values of the Δ_t's. For example, try this when $\Delta_1 = 2$, $\Delta_2 = 5$, and $\Delta_3 = 3$. Describe the behavior you observe in the table. Can you find any "reasonable" Δ_t's that induce *positive* production levels in week 3?

34. Bloomington Brewery produces beer and ale. Beer sells for $5 per barrel, and ale sells for $2 per barrel. Producing a barrel of beer requires 5 pounds of corn and 2 pounds of hops. Producing a barrel of ale requires 2 pounds of corn and 1 pound of hops. The brewery has 60 pounds of corn and 25 pounds of hops.
   a. Use Solver to maximize Bloomington Brewery's revenue.
   b. Confirm graphically that the solution in part **a** maximizes Bloomington Brewery's revenue.

35. Starting with the optimal solution to the previous problem, use SolverTable to either substantiate or refute the following statements: The availability of corn can decrease by any amount (up to 60 pounds), and each unit decrease will cost Bloomington Brewery the same amount in terms of lost revenue. On the other hand, increases in the availability of corn do not have a constant effect on total revenue; the first few extra units have a larger effect than subsequent units.

36. For a telephone survey, a marketing research group needs to contact at least 150 wives, 120 husbands, 100 single adult males, and 110 single adult females. It costs $2 to make a daytime call and (because of higher labor costs) $5 to make an evening call. The file **P14_36.xlsx** lists the results that can be expected. For example, 30% of all daytime calls are answered by a wife, and 15% of all evening calls are answered by a single male. Because of a limited staff, at most half of all phone calls can be evening calls. Determine how to minimize the cost of completing the survey.

37. Starting with the optimal solution to the previous problem, use the SolverTable add-in to investigate changes in the unit cost of either type of call. Specifically, investigate changes in the cost of a daytime call, with the cost of an evening call fixed, to see when (if ever) *only* daytime calls or *only* evening calls will be made. Then repeat the analysis by changing the cost of an evening call and keeping the cost of a daytime call fixed.

38. Woodco manufactures tables and chairs. Each table and chair must be made entirely out of oak or entirely out of pine. A total of 150 board feet of oak and 210 board feet of pine are available. A table requires either 17 board feet of oak or 30 board feet of pine, and a chair requires either 5 board feet of oak or 13 board feet of pine. Each table can be sold for $40, and each chair for $15. Determine how Woodco can maximize its revenue.

39. Referring to the previous problem, suppose you want to investigate the effects of simultaneous changes in the selling prices of the products. Specifically, you want to see what happens to the total revenue when the selling prices of oak products change by a factor $1 + k_1$ and the selling prices of pine products change by a factor $1 + k_2$. Revise your model from the previous problem so that you can use SolverTable to investigate changes in total revenue as k_1 and k_2 both vary from -0.3 to 0.3 in increments of 0.1. Can you conclude that total revenue changes *linearly* within this range?

40. Alden Enterprises produces two products. Each product can be produced on either of two machines. The time (in hours) required to produce each product on each machine is listed in the file **P14_40.xlsx**. Each month, 500 hours of time are available on each machine. Each month, customers are willing to buy up to the quantities of each product at the prices also given in the file **P14_40.xlsx**. The company's goal is to maximize the revenue obtained from selling units during the next 2 months. Determine how it can meet this goal. Assume that Alden will not produce any units in either month that it cannot sell in that month.

41. Referring to the previous problem, suppose Alden wants to see what happens if customer demands for each product in each month simultaneously change by a factor $1 + k$. Revise the model so that you can use SolverTable to investigate the effect of this change on total revenue as k varies from -0.3 to 0.3 in increments of 0.1. Does revenue change in a linear manner over this range? Can you explain intuitively why it changes in the way it does?

42. There are three factories on the Momiss River: 1, 2, and 3. Each emits two types of pollutants, labeled P_1 and P_2, into the river. If the waste from each factory is processed, the pollution in the river can be reduced. It costs $15 to process a ton of factory 1 waste, and each ton processed reduces the amount of P_1 by 0.10 ton and the amount of P_2 by 0.45 ton. It costs $10 to process a ton of factory 2 waste, and each ton processed reduces the amount of P_1 by 0.20 ton and the amount of P_2 by 0.25 ton. It costs $20 to process a ton of factory 3 waste, and each ton processed reduces the amount of P_1 by 0.40 ton and the amount of P_2 by 0.30 ton. The state wants to reduce the amount of P_1 in the river by at least 30 tons and the amount of P_2 by at least 40 tons.

a. Use Solver to determine how to minimize the cost of reducing pollution by the desired amounts.

b. Are the LP assumptions (proportionality, additivity, divisibility) reasonable in this problem?

43. Referring to the previous problem, suppose you want to investigate the effects of increases in the minimal reductions required by the state. Specifically, you want to see what happens to the amounts of waste processed at the three factories and the total cost if both requirements (currently 30 and 40 tons, respectively) are increased by the *same* percentage. Revise your model so that you can use the SolverTable add-in to investigate these changes when the percentage increase varies from 10% to 100% in increments of 10%. Do the amounts processed at the three factories and the total cost change in a linear manner?

Level B

44. Truckco manufactures two types of trucks, types 1 and 2. Each truck must go through the painting shop and the assembly shop. If the painting shop were completely devoted to painting type 1 trucks, 800 per day could be painted, whereas if the painting shop were completely devoted to painting type 2 trucks, 700 per day could be painted. If the assembly shop were completely devoted to assembling truck 1 engines, 1500 per day could be assembled, and if the assembly shop were completely devoted to assembling truck 2 engines, 1200 per day could be assembled. It is possible, however, to paint *both* types of trucks in the painting shop. Similarly, it is possible to assemble both types in the assembly shop. Each type 1 truck contributes $300 to profit; each type 2 truck contributes $500. Use Solver to maximize Truckco's profit. (*Hint:* One approach, but not the only approach, is to try a graphical procedure first and then deduce the constraints from the graph.)

45. U.S. Labs manufactures mechanical heart valves from the heart valves of pigs. Different heart operations require valves of different sizes. U.S. Labs purchases pig valves from three different suppliers. The cost and size mix of the valves purchased from each supplier are given in the file **P14_45.xlsx**. Each month, U.S.

Labs places an order with each supplier. At least 500 large, 300 medium, and 300 small valves must be purchased each month. Because of the limited availability of pig valves, at most 500 valves per month can be purchased from each supplier. Use Solver to determine how U.S. Labs can minimize the cost of acquiring the needed valves.

46. Referring to the previous problem, suppose U.S. Labs wants to investigate the effect on total cost of increasing its minimal purchase requirements each month. Specifically, it wants to see how total cost changes as the minimal purchase requirements of large, medium, and small valves all increase from their values in the previous problem by the *same* percentage. Revise your model so that SolverTable can be used to investigate these changes when the percentage increase varies from 2% to 20% in increments of 2%. Explain intuitively what happens when this percentage is at least 16%.

47. Sailco Corporation must determine how many sailboats to produce during each of the next four quarters. The demand during each of the next four quarters is as follows: first quarter, 40 sailboats; second quarter, 60 sailboats; third quarter, 75 sailboats; fourth quarter, 25 sailboats. Sailco must meet demands on time. At the beginning of the first quarter, Sailco has an inventory of 10 sailboats. At the beginning of each quarter, Sailco must decide how many sailboats to produce during that quarter. For simplicity, we assume that sailboats manufactured during a quarter can be used to meet demand for that quarter. During each quarter, Sailco can produce up to 40 sailboats with regular-time labor at a total cost of $400 per sailboat. By having employees work overtime during a quarter, Sailco can produce additional sailboats with overtime labor at a total cost of $450 per sailboat. At the end of each quarter (after production has occurred and the current quarter's demand has been satisfied), a holding cost of $20 per sailboat is incurred. Determine a production schedule to minimize the sum of production and inventory holding costs during the next four quarters.

48. Referring to the previous problem, suppose Sailco wants to see whether any changes in the $20 holding cost per sailboat could induce the company to carry more or less inventory. Revise your model so that SolverTable can be used to investigate the effects on ending inventory during the 4-month interval of systematic changes in the unit holding cost. (Assume that even though the unit holding cost changes, it is still constant over the 4-month interval.) Are there any (nonnegative) unit holding costs that would induce Sailco to hold *more* inventory than it holds when the holding cost is $20? Are there any unit holding costs that would induce Sailco to hold *less* inventory than it holds when the holding cost is $20?

49. During the next 2 months General Cars must meet (on time) the following demands for trucks and cars: month 1, 400 trucks and 800 cars; month 2, 300 trucks and 300 cars. During each month at most 1000 vehicles can be produced. Each truck uses 2 tons of steel, and each car uses 1 ton of steel. During month 1, steel costs $400 per ton; during month 2, steel costs $600 per ton. At most 2500 tons of steel can be purchased each month. (Steel can be used only during the month in which it is purchased.) At the beginning of month 1, 100 trucks and 200 cars are in the inventory. At the end of each month, a holding cost of $150 per vehicle is assessed. Each car gets 20 mpg, and each truck gets 10 mpg. During each month, the vehicles produced by the company must average at least 16 mpg. Determine how to meet the demand and mileage requirements at minimum total cost.

50. Referring to the previous problem, check how sensitive the total cost is to the 16 mpg requirement by using SolverTable. Specifically, let this requirement vary from 14 mpg to 18 mpg in increments of 0.25 mpg, and write a short report of your results. In your report, explain intuitively what happens when the requirement is greater than 17 mpg.

51. The Deckers Clothing Company produces shirts and pants. Each shirt requires 2 square yards of cloth, and each pair of pants requires 3 square yards of cloth. During the next 2 months the following demands for shirts and pants must be met (on time): month 1, 1000 shirts and 1500 pairs of pants; month 2, 1200 shirts and 1400 pairs of pants. During each month the following resources are available: month 1, 9000 square yards of cloth; month 2, 6000 square yards of cloth. (Cloth that is available during month 1 and is not used can be used during month 2.) During each month it costs $4 to make an article of clothing with regular-time labor and $8 with overtime labor. During each month a total of at most 2500 articles of clothing can be produced with regular-time labor, and an unlimited number of articles of clothing can be produced with overtime labor. At the end of each month, a holding cost of $3 per article of clothing is assessed. Determine how to meet demands for the next 2 months (on time) at minimum cost. Assume that 100 shirts and 200 pairs of pants are available at the beginning of month 1.

52. Referring to the previous problem, use SolverTable to investigate the effect on total cost of two *simultaneous* changes. The first change is to allow the ratio of overtime to regular time production cost (currently $8/$4 = 2) to decrease from 20% to 80% in increments of 20%, while keeping the regular time cost at $4. The second change is to allow the production capacity *each* month (currently 2500) to decrease by 10% to 50% in increments of 10%. The idea here is that less regular time capacity is available, but

overtime becomes relatively cheaper. Is the net effect on total cost positive or negative?

53. Each year, Comfy Shoes faces demands (which must be met on time) for pairs of shoes as shown in the file **P14_53.xlsx**. Employees work three consecutive quarters and then receive one quarter off. For example, a worker might work during quarters 3 and 4 of one year and quarter 1 of the next year. During a quarter in which an employee works, he or she can produce up to 500 pairs of shoes. Each worker is paid $5000 per quarter. At the end of each quarter, a holding cost of $10 per pair of shoes is assessed. Determine how to minimize the cost per year (labor plus holding) of meeting the demands for shoes. To simplify the model, assume that at the end of each year, the ending inventory is 0. (*Hint*: You can assume that a given worker gets the *same* quarter off during each year.)

54. Referring to the previous problem, suppose Comfy Shoes can pay a flat fee for a training program that increases the productivity of all of its workers. Use SolverTable to see how much the company would be willing to pay for a training program that increases worker productivity from 500 pairs of shoes per quarter to P pairs of shoes per quarter, where P varies from 525 to 700 in increments of 25.

55. A company must meet (on time) the following demands: quarter 1, 3000 units; quarter 2, 2000 units; quarter 3, 4000 units. Each quarter, up to 2700 units can be produced with regular-time labor, at a cost of $40 per unit. During each quarter, an unlimited number of units can be produced with overtime labor, at a cost of $60 per unit. Of all units produced, 20% are unsuitable and cannot be used to meet demand. Also, at the end of each quarter, 10% of all units on hand spoil and cannot be used to meet any future demands. After each quarter's demand is satisfied and spoilage is accounted for, a cost of $15 per unit is assessed against the quarter's ending inventory. Determine how to minimize the total cost of meeting the demands of the next 3 quarters. Assume that 1000 usable units are available at the beginning of quarter 1.

56. Referring to the previous problem, the company wants to know how much money it would be worth to decrease the percentage of unsuitable items and/or the percentage of items that spoil. Write a short report that provides relevant information. Base your report on three uses of SolverTable: (1) where the percentage of unsuitable items decreases and the percentage of items that spoil stays at 10%; (2) where the percentage of unsuitable items stays at 20% and the percentage of items that spoil decreases; and (3) where both percentages decrease. Does the sum of the separate effects on total cost from the first two tables equal the combined effect from the third table? Include an answer to this question in your report.

57. A pharmaceutical company manufactures two drugs at Los Angeles and Indianapolis. The cost of manufacturing a pound of each drug depends on the location, as indicated in the file **P14_57.xlsx**. The machine time (in hours) required to produce a pound of each drug at each city is also shown in this table. The company must produce at least 1000 pounds per week of drug 1 and at least 2000 pounds per week of drug 2. It has 500 hours per week of machine time at Indianapolis and 400 hours per week at Los Angeles.

   a. Determine how the company can minimize the cost of producing the required drugs.

   b. Use SolverTable to determine how much the company would be willing to pay to purchase a combination of *A* extra hours of machine time at Indianapolis and *B* extra hours of machine time at Los Angeles, where *A* and *B* can be any positive multiples of 10 up to 50.

58. A company manufactures two products on two machines. The number of hours of machine time and labor depends on the machine and product as shown in the file **P14_58.xlsx**. The cost of producing a unit of each product depends on which machine produces it. These unit costs also appear in the file **P14_58.xlsx**. There are 200 hours available on each of the two machines, and there are 400 labor hours available. This month at least 200 units of product 1 and at least 240 units of product 2 must be produced. Also, at least half of the product 1 requirement must be produced on machine 1, and at least half of the product 2 requirement must be produced on machine 2.

   a. Determine how the company can minimize the cost of meeting this month's requirements.

   b. Use SolverTable to see how much the "at least half" requirements are costing the company. Do this by changing *both* of these requirements from "at least half" to "at least *x* percent," where *x* can be any multiple of 5% from 0% to 50%.

APPENDIX INFORMATION ON SOLVERS

Microsoft Office (or Excel) ships with a built-in version of Solver. This version and all other versions of Solver have been developed by Frontline Systems, not Microsoft. When you install Office (or Excel), you have the option of installing or not installing Solver. In most cases, a "typical" install should install Solver. To check whether Solver is installed on your system, open Excel, select the Office Button, select Excel Options, select Add-Ins, and click on Go. If there is a Solver item in the list, then Solver has been installed. (To actually add it in, make sure this item is checked.) Otherwise, you need to run the Office Setup program with the Add/Remove feature to install Solver. For users of previous versions of Excel (2003 or earlier), the actual Solver add-in file is a different one in Excel 2007. In previous versions, it was Solver.xla; now it is Solver.xlam. However, the functionality hasn't changed.

The built-in version of Solver is able to solve most problems you are likely to encounter. However, it does have one important limitation you should be aware of: it allows only 200 changing cells. This might sound like plenty, but many real-world problems go well beyond 200 changing cells. If you want to solve larger problems, you will need to purchase one of Frontline's commercial versions of Solver. For more information, check Frontline Systems' Web site at http://www.solver.com.

Shelby Shelving is a small company that manufactures two types of shelves for grocery stores. Model S is the standard model, and model LX is a heavy-duty model. Shelves are manufactured in three major steps: stamping, forming, and assembly. In the stamping stage, a large machine is used to stamp (i.e., cut) standard sheets of metal into appropriate sizes. In the forming stage, another machine bends the metal into shape. Assembly involves joining the parts with a combination of soldering and riveting. Shelby's stamping and forming machines work on both models of shelves. Separate assembly departments are used for the final stage of production.

The file **Shelby Shelving.xlsx** contains relevant data for Shelby. (See Figure 14.38.) The hours required on each machine for each unit of product are shown in the range B5:C6 of the Accounting Data sheet. For example, the production of one model S shelf requires 0.25 hour on the forming machine. Both the stamping and forming machines can operate for 800 hours each month. The model S assembly department has a monthly capacity of 1900 units. The model LX assembly department has a monthly capacity of only 1400 units. Currently Shelby is producing and selling 400 units of model S and 1400 units of model LX per month.

Model S shelves are sold for $1800, and model LX shelves are sold for $2100. Shelby's operation is fairly small in the industry, and management at Shelby believes it cannot raise prices beyond these levels because of the competition. However, the marketing department believes that Shelby can sell as much as it can produce at these prices. The costs of production are summarized in the Accounting Data sheet. As usual, values in blue cells are given, whereas other values are calculated from these.

Management at Shelby just met to discuss next month's operating plan. Although the shelves are selling well, the overall profitability of the company is a concern. The plant's engineer suggested that the current production of model S shelves be cut back. According to him, "Model S shelves are sold for $1800 per unit, but our costs are $1839. Even though we're selling only 400 units a month, we're losing money on each one. We should decrease production of model S." The controller disagreed. He said that the problem was the model S assembly department trying to absorb a large overhead with a small production volume. "The model S units are making a contribution to overhead. Even though production doesn't cover all of the fixed costs, we'd be worse off with lower production."

Figure 14.38 Accounting Data for Shelby

	A	B	C	D	E	F	G	H	I
1	Shelby Shelving Data for Current Production Schedule								
2									
3	Machine requirements (hours per unit)					Given monthly overhead cost data			
4		Model S	Model LX	Available			Fixed	Variable S	Variable LX
5	Stamping	0.3	0.3	800		Stamping	$125,000	$80	$90
6	Forming	0.25	0.5	800		Forming	$95,000	$120	$170
7						Model S Assembly	$80,000	$165	$0
8		Model S	Model LX			Model LX Assembly	$85,000	$0	$185
9	Current monthly production	400	1400						
10						Standard costs of the shelves -- based on the current production levels			
11	Hours spent in departments						Model S	Model LX	
12		Model S	Model LX	Totals		Direct materials	$1,000	$1,200	
13	Stamping	120	420	540		Direct labor:			
14	Forming	100	700	800		Stamping	$35	$35	
15						Forming	$60	$90	
16	Percentages of time spent in departments					Assembly	$80	$85	
17		Model S	Model LX			Total direct labor	$175	$210	
18	Stamping	22.2%	77.8%			Overhead allocation			
19	Forming	12.5%	87.5%			Stamping	$149	$159	
20						Forming	$150	$229	
21	Unit selling price	$1,800	$2,100			Assembly	$365	$246	
22						Total overhead	$664	$635	
23	Assembly capacity	1900	1400			Total cost	$1,839	$2,045	

Your job is to develop an LP model of Shelby's problem, then run Solver, and finally make a recommendation to Shelby management, with a short verbal argument supporting the engineer or the controller.

Notes on Accounting Data Calculations

The fixed overhead is distributed using activity-based costing principles. For example, at current production levels, the forming machine spends 100 hours on model S shelves and 700 hours on model LX shelves. The forming machine is used 800 hours of the month, of which 12.5% of the time is spent on model S shelves and 87.5% is spent on model LX shelves. The $95,000 of fixed overhead in the forming department is distributed as $11,875 (= 95,000 × 0.125) to model S shelves and $83,125 (= 95,000 × 0.875) to model LX shelves. The fixed overhead per unit of output is allocated as $29.69 (= 11,875/400) for model S and $59.38 (= 83,125/1400) for model LX. In the calculation of the standard overhead cost, the fixed and variable costs are added together, so that the overhead cost for the forming department allocated to a model S shelf is $149.69 (= 29.69 + 120, shown rounded up to $150). Similarly, the overhead cost for the forming department allocated to a model LX shelf is $229.38 (= 59.38 + 170, shown rounded down to $229). ∎

After graduating from business school, George Clark went to work for a Big Six accounting firm in San Francisco. Because his hobby has always been wine making, when he had the opportunity a few years later he purchased 5 acres plus an option to buy 35 additional acres of land in Sonoma Valley in Northern California. He plans eventually to grow grapes on that land and make wine with them. George knows that this is a big undertaking and that it will require more capital than he has at the present. However, he figures that if he persists, he will be able to leave accounting and live full time from his winery earnings by the time he is 40.

Because wine making is capital-intensive and because growing commercial-quality grapes with a full yield of 5 tons per acre takes at least 8 years, George is planning to start small. This is necessitated by both his lack of capital and his inexperience in wine making on a large scale, although he has long made wine at home. His plan is first to plant the grapes on his land to get the vines started. Then he needs to set up a small trailer where he can live on weekends while he installs the irrigation system and does the required work to the vines, such as pruning and fertilizing. To help maintain a positive cash flow during the first few years, he also plans to buy grapes from other nearby growers so he can make his own label wine. He proposes to market it through a small tasting room that he will build on his land and keep open on weekends during the spring–summer season.

To begin, George is going to use $10,000 in savings to finance the initial purchase of grapes from which he will make his first batch of wine. He is also thinking about going to the Bank of Sonoma and asking for a loan. He knows that if he goes to the bank, the loan officer will ask for a business plan; so he is trying to pull together some numbers for himself first. This way he will have a rough notion of the profitability and cash flows associated with his ideas before he develops a formal plan with a pro forma income statement and balance sheet. He has decided to make the preliminary planning horizon 2 years and would like to estimate the profit over that period. His most immediate task is to decide how much of the $10,000 should be allocated to purchasing grapes for the first year and how much to purchasing grapes for the second year. In addition, each year he must decide how much he should allocate to purchasing grapes to make his favorite Petite Sirah and how much to purchasing grapes to make the more popular Sauvignon Blanc that seems to have been capturing the attention of a wider market during the last few years in California.

In the first year, each bottle of Petite Sirah requires $0.80 worth of grapes and each bottle of Sauvignon Blanc uses $0.70 worth of grapes. For the second year, the costs of the grapes per bottle are $0.75 and $0.85, respectively.

George anticipates that his Petite Sirah will sell for $8.00 a bottle in the first year and for $8.25 in the second year, while his Sauvignon Blanc's price remains the same in both years at $7.00 a bottle.

Besides the decisions about the amounts of grapes purchased in the 2 years, George must make estimates of the sales levels for the two wines during the 2 years. The local wine-making association has told him that marketing is the key to success in any wine business; generally, demand is directly proportional to the amount of effort spent on marketing. Thus, since George cannot afford to do any market research about sales levels due to his lack of capital, he is pondering how much money he should spend to promote each wine each year. The wine-making association has given him a rule of thumb that relates estimated demand to the amount of money spent on advertising. For instance, they estimate that for each dollar spent in the first year promoting the Petite Sirah, a demand for five bottles will be created; and for each dollar spent in the second year, a demand for six bottles will result. Similarly, for each dollar spent on advertising for the Sauvignon Blanc in the first year, up to eight bottles can be sold; and for each dollar spent in the second year, up to ten bottles can be sold.

The initial funds for the advertising will come from the $10,000 savings. Assume that the cash earned from wine sales in the first year is available in the second year.

A personal concern George has is that he maintain a proper balance of wine products so that he

[15]This case was written by William D. Whisler, California State University, Hayward.

will be well positioned to expand his marketing capabilities when he moves to the winery and makes it his full-time job. Thus, in his mind it is important to ensure that the number of bottles of Petite Sirah sold each year falls in the range between 40% and 70% of the overall number of bottles sold.

Questions

1. George needs help to decide how many grapes to buy, how much money to spend on advertising, how many bottles of wine to sell, and how much profit he can expect to earn over the 2-year period. Develop a spreadsheet LP model to help him.

2. Solve the linear programming model formulated in Question 1.

The following questions should be attempted only after Questions 1 and 2 have been answered correctly.

3. After showing the business plan to the Bank of Sonoma, George learns that the loan officer is concerned about the market prices used in estimating the profits; recently it has been forecasted that Chile and Australia will be flooding the market with high-quality, low-priced white wines over the next couple of years. In particular, the loan officer estimates that the price used for the Sauvignon Blanc in the second year is highly speculative and realistically might be only half the price George calculated. Thus, the bank is nervous about lending the money because of the big effect such a decrease in price might have on estimated profits. What do you think?

4. Another comment the loan officer of the Bank of Sonoma has after reviewing the business plan is: "I see that you do have an allowance in your calculations for the carryover of inventory of unsold wine from the first year to the second year, but you do not have any cost associated with this. All companies must charge something for holding inventory, so you should redo your plans to allow for this." If the holding charges are $0.10 per bottle per year, how much, if any, does George's plan change?

5. The president of the local grape growers' association mentions to George that there is likely to

be a strike soon over the unionization of the grape workers. (Currently they are not represented by any union.) This means that the costs of the grapes might go up by anywhere from 50% to 100%. How might this affect George's plan?

6. Before taking his business plan to the bank, George had it reviewed by a colleague at the accounting firm where he works. Although his friend was excited about the plan and its prospects, he was dismayed to learn that George had not used present value in determining his profit. "George, you are an accountant and must know that money has a time value; and although you are only doing a 2-year planning problem, it still is important to calculate the present value profit." George replies, "Yes, I know all about present value. For big investments over long time periods, it is important to consider. But in this case, for a small investment and only a 2-year time period, it really doesn't matter." Who is correct, George or his colleague? Why? Use an 8% discount factor in answering this question. Does the answer change if a 6% or 10% discount rate is used? Use a spreadsheet to determine the coefficients of the objective function for the different discount rates.

7. Suppose that the Bank of Sonoma is so excited about the prospects of George's wine-growing business that they offer to lend him an extra $10,000 at their best small business rate—28% plus a 10% compensating balance.[17] Should he accept the bank's offer? Why or why not?

8. Suppose that the rule of thumb George was given by the local wine-making association is incorrect. Assume that the number of bottles of Petite Sirah sold in the first and second years is at most four for each dollar spent on advertising. And likewise for the Sauvignon Blanc, assume that it can be at most only five in years one and two.

9. How much could profits be increased if George's personal concerns (that Petite Sirah sales should account for between 40% and 70% of overall sales) are ignored? ∎

---

[17]The compensating balance requirement means that only $9,000 of the $10,000 loan is available to George; the remaining $1,000 remains with the bank.

© Ryan McVay/Photodisc/Getty Images

CHAPTER
15

Optimization Modeling: Applications

GLOBAL SUPPLY CHAIN MODELING AT DIGITAL EQUIPMENT CORPORATION

Many optimization models can be characterized as **logistics problems**—that is, problems of finding the least expensive way to transport products from their origin to their destination. In addition, real

847

logistics problems are often coupled with manufacturing or plant location decisions; the company must decide where to locate its manufacturing plants and what products to produce at each plant. Computer manufacturer Digital Equipment Corporation (DEC) faced such a problem, as reported by Arntzen et al. (1995) in "Global Supply Chain Management at Digital Equipment Corporation." DEC faces a huge global manufacturing and distribution problem with its wide range of products (mainframe computers, mini-computers, PCs, and many types of computer parts and peripherals). It must decide where (or whether) to manufacture these products and how to get them to its customers around the world in the most economical manner.

Until the late 1980s DEC specialized primarily in mainframes and minicomputers, using a manufacturing and distribution system that had proved very successful for over 20 years. But as PCs revolutionized the industry, DEC realized that it had to change—quickly and radically—if it wanted to remain a thriving company. The company had too many plants and too much overhead, and too many groups within DEC were making decisions without central coordination. In 1989 the company began to redesign its supply and delivery network and to reengineer its manufacturing and logistics processes. A key step in these corporate changes was the development of the Global Supply Chain Model (GSCM), an extremely complex linear programming model.[1] Since that time, DEC has used GSCM to perform thousands of optimizations in scores of studies.

The typical models run with GSCM are huge. They generally contain from 2000 to 6000 constraints and from 5000 to 20,000 decision variables. (They are *not* suitable for spreadsheets!) The objective typically minimizes total cost, where total cost includes production costs, inventory holding costs, facility material handling costs, taxes, facility fixed charges, production line fixed costs, transportation costs, and duty costs. The constraints include customer demand requirements, "balance" constraints for production and inventory, limits on the weight of products through the facilities, production capacities, storage capacities, and others. Also, the models become even more complicated because of multiple products, multiple time periods (planning for four consecutive quarters, for example), and the complexities of international trade. Nevertheless, by taking advantage of the special structure of these models and the advanced software that is now available, DEC is able to solve these models routinely.

To illustrate, DEC ran a large study during 1992 to determine the optimal supply chain design for all of DEC's manufacturing. The study recommended an 18-month plan to restructure the manufacturing infrastructure completely to cut costs. Specifically, it recommended that the number of worldwide plants be reduced from 33 to 12, it called for the three basic customer regions (Pacific Rim, Americas, and Europe) to be served primarily by plants within their own regions, and it included a quarter-by-quarter implementation plan. This 18-month plan has since been implemented. By spring 1994 it led to a decrease of $167 million in manufacturing costs (with another $160 million expected by June 1995) and a decrease of over $200 million in logistics costs. This is quite impressive considering that the number of units manufactured and shipped increased dramatically during this same time period. ■

15.1 INTRODUCTION

In a survey of Fortune 500 firms, 85% of those responding said that they use linear programming (LP). In this chapter we discuss some of the LP models that are most often applied to real-world applications. Some typical examples include:

[1]The GSCM is actually more than an LP model; it is a mixed-integer model with 0–1 (binary) variables for the plant location decisions.

- scheduling bank clerks for check encoding
- optimizing the operation of an oil refinery
- planning dairy production at a creamery
- scheduling production of fiberglass products at Owens-Corning Fiberglass
- optimizing a Wall Street firm's bond portfolio

Actually, these problems are just a sampling of the types of problems we will model in this chapter. There are two basic goals in this chapter. The first is to illustrate some of the many real applications that can take advantage of LP. You will see that these applications cover a wide range, from oil production to worker scheduling to cash management. The second goal is to increase your facility in modeling LP problems on a spreadsheet. We present a few principles that will help you model a wide variety of problems. The best way to learn, however, is to see many examples and work through numerous problems. In short, mastering the art of LP spreadsheet modeling takes hard work and practice. You will have plenty of opportunity to do both with the material in this chapter.

Although a wide variety of problems can be formulated as *linear* programming models, there are some that cannot. Either they require *integer* variables or they are *nonlinear* in their decision variables. We include examples of integer programming and nonlinear programming models in this chapter, just to give a taste of what's involved. We see that the modeling process for these types of problems is not much different than for LP problems. Once the models are formulated, Excel's Solver can be used to solve them. Then SolverTable can be used to perform sensitivity analysis. However, we point out that these non-LP problems are inherently more difficult to solve. Solver must use more complex algorithms, and it is not always guaranteed to find the correct solution. As long as you are aware of this, you will see that Excel's Solver provides the power to solve a great variety of realistic business problems.

Although there is a tremendous amount of theory behind the *algorithms* that solve these problems, the modeling process itself is fairly straightforward and is learned best by seeing a lot of examples. Therefore, we proceed in this chapter by modeling (and then solving) a diverse class of problems that arise in business. The exercises scattered throughout the chapter provide even more examples of how linear programming and its integer and nonlinear extensions can be applied.

All of these models can benefit from sensitivity analysis, either done formally with the SolverTable add-in or informally by changing one or more inputs and rerunning Solver. To keep the chapter from getting too long, we present only a few of the many possible sensitivity analyses. However, we stress that in real applications, the model development is just part of the overall analysis. It is usually followed by extensive sensitivity analysis.

15.2 WORKFORCE SCHEDULING MODELS

Many organizations must determine how to schedule employees to provide adequate service. The following example illustrates how to use LP to schedule employees on a daily basis.

EXAMPLE | **15.1 POSTAL EMPLOYEE SCHEDULING**

A post office requires different numbers of full-time employees on different days of the week. The number of full-time employees required each day is given in Table 15.1. Union rules state that each full-time employee must work 5 consecutive days and then receive 2 days off. For example, an employee who works Monday to Friday must be off on

Saturday and Sunday. The post office wants to meet its daily requirements using only full-time employees. Its objective is to minimize the number of full-time employees that must be hired.

Table 15.1   Employee Requirements for Post Office

Day of Week	Minimum Number of Employees Required
Monday	17
Tuesday	13
Wednesday	15
Thursday	19
Friday	14
Saturday	16
Sunday	11

Objective   To develop an LP spreadsheet model that relates 5-day shift schedules to daily numbers of employees available, and to use Solver on this model to find a schedule that uses the fewest number of employees and meets all daily workforce requirements.

WHERE DO THE NUMBERS COME FROM?

In real employee scheduling problems much of the work involves forecasting and queueing analysis to obtain worker requirements. This must be done before any schedule optimizing can be accomplished.

The only inputs we need for this problem are the minimum employee requirements in Table 15.1, but these are not necessarily easy to obtain. They would probably be obtained through a combination of two quantitative techniques: forecasting (Chapter 13) and queueing analysis (not covered in this book). The postal office would first use historical data to forecast customer and mail arrival patterns throughout a typical week. It would then use queueing analysis to translate these arrival patterns into worker requirements on a daily basis. Actually, we have kept the problem relatively simple by considering only *daily* requirements. In a realistic setting, the organization might forecast worker requirements on an hourly or even a 15-minute basis.

Solution

The key to this model is choosing the correct changing cells.

The variables and constraints for this problem appear in Table 15.2. The trickiest part is identifying the appropriate decision variables. Many people believe the decision variables should be the numbers of employees working on the various days of the week. Clearly, we need to know these values. However, it is not enough to specify, say, that 18 employees are working on Monday. The problem is that we don't know when these 18 employees start their 5-day shifts. Without this knowledge, it is impossible to implement the 5-consecutive-day, 2-day-off requirement. (If you don't believe this, try developing your own model with the "wrong" decision variables. You will eventually reach a dead end.)

The trick is to define the decision variables as the numbers of employees working each of the 7 possible 5-day shifts. For example, we need to know the number of employees who work Monday through Friday. By knowing the values of these decision variables, we can calculate the other output variables we need. For example, the number working on Thursday is the total of those who begin their 5-day shifts on Sunday, Monday, Tuesday, Wednesday, and Thursday.

Note that this is a "wrap-around" problem. We assume that the daily requirements in Table 15.1 and the worker schedules continue week after week. So, for example, if we find that 8 employees are assigned to the Thursday through Monday shift, then these employees always wrap around from one week to the next on their 5-day shift.

Table 15.2 Variables and Constraints for Postal Scheduling Problem

Input variables	Minimum required number of workers each day
Decision variables (changing cells)	Number of employees working each of the 5-day shifts (defined by their first day of work)
Objective (target cell)	Total number of employees on the payroll
Other calculated variables	Number of employees working each day
Constraints	Employees working $\geq$ Employees required

DEVELOPING THE SPREADSHEET MODEL

The spreadsheet model for this problem is shown in Figure 15.1. (See the file **Worker Scheduling.xlsx**.) To form this spreadsheet, proceed as follows.

Figure 15.1 Postal Scheduling Model with Optimal Solution

	A	B	C	D	E	F	G	H	I	J	K
1	Worker scheduling model								Range names used		
2									Employees_available	=Model!$B$23:$H$23	
3	Decision variables: number of employees starting their five-day shift on various days								Employees_required	=Model!$B$25:$H$25	
4	Mon	6.33							Employees_Starting	=Model!$B$4:$B$10	
5	Tue	5.00							Total_employees	=Model!$B$28	
6	Wed	0.33									
7	Thu	7.33									
8	Fri	0.00									
9	Sat	3.33									
10	Sun	0.00									
11											
12	Result of decisions: number of employees working on various days (along top) who started their shift on various days (along side)										
13		Mon	Tue	Wed	Thu	Fri	Sat	Sun			
14	Mon	6.33	6.33	6.33	6.33	6.33					
15	Tue		5.00	5.00	5.00	5.00	5.00				
16	Wed			0.33	0.33	0.33	0.33	0.33			
17	Thu	7.33			7.33	7.33	7.33	7.33			
18	Fri	0.00	0.00			0.00	0.00	0.00			
19	Sat	3.33	3.33	3.33			3.33	3.33			
20	Sun	0.00	0.00	0.00	0.00			0.00			
21											
22	Constraint on worker availabilities										
23	Employees available	17.00	14.67	15.00	19.00	19.00	16.00	11.00			
24		>=	>=	>=	>=	>=	>=	>=			
25	Employees required	17	13	15	19	14	16	11			
26											
27	Objective to maximize										
28	Total employees	22.33									

1 **Inputs and range names.** Enter the number of employees needed on each day of the week (from Table 15.1) in the shaded range, and create the range names shown.

2 **Employees beginning each day.** Enter *any* trial values for the number of employees beginning work on each day of the week in the Employees_starting range. These beginning days determine the possible 5-day shifts. For example, the employees in cell B4 work Monday through Friday.

3 **Employees on hand each day.** The key to this solution is to realize that the numbers in the Employees_starting range—the changing cells—do not represent the number of workers who will show up each day. As an example, the number in B4 who start on Monday work Monday through Friday. Therefore, enter the formula

=$B$4

in cell B14 and copy it across to cell F14. Proceed similarly for rows 15–20, being careful to take "wrap arounds" into account. For example, the workers starting on Thursday work Thursday through Sunday, plus Monday. Then calculate the total number who show up on each day by entering the formula

=SUM(B14:B20)

in cell B23 and copying it across to cell H23.

Excel Tip: *Ctrl-Enter Shortcut*
*You often enter a "typical" formula into a cell and then copy it many times throughout this book. To do this efficiently, highlight the entire range, here B23:H23. Then enter the typical formula, here =SUM(B14:B20), and press **Ctrl-Enter**. This has the same effect as copying, but it is quicker.*

④ Total employees. Calculate the total number of employees in cell B28 with the formula

=SUM(Employees_starting)

Note that there is no double-counting in this sum. For example, the employees in cells B4 and B5 are *not* the same people.

At this point, you might want to try experimenting with the numbers in the changing cell range to see whether you can "guess" an optimal solution (without looking at Figure 15.1). It is not that easy! Each worker who starts on a given day works the next 4 days as well, so when you find a solution that meets the minimal requirements for the various days, you usually have a few more workers available on some days than are needed.

USING SOLVER

Invoke Solver and fill out its main dialog box as shown in Figure 15.2. Also, check the Assume Linear Model and Assume Non-Negativity options in the Options dialog box.

Figure 15.2
Solver Dialog Box for Postal Model

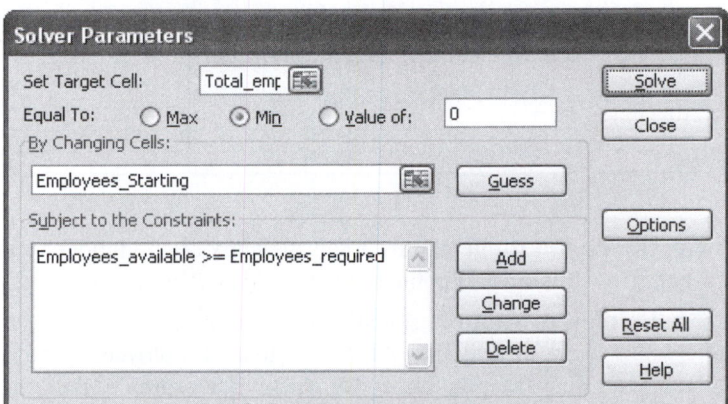

Discussion of the Solution

The optimal solution shown in Figure 15.1 has one drawback: It requires the number of employees starting work on some days to be a fraction. Because part-time employees are not allowed, this solution is unrealistic. However, it is simple to add integer constraints on the changing cells. We fill in a new constraint as shown in Figure 15.3 and then reoptimize. This produces the optimal integer solution shown in Figure 15.4.

Figure 15.3

Solver Dialog Box with Integer Constraint

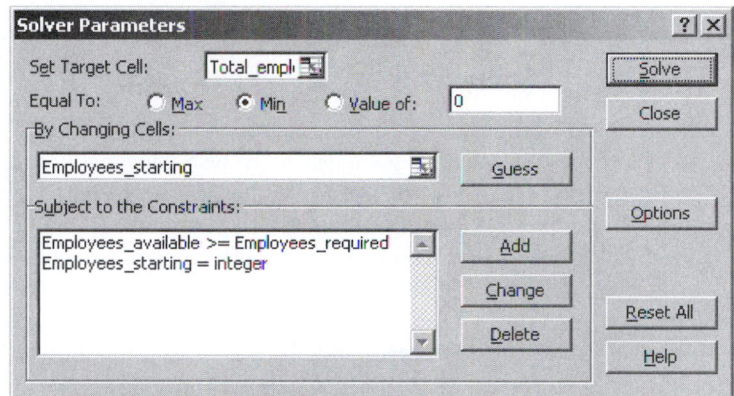

Figure 15.4 Optimal Integer Solution to Postal Scheduling Model

	A	B	C	D	E	F	G	H	I	J	K
1	Worker scheduling model								Range names used		
2									Employees_available	=Model!$B$23:$H$23	
3	Decision variables: number of employees starting their five-day shift on various days								Employees_required	=Model!$B$25:$H$25	
4	Mon	6							Employees_Starting	=Model!$B$4:$B$10	
5	Tue	6							Total_employees	=Model!$B$28	
6	Wed	0									
7	Thu	7									
8	Fri	0									
9	Sat	4									
10	Sun	0									
11											
12	Result of decisions: number of employees working on various days (along top) who started their shift on various days (along side)										
13		Mon	Tue	Wed	Thu	Fri	Sat	Sun			
14	Mon	6	6	6	6	6					
15	Tue		6	6	6	6	6				
16	Wed			0	0	0	0	0			
17	Thu	7			7	7	7	7			
18	Fri	0	0			0	0	0			
19	Sat	4	4	4			4	4			
20	Sun	0	0	0	0			0			
21											
22	Constraint on worker availabilities										
23	Employees available	17	16	16	19	19	17	11			
24		>=	>=	>=	>=	>=	>=	>=			
25	Employees required	17	13	15	19	14	16	11			
26											
27	Objective to maximize										
28	Total employees	23									

The changing cells in the optimal solution indicate the numbers of workers who start their 5-day shifts on the various days. We can then look at the *columns* of the B14:H20 range to see which employees are working on any given day. This optimal solution is typical in scheduling problems. Due to a labor constraint—each employee must work 5 consecutive days and then have 2 days off—it is typically impossible to meet the minimum employee requirements exactly. To ensure that there are enough employees available on busy days, it is often necessary to have more than enough on hand on light days.

Another interesting aspect of this problem is that if you solve this problem on your own PC, you might get a *different* schedule that is still optimal—that is, it still uses a total of 23 employees and meets all constraints. This is a case of **multiple optimal solutions** and it is not at all uncommon in LP problems. In fact, it is typically good news for a manager, who can then choose among the optimal solutions using other, possibly nonquantitative criteria.[2]

Technical Note: Solver Tolerance Setting

One technical comment about integer constraints concerns Solver's **Tolerance** setting. The idea is as follows. As Solver searches for the best integer solution, it is often able to find a "good" solution fairly quickly, but it often has to spend a lot of time finding slightly better solutions. A *nonzero* tolerance setting allows it to quit early. The default tolerance setting is 0.05. This means that if Solver finds a feasible solution that is guaranteed to have an objective value no more than 5% from the optimal value, it will quit and report this "good" solution (which might even be the *optimal* solution). Therefore, if you keep this default tolerance value, your integer solutions will sometimes not be optimal, but they will be close. If you want to ensure that you get an optimal solution, you can change the Solver tolerance value to 0. (For the standard Solver that accompanies Excel, this setting is directly under the Solver Options. If you use the Premium Solver, you can find the setting by clicking on the Solver Options button, then on the Integer Options button.)

Sensitivity Analysis

The most obvious type of sensitivity analysis involves examining how the work schedule and the total number of employees change as the number of employees required each day changes. Suppose the number of employees needed on each day of the week increases by 2, 4, or 6. How does this change the total number of employees needed? We can answer this by using SolverTable, but we first have to alter the model slightly, as shown in Figure 15.5. The problem is that we want to increase *each* of the daily minimal required values by the same amount. Therefore, we move the original requirements up to row 12, enter a trial value for the extra number required per day in cell K12, enter the formula **=B12+$K$12** in cell B27, and then copy this formula across to cell H27. Now we can use the one-way SolverTable option, using the Extra cell as the single input, letting it vary from 0 to 6 in increments of 2, and specifying the Total_employees cell as the single output cell.

The results appear in rows 34 through 37 of Figure 15.5. When the requirement increases by 2 each day, only 2 extra employees are necessary (scheduled appropriately). However, when the requirement increases by 4 each day, *more* than 4 extra employees are necessary. The same is true when the requirement increases by 6 each day. This might surprise you at first, but there is an intuitive explanation: Each extra worker works only 5 days of the week.

Note that we did not use Solver's sensitivity report here for two reasons. First, Solver does not offer a sensitivity report for models with integer constraints. Second, even if we deleted the integer constraints, Solver's sensitivity report is not suited for questions about *multiple* input changes, as we asked here. It is used primarily for questions about one-at-a-time changes to inputs, such as a change to a *specific* day's worker requirement. In this sense, SolverTable is a more flexible tool.

---

[2]It is usually difficult to tell whether there are multiple optimal solutions. You typically discover this by rerunning Solver from different starting solutions.

Figure 15.5 Sensitivity Analysis for Postal Model

	A	B	C	D	E	F	G	H	I	J	K
1	Worker scheduling model								Range names used		
2									Employees_available	=Model!$B$23:$H$23	
3	Decision variables: number of employees starting their five-day shift on various days								Employees_required	=Model!$B$25:$H$25	
4	Mon	6							Employees_Starting	=Model!$B$4:$B$10	
5	Tue	6							Total_employees	=Model!$B$28	
6	Wed	0									
7	Thu	7									
8	Fri	0									
9	Sat	4									
10	Sun	0									
11											
12	Employees required (original values)	17	13	15	19	14	16	11		Extra required each day	0
13											
14	Result of decisions: number of employees working on various days (along top) who started their shift on various days (along side)										
15		Mon	Tue	Wed	Thu	Fri	Sat	Sun			
16	Mon	6	6	6	6	6					
17	Tue		6	6	6	6	6				
18	Wed			0	0	0	0	0			
19	Thu	7			7	7	7	7			
20	Fri	0	0			0	0	0			
21	Sat	4	4	4			4	4			
22	Sun	0	0	0	0			0			
23											
24	Constraint on worker availabilities										
25	Employees available	17	16	16	19	19	17	11			
26		>=	>=	>=	>=	>=	>=	>=			
27	Employees required	17	13	15	19	14	16	11			
28											
29	Objective to maximize										
30	Total employees	23									
31											
32	Sensitivity of total employees to extra required each day										
33		$B$30									
34	0	23									
35	2	25									
36	4	28									
37	6	31									

MODELING ISSUES

1. The postal employee scheduling example is called a **static** scheduling model because we assume that the post office faces the same situation each week. In reality, demands change over time, workers take vacations in the summer, and so on, so the post office does not face the same situation each week. **Dynamic** scheduling models are discussed in the Section 15.5.

Heuristic solutions are often close to optimal, but they are never guaranteed to be optimal.

2. If you wanted to develop a weekly scheduling model for a supermarket or a fast-food restaurant, the number of variables could be very large and optimization software such as Solver might have difficulty finding an exact solution. In such cases, heuristic methods (essentially clever trial-and-error algorithms) can often be used to find a good solution to the problem. Love and Hoey (1990) indicate how this can be done for a particular staff scheduling example.

3. Our model can easily be expanded to handle part-time employees, the use of overtime, and alternative objectives such as maximizing the number of weekend days off received by employees. You can explore such extensions in the problems. ■

PROBLEMS

Level A

1. Modify the post office model so that employees are paid $10 per hour on weekdays and $15 per hour on weekends. Change the objective so that you now minimize the weekly payroll. (You can assume that each employee works 8 hours per day.) Is the previous optimal solution still optimal?

2. How much influence can the worker requirements for one, two, or three days have on the weekly schedule in the post office example? You are asked to explore this in the following questions.

a. Let Monday's requirements change from 17 to 25 in increments of 1. Use SolverTable to see how the total number of employees changes.

b. Suppose the Monday and Tuesday requirements can each, independently of one another, increase from 1 to 8 in increments of 1. Use a two-way SolverTable to see how the total number of employees changes.

c. Suppose the Monday, Tuesday, and Wednesday requirements each increase by the *same* amount, where this increase can be from 1 to 8 in increments of 1. Use a one-way SolverTable to investigate how the total number of employees changes.

3. In the post office example, suppose that each full-time employee works 8 hours per day. Thus, Monday's requirement of 17 workers can be viewed as a requirement of 8(17) = 136 hours. The post office can meet its daily labor requirements by using both full-time and part-time employees. During each week a full-time employee works 8 hours a day for 5 consecutive days, and a part-time employee works 4 hours a day for 5 consecutive days. A full-time employee costs the post office $15 per hour, whereas a part-time employee (with reduced fringe benefits) costs the post office only $10 per hour. Union requirements limit part-time labor to 25% of weekly labor requirements.

a. Modify the model as necessary, and then use Solver to minimize the post office's weekly labor costs.

b. Use SolverTable to determine how a change in the part-time labor limitation (currently 25%) influences the optimal solution.

Level B

4. In the post office example, suppose the employees want more flexibility in their schedules. They want to be allowed to work 5 consecutive days followed by 2 days off *or* to work 3 consecutive days followed by a day off followed by 2 consecutive days followed by another day off. Modify the original model (with integer constraints) to allow this flexibility. Might this be a good deal for management as well as labor? Explain.

5. In the post office example, suppose that the post office can force employees to work 1 day of overtime each week on the day immediately following this 5-day shift. For example, an employee whose regular shift is Monday to Friday can also be required to work on Saturday. Each employee is paid $100 a day for each of the first 5 days worked during a week and $124 for the overtime day (if any). Determine how the post office can minimize the cost of meeting its weekly work requirements.

6. Suppose the post office has 25 full-time employees and is not allowed to hire or fire any of them. Determine a schedule that maximizes the number of weekend days off received by these employees.

15.3 BLENDING MODELS

In many situations, various inputs must be blended to produce desired outputs. In many of these situations, LP can find the optimal combination of outputs as well as the "mix" of inputs that are used to produce the desired outputs. Some examples of blending models follow.

Inputs	Outputs
Meat, filler, water	Different types of sausage
Various types of oil	Heating oil, gasolines, aviation fuels
Carbon, iron, molybdenum	Different types of steels
Different types of pulp	Different kinds of recycled paper

The next example illustrates how to model a typical blending problem in Excel. Although this example is small relative to blending problems in real applications, we think you will agree that it is fairly complex. If you are able to guess the optimal solution, your intuition is much better than ours!

EXAMPLE | **15.2 BLENDING AT CHANDLER OIL**

Chandler Oil has 5000 barrels of crude oil 1 and 10,000 barrels of crude oil 2 available. Chandler sells gasoline and heating oil. These products are produced by blending together the two crude oils. Each barrel of crude oil 1 has a "quality level" of 10 and each barrel of crude oil 2 has a quality level of 5.[3] Gasoline must have an average quality level of at least 8, whereas heating oil must have an average quality level of at least 6. Gasoline sells for $25 per barrel, and heating oil sells for $20 per barrel. We assume that demand for heating oil and gasoline is unlimited, so that all of Chandler's production can be sold. Chandler wants to maximize its revenue from selling gasoline and heating oil.

Objective To develop an LP spreadsheet model that relates a detailed blending plan to relevant quantities on crude oil inputs and gasoline/heating oil outputs, and to use Solver to find the revenue-maximizing plan that meets quality constraints and stays within limits on crude oil availabilities.

WHERE DO THE NUMBERS COME FROM?

Most of the inputs for this problem should be easy to obtain.

- The selling prices for outputs are dictated by market pressures.
- The availabilities of inputs are based on crude supplies from the suppliers.
- The quality levels of crude oils are known from chemical analysis, whereas the required quality levels for outputs are specified by Chandler, probably in response to competitive or regulatory pressures.

Solution

In typical blending problems, the correct decision variables are the amounts of each input blended into each output.

The variables and constraints required for this blending model are listed in Table 15.3. The key to a successful model of this problem is the selection of the appropriate decision variables. Many people, when asked what decision variables should be used, specify the amounts of the two crude oils used and the amounts of the two products produced. However, this is not enough! The problem is that this information doesn't tell Chandler how to *make* the outputs from the inputs. What we need instead is a blending plan: how much of each input to use in the production of a barrel of each output. Once you understand that this blending plan is the basic decision, then all other output variables follow in a straightforward manner.

Table 15.3 **Variables and Constraints for Blending Model**

Input variables	Unit selling prices, availabilities of inputs, quality levels of inputs, required quality levels of outputs
Decision variables (changing cells)	Barrels of each input used to produce each output
Objective (target cell)	Revenue from selling gasoline and heating oil
Other calculated variables	Barrels of inputs used, barrels of outputs produced (and sold), quality obtained and quality required for outputs
Constraints	Barrels of inputs used ≤ Barrels available
	Quality of outputs obtained ≥ Quality required

A secondary, but very important, issue in typical blending problems is how to implement the "quality" constraints. [The constraints here are in terms of quality. In other blending problems they are often expressed in terms of percentages of some ingredient(s). For example, a typical quality constraint might be that some output can contain no more than 2% sulfur. Such constraints are typical of blending problems.] When we explain how to develop the spreadsheet model, we will discuss the preferred way to implement quality constraints.

[3]To avoid getting into an overly technical discussion, we use the generic term *quality level*. In real oil blending, qualities of interest might be octane rating, viscosity, and others.

DEVELOPING THE SPREADSHEET MODEL

The spreadsheet model for this problem appears in Figure 15.6. (See the file **Blending Oil.xlsx**.) To set it up, proceed as follows.

Figure 15.6 Chandler Oil Blending Model

	A	B	C	D	E	F	G	H
1	Chandler oil blending model					Range names used		
2						Barrels_available	=Model!$F$16:$F$17	
3	Monetary inputs	Gasoline	Heating oil			Barrels_used	=Model!$D$16:$D$17	
4	Selling price/barrel	$25.00	$20.00			Blending_plan	=Model!$B$16:$C$17	
5						Quality_points_obtained	=Model!$B$22:$C$22	
6	Quality level per barrel of crudes					Quality_points_required	=Model!$B$24:$C$24	
7	Crude oil 1	10				Revenue	=Model!$B$27	
8	Crude oil 2	5						
9								
10	Required quality level per barrel of product							
11		Gasoline	Heating oil					
12		8	6					
13								
14	Blending plan (barrels of crudes in each product)							
15		Gasoline	Heating oil	Barrels used		Barrels available		
16	Crude oil 1	3000	2000	5000	<=	5000		
17	Crude oil 2	2000	8000	10000	<=	10000		
18	Barrels sold	5000	10000					
19								
20	Constraints on quality							
21		Gasoline	Heating oil					
22	Quality points obtained	40000	60000					
23		>=	>=					
24	Quality points required	40000	60000					
25								
26	Objective to maximize							
27	Revenue	$325,000						

From here on, the solutions shown, such as in Figure 15.6, are optimal. However, remember that you can start with any solution. It doesn't even need to be feasible.

1 **Inputs and range names.** Enter the unit selling prices, quality levels for inputs, required quality levels for outputs, and availabilities of inputs in the shaded ranges. Then name the ranges as indicated.

2 **Inputs blended into each output.** As we discussed, the quantities Chandler must specify are the barrels of each input used to produce each output. Therefore, enter *any* trial values for these quantities in the Blending_plan range. For example, the value in cell B16 is the amount of crude oil 1 used to make gasoline and the value in cell C16 is the amount of crude oil 1 used to make heating oil. The Blending_plan range contains the changing cells.

3 **Inputs used and outputs sold.** We need to calculate the row sums (in column D) and column sums (in row 18) of the Blending_plan range. There is a quick way to do this. Just highlight both the row and column where the sums will go (highlight one, then hold down the Ctrl key and highlight the other), and click on the Summation (Σ) button on the main Excel toolbar. This creates SUM formulas in each highlighted cell.

4 **Quality achieved.** Keeping track of the quality level of gasoline and heating oil in the Quality_points_obtained range is tricky. Begin by calculating for each output the number of "quality points" (QP) in the inputs used to produce this output:

$$QP \text{ in gasoline} = 10 \text{ (Oil 1 in gasoline)} + 5 \text{ (Oil 2 in gasoline)}$$

$$QP \text{ in heating oil} = 10 \text{ (Oil 1 in heating oil)} + 5 \text{ (Oil 2 in heating oil)}$$

For the gasoline produced to have a quality level of at least 8, we must have

$$\text{QP in gasoline} \geq 8 \text{ (Gasoline sold)} \tag{15.1}$$

For the heating oil produced to have a quality level of at least 6, we must have

$$\text{QP in heating oil} \geq 6 \text{ (Heating oil sold)} \tag{15.2}$$

To implement inequalities (15.1) and (15.2), calculate the QP for gasoline in cell B22 with the formula

=SUMPRODUCT(B16:B17, $B$7:$B$8)

Then copy this formula to cell C22 to generate the QP for heating oil.

5 **Quality required.** Calculate the required quality points for gasoline and heating oil in cells B24 and C24. Specifically, determine the required quality points for gasoline in cell B24 with the formula

=B12*B18

Then copy this formula to cell C24 for heating oil.

6 **Revenue.** Calculate the total revenue in cell B27 with the formula

=SUMPRODUCT(B4:C4,B18:C18)

USING SOLVER

To solve Chandler's problem with Solver, fill out the main Solver dialog box as shown in Figure 15.7. As usual, check the Assume Linear Model and Assume Non-Negative options before optimizing. You should obtain the optimal solution shown in Figure 15.6.

Figure 15.7
Solver Dialog Box
for Blending Model

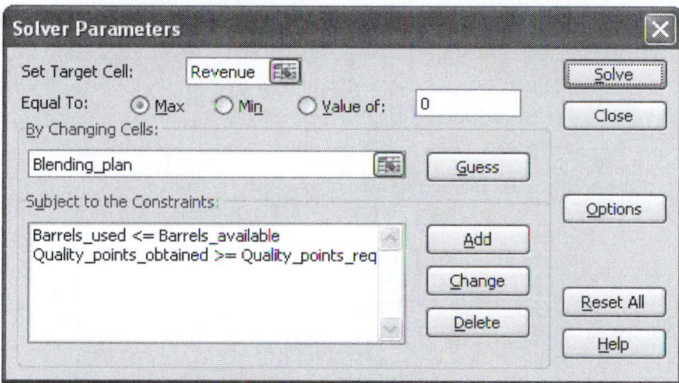

Discussion of the Solution

The optimal solution implies that Chandler should make 5000 barrels of gasoline with 3000 barrels of crude oil 1 and 2000 barrels of crude oil 2. The company should also make 10,000 barrels of heating oil with 2000 barrels of crude oil 1 and 8000 barrels of crude oil 2. With this blend, Chandler will obtain a revenue of $325,000. As stated previously, we believe this problem is sufficiently complex to defy intuition. Clearly, gasoline is more profitable per barrel than heating oil, but given the crude availability and the quality constraints, it turns out that Chandler should sell twice as much heating oil as gasoline. This would have been very difficult to guess ahead of time.

Sensitivity Analysis

We perform two typical sensitivity analyses on the Chandler blending model. In each, we see how revenue and the amounts of the outputs produced (and sold) vary. In the first analysis, we use the unit selling price of gasoline as the input and let it vary from $20 to $80 in increments of $5. The SolverTable results appear in Figure 15.8. Two things are of interest. First, as the price of gasoline increases, Chandler produces more gasoline and less heating oil, exactly as we would expect. Second, the revenue always increases, as the changes in column E indicate.

Figure 15.8

Sensitivity to the Selling Price of Gasoline

	A	B	C	D	E
29	Sensitivity of outputs sold and revenue to selling price of gasoline				
30		$B$18	$C$18	$B$27	Increase
31	20	5000	10000	$300,000	
32	25	5000	10000	$325,000	$25,000
33	30	5000	10000	$350,000	$25,000
34	35	5000	10000	$375,000	$25,000
35	40	5000	10000	$400,000	$25,000
36	45	5000	10000	$425,000	$25,000
37	50	5000	10000	$450,000	$25,000
38	55	5000	10000	$475,000	$25,000
39	60	8333	0	$500,000	$25,000
40	65	8333	0	$541,667	$41,667
41	70	8333	0	$583,333	$41,667
42	75	8333	0	$625,000	$41,667
43	80	8333	0	$666,667	$41,667

In the second sensitivity analysis we vary the availability of crude 1 from 2000 barrels to 20,000 barrels in increments of 1000 barrels. The resulting SolverTable output appears in Figure 15.9. These results make sense if we analyze them carefully. First, the revenue increases, but at a decreasing rate, as more crude 1 is available. This is a common occurrence in LP models. As more of a resource is made available, revenue can only increase or remain the same, but each extra unit of the resource produces less (or at least no more) revenue than the previous unit. Second, the amount of gasoline produced increases, whereas the amount of heating oil produced decreases. Here is the reason: Crude 1 has a higher quality than crude 2, and gasoline requires higher quality. Gasoline also sells for a higher price. Therefore, as more crude 1 is available, Chandler can produce more gasoline, receive more revenue, and still meet quality standards.

Figure 15.9

Sensitivity to the Availability of Crude 1

	G	H	I	J	K	L
29	Sensitivity of outputs sold and revenue to availability of crude 1					
30		$B$18	$C$18	$B$27	Increase	
31	2000	0	10000	$200,000		
32	3000	1000	12000	$265,000	$65,000	
33	4000	3000	11000	$295,000	$30,000	
34	5000	5000	10000	$325,000	$30,000	
35	6000	7000	9000	$355,000	$30,000	
36	7000	9000	8000	$385,000	$30,000	
37	8000	11000	7000	$415,000	$30,000	
38	9000	13000	6000	$445,000	$30,000	
39	10000	15000	5000	$475,000	$30,000	
40	11000	17000	4000	$505,000	$30,000	
41	12000	19000	3000	$535,000	$30,000	
42	13000	21000	2000	$565,000	$30,000	
43	14000	23000	1000	$595,000	$30,000	
44	15000	25000	0	$625,000	$30,000	
45	16000	26000	0	$650,000	$25,000	
46	17000	27000	0	$675,000	$25,000	
47	18000	28000	0	$700,000	$25,000	
48	19000	29000	0	$725,000	$25,000	
49	20000	30000	0	$750,000	$25,000	

Could we also answer these sensitivity questions with Solver's sensitivity report, shown in Figure 15.10? Consider the sensitivity to the change in the price of gasoline. The first and third rows of the top table in this report are for sensitivity to the objective coefficients of decision variables involving gasoline. The problem is that when we change the price of gasoline, we automatically change *both* of these coefficients. The reason is that we sum these two decision variables to calculate the amount of gasoline sold, which we then multiply by the unit price of gasoline in the objective. However, Solver's sensitivity report is valid only for one-at-a-time coefficient changes. Therefore, it cannot answer our question.

Figure 15.10
Sensitivity Report for Blending Model

Cell	Name	Final Value	Reduced Cost	Objective Coefficient	Allowable Increase	Allowable Decrease
Adjustable Cells						
$B$16	Crude oil 1 Gasoline	3000	0	25	58.333	8.333
$C$16	Crude oil 1 Heating oil	2000	0	20	8.333	58.333
$B$17	Crude oil 2 Gasoline	2000	0	25	87.5	6.25
$C$17	Crude oil 2 Heating oil	8000	0	20	6.25	14.583

Cell	Name	Final Value	Shadow Price	Constraint R.H. Side	Allowable Increase	Allowable Decrease
Constraints						
$D$16	Crude oil 1 Barrels used	5000	30.0	5000	10000	2500
$D$17	Crude oil 2 Barrels used	10000	17.5	10000	10000	6666.667
$B$22	Quality points obtained Gasoline	40000	-2.5	0	5000	20000
$C$22	Quality points obtained Heating oil	60000	-2.5	0	10000	6666.667

In contrast, the first row of the bottom table in Figure 15.10 complements the SolverTable sensitivity analysis on the availability of crude 1. It shows that if the availability increases by no more than 10,000 barrels or decreases by no more than 2500 barrels, then the shadow price stays at $30 per barrel—that is, the same $30,000 increase in profit per 1000 barrels we saw in Figure 15.9. Beyond that range, the sensitivity report indicates only that the shadow price will change. The SolverTable results indicate *how* it changes. For example, when crude 1 availability increases beyond 15,000 barrels, the SolverTable results indicate that the shadow price decreases to $25 per barrel.

A Caution About Blending Constraints

Blending models usually have various "quality" constraints, often expressed as required percentages of various ingredients. To keep these models linear (and avoid dividing by 0), it is important to clear denominators.

Before concluding this example, we discuss why our model is linear. The key is our implementation of the quality constraints, as shown in inequalities (15.1) and (15.2). To keep a model linear, each side of an inequality constraint must be a constant, the product of a constant and a variable, or a sum of such products. If we implement the quality constraints as in inequalities (15.1) and (15.2), we indeed get linear constraints. However, it is arguably more natural to rewrite this type of constraint by dividing through by the amount sold. For example, the modified gasoline constraint would be

$$\frac{QP \text{ in gasoline}}{\text{Gasoline sold}} \geq 8 \qquad (15.3)$$

Although this form of the constraint is perfectly valid—and is possibly more natural to many users—it suffers from two drawbacks. First, it makes the model nonlinear. This is because the left-hand side is no longer a sum of products; it involves a quotient. We prefer linear models whenever possible. Second, suppose it turned out that Chandler's optimal solution called for *no* gasoline at all. Then we would be dividing by 0 in inequality (15.3), and this would cause an error in Excel. Because of these two drawbacks, the moral is to clear denominators in all such blending constraints. ∎

MODELING ISSUES

In reality, a company using a blending model would run the model periodically (each day, say) and set production on the basis of the current inventory of inputs and the current forecasts of demands and prices. Then the forecasts and the input levels would be updated, and the model would be run again to determine the next day's production. ∎

PROBLEMS

Level A

7. Use SolverTable in Chandler's blending model to see whether, by increasing the selling price of gasoline, you can get an optimal solution that produces only gasoline, no heating oil. Then use SolverTable again to see whether, by increasing the selling price of heating oil, you can get an optimal solution that produces only heating oil, no gasoline.

8. Use SolverTable in Chandler's blending model to find the shadow price of crude oil 1—that is, the amount Chandler would be willing to spend to acquire more crude oil 1. Does this shadow price change as Chandler keeps getting more of crude oil 1? Answer the same questions for crude oil 2.

9. How sensitive is the optimal solution (barrels of each output sold and profit) to the required quality points? Answer this by running a two-way SolverTable with these three outputs. You can choose the values of the two inputs to vary.

10. In Chandler's blending model suppose there is a chemical ingredient, which we'll call CI, that both gasoline and heating oil need. At least 3% of every barrel of gasoline must be CI, and at least 5% of every barrel of heating oil must be CI. Suppose that 4% of all crude oil 1 is CI and 6% of all crude oil 2 is CI. Modify the model to incorporate the constraints on CI, and then optimize. Don't forget to clear denominators.

11. As we have formulated Chandler's blending model, a barrel of any input results in a barrel of output. However, in a real blending problem there can be losses. Suppose a barrel of input results in only a fraction of a barrel of output. Specifically, each barrel of either crude oil used for gasoline results in only 0.95 barrel of gasoline, and each barrel of either crude used for heating oil results in only 0.97 barrel of heating oil. Modify the model to incorporate these losses, and reoptimize.

Level B

12. We warned you about clearing denominators in the quality constraints. This problem indicates what happens if you don't do so.
   a. Implement the quality constraints as indicated in inequality (15.3) of the text. Then run Solver with Assume Linear Model checked. What happens? What if you uncheck the Assume Linear Model option?
   b. Repeat part **a**, but increase the selling price of heating oil to $40 per barrel. What happens now? Does it matter whether you check or uncheck the Assume Linear Model option? Why?

15.4 LOGISTICS MODELS

In many situations a company produces products at locations called **supply points** and ships these products to customer locations called **demand points**. Typically, each supply point has a limited capacity that it can ship, and each customer must receive a required quantity of the product. Spreadsheet models can be used to determine the minimum-cost shipping method for satisfying customer demands.

15.4.1 Transportation Models

We begin by assuming that the only possible shipments are those directly from a supply point to a demand point. That is, no shipments between supply points or between demand points are possible. Such a problem is called a **transportation problem**.

15.3 SHIPPING CARS FROM PLANTS TO REGIONS OF THE COUNTRY

The Grand Prix Automobile Company manufactures automobiles in three plants and then ships them to four regions of the country. The plants can supply the amounts listed in the right column of Table 15.4. The customer demands by region are listed in the bottom row of this table, and the unit costs of shipping an automobile from each plant to each region are listed in the middle of the table. Grand Prix wants to find the lowest-cost shipping plan for meeting the demands of the four regions without exceeding the capacities of the plants.

Table 15.4 **Input Data for Grand Prix Example**

	Region 1	Region 2	Region 3	Region 4	Capacity
Plant 1	131	218	266	120	450
Plant 2	250	116	263	278	600
Plant 3	178	132	122	180	500
Demand	450	200	300	300	

Objective To develop a spreadsheet optimization model that finds the least-cost way of shipping the automobiles from plants to regions that stays within plant capacities and meets regional demands.

WHERE DO THE NUMBERS COME FROM?

A typical transportation problem requires three sets of numbers: capacities (or supplies), demands (or requirements), and unit shipping (and possibly production) costs. We discuss each of these next.

- The capacities indicate the most each plant can supply in a given amount of time—a month, say—under current operating conditions. In some cases it might be possible to increase the "base" capacities, by using overtime, for example. In such cases we could modify the model to determine the amounts of additional capacity to use (and pay for).

- The customer demands are typically estimated from some type of forecasting model (as discussed in Chapter 13). The forecasts are often based on historical customer demand data.

- The unit shipping costs come from a transportation cost analysis—how much does it really cost to send a single automobile from any plant to any region? This is not an easy question to answer, and it requires an analysis of the best mode of transportation (railroad, ship, or truck, say). However, companies typically have the required data. Actually, the unit "shipping" cost can also include the unit production cost at each plant. However, if this cost is the same across all plants, as we are tacitly assuming here, it can be omitted from the model.

Solution

The variables and constraints required for this model are listed in Table 15.5. We must know the amounts sent out of the plants and the amounts sent to the regions. However, these aggregate quantities are not directly the decision variables. The company must decide exactly the number of autos to send from each plant to each region—a shipping plan.

Table 15.5 Variables and Constraints for Transportation Model

Input variables	Plant capacities, regional demands, unit shipping costs
Decision variables (changing cells)	Number of autos sent from each plant to each region
Objective (target cell)	Total shipping cost
Other calculated variables	Number sent out of each plant, number sent to each region
Constraints	Number sent out of each plant ≤ Plant capacity
	Number sent to each region ≥ Region demand

Representing as a Network Model

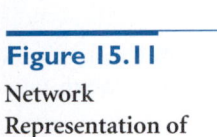

In a transportation problem all flows go from left to right— from origins to destinations. We see more complex network structures in Section 15.4.2.

A network diagram of this model appears in Figure 15.11. This diagram is typical of network models. It consists of nodes and arcs. A **node**, indicated by a circle, generally represents a geographical location. In this case the nodes on the left correspond to plants, and the nodes on the right correspond to regions. An **arc**, indicated by an arrow, generally represents a route for getting a product from one node to another. Here, the arcs all go from a plant node to a region node—from left to right.

The problem data fit nicely on such a diagram. The capacities are placed next to the plant nodes, the demands are placed next to the region nodes, and the unit shipping costs are placed on the arcs. The decision variables are usually called **flows**. They represent the amounts shipped on the various arcs. Sometimes (although not in this problem), there are upper limits on the flows on some or all of the arcs. These upper limits are called **arc capacities**, and they can also be shown on the diagram.[4]

Figure 15.11

Network Representation of Grand Prix Problem

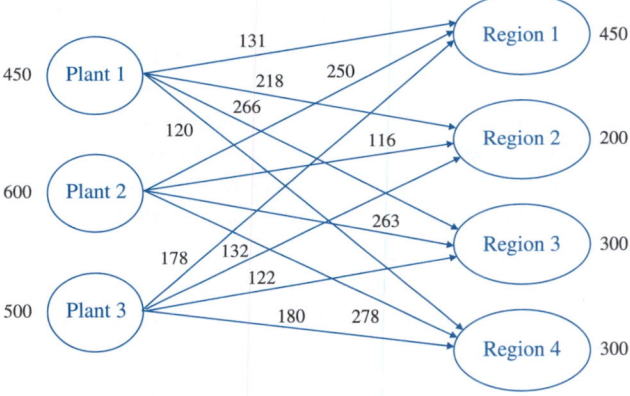

DEVELOPING THE SPREADSHEET MODEL

The spreadsheet model appears in Figure 15.12. (See the file **Transportation 1.xlsx**.) To develop this model, perform the following steps.

---

[4]There can even be lower limits, other than 0, on certain flows, but we don't consider any such models here.

Figure 15.12 Grand Prix Transportation Model

	A	B	C	D	E	F	G	H	I	J	K
1	Grand Prix transportation model								Range names used:		
2									Capacity	=Model!$I$13:$I$15	
3	Unit shipping costs								Demand	=Model!$C$18:$F$18	
4			To						Shipping_Plan	=Model!$C$13:$F$15	
5			Region 1	Region 2	Region 3	Region 4			Total_cost	=Model!$B$21	
6	From	Plant 1	$131	$218	$266	$120			Total_received	=Model!$C$16:$F$16	
7		Plant 2	$250	$116	$263	$278			Total_shipped	=Model!$G$13:$G$15	
8		Plant 3	$178	$132	$122	$180					
9											
10	Shipping plan, and constraints on supply and demand										
11			To								
12			Region 1	Region 2	Region 3	Region 4	Total shipped		Capacity		
13	From	Plant 1	150	0	0	300	450	<=	450		
14		Plant 2	100	200	0	0	300	<=	600		
15		Plant 3	200	0	300	0	500	<=	500		
16		Total received	450	200	300	300					
17			>=	>=	>=	>=					
18		Demand	450	200	300	300					
19											
20	Objective to minimize										
21	Total cost	$176,050									

① Inputs.[5] Enter the unit shipping costs, plant capacities, and region demands in the shaded ranges.

② Shipping plan. Enter any trial values for the shipments from plants to regions in the Shipping_plan range. These are the changing cells. Note that we model this as a rectangular range with exactly the same shape as the range where the unit shipping costs are entered. This is natural, and it simplifies the formulas in the following steps.

③ Numbers shipped from plants. We need to calculate the amount shipped out of each plant with row sums in the range G13:G15. To do this most easily, highlight this range and click on the summation (Σ) toolbar button.

④ Amounts received by regions. We also need to calculate the amount shipped to each region with column sums in the range C16:F16. Again, do this by highlighting the range and clicking on the summation button.

⑤ Total shipping cost. Calculate the total cost of shipping power from the plants to the regions in the Total_cost cell with the formula

=SUMPRODUCT(C6:F8,Shipping_plan)

This formula sums all products of unit shipping costs and amounts shipped. We see the benefit of placing unit shipping costs and amounts shipped in similar-size rectangular ranges—we can then use the SUMPRODUCT function.

USING SOLVER

Invoke Solver with the settings shown in Figure 15.13. As usual, check the Assume Linear Model and Assume Non-Negative options before optimizing.

It is typical in transportation models, especially large models, that only a relatively few of the possible routes are used.

Discussion of the Solution

The Solver solution appears in Figure 15.12 and is illustrated graphically in Figure 15.14. The company incurs a total shipping cost of $176,050 by using the shipments listed in Figure 15.14. Except for the six routes shown, no other routes are used. Most of the

[5]From here on, we might not remind you about creating range names, but we will continue to list our suggested range names on the spreadsheet.

shipments occur on the low-cost routes, but this is not always the case. For example, the route from plant 2 to region 1 is relatively expensive, and it is used. On the other hand, the route from plant 3 to region 2 is relatively cheap, but it is not used. A good shipping plan tries to use cheap routes, but it is constrained by capacities and demands.

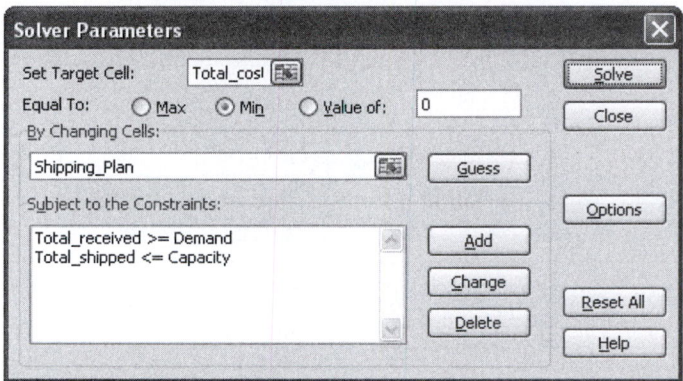

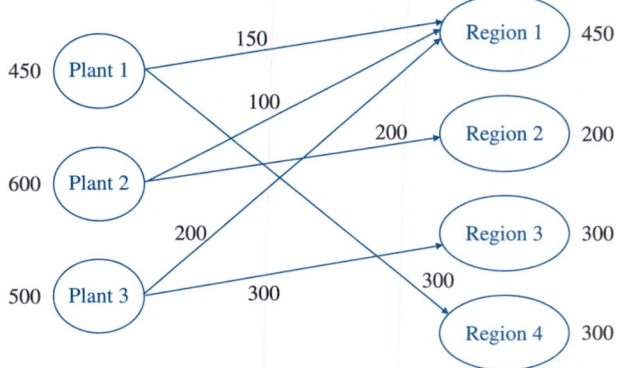

Note that the available capacity is not all used. The reason is that total capacity is 1550, whereas total demand is only 1250. Even though we constrained the demand constraints to be of the "≥" type, there is clearly no reason to send the regions more than they request because it only increases shipping costs. Therefore, we send them the minimal amounts they request and no more. In fact, we could have expressed the demand constraints as "=" constraints, and we would have obtained exactly the same solution.

Sensitivity Analysis

There are many sensitivity analyses we could perform on the basic transportation model. For example, we could vary any one of the unit shipping costs, capacities, or demands. The effect of any such change in a single input is captured nicely in Solver's sensitivity report, shown in Figure 15.15. The top part indicates the effects of changes in the unit shipping costs. The results here are typical. For all routes with positive flows, the corresponding reduced cost is 0, whereas for all routes not currently being used, the reduced cost indicates how much less the unit shipping cost would have to be before the company would start shipping along it. For example, if the unit shipping cost from plant 2 to region 3 decreased by more than $69, then this route would become attractive.

Figure 15.15

Solver's Sensitivity Report for Transportation Model

				Final	Reduced	Objective	Allowable	Allowable
	A	B	C	D	E	F	G	H
6		Adjustable Cells						
7					Final	Reduced	Objective	Allowable	Allowable
8		Cell	Name		Value	Cost	Coefficient	Increase	Decrease
9		$C$13	Plant 1 Region 1		150	0	131	119	13
10		$D$13	Plant 1 Region 2		0	221	218	1E+30	221
11		$E$13	Plant 1 Region 3		0	191	266	1E+30	191
12		$F$13	Plant 1 Region 4		300	0	120	13	239
13		$C$14	Plant 2 Region 1		100	0	250	39	72
14		$D$14	Plant 2 Region 2		200	0	116	88	116
15		$E$14	Plant 2 Region 3		0	69	263	1E+30	69
16		$F$14	Plant 2 Region 4		0	39	278	1E+30	39
17		$C$15	Plant 3 Region 1		200	0	178	13	69
18		$D$15	Plant 3 Region 2		0	88	132	1E+30	88
19		$E$15	Plant 3 Region 3		300	0	122	69	194
20		$F$15	Plant 3 Region 4		0	13	180	1E+30	13
21									
22		Constraints							
23					Final	Shadow	Constraint	Allowable	Allowable
24		Cell	Name		Value	Price	R.H. Side	Increase	Decrease
25		$G$13	Plant 1 Total shipped		450	-119	450	100	150
26		$G$14	Plant 2 Total shipped		300	0	600	1E+30	300
27		$G$15	Plant 3 Total shipped		500	-72	500	100	200
28		$C$16	Total received Region 1		450	250	450	300	100
29		$D$16	Total received Region 2		200	116	200	300	200
30		$E$16	Total received Region 3		300	194	300	200	100
31		$F$16	Total received Region 4		300	239	300	150	100

The bottom part of this report is useful because of its shadow prices. For example, we know that plants 1 and 3 are shipping all of their capacity, so the company would benefit from having more capacity at these plants. In particular, the report indicates that each extra unit of capacity at plant 1 is worth $119, and each extra unit of capacity at plant 3 is worth $72. However, because the allowable increase for each of these is 100, we know that after an increase in capacity of 100 at either plant, further increases will probably be worth less than the stated shadow prices.

The key to this sensitivity analysis is to modify the model slightly before running SolverTable.

One interesting analysis that cannot be performed with Solver's sensitivity report is to keep shipping costs and capacities constant and allow all of the demands to change by a certain percentage (positive or negative). To perform this analysis, we use SolverTable, with the varying percentage as the single input. Then we can keep track of the total cost and any particular amounts shipped of interest. The key to doing this correctly is to modify the model slightly before running SolverTable. The appropriate modifications appear in Figure 15.16. (See the second sheet of the finished **Transportation 1** file.) Now we store the original demands in row 10, we enter a percent increase in cell I10, and we enter *formulas* in the Demand range in row 20. For example, the formula in cell C20 is =C10*(1+$I$10). Then we run SolverTable with cell I10 as the single input cell, allowing it to vary from −20% to 30% in increments of 5%, and we keep track of total cost. As the table shows, the total shipping cost increases at an increasing rate as the demands increase. However, at some point the problem becomes infeasible. As soon as the total demand is greater than the total capacity, it is impossible to meet all demand.

An Alternative Model

The transportation model in Figure 15.12 is a very natural one. If we consider the graphical representation in Figure 15.11, we note that all arcs go from left to right, that is, from plants to regions. Therefore, the rectangular range of shipments allows us to calculate shipments out of plants as row sums and shipments into regions as column sums. In anticipation of later models in this chapter, however, where the graphical network can be more complex, we present an alternative model of the transportation problem. (See the file **Transportation 2.xlsx.**)

Figure 15.16
Sensitivity Analysis to Percentage Changes in All Demands

	A	B	C	D	E	F	G	H	I
1	Grand Prix transportation model								
2									
3	Unit shipping costs								
4			To						
5			Region 1	Region 2	Region 3	Region 4			
6	From	Plant 1	$131	$218	$266	$120			
7		Plant 2	$250	$116	$263	$278			
8		Plant 3	$178	$132	$122	$180			
9								Input for SolverTable	
10	Original demands		450	200	300	300		% change	0%
11									
12	Shipping plan, and constraints on supply and demand								
13			To						
14			Region 1	Region 2	Region 3	Region 4	Total shipped		Capacity
15	From	Plant 1	150	0	0	300	450	<=	450
16		Plant 2	100	200	0	0	300	<=	600
17		Plant 3	200	0	300	0	500	<=	500
18		Total received	450	200	300	300			
19			>=	>=	>=	>=			
20		Demand	450	200	300	300			
21									
22	Objective to minimize								
23	Total cost	$176,050							
24									
25	Sensitivity of total cost to percentage change in each of the demands								
26		$B$23							
27	-20%	$130,850							
28	-15%	$140,350							
29	-10%	$149,850							
30	-5%	$162,770							
31	0%	$176,050							
32	5%	$189,330							
33	10%	$202,610							
34	15%	$215,890							
35	20%	$229,170							
36	25%	Not feasible							
37	30%	Not feasible							

First, it is useful to introduce some additional network terminology. We already defined flows as the amounts shipped on the various arcs. The direction of the arcs indicates which way the flows are allowed to travel. An arc pointed into a node is called an **inflow**, whereas an arrow pointed out of a node is called an **outflow**. In the basic transportation model, all outflows originate from suppliers, and all inflows go toward demanders. However, general networks can have both inflows and outflows for any given node.

With this general structure in mind, the typical network model has one changing cell per arc. It indicates how much (if any) to send along that arc in the direction of the arrow. Therefore, it is often useful to model network problems by listing all of the arcs and their corresponding flows in one long list. Then we can deal with constraints in a separate section of the spreadsheet. Specifically, for each node in the network, there is a **flow balance constraint**. These flow balance constraints for the basic transportation model are simply the supply and demand constraints we have already discussed, but they can be more general for other network models, as we discuss in the next subsection.

Although this model is possibly less natural than the original model, it generalizes much better to other network models in this chapter.

The alternative model of the Grand Prix problem appears in Figure 15.17. In the range A5:C16, we manually enter the plant and region indexes and the associated unit shipping costs. Each row in this range corresponds to an arc in the network. For example, row 12 corresponds to the arc from plant 2 to region 4, with unit shipping cost $278. Then we create a column of changing cells for the flows in column D. (If there were arc capacities, we would place them to the right of the flows.)

Figure 15.17 Alternative Model of Transportation Problem

	A	B	C	D	E	F	G	H	I	J	K	L	M
1	Grand Prix transportation model: a more general network formulation										Range names used:		
2											Capacity	=Model!$I$6:$I$8	
3	Network structure and flows					Flow balance constraints					Demand	=Model!$I$12:$I$15	
4	Origin	Destination	Unit cost	Flow		Capacity constraints					Destination	=Model!$B$5:$B$16	
5	1	1	131	150		Plant	Outflow		Capacity		Flow	=Model!$D$5:$D$16	
6	1	2	218	0		1	450	<=	450		Inflow	=Model!$G$12:$G$15	
7	1	3	266	0		2	300	<=	600		Origin	=Model!$A$5:$A$16	
8	1	4	120	300		3	500	<=	500		Outflow	=Model!$G$6:$G$8	
9	2	1	250	100							Total_Cost	=Model!$B$19	
10	2	2	116	200		Demand constraints							
11	2	3	263	0		Region	Inflow		Demand				
12	2	4	278	0		1	450	>=	450				
13	3	1	178	200		2	200	>=	200				
14	3	2	132	0		3	300	>=	300				
15	3	3	122	300		4	300	>=	300				
16	3	4	180	0									
17													
18	Objective to minimize												
19	Total Cost	$176,050											

The flow balance constraints are conceptually straightforward. Each cell in the Outflow and Inflow ranges in column G contains the appropriate sum of flows. For example, cell G6, the outflow from plant 1, represents the sum of cells D5 through D8, whereas cell G12, the inflow to plant 1, represents the sum of cells D5, D9, and D13. Fortunately, there is an easy way to enter these summation formulas.[6] We use Excel's built-in SUMIF function, in the form =SUMIF(*CompareRange,Criteria,SumRange*). For example, the formula in cell G6 is

=SUMIF(Origin,F6,Flow)

This formula compares the plant number in cell F6 to the Origin range in column A and sums all flows where they are equal—that is, it sums all flows out of plant 1. By copying this formula down to cell G8, we obtain the flows out of the other plants. For flows into regions, we enter the similar formula

=SUMIF(Destination,F12,Flow)

in cell G12 to sum all flows into region 1, and we copy it down to cell G15 for flows into the other regions. In general, the SUMIF function finds all cells in the first argument that satisfy the criterion in the second argument and then sums the corresponding cells in the third argument. It is a very handy function, especially for network modeling.

Excel Function: *SUMIF*
The SUMIF function is useful for summing values in a certain range if cells in a related range satisfy given conditions. It has the syntax =SUMIF(**compareRange,criterion,sumRange**), *where compareRange and sumRange are similar-size ranges. This formula checks each cell in compareRange to see whether it satisfies the criterion. If it does, it adds the corresponding value in sumRange to the overall sum. For example,* =SUMIF(A12:A23,1,D12:D23) *sums all values in the range D12:D23 where the corresponding cell in the range A12:A23 has the value 1.*

---

[6]Try entering these formulas manually, even for a 3 × 4 transportation model, and you will see why we use the SUMIF function!

This use of the SUMIF function, along with the list of origins, destinations, unit costs, and flows in columns A through D, is the key to the model. The rest is straightforward. We calculate the total cost as the SUMPRODUCT of unit costs and flows, and we set up the Solver dialog box as shown in Figure 15.18.

Figure 15.18

Solver Dialog Box for Alternative Transportation Model

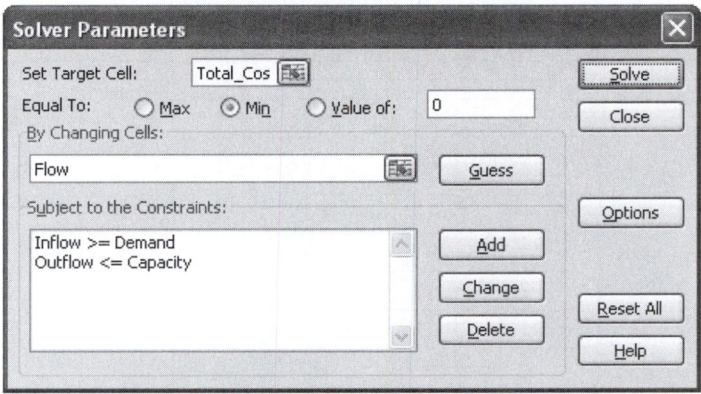

The alternative network model not only accommodates more general networks, but it is more efficient in that it has the fewest number of changing cells.

This alternative model generalizes nicely to other network problems. Essentially, it shows that all network models look alike. There is an additional benefit from this alternative model. Suppose that flows from certain plants to certain regions are not allowed. (Maybe no roads exist.) It is not easy to disallow such routes in the original model. The usual trick is to allow the "disallowed" routes but to impose extremely large unit shipping costs on them. This works, but it is wasteful because it adds changing cells that do not really belong in the model. However, the alternative network model simply omits arcs that are not allowed. For example, if the route from plant 2 to region 4 is not allowed, we simply omit the data in the range A12:D12. This creates a model with exactly as many changing cells as allowable arcs. This additional benefit can be very valuable when the number of potential arcs in the network is huge—even though the vast majority of them are disallowed—and this is exactly the situation in many large network models.

We do not necessarily recommend this more general network model for simple transportation problems. In fact, we believe it is less natural than the original model in Figure 15.12. However, it paves the way for the more complex network problems discussed next. ■

MODELING ISSUES

Depending on how you treat the demand constraints, you can get several varieties of the basic transportation model.

1. The customer demands in typical transportation problems can be handled in one of two ways. First, we can think of these forecasted demands as minimal requirements that must be sent to the customers. This is how we treated regional demands here. For example, we constrained the amount shipped to region 1 to be at least 450. Alternatively, we could consider the demands as maximal sales quantities, the most each region can sell. Then we would constrain the amounts sent to the regions to be less than or equal to the forecasted demands. Whether we express the demand constraints as "≥" or "≤" (or even "=") constraints depends on the context of the problem—do the dealers need at least this many, do they need exactly this many, or can they sell only this many?

2. If all the supplies and demands for a transportation problem are integers, then the optimal Solver solution automatically has integer-valued shipments. We do not have

to add explicit integer constraints. This is a very important benefit. It allows us to use the "fast" simplex method rather than much slower integer algorithms.

3. Shipping costs are often nonlinear (and "nonsmooth") due to quantity discounts. For example, if it costs $3 per item to ship up to 100 items between locations and $2 per item for each additional item, the proportionality assumption of LP is violated and the transportation model we have developed is nonlinear. Shipping problems that involve quantity discounts are generally quite difficult to solve.

4. Excel's Solver uses the simplex method to solve transportation problems. There is a streamlined version of the simplex method, called the **transportation simplex method**, that is much more efficient than the ordinary simplex method for transportation problems. Large transportation problems are usually solved with the transportation simplex method. See Winston (2003) for a discussion of the transportation simplex method. ■

15.4.2 Minimum Cost Network Flow Models

The objective of many real-world network models is to ship goods from one set of locations to another set of locations at minimum cost, subject to various constraints. There are many variations of these models. The simplest models include a single product that must be shipped via one mode of transportation (truck, for example) in a particular period of time. More complex models—and much larger ones—can include multiple products, multiple modes of transportation, and/or multiple time periods. We refer to this general class of problems as **minimum cost network flow** problems. We discuss one such problem in this section.

Basically, the general minimum cost network flow problem is like the transportation problem except for two possible differences. First, arc capacities are often imposed on some or all of the arcs. These become simple upper bound constraints in the model. Second and more significant, there can be inflows *and* outflows associated with any node. Nodes are generally categorized as **suppliers**, **demanders**, and **transshipment points**. A supplier is a location that starts with a certain supply (or possibly a capacity for supplying). A demander is the opposite; it requires a certain amount to end up there. A transshipment point is a location where goods simply pass through.

The best way to think of these categories is in terms of **net inflow** and **net outflow**. The net inflow for any node is defined as total inflow minus total outflow for that node. The net outflow is the negative of this, total outflow minus total inflow. Then a supplier is a node with positive net outflow, a demander is a node with positive net inflow, and a transshipment point is a node with net outflow (and net inflow) equal to 0. It is important to realize that inflows are sometimes allowed to suppliers, but their *net* outflows must be positive. Similarly, outflows from demanders are sometimes allowed, but their *net* inflows must be positive. For example, if Cincinnati and Memphis are manufacturers (suppliers) and Dallas and Phoenix are retail locations (demanders), then it is possible that flow could go from Cincinnati to Memphis to Dallas to Phoenix.

There are typically two types of constraints in minimum cost network flow models (other than nonnegativity of flows). The first type represents the arc capacity constraints, which are simple upper bounds on the arc flows. The second type represents the flow balance constraints, one for each node. For a supplier, this constraint is typically of the form **Net Outflow = Capacity** or possibly **Net Outflow ≤ Capacity**. For a demander, it is typically of the form **Net Inflow >= Demand** or possibly **Net Inflow = Demand**. For a transshipment point, it is of the form **Net Inflow = 0** (which is equivalent to **Net Outflow = 0**, whichever you prefer).

If we represent the network graphically, then it is easy to "see" these constraints. We simply examine the flows on the arrows leading into and out of the various nodes. We illustrate the typical situation in the following example.

15.4 PRODUCING AND SHIPPING TOMATO PRODUCTS AT REDBRAND

The RedBrand Company produces a tomato product at three plants. This product can be shipped directly to the company's two customers or it can first be shipped to the company's two warehouses and then to the customers. Figure 15.19 is a network representation of RedBrand's problem. Nodes 1, 2, and 3 represent the plants (these are the suppliers, denoted by S), nodes 4 and 5 represent the warehouses (these are the transshipment points, denoted by T), and nodes 6 and 7 represent the customers (these are the demanders, denoted by D). Note that we allow the possibility of some shipments among plants, among warehouses, and among customers. Also, some arcs have arrows on both ends. This means that flow is allowed in either direction.

Figure 15.19

Graphical Representation of RedBrand Logistics Model

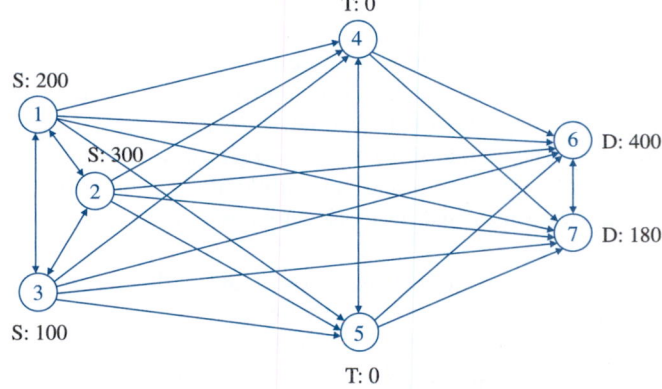

The cost of producing the product is the same at each plant, so RedBrand is concerned with minimizing the total shipping cost incurred in meeting customer demands. The production capacity of each plant (in tons per year) and the demand of each customer are shown in Figure 15.19. For example, plant 1 (node 1) has a capacity of 200, and customer 1 (node 6) has a demand of 400. In addition, the cost (in thousands of dollars) of shipping a ton of the product between each pair of locations is listed in Table 15.6, where a blank indicates that RedBrand cannot ship along that arc. We also assume that at most 200 tons of the product can be shipped between any two nodes. This is the common arc capacity. RedBrand wants to determine a minimum-cost shipping schedule.

Table 15.6 Shipping Costs for RedBrand Example

From node	To node						
	1	2	3	4	5	6	7
1		5.0	3.0	5.0	5.0	20.0	20.0
2	9.0		9.0	1.0	1.0	8.0	15.0
3	0.4	8.0		1.0	0.5	10.0	12.0
4					1.2	2.0	12.0
5				0.8		2.0	12.0
6							1.0
7						7.0	

Objective   To find the minimum-cost way to ship the tomato product from suppliers to customers, possibly through warehouses, so that customer demands are met and supplier capacities are not exceeded.

WHERE DO THE NUMBERS COME FROM?

The network configuration itself would come from geographical considerations—which routes are physically possible (or sensible) and which are not. The numbers themselves would be derived as in the Grand Prix automobile example. (See Example 15.3 for further discussion.)

Solution

Other than arc capacity constraints, the only constraints are flow balance constraints.

The variables and constraints for RedBrand's model are listed in Table 15.7. The key to the model is handling the flow balance constraints. We see exactly how to implement these when we give step-by-step instructions for developing the spreadsheet model. However, it is not enough, say, to specify that the flow out of plant 2 is less than or equal to the capacity of plant 2. The reason is that there might also be flow *into* plant 2 (from another plant). Therefore, the correct flow balance constraint for plant 2 is that the flow out of it must be less than or equal to its capacity plus any flow into it. Equivalently, the *net* flow out of plant 2 must be less than or equal to its capacity.

Table 15.7   Variables and Constraints for RedBrand Logistics Model

Input variables	Plant capacities, customer demands, unit shipping costs on allowable arcs, common arc capacity
Decision variables (changing cells)	Shipments on allowed arcs
Objective (target cell)	Total cost
Other calculated variables	Flows into and out of nodes
Constraints	Flow on each arc ≤ Common arc capacity
	Flow balance at each node

DEVELOPING THE SPREADSHEET MODEL

To set up the spreadsheet model, proceed as follows. (See Figure 15.20 and the file **RedBrand Logistics 1.xlsx**. Also, refer to the network in Figure 15.19.)

1   **Origins and destinations.** Enter the node numbers (1 to 7) for the origins and destinations of the various arcs in the range A8:B33. Note that the disallowed arcs are not entered in this list.

2   **Input data.** Enter the unit shipping costs (in thousands of dollars), the common arc capacity, the plant capacities, and the customer demands in the shaded ranges. Again, only the nonblank entries in Table 15.6 are used to fill up the column of unit shipping costs.

3   **Flows on arcs.** Enter *any* initial values for the flows in the range D8:D33. These are the changing cells.

4   **Arc capacities.** To indicate a common arc capacity for all arcs, enter the formula

=$B$4

in cell F8 and copy it down column F.

Figure 15.20 Spreadsheet Model for RedBrand Problem

	A	B	C	D	E	F	G	H	I	J	K
1	RedBrand shipping model										
2											
3	Inputs										
4	Common arc capacity		200								
5											
6	Network structure, flows, and arc capacity constraints							Node balance constraints			
7	Origin	Destination	Unit Cost	Flow		Arc Capacity		Plant constraints			
8	1	2	5	0	<=	200		Node	Plant net outflow		Plant capacity
9	1	3	3	180	<=	200		1	180	<=	200
10	1	4	5	0	<=	200		2	300	<=	300
11	1	5	5	0	<=	200		3	99.99999997	<=	100
12	1	6	20	0	<=	200					
13	1	7	20	0	<=	200		Warehouse constraints			
14	2	1	9	0	<=	200		Node	Warehouse net outflow		Required
15	2	3	9	0	<=	200		4	2.54659E-08	=	0
16	2	4	1	120	<=	200		5	1.89488E-10	=	0
17	2	5	1	0	<=	200					
18	2	6	8	180	<=	200		Customer constraints			
19	2	7	15	0	<=	200		Node	Customer net inflow		Customer demand
20	3	1	0.4	0	<=	200		6	400	>=	400
21	3	2	8	0	<=	200		7	180	>=	180
22	3	4	1	80	<=	200					
23	3	5	0.5	200	<=	200		Range names used			
24	3	6	10	0	<=	200		Arc_Capacity	=Model!$F$8:$F$33		
25	3	7	12	0	<=	200		Customer_demand	=Model!$K$20:$K$21		
26	4	5	1.2	0	<=	200		Customer_net_inflow	=Model!$I$20:$I$21		
27	4	6	2	200	<=	200		Destination	=Model!$B$8:$B$33		
28	4	7	12	0	<=	200		Flow	=Model!$D$8:$D$33		
29	5	4	0.8	0	<=	200		Origin	=Model!$A$8:$A$33		
30	5	6	2	200	<=	200		Plant_capacity	=Model!$K$9:$K$11		
31	5	7	12	0	<=	200		Plant_net_outflow	=Model!$I$9:$I$11		
32	6	7	1	180	<=	200		Total_cost	=Model!$B$36		
33	7	6	7	0	<=	200		Unit_Cost	=Model!$C$8:$C$33		
34								Warehouse_net_outflow	=Model!$I$15:$I$16		
35	Objective to minimize										
36	Total cost		$3,260								

⑤ Flow balance constraints. Nodes 1, 2, and 3 are supply nodes, nodes 4 and 5 are transshipment points, and nodes 6 and 7 are demand nodes. Therefore, set up the left sides of the flow balance constraints appropriately for these three cases. Specifically, enter the net *outflow* for node 1 in cell I9 with the formula

=SUMIF(Origin,H9,Flow)-SUMIF(Destination,H9,Flow)

We generally prefer positive numbers on right-hand sides of constraints. This is why we calculate net outflows for plants and net inflows for customers.

and copy it down to cell I11. This formula subtracts flows into node 1 from flows out of node 1 to obtain net outflow for node 1. Next, copy this *same* formula to cells I15 and I16 for the warehouses. (Remember that for transshipment nodes, the left side of the constraint can be net outflow *or* net inflow, whichever you prefer. The reason is that if net outflow is 0, then net inflow must also be 0.) Finally, enter the net *inflow* for node 6 in cell I20 with the formula

=SUMIF(Destination,H20,Flow)-SUMIF(Origin,H20,Flow)

and copy it to cell I21. This formula subtracts flows out of node 6 from flows into node 6 to obtain the net inflow for node 6.

⑥ Total shipping cost. Calculate the total shipping cost (in thousands of dollars) in cell B36 with the formula

=SUMPRODUCT(Unit_cost,Flow)

USING SOLVER

The Solver dialog box should be set up as in Figure 15.21. We want to minimize total shipping costs, subject to the three types of flow balance constraints and the arc capacity constraints.

Discussion of the Solution

The optimal solution in Figure 15.20 indicates that RedBrand's customer demand can be satisfied with a shipping cost of $3,260,000. This solution appears graphically in Figure 15.22.

Note in particular that plant 1 produces 180 tons (under capacity) and ships it all to plant 3, not directly to warehouses or customers. Also, note that all shipments from the warehouses go directly to customer 1. Then customer 1 ships 180 tons to customer 2. We purposely chose unit shipping costs (probably unrealistic ones) to produce this type of behavior, just to show that it *can* occur. As you can see, the costs of shipping from plant 1 directly to warehouses or customers are relatively large compared to the cost of shipping directly to plant 3. Similarly, the costs of shipping from plants or warehouses directly to customer 2 are prohibitive. Therefore, RedBrand should ship to customer 1 and let customer 1 forward some of its shipment to customer 2.

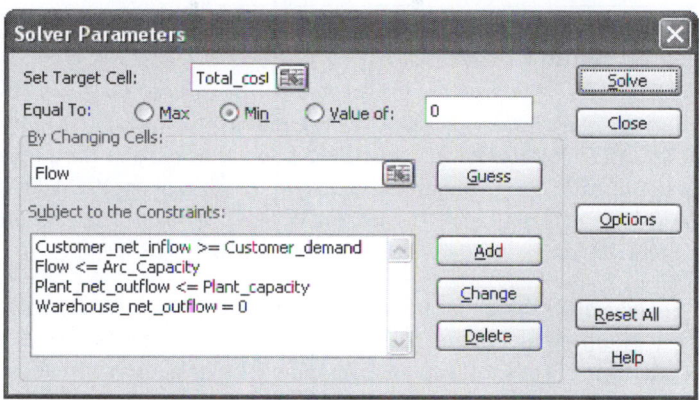

Figure 15.21
Solver Dialog Box for RedBrand Model

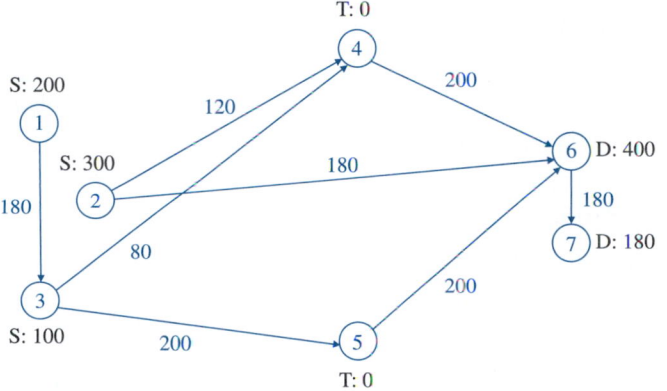

Figure 15.22
Optimal Flows for RedBrand Example

Sensitivity Analysis

How much effect does the arc capacity have on the optimal solution? Currently, we see that three of the arcs with positive flow are at the arc capacity of 200. We can use SolverTable to see how sensitive this number and the total cost are to the arc capacity.[7] In this case the single input cell for SolverTable is cell B4, which we vary from 150 to 300 in increments of 25. We keep track of two outputs: total cost and the number of arcs at arc capacity. As before, if we want to keep track of an output that does not already exist, we create it with an appropriate formula in a new cell before running SolverTable. This is shown in Figure 15.23. The formula in cell B39 is **=COUNTIF(Flow,B4)**. This formula counts the arcs with flow equal to arc capacity. (See the finished version of the file for a note about this formula.)

---

[7]Note that Solver's sensitivity report would not answer our question. This report is useful only for one-at-a-time changes in inputs, and here we are simultaneously changing the upper limit for *each* flow. However, this report (its bottom section) could be used to assess the effects of changes in plant capacities or customer demands.

Figure 15.23 Sensitivity to Arc Capacity

	A	B	C
38	Additional output variable (for sensitivity analysis)		
39	Arcs at capacity	2	
40			
41	Sensitivity of total cost and arcs at capacity to arc capacity		
42		$B$36	$B$39
43	150	$4,120	6
44	175	$3,643	6
45	200	$3,260	3
46	225	$2,998	3
47	250	$2,735	3
48	275	$2,473	3
49	300	$2,320	2

Excel Function: *COUNTIF*

The COUNTIF function counts the number of values in a given range that satisfy some criterion. The syntax is =COUNTIF(range,criterion). For example, the formula =COUNTIF(D8:D33,150) counts the number of cells in the range D8:D33 that contain the value 150. This formula could also be entered as =COUNTIF(D8:D33,"=150"). Similarly, the formula =COUNTIF(D8:D33,">=100") counts the number of cells in this range with values greater than or equal to 100.[8]

The SolverTable output is what we would expect. As the arc capacity decreases, more flows bump up against it, and the total cost increases. But even when the arc capacity is increased to 300, two flows are constrained by it. In this sense, even this large an arc capacity costs RedBrand money.

Variations of the Model

There are many variations of the RedBrand shipping problem that can be handled by a network model. We briefly consider two possible variations. First, suppose that RedBrand ships two products along the given network. We assume that the unit shipping costs are the

Figure 15.24 RedBrand Model with Two Products

	A Origin	B Destination	C Unit Cost	D Flow product 1	E Flow product 2	F Total flow	G	H Arc Capacity	I	J Node	K Net outflow product 1	L Net outflow product 2	M	N Capacity product 1	O Capacity product 2
1	RedBrand shipping model with two products competing for arc capacity														
2															
3	Inputs														
4	Common arc capacity	300													
5															
6	Network structure, flows, and arc capacity constraints									Node balance constraints					
7	Origin	Destination	Unit Cost	Flow product 1	Flow product 2	Total flow		Arc Capacity		Plant constraints					
8	1	2	5	0	0	0	<=	300		Node	Net outflow product 1	Net outflow product 2		Capacity product 1	Capacity product 2
9	1	3	3	160	140	300	<=	300		1	180	140	<=	200	200
10	1	4	5	20	0	20	<=	300		2	300	100	<=	300	100
11	1	5	5	0	0	0	<=	300		3	100	100	<=	100	100
12	1	6	20	0	0	0	<=	300							
13	1	7	20	0	0	0	<=	300		Warehouse constraints					
14	2	1	9	0	0	0	<=	300		Node	Net outflow product 1	Net outflow product 2		Required product 1	Required product 2
15	2	3	9	0	0	0	<=	300		4	0	0	=	0	0
16	2	4	1	100	0	100	<=	300		5	0	0	=	0	0
17	2	5	1	0	0	0	<=	300							
18	2	6	8	200	100	300	<=	300		Customer constraints					
19	2	7	15	0	0	0	<=	300		Node	Net inflow product 1	Net inflow product 2		Demand product 1	Demand product 2
20	3	1	0.4	0	0	0	<=	300		6	400	200	>=	400	200
21	3	2	8	0	0	0	<=	300		7	180	140	>=	180	140
22	3	4	1	0	180	180	<=	300							
23	3	5	0.5	240	60	300	<=	300							
24	3	6	10	0	0	0	<=	300							
25	3	7	12	20	0	20	<=	300							
26	4	5	1.2	0	0	0	<=	300							
27	4	6	2	120	180	300	<=	300							
28	4	7	12	0	0	0	<=	300							
29	5	4	0.8	0	0	0	<=	300							
30	5	6	2	240	60	300	<=	300							
31	5	7	12	0	0	0	<=	300							
32	6	7	1	160	140	300	<=	300							
33	7	6	7	0	0	0	<=	300							
34															
35	Objective to minimize														
36	Total cost	$5,570													

---

[8]The COUNTIF and SUMIF functions are limited in that they allow only one condition, such as ">=10". For this reason, Microsoft added two new functions in Excel 2007, COUNTIFS and SUMIFS, that allow multiple conditions. Check them out in online help!

same for both products (although this assumption could easily be relaxed), but the arc capacity, which we now change to 300, represents the maximum flow of *both* products that can flow on any arc. In this sense, the two products are competing for arc capacity. Each plant has a separate production capacity for each product, and each customer has a separate demand for each product.

There are endless variations of this basic minimum cost network flow model, corresponding to the many types of real-world shipping problems.

The spreadsheet model for this variation appears in Figure 15.24. (See the file **RedBrand Logistics 2.xlsx**.) Very little in the original model must be changed. We need to (1) have two columns of changing cells (columns D and E), (2) apply the previous logic to both products separately in the flow balance constraints, and (3) apply the arc capacities to the *total* flows in column F (which are the sums of flows in columns D and E). The modified Solver dialog box is shown in Figure 15.25. Note that we have range-named blocks of cells for the flow balance constraints. For example, the ranges K9:L11 and N9:O11 are named Plant_net_outflow and Plant_capacity. Then we can use these entire blocks to specify the capacity constraints for both products with the single entry **Plant_net_outflow ≤=Plant_capacity** in the Solver dialog box. This is another example of planning the spreadsheet layout so that the resulting model is as efficient and readable as possible.

Figure 15.25

Solver Dialog Box for Two-Product Model

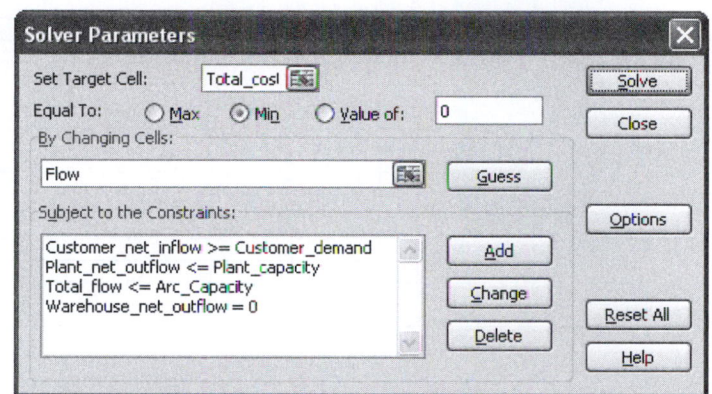

A second variation of the model is appropriate for perishable goods, such as fruit. (See the file **RedBrand Logistics 3.xlsx**.) We again assume that there is a single product, but some percentage of the product that is shipped to warehouses perishes and cannot be sent to customers. This means that the total inflow to a warehouse is *greater than* the total outflow from the warehouse. We model this behavior as shown in Figure 15.26. (The corresponding Solver dialog box, not shown here, is the same as in the original RedBrand model.) The "shrinkage factor" in cell B5, the percentage that does *not* spoil in the warehouses, becomes a new input. It is then incorporated into the warehouse flow balance constraints by entering the formula

=SUMIF(Origin,H16,Flow)-$B$5*SUMIF(Destination,H16,Flow)

in cell I16 and copying to cell I17. This formula says that what goes out (the first term) is 90% of what goes in. The other 10% perishes. Of course, shrinkage results in a larger total cost—about 20% larger—than in the original RedBrand model.

Interestingly, however, some units are still sent to both warehouses, and the entire capacity of all plants is now used. Finally, you can check that a feasible solution exists even for a shrinkage factor of 0% (where everything sent to warehouses disappears). As you might guess, the solution then is to send everything directly from plants to customers—at a steep cost.

Figure 15.26 RedBrand Model with Shrinkage

	A	B	C	D	E	F	G	H	I	J	K
1	RedBrand shipping model with shrinkage at warehouses										
2											
3	Inputs										
4	Common arc capacity	200									
5	Shrinkage factor	90%									
6											
7	Network formulation							Node balance constraints			
8		Origin	Destination	Unit Cost	Flow		Arc Capacity	Plant constraints			
9		1	2	5	0	<=	200	Node	Plant net outflow		Plant capacity
10		1	3	3	200	<=	200	1	200	<=	200
11		1	4	5	0	<=	200	2	300	<=	300
12		1	5	5	0	<=	200	3	100	<=	100
13		1	6	20	0	<=	200				
14		1	7	20	0	<=	200	Warehouse constraints			
15		2	1	9	0	<=	200	Node	Warehouse net outflow		Required
16		2	3	9	0	<=	200	4	0	=	0
17		2	4	1	0	<=	200	5	0	=	0
18		2	5	1	100	<=	200				
19		2	6	8	200	<=	200	Customer constraints			
20		2	7	15	0	<=	200	Node	Customer net inflow		Customer demand
21		3	1	0.4	0	<=	200	6	400	>=	400
22		3	2	8	0	<=	200	7	180	>=	180
23		3	4	1	0	<=	200				
24		3	5	0.5	100	<=	200				
25		3	6	10	200	<=	200				
26		3	7	12	0	<=	200				
27		4	5	1.2	0	<=	200				
28		4	6	2	0	<=	200				
29		4	7	12	0	<=	200				
30		5	4	0.8	0	<=	200				
31		5	6	2	180	<=	200				
32		5	7	12	0	<=	200				
33		6	7	1	180	<=	200				
34		7	6	7	0	<=	200				
35											
36	Objective to minimize										
37	Total cost	$4,890									

MODELING ISSUES

1. Excel's Solver uses the simplex method to solve network flow models. However, the simplex method can be simplified dramatically for these types of models. The simplified version of the simplex method, called the **network simplex method**, is much more efficient than the ordinary simplex method. Specialized computer codes have been written to implement the network simplex method, and all large network flow problems are solved by using the network simplex method. This is fortunate because real network models can be extremely large. See Winston (2003) for a discussion of this method.

2. If the given supplies and demands for the nodes are integers and all arc capacities are integers, then the network flow model always has an optimal solution with all integer flows. Again, this is very fortunate for large problems—we get integer solutions "for free" without having to use an integer programming algorithm. Note, however, that this "integers for free" benefit is guaranteed only for the "basic" network flow model, as in the original RedBrand model. When we modify the model, by adding a shrinkage factor, say, the optimal solution is no longer guaranteed to be integer-valued. ∎

Distribution in Nu-kote International's Network

LeBlanc et al. (2002) used a linear programming transportation model like the one in Section 5.3 to analyze distribution in Nu-kote International's network of vendors, manufacturing plants, warehouses, and customers. Nu-kote, a manufacturer of inkjet, laser, and toner cartridges, saves approximately $1 million annually as a result of this model. The LP has nearly 6,000 variables and 2,500 constraints. Total time available for data collection and model development and verification was limited to only six weeks. It is a tribute to the efficiency and user-friendliness of Microsoft Excel that all of this was completed within this time frame. ■

PROBLEMS

Level A

13. In the original RedBrand problem, suppose the plants cannot ship to each other and the customers cannot ship to each other. Modify the model appropriately, and reoptimize. How much does the total cost increase because of these disallowed routes?

14. Modify the original RedBrand problem so that all flows must be from plants to warehouses and from warehouses to customers. Disallow all other arcs. How much does this restriction cost RedBrand, relative to the original optimal shipping cost?

15. In the original RedBrand problem, the costs for shipping from plants or warehouses to customer 2 were purposely made high so that it would be optimal to ship to customer 1 and then let customer 1 ship to customer 2. Use SolverTable appropriately to do the following. Decrease the unit shipping costs from plants and warehouses to customer 1, all by the same amount, until it is no longer optimal for customer 1 to ship to customer 2. Describe what happens to the optimal shipping plan at this point.

16. In the original RedBrand problem we assume a constant arc capacity, the same for all allowable arcs. Modify the model so that each arc has its own arc capacity. You can make up the arc capacities.

17. Continuing the previous problem, make the problem even more general by allowing upper bounds (arc capacities) *and* lower bounds for the flows on the allowable arcs. Some of the upper bounds can be very large numbers, effectively indicating that there is no arc capacity for these arcs, and the lower bounds can be 0 or positive. If they are positive, then they indicate that some positive flow must occur on these arcs. Modify the model appropriately to handle these upper and lower bounds. You can make up the upper and lower bounds.

18. Expand the RedBrand two-product spreadsheet model so that there are now three products competing for the arc capacity. You can make up the required input data.

19. In the RedBrand two-product problem, we assumed that the unit shipping costs are the same for both products. Modify the spreadsheet model so that each product has its own unit shipping costs. You can assume that the original unit shipping costs apply to product 1, and you can make up new unit shipping costs for product 2.

Level B

20. How difficult is it to expand the original RedBrand model? Answer this by adding a new plant, two new warehouses, and three new customers, and modify the spreadsheet model appropriately. You can make up the required input data.

21. In the RedBrand problem with shrinkage, change the assumptions. Now instead of assuming that there is some shrinkage at the warehouses, assume that there is shrinkage in delivery along each route. Specifically, assume that a certain percentage of the units sent along each arc perish in transit—from faulty refrigeration, say—and this percentage can differ from one arc to another. Modify the model appropriately to take this type of behavior into account. You can make up the shrinkage factors, and you can assume that arc capacities apply to the amounts originally shipped, not to the amounts after shrinkage. (Make sure your input data permit a *feasible* solution. After all, if there is too much shrinkage, it will be impossible to meet demands with available plant capacity. Increase the plant capacities if necessary.)

22. Consider a modification of the original RedBrand problem where there are *N* plants, *M* warehouses, and *L* customers. Assume that the only allowable arcs are from plants to warehouses and from warehouses to customers. If *all* such arcs are allowable—all plants can ship to all warehouses and all warehouses can ship to all customers—how many changing cells are in the spreadsheet model? Keeping in mind that Excel's Solver can handle at most 200 changing cells, provide some combinations of N, M, and L that will just barely stay within Solver's limit.

23. Continuing the previous problem, develop a sample model with your own choices of N, M, and L that barely stay within Solver's limit. You can make up any input data. The important point here is the layout and formulas of the spreadsheet model.

15.5 AGGREGATE PLANNING MODELS

In this section we extend the production planning model discussed in Example 14.3 of the previous chapter to include a situation where the number of workers available influences the possible production levels. We allow the workforce level to be modified each period through the hiring and firing of workers. Such models, where we determine workforce levels and production schedules for a multiperiod time horizon, are called **aggregate planning** models. There are many aggregate planning models we could develop, depending on the detailed assumptions we make. We consider a fairly simple version and then ask you to modify it in the problems.

EXAMPLE | **15.5 WORKER AND PRODUCTION PLANNING AT SURESTEP**

During the next 4 months the SureStep Company must meet (on time) the following demands for pairs of shoes: 3000 in month 1; 5000 in month 2; 2000 in month 3; and 1000 in month 4. At the beginning of month 1, 500 pairs of shoes are on hand, and SureStep has 100 workers. A worker is paid $1500 per month. Each worker can work up to 160 hours a month before he or she receives overtime. A worker can work up to 20 hours of overtime per month and is paid $13 per hour for overtime labor. It takes 4 hours of labor and $15 of raw material to produce a pair of shoes. At the beginning of each month, workers can be hired or fired. Each hired worker costs $1600, and each fired worker costs $2000. At the end of each month, a holding cost of $3 per pair of shoes left in inventory is incurred. Production in a given month can be used to meet that month's demand. SureStep wants to use LP to determine its optimal production schedule and labor policy.

Objective To develop an LP spreadsheet model that relates workforce and production decisions to monthly costs, and to use Solver to find the minimum-cost solution that meets forecasted demands on time and stays with limits on overtime hours and production capacity.

WHERE DO THE NUMBERS COME FROM?

There are a number of required inputs for this type of problem. Some, including initial inventory, holding costs, and demands, are similar to requirements for Example 14.3 in the previous chapter, so we won't discuss them again here. Others might be obtained as follows:

■ The data on the current number of workers, the regular hours per worker per month, the regular hourly wage rates, and the overtime hourly rate, should be well known. The maximum number of overtime hours per worker per month is probably either the result of a policy decision by management or a clause in the workers' contracts.

- The costs for hiring and firing a worker are not trivial. The hiring cost includes training costs and the cost of decreased productivity due to the fact that a new worker must learn the job (the "learning curve" effect). The firing cost includes severance costs and costs due to loss of morale. Neither the hiring nor the firing cost would be simple to estimate accurately, but the human resources department should be able to estimate their values.

- The unit production cost is a combination of two inputs, the raw material cost per pair of shoes and the labor hours per pair of shoes. The raw material cost is the going rate from the supplier(s). The labor hours per pair of shoes represents the "production function"—the average labor required to produce a unit of the product. The operations managers should be able to supply this number.

Solution

The key to this model is choosing the correct changing cells—the decision variables that determine all outputs.

The variables and constraints for this aggregate planning model are listed in Table 15.8. As we see, there are a lot of variables to keep track of. In fact, the most difficult aspect of modeling this problem is knowing which variables the company gets to choose—the decision variables—and which variables are *determined* by these decisions. It should be clear that the company gets to choose the number of workers to hire and fire and the number of shoes to produce. Also, because management sets only an upper limit on overtime hours, it gets to decide how many overtime hours to use within this limit. But once it decides the values of these variables, everything else is determined. We show how these are determined through detailed cell formulas, but you should mentally go through the list of "Other calculated variables" in the table and deduce how they are determined by the decision variables. Also, you should also convince yourself that the three constraints we have listed are the ones, and the only ones, that are required.

Table 15.8   **Variables and Constraints for Aggregate Planning Problem**

Input variables	Initial inventory of shoes, initial number of workers, number and wage rate of regular hours, maximum number and wage rate of overtime hours, hiring and firing costs, data for unit production and holding costs, forecasted demands
Decision variables (changing cells)	Monthly values for number of workers hired and fired, number of shoes produced, and overtime hours used
Objective (target cell)	Total cost
Other calculated variables	Monthly values for workers on hand before and after hiring/firing, regular hours available, maximum overtime hours available, total production hours available, production capacity, inventory on hand after production, ending inventory, and various costs
Constraints	Overtime labor hours used $\leq$ Maximum overtime hours allowed
	Production $\leq$ Capacity
	Inventory on hand after production $\geq$ Demand

DEVELOPING THE SPREADSHEET MODEL

The spreadsheet model appears in Figure 15.27. (See the file **Aggregate Planning 1.xlsx**.) It can be developed as follows.

This is common in multiperiod problems. We usually have to relate a beginning value in one period to an ending value from the previous period.

1 **Inputs and range names.** Enter the input data in the range B4:B14 and the Forecasted_demand range. Also, create the range names listed.

2 **Production, hiring and firing plan.** Enter *any* trial values for the number of pairs of shoes produced each month, the overtime hours used each month, the workers hired each month, and the workers fired each month. These four ranges, in rows 18, 19, 23, and 30, comprise the changing cells.

3 **Workers available each month.** In cell B17 enter the initial number of workers available with the formula

=B5

Because the number of workers available at the beginning of any other month (before hiring and firing) is equal to the number of workers from the previous month, enter the formula

=B20

Figure 15.27   SureStep Aggregate Planning Model

	A	B	C	D	E	F	G	H	I
1	SureStep aggregate planning model								
2									
3	Input data						Range names used:		
4	Initial inventory of shoes	500					Forecasted_demand	=Model!$B$36:$E$36	
5	Initial number of workers	100					Inventory_after_production	=Model!$B$34:$E$34	
6	Regular hours/worker/month	160					Maximum_overtime_labor_hours_available	=Model!$B$25:$E$25	
7	Maximum overtime hours/worker/month	20					Overtime_labor_hours_used	=Model!$B$23:$E$23	
8	Hiring cost/worker	$1,600					Production_capacity	=Model!$B$32:$E$32	
9	Firing cost/worker	$2,000					Shoes_produced	=Model!$B$30:$E$30	
10	Regular wages/worker/month	$1,500					Total_cost	=Model!$F$46	
11	Overtime wage rate/hour	$13					Workers_fired	=Model!$B$19:$E$19	
12	Labor hours/pair of shoes	4					Workers_hired	=Model!$B$18:$E$18	
13	Raw material cost/pair of shoes	$15							
14	Holding cost/pair of shoes in inventory/month	$3							
15									
16	Worker plan	Month 1	Month 2	Month 3	Month 4				
17	Workers from previous month	100	94	93	50				
18	Workers hired	0	0	0	0				
19	Workers fired	6	1	43	0				
20	Workers available after hiring and firing	94	93	50	50		Notes: We originally omitted integer constraints on workers hired and fired, and Solver found a noninteger solution with no problems. Then we added these integer constraints and Solver reported "no feasible solution." So we tried checking the Automatic Scaling in Solver's Options dialog box, and we got the solution shown here.		
21									
22	Regular-time hours available	15040	14880	8000	8000				
23	Overtime labor hours used	0	80	0	0				
24		<=	<=	<=	<=				
25	Maximum overtime labor hours available	1880	1860	1000	1000				
26									
27	Total hours for production	15040	14960	8000	8000				
28									
29	Production plan	Month 1	Month 2	Month 3	Month 4				
30	Shoes produced	3760	3740	2000	1000				
31		<=	<=	<=	<=				
32	Production capacity	3760	3740	2000	2000				
33									
34	Inventory after production	4260	5000	2000	1000				
35		>=	>=	>=	>=				
36	Forecasted demand	3000	5000	2000	1000				
37	Ending inventory	1260	0	0	0				
38									
39	Monetary outputs	Month 1	Month 2	Month 3	Month 4	Totals			
40	Hiring cost	$0	$0	$0	$0	$0			
41	Firing cost	$12,000	$2,000	$86,000	$0	$100,000			
42	Regular-time wages	$141,000	$139,500	$75,000	$75,000	$430,500			
43	Overtime wages	$0	$1,040	$0	$0	$1,040			
44	Raw material cost	$56,400	$56,100	$30,000	$15,000	$157,500			
45	Holding cost	$3,780	$0	$0	$0	$3,780			
46	Totals	$213,180	$198,640	$191,000	$90,000	$692,820	← Objective to minimize		

in cell C17 and copy it to the range D17:E17. Then in cell B20 calculate the number of workers available in month 1 (after hiring and firing) with the formula

=B17+B18-B19

and copy this formula to the range C20:E20 for months 2 through 4.

4 **Overtime capacity.** Because each available worker can work up to 20 hours of overtime in a month, enter the formula

=$B$7*B20

in cell B25 and copy it to the range C25:E25.

5 **Production capacity.** Because each worker can work 160 regular-time hours per month, calculate the regular-time hours available in month 1 in cell B22 with the formula

=$B$6*B20

and copy it to the range C22:E22 for the other months. Then calculate the total hours available for production in cell B27 with the formula

=SUM(B22:B23)

and copy it to the range C27:E27 for the other months. Finally, because it takes 4 hours of labor to make a pair of shoes, calculate the production capacity in month 1 by entering the formula

=B27/$B$12

in cell B32 and copy it to the range C32:E32.

6 **Inventory each month.** Calculate the inventory after production in month 1 (which is available to meet month 1 demand) by entering the formula

=B4+B30

in cell B34. For any other month, the inventory after production is the previous month's ending inventory plus that month's production, so enter the formula

=B37+C30

in cell C34 and copy it to the range D34:E34. Then calculate the month 1 ending inventory in cell B37 with the formula

=B34-B36

and copy it to the range C37:E37.

7 **Monthly costs.** Calculate the various costs shown in rows 40 through 45 for month 1 by entering the formulas

=$B$8*B18

=$B$9*B19

=$B$10*B20

=$B$11*B23

=$B$13*B30

=$B$14*B37

In Example 14.3 from the previous chapter, production capacities were given inputs. Now they are based on the size of the workforce, which itself is a decision variable.

in cells B40 through B45. Then copy the range B40:B45 to the range C40:E45 to calculate these costs for the other months.

8 **Totals.** In row 46 and column F, use the SUM function to calculate cost totals, with the value in F46 being the overall total cost.

Excel Tip: *Calculating Row and Column Sums Quickly*
A common operation in spreadsheet models is to calculate row and column sums for a rectangular range, as we did for costs in step 8. There is a very quick way to do this. Highlight the row and column where the sums will go (remember to press the Ctrl key to highlight nonadjacent ranges) and click on the summation (Σ) toolbar button. This enters all of the sums automatically. It even calculates the "grand sum" in the corner (cell F46 in the example) if you highlight this cell.

USING SOLVER

The Solver dialog box should be filled in as shown in Figure 15.28. Note that the changing cells include four separate named ranges. To enter these in the dialog box, drag the four ranges, keeping your finger on the Ctrl key. (Alternatively, you can drag a range, type comma, drag a second range, type another comma, and so on.) As usual, you should also check the Assume Linear Model and Assume Non-Negative options before optimizing.

Figure 15.28
Solver Dialog Box
for SureStep Model

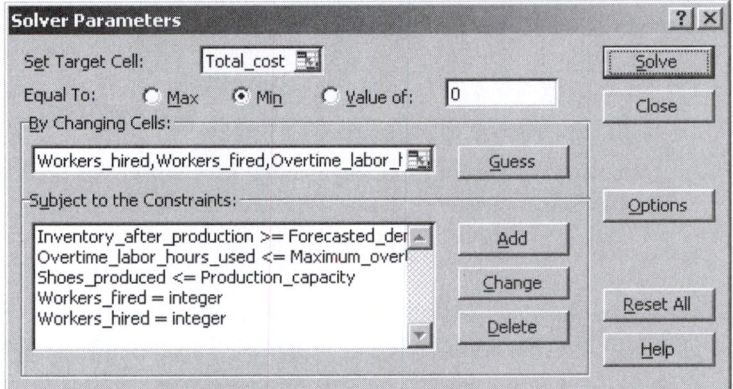

Note that we entered integer constraints on the numbers hired and fired. We could also constrain the numbers of shoes produced to be integers. However, integer constraints typically require longer solution times. Therefore, it is often best to omit such constraints, especially when the optimal values are fairly large, such as the production quantities in this model. If the solution then has noninteger values, we can usually round them to integers for a solution that is at least close to the optimal integer solution.

Discussion of the Solution

The optimal solution is given in Figure 15.27. Observe that SureStep should never hire any workers, and it should fire 6 workers in month 1, 1 worker in month 2, and 43 workers in month 3. Eighty hours of overtime are used, but only in month 2. The company produces over 3700 pairs of shoes during each of the first 2 months, 2000 pairs in month 3, and 1000 pairs in month 4. A total cost of $692,820 is incurred. The model will recommend overtime hours only when regular-time production capacity is exhausted. This is because overtime labor is more expensive.

Because integer constraints make a model harder to solve, use them sparingly—only when they are really needed.

Again, we would probably not force the number of pairs of shoes produced each month to be an integer. It makes little difference whether the company produces 3760 or 3761 pairs of shoes during a month, and forcing each month's shoe production to be an integer can greatly increase the time the computer needs to find an optimal solution. On the other hand, it is somewhat more important to ensure that the number of workers hired and fired each month is an integer, given the small numbers of workers involved.

Finally, if you want to ensure that Solver finds the optimal solution in a problem where some or all of the changing cells must be integers, it is a good idea to go into Options (in the Solver dialog box) and set the tolerance to 0. Otherwise, Solver might stop when it finds a solution that is only *close* to optimal.

Sensitivity Analysis

There are many sensitivity analyses we could perform on this final SureStep model. We illustrate one of them with SolverTable, where we see how the overtime hours used and the total cost vary with the overtime wage rate.[9] The results appear in Figure 15.29. As we see, when wage rate is really low, we use considerably more overtime hours, whereas when it is sufficiently large, we use no overtime hours. It is not surprising that the company uses much more overtime when the overtime rate is $7 or $9 per hour. The *regular*-time wage rate is $9.375 per hour (=1500/160). Of course, it is not likely that the company would pay *less* per hour for overtime than for regular time!

Figure 15.29
Sensitivity to Overtime Wage Rate

	A	B	C	D	E	F
48	Sensitivity of overtime hours used and total cost to overtime wage rate					
49		$B$23	$C$23	$D$23	$E$23	$F$46
50	7	1620	1660	0	0	$684,755
51	9	80	1760	0	0	$691,180
52	11	0	80	0	0	$692,660
53	13	0	80	0	0	$692,820
54	15	0	80	0	0	$692,980
55	17	0	80	0	0	$693,140
56	19	0	0	0	0	$693,220
57	21	0	0	0	0	$693,220

The Rolling Planning Horizon Approach

In reality, an aggregate planning model is usually implemented via a rolling planning horizon. To illustrate, we assume that SureStep works with a 4-month planning horizon. To implement the SureStep model in the rolling planning horizon context, we view the "demands" as forecasts and solve a 4-month model with these forecasts. However, we implement only the month 1 production and work scheduling recommendation. Thus (assuming that the numbers of workers hired and fired in a month must be integers and that shortages are not allowed) SureStep should hire no workers, fire 6 workers, and produce 3760 pairs of shoes with regular-time labor in month 1. Next, we observe month 1's actual demand. Suppose it is 2950. Then SureStep begins month 2 with 1310 (= 4260 − 2950) pairs of shoes and 94 workers. We would now enter 1310 in cell B4 and 94 in cell B5 (referring to Figure 15.27). Then we would replace the demands in the Demand range with the updated forecasts for the *next* 4 months. Finally, we would rerun Solver and use the production levels and hiring and firing recommendations in column B as the production level and workforce policy for month 2.

[9]As we mentioned in Example 15.2, Solver's sensitivity report isn't even available here because of the integer constraints.

Model with Backlogging Allowed

The term backlogging means that the customer's demand is met at a later date. The term backordering means the same thing.

In many situations, backlogging of demand is allowed—that is, customer demand can be met later than it occurs. We now show how to modify the SureStep model to include the option of backlogging demand. We assume that at the end of each month a cost of $20 is incurred for each unit of demand that remains unsatisfied at the end of the month. This is easily modeled by allowing a month's ending inventory to be negative. For example, if month 1's ending inventory is -10, a shortage cost of $200 (and no holding cost) is incurred. To ensure that SureStep produces any shoes at all, we constrain month 4's ending inventory to be nonnegative. This implies that all demand is *eventually* satisfied by the end of the 4-month planning horizon. We now need to modify the monthly cost computations to incorporate costs due to shortages.

There are actually several modeling approaches to this backlogging problem. We show the most natural approach in Figure 15.30. (See the file **Aggregate Planning 2.xlsx**.) To begin, we enter the per-unit monthly shortage cost in cell B15. (We inserted a new row for this cost input.) Note in row 38 how the ending inventory in months 1 through 3 can be

Figure 15.30 Nonlinear SureStep Model with Backlogging Using IF Functions

	A	B	C	D	E	F	G	H	I
1	SureStep aggregate planning model with backlogging: a nonsmooth model Solver might not handle correctly								
2									
3	**Input data**						Range names used:		
4	Initial inventory of shoes	500					Forecasted_demand_4	=Model!$E$37	
5	Initial number of workers	100					Inventory_after_production_4	=Model!$E$35	
6	Regular hours/worker/month	160					Maximum_overtime_labor_hours_available	=Model!$B$26:$E$26	
7	Maximum overtime hours/worker/month	20					Overtime_labor_hours_used	=Model!$B$24:$E$24	
8	Hiring cost/worker	$1,600					Production_capacity	=Model!$B$33:$E$33	
9	Firing cost/worker	$2,000					Shoes_produced	=Model!$B$31:$E$31	
10	Regular wages/worker/month	$1,500					Total_cost	=Model!$F$48	
11	Overtime wage rate/hour	$13					Workers_fired	=Model!$B$20:$E$20	
12	Labor hours/pair of shoes	4					Workers_hired	=Model!$B$19:$E$19	
13	Raw material cost/pair of shoes	$15							
14	Holding cost/pair of shoes in inventory/month	$3							
15	Shortage cost/pair of shoes/month	$20							
16									
17	**Worker plan**	Month 1	Month 2	Month 3	Month 4				
18	Workers from previous month	100	94	93	38				
19	Workers hired	0	0	0	0				
20	Workers fired	6	1	55	0				
21	Workers available after hiring and firing	94	93	38	38				
22									
23	Regular-time hours available	15040	14880	6080	6080				
24	Overtime labor hours used	0	0	0	0				
25		<=	<=	<=	<=				
26	Maximum overtime labor hours available	1880	1860	760	760				
27									
28	Total hours for production	15040	14880	6080	6080				
29									
30	**Production plan**	Month 1	Month 2	Month 3	Month 4				
31	Shoes produced	3760	3720	1520	1500				
32		<=	<=	<=	<=				
33	Production capacity	3760	3720	1520	1520				
34									
35	Inventory after production	4260	4980	1500	1000				
36					>=				
37	Forecasted demand	3000	5000	2000	1000				
38	Ending inventory	1260	-20	-500	0				
39							Note that we use IF functions in rows 46 and 47 to capture the holding and shortage costs. These IF functions make the model nonlinear (and "nonsmooth"), and Solver can't handle these functions in a predictable manner. We just got lucky here! Try changing the unit shortage cost in cell B15 to $40 and rerun Solver. Then you won't be so lucky -- Solver will converge to a solution that is pretty far from optimal.		
40	**Monetary outputs**	Month 1	Month 2	Month 3	Month 4	Totals			
41	Hiring cost	$0	$0	$0	$0	$0			
42	Firing cost	$12,000	$2,000	$110,000	$0	$124,000			
43	Regular-time wages	$141,000	$139,500	$57,000	$57,000	$394,500			
44	Overtime wages	$0	$0	$0	$0	$0			
45	Raw material cost	$56,400	$55,800	$22,800	$22,500	$157,500			
46	Holding cost	$3,780	$0	$0	$0	$3,780			
47	Shortage cost	$0	$400	$10,000	$0	$10,400			
48	Totals	$213,180	$197,700	$199,800	$79,500	$690,180	← Objective to minimize		

positive (leftovers) or negative (shortages). We can account correctly for the resulting costs with IF functions in rows 46 and 47. For holding costs, enter the formula

=IF(B38>0,$B$14*B38,0)

in cell B46 and copy it across. For shortage costs, enter the formula

=IF(B38<0,–$B$15*B38,0)

in cell B47 and copy it across. (The minus sign makes this a *positive* cost.)

Although these formulas accurately compute holding and shortage costs, the IF functions make the target cell a *nonlinear* function of the changing cells, and we must use Solver's GRG nonlinear algorithm, as indicated in Figure 15.31, where the Assume Linear Model box is *not* checked.[10] (How do you know the model is nonlinear? Although there is a mathematical reason, it is easier to try running Solver with the Assume Linear Model box checked. Solver will then *inform* you that the model is not linear.)

We ran Solver with this setup from a variety of initial solutions in the changing cells, and it always found the solution shown in Figure 15.30. It turns out that this is indeed the optimal solution, but we were lucky. When certain functions, including IF, MIN, MAX, and ABS, are used to relate the target cell to the changing cells, the resulting model becomes not only nonlinear but "nonsmooth." Essentially, nonsmooth functions can have sharp edges or discontinuities. Solver's GRG nonlinear algorithm can handle "smooth" nonlinearities, as we see in Section 15.8, but it has trouble with nonsmooth functions. Sometimes it gets lucky, as it did here, and other times it finds a nonoptimal solution that is not even close to the optimal solution. For example, we changed the unit shortage cost from $20 to $40 and reran Solver. Starting from a solution where all changing cells contain 0, Solver stopped at a solution with total cost $725,360, even though the optimal solution has total cost $692,820. In other words, we weren't so lucky on this problem.

Figure 15.31
GRG Nonlinear Algorithm: Assume Linear Model Box Not Checked

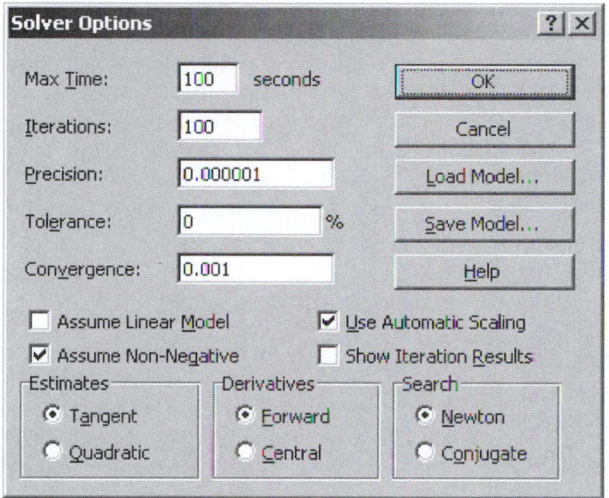

The moral is that you should avoid these nonsmooth functions in optimization models if at all possible. If you *do* use them, as we have done here, then you should run Solver several times, starting from different initial solutions. There is still absolutely no guarantee that you will get the optimal solution, but you will see more evidence of how Solver is progressing.

---

[10]GRG stands for generalized reduced gradient. This is a technical term for the mathematical algorithm used.

Solver Tip: *Nonsmooth Functions*

There is nothing inherently wrong with using IF, MIN, MAX, ABS, and other nonsmooth functions in spreadsheet optimization models. The only problem is that Solver cannot handle these functions in a predictable manner.

There are sometimes alternatives to using IF, MIN, MAX, and ABS functions that make a model linear. Unfortunately, these alternatives are often far from intuitive, and we do not cover them here. (If you are interested, we have included the "linearized" version of the backlogging model in the file **Aggregate Planning 3.xlsx**.) Alternatively, nonsmooth functions can be handled with a totally different kind of algorithm, called a **genetic algorithm**, and Frontline's Premium Solver includes an Evolutionary Solver that implements a genetic algorithm. However, we do not cover genetic algorithms in this book. ■

MODELING ISSUES

1. Silver et al. (1998) recommend that when demand is seasonal, the planning horizon should extend beyond the next seasonal peak.

2. Beyond a certain point, the cost of using extra hours of overtime labor increases because workers become less efficient. We haven't modeled this type of behavior, but it would make the model nonlinear. ■

PROBLEMS

Level A

24. Extend SureStep's original (no backlogging) aggregate planning model from 4 to 6 months. Try several different values for demands in months 5 and 6, and run Solver for each. Is your optimal solution for the *first* 4 months the same as the one in the example?

25. The current solution to SureStep's no-backlogging aggregate planning model does quite a lot of firing. Run a one-way SolverTable with the firing cost as the input variable and the numbers fired as the outputs. Let the firing cost increase from its current value to double that value in increments of $400. Do high firing costs eventually induce the company to fire fewer workers?

26. SureStep is currently getting 160 regular-time hours from each worker per month. This is actually calculated from 8 hours per day times 20 days per week. For this, they are paid $9.375 per hour (=1500/160). Suppose workers can change their contract so that they have to work only 7.5 hours per day regular time—everything above this becomes overtime—and their regular-time wage rate increases to $10 per hour. They will still work 20 days per month. Does this change the optimal no-backlogging solution?

27. Suppose SureStep could begin a machinery upgrade and training program to increase its worker productivity. This program would result in the following values of labor hours per pair of shoes over the next 4 months: 4, 3.9, 3.8, and 3.8. How much would this new program be worth to SureStep, at least for this 4-month planning horizon with no backlogging? How might you evaluate the program's worth *beyond* the next 4 months?

Level B

28. In the current no-backlogging problem SureStep doesn't hire any workers, and it uses almost no overtime. This is evidently because of low demand. Change the demands to 6000, 8000, 5000, and 3000, and reoptimize. Is there now hiring and overtime? With this new demand pattern, explore the trade-off between hiring and overtime by running a two-way SolverTable. As inputs, use the hiring cost per worker and the maximum overtime hours allowed per worker per month, varied as you see fit. As outputs, use the total number of workers hired over the 4 months and the total number of overtime hours used over the 4 months. Write up your results in a short memo to SureStep management.

29. In the SureStep no-backlogging problem, change the demands so that they become 6000, 8000, 5000, 3000. Also, change the problem slightly so that newly hired workers take 6 hours to produce a pair of shoes during their first month of employment. After that, they take only 4 hours per pair of shoes. Modify the model appropriately, and use Solver to find the optimal solution.

30. We saw that the "natural" way to model SureStep's backlogging model, with IF functions, leads to a non-smooth model that Solver has difficulty handling. There is another version of the problem that is also difficult for Solver. Suppose SureStep wants to meet all demand on time (no backlogging), but it wants to keep its employment level as constant across time as possible. To induce this, it charges a cost of $1000 each month on the absolute difference between the beginning number of workers and the number after hiring and firing—that is, the absolute difference between the values in rows 17 and 20 of the original spreadsheet model. Implement this extra cost in the model in the "natural" way, using the ABS function. Using demands of 6000, 8000, 5000, and 3000, see how well Solver does in trying to solve this non-smooth model. Try several initial solutions, and see whether Solver gets the same optimal solution from each of them.

15.6 FINANCIAL MODELS

The majority of optimization examples described in management science textbooks are in the area of operations: scheduling, blending, logistics, aggregate planning, and others. This is probably warranted, because many of the most successful management science applications in the real world have been in these areas. However, optimization and other management science methods have also been applied successfully in a number of financial areas, and they deserve recognition. We discuss several of these applications throughout this book. In this section we begin the discussion with two typical applications of LP in finance. The first involves investment strategy. The second involves pension fund management.

EXAMPLE | **15.6 FINDING AN OPTIMAL INVESTMENT STRATEGY AT BARNEY-JONES**

At the present time, the beginning of year 1, the Barney-Jones Investment Corporation has $100,000 to invest for the next 4 years. There are five possible investments, labeled A through E. The timing of cash outflows and cash inflows for these investments is somewhat irregular. For example, to take part in investment A, cash must be invested at the beginning of year 1, and for every dollar invested, there are returns of $0.50 and $1.00 at the beginnings of years 2 and 3. Similar information for the other investments are as follows, where all returns are per dollar invested:

- Investment B: Invest at the beginning of year 2, receive returns of $0.50 and $1.00 at the beginnings of years 3 and 4

- Investment C: Invest at the beginning of year 1, receive return of $1.20 at the beginning of year 2

- Investment D: Invest at the beginning of year 4, receive return of $1.90 at the beginning of year 5

- Investment E: Invest at the beginning of year 3, receive return of $1.50 at the beginning of year 4

We assume that any amounts can be invested in these strategies and that the returns are the same for each dollar invested. However, to create a diversified portfolio, Barney-Jones decides to limit the amount put into any investment to $75,000. The company wants an investment strategy that maximizes the amount of cash on hand at the beginning of year 5. At the beginning of any year, it can invest only cash on hand, which includes returns from previous investments. Any cash not invested in any year can be put in a short-term money market account that earns 3% annually.

Objective   To develop an LP spreadsheet model that relates investment decisions to total ending cash, and to use Solver to find the strategy that maximizes ending cash and invests no more than a given amount in any one investment.

WHERE DO THE NUMBERS COME FROM?

There is no mystery here. We assume that the terms of each investment are spelled out, so that Barney-Jones knows exactly when money must be invested and what the amounts and timing of returns will be. Of course, this would not be the case for many real-world investments, such as money put into the stock market, where considerable uncertainty is involved. We consider one such example of investing with uncertainty when we study portfolio optimization in Section 15.8.

Solution

There are often multiple equivalent ways to state a constraint. You can choose the one that is most natural for you.

The variables and constraints for this investment model are listed in Table 15.9. On the surface, this problem looks to be very straightforward. We must decide how much to invest in the available investments at the beginning of each year, and we can use only the cash available. If you try modeling this problem without our help, however, we suspect that you will have some difficulty. It took us a few tries to get a "nice" model, one that is easy to read and one that generalizes to other similar investment problems. By the way, the second constraint in the table can be expressed in two ways. It can be expressed as shown, where the cash on hand *after* investing is nonnegative, or it can be expressed as "cash on hand at the beginning of any year must be greater than or equal to cash invested that year." These are equivalent. The one you choose is a matter of taste.

Table 15.9   **Variables and Constraints for Investment Model**

Input variables	Timing of investments and returns, initial cash, maximum amount allowed in any investment, money market rate on cash
Decision variables (changing cells)	Amounts to invest in investments
Objective (target cell)	Ending cash at the beginning of year 5
Other calculated variables	Cash available at the beginning of years 2–4
Constraints	Amount in any investment ≤ Max investment amount
	Cash on hand after investing each year ≥ 0

DEVELOPING THE SPREADSHEET MODEL

The spreadsheet model for this investment problem appears in Figure 15.32. (See the file **Investing.xlsx**.) To set up this spreadsheet, proceed as follows.

Figure 15.32 Spreadsheet Model for Investment Problem

	A	B	C	D	E	F	G	H	I	J
1	Investments with irregular timing of returns							Range names used		
2								Cash_after_investing	=Model!$E$32:$E$35	
3	Inputs							Dollars_invested	=Model!$B$26:$F$26	
4	Initial amount to invest	$100,000						Final_cash	=Model!$B$38	
5	Maximum per investment	$75,000						Maximum_per_investment	=Model!$B$28:$F$28	
6	Interest rate on cash	3%								
7										
8	Cash outlays on investments (all incurred at beginning of year)									
9		Investment								
10	Year	A	B	C	D	E				
11	1	$1.00	$0.00	$1.00	$0.00	$0.00				
12	2	$0.00	$1.00	$0.00	$0.00	$0.00				
13	3	$0.00	$0.00	$0.00	$0.00	$1.00				
14	4	$0.00	$0.00	$0.00	$1.00	$0.00				
15										
16	Cash returns from investments (all incurred at beginning of year)									
17		Investment								
18	Year	A	B	C	D	E				
19	1	$0.00	$0.00	$0.00	$0.00	$0.00				
20	2	$0.50	$0.00	$1.20	$0.00	$0.00				
21	3	$1.00	$0.50	$0.00	$0.00	$0.00				
22	4	$0.00	$1.00	$0.00	$0.00	$1.50				
23	5	$0.00	$0.00	$0.00	$1.90	$0.00				
24										
25	Investment decisions									
26	Dollars invested	$64,286	$75,000	$35,714	$75,000	$75,000				
27		<=	<=	<=	<=	<=				
28	Maximum per investment	$75,000	$75,000	$75,000	$75,000	$75,000				
29										
30	Constraints on cash balance									
31	Year	Beginning cash	Returns from investments	Cash invested	Cash after investing					
32	1	$100,000	$0	$100,000	$0	>=	0			
33	2	$0	$75,000	$75,000	-$0	>=	0			
34	3	-$0	$101,786	$75,000	$26,785	>=	0			
35	4	$27,589	$187,500	$75,000	$140,089	>=	0			
36	5	$144,292	$142,500							
37										
38	Final cash	$286,792	←	Objective to maximize: final cash at beginning of year 5						

Note how the two input tables at the top of the spreadsheet allow us to use, and copy, the SUMPRODUCT function for cash outflows and inflows. Careful spreadsheet planning can often greatly simplify the necessary formulas.

1 **Inputs and range names.** As usual, enter the given inputs in the shaded ranges and name the ranges indicated. Pay particular attention to the two shaded tables. This is probably the first model we have encountered where model development is affected significantly by the way we enter the inputs, specifically, the information about the investments. We suggest separating cash outflows from cash inflows, as shown in the two ranges B11:F14 and B19:F23. The top table indicates when we invest, where a 0 indicates no possible investment, and a 1 indicates a dollar of investment. The bottom table then indicates the amounts and timing of returns per dollar invested.

2 **Investment amounts.** Enter *any* trial values in the Dollars_invested range. This range contains the changing cells. Also put a link to the maximum investment amount per investment by entering the formula

=$B$5

in cell B28 and copying it across.

3 **Cash balances and flows.** The key to the model is the section in rows 32 through 36. For each year, we need to calculate the beginning cash held from the previous year, the returns from investments that are due in that year, the investments made in that year, and cash balance after investments. Begin by entering the initial cash in cell B32 with the formula

=B4

Moving across, calculate the return due in year 1 in cell C32 with the formula

=SUMPRODUCT(B19:F19,Dollars_invested)

Admittedly, no returns come due in year 1, but this formula can be copied down column C for other years. Next, calculate the total amount invested in year 1 in cell D32 with the formula

=SUMPRODUCT(B11:F11,Dollars_invested)

Now find the cash balance after investing in year 1 in cell E32 with the formula

=B32+C32-D32

The only other required formula is the formula for the cash available at the beginning of year 2. Because any cash not invested earns 3% interest, enter the formula

=E32*(1+$B$6)

in cell B33. This formula, along with those in cells C32, D32, and E32, can now be copied down. (The 0's in column G are entered manually to remind us of the nonnegativity constraint on cash after investing.)

Always look at the Solver solution for signs of implausibility. This can often lead you to an error in your model.

④ **Ending cash.** The ending cash at the beginning of year 5 is sum of the amount in the money market and any returns that come due in year 5. Calculate this sum with the formula

=SUM(B36:C36)

in cell B38. (*Note*: Here is the type of error to watch out for. We originally failed to calculate the return in cell C36 and mistakenly used the beginning cash in cell B36 as the target cell. We realized our error when the optimal solution called for no money in investment D, which is clearly an attractive investment. The moral is that you can often catch errors by looking at the *plausibility* of your optimal solution.)

Review of the Model

Take a careful look at this model and how it has been set up. There are undoubtedly many alternative ways to model this problem, but the attractive feature of our model is the way the tables of inflows and outflows in rows 11 through 14 and 19 through 23 allow us to copy formulas for returns and investment amounts in columns C and D of rows 32 through 35. In fact, this same model setup, with only minor modifications, will work for *any* set of investments, regardless of the timing of investments and their returns. This is a quality you should strive for in your own spreadsheet models: generalizability.

USING SOLVER

To find the optimal investment strategy, fill in the main Solver dialog box as shown in Figure 15.33, check the Assume Linear Model and Assume Non-Negative options, and optimize. Note that the explicit nonnegativity constraint in Figure 15.33 is necessary, even though we check the Assume Non-Negative option. Again, this is because the Assume Non-Negative option covers only the changing cells. If we want other output cells to be nonnegative, we must add such constraints explicitly.

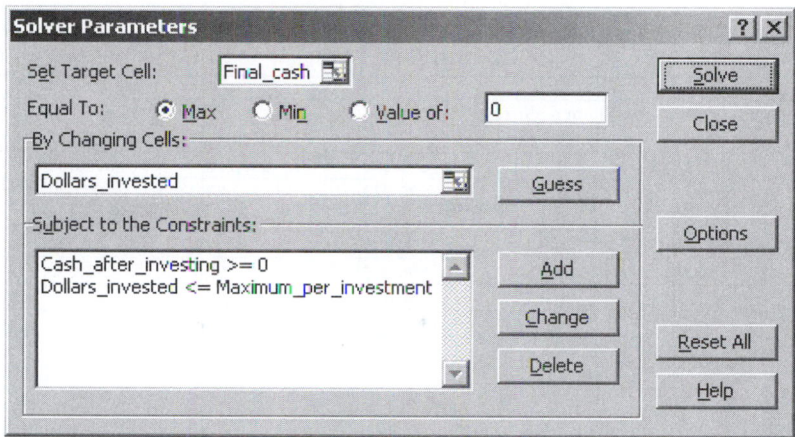

Figure 15.33
Solver Dialog Box
for Investment
Model

Discussion of the Results

The optimal solution appears in Figure 15.32. Let's follow the cash. The company spends all of its cash in year 1 on the two available investments, A and C ($64,286 in A, $35,714 in C). A total of $75,000 in returns from these investments is available in year 2, and all of this is invested in investment B. (The minus signs in cells E33 and B34 are due to roundoff error. The values in these cells are very small negative numbers, but they are equal to 0 for all practical purposes.) At the beginning of year 3, a total of $101,786 is available from investment A and B returns, and $75,000 of this invested in investment E. This leaves $26,786 for the money market, which grows to $27,589 at the beginning of year 4. In addition, returns totaling $187,500 from investments B and E come due in year 4. Of this total cash of $215,089, $75,000 is invested in investment D, and the rest, $140,089, is put in the money market. The return from investment D, $142,500, plus the money available from the money market, $144,292, equals the final cash in the target cell, $286,792.

Sensitivity Analysis

Constraints always have the potential to "penalize" the objective to some extent. SolverTable is a perfect tool for finding the magnitude of this penalty.

A close look at the optimal solution in Figure 15.32 indicates that Barney-Jones is really "penalizing" itself by imposing a maximum of $75,000 per investment. This upper limit is forcing the company to put cash into the money market fund, despite this fund's low rate of return. Therefore, a natural sensitivity analysis is to see how the optimal solution changes as this maximum value changes. We performed this sensitivity analysis with a one-way SolverTable, shown in Figure 15.34.[11] It uses the maximum in cell B5 as the input cell, varied from $75,000 to $225,000 in increments of $25,000, and keeps track of the optimal changing cells and target cell. As we see, the final cash (column G) grows steadily as we allow the maximum investment amount to increase. This is because the company can take greater advantage of the attractive investments and put less in the money market.

---

[11]Because Solver's sensitivity reports do not help answer our specific sensitivity questions in this example or the next example, we discuss only the SolverTable results.

Figure 15.34 Sensitivity of Optimal Solution to Maximum Investment Amount

	A	B	C	D	E	F	G
40	Sensitivity of optimal solution to maximum per investment						
41		$B$26	$C$26	$D$26	$E$26	$F$26	$B$38
42	75000	$64,286	$75,000	$35,714	$75,000	$75,000	$285,118
43	100000	$61,538	$76,923	$38,462	$100,000	$100,000	$319,462
44	125000	$100,000	$50,000	$0	$125,000	$125,000	$352,250
45	150000	$100,000	$50,000	$0	$150,000	$125,000	$374,250
46	175000	$100,000	$50,000	$0	$175,000	$125,000	$396,250
47	200000	$100,000	$50,000	$0	$200,000	$125,000	$418,250
48	225000	$100,000	$50,000	$0	$225,000	$125,000	$440,250

To perform sensitivity on an output variable not calculated explicitly in your spreadsheet model, calculate it in some unused portion of the spreadsheet before running SolverTable.

We go one step further with the two-way SolverTable in Figure 15.35. Here we allow both the maximum investment amount and the money market rate to vary, and we keep track of the maximum amount ever put in the money market. Because this latter amount is not calculated in the spreadsheet model, we calculate it with the formula **=MAX(Cash_after_investing)** in cell B51 and then use it as the output cell for SolverTable. In every case, even with a large maximum investment amount and a low money market rate, the company puts *some* money in the money market. The reason is simple. Even when the maximum investment amount is $225,000, the company evidently has more cash than this to invest at some point (probably at the beginning of year 4). Therefore, it will have to put some of it in the money market. ∎

Figure 15.35 Sensitivity of Maximum in Money Market to Two Inputs

	A	B	C	D	E	F	G	H
51	Maximum in money market	$140,089	←	Extra output for use in sensitivity analysis below				
52								
53	Sensitivity of maximum placed in money market to interest rate on cash and maximum per investment							
54	$B$51	75000	100000	125000	150000	175000	200000	225000
55	0.5%	$139,420	$126,923	$112,500	$87,500	$62,500	$37,500	$12,500
56	1.0%	$139,554	$126,923	$112,500	$87,500	$62,500	$37,500	$12,500
57	1.5%	$139,688	$126,923	$112,500	$87,500	$62,500	$37,500	$12,500
58	2.0%	$139,821	$126,923	$112,500	$87,500	$62,500	$37,500	$12,500
59	2.5%	$139,955	$126,923	$112,500	$87,500	$62,500	$37,500	$12,500
60	3.0%	$140,089	$126,923	$112,500	$87,500	$62,500	$37,500	$12,500
61	3.5%	$140,223	$126,923	$112,500	$87,500	$62,500	$37,500	$12,500
62	4.0%	$140,357	$126,923	$112,500	$87,500	$62,500	$37,500	$12,500
63	4.5%	$140,491	$126,923	$112,500	$87,500	$62,500	$37,500	$12,500

The following example illustrates a common situation where fixed payments are due in the future and current funds must be allocated and invested so that their returns are sufficient to make the payments. We put this in a pension fund context.

EXAMPLE 15.7 MANAGING A PENSION FUND AT ARMCO

James Judson is the financial manager in charge of the company pension fund at Armco Incorporated. James knows that the fund must be sufficient to make the payments listed in Table 15.10. Each payment must be made on the first day of each year. James is going to finance these payments by purchasing bonds. It is currently January 1, 2008, and three bonds are available for immediate purchase. The prices and coupons for the bonds are as follows. (All coupon payments are received on January 1 and arrive in time to meet cash demands for the date on which they arrive.)

- Bond 1 costs $980 and yields a $60 coupon in the years 2009 through 2012 and a $1060 payment on maturity in the year 2013.

- Bond 2 costs $970 and yields a $65 coupon in the years 2009 through 2018 and a $1065 payment on maturity in the year 2019.

- Bond 3 costs $1050 and yields a $75 coupon in the years 2009 through 2021 and a $1075 payment on maturity in the year 2022.

James must decide how much cash to allocate (from company coffers) to meet the initial $11,000 payment and buy enough bonds to make future payments. He knows that any excess cash on hand can earn an annual rate of 4% in a fixed-rate account. How should he proceed?

Table 15.10   Payments for Pension Problem

Year	Payment	Year	Payment	Year	Payment
2008	$11,000	2013	$18,000	2018	$25,000
2009	$12,000	2014	$20,000	2019	$30,000
2010	$14,000	2015	$21,000	2020	$31,000
2011	$15,000	2016	$22,000	2021	$31,000
2012	$16,000	2017	$24,000	2022	$31,000

Objective   To develop an LP spreadsheet model that relates initial allocation of money and bond purchases to future cash availabilities, and to use Solver to minimize the initialize allocation of money required to meet all future pension fund payments.

WHERE DO THE NUMBERS COME FROM?

As in the previous financial example, the inputs are fairly easy to obtain. A pension fund has known liabilities that must be met in future years, and information on bonds and fixed-rate accounts is widely available.

Solution

Although it doesn't occur very often, it is perfectly acceptable to make the target cell one of the changing cells. In fact, this is the key to the current model.

The variables and constraints required for this pension fund model are listed in Table 15.11. When modeling this problem, we see a new twist that involves the money James must allocate in 2008 for his funding problem. It is clear that he must decide how many bonds of each type to purchase in 2008 (note that no bonds are purchased *after* 2008), but he must also decide how much money to allocate from company coffers. This allocated money has to cover the initial pension payment in 2008 *and* the bond purchases. In addition, James wants to find the *minimum* allocation that will suffice. Therefore, this initial allocation serves two roles in the model. It is a decision variable *and* it is the objective we want to minimize. In terms of spreadsheet modeling, it is perfectly acceptable to make the target cell one of the changing cells, and we do so here. You might not see this in many models—because the objective typically involves a linear combination of several decision variables—but it is occasionally the most natural way to proceed.

Table 15.11   Variables and Constraints for Pension Model

Input variables	Pension payments, information on bonds, fixed interest rate on cash
Decision variables (changing cells)	Money to allocate in 2008, numbers of bonds to purchase in 2008
Object (target cell)	Money to allocate in 2008 (minimize)
Other calculated variables	Cash available to meet pension payments each year
Constraints	Cash available for payments ≥ Payment amounts

DEVELOPING THE SPREADSHEET MODEL

The completed spreadsheet model is shown in Figure 15.36. (See the file **Pension Fund Management.xlsx**.) You can create it with the following steps.

Figure 15.36 Spreadsheet Model for Pension Fund Management

	A	B	C	D	E	F	G	H	I	J	K	L	M	N	O	P
1	Pension fund management															
2																
3	Costs (in 2008) and income (in other years) from bonds															
4	Year	2008	2009	2010	2011	2012	2013	2014	2015	2016	2017	2018	2019	2020	2021	2022
5	Bond 1	$980	$60	$60	$60	$60	$1,060									
6	Bond 2	$970	$65	$65	$65	$65	$65	$65	$65	$65	$65	$65	$1,065			
7	Bond 3	$1,050	$75	$75	$75	$75	$75	$75	$75	$75	$75	$75	$75	$75	$75	$1,075
8																
9	Interest rate	4%														
10																
11	Number of bonds (allowing fractional values) to purchase in 2008															
12	Bond 1	73.69														
13	Bond 2	77.21														
14	Bond 3	28.84														
15																
16	Money allocated	$197,768	←	Objective to minimize, also a changing cell												
17																
18	Constraints to meet payments															
19	Year	2008	2009	2010	2011	2012	2013	2014	2015	2016	2017	2018	2019	2020	2021	2022
20	Amount available	$20,376	$21,354	$21,332	$19,228	$16,000	$85,298	$77,171	$66,639	$54,646	$41,133	$25,000	$84,390	$58,728	$31,000	$31,000
21		>=	>=	>=	>=	>=	>=	>=	>=	>=	>=	>=	>=	>=	>=	>=
22	Amount required	$11,000	$12,000	$14,000	$15,000	$16,000	$18,000	$20,000	$21,000	$22,000	$24,000	$25,000	$30,000	$31,000	$31,000	$31,000
23																
24	Range names used:															
25	Amount_available	=Model!$B$20:$P$20														
26	Amount_required	=Model!$B$22:$P$22														
27	Bonds_purchased	=Model!$B$12:$B$14														
28	Money_allocated	=Model!$B$16														

> The value in cell B16 is the money allocated to make the 2008 payment and buy bonds in 2008. It is both a changing cell and the target cell to minimize.

1 **Inputs and range names.** Enter the given data in the shaded cells and name the ranges as indicated. Note that we have entered the bond costs in the range B5:B7 as *positive* quantities. Some financial analysts might prefer that they be entered as negative numbers, indicating outflows. It doesn't really matter, however, as long as we are careful with spreadsheet formulas later on.

Always document your spreadsheet conventions as clearly as possible.

2 **Money allocated and bonds purchased.** As we discussed previously, the money allocated in 2008 and the numbers of bonds purchased are both decision variables, so enter *any* values for these in the Money_allocated and Bonds_purchased ranges. Note that we had to modify our color-coding convention for the Money_allocated cell. Because it is both a changing cell and the target cell, we color it red but add a note to emphasize that it is the objective to maximize.

3 **Cash available to make payments.** In 2008, the only cash available is the money initially allocated minus cash used to purchase bonds. Calculate this quantity in cell B20 with the formula

=Money_allocated-SUMPRODUCT(Bonds_purchased,B5:B7)

For all other years, the cash available comes from two sources: excess cash invested at the fixed interest rate the year before and payments from bonds. Calculate this quantity for 2009 in cell C20 with the formula

=(B20-B22)*(1+$B$9)+SUMPRODUCT(Bonds_purchased,C5:C7)

and copy it across row 20 for the other years.

As you see, this model is fairly straightforward to develop once you understand the role of the amount allocated in cell B16. However, we have often given this problem as an assignment to our students, and many fail to deal correctly with the amount allocated. (They usually forget to make it a changing cell.) So make sure you understand what we have done, and why we have done it this way.

USING SOLVER

The main Solver dialog box should be filled out as shown in Figure 15.37. As usual, the Assume Linear Model and Assume Non-Negative options should be checked before optimizing. Once again, notice that the Money_allocated cell is both the target cell and one of the changing cells.

Figure 15.37

Solver Dialog Box for Pension Model

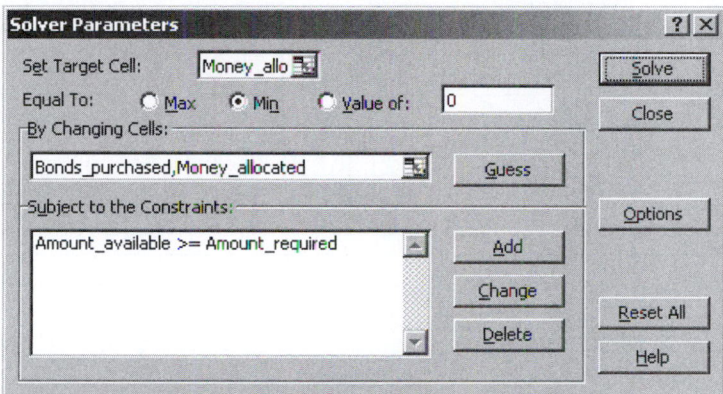

Discussion of the Solution

The optimal solution appears in Figure 15.36. You might argue that the numbers of bonds purchased should be constrained to integer values. We tried this and the optimal solution changed very little: The optimal numbers of bonds to purchase changed to 74, 79, and 27, and the optimal money to allocate increased to $197,887. With this integer solution, shown in Figure 15.38, James sets aside $197,887 initially. Any less than this would not work—he couldn't make enough from bonds to meet future pension payments. All but $20,387 of this (see cell B20) is spent on bonds, and of the $20,387, $11,000 is used to make the 2008 pension payment. After this, the amounts in row 20, which are always sufficient to make the payments in row 22, are composed of returns from bonds and cash, with interest, from the previous year. Even more so than in previous examples, we see no way to "guess" this optimal solution. The timing of bond returns and the irregular pension payments make a spreadsheet optimization model an absolute necessity.

Sensitivity Analysis

Because the bond information and pension payments are evidently fixed, we see only one promising direction for sensitivity analysis: on the fixed interest rate in cell B9. We tried this, allowing this rate to vary from 2% to 6% in increments of 0.5%, and we kept track of the optimal changing cells, including the target cell. The results appear in Figure 15.39. They indicate that as the interest rate increases, James can get by with fewer bonds of types 1 and 2, and he can allocate less money for the problem. The reason is that he is making more interest on excess cash.

Figure 15.38 Optimal Integer Solution for Pension Model

	A	B	C	D	E	F	G	H	I	J	K	L	M	N	O	P
1	Pension fund management															
2																
3	Costs (in 2008) and income (in other years) from bonds															
4	Year	2008	2009	2010	2011	2012	2013	2014	2015	2016	2017	2018	2019	2020	2021	2022
5	Bond 1	$980	$60	$60	$60	$60	$1,060									
6	Bond 2	$970	$65	$65	$65	$65	$65	$65	$65	$65	$65	$65	$1,065			
7	Bond 3	$1,050	$75	$75	$75	$75	$75	$75	$75	$75	$75	$75	$75	$75	$75	$1,075
8																
9	Interest rate	4%														
10																
11	Number of bonds (allowing fractional values) to purchase in 2008															
12	Bond 1	74.00														
13	Bond 2	79.00														
14	Bond 3	27.00														
15								The value in cell B16 is the money allocated to make the 2008								
16	Money allocated	$197,887	←	Objective to minimize, also a changing cell				payment and buy bonds in 2008. It is both a changing cell and the								
17								target cell to minimize.								
18	Constraints to meet payments															
19	Year	2008	2009	2010	2011	2012	2013	2014	2015	2016	2017	2018	2019	2020	2021	2022
20	Amount available	$20,387	$21,363	$21,337	$19,231	$16,000	$85,600	$77,464	$66,923	$54,919	$41,396	$25,252	$86,422	$60,704	$32,917	$31,019
21		>=	>=	>=	>=	>=	>=	>=	>=	>=	>=	>=	>=	>=	>=	>=
22	Amount required	$11,000	$12,000	$14,000	$15,000	$16,000	$18,000	$20,000	$21,000	$22,000	$24,000	$25,000	$30,000	$31,000	$31,000	$31,000
23																
24	Range names used:															
25	Amount_available	=Model!$B$20:$P$20														
26	Amount_required	=Model!$B$22:$P$22														
27	Bonds_purchased	=Model!$B$12:$B$14														
28	Money_allocated	=Model!$B$16														

Figure 15.39

Sensitivity to Fixed Interest Rate

	A	B	C	D	E
30	Sensitivity to interest rate				
31		$B$12	$B$13	$B$14	$B$16
32	2.0%	77.12	78.71	28.84	$202,010
33	2.5%	76.24	78.33	28.84	$200,930
34	3.0%	75.37	77.95	28.84	$199,863
35	3.5%	74.53	77.58	28.84	$198,809
36	4.0%	73.69	77.21	28.84	$197,768
37	4.5%	72.88	76.84	28.84	$196,741
38	5.0%	72.09	76.49	28.84	$195,727
39	5.5%	71.30	76.13	28.84	$194,725
40	6.0%	70.54	75.78	28.84	$193,737

ADDITIONAL APPLICATIONS

Using LP to Optimize Bond Portfolios

Many Wall Street firms buy and sell bonds. Rohn (1987) developed a bond selection model that maximizes profit from bond purchases and sales subject to constraints that minimize the firm's risk exposure. The method used to model this situation is closely related to the method we used to model the Barney-Jones problem. ■

PROBLEMS

Level A

31. Modify the Barney-Jones investment problem so that there is a minimum amount that must be put into any investment, although this minimum can vary by investment. For example, the minimum amount for investment A might be $0, whereas the minimum amount for investment D might be $50,000. These minimum

amounts should be inputs; you can make up any values you like. Run Solver on your modified model.

32. In the Barney-Jones investment problem, increase the maximum amount allowed in any investment to $150,000. Then run a one-way sensitivity analysis to the money market rate on cash. Capture one output variable: the maximum amount of cash ever put in the money market. You can choose any reasonable range for varying the money market rate.

33. We claimed that our model for Barney-Jones is generalizable. Try generalizing it to the case where there are two more potential investments, F and G. Investment F requires a cash outlay in year 2 and returns $0.50 in *each* of the next 4 years. Investment G requires a cash outlay in year 3 and returns $0.75 in each of years 5, 6, and 7. Modify the model as necessary, making the objective the final cash after year 7.

34. In our Barney-Jones spreadsheet model we ran investments across columns and years down rows. Many financial analysts seem to prefer the opposite. Modify the spreadsheet model so that years go across columns and investments go down rows. Run Solver to ensure that your modified model is correct! (We suggest three possible ways to do this, and you can experiment to see which you prefer. First, you could basically start over on a blank worksheet. Second, you could use the Edit/Copy and then Edit/Paste Special with the Transpose option. Third, you could use Excel's TRANSPOSE function.)

35. In the pension fund problem, suppose there is a fourth bond, bond 4. Its unit cost in 2008 is $1020, it returns coupons of $70 in years 2009 through 2014 and a payment of $1070 in 2015. Modify the model to incorporate this extra bond, and reoptimize. Does the solution change—that is, should James purchase any of bond 4?

36. In the pension fund problem, suppose there is an upper limit of 60 on the number of bonds of any particular type that can be purchased. Modify the model to incorporate this extra constraint and then reoptimize. How much more money does James need to allocate initially?

37. In the pension fund problem, suppose James has been asked to see how the optimal solution will change if the required payments in years 2015 through 2022 all increase by the same percentage, where this percentage could be anywhere from 5% to 25%. Use an appropriate one-way SolverTable to help him out, and write a memo describing the results.

38. Our pension fund model is streamlined, perhaps too much. It does all of the calculations concerning cash

flows in row 20. James decides he would like to "break these out" into several rows of calculations: Beginning cash (for 2008, this is the amount allocated; for other years, it is the unused cash, plus interest, from the previous year), Amount spent on bonds (positive in 2008 only), Amount received from bonds (positive for years 2009 through 2022 only), Cash available for making pension fund payments, and (below the Amount required row) Cash left over (amount invested in the fixed interest rate). Modify the model by inserting these rows, enter the appropriate formulas, and run Solver. You should obtain the same result, but you get more detailed information.

Level B

39. Suppose the investments in the Barney-Jones problem sometimes require cash outlays in more than one year. For example, a $1 investment in investment B might require $0.25 to be spent in year 1 and $0.75 to be spent in year 2. Does our model easily accommodate such investments? Try it with some cash outlay data you make up, run Solver, and interpret your results.

40. In the pension fund problem, we know that if the amount of money initially is *less* than the amount found by Solver, then James will not be able to meet all of the pension fund payments. Use the current model to demonstrate that this is true. To do so, enter a value less than the optimal value into cell B16. Then run Solver, but remove the Money_allocated cell as a changing cell and as the target cell. (If there is no target cell, Solver simply tries to find a solution that satisfies all of the constraints.) What do you find?

41. Continuing the previous problem in a slightly different direction, continue to use the Money_allocated cell as a changing cell, and add a constraint that it must be less than or equal to any value, such as $195,000, that is less than its current optimal value. With this constraint, James will again not be able to meet all of the pension fund payments. Create a new target cell to minimize the total amount of payments not met. The easiest way to do this is with IF functions. Unfortunately, this makes the model nonsmooth, and Solver might have trouble finding the optimal solution. Try it and see.

15.7 INTEGER PROGRAMMING MODELS

In this section we see how some problems can be modeled using 0–1 variables (and possibly other integer variables). A **0–1 variable** is a variable that must equal 0 or 1. Usually a 0–1 variable corresponds to an activity that is or is not undertaken. If the 0–1 variable corresponding to the activity equals 0, then the activity is not undertaken; if it equals 1, the activity is undertaken. A 0–1 variable is also called a **binary variable**.

Optimization models in which some or all of the variables must be integers are known as **integer programming** (IP) models. We have already seen examples in our discussion of scheduling postal workers and aggregate planning at SureStep. In this section we illustrate some of the "tricks of the trade" that are needed to formulate IP models of complex situations. You should be aware that a spreadsheet Solver typically has a much harder time solving an IP problem than an LP problem! In fact, Solver is unable to solve some IP problems, even when they have an optimal solution. The reason is that these problems are inherently difficult to solve, no matter what software package is used. However, as we see in this section, our ability to model complex problems increases tremendously when we are able to use IP, particularly with 0–1 variables.

15.7.1 Capital Budgeting Models

Perhaps the simplest IP model is the following capital budgeting example. It perfectly illustrates the "go–no go" nature of many IP models.

| EXAMPLE | 15.8 SELECTING INVESTMENTS AT TATHAM |

The Tatham Company is considering seven investments. The cash required for each investment and the net present value (NPV) each investment adds to the firm are listed in Table 15.12. The cash available for investment is $15,000. Tatham wants to find the investment policy that maximizes its NPV. The crucial assumption here is that if Tatham wishes to take part in any of these investments, it must go "all the way." It cannot, for example, go halfway in investment 1 by investing $2500 and realizing an NPV of $8000. In fact, if partial investments were allowed, we wouldn't need IP; we could use LP.

Table 15.12   Data for Capital Budgeting Example

Investment	Cash Required	NPV
1	$5000	$16,000
2	$2500	$8000
3	$3500	$10,000
4	$6000	$19,500
5	$7000	$22,000
6	$4500	$12,000
7	$3,000	$7,500

Objective   To use binary IP to find the set of investments that stays within budget and maximizes total NPV.

WHERE DO THE NUMBERS COME FROM?

The initial required cash and the available budget are easy to obtain. It is undoubtedly harder to obtain the NPV for each investment. Here we require a time sequence of anticipated cash inflows from the investments, and we need a discount factor. We might even use simulation to estimate these NPVs. In any case, estimation of the required NPVs would definitely put the financial analysts to work.

Solution

The variables and constraints required for this model are listed in Table 15.13. The most important part is that the decision variables must be binary, where a 1 means an investment is undertaken and a 0 means it is not. These variables cannot have fractional values such as 0.5, because we do not allow partial investments—the company has to go all the way or not at all. Note in this table that we specify the binary restriction in the second row, not the last row. We do this throughout this chapter. However, when we set up the Solver dialog box, we add explicit binary constraints in the constraints section.

Table 15.13   **Variables and Constraints for Capital Budgeting Model**

Input variables	Initial cash required for investments, NPVs from investments, budget
Decision variables (changing cells)	Whether to invest (binary variables)
Objective (target cell)	Total NPV
Other calculated variables	Total initial cash invested
Constraints	Total initial cash invested ≤ Budget

DEVELOPING THE SPREADSHEET MODEL

To form the spreadsheet model, which is shown in Figure 15.40, proceed as follows. (See the file **Capital Budgeting 1.xlsx**.)

Figure 15.40   Capital Budgeting Model

	A	B	C	D	E	F	G	H	I	J	K	L	M
1	Tatham capital budgeting model										Range names used:		
2											Amount_invested	=Model!$B$14	
3	Input data on potential investments										Budget	=Model!$D$14	
4	Investment	1	2	3	4	5	6	7			Investment_levels	=Model!$B$10:$H$10	
5	Investment cost	$5,000	$2,500	$3,500	$6,000	$7,000	$4,500	$3,000			Total_NPV	=Model!$B$17	
6	NPV	$16,000	$8,000	$10,000	$19,500	$22,000	$12,000	$7,500					
7	NPV per investment dollar	3.20	3.20	2.86	3.25	3.14	2.67	2.50					
8													
9	Decisions: whether to invest												
10	Investment levels	1	1	0	0	1	0	0					
11													
12	Budget constraint												
13		Amount invested		Budget									
14		$14,500	<=	$15,000									
15													
16	Objective to maximize												
17	Total NPV	$46,000											

A SUMPRODUCT formula, where one of the ranges comprises 0's and 1's, really just sums the values in the other range that "match up" with the 1's.

1   **Inputs.** Enter the initial cash requirements, the NPVs, and the budget in the shaded ranges.

2   **0–1 values for investments.** Enter *any* trial 0–1 values for the investments in the Investment_levels range. Actually, you can even enter fractional values such as 0.5 in these cells. The Solver constraints will eventually force them to be 0 or 1.

3   **Cash invested.** Calculate the total cash invested in cell B14 with the formula

=SUMPRODUCT(B5:H5,Investment_levels)

Note that this formula "picks up" the costs *only* for those investments with 0–1 variables equal to 1. To see this, think how the SUMPRODUCT function works when one of its ranges is a range of 0's and 1's. It effectively sums the cells in the other range corresponding to the 1's.

4   **NPV contribution.** Calculate the NPV contributed by the investments in cell B17 with the formula

=SUMPRODUCT(B6:H6,Investment_levels)

Again, this picks up only the NPVs of the investments with 0–1 variables equal to 1.

Excel's Solver makes it easy to specify binary constraints, just by clicking on the "bin" option.

The Solver dialog box appears in Figure 15.41. We want to maximize the total NPV, subject to staying within the budget. However, we also need to *constrain* the changing cells to be 0–1. Fortunately, Solver makes this simple, as shown in the dialog box in Figure 15.42. We add a constraint with Investments in the left box and choose the "bin" option in the middle box. The "binary" in the right box is then added automatically. Note that if *all* changing cells are binary, we do not need to check Solver's Assume Non-Negative option (because 0 and 1 are certainly nonnegative), but we should still check the Assume Linear Model option if the model is linear, as it is here.

Figure 15.41

Solver Dialog Box for Capital Budgeting Model

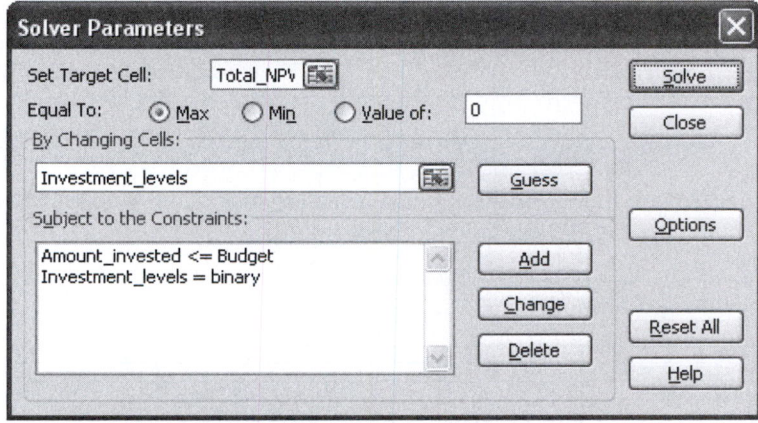

Figure 15.42

Specifying a Binary Constraint

Discussion of the Solution

The optimal solution in Figure 15.40 indicates that Tatham can obtain a maximum NPV of $46,000 by selecting investments 1, 2, and 5. These three investments consume only $14,500 of the available budget, with $500 left over. However, this $500 is not enough—because of the "investing all the way" requirement—to invest in any of the remaining investments.

If we rank Tatham's investments on the basis of NPV per dollar invested (see row 7 of Figure 15.40), the ranking from best to worst is 4, 1, 2, 5, 3, 6, 7. Using your economic intuition, you might expect the investments to be chosen in this order—until the budget runs out. However, the optimal solution does not do this. It selects the second-, third-, and fourth-best investments, but it ignores the best. To understand why it does this, imagine investing in the order from best to worst, according to row 7, until the budget allows no more. By the time you have invested in investments 4, 1, and 2, you will have consumed $13,500 of the budget, and the remainder, $1500, is not sufficient to invest in any of the rest. This strategy provides an NPV of only $43,500. A smarter strategy, the optimal solution from Solver, gains you an extra $2500 in NPV.

Sensitivity Analysis

SolverTable can be used on models with binary variables exactly as we have used it in previous models. Here we see how the total NPV varies as the budget increases. We select the Budget cell as the single input cell, allow it to vary from $15,000 to $25,000 in increments of $1000, and keep track of the total NPV, the amount of the budget used, and the binary variables. The results are given in Figure 15.43. Clearly, Tatham can achieve a larger NPV with a larger budget, but as the numbers and the chart show, each extra $1000 of budget does *not* have the same effect on total NPV. The first $1000 increase to the budget adds $3500 to total NPV, the next two $1000 increases add $4000 each, the next two $1000 increases add $2000 each, and so on. Note also how the selected investments vary quite a lot as the budget increases. This somewhat strange behavior is due to the "lumpiness" of the inputs and the all-or-nothing nature of the problem.

Figure 15.43   Sensitivity to Budget

	A	B	C	D	E	F	G	H	I	J
19	Sensitivity of total NPV, amount invested, and investments to budget									
20	Budget	Total NPV	Amt invested	Invest1	Invest2	Invest3	Invest4	Invest5	Invest6	Invest7
21		$B$17	$B$14	$B$10	$C$10	$D$10	$E$10	$F$10	$G$10	$H$10
22	15000	$46,000	$14,500	1	1	0	0	1	0	0
23	16000	$49,500	$15,500	0	1	0	1	1	0	0
24	17000	$53,500	$17,000	1	1	1	1	0	0	0
25	18000	$57,500	$18,000	1	0	0	1	1	0	0
26	19000	$59,500	$19,000	0	1	1	1	1	0	0
27	20000	$61,500	$20,000	0	1	0	1	1	1	0
28	21000	$65,500	$20,500	1	1	0	1	1	0	0
29	22000	$67,500	$21,500	1	0	1	1	1	0	0
30	23000	$69,500	$22,500	1	0	0	1	1	1	0
31	24000	$75,500	$24,000	1	1	1	1	1	0	0
32	25000	$77,500	$25,000	1	1	0	1	1	1	0

Total NPV versus Budget

Effect of Solver Tolerance Setting

When the Tolerance setting is 5% instead of 0%, Solver's solution might not be optimal, but it will be close.

To illustrate the effect of the Solver Tolerance setting, compare the SolverTable results in Figure 15.44 with those in Figure 15.43. Each is for the Tatham capital budgeting model, but Figure 15.44 uses Solver's default tolerance of 5%, whereas Figure 15.43 uses a tolerance of 0%. The four shaded cells in Figure 15.44 indicate *lower* total NPVs than the corresponding cells in Figure 15.43. In these four cases, Solver stopped short of finding the true optimal solutions because it found solutions within the 5% tolerance and then quit.

Figure 15.44 Results with Tolerance at 5%

	A	B	C	D	E	F	G	H	I	J
19	Sensitivity of total NPV, amount invested, and investments to budget									
20	Budget	Total NPV	Amt invested	Invest1	Invest2	Invest3	Invest4	Invest5	Invest6	Invest7
21		$B$17	$B$14	$B$10	$C$10	$D$10	$E$10	$F$10	$G$10	$H$10
22	15000	$45,500	$15,000	1	0	0	0	1	0	1
23	16000	$49,500	$15,500	0	1	0	1	1	0	0
24	17000	$53,500	$17,000	1	1	1	1	0	0	0
25	18000	$57,500	$18,000	1	0	0	1	1	0	0
26	19000	$59,500	$19,000	0	1	1	1	1	0	0
27	20000	$60,000	$20,000	1	0	1	0	1	1	0
28	21000	$65,500	$20,500	1	1	0	1	1	0	0
29	22000	$65,500	$20,500	1	1	0	1	1	0	0
30	23000	$68,000	$22,500	1	1	1	0	1	1	0
31	24000	$75,500	$24,000	1	1	1	1	1	0	0
32	25000	$77,500	$25,000	1	1	0	1	1	1	0

MODELING ISSUES

1. The following modifications of the capital budgeting example can be handled easily. You are asked to explore similar modifications in the problems.

   - Suppose that at most two projects can be selected. In this case we add a constraint that the sum of the 0–1 variables for the investments is less than or equal to 2. This constraint is satisfied if 0, 1, or 2 investments are chosen, but it is violated if 3 or more investments are chosen.

   - Suppose that if investment 2 is selected, then investment 1 must also be selected. In this case we add a constraint saying that the 0–1 variable for investment 1 is greater than or equal to the 0–1 variable for investment 2. This constraint rules out the one possibility that is not allowed—where investment 2 is selected but investment 1 is not.

   - Suppose that either investment 1 or investment 3 (or both) *must* be selected. In this case we add a constraint that the sum of the 0–1 variables for investments 1 and 3 must be greater than or equal to 1. This rules out the one possibility that is not allowed—where both of these 0–1 variables are 0, so that neither investment is selected.

2. Capital budgeting models with multiple periods can also be handled. Figure 15.45 shows one possibility. (See the **Capital Budgeting 2.xlsx** file.) The costs in rows 5 and 6 are *both* incurred if any given investment is selected. Now there are two budget constraints, one in each year, but otherwise the model is exactly as before. Note that some investments could have a cost of 0 in year 1 and a positive cost in year 2. This would effectively mean that these investments are undertaken in year 2 rather than year 1. Also, it would be easy to modify the model to incorporate costs in years 3, 4, and so on.

3. If Tatham could choose a *fractional* amount of an investment, then we could maximize its NPV by deleting the binary constraint. The optimal solution to the resulting LP model has a total NPV of $48,714. All of investments 1, 2, and 4, and 0.214 of investment 5 are chosen. Note that there is no way to round the changing cell values from this LP solution to obtain the optimal IP solution. Sometimes the solution to an IP model *without* the integer constraints bears little resemblance to the optimal IP solution.

4. Any IP involving 0–1 variables with only one constraint is called a **knapsack problem**. Think of the problem faced by a hiker going on an overnight hike. For

example, imagine that the hiker's knapsack can hold only 14 pounds, and she must choose which of several available items to take on the hike. The benefit derived from each item is analogous to the NPV of each project, and the weight of each item is analogous to the cash required by each investment. The single constraint is analogous to the budget constraint—that is, only 14 pounds can fit in the knapsack. In a knapsack problem the goal is to get the most value in the knapsack without overloading it. ■

Figure 15.45 A Two-Period Capital Budgeting Model

	A	B	C	D	E	F	G	H	I	J	K	L
1	Tatham two-period capital budgeting model									Range names used:		
2										Amount_invested	=Model!$B$14:$B$15	
3	Input data on potential investments									Budget	=Model!$D$14:$D$15	
4	Investment	1	2	3	4	5	6	7		Investment_levels	=Model!$B$10:$H$10	
5	Year 1 cost	$5,000	$2,500	$3,500	$6,500	$7,000	$4,500	$3,000		Total_NPV	=Model!$B$18	
6	Year 2 cost	$2,000	$1,500	$2,000	$0	$500	$1,500	$0				
7	NPV	$16,000	$8,000	$10,000	$20,000	$22,000	$12,000	$8,000				
8												
9	Decisions: whether to invest											
10	Investment levels	1	1	0	1	0	0	0				
11												
12	Budget constraints											
13		Amount invested		Budget								
14		$14,000	<=	$14,000								
15		$3,500	<=	$4,500								
16												
17	Objective to maximize											
18	Total NPV	$44,000										

15.7.2 Fixed-Cost Models

In many situations a fixed cost is incurred if an activity is undertaken at *any positive* level. This cost is independent of the level of the activity and is known as a **fixed cost** (or fixed charge). Here are three examples of fixed costs:

■ Construction of a warehouse incurs a fixed cost that is the same whether the warehouse is used at a low or a high level.

■ A cash withdrawal from a bank incurs a fixed cost, independent of the size of the withdrawal, due to the time spent at the bank.

■ A machine that is used to make several products must be set up for the production of each product. No matter how many units of a product the company produces, it incurs the same fixed cost (lost production due to the setup time) for making the product.

In these examples a fixed cost is incurred if an activity is undertaken at any positive level, whereas zero fixed cost is incurred if the activity is not undertaken at all. Although it might not be obvious, this feature makes the problem inherently *nonlinear*, which means that a straightforward application of LP is not possible. However, the following example illustrates how a clever use of 0–1 variables can result in a *linear* model.

EXAMPLE | **15.9 TEXTILE MANUFACTURING AT GREAT THREADS**

The Great Threads Company is capable of manufacturing shirts, shorts, pants, skirts, and jackets. Each type of clothing requires that Great Threads have the appropriate type of machinery available. The machinery needed to manufacture each type of clothing must be rented at the weekly rates shown in Table 15.14. This table also lists the amounts of cloth and labor required per unit of clothing, as well as the sales price and the unit variable cost for each type of clothing. There are 4000 labor hours and 4500 square yards (sq yd) of cloth available in a given week. The company wants to find a solution that maximizes its weekly profit.

Table 15.14 Data for Great Threads Example

	Rental Cost	Labor Hours	Cloth (sq yd)	Sales Price	Unit Variable Cost
Shirts	$1500	2.0	3.0	$35	$20
Shorts	$1200	1.0	2.5	$40	$10
Pants	$1600	6.0	4.0	$65	$25
Skirts	$1500	4.0	4.5	$70	$30
Jackets	$1600	8.0	5.5	$110	$35

Objective To develop a linear model with binary variables that can be used to maximize the company's profit, correctly accounting for fixed costs and staying within resource availabilities.

WHERE DO THE NUMBERS COME FROM?

Except for the fixed costs, this is the same basic problem as the product mix problem (Example 14.2) in Chapter 14. Therefore, the same discussion there about input variables applies here. As for the fixed costs, these would simply be the given rental rates for the machinery.

Solution

The variables and constraints required for this model are listed in Table 15.15. We first note that the cost of producing x shirts during a week is 0 if $x = 0$, but it is $1500 + 20x$ if $x > 0$. This cost structure violates the proportionality assumption (discussed in the previous chapter) that is needed for a linear model. If proportionality were satisfied, then the cost of making, say, 10 shirts would be double the cost of making 5 shirts. However, because of the fixed cost, the total cost of making 5 shirts is $1600, and the cost of making 10 shirts is only $1700. This violation of proportionality requires us to resort to 0–1 variables to obtain a *linear* model. These 0–1 variables allow us to model the fixed costs correctly, as explained in detail here.

Table 15.15 Variables and Constraints for Fixed-Cost Model

Input variables	Fixed rental costs, resource usages (labor hours, cloth) per unit of clothing, sales prices, unit variable costs, resource availabilities
Decision variables (changing cells)	Whether to produce any of each clothing (binary), how much of each clothing to produce
Objective (target cell)	Profit
Other calculated variables	Resources used, upper limits on amounts to produce, total revenue, total variable cost, total fixed cost
Constraints	Amount produced ≤ Logical upper limit (capacity) Resources used ≤ Resources available

DEVELOPING THE SPREADSHEET MODEL

The spreadsheet model, shown in Figure 15.46, can now be formulated as follows. (See the file **Fixed Cost Manufacturing.xlsx**.)

Figure 15.46 Fixed-Cost Clothing Model

	A	B	C	D	E	F	G	H	I	J	K
1	Great Threads fixed cost clothing model								Range names used:		
2									Logical_upper_limit	=Model!$B$18:$F$18	
3	Input data on products								Produce_any?	=Model!$B$14:$F$14	
4		Shirts	Shorts	Pants	Skirts	Jackets			Profit	=Model!$B$29	
5	Labor hours/unit	2	1	6	4	8			Resource_available	=Model!$D$22:$D$23	
6	Cloth (sq. yd.)/unit	3	2.5	4	4.5	5.5			Resource_used	=Model!$B$22:$B$23	
7									Units_produced	=Model!$B$16:$F$16	
8	Selling price/unit	$35	$40	$65	$70	$110					
9	Variable cost/unit	$20	$10	$25	$30	$35					
10	Fixed cost for equipment	$1,500	$1,200	$1,600	$1,500	$1,600					
11											
12	Production plan, constraints on capacity										
13		Shirts	Shorts	Pants	Skirts	Jackets					
14	Produce any?	0	1	0	0	1					
15											
16	Units produced	0	965.52	0	0	379.31					
17		<=	<=	<=	<=	<=					
18	Logical upper limit	0.00	1800.00	0.00	0.00	500.00					
19											
20	Constraints on resources										
21		Resource used		Available							
22	Labor hours	4000.00	<=	4000							
23	Cloth	4500.00	<=	4500							
24											
25	Monetary outputs										
26	Revenue	$80,345									
27	Variable cost	$22,931									
28	Fixed cost for equipment	$2,800									
29	Profit	$54,614	←	Objective to maximize							

1 **Inputs.** Enter the given inputs in the shaded ranges.

2 **Binary values for clothing types.** Enter *any* trial values for the 0–1 variables for the various clothing types in the Produce_any? range. For example, if you enter a 1 in cell C14, you are implying that *some* shorts are produced. More importantly, you are implying that the machinery for making shorts is rented and its fixed cost is incurred.

3 **Production quantities.** Enter *any* trial values for the numbers of the various clothing types produced in the Units_produced range. At this point you could enter "illegal" values, such as 0 in cell B14 and a positive value in cell B16. We say this is illegal because it implies that the company produces some shirts but avoids the fixed cost of the machinery for shirts. However, Solver will eventually disallow such illegal combinations.

4 **Labor and cloth used.** In cell B22 enter the formula

=SUMPRODUCT(B5:F5,Units_produced)

to calculate total labor hours, and copy this to cell B23 for cloth.

5 **Effective capacities.** Now we come to the tricky part of the formulation. We need to ensure that if any of a given type of clothing is produced, then its 0–1 variable equals 1. This ensures that the model incurs the fixed cost of renting the machine for this type of clothing. We could easily implement these constraints with IF statements. For example, to implement the constraint for shirts, we could enter the following formula in cell B14:

=IF(B16>0,1,0)

However, Excel's Solver is unable to deal with IF functions predictably. Therefore, we instead model the fixed-cost constraints as follows:

$$\text{Shirts produced} \leq \text{Maximum capacity} \times (0\text{–}1 \text{ variable for shirts}) \tag{15.4}$$

There are similar inequalities for the other types of clothing.

Here is the logic behind inequality (15.4). If the 0–1 variable for shirts is 0, then the right-hand side of the inequality is 0, which means that the left side must be 0—no shirts can be produced. That is, if the 0–1 variable for shirts is 0, so that no fixed cost for shirts is incurred, then inequality (15.4) does not allow Great Threads to "cheat" and produce a positive number of shirts. On the other hand, if the 0–1 variable for shirts is 1, then the inequality is certainly true and is essentially redundant. It simply states that the number of shirts produced must be no greater than the *maximum* number that could be produced. Inequality (15.4) rules out the one case we want it to rule out—namely, that Great Threads produces shirts but avoids the fixed cost.

To implement inequality (15.4), we need a maximum capacity—an upper limit on the number of shirts that *could* be produced. To obtain this, suppose the company puts all of its resources into producing shirts. Then the number of shirts that can be produced is limited by the smaller of

$$\frac{\text{Available labor hours}}{\text{Labor hours per shirt}}$$

and

$$\frac{\text{Available square yards of cloth}}{\text{Square yards of cloth per shirt}}$$

Therefore, the smaller of these—the most limiting—can be used as the maximum needed in inequality (15.4).

To implement this logic, calculate the "effective capacity" for shirts in cell B18 with the formula

=B14*MIN($D$22/B5,$D$23/B6)

Then copy this formula to the range C16:F16 for the other types of clothing.[12] By the way, this MIN formula causes no problems for Solver because it does not involve *changing* cells, only input cells.

6 **Monetary values.** Calculate the total sales revenue and the total variable cost by entering the formula

=SUMPRODUCT(B8:F8,Units_produced)

in cell B26 and copying it to cell B27. Then calculate the total fixed cost in cell B28 with the formula

=SUMPRODUCT(B10:F10,Produce_any?)

Note that this formula picks up the fixed costs only for those products with 0–1 variables equal to 1. Finally, calculate the total profit in cell B29 with the formula

=B26-B27-B28

USING SOLVER

The Solver dialog box is shown in Figure 15.47. We maximize profit, subject to using no more labor hours or cloth than are available, and we ensure that production is less than or equal to "effective" capacity. The key is that this effective capacity is 0 if we decide to produce none of a given type of clothing. As usual, check the Assume Linear Model and Assume Non-Negative boxes under Solver options, and set the tolerance to 0.

[12] Why not set the upper limit on shirts equal to a huge number like 1,000,000? The reason is that Solver works most efficiently when the upper limit is as "tight"—that is, as low—as possible. A tighter upper limit means fewer potential feasible solutions for Solver to search through. Here's an analogy. If you were trying to locate a criminal, which would be easier: (1) if you were told that he was somewhere in Texas, or (2) if you were told he was somewhere in Dallas?

Figure 15.47
Solver Dialog Box for Fixed-Cost Model

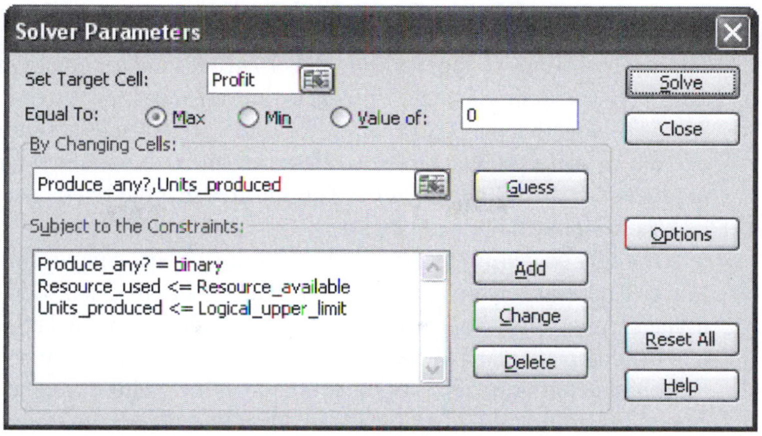

Solver Parameters

Set Target Cell: Profit

Equal To: ⊙ Max ○ Min ○ Value of: 0

By Changing Cells:
Produce_any?,Units_produced

Subject to the Constraints:
Produce_any? = binary
Resource_used <= Resource_available
Units_produced <= Logical_upper_limit

[Solve] [Close] [Guess] [Options] [Add] [Change] [Delete] [Reset All] [Help]

Although Solver finds the optimal solution automatically, you should understand the effect of the logical upper bound constraint on production. It rules out a solution such as the one shown in Figure 15.48. This solution calls for a positive production level of pants but does not incur the fixed cost of the pants equipment. The logical upper bound constraint rules this out because it prevents a positive value in row 16 if the corresponding binary value in row 14 is 0. In other words, if the company wants to produce some pants, then the constraint in inequality (15.4) forces the associated binary variable to be 1, thus incurring the fixed cost for pants.

Note that inequality (15.4) does *not* rule out the situation we see for skirts, where the binary value is 1 and the production level is 0. However, Solver will never choose this type of solution as optimal. Solver recognizes that the binary value in this case can be changed to 0, so that no skirt equipment is rented and its fixed cost is not incurred.

Figure 15.48 An Illegal (and Nonoptimal) Solution

	A	B	C	D	E	F	G	H	I	J	K
1	Great Threads fixed cost clothing model								Range names used:		
2									Logical_upper_limit	=Model!$B$18:$F$18	
3	Input data on products								Produce_any?	=Model!$B$14:$F$14	
4		Shirts	Shorts	Pants	Skirts	Jackets			Profit	=Model!$B$29	
5	Labor hours/unit	2	1	6	4	8			Resource_available	=Model!$D$22:$D$23	
6	Cloth (sq. yd.)/unit	3	2.5	4	4.5	5.5			Resource_used	=Model!$B$22:$B$23	
7									Units_produced	=Model!$B$16:$F$16	
8	Selling price/unit	$35	$40	$65	$70	$110					
9	Variable cost/unit	$20	$10	$25	$30	$35					
10	Fixed cost for equipment	$1,500	$1,200	$1,600	$1,500	$1,600					
11											
12	Production plan, constraints on capacity										
13		Shirts	Shorts	Pants	Skirts	Jackets					
14	Produce any?	0	1	0	1	1					
15											
16	Units produced	0	965.52	450	0	379.31					
17		<=	<=	<=	<=	<=					
18	Logical upper limit	0.00	1800.00	0.00	1000.00	500.00					
19											
20	Constraints on resources										
21		Resource used		Available							
22	Labor hours	6700.00	<=	4000							
23	Cloth	6300.00	<=	4500							
24											
25	Monetary outputs										
26	Revenue	$109,595									
27	Variable cost	$34,181									
28	Fixed cost for equipment	$4,300									
29	Profit	$71,114	←	Objective to maximize							

Discussion of the Solution

The optimal solution appears in Figure 15.46. It indicates that Great Threads should produce about 966 shorts and 379 jackets, but no shirts, pants, or skirts. The total profit is $54,614. Note that the 0–1 variables for shirts, pants, and skirts are all 0, which forces production of these products to be 0. However, the 0–1 variables for shorts and jackets, the products that are produced, are 1. This ensures that the fixed cost of producing shorts and jackets is included in the total cost.

It might be helpful to think of this solution as occurring in two stages. In the first stage Solver determines which products to produce—in this case, shorts and jackets only. Then in the second stage, Solver decides how *many* shorts and jackets to produce. If you know that the company plans to produce shorts and jackets only, you could then ignore the fixed costs and determine the best production quantities with the same product mix model discussed in Example 14.2 of Chapter 14. Of course, these two stages—deciding which products to produce and how many of each to produce—are interrelated, and Solver considers both of them in its solution process.

As always, adding constraints can only make the objective worse. In this case, it means decreased profit.

The Great Threads management might not be very excited about producing shorts and jackets only. Suppose the company wants to ensure that at least three types of clothing are produced at positive levels. One approach is to add another constraint—namely, that the sum of the 0–1 values in row 14 is greater than or equal to 3. You can check, however, that when this constraint is added and Solver is rerun, the 0–1 variable for skirts becomes 1, but no skirts are produced! Shorts and jackets are more profitable than skirts, so only shorts and jackets are produced. (See Figure 15.49.) The new constraint forces Great Threads to rent an extra piece of machinery (for skirts), but it doesn't force the company to use it. To force the company to produce some skirts, we would also need to add a constraint on the value in E16, such as E16>=100. Any of these additional constraints will cost Great Threads money, but if, as a matter of policy, the company wants to produce more than two types of clothing, this is its only option.

Figure 15.49 Great Threads Model with Extra Constraint

	A	B	C	D	E	F	G	H	I
1	Great Threads fixed cost clothing model								
2									
3	Input data on products								
4		Shirts	Shorts	Pants	Skirts	Jackets			
5	Labor hours/unit	2	1	6	4	8			
6	Cloth (sq. yd.)/unit	3	2.5	4	4.5	5.5			
7									
8	Selling price/unit	$35	$40	$65	$70	$110			
9	Variable cost/unit	$20	$10	$25	$30	$35			
10	Fixed cost for equipment	$1,500	$1,200	$1,600	$1,500	$1,600			
11									
12	Production plan, constraints on capacity								
13		Shirts	Shorts	Pants	Skirts	Jackets	Sum		Required
14	Produce any?	0	1	0	1	1	3	>=	3
15									
16	Units produced	0	965.52	0	0	379.31			
17		<=	<=	<=	<=	<=			
18	Logical upper limit	0.00	1800.00	0.00	1000.00	500.00			
19									
20	Constraints on resources								
21		Resource used			Available				
22	Labor hours	4000.00	<=		4000				
23	Cloth	4500.00	<=		4500				
24									
25	Monetary outputs								
26	Revenue	$80,345							
27	Variable cost	$22,931							
28	Fixed cost for equipment	$4,300							
29	Profit	$53,114	←	Objective to maximize					

Sensitivity Analysis

Because the optimal solution currently calls for only shorts and jackets to be produced, an interesting sensitivity analysis is to see how much "incentive" is required for other products to be produced. One way to check this is to increase the sales price for a nonproduced product such as skirts in a one-way SolverTable. We did this, keeping track of all binary variables and profit, with the results shown in Figure 15.50. When the sales price for skirts is $85 or less, the company continues to produce only shorts and jackets. However, when the sales price is $90 or greater, the company stops producing shorts and jackets and produces *only* skirts. You can check that the optimal production quantity of skirts is 1000 when the sales price of skirts is any value $90 or above. The only reason that the profits in Figure 15.50 increase from row 37 down is that the revenues from these 1000 skirts increase.

Figure 15.50

Sensitivity of Binary Variables to Unit Revenues of Shorts and Pants

	A	B	C	D	E	F	G
31	Sensitivity of binary variables and profit to unit revenue from skirts						
32		$B$14	$C$14	$D$14	$E$14	$F$14	$B$29
33	70	0	1	0	0	1	$54,614
34	75	0	1	0	0	1	$54,614
35	80	0	1	0	0	1	$54,614
36	85	0	1	0	0	1	$54,614
37	90	0	0	0	1	0	$58,500
38	95	0	0	0	1	0	$63,500
39	100	0	0	0	1	0	$68,500

A Model with IF Functions

In case you are still not convinced that the binary variable approach is required, and you think IF functions could be used instead, take a look at the last sheet in the finished version of the file. The resulting model *looks* the same as in Figure 15.46, but it incorporates the following changes:

- We no longer use the binary range as part of the changing cells range. Instead, we enter the formula **=IF(B16>0,1,0)** in cell B14 and copy it across to cell F14. Logically, this probably appears more natural. If a production quantity is positive, then a 1 is entered in row 14, which means that the fixed cost is incurred.

- We model the effective capacities in row 18 with IF functions. Specifically, we enter the formula **=IF(B16>0,MIN($D$22/B5,$D$23/B6),0)** in cell B18 and copy it across to cell F18.

- We change the Solver dialog box so that it appears as in Figure 15.51. The Produce_any? range is not part of the changing cells range, and there is no binary constraint. We also uncheck the Assume Linear Model box in Solver's options because the IF functions make the model nonlinear.

Figure 15.51

Solver Dialog Box When IF Functions Are Used

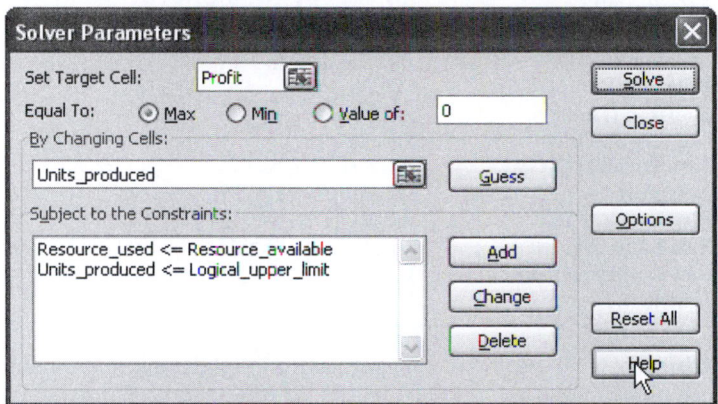

When we ran Solver on this modified model, we found inconsistent results, depending on the initial production quantities entered in row 16. For example, when we entered initial values all equal to 0, the Solver solution was exactly that—all 0's. Of course, this solution is *terrible* because it leads to a profit of $0. However, when we entered initial production quantities all equal to 100, Solver found the correct optimal solution, the same as in Figure 15.46. Was this just lucky? To check, we tried another initial solution, where the production quantities for shorts and jackets were 0, and the production quantities for shirts, pants, and skirts were all 500. In this case Solver found a solution where only skirts are produced. Of course, we know this is not optimal.

The moral is that the IF-function approach is not the way to go. Its success depends strongly on the initial values we enter in the changing cells, and this requires us to make very good guesses. The binary approach ensures that we get the correct solution. ■

15.7.3 Set-Covering Models

In a set-covering model, each member of a given set (set 1) must be "covered" by an acceptable member of another set (set 2). The objective in a set-covering problem is to minimize the number of members in set 2 necessary to cover all the members in set 1. For example, set 1 might consist of all the cities in a county and set 2 might consist of the cities in which a fire station is located. A member of set 2 "covers" a city in set 1 if the fire station is located within, say, 10 minutes of the city. The goal is to minimize the number of fire stations needed to cover all cities. Set-covering models have been applied to areas as diverse as airline crew scheduling, truck dispatching, political redistricting, and capital investment. The following is a typical example of a set-covering model.

EXAMPLE **15.10 HUB LOCATION AT WESTERN AIRLINES**

Western Airlines has decided that it wants to design a "hub" system in the United States. Each hub is used for connecting flights to and from cities within 1000 miles of the hub. Western runs flights among the following cities: Atlanta, Boston, Chicago, Denver, Houston, Los Angeles, New Orleans, New York, Pittsburgh, Salt Lake City, San Francisco, and Seattle. The company wants to determine the smallest number of hubs it will need to cover all of these cities, where a city is "covered" if it is within 1000 miles of at least one hub. Table 15.16 lists the cities that are within 1000 miles of other cities.

Table 15.16   Data for Western Set-Covering Example

	Cities Within 1000 Miles
Atlanta (AT)	AT, CH, HO, NO, NY, PI
Boston (BO)	BO, NY, PI
Chicago (CH)	AT, CH, NY, NO, PI
Denver (DE)	DE, SL
Houston (HO)	AT, HO, NO
Los Angeles (LA)	LA, SL, SF
New Orleans (NO)	AT, CH, HO, NO
New York (NY)	AT, BO, CH, NY, PI
Pittsburgh (PI)	AT, BO, CH, NY, PI
Salt Lake City (SL)	DE, LA, SL, SF, SE
San Francisco (SF)	LA, SL, SF, SE
Seattle (SE)	SL, SF, SE

Objective   To develop a binary model to find the minimum number of hub locations that can cover all cities.

WHERE DO THE NUMBERS COME FROM?

Western has evidently made a policy decision that its hubs will cover only cities within a 1000-mile radius. Then the cities covered by any hub location can be found from a map. (In a later sensitivity analysis, we explore how the solution changes when we allow the coverage distance to vary.)

Solution

The variables and constraints for this set-covering model are listed in Table 15.17 The model is straightforward. We use a binary variable for each city to indicate whether a hub is located there. Then we calculate the number of hubs that cover each city and require it to be at least 1. There are no monetary costs in this version of the problem. We simply minimize the number of hubs.

Table 15.17   Variables and Constraints for Set-Covering Model

Input variables	Cities within 1000 miles of one another
Decision variables (changing cells)	Locations of hubs (binary)
Objective (target cell)	Number of hubs
Other calculated variables	Number of hubs covering each city
Constraints	Number of hubs covering a city $\geq$ 1

DEVELOPING THE SPREADSHEET MODEL

The spreadsheet model for Western is shown in Figure 15.52. (See the file **Locating Hubs 1.xlsx**.) It can be developed as follows.

Figure 15.52   Airline Hub Set-Covering Model

	A	B	C	D	E	F	G	H	I	J	K	L	M	N	O	P	Q
1	Western Airlines hub location model																
2																	
3	Input data: which cities are covered by which potential hubs														Range names used:		
4		Potential hub													Hubs_covered_by	=Model!$B$25:$B$36	
5	City		AT	BO	CH	DE	HO	LA	NO	NY	PI	SL	SF	SE		Total_hubs	=Model!$B$39
6	AT		1	0	1	0	1	0	1	1	1	0	0	0		Used_as_hub?	=Model!$B$21:$M$21
7	BO		0	1	0	0	0	0	0	1	1	0	0	0				
8	CH		1	0	1	0	0	0	1	1	1	0	0	0				
9	DE		0	0	0	1	0	0	0	0	0	1	0	0				
10	HO		1	0	0	0	1	0	1	0	0	0	0	0				
11	LA		0	0	0	0	0	1	0	0	0	1	1	0				
12	NO		1	0	1	0	1	0	1	0	0	0	0	0				
13	NY		1	1	1	0	0	0	0	1	1	0	0	0				
14	PI		1	1	1	0	0	0	0	1	1	0	0	0				
15	SL		0	0	0	1	0	0	0	0	0	1	1	1				
16	SF		0	0	0	0	0	1	0	0	0	1	1	1				
17	SE		0	0	0	0	0	0	0	0	0	1	1	1				
18																		
19	Decisions: which cities to use as hubs																
20			AT	BO	CH	DE	HO	LA	NO	NY	PI	SL	SF	SE				
21	Used as hub?		0	0	0	0	1	0	0	1	0	1	0	0				
22																		
23	Constraints that each city must be covered by at least one hub																
24	City	Hubs covered by		Required													
25	AT	2	>=	1													
26	BO	1	>=	1													
27	CH	1	>=	1													
28	DE	1	>=	1													
29	HO	1	>=	1													
30	LA	1	>=	1													
31	NO	1	>=	1													
32	NY	1	>=	1													
33	PI	1	>=	1													
34	SL	1	>=	1													
35	SF	1	>=	1													
36	SE	1	>=	1													
37																		
38	Objective to minimize																
39	Total hubs	3															

Note that there are multiple optimal solutions to this model, all of which require a total of 3 hubs. You might get a different solution from the one shown here.

① Inputs. Enter the information from Table 15.16 in the shaded range. A 1 in a cell indicates that the column city covers the row city, whereas a 0 indicates that the column city does not cover the row city. For example, the three 1's in row 7 indicate that Boston, New York, and Pittsburgh are the only cities within 1000 miles of Boston.

② 0–1 values for hub locations. Enter *any* trial values of 0's or 1's in the Used_as_hub? range to indicate which cities are used as hubs. These are the changing cells.

③ Cities covered by hubs. We now determine the number of hubs that cover each city. Specifically, calculate the total number of hubs within 1000 miles of Atlanta in cell B25 with the formula

=SUMPRODUCT(B6:M6,Used_as_hub?)

For any 0–1 values in the changing-cells range, this formula "picks up" the number of hubs that cover Atlanta. Then copy this to the rest of the Hubs_covered_by range. Note that a value in the Hubs_covered_by range can be 2 or greater. This indicates that a city is within 1000 miles of multiple hubs.

④ Number of hubs. Calculate the total number of hubs used in cell B39 with the formula

=SUM(Used_as_hub?)

USING SOLVER

The Solver dialog box should appear as in Figure 15.53. We minimize the total number of hubs, subject to covering each city by at least one hub and ensuring that the changing cells are binary. As usual, the Assume Linear Model option should be checked.

Figure 15.53

Solver Dialog Box for Set-Covering Model

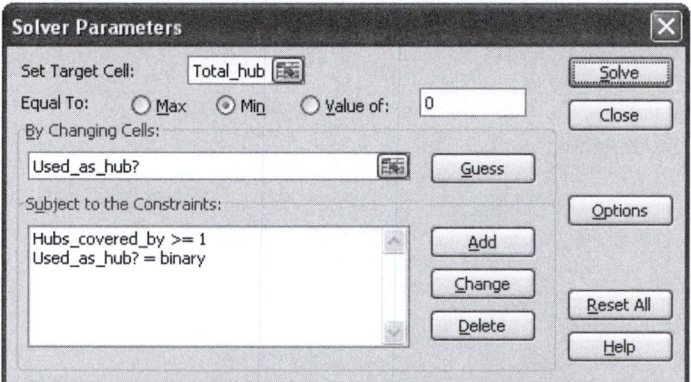

Discussion of the Solution

Figure 15.54 is a graphical representation of the optimal solution, where the double ovals indicate hub locations and the large circles indicate ranges covered by the hubs. (These large circles are not drawn to scale. In reality, they should be circles of radius 1000 miles centered at the hubs.) Three hubs—in Houston, New York, and Salt Lake City—are needed.[13] Would you have guessed this? The Houston hub covers Houston, Atlanta, and New Orleans. The New York hub covers Atlanta, Pittsburgh, Boston, New York, and Chicago. The Salt Lake City hub covers Denver, Los Angeles, Salt Lake City, San Francisco, and Seattle. Note that Atlanta is the only city covered by two hubs; it can be serviced by New York or Houston.

---

[13]There are multiple optimal solutions for this model, all requiring three hubs, so you might obtain a different solution from ours.

Figure 15.54

Graphical Solution
to Set-Covering
Model

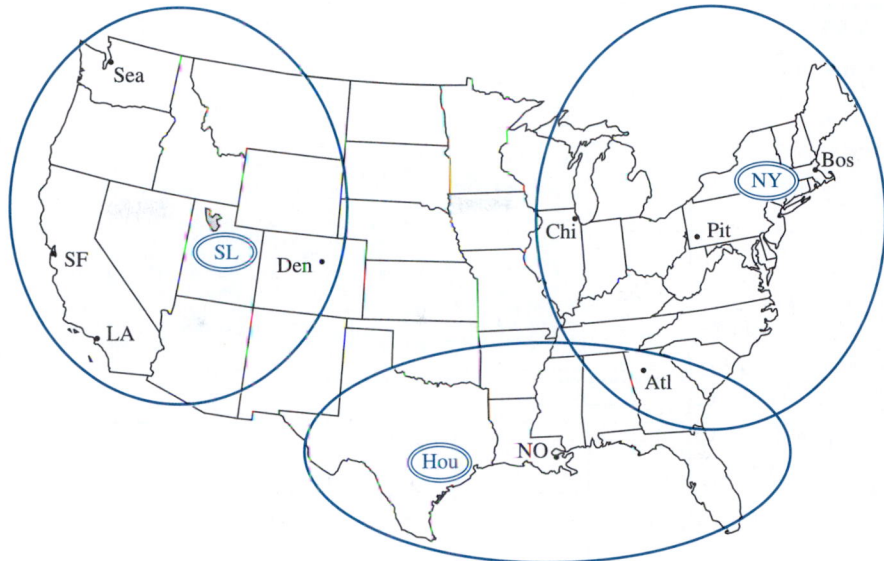

Sensitivity Analysis

An interesting sensitivity analysis for Western's problem is to see how the solution is affected by the mile limit. Currently, a hub can service all cities within 1000 miles. What if the limit were 800 or 1200 miles, say? To answer this question, we must first collect data on actual distances among all of the cities. Once we have a matrix of these distances, we can build the 0–1 matrix, corresponding to the range B6:M17 in Figure 15.52, with IF functions. The modified model appears in Figure 15.55. (See the file **Locating Hubs 2.xlsx**.) The typical formula in B24 is **=IF(B8<=$B$4,1,0)**, which is then copied to the rest of the B24:M35 range.[14] We then run SolverTable, selecting cell B4 as the single input cell, letting it vary from 800 to 1200 in increments of 100, and keeping track of where the hubs are located and the number of hubs. The SolverTable results at the bottom show the effect of the mile limit. When this limit is lowered to 800 miles, 4 hubs are required, but when it is increased to 1100 or 1200, only 2 hubs are required. By the way, the solution shown for the 1000-mile limit is different from the previous solution in Figure 15.52, but it still requires 3 hubs.

ADDITIONAL APPLICATIONS

Station Staffing at Pan Am

Like many other airlines, Pan Am has used management science to determine optimal staffing levels for its support staff (for ticket counters, baggage loading and unloading, mechanical maintenance, and so on). Schindler and Semmel (1993) describe how Pan Am used a set-covering model to determine flexible shifts of full-time and part-time personnel in the United States, Central and South America, and Europe. The model allowed the company to reduce its deployment of staff by up to 11% in work-hour requirements and suggested how existing staff could be used more efficiently. ∎

---

[14]We have warned you about using IF functions in Solver models. However, the current use affects only the *inputs* to the problem, not quantities that depend on the changing cells. Therefore, it causes no problems.

Figure 15.55
Sensitivity to Mile Limit

	A	B	C	D	E	F	G	H	I	J	K	L	M	N	O	P	Q
1	Western Airlines hub location model with distances														Range names used:		
2															Hubs_covered_by	=Model!$B$43:$B$54	
3	Input data														Total_hubs	=Model!$B$57	
4	Mile limit	1000													Used_as_hub?	=Model!$B$39:$M$39	
5																	
6	Distance from each city to each other city																
7			AT	BO	CH	DE	HO	LA	NO	NY	PI	SL	SF	SE			
8	AT		0	1037	674	1398	789	2182	479	841	687	1878	2496	2618			
9	BO		1037	0	1005	1949	1804	2979	1507	222	574	2343	3095	2976			
10	CH		674	1005	0	1008	1067	2054	912	802	452	1390	2142	2013			
11	DE		1398	1949	1008	0	1019	1059	1273	1771	1411	504	1235	1307			
12	HO		789	1804	1067	1019	0	1538	356	1608	1313	1438	1912	2274			
13	LA		2182	2979	2054	1059	1538	0	1883	2786	2426	715	379	1131			
14	NO		479	1507	912	1273	356	1883	0	1311	1070	1738	2249	2574			
15	NY		841	222	802	1771	1608	2786	1311	0	368	2182	2934	2815			
16	PI		687	574	452	1411	1313	2426	1070	368	0	1826	2578	2465			
17	SL		1878	2343	1390	504	1438	715	1738	2182	1826	0	752	836			
18	SF		2496	3095	2142	1235	1912	379	2249	2934	2578	752	0	808			
19	SE		2618	2976	2013	1307	2274	1131	2574	2815	2465	836	808	0			
20																	
21	Which cities are covered by which potential hubs with this mile limit																
22		Potential hub															
23	City		AT	BO	CH	DE	HO	LA	NO	NY	PI	SL	SF	SE			
24	AT		1	0	1	0	1	0	1	1	1	0	0	0			
25	BO		0	1	0	0	0	0	0	1	1	0	0	0			
26	CH		1	0	1	0	0	0	1	1	1	0	0	0			
27	DE		0	0	0	1	0	0	0	0	0	1	0	0			
28	HO		1	0	0	0	1	0	1	0	0	0	0	0			
29	LA		0	0	0	0	0	1	0	0	0	1	1	0			
30	NO		1	0	1	0	1	0	1	0	0	0	0	0			
31	NY		1	1	1	0	0	0	0	1	1	0	0	0			
32	PI		1	1	1	0	0	0	0	1	1	0	0	0			
33	SL		0	0	0	1	0	1	0	0	0	1	1	1			
34	SF		0	0	0	0	0	1	0	0	0	1	1	1			
35	SE		0	0	0	0	0	0	0	0	0	1	1	1			
36																	
37	Decisions: which cities to use as hubs																
38			AT	BO	CH	DE	HO	LA	NO	NY	PI	SL	SF	SE			
39	Used as hub?		0	0	0	0	1	0	0	1	0	1	0	0			
40																	
41	Constraints that each city must be covered by at least one hub																
42	City	Hubs covered by		Required													
43	AT	2	>=	1													
44	BO	1	>=	1													
45	CH	1	>=	1													
46	DE	1	>=	1													
47	HO	1	>=	1													
48	LA	1	>=	1													
49	NO	1	>=	1													
50	NY	1	>=	1													
51	PI	1	>=	1													
52	SL	1	>=	1													
53	SF	1	>=	1					Note: There are multiple optimal solutions to these							
54	SE	1	>=	1					problems, so don't be surprised if you don't get exactly							
55									the same hub locations as shown here.							
56	Objective to minimize																
57	Total hubs	3															
58																	
59	Sensitivity of total hubs and their locations to the mile limit																
60	Mile limit		AT	BO	CH	DE	HO	LA	NO	NY	PI	SL	SF	SE	Total		
61			$B$39	$C$39	$D$39	$E$39	$F$39	$G$39	$H$39	$I$39	$J$39	$K$39	$L$39	$M$39	$B$57		
62	800		1	1	0	0	0	0	0	0	0	1	0	1	4		
63	900		0	0	0	0	1	0	0	1	0	1	0	0	3		
64	1000		0	1	0	0	0	1	0	0	0	1	0	0	3		
65	1100		0	0	1	0	0	0	0	0	0	0	1	0	2		
66	1200		0	0	1	0	0	0	0	0	0	0	0	1	2		

PROBLEMS

Level A

42. Solve the following modifications of the capital budgeting model in Figure 15.40. (Solve each part independently of the others.)

a. Suppose that at most two of projects 1 through 5 can be selected.

b. Suppose that if investment 1 is selected, then investment 3 must also be selected.

c. Suppose that at least one of investments 6 and 7 *must* be selected.

d. Suppose that investment 2 can be selected only if *both* investments 1 and 3 are selected.

43. In the capital budgeting model in Figure 15.40, we supplied the NPV for each investment. Suppose instead that you are given only the streams of cash inflows from each investment shown in the file **P15_43.xlsx**. This file also shows the cash requirements and the budget. You can assume that (1) all cash outflows occur at the beginning of year 1, (2) all cash inflows occur at the ends of their respective years, and (3) the company uses a 10% discount rate for calculating its NPVs. Which investments should the company make?

44. Solve the previous problem using the input data in the file **P15_44.xlsx**.

45. Solve Problem 43 with the extra assumption that the investments can be grouped naturally as follows: 1–4, 5–8, 9–12, 13–16, and 17–20.
   a. Find the optimal investments when at most one investment from each group can be selected.
   b. Find the optimal investments when at least one investment from each group must be selected. (If the budget isn't large enough to permit this, increase the budget to a larger value.)

46. In the capital budgeting model in Figure 15.40, investment 4 has the largest ratio of NPV to cash requirement, but it is not selected in the optimal solution. How much NPV is lost if Tatham is *forced* to select investment 4? Answer by solving a suitably modified model.

47. As it currently stands, investment 7 in the capital budgeting model in Figure 15.40 has the lowest ratio of NPV to cash requirement, 2.5. Keeping this same ratio, can you change the cash requirement and NPV for investment 7 in such a way that it *is* selected in the optimal solution? Does this lead to any general insights? Explain.

48. Expand the capital budgeting model in Figure 15.40 so that there are now 20 possible investments. You can make up the data on cash requirements, NPVs, and the budget. However, use the following guidelines:
   ■ The cash requirements and NPVs for the various investments can vary widely, but the ratio of NPV to cash requirement should be between 2.5 and 3.5 for each investment.
   ■ The budget should be such that somewhere between 5 and 10 of the investments can be selected.

49. Suppose in the capital budgeting model in Figure 15.40 that each investment requires $2000 during year 2 and only $5000 is available for investment during year 2.
   a. Assuming that available money uninvested at the end of year 1 cannot be used during year 2, what combination of investments maximizes NPV?
   b. Suppose that any uninvested money at the end of year 1 is available for investment in year 2. Does your answer to part **a** change?

50. How difficult is it to expand the Great Threads model to accommodate another type of clothing? Answer by assuming that the company can also produce sweatshirts. The rental cost for sweatshirt equipment is

$1100, the variable cost per unit and the selling price are $15 and $45, respectively, and each sweatshirt requires 1 labor hour and 3.5 square yards of cloth.

51. Referring to the previous problem, if it is optimal for the company to produce sweatshirts, use SolverTable to see how much larger the fixed cost of sweatshirt machinery would have to be before the company would *not* produce any sweatshirts. However, if the solution to the previous problem calls for no sweatshirts to be produced, use SolverTable to see how much lower the fixed cost of sweatshirt machinery would have to be before the company *would* start producing sweatshirts.

52. In the Great Threads model, we didn't constrain the production quantities in row 16 to be integers, arguing that any fractional values could be safely rounded to integers. See whether this is true. Constrain these quantities to be integers and then run Solver. Are the optimal integer values the same as the rounded fractional values in Figure 15.46?

53. In the optimal solution to the Great Threads model, the labor hour and cloth constraints are both binding—the company is using all it has.
   a. Use SolverTable to see what happens to the optimal solution when the amount of available cloth increases from its current value. (You can choose the range of input values to use.) Capture all of the changing cells, the labor hours and cloth used, and the profit as outputs in the table. The real issue here is whether the company can profitably use more cloth when it is already constrained by labor hours.
   b. Repeat part **a**, but reverse the roles of labor hours and cloth. That is, use the available labor hours as the input for SolverTable.

54. In the optimal solution to the Great Threads model, no pants are produced. Suppose Great Threads has an order for 300 pairs of pants that *must* be produced. Modify the model appropriately and use Solver to find the new optimal solution. (Is it enough to put a lower bound of 300 on the production quantity in cell D16? Will this automatically force the binary value in cell D14 to be 1? Explain.) How much profit does the company lose because of having to produce pants?

55. In the original Western set-covering model in Figure 15.52, we assumed that each city must be covered by at least one hub. Suppose that for added flexibility in flight routing, Western requires that each city must be covered by at least two hubs. How do the model and optimal solution change?

56. In the original Western set-covering model in Figure 15.52, we used the number of hubs as the objective to minimize. Suppose instead that there is a fixed cost of locating a hub in any city, where these fixed costs can possibly vary across cities. Make up some reasonable fixed costs, modify the model appropriately, and use Solver to find the solution that minimizes the sum of fixed costs.

57. Set-covering models such as the original Western model in Figure 15.52 often have multiple optimal solutions. See how many alternative optimal solutions you can find. Of course, each must use three hubs because we know this is optimal. (*Hint*: Use various initial values in the changing cells and then run Solver repeatedly.)[15]

58. How hard is it to expand a set-covering model to accommodate new cities? Answer this by modifying the model in Figure 15.55. (See the file **Locating Hubs 2.xlsx**.) Add several cities that must be served: Memphis, Dallas, Tucson, Philadelphia, Cleveland, and Buffalo. You can look up the distances from these cities to each other and to the other cities in a reference book (or on the Web), or you can make up approximate distances.
  a. Modify the model appropriately, assuming that these new cities must be covered *and* are candidates for hub locations.
  b. Modify the model appropriately, assuming that these new cities must be covered but are *not* candidates for hub locations.

Level B

59. The models in this section are often called *combinatorial* models because each solution is a combination of the various 0's and 1's, and there are only a finite number of such combinations. For the capital budgeting model in Figure 15.40, there are 7 investments, so there are $2^7 = 128$ possible solutions (some of which are infeasible). This is a fairly large number, but not *too* large. Solve the model *without* Solver by listing all 128 solutions. For each, calculate the total cash requirement and total NPV for the model. Then manually

choose the one that stays within the budget and has the largest NPV.

60. Make up an example, as described in Problem 48, with 20 possible investments. However, do it so the ratios of NPV to cash requirement are in a very tight range, from 3 to 3.2. Then use Solver to find the optimal solution when the Solver tolerance is set to its default value of 5%, and record the solution. Next, solve again with the tolerance set to 0. Do you get the same solution? Try this on a few more instances of the model, where you keep tinkering with the inputs. The question is whether the tolerance matters in these types of "close call" problems.

61. In the Great Threads model, we found an upper bound on production of any clothing type by calculating the amount that could be produced if *all* of the resources were devoted to this clothing type.
  a. What if we instead used a very large value such as 1,000,000 for this upper bound? Try it and see whether you get the same optimal solution.
  b. Explain why *any* such upper bound is required. Exactly what role does it play in the model, as we have formulated it?

62. In the last sheet of the finished version of the Fixed Cost Manufacturing file, we illustrated one way to model the Great Threads problem with IF functions, and we saw that this approach didn't work. Try a slightly different approach here. Eliminate the binary variables in row 14 altogether, and eliminate the upper bounds in row 18 and the corresponding upper bound constraints in the Solver dialog box. (The only constraints are now the resource availability constraints.) However, use IF functions to calculate the total fixed cost of renting equipment, so that if the amount of any clothing type is positive, then its fixed cost is added to the total fixed cost. Is Solver able to handle this model? Does it depend on the initial values in the changing cells? (Don't forget to uncheck the Assume Linear Model box.)

15.8 NONLINEAR MODELS

In many optimization problems the objective function and/or the constraints are not linear functions of the decision variables. Such an optimization problem is called a **nonlinear programming problem** (NLP). In this section we discuss how to use Excel's Solver to find optimal solutions to NLPs. We then discuss a couple of interesting applications, including the important portfolio optimization model.

15.8.1 Basic Ideas of Nonlinear Optimization

When we solve an LP problem with Solver, we can guarantee that the solution obtained is an optimal solution. When we solve an NLP problem, however, it is very possible that

[15]One of our colleagues at Indiana University, Vic Cabot, now deceased, worked for years trying to develop a general algorithm (other than trial and error) for finding *all* alternative optimal solutions to optimization models. It turns out that this is a very difficult problem—and one that Vic never totally solved.

Solver will obtain the wrong answer. This is because a nonlinear function can have a local optimal solution that is not the global optimal solution. A **local** optimal solution is one that is better than all nearby points, whereas a **global** optimum is the one that beats all points in the entire feasible region. If there are indeed one or more local optimal solutions that are not globally optimal, then it is entirely possible for Solver to end up at one of them. Unfortunately, this is not what we want; we want the global optimum.

There are mathematical conditions that guarantee the Solver solution is indeed the global optimum we are seeking. However, these conditions are difficult to understand, and they are often difficult to check. A much simpler approach is to run Solver several times, each time with different starting values in the changing cells. In general, if Solver obtains the same optimal solution in all cases, we can be fairly confident—but still not absolutely sure—that we have found the optimal solution to the NLP. On the other hand, if we try different starting values for the changing cells and obtain several different solutions, then we should keep the "best" solution we have found. That is, we should keep the solution with the lowest objective value (for a minimization problem) or the highest objective value (for a maximization problem).

15.8.2 Managerial Economics Models

Many problems that are discussed in managerial economics are nonlinear but can be solved with Solver. We illustrate one such peak-load pricing example in this section.

EXAMPLE | **15.11 PEAK-LOAD PRICING AT FLORIDA POWER AND LIGHT**

Florida Power and Light (FPL) faces demands during both peak-load and off-peak times. FPL must determine the price per kilowatt hour (kwh) to charge during both peak-load and off-peak periods. The daily demand for power during each period (in kwh) is related to price as follows:

$$D_p = 60 - 0.5P_p + 0.1P_o \tag{15.5}$$

$$D_o = 40 - P_o + 0.1P_p \tag{15.6}$$

Here, D_p and P_p are demand and price during peak-load times, whereas D_o and P_o are demand and price during off-peak times. Note that we are now using *linear* demand functions. Also, note from the signs of the coefficients that an increase in the peak-load price decreases the demand for power during the peak-load period but *increases* the demand for power during the off-peak period. Similarly, an increase in the price for the off-peak period decreases the demand for the off-peak period but *increases* the demand for the peak-load period. In economic terms, this implies that peak-load power and off-peak power are *substitutes* for one another. In addition, it costs FPL $10 per day to maintain 1 kwh of capacity. The company wants to determine a pricing strategy and a capacity level that maximize its daily profit.

Objective   To use a nonlinear model to determine prices and capacity when there are two different daily usage patterns, peak-load and off-peak.

WHERE DO THE NUMBERS COME FROM?

A cost accountant should be able to estimate the unit cost of capacity. The real difficulty here would be to estimate the demand functions in equations (15.5) and (15.6). This would require either sufficient historical data on prices and demands (for both peak-load and off-peak periods) or educated guesses from management.

Solution

The variables and constraints for this model are listed in Table 15.18. The company must decide on two prices, and it must determine the amount of capacity to maintain. Because this capacity level, once determined, is relevant for peak-load and off-peak periods, it must be large enough to meet demands for both periods. This is the reasoning behind the constraint.

Table 15.18   Variables and Constraints for Peak-Load Pricing Model

Input variables	Parameters of demand functions, unit cost of capacity
Decision variables (changing cells)	Peak-load and off-peak prices, capacity
Objective (target cell)	Profit
Other calculated variables	Peak-load and off-peak demands, revenue, cost of capacity
Constraints	Demands ≤ Capacity

Due to the relationships between the demand and price variables, it is not at all obvious what FPL should do. The pricing decisions determine demand, and larger demand requires larger capacity, which costs money. In addition, revenue is price multiplied by demand, so it is not clear whether price should be low or high to increase revenue.

DEVELOPING THE SPREADSHEET MODEL

The spreadsheet model appears in Figure 15.56. (See the file **Peak-Load Pricing.xlsx**.) It can be developed as follows.

Figure 15.56

Peak-Load Pricing Model

	A	B	C	D	E	F	G	H
1	Florida Power & Light peak-load pricing model					Range names used:		
2						Capacity	=Model!$B$15	
3	Input data					Common_Capacity	=Model!$B$21:$C$21	
4	Coefficients of demand functions					Demands	=Model!$B$19:$C$19	
5		Constant	Peak price	Off-peak price		Prices	=Model!$B$13:$C$13	
6	Peak-load demand	60	-0.5	0.1		Profit	=Model!$B$26	
7	Off-peak demand	40	0.1	-1				
8								
9	Cost of capacity/kwh	$10						
10								
11	Decisions							
12		Peak-load	Off-peak					
13	Prices	$70.31	$26.53					
14								
15	Capacity	27.50						
16								
17	Constraints on demand							
18		Peak-load	Off-peak					
19	Demand	27.50	20.50					
20		<=	<=					
21	Capacity	27.50	27.50					
22								
23	Monetary summary							
24	Revenue	$2,477.30						
25	Cost of capacity	$275.00						
26	Profit	$2,202.30						

1 **Inputs.** Enter the parameters of the demand functions and the cost of capacity in the shaded ranges.

2 **Prices and capacity level.** Enter *any* trial prices (per kwh) for peak-load and off-peak power in the Prices range, and enter *any* trial value for the capacity level in the Capacity cell. These are the three values FPL has control over, so they become the changing cells.

3 **Demands.** Calculate the demand for the peak-load period by substituting into equation (15.5). That is, enter the formula

=B6+SUMPRODUCT(Prices,C6:D6)

in cell B19. Similarly, enter the formula

=B7+SUMPRODUCT(Prices,C7:D7)

in cell C19 for the off-peak demand.

4 **Copy capacity.** To indicate the capacity constraints, enter the formula

=Capacity

in cells B21 and C21. The reason for creating these links is that we want the two demand cells in row 19 to be paired with two capacity cells in row 21, so that we can specify the Solver constraints appropriately. (Solver doesn't allow us to have a "two versus one" constraint like B19:C19 <= B15.)

5 **Monetary values.** Calculate the daily revenue, cost of capacity, and profit in the corresponding cells with the formulas

=SUMPRODUCT(Demands,Prices)

=Capacity*B9

and

=B24-B25

USING SOLVER

The Solver dialog box should be filled in as shown in Figure 15.57. We maximize profit by setting appropriate prices and capacity, and we ensure that demand never exceeds the capacity. Logically, we should also check Solver's Assume Non-Negative box (prices and capacity cannot be negative), but we should *not* check the Assume Linear Model box. This is because we are multiplying prices by demands, which are functions of prices, so that profit is a nonlinear function of the prices.

Figure 15.57

Solver Dialog Box
for Peak-Load
Pricing Model

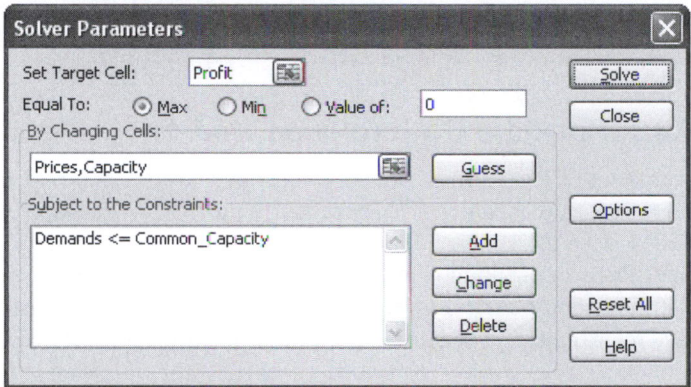

Discussion of the Solution

The Solver solution in Figure 15.56 indicates that FPL should charge $70.31 per kwh during the peak-load period and $26.53 during the off-peak-load period. These prices generate demands of 27.5 (peak-load) and 20.5 (off-peak), so that a capacity of 27.5 kwh is required. The cost of this capacity is $275. When this is subtracted from the revenue of $2477.30, the daily profit becomes $2202.30.

Varying the changing cells slightly from their optimal values sometimes provides insight into the optimal solution.

To gain some insight into this solution, consider what happens if FPL changes the peak-load price slightly from its optimal value of $70.31. If FPL decreases the price to $70, say, you can check that the peak-load demand increases to 27.65 and the off-peak demand decreases to 20.47. The net effect is that revenue increases slightly, to $2478.78. However, the peak-load demand is now greater than capacity, so FPL must increase its capacity from 27.50 to 27.65. This costs an extra $1.50, which more than offsets the increase in revenue. A similar chain of effects occurs if FPL increases the peak price to $71. In this case, peak-load demand decreases, off-peak demand increases, and total revenue decreases. Although FPL can get by with lower capacity, the net effect is slightly less profit. Fortunately, Solver evaluates all of these trade-offs for us when it finds the optimal solution.

Is the Solver Solution Optimal?

It is not difficult to show that the constraints for this model are linear and the objective is concave. This is enough to guarantee that there are no local maxima that are not globally optimal. In short, this guarantees that the Solver solution is optimal.

Sensitivity Analysis

To gain even more insight, we use SolverTable to see the effects of changing the unit cost of capacity, which we allow to vary from $5 to $15 in increments of $1. The results appear in Figure 15.58. They indicate that as the cost of capacity increases, the peak-load price increases, the off-peak price stays constant, the amount of capacity decreases, and profit decreases. The latter two effects are probably intuitive, but we challenge you to explain the effects on price. In particular, why does the peak-load price *increase*, and why doesn't the off-peak price increase as well?

Figure 15.58

Sensitivity to Cost of Capacity

	A	B	C	D	E
28	Sensitivity of changing cells and profit to cost of capacity				
29			$B$13	$C$13	$B$15	$B$26
30		5	$67.81	$26.53	28.75	$2,342.92
31		6	$68.31	$26.53	28.50	$2,314.30
32		7	$68.81	$26.53	28.25	$2,285.92
33		8	$69.31	$26.53	28.00	$2,257.80
34		9	$69.81	$26.53	27.75	$2,229.92
35		10	$70.31	$26.53	27.50	$2,202.30
36		11	$70.81	$26.53	27.25	$2,174.92
37		12	$71.31	$26.53	27.00	$2,147.80
38		13	$71.81	$26.53	26.75	$2,120.92
39		14	$72.31	$26.53	26.50	$2,094.30
40		15	$72.81	$26.53	26.25	$2,067.92

15.8.3 Portfolio Optimization Models

Given a set of investments, how do financial analysts determine the portfolio that has the lowest risk and yields a high expected return? This question was answered by Harry Markowitz in the 1950s. For his work on this and other investment topics, he received the Nobel Prize in economics in 1991. The ideas discussed in this section are the basis for most methods of *asset allocation* used by Wall Street firms. Asset allocation models are used, for example, to determine the percentage of assets to invest in stocks, gold, and

Treasury bills. Before proceeding, however, we need to discuss some important formulas involving the expected value and variance of sums of random variables.

Weighted Sums of Random Variables[16]

Let R_i be the (random) return earned during a year on a dollar invested in investment i. For example, if $R_i = 0.10$, a dollar invested at the beginning of the year grows to \$1.10 at the end of the year, whereas if $R_i = -0.20$, a dollar invested at the beginning of the year decreases in value to \$0.80. We assume that n investments are available. Let x_i be the fraction of our money invested in investment i. We assume that $x_1 + x_2 + \cdots + x_n = 1$, so that all of our money is invested. (To prevent shorting a stock—that is, selling shares we don't own—we assume that $x_i \geq 0$.) Then the annual return on our investments is given by the random variable R_p, where

$$R_p = R_1 x_1 + R_2 x_2 + \cdots + R_n x_n$$

(The subscript p on R_p stands for "portfolio.")

Let μ_i be the expected value (also called the mean) of R_i, let σ_i^2 be the variance of R_i (so that σ_i is the standard deviation of R_i), and let ρ_{ij} be the correlation between R_i and R_j. To do any work with investments, you must understand how to use the following formulas, which relate the data for the individual investments to the expected return and the variance of return for a *portfolio* of investments.

$$\text{Expected value of } R_p = \mu_1 x_1 + \mu_2 x_2 + \cdots + \mu_n x_n \tag{15.7}$$

$$\text{Variance of } R_p = \sigma_1^2 x_1^2 + \sigma_2^2 x_2^2 + \cdots + \sigma_n^2 x_n^2 + \sum_{ij} \rho_{ij}\sigma_i\sigma_j x_i x_j \tag{15.8}$$

The latter summation in the variance formula is over all pairs of investments. The quantities in equations (15.7) and (15.8) are extremely important in portfolio selection because of the risk–return trade-off investors need to make. All investors want to choose portfolios with high return, measured by the expected value in equation (15.7), but they also want portfolios with low risk, usually measured by the variance in equation (15.8).

We can rewrite equation (15.8) slightly by using *covariances* instead of correlations. The covariance between two stock returns is another measure of the relationship between the two returns, but unlike a correlation, it is *not* scaled to be between -1 and $+1$. This is because covariances are affected by the units in which the returns are measured.

Although a covariance is a somewhat less intuitive measure than a correlation, it is used so frequently by financial analysts that we use it here as well. If c_{ij} is the estimated covariance between stocks i and j, then $c_{ij} = r_{ij}s_i s_j$. Using this equation and the fact that the correlation between any stock and itself is 1, we can also write $c_{ii} = s_i^2$ for each stock i. Therefore, an equivalent form of equation (15.8) is the following equation (15.9):

$$\text{Estimated variance of } R_p = \sum_{i,j} c_{ij} x_i x_j \tag{15.9}$$

As we see in the portfolio optimization example, this allows us to calculate the portfolio variance very easily with Excel's matrix functions.

---

[16]The material was covered in Chapter 5, but it is included here for those who did not cover Chapter 5.

Matrix Functions in Excel

Equation (15.9) for the variance of portfolio return looks intimidating, particularly if there are many potential investments. Fortunately, we can take advantage of two built-in Excel matrix functions to simplify our work. In this subsection we illustrate how to use Excel's MMULT (matrix multiplication) and TRANSPOSE functions. Then in the next subsection we put these to use in the portfolio selection model.

A **matrix** is a rectangular array of numbers. We say a matrix is an $i \times j$ matrix if it consists of i rows and j columns. For example,

$$A = \begin{pmatrix} 1 & 2 & 3 \\ 4 & 5 & 6 \end{pmatrix}$$

is a 2×3 matrix, and

$$B = \begin{pmatrix} 1 & 2 \\ 3 & 4 \\ 5 & 6 \end{pmatrix}$$

is a 3×2 matrix. If the matrix has only a single row, we call it a **row vector**. Similarly, if it has only a single column, we call it a **column vector**.

If matrix A has the same number of columns as matrix B has rows, then we can construct the **matrix product** of A and B, denoted AB. The entry in row i, column j of the product AB is obtained by summing the products of the elements in row i of A with the corresponding elements in column j of B. If A is an $i \times k$ matrix and B is a $k \times j$ matrix, then AB is an $i \times j$ matrix.

For example, if

$$A = \begin{pmatrix} 1 & 2 & 3 \\ 2 & 4 & 5 \end{pmatrix}$$

and

$$B = \begin{pmatrix} 1 & 2 \\ 3 & 4 \\ 5 & 6 \end{pmatrix}$$

then AB is the following 2×2 matrix:

$$AB = \begin{pmatrix} 1(1) + 2(3) + 3(5) & 1(2) + 2(4) + 3(6) \\ 2(1) + 4(3) + 5(5) & 2(2) + 4(4) + 5(6) \end{pmatrix} = \begin{pmatrix} 22 & 28 \\ 39 & 50 \end{pmatrix}$$

The Excel MMULT function performs matrix multiplication in a single step. The spreadsheet in Figure 15.59 indicates how to multiply matrices of different sizes. (See the file **Matrix Multiplication.xlsx**.) For example, to multiply matrix 1 by matrix 2 (which is possible because matrix 1 has 3 columns and matrix 2 has 3 rows), we select the range B13:C14, type the formula

=MMULT(B4:D5,B7:C9)

and press Ctrl-Shift-Enter (all three keys at once). Note that we selected a range with 2 rows because matrix 1 has 2 rows, and we selected a range with 2 columns because matrix 2 has 2 columns.

Figure 15.59 Examples of Matrix Multiplication in Excel

	A	B	C	D	E	F	G	H	I	J	K	L	M	N
1	Matrix multiplication in Excel													
2														
3	Typical multiplication of two matrices							Multiplication of a matrix and a column						
4	Matrix 1	1	2	3				Column 1	2					
5		2	4	5					3					
6									4					
7	Matrix 2	1	2											
8		3	4					Matrix 1 times Column 1, with formula =MMULT(B4:D5,I4:I6)						
9		5	6					Select range with 2 rows, 1 column, enter formula, press Ctrl-Shift-Enter						
10									20					
11	Matrix 1 times Matrix 2, with formula =MMULT(B4:D5,B7:C9)								36					
12	Select range with 2 rows, 2 columns, enter formula, press Ctrl-Shift-Enter.													
13		22	28					Multiplication of a row and a matrix						
14		39	50					Row 1	4	5				
15														
16	Multiplication of a quadratic form (row times matrix times column)							Row 1 times Matrix 1, with formula =MMULT(I14:J14,B4:D5)						
17	Matrix 3	2	1	3				Select range with 1 row, 3 columns, enter formula, press Ctrl-Shift-Enter						
18		1	-1	0					14	28	37			
19		3	0	4										
20								Multiplication of a row and a column						
21	Transpose of Column 1 times Matrix 3 times Column 1							Row 2	1	6	3			
22	Formula is =MMULT(TRANSPOSE(I4:I6),MMULT(B17:D19,I4:I6))													
23	Select range with 1 row, 1 column, enter formula, press Ctrl-Shift-Enter							Row 2 times Column 1, with formula =MMULT(I22:K22,I4:I6)						
24		123						Select range with 1 row, 1 column, enter formula, press Ctrl-Shift-Enter						
25									32					
26	Notes on quadratic form example:													
27	Two MMULT's are required because MMULT works on only two ranges at a time.													
28	TRANSPOSE is needed to change a column into a row.													

The matrix multiplication in cell B24 indicates that (1) we can multiply three matrices together by using MMULT twice, and (2) we can use the TRANSPOSE function to convert a column vector to a row vector (or vice versa), if necessary. Here, we want to multiply Column 1 by the product of Matrix 3 and Column 1. However, Column 1 is 3×1, and Matrix 3 is 3×3, so Column 1 times Matrix 3 doesn't work. Instead, we must transpose Column 1 to make it 1×3. Then the result of multiplying all three together is a 1×1 matrix (a number). We calculate it by selecting cell B24, typing the formula

=MMULT(TRANSPOSE(I4:I6),MMULT(B17:D19,I4:I6))

and pressing Ctrl-Shift-Enter. We use MMULT twice in this formula because it can multiply only *two* matrices at a time.

Excel Function: *MMULT*

The MMULT and TRANSPOSE functions are useful for matrix operations. They are called array functions because they return results to an entire range, not just a single cell. The MMULT function multiplies two matrices and has the syntax =MMULT(range1,range2), where range1 must have as many columns as range2 has rows. To use this function, highlight a range that has as many rows as range1 and as many columns as range2, type the formula, and press Ctrl-Shift-Enter. The resulting formula will have curly brackets around it in the Excel formula bar. You should not type these curly brackets. Excel enters them automatically to remind you that this is an array formula.

The Portfolio Selection Model

Most investors have two objectives in forming portfolios: to obtain a large expected return and to obtain a small variance (to minimize risk). The problem is inherently nonlinear because variance is nonlinear. The most common way of handling this two-objective problem is to specify a minimal expected return that we require and then minimize the variance subject to the constraint on the expected return. The following example illustrates how we can use Solver to do this.

15.12 PORTFOLIO OPTIMIZATION AT PERLMAN & BROTHERS

Perlman & Brothers, an investment company, intends to invest a given amount of money in three stocks. From past data, the means and standard deviations of annual returns have been estimated as shown in Table 15.19. The correlations between the annual returns on the stocks are listed in Table 15.20. The company wants to find a minimum-variance portfolio that yields an expected annual return of at least 0.12.

Table 15.19   Estimated Means and Standard Deviations of Stock Returns

Stock	Mean	Standard Deviation
1	0.14	0.20
2	0.11	0.15
3	0.10	0.08

Table 15.20   Estimated Correlations Between Stock Returns

Combination	Correlation
Stocks 1 and 2	0.6
Stocks 1 and 3	0.4
Stocks 2 and 3	0.7

Objective   To use NLP to find the portfolio of the three stocks that minimizes the risk, measured by portfolio variance, subject to achieving an expected return of at least 0.12.

WHERE DO THE NUMBERS COME FROM?

Financial analysts typically estimate the required means, standard deviations, and correlations for stock returns from historical data. However, you should be aware that there is no guarantee that these estimates, based on *historical* return data, are relevant for *future* returns. If the analysts have new information about the stocks, they should incorporate this new information into their estimates.

Solution

The variables and constraints for this model are listed in Table 15.21. One interesting aspect of this model is that we do *not* have to specify the amount of money invested—it could be $100, $1000, $1,000,000, or any other amount. The model determines the *fractions* of this amount to invest in the various stocks, and these fractions are then relevant for any investment amount. All we require is that the fractions sum to 1, so that all of the money is invested. Besides this, we require *nonnegative* fractions to prevent shorting stocks.[17] We also require that the expected return from the portfolio be at least as large as the specified minimal required expected return.

---

[17]If you want to allow shorting, do not check the Assume Non-Negative box in Solver options.

Table 15.21 Variables and Constraints for Portfolio Optimization Model

Input variables	Means, standard deviations, and correlations for stock returns, minimum required expected portfolio return
Decision variables (changing cells)	Fractions invested in the various stocks
Objective (target cell)	Portfolio variance (minimize)
Other calculated variables	Covariances between stock returns, total fraction of money invested, expected portfolio return
Constraints	Total fraction invested = 1
	Expected portfolio return ≥ Minimum required expected portfolio return

DEVELOPING THE SPREADSHEET MODEL

The individual steps are now listed. (See Figure 15.60 and the file **Portfolio Selection.xlsx**.)

Figure 15.60   Portfolio Optimization Model

	A	B	C	D	E	F	G	H	I
1	Portfolio selection model					Range names used:			
2						Actual_return	=Model!$B$23		
3	Stock input data					Fractions_to_invest	=Model!$B$15:$D$15		
4		Stock 1	Stock 2	Stock 3		Portfolio_variance	=Model!$B$25		
5	Mean return	0.14	0.11	0.1		Required_return	=Model!$D$23		
6	StDev of return	0.2	0.15	0.08		Total_invested	=Model!$B$19		
7									
8	Correlations	Stock 1	Stock 2	Stock 3		Covariances	Stock 1	Stock 2	Stock 3
9	Stock 1	1	0.6	0.4		Stock 1	0.04	0.018	0.0064
10	Stock 2	0.6	1	0.7		Stock 2	0.018	0.0225	0.0084
11	Stock 3	0.4	0.7	1		Stock 3	0.0064	0.0084	0.0064
12									
13	Investment decisions								
14		Stock 1	Stock 2	Stock 3					
15	Fractions to invest	0.500	0.000	0.500					
16									
17	Constraint on investing everything								
18		Total invested		Required value					
19		1.00	=	1					
20									
21	Constraint on expected portfolio return								
22		Actual return		Required return					
23		0.12	>=	0.12					
24									
25	Portfolio variance	0.0148							
26	Portfolio stdev	0.1217							

1 Inputs. Enter the inputs in the shaded ranges. These include the estimates of means, standard deviations, and correlations, as well as the required expected return.

2 Fractions invested. Enter *any* trial values in the Fractions_to_invest range for the fractions of Perlman's money placed in the three investments. Then sum these with the SUM function in cell B19.

3 Expected annual return. Use equation (15.7) to compute the expected annual return in cell B23 with the formula

=SUMPRODUCT(B5:D5,Fractions_to_invest)

④ **Covariance matrix.** We want to use equation (15.9) to calculate the portfolio variance. To do this, we must first calculate a matrix of covariances. Using the general formula for covariance, $c_{ij} = r_{ij}s_i s_j$ (which holds even when $i = j$ since $r_{ii} = 1$), we can calculate these from the inputs, using lookups. Specifically, enter the formula

=HLOOKUP($F9,$B$4:$D$6,3)*B9*HLOOKUP(G$8,$B$4:$D$6,3)

in cell G9, and copy it to the range G9:I11. (This formula is a bit tricky, so take a close look at it. The term B9 captures the relevant correlation. The two HLOOKUP terms capture the appropriate standard deviations.)

⑤ **Portfolio variance.** Although we don't go into the mathematical details, it can be shown that the summation in equation (15.9) is really the product of three matrices: a row of fractions invested times the covariance matrix times a column of fractions invested. To calculate it, enter the formula

=MMULT(Fractions_to_invest,MMULT(G9:I11,TRANSPOSE(Fractions_to_invest)))

in cell B25 and press Ctrl-Shift-Enter. (Remember that Excel puts curly brackets around this formula. You should *not* type these curly brackets.) Note that this formula uses two MMULT functions. Again, this is because MMULT can multiply only two matrices at a time. Therefore, we first multiply the last two matrices and then multiply this product by the first matrix.

⑥ **Portfolio standard deviation.** Most financial analysts talk in terms of portfolio *variance*. However, it is probably more intuitive to talk about portfolio *standard deviation* because it is in the same units as the returns. We calculate the standard deviation in cell B26 with the formula

=SQRT(Portfolio_variance)

Actually, we could use either cell B25 or B26 as the target cell to minimize. Minimizing the square root of a function is equivalent to minimizing the function itself.

USING SOLVER

The completed Solver dialog box should appear as in Figure 15.61. The constraints specify that the expected return must be at least as large as the minimum required return, and all of the company's money must be invested. We constrain the changing cells to be nonnegative (to avoid short selling), but because of the squared terms in the variance formula, we do *not* check the Assume Linear Model option.

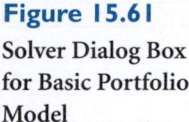

Figure 15.61

Solver Dialog Box for Basic Portfolio Model

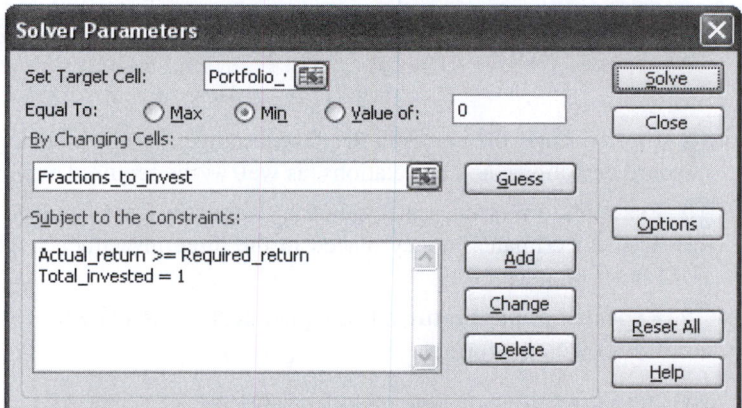

Discussion of the Solution

The solution in Figure 15.60 indicates that the company should put half of its money in each of stocks 1 and 3, and it should not invest in stock 2 at all. This might be somewhat surprising, given that the ranking of riskiness of the stocks is 1, 2, 3, with stock 1 being the most risky but also having the highest expected return. However, the correlations play an important role in portfolio selection, so we can usually not guess the optimal portfolio on the basis of the means and standard deviations of stock returns alone.

We can interpret the portfolio standard deviation of 0.1217 in a probabilistic sense. Specifically, if we believe that stock returns are approximately *normally* distributed, then the probability is about 0.68 that the actual portfolio return will be within 1 standard deviation of the expected return, and the probability is about 0.95 that the actual portfolio return will be within 2 standard deviations of the expected return. Given that the expected return is 0.12, this implies a lot of risk—2 standard deviations below this mean is a *negative* return (or loss) of slightly more than 0.12!

Is the Solver Solution Optimal?

The constraints for this model are linear, and it can be shown that the portfolio variance is a *convex* function of the investment fractions. This is sufficient to guarantee that the Solver solution is indeed optimal.

Sensitivity Analysis

This model begs for a sensitivity analysis on the minimum required return. When the company requires a larger expected return, it must assume a larger risk. We see how this occurs in Figure 15.62. We use SolverTable with cell D23 as the single input cell, allowing it to vary from 0.10 to 0.14 in increments of 0.005. Note that values outside this range are of little interest. Stock 3 has the minimum expected return, 0.10, and stock 1 has the highest expected return, 0.14, so no portfolio can have an expected return outside of this range.

Figure 15.62

The Efficient Frontier

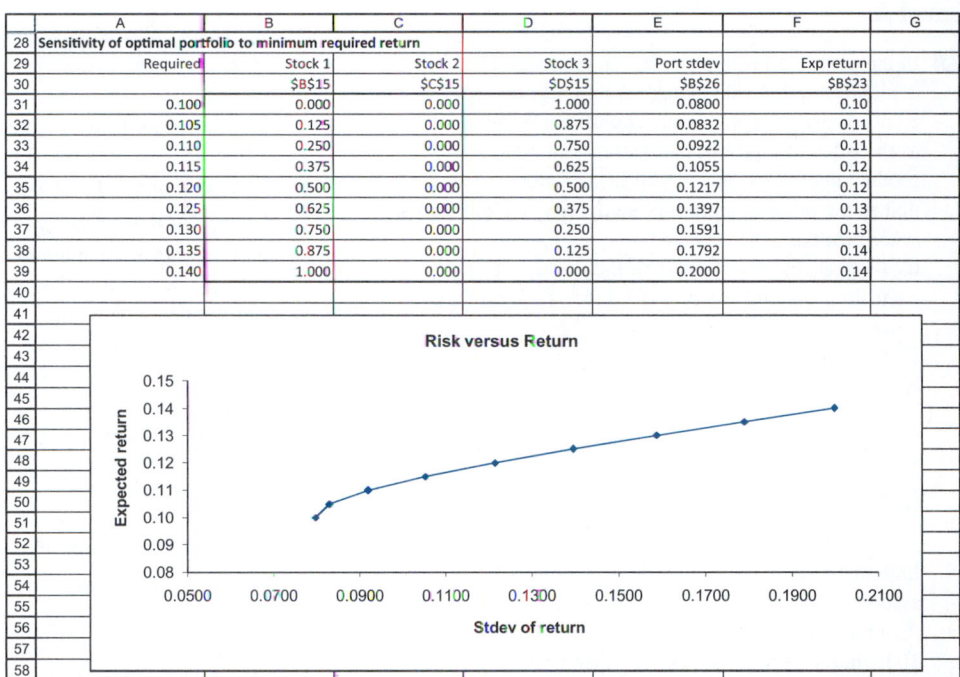

	A	B	C	D	E	F	G
28	Sensitivity of optimal portfolio to minimum required return						
29	Required	Stock 1	Stock 2	Stock 3	Port stdev	Exp return	
30		$B$15	$C$15	$D$15	$B$26	$B$23	
31	0.100	0.000	0.000	1.000	0.0800	0.10	
32	0.105	0.125	0.000	0.875	0.0832	0.11	
33	0.110	0.250	0.000	0.750	0.0922	0.11	
34	0.115	0.375	0.000	0.625	0.1055	0.12	
35	0.120	0.500	0.000	0.500	0.1217	0.12	
36	0.125	0.625	0.000	0.375	0.1397	0.13	
37	0.130	0.750	0.000	0.250	0.1591	0.13	
38	0.135	0.875	0.000	0.125	0.1792	0.14	
39	0.140	1.000	0.000	0.000	0.2000	0.14	

The results indicate that the company should put more and more into risky stock 1 as the required return increases—and stock 2 continues to be unused. The accompanying X-Y chart (with the option to "connect the dots") shows the risk–return trade-off. As the company assumes more risk, as measured by portfolio standard deviation, the expected return increases, but at a decreasing rate.

The curve in this chart is called the **efficient frontier**. Points on the efficient frontier can be achieved by appropriate portfolios. Points below the efficient frontier can be achieved, but they are not as good as points on the efficient frontier because they have a lower expected return for a given level of risk. In contrast, points above the efficient frontier are unachievable—the company cannot achieve this high an expected return for a given level of risk. ∎

MODELING ISSUES

1. Typical real-world portfolio selection problems involve a large number of potential investments, certainly many more than three. This admittedly requires more input data, particularly for the correlation matrix, but the basic model does not change at all. In particular, the matrix formula for portfolio variance is exactly the same. This shows the power of using Excel's matrix functions. Without them, the formula for portfolio variance would be a long involved sum.

2. If Perlman is allowed to short a stock, we simply allow the fraction invested in that stock to be negative. To implement this, we eliminate the nonnegativity constraints on the changing cells.

3. An alternative objective might be to minimize the probability that the portfolio loses money. We illustrate this possibility in one of the problems. ∎

PROBLEMS

Level A

63. In the peak-load pricing model in Example 15.11, the demand functions have positive and negative coefficients of prices. The negative coefficients indicate that as the price of a product increases, demand for *that* product decreases. The positive coefficients indicate that as the price of a product increases, demand for the *other* product increases.

    a. Increase the magnitudes of the negative coefficients from -0.5 and -1 to -0.7 and -1.2, and then rerun Solver. Are the changes in the optimal solution intuitive? Explain.

    b. Increase the magnitudes of the positive coefficients from 0.1 and 0.1 to 0.3 and 0.3, and then rerun Solver. Are the changes in the optimal solution intuitive? Explain.

    c. Make the changes in parts **a** and **b** simultaneously, and then rerun Solver. What happens now?

64. In the peak-load pricing model in Example 15.11, we assumed that the capacity level is a decision variable. Assume now that capacity has already been set at 30 kwh. (Note that the cost of capacity is now a sunk

cost, so it is irrelevant to the decision problem.) Change the model appropriately and run Solver. Then use SolverTable to see how sensitive the optimal solution is to the capacity level, letting it vary over some relevant range. Does it appear that the optimal prices will be set so that demand is always equal to capacity for at least one of the two periods of the day?

65. For each of the following, answer whether it makes sense to multiply the matrices of the given sizes. In each case where it makes sense, demonstrate an example in Excel, where you can make up the numbers.

    a. AB, where A is 3×4 and B is 4×1

    b. AB, where A is 1×4 and B is 4×1

    c. AB, where A is 4×1 and B is 1×4

    d. AB, where A is 1×4 and B is 1×4

    e. ABC, where A is 1×4, B is 4×4, and C is 4×1

    f. ABC, where A is 3×3, B is 3×3, and C is 3×1

    g. $A^T B$, where A is 4×3 and B is 4×3, and A^T denotes the transpose of A

66. Add a new stock, stock 4, to the model in Example 15.12. Assume that the estimated mean and standard deviation of return for stock 4 are 0.125 and 0.175, respectively. Also, assume the correlations between stock 4 and the original three stocks are 0.3, 0.5, and 0.8. Run Solver on the modified model, where the required expected portfolio return is again 0.12. Is stock 4 in the optimal portfolio? Then run SolverTable as in the example. Is stock 4 in any of the optimal portfolios on the efficient frontier?

67. In the model in Example 15.12, stock 2 is not in the optimal portfolio. Use SolverTable to see whether it ever enters the optimal portfolio as its correlations with stocks 1 and 3 vary. Specifically, use a two-way SolverTable with two inputs, the correlations between stock 2 and stocks 1 and 3, each allowed to vary from 0.1 to 0.9 in increments of 0.1. Capture as outputs the three changing cells. Discuss the results. (*Note*: You'll have to change the model slightly. For example, if you use cells B10 and C11 as the two SolverTable input cells, you'll have to ensure that cells C9 and D10 change accordingly. This is easy. Just put formulas in these latter two cells.)

68. The stocks in Example 15.12 are all *positively* correlated. What happens when they are *negatively* correlated? Answer for each of the following scenarios. In each case, two of the three correlations are the negatives of their original values. Discuss the differences between the optimal portfolios in these three scenarios.
   a. Change the signs of the correlations between stocks 1 and 2 and between stocks 1 and 3. (Here, stock 1 tends to go in a different direction from stocks 2 and 3.)
   b. Change the signs of the correlations between stocks 1 and 2 and between stocks 2 and 3. (Here, stock 2 tends to go in a different direction from stocks 1 and 3.)
   c. Change the signs of the correlations between stocks 1 and 3 and between stocks 2 and 3. (Here, stock 3 tends to go in a different direction from stocks 1 and 2.)

69. The file **P15_69.xlsx** contains historical monthly returns for 28 companies. For each company, calculate the estimated mean return and the estimated variance of return. Then calculate the estimated correlations between the companies' returns. Note that "return" here means *monthly* return. (*Hint*: Make life easy for yourself by using StatTools's Summary Statistics capabilities.)

70. This problem continues using the data from the previous problem. The file **P15_70.xlsx** includes all of the previous data. It also contains fractions in row 3 for creating a portfolio. These fractions are currently all equal to 1/28, but they can be changed to any values you like, so long as they continue to sum to 1. For any such fractions, find the estimated mean, variance, and standard deviation of the resulting portfolio return.

Level B

71. Continuing the previous problem, find the portfolio that achieves an expected monthly return of at least 0.01% and minimizes portfolio variance. Then use SolverTable to sweep out the efficient frontier, as in Example 15.12. Create a chart of this efficient frontier from your SolverTable results. What are the relevant lower and upper limits on the required expected monthly return?

72. In many cases we can assume that the portfolio return is at least approximately *normally* distributed. Then we can use Excel's NORMDIST function to calculate the probability that the portfolio return is negative. The relevant formula is =**NORMDIST(0,*mean*,*stdev*,1)**, where *mean* and *stdev* are the expected portfolio return and standard deviation of portfolio return, respectively.
   a. Modify the model in Example 15.12 slightly, and then run Solver, to find the portfolio that achieves at least a 0.12 expected return and minimizes the probability of a negative return. Do you get the same optimal portfolio as before? What is the probability that the return from this portfolio will be negative?
   b. Using the model in part **a**, proceed as in Example 15.12 to use SolverTable and create a chart of the efficient frontier. However, this time put the probability of a negative return on the horizontal axis.

15.9 CONCLUSION

In this chapter we have formulated spreadsheet optimization models of many diverse problems. No standard procedure can be used to attack all problems. However, there are several keys to most formulations.

   1. First, determine the changing cells. For example, in blending problems it is important to realize that the changing cells are the amounts of inputs used to produce outputs, and in the post office scheduling example, it is important to realize that the changing cells are the number of people who start their 5-day shift each day of the week.

2. Set up the spreadsheet model so that you can easily compute what you wish to maximize or minimize (usually profit or cost). For example, in the aggregate planning model it is a good idea to compute total cost by calculating the monthly cost of the various activities in separate rows and then summing the subtotals.

3. Set up the spreadsheet so that the relationships between the cells in the spreadsheet and the constraints of the problem are readily apparent. For example, in the post office scheduling model it is convenient to compute the number of people working each day of the week adjacent to the minimum required number of people for each day of the week.

4. Optimization models do not always fall into ready-made categories. A problem might involve a combination of the ideas we discussed in the inventory scheduling, blending, and aggregate planning examples. In fact, many real applications are not strictly analogous to any of the models we have discussed. However, the exposure to the models in this chapter should give you the insights you need to solve a wide variety of interesting problems.

Summary of Key Terms

Term	Explanation	Page
Workforce scheduling models	Models for choosing the staffing levels to meet workload requirements	849
Multiple optimal solutions	Situation where several solutions obtain the same optimal objective value	854
Blending models	Models where inputs must be mixed in the right proportions to produce outputs	856
Logistics models	Models where goods must be shipped from one set of locations to another at minimal cost	862
Aggregate planning models	Models where workforce levels and production levels must be set to meet customer demand	880
Dynamic financial models	Models where financial instruments such as loan amounts must be set to meet specified cash balances or other constraints	889
Integer programming models	Models where at least some of the decision variables must be integers	899
Binary variables	Integer variables that must be 0 or 1; used to indicate whether an activity takes place	899
Capital budgeting models	Models where a subset of investment activities is chosen from a set of possible activities	900
Fixed-cost models	Models where fixed costs are incurred for various activities if they are done at *any* positive level	905
Set-covering models	Models where members of one set must be selected to "cover" members of another set	912
Nonlinear programming models	Models where either the objective function or the constraints (or both) are nonlinear functions of the decision variables	918
Global optima	Solutions that are the best in the entire feasible region	919
Local optima	Solutions that are better than all nearby solutions (but might not be optimal globally)	919
Managerial economics models	Models such as optimal pricing models that arise in managerial economics applications	919
Portfolio optimization models	Models that attempt to find the portfolio of securities that achieves the best balance between risk and return	922

PROBLEMS

Conceptual Exercises

C.1. Distinguish between a *static* and a *dynamic* optimization model.

C.2. Explain why it is problematic to include a constraint such as the following in an LP model for a blending problem:

$$\frac{\text{Total octane in gasoline 1 blend}}{\text{Barrels of gasoline 1 blended daily}} \geq 10$$

C.3. "It is essential to constrain all shipments in a transportation problem to have integer values to ensure that the optimal LP solution consists entirely of integer-valued shipments." Is this statement true or false? Explain your choice.

C.4. What is the relationship between transportation problems and minimum cost network flow problems? Carefully explain how these two types of linear optimization models are similar and how they are different.

C.5. Suppose that you formulate and solve an integer programming model with a cost-minimization objective. Assume that the optimal solution yields a target cell value of $500,000. Now, consider the same linear optimization model without the integer restrictions. That is, suppose that you drop the requirement that the changing cells are integer-valued and re-optimize with Solver. How does the optimal target cell value for this modified model (called the *LP relaxation* of the IP model) compare to the original total cost value of $500,000? Explain your answer.

Level A

73. A bus company believes that it will need the following numbers of bus drivers during each of the next 5 years: 60 drivers in year 1; 70 drivers in year 2; 50 drivers in year 3; 65 drivers in year 4; 75 drivers in year 5. At the beginning of each year, the bus company must decide how many drivers to hire or fire. It costs $4000 to hire a driver and $2000 to fire a driver. A driver's salary is $10,000 per year. At the beginning of year 1 the company has 50 drivers. A driver hired at the beginning of a year can be used to meet the current year's requirements and is paid full salary for the current year.
   a. Determine how to minimize the bus company's salary, hiring, and firing costs over the next 5 years.
   b. Use SolverTable to determine how the total number hired, total number fired, and total cost change as the unit hiring and firing costs *each* increase by the same percentage.

74. NewAge Pharmaceuticals produces the drug NasaMist from four chemicals. Today, the company must produce 1000 pounds of the drug. The three active ingredients in NasaMist are A, B, and C. By weight, at least 8% of NasaMist must consist of A, at least 4% of B, and at least 2% of C. The cost per pound of each chemical and the amount of each active ingredient in 1 pound of each chemical are given in the file **P15_74.xlsx**. It is necessary that at least 100 pounds of chemical 2 be used.
   a. Determine the cheapest way of producing today's batch of NasaMist.
   b. Use SolverTable to see how much the percentage of requirement of A is really costing NewAge. Let the percentage required vary from 6% to 12%.

75. A bank is attempting to determine where its assets should be invested during the current year. At present, $500,000 is available for investment in bonds, home loans, auto loans, and personal loans. The annual rates of return on each type of investment are known to be the following: bonds, 10%; home loans, 16%; auto loans, 13%; personal loans, 20%. To ensure that the bank's portfolio is not too risky, the bank's investment manager has placed the following three restrictions on the bank's portfolio:
   - The amount invested in personal loans cannot exceed the amount invested in bonds.
   - The amount invested in home loans cannot exceed the amount invested in auto loans.
   - No more than 25% of the total amount invested can be in personal loans.

Help the bank maximize the annual return on its investment portfolio.

76. Bullco blends silicon and nitrogen to produce two types of fertilizers. Fertilizer 1 must be at least 40% nitrogen and sells for $70 per pound. Fertilizer 2 must be at least 70% silicon and sells for $40 per pound. Bullco can purchase up to 8000 pounds of nitrogen at $15 per pound and up to 10,000 pounds of silicon at $10 per pound.
   a. Assuming that all fertilizer produced can be sold, determine how Bullco can maximize its profit.
   b. Use SolverTable to explore the effect on profit of changing the minimum percentage of nitrogen required in fertilizer 1.
   c. Suppose the availabilities of nitrogen and silicon both increase by the same percentage from their current values. Use SolverTable to explore the effect of this change on profit.

77. Linear programming models are used by many Wall Street firms to select a desirable bond portfolio. The following is a simplified version of such a model. Solodrex is considering investing in four bonds; $1 million is available for investment. The expected annual return, the worst-case annual return on each bond, and the "duration" of each bond are given in the file **P15_77.xlsx**. (The duration of a bond is a measure of the bond's sensitivity to interest rates.) Solodrex wants to maximize the expected return from its bond investments, subject to three constraints:

- The worst-case return of the bond portfolio must be at least 8%.
- The average duration of the portfolio must be at most 6. For example, a portfolio that invests $600,000 in bond 1 and $400,000 in bond 4 has an average duration of $[600,000(3) + 400,000(9)]/1,000,000 = 5.4$
- Because of diversification requirements, at most 40% of the total amount invested can be invested in a single bond.

Determine how Solodrex can maximize the expected return on its investment.

78. At the beginning of year 1, you have $10,000. Investments A and B are available; their cash flows are shown in the file **P15_78.xlsx**. Assume that any money not invested in A or B earns interest at an annual rate of 8%.
   a. Determine how to maximize your cash on hand in year 4.
   b. Use SolverTable to determine how a change in the year 3 yield for investment A changes the optimal solution to the problem.
   c. Use SolverTable to determine how a change in the yield of investment B changes the optimal solution to the problem.

79. Carrington Oil produces gas 1 and gas 2 from two types of crude oil: crude 1 and crude 2. Gas 1 is allowed to contain up to 4% impurities, and gas 2 is allowed to contain up to 3% impurities. Gas 1 sells for $8 per barrel, whereas gas 2 sells for $12 per barrel. Up to 4200 barrels of gas 1 and up to 4300 barrels of gas 2 can be sold. The cost per barrel of each crude, their availability, and the level of impurities in each crude are listed in the file **P15_79.xlsx**. Before blending the crude oil into gas, any amount of each crude can be "purified" for a cost of $0.50 per barrel. Purification eliminates half of the impurities in the crude oil.
   a. Determine how to maximize profit.
   b. Use SolverTable to determine how an increase in the availability of crude 1 affects the optimal profit.
   c. Use SolverTable to determine how an increase in the availability of crude 2 affects the optimal profit.
   d. Use SolverTable to determine how a change in the profitability of gas 2 changes profitability and the types of gas produced.

80. The government is auctioning off oil leases at two sites: 1 and 2. At each site 100,000 acres of land are to be auctioned. Cliff Ewing, Blake Barnes, and Alexis Pickens are bidding for the oil. Government rules state that no bidder can receive more than 40% of the land

being auctioned. Cliff has bid $1000 per acre for site 1 land and $2000 per acre for site 2 land. Blake has bid $900 per acre for site 1 land and $2200 per acre for site 2 land. Alexis has bid $1100 per acre for site 1 land and $1900 per acre for site 2 land.
   a. Determine how to maximize the government's revenue.
   b. Use SolverTable to see how changes in the government's rule on 40% of all land being auctioned affect the optimal revenue. Why can the optimal revenue not decrease if this percentage required increases? Why can the optimal revenue not increase if this percentage required decreases?

81. General Ford produces cars in Los Angeles and Detroit and has a warehouse in Atlanta. The company supplies cars to customers in Houston and Tampa. The costs of shipping a car between various points are listed in the file **P15_81.xlsx**, where a dash means that a shipment is not allowed. Los Angeles can produce up to 1100 cars, and Detroit can produce up to 2900 cars. Houston must receive 2400 cars, and Tampa must receive 1500 cars.
   a. Determine how to minimize the cost of meeting demands in Houston and Tampa.
   b. Modify the answer to part a if shipments between Los Angeles and Detroit are not allowed.
   c. Modify the answer to part a if shipments between Houston and Tampa are allowed at a cost of $5 per car.

82. Sunco Oil produces oil at two wells. Well 1 can produce up to 150,000 barrels per day, and well 2 can produce up to 200,000 barrels per day. It is possible to ship oil directly from the wells to Sunco's customers in Los Angeles and New York. Alternatively, Sunco could transport oil to the ports of Mobile and Galveston and then ship it by tanker to New York or Los Angeles. Los Angeles requires 160,000 barrels per day, and New York requires 140,000 barrels per day. The costs of shipping 1000 barrels between various locations are shown in the file **P15_82.xlsx**, where a dash indicates shipments that are not allowed. Determine how to minimize the transport costs in meeting the oil demands of Los Angeles and New York.

83. Based on Bean et al. (1987). Boris Milkem's firm owns six assets. The expected selling price (in millions of dollars) for each asset is given in the file **P15_83.xlsx**. For example, if asset 1 is sold in year 2, the firm receives $20 million. To maintain a regular cash flow, Milkem must sell at least $20 million of assets during year 1, at least $30 million worth during year 2, and at least $35 million worth during year 3. Determine how Milkem can maximize his total revenue from assets sold during the next 3 years. In implementing this model, how might the idea of a rolling planning horizon be used?

84. Based on Sonderman and Abrahamson (1985). In treating a brain tumor with radiation, physicians want the maximum amount of radiation possible to bombard the tissue containing the tumors. The constraint is, however, that there is a maximum amount of radiation that normal tissue can handle without suffering tissue damage. Physicians must therefore decide how to aim the radiation so as to maximize the radiation that hits the tumor tissue subject to the constraint of not damaging the normal tissue. As a simple example of this situation, suppose there are six types of radiation beams (beams differ in where they are aimed and their intensity) that can be aimed at a tumor. The region containing the tumor has been divided into six regions: three regions contain tumors and three contain normal tissue. The amount of radiation delivered to each region by each type of beam is shown in the file **P15_84.xlsx**. If each region of normal tissue can handle at most 60 units of radiation, which beams should be used to maximize the total amount of radiation received by the tumors?

85. Fruit Computer produces two types of computers: Pear computers and Apricot computers. The relevant data are given in the file **P15_85.xlsx**. The equipment cost is a fixed cost; it is incurred if any of this type of computer is produced. A total of 3000 chips and 1200 hours of labor are available.
   a. Determine how Fruit can maximize its profit.
   b. Use SolverTable to analyze the effect on the optimal solution of a change in the selling price of Pear computers. Do the same for the selling price of Apricot computers.

86. Heinsco produces tomato sauce at five different plants. The tomato sauce is then shipped to one of three warehouses, where it is stored until it is shipped to one of the company's four customers. All of the inputs for the problem are given in the file **P15_86.xlsx**, as follows:
   - The plant capacities (in tons)
   - The cost per ton of producing tomato sauce at each plant and shipping it to each warehouse
   - The cost of shipping a ton of sauce from each warehouse to each customer
   - The customer requirements (in tons) of sauce
   - The fixed annual cost of operating each plant and warehouse

Heinsco must decide which plants and warehouses to open, and which routes from plants to warehouses and from warehouses to customers to use. All customer demand must be met. A given customer's demand can be met from more than one warehouse, and a given plant can ship to more than one warehouse.
   a. Determine the minimum-cost method for meeting customer demands.
   b. Use SolverTable to see how a change in the capacity of plant 1 affects the total cost.

   c. Use SolverTable to see how a change in the customer 2 demand affects the total cost.

87. Consider three investments. You are given the following means, standard deviations, and correlations for the annual return on these three investments. The means are 0.12, 0.15, and 0.20. The standard deviations are 0.20, 0.30, and 0.40. The correlation between stocks 1 and 2 is 0.65, between stocks 1 and 3 is 0.75, and between stocks 2 and 3 is 0.41. You have $10,000 to invest and can invest no more than half of your money in any single stock. Determine the minimum-variance portfolio that yields an expected annual return of at least 0.14.

88. I have $1000 to invest in three stocks. Let R_i be the random variable representing the annual return on $1 invested in stock i. For example, if $R_i = 0.12$, then $1 invested in stock i at the beginning of a year is worth $1.12 at the end of the year. The means are $E(R_1) = 0.14$, $E(R_2) = 0.11$, and $E(R_3) = 0.10$. The variances are $Var\ R_1 = 0.20$, $Var\ R_2 = 0.08$, and $Var\ R_3 = 0.18$. The correlations are $r_{12} = 0.8$, $r_{13} = 0.7$, and $r_{23} = 0.9$. Determine the minimum-variance portfolio that attains an expected annual return of at least 0.12.

Level B

89. The risk index of an investment can be obtained by taking the absolute values of percentage changes in the value of the investment for each year and averaging them. Suppose you are trying to determine what percentage of your money you should invest in T-bills, gold, and stocks. The file **P15_89.xlsx** lists the annual returns (percentage changes in value) for these investments for the years 1968 through 1988. Let the risk index of a portfolio be the weighted average of the risk indices of these investments, where the weights are the fractions of the portfolio assigned to the investments. Suppose that the amount of each investment must be between 20% and 50% of the total invested. You would like the risk index of your portfolio to equal 0.15, and your goal is to maximize the expected return on your portfolio. Determine the maximum expected return on your portfolio, subject to the stated constraints. Use the average return earned by each investment during the years 1968 through 1988 as your estimate of expected return.

90. Broker Sonya Wong is currently trying to maximize her profit in the bond market. Four bonds are available for purchase and sale at the bid and ask prices shown in the file **P15_90.xlsx**. Sonya can buy up to 1000 units of each bond at the ask price or sell up to 1000 units of each bond at the bid price. During each of the next 3 years, the person who sells a bond will pay the owner of the bond the cash payments listed in the file **P15_90.xlsx**. Sonya's goal is to maximize her revenue from selling bonds minus her payment for buying bonds, subject to the constraint that after each year's payments are received, her current cash position (due only to cash payments from bonds and not purchases or sales of bonds) is nonnegative. Note that her current cash position can depend on past coupons and that cash accumulated at the end of each year earns 11% annual interest. Determine how to maximize net profit from buying and selling bonds, subject to the constraints previously described. Why do you think we limit the number of units of each bond that can be bought or sold?

91. The ZapCon Company is considering investing in three projects. If it fully invests in a project, the realized cash flows (in millions of dollars) will be as listed in the file **P15_91.xlsx**. For example, project 1 requires a cash outflow of $3 million today and returns $5.5 million 3 years from now. Today ZapCon has $2 million in cash. At each time point (0, 0.5, 1, 1.5, 2, and 2.5 years from today), the company can, if desired, borrow up to $2 million at 3.5% (per 6 months) interest. Leftover cash earns 3% (per 6 months) interest. For example, if after borrowing and investing at time 0, ZapCon has $1 million, it would receive $30,000 in interest at time 0.5 year. The company's goal is to maximize cash on hand after cash flows 3 years from now are accounted for. What investment and borrowing strategy should it use? Assume that the company can invest in a fraction of a project. For example, if it invests in 0.5 of project 3, it has cash outflows of −$1 million at times 0 and 0.5.

92. You are a CFA (chartered financial analyst). An overextended client has come to you because she needs help paying off her credit card bills. She owes the amounts on her credit cards listed in the file **P15_92.xlsx**. The client is willing to allocate up to $5000 per month to pay off these credit cards. All cards must be paid off within 36 months. The client's goal is to minimize the total of all her payments. To solve this problem, you must understand how interest on a loan works. To illustrate, suppose the client pays $5000 on Saks during month 1. Then her Saks balance at the beginning of month 2 is 20,000 − [5000 − 0.005(20,000)]. This follows because she incurs 0.005(20,000) in interest charges on her Saks card during month 1. Help the client solve her problem. Once you have solved this problem, give an intuitive explanation of the solution found by Solver.

93. The Wild Turkey Company produces two types of turkey cutlets for sale to fast-food restaurants. Each type of cutlet consists of white meat and dark meat. Cutlet 1 sells for $4 per pound and must consist of at least 70% white meat. Cutlet 2 sells for $3 per pound

and must consist of at least 60% white meat. At most 50 pounds of cutlet 1 and 30 pounds of cutlet 2 can be sold. The two types of turkey used to manufacture the cutlets are purchased from the GobbleGobble Turkey Farm. Each type 1 turkey costs $10 and yields 5 pounds of white meat and 2 pounds of dark meat. Each type 2 turkey costs $8 and yields 3 pounds of white meat and 3 pounds of dark meat. Determine how to maximize Wild Turkey's profit.

94. Each hour from 10 A.M. to 7 P.M., Bank One receives checks and must process them. Its goal is to process all checks the same day they are received. The bank has 13 check processing machines, each of which can process up to 500 checks per hour. It takes one worker to operate each machine. Bank One hires both full-time and part-time workers. Full-time workers work 10 A.M. to 6 P.M., 11 A.M. to 7 P.M., or noon to 8 P.M. and are paid $160 per day. Part-time workers work either 2 P.M. to 7 P.M. or 3 P.M. to 8 P.M. and are paid $75 per day. The numbers of checks received each hour are listed in the file **P15_94.xlsx**. In the interest of maintaining continuity, Bank One believes that it must have at least 3 full-time workers under contract. Develop a work schedule that processes all checks by 8 P.M. and minimizes daily labor costs.

95. Oilco has oil fields in San Diego and Los Angeles. The San Diego field can produce up to 500,000 barrels per day, and the Los Angeles field can produce up to 400,000 barrels per day. Oil is sent from the fields to a refinery, either in Dallas or in Houston. (Assume that each refinery has unlimited capacity.) To refine 100,000 barrels costs $700 at Dallas and $900 at Houston. Refined oil is shipped to customers in Chicago and New York. Chicago customers require 400,000 barrels per day, and New York customers require 300,000 barrels per day. The costs of shipping 100,000 barrels of oil (refined or unrefined) between cities are shown in the file **P15_95.xlsx**.
    a. Determine how to minimize the total cost of meeting all demands.
    b. If each refinery had a capacity of 380,000 barrels per day, how would you modify the model in part **a**?

96. Powerhouse produces capacitors at three locations: Los Angeles, Chicago, and New York. Capacitors are shipped from these locations to public utilities in five regions of the country: northeast (NE), northwest (NW), midwest (MW), southeast (SE), and southwest (SW). The cost of producing and shipping a capacitor from each plant to each region of the country is given in the file **P15_96.xlsx**. Each plant has an annual production capacity of 100,000 capacitors. Each year, each region of the country must receive the following number of capacitors: NE, 55,000; NW, 50,000; MW, 60,000; SE, 60,000; SW, 45,000. Powerhouse believes that shipping costs are too high, and it is therefore

considering building one or two more production plants. Possible sites are Atlanta and Houston. The costs of producing a capacitor and shipping it to each region of the country are also given in the file **P15_96.xlsx**. It costs $3 million (in current dollars) to build a new plant, and operating each plant incurs a fixed cost (in addition to variable shipping and production costs) of $50,000 per year. A plant at Atlanta or Houston will have the capacity to produce 100,000 capacitors per year. Assume that future demand patterns and production costs will remain unchanged. If costs are discounted at a rate of 12% per year, how can Powerhouse minimize the net present value (NPV) of all costs associated with meeting current and future demands?

97. Based on Bean et al. (1988). Simon's Mall has 10,000 square feet of space to rent and wants to determine the types of stores that should occupy the mall. The minimum number and maximum number of each type of store (along with the square footage of each type) are given in the file **P15_97.xlsx**. The annual profit made by each type of store depends on how many stores of that type are in the mall. This dependence is also given in the file **P15_97.xlsx** (where all profits are in units of $10,000). For example, if there are two department stores in the mall, each department store will earn $210,000 profit per year. Each store pays 5% of its annual profit as rent to Simon's. Determine how Simon can maximize its rental income from the mall.

98. It is currently the beginning of 2003. Gotham City is trying to sell municipal bonds to support improvements in recreational facilities and highways. The face values (in thousands of dollars) of the bonds and the due dates at which principal comes due are listed in the file **P15_98.xlsx**. (The due dates are the *beginnings* of the years listed.) The Gold and Silver Company (GS) wants to underwrite Gotham City's bonds. A proposal to Gotham for underwriting this issue consists of the following: (1) an interest rate, 3%, 4%, 5%, 6%, or 7%, for each bond, where coupons are paid annually, and (2) an up-front premium paid by GS to Gotham City. GS has determined the set of fair prices (in thousands of dollars) for the bonds listed in the file **P15_98.xlsx**. For example, if GS underwrites bond 2 maturing in 2006 at 5%, it will charge Gotham City $444,000 for that bond. GS is constrained to use at most three different interest rates. GS wants to make a profit of at least $46,000, where its profit is equal to the sale price of the bonds minus the face value of the bonds minus the premium GS pays to Gotham City. To maximize the chance that GS will get Gotham City's business, GS wants to minimize the total cost of the bond issue to Gotham City, which is equal to the total interest on the bonds minus the premium paid by GS. For example, if the year 2005 bond (bond 1) is issued at a 4% rate, then Gotham City must pay 2 years of coupon interest: $2(0.04)(\$700,000) = \$56,000$. What assignment of interest rates to each bond and up-front premiums ensure that GS will make the desired profit (assuming it gets the contract) and maximize the chance of GS getting Gotham City's business?

This problem deals with strategic planning issues for a large company.[18] The main issue is planning the company's production capacity for the coming year. At issue is the overall level of capacity and the type of capacity—for example, the degree of *flexibility* in the manufacturing system. The main tool used to aid the company's planning process is a mixed integer programming model. A *mixed* integer program has both integer and continuous variables.

Problem Statement

The Giant Motor Company (GMC) produces three lines of cars for the domestic (U.S.) market: Lyras, Libras, and Hydras. The Lyra is a relatively inexpensive subcompact car that appeals mainly to first-time car owners and to households using it as a second car for commuting. The Libra is a sporty compact car that is sleeker, faster, and roomier than the Lyra. Without any options, the Libra costs slightly more than the Lyra; additional options increase the price further. The Hydra is the luxury car of the GMC line. It is significantly more expensive than the Lyra and Libra, and it has the highest profit margin of the three cars.

Retooling Options for Capacity Expansion

Currently GMC has three manufacturing plants in the United States. Each plant is dedicated to producing a single line of cars. In its planning for the coming year, GMC is considering the retooling of its Lyra and/or Libra plants. Retooling either plant would represent a major expense for the company. The retooled plants would have significantly increased production capacities. Although having greater *fixed* costs, the retooled plants would be more efficient and have lower *marginal* production costs—that is, higher *marginal* profit contributions. In addition, the retooled plants would be *flexible*: They would have the capability of producing more than one line of cars.

The characteristics of the current plants and the retooled plants are given in Table 15.22. The retooled

[18]The idea for this case came from Eppen, Martin, and Schrage, "A Scenario Approach to Capacity Planning." *Operations Research* 37, no. 4 (July–August 1989): 517–527.

Lyra and Libra plants are prefaced by the word *new*. The fixed costs and capacities in Table 15.22 are given on an annual basis. A dash in the profit margin section indicates that the plant cannot manufacture that line of car. For example, the new Lyra plant would be capable of producing both Lyras and Libras but not Hydras. The new Libra plant would be capable of producing any of the three lines of cars. Note, however, that the new Libra plant has a slightly lower profit margin for producing Hydras than the Hydra plant. The flexible new Libra plant is capable of producing the luxury Hydra model but is not quite as efficient as the current Hydra plant that is dedicated to Hydra production.

The fixed costs are annual costs that are incurred by GMC independent of the number of cars that are produced by the plant. For the current plant configurations, the fixed costs include property taxes, insurance, payments on the loan that was taken out to construct the plant, and so on. If a plant is retooled, the fixed costs will include the previous fixed costs plus the additional cost of the renovation. The additional renovation cost will be an annual cost representing the cost of the renovation amortized over a long period.

Demand for GMC Cars

Short-term demand forecasts have been very reliable in the past and are expected to be reliable in the future. (Longer-term forecasts are not so accurate.) The demand for GMC cars for the coming year is given in Table 15.23.

A quick comparison of plant capacities and demands in Tables 15.22 and 15.23 indicates that GMC is faced with insufficient capacity. Partially offsetting the lack of capacity is the phenomenon of **demand diversion**. If a potential car buyer walks into a GMC dealer showroom wanting to buy a Lyra but the dealer is out of stock, frequently the salesperson can convince the customer to purchase the better Libra car, which is in stock. Unsatisfied demand for the Lyra is said to be *diverted* to the Libra. Only rarely in this situation can the salesperson convince the customer to switch to the luxury Hydra model.

From past experience GMC estimates that 30% of unsatisfied demand for Lyras is diverted to demand for Libras and 5% to demand for Hydras. Similarly, 10% of unsatisfied demand for Libras is diverted to demand for Hydras. For example, if the demand for Lyras is 1,400,000 cars, then the unsatisfied demand will be 400,000 if no capacity is added. Out of this unsatisfied demand, 120,000 (= 400,000 × 0.3) will materialize as demand for Libras, and 20,000 (= 400,000 × 0.05) will materialize as demand for Hydras. Similarly, if the demand for Libras is 1,220,000 cars (1,100,000 original demand plus 120,000 demand diverted from Lyras), then the unsatisfied demand for Lyras would be 420,000 if no capacity is added. Out of this unsatisfied demand, 42,000 (= 420,000 × 0.1) will materialize as demand for Hydras. All other unsatisfied demand is lost to competitors. The pattern of demand diversion is summarized in Table 15.24.

Question

GMC wants to decide whether to retool the Lyra and Libra plants. In addition, GMC wants to determine its production plan at each plant in the coming year. Based on the previous data, formulate a mixed integer programming model for solving GMC's production planning–capacity expansion problem for the coming year. The file **GMC Retooling.xlsx** gets you started.

Table 15.22

Plant Characteristics

	Lyra	Libra	Hydra	New Lyra	New Libra
Capacity (in 1000s)	1000	800	900	1600	1800
Fixed cost (in $millions)	2000	2000	2600	3400	3700

	Profit Margin by Car Line (in $1000s)				
Lyra	2	—	—	2.5	2.3
Libra	—	3	—	3.0	3.5
Hydra	—	—	5	—	4.8

Table 15.23

Demand for GMC Cars

	Demand (in 1000s)
Lyra	1400
Libra	1100
Hydra	800

Table 15.24

Demand Diversion Matrix

	Lyra	Libra	Hydra
Lyran	NA	0.3	0.05
Libra	0	NA	0.10
Hydra	0	0.0	NA

K ate Torelli, a security analyst for LionFund, has identified a gold mining stock (ticker symbol GMS) as a particularly attractive investment. Torelli believes that the company has invested wisely in new mining equipment. Furthermore, the company has recently purchased mining rights on land that has high potential for successful gold extraction. Torelli notes that gold has underperformed the stock market in the last decade and believes that the time is ripe for a large increase in gold prices. In addition, she reasons that conditions in the global monetary system make it likely that investors may once again turn to gold as a safe haven in which to park assets. Finally, supply and demand conditions have improved to the point where there could be significant upward pressure on gold prices.

GMS is a highly leveraged company, so it is quite a risky investment by itself. Torelli is mindful of a passage from the annual report of a competitor, Baupost, which has an extraordinarily successful investment record: "Baupost has managed a decade of consistently profitable results despite, and perhaps in some respect due to, consistent emphasis on the avoidance of downside risk. We have frequently carried both high cash balances and costly market hedges. Our results are particularly satisfying when considered in the light of this sustained risk aversion." She would therefore like to *hedge* the stock purchase—that is, reduce the risk of an investment in GMS stock.

Currently GMS is trading at $100 per share. Torelli has constructed seven scenarios for the price of GMS stock 1 month from now. These scenarios and corresponding probabilities are shown in Table 15.25.

To hedge an investment in GMS stock, Torelli can invest in other securities whose prices tend to move in the direction opposite to that of GMS stock. In particular, she is considering over-the-counter put options on GMS stock as potential hedging instruments. The value of a put option increases as the price of the underlying stock decreases. For example, consider a put option with a strike price of $100 and a time to expiration of 1 month. This means that the owner of the put has the right to sell GMS stock at

$100 per share 1 month in the future. Suppose that the price of GMS falls to $80 at that time. Then the holder of the put option can exercise the option and receive $20 (= 100 − 80). If the price of GMS falls to $70, the option would be worth $30 (= 100 − 70). However, if the price of GMS rises to $100 or more, the option expires worthless.

Torelli called an options trader at a large investment bank for quotes. The prices for three (European-style) put options are shown in Table 15.26. Torelli wishes to invest $10 million in GMS stock and put options.

Questions

1. Based on Torelli's scenarios, what is the expected return of GMS stock? What is the standard deviation of the return of GMS stock?

2. After a cursory examination of the put option prices, Torelli suspects that a good strategy is to buy one put option A for each share of GMS stock purchased. What are the mean and standard deviation of return for this strategy?

3. Assuming that Torelli's goal is to minimize the standard deviation of the portfolio return, what is the optimal portfolio that invests all $10 million? (For simplicity, assume that fractional numbers of stock shares and put options can be purchased. Assume that the amounts invested in each security must be nonnegative. However, the number of options purchased need *not* equal the number of shares of stock purchased.) What are the expected return and standard deviation of return of this portfolio? How many shares of GMS stock and how many of each put option does this portfolio correspond to?

4. Suppose that short selling is permitted—that is, the nonnegativity restrictions on the portfolio weights are removed. Now what portfolio minimizes the standard deviation of return?

(*Hint:* A good way to attack this problem is to create a table of security returns, as indicated in Table 15.27. Only a few of the table entries are shown. To correctly compute the standard deviation

of portfolio return, you will need to incorporate the
scenario probabilities. If r_i is the portfolio return in
scenario i, and p_i is the probability of scenario i, then
the standard deviation of portfolio return is

$$\sqrt{\sum_{i=1}^{7} p_i(r_i - \mu)^2}$$

where $\mu = \Sigma^{7}_{i=1} p_i r_i$ is the expected portfolio return.)

Table 15.25   Scenarios and Probabilities for GMS Stock in 1 Month

	Scenario 1	Scenario 2	Scenario 3	Scenario 4	Scenario 5	Scenario 6	Scenario 7
Probability	0.05	0.10	0.20	0.30	0.20	0.10	0.05
GMS stock price	150	130	110	100	90	80	70

Table 15.26   Put Option Prices (Today) for GMS Case Study

	Put Option A	Put Option B	Put Option C
Strike Price	90	100	110
Option Price	$2.20	$6.40	$12.50

Table 15.27   Table of Security Returns

	GMS Stock	Put Option A	Put Option B	Put Option C
Scenario 1			−100%	
2	30%			
⋮				
7				220%

Durham Asset Management (DAM) is a small firm with 50 employees that manages the pension funds of small to medium-sized companies.[19] Durham was founded in 1975 and has grown considerably throughout the years. Initially, DAM managed the pension funds of three small companies whose asset values totaled $30 million. By 1991 DAM's funds under management were valued at $2 billion.

James Franklin is a senior vice president at DAM, in charge of managing the equity portion of one of its largest pension funds. Franklin meets on a quarterly basis with company officials who supervise his decisions and oversee his performance. His work is measured on several levels, including both subjective and objective criteria. The subjective criteria include estimates of the quality of research reports. The objective criteria include the actual performance of Franklin's portfolio relative to a customized index of companies in DAM's investment universe. Franklin attempts to "beat" the index not by trying to time market moves, but by investing more heavily in those companies he expects to outperform the customized index and less heavily in those companies he expects to underperform the index.

Franklin has several research analysts who are charged with following the performance of several companies within specific industries. The research analysts prepare reports that analyze the past performance of the companies and prepare projections of future performance. The projections include assessments of the "most likely" or average performance anticipated over the next month.

Franklin analyzes their findings and often asks for additional information or suggests modifications to the analyses. After a period of careful review, the final forecasts for the next month are assembled and summarized. Each month the analysts' forecasts are compared to the actual results. Annual bonuses for the analysts are based in part on the comparison of these numbers.

It is now late December 1991, and the projections for January 1992 are indicated in Table 15.28. The projections have been made for 15 U.S. companies divided into five industry groups. The five industry groups are metals, retail, computer, automotive, and aviation. Franklin would like to use the portfolio optimization approach to see what portfolios it would recommend. He has data containing end-of-month prices for the last two years for each of the companies. The data are contained in the spreadsheet **Durham Asset Management.xlsx**. Also included in the spreadsheet is information about dividends and stock splits. Using this data James constructs a history of 24 monthly returns for each of the 15 companies.

The past data provide useful information about the volatility (standard deviation) of stock returns. They also give useful information about the degree of association (correlation) of returns between pairs of stocks. However, average returns from the past do not tend to be good predictors of future average returns. Rather than using the raw historical data directly, Franklin creates 24 future return scenarios by adjusting the 24 historical returns. The adjustments are made so that the means of the future scenario returns are consistent with the forecasts from Table 15.28. The adjustments are also made so that the volatilities and correlations of the future scenario returns are the same as in the historical data.

The exact procedure that Franklin uses for developing future scenario returns is described next. Let r^0_{ij} denote the historical return of security j in month i (for $j = 1,...,15$ and $i = 1,...,24$). Suppose that the average historical return of security j is μ_j^0. For security j, denote the forecasted mean return in Table 15.19 by μ_j. (For example, $\mu_1 = 0.6\%$ and $\mu_2 = 0.9\%$, where the index 1 refers to ALCOA and 2 refers to Reynolds Metals.) Franklin creates the future scenario return r_{ij} for security j in scenario i using the following equation:

$$r_{ij} = r^0_{ij} + \mu_j - \mu_j^0 \qquad (15.10)$$

Franklin assumes that any of the scenarios defined by equation (15.10) can occur with equal probability. DAM's policy is never to invest more than 30% of the funds in any one industry group. Franklin measures the risk of a portfolio by its standard deviation of return. He then solves a portfolio optimization model for various minimum levels of mean return to see

[19]Thanks to Ziv Katalan and Aliza Schachter for assistance in developing this case.

which portfolios are recommended. After analyzing the trade-off between risk and return, Franklin makes a judgment as to which portfolio to hold for the coming month.

Questions

1. Use the information in the **Durham Asset Management.xlsx** file to create a history of 24 monthly returns for the 15 companies. Compute the historical average return of each stock. In particular, what was the historical return of ALCOA from 12/29/89 to 1/31/90? What was the historical return of Boeing from 5/31/90 to 6/29/90? Explain how you account for dividends and stock splits in computing monthly returns.

2. Develop 24 future scenario returns using equation (15.10). What is the explanation underlying it? In particular, what is the return of ALCOA if scenario 1 occurs? What is the return of Reynolds Metals if scenario 3 occurs?

3. Compute and graph the mean–standard deviation efficient frontier. Compute at least six points on the efficient frontier (including the minimum standard deviation and maximum expected return points). Create a table of results showing the following for each of your points on the efficient frontier: (1) the optimal portfolio weights, (2) mean portfolio return, and (3) standard deviation. (Briefly explain the equations and optimization model used in the spreadsheet.)

Table 15.28 Projections for January 1992 for DAM Case Study

Company	Forecasted Mean Return
Aluminum Co. of America (ALCOA)	0.6%
Reynolds Metals	0.9%
Alcan Aluminum, Ltd.	0.8%
Wal-Mart Store, Inc.	1.5%
Sears, Roebuck & Co.	0.8%
Kmart Corporation	1.3%
International Business Machines (IBM)	0.4%
Digital Equipment Corporation (DEC)	1.1%
Hewlett Packard Co.(HP)	0.7%
General Motors Corp. (GM)	1.2%
Ford Motor Co. (FORD)	0.9%
Chrysler Corp.	1.3%
Boeing Co.	0.3%
McDonnell Douglas Corp.	0.2%
United Technologies Corp.	0.7%

CHAPTER

16

Introduction to Simulation Modeling

© Sherwin Crasto/Reuters/Landov

CALL PROCESSING SIMULATION AT AT&T

Simulation is a versatile tool that allows companies to ask many what-if questions about changes in their systems without actually changing the systems themselves. As reported in the article "AT&T's Call Processing Simulator (CAPS) Operational Design for Inbound Call Centers" by Brigandi et al. (1994), AT&T has used a simulation model called CAPS to help its corporate customers design and operate their call centers. These call centers are the locations into which customers phone, usually using 800 numbers, for customer service, telephone shopping, and other services. The system that is used to handle these calls—the way calls are routed to agents, the number of lines open, the prerecorded messages given to customers, the way customer queues are handled, and so on—can be extremely complex and difficult to understand, let alone optimize. Therefore, AT&T developed the CAPS simulation tool to simulate a variety of operating policies for its corporate customers. AT&T reports that it has used this tool to regain more than $1 billion from a customer base of approximately 2000 corporate customers per year. The CAPS tool has improved the customers' call-center operations dramatically and has helped sell these customers on further AT&T services.

As an example, a major airline's reservation system was supported by 19 separate call centers located near domestic and international airports. In 1992, the airline decided to consolidate its reservations centers. AT&T helped the airline by running a series of CAPS studies to determine the characteristics of efficient, load-balanced call centers that would accomplish the airline's goals. The airline was particularly interested in reducing its 10% blocked-call rate while using its resources more efficiently. The result of the CAPS studies was a $25 million savings in the airline's reservations call-center operations costs and an ability to handle approximately 3000 more reservation sales calls per day. At the same time, AT&T strengthened its position as the 800-number service communications carrier of choice with the airline. Its annual billed network services for the airline increased by 5% on a base of $49 million. ∎

16.1 INTRODUCTION

A simulation model is a computer model that imitates a real-life situation. It is like other mathematical models, but it explicitly incorporates uncertainty in one or more input variables. When we run a simulation, we allow these random input variables to take on various values, and we keep track of any resulting output variables of interest. In this way, we are able to see how the outputs vary as a function of the varying inputs.

The fundamental advantage of a simulation model is that it shows us an entire distribution of results, not simply a single bottom-line result. As an example, suppose an automobile manufacturer is planning to develop and market a new model car. The company is ultimately interested in the net present value (NPV) of the profits from this car over the next 10 years. However, there are many uncertainties surrounding this car, including the yearly customer demands for it, the cost of developing it, and others. We could develop a spreadsheet model for the 10-year NPV, using our best guesses for these uncertain quantities. We could then report the NPV based on these *best guesses*, with the implicit understanding that this best-guess NPV is going to occur. However, this analysis would be incomplete and probably misleading—after all, how can we be certain that any *specific* value of NPV will occur? It is much better to treat the uncertainty explicitly with a simulation model. This involves entering probability distributions for the uncertain quantities and seeing how the NPV varies as the uncertain quantities vary.

Each different set of values for the uncertain quantities can be considered a scenario. Simulation allows us to generate many scenarios, each leading to a particular NPV. In the end, we see a whole distribution of NPVs, not a single best guess. We can see what the NPV will be on average, and we can also see worst-case and best-case results.

Simulation models are also useful for determining how sensitive a system is to changes in operating conditions. For example, we might simulate the operations of a supermarket. Once the simulation model has been developed, we can then run it (with suitable modifications) to ask a number of what-if questions. For example, if the supermarket experiences a 20% increase in business, what will happen to the average time customers must wait for service?

A huge benefit of computer simulation is that it enables us to answer these types of what-if questions without actually changing (or building) a physical system. For example, the supermarket might want to experiment with the number of open registers to see the effect on customer waiting times. The only way it can *physically* experiment with more registers than it currently owns is to purchase more equipment. Then if it determines that this equipment is not a good investment—customer waiting times do not decrease appreciably—the company is stuck with expensive equipment it doesn't need. Computer simulation is a much less expensive alternative. It provides the company with an electronic replica of what would happen *if* the new equipment were purchased. Then, if the simulation indicates that the new equipment is worth the cost, the company can be confident that purchasing it is the right decision. Otherwise, it can abandon the idea of the new equipment *before* the equipment has been purchased.

Spreadsheet simulation modeling is quite similar to the other modeling applications in this book. We begin with input variables and then relate these with appropriate Excel formulas to produce output variables of interest. The main difference is that simulation uses *random* numbers to drive the whole process. These random numbers are generated with special functions that we discuss in detail. Each time the spreadsheet recalculates, all of the random numbers change. This gives us the ability to model the logical process once and then use Excel's recalculation ability to generate many different scenarios. By collecting the data from these scenarios, we see the most likely values of the outputs and we see the best-case and worst-case scenarios values of the outputs.

In this chapter we illustrate spreadsheet models that can be developed with the basic Excel package. However, because simulation is becoming such an important tool for analyzing real problems, add-ins to Excel have been developed to streamline the process of developing and analyzing simulation models. Therefore, we also introduce @RISK, one of the most popular simulation add-ins. This add-in not only augments the simulation capabilities of Excel, but it also enables users to analyze models much more quickly and easily.

The purpose of this chapter is to introduce basic simulation concepts, show how simulation models can be developed in Excel, and demonstrate the capabilities of the @RISK add-in. Then in the next chapter, armed with the necessary simulation tools, we explore a number of interesting and useful simulation models.

16.2 REAL APPLICATIONS OF SIMULATION

There are many published applications of simulation. These cover a wide variety of topics, as we discuss briefly in this section.

Burger King developed a simulation model for its restaurants [see Swart and Donno (1981)]. This model was used to answer business questions such as whether the restaurant should open a second drive-through window, and how much customer waiting times would increase if a new sandwich were added to the menu.

Many companies (Cummins Engine, Merck, Procter & Gamble, Kodak, and United Airlines, to name a few) have used simulation to determine which of several possible investment projects they should choose. This is often referred to as **risk analysis**. As an example, consider a situation where a company must choose a single investment. If the future cash flows for each investment project are known with certainty, then most companies advocate choosing the investment with the largest NPV. However, if future cash flows are not known with certainty, then it is not clear how to choose between competing projects. Using simulation, we can obtain a distribution of the NPV for a project. Then we can answer such questions as:

- Which project is the riskiest?

- What is the probability that an investment will yield at least a 20% return?

- What is the probability that the NPV of an investment will be less than −$1 billion— that is, a loss of more than $1 billion?

To illustrate the use of simulation in corporate finance, we refer to Norton (1994). This article describes a simulation model that was used by Merck, the world's largest drug company, to determine whether Merck should pay $6.6 billion to acquire Medco, a mail-order drug company. The model's inputs included the following:

- Possible scenarios for the future of the U.S. health-care system, such as a single-payer system, universal coverage, and so forth

- Possible future changes in the mix of generic and brand-name drugs

- Probability distributions of profit margins for each product
- Assumptions about competitors' reactions to a merger with Medco

A simulation of the Merck model was performed to see how the merger would perform under various possible scenarios. As Merck's CFO, Judy Lewent, said, "Monte Carlo techniques are a very, very powerful tool to get a more intelligent look at a range of outcomes. It's almost never useful in this kind of environment to build a single bullet forecast." The simulation results indicated that the merger with Medco would benefit Merck regardless of the type of health insurance plan (if any) the federal government enacted.

Other applications of simulation include the following:

- Companies must constantly make inventory-ordering decisions in the face of unknown demand. In special cases, analytic (nonsimulation) models can be used to help make decisions. However, when the problems become more complex, simulation often provides the only feasible solution method. We consider a typical ordering model in this chapter.

- Firms must often bid against competitors to win a contract. If a firm's bid is too low, it will probably win the contract, but it will make very little profit on the contract. On the other hand, if the firm bids too high, it will probably not win the contract at all. The firm must decide how much to bid, although the competitors' bids are uncertain. In the next chapter we develop a simulation model that can help a firm choose the bid amount that maximizes its expected profit. This provides a different approach to the bidding problem than the one we discussed in Example 7.1 of Chapter 7.

- Large corporate projects can frequently be divided into smaller activities. (A prime example is the Apollo space mission.) To create the project's schedule, the company must estimate the length of time required to finish the project. It is certainly realistic to assume that these times can be estimated only with probability distributions. In this case simulation is required.

16.3 PROBABILITY DISTRIBUTIONS FOR INPUT VARIABLES

In spreadsheet simulation models, input cells can contain random numbers. Any output cells then vary as these random inputs change.

In this section we discuss the "building blocks" of spreadsheet simulation models. All spreadsheet simulation models are similar to the spreadsheet models we have developed in previous chapters. They have a number of cells that contain values of input variables. The other cells then contain formulas that embed the logic of the model and eventually lead to the output variable(s) of interest. The primary difference between the spreadsheet models we have developed so far and simulation models is that at least one of the input variable cells in a simulation model contains *random* numbers. We can make these random numbers change by recalculating the spreadsheet. Each time the spreadsheet recalculates, the new random values of the inputs produce new values of the outputs. This is the essence of simulation—seeing how outputs vary as random inputs change.

Excel Tip: *Recalculation Key*
The easiest way to make a spreadsheet recalculate is to press the F9 key. This is often called the "recalc" key.

Technically speaking, we do not actually enter random numbers in input cells; we enter *probability distributions*. In general, a probability distribution indicates the possible values of a variable and the probabilities of these values. As a very simple example, we might indicate by an appropriate formula (to be described later) that we want a probability distribution with possible values 50 and 100, and corresponding probabilities 0.7 and 0.3. The effect of this is that if we then press the F9 key repeatedly and watch this input cell, we will see the value 50 about 70% of the time and the value 100 about 30% of the time. No other values besides 50 and 100 will appear.

When we enter a given probability distribution in a random input cell, we are describing the possible values and the probabilities of these values that we believe mirror reality. There are many probability distributions to choose from, and we always attempt to choose an *appropriate* distribution for each specific problem. This is not necessarily an easy task. Therefore, we address it in this section by answering several key questions:

- What types of probability distributions are available, and why do we choose one probability distribution rather than another in an actual simulation model?

- Which probability distributions can we use in simulation models, and how do we invoke them with Excel formulas?

In later sections we address one additional question: Does the choice of input probability distribution really matter—that is, does it have a large effect on the *outputs* from the simulation?

Types of Probability Distributions

It is useful to think of a toolbox that contains the probability distributions you know and understand. As you obtain more experience in simulation modeling, you will naturally add probability distributions to this toolbox that you can then use in *future* simulation models. We begin by adding a few useful probability distributions to this toolbox. However, before adding any specific distributions, we look at some important characteristics of probability distributions in general. These include the following distinctions:

- Discrete versus continuous
- Symmetric versus skewed
- Bounded versus unbounded
- Positive versus not necessarily positive

Discrete versus Continuous

A probability distribution is **discrete** if it has a finite number of possible values.[1] For example, if we throw two dice and look at the sum of the faces showing, there are only 11 discrete possibilities: the integers 2 through 12. In contrast, a probability distribution is **continuous** if its possible values are essentially some continuum. An example is the amount of rain that falls during a month in Indiana. It could be any decimal value from 0 to, say, 15 inches.

The graph of a discrete distribution is a series of spikes, as shown in Figure 16.1.[2] The height of each spike is the probability of the corresponding value. That's all there is to it. You can have as many possible values as you like, and their probabilities can be any positive numbers that sum to 1.

The heights above a density function are not probabilities, but they still indicate relative likelihoods of the possible values.

In contrast, a continuous distribution is characterized by a **density function**, a smooth curve as shown in Figure 16.2. There are two important properties of density functions. First, the height of the density curve above any point is not actually a probability—that is, it is not necessarily between 0 and 1. However, the heights still indicate relative likelihoods. For example, the height of the density above 12 is about 5 times as large as the height above 6 in the figure. Therefore, a random number from this distribution is about 5 times as likely to be near 12 as to be near 6.

---

[1] Actually, it is possible for a discrete variable to have a "countably infinite" number of possible values, such as all the nonnegative integers 0, 1, 2, and so on. However, this is not an important distinction for practical applications.
[2] This figure and several later figures have been captured from Palisade's @RISK program. This program, which is included on the CD-ROM that accompanies this book, is discussed later in the chapter.

Figure 16.1

A Typical Discrete
Probability
Distribution

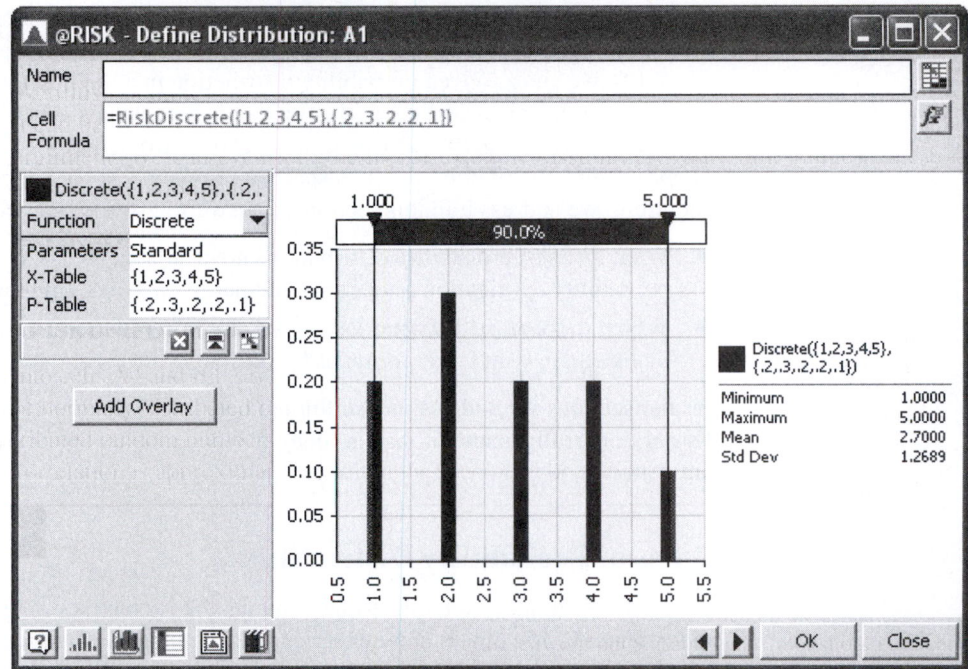

Second, probabilities for continuous distributions are found as areas under the density curve. Specifically, the probability of being between 6 and 12 in Figure 16.2 is the shaded area between the vertical lines at 6 and 12. Density functions are always scaled so that the *entire* area under the density is 1. This means that any particular area, such as the area between 6 and 12, is always a value between 0 and 1—that is, a probability. We do not actually calculate areas under particular density functions because this typically requires integral calculus. However, it is important that you understand conceptually that probabilities are areas under the density.

> A continuous distribution is described by a **density function**. Heights above the density function indicate relative likelihoods but are not necessarily values between 0 and 1. Probabilities are found as areas under the density function.

Sometimes it is convenient to treat a discrete probability distribution as continuous, and vice versa. For example, consider a student's random score on an exam that has 1000 possible points. If the grader scores each exam to the nearest integer, then even though the score is really discrete with many possible integer values, it is probably more convenient to model its distribution as a continuum. Continuous probability distributions are typically more intuitive and easier to work with than discrete distributions in cases such as this, where there are many possible values. In contrast, we sometimes "discretize" continuous distributions for simplicity. As an example, consider a random interest rate with possible values in the continuum from 5% to 15%. We might model this with a discrete probability distribution with possible values 5%, 7.5%, 10%, 12.5%, and 15%. Although this is not as common as going the other way—from discrete to continuous—it is often done by simulation modelers.

Symmetric versus Skewed

A probability distribution is **symmetric** (around some point) if the distribution to the left of the point is a mirror image of the distribution to the right of the point. Otherwise, the distribution is **skewed**. If a distribution is skewed, then we say it is **skewed to the right** (or **positively skewed**) if the "longer tail" is the right tail. Otherwise, we say the distribution is **skewed to the left** (or **negatively skewed**). The distribution in Figure 16.2 is symmetric, the distribution in Figure 16.3 is skewed to the right, and the distribution in Figure 16.4 is skewed to the left.

Figure 16.2

A Typical Continuous Probability Distribution

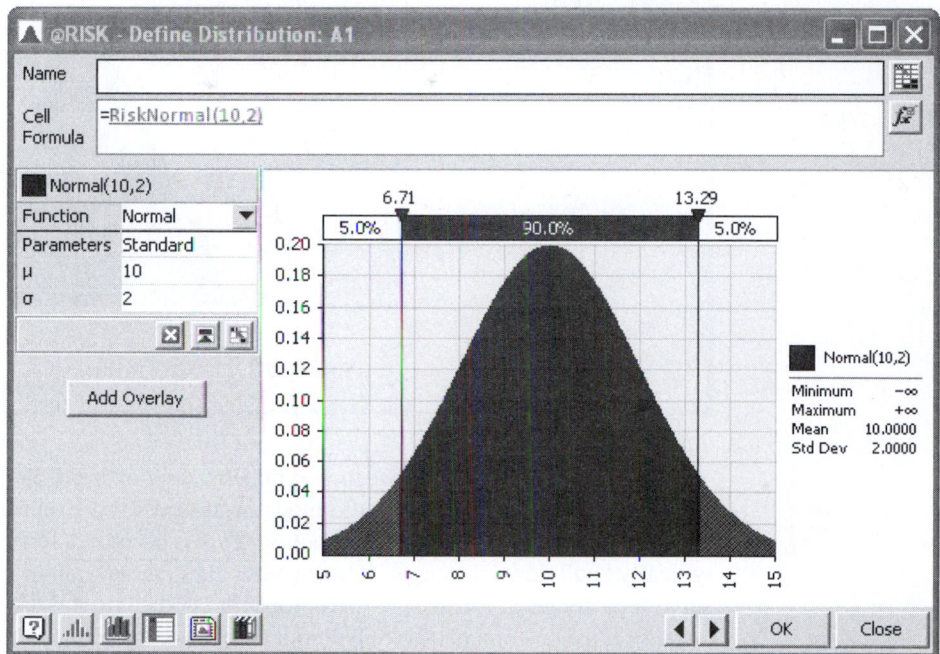

Figure 16.3

A Positively Skewed Probability Distribution

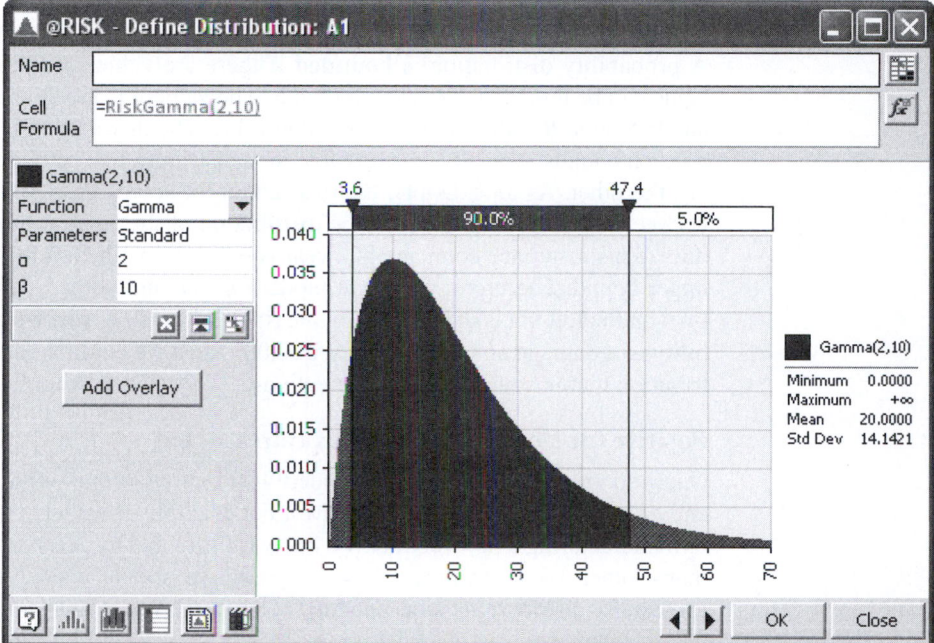

Figure 16.4

A Negatively Skewed
Probability
Distribution

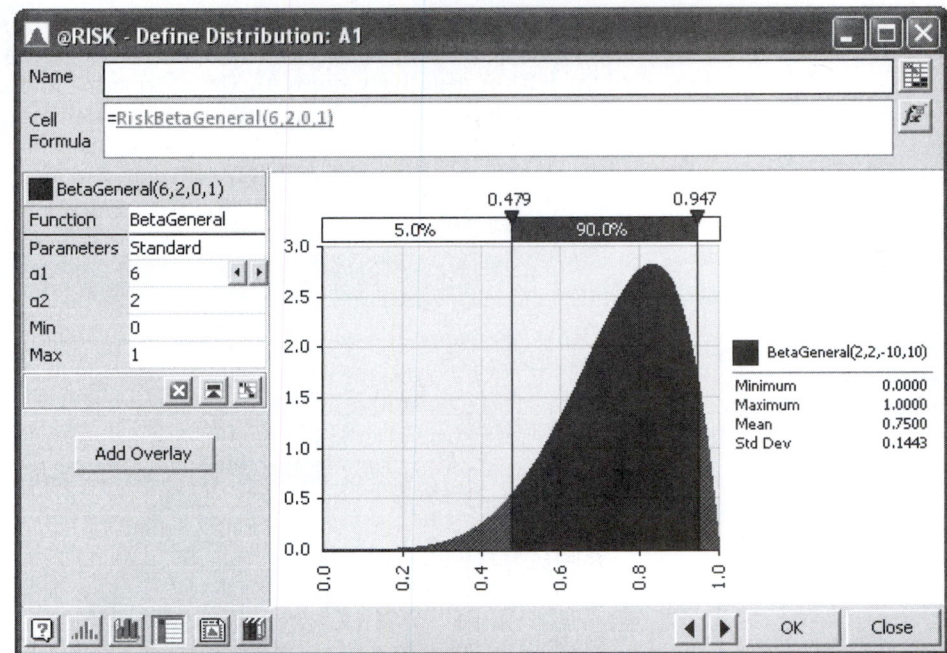

We typically choose between a symmetric and skewed distribution on the basis of realism. For example, if we want to model a student's score on a 100-point exam, we will probably choose a left-skewed distribution. This is because a few poorly prepared students typically "pull down the curve." On the other hand, if we want to model the time it takes to serve a customer at a bank, we will probably choose a right-skewed distribution. This is because most customers take only a minute or two, but a few customers take a long time. Finally, if we want to model the monthly return on a stock, we might choose a distribution symmetric around 0, reasoning that the stock return is just as likely to be positive as negative and there is no obvious reason for skewness one way or the other.

Bounded versus Unbounded

A probability distribution is **bounded** if there are values A and B such that no possible value can be less than A or greater than B. The value A is then the *minimum* possible value, and the value B is the *maximum* possible value. The distribution is **unbounded** if there are no such bounds. Actually, it is possible for a distribution to be bounded in one direction but not the other. As an example, the distribution of scores on a 100-point exam is bounded between 0 and 100. In contrast, the distribution of the amount of damages Mr. Jones submits to his insurance company in a year is bounded on the left by 0, but there is no natural upper bound. Therefore, we might model this amount with a distribution that is bounded by 0 on the left but is unbounded on the right. Alternatively, if we believe there is no possibility of a damage amount over, say, $20,000, then we could model this amount with a distribution that is bounded in both directions.

Positive (or Nonnegative) versus Unrestricted

One important special case of bounded distributions occurs with variables that are inherently *positive* (or possibly *nonnegative*). For example, if we want to model the random cost of manufacturing a new product, we know for sure that this cost must be positive. There are many other such examples. In each case, we should model the randomness with a probability distribution that is bounded below by 0. We do not want to allow negative values because they make no practical sense.

Common Probability Distributions

Think of the Probability Distributions.xlsx file as a "dictionary" of the most commonly used distributions. Keep it handy for reference.

A family of distributions has a common name, such as "normal." Each member of the family is specified by one or more numerical parameters.

Now that we know the *types* of probability distributions available, we add some common probability distributions to our toolbox. To help you learn and explore these, we developed the file **Probability Distributions.xlsx**. Each sheet in this file illustrates a particular probability distribution. It describes the general characteristics of the distribution, it indicates how you can generate random numbers from the distribution, either with Excel's built-in functions or with @RISK functions, and it includes histograms of these distributions from simulated data to illustrate their shapes.[3]

It is important to realize that each of the following distributions is really a *family* of distributions. Each member of the family is specified by one or more parameters. For example, there is not a *single* normal distribution; there is a normal distribution for each possible mean and standard deviation we specify. Therefore, when you try to find an appropriate input probability distribution in a simulation model, you first have to choose an appropriate family, and then you have to select an appropriate member of that family.

Uniform Distribution

The uniform distribution is the "flat" distribution illustrated in Figure 16.5. It is bounded by a minimum and a maximum, and all values between these two extremes are equally likely. You can think of this as the "I have no idea" distribution. For example, a manager might realize that a building cost is uncertain. If she can state only that, "I know the cost will be between $20,000 and $30,000, but other than this, I have no idea what the cost will be," then a uniform distribution from $20,000 to $30,000 is a natural choice. However, even though some people do use the uniform distribution in such cases, we don't believe these situations are very common or realistic. If the manager really thinks about it, she can probably provide more information about the uncertain cost, such as, "The cost is more likely to be close to $25,000 than to either of the extremes." Then some distribution other than the uniform is more appropriate.

Figure 16.5

The Uniform Distribution

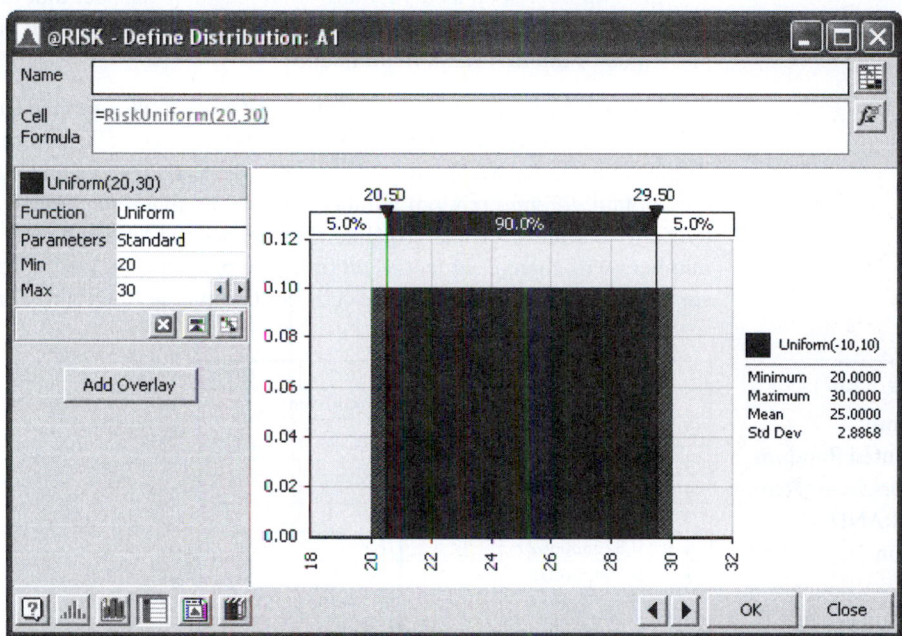

[3]In later sections of this chapter, and all through the next chapter, we discuss much of @RISK's functionality. For this section, the only functionality we use is @RISK's collection of functions, such as RISKNORMAL and RISKTRIANG, for generating random numbers from various probability distributions. You can skim the details of these functions for now and refer back to them as necessary in later sections.

Regardless of whether the uniform distribution is an appropriate candidate as an input distribution, it is important for another reason. All spreadsheet packages are capable of generating random numbers uniformly distributed between 0 and 1. These are the "building blocks" of all simulated random numbers, in that random numbers from all other probability distributions are generated from these building blocks.

In Excel, we can generate a random number between 0 and 1 by entering the formula

=RAND()

in any cell. (The parentheses to the right of RAND indicate that this is an Excel function with no arguments. These parentheses must be included.)

The RAND function is Excel's "building block" function for generating random numbers.

Excel Function: *RAND*

To generate a random number equally likely to be anywhere between 0 and 1, enter the formula =RAND() into any cell. Press the F9 key to make it change randomly.

In addition to being between 0 and 1, the numbers created by this function have two properties that we would expect "random" numbers to have.

- **Uniform property.** Each time we enter the RAND function in a cell, all numbers between 0 and 1 have the same chance of occurring. This means that approximately 10% of the numbers generated by the RAND function will be between 0.0 and 0.1; 10% of the numbers will be between 0.65 and 0.75; 60% of the numbers will be between 0.20 and 0.80; and so on. This property explains why we say the random numbers are *uniformly distributed* between 0 and 1.

- **Independence property.** Different random numbers generated by the computer are *probabilistically independent*. This implies that when we generate a random number in cell A5, say, it has no effect on the values of any other random numbers generated in the spreadsheet. For example, if one call to the RAND function yields a large random number such as 0.98, there is no reason to suspect that the next call to RAND will yield an abnormally small (or large) random number; it is unaffected by the value of the first random number.

To illustrate the RAND function, open a new workbook, enter the formula =RAND() in cell A4, and copy it to the range A4:A503. This generates 500 random numbers. Figure 16.6 displays the values we obtained. However, when you try this on your PC, you will undoubtedly obtain *different* random numbers. This is an inherent characteristic of simulation—no two answers are ever exactly alike. Now press the "recalc" (F9) key. All of the random numbers will change. In fact, each time you press the F9 key or do anything to make your spreadsheet recalculate, all of the cells containing the RAND function will change.

Figure 16.6

Uniformly Distributed Random Numbers Generated by the RAND Function

	A	B	C	D
1	500 random numbers from RAND function			
2				
3	Random #			
4	0.639741246			
5	0.977449085			
6	0.826336662			
7	0.794236038			
8	0.326052217			
9	0.540446013			
10	0.012582316			
501	0.868540879			
502	0.297930515			
503	0.960969187			

A histogram of the 500 random numbers for our illustration is shown in Figure 16.7. (Again, if you try this on your PC, the shape of your histogram will not be identical to the one shown in Figure 16.7 because it will be based on *different* random numbers.) From property 1, we would expect *equal* numbers of observations in the 10 categories. Although the heights of the bars are not exactly equal, the differences are due to chance—not to a faulty random number generator.

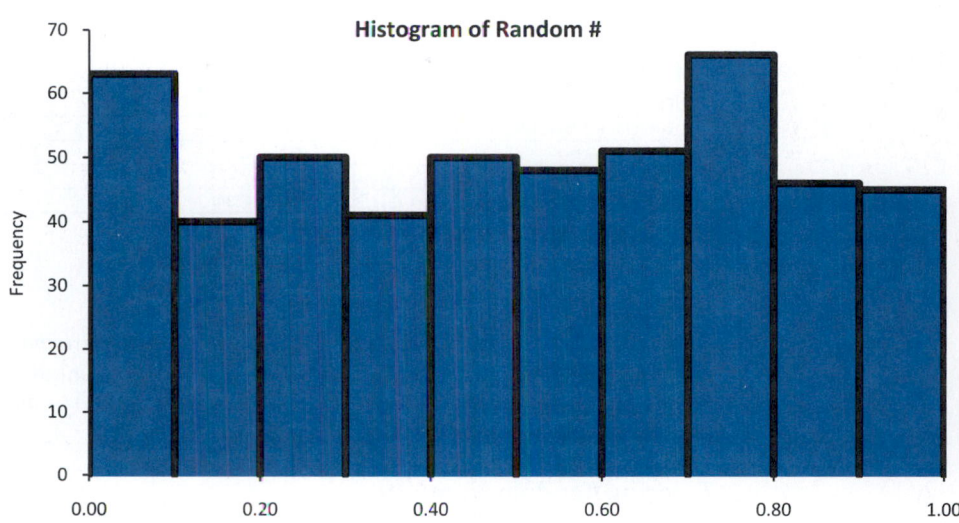

Technical Excel Note: *Pseudo-random Numbers*

*The "random" numbers generated by the RAND function (or by any other package's random number generator) are not really random. They are sometimes called **pseudo-random numbers**. Each successive random number follows the previous random number by a complex arithmetic operation. If you happen to know the details of this arithmetic operation, you can predict ahead of time exactly which random numbers will be generated by the RAND function. This is quite different from using a "true" random mechanism, such as spinning a wheel, to get the next random number—a mechanism that would be impractical to implement on a computer. Mathematicians and computer analysts have studied many ways to produce random numbers that have the two properties we just discussed, and they have developed many competing random number generators such as the RAND function in Excel. The technical details need not concern us. The important point is that these random number generators produce numbers that are useful for simulation modeling.*

It is simple to generate a uniformly distributed random number with a minimum and maximum other than 0 and 1. For example, the formula

=200+100*RAND()

generates a number uniformly distributed between 200 and 300. (Make sure you see why.) Alternatively, we could use the @RISK formula[4]

=RISKUNIFORM(200,300)

You can take a look at this and other properties of the uniform distribution on the Uniform sheet in the **Probability Distributions.xlsx** file. (See Figure 16.8.)

---

[4]As we have done with other Excel functions, we capitalize the @RISK functions, such as RISKUNIFORM, in the text. However, this is not necessary when you enter the formulas in Excel.

Figure 16.8

Properties of
Uniform
Distribution

	A	B	C	D	E	F	G	H
1	Uniform distribution							
2								
3	Characteristics							
4	Continuous							
5	Symmetric							
6	Bounded in both directions							
7	Not necessarily positive (depends on bounds)							
8								
9	Parameters							
10	MinVal	50						
11	MaxVal	100						
12								
13	Excel		Example					
14	=MinVal + (MaxVal-MinVal)*RAND()		59.903648					
15								
16	@RISK							
17	=RISKUNIFORM(MinVal,MaxVal)		80.584134					

> This is a flat distribution between two values, labeled here MinVal and MaxVal. Note that if MinVal=0 and MaxVal=1, then we can just use Excel's RAND function.

@RISK Function: *RISKUNIFORM*

To generate a random number from any uniform distribution, enter the formula =RISKUNIFORM(MinVal,MaxVal) in any cell. Here, MinVal and MaxVal are the minimum and maximum possible values. Note that if MinVal is 0 and MaxVal is 1, this function is equivalent to Excel's RAND function.

Freezing Random Numbers

The automatic recalculation of random numbers can be useful sometimes and annoying at other times. There are situations when we want the random numbers to stay fixed—that is, we want to "freeze" them at their current values. The following three-step method does this.

1. **Select the range.** Select the range that you want to freeze, such as A4:A503 in Figure 16.6.

2. **Copy.** Use the Copy command to copy this range.

3. **Paste Special with Values.** With the same range still selected, select the Paste Values option from the Paste dropdown on the Home ribbon. This procedure pastes a copy of the range onto itself, except that the entries are now numbers, not formulas. Therefore, whenever the spreadsheet recalculates, these numbers do not change.

Random numbers that have been frozen do not change when you press the F9 key.

Each sheet in the **Probability Distributions.xlsx** file has a list of 500 random numbers that have been frozen. We created the histograms in the sheets based on the frozen random numbers. However, we encourage you to enter "live" random numbers in column B over our frozen ones and see how the histogram changes when you press F9.

USING @RISK TO EXPLORE PROBABILITY DISTRIBUTIONS[5]

The **Probability Distributions.xlsx** file illustrates a few frequently used probability distributions, and it shows the formulas required to generate random numbers from these distributions. Another option is to use Palisade's @RISK add-in, which allows us to experiment with probability distributions. Essentially, it allows us to see the shapes of various distributions and to calculate probabilities for them, all in a graphical, user-friendly interface.

---

[5]Palisade previously offered a standalone program called RISKview for exploring probability distributions, and we discussed it in the previous edition. However, Palisade has decided to discontinue RISKview and instead incorporate its functionality into @RISK.

To run @RISK, click on the Windows Start button, go to the Programs tab, locate the Palisades DecisionTools suite, and select @RISK. Select a blank cell in your worksheet, and then click on Define Distributions on the @RISK ribbon. Double-click on one of the distributions (we chose uniform, as shown in Figure 16.9) and change the parameters to the ones you want (we chose a minimum of 75 and a maximum of 150). Now you see the shape of the distribution and a few summary measure to the right. For example, you see that the mean and standard deviation of this uniform distribution are 112.5 and 21.651.

Figure 16.9

@RISK Illustration of Uniform Distribution

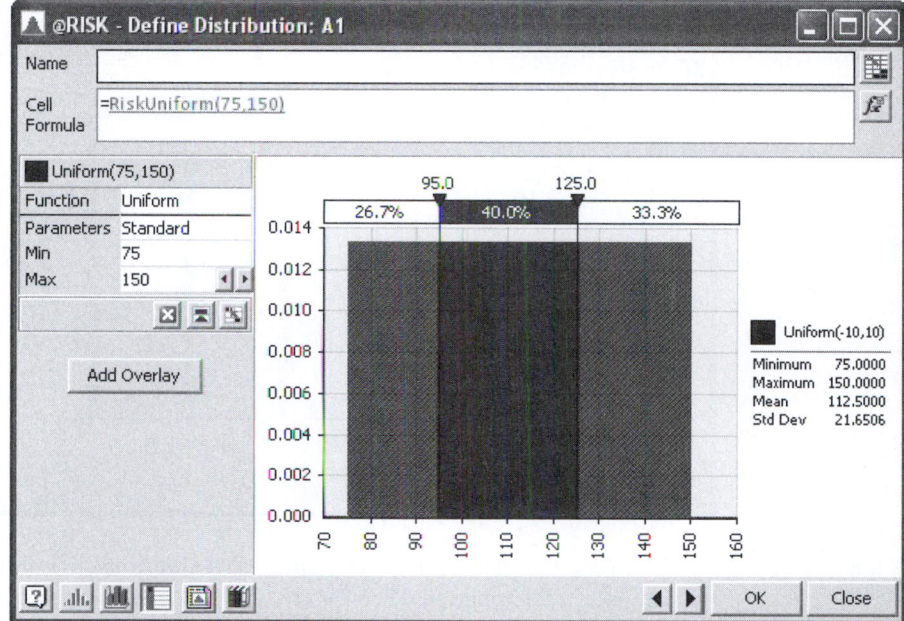

From here, everything is interactive. Suppose you want to find the probability that a value from this distribution is less than 95. You can drag the left-hand "slider" in the diagram (the vertical line with the triangle at the top) to the position 95, as shown in Figure 16.9. You see immediately that the left-hand probability is 0.267. Similarly, if you want the probability that a value from this distribution is greater than 125, you can drag the right-hand slider to the position 125 to see that the required probability is 0.3333.

The interactive capabilities of @RISK's Define Distributions window, with its sliders, make it perfect for finding probabilities or percentiles for any given distribution.

You can also enter probabilities instead of values. For example, if you want the value such that there is probability 0.10 to the left of it—the 10th percentile—enter 10% in the left space above the chart. You will see that the corresponding value is 82.5. Similarly, if you want the value such that there is probability 0.10 to the right of it, enter 10% in the right space above the chart, and you will see that the corresponding value is 142.5.

We like @RISK's Define Distributions window because it is quick and easy. We urge you to use it and experiment with some of its options. By the way, you can click on the fifth button from the left at the bottom of this window to copy the chart into an Excel worksheet. However, you then lose the interactive capabilities, such as moving the sliders.

Discrete Distribution

A discrete distribution is useful for many situations, either when the uncertain quantity is not really continuous (the number of televisions demanded, for example) or when you want a discrete approximation to a continuous variable. All you need to do is specify the possible values and their probabilities, making sure that the probabilities sum to 1.

Because of this flexibility in specifying values and probabilities, discrete distributions can have practically any shape.

As an example, suppose a manager estimates that the demand for a particular brand of television during the coming month will be 10, 15, 20, or 25 with respective probabilities 0.1, 0.3, 0.4, and 0.2. This is a typical discrete distribution, and it is illustrated in Figure 16.10.

Figure 16.10

Discrete Distribution (from @RISK)

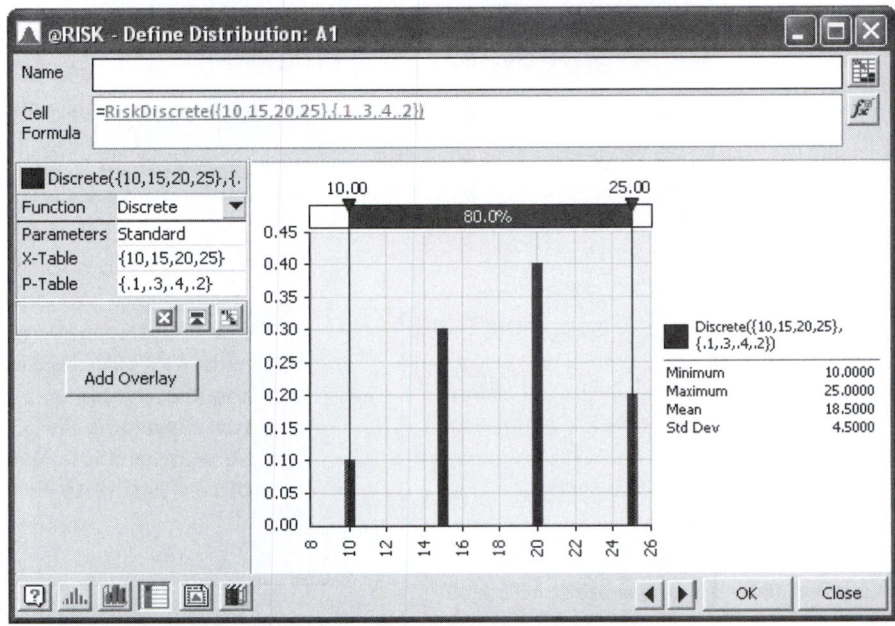

@RISK's way of generating a discrete random number is much simpler and more intuitive than Excel's "native" method that requires cumulative probabilities and a lookup function.

The Discrete sheet of the **Probability Distributions.xlsx** file indicates how to work with a discrete distribution. (See Figure 16.11.) As we see, there are two quite different ways to generate a random number from this distribution in Excel. We discuss the "Excel" way in detail in Section 16.4. For now, we simply mention that this is one case (of many) where it is much easier to generate random numbers with @RISK functions than with built-in Excel functions. Assuming that @RISK is loaded, all we need to do is enter the function RISKDISCRETE with two arguments, a list of possible values and a list of their probabilities, as in

=RISKDISCRETE(B11:B14,C11:C14)

The Excel way, which requires cumulative probabilities and a lookup table, requires more work and is harder to remember.

@RISK Function: *RISKDISCRETE*
*To generate a random number from any discrete probability distribution, enter the formula =RISKDISCRETE(**valRange,probRange***) into any cell. Here* valRange *is the range where the possible values are stored, and* probRange *is the range where their probabilities are stored.*

The selected input distributions for any simulation model reflect historical data and an analyst's best judgment as to what will happen in the future.

At this point, a relevant question is, Why would a manager choose this particular discrete distribution? First, it is clearly an approximation. After all, if it is possible to have demands of 20 and 25, why aren't demands of 22 or 24 possible? Here, the manager approximates a discrete distribution with *many* possible values—all integers from 0 to 50, say—with a discrete distribution with a few well-chosen values. This is common in simulation modeling. Second, where do the probabilities come from? They are probably a blend of historical data (perhaps demand was near 15 in 30% of previous months) and the manager's subjective feelings about demand *next* month.

Figure 16.11

Properties of a
Discrete
Distribution

	A	B	C	D	E	F	G	H	I
1	General discrete distribution								
2									
3	Characteristics								
4	Discrete				This can have any shape, depending				
5	Can be symmetric or skewed (or bumpy, i.e., basically any shape)				on the list of possible values and their				
6	Bounded in both directions				probabilities.				
7	Not necessarily positive (depends on possible values)								
8									
9	Parameters				Lookup table required for Excel method				
10		Values	Probabilities		CumProb	Value			
11		10	0.1		0	10			
12		15	0.3		0.1	15			
13		20	0.4		0.4	20			
14		25	0.2		0.8	25			
15									
16	Excel		Example						
17	=VLOOKUP(RAND(),LookupTable,2)		10						
18									
19	@RISK								
20	=RISKDISCRETE(Values,Probs)		20						

Normal Distribution

The normal distribution is the familiar bell-shaped curve that is the hallmark of statistics. (See Figure 16.12.) It is also useful in simulation modeling as a continuous input distribution. However, it is not always the most appropriate distribution. It is symmetric, which can be a drawback when a skewed distribution is more realistic. Also, it allows negative values, which are not appropriate in many situations. For example, the demand for televisions cannot be negative. Fortunately, this possibility of negative values is often not a problem. The two parameters of a normal distribution are its mean and standard deviation. Suppose you generate a normally distributed random number with mean 100 and standard deviation 20. Then, as you should recall from Chapter 6, there is almost no chance of having values more than 3 standard deviations to the left of the mean. Therefore, negative values will virtually never occur in this situation.

Normally distributed random numbers will almost certainly be within 3 standard deviations of the mean.

Figure 16.12

Normal Distribution
(from @RISK)

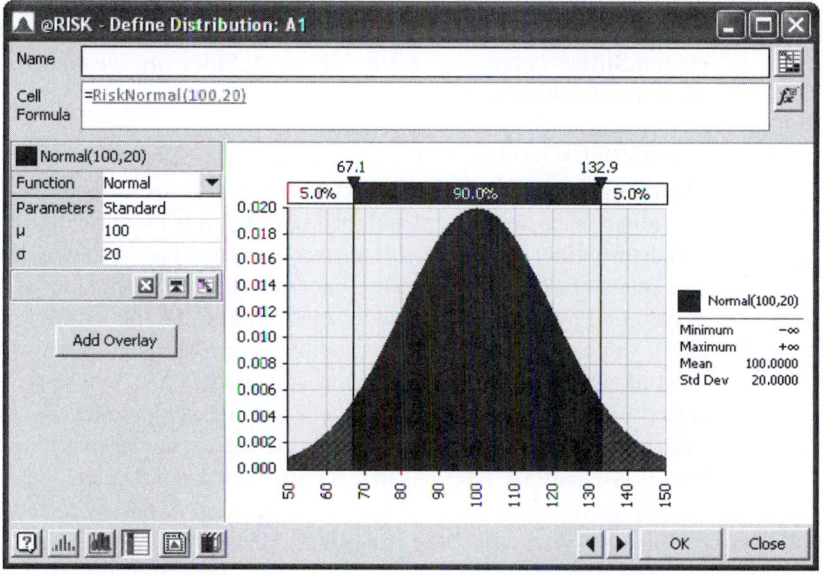

A tip-off that a normal distribution might be an appropriate candidate for an input variable is a statement such as, "We believe the most likely value of demand is 100, the chances are about 95% that demand will be no more than 40 units on either of side of this most likely value, and the shape of the distribution is symmetric around this most likely value." Because a normally distributed value is within 2 standard deviations of its mean with probability 0.95, this statement translates easily to a mean of 100 and a standard deviation of 20. We do not imply that a normal distribution is the *only* candidate for distribution of demand, but the statement naturally leads us to this distribution.

The Normal sheet in the **Probability Distributions.xlsx** file indicates how we can generate normally distributed random numbers in Excel, either with or without @RISK. (See Figure 16.13.) This is one case where an add-in is not really necessary—the formula

=NORMINV(RAND(),*Mean*,*Stdev*)

will always work. Still, this is not nearly as easy to remember as @RISK's formula

=RISKNORMAL(*Mean*,*Stdev*)

Figure 16.13

Properties of the Normal Distribution

	A	B	C	D	E	F	G	H
1	Normal distribution							
2								
3	Characteristics							
4	Continuous							
5	Symmetric (bell-shaped)							
6	Unbounded in both directions							
7	Is both positive and negative							
8								
9	Parameters							
10	Mean		100					
11	Stdev		10					
12								
13	Excel		Example					
14	=NORMINV(RAND(),Mean,Stdev)		90.18632693					
15								
16	@RISK							
17	=RISKNORMAL(Mean,Stdev)		89.35430818					

This is the familiar bell-shaped curve, defined by two parameters: the mean and the standard deviation.

@RISK Function: *RISKNORMAL*

To generate a normally distributed random number, enter the formula =RISKNORMAL **(Mean,Stdev)** *in any cell. Here,* Mean *and* Stdev *are the mean and standard deviation of the normal distribution.*

Triangular Distribution

A triangular distribution is a good choice in many simulation models because it is flexible and its parameters are easy to understand.

The triangular distribution is somewhat similar to the normal distribution in that its density function rises to some point and then falls, but it is more flexible and intuitive than the normal distribution. Therefore, it is an excellent candidate for many continuous input variables. The shape of a triangular density function is literally a triangle, as shown in Figure 16.14. It is specified by three easy-to-understand parameters: the minimum possible value, the most likely value, and the maximum possible value. The high point of the triangle is above the most likely value. Therefore, if a manager states, "We believe the most likely development cost is $1.5 million, and we don't believe the development cost could possibly be less than $1.2 million or greater than $2.1 million," the triangular distribution with these three parameters is a natural choice. As in this numerical example, note that the triangular distribution can be skewed if the mostly likely value is closer to one extreme than another. Of course, it can also be symmetric if the most likely value is right in the middle.

The Triangular sheet of the **Probability Distributions.xlsx** file indicates how to generate random values from this distribution. (See Figure 16.15.) As we see, there is no way to do it with native Excel (at least not without a lot of trickery). However, it is easy with @RISK, using the RISKTRIANG function, as in

=RISKTRIANG(B10,B11,B12)

Figure 16.14

Triangular
Distribution
(from @RISK)

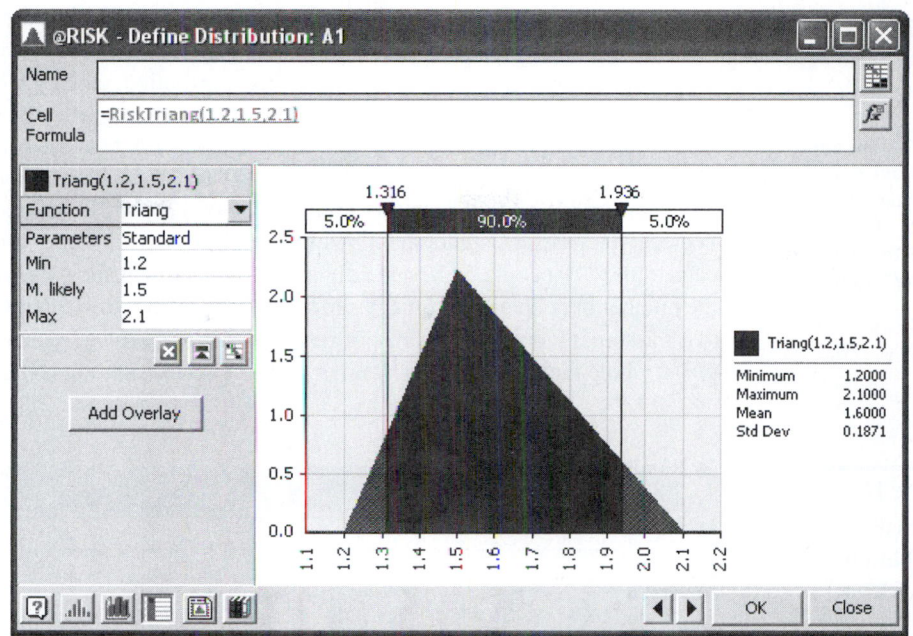

All we need to feed this function are the minimum value, the most likely value, and the maximum value—in this order and separated by commas. You will see this function in many of our examples. Just remember that it has an "abbreviated" spelling: **RISKTRIANG**, not RISKTRIANGULAR.

Figure 16.15

Properties of the
Triangular
Distribution

	A	B	C	D	E	F	G	H	I
1	**Triangular distribution**								
2									
3	**Characteristics**			The density of this distribution is literally a triangle. The "top" of the					
4	Continuous			triangle is above the most likely value, and the base of the triangle					
5	Can be symmetric or skewed in either direction			extends from the minimum value to the maximum value. It is					
6	Bounded in both directions			intuitive for nontechnical people because the three parameters are					
7	Not necessarily positive (depends on bounds)			meaningful.					
8									
9	**Parameters**								
10	Min	50							
11	MostLikely	85							
12	Max	100							
13									
14	**Excel**								
15	There is no easy way to do it. This is a case where we need an add-in.								
16									
17	**@RISK**		Example						
18	=RISKTRIANG(Min,MostLikely,Max)		75.77332227						

@RISK Function: *RISKTRIANG*

*To generate a random number from a triangular distribution, enter the formula =**RISKTRIANG** (**MinVal,MLVal,MaxVal**) in any cell. Here, MinVal is the minimum possible value, MLVal is the most likely value, and MaxVal is the maximum value.*

Binomial Distribution

The binomial distribution is a discrete distribution, but unlike the "general" discrete distribution we discussed previously, the binomial distribution applies to a very specific situation.

This is when a number of independent and identical "trials" occur, where each trial results in a "success" or "failure," and we want to generate the random number of successes in these trials. There are two parameters of this distribution, usually labeled n and p. Here, n is the number of trials and p is the probability of success on each trial.

As an example, suppose an airline company sells 170 tickets for a flight and estimates that 80% of the people with tickets will actually show up for the flight. How many people will actually show up? We could state that *exactly* 80% of 170, or 136 people, will show up, but this neglects the inherent randomness. A more realistic way to model this situation is to say that each of the 170 people, independently of one another, will show up with probability 0.8. Then the number of people who actually show up is binomially distributed with $n = 170$ and $p = 0.8$ (This assumes independent behavior across passengers, which might not be the case, for example, if whole families either show up or don't.) This distribution is illustrated in Figure 16.16.

A random number from a binomial distribution indicates the number of "successes" in a certain number of identical "trials."

Figure 16.16

Binomial Distribution (from @RISK)

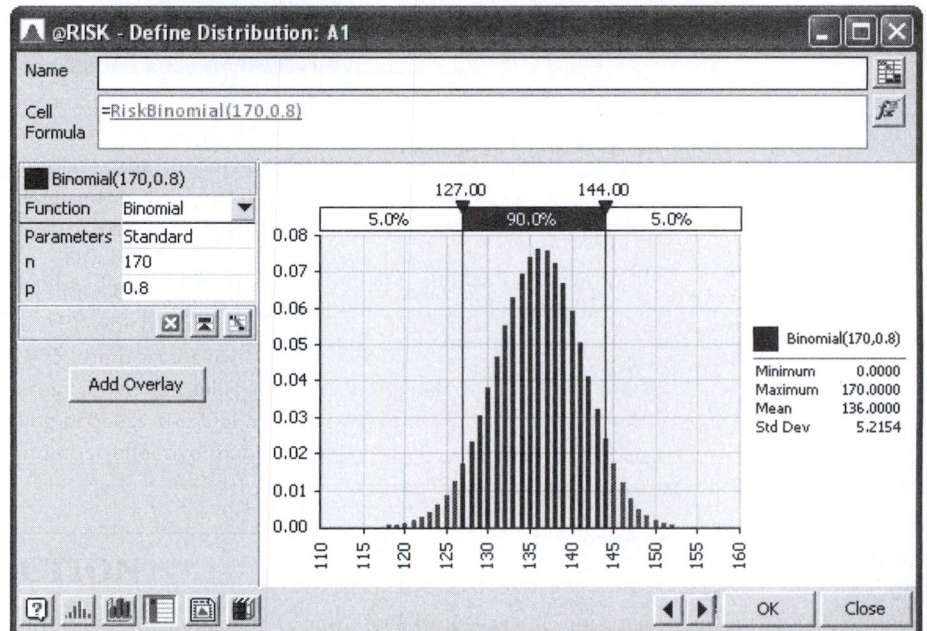

The Binomial sheet of the **Probability Distributions.xlsx** file indicates how to generate random numbers from this distribution. (See Figure 16.17.) Although it is possible to do this with native Excel, using the built-in CRITBINOM function and the RAND function, it is not very intuitive or easy to remember. Clearly, the @RISK way is preferable. In the airline example, we would generate the number who show up with the formula

=RISKBINOMIAL(170,0.8)

Note that the histogram in this figure is approximately bell-shaped. This is no accident. When the number of trials n is reasonably large and p isn't too close to 0 or 1, the binomial distribution can be well approximated by the normal distribution.

@RISK Function: *RISKBINOMIAL*
To generate a random number from a binomial distribution, enter the formula =RISKBINOMIAL(NTrials,PSuccess) in any cell. Here, NTrials is the number of trials, and PSuccess is the probability of a "success" on each trial.

Figure 16.17

Properties of the Binomial Distribution

	A	B	C	D	E	F	G	H
1	**Binomial distribution**							
2								
3	**Characteristics**			This distribution is of the number of "successes" in a given number of identical, independent trials, when the probability of success is constant on each trial.				
4	Discrete							
5	Can be symmetric or skewed							
6	Bounded below by 0, bounded above by Ntrials							
7	Nonnegative							
8								
9	**Parameters**							
10	NTrials	170						
11	PSuccess	0.8						
12								
13	**Excel**		Example					
14	=CRITBINOM(NTrials,PSuccess,RAND())		142					
15	This will generate the number of successes in NTrials, with PSuccess as the probability of success on each trial							
16								
17	**@RISK**							
18	=RISKBINOMIAL(NTrials,PSuccess)		134					

PROBLEMS

Level A

1. Use the RAND function and the Copy command to generate a set of 100 random numbers.
   a. What fraction of the random numbers are smaller than 0.5?
   b. What fraction of the time is a random number less than 0.5 followed by a random number greater than 0.5?
   c. What fraction of the random numbers are larger than 0.8?
   d. Freeze these random numbers. However, instead of pasting them over the original random numbers, paste them onto a new range. Then press the F9 recalculate key. The original random numbers should change, but the pasted copy should remain the same.

2. Use Excel's functions (not @RISK) to generate 1000 random numbers from a normal distribution with mean 100 and standard deviation 10. Then freeze these random numbers.
   a. Calculate the mean and standard deviation of these random numbers. Are they approximately what you would expect?
   b. What fraction of these random numbers are within k standard deviations of the mean? Answer for $k = 1$; for $k = 2$; for $k = 3$. Are the answers close to what they should be (as you learned in Chapter 6)?
   c. Create a histogram of the random numbers using 10 to 15 categories of your choice. Does this histogram have approximately the shape you would expect?

3. Use @RISK to draw a uniform distribution from 400 to 750. Then answer the following questions.
   a. What are the mean and standard deviation of this distribution?
   b. What are the 5th and 95th percentiles of this distribution?
   c. What is the probability that a random number from this distribution is less than 450?
   d. What is the probability that a random number from this distribution is greater than 650?
   e. What is the probability that a random number from this distribution is between 500 and 700?

4. Use @RISK to draw a normal distribution with mean 500 and standard deviation 100. Then answer the following questions.
   a. What is the probability that a random number from this distribution is less than 450?
   b. What is the probability that a random number from this distribution is greater than 650?
   c. What is the probability that a random number from this distribution is between 500 and 700?

5. Use @RISK to draw a triangular distribution with parameters 300, 500, and 900. Then answer the following questions.
   a. What are the mean and standard deviation of this distribution?
   b. What are the 5th and 95th percentiles of this distribution?
   c. What is the probability that a random number from this distribution is less than 450?
   d. What is the probability that a random number from this distribution is greater than 650?
   e. What is the probability that a random number from this distribution is between 500 and 700?

6. Use @RISK to draw a binomial distribution that results from 50 trials with probability of success 0.3 on each trial, and use it to answer the following questions.
   a. What are the mean and standard deviation of this distribution?
   b. You have to be more careful in interpreting @RISK probabilities with a discrete distribution such as this binomial. For example, if you move the left slider to 11, you find a probability of 0.139 to the left of it. But is this the probability of "less than 11" or "less than or equal to 11"? One way to check is to use Excel's BINOMDIST function. The formula $=\text{BINOMDIST}(k,n,p,1)$ calculates the probability that a binomial random number with parameters n and p is less than or equal to k. (The last argument, 1, ensures that you get a *cumulative* probability.) Use this function to interpret the 0.139 value from @RISK.
   c. Using part **b** to guide you, use @RISK to find the probability that a random number from this distribution will be greater than 17. Check your answer by using the BINOMDIST function appropriately in Excel.

7. Use @RISK to draw a triangular distribution with parameters 200, 300, and 600. Then superimpose a normal distribution on this drawing, choosing the mean and standard deviation to match those from the triangular distribution. (Click on the Add Overlay button to get a choice of distributions to superimpose.)
   a. What are the 5th and 95th percentiles for these two distributions?
   b. What is the probability that a random number from the triangular distribution is less than 400? What is this probability for the normal distribution?
   c. Experiment with the sliders to answer other questions like in part **b**. Would you conclude that these two distributions differ most in the extremes (right or left) or in the middle? Explain.

8. We all hate to bring change to a store. By using random numbers, we could eliminate the need for change and give the store and the customer a fair deal. This problem indicates how it could be done.
   a. Suppose that you buy something for $0.20. How could you use random numbers (built into the cash register system) to decide whether you should pay $1.00 or nothing? This would eliminate the need for change!
   b. If you bought something for $9.60, how would you use random numbers to eliminate the need for change?

c. In the long run, why is this method fair to both the store and the customers? Would you personally (as a customer) be willing to abide by such a system?

Level B

9. A company is about to develop and then market a new product. It wants to build a simulation model for the entire process, and one key uncertain input is the development cost. For each of the following scenarios, choose an "appropriate" distribution, together with its parameters, justify your choice in words, and use @RISK to draw your chosen distribution.
   a. Company experts have no idea what the distribution of the development cost is. All they can state is that "we are 95% sure it will be at least $450,000," and "we are 95% sure it will be no more than $650,000."
   b. Company experts can still make the same two statements as in part **a**, but now they can also state that "we believe the distribution is symmetric, reasonably bell-shaped, and its most likely value is about $550,000."
   c. Company experts can still make the same two statements as in part **a**, but now they can also state that "we believe the distribution is skewed to the right, and its most likely value is about $500,000."

10. Continuing the preceding problem, suppose that another key uncertain input is the development time, which is measured in an *integer* number of months. For each of the following scenarios, choose an "appropriate" distribution, together with its parameters, justify your choice in words, and use @RISK to draw your chosen distribution.
    a. Company experts believe the development time will be from 6 to 10 months, but they have absolutely no idea which of these will result.
    b. Company experts believe the development time will be from 6 to 10 months. They believe the probabilities of these five possible values will increase linearly to a most likely value at 8 months and will then decrease linearly.
    c. Company experts believe the development time will be from 6 to 10 months. They believe that 8 months is twice as likely as either 7 months or 9 months and that either of these latter possibilities is three times as likely as either 6 months or 10 months.

16.4 SIMULATION WITH BUILT-IN EXCEL TOOLS

In this section we show how spreadsheet simulation models can be developed and analyzed with Excel's built-in tools without using add-ins. As we will see, this is certainly possible, but it presents two problems. First, the @RISK functions illustrated in the

Probability Distributions.xlsx file are not available. We are able to use only Excel's RAND function and transformations of it to generate random numbers from various probability distributions. Second, there is a bookkeeping problem. Once we build an Excel model with output cells linked to appropriate random input cells, we can press the F9 key as often as we like to see how the outputs vary. However, how do we keep track of these output values and summarize them? This bookkeeping feature is the real strength of a simulation add-in such as @RISK. We will see that it can be done with Excel, usually with data tables, but the summarization of the resulting data is completely up to the user—you!

To illustrate the procedure, we analyze a simple "news vendor" problem. This problem occurs when a company (such as a news vendor) must make a one-time purchase of a product (such as a newspaper) to meet customer demands for a certain period of time. If the company orders too few newspapers, it will lose potential profit by not having enough on hand to satisfy its customers. If it orders too many, it will have newspapers left over at the end of the day that, at best, can be sold at a loss. The following example illustrates this basic problem in a slightly different context.

EXAMPLE | **16.1 ORDERING CALENDARS AT WALTON BOOKSTORE**

In August, Walton Bookstore must decide how many of next year's nature calendars to order. Each calendar costs the bookstore $7.50 and sells for $10. After January 1, all unsold calendars will be returned to the publisher for a refund of $2.50 per calendar. Walton believes that the number of calendars it can sell by January 1 follows the probability distribution shown in Table 16.1. Walton wants to develop a simulation model to help it decide how many calendars to order.

Table 16.1 Probability Distribution of Demand for Walton Example

Demand	Probability
100	0.30
150	0.20
200	0.30
250	0.15
300	0.05

Objective To use built-in Excel tools—including the RAND function and data tables, but no add-ins—to simulate profit for several order quantities and ultimately choose the "best" order quantity.

WHERE DO THE NUMBERS COME FROM?

The monetary values are straightforward. The numbers in Table 16.1 are the key to the simulation model. They are discussed in more detail next.

Solution

We first discuss the probability distribution in Table 16.1. It is a discrete distribution with only five possible values: 100, 150, 200, 250, and 300. In reality, it is clear that other values of demand are possible. For example, there could be demand for exactly 187 calendars. In spite of its apparent lack of realism, we use this discrete distribution for two reasons. First, its simplicity is a nice feature to get us started with simulation modeling. Second, discrete distributions are often used in real business simulation models. Even though the discrete distribution is only an *approximation* to reality, it can still give us important insights into the actual problem.

As for the probabilities listed in Table 16.1, they are typically drawn from historical data or (if historical data are lacking) educated guesses. In this case, the manager of Walton Bookstore has presumably looked at demands for calendars in previous years, and he has used any information he has about the market for next year's calendars to estimate, for example, that the probability of a demand for 200 calendars is 0.30. The five probabilities in this table *must* sum to 1. Beyond this requirement, we want them to be as reasonable and consistent with reality as possible.

Another important point to realize is that this is really a decision problem under uncertainty. Walton must choose an order quantity *before* knowing the demand for calendars. Unfortunately, we cannot use Solver because of the uncertainty.[6] Therefore, we develop a simulation model for any *fixed* order quantity. Then we run this simulation model with various order quantities to see which one appears to be best.

DEVELOPING THE SIMULATION MODEL

Now we discuss the ordering model. For any fixed order quantity, we show how Excel can be used to simulate 1000 replications (or any other number of replications). Each replication is an independent replay of the events that occur. To illustrate, suppose we want to simulate profit if Walton orders 200 calendars. Figure 16.18 illustrates the results obtained by simulating 1000 independent replications for this order quantity. (See the file **Walton Bookstore 1.xlsx**.) Note that there are a number of hidden rows in Figure 16.18. This is the case for several of the spreadsheet figures in this chapter. To develop this model, use the following steps.

1 **Inputs.** Enter the cost data in the range B4:B6, the probability distribution of demand in the range E5:F9, and the proposed order quantity, 200, in cell B9. Pay particular attention to the way the probability distribution is entered (and compare to the Discrete sheet in the **Probability Distributions.xlsx** file). Columns E and F contain the possible demand values and the probabilities from Table 16.1. It is also necessary (see step 3 for the reasoning) to have the cumulative probabilities in column D. To obtain these, first enter the value 0 in cell D5. Then enter the formula

=F5+D5

in cell D6 and copy it to the range D7:D9.

2 **Generate random numbers.** Enter a random number in cell B19 with the formula

=RAND()

and copy this to the range B20:B1018.

3 **Generate demands.** The key to the simulation is the generation of the customer demands in the range C19:C1018 from the random numbers in column B and the probability distribution of demand. Here is how it works. We divide the interval from 0 to 1 into five segments: 0.0 to 0.3 (length 0.3), 0.3 to 0.5 (length 0.2), 0.5 to 0.8 (length 0.3), 0.8 to 0.95 (length 0.15), and 0.95 to 1.0 (length 0.05). Note that these lengths are the probabilities of the various demands. Then we associate a demand with each random number, depending on which interval the random number falls in. For example, if a random number is 0.5279, this falls in the third interval, so we associate the third possible demand value, 200, with this random number.

[6]Palisade Corporation has another Excel add-in called RiskOptimizer that can be used for optimization in a simulation model. However, we do not discuss this software here, even though it *is* included on the CD-ROM.

Figure 16.18 Walton Bookstore Simulation Model

	A	B	C	D	E	F	G	H	I	J	K
1	Simulation of Walton's bookstore								Range names used:		
2									LookupTable	=Model!$D$5:$F$9	
3	Cost data			Demand distribution					Order_quantity	=Model!$B$9	
4	Unit cost	$7.50		Cum Prob	Demand	Probability			Profit	=Model!$G$19:$G$1018	
5	Unit price	$10.00		0.00	100	0.30			Unit_cost	=Model!$B$4	
6	Unit refund	$2.50		0.30	150	0.20			Unit_price	=Model!$B$5	
7				0.50	200	0.30			Unit_refund	=Model!$B$6	
8	Decision variable			0.80	250	0.15					
9	Order quantity	200		0.95	300	0.05					
10											
11	Summary measures for simulation below										
12	Average profit	$204.13		95% confidence interval for expected profit							
13	Stdev of profit	$328.04		Lower limit	$183.79						
14	Minimum profit	-$250.00		Upper limit	$224.46						
15	Maximum profit	$500.00									
16											
17	Simulation								Distribution of profit		
18	Replication	Random #	Demand	Revenue	Cost	Refund	Profit		Value	Frequency	
19	1	0.2249	100	$1,000	$1,500	$250	-$250		-250	299	
20	2	0.6693	200	$2,000	$1,500	$0	$500		125	191	
21	3	0.4164	150	$1,500	$1,500	$125	$125		500	510	
22	4	0.7562	200	$2,000	$1,500	$0	$500				
23	5	0.1581	100	$1,000	$1,500	$250	-$250				
24	6	0.0579	100	$1,000	$1,500	$250	-$250				
25	7	0.7452	200	$2,000	$1,500	$0	$500				
26	8	0.3717	150	$1,500	$1,500	$125	$125				
27	9	0.5077	200	$2,000	$1,500	$0	$500				
28	10	0.6669	200	$2,000	$1,500	$0	$500				
1012	994	0.7689	200	$2,000	$1,500	$0	$500				
1013	995	0.8861	250	$2,000	$1,500	$0	$500				
1014	996	0.4036	150	$1,500	$1,500	$125	$125				
1015	997	0.4092	150	$1,500	$1,500	$125	$125				
1016	998	0.5055	200	$2,000	$1,500	$0	$500				
1017	999	0.2457	100	$1,000	$1,500	$250	-$250				
1018	1000	0.3484	150	$1,500	$1,500	$125	$125				

The easiest way to implement this procedure is to use a VLOOKUP function. To do this, we create a "lookup table" in the range D5:E9 (range-named LookupTable). This table has the cumulative probabilities in column D and the possible demand values in column E. In fact, the whole purpose of the cumulative probabilities in column D is to allow us to use the VLOOKUP function. To generate the simulated demands, enter the formula

=VLOOKUP(B19,LookupTable,2)

This rather cumbersome procedure for generating a discrete random number is greatly simplified when we use @RISK.

in cell C19 and copy it to the range C20:C1018. For each random number in column B, this function compares the random number to the values in D5:D9 and returns the appropriate demand from E5:E9.

This step is the key to the simulation, so make sure you understand exactly what it entails. The rest is "bookkeeping," as we illustrate in the following steps. First, however, we note that a separate column for the random numbers in column B is not really necessary. They could be included in the VLOOKUP function directly, as in

=VLOOKUP(RAND(),LookupTable,2)

4 Revenue. Once the demand is known, the number of calendars sold is the smaller of the demand and the order quantity. For example, if 150 calendars are demanded, 150 will be sold. But if 250 are demanded, only 200 can be sold (because Walton orders only 200). Therefore, to calculate the revenue in cell D19, enter the formula

=Unit_price*MIN(C19,Order_quantity)

5 Ordering cost. The cost of ordering the calendars does not depend on the demand; it is the unit cost multiplied by the number ordered. Calculate this cost in cell E19 with the formula

=Unit_cost*Order_quantity

6 Refund. If the order quantity is greater than the demand, there is a refund of $2.50 for each calendar left over; otherwise, there is no refund. Therefore, calculate the refund in cell F19 with the formula

=Unit_refund*MAX(Order_quantity-C19,0)

For example, if demand is 150, then 50 calendars are left over, and this MAX is 50, the larger of 50 and 0. However, if demand is 250, then no calendars are left over, and this MAX is 0, the larger of −50 and 0. (This calculation could also be accomplished with an IF function instead of a MAX function.)

7 Profit. Calculate the profit in cell G19 with the formula

=D19-E19+F19

8 Copy to other rows. Do the same bookkeeping for the other 999 replications by copying the range D19:G19 to the range D20:G1018.

9 Summary measures. Each profit value in column G corresponds to one randomly generated demand. We usually want to see how these vary from one replication to another. First, calculate the average and standard deviation of the 1000 profits in cells B12 and B13 with the formulas

=AVERAGE(Profit)

and

=STDEV(Profit)

Similarly, calculate the smallest and largest of the 1000 profits in cells B14 and B15 with the MIN and MAX functions.

10 Confidence interval for expected profit. Calculate a 95% confidence interval for the expected profit in cells E13 and E14 with the formulas

=B12−1.96*B13/SQRT(1000)

and

=B12+1.96*B13/SQRT(1000)

(See the next section on confidence intervals for details.)

11 Distribution of simulated profits. There are only three possible profits, −$250, $125, or $500 (depending on whether demand is 100, 150, or at least 200—see the following discussion). We can use the COUNTIF function to count the number of times each of these possible profits is obtained. To do so, enter the formula

=COUNTIF(Profit,I19)

in cell J19 and copy it down to cell J21.

Discussion of the Simulation Results

At this point, it is a good idea to stand back and see what we have accomplished. First, in the body of the simulation, rows 19 through 1018, we randomly generated 1000 possible demands and the corresponding profits. Because there are only five possible demand values (100, 150, 200, 250, and 300), there are only five possible profit values: −$250, $125, $500, $500, and $500. Also, note that for the order quantity 200, the profit is $500 regardless of whether demand is 200, 250, or 300. (Make sure you understand why.) A tally of the profit values in these rows, including the hidden rows, indicates that there are 299 rows with profit equal to −$250 (demand 100), 191 rows with profit equal to $125 (demand 150), and 510 rows with profit equal to $500 (demand 200, 250, or 300). The average of these 1000 profits is $204.13, and their standard deviation is $328.04. (Again, remember that your answers will probably differ from these because your random numbers will probably differ from those shown in Figure 16.18.)

For this particular model, the output distribution is also discrete: There are only three possible profits for an order quantity of 200.

Typically, we want a simulation model to capture one or more output variables, such as profit. These output variables depend on random inputs, such as demand. Our goal is to estimate the probability distributions of the outputs. In the Walton simulation we estimate the probability distribution of profit to be

$$P(\text{Profit} = -\$250) = 299/1000 = 0.299$$

$$P(\text{Profit} = \$125) = 191/1000 = 0.191$$

$$P(\text{Profit} = \$500) = 510/1000 = 0.510$$

We also estimate the mean of this distribution to be $204.13 and its standard deviation to be $328.04. It is important to realize that if the entire simulation were run again with *different* random numbers (such as the ones you might have generated on your PC), the answers would be slightly different. This is the primary reason for the confidence interval in cells E13 and E14. This interval expresses our uncertainty about the *mean* of the profit distribution. Our best guess for this mean is the average of the 1000 profits we happened to observe. However, because the corresponding confidence interval is somewhat wide, from $183.79 to $224.46, we are not at all sure of the *true* mean of the profit distribution. We are only 95% confident that the true mean is within this interval. If we run this simulation again with different random numbers, the average profit might be quite different from the average profit we observed, $204.13, and the other summary statistics will probably also be different.

Notes about Confidence Intervals

The confidence interval provides a measure of accuracy of the mean profit, as estimated from the simulation.

It is common in computer simulations to estimate the mean of some distribution by the average of the simulated observations, just as we estimated the mean of the profit distribution by the average of 1000 profits. The usual practice is then to accompany this estimate with a **confidence interval**, which indicates the accuracy of the estimate. You should recall from Chapter 9 that to obtain a confidence interval for the mean, you start with the estimated mean and then add and subtract a multiple of the **standard error** of the estimated mean. If we denote the estimated mean (that is, the average) by $\overline{X}$, we have the following formula.

> **Confidence Interval for the Mean**
>
> $$\overline{X} \pm (\text{Multiple} \times \text{Standard Error of } \overline{X})$$

We repeat these basic facts about confidence intervals from Chapter 9 here for your convenience.

The standard error of $\overline{X}$ is the standard deviation of the observations divided by the square root of n, the number of observations:

Standard Error of $\overline{X}$

$$s/\sqrt{n}$$

Here, s is the symbol for the standard deviation of the observations. We obtain it with the STDEV function in Excel.

The "multiple" in the confidence interval formula depends on the confidence level and the number of observations. If the confidence level is 95%, for example, then the multiple is usually very close to 2, so a good guideline is to go out 2 standard errors on either side of the average to obtain an approximate 95% confidence interval for the mean.

Approximate 95% Confidence Interval for the Mean

$$\overline{X} \pm 2s/\sqrt{n}$$

To be more precise, if n is reasonably large, which is almost always the case in simulations, the central limit theorem from statistics implies that the correct multiple is the number from the standard normal distribution that cuts off probability 0.025 in each tail. This is a famous number in statistics: 1.96. Because 1.96 is very close to 2, it is acceptable for all practical purposes to use 2 instead of 1.96 when forming the confidence interval. (Note that this would be a different multiple if, say, we were using a 90% or a 99% confidence level rather than a 95% level.)

The idea is to choose the number of iterations large enough so that the resulting confidence interval will be sufficiently narrow.

Analysts often plan a simulation so that the confidence interval for the mean of some important output will be sufficiently narrow. The reasoning is that narrow confidence intervals imply more precision about the estimated mean of the output variable. If the confidence level is fixed at some value such as 95%, then the only way to narrow the confidence interval is to simulate more replications. Assuming that the confidence level is 95%, the following value of n is required to ensure that the resulting confidence interval will have half-length approximately equal to some specified value B:

Sample Size Determination

$$n = \frac{4 \times (\text{Estimated standard deviation})^2}{B^2}$$

To use this formula, we must have an estimate of the standard deviation of the output variable. For example, in the Walton simulation we saw that with $n = 1000$, the resulting 95% confidence interval for the mean profit has half-length ($224.46 - $183.99)/2 = $20.33. Suppose that we want to reduce this half-length to $12.50—that is, we want $B = $12.50. We do not know the exact standard deviation of the profit distribution, but we can estimate it from the simulation as $328.04. Therefore, to obtain the required confidence interval half-length B, we need to simulate n replications, where

$$n = \frac{4(328.04)^2}{12.50^2} \approx 2755$$

(When this formula produces a noninteger, it is common to round upward.) The claim, then, is that if we rerun the simulation with 2755 replications rather than 1000 replications, the half-length of the 95% confidence interval for the mean profit will be close to $12.50.

Finding the Best Order Quantity

We are not yet finished with the Walton example. So far, we have run the simulation for only a single order quantity, 200. Walton's ultimate goal is to find the best order quantity. Even this statement must be clarified. What do we mean by "best?" As in Chapter 7, we use the *expected* profit as our optimality criterion—that is, EMV—but we see that other characteristics of the profit distribution could influence our decision. We can obtain the required outputs with a data table. Specifically, we use a data table to rerun the simulation for other order quantities. We show this data table in Figure 16.19. (This is still part of the finished version of the **Walton Bookstore 1.xlsx** file.)

Figure 16.19

Data Table for
Walton Bookstore
Simulation

	L	M	N	O
17	Data table for average profit versus order quantity			
18	Order quantity	AvgProfit		
19		$204.13		
20	100	$250.00		
21	125	$256.44		
22	150	$262.88		
23	175	$233.50		
24	200	$204.13		
25	225	$120.19		
26	250	$36.25		
27	275	($76.00)		
28	300	($188.25)		

To optimize in simulation models, try various values of the decision variable(s) and run the simulation for each of them.

To create this table, enter the trial order quantities shown in the range A1023:A1031, enter the link **=B12** to the average profit in cell B12, and select the data table range, L19:M28. Then select Data Table from the What-If Analysis dropdown, specifying that the column input cell is B9. (See Figure 16.18.) Finally, construct a column chart of the average profits in the data table, as in Figure 16.20. Note that an order quantity of 150 appears to maximize the average profit. Its average profit of $262.88 is slightly higher than the average profits from nearby order quantities and much higher than the profit gained from an order of 200 or more calendars. However, again keep in mind that this is a simulation, so that all of these average profits depend on the particular random numbers we generated. If we rerun the simulation with different random numbers, it is conceivable that some other order quantity could be best.

To Freeze or Not to Freeze

In developing this simulation model, we didn't instruct you to freeze the random numbers in column B. The effect is that every time you press the F9 key or make any change to your spreadsheet model, a new set of simulated answers (including those in the data table) appear. Depending on the speed of your computer, this recalculation can take a few seconds, even for a relatively small simulation. For larger simulations, the recalculation time can be quite lengthy, which is one of the primary reasons you might want to freeze your random numbers.

However, the drawback is that once the random numbers are frozen, you are stuck with that particular set of random numbers. We typically do not freeze the random numbers. This way we are able to generate many different scenarios simply by pressing the F9 key.

Using a Data Table to Repeat Simulations

The Walton simulation is a particularly simple "one-line" simulation model. We are able to capture all of the logic—generating a demand and calculating the corresponding profit—in a single row. Then to replicate the simulation, we simply copy this row down as far as we like. Many simulation models are significantly more complex and require more than one row to capture the logic. Nevertheless, they still result in one or more output quantities (such as profit) that we want to replicate. We now illustrate another method that is more general (still using the Walton example). It uses a data table to generate the replications. Refer to Figure 16.21 and the file **Walton Bookstore 2.xlsx**.

Figure 16.20

Average Profit versus Order Quantity

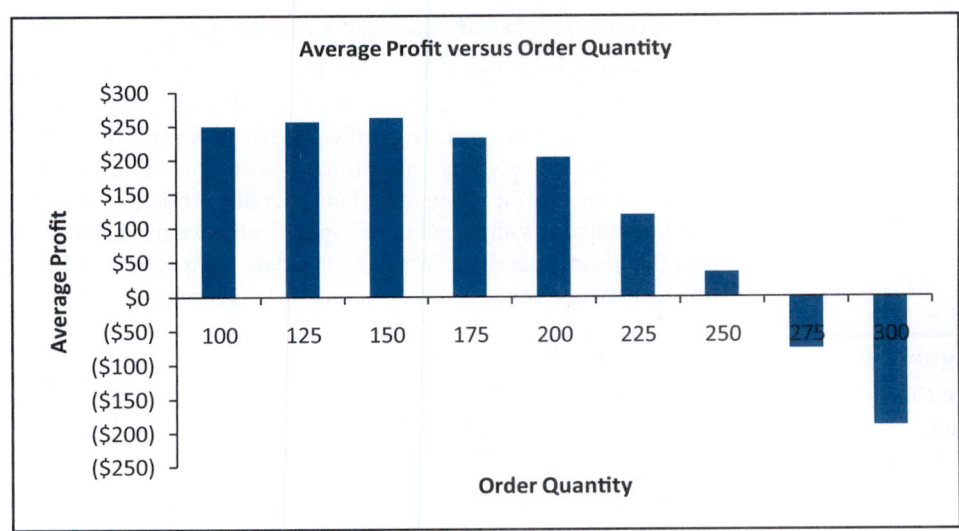

Figure 16.21 Using a Data Table to Simulate Replications

	A	B	C	D	E	F	G	H	I	J	K
1	Simulation of Walton's bookstore										
2											
3	Cost data			Demand distribution				Range names used:			
4	Unit cost	$7.50		CumProb	Demand	Probability		LookupTable	=Model!$D$5:$F$9		
5	Unit price	$10.00		0.00	100	0.30		Order_quantity	=Model!$B$9		
6	Unit refund	$2.50		0.30	150	0.20		Profit	=Model!$B$24:$B$1023		
7				0.50	200	0.30		Unit_cost	=Model!$B$4		
8	Decision variable			0.80	250	0.15		Unit_price	=Model!$B$5		
9	Order quantity	200		0.95	300	0.05		Unit_refund	=Model!$B$6		
10											
11	Summary measures from simulation below										
12	Average	$203.75		95% confidence interval for expected profit							
13	StDev	$324.03		Lower limit	$183.67						
14	Minimum	-$250.00		Upper limit	$223.83						
15	Maximum	$500.00									
16											
17	Simulation										
18		Demand	Revenue	Cost	Refund	Profit					
19		100	$1,000	$1,500	$250	-$250					
20											
21	Data table for replications, each shows profit from that replication										
22	Replication	Profit									
23		-$250									
24	1	$500									
25	2	-$250									
26	3	$500									
27	4	$500									
28	5	$500									
29	6	-$250									
30	7	-$250									
31	8	-$250									
32	9	-$250									
33	10	$500									
1017	994	-$250									
1018	995	-$250									
1019	996	$500									
1020	997	$500									
1021	998	-$250									
1022	999	-$250									
1023	1000	$500									

Through row 19, this model is exactly like the previous model. That is, we use the given data at the top of the spreadsheet to construct a typical "prototype" of the simulation in row 19. Actually, we use our earlier suggestion. We eliminate an explicit random number cell and enter the formula

=VLOOKUP(RAND(),LookupTable,2)

for demand in cell B19. Also, we use the following convention: We color any random quantity, in this case demand, green. This is totally optional. We do it only to remind ourselves that this cell contains a random number.

Note that we no longer copy this row 19 down—and we definitely do *not* freeze the cell with the random number, cell B19. Instead, we form a data table in the range A23:B1023 to replicate the basic simulation 1000 times. In column A we list the replication numbers, 1–1000. The formula in cell B23 is **=F19**. This forms a link to the profit from the prototype row for use in the data table. Then we create a data table and enter *any blank cell* (such as C23) as the column input cell. (No row input cell is necessary, so its box should be left empty.) This tricks Excel into repeating the row 19 calculations 1000 times, each time with a new random number, and reporting the profits in column B of the data table. (If we wanted to see other simulated quantities, such as revenue, for each replication, we could add extra output columns to the data table.)

Excel Tip: *How Data Tables Work*

To understand this procedure, you must understand exactly how data tables work. When we create a data table, Excel takes each value in the left column of the data table (here, column A), substitutes it into the cell we designate as the column input cell, recalculates the spreadsheet, and returns the "bottom line" value (or values) we have requested in the top row of the data table (such as profit). It might seem silly to substitute each replication number from column A into a blank cell such as cell C23, but this part is really irrelevant. The important part is the recalculation. Each recalculation leads to a new random demand and the corresponding profit, and these profits are the quantities we want. Of course, this means that we should not freeze the quantity in cell B19 before forming the data table. The whole point of the data table is to use a different random number for each replication, and this will occur only if the random demand in row 19 is left unfrozen.

Excel Tip: *Recalculation Mode*

Here is a useful Excel tip for speeding up recalculation. Select the Office button, then Excel Options, and then the Formulas group. Under the Calculation options, click on the Automatic Except for data tables option, and click on OK. Now when you change anything in your spreadsheet, everything will recalculate in the usual way except data tables. Data tables will not recalculate until you intentionally press the F9 key. Data tables can require a lot of computing time, so this option can be very useful. However, be aware that if you set this option and then form a data table, you will have to press F9 to make the data table recalculate the first time. Otherwise, you will see the same output value the whole way down the data table.

Using a Two-Way Data Table

We can carry this method one step further to see how the profit depends on the order quantity. Here we use a two-way data table with the replication number along the side and possible order quantities along the top. See Figure 16.22 and the file **Walton Bookstore 3.xlsx**. Now the data table range is A23:J1023, and the driving formula, entered in cell A23, is again the link **=F19**. The column input cell should again be *any blank cell*, and the row input cell should be B9 (the order quantity). Each cell in the body of the data table shows a simulated profit for a particular replication and a particular order quantity, and each is based on a *different* random demand.

Figure 16.22 Using a Two-Way Data Table for the Simulation Model

	A	B	C	D	E	F	G	H	I	J
1	Simulation of Walton's bookstore									
2										
3	Cost data			Demand distribution				Range names used:		
4	Unit cost	$7.50		CumProb	Demand	Probability		LookupTable	=Model!$D$5:$F$9	
5	Unit price	$10.00		0.00	100	0.30		Order_quantit	=Model!$B$9	
6	Unit refund	$2.50		0.30	150	0.20		Unit_cost	=Model!$B$4	
7				0.50	200	0.30		Unit_price	=Model!$B$5	
8	Decision variable			0.80	250	0.15		Unit_refund	=Model!$B$6	
9	Order quantity	200		0.95	300	0.05				
10										
11	Summary measures of simulated profits for each order quantity									
12				Order quantity						
13		100	125	150	175	200	225	250	275	300
14	Average profit	$250.00	$237.50	$255.00	$223.75	$140.00	$67.50	$55.00	-$70.00	-$300.00
15	Stdev profit	$0.00	$92.79	$176.70	$233.54	$346.85	$346.69	$449.74	$441.70	$460.84
16										
17	Simulation									
18		Demand	Revenue	Cost	Refund	Profit				
19		100	$1,000	$1,500	$250	-$250				
20										
21	Data table showing profit for replications with various order quantities									
22	Replication			Order quantity						
23	($250.00)	100	125	150	175	200	225	250	275	300
24	1	$250	$313	$375	$438	-$250	375	-500	500	-750
25	2	$250	$125	$0	-$125	$500	-375	-500	500	-750
26	3	$250	$313	$375	$438	-$250	-375	625	-625	-750
27	4	$250	$125	$375	-$125	-$250	0	-125	125	-750
28	5	$250	$313	$375	-$125	$500	-375	-500	-250	-375
29	6	$250	$313	$375	$250	-$250	0	-500	-625	0
30	7	$250	$125	$375	-$125	$125	562.5	250	687.5	0
31	8	$250	$313	$375	-$125	-$250	0	250	-625	-375
32	9	$250	$313	$0	$250	$125	0	-500	500	-750
1019	996	$250	$125	$0	$438	$500	562.5	-500	-250	0
1020	997	$250	$313	$375	$438	$500	375	-125	125	-750
1021	998	$250	$313	$375	$438	$500	-375	250	125	0
1022	999	$250	$313	$375	$438	$125	-375	-500	-250	-750
1023	1000	$250	$313	$375	$438	$500	375	-125	-625	0

Figure 16.23

Column Chart of Average Profits for Different Order Quantities

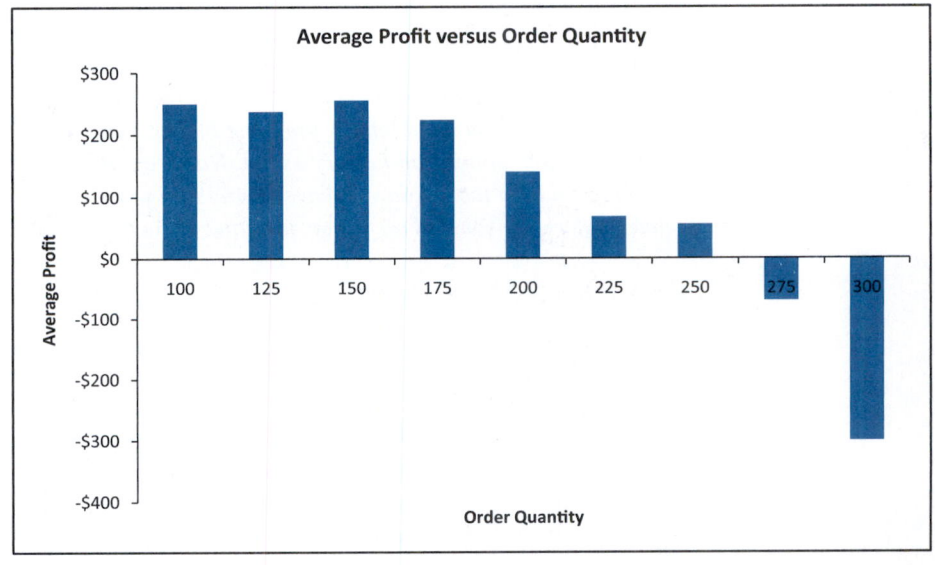

By averaging the numbers in each column of the data table (see row 14), we again see that 150 appears to be the best order quantity. It is also helpful to construct a column chart of these averages, as in Figure 16.23. Now, however, assuming you have not frozen anything, the data table and the corresponding chart will change each time you press the F9 key. To see whether 150 is always the best order quantity, you can press the F9 key and see whether the bar above 150 continues to be the highest. ∎

By now you should appreciate the usefulness of data tables in spreadsheet simulations. They allow us to take a "prototype" simulation and replicate its key results as often as we like. This method makes summary statistics (over the entire group of replications) and corresponding charts fairly easy to obtain. Nevertheless, it takes some work to create the data tables and charts. In the next section we see how the @RISK add-in does a lot of this work for us.

PROBLEMS

Level A

11. Suppose you own an expensive car and purchase auto insurance. This insurance has a $1000 deductible, so that if you have an accident and the damage is less than $1000, you pay for it out of your pocket. However, if the damage is greater than $1000, you pay the first $1000 and the insurance pays the rest. In the current year there is probability 0.025 of your having an accident. If you have an accident, the damage amount is normally distributed with mean $3000 and standard deviation $750.

  a. Use Excel and a one-way data table to simulate the amount you have to pay for damages to your car. Run 5000 iterations. Then find the average amount you pay, the standard deviation of the amounts you pay, and a 95% confidence interval for the average amount you pay. (Note that many of the amounts you pay will be 0 because you have no accidents.)

  b. Continue the simulation in part **a** by creating a two-way data table, where the row input is the deductible amount, varied from $500 to $2000 in multiples of $500. Now find the average amount you pay, the standard deviation of the amounts you pay, and a 95% confidence interval for the average amount you pay for each deductible amount.

  c. Do you think it is reasonable to assume that damage amounts are *normally* distributed? What would you criticize about this assumption? What might you suggest instead?

12. In August 2007, a car dealer is trying to determine how many 2008 cars to order. Each car ordered in August 2007 costs $10,000. The demand for the dealer's 2008 models has the probability distribution shown in the file **P16_12.xlsx**. Each car sells for $15,000. If demand for 2008 cars exceeds the number of cars ordered in August, the dealer must reorder at a cost of $12,000 per car. Excess cars can be disposed of at $9000 per car. Use simulation to determine how many cars to order in

August. For your optimal order quantity, find a 95% confidence interval for the expected profit.

13. In the Walton Bookstore example, suppose that Walton receives no money for the first 50 excess calendars returned but receives $2.50 for every calendar after the first 50 returned. Does this change the optimal order quantity?

14. A sweatshirt supplier is trying to decide how many sweatshirts to print for the upcoming NCAA basketball championships. The final four teams have emerged from the quarterfinal round, and there is now a week left until the semifinals, which are then followed in a couple of days by the finals. Each sweatshirt costs $10 to produce and sells for $25. However, in 3 weeks, any leftover sweatshirts will be put on sale for half price, $12.50. The supplier assumes that the demand for his sweatshirts during the next 3 weeks (when interest is at its highest) has the distribution shown in the file **P16_14.xlsx**. The residual demand, after the sweatshirts have been put on sale, has the distribution also shown in this file. The supplier, being a profit maximizer, realizes that every sweatshirt sold, even at the sale price, yields a profit. However, he also realizes that any sweatshirts produced but not sold (even at the sale price) must be thrown away, resulting in a $10 loss per sweatshirt. Analyze the supplier's problem with a simulation model.

Level B

15. In the Walton Bookstore example with a discrete demand distribution, explain why an order quantity other than one of the possible demands cannot maximize the expected profit. (*Hint:* Consider an order of 190 calendars. If this maximizes expected profit, then it must yield a higher expected profit than an order of 150 or 100. But then an order of 200 calendars must also yield a larger expected profit than 190 calendars. Why?)

16.5 INTRODUCTION TO @RISK

Spreadsheet simulation modeling has become extremely popular in recent years, both in the academic and corporate communities. Much of the reason for this popularity is due to simulation add-ins such as @RISK. There are two primary advantages to using such an add-in. First, an add-in gives us easy access to many probability distributions we might want to use in our simulation models. We already saw in Section 16.3 how the RISKDISCRETE, RISKNORMAL, and RISKTRIANG functions, among others, are easy to use and remember. Second, an add-in allows us to perform simulations much more easily than is possible with Excel alone. To replicate a simulation in Excel, we typically need to build a data table. Then we have to calculate summary statistics, such as averages, standard deviations, and percentiles, with built-in Excel functions. If we want graphs to enhance the analysis, we have to create them. In short, we have to perform a number of time-consuming steps for each simulation. Simulation add-ins such as @RISK perform much of this work for us automatically.

@RISK provides a number of functions for simulating from various distributions, and it takes care of all the bookkeeping in spreadsheet simulations. Simulating without @RISK in Excel requires much more work for the user.

Although we will focus on on @RISK in this book, it is not the only available simulation add-in for Excel. A worthy competitor is Crystal Ball, developed by Decisioneering (http://www.decisioneering.com). Crystal Ball has much of the same functionality as @RISK. In addition, because of the relative ease of developing "home-grown" applications in Excel with Excel's built-in macro language Visual Basic for Applications (VBA), some individuals are developing their own simulation add-ins for Excel. However, we have a natural bias for @RISK—we have been permitted by its developer, Palisade Corporation (http://www.palisade.com), to include it in the CD-ROM that is packaged with this book. If it were not included, you would have to purchase it from Palisade at a fairly steep price. Indeed, Microsoft Office does not include @RISK, Crystal Ball, or any other simulation add-in—you must purchase them separately.

@RISK Features

Here is an overview of some of @RISK's features. We discuss all of these in more detail later in this section.

1. @RISK contains a number of functions such as RISKNORMAL and RISKDISCRETE that make it easy to generate observations from the most important probability distributions. We discussed these in Section 16.3.

2. You can specify any cell or range of cells in your simulation model as **output cells**. When you run the simulation, @RISK automatically keeps summary measures (averages, standard deviations, percentiles, and others) from the values generated in these output cells across the replications. It also creates graphs such as histograms based on these values. In other words, @RISK takes care of tedious bookkeeping operations for you.

3. @RISK has a special function, RISKSIMTABLE, that allows you to run the same simulation several times, using a different value of some key input variable each time. This input variable is typically a decision variable. For example, suppose that you would like to simulate an inventory ordering policy (as in the Walton Bookstore example). Your ultimate purpose is to compare simulation outputs across a number of possible order quantities such as 100, 150, 200, 250, and 300. If you use an appropriate formula involving the RISKSIMTABLE function, the entire simulation is performed for each of these order quantities separately—with one click of a button. You can then compare the outputs to choose the "best" order quantity.

Loading @RISK

To build simulation models with @RISK, you need to have Excel open with @RISK added in. The first step, if you have not already done so, is to install the Palisade DecisionTools suite with the Setup program on the CD-ROM that is packaged with this book. Then you can load @RISK by clicking on the Windows Start button, selecting the Programs group, selecting the Palisade DecisionTools group, and finally selecting the @RISK item. If Excel is already open, this loads @RISK inside Excel. If Excel is not yet open, this launches Excel and @RISK simultaneously.[7] After @RISK is loaded, you see an @RISK tab and the corresponding @RISK ribbon in Figure 16.24.[8]

Figure 16.24   @RISK Toolbar

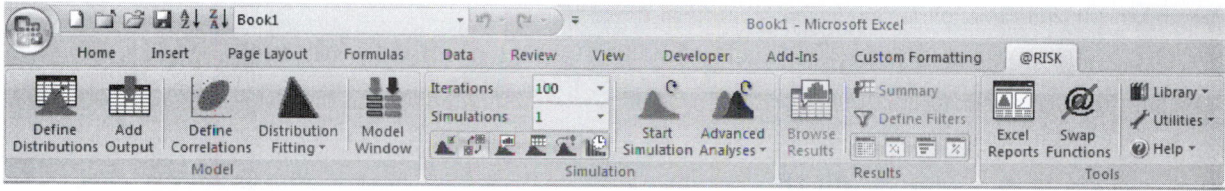

@RISK Models with a Single Random Input Variable

The majority of the work (and thinking) goes into developing the model. Setting up up @RISK and then running it are relatively easy.

In the remainder of this section we illustrate some of @RISK's functionality by revisiting the Walton Bookstore example. Then in the next chapter, we use @RISK to help develop a number of interesting simulation models. Throughout our discussion, you should keep one very important idea in mind. The development of a simulation model is basically a two-step procedure. The first step is to build the model itself. This step requires you to build in all of the logic that transforms inputs (including @RISK functions such as RISKDISCRETE) into outputs (such as profit). This is where most of the work and thinking go, exactly as in models from previous chapters, and @RISK cannot do this for you. It is *your* job to enter the formulas that link inputs to outputs appropriately. However, once this logic has been incorporated, @RISK takes over in the second step. It automatically replicates your model, with different random numbers on each replication, and it reports any summary measures that you request in tabular or graphical form. Therefore, @RISK can greatly decrease the amount of "busy work" you need to do, but it is not a magic bullet!

We begin by analyzing an example with a single random input variable.

EXAMPLE   16.2 USING @RISK AT WALTON BOOKSTORE

Recall that Walton Bookstore buys calendars for $7.50, sells them at the regular price of $10, and gets a refund of $2.50 for all calendars that cannot be sold. In contrast to Example 16.1, we now assume that Walton estimates a triangular probability distribution for demand, where the minimum, most likely, and maximum values of demand are 100, 175, and 300, respectively. The company wants to use this probability distribution, together with @RISK, to simulate the profit for any particular order quantity. It eventually wants to find the "best" order quantity.

---

[7]We have had the best luck when we (1) close other applications we are not currently using, and (2) launch Excel and @RISK together by starting @RISK. However, it is also possible to start @RISK *after* Excel is already running.

[8]If you are used to the previous version (4.5) of @RISK, you are in for some surprises with the new version (5.0) packaged with this book. The main differences are in where you find your results, as we explain shortly. However, the model building step–usually the most time-consuming and difficult step—is no different from before.

This is the same Walton Bookstore model as before, except that we now use a triangular distribution for demand.

Objective To learn about @RISK's basic functionality by revisiting the Walton Bookstore problem.

WHERE DO THE NUMBERS COME FROM?

The monetary values are the same as before. The parameters of the triangular distribution of demand are probably Walton's best subjective estimates, possibly guided by its experience with previous calendars.

Solution

We use this example to illustrate the most important features of @RISK. We first see how it helps us to implement an appropriate input probability distribution for demand. Then we use it to build a simulation model for a specific order quantity and generate outputs from this model. Finally, we see how the RISKSIMTABLE function enables us to simultaneously generate outputs from several order quantities so that we can choose a "best" order quantity.

DEVELOPING THE SIMULATION MODEL

The spreadsheet model for profit is essentially the same as we developed previously *without* @RISK, as shown in Figure 16.25. (See the file **Walton Bookstore 4.xlsx**.) The only new things to be aware of are the following.

1 **Input distribution.** To generate a random demand, enter the formula

=ROUND(RISKTRIANG(E4,E5,E6),0)

in cell B13 for the random demand. This uses the RISKTRIANG function to generate a demand from the given input distribution. (As before, we continue to color random input cells green.) We also use Excel's ROUND function to round demand to the nearest integer. Recall from our discussion in Section 16.3 that Excel has no built-in functions to generate random numbers from a triangular distribution, but it is easy with @RISK.

Figure 16.25

Simulation Model with a Fixed Order Quantity

	A	B	C	D	E	F	G	H	I	J
1	Simulation of Walton's Bookstore using @RISK							Range names used:		
2								Order_quantity	=Model!$B$9	
3	Cost data			Demand distribution - triangular				Profit	=Model!$F$13	
4	Unit cost	$7.50		Minimum	100			Unit_cost	=Model!$B$4	
5	Unit price	$10.00		Most likely	175			Unit_price	=Model!$B$5	
6	Unit refund	$2.50		Maximum	300			Unit_refund	=Model!$B$6	
7										
8	Decision variable									
9	Order quantity	200								
10										
11	Simulation									
12		Demand	Revenue	Cost	Refund	Profit				
13		189	$1,890	$1,500	$28	$418				
14										
15	Summary measures of profit from @RISK - based on 1000 iterations									
16	Minimum	-$235.00								
17	Maximum	$500.00								
18	Average	$337.51								
19	Standard deviation	$189.06								
20	5th percentile	-$47.50								
21	95th percentile	$500.00								
22	P(profit <= 300)	0.360								
23	P(profit > 400)	0.516								

2 Output cell. When we run the simulation, we want @RISK to keep track of profit. In @RISK's terminology, we need to designate the Profit cell, F13, as an **output cell**. To do this, select cell F13 and then click on the Add Output button on the @RISK ribbon. (See Figure 16.24.) This adds **RISKOUTPUT(*"label"*)+** to the cell's formula. (Here, "label" is a label that @RISK uses for its reports. In this case it makes sense to use "Profit" as the label.) The formula in cell F13 changes from

=C13+E13-D13

to

=RISKOUTPUT("Profit")+C13+E13-D13

The RISKOUTPUT function indicates that a cell is an output cell, so that @RISK will keep track of its values throughout the simulation.

The plus sign following RISKOUTPUT does *not* indicate addition. It is simply @RISK's way of indicating that we want to keep track of the value in this cell (for reporting reasons) as the simulation progresses. Any number of cells can be designated in this way as output cells. They are typically the "bottom line" values of primary interest. We color such cells gray for emphasis.

3 Summary functions. There are several places where you can store @RISK results. One of these is to use @RISK statistical functions to place results right in your model worksheet. @RISK provides several functions for summarizing output values. We illustrate some of these in the range B16:B23 of Figure 16.25. They contain the formulas

=RISKMIN(Profit)

=RISKMAX(Profit)

=RISKMEAN(Profit)

=RISKSTDDEV(Profit)

=RISKPERCENTILE(Profit,0.05)

=RISKPERCENTILE(Profit,0.95)

=RISKTARGET(Profit,300)

and

=1-RISKTARGET(Profit,400)

These @RISK summary functions allow you to show simulation results on the same sheet as the model. However, they are totally optional.

The values in these cells are not meaningful until you run the simulation. However, once the simulation runs, these formulas capture summary statistics of profit. For example, RISKMEAN calculates the average of the 1000 simulated profits, RISKPERCENTILE finds the value such that the specified percentage of simulated profits are less than or equal to this value, and RISKTARGET finds the percentage of simulated profits less than or equal to the specified value. Although these same summary statistics also appear in other @RISK reports, it is sometimes handy to have them in the same worksheet as the model.

Running the Simulation

Now that we have developed the model for Walton, the rest is straightforward. The procedure is always the same: (1) specify simulation settings, (2) run the simulation, and (3) examine the results.

Figure 16.26

Simulation Group
on @RISK Ribbon

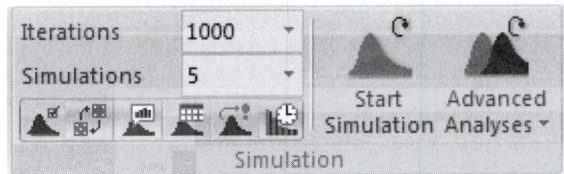

1 **Simulation settings.** We must first choose some simulation settings. To do so, the buttons on the left of the Simulation group (see Figure 16.26) are useful. We typically do the following:

- Set Iterations to a number such as 1000. (@RISK calls "replications" iterations.) Any number could be used, but because the educational version of @RISK allows only 1000 uninterrupted iterations, we typically choose 1000.

- Set Simulations to 1. In a later section, we'll see why you might want to request multiple simulations.

- Click on the "dice" button so that it becomes orange. This button is actually a toggle for what appears on your worksheet. If it is orange, the setting is called "Monte Carlo" and all random cells appear random (they change when you press the F9 key). If it is blue, only the *means* appear in random input cells and the F9 key has no effect. We prefer the Monte Carlo setting, although it has no effect on how the simulation is actually run.

- Many more settings are available by clicking on the button to the left of the "dice" button, but the ones we mentioned should suffice. In addition, more permanent settings can be chosen from Application Settings under Utilities on the @RISK ribbon. Figure 16.27 shows three particular settings we suggest: (1) Place Reports In: Active Workbook (rather than a new workbook), (2) Iterations: 1000, and (3) Standard Recalc: Random Values (which saves you from having to click on the "dice" button each time).

Figure 16.27

Application Settings
Under @RISK
Utilities

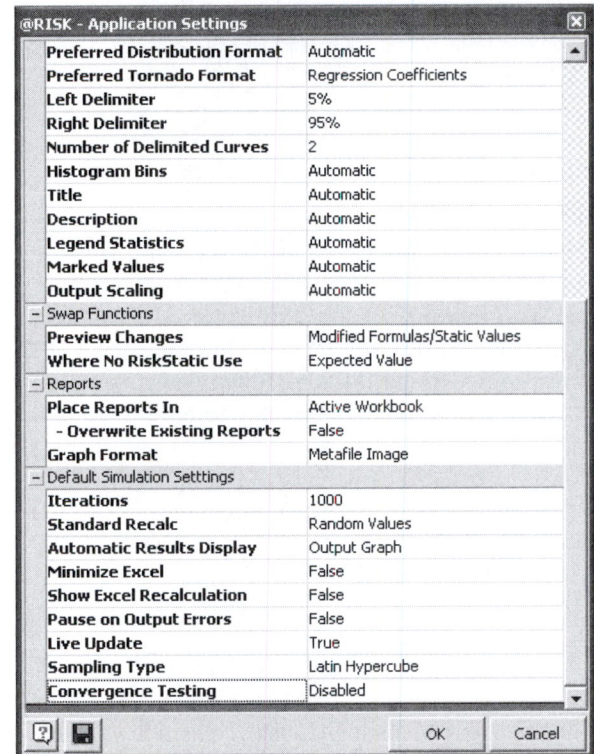

@RISK TECHNICAL ISSUE: *Latin Hypercube Sampling*

Leave Latin Hypercube sampling on. It produces more accurate results.

One setting you shouldn't change is the Sampling Type (available from the button to the left of the "dice" button). It should remain at the default Latin Hypercube setting. This is a more efficient option than the other (Monte Carlo) option because it produces a more accurate estimate of the profit distribution. In fact, we were surprised how accurate it is. In repeated runs of this model, always using different random numbers, we virtually always got a mean profit within a few pennies of \$337.50. It turns out that this is the true mean profit for this input distribution of demand. Amazingly, simulation estimates it correctly—almost exactly—on virtually every run! Unfortunately, this means that a confidence interval for the mean, based on @RISK's outputs and the usual confidence interval formula (which assumes Monte Carlo sampling), is much wider (more pessimistic) than it should be. Therefore, we do not even calculate such confidence intervals from here on.

2 **Run the simulation.** To run the simulation, simply click on the Start Simulation on the @RISK ribbon. When you do so, @RISK repeatedly generates a random number for each random input cell, recalculates the worksheet, and keeps track of all output cell values. You can watch the progress at the bottom left of the screen. (*Note:* Palisade has informed us that Excel 2007 does repetitive calculations much more slowly than in Excel 2003, so if you're used to @RISK simulations running very quickly, be patient. The "problem" will hopefully have been fixed in a Microsoft Office service pack by the time you read this.)

3 **Examine the Results.** The big questions are (1) which results you want and (2) where you want them. @RISK provides a lot of possibilities, and we mention only our favorites.

- You can ask for summary measures right in your model worksheet by using the @RISK statistical functions, such as RISKMEAN, that we discussed earlier.

For a quick histogram of an output or input, select the output or input cell and click on @RISK's Browse Results button.

- The quickest way to get results is to select an input or output cell (we chose the profit cell, F13) and then click on the Browse Results button on the @RISK ribbon. (See Figure 16.28.) This shows an interactive histogram of the selected value, as shown in Figure 16.29. You can move the sliders on this histogram to see probabilities of various outcomes. Note that the window you see from Browse Results is temporary—it goes away when you click on Close. You can make a permanent copy of the chart by clicking on the third button from the left (see the bottom of Figure 16.29) and choosing one of the copy options.

Figure 16.28

Results and Tools Groups on @RISK Ribbon

@RISK Tip: *Saving Graphs and Tables*

When you run a simulation with @RISK and then save your file, it asks whether you want to save your graphs and tables. We suggest that you save them. This makes your file slightly larger, but when you reopen it, the temporary graphs and tables, such as the histogram in Figure 16.29, will still be available. Otherwise, you will have to rerun the simulation.

Figure 16.29

Interactive
Histogram of Profit
Output

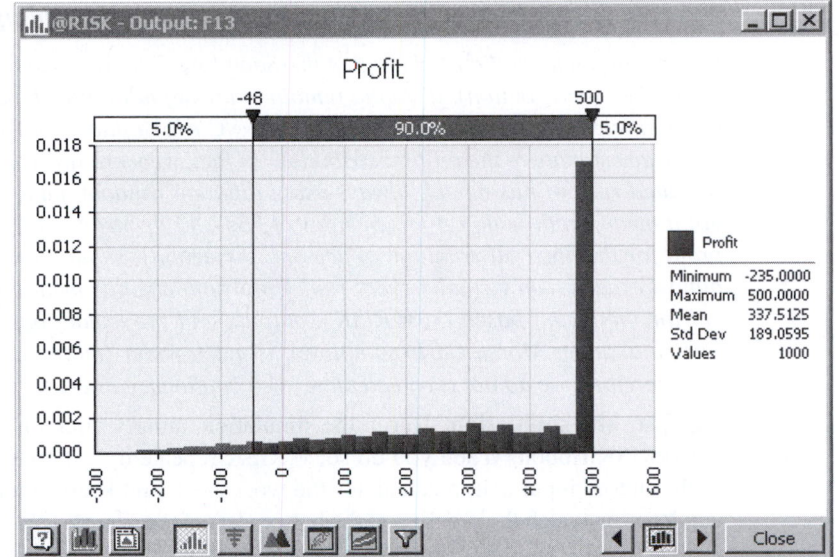

- You can click on the Summary button (again, see Figure 16.28) to see the temporary window in Figure 16.30 with the summary measures for Profit. In general, this report shows the summary for *all* designated inputs and outputs. By default, this Results Summary window shows a mini histogram for each output and a number of numerical summary measures. However, it is easy to customize. If you right-click on this table and choose Columns for Table, you can check or uncheck any of the options. For future screenshots in this book, we elected *not* to show the Graph and Errors columns, but instead to show median and standard deviation columns.

Figure 16.30   Summary Table of Profit Output

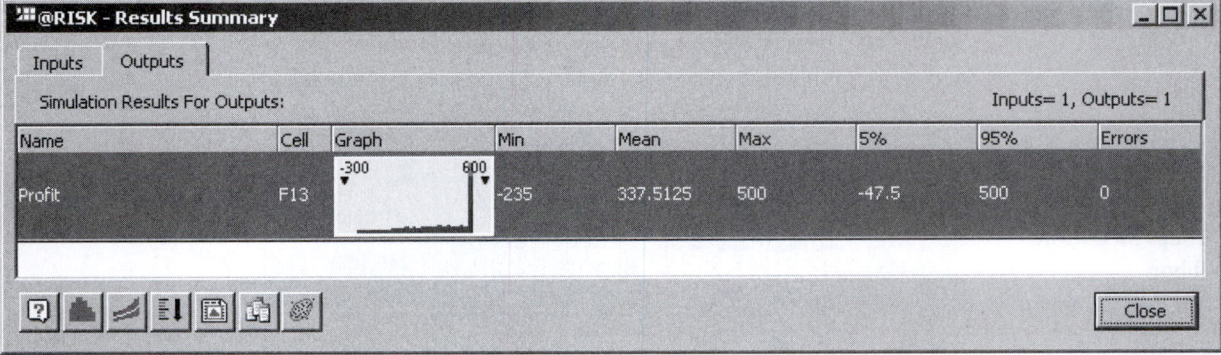

- You can click on the Excel Reports button (again, see Figure 16.28) to choose from a number of reports that are placed on new worksheets. This is a good option if you want permanent (but non-interactive) copies of reports in your workbook. As an example, Figure 16.31 shows (part of) the Detailed Statistics report you can request. It has the same information as the summary report in Figure 16.30, plus a lot more.

Figure 16.31

@RISK Detailed
Statistics Report

	B	C	D
1	**@Risk Detailed Statistics**		
2	**Performed By:** Chris Albright		
3	**Date:** Monday, October 08, 2007 2:33:55 PM		
4			
5			
6	Name	Profit	Demand
7	Description	Output	RiskTriang(E4,E5,E6)
8	Cell	Model!F13	Model!B13
9	Minimum	-235	101.946
10	Maximum	500	296.6687
11	Mean	337.5125	191.6672
12	Std Deviation	189.0595	41.2748
13	Variance	35743.51	1703.609
14	Skewness	-0.9482242	0.2363251
15	Kurtosis	2.792944	2.404146
16	Errors	0	0
17	Mode	290	173.9869
18	5% Perc	-47.5	127.369
19	10% Perc	42.5	138.6223
20	15% Perc	102.5	147.3225
21	20% Perc	162.5	154.7333
22	25% Perc	207.5	161.1572
23	30% Perc	252.5	166.99
24	35% Perc	290	172.4364

Discussion of the Simulation Results

The strength of @RISK is that it keeps track of any outputs you specify and then allows you to show the corresponding results as graphs or tables, in temporary windows or in permanent worksheets. As we have seen, @RISK gives you several options for displaying results, and we encourage you to explore the possibilities. However, don't lose sight of the overall goal: You want to see how outputs vary as the random inputs vary, and you want reports that "tell the story" most effectively. For this particular example, the results in Figures 16.25, 16.29, 16.30, and 16.31 allow us to conclude the following:

- The smallest simulated profit (out of 1000) was −$235, the largest was $500, the average was $337.51, and the standard deviation of the 1000 profits was $189.06. Five percent of the simulated profits were −$47.50 or below, and 95 percent were $500 or above. Also, 36% of the profits were less than or equal to $300, and 51.6% were larger than $400. (See Figure 16.25. These results are also available from the summary table in Figure 16.30 or the detailed statistics report in Figure 16.31. In particular, the bottom of the detailed statistics report, not shown in the figure, allows you to ask for any percentiles or "target" values.)

- The profit distribution, for this particular order quantity, is extremely skewed to the left, with a large bar at $500. (See Figure 16.29.) Do you see why? It's because profit is exactly $500 if demand is greater than or equal to the order quantity, 200. In other words, the probability that profit is $500 equals the probability that demand is at least 200. (This probability is 0.4.) Lower demands result in decreasing profits, which explains the gradual decline in the histogram from right to left.

USING RISKSIMTABLE

Walton's ultimate goal is to choose an order quantity that provides a large average profit. We could rerun the simulation model several times, each time with a different order quantity in the order quantity cell, and compare the results. However, this has two drawbacks.

First, it takes a lot of time and work. The second drawback is more subtle. Each time we run the simulation, we get a *different* set of random demands. Therefore, one of the order quantities could win the contest just by luck. For a fairer comparison, it is better to test each order quantity on the *same* set of random demands.

The RISKSIMTABLE function in @RISK enables us to obtain a fair comparison quickly and easily. We illustrate this function in Figure 16.32. (See the file **Walton Bookstore 5.xlsx**.) There are two modifications to the previous model. The first is that we have listed order quantities we want to test in row 9. (We chose these as representative order quantities. You could change, or add to, this list.) Second, instead of entering a *number* in cell B9, we enter the *formula*

=**RISKSIMTABLE(D9:H9)**

The RISKSIMTABLE function allows us to run several simulations at once—one for each value of some variable (usually a decision variable).

Figure 16.32

Model with a RISKSIMTABLE Function

	A	B	C	D	E	F	G	H	I	J	K
1	Simulation of Walton's Bookstore using @RISK								Range names used:		
2									Order_quantity	=Model!$B$9	
3	Cost data			Demand distribution - triangular					Profit	=Model!$F$13	
4	Unit cost	$7.50		Minimum	100				Unit_cost	=Model!$B$4	
5	Unit price	$10.00		Most likely	175				Unit_price	=Model!$B$5	
6	Unit refund	$2.50		Maximum	300				Unit_refund	=Model!$B$6	
7											
8	Decision variable			Order quantities to try							
9	Order quantity	150		150	175	200	225	250			
10											
11	Simulated quantities										
12		Demand	Revenue	Cost	Refund	Profit					
13		180	$1,500	$1,125	$0	$375					
14											
15	Summary measures of profit from @RISK - based on 1000 iterations for each simulation										
16	Simulation	1	2	3	4	5					
17	Order quantity	150	175	200	225	250					
18	Minimum	$15.00	-$110.00	-$235.00	-$360.00	-$485.00					
19	Maximum	$375.00	$437.50	$500.00	$562.50	$625.00					
20	Average	$354.16	$367.19	$337.48	$270.32	$175.02					
21	Standard deviation	$58.98	$121.88	$189.07	$247.08	$287.01					
22	5th percentile	$202.50	$77.50	-$47.50	-$172.50	-$297.50					
23	95th percentile	$375.00	$437.50	$500.00	$562.50	$625.00					

Note that the list does not need to be entered in the spreadsheet (although we believe this is a good idea). We could instead enter the formula

=**RISKSIMTABLE({150,175,200,225,250})**

where the list of numbers must be enclosed in curly brackets. In either case, the worksheet displays the first member of the list, 150, and the corresponding calculations for this first order quantity. However, the model is now set up to run the simulation for *all* order quantities in the list.

To implement this, only one setting needs to be changed. As before, enter 1000 for the number of iterations, but this time enter 5 for the number of simulations. @RISK then runs 5 simulations of 1000 iterations each, one simulation for each order quantity in the list, and it uses the *same* 1000 random demands for each simulation.

@RISK Function: *RISKSIMTABLE*

To run several simulations all at once, enter the formula =*RISKSIMTABLE* **(InputRange)** *in any cell. Here,* InputRange *refers to a list of the values to be simulated, such as various order quantities. Before running the simulation, make sure the number of simulations is set to the number of values in the* InputRange *list.*

We can again get results from the simulation in various ways. Here are some possibilities.

- We can enter the same @RISK statistical functions in cells in the model worksheet, as shown in rows 18–23 of Figure 16.32. The trick is to realize that each such function can have a last argument that specifies the simulation number. For example, the formulas in cells C20 and C22 are

=**RISKMEAN(Profit,C16)**

and

=**RISKPERCENTILE(Profit,0.05,C16)**

Remember that the results in these cells are meaningless until you run the simulation.

■ We can select the Profit cell and click on Browse Results to see a histogram of profits, as shown in Figure 16.33. By default, the histogram shown is for the *first* simulation, where the order quantity is 150. However, if you click on the red button with the pound sign, you can select any of the simulations. As an example, Figure 16.34 shows the histogram of profits for the fifth simulation, where the order quantity is 250. (Do you see why these two histograms are so different? When the order quantity is 150, there is a high probability of selling out; hence the spike on the right is large. But the probability of selling out with an order quantity of 250 is much lower; hence its spike on the right is much less dominant.)

Figure 16.33

Histogram of Profit with Order Quantity 150

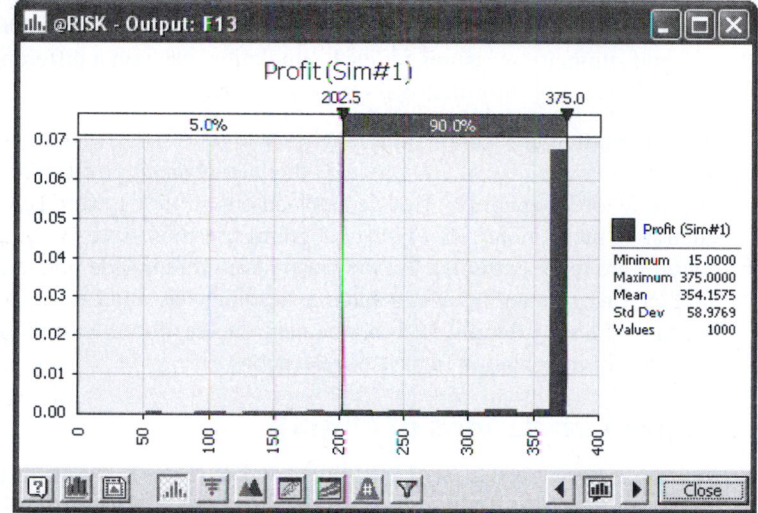

Figure 16.34

Histogram of Profit with Order Quantity 250

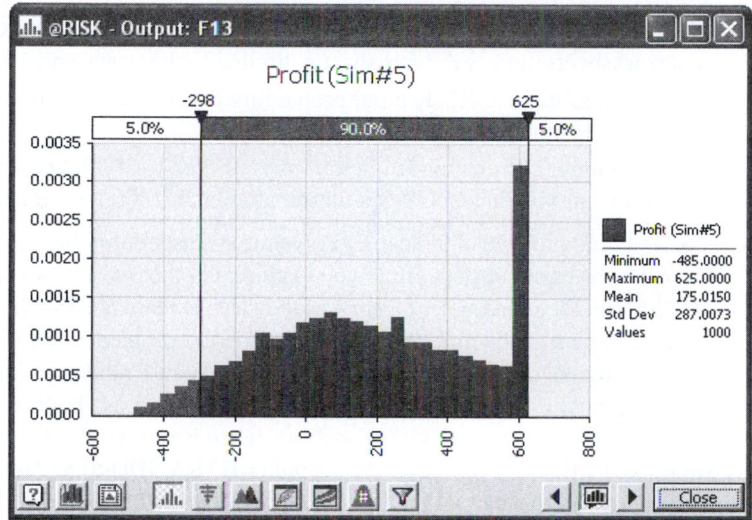

- We can click on the Summary button to get the results from all simulations shown in Figure 16.35. (These results match those in Figure 16.32.)

Figure 16.35 Summary Report for All Five Simulations

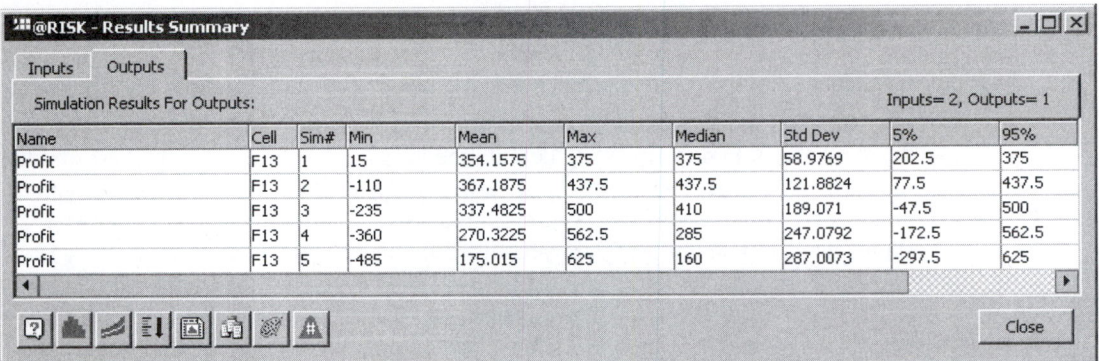

- We can click on Excel Reports to get any of a number of reports on permanent worksheets. Specifically, we suggest you try Quick Reports. This produces several graphs and summary measures for each simulation, each on a different worksheet. This provides a lot of information for almost no work!

For this particular example, the results in Figures 16.32–16.35 are illuminating. We see that an order quantity of 200 provides the largest *mean* profit. However, is this necessarily the "best" order quantity? This depends on our attitude toward risk. Certainly, larger order quantities incur more risk (their histograms are more spread out, their 5th and 95th percentiles are more extreme), but they also have more upside potential. On the other hand, a smaller order quantity, while having a somewhat smaller mean, might be preferable because of less variability. It is *not* an easy choice, but at least the simulation results gives us plenty of information to base our decision on.

Some Limitations of @RISK

The educational version of @RISK included with the book has some limitations you should be aware of. (If you want to spend several hundred dollars, you can purchase the commercial version of @RISK without these limitations.)

- The simulation model must be contained in a single workbook with at most four worksheets, and each worksheet is limited to 300 rows and 100 columns.
- The number of @RISK input probability distribution functions, such as RISKNORMAL, is limited to 100.
- The number of unattended iterations is limited to 1000. You can request more than 1000, but you have to click a button after each 1000 iterations.

To avoid potential problems, close all other workbooks when running an @RISK model.

The first limitation shouldn't cause problems, at least not for the model sizes discussed in this book. However, we strongly urge you to close all other workbooks when you are running an @RISK simulation model, *especially* if they also contain @RISK functions. The second limitation can be a problem, especially in multiperiod problems. For example, if you are simulating 52 weeks of a year, and each week requires two random inputs, you are already over the 100-function limit. One way to get around this is to use built-in Excel functions for random inputs rather than @RISK functions whenever possible. For example, if you want to simulate the flip of a fair coin, the formula **=IF(RAND()<0.5,"Heads","Tails")** works just as well as the formula **=IF(RISKUNIFORM(0,1)<0.5,"Heads","Tails")**, but the former doesn't count against the 100-function limit.

@RISK Models with Several Random Input Variables

We conclude this section with another modification of the Walton Bookstore example. To this point, there has been a single random variable, demand. Often there are several random variables, each reflecting some uncertainty, and we want to include each of these in the simulation model. The following example illustrates how this can be done, and it also illustrates a very useful feature of @RISK, its sensitivity analysis.

EXAMPLE **16.3 ADDITIONAL UNCERTAINTY AT WALTON BOOKSTORE**

As in the previous Walton Bookstore example, Walton needs to place an order for next year's calendar. We continue to assume that the calendars sell for $10 and customer demand for the calendars at this price is triangularly distributed with minimum value, most likely value, and maximum value equal to 100, 175, and 300. However, there are now two other sources of uncertainty. First, the maximum number of calendars Walton's supplier can supply is uncertain and is modeled with a triangular distribution. Its parameters are 125 (minimum), 200 (most likely), and 250 (maximum). Once Walton places an order, the supplier will charge $7.50 per calendar *if* he can supply the entire Walton order. Otherwise, he will charge only $7.25 per calendar. Second, unsold calendars can no longer be returned to the supplier for a refund. Instead, Walton will put them on sale for $5 apiece after January 1. At that price, Walton believes the demand for leftover calendars is triangularly distributed with parameters 0, 50, and 75. Any calendars *still* left over, say, after March 1, will be thrown away. Walton again wants to use simulation to analyze the resulting profit for various order quantities.

Objective To develop and analyze a simulation model with multiple sources of uncertainty using @RISK, and to introduce @RISK's sensitivity analysis features.

WHERE DO THE NUMBERS COME FROM?

As in Example 16.2, the monetary values are straightforward, and the parameters of the triangular distributions are probably educated guesses, possibly based on experience with previous calendars.

Solution

As always, we first need to develop the model. Then we can run the simulation with @RISK and examine the results.

DEVELOPING THE SIMULATION MODEL

The completed model is in Figure 16.36. (See the file **Walton Bookstore 6.xlsx**.) The model itself requires a bit more logic than the previous Walton model. It can be developed with the following steps.

1 Random inputs. There are three random inputs in this model: the most the supplier can supply Walton, the customer demand when the selling price is $10, and the customer demand for sale-price calendars. Generate these in cells B14, E14, and H14 (using the ROUND function to obtain integers) with the RISKTRIANG function. Specifically, the formulas in cells B14, E14, and H14 are

=ROUND(RISKTRIANG(I5,I6,I7),0)

=ROUND(RISKTRIANG (E5,E6,E7),0)

and

=ROUND(RISKTRIANG (F5,F6,F7),0)

Figure 16.36

@RISK Simulation Model with Three Random Inputs

	A	B	C	D	E	F	G	H	I	J	K	L	M
1	Simulation of Walton's Bookstore using @RISK										Range names used:		
2											Order_quantity	=Model!$B$10	
3	Cost data			Demand distribution: triangular							Profit	=Model!$J$14	
4	Unit cost 1	$7.50			Regular price	Sale price		Supply distribution: triangular			Regular_price	=Model!$B$6	
5	Unit cost 2	$7.25		Minimum	100	0		Minimum	125		Sale_price	=Model!$B$7	
6	Regular price	$10.00		Most likely	175	50		Most likely	200		Unit_cost_1	=Model!$B$4	
7	Sale price	$5.00		Maximum	300	75		Maximum	250		Unit_cost_2	=Model!$B$5	
8													
9	Decision variable			Order quantities to try									
10	Order quantity	150		150	175	200	225	250					
11													
12	Simulated quantities					At regular price		At sale price					
13		Maximum supply	Actual supply	Cost	Demand	Revenue	Left over	Demand	Revenue	Profit			
14		172	150	$1,125	192	$1,500	0	59	$0	$375			
15													
16	Summary measures of profit from @RISK - based on 1000 iterations for each simulation												
17	Simulation	1	2	3	4	5							
18	Order quantity	150	175	200	225	250							
19	Minimum	$15.00	-$172.50	-$360.00	-$394.00	-$394.00							
20	Maximum	$409.75	$478.50	$547.25	$616.00	$671.00							
21	Average	$361.57	$389.55	$394.50	$395.03	$397.62							
22	Standard deviation	$43.51	$94.74	$148.51	$176.27	$178.58							
23	5th percentile	$265.00	$182.50	$55.00	$11.50	$14.25							
24	95th percentile	$375.00	$456.50	$528.00	$577.50	$588.50							

Note that in cell H14, we generate the random *potential* demand for calendars at the sale price even though there might not be any calendars left to put on sale.

2 Actual supply. The number of calendars supplied to Walton is the smaller of the number ordered and the maximum the supplier is able to supply. Calculate this value in cell C14 with the formula

=MIN(B14,Order_quantity)

3 Order cost. Walton gets the reduced price, $7.25, if the supplier cannot supply the entire order. Otherwise, Walton must pay $7.50 per calendar. Therefore, calculate the total order cost in cell D14 with the formula (using the obvious range names)

=IF(B14>=Order_quantity,Unit_cost_1,Unit_cost_2)*C14

4 Other quantities. The rest of the model is straightforward. Calculate the revenue from regular-price sales in cell F14 with the formula

=Regular_price*MIN(C14,E14)

Calculate the number left over after regular-price sales in cell G14 with the formula

=MAX(C14-E14,0)

Calculate the revenue from sale-price sales in cell I14 with the formula

=Sale_price*MIN(G14,H14)

Finally, calculate profit and designate it as an output cell for @RISK in cell J14 with the formula

=RISKOUTPUT("Profit")+F14+I14-D14

We could also designate other cells (the revenue cells, for example) as output cells, but we have chosen to have a single output cell, Profit.

5 Order quantities. As before, enter a RISKSIMTABLE function in cell B10 so that Walton can try different order quantities. Specifically, enter the formula

=RISKSIMTABLE(D10:H10)

in cell B10.

Running the Simulation

On each iteration, @RISK generates a new set of random inputs and calculates the corresponding output(s).

As always, the next steps are to specify the simulation settings (we chose 1000 iterations and 5 simulations), and run the simulation. It is important to realize what @RISK does when it runs a simulation, especially when there are several random input cells. For each iteration, @RISK generates a random value for each input variable *independently*. In this example, it generates a maximum supply in cell B14 from one triangular distribution, it generates a regular-price demand in cell E14 from another triangular distribution, and it generates a sale-price demand in cell H14 from a third triangular distribution. With these input values, it then calculates profit. For each order quantity, it then iterates this procedure 1000 times and keeps track of the corresponding profits.[9]

Discussion of the Simulation Results

Selected results are given in Figures 16.36 (at the bottom) and 16.37, the profit histogram for an order quantity of 200. (The histograms for the other order quantities are similar to what we've seen before, with more skewness to the left and a larger spike to the right as the order quantity decreases.) For this particular order quantity, they indicate an average profit of about $395, a 5th percentile of $55, a 95th percentile of $528, and a distribution of profits that is again skewed to the left.

Figure 16.37

Histogram of Simulated Profits for Order Quantity 200

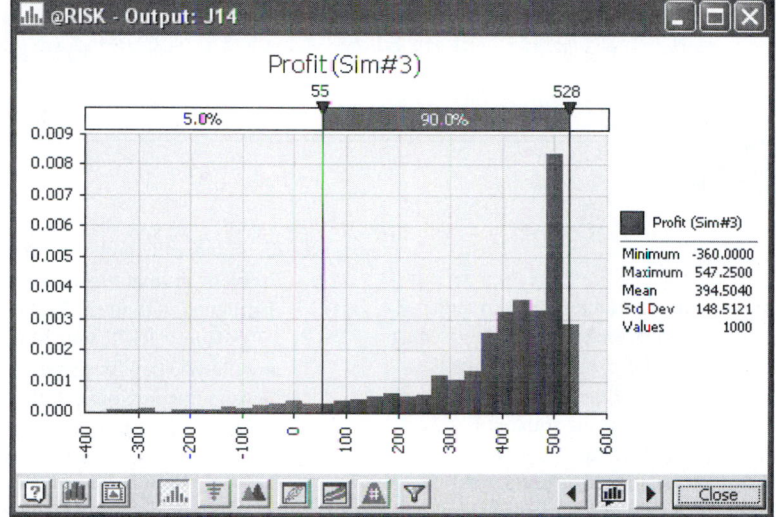

Sensitivity Analysis

We now demonstrate a feature of @RISK that is particularly useful when there are several random input cells. This feature lets us see which of these inputs is most related to, or *correlated* with, an output cell. To perform this analysis, select the profit cell, J14, and click on the Browse Results button. You see a histogram of profit in a temporary window, as we've already discussed, with a number of buttons at the bottom of the window. Click on the red button with the pound sign to select a simulation. We chose #3, where the order quantity is 200. Then click on the "tornado" button (the fifth button from the left) and choose Correlation Coefficients. This produces the chart in Figure 16.38. (The Regression option produces similar results, but we believe the Correlation option is easier to understand.)

This figure shows graphically and numerically how each of the random inputs correlates with profit: the higher the (magnitude of the) correlation, the stronger the relationship between that input and profit. In this sense, we see that the regular-price demand has by far the largest effect on profit. The other two inputs, maximum supply and sale-price demand, are nearly uncorrelated with profit, so they are much less important. Identifying important input variables is important for real applications. If a random input is highly correlated with an important output, then it might be worth the time and money to learn more about this input and possibly reduce the amount of uncertainty involving it.

[9]It is also possible to *correlate* the inputs, as we demonstrate in the next section.

Figure 16.38

Tornado Graph for
Sensitivity Analysis

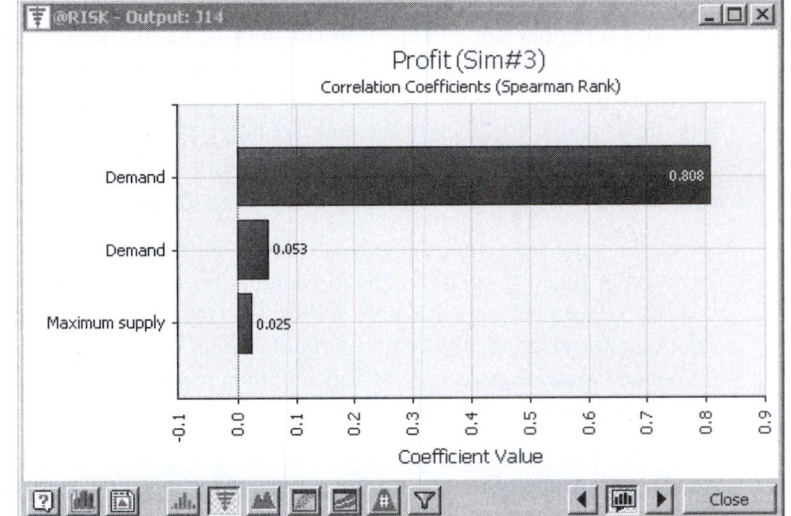

A tornado chart
allows you to see
which of the random
inputs have large
effects on an output.

PROBLEMS

Level A

16. If you add several normally distributed random numbers, the result is normally distributed, where the mean of the sum is the sum of the individual means, and the variance of the sum is the sum of the individual variances. (Remember that variance is the square of standard deviation.) This is a difficult result to prove mathematically, but it is easy to demonstrate with simulation. To do so, run a simulation where you add three normally distributed random numbers, each with mean 100 and standard deviation 10. Your single output variable should be the sum of these three numbers. Verify with @RISK that the distribution of this output is approximately normal with mean 300 and variance 300 (hence, standard deviation $\sqrt{300} = 17.32$).

17. In Problem 11, suppose that the damage amount is triangularly distributed with parameters 500, 1500, and 7000. That is, the damage in an accident can be as low as $500 or as high as $7000, the most likely value is $1500, and there is definite skewness to the right. (It turns out, as you can verify in @RISK, that the mean of this distribution is $3000, the same as in Problem 11.) Use @RISK to simulate the amount you pay for damage. Run 5000 iterations. Then answer the following questions. In each case, explain how the indicated event would occur.
  a. What is the probability that you pay a positive amount but less than $250?
  b. What is the probability that you pay more than $500?
  c. What is the probability that you pay exactly $1000 (the deductible)?

18. Continuing the previous problem, assume, as in Problem 11, that the damage amount is *normally* distributed with mean $3000 and standard deviation $750. Run @RISK with 5000 iterations to simulate the amount you pay for damage. Compare your results with those in the previous problem. Does it appear to matter whether you assume a triangular distribution or a normal distribution for damage amounts? Why isn't this a totally fair comparison? (*Hint*: Use @RISK to find the standard deviation for the triangular distribution.)

19. In Problem 12, suppose that the demand for cars is normally distributed with mean 100 and standard deviation 15. Use @RISK to determine the "best" order quantity—that is, the one with the largest mean profit. Using the statistics and/or graphs from @RISK, discuss whether this order quantity would be considered best by the car dealer. (The point is that a decision maker can use more than just *mean* profit in making a decision.)

20. Use @RISK to analyze the sweatshirt situation in Problem 14. Do this for the discrete distributions given in the problem. Then do it for normal distributions. For the normal case, assume that the regular demand is normally distributed with mean 9800 and standard deviation 1300 and that the demand at the reduced price is normally distributed with mean 3800 and standard deviation 1400.

Level B

21. Although the normal distribution is a reasonable input distribution in many situations, it does have two potential drawbacks: (1) it allows negative values, even though they may be extremely improbable, and (2) it is a symmetric distribution. Many situations are modeled better with a distribution that allows only positive values and is skewed to the right. Two of these are the gamma and lognormal distributions, and @RISK enables you to generate observations from each of these distributions. The @RISK function for the gamma distribution is RISKGAMMA, and it takes two arguments, as in **=RISKGAMMA(3,10)**. The first argument, which must be positive, determines the shape. The smaller it is, the more skewed the distribution is to the right; the larger it is, the more symmetric the distribution is. The second argument determines the scale, in the sense that the product of it and the first argument equals the mean of the distribution. (The

mean above is 30.) Also, the product of the second argument and the square root of the first argument is the standard deviation of the distribution. (Above, it is $\sqrt{3}(10) = 17.32$.) The @RISK function for the lognormal distribution is RISKLOGNORM. It has two arguments, as in **=RISKLOGNORM(40,10)**. These arguments are the mean and standard deviation of the distribution. Rework Example 16.2 for the following demand distributions. Do the simulated outputs have any different qualitative properties with these skewed distributions than with the triangular distribution used in the example?

a. Gamma distribution with parameters 2 and 85
b. Gamma distribution with parameters 5 and 35
c. Lognormal distribution with mean 170 and standard deviation 60

16.6 THE EFFECTS OF INPUT DISTRIBUTIONS ON RESULTS

In Section 16.3 we discussed input distributions. The randomness in input variables causes the variability in the output variables. We now briefly explore whether the choice of input distribution(s) makes much difference in the distribution of an output variable such as profit. This is an important question. If the choice of input distributions doesn't matter much, then we do not need to agonize over this choice. However, if it *does* make a difference, then we have to be more careful about choosing the most appropriate input distribution for any particular situation. Unfortunately, it is impossible to answer the question definitively. The best we can say in general is, "It depends." Some models are more sensitive to changes in the shape or parameters of input distributions than others. Still, the issue is worth exploring.

We discuss two types of sensitivity analysis in this section. First, we see whether the shape of the input distribution matters. In the Walton Bookstore example, we have been assumed a triangularly distributed demand with some skewness. Do we get basically the same results if we try another input distribution such as the normal distribution? Second, we see whether the *independence* of input variables that we have implicitly assumed to this point is crucial to the output results. Many random quantities in real situations are *not* independent; they are positively or negatively correlated. Fortunately, @RISK enables us to build correlation into a model. We analyze the effect of this correlation.

Effect of the Shape of the Input Distribution(s)

We first explore the effect of the shape of the input distribution(s). As the following example indicates, if we make a "fair" comparison, the shape can have a relatively minor effect.

| EXAMPLE | **16.4 EFFECT OF DEMAND DISTRIBUTION AT WALTON'S** |

We continue to explore the demand for calendars at Walton Bookstore. We keep the same unit cost, unit price, and unit refund for leftovers as in Example 16.2. However, in that example we assumed a triangular distribution for demand with parameters 100, 175, and 300. Assuming that Walton orders 200 calendars, is the distribution of profit affected if we instead assume a *normal* distribution of demand?

Objective   To see whether a triangular distribution with some skewness gives the same profit distribution as a normal distribution for demand.

WHERE DO THE NUMBERS COME FROM?

The numbers here are the same as in Example 16.2. However, as discussed next, we choose the parameters of the normal distribution to provide a "fair" comparison with the triangular distribution we used earlier.

Solution

It is important in this type of analysis to make a fair comparison. When we select a normal distribution for demand, we must choose a mean and standard deviation for this distribution. Which values should we choose? It seems only fair to choose the *same* mean and standard deviation that the triangular distribution has. To find the mean and standard deviation for a triangular distribution with given minimum, most likely, and maximum values, we can take advantage of @RISK's Define Distributions window. Select any blank cell, click on the Define Distribution button, select the triangular distribution, and enter the parameters 100, 175, and 300. We see that the mean and standard deviation are 191.67 and 41.248, respectively. Therefore, for a fair comparison we will use the normal distribution with mean 191.67 and standard deviation 41.248. In fact, @RISK allows us to see a comparison of these two distributions, as in Figure 16.39. To get this chart, click on the Add Overlay button, select the normal distribution from the gallery, and enter 191.67 and 41.248 as its mean and standard deviation.

Figure 16.39

Triangular and Normal Distributions for Demand

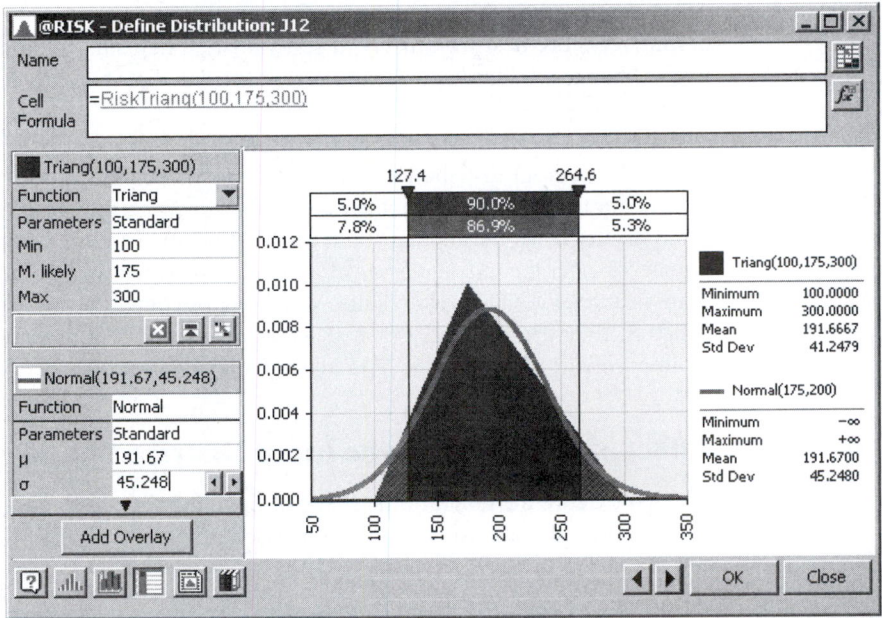

For a fair comparison of alternative input distributions, the distributions should have (at least approximately) equal means and standard deviations.

DEVELOPING THE SIMULATION MODEL

The logic in this model is almost exactly the same as before. (See Figure 16.40 and the file **Walton Bookstore 7.xlsx**.) However, a clever use of the RISKSIMTABLE function allows us to run two simulations at once, one for the triangular distribution and one for the corresponding normal distribution. The two steps required are as follows.

Figure 16.40 @RISK Model for Comparing Two Input Distributions

	A	B	C	D	E	F	G	H	I	J	K	L	M
1	Simulation of Walton's Bookstore using @RISK - two possible demand distributions										Range names used:		
2											Order_quantity	=Model!$B$9	
3	Cost data			Demand distribution 1 - triangular			Demand distribution 2 - normal				Profit	=Model!$F$15	
4	Unit cost	$7.50		Minimum	100		Mean	191.67			Unit_cost	=Model!$B$4	
5	Unit price	$10.00		Most likely	175		Stdev	41.248			Unit_price	=Model!$B$5	
6	Unit refund	$2.50		Maximum	300						Unit_refund	=Model!$B$6	
7													
8	Decision variable												
9	Order quantity	200											
10													
11	Demand distribution to use	1	←	Formula is =RiskSimtable({1,2})									
12													
13	Simulated quantities												
14		Demand	Revenue	Cost	Refund	Profit							
15		132	$1,320	$1,500	$170	-$10							
16													
17	Summary measures of profit from @RISK - based on 1000 iterations for each simulation												
18	Simulation	1	2										
19	Distribution	Triangular	Normal										
20	Minimum	-$242.50	-$640.00										
21	Maximum	$500.00	$500.00										
22	Average	$337.52	$342.79										
23	Standard deviation	$189.07	$201.85										
24	5th percentile	-$47.50	-$70.00										
25	95th percentile	$500.00	$500.00										

As you continue to use @RISK, look for ways to use the RISKSIMTABLE function. It can really improve your efficiency because it allows you to run several simulations at once.

1 **RISKSIMTABLE function.** We index the two distributions as 1 and 2. To indicate that we want to run the simulation with both of them, enter the formula

=RISKSIMTABLE({1,2})

in cell B11. Note that when we enter actual numbers in this function, rather than cell references, @RISK requires us to put curly brackets around the list of numbers.

2 **Demand.** When the value in cell B11 is 1, we want the demand distribution to be triangular. When it is 2, we want the distribution to be normal. Therefore, enter the formula

=ROUND(IF(B11=1,RISKTRIANG(E4,E5,E6),RISKNORMAL(H4,H5)),0)

in cell B15. Again, the effect is that the first simulation will use the triangular distribution, and the second will use the normal distribution.

Running the Simulation

The only @RISK setting to change is the number of simulations. It should now be set to 2, the number of values in the RISKSIMTABLE formula. Other than this, we run the simulation exactly as before.

Discussion of the Simulation Results

The comparison is shown numerically in Figure 16.41 and graphically in Figure 16.42. As we see, there is more chance of really low profits when the demand distribution is normal, whereas each simulation results in the same maximum profit. Both of these statements make sense. The normal distribution, being unbounded on the left, allows for very low demands, and these occasional low demands result in very low profits. On the other side, Walton's maximum profit is $500 regardless of the input distribution (provided it allows demands greater than the order quantity). This occurs when Walton's sells all it orders, in which case excess demand has no effect on profit.

Figure 16.41   Summary Results for Comparison Model

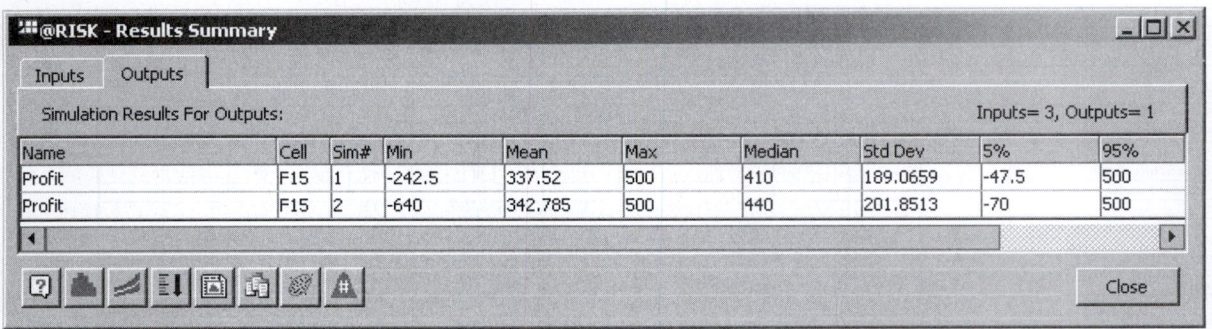

Figure 16.42   Graphical Results for Comparison Model

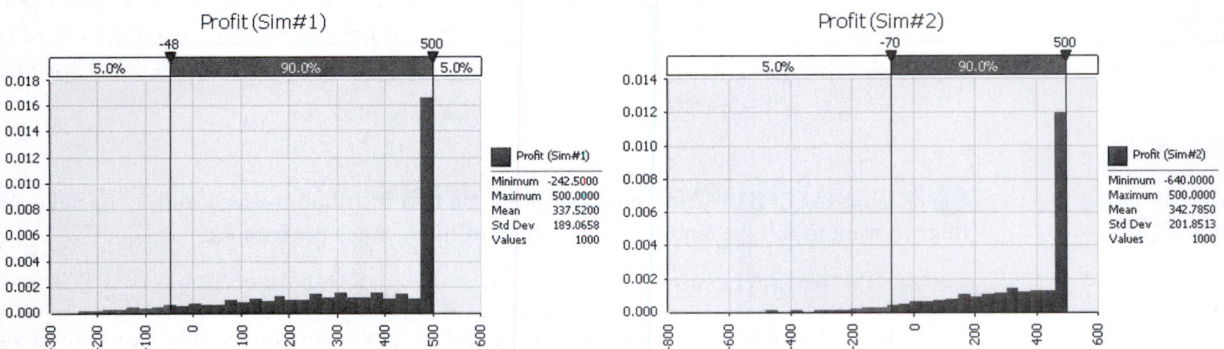

Nevertheless, it is probably safe to conclude that the profit distribution in this model is not greatly affected by the choice of demand distribution, at least not when (1) the candidate input distributions have the same mean and standard deviation, and (2) their shapes are not too dissimilar. We would venture to guess that this general conclusion about insensitivity of output distributions to shapes of input distributions can be made in many simulation models. However, it is always worth checking, as we have done here, especially when there is a lot of money at stake! ■

Effect of Correlated Input Variables

Input variables in real-world problems are often correlated, which makes the material in this section particularly important.

Until now, all of the random numbers we have generated with @RISK functions have been probabilistically independent. This means, for example, that if a random value in one cell is much larger than its mean, the random values in other cells are completely unaffected. They are no more likely to be abnormally large or small than if the first value had been average or less than average. Sometimes, however, this independence is unrealistic. Therefore, we want the random numbers to be correlated in some way. If they are positively correlated, then large numbers tend to go with large numbers, and small with small. If they are negatively correlated, then large tend to go with small and small with large. As an example, we might expect daily stock price changes for two companies in the same industry to be positively correlated. If the price of one oil company increases, we might expect the price of another oil company to increase as well. @RISK allows us to build in this correlated behavior with the RISKCORRMAT function, as we illustrate in the following continuation of the Walton example.

16.5 CORRELATED DEMANDS FOR TWO CALENDARS AT WALTON'S

Suppose that Walton Bookstore must order two different calendars. To simplify the example, we assume that the calendars each have the same unit cost, unit selling price, and unit refund value as in previous examples. Also, we assume that each has a triangularly distributed demand with parameters 100, 175, and 300. However, we now assume they are "substitute" products, so that their demands are negatively correlated. This simply means that if a customer buys one, the customer is not likely to buy the other. Specifically, we assume a correlation of −0.9 between the two demands. How does this correlation affect the distribution of profit, as compared to the situation where the demands are uncorrelated (correlation 0) or very positively correlated (correlation 0.9)?

Objective To see how @RISK enables us to simulate correlated demands, and to see the effect of correlated demands on profit.

WHERE DO THE NUMBERS COME FROM?

The only new input here is the correlation. It is probably negative because the calendars are probably substitute products, but it is a difficult number to estimate accurately. This is a good candidate for a sensitivity analysis.

Solution

The key to building in correlation is @RISK's RISKCORRMAT (correlation matrix) function. To use this function, we must include a correlation matrix in the model, as shown in the range J5:K6 of Figure 16.43. (See the file **Walton Bookstore 8.xlsx**.) A correlation matrix must always have 1's along its diagonal (because a variable is always perfectly correlated with itself) and the correlations between variables elsewhere. Also, the matrix must be symmetric, so that the correlations above the diagonal are a mirror image of those below it. (We enforce this by entering the *formula* **=J6** in cell K5.)

Figure 16.43 Simulation Model with Correlations

	A	B	C	D	E	F	G	H	I	J	K
1	Simulation of Walton's Bookstore using @RISK - correlated demands										
2											
3	Cost data - same for each product			Demand distribution for each product- triangular					Correlation matrix between demands		
4	Unit cost	$7.50		Minimum	100					Product 1	Product 2
5	Unit price	$10.00		Most likely	175				Product 1	1	-0.9
6	Unit refund	$2.50		Maximum	300				Product 2	-0.9	1
7							Note RISKSIMTABLE				
8	Decision variables						function in cell J6.		Possible correlations to try		
9	Order quantity 1	200								-0.9	0	0.9
10	Order quantity 2	200									
11									Range names used:		
12	Simulated quantities								Order_quantity_1	=Model!$B$9	
13		Demand	Revenue	Cost	Refund	Profit			Order_quantity_2	=Model!$B$10	
14	Product 1	222	$2,000	$1,500	$0	$500			Profit	=Model!$F$16	
15	Product 2	216	$2,000	$1,500	$0	$500			Unit_cost	=Model!$B$4	
16	Totals	438	$4,000	$3,000	$0	$1,000			Unit_price	=Model!$B$5	
17									Unit_refund	=Model!$B$6	
18	Summary measures of profit from @RISK - based on 1000 iterations										
19	Simulation	1	2	3							
20	Correlation	-0.9	0	0.9							
21	Minimum	$272.50	-$275.00	-$432.50							
22	Maximum	$1,000.00	$1,000.00	$1,000.00							
23	Average	$675.00	$675.00	$675.00							
24	Standard deviation	$157.76	$262.88	$365.51							
25	5th percentile	$392.50	$197.50	-$72.50							
26	95th percentile	$925.00	$1,000.00	$1,000.00							

The RISKCORRMAT function is "tacked on" as an extra argument to a typical random @RISK function.

To enter random values in any cells that are correlated, we start with a typical @RISK formula, such as

=RISKTRIANG(E4,E5,E6).

Then we add an extra argument, the RISKCORRMAT function, as follows:

=RISKTRIANG(E4,E5,E6,RISKCORRMAT(J5:K6,1))

The first argument of the RISKCORRMAT function is the correlation matrix range. The second is an index of the variable. In our case, the first calendar demand has index 1, and the second has index 2.

@RISK Function: *RISKCORRMAT*

This function enables us to correlate two or more input variables in an @RISK model. The function has the form **RISKCORRMAT(CorrMat,Index)***, where* CorrMat *is a matrix of correlations and* Index *is an index of the variable being correlated to others. For example, if there are three correlated variables,* Index *is 1 for the first variable, 2 for the second, and 3 for the third. The RISKCORRMAT function is not entered by itself. Rather, it is entered as the last argument of a random @RISK function, such as* =**RISKTRIANG(10,15,30,RISKCORRMAT(CorrMat,2))**.

DEVELOPING THE SIMULATION MODEL

Armed with this knowledge, the simulation model in Figure 16.43 is straightforward. It can be developed as follows.

1 **Inputs.** Enter the inputs in the blue ranges in columns B and E.

2 **Correlation matrix.** For the correlation matrix in the range J5:H6, enter 1's on the diagonal, and enter the formula

=J6

in cell K5. Then, because we want to compare the results for several correlations (those in the range I9:K9), enter the formula

=RISKSIMTABLE(I9:K9)

in cell J6. This allows us to simultaneously simulate negatively correlated demands, uncorrelated demands, and positively correlated demands.

3 **Order quantities.** We assume the company orders the *same* number of each calendar, 200, so enter this value in cells B9 and B10. However, the simulation is set up so that you can experiment with any order quantities in these cells, including unequal values.

4 **Correlated demands.** Generate correlated demands by entering the formula

=ROUND(RISKTRIANG(E4,E5,E6,RISKCORRMAT(J5:K6,1)),0)

in cell B14 for demand 1 and the formula

=ROUND(RISKTRIANG(E4,E5,E6, RISKCORRMAT(J5:K6,2)),0)

in cell B15 for demand 2. The only difference between these is the index of the variable being generated. The first has index 1; the second has index 2.

5 **Other formulas.** The other formulas in rows 14 and 15 are identical to ones we developed in previous examples, so we won't discuss them again here. The quantities in row 16 are simply sums of rows 14 and 15. Also, the only @RISK output we specified is the total profit in cell F16.

Running the Simulation

We set up and run @RISK exactly as before. For this example, we set the number of iterations to 1000 and the number of simulations to 3 (because we are trying three different correlations).

Discussion of the Simulation Results

Selected numerical and graphical results are shown in Figures 16.44 and 16.45. You will probably be surprised to see that the *mean* total profit is the same, regardless of the correlation. This is no coincidence. In each of the three simulations, @RISK uses the *same* random numbers, but it "shuffles" them in different orders to get the correct correlations. This means that averages are unaffected. (The idea is that the average of the numbers 30, 26, and 48 is the same as the average of the numbers 48, 30, and 26.)

Figure 16.44   Summary Results for Correlated Model

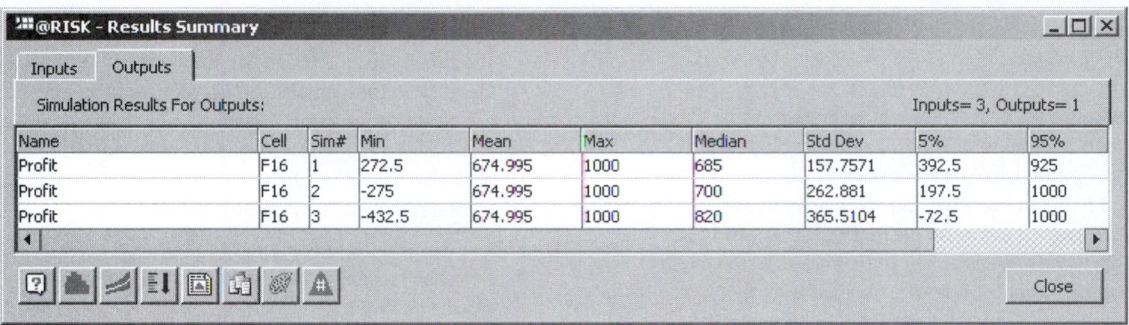

Figure 16.45   Graphical Results for Correlated Model

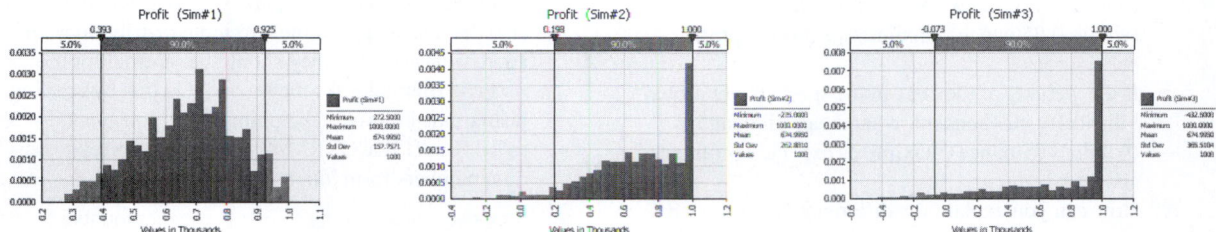

However, the correlation has a definite effect on the *distribution* of total profit. We can see this in Figure 16.44, for example, where the standard deviation of total profit increases as the correlation goes from negative to zero to positive. This same increase in variability is apparent in the histograms in Figure 16.45. Do you see intuitively why this increase in variability occurs? It is basically the "Don't put all of your eggs in one basket" effect. When the correlation is negative, high demands for one product tend to cancel low demands for the other product, so extremes in profit are rare. However, when the correlation is positive, high demands for the two products tend to go together, as do low demands. These make extreme profits on either end much more likely.

This same phenomenon would occur if we simulated an investment portfolio containing two stocks. When the stocks are positively correlated, the portfolio is much riskier (more variability) than when they are negatively correlated. Of course, this is the idea behind the advice that investors should diversify their portfolios. ∎

We illustrated the RISKCORRMAT function for triangularly distributed values. However, it can be used with any of @RISK's distributions by tacking on RISKCORRMAT as a last argument. We can even mix them. For example, assuming CMat is the range name for a 2×2 correlation matrix, we could enter the formulas

With the RISKCORRMAT function, we can correlate random numbers from any distributions.

=RISKNORMAL(10,2,RISKCORRMAT(CMat,1))

and

=RISKUNIFORM(100,200,RISKCORRMAT(CMat,2))

into cells A4 and B4, say, and then copy them down. In this case @RISK generates a sequence of normally distributed random numbers in column A and another sequence of uniformly distributed random numbers in column B. Then it shuffles them in some complex way until their correlation is approximately equal to the specified correlation in the correlation matrix. ∎

PROBLEMS

Level A

22. Bottleco produces six-packs of soda cans. Each can is supposed to contain at least 12 ounces of soda. If the total weight in a six-pack is under 72 ounces, Bottleco is fined $100 and receives no sales revenue for the six-pack. Each six-pack sells for $3.00. It costs Bottleco $0.02 per ounce of soda put in the cans. Bottleco can control the mean fill rate of its soda-filling machines. The amount put in each can by a machine is normally distributed with standard deviation 0.10 ounce.
    a. Assume that the weight of each can in a six-pack has a 0.8 correlation with the weight of the other cans in the six-pack. What mean fill quantity (within 0.05 ounce) maximizes expected profit per six-pack?
    b. If the weights of the cans in the six-pack are probabilistically independent, what mean fill quantity (within 0.05 ounce) maximizes expected profit per six-pack?
    c. How can you explain the difference in the answers to parts **a** and **b**?

23. When you use @RISK's correlation feature to generate correlated random numbers, how can you verify that they are correlated? Try the following. Use the RISKCORRMAT function to generate two normally distributed random numbers, each with mean 100 and standard deviation 10, and with correlation 0.7. To run a simulation, you need an output variable, so sum these two numbers and designate the sum as an output variable. Now run @RISK with 500 iterations. Click on @RISK's Excel Reports button and check the Simulation Data option to see the actual simulated data.
    a. Use Excel's CORREL function to calculate the correlation between the two input variables. It

should be close to 0.7. Then create a scatterplot of these two input variables. The plot should indicate a definite positive relationship.
    b. Are the two input variables correlated with the output? Use Excel's CORREL function to find out. Interpret your results intuitively.

24. Repeat the previous problem, but make the correlation between the two inputs equal to -0.7. Explain how the results change.

25. Repeat Problem 23, but now make the second input variable triangularly distributed with parameters 50, 100, and 500. This time, verify not only that the correlation between the two inputs is approximately 0.7, but also that the shapes of the two input distributions are approximately what they should be: normal for the first and triangular for the second. Do this by creating histograms in Excel. The point is that you can use @RISK's RISKCORRMAT function to correlate random numbers from *different* distributions.

26. Suppose you are going to invest equal amounts in three stocks. The annual return from each stock is normally distributed with mean 0.01 (1%) and standard deviation 0.06. The annual return on your portfolio, the output variable of interest, is the average of the three stock returns. Run @RISK, using 1000 iterations, on each of the following scenarios.
    a. The three stock returns are highly correlated. The correlation between each pair is 0.9.
    b. The three stock returns are practically independent. The correlation between each pair is 0.1.
    c. The first two stocks are moderately correlated. The correlation between their returns is 0.4. The third stock's return is negatively correlated with the other two. The correlation between its return and each of the first two is -0.8.

d. Compare the portfolio distributions from @RISK for these three scenarios. What do you conclude?

e. You might think of a fourth scenario, where the correlation between each *pair* of returns is a large negative number such as −0.8. But explain intuitively why this makes no sense. Try running the simulation with these negative correlations to see what happens.

27. The effect of the shapes of input distributions on the distribution of an output can depend on the output function. For this problem, assume there are 10 input variables. We want to compare the case where these 10 inputs each have a normal distribution with mean 1000 and standard deviation 250 to the case where they each have a triangular distribution with parameters 600, 700, and 1700. (You can check with @RISK's Define Distributions window that even though this triangular distribution is very skewed, it has the same mean and approximately the same standard deviation as the normal distribution.) For each of the following outputs, run @RISK twice, once with the normally distributed inputs and once with the triangularly distributed inputs, and comment on the differences between the resulting output distributions. For each simulation run 10,000 iterations.

a. Let the output be the *average* of the inputs.

b. Let the output be the *maximum* of the inputs.

c. Calculate the average of the inputs. Let the output be the minimum of the inputs if this average is less than 1000; otherwise, let the output be the maximum of the inputs.

Level B

28. The Business School at State University currently has three parking lots, each containing 155 spaces. Two hundred faculty members have been assigned to each lot. On a peak day, an average of 70% of all lot 1 parking sticker holders show up, an average of 72% of all lot 2 parking sticker holders show up, and an average of 74% of all lot 3 parking sticker holders show up.

a. Given the current situation, estimate the probability that on a peak day, at least one faculty member with a sticker will be unable to find a spot. Assume that the number who show up at each lot is independent of the number who show up at the other two lots. (*Hint*: Use the RISKBINOMIAL function.)

b. Now suppose the numbers of people who show up at the three lots are correlated (correlation 0.9). Does your solution work as well? Why or why not?

16.7 CONCLUSION

Simulation has traditionally not received the attention it deserves in management science courses. The primary reason for this has been the lack of easy-to-use simulation software. Now with Excel's built-in simulation capabilities, plus powerful and affordable add-ins such as @RISK, simulation is receiving its rightful emphasis. The world is full of uncertainty, which is what makes simulation so valuable. Simulation models provide important insights that are missing in models that do not incorporate uncertainty explicitly. In addition, simulation models are relatively easy to understand and develop. Therefore, we suspect that simulation models (together with optimization models) will soon be the primary emphasis of many management science courses—if they are not already. In this chapter we have illustrated the basic ideas of simulation, how to perform simulation with Excel built-in tools, and how @RISK greatly enhances Excel's basic capabilities. In the next chapter we build on this knowledge to develop and analyze simulation models in a variety of business areas.

Summary of Key Terms

Term	Explanation	Excel	Page	Equation Number
Simulation models	Models with random inputs that affect one or more outputs, where the randomness is modeled explicitly		946	
F9 key	The "recalc" key, used to make a spreadsheet recalculate	Press the F9 key	948	

(continued)

Term	Explanation	Excel	Page	Equation Number
Probability distributions for input variables	Specification of the possible values and their likelihoods for random input variables; these must be specified in any simulation model		948	
Density function	Function that indicates the probability distribution of a continuous random variable; probabilities are areas under the density		949	
Uniform distribution	The flat distribution, where all values in a bounded continuum are equally likely		953	
RAND function	Excel's built-in random number generator; generates uniform random numbers between 0 and 1	=RAND()	954	
Freezing random numbers	Changing "volatile" random numbers into "fixed" numbers	Copy range, paste it onto itself with the Paste Values option	956	
@RISK random functions	A set of functions, including RISKNORMAL and RISKTRIANG, for generating random numbers from various distributions	=RISKNORMAL (*mean,stdev*) or =RISKTRIANG (*min,mostlikely,max*), for example	956–961	
Discrete distribution	A general distribution where a discrete number of possible values and their probabilities are specified		957	
Normal distribution	The familiar bell-shaped distribution, specified by a mean and a standard deviation		959	
Triangular distribution	Literally a triangle-shaped distribution, specified by a minimum value, a most likely value, and a maximum value		960	
Binomial distribution	The random number of "successes" in a given number of independent "trials," where each trial has the same probability of success		961	
Confidence interval	An interval around an estimate of some parameter, such that we are very confident the true value of the parameter is within the interval		969	
Replicating with Excel only	Useful when an add-in such as @RISK is not available	Develop simulation model, use a data table with any blank Column Input cell to replicate one or more outputs	971	
@RISK	A useful simulation add-in developed by Palisade	Has its own ribbon in Excel	976	

(continued)

Term	Explanation	Excel	Page	Equation Number
RISKSIMTABLE function	Used to run an @RISK simulation model for several values of some variable, often a decision variable	=RISKSIMTABLE(*list*)	976	
RISKOUTPUT function	Used to indicate that a cell contains an output that will be tracked by @RISK	=RISKOUTPUT ("Profit")+Revenue-Cost, for example	979	
Latin hypercube sampling	An efficient way of simulating random numbers for a simulation model, where the results are more accurate than with other sampling methods		981	
Correlated inputs	Random quantities, such as returns from stocks in the same industry, that tend to go together (or possibly go in opposite directions from one another)		994	
RISKCORRMAT function	Used to correlate two or more random input variables	=RISKNORMAL (100,10, RISKCORRMAT (*CorrMat*,2)), for example	996	

PROBLEMS

Level A

29. Six months before its annual convention, the American Medical Association must determine how many rooms to reserve. At this time, the AMA can reserve rooms at a cost of $100 per room. The AMA believes the number of doctors attending the convention will be normally distributed with a mean of 5000 and a standard deviation of 1000. If the number of people attending the convention exceeds the number of rooms reserved, extra rooms must be reserved at a cost of $160 per room.

    a. Use simulation with @RISK to determine the number of rooms that should be reserved to minimize the expected cost to the AMA.

    b. Rework part **a** for the case where the number attending has a triangular distribution with minimum value 2000, maximum value 7000, and most likely value 5000. Does this change the substantive results from part **a**?

30. You have made it to the final round of "Let's Make a Deal." You know that there is $1 million prize behind either door 1, door 2, or door 3. It is equally likely that the prize is behind any of the three doors. The two doors without a prize have nothing behind them. You randomly choose door 2. Before you see whether the prize is behind door 2, host Monty Hall opens a door that has no prize behind it. To be specific, suppose that

before door 2 is opened, Monty reveals that there is no prize behind door 3. You now have the opportunity to switch and choose door 1. Should you switch? Use a spreadsheet to simulate this situation 1000 times. For each replication use an @RISK function to generate the door behind which the prize sits. Then use another @RISK function to generate the door that Monty will open. Assume that Monty plays as follows: Monty knows where the prize is and will open an empty door, but he cannot open door 2. If the prize is really behind door 2, Monty is equally likely to open door 1 or door 3. If the prize is really behind door 1, Monty must open door 3. If the prize is really behind door 3, Monty must open door 1.

31. A new edition of our management science textbook will be published a year from now. Our publisher currently has 2000 copies on hand and is deciding whether to do another printing before the new edition comes out. The publisher estimates that demand for the book during the next year is governed by the probability distribution in the file **P16_31.xlsx**. A production run incurs a fixed cost of $50,000 plus a variable cost of $50 per book printed. Books are sold for $80 per book. Any demand that cannot be met incurs a penalty cost of $10 per book, due to loss of goodwill. Half of any leftover books can be sold to Barnes and Noble for $35 per book. Our publisher is interested in maximizing expected profit. The following print-run sizes are under consideration: 0 (no production run), 1000, 2000, 4000, 6000, and 8000. What decision would you recommend? Use simulation with at least 100 replications. For your optimal decision, our publisher can be 90% certain that the actual profit associated with remaining sales of the current edition will be between what two values?

32. It is equally likely that annual unit sales for Widgetco's widgets will be low or high. If sales are low (60,000), the company can sell the product for $10 per unit. If sales are high (100,000), a competitor will enter and Widgetco can sell the product for only $8 per unit. The variable cost per unit has a 25% chance of being $6, a 50% chance of being $7.50, and a 25% chance of being $9. Annual fixed costs are $30,000.
   a. Use simulation to estimate Widgetco's expected annual profit.
   b. Construct a 95% confidence interval for Widgetco's annual expected profit.
   c. Now suppose that annual unit sales, variable cost, and unit price are equal to their respective expected values—that is, there is no uncertainty. Determine Widgetco's annual profit for this scenario.
   d. Can you conclude from the results in parts a and c that the expected profit from a simulation is equal to the profit from the scenario where each input assumes its expected value? Explain.

33. W. L. Brown, a direct marketer of women's clothing, must determine how many telephone operators to schedule during each part of the day. W. L. Brown estimates that the number of phone calls received each hour of a typical 8-hour shift can be described by the probability distribution in the file **P16_33.xlsx**. Each operator can handle 15 calls per hour and costs the company $20 per hour. Each phone call that is not handled is assumed to cost the company $6 in lost profit. Considering the options of employing 6, 8, 10, 12, 14, or 16 operators, use simulation to determine the number of operators that minimizes the expected hourly cost (labor costs plus lost profits).

34. Assume that all of your job applicants must take a test, and that the scores on this test are normally distributed. The "selection ratio" is the cutoff point you use in your hiring process. For example, a selection ratio of 20% means that you will accept applicants for jobs who rank in the top 20% of all applicants. If you choose a selection ratio of 20%, the average test score of those selected will be 1.40 standard deviations above average. Use simulation to verify this fact, proceeding as follows.
   a. Show that if you want to accept only the top 20% of all applicants, you should accept applicants whose test scores are at least 0.842 standard deviation above average. (No simulation is required here. Just use the appropriate Excel normal function.)
   b. Now generate 1000 test scores from a normal distribution with mean 0 and standard deviation 1. The average test score of those selected is the average of the scores that are at least 0.842. To determine this, use Excel's DAVERAGE function. To do so, put the heading Score in cell A3, generate the 1000 test scores in the range A4:A1003, and name the range A3:A1003 Data. In cells C3 and C4, enter the *labels* Score and >0.842. (The range C3:C4 is called the *criterion* range.) Then calculate the average of all applicants who will be hired by entering the formula =DAVERAGE(Data, "Score", C3:C4) in any cell. This average should be close to the theoretical average, 1.40. This formula works as follows. Excel finds all observations in the Data range that satisfy the criterion described in the range C3:C4 (Score>0.842). Then it averages the values in the Score column (the second argument of DAVERAGE) corresponding to these entries. Look in online help for more about Excel's database functions.
   c. What information would you need to determine an "optimal" selection ratio? How could you determine an optimal selection ratio?

35. Lemington's is trying to determine how many Jean Hudson dresses to order for the spring season. Demand for the dresses is assumed to follow a normal distribution with mean 400 and standard deviation 100. The contract between Jean Hudson and Lemington's works as follows. At the beginning of the season, Lemington's reserves x units of capacity. Lemington's must take delivery for at least $0.8x$ dresses and can, if desired, take delivery on up to x dresses. Each dress sells for $160 and Jean charges $50 per dress. If Lemington's does not take delivery on all x dresses, it owes Jean a $5 penalty for each unit of reserved capacity that is unused. For example, if Lemington's orders 450 dresses and demand is for 400 dresses, then Lemington's will receive 400 dresses and owe Jean 400($50) + 50($5). How many units of capacity should Lemington's reserve to maximize its expected profit?

36. Dilbert's Department Store is trying to determine how many Hanson T-shirts to order. Currently the shirts are sold for $21.00, but at later dates the shirts will be offered at a 10% discount, then a 20% discount, then a 40% discount, then a 50% discount, and finally a 60% discount. Demand at the full price of $21.00 is believed to be normally distributed with mean 1800 and standard deviation 360. Demand at various discounts is assumed to be a multiple of full-price demand. These multiples, for discounts of 10%, 20%, 40%, 50%, and 60% are, respectively, 0.4, 0.7, 1.1, 2, and 50. For example, if full-price demand is 2500, then at a 10% discount, customers would be willing to buy 1000 T-shirts. The unit cost of purchasing T-shirts depends on the number of T-shirts ordered, as shown in the file **P16_36.xlsx**. Use

simulation to see how many T-shirts Dilbert's should order. Model the problem so that Dilbert's first orders some quantity of T-shirts, then discounts deeper and deeper, as necessary, to sell all of the shirts.

Level B

37. The annual return on each of four stocks for each of the next 5 years is assumed to follow a normal distribution, with the mean and standard deviation for each stock, as well as the correlations between stocks, listed in the file **P16_37.xlsx**. We believe that the stock returns for these stocks in a given year are correlated, according to the correlation matrix given, but we believe the returns in different years are uncorrelated. For example, the returns for stocks 1 and 2 in year 1 have correlation 0.55, but the correlation between the return of stock 1 in year 1 and the return of stock 1 in year 2 is 0, and the correlation between the return of stock 1 in year 1 and the return of stock 2 in year 2 is also 0. The file has the formulas you might expect for this situation entered in the range C20:G23. You can check how the RISKCORRMAT function has been used in these formulas. Just so that we have an @RISK output cell, we calculate the average of all returns in cell B25 and designate it as an @RISK output. (This cell is not really important for the problem, but we include it because @RISK requires at least one output cell.)
    a. Using the model exactly as it stands, run @RISK with 1000 iterations. The question is whether the correlations in the simulated data are close to what we expect. To find out, go to @RISK's Report Settings and check the Input Data option before you run the simulation. This gives you all of the simulated returns on a new sheet. Then calculate correlations for all pairs of columns in the resulting Inputs Data Report sheet. (We recommend instead that you use the StatTools add-in included with this book to create a matrix of all correlations.) Comment on whether the correlations are different from what you expect.
    b. Recognizing that this is a common situation (correlation within years, no correlation across years), @RISK allows you to model it by adding a *third* argument to the RISKCORRMAT function: the year index in row 19 of the **P16_37.xlsx** file. For example, the RISKCORRMAT part of the formula in cell C20 becomes =RISKNORMAL($B5,$C5, RISKCORRMAT($B$12:$E$15,$B20,C$19)). Make this change to the formulas in the range C20:G23, rerun the simulation, and redo the correlation analysis in part **a**. Verify that the correlations between inputs are now more in line with what you expect.

38. It is surprising (but true) that if 23 people are in the same room, there is about a 50% chance that at least

two people will have the same birthday. Suppose you want to estimate the probability that if 30 people are in the same room, at least two of them will have the same birthday. You can proceed as follows.
    a. Generate the "birthdays" of 30 different people. Ignoring the possibility of a leap year, each person has a 1/365 chance of having a given birthday (label the days of the year 1, 2,...,365). You can use a formula involving the RANDBETWEEN function to generate birthdays.
    b. Once you have generated 30 people's birthdays, how can you tell whether at least two people have the same birthday? The key here is to use Excel's RANK function. (You can learn how to use this function with Excel's online help.) This function returns the rank of a number relative to a given group of numbers. In the case of a tie, two numbers are given the same rank. For example, if the set of numbers is 4, 3, 2, 5, the RANK function returns 2, 3, 4, 1. If the set of numbers is 4, 3, 2, 4, the RANK function returns 1, 3, 4, 1.
    c. After using the RANK function, you should be able to determine whether at least two of the 30 people have the same birthday.

39. United Electric (UE) sells refrigerators for $400 with a 1-year warranty. The warranty works as follows. If any part of the refrigerator fails during the first year after purchase, UE replaces the refrigerator for an average cost of $100. As soon as a replacement is made, another 1-year warranty period begins for the customer. If a refrigerator fails outside the warranty period, we assume that the customer immediately purchases another UE refrigerator. Suppose that the amount of time a refrigerator lasts follows a normal distribution with a mean of 1.8 years and a standard deviation of 0.3 year.
    a. Estimate the average profit per year UE earns from a customer.
    b. How could the approach of this problem be used to determine the optimal warranty period?

40. A Tax Saver Benefit (TSB) plan allows you to put money into an account at the beginning of the calendar year that can be used for medical expenses. This amount is not subject to federal tax—hence the phrase TSB. As you pay medical expenses during the year, you are reimbursed by the administrator of the TSB until the TSB account is exhausted. From that point on, you must pay your medical expenses out of your own pocket. On the other hand, if you put more money into your TSB than the medical expenses you incur, this extra money is lost to you. Your annual salary is $80,000 and your federal income tax rate is 30%.
    a. Assume that your medical expenses in a year are normally distributed with mean $2000 and standard deviation $500. Build an @RISK model in which the output is the amount of money left to you after

paying taxes, putting money in a TSB, and paying any extra medical expenses. Experiment with the amount of money put in the TSB, using a RISKSIMTABLE function.

b. Rework part **a**, but this time assume a gamma distribution for your annual medical expenses. Use 16 and 125 as the two parameters of this distribution. These imply the same mean and standard deviation as in part a, but the distribution of medical expenses is now skewed to the right, which is probably more realistic. Using simulation, see whether you should now put more or less money in a TSB than in the symmetric case in part **a**.

41. At the beginning of each week, a machine is in one of four conditions: 1 = excellent; 2 = good; 3 = average; 4 = bad. The weekly revenue earned by a machine in state 1, 2, 3, or 4 is $100, $90, $50, or $10, respectively. After observing the condition of the machine at the beginning of the week, the company has the option, for a cost of $200, of instantaneously replacing the machine with an excellent machine. The quality of the machine deteriorates over time, as shown in the file **P16_41.xlsx**. Four maintenance policies are under consideration:

- Policy 1: Never replace a machine.
- Policy 2: Immediately replace a bad machine.
- Policy 3: Immediately replace a bad or average machine.
- Policy 4: Immediately replace a bad, average, or good machine.

Simulate each of these policies for 50 weeks (using 250 iterations each) to determine the policy that maximizes expected weekly profit. Assume that the machine at the beginning of week 1 is excellent.

42. Simulation can be used to illustrate a number of results from statistics that are difficult to understand with non-simulation arguments. One is the famous central limit theorem, which says that if you sample enough values from any population distribution and then average these values, the resulting average will be approximately normally distributed. Confirm this by using @RISK with the following population distributions (run a separate simulation for each): (a) discrete with possible values 1 and 2 and probabilities 0.2 and 0.8; (b) exponential with mean 1 (use the RISKEXPON function with the single argument 1); (c) triangular with minimum, most likely, and maximum values equal to 1, 9, and 10. (Note that each of these distributions is very nonnormal.) Run each simulation with 10 values in each average, and run 1000 iterations to simulate 1000 averages. Create a histogram of the averages to see whether it is indeed bell-shaped. Then repeat, using 30 values in each average. Are the histograms based on 10 values qualitatively different from those based on 30?

43. In statistics we often use observed data to test a hypothesis about a population or populations. The basic method uses the observed data to calculate a test statistic (a single number). If the magnitude of this test statistic is sufficiently large, we reject the "null" hypothesis in favor of the "research" hypothesis. As an example, consider a researcher who believes teenage girls sleep longer than teenage boys on average. She collects observations on $n = 40$ randomly selected girls and $n = 40$ randomly selected boys. (We assume that each observation is the average sleep time over several nights for a given person.) The averages are

$\overline{X}_1 = 7.9$ hours for the girls and $\overline{X}_2 = 7.6$ hours

for the boys. The standard deviation of the 40 observations for girls is $s_1 = 0.5$ hour; for the boys it is $s_2 = 0.7$ hour. The researcher, consulting Chapter 10, then calculates the test statistic

$$\frac{\overline{X}_1 - \overline{X}_2}{\sqrt{s_1^2/40 + s_2^2/40}} = \frac{7.9 - 7.6}{\sqrt{0.25/40 + 0.49/40}} = 2.206$$

Based on the fact that 2.206 is "large," she claims that her research hypothesis is confirmed—girls do sleep longer than boys.

You are skeptical of this claim, so you check it out by running a simulation. In your simulation you assume that girls and boys have the *same* mean and standard deviation of sleep times in the entire population, say, 7.7 and 0.6. You also assume that the distribution of sleep times is normal. Then you repeatedly simulate observations of 40 girls and 40 boys from this distribution and calculate the test statistic. The question is whether the observed test statistic, 2.206, is "extreme." If it is larger than most or all of the test statistics you simulate, then the researcher is justified in her claim; otherwise, this large a statistic could have happened just by chance, even if the girls and boys have identical population means. Use @RISK to see which is the case.

Modeling Problems

44. Big Hit Video must determine how many copies of a new video to purchase. Assume that the company's goal is to purchase a number of copies that maximizes its expected profit from the video during the next year. Describe how you would use simulation to solve this problem. To simplify matters, assume that each time a tape is rented, it is rented for one day.

45. Many people who are involved in a small auto accident do not file a claim because they are afraid their insurance premiums will be raised. Suppose that City Farm Insurance has three rates. If you file a claim, you are moved to the next higher rate. How might you use simulation to determine whether a particular claim should be filed?

46. A building contains 1000 lightbulbs. Each bulb lasts at most 5 months. The company maintaining the building is trying to decide whether it is worthwhile to practice a "group replacement" policy. Under a group replacement policy, all bulbs are replaced every T months (where T is to be determined). Also, bulbs are replaced when they burn out. Assume that it costs $0.05 to replace each bulb during a group replacement and $0.20 to replace each burned-out bulb if it is replaced individually. How would you use simulation to determine whether a group replacement policy is worthwhile?

47. We are constantly hearing reports on the nightly news about natural disasters—droughts in Texas, hurricanes in Florida, floods in California, and so on. We often hear that one of these was the "worst in over 30 years," or some such statement. Are natural disasters getting worse these days, or does it just appear so? How might you use simulation to answer this question? Here is one possible approach. Imagine that there are N areas of the country (or the world) that tend to have, to some extent, various types of weather phenomena each year. For example, hurricanes are always a potential problem for Florida. You might model the severity of the problem for any area in any year by a normally distributed random number with mean 0 and standard deviation 1, where negative values are interpreted as mild years and positive values are interpreted as severe years. (We suggest the normal distribution, but there is no reason other distributions couldn't be used instead.) Then you could simulate such values for all areas over a period of many years and keep track, say, of whether any of the areas have worse conditions in the current year than they have had in the past 30 years. What might you keep track of? How might you interpret your results?

Egress, Inc., is a small company that designs, produces, and sells ski jackets and other coats. The creative design team has labored for weeks over its new design for the coming winter season. It is now time to decide how many ski jackets to produce in this production run. Because of the lead times involved, no other production runs will be possible during the season. Predicting ski jacket sales months in advance of the selling season can be quite tricky. Egress has been in operation for only 3 years, and its ski jacket designs were quite successful in two of those years. Based on realized sales from the last 3 years, current economic conditions, and professional judgment, twelve Egress employees have independently estimated demand for their new design for the upcoming season. Their estimates are listed in Table 16.2.

Table 16.2   Estimated Demands

14,000	16,000
13,000	8000
14,000	5000
14,000	11,000
15,500	8000
10,500	15,000

To assist in the decision on the number of units for the production run, management has gathered the data in Table 16.3. Note that S is the price Egress charges retailers. Any ski jackets that do not sell during the season can be sold by Egress to discounters for V per jacket. The fixed cost of plant and equipment is F. This cost is incurred regardless of the size of the production run.

Table 16.3   Monetary Values

Variable production cost per unit (C):	$80
Selling price per unit (S):	$100
Salvage value per unit (V):	$30
Fixed production cost (F):	$100,000

Questions

1. Egress management believes that a normal distribution is a reasonable model for the unknown demand in the coming year. What mean and standard deviation should Egress use for the demand distribution?

2. Use a spreadsheet model to simulate 1000 possible outcomes for demand in the coming year. Based on these scenarios, what is the expected profit if Egress produces $Q = 7800$ ski jackets? What is the expected profit if Egress produces $Q = 12,000$ ski jackets? What is the standard deviation of profit in these two cases?

3. Based on the same 1000 scenarios, how many ski jackets should Egress produce to maximize expected profit? Call this quantity Q.

4. Should Q equal mean demand or not? Explain.

5. Create a histogram of profit at the production level Q. Create a histogram of profit when the production level Q equals mean demand. What is the probability of a loss greater than $100,000 in each case? ■

Management of Ebony, a leading manufacturer of bath soap, is trying to control its inventory costs. The weekly cost of holding one unit of soap in inventory is $30 (one unit is 1000 cases of soap). The marketing department estimates that weekly demand averages 120 units, with a standard deviation of 15 units, and is reasonably well modeled by a normal distribution. If demand exceeds the amount of soap on hand, those sales are *lost*—that is, there is no backlogging of demand. The production department can produce at one of three levels: 110, 120, or 130 units per week. The cost of changing the production level from one week to the next is $3000.

Management would like to evaluate the following production policy. If the current inventory is less than $L = 30$ units, then produce 130 units in the next week. If the current inventory is greater than $U = 80$ units, then produce 110 units in the next week. Otherwise, continue at the previous week's production level.

Ebony currently has 60 units of inventory on hand. Last week's production level was 120.

Questions

1. Create a spreadsheet to simulate 52 weeks of operation at Ebony. Graph the inventory of soap over time. What is the total cost (inventory cost plus production change cost) for the 52 weeks?

2. Use a simulation of 500 iterations to estimate the average 52-week cost with values of U ranging from 30 to 80 in increments of 10. Keep $L = 30$ for every trial.

3. Calculate the sample mean and standard deviation of the 52-week cost under each policy. Using those results, construct 95% confidence intervals for the average 52-week cost for each value of U. Graph the average 52-week cost versus U. What is the best value of U for $L = 30$?

4. What other production policies might be useful to investigate? ∎

Simulation Models

AUTOMATING OPERATIONS AT THE UNITED STATES POSTAL SERVICE

One of the key benefits of simulation methodology is that it allows a company to see how important outputs respond to various scenarios. Each scenario, which is determined by certain inputs and operating policies, can be simulated, and statistics can be collected. By running enough scenarios, the company obtains useful information about which inputs and policies tend to produce the best outputs. This methodology was used in the 1980s by the United States Postal Service (USPS), as described in the article "Management Science in Automating Postal Operations: Facility and Equipment Planning in the United States Postal Service" by Cebry et al. (1992). At the time, the USPS was faced with increasing competitive pressure from a variety of competitors, including other advertising media, alternative retail and delivery companies, and electronic mail. Automation technology was identified as the only way to handle an increase in mail volume, to maintain cost competitiveness, and to provide adequate service.

The process of getting mail from the sender to the receiver is an extremely complex one. Mail enters the process as a mixed product—many types of mail addressed in various ways to many geographical regions—and it must be sorted in several stages before it can eventually reach the proper destination. The USPS recognized the need for automated equipment to speed up this process and to save on labor costs. In fact, by the early 1980s it had purchased optical character recognition (OCR) machines that could identify the destination (at least on some mail) and attach a bar code corresponding to the ZIP code to the mail. It had also purchased bar code sensing machines that could read these bar codes and automatically help sort the mail. Part of the cost-effectiveness of these new machines relied on heavy use by businesses of the new nine-digit ZIP codes. Unfortunately, businesses were somewhat slow to use the nine-digit codes.

At about this time, the USPS realized that it needed to use management science methods to utilize its existing automation equipment most effectively and to plan appropriately for the future. It hired a consulting company, Kenan Systems Corporation, to help compare automation alternatives. The result was META, a simulation model that quantifies the impacts of changes in mail processing and delivery operations. The META model is very complex, but it can be described briefly as follows.

Mail of various types and of various volumes enters the system and progresses through a number of "links." Each of the links is one step in the overall sorting process that gets the mail from its origin to its final destination. The META model takes as its inputs various mail streams (types of mail with similar characteristics) and routes these streams through the links of the sorting process according to user-specified rules. For example, a rule might specify which mail streams receive highest priority on certain automation equipment at each link. Each set of mail streams and each set of rules corresponds to a single scenario in the simulation model. Given a typical scenario, the model simulates the throughput of the system, the number of errors made, the amount of labor required, and the total cost. These outputs are then compared to identify the best policies for the USPS to implement.

The META model, first developed in 1985, has proved to be extremely useful and versatile. Using this simulation tool, the USPS formulated a corporate automation plan (CAP), which was first released in 1989. By the time CAP was to be fully implemented in 1995, the postal service expected it to save 100,000 work years annually, which translates to over $4 billion. Just as important, by using the model as part of an ongoing planning process, the USPS ensured that it would implement future technologies in a timely and cost-effective manner. ∎

17.1 INTRODUCTION

In the previous chapter we introduced most of the important concepts for developing and analyzing spreadsheet simulation models. We also discussed many of the available features in the powerful simulation add-in, @RISK, that accompanies this book. Now we apply the tools to a wide variety of problems that can be analyzed by simulation. For convenience, we group the applications into four general areas: (1) operations models, (2) financial models, (3) marketing models, and (4) games of chance. The only overriding theme in this chapter is that simulation models can yield important insights in all of these areas. You do not need to cover all of the models in this chapter or cover them in the order in which they are presented. Rather, you can cover the ones of most interest to you and in practically any order.

17.2 OPERATIONS MODELS

Whether we are discussing the operations of a manufacturing or a service company, there is likely to be uncertainty that can be modeled by simulation. In this section we look at examples of bidding for a government contract (uncertainty in the bids by competitors), warranty costs (uncertainty in the time until failure of an appliance), and drug production (uncertainty in the yield).

Bidding for Contracts

In situations where a company must bid against competitors, simulation can often be used to determine the company's optimal bid. Usually the company does not know what its competitors will bid, but it might have an idea about the range of the bids its competitors will choose. In this section we show how to use simulation to determine a bid that maximizes the company's expected profit.

EXAMPLE   **17.1 BIDDING FOR A GOVERNMENT CONTRACT**

The Miller Construction Company is trying to decide whether to make a bid on a construction project. Miller believes it will cost the company $10,000 to complete the project (if it wins the contract), and it will cost $350 to prepare a bid. However, there is uncertainty about each of these. Upon further reflection, Miller assesses that the cost to complete the project has a triangular distribution with minimum, most likely, and maximum values $9000, $10,000, and $15,000. Similarly, Miller assesses that the cost to prepare a bid has a triangular distribution with parameters $300, $350, and $500. (Note the skewness in these distributions. Miller recognizes that cost overruns are much more likely than cost underruns.) Up to four potential competitors are going to bid against Miller. The lowest bid will win the contract, and the winner will then be given the winning bid amount to complete the project. Based on past history, Miller believes that each competitor will bid, independently of the others, with probability 0.5. Miller also believes that each competitor's bid will be a multiple of its (Miller's) *most likely* cost to complete the project, where this multiple has a triangular distribution with minimum, most likely, and maximum values 0.9, 1.3, and 1.8, respectively. If Miller decides to prepare a bid, its bid amount will be a multiple of $500 in the range $10,500 to $15,000. The company wants to use simulation to determine which strategy to use to maximize its expected profit.

Objective   To simulate the profit to Miller from any particular bid, and to see which bid amount is best.

WHERE DO THE NUMBERS COME FROM?

The data required here are the distributions of Miller's costs and the competitors' bids. Triangular distributions are chosen for simplicity, although Miller could try other types of distributions. The parameters of these distributions are probably educated guesses, possibly based on previous contracts and previous bidding experience against these same competitors.

Solution

The logic is straightforward. We first simulate the number of competitors who will bid and then simulate their bids. Then for any bid Miller makes, we see whether Miller wins the contract, and if so, what its profit is.

DEVELOPING THE SIMULATION MODEL

The simulation model appears in Figure 17.1. (See the file **Contract Bidding.xlsx**.) It can be developed with the following steps. (Note that this model does not check the possibility of Miller not bidding at all. But this case is easy. If Miller opts not to bid, the profit is a certain $0.)

1 **Inputs.** Enter the inputs in the blue cells.

Figure 17.1
Bidding Simulation
Model

	A	B	C	D	E	F	G	H	I	J	K	L	M
1	Bidding for a contract												
2													
3	Inputs												
4	Miller's costs, triangular distributed	Min	Most likely	Max									
5	Cost to prepare a bid	$300	$350	$500									
6	Cost to complete project	$9,000	$10,000	$15,000									
7													
8	Number of potential competitors	4											
9	Probability a given competitor bids	0.5											
10													
11	Parameters of triangular distributions for each competitor's bid (expressed as multiple of Miller's most likely cost to complete project)												
12	Min	0.9											
13	Most likely	1.3											
14	Max	1.8											
15				Possible bids for Miller									
16	Miller's bid	$10,500		$10,500	$11,000	$11,500	$12,000	$12,500	$13,000	$13,500	$14,000	$14,500	$15,000
17													
18	Simulation												
19	Miller's cost to prepare a bid	$359											
20	Miller's cost to complete project	$11,279											
21	Number of competing bids	1											
22	Competitor index	1	2	3	4								
23	Competitors' bids	$15,697											
24	Minimum competitor bid	$15,697											
25													
26	Miller wins bid? (1 if yes, 0 if no)	1											
27	Miller's profit	-$1,138											

Recall that the RISKSIMTABLE function allows you to run a separate simulation for each value in its list.

2 **Miller's bid.** We can test all of Miller's possible bids simultaneously with the RISKSIMTABLE function. To set up for this, enter the formula

=RISKSIMTABLE(D16:M16)

in cell B16. As with all uses of this function, the spreadsheet shows the simulated values for the *first* bid, $10,500. However, when we run the simulation, we see outputs for all of the bids.

3 **Miller's costs.** Generate Miller's cost to prepare a bid in cell B19 with the formula

=RISKTRIANG(B5,C5,D5)

Then copy this to cell B20 to generate Miller's cost to complete the project.

4 **Competitors and their bids.** First, generate the random number of competitors who bid. This has a binomial distribution with 4 trials and probability of "success" equal to 0.5 for each trial, so enter the formula

=RISKBINOMIAL(B8,B9)

in cell B21. Then generate random bids for the competitors who bid in row 23 by entering the formula

=IF(B22<=$B$21,RISKTRIANG($B$12,$B$13,$B$14)*$C$6," ")

in cell B23 and copying across. (Remember that the random value is the *multiple* of Miller's most likely cost to complete the project.) Calculate the smallest of these (if there are any) in cell B24 with the formula

=IF(B21>=1,MIN(B23:E23)," ")

Of course, Miller will not see these other bids until it has submitted its own bid.

5 **Win contract?** See whether Miller wins the bid by entering the formula

=IF(OR(B16<B24,B21=0),1,0)

in cell B26. Here, 1 means that Miller wins the bid, and 0 means a competitor wins the bid. Then designate this cell as an @RISK output cell. Recall that to designate a cell as an @RISK output cell, you select the cell and then click on the Add Output button on @RISK's ribbon. You can then "name" this output appropriately. We used the name "Win bid."

6 **Miller's profit.** If Miller submits a bid, the bid cost is lost for sure. Beyond that, the profit to Miller is the bid amount minus the cost of completing the project if the bid is won. Otherwise, Miller makes nothing. So enter the formula

=IF(B26=1,B16-B20,0)−B19

in cell B27. Then designate this cell as an additional @RISK output cell. (We named it "Profit.")

Running the Simulation

We set the number of iterations to 1000, and we set the number of simulations to 10 because there are 10 bid amounts Miller wants to test.

Discussion of the Simulation Results

The summary results appear in Figure 17.2. For each simulation—that is, each bid amount—there are two outputs: 1 or 0 to indicate whether Miller wins the contract and Miller's profit. The only interesting results for the 0/1 output are in the Mean column, which shows the fraction of iterations that resulted in 1's. So we see, for example, that if Miller bids $12,000 (simulation #4), the probability of winning the bid is estimated to be 0.587. This probability clearly decreases as Miller's bid increases.

Figure 17.2
Summary Results from @RISK

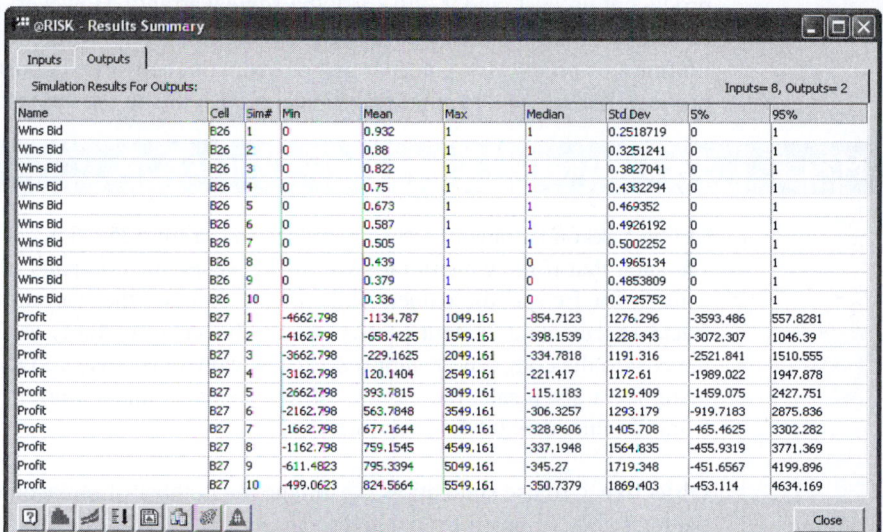

In terms of net profit, if we concentrate only on the Mean column, then a bid amount of $13,000 (simulation #6) is clearly the best. But as the other numbers in this figure indicate, the mean doesn't tell the whole story. For example, if Miller bids $13,000, it could win the bid but still lose a considerable amount of money because of cost overruns. The histogram of profit in Figure 17.3 indicates this more clearly. It shows that in spite of the positive mean, most outcomes are negative!

So what should Miller do? If it doesn't bid at all, its profit is $0 for sure. If Miller is an *expected* profit maximizer, then the fact that several of the means in Figure 17.2 are positive indicates that bidding is better than not bidding, with a bid of $13,000 being the best bid. However, potential cost overruns and the corresponding losses are certainly a concern. Depending on Miller's degree of risk aversion, the company might decide to (1) not bid at all, or (2) bid higher than $13,000 to minimize its worse loss. Still, we would caution Miller not to be *too* conservative. Rather than focusing on the Min (worst case) column in Figure 17.2, we would suggest focusing on the 5% column. This shows nearly how bad things could get (5% of the time it would be worse than this), and this fifth percentile remains nearly constant for higher bids.

Figure 17.3

Summary Results
for Profit Output

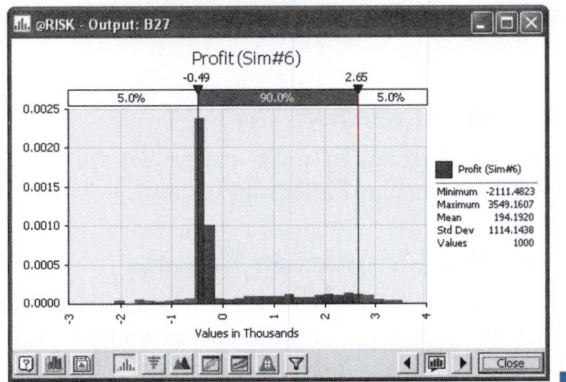

Warranty Costs

When you buy a new product, it usually carries a warranty. A typical warranty might state that if the product fails within a certain period such as 1 year, then you will receive a new product at no cost, and it will carry the *same* warranty. However, if the product fails after the warranty period, then you have to bear the cost of replacing the product. Due to random lifetimes of products, we need a way to estimate the warranty costs (to the company) of a product. We see how simulation can accomplish this in the next example.

EXAMPLE | **17.2 WARRANTY COSTS FOR A CAMERA**

The Yakkon Company sells a popular camera for $250. This camera carries a warranty such that if the camera fails within 1.5 years, the company gives the customer a new camera for free. If the camera fails after 1.5 years, the warranty is no longer in effect. Every replacement camera carries exactly the same warranty as the original camera, and the cost to the company of supplying a new camera is always $185. Use simulation to estimate, for a given sale, the number of replacements under warranty and the NPV of profit from the sale, using a discount rate of 12%.

Objective   To use simulation to estimate the number of replacements under warranty and the total NPV of profit from a given sale.

WHERE DO THE NUMBERS COME FROM?

The warranty information is a policy decision made by the company. The hardest input to estimate is the probability distribution of the lifetime of the product. We discuss this next.

Solution

The gamma distribution is a popular distribution, especially when we want a right-skewed distribution of a nonnegative quantity.

The only randomness in this problem concerns the time until failure of a new camera. Yakkon could estimate the distribution of time until failure from historical data. This would probably indicate a right-skewed distribution, as shown in Figure 17.4. If you look through the list of distributions available in @RISK under Define Distributions, you will see several with this same basic shape. The one shown in Figure 17.4 is a commonly used distribution called the **gamma** distribution. For variety (and realism), we use this distribution in this example, although other choices such as the triangular are certainly possible.

Selecting a Gamma Distribution

The gamma distribution is characterized by two parameters, α and β. These determine its exact shape and location. It can be shown that the mean and standard deviation are

You can learn about distributions from @RISK's Define Distribution window

$\mu = \alpha\beta$ and $\sigma = \sqrt{\alpha}\beta$. Alternatively, if we have desired values of the mean and standard deviation, we can solve these equations for α and β to give us the desired mean and standard deviation. This leads to $\alpha = \mu^2/\sigma^2$ and $\beta = \sigma^2/\mu$. So, for example, if we want a gamma distribution with mean 2.5 and standard deviation 1 (which in this example would be based on camera lifetime data from the past), we should choose $\alpha = 2.5^2/1^2 = 6.25$ and $\beta = 1^2/2.5 = 0.4$. These are the values shown in Figure 17.4 and the ones we will use for this example. The values in the figure (from @RISK) imply that the probability of failure before 1.5 years is about 0.15, so that the probability of failure out of warranty is about 0.85.

Figure 17.4

Right-Skewed Gamma Distribution

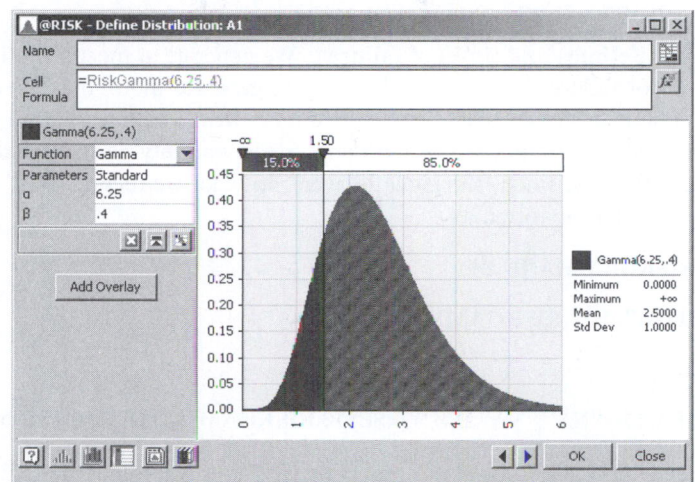

DEVELOPING THE SIMULATION MODEL

The simulation model appears in Figure 17.5. (See the file **Warranty Costs.xlsx**.) The particular random numbers in this figure indicate an example (a rather unusual one) where there are two failures within warranty. However, because the lifetime of the second replacement (cell D17) is greater than 1.5, the company incurs only two replacement costs, as shown in cells B19 and C19. The model can be developed with the following steps.

Figure 17.5

Warranty Simulation Model

	A	B	C	D	E	F
1	Warranty costs for camera					
2						
3	Inputs					
4	Parameters of time to failure distribution of any new camera (Gamma)					
5	Desired mean	2.5				
6	Desired stdev	1				
7	Implied alpha	6.250				
8	Implied beta	0.400				
9						
10	Warranty period	1.5				
11	Cost of new camera (to customer)	$250				
12	Replacement cost (to company)	$185				
13	Discount rate	12%				
14						
15	Simulation of new camera and its replacements (if any)					
16	Camera	1	2	3	4	5
17	Lifetime	0.925	1.351	1.698	NA	NA
18	Time of failure	0.925	2.276	3.974	NA	NA
19	Cost to company	185	185	0	0	0
20	Discounted cost	166.59	142.94	0.00	0.00	0.00
21						
22	Failures within warranty	2				
23	NPV of profit from customer	($244.53)				

① **Inputs.** Enter the inputs in the blue cells.

② **Parameters of gamma distribution.** As we discussed previously, if we enter a desired mean and standard deviation (in cells B5 and B6), then we have to calculate the parameters of the gamma distribution. Do this by entering the formulas

=B5^2/B6^2

and

=B6^2/B5

in cells B7 and B8.

③ **Lifetimes and times of failures.** We generate at most 5 lifetimes and corresponding times of failures. Why only 5? We could generate more, but it is extremely unlikely that this same customer would experience more than 5 failures within warranty, so 5 suffices. As soon as a lifetime is greater than 1.5, the warranty period, we do not generate any further lifetimes, since "the game is over"; instead, we record "NA" in row 17. With this in mind, enter the formulas

=RISKGAMMA(B7,B8)

=IF(B17<B10,RISKGAMMA(B7,B8),"NA")

and

=IF(C17="NA","NA",IF(C17<$B$10,RISKGAMMA($B$7,$B$8),"NA"))

in cells B17, C17, and D17, and copy the latter formula to cells E17 and F17. These formulas guarantee that once "NA" is recorded in a cell, all cells to its right will also contain "NA." To get the actual times of failures, relative to time 0 when the customer originally purchases the camera, enter the formulas

=B17

and

=IF(C17="NA","NA",B18+C17)

in cells B18 and C18, and copy the latter across row 18. These values will be used for the NPV calculation because for NPV we need to know exactly when cash flows occur.

@RISK Function: *RISKGAMMA*

*To generate a random number from the gamma distribution, use the RISKGAMMA function in the form =**RISKGAMMA**(alpha,beta). The mean and standard deviation of this distribution are $\mu = \alpha\beta$ and $\sigma = \sqrt{\alpha\beta}$. Equivalently, we have $\alpha = \mu^2/\sigma^2$ and $\beta = \sigma^2/\mu$.*

④ **Costs and discounted costs.** In row 19 we enter the replacement cost ($185) or 0, depending on whether a failure occurs within warranty, and in row 20 we discount these costs back to time 0, using the failure times in row 18. To do this, enter the formulas

Excel's NPV function can be used only for cash flows that occur at the ends of the respective years. Otherwise, we have to discount cash flows "manually."

=IF(B17<B10,B12,0)

and

=IF(C17="NA",0,IF(C17<$B$10,$B$12,0))

in cells B19 and C19, and copy this latter formula across row 19. Then enter the formula

=IF(B19>0,B19/(1+$B$13)^B18,0)

in cell B20 and copy it across row 20. This formula uses that well-known fact that the present value of a cash flow at time t is the cash flow multiplied by $1/(1 + r)^t$, where r is the discount rate.

5 **Outputs.** Calculate two outputs, the number of failures within warranty and the NPV of profit, with the formulas

=COUNTIF(B19:F19,">0")

and

=B11−B12−SUM(B20:F20)

in cells B22 and B23. Then designate these two cells as @RISK output cells. Note that the NPV is the margin from the sale (undiscounted) minus the sum of the discounted costs from replacements under warranty.

Running the Simulation

The @RISK setup is typical. We run 1000 iterations of a *single* simulation (because there is no RISKSIMTABLE function).

Discussion of the Simulation Results

The @RISK summary statistics and histograms for the two outputs appear in Figures 17.6, 17.7, and 17.8. They show a pretty clear picture. About 85% of the time, there are no failures under warranty and the company makes a profit of $65, the margin from the camera sale. However, there is about a 12.9% chance of exactly 1 failure under warranty, in which case the company's NPV of profit will be an approximate $100 loss. Additionally, there is about a 2.1% chance that there will be even more failures under warranty, in which case the loss will be even greater. Note that in our 1000 iterations, the maximum number of failures under warranty was 3, and the maximum net loss was $357.70. On average, the NPV of profit was $37.62.

Figure 17.6 @RISK Summary Statistics for Warranty Model

Name	Cell	Min	Mean	Max	Median	Std Dev	5%	95%
Failures	B22	0	0.172	3	0	0.4342863	0	1
NPV of profit	B23	-357.7041	37.62433	65	65	68.36123	-99.56981	65

@RISK - Results Summary — Inputs | Outputs — Simulation Results For Outputs: — Inputs= 5, Outputs= 2 — Close

These results indicate that Yakkon is not suffering terribly from warranty costs. However, there are several ways the company could decrease the effects of warranty costs. First, it could increase the price of the camera. Second, it could decrease the warranty period, say, from 1.5 years to 1 year. Third, it could change the terms of the warranty. For example, it could stipulate that if the camera fails within a year, the customer gets a new camera for free, whereas if the time to failure is between 1 and 1.5 years, the customer pays some pro rata share of the replacement cost. Finally, it could try to sell the customer an extended warranty—at a hefty price. We ask you to explore these possibilities in the problems.

Figure 17.7

Histogram of
Number of Failures

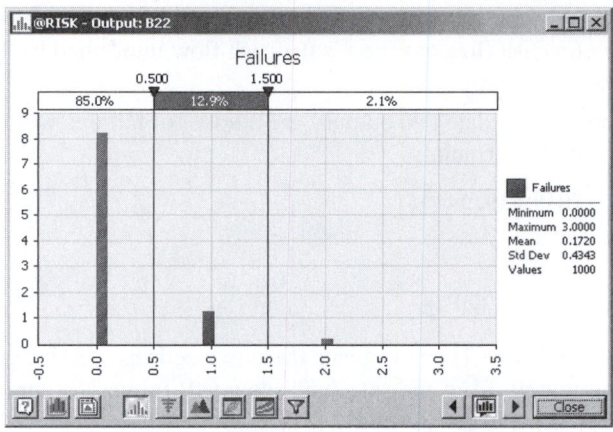

Figure 17.8

Histogram of NPV
of Profit

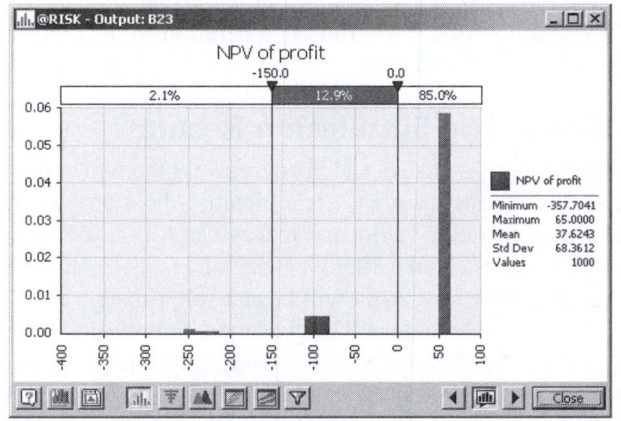

Drug Production with Uncertain Yield

In many manufacturing settings, products are produced in batches, and the usable *yields* from these batches are uncertain. This is particularly true in the drug industry. The following example illustrates how a drug manufacturer can take this uncertainty into account when planning production.

EXAMPLE | **17.3 TRYING TO MEET AN ORDER DUE DATE AT WOZAC**

The Wozac Company is a drug manufacturing company. Wozac has recently accepted an order from its best customer for 8000 ounces of a new miracle drug, and Wozac wants to plan its production schedule to meet the customer's promised delivery date of December 1, 2008. There are three sources of uncertainty that make planning difficult. First, the drug must be produced in batches, and there is uncertainty in the time required to produce a batch, which could be anywhere from 5 to 11 days. This uncertainty is described by the discrete distribution in Table 17.1. Second, the yield (usable quantity) from any batch is uncertain. Based on historical data, Wozac believes the yield can be modeled by a triangular distribution with minimum, most likely, and maximum values equal to 600, 1000, and 1100 ounces, respectively. Third, all batches must go through a rigorous inspection once they are completed. The probability that a typical batch passes inspection is only 0.8.

With probability 0.2, the batch fails inspection, and *none* of it can be used to help fill the order. Wozac wants to use simulation to help decide how many days prior to the due date it should begin production.

Table 17.1   Distribution of Days to Complete a Batch

Days	Probability
5	0.05
6	0.10
7	0.20
8	0.30
9	0.20
10	0.10
11	0.05

Objective   To use simulation to learn when Wozac should begin production for this order so that there is a high probability of completing it by the due date.

WHERE DO THE NUMBERS COME FROM?

The important inputs here are the probability distributions of the time to produce a batch, the yield from a batch, and the inspection result. The probabilities we have assumed would undoubtedly be based on previous production data. For example, the company might have observed that about 80% of all batches in the past passed inspection. Of course, a *discrete* distribution is natural for the number of days to produce a batch, and a *continuous* distribution is appropriate for the yield from a batch.

Solution

The idea is to simulate successive batches—their days to complete, their yields, and whether they pass inspection—and keep a running total of the usable ounces obtained so far. We then use IF functions to check whether the order is complete or another batch is required. We simulate only as many as batches as are required to meet the order, and we keep track of the days required to produce all of these batches. In this way we can "back up" to see when production must begin to meet the due date. For example, if the simulation indicates that the order takes 96 days to complete, then production must begin on August 27, 2008, 96 days before the due date. (For simplicity, we assume that production occurs 7 days a week.)

DEVELOPING THE SIMULATION MODEL

The completed model appears in Figure 17.9. (See the file **Drug Production.xlsx**.) It can be developed as follows.

1 **Inputs.** Enter all of the inputs in the blue cells.

2 **Batch indexes.** We do not know ahead of time how many batches will be required to fill the order. We want to have enough rows in the simulation to cover the worst case that is likely to occur. After some experimentation we found that 25 batches are almost surely enough. Therefore, enter the batch indexes 1 through 25 in column A of the simulation section. (If 25 were not enough, we could always add more rows.) The idea, then, is to fill the *entire* range B25:F49 with formulas. However, we use IF functions in these formulas so that if enough has already been produced to fill the order, blanks are inserted in the remaining cells. For example, the scenario shown in Figure 17.9 is one where 12 batches were required, so blanks appear below row 36.

Figure 17.9 Drug Production Simulation Model

	A	B	C	D	E	F	G	H	I	J	K	L
1	Planning production of a drug											
2												
3	Input section											
4	Amount required (ounces)	8000			Assumptions:							
5	Promised delivery date	12/01/08			The drug is produced in similar-sized batches, although the yield in each							
6					batch is random. Also, the number of days to produce a batch is random.							
7	Distribution of days needed to produce a batch (discrete)				Each batch is inspected, and if it doesn't pass inspection, none of that batch							
8		Days	Probability		can be used.							
9		5	0.05									
10		6	0.10									
11		7	0.20									
12		8	0.30									
13		9	0.20									
14		10	0.10									
15		11	0.05									
16												
17	Distribution of yield (ounces) from each batch (triangular)											
18		Min	Most likely	Max								
19		600	1000	1100								
20												
21	Probability of passing inspection	0.8										
22												
23	Simulation model							Summary measures				
24	Batch	Days	Yield	Pass?	CumYield	Enough?		Batches required	12			
25	1	6	982.4	Yes	982.4	Not yet		Days to complete	94			
26	2	8	902.4	Yes	1884.8	Not yet		Day to start	8/29/08			
27	3	8	887.8	No	1884.8	Not yet						
28	4	5	830.6	Yes	2715.4	Not yet		@Risk summary outputs				
29	5	10	794.2	Yes	3509.6	Not yet		Max batches reqd	20			
30	6	8	872.5	Yes	4382.1	Not yet						
31	7	8	768.4	Yes	5150.5	Not yet		Avg days reqd	94	8/29/08		
32	8	8	651.0	Yes	5801.5	Not yet		Min days reqd	59	10/3/08		
33	9	9	879.3	No	5801.5	Not yet		Max days reqd	160	6/24/08		
34	10	7	690.6	Yes	6492.1	Not yet		5th perc days reqd	72	9/20/08		
35	11	8	941.0	Yes	7433.0	Not yet		95th perc days reqd	121	8/2/08		
36	12	9	897.6	Yes	8330.6	Yes						
37	13							Probability of meeting due date for several starting dates				
38	14								7/15/08	0.991		
39	15								8/1/08	0.954		
40	16								8/15/08	0.845		
41	17								9/1/08	0.469		
42	18								9/15/08	0.120		
43	19											
44	20											
45	21											
46	22											
47	23											
48	24											
49	25											

3 Days for batches. Simulate the days required for batches in column B. To do this, enter the formulas

=RISKDISCRETE(B9:B15,C9:C15)

and

=IF(OR(F25="Yes",F25=""),"",RISKDISCRETE($B$9:$B$15,$C$9:$C$15))

in cell B25 and B26, and copy the latter formula down to cell B49. Note how the IF function enters a blank in this cell if either of two conditions is true: the order was just completed in the previous batch or it has been completed for some time. Similar logic appears in later formulas.

4 Batch yields. Simulate the batch yields in column C. To do this, enter the formulas

=RISKTRIANG(B19,C19,D19)

and

=IF(OR(F25="Yes",F25=""),"",RISKTRIANG($B$19,$C$19,$D$19))

in cells C25 and C26, and copy the latter formula down to cell C49.

⑤ Pass inspection? Check whether each batch passes inspection with the formulas

=IF(RAND()<B21, "Yes","No")

and

=IF(OR(F25="Yes",F25=""),"",IF(RAND()<$B$21, "Yes","No"))

in cells D25 and D26, and copy the latter formula down to cell D49. Note that we could use @RISK's RISKUNIFORM(0,1) function instead of RAND(), but there is no real advantage to doing so. They are essentially equivalent. (Besides, the educational version of @RISK imposes an upper limit of 100 "RISK" input functions per model, so it is often a good idea to substitute built-in Excel functions when possible.)

⑥ Order filled? We keep track of the cumulative usable production and whether the order has been filled in columns E and F. First, enter the formulas

=IF(D25="Yes",C25,0)

and

=IF(E25>=B4, "Yes","Not yet")

in cells E25 and F25 for batch 1. Then enter the general formulas

=IF(OR(F25="Yes",F25=""),"",IF(D26="Yes",C26+E25,E25))

and

=IF(OR(F25="Yes",F25=""),"",IF(E26>=$B$4,"Yes","Not yet"))

in cells E26 and F26, and copy them down to row 49. Note that the entry in column F is "Not enough" if the order is not yet complete. In the row that completes the order, it changes to "Yes," and then it is blank in succeeding rows.

⑦ Summary measures. Calculate the batches and days required in cells I24 and I25 with the formulas

=COUNT(B25:B49)

and

=SUM(B25:B49)

These are the two cells we use as output cells for @RISK, so designate them as such. Also, calculate the day the order should be started to just meet the due date in cell I26 with the formula

=B5−I25

This formula uses "date subtraction" to find an elapsed time. (Again, we assume for simplicity that production occurs every day of the week.)

This completes the simulation model development. The other entries in columns H through J are explained shortly.

Running the Simulation

We set the number of iterations to 1000 and the number of simulations to 1, and then run the simulation as usual.

We can use Excel's RAND function inside an IF function to simulate whether some event occurs or does not occur.

Date subtraction in Excel allows us to calculate the number of days between two given dates.

Discussion of the Simulation Results

After running the simulation, we obtain the histograms of the number of batches required and the number of days required in Figures 17.10 and 17.11.

Figure 17.10

Histogram of
Batches Required

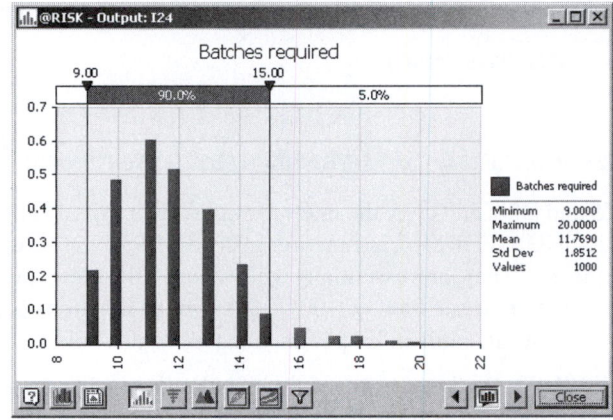

Figure 17.11

Histogram of Days
Required

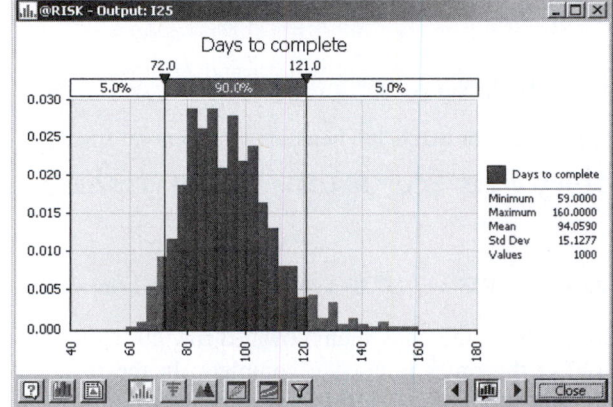

How should Wozac use this information? The key questions are (1) How many batches will be required?, and (2) When should we start production? To answer these questions, it is helpful to use several of @RISK's statistical functions. Recall that these functions can be entered directly into the Excel model worksheet. (Also, recall that they provide useful information only *after* the simulation has been run.) These functions provide no new information we didn't already have from other @RISK windows, but they allow us to see (and manipulate) this information directly in our spreadsheet.

For the first question, we enter the formula

=RISKMAX(I24)

in cell I29. (Refer to Figure 17.9.) It shows that the worst case from the 1000 iterations, in terms of batches required, is 20 batches. (If this maximum were 25, we would add more rows to the simulation model and run the simulation again!)

We can answer the second question in two ways. First, we can calculate summary measures for days required and then back up from the due date. We do this in the range I31:J35. The formulas in column I are

=INT(RISKMEAN(I25))

=RISKMIN(I25)

=RISKMAX(I25)

=RISKPERCENTILE(I25,0.05)

and

=RISKPERCENTILE(I25,0.95)

(The first uses the INT function to produce an integer.) We then subtract each of these from the due date to obtain the potential starting dates in column J. Wozac should realize the pros and cons of these starting dates. For example, if the company wants to be 95% sure of meeting the due date, it should start production on August 2. In contrast, if Wozac starts production on September 20, there is only a 5% chance of meeting the due date.

Alternatively, we can get a more direct answer to our question by using @RISK's RISKTARGET function. This allows us to find the probability of meeting the due date for *any* starting date, such as the trial dates in the range H38:H42. We enter the formula

=RISKTARGET(I25,$B$4−H38)

Using @RISK summary functions such as RISKMEAN, RISKPERCENTILE, and others allows us to capture simulation results in the same worksheet as the simulation model. These functions do not provide relevant results until the simulation is run.

in cell I38 and copy it down. This function returns the fraction of iterations where the (random) value in the first argument is less than or equal to the (fixed) value in the second argument. For example, we see that 84.5% of the iterations have a value of days required less than or equal to 108, the number of days from August 15 to the due date.

What is our recommendation to Wozac? We suggest going with the 95th percentile—begin production on August 2. Then there is only a 5% chance of failing to meet the due date. But the table in the range H38:I42 also provides useful information. For each potential starting date, Wozac can see the probability of meeting the due date. ∎

PROBLEMS

Level A

1. In Example 17.1, the possible profits vary from negative to positive for each of the 10 possible bids examined.
   a. For each of these, use @RISK's RISKTARGET function to find the probability that Miller's profit is positive. Do you believe these results should have any bearing on Miller's choice of bid?
   b. Use @RISK's RISKPERCENTILE function to find the 10th percentile for each of these bids. Can you explain why the percentiles have the values you obtain?

2. If the number of competitors in Example 17.1 doubles, how does the optimal bid change?

3. Referring to Example 17.1, if the average bid for each competitor stays the same, but their bids exhibit less variability, does Miller's optimal bid increase or decrease? To study this question, assume that each competitor's bid, expressed as a multiple of Miller's cost to complete the project, follows each of the following distributions.
   a. Triangular with parameters 1.0, 1.3, and 2.4

   b. Triangular with parameters 1.2, 1.3, and 2.2
   c. Use @RISK's Define Distributions window to see that the distributions in parts **a** and **b** have the same mean as the original triangular distribution in the example, but smaller standard deviations. What is the common mean? Why is it not the same as the most likely value, 1.3?

4. In the warranty example, Example 17.2, we introduced the gamma distribution to model the right skewness of the lifetime distribution. Experiment to see whether we could have used the triangular distribution instead. Let its minimum value be 0, and choose its most likely and maximum values so that this triangular distribution has approximately the same mean and standard deviation as the gamma distribution in the example. (Use @RISK's Define Distributions window and trial and error to do this.) Then run the simulation and comment on similarities or differences between your outputs and the outputs in the example.

5. See how sensitive the results in the warranty example, Example 17.2, are to the following changes. For each part, make the change indicated, run the simulation, and comment on any differences between your outputs and the outputs in the example.

a. The cost of a new camera is increased to $300.

b. The warranty period is decreased to 1 year.

c. The terms of the warranty are changed. If the camera fails within 1 year, the customer gets a new camera for free. However, if the camera fails between 1 year and 1.5 years, the customer pays a pro rata share of the new camera, going linearly from 0 to full price. For example, if it fails at 1.2 years, which is 40% of the way from 1 to 1.5, the customer pays 40% of the full price.

d. The customer pays $50 up front for an extended warranty. This extends the warranty to 3 years. This extended warranty is just like the original, so that if the camera fails within 3 years, the customer gets a new camera for free.

6. In the drug production example, Example 17.3, we commented on the 95th percentile on days required in cell I35 and the corresponding date in cell J35. If the company begins production on this date, then it is 95% sure to complete the order by the due date. We found this date to be August 2. Do you always get this answer? Find out by (1) running the simulation 10 more times, each with 1000 iterations, and finding the 95th percentile and corresponding date in each, and (2) running the simulation once more, but with 10,000 iterations. Comment on the difference between simulations 1 and 2 in terms of accuracy. Given these results, when would you recommend that production should begin?

7. In the drug production example, Example 17.3, suppose we want to run 5 simulations, where we vary the probability of passing inspection from 0.6 to 1.0 in increments of 0.1. Use the RISKSIMTABLE function appropriately to do this. Comment on the effect of this parameter on the key outputs. In particular, does the probability of passing inspection have a big effect on when production should start? (*Note*: When this probability is low, it might be necessary to produce more than 25 batches, the maximum we built into our model. Check whether this maximum should be increased.)

17.3 FINANCIAL MODELS

There are many financial applications where simulation can be applied. Future cash flows, future stock prices, and future interest rates are some of the many uncertain variables financial analysts must deal with. In every direction they turn, they see uncertainty. In this section we analyze a few typical financial applications that can benefit from simulation modeling.

Financial Planning Models

Many companies, such as GM, Eli Lilly, Procter & Gamble, and Pfizer, use simulation in their capital budgeting and financial planning processes. Simulation can be used to model the uncertainty associated with future cash flows. In particular, simulation can be used to answer questions such as the following:

■ What are the mean and variance of a project's net present value (NPV)?

■ What is the probability that a project will have a negative NPV?

■ What are the mean and variance of a company's profit during the next fiscal year?

■ What is the probability that a company will have to borrow more than $2 million during the next year?

The following example illustrates how simulation can be used to evaluate an investment opportunity.

EXAMPLE | **17.4 DEVELOPING A NEW CAR AT GF AUTO**

General Ford (GF) Auto Corporation is developing a new model of compact car. This car is assumed to generate sales for the next 5 years. GF has gathered information about the following quantities through focus groups with the marketing and engineering departments.

- **Fixed cost of developing car.** This cost is assumed to $1.4 billion. The fixed cost is incurred at the beginning of year 1, before any sales are recorded.

- **Margin per car.** This is the unit selling price minus the variable cost of producing a car. GF assumes that in year 1, the margin will be $5000. Every other year, GF assumes the margin will decrease by 4%.[1]

- **Sales.** The demand for the car is the uncertain quantity. In its first year, GF assumes sales—number of cars sold—will be triangularly distributed with parameters 100,000, 150,000, and 170,000. Every year after that, the company assumes that sales will decrease by some percentage, where this percentage is triangularly distributed with parameters 5%, 8%, and 10%. GF also assumes that the percentage decreases in successive years are independent of one another.

- **Depreciation and taxes.** The company will depreciate its development cost on a straight-line basis over the lifetime of the car. The corporate tax rate is 40%.

- **Discount rate.** GF figures its cost of capital at 15%.

Given these assumptions, GF wants to develop a simulation model that will evaluate its NPV of after-tax cash flows for this new car over the 5-year time horizon.

Objective   To simulate the cash flows from the new car model, from the development time to the end of its life cycle, so that GF can estimate the NPV of after-tax cash flows from this car.

WHERE DO THE NUMBERS COME FROM?

There are many inputs to this problem. As we indicated, they are probably obtained from experts within the company and from focus groups of potential customers.

Solution

This model is like most financial multiyear spreadsheet models. The completed model extends several years to the right, but most of the work is for the first year or two. From that point, we simply copy to the other years to complete the model.

DEVELOPING THE SIMULATION MODEL

The simulation model for GF appears in Figure 17.12. (See the file **New Car Development.xlsx.**) It can be formed as follows.

1 Inputs. Enter the various inputs in the blue cells.

2 Unit sales. Generate first-year sales in cell B12 with the formula

=RISKTRIANG(E5,F5,G5)

Then generate the reduced sales in later years by entering the formula

=B12*(1−RISKTRIANG($E$6,$F$6,$G$6))

in cell C12 and copying it across row 12. Note that each sales figure is a random fraction of the *previous* sales figure.

---

[1] The margin decreases because we assume variable costs tend to increase through time, whereas selling prices tend to remain fairly constant through time.

Figure 17.12   GF Auto Simulation Model

	A	B	C	D	E	F	G
1	New car simulation						
2							
3	Inputs			Parameters of triangular distributions			
4	Fixed development cost	$1,400,000,000			Min	Most likely	Max
5	Year 1 contribution	$5,000		Year 1 sales	100000	150000	170000
6	Annual decrease in contribution	4%		Annual decay rate	5%	8%	10%
7	Tax rate	40%					
8	Discount rate	15%					
9							
10	Simulation						
11	End of year	1	2	3	4	5	
12	Unit sales	129137	118721	109417	102122	92835	
13	Unit contribution	$5,000	$4,800	$4,608	$4,424	$4,247	
14	Revenue minus variable cost	$645,687,270	$569,859,933	$504,193,828	$451,754,559	$394,245,786	
15	Depreciation	$280,000,000	$280,000,000	$280,000,000	$280,000,000	$280,000,000	
16	Before tax profit	$365,687,270	$289,859,933	$224,193,828	$171,754,559	$114,245,786	
17	After tax profit	$219,412,362	$173,915,960	$134,516,297	$103,052,736	$68,547,472	
18	Cash flow	$499,412,362	$453,915,960	$414,516,297	$383,052,736	$348,547,472	
19							
20	NPV of cash flows	$42,349,830					

3 **Contributions.** Calculate the unit contributions in row 13 by entering the formulas

=B5

and

=B13*(1−$B$6)

in cells B13 and C13, and copying the latter across. Then calculate the contributions in row 14 as the product of the corresponding values in rows 12 and 13.

4 **Depreciation.** Calculate the depreciation each year in row 15 as the development cost in cell B4 divided by 5. This is exactly what "straight-line depreciation" means.

5 **Before-tax and after-tax profits.** To calculate the before-tax profit in any year, we subtract the depreciation from total contribution, so each value in row 16 is the difference between the corresponding values in rows 14 and 15. The reason is that depreciation isn't taxed. To calculate the after-tax profits in row 17, we multiply each before-tax profit by 1 minus the tax rate in cell B7. Finally, each cash flow in row 18 is the sum of the corresponding values in rows 15 and 17. Here we add depreciation back to get the cash flow.

We subtract depreciation to get before-tax profit, but we then add it back after taxes have been deducted.

6 **NPV.** Calculate the NPV of cash flows in cell B20 with the formula

=−B4+NPV(B8,B18:F18)

and designate it as an @RISK output cell (the only output cell). Here, we are assuming that the development cost is incurred right now, so that it isn't discounted, and that all other cash flows occur at the ends of the respective years. This allows us to use the NPV function directly.

Running the Simulation

We set the number of iterations to 1000 and the number of simulations to 1, and then run the simulation as usual.

Discussion of the Simulation Results

After running @RISK, we obtain the summary measures for total NPV in Figure 17.13 and the histogram in Figure 17.14. These results are somewhat comforting, but also a cause of concern, for GF. On the bright side, the mean NPV is about $135 million, and there is some chance that the NPV could go well above that figure, even up to almost $400 million. However, there is also a dark side as shown by the two sliders in the histogram. We placed one slider over an NPV of 0. As the histogram indicates, there is about an 84% chance of a positive NPV, but there is about a 16% chance of it being negative. The second slider is positioned at its default 5 percentile setting. Financial analysts often call this percentile the **value at risk**, or **VAR**, because it indicates nearly the worst possible outcome. From this simulation, we see that GF's VAR is approximately an $87 million loss.

Figure 17.13   Summary Measures for Total NPV

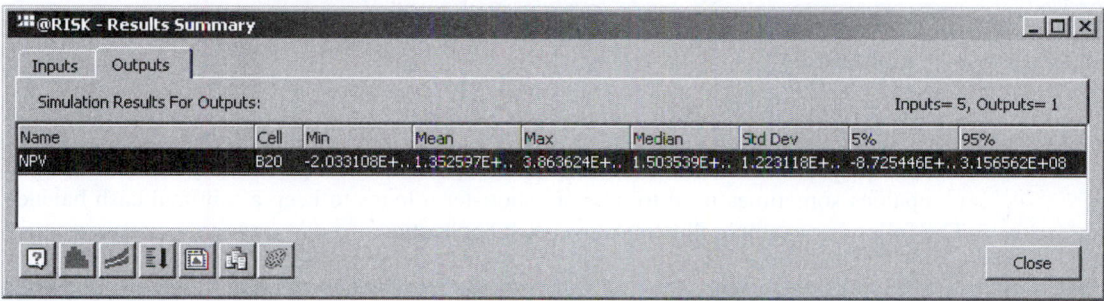

Figure 17.14

Histogram of
Total NPV

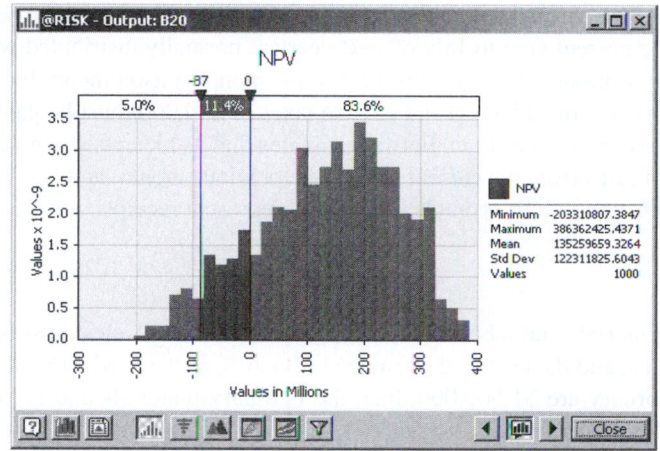

> The **value at risk**, or **VAR**, is the 5th percentile of a distribution, and it is often used in financial models. It indicates nearly the worst possible outcome.

Financial analysts typically look at VAR to see how bad—or more precisely, almost how bad— things could get.

What is most responsible for this huge variability in NPV, the variability in first-year sales or the variability in annual sales decreases? We can answer this with @RISK's tornado chart. (See Figure 17.15.) To get this chart, click on the tornado button below the histogram in Figure 17.14 and select the Correlation option. This chart answers our question emphatically. Variability in first-year sales is by far the largest influence on NPV. It correlates almost perfectly with NPV. The annual decreases in sales are not unimportant, but they have much less effect on NPV. If GF wants to get a more favorable NPV distribution, it should do all it can to boost first-year sales—and make the first-year sales distribution less variable.

Figure 17.15

Tornado Chart for NPV

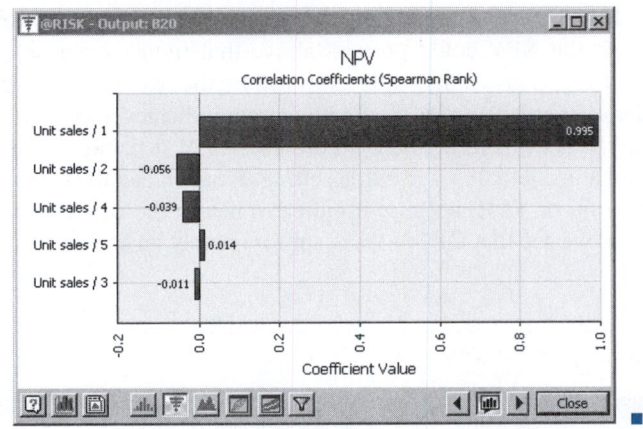

A tornado chart lets you see which random inputs have the most effect on a specified output.

Cash Balance Models

All companies track their cash balance through time. As specific payments come due, companies sometimes need to take out short-term loans to keep a minimal cash balance. The following example illustrates one such application.

EXAMPLE | **17.5 MAINTAINING A MINIMAL CASH BALANCE AT ENTSON**

The Entson Company believes that its monthly sales during the period from November of the current year to July of next year are normally distributed with the means and standard deviations given in Table 17.2. Each month Entson incurs fixed costs of $250,000. In March taxes of $150,000 and in June taxes of $50,000 must be paid. Dividends of $50,000 must also be paid in June. Entson estimates that its receipts in a given month are a weighted sum of sales from the current month, the previous month, and two months ago with weights 0.2, 0.6, and 0.2. In symbols, if R_t and S_t represent receipts and sales in month t, then

$$R_t = 0.2S_{t-2} + 0.6S_{t-1} + 0.2S_t \qquad (17.1)$$

The materials and labor needed to produce a month's sales must be purchased 1 month in advance, and the cost of these averages to 80% of the product's sales. For example, if sales in February are $1,500,000, then the February materials and labor costs are $1,200,000, but these must be paid in January.

Table 17.2   Monthly Sales (in Thousands of Dollars) for Entson

	Nov.	Dec.	Jan.	Feb.	Mar.	Apr.	May	Jun.	Jul.
Mean	1500	1600	1800	1500	1900	2600	2400	1900	1300
Standard Deviation	70	75	80	80	100	125	120	90	70

At the beginning of January, Entson has $250,000 in cash. The company wants to ensure that each month's ending cash balance never falls below $250,000. This means that Entson might have to take out short-term (one-month) loans. For example, if the ending cash balance at the end of March is $200,000, Entson will take out a loan for $50,000, which it will then pay back (with interest) one month later. The interest rate on a short-term loan is 1% per month. At the beginning of each month, Entson earns interest of 0.5% on its cash balance. The company wants to use simulation to estimate the maximum loan it will need to take out to meet its desired minimum cash balance. Entson also wants to analyze how its loans will vary through time, and it wants to estimate the total interest paid on these loans.

Objective To simulate Entson's cash flows and the loans the company must take out to meet a minimum cash balance.

WHERE DO THE NUMBERS COME FROM?

Although there are many monetary inputs in the problem statement, they should all be easily accessible. Of course, Entson chooses the minimum cash balance of $250,000 as a matter of company policy.

Solution

There is a considerable amount of bookkeeping in this simulation, so it is a good idea to list the events in chronological order that occur each month. We assume the following:

- Entson observes its beginning cash balance.
- Entson receives interest on its beginning cash balance.
- Receipts arrive and expenses are paid (including payback of the previous month's loan, if any, with interest).
- If necessary, Entson takes out a short-term loan.
- The final cash balance is observed, which becomes next month's beginning cash balance.

DEVELOPING THE SIMULATION MODEL

The completed simulation model appears in Figure 17.16. (See the file **Cash Balance.xlsx**.) It requires the following steps.

1 **Inputs.** Enter the inputs in the blue cells. Note that we simulate loans (in row 42) only for the period from January to June of next year. However, we need sales figures (in row 28) in November and December of the current year to generate receipts for January and February. Also, we need July sales for next year to generate the material and labor costs paid in June.

2 **Actual sales.** Generate the sales in row 28 by entering the formula

=RISKNORMAL(B6,B7)

in cell B28 and copying across.

3 **Beginning cash balance.** For January of next year, enter the cash balance with the formula

=B19

in cell D31. Then for the other months enter the formula

=D43

in cell E31 and copy it across row 31. This reflects that the beginning cash balance for one month is the final cash balance from the previous month.

Figure 17.16
Cash Balance
Simulation Model

	A	B	C	D	E	F	G	H	I	J
1	Entson cash balance simulation									
2						All monetary values are in $1000s.				
3	Inputs									
4	Distribution of monthly sales (normal)									
5		Nov	Dec	Jan	Feb	Mar	Apr	May	Jun	Jul
6	Mean	1500	1600	1800	1500	1900	2600	2400	1900	1300
7	St Dev	70	75	80	80	100	125	120	90	70
8										
9	Monthly fixed cost			250	250	250	250	250	250	
10	Tax, dividend expenses			0	0	150	0	0	100	
11										
12	Receipts in any month are of form: A*(sales from 2 months ago)+B*(previous month's sales)+C*(current month's sales), where:									
13		A	B	C						
14		0.2	0.6	0.2						
15										
16	Cost of materials and labor for next month, spent this month, is a percentage of product's sales from next month, where the percentage is:									
17		80%								
18										
19	Initial cash in January	250								
20	Minimum cash balance	250								
21										
22	Monthly interest rates									
23	Interest rate on loan	1.0%								
24	Interest rate on cash	0.5%								
25										
26	Simulation									
27		Nov	Dec	Jan	Feb	Mar	Apr	May	Jun	Jul
28	Actual sales	1488.324	1536.407	1821.793	1454.789	2023.135	2596.600	2449.972	2004.528	1310.329
29										
30	Cash, receipts									
31	Beginning cash balance			250.000	421.286	250.000	250.000	250.000	250.000	
32	Interest on cash balance			1.250	2.106	1.250	1.250	1.250	1.250	
33	Receipts			1583.867316	1691.314966	1641.858901	2024.158547	2452.581126	2390.2086	
34	Costs									
35	Fixed costs			250	250	250	250	250	250	
36	Tax, dividend expenses			0	0	150	0	0	100	
37	Material, labor expenses			1163.831	1618.508	2077.280	1959.977	1603.623	1048.263	
38	Loan payback (principal)				0.000	3.800	838.009	1030.958	441.059	0.000
39	Loan payback (interest)				0.000	0.038	8.380	10.310	4.411	0.000
40										
41	Cash balance before loan			421.286	246.200	-588.009	-780.958	-191.059	797.726	
42	Loan amount (if any)			0.000	3.800	838.009	1030.958	441.059	0.000	
43	Final cash balance			421.286	250.000	250.000	250.000	250.000	797.726	
44										
45	Maximum loan	1030.958								
46	Total intest on loans	23.138								

4 **Incomes.** Entson's incomes (interest on cash balance and receipts) are entered in rows 32 and 33. To calculate these, enter the formulas

=$B$24*D31

and

=SUMPRODUCT($B$14:$D$14,B28:D28)

in cells D32 and D33 and copy them across rows 32 and 33. This latter formula, which is based on equation (17.1), multiplies the fixed weights in row 14 by the relevant sales and adds these products to calculate receipts.

5 **Expenses.** Entson's expenses (fixed costs, taxes and dividends, material and labor costs, and payback of the previous month's loan) are entered in rows 35 through 39. Calculate these by entering the formulas

=D9

=D10

=$B$17*E28

=D42

and

$$=D42*\$B\$23$$

in cells D35, D36, D37, E38, and E39 and copying these across rows 35 through 39. (For the loan payback, we are assuming that no loan payback is due in January.)

The loan amounts are determined by the random cash inflows and outflows and the fact that Entson's policy is to maintain a minimum cash balance.

6 **Cash balance before loan.** Calculate the cash balance before the loan (if any) by entering the formula

$$=SUM(D31:D33)-SUM(D35:D39)$$

in cell D41 and copying it across row 41.

7 **Amount of loan.** If the value in row 41 is below the minimum cash balance ($250,000), Entson must borrow enough to bring the cash balance up to this minimum. Otherwise, no loan is necessary. Therefore, enter the formula

$$=MAX(\$B\$20-D41,0)$$

in cell D42 and copy it across row 42. (We could use an IF function, rather the MAX function, to accomplish the same result.)

8 **Final cash balance.** Calculate the final cash balance by entering the formula

$$=D41+D42$$

in cell D43 and copying it across row 43.

9 **Maximum loan, total interest.** Calculate the maximum loan from January to June in cell B45 with the formula

$$=MAX(D42:I42)$$

Then calculate the total interest paid on all loans in cell B46 with the formula

$$=SUM(E39:J39)$$

An @RISK output range, as opposed to a single output cell, allows us to obtain a summary chart that shows the whole simulated range at once. This range is typically a time series.

10 **Output range.** In the usual way, designate cells B45 and B46 as output cells. Also, designate the entire range of loans, D42:I42, as an output range. To do this, highlight this range and click on the @RISK Add Output button. It will ask you for a name of the output. We suggest "Loans." Then a typical formula in this range, such as the formula for cell E42, will be

$$=RISKOUTPUT(\text{“Loans”},2) + MAX(\$B\$20-E41,0)$$

This indicates that cell E42 is the second cell in the Loans output range.

Running the Simulation

We set the number of iterations to 1000 and the number of simulations to 1. We then run the simulation in the usual way.

Discussion of the Simulation Results

After running the simulation, we obtain the summary results in Figure 17.17. They indicate that the maximum loan varies considerably, from a low of about $461,000 to a high of about $1,534,000. The average is about $952,500. We also see that Entson is spending close to $20,000 on average in interest on the loans, although the actual amounts vary considerably from one iteration to another.

Figure 17.17

Summary Measures
for Simulation

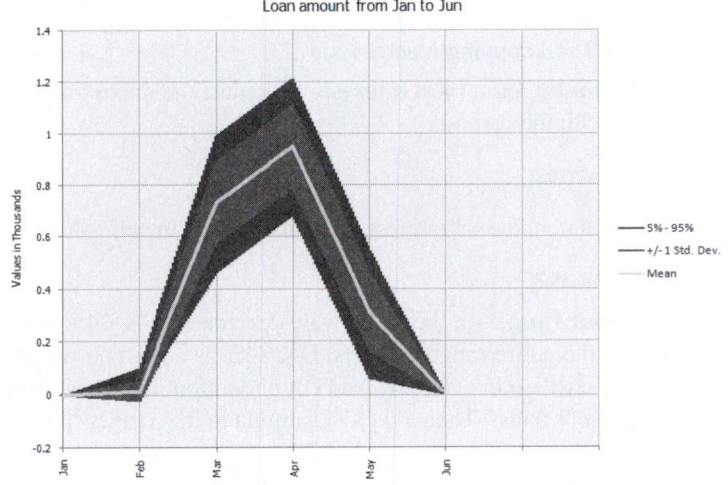

	@RISK - Results Summary							
Inputs	Outputs							

Simulation Results For Outputs: Inputs= 9, Outputs= 8

Name	Cell	Min	Mean	Max	Median	Std Dev	5%	95%
– Range: Loans								
Loan amount (if any) / Jan	D42	0	0.3120223	64.81628	0	3.559813	0	0
Loan amount (if any) / Feb	E42	0	14.54189	351.7782	0	39.7943	0	102.3367
Loan amount (if any) / Mar	F42	201.7258	734.8561	1194.72	736.7593	157.588	462.1605	992.7601
Loan amount (if any) / Apr	G42	461.3435	950.9836	1534.026	955.7982	163.0347	682.6968	1212.633
Loan amount (if any) / May	H42	0	309.9905	826.8547	308.2774	147.6159	60.40136	547.5947
Loan amount (if any) / Jun	I42	0	0	0	0	0	0	0
– Range: <none>								
Maximum loan	B45	461.3435	952.5247	1534.026	955.976	161.0774	687.219	1212.633
Total interest	B46	7.421526	20.10684	33.60012	20.13556	4.273962	13.28679	27.12564

We can also gain insights from the summary trend chart of the series of loans, shown in Figure 17.18. To get this chart, click on the third button at the bottom of the Results Summary window in Figure 17.17. (This button is also available in any histogram window.) This chart clearly shows how the loans vary through time. The middle line is the expected loan amount. The inner bands extend to 1 standard deviation on each side of the mean, and the outer bands extend to the 5th and 95th percentiles. (@RISK lets you customize these bands in a number of ways by right-clicking on the chart.) We see that the largest loans will be required in March and April.

Figure 17.18

Summary Chart
of Loans
Through Time

Is it intuitively clear why the required loans peak in March and April? After all, why should Entson need money in months when its sales tend to be relatively high? There are two factors working here. First, Entson has to pay its costs early. For example, it has to pay 80% of its April sales for labor and material expenses in March. Second, most of its receipts arrive late. For example, 80% of its receipts from sales in March are not received until *after* March. Therefore, the answer to our question is that the timing and amounts of loans are fairly complex. Of course, this is why Entson goes to the trouble of building a simulation model! ∎

Investment Models

Individual investors typically want to choose investment strategies that meet some prespecified goal. The following example is typical. Here, a person wants to meet a retirement goal, starting at an early age.

EXAMPLE | **17.6 INVESTING FOR RETIREMENT**

Attorney Sally Evans has just begun her career. At age 25, she has 40 years until retirement, but she realizes that now is the time to start investing. She plans to invest $1000 at the beginning of each of the next 40 years. Each year, she plans to put fixed percentages—the same each year—of this $1000 into stocks, Treasury bonds (T-bonds), and Treasury bills (T-bills). However, she is not sure which percentages to use. (We call these percentages *investment weights*.) She does have historical annual returns from stocks, T-bonds, and T-bills from 1946 to 2001. These are listed in the file **Retirement Planning.xlsx**. This file also includes inflation rates for these years. For example, for 1993 the annual returns for stocks, T-bonds, and T-bills were 9.99%, 18.24%, and 2.90%, respectively, and the inflation rate was 2.75%. Sally would like to use simulation to help decide what investment weights to use, with the objective of achieving a large investment value, in *today's* dollars, at the end of 40 years.

Objective   To use simulation to estimate the value of Sally's future investments, in today's dollars, from several investment strategies in T-bills, T-bonds, and stocks.

WHERE DO THE NUMBERS COME FROM?

Historical returns and inflation rates, such as those quoted here, are widely available on the Web. In fact, you might want to get more recent data for use in the model.

Solution

We simulate future scenarios by randomly choosing past scenarios, giving higher probabilities to more recent scenarios.

The most difficult modeling aspect is settling on a way to use historical returns and inflation factors to generate *future* values of these quantities. We use a "scenario" approach. We think of each historical year as a possible scenario, where the scenario specifies the returns and inflation factor for that year. Then for any future year, we randomly choose one of these scenarios. It seems intuitive that more recent scenarios ought to have a greater chance of being chosen. To implement this idea, we give a weight (not to be confused with the investment weights) to each scenario, starting with weight 1 for 2001. Then the weight for any year is a "damping factor" multiplied by the weight from the next year. For example, the weight for 1996 is the damping factor multiplied by the weight for 1997. To change these weights to probabilities, we divide each weight by the sum of all the weights. The damping factor we illustrate is 0.98. Others could be used instead, and we are frankly not sure which produces the most realistic results. (This is an important question for financial research!)

Without a package like RiskOptimizer, we cannot find the "best" set of investment weights, but the simulation model lets us experiment with various sets of weights.

The other difficult part of the solution is knowing which investment weights to try. This is really an optimization problem—find three weights that add to 1 and produce the largest mean final cash. Palisade has another software package, RiskOptimizer, that solves this type of optimization–simulation problem. However, we simply try several sets of weights, where some percentage is put into stocks and the remainder is split evenly between T-bonds and T-bills, and see which does best. You can try other sets if you like.

DEVELOPING THE SIMULATION MODEL

The historical data and the simulation model (each with some rows hidden) appear in Figures 17.19 and 17.20. (Again, see the **Retirement Planning.xlsx** file.) It can be developed as follows.

Figure 17.19

Historical Data,
Inputs, and
Probabilities

	A	B	C	D	E	F	G
18	**Historical data and probabilities**						
19	Year	T-Bills	T-Bonds	Stocks	Inflation	ProbWts	Probability
20	1946	0.0035	-0.0010	-0.0807	0.1817	0.3292	0.0097
21	1947	0.0050	-0.0263	0.0571	0.0901	0.3359	0.0099
22	1948	0.0081	0.0340	0.0550	0.0271	0.3428	0.0101
23	1949	0.0110	0.0645	0.1879	-0.0180	0.3497	0.0103
24	1950	0.0120	0.0006	0.3171	0.0579	0.3569	0.0105
52	1978	0.0718	-0.0116	0.0656	0.0903	0.6283	0.0186
53	1979	0.1038	-0.0122	0.1844	0.1331	0.6412	0.0189
54	1980	0.1124	-0.0395	0.3242	0.1240	0.6543	0.0193
55	1981	0.1471	0.0185	-0.0491	0.0894	0.6676	0.0197
56	1982	0.1054	0.4035	0.2141	0.0387	0.6812	0.0201
57	1983	0.0880	0.0068	0.2251	0.0380	0.6951	0.0205
58	1984	0.0985	0.1543	0.0627	0.0395	0.7093	0.0209
59	1985	0.0772	0.3097	0.3216	0.0377	0.7238	0.0214
60	1986	0.0616	0.2444	0.1847	0.0113	0.7386	0.0218
61	1987	0.0547	-0.0269	0.0523	0.0441	0.7536	0.0223
62	1988	0.0635	0.0967	0.1681	0.0442	0.7690	0.0227
63	1989	0.0837	0.1811	0.3149	0.0465	0.7847	0.0232
64	1990	0.0781	0.0618	-0.0317	0.0611	0.8007	0.0236
65	1991	0.0560	0.1930	0.3055	0.0306	0.8171	0.0241
66	1992	0.0351	0.0805	0.0767	0.0290	0.8337	0.0246
67	1993	0.0290	0.1824	0.0999	0.0275	0.8508	0.0251
68	1994	0.0390	-0.0777	0.0131	0.0267	0.8681	0.0256
69	1995	0.0560	0.2348	0.3720	0.0250	0.8858	0.0262
70	1996	0.0514	0.0143	0.2382	0.0330	0.9039	0.0267
71	1997	0.0491	0.0994	0.3186	0.0170	0.9224	0.0272
72	1998	0.0516	0.1492	0.2834	0.0160	0.9412	0.0278
73	1999	0.0439	-0.0825	0.2089	0.0270	0.9604	0.0284
74	2000	0.0537	0.1666	-0.0903	0.0340	0.9800	0.0289
75	2001	0.0573	0.0557	-0.1185	0.0160	1.0000	0.0295
76					Sums -->	33.8702	1.0000

1 **Inputs.** Enter the data in the blue regions of Figures 17.19 and 17.20.

2 **Weights.** The investment weights we use for the model are in rows 10 through 12. (For example, the first set puts 80% in stocks and 10% in each of T-bonds and T-bills.) We can simulate all three sets of weights simultaneously with a RISKSIMTABLE and VLOOKUP combination as follows. First, enter the formula

=RISKSIMTABLE({1,2,3})

in cell A16. Then enter the formula

=VLOOKUP($A$16,LTable1,2)

in cell B16 and copy it to cells C16 and D16. Then modify the formulas in these latter two cells, changing the last argument of the VLOOKUP to 3 and 4, respectively. For example, the formula in cell D16 should end up as

=VLOOKUP($A$16,LTable1,4)

The effect is that we will run three simulations, one for each set of weights in rows 10 through 12.

3 **Probabilities.** Enter value 1 in cell F75. Then enter the formula

=$B$4*F75

in cell F74 and copy it *up* to cell F20. Sum these values with the SUM function in cell F76. Then to convert them to probabilities (numbers that add to 1), enter the formula

=F20/$F$76

Figure 17.20 Simulation Model

	A	B	C	D	E	F	G	H	I	J	K	L	M	N	O	P	Q
1	Planning for retirement																
2																	
3	Inputs								Range names used:								
4	Damping factor	0.98							LTable1	=Model!$A$10:$D$12							
5	Yearly investment	$1,000							LTable2	=Model!$A$20:$E$75							
6	Planning horizon	40	years						Weights	=Model!$B$16:$D$16							
7																	
8	Alternative sets of weights to test																
9		Index	T-Bills	T-Bonds	Stocks												
10		1	0.10	0.10	0.80												
11		2	0.20	0.20	0.60												
12		3	0.30	0.30	0.40												
13																	
14	Weights used								Output from simulation below								
15		Index	T-Bills	T-Bonds	Stocks				Final cash (today's dollars)	$72,757							
16		1	0.10	0.10	0.80												
17													Column offset for lookup2				
18	Historical data and probabilities								Simulation model								
19	Year	T-Bills	T-Bonds	Stocks	Inflation	ProbWts	Probability		Future year	Beginning cash	Scenario	T-Bills	T-Bonds	Stocks	Inflation	Ending cash	Deflator
												2	3	4	5		
20	1946	0.0035	-0.0010	-0.0807	0.1817	0.3292	0.0097		1	$1,000	1995	1.0560	1.2348	1.3720	1.0250	1327	0.976
21	1947	0.0050	-0.0263	0.0571	0.0901	0.3359	0.0099		2	2327	1988	1.0635	1.0967	1.1681	1.0442	2677	0.934
22	1948	0.0081	0.0340	0.0550	0.0271	0.3428	0.0101		3	3677	1990	1.0781	1.0618	0.9683	1.0611	3635	0.881
23	1949	0.0110	0.0645	0.1879	-0.0180	0.3497	0.0103		4	4635	1982	1.1054	1.4035	1.2141	1.0387	5665	0.848
24	1950	0.0120	0.0006	0.3171	0.0579	0.3569	0.0105		5	6665	1968	1.0521	0.9974	1.1106	1.0472	7287	0.809
52	1978	0.0718	-0.0116	0.0656	0.0903	0.6283	0.0186		33	145741	1954	1.0086	1.0719	1.5262	0.9950	208266	0.195
53	1979	0.1038	-0.0122	0.1844	0.1331	0.6412	0.0189		34	209266	1966	1.0476	1.0365	0.8994	1.0335	194184	0.189
54	1980	0.1124	-0.0395	0.3242	0.1240	0.6543	0.0193		35	195184	1983	1.0880	1.0068	1.2251	1.0380	232183	0.182
55	1981	0.1471	0.0185	-0.0491	0.0894	0.6676	0.0197		36	233183	1950	1.0120	1.0006	1.3171	1.0579	292631	0.172
56	1982	0.1054	0.4035	0.2141	0.0387	0.6812	0.0201		37	293631	1958	1.0154	0.9390	1.4336	1.0176	394147	0.169
57	1983	0.0880	0.0068	0.2251	0.0380	0.6951	0.0205		38	395147	2000	1.0537	1.1666	0.9097	1.0340	375307	0.163
58	1984	0.0985	0.1543	0.0627	0.0395	0.7093	0.0209		39	376307	1988	1.0635	1.0967	1.1681	1.0442	432941	0.156
59	1985	0.0772	0.3097	0.3216	0.0377	0.7238	0.0214		40	433941	1993	1.0290	1.1824	1.0999	1.0275	477795	0.152

in cell G20 and copy it down to cell G75. Note how the probabilities for more recent years are considerably larger. When we randomly select scenarios, the recent years will have a greater chance of being chosen. (The SUM formula in cell G76 simply confirms that the probabilities sum to 1.)

4 Scenarios. Moving to the model in Figure 17.20, we want to simulate 40 scenarios in columns K through O, one for each year of Sally's investing. To do this, enter the formulas

=RISKDISCRETE($A$20:$A$75,$G$20:$G$75)

and

=1+VLOOKUP($K20,LTable2,L$18)

in cells K20 and L20, and then copy this latter formula to the range M20:O20. Make sure you understand how the RISKDISCRETE and VLOOKUP functions combine to achieve our goal. (Also, check the list of range names we have used at the top of Figure 17.20.) The RISKDISCRETE randomly generates a year from column A, using the probabilities in column G. Then the VLOOKUP captures the data from this year. (We add 1 to the VLOOKUP to get a value such as 1.08, rather than 0.08.) This is the key to the simulation. (Do you see why we don't use Excel's RANDBETWEEN function to generate the years in column K? The reason is that this function makes all possible years equally likely, and we want more recent years to be *more* likely.)

5 Beginning, ending cash. The bookkeeping part is straightforward. Begin by entering the formula

=B5

in cell J20 for the initial investment. Then enter the formulas

=J20*SUMPRODUCT(Weights,L20:N20)

and

=$B$5+P20

in cells P20 and J21 for ending cash in the first year and beginning cash in the second year. The former shows how the beginning cash grows in a given year. You should think through it carefully. The latter implies that Sally reinvests her previous money, plus she invests an additional $1000. Copy these formulas down columns J and P.

6 **Deflators.** We eventually want to deflate future dollars to today's dollars. The proper way to do this is to calculate deflators (also called deflation factors). Do this by entering the formula

=1/O20

in cell Q20. Then enter the formula

=Q20/O21

in cell Q21 and copy it down. The effect is that the deflator for future year 20, say, in cell Q39, is 1 divided by the product of all 20 inflation factors up through that year. (This is similar to discounting for the time value of money, but the relevant discount rate, now the inflation rate, varies from year to year.)

7 **Final cash.** Calculate the final value *in today's dollars* in cell K15 with the formula

=P59*Q59

Then designate this cell as an @RISK output cell.

Running the Simulation

Set the number of iterations to 1000 and the number of simulations to 3 (one for each set of investment weights we want to test). Then run the simulation as usual.

Discussion of the Simulation Results

Summary results appear in Figure 17.21. The first simulation, which invests the most heavily in stocks, is easily the winner. Its mean final cash, close to $181,000 in today's dollars, is much greater than the means for the other two sets of weights. The first simulation also has a *much* larger upside potential (its 95th percentile is well over $400,000), and even its downside is slightly better than the others: Its 5th percentile is the best, and its minimum is only slightly worse than the minimum for the third set of weights.

Nevertheless, the histogram for simulation 1 (put 80% in stocks), shown in Figure 17.22, indicates a lot of variability—and skewness—in the distribution of final cash. As in Example 17.4, the concept of value at risk (VAR) is useful. Recall that VAR is defined as the 5th percentile of a distribution and is often the value investors worry about. Perhaps Sally should rerun the simulation with different investment weights, with an eye on the weights that increase her VAR. Right now it is close to $43,000—not too good considering that she invests $40,000 total. She might not like the prospect of a 5% chance of ending up with no more than this! We also encourage you to try running this simulation with other investment weights, both for the 40-year horizon and (after modifying the spreadsheet model slightly) for shorter time horizons such as 10 or 15 years. Even though the stock strategy appears to be best for a long horizon, it is not necessarily guaranteed to dominate for a shorter time horizon.

Figure 17.21
Summary Results from @RISK

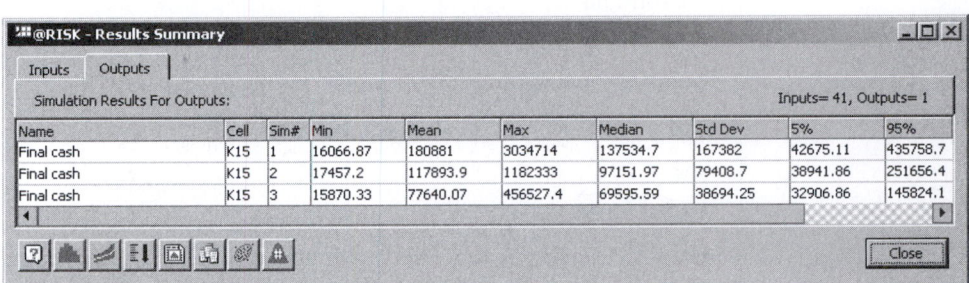

Name	Cell	Sim#	Min	Mean	Max	Median	Std Dev	5%	95%
Final cash	K15	1	16066.87	180881	3034714	137534.7	167382	42675.11	435758.7
Final cash	K15	2	17457.2	117893.9	1182333	97151.97	79408.7	38941.86	251656.4
Final cash	K15	3	15870.33	77640.07	456527.4	69595.59	38694.25	32906.86	145824.1

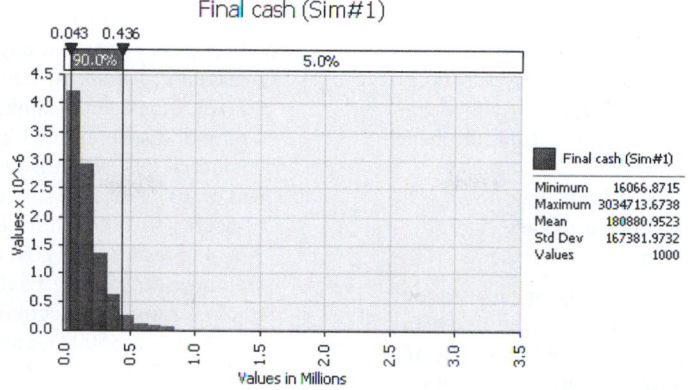

Figure 17.22

Histogram of Final Cash with 80% in Stocks

Final cash (Sim#1)

Minimum	16066.8715
Maximum	3034713.6738
Mean	180880.9523
Std Dev	167381.9732
Values	1000

PROBLEMS

Level A

8. Rerun the new car simulation from Example 17.4, but now introduce uncertainty into the fixed development cost. Let it be triangularly distributed with parameters $1.2 billion, $1.3 billion, and $1.7 billion. (You can check that the mean of this distribution is $1.4 billion, the same as the cost given in the example.) Comment on the differences between your output and those in the example. Would you say these differences are "important" for the company?

9. Rerun the new car simulation from Example 17.4, but now use the RISKSIMTABLE function appropriately to simulate discount rates of 7.5%, 10%, 12.5%, and 15%. Comment on how the outputs change as the discount rate decreases from the value we used, 15%.

10. In the cash balance model from Example 17.5, the timing is such that some receipts are delayed by 1 or 2 months, and the payments for materials and labor must be made a month in advance. Change the model so that all receipts are received immediately, and payments made this month for materials and labor are 80% of sales *this* month (not next month). The period of interest is again January through June. Rerun the simulation, and comment on any differences between your outputs and those from the example.

11. In the cash balance model from Example 17.5, is the $250,000 minimum cash balance requirement really "costing" the company very much? Find out by rerunning the simulation with minimum required cash balances of $50,000, $100,000, $150,000, and $200,000. Use the RISKSIMTABLE function to run all simulations at once. Comment on the outputs from these simulations. In particular, comment on whether the company appears to be "better off" with a lower minimum cash balance.

12. Run the retirement model from Example 17.6 with a damping factor of 1.0 (instead of 0.98), again using the same three sets of investment weights. Explain in words what it means, in terms of the simulation, to have a damping factor of 1. Then comment on the differences, if any, between your simulation results and those in the example.

13. The simulation output from Example 17.6 indicates that an investment heavy in stocks produces the best results. Would it be better to invest *entirely* in stocks? Find out by rerunning the simulation. Is there any apparent downside to this strategy?

14. Modify the model from Example 17.6 so that you use only the years 1970 to 2001 of historical data. Run the simulation for the same three sets of investment weights. Comment on whether your results differ in any important way from those in the example.

15. Referring to the retirement example in Example 17.6, rerun the model for a planning horizon of 10 years; 15 years; 25 years. For each, try to find the set of investment weights that maximize the VAR (the 5th percentile) of final cash in today's dollars. Does it appear that a portfolio heavy in stocks is better for long horizons but not for shorter horizons?

Level B

16. Change the new car simulation from Example 17.4 as follows. It is the same as before for years 1 through 5, including depreciation through year 5. However, the car might sell through year 10. Each year *after* year 5, the company examines sales. If fewer than 90,000 cars were sold that year, there is a 50% chance the car won't be sold after that year. Modify the model and run the simulation. Keep track of two outputs: NPV (through year 10) and the number of years of sales.

17. Based on Kelly (1956). You currently have $100. Each week you can invest any amount of money you currently have in a risky investment. With probability 0.4, the amount you invest is tripled (e.g., if you invest $100, you increase your asset position by $300), and, with probability 0.6, the amount you invest is lost. Consider the following investment strategies:

- Each week invest 10% of your money.
- Each week invest 30% of your money.
- Each week invest 50% of your money.

Use @RISK to simulate 100 weeks of each strategy 1000 times. Which strategy appears to be best? (In general, if you can multiply your investment by M with probability p and lose your investment with probability q, you should invest a fraction $[p(M - 1) - q]/(M - 1)$ of your money each week. This strategy maximizes the expected growth rate of your fortune and is known as the **Kelly criterion**.) [*Hint*: If an initial wealth of I dollars grows to F dollars in 100 weeks, then the weekly growth rate, labeled r, satisfies $F = (1 + r)^{100} I$, so that $r = (F/I)^{1/100} - 1$.]

18. Amanda has 30 years to save for her retirement. At the beginning of each year, she puts $5000 into her retirement account. At any point in time, all of Amanda's retirement funds are tied up in the stock market. Suppose the annual return on stocks follows a normal distribution with mean 12% and standard deviation 25%. What is the probability that at the end of 30 years, Amanda will have reached her goal of having $1,000,000 for retirement? Assume that if Amanda reaches her goal *before* 30 years, she will stop investing. (*Hint*: Each year you should keep track of Amanda's beginning cash position—for year 1, this is $5000—and Amanda's ending cash position. Of course, Amanda's ending cash position for a given year is a function of her beginning cash position and the return on stocks for that year. To estimate the probability that Amanda meets her goal, use an IF statement that returns 1 if she meets her goal and 0 otherwise.)

17.4 MARKETING MODELS

There are plenty of opportunities for marketing departments to use simulation. They face uncertainty in the brand-switching behavior of customers, the entry of new brands into the market, customer preferences for different attributes of products, the effects of advertising on sales, and so on. We examine some interesting marketing applications of simulation in this section.

Models of Customer Loyalty

What is a loyal customer worth to a company? This is an extremely important question for companies. (It is an important part of customer relationship management, or CRM, currently one of the hottest topics in marketing.) Companies know that if customers become dissatisfied with the company's product, they are likely to switch and never return. Marketers refer to this customer loss as **churn**. The loss in profit from churn can be large, particularly since long-standing customers tend to be more profitable in any given year than new customers. The following example uses a reasonable model of customer loyalty and simulation to estimate the worth of a customer to a company. It is based on the excellent discussion of customer loyalty in Reichheld (1996).

EXAMPLE | **17.7 THE LONG-TERM VALUE OF A CUSTOMER AT CCAMERICA**

CCAmerica is a credit card company that does its best to gain customers and keep their business in a highly competitive industry. The first year a customer signs up for service typically results in a loss to the company because of various administrative expenses. However, after the first year, the profit from a customer is typically positive, and this profit tends to increase through the years. The company has estimated the mean profit from a typical customer to be as shown in column B of Figure 17.23. For example, the company expects to lose $40 in the customer's first year but to gain $87 in the fifth year—provided that the customer stays loyal that long. For modeling purposes, we assume that the *actual* profit from a customer in the customer's nth year of service is normally distributed with mean shown in Figure 17.23 and standard deviation equal to 10% of the mean. At the end of each year, the customer leaves the company, never to return, with probability 0.15, the **churn rate**. Alternatively, the customer stays with probability 0.85, the **retention rate**. The company wants to estimate the NPV of the net profit from any such customer who has just signed up for service at the beginning of year 1, at a discount rate of 15%, assuming that the cash flow occurs in the middle of the year.[2] It also wants to see how sensitive this NPV is to the retention rate.

Figure 17.23

Mean Profit as a Function of Years as Customer

	A	B
9	**Estimated means**	
10	Year	Mean Profit(if still here)
11	1	($40.00)
12	2	$66.00
13	3	$72.00
14	4	$79.00
15	5	$87.00
16	6	$92.00
17	7	$96.00
18	8	$99.00
19	9	$103.00
20	10	$106.00
21	11	$111.00
22	12	$116.00
23	13	$120.00
24	14	$124.00
25	15	$130.00
26	16	$137.00
27	17	$142.00
28	18	$148.00
29	19	$155.00
30	20	$161.00
31	21	$161.00
32	22	$161.00
33	23	$161.00
34	24	$161.00
35	25	$161.00
36	26	$161.00
37	27	$161.00
38	28	$161.00
39	29	$161.00
40	30	$161.00

Objective   To use simulation to find the NPV of a customer and to see how this varies with the retention rate.

WHERE DO THE NUMBERS COME FROM?

The numbers in Figure 17.23 are undoubtedly averages, based on historical records of many customers. To build in randomness for any *particular* customer, we need a probability distribution around the numbers in this figure. We arbitrarily chose a normal distribution centered on the historical average and a standard deviation of 10% of the average. These are educated guesses. Finally, the churn rate is a number very familiar to marketing people, and it can also be estimated from historical customer data.

[2]This makes the NPV calculation slightly more complex, but it is probably more realistic than our usual assumption that cash flows occur at the *ends* of the years.

Solution

The idea is to keep simulating profits (or a loss in the first year) for the customer until the customer churns. We simulate 30 years of potential profits.

DEVELOPING THE SIMULATION MODEL

The simulation model appears in Figure 17.24. (See the file **Customer Loyalty.xlsx.**) It can be developed with the following steps.

1 **Inputs.** Enter the inputs in the blue cells.

2 **Retention rate.** Although an 85% retention rate was given in the statement of the problem, we investigate retention rates from 75% to 95%, as shown in row 4. To run a separate simulation for each of these, enter the formula

=RISKSIMTABLE(D4:H4)

in cell B4.

Figure 17.24 Customer Loyalty Model

	A	B	C	D	E	F	G	H	I	J
1	Customer loyalty model in the credit card industry									
2										
3	Inputs			Retention rates to try						
4	Retention rate	0.75		0.75	0.80	0.85	0.90	0.95		
5	Discount rate	0.15								
6	Stdev % of mean	10%								
7										
8										
9	Estimated means		Simulation				Outputs			
10		Year	Mean Profit(if still here)	Quits at end of year?	Actual profit	Discounted profit	NPV	$17.94		
11		1	($40.00)	No	($43.14)	($40.23)	Years loyal	2		
12		2	$66.00	Yes	$71.74	$58.17				
13		3	$72.00		$0.00	$0.00	Means			
14		4	$79.00		$0.00	$0.00	Simulation	Retention rate	NPV	Years loyal
15		5	$87.00		$0.00	$0.00	1	0.75	$101.74	4.10
16		6	$92.00		$0.00	$0.00	2	0.80	$134.32	5.09
17		7	$96.00		$0.00	$0.00	3	0.85	$182.63	6.61
18		8	$99.00		$0.00	$0.00	4	0.90	$253.87	9.68
19		9	$103.00		$0.00	$0.00	5	0.95	$368.45	15.95
20		10	$106.00		$0.00	$0.00				
21		11	$111.00		$0.00	$0.00				
22		12	$116.00		$0.00	$0.00				
23		13	$120.00		$0.00	$0.00				
24		14	$124.00		$0.00	$0.00				
25		15	$130.00		$0.00	$0.00				
26		16	$137.00		$0.00	$0.00				
27		17	$142.00		$0.00	$0.00				
28		18	$148.00		$0.00	$0.00				
29		19	$155.00		$0.00	$0.00				
30		20	$161.00		$0.00	$0.00				
31		21	$161.00		$0.00	$0.00				
32		22	$161.00		$0.00	$0.00				
33		23	$161.00		$0.00	$0.00				
34		24	$161.00		$0.00	$0.00				
35		25	$161.00		$0.00	$0.00				
36		26	$161.00		$0.00	$0.00				
37		27	$161.00		$0.00	$0.00				
38		28	$161.00		$0.00	$0.00				
39		29	$161.00		$0.00	$0.00				
40		30	$161.00		$0.00	$0.00				

As usual, Excel's RAND function can be used inside an IF statement to determine whether a given event occurs.

3 **Timing of churn.** In column C, we use simulation to discover when the customer churns. This column will contain a sequence of No's, followed by a Yes, and then a sequence of blanks. To generate these, enter the formulas

=IF(RAND()<1−B4,"Yes","No")

and

=IF(OR(C11="",C11="Yes"),"",IF(RAND()<1−$B$4,"Yes","No"))

in cells C11 and C12, and copy the latter formula down column C. Study these formulas carefully to see how the logic works. Note that they do not rely on @RISK functions. Excel's RAND function can be used any time we want to simulate whether an event occurs.

4 **Actual and discounted profits.** Profits (or a loss in the first year) occur as long as there is not a blank in column C. Therefore, simulate the actual profits by entering the formula

Careful discounting is required if cash flows occur in the middle of a year.

=IF(C11<>"",RISKNORMAL(B11,$B$6*ABS(B11)),0)

in cell D11 and copying it down. (The absolute value function, ABS, is required in case any of the cash flows are negative. A normal distribution cannot have a *negative* standard deviation.) Then discount these appropriately in column E by entering the formula

=D11/(1+$B$5)^(A11−0.5)

in cell E11 and copying it down. Note how the exponent of the denominator accounts for the cash flow in the *middle* of the year.

5 **Outputs.** We will actually keep track of two outputs, the total NPV and the number of years the customer stays with the company. Calculate the NPV in cell H10 by summing the discounted values in column E. (They have already been discounted, so the NPV function is not needed.) To find the number of years the customer is loyal, note that it will always be the number of No's in column C, plus 1. Therefore, calculate it in cell H11 with the formula

=COUNTIF(C11:C40,"No")+1

Finally, designate both of cells H10 and H11 as @RISK output cells.

Running the Simulation

Set the number of iterations to 1000 and the number of simulations to 5 (one for each potential retention rate). Then run the simulation as usual.

Discussion of the Simulation Results

Varying the retention rate can have a large impact on the value of a customer.

Summary results for all five retention rates and the histogram for an 85% retention rate appear in Figures 17.25 and 17.26. The histogram indicates that there is almost a 14% chance that the NPV will be negative, whereas the chance that it will be above $300 is over 26%. We also see from the summary measures that the mean NPV and the mean number of years loyal are quite sensitive to the retention rate.

To follow up on this observation, we used the RISKMEAN function to capture the means in columns I and J of the model sheet and then created a line chart of them as a function of the retention rate. (See Figure 17.27.) This line chart shows the rather dramatic effect the retention rate can have on the value of a customer. For example, if it increases from the current 85% to 90%, the mean NPV increases by about 39%. If it increases from 85% to 95%, the mean NPV increases by over 100%. In the other direction, if the retention rate decreases from 85% to 80%, the mean NPV decreases by about 27%. This is why credit card companies are so anxious to keep their customers.

Figure 17.25 Summary Results for Customer Loyalty Model

@RISK - Results Summary

Inputs | Outputs

Simulation Results For Outputs: | Inputs= 31, Outputs= 2

Name	Cell	Sim#	Min	Mean	Max	Median	Std Dev	5%	95%
NPV	H10	1	-47.40235	101.736	557.2523	67.44688	134.1185	-40.44756	375.1754
NPV	H10	2	-47.11087	134.321	561.9925	105.1464	151.9073	-39.6735	437.8878
NPV	H10	3	-44.84556	182.6265	574.3201	153.4405	169.8054	-38.66203	488.9123
NPV	H10	4	-45.87011	253.8659	599.3862	252.6532	191.7656	-36.62914	552.2297
NPV	H10	5	-43.82383	368.4498	606.0264	427.0797	191.8821	10.73628	572.7899
Years loyal	H11	1	1	4.101	26	3	3.526079	1	11
Years loyal	H11	2	1	5.087	31	4	4.638205	1	15
Years loyal	H11	3	1	6.605	31	5	5.681307	1	18
Years loyal	H11	4	1	9.681	31	7	8.160136	1	30
Years loyal	H11	5	1	15.952	31	14	10.53711	2	31

Close

Figure 17.26

Histogram of NPV for an 85% Retention Rate

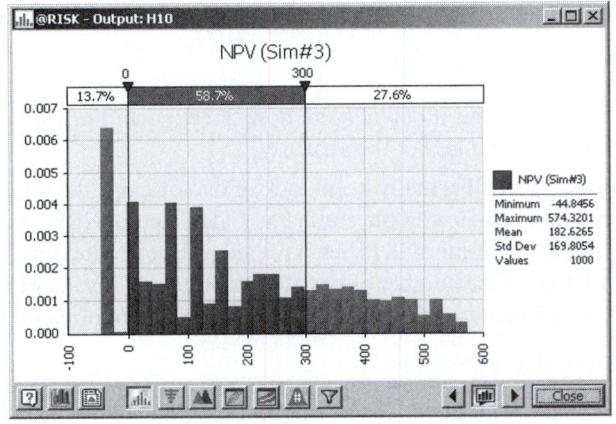

Figure 17.27

Sensitivity of Outputs to the Retention Rate

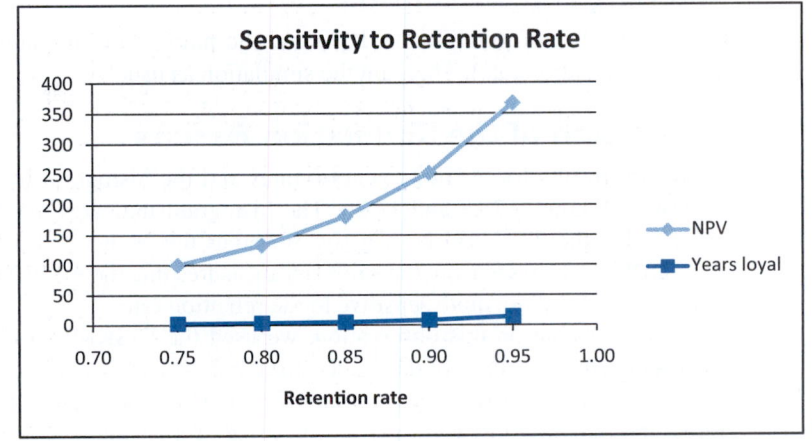

The following example is a variation of the previous example. We now investigate the effect of offering a customer an incentive to remain loyal. We also change the model to allow previous customers to rejoin our company.

EXAMPLE | 17.8 REDUCING CHURN AT AOSN

We are all aware of the fierce competition by Internet Service Providers (ISPs) to get our business. For example, MSN is always trying to attract AOL's customers, and vice versa. Some even give away prizes to entice us to sign up for a guaranteed length of time. This example is based on one such offer. We assume that an ISP named AOSN is willing to give a customer a free PC, at a cost of $700 to AOSN, if the customer signs up for a guaranteed 3 years of service. During that time, the cost of service to the customer is a constant $21.95 per month, or $263.40 annually. After 3 years, we assume the cost of service increases by 3% annually. We assume that in any year after the guaranteed 3 years, the probability is 0.7 that the customer will stay with AOSN. As in the previous example, this is the retention rate. We also assume that if a customer has switched to another ISP, there is always a probability of 0.1 that the customer will (without any free PC offer) willingly join AOSN. AOSN wants to see whether, in terms of NPV with a 10% discount rate, this offer makes financial sense. It also wants to see how the NPV varies with the retention rate.

Objective To use simulation to estimate whether it makes sense for an ISP to give away a free PC for a promise of at least 3 years of customer loyalty, and to see how the answer varies with the retention rate.

WHERE DO THE NUMBERS COME FROM?

In the previous example we discussed the switching rates, which would be estimated from extensive customer data. The other data in the problem statement are straightforward to obtain.

Solution

The solution strategy is similar to the previous example. We use IF functions to check whether a customer is currently getting service from AOSN. There are two differences, however. First, we need to modify the logic so that a customer can leave AOSN *or* return. Second, we run two side-by-side simulations: one for a customer who has just accepted a free PC for a guaranteed 3-year subscription and the other for a customer who is not currently an AOSN customer and does *not* accept such an offer. By comparing these, we can see whether the free PC is worth its cost to AOSN.

DEVELOPING THE SIMULATION MODEL

The completed simulation model appears in Figure 17.28. (See the file **Free PC Value.xlsx**.) It can be developed with the following steps.

1 **Inputs.** Enter the given data in the blue cells.

2 **Retention rate.** We will test the retention rates in row 4 with five separate simulations, so enter the formula

=RISKSIMTABLE(D4:H4)

in cell B4.

3 **Subscription prices.** Enter a link to the current subscription price from cell B6 in cells B19 through B21. Then calculate the increasing subscription costs with the formula

=B21*(1+$B$8)

in cell B22, copied down column B. For these latter years, the subscription increases by 3% annually.

Figure 17.28   Simulation Model of Free PC

	A	B	C	D	E	F	G	H	I	J	K	L	M
1	Estimating value of giving away free PC to get loyal customer												
2													
3	Inputs			Retention rates to try									
4	Retention rate	0.5		0.5	0.6	0.7	0.8	0.9					
5	Switchback rate	0.1											
6	Cost of PC	$700											
7	Yearly subscription cost	$263.40											
8	Annual cost increase	3%											
9	Discount rate	10%											
10													
11	Outputs from simulation below			Probability of difference being positive									
12	NPV with PC	$428.79		Simulation	1	2	3	4	5				
13	NPV without PC	$288.45		Retention rate	0.5	0.6	0.7	0.8	0.9				
14	Difference	$140.34		Pr(positive)	0.347	0.400	0.467	0.501	0.600				
15													
16	Simulation			With Free PC				Without free PC					
17		End of year	Subscription cost	With us?	Quit?	Switch to us?	Revenue	With us?	Quit?	Switch to us?	Revenue		Random numbers for:
18		0					($700)						Quitting	Switching
19		1	$263.40	Yes	No	No	$263.40	No	No	No	$0.00		0.073137	0.819553
20		2	$263.40	Yes	No	No	$263.40	No	No	No	$0.00		0.191073	0.788467
21		3	$263.40	Yes	No	No	$263.40	No	No	No	$0.00		0.156098	0.539344
22		4	$271.30	Yes	Yes	No	$271.30	No	No	No	$0.00		0.7632	0.237589
23		5	$279.44	No	No	No	$0.00	No	No	No	$0.00		0.231037	0.970496
24		6	$287.82	No	No	No	$0.00	No	No	No	$0.00		0.035589	0.810818
25		7	$296.46	No	No	No	$0.00	No	No	No	$0.00		0.077157	0.671465
26		8	$305.35	No	No	No	$0.00	No	No	No	$0.00		0.695741	0.670606
27		9	$314.51	No	No	No	$0.00	No	No	No	$0.00		0.393822	0.475298
28		10	$323.95	No	No	No	$0.00	No	No	No	$0.00		0.003606	0.717069
29		11	$333.67	No	No	No	$0.00	No	No	No	$0.00		0.369943	0.284277
30		12	$343.68	No	No	Yes	$0.00	No	No	Yes	$0.00		0.777977	0.023854
31		13	$353.99	Yes	No	No	$353.99	Yes	No	No	$353.99		0.053296	0.543153
32		14	$364.61	Yes	No	No	$364.61	Yes	No	No	$364.61		0.320396	0.77635
33		15	$375.55	Yes	Yes	No	$375.55	Yes	Yes	No	$375.55		0.692112	0.38566
34		16	$386.81	No	No	No	$0.00	No	No	No	$0.00		0.322743	0.273569
35		17	$398.42	No	No	No	$0.00	No	No	No	$0.00		0.104524	0.905263
36		18	$410.37	No	No	No	$0.00	No	No	No	$0.00		0.386579	0.454987
37		19	$422.68	No	No	No	$0.00	No	No	No	$0.00		0.878338	0.40961
38		20	$435.36	No	No	No	$0.00	No	No	No	$0.00		0.21904	0.932583
39		21	$448.42	No	No	No	$0.00	No	No	No	$0.00		0.568445	0.115218
40		22	$461.87	No	No	No	$0.00	No	No	No	$0.00		0.310568	0.546483
41		23	$475.73	No	No	No	$0.00	No	No	No	$0.00		0.593845	0.810983
42		24	$490.00	No	No	No	$0.00	No	No	No	$0.00		0.915499	0.378981
43		25	$504.70	No	No	No	$0.00	No	No	No	$0.00		0.371658	0.863412
44		26	$519.84	No	No	No	$0.00	No	No	No	$0.00		0.964949	0.728986
45		27	$535.44	No	No	No	$0.00	No	No	No	$0.00		0.175341	0.88567
46		28	$551.50	No	No	No	$0.00	No	No	No	$0.00		0.596402	0.544829
47		29	$568.05	No	No	No	$0.00	No	No	No	$0.00		0.843877	0.188536
48		30	$585.09	No	No	No	$0.00	No	No	No	$0.00		0.390914	0.963068

4 **Random numbers.** Columns C through F are for a customer who accepts a free PC, whereas columns G through J are for a customer who does not accept such an offer. To compare these fairly, they should use the *same* random numbers for generating switching behavior. Therefore, enter two columns of random numbers with the RAND function in columns L and M. The first set in column L will be used to see whether the customer quits AOSN in any year, whereas the second set in column M will be used to see whether the customer switches back to AOSN in any given year.

Using common random numbers for two side-by-side simulations is a good practice. It results in a fairer comparison.

5 **Switching with free PC.** To understand columns C through E, each cell in column C indicates whether the customer is with AOSN during that year. If "Yes," then a "Yes" is possible in column D, meaning that the customer quits AOSN at the end of the year. If "No," then a "Yes" is possible in column E, meaning that the customer switches back to AOSN at the end of the year. (The meaning is the same in columns G through I.) For a customer who accepts a free PC, fill in columns C, D, and E as follows. Enter "Yes" in cells C19 through C21 and "No" in cells D19, D20, and E19 through E21. (This customer is not *allowed* to switch during the first 3 years.) Then enter the formulas

=IF(D21="Yes","No",IF(E21="Yes","Yes",C21))

=IF(L21<B4,"No","Yes")

and

=IF(C22="Yes","No",IF(M22<$B$5,"Yes","No"))

in cells C22, D21, and E22, and copy these down their respective columns. These formulas allow the customer to switch back and forth after 3 years.

6 **Switching with no free PC.** The logic for the customer in columns G through I is almost the same. Now we assume that the customer is not with AOSN in year 0, so enter the formula

=IF(RAND()<B5,"Yes","No")

in cell G19 to see whether she might join AOSN of her own accord in year 1. Then enter the same logic for the other cells in columns G through I as in the previous step, referring to the *same* random numbers in columns L and M.

7 **Revenue.** Enter a link to the cost of the PC in cell F18, but make it negative. Then enter the formula

=IF(C19="Yes",$B19,0)

in cell F19, and copy it to the ranges F19:F48 and J19:J48—the logic is equivalent for both customers.

8 **NPV.** We assume that all cash flows are at the *ends* of the respective years, so enter the formulas

=F18+NPV(B9,F19:F48)

=NPV(B9,J19:J48)

and

=B12−B13

in cells B12, B13, and B14, and designate each of these as @RISK output cells. Note that the first includes the cost (to AOSN) of the PC, whereas the second does not. We are particularly interested in the difference, in cell B14. If it tends to be positive, then the free PC is worth the cost to AOSN.

Running the Simulation

Set up @RISK to run 1000 iterations and 5 simulations, one for each retention rate to be tested. Then run the simulation as usual.

Discussion of the Simulation Results

Selected results appear in Figures 17.29 and 17.30. The summary statistics indicate that the mean difference between the two NPVs is positive except for the lowest retention rate, 0.5. However, in all cases, this difference in NPV varies from more than $1000 negative to more than $1000 positive. This indicates that for some customers, the free PC offer will make money, whereas for others it will lose money. Another way to view the results is by the probabilities of positive differences in NPV, shown in the range E13:I13 of Figure 17.28. (We found these with the RISKTARGET function.) With retention rates of 0.5, 0.6, and 0.7, there is actually less than a 50–50 chance that the difference will be positive. If the actual retention rate is 0.7, perhaps AOSN ought to rethink its free PC strategy. In a purely financial sense, it is not a clear winner.

Figure 17.29

Summary Statistics from @RISK

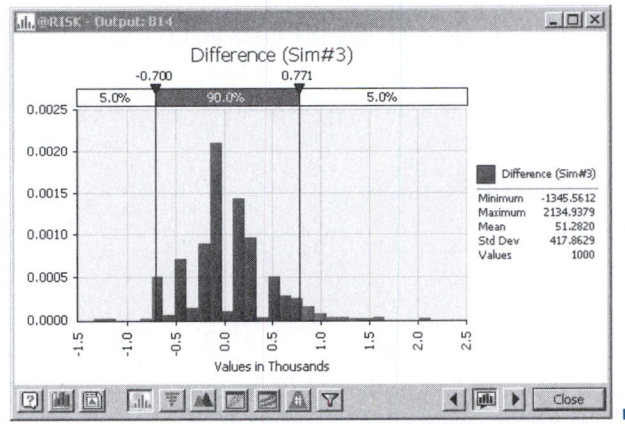

Name	Cell	Sim#	Min	Mean	Max	Median	Std Dev	5%	95%
NPV with PC	B12	1	-44.96318	462.9238	1588.01	425.2642	318.2812	15.63218	1057.47
NPV with PC	B12	2	-44.96318	563.7779	1786.695	519.1096	365.9869	57.57441	1227.422
NPV with PC	B12	3	-44.96318	742.6642	2242.521	702.8228	442.1791	67.39185	1507.819
NPV with PC	B12	4	-44.96318	1002.5	2373.562	953.2783	540.6018	140.3397	1975.322
NPV with PC	B12	5	-44.96318	1477.501	2373.562	1544.087	615.0246	313.8506	2373.562
NPV without PC	B13	1	0	485.2859	1988.479	421.2366	358.1426	35.80929	1181.173
NPV without PC	B13	2	0	546.7148	2187.121	479.2117	394.0594	38.24294	1324.52
NPV without PC	B13	3	0	691.3823	2645.111	607.2047	489.261	38.24294	1583.361
NPV without PC	B13	4	0	879.9634	2834.938	814.0509	591.4378	33.53052	1987.767
NPV without PC	B13	5	0	1195.121	3073.562	1139.288	752.2802	38.24294	2512.381
Difference	B14	1	-936.0626	-22.36205	1358.172	-44.96318	292.9265	-502.1037	476.3199
Difference	B14	2	-1175.517	17.06311	1454.185	-44.96318	347.9307	-502.1037	628.4503
Difference	B14	3	-1345.561	51.28196	2134.938	-44.96318	417.8629	-700	770.8997
Difference	B14	4	-1544.111	122.5365	1975.322	96.1647	542.0587	-700	1146.129
Difference	B14	5	-2175.116	282.3794	2373.562	140.3397	677.4404	-700	1544.087

Figure 17.30

Histogram of the Difference in NPV for a 70% Retention Rate

Market Share Models

We conclude this marketing section with a fairly simple model of market share behavior. This model is based on the type of competition faced by two dominant brands in an industry, such as Coca-Cola and Pepsi. We ignore all other brands. Each quarter, one of the companies wins market share from the other in a random manner, although this behavior depends largely on how much each company promotes its product. The timing of promotions is the key to the model.

EXAMPLE **17.9 ESTIMATING DYNAMIC MARKET SHARE WITH TWO DOMINANT BRANDS**

We assume that there are two dominant companies in the soft drink industry: "us" and "them." For this example, we view everything from the point of view of "us." We start with a 45% market share. During each of the next 20 quarters, each company promotes its product to some extent. To make the model simple, we assume that each company each quarter either promotes at a "regular" level or at a "blitz" level. Depending on each company's promotional behavior in a given month, the change in our market share from this month to the next is triangularly distributed, with parameters given in Table 17.3. For example, if we blitz and they don't, then we could lose as much as 1% market share, we could gain as much as 6% market share, and our most likely outcome is an increase of 2% market share. We want to develop a simulation model that allows us to gauge the long-term change in our market share for any pattern of blitzing employed by us and them.

Table 17.3   Parameters of Market Share Change Distributions

Blitzer	Minimum	Most Likely	Maximum
Neither	−0.03	0.00	0.03
Both	−0.05	0.00	0.05
Only us	−0.01	0.02	0.06
Only them	−0.06	−0.02	0.01

Objective   To develop a simulation model that allows us to see how our market share will change through time for any pattern of blitzing by the two companies.

WHERE DO THE NUMBERS COME FROM?

Even if there are only two levels of advertising—and this is itself an obvious approximation to reality—the numbers in Table 17.3 are probably educated guesses at best. It is difficult to gauge the effects of advertising on market share, and many management science models have been developed to do so. However, marketers can use such models, along with their intuition, to make the required estimates.

Solution

The idea is that we will enter *any* pattern of blitzing, indicated by 0's and 1's, of the two companies, simulate the corresponding changes in market shares, and then track our market share through the 20-quarter period. Once the simulation has been developed, we can then use it as a tool to analyze various blitzing patterns.

DEVELOPING THE SIMULATION MODEL

The completed simulation model (with several hidden columns) appears in Figure 17.31. (See the file **Market Share.xlsx**.) The following steps are required to develop it.

1 **Inputs.**   Enter the inputs in the blue ranges.

2 **Blitz pattern.**   Enter any sequence of 0's and 1's in rows 15 and 16. The 1's indicate blitz promotions. In reality, our company has no control over the pattern in row 16, and although we can choose the pattern in row 15, we probably have to choose it *before* observing their pattern in row 16. We arbitrarily entered a pattern where the 1's and 0's alternate for each company, and the two companies are "out of step" with one another. However, this is just for illustration.

3 **Possible market share changes.**   It will simplify matters to generate the *possible* market share changes in rows 21 through 24. These are then used as needed in row 28. To generate these random changes, enter the formula

=RISKTRIANG($B8,$C8,$D8)

in cell B21, and copy it to the range B21:U24.

Figure 17.31 Market Share Simulation Model

	A	B	C	D	E	F	G	H	S	T	U
1	Market share model										
2											
3	Inputs										
4	Our current market share	45%									
5											
6	Parameters of triangular distribution of change in our market share - depends on who has a big promotional campaign										
7		Minimum	Most likely	Maximum							
8	Neither	-0.03	0	0.03							
9	Both	-0.05	0	0.05							
10	Only us	-0.01	0.02	0.06							
11	Only them	-0.06	-0.02	0.01							
12											
13	Promotional campaigns (1 if promote, 0 if not) - enter any patterns you want to test in the following two rows										
14	Quarter	1	2	3	4	5	6	7	18	19	20
15	Us	0	1	0	1	0	1	0	1	0	1
16	Them	1	0	1	0	1	0	1	0	1	0
17											
18	Simulation										
19	Possible changes in our market share										
20	Quarter	1	2	3	4	5	6	7	18	19	20
21	Neither promote	0.60%	0.64%	-0.11%	-1.74%	-0.24%	-0.61%	0.12%	0.03%	-1.99%	-0.08%
22	Both promote	0.96%	-0.20%	-0.53%	1.91%	1.95%	-1.15%	1.62%	-2.04%	-1.24%	-0.43%
23	Only we promote	3.65%	0.70%	2.84%	0.19%	1.27%	3.07%	3.44%	1.23%	4.79%	-0.73%
24	Only they promote	-0.10%	-2.03%	-2.18%	-0.91%	-1.07%	-2.58%	0.05%	-3.85%	-0.13%	-4.06%
25											
26	Tracking our market share										
27	Beginning market share	45.00%	44.90%	45.61%	43.43%	43.62%	42.55%	45.62%	41.79%	43.02%	42.89%
28	Change in our market share	-0.10%	0.70%	-2.18%	0.19%	-1.07%	3.07%	0.05%	1.23%	-0.13%	-0.73%
29	Ending market share	44.90%	45.61%	43.43%	43.62%	42.55%	45.62%	45.67%	43.02%	42.89%	42.16%

4 **Our market share.** We track our market share in rows 27 through 29. There are really only two ideas here. First, our beginning market share in any quarter is our ending market share from the previous quarter. Second, the change in our market share in any quarter is one of the values in rows 21 through 24, depending on who blitzes that quarter. This requires a nested IF formula. Start by entering a link to our current market share (from cell B4) in cell B27. Then enter the formulas

=IF(AND(B16=0,B15=0),B21,IF(AND(B16=1,B15=1),B22,IF(AND(B16=0,B15=1),B23,B24)))

=B27+B28

and

=B29

in cells B28, B29, and C27, and copy all of these across. Again, the nested IF simply records the appropriate market share change for that quarter from rows 21 through 24.

5 **Output range.** We designate the entire 20-quarter range in row 29 as an output range, so highlight this range and click on the @RISK Add Output button. We suggest that you name this output range "Market share."

Running the Simulation

We set @RISK to run 1000 iterations for a single simulation. However, unlike previous examples, the point here is not so much to see results for any particular simulation run, but rather to use the simulation model as a tool for analysis. That is, we can play any "game" we want by seeing how a blitzing strategy for "us" does against a given blitzing strategy for "them." For example, in the file **Market Share Random 10.xlsx,** we entered formulas in their row 16 that guarantee exactly 10 randomly placed

1's.[3] This would be relevant if we believe they are going to blitz half of the time, but we have no idea when. Now we can try any strategy we want and run the resulting simulation.

Discussion of the Simulation Results

These results represent only one possibility. Other patterns of blitzes will certainly lead to different results.

Figure 17.32 shows the summary graph of our market share through time when we react to their "random 10" strategy by blitzing in the middle 12 quarters, Q5 through Q16. That is, we blitz two more quarters than they do, and we do our blitzing consecutively. The results are not unexpected. Because we blitz two more quarters than they do, we tend to gain market share—our average market share after 20 quarters is close to 50%, up from the initial 45%. However, the shape of this summary graph clearly shows what happens to our market share when we do not blitz and there is a chance that they do.

Figure 17.32

Summary Chart for Our "Middle 12" Strategy Versus Their "Random 10" Strategy

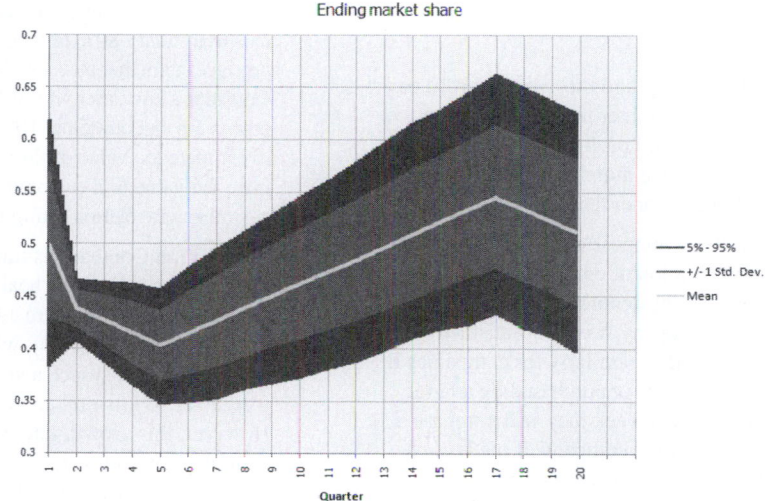

This example indicates quite clearly how a simulation model can be used as a tool to analyze all sorts of scenarios. In this case, the purpose is not to run a simulation once and then report these specific results. Rather, it is to run the simulation many times, tweaking various parameters on each run, to see what insights we can gain. ∎

PROBLEMS

Level A

19. Suppose that Coke and Pepsi are fighting for the cola market. Each week each person in the market buys one case of Coke or Pepsi. If the person's last purchase was Coke, there is a 0.90 probability that this person's next purchase will be Coke; otherwise, it will be Pepsi. (We are considering only two brands in the market.) Similarly, if the person's last purchase was Pepsi, there is a 0.80 probability that this person's next purchase will be Pepsi; otherwise, it will be Coke. Currently half of all people purchase Coke, and the other half purchase Pepsi. Simulate one year of sales in the cola market and estimate each company's average weekly market share. Do this by assuming that the total

market size is fixed at 100 customers. (*Hint*: Use the RISKBINOMIAL function.)

20. Seas Beginning sells clothing by mail order. An important question is when to strike a customer from their mailing list. At present, they strike a customer from their mailing list if a customer fails to order from six consecutive catalogs. They want to know whether striking a customer from their list after a customer fails to order from four consecutive catalogs results in a higher profit per customer. The following data are available:

- If a customer placed an order the last time she received a catalog, then there is a 20% chance she will order from the next catalog.

---

[3]These formulas are interesting in their own right. How can we randomly enter 0's and 1's and guarantee that exactly half are 1's? The idea is that if there is a 1 in Q1, then the probability of a 1 in Q2 should be 9/19. However, if there is a 0 in Q1, then the probability of a 1 in Q2 should be 10/19. See if you can do it!

- If a customer last placed an order one catalog ago, there is a 16% chance she will order from the next catalog she receives.
- If a customer last placed an order two catalogs ago, there is a 12% chance she will order from the next catalog she receives.
- If a customer last placed an order three catalogs ago, there is an 8% chance she will order from the next catalog she receives.
- If a customer last placed an order four catalogs ago, there is a 4% chance she will order from the next catalog she receives.
- If a customer last placed an order five catalogs ago, there is a 2% chance she will order from the next catalog she receives.

It costs $1 to send a catalog, and the average profit per order is $15. Assume a customer has just placed an order. To maximize expected profit per customer, would Seas Beginning make more money canceling such a customer after six nonorders or four nonorders?

21. Based on Babich (1992). Suppose that each week each of 300 families buys a gallon of orange juice from company A, B, or C. Let p_A denote the probability that a gallon produced by company A is of unsatisfactory quality, and define p_B and p_C similarly for companies B and C. If the last gallon of juice purchased by a family is satisfactory, then the next week they will purchase a gallon of juice from the same company. If the last gallon of juice purchased by a family is not satisfactory, then the family will purchase a gallon from a competitor. Consider a week in which A families have purchased juice A, B families have purchased juice B, and C families have purchased juice C. Assume that families that switch brands during a period are allocated to the remaining brands in a manner that is proportional to the current market shares of the other brands. Thus, if a customer switches from brand A, there is probability $B/(B + C)$ that he will switch to brand B and probability $C/(B + C)$ that he will switch to brand C. Suppose that the market is currently divided equally: 100 families for each of the three brands.
    a. After a year, what will the market share for each firm be? Assume $p_A = 0.10$, $p_B = 0.15$, and $p_C = 0.20$. (Hint: You will need to use the RISKBINOMIAL function to see how many people switch from A and then use the RISKBINOMIAL function again to see how many switch from A to B and from A to C.)
    b. Suppose a 1% increase in market share is worth $10,000 per week to company A. Company A believes that for a cost of $1 million per year it can cut the percentage of unsatisfactory juice cartons in half. Is this worthwhile? (Use the same values of p_A, p_B, and p_C as in part a.)

Level B

22. Suppose that GLC earns a $4000 profit each time a person buys a car. We want to determine how the expected profit earned from a customer depends on the quality of GLC's cars. We assume a typical customer will purchase 10 cars during her lifetime. She will purchase a car now (year 1) and then purchase a car every 5 years—during year 6, year 11, and so on. For simplicity, we assume that Hundo is GLC's only competitor. We also assume that if the consumer is satisfied with the car she purchases, she will buy her next car from the same company, but if she is not satisfied, she will buy her next car from the other company. Hundo produces cars that satisfy 80% of its customers. Currently, GLC produces cars that also satisfy 80% of its customers. Consider a customer whose first car is a GLC car. If profits are discounted at 10% annually, use simulation to estimate the value of this customer to GLC. Also estimate the value of a customer to GLC if it can raise its customer satisfaction rating to 85%; to 90%; to 95%.

23. The Mutron Company is thinking of marketing a new drug used to make pigs healthier. At the beginning of the current year, there are 1,000,000 pigs that could use the product. Each pig will use Mutron's drug or a competitor's drug once a year. The number of pigs is forecasted to grow by an average of 5% per year. However, this growth rate is not a sure thing. Mutron assumes that each year's growth rate is an independent draw from a normal distribution, with probability 0.95 that the growth rate will be between 3% and 7%. Assuming it enters the market, Mutron is not sure what its share of the market will be during year 1, so it models this with a triangular distribution. Its worst-case share is 20%, its most likely share is 40%, and its best-case share is 70%. In the absence of any new competitors entering this market (in addition to itself), Mutron believes its market share will remain the same in succeeding years. However, there are three potential entrants (in addition to Mutron). At the beginning of each year, each entrant that has not already entered the market has a 40% chance of entering the market. The year after a competitor enters, Mutron's market share will drop by 20% for each new competitor who entered. For example, if two competitors enter the market in year 1, Mutron's market share in year 2 will be reduced by 40% from what it would have been with no entrants. Note that if all three entrants have entered, there will be no more entrants. Each unit of the drug sells for $2.20 and incurs a variable cost of $0.40. Profits are discounted by 10% annually.
    a. Assuming that Mutron enters the market, use simulation to find its net present value (NPV) for the next 10 years from the drug.
    b. Again assuming that Mutron enters the market, it can be 95% certain that its actual NPV from the drug is between what two values?

17.5 SIMULATING GAMES OF CHANCE

We realize that this is a book about "business" applications. However, it is instructive (and fun) to see how simulation can be used to analyze games of chance, including sports contests. Indeed, many analysts refer to the "Monte Carlo" simulation, and you can guess where that name comes from—the gambling casinos of Monte Carlo.

Simulating the Game of Craps

Most games of chance are great candidates for simulation since they are, by their very nature, driven by randomness. In this section we examine one such game that is extremely popular in the gambling casinos: the game of craps. In its most basic form, the game of craps is played as follows. A player rolls two dice and observes the sum of the two sides turned up. If this sum is 7 or 11, the player wins immediately. If the sum is 2, 3, or 12, the player loses immediately. Otherwise, if this sum is any other number (4, 5, 6, 8, 9, or 10), that number becomes the player's "point." Then the dice are thrown repeatedly until the sum is the player's point or 7. In case the player's point occurs before a 7, the player wins. But if a 7 occurs before the point, the player loses. The following example uses simulation to determine the properties of this game.

EXAMPLE **17.10 ESTIMATING THE PROBABILITY OF WINNING AT CRAPS**

Joe Gamble loves to play craps at the casinos. He suspects that his chances of winning are less than 50–50, but he wants to find the probability that he wins a single game of craps.

Objective To use simulation to find the probability of winning a single game of craps.

WHERE DO THE NUMBERS COME FROM?

There are no input numbers here, only the rules of the game.

Solution

We simulate a single game. By running this simulation for many iterations, we find the probability that Joe wins a single game of craps. If his intuition is correct (and surely it must be, or the casino could not stay in business), this probability is less than 0.5.

DEVELOPING THE SIMULATION MODEL

The simulation model is for a single game. (See Figure 17.33 and the file **Craps.xlsx**.) There is a subtle problem here: We do not know how many tosses of the dice are necessary to determine the outcome of a single game. Theoretically, the game could continue forever, with the player waiting for his point or a 7. However, it is extremely unlikely that more than, say, 40 tosses are necessary in a single game. (This can be shown by a probability argument, but we do not present it here.) Therefore, we simulate 40 tosses and use only those that are necessary to determine the outcome of a single game. The steps required to simulate a single game are as follows.

Figure 17.33 Simulation of Craps Game

	A	B	C	D	E	F	G	H	I	J
1	Craps Simulation									
2										
3	Simulated tosses									
4	Toss	Die 1	Die 2	Sum	Win on this toss?	Lose on this toss?	Continue?		Summary results from simulation	
5	1	4	4	8	0	0	Yes		Win? (1 if yes, 0 if no)	0
6	2	6	6	12	0	0	Yes		Number of tosses	6
7	3	4	5	9	0	0	Yes			
8	4	2	3	5	0	0	Yes		Pr(winning)	0.491
9	5	1	2	3	0	0	Yes		Expected number of tosses	3.392
10	6	6	1	7	0	1	No			
11	7	1	4	5						
12	8	2	4	6						
13	9	3	4	7						
14	10	3	5	8						
15	11	2	4	6						
16	12	3	5	8						
42	38	6	6	12						
43	39	6	2	8						
44	40	2	2	4						

1 **Simulate tosses.** Simulate the results of 40 tosses in the range B5:D44 by entering the formula

=RANDBETWEEN(1,6)

in cells B5 and C5 and the formula

=SUM(B5:C5)

in cell D5. Then copy these to the range B6:D44. (Note: The RANDBETWEEN function is new to Excel 2007. It generates a random integer between the two specified values such that all values are equally likely, so it is perfect for tossing a die. We could also have used @RISK's RISKDUNIFORM function, as we did in the previous edition.)

Excel Function: *RANDBETWEEN*
The function RANDBETWEEN in the form **=RANDBETWEEN(N1,N2)** generates a random integer from N1 to N2, with each possibility being equally likely.

@RISK Function: *RISKDUNIFORM*
The @RISK function RISKDUNIFORM in the form **=RISKDUNIFORM({List})** generates a random member of a given list, so that each member of the list has the same chance of being chosen. Here List is a list of values separated by commas.

2 **First toss outcome.** Determine the outcome of the first toss with the formulas

=IF(OR(D5=7,D5=11),1,0)

=IF(OR(D5=2,D5=3,D5=12),1,0)

and

=IF(AND(E5=0,F5=0),"Yes","No")

As in many spreadsheet simulation models, the concepts in this model are simple. The key is careful bookkeeping.

in cells G5, H5, and I5. Note that we use the OR condition to check whether Joe wins right away (in which case a 1 is recorded in cell G5). Similarly, the OR condition in cell H5 checks whether he loses right away. In cell I5, we use the AND condition to check whether both cells G5 and H5 are 0, in which case the game continues. Otherwise, the game is over.

3 **Outcomes of other tosses.** Assuming the game continues beyond the first toss, Joe's point is the value in cell D5. Then we are waiting for a toss to have the value in cell D5 or 7, whichever occurs first. To implement this logic, enter the formulas

=IF(OR(G5="No",G5=""),"",IF(D6=$D$5,1,0))

=IF(OR(G5="No",G5=""),"",IF(D6=7,1,0))

and

$$=IF(OR(G5=\text{``No''},G5=\text{``''}),\text{``''},IF(AND(E6=0,F6=0),\text{``Yes''},\text{``No''}))$$

in cells G6, H6, and I6, and copy these to the range G7:I44. The OR condition in each formula checks whether the game just ended on the previous toss or has been over for some time, in which case blanks are entered. Otherwise, the first two formulas check whether Joe wins or loses on this toss. If both of these return 0, the third formula returns "Yes" (and the game continues). Otherwise, it returns "No" (and the game has just ended).

4 **Game outcomes.** We keep track of two aspects of the game in @RISK output cells: whether Joe wins or loses and how many tosses are required. To find these, enter the formulas

$$=SUM(E5:E44)$$

and

$$=COUNT(E5:E44)$$

in cells J5 and J6, and designate each of these as an @RISK output cell. Note that both functions, SUM and COUNT, ignore blank cells.

5 **Simulation summary.** Although we get summary measures in the various @RISK results windows when we run the simulation, it is useful to see some key summary measures right on the model sheet. To obtain these, enter the formula

$$=RISKMEAN(J5)$$

in cell J8 and copy it to cell J9. As the labels indicate, the RISKMEAN in cell J8, being an average of 0's and 1's, is just the fraction of iterations where Joe wins. The average in cell J9 is the average number of tosses until the game's outcome is determined.

Recall that the mean (or average) of a sequence of 0's and 1's is the fraction of 1's in the sequence. This can typically be interpreted as a probability.

Running the Simulation

We set the number of iterations to 10,000 (partly for variety and partly to obtain a very accurate answer) and the number of simulations to 1. Then we run the simulation as usual.

Discussion of the Simulation Results

Perhaps surprisingly, the probability of winning in craps is 0.493, only slightly less than 0.5.

After running @RISK, we obtain the summary results in cells J8 and J9 of Figure 17.33 (among others). Our main interest is in the average in cell J8. It represents our best estimate of the probability of winning, 0.491. (It can be shown with a probability argument that the exact probability of winning in craps is 0.493.) We also see that the average number of tosses needed to determine the outcome of a game was 3.392. (The maximum number of tosses ever needed was 30.) ∎

Simulating the NCAA Basketball Tournament

Each year the suspense reaches new levels as "March Madness" approaches, the time of the NCAA Basketball Tournament. Which of the 64 teams in the tournament will reach the "Sweet Sixteen," which will go on to the prestigious "Final Four," and which team will be crowned champion? The excitement at Indiana University is particularly high, given the strong basketball tradition here, so it has become a yearly tradition at IU (at least for the authors) to simulate the NCAA Tournament right after the 64-team field has been announced. We share that simulation in the following example.

EXAMPLE | **17.11 MARCH MADNESS**

As of press time for this book, the most recent NCAA Basketball Tournament was the 2007 tournament, won by the University of Florida (for the second year in a row). Of course, on the Sunday evening when the 64-team field was announced, we did not know which team would win. All we knew were the pairings (which teams would play which other teams) and the team ratings, based on Jeff Sagarin's nationally syndicated rating system. We show how to simulate the tournament and keep a tally of the winners.

Objective To simulate the 64-team NCAA basketball tournament and keep a tally on the number of times each team wins the tournament.

WHERE DO THE NUMBERS COME FROM?

As soon as you learn the pairings for the *next* NCAA tournament, you can visit Sagarin's site at http://www.usatoday.com/sports/sagarin.htm#hoop for the latest ratings.

Solution

We model the point spread as normally distributed, with mean equal to the difference between the Sagarin ratings and standard deviation 10.

We need to make one probabilistic assumption. From that point, it is a matter of "playing out" the games and doing the required bookkeeping. To understand this probabilistic assumption, suppose team A plays team B and Sagarin's ratings for these teams are, say, 85 and 78. Then Sagarin predicts that the actual point differential in the game (team A's score minus team B's score) will be the difference between the ratings, 7.[4] We take this one step further. We assume the *actual* point differential is normally distributed with mean equal to Sagarin's prediction, 7, and standard deviation 10. (Why 10? This is an estimate based on an extensive analysis of historical data.) Then if the actual point differential is positive, team A wins. If it is negative, team B wins.

DEVELOPING THE SIMULATION MODEL

We only outline the simulation model. You can see the full details in the file **March Madness.xlsm**. (It includes the data for the 2007 tournament, but you can easily modify it for future tournaments by following the directions on the sheet.) The entire simulation is on a single Model sheet. Columns A through C list team indexes, team names, and Sagarin ratings. If two teams are paired in the first round, they are placed next to one another in the list. Also, all teams in a given region are listed together. (The regions are color-coded.) Columns K through Q contains the simulation. The first-round results are at the top, the second round results are below these, and so on. Winners from one round are automatically carried over to the next round with appropriate formulas. Selected portions of the Model sheet appear in Figures 17.34 and 17.35. We now describe the essential features of the model.

1 **Teams and ratings.** We first enter the teams and their ratings, as shown in Figure 17.34. Most of the teams shown here were in the East region in the 2007 tournament. North Carolina played Eastern Kentucky in the first round, Marquette played Michigan State, and so on.

---

[4]In general, there is also a home-court advantage, but we assume all games in the tournament are on "neutral" courts, so that there is no advantage to either team.

Figure 17.34

Teams and Sagarin Ratings

	A	B	C	D	E	F	G	H	I
1	Simulation of NCAA men's 2007 basketball tournament, using Sagarin ratings								
2									
3	Final Sagarin ratings of teams								
4	Index	Team	Rating						
5	1	North Carolina	93.48						
6	2	Eastern Kentucky	71.35						
7	3	Marquette	84.35						
8	4	Michigan State	85.75						
9	5	Southern Cal	84.62						
10	6	Arkansas	83.90						
11	7	Texas	86.67						
12	8	New Mexico St.	78.97		East regional				
13	9	Vanderbilt	82.52						
14	10	George Washington	79.99						
15	11	Washington St.	85.71						
16	12	Oral Roberts	77.45						
17	13	Boston College	84.63						
18	14	Texas Tech	81.27		Assumption: The actual point spread for each				
19	15	Georgetown	90.02		game is normally distributed with mean equal to				
20	16	Belmont	75.28		difference between Sagarin ratings, standard				
21	17	Ohio St.	92.77		deviation 10.				
22	18	C. Conn. St.	69.89						
23	19	BYU	83.62						
24	20	Xavier	83.71						
25	21	Tennessee	85.28						
26	22	Long Beach St.	78.05						
27	23	Virginia	83.97						
28	24	Albany	75.52		South regional				
29	25	Louisville	84.65						

Figure 17.35

NCAA Basketball Simulation Model (Last 3 Rounds Only)

	K	L	M	N	O	P	Q
124	Results of Round 4						
125	Game	Indexes	Teams	Predicted	Simulated	Index of winner	Winner
126	1	5	Southern Cal	-5.4	-15.09	15	Georgetown
127		15	Georgetown				
128	1	17	Ohio St.	7.97	10.88	17	Ohio St.
129		30	Creighton				
130	1	39	Maryland	-3.37	-4.77	47	Wisconsin
131		47	Wisconsin				
132	1	51	Kentucky	-4.76	0.67	51	Kentucky
133		63	UCLA				
134							
135	Semifinals						
136	Game	Indexes	Teams	Predicted	Simulated	Index of winner	Winner
137	1	15	Georgetown	-2.75	-5.83	17	Ohio St.
138		17	Ohio St.				
139	2	47	Wisconsin	4.96	11.95	47	Wisconsin
140		51	Kentucky				
141							
142	Finals						
143	Game	Indexes	Teams	Predicted	Simulated	Index of winner	Winner
144	1	17	Ohio St.	1.66	4.41	17	Ohio St.
145		47	Wisconsin				

2 **Simulate rounds.** Jumping ahead to the fourth-round simulation in Figure 17.35, we capture the winners from the previous round 3 and then simulate the games in round 4. The key formulas are in columns N and O. For example, the formulas in cells N126 and O126 are

=VLOOKUP(L126,LTable,3)−VLOOKUP(L127,LTable,3)

and

=RISKNORMAL(N126,10)

The first of these looks up the ratings of the two teams involved (in this case, Southern Cal and Georgetown) and subtracts them to get the predicted point spread. The second formula simulates a point spread with the predicted point spread as its mean. The rest of the formulas do the appropriate bookkeeping. You can view the details in the file.

3 **Outputs.** As shown by the boxed-in cells in Figure 17.35, we designate seven cells as @RISK output cells: the index of the winner, the indexes of the two finalists, and the indexes of the four semifinalists (the Final Four teams). However, the results we really want are tallies, such as the number of iterations where Duke (or any other team) wins the tournament. This takes some planning. In the @RISK Excel Reports dialog box, if we check the Simulation Data option, we get a sheet called Data that lists the values of all @RISK output cells for *each* of the iterations. (We used 1000 iterations.) Once we have these, we can use COUNTIF functions to tally the number of wins (or finalist or semifinalist appearances) for each team, right in the original Model sheet.

Some of these tallies appear in Figure 17.36. For example, the formula in cell U5 is

=COUNTIF('Data'!$I$8:$I$1007,S5)

In this case, the range I8:I1007 of the Data sheet contains the indexes of the 1000 winners, so this formula simply counts the number of these that are index 1.[5] As you can see, the top-rated team in the East region, North Carolina, won the tournament in 167 of the 1000 iterations and reached the Final Four almost half of the time. In contrast, the lowly rated Eastern Kentucky did not make the Final Four in any of the 1000 iterations.

The Simulation Data report in @RISK lists the outputs from each iteration of the simulation, which allows us to tally the winners.

Figure 17.36

Tally of Winners

	S	T	U	V	W
1		Update formulas for tallies			
2					
3	Tally of winners, finalists, and semifinalists				
4	Index	Team	Winner	Finalist	Semifinalist
5	1	North Carolina	167	275	473
6	2	Eastern Kentucky	0	0	0
7	3	Marquette	3	8	33
8	4	Michigan State	2	7	17
9	5	Southern Cal	3	6	26
10	6	Arkansas	1	4	19
11	7	Texas	6	16	62
12	8	New Mexico St.	0	0	0
13	9	Vanderbilt	2	6	18
14	10	George Washington	0	0	8
15	11	Washington St.	9	21	56
16	12	Oral Roberts	0	0	2
17	13	Boston College	2	10	23
18	14	Texas Tech	1	1	4
19	15	Georgetown	68	137	258
20	16	Belmont	0	0	1

PROBLEMS

Level A

24. The game of Chuck-a-Luck is played as follows: You pick a number between 1 and 6 and toss three dice. If your number does not appear, you lose $1. If your number appears x times, you win x. On the average, how much money will you win or lose on each play of the game? Use simulation to find out.

25. A **martingale** betting strategy works as follows. We begin with a certain amount of money and repeatedly play a game in which we have a 40% chance of winning any bet. In the first game, we bet $1. From then

on, every time we win a bet, we bet $1 the next time. Each time we lose, we double our previous bet. Currently we have $63. Assume we have unlimited credit, so that we can bet more money than we have. Use simulation to estimate the profit we will have earned after playing the game 50 times.

Level B

26. Based on Morrison and Wheat (1984). When his team is behind late in the game, a hockey coach usually waits until there is one minute left before pulling the

[5]Unfortunately, each time we rerun the simulation, the Data sheet is deleted and then recreated, which messes up the references in the tally formulas. Therefore, we created a macro to update these formulas. You can run the macro by clicking on the button at the top of Figure 17.36.

goalie. Actually, coaches should pull their goalies much sooner. Suppose that if both teams are at full strength, each team scores an average of 0.05 goal per minute. Also, suppose that if you pull your goalie you score an average of 0.08 goal per minute while your opponent scores an average of 0.12 goal per minute. Suppose you are one goal behind with 5 minutes left in the game. Consider the following two strategies:

- Pull your goalie if you are behind at any point in the last 5 minutes of the game; put him back in if you tie the score.
- Pull your goalie if you are behind at any point in the last minute of the game; put him back in if you tie the score.

Which strategy maximizes your chance of winning or tying the game? Simulate the game using 10-second increments of time. Use the @RISKBINOMIAL function to determine whether a team scores a goal in a given 10-second segment. This is reasonable because the probability of scoring two or more goals in a 10-second period is near 0.

27. You are playing Andy Roddick in tennis, and you have a 42% chance of winning each point. (You are *good*!)
   a. Use simulation to estimate the probability you will win a particular game. Note that the first player to score at least 4 points and have at least 2 more points than his or her opponent wins the game.
   b. Use simulation to determine your probability of winning a set. Assume that the first player to win 6 games wins the set if he or she is at least 2 games ahead; otherwise, the first player to win 7 games wins the set. (We substitute a single game for the usual tiebreaker.)
   c. Use simulation to determine your probability of winning a match. Assume that the first player to win 3 sets wins the match.

17.6 CONCLUSION

We claimed in the previous chapter that spreadsheet simulation, especially together with an add-in like @RISK, is a very powerful tool. After seeing the examples in this chapter, you should now appreciate how powerful and flexible simulation can be. Unlike Solver optimization models, where we often make simplifying assumptions to achieve linearity, say, we allow virtually anything in simulation models. All we need to do is relate output cells to input cells with appropriate formulas, where any of the input cells can contain probability distributions to reflect uncertainty. The results of the simulation then show how bad things can get, how good they can get, and what we might expect on average. It is no wonder that companies like GM, Eli Lilly, and many others are increasingly relying on simulation models to analyze their corporate operations.

Summary of Key Terms

Term	Explanation	Excel	Page	Equation Number
Gamma distribution	Right-skewed distribution of nonnegative values useful for many quantities such as the lifetime of an appliance		1014	
RISKGAMMA function	Implements the gamma distribution in @RISK	=RISKGAMMA (*alpha,beta*)	1016	
Value at risk (VAR)	Fifth percentile of distribution of some output, usually a monetary output; indicates nearly how bad the output could be		1027	
Churn	When customers stop buying our product or service and switch to a competitor		1038	

(continued)

Term	Explanation	Excel	Page	Equation Number
RISKDUNIFORM function	Generates a random number from a discrete set of possible values, where each has the same probability	=RISKDUNIFORM ({1,2,3,4}), for example	1052	
RANDBETWEEN function	Generates a random integer between two limits, where each is equally likely	=RANDBETWEEN (1,6), for example	1052	

PROBLEMS

Level A

28. You now have $3. You will toss a fair coin four times. Before each toss you can bet any amount of your money (including none) on the outcome of the toss. If heads comes up, you win the amount you bet. If tails comes up, you lose the amount you bet. Your goal is to reach $6. It turns out that you can maximize your chance of reaching $6 by betting either the money you have on hand or $6 minus the money you have on hand, whichever is smaller. Use simulation to estimate the probability that you will reach your goal.

29. You now have $1000, all of which is invested in a sports team. Each year there is a 60% chance that the value of the team will increase by 60% and a 40% chance that the value of the team will decrease by 60%. Estimate the mean and median value of your investment after 100 years. Explain the large difference between the estimated mean and median.

30. Suppose you have invested 25% of your portfolio in four different stocks. The mean and standard deviation of the annual return on each stock are as shown in the file **P17_30.xlsx**. The correlations between the annual returns on the four stocks are also shown in this file.
   a. What is the probability that your portfolio's annual return will exceed 20%?
   b. What is the probability that your portfolio will lose money during the course of a year?

31. A ticket from Indianapolis to Orlando on Deleast Airlines sells for $150. The plane can hold 100 people. It costs Deleast $8000 to fly an empty plane. Each person on the plane incurs variable costs of $30 (for food and fuel). If the flight is overbooked, anyone who cannot get a seat receives $300 in compensation. On average, 95% of all people who have a reservation show up for the flight. To maximize expected profit, how many reservations for the flight should Deleast book? (*Hint*: The function RISKBINOMIAL can be used to simulate the number who show up. It takes two arguments: the number of reservations booked and the probability that any ticketed person shows up.)

32. Based on Marcus (1990). The Balboa mutual fund has beaten the Standard and Poor's 500 during 11 of the last 13 years. People use this as an argument that you can "beat the market." Here is another way to look at it that shows that Balboa's beating the market 11 out of 13 times is not unusual. Consider 50 mutual funds, each of which has a 50% chance of beating the market during a given year. Use simulation to estimate the probability that over a 13-year period the "best" of the 50 mutual funds will beat the market for at least 11 out of 13 years. This probability turns out to exceed 40%, which means that the best mutual fund beating the market 11 out of 13 years is not an unusual occurrence!

33. You have been asked to simulate the cash inflows to a toy company for the next year. Monthly sales are independent random variables. Mean sales for the months January through March and October through December are $80,000, and mean sales for the months April through September are $120,000. The standard deviation of each month's sales is 20% of the month's mean sales. We model the method used to collect monthly sales as follows:
   ■ During each month a certain fraction of new sales will be collected. All new sales not collected become 1 month overdue.
   ■ During each month a certain fraction of 1-month overdue sales is collected. The remainder becomes 2 months overdue.
   ■ During each month a certain fraction of 2-month overdue sales is collected. The remainder is written off as bad debts.

   You are given the information in the file **P17_33.xlsx** from some past months. Using this information, build a simulation model that generates the total cash inflow for each month. Develop a simple forecasting model and build the error of your forecasting model into the simulation. Assuming that there are $120,000 of 1-month-old sales outstanding and $140,000 of 2-month-old sales outstanding during January, you are 95% sure that total cash inflow for the year will be between what two values?

34. Consider a device that requires two batteries to function. If either of these batteries dies, the device will not work. Currently there are two brand-new batteries in the device, and there are three extra brand-new batteries. Each battery, once it is placed in the device, lasts a random amount of time that is triangularly distributed with parameters 15, 18, and 25 (all expressed in hours). When any of the batteries in the device dies, it is immediately replaced by an extra (if an extra is still available). Use @RISK to simulate the time the device can last with the batteries currently available.

35. Consider a drill press containing three drill bits. The current policy (called **individual replacement**) is to replace a drill bit when it fails. The firm is considering changing to a **block replacement** policy in which all three drill bits are replaced whenever a single drill bit fails. Each time the drill press is shut down, the cost is $100. A drill bit costs $50, and the variable cost of replacing a drill bit is $10. Assume that the time to replace a drill bit is negligible. Also, assume that the time until failure for a drill bit follows an exponential distribution with a mean of 100 hours. This can be modeled in @RISK with the formula **=RISKEXPON(100)**. Determine which replacement policy (block or individual replacement) should be implemented.

36. Freezco sells refrigerators. Any refrigerator that fails before it is 3 years old is replaced for free. Of all refrigerators, 3% fail during their first year of operation; 5% of all 1-year-old refrigerators fail during their second year of operation; and 7% of all 2-year-old refrigerators fail during their third year of operation.
    a. Estimate the fraction of all refrigerators that will have to be replaced.
    b. It costs $500 to replace a refrigerator, and Freezco sells 10,000 refrigerators per year. If the warranty period were reduced to 2 years, how much per year in replacement costs would be saved?

37. The annual demand for Prizdol, a prescription drug manufactured and marketed by the NuFeel Company, is normally distributed with mean 50,000 and standard deviation 12,000. We assume that demand during each of the next 10 years is an independent random number from this distribution. NuFeel needs to determine how large a Prizdol plant to build to maximize its expected profit over the next 10 years. If the company builds a plant that can produce x units of Prizdol per year, it will cost $16 for each of these x units. NuFeel will produce only the amount demanded each year, and each unit of Prizdol produced will sell for $3.70. Each unit of Prizdol produced incurs a variable production cost of $0.20. It costs $0.40 per year to operate a unit of capacity.
    a. Among the capacity levels of 30,000, 35,000, 40,000, 45,000, 50,000, 55,000, and 60,000 units per year, which level maximizes expected profit? Use simulation to answer this question.
    b. Using the capacity from your answer to part **a**, NuFeel can be 95% certain that *actual* profit for the 10-year period will be between what two values?

38. We are trying to determine the proper capacity level for a new electric car. A unit of capacity gives us the potential to produce one car per year. It costs $10,000 to build a unit of capacity and the cost is charged equally over the next 5 years. It also costs $400 per year to maintain a unit of capacity (whether or not it is used). Each car sells for $14,000 and incurs a variable production cost of $10,000. The annual demand for the electric car during each of the next 5 years is believed to be normally distributed with mean 500,000 and standard deviation 100,000. The demands during different years are assumed to be independent. Profits are discounted at a 10% annual interest rate. We are working with a 5-year planning horizon. Capacity levels of 300,000, 400,000, 500,000, 600,000 and 700,000 are under consideration.
    a. Assuming that we are risk neutral, use simulation to find the optimal capacity level.
    b. Using the answer to part **a**, there is a 5% chance that the *actual* discounted profit will exceed what value?
    c. Using the answer to part **a**, there is a 5% chance that the *actual* discounted profit will be less than what value?
    d. If we are risk averse, how might the optimal capacity level change?

Level B

39. Consider an oil company that bids for the rights to drill in offshore areas. The value of the right to drill in a given offshore area is highly uncertain, as are the bids of the competitors. This problem demonstrates the "winner's curse." The winner's curse states that the optimal bidding strategy entails bidding a substantial amount below your assumed value of the product for which you are bidding. The idea is that if you do not bid under your assumed value, your uncertainty about the actual value of the product will often lead you to win bids for products on which you (after paying your high bid) lose money. Suppose Royal Conch Oil (RCO) is trying to determine a profit-maximizing bid for the right to drill on an offshore oil site. The actual value of the right to drill is unknown, but it is equally likely to be any value between $10 million and $110 million. Seven competitors will bid against RCO. Each bidder's (including RCO's) estimate of the value of the drilling rights is equally likely to be any number between 50% and 150% of the actual value. Based on past history, RCO believes that each competitor is equally likely to bid between 40% and 60% of its value estimate. Given this information, what fraction (within 0.05) of RCO's estimated value should it bid to maximize its expected profit? (*Note*: Use the

RISKUNIFORM function to model the actual value of the field and the competitors' bids.)

40. We begin year 1 with $500. At the beginning of each year, we put half of our money under our mattress and invest the other half in Whitewater stock. During each year, there is a 50% chance that the Whitewater stock will double, and there is a 50% chance that we will lose half of our investment. To illustrate, if the stock doubles during the first year, we will have $375 under the mattress and $375 invested in Whitewater during year 2. We want to estimate our annual return over a 50-year period. If we end with F dollars, then our annual return is $(F/500)^{1/50} - 1$. For example, if we end with $10,000, our annual return is $20^{1/50} - 1 = 0.062$, or 6.2%. Run 1000 replications of an appropriate simulation. Based on the results, we can be 95% certain that our annual return will be between what two values?

41. Mary Higgins is a freelance writer with enough spare time on her hands to play the stock market fairly seriously. Each morning she observes the change in stock price of a particular stock and decides whether to buy or sell, and if so, how many shares to buy or sell. We assume that on day 1, she has $100,000 cash to invest and that she spends part of this to buy her first 500 shares of the stock at the current price of $50 per share. From that point on, she follows a fairly simple "buy low, sell high" strategy. Specifically, if the price has increased three days in a row, she sells 25% of her shares of the stock. If the price has increased two days in a row (but not three), she sells 10% of her shares. In the other direction, if the price has decreased three days in a row, she buys 25% more shares, whereas if the price has decreased only two days in a row, she buys 10% more shares. We assume a fairly simple model of stock price changes, as described in the file **P17_41.xlsx**. Each day the price can change by as much as $2 in either direction, and the probabilities depend on the previous price change: decrease, increase, or no change. Build a simulation model of this strategy for a period of 75 trading days. (You can assume that the stock price on each of the previous two days was $49.) Decide on interesting @RISK output cells, and then run @RISK for 500 iterations and report your findings.

42. You are considering a 10-year investment project. At present, the expected cash flow each year is $1000. Suppose, however, that each year's cash flow is normally distributed with mean equal to *last* year's actual cash flow and standard deviation $100. For example, suppose that the actual cash flow in year 1 is $1200. Then year 2 cash flow is normal with mean $1200 and standard deviation $100. Also, at the end of year 1, your best guess is that each later year's expected cash flow will be $1200.

   a. Estimate the mean and standard deviation of the NPV of this project. Assume that cash flows are discounted at a rate of 10% per year.

   b. Now assume that the project has an abandonment option. At the end of each year you can abandon the project for the value given in the file **P17_42.xlsx**. For example, suppose that year 1 cash flow is $400. Then at the end of year 1, you expect cash flow for each remaining year to be $400. This has an NPV of less than $6200, so you should abandon the project and collect $6200 at the end of year 1. Estimate the mean and standard deviation of the project with the abandonment option. How much would you pay for the abandonment option? (*Hint*: You can abandon a project at most once. Thus in year 5, for example, you abandon only if the sum of future expected NPVs is less than the year 5 abandonment value *and* the project has not yet been abandoned. Also, once you abandon the project, the actual cash flows for future years are 0. So the future cash flows after abandonment should disappear.)

43. Toys For U is developing a new Hannah Montana doll. The company has made the following assumptions:
   - It is equally likely that the doll will sell for 2, 4, 6, 8, or 10 years.
   - At the beginning of year 1, the potential market for the doll is 1 million. The potential market grows by an average of 5% per year. Toys For U is 95% sure that the growth in the potential market during any year will be between 3% and 7%. It uses a normal distribution to model this.
   - The company believes its share of the potential market during year 1 will be at worst 20%, most likely 40%, and at best 50%. It uses a triangular distribution to model this.
   - The variable cost of producing a doll during year 1 is equally likely to be $4 or $6.
   - Each year the selling price and variable cost of producing the doll will increase by 5%. The current selling price is $10.
   - The fixed cost of developing the doll (which is incurred right away, at time 0) is equally likely to be $4, $8, or $12 million.
   - Right now there is one competitor in the market. During each year that begins with 4 or fewer competitors, there is a 20% chance that a new competitor will enter the market.
   - We determine year t sales (for $t > 1$) as follows. Suppose that at the end of year $t - 1$, n competitors are present. Then we assume that during year t, a fraction $0.9 - 0.1n$ of the company's loyal customers (last year's purchasers) will buy a doll during this year, and a fraction $0.2 - 0.04n$ of customers currently in the market who did not purchase a doll last year will purchase a doll from the company this year. We can now generate a prediction for year t sales. Of course, this prediction will not be exactly correct. We assume that it is sure to be accurate within 15%, however. (There are different ways to model this. You can choose any method that is reasonable.)

a. **Use** @RISK to estimate the expected NPV of this project.

b. Use the percentiles in @RISK's output to find an interval such that you are 95% certain that the company's *actual* NPV will be within this interval.

44. Dord Motors is considering whether to introduce a new model called the Racer. The profitability of the Racer depends on the following factors:

    - The fixed cost of developing the Racer is equally likely to be $3 or $5 billion.
    - Year 1 sales are normally distributed with mean 200,000 and standard deviation 50,000. Year 2 sales are normally distributed with mean equal to actual year 1 sales and standard deviation 50,000. Year 3 sales are normally distributed with mean equal to actual year 2 sales and standard deviation 50,000.
    - The selling price in year 1 is $13,000. The year 2 selling price will be 1.05[year 1 price + $30(% diff1)] where % diff1 is the percentage by which actual year 1 sales differ from expected year 1 sales. The 1.05 factor accounts for inflation. For example, if the year 1 sales figure is 180,000, which is 10% below the expected year 1 sales, then the year 2 price will be 1.05[13,000 + 30(−10)] = $13,335. Similarly, the year 3 price will be 1.05[year 2 price + $30(% diff2)] where % diff2 is the percentage by which actual year 2 sales differ from expected year 2 sales.
    - The variable cost is equally likely to be $5000, $6000, $7000, or $8000 during year 1 and is assumed to increase by 5% each year.

    Your goal is to estimate the NPV of the new car during its first 3 years. Assume that cash flows are discounted at 10%. Simulate 1000 trials and estimate the mean and standard deviation of the NPV for the first 3 years of sales. Also, determine an interval such that you are 95% certain that the NPV of the Racer during its first 3 years of operation will be within this interval.

45. Rerun the simulation from the previous problem, but now assume that the fixed cost of developing the Racer is triangularly distributed with minimum, most likely, and maximum values $3, $4, and $5 billion. Also, assume that the variable cost per car in year 1 is triangularly distributed with minimum, most likely, and maximum values $5000, $7000, and $8000.

46. Truckco produces the OffRoad truck. The company wants to gain information about the discounted profits earned during the next 3 years. During a given year, the total number of trucks sold in the United States is $500{,}000 + 50{,}000G - 40{,}000I$, where G is the percentage increase in gross domestic product during the year and I is the percentage increase in the consumer price index during the year. During the next 3 years, Value Line has made the predictions listed in the file **P17_46.xlsx**. In the past, 95% of Value Line's G predictions have been accurate within 6%, and 95% of Value Line's I predictions have been accurate within

5%. We assume that the actual G and I values are normally distributed each year.

At the beginning of each year, a number of competitors might enter the trucking business. The probability distribution of the number of competitors that will enter the trucking business is also given in the file **P17_46.xlsx**. Before competitors join the industry at the beginning of year 1, there are two competitors. During a year that begins with n competitors (after competitors have entered the business, but before any have left), OffRoad will have a market share given by $0.5(0.9)^n$. At the end of each year, there is a 20% chance that any competitor will leave the industry. The selling price of the truck and the production cost per truck are also given in the file **P17_46.xlsx**. Simulate 1000 replications of Truckco's profit for the next 3 years. Estimate the mean and standard deviation of the discounted 3-year profits, using a discount rate of 10%. You can use Excel's NPV function here. Do the same if there is the probability that any competitor leaves the industry during any year increases to 50%.

47. Suppose you buy an electronic device that you operate continuously. The device costs you $100 and carries a 1-year warranty. The warranty states that if the device fails during its first year of use, you get a new device for no cost, and this new device carries exactly the same warranty. However, if it fails after the first year of use, the warranty is of no value. You need this device for the next 6 years. Therefore, any time the device fails outside its warranty period, you pay $100 for another device of the same kind. (We assume the price does not increase during the 6-year period.) The time until failure for a device is gamma distributed with parameters $\alpha = 2$ and $\beta = 0.5$. (This implies a mean of 1 year.) Use @RISK to simulate the 6-year period. Include as outputs (1) your total cost, (2) the number of failures during the warranty period, and (3) the number of devices owned during the 6-year period.

48. Rework the previous problem for a case in which the 1-year warranty requires you to pay for the new device even if failure occurs during the warranty period. Specifically, if the device fails at time t, measured relative to the time it went into use, you must pay $100t$ for a new device. For example, if the device goes into use at the beginning of April and fails 9 months later, at the beginning of January, you must pay $75. The reasoning is that you got 9/12 of the warranty period for use, so you should pay that fraction of the total cost for the next device. As before, however, if the device fails outside the warranty period, you must pay the full $100 cost for a new device.

49. Based on Hoppensteadt and Peskin (1992). The following model (the Reed–Frost model) is often used to model the spread of an infectious disease. Suppose that at the beginning of period 1, the population

consists of 5 diseased people (called infectives) and 95 healthy people (called susceptibles). During any period there is a 0.05 probability that a given infective person will encounter a particular susceptible. If an infective encounters a susceptible, there is a 0.5 probability that the susceptible will contract the disease. An infective lives an average of 10 periods with the disease. To model this, we assume that there is a 0.10 probability that an infective dies during any given period. Use @RISK to model the evolution of the population over 100 periods. Use your results to answer the following questions. [*Hint*: During any period there is a probability $0.05(0.50) = 0.025$ that an infective will infect a particular susceptible. Thus the probability that a particular susceptible is not infected during a period is $(1 - 0.025)^n$, where n is the number of infectives present at the end of the previous period.]

a. What is the probability that the population will die out?
b. What is the probability that the disease will die out?
c. On the average, what percentage of the population is infected by the end of period 100?
d. Suppose that people use infection "protection" during encounters. The use of protection reduces the probability that a susceptible will contract the disease during a single encounter with an infective from 0.50 to 0.10. Now answer parts **a** through **c** under the assumption that everyone uses protection.

50. Chemcon has taken over the production of Nasacure from a rival drug company. Chemcon must build a plant to produce Nasacure by the beginning of 2007. Once the plant is built, the plant's capacity cannot be changed. Each unit sold brings in $10 in revenue. The fixed cost (in dollars) of producing a plant that can produce x units per year of the drug is $5,000,000 + 10x$. This cost is assumed to be incurred at the end of 2007. In fact, we assume that all cost and sales cash flows are incurred at the ends of the respective years. If a plant of capacity x is built, the variable cost of producing a unit of Nasacure is $6 - 0.1(x - 1,000,000)/100,000$. For example, a plant capacity of 1,100,000 units has a variable cost of $5.90. Each year a plant operating cost of $1 per unit of capacity is also incurred. Based on a forecasting sales model from the previous 10 years, Chemcon forecasts that demand in year t, D_t, is related to the demand in the previous year, D_{t-1}, by the equation $D_t = 67,430 + 0.985D_{t-1} + e_t$ where e_t is a random term that is normally distributed with mean 0 and standard deviation 29,320. The demand in 2006 was 1,011,000 units. If demand for a year exceeds production capacity, all demand in excess of plant capacity is lost. Chemcon wants to determine a capacity level that maximizes expected discounted profits (using an interest rate of 10%) for the time period 2007 through 2016. Use simulation to help it do so.

51. The Tinkan Company produces 1-pound cans for the Canadian salmon industry. Each year the salmon spawn during a 24-hour period and must be canned immediately. Tinkan has the following agreement with the salmon industry. The company can deliver as many cans as it chooses. Then the salmon are caught. For each can by which Tinkan falls short of the salmon industry's needs, the company pays the industry a $2 penalty. Cans cost Tinkan $1 to produce and are purchased for $2 per can. If any cans are left over, they are returned to Tinkan and the company reimburses the industry $2 for each extra can. These extra cans are put in storage for next year. Each year a can is held in storage, a carrying cost equal to 20% of the can's production cost is incurred. It is well known that the number of salmon harvested during a year is strongly related to the number of salmon harvested the previous year. In fact, using past data, Tinkan estimates that the harvest size in year t, H_t (measured in the number of cans required), is related to the harvest size in the previous year, H_{t-1}, by the equation $H_t = H_{t-1}e_t$ where e_t is normally distributed with mean 1.02 and standard deviation 0.10.

Tinkan plans to use the following production strategy. For some value of x, it produces enough cans at the beginning of year t to bring its inventory up to $x + \hat{H}_t$, where $\hat{H}_t$ is the predicted harvest size in year t. Then it delivers these cans to the salmon industry. For example, if it uses $x = 100,000$, the predicted harvest size is 500,000 cans, and 80,000 cans are already in inventory, then Tinkan produces and deliver 520,000 cans. Given that the harvest size for the previous year was 550,000 cans, use simulation to help Tinkan develop a production strategy that maximizes its expected profit over the next 20 years.

52. You are unemployed and 21 years old and searching for a job. Until you accept a job offer, the following situation occurs. At the beginning of each year, you receive a job offer. The annual salary associated with the job offer is equally likely to be any number between $20,000 and $100,000. You must immediately choose whether to accept the job offer. If you accept an offer with salary x, you receive x per year while you work (we assume you retire at age 70), including the current year. Assume that cash flows are discounted so that a cash flow received 1 year from now has a present value of 0.9. You have adopted the following policy. You will accept the first job offer that exceeds w dollars.

a. Use simulation to determine the value of w (within $10,000) that maximizes the expected NPV of earnings you will receive the rest of your working life?
b. Repeat part **a**, assuming now that you get a 3% raise in salary every year after the first year you accept the job.

Your next-door neighbor, Scott Jansen, has a 12-year-old daughter, and he wants to pay the tuition for her first year of college 6 years from now. The tuition for the first year will be $17,500. Scott has gone through his budget and finds that he can invest $200 per month for the next 6 years. Scott has opened accounts at two mutual funds. The first fund follows an investment strategy designed to match the return of the S&P 500. The second fund invests in short-term Treasury bills. Both funds have very low fees.

Scott has decided to follow a strategy in which he contributes a fixed fraction of the $200 to each fund. An adviser from the first fund suggested that each month he invest 80% of the $200 in the S&P 500 fund and the other 20% in the T-bill fund. The adviser explained that the S&P 500 has averaged much larger returns than the T-bill fund. Even though stock returns are risky investments in the short run, the risk would be fairly minimal over the longer 6-year period. An adviser from the second fund recommended just the opposite: invest 20% in the S&P 500 fund and 80% in T-bills, he said. Treasury bills are backed by the United States government. If you follow this allocation, he said, your average return will be lower, but at least you will have enough to reach your $17,500 target in 6 years.

Not knowing which adviser to believe, Scott has come to you for help.

Questions

1. The file **Investing for College.xlsx** contains 261 monthly returns of the S&P 500 and Treasury bills from January 1970 through September 1991. (If you can find more recent data on the Web, feel free to use it.) Suppose that in each of the next 72 months (6 years), it is equally likely that any of the historical returns will occur. Develop a spreadsheet model to simulate the two suggested investment strategies over the 6-year period. Plot the value of each strategy over time for a single iteration of the simulation. What is the total value of each strategy after 6 years? Do either of the strategies reach the target?

2. Simulate 1000 iterations of the two strategies over the 6-year period. Create a histogram of the final fund values. Based on your simulation results, which of the two strategies would you recommend? Why?

3. Suppose that Scott needs to have $19,500 to pay for the first year's tuition. Based on the same simulation results, which of the two strategies would you recommend now? Why?

4. What other real-world factors might be important to consider in designing the simulation and making a recommendation? ∎

An investor is considering the purchase of zero-coupon U.S. Treasury bonds. A 30-year zero-coupon bond yielding 8% can be purchased today for $9.94. At the end of 30 years, the owner of the bond will receive $100. The yield of the bond is related to its price by the following equation:

$$P = \frac{100}{(1 + y)^t}$$

Here, P is the price of the bond, y is the yield of the bond, and t is the maturity of the bond measured in years. Evaluating this equation for $t = 30$ and $y = 0.08$ gives $P = 9.94$.

The investor is planning to purchase a bond today and sell it 1 year from now. The investor is interested in evaluating the *return* on the investment in the bond. Suppose, for example, that the yield of the bond 1 year from now is 8.5%. Then the price of the bond 1 year later will be $9.39 $[= 100/(1 + 0.085)^{29}]$. The time remaining to maturity is $t = 29$ because 1 year has passed. The return for the year is -5.54% $[= (9.39 - 9.94)/9.94]$.

In addition to the 30-year-maturity zero-coupon bond, the investor is considering the purchase of zero-coupon bonds with maturities of 2, 5, 10, or 20 years. All of the bonds are currently yielding 8.0%. (Bond investors describe this as a *flat yield curve*.) The investor cannot predict the future yields of the bonds with certainty. However, the investor believes that the yield of each bond 1 year from now can be modeled by a normal distribution with a mean of 8% and a standard deviation of 1%.

Questions

1. Suppose that the yields of the five zero-coupon bonds are all 8.5% 1 year from today. What are the returns of each bond over the period?

2. Using a simulation with 1000 iterations, estimate the expected return of each bond over the year. Estimate the standard deviations of the returns.

3. Comment on the following statement: "The expected yield of the 30-year bond 1 year from today is 8%. At that yield, its price would be $10.73. The return for the year would be 8% $[= (10.73 - 9.94)/9.94]$. Hence, the average return for the bond should be 8% as well. A simulation isn't really necessary. Any difference between 8% and the answer in Question 2 must be due to simulation error." ■

Statistical Reporting

A.1 INTRODUCTION

By now, you have learned a wide variety of statistical tools, ranging from simple charts and descriptive measures to more complex tools such as regression and time series analysis. We suspect that all of you will be required to use some of these tools in your later coursework and in your eventual jobs. This means that you will not only need to understand the statistical tools and apply them correctly, but you will also have to write reports of your analyses for someone else—an instructor, a boss, or a client—to read. Unfortunately, the best statistical analysis is worth little if the report is written poorly. A good report must be accurate from a statistical point of view, but maybe even more important, it must be written in clear, concise English.[1]

As instructors, we know from experience that statistical report writing is the downfall of many students in statistics courses. Many students appear to believe that they will be evaluated entirely on whether the numbers are right and that the quality of the write-up is at best secondary. This is simply not true. It is not true in an academic environment, and it is certainly not true in a business environment. Managers and executives in business are very busy people who have little time or patience to wade through poorly written reports. In fact, if a report starts out badly, the remainder will probably not be read at all. Only when it is written clearly, concisely, and accurately will it have a chance of making any impact. Stated simply, a statistical analysis is often worthless if not reported well.

The goals of this brief appendix are to list several suggestions for writing good reports and to provide examples of good reports based on analyses we have done in previous chapters. You have undoubtedly had many classes in writing throughout your school years, and we cannot hope to make you a good writer if you have not already developed good basic writing skills. However, we can do three things to make you a competent statistical report writer. First, we can motivate you to spend time on your report writing by stressing how important it is in the business world. Indeed, we believe that poor writing often occurs because writers do not believe the quality of their writing makes any difference to anyone. However, we promise you that it does make a difference in the business world—your job might depend on it! Second, we can list several suggestions for improving your statistical report writing. Once you believe that good writing is really important, these tips might be all you need to help you improve your report writing significantly. Finally, we can provide examples of good reports based on examples from this book. Some people learn best by example, so these "templates" should come in very handy.

---

[1]This appendix discusses report *writing*. However, we acknowledge that oral presentation of statistical analysis is also very important. Fortunately, virtually all of our suggestions for good report writing carry over to making effective presentations. Also, we focus here on *statistical* reporting. The same comments are relevant for other quantitative reports, such as those dealing with optimization models or simulation.

There is no single best way to write a statistical report. Just as there are many different methods for writing a successful novel or a successful biography, there are many different methods for writing a successful statistical report. The examples we provide look good to us, but you might want to change them according to your own tastes—or maybe even improve on them. Nevertheless, there are some bad habits that practically all readers will object to, and there are some good habits that will make your writing more effective. We list several suggestions here and expand on them in the next section.

Planning

- Clarify the objective
- Develop a clear plan
- Give yourself enough time

Developing a report

- Write a quick first draft
- Edit and proofread
- Give your report a professional look

Be clear

- Provide sufficient background information
- Tailor statistical explanations to your audience
- Place charts and tables in the body of the report

Be concise

- Let charts do the talking
- Be selective in the computer outputs you include

Be precise

- List assumptions and potential limitations
- Limit the decimal places
- Report the results fairly
- Get advice from an expert

A.2 SUGGESTIONS FOR GOOD STATISTICAL REPORTING

To some extent, the habits that make someone a good statistical report writer are the same habits that make someone a good writer in general. Good writing is good writing! However, there are some specific aspects of good statistical reporting that do not apply to other forms of writing. In this section we list several suggestions for becoming a good writer in general and for becoming a good statistical report writer in particular.

A.2.1 Planning

Clarify the objective When you write a statistical report, you are probably writing it *for* someone—an instructor, a boss, or maybe even a client. Make sure you know exactly what this other person wants, so that you do not write the wrong report (or perform the wrong statistical analysis). If there is any doubt in your mind about the objective of the report, clarify it with the other person before proceeding. Do not just assume that coming close to the target objective is good enough.

Develop a clear plan Before you start writing the report, make a plan for how you are going to organize it. This can be a mental plan, especially if the report is short and straight-forward, or it can be a more formal written outline. Think about the "best" length for the report. It should be long enough to cover the important points, but it should not be verbose. Think about the overall organization of the report and how you can best divide it into sections (if separate sections are appropriate). Think about the computer outputs you need to include (and those you can exclude) to make your case as strong as possible. Think about the audience for whom you are writing and what level of detail they will demand or will be able to comprehend. If you have a clear plan before you begin writing, the writing itself will flow much more smoothly and easily than if you make up a plan as you go. Most effective statistical reports essentially follow the outline below. We recommend that you try it.

- Executive summary
- Problem description
- Data description
- Statistical methodology
- Results and conclusions

Give yourself enough time If you plan to follow the suggestions we list here, you need to give yourself time to do the job properly. If the report is due first thing Monday morning and you begin writing it on Sunday evening, your chances of producing anything of high quality are slim. Get started early, and don't worry if your first effort is not perfect. If you produce *something* a week ahead of time, you'll have plenty of time to polish it in time for the deadline.

A.2.2 Developing a Report

Write a quick first draft We have all seen writers in movies who agonize over the first sentence of a novel, and we suspect many of you suffer the same problem when writing a report. You want to get it exactly right the first time through, so you agonize over every word. We suggest writing the first draft as quickly as possible—just get *something* down in writing—and then worry about fixing it up with careful editing later on. The worst thing many of us face as writers is a blank piece of paper (or a blank computer document). Once there is something written, even if it is only in preliminary form, the hard part is over and the perfecting can begin.

Edit and proofread The secret of good writing is rewriting! We believe this suggestion (when coupled with the previous suggestion) can have the most immediate impact on the quality of your writing—and it is relatively easy to do. With today's software, there is no excuse for not editing and checking thoroughly, yet we are constantly amazed at how many people fail to do so. Spell checkers and grammar checkers are available in all of the popular word processors, and although they do not catch all errors, they should definitely be used. Then the real editing task can begin. A report that contains no spelling or grammatical errors is not necessarily well written. We believe a good practice, given enough time and planning, is to write a report and then reread it with a critical eye in a day or two. Better yet, get a knowledgeable friend to read it. Often the wording you thought was fine the first time around will sound awkward or confusing on a second reading. If this is the case, rewrite it! And don't just change a word or two. If a sentence sounds really awkward or a paragraph does not get your point across, don't be afraid to delete the whole thing and explore better ways of structuring it. Finally, proofread the final copy at least once, preferably more than once. Just remember that this report has *your* name on it, and any careless spelling or grammar mistakes will reflect badly on you. Admittedly, this editing and proofreading process can be time-consuming, but it can also be very rewarding when you realize how much better the final report reads.

Give your report a professional look   We are not necessarily fans of the glitz that today's software enables (fancy colored fonts, 3-D charts, and so on), and we suspect that many writers spend too much time on glitz as opposed to substance. Nevertheless, it is important to give your reports a professional look. If nothing else, an attractive report makes a good first impression, and a first impression matters. It indicates to the reader that you have spent some time on the report and that there *might* be something inside worth reading. Of course, the fanciest report in the world cannot overcome a lack of substance, but at least it will gain you some initial respect. A sloppy report, even if it presents a great statistical analysis, might never be read at all! In any case, leave the glitz until last. Spend sufficient time to ensure that your report reads well and makes the points you want to make. Then you can have some fun "dressing it up."

A.2.3 Be Clear

How many times have you read a passage from a book, only to find that you need to read it again—maybe several times—because you keep losing your train of thought? It could be that you were daydreaming about something else, but it could also be that the writing itself is not clear. If a report is written clearly, the chances are that you will pick up its meaning on the first reading. Therefore, strive for clarity in your own writing. Avoid long, involved sentence structure. Don't beat around the bush, but come right out and say what you mean to say. Make sure each paragraph has a single theme that hangs together. Don't use jargon (unless you define it explicitly) that your intended readers are unlikely to understand. And, of course, read and reread what you have written—that is, edit it—to ensure that your writing is as clear as you thought.

Provide sufficient background information   After working on a statistical analysis for weeks or even months, you might lose sight of the fact that others are not as familiar with the project as you are. Make sure you include enough background information to bring the reader up to speed on the context of your report. As instructors, we have read through the fine details of many student reports without knowing exactly what the overall report is all about. Don't put your readers in this position.

Tailor statistical explanations to your audience   Once you begin writing the "analysis" section of a statistical report, you will probably start wondering how much explanation you need to include. For example, if you are describing the results of a regression analysis, you certainly want to mention the R^2 value, the standard error of estimate, and the regression coefficients, but do you need to explain the *meaning* of these statistical concepts? This depends entirely on your intended audience. If this report is for a statistics class, your instructor is certainly familiar with the statistical concepts, and you do not need to define them in your report. But if your report is for a nontechnical boss who knows very little about statistics beyond means and medians, a bit of explanation is certainly useful. Even in this case, however, keep in mind that your task is not to write a statistics textbook; it is to analyze a particular problem for your boss. So keep the statistical explanations brief, and get on with the analysis.

Place charts and tables in the body of the report   This is a personal preference and can be disputed, but we favor placing charts and tables in the body of the report, right next to where they are referenced, rather than at the back of the report in an appendix. This way, when readers see a reference to Figure 3 or Table 2 in the body of the report, they do not have to flip through pages to find Figure 3 or Table 2. Given the options in today's word processors, this can be done in a visually attractive manner with very little extra work.

A.2.4 Be Concise

Statistical report writing is not the place for the flowery language used in novels. Your readers want to get straight to the point, and they typically have no patience for verbose reports. Make sure each paragraph, each sentence, and even each word has a purpose, and delete everything that is extraneous. This is the time where you can put critical editing to good use. Just remember that many professionals have a one-page rule—they refuse to read anything that does not fit on a single page. You might be surprised at how much you can say on a single page once you realize that this is the limit of your allotted space.

Let charts do the talking   After writing this book, we are the first to admit that it can sometimes be very difficult to explain a statistical result in a clear, concise, and precise manner. It is sometimes easy to get mired in a tangle of words, even when the statistical concepts are fairly simple. This is where charts can help immensely. A well-constructed chart can be a great substitute for a long drawn-out sentence or paragraph. For example, we have seen many confusing discussions of interaction effects in regression or two-way ANOVA studies, although an accompanying chart of interactions makes the results clear and simple to understand. Do not omit the accompanying verbal explanations completely, but keep them short and refer instead to the charts.

Be selective in the computer outputs you include   With today's statistical software, it is easy to produce masses of numerical outputs and accompanying charts. There is unfortunately a tendency to include everything the computer spews out—often in an appendix to the report. Worse yet, there are often no references to some of these outputs in the body of the report; the outputs are just there, supposedly self-explanatory to the intended reader. This is a bad practice. Be selective in the outputs you include in your report, and don't be afraid to alter them (with a text processor or a graphics package, say) to help clarify your points. Also, if you believe a table or chart is really important enough to include in the report, be sure to refer to it in some way in your write-up. For example, you might say, "We can see from the chart in Figure 3 that men over 50 years old are much more likely to try our product than women under 50 years old." This observation is probably clear from the chart in Figure 3—this is probably why you *included* Figure 3—but you should definitely bring attention to it in your write-up.

A.2.5 Be Precise

Statistics is a science, as well as an art. The way a statistical concept or result is explained can affect its meaning in a critical way. Therefore, try to use very precise language in your statistical reports. If you are unsure of the most precise wording, look at the wording used in this book (or another statistics book) for guidance. For example, if you are reporting a confidence interval, don't report, "The probability is 95% that the sample mean is between 97.3 and 105.4." This might sound good enough, but it is not really correct. A more precise statement is, "We are 95% confident that the true but unobserved population mean is between 97.3 and 105.4." Of course, you must understand a statistical result (and sometimes the theory behind it) before you can report it precisely, but we suspect that imprecise statements are often due to laziness, not lack of understanding. Make the effort to phrase your statistical statements as precisely as possible.

List assumptions and potential limitations Many of the statistical procedures we have discussed rely on certain assumptions to hold. For example, in standard regression analysis there are assumptions about equal error variance, lack of residual autocorrelation, and normality of the residuals. If your analysis relies on certain assumptions for validity, mention these in your report, especially when there is evidence that they are violated. In fact, if they appear to be violated, warn the reader about the possible limitations of your results. For example, a confidence interval reported at the 95% level might really, due to the violation of an equal variance assumption, be valid at only the 80% or 85% level. Don't just ignore assumptions—with the implication that they do not matter.

Limit the decimal places We are continually surprised at the number of students who quote statistical results (directly from computer outputs, of course) to 5–10 decimal places, even when the original data are given with much less precision. For example, when forecasting sales a year from now, given historical sales data like $3440, $4120, and so on, some people quote a forecast such as $5213.2345. Who are they kidding? Statistical methods are exact only up to a certain limit. If you quote a forecast like $5213.2345, just because this is what appears in your computer output, you are not gaining precision; you are showing your lack of understanding of the limits of the statistical methodology. If you instead quote a forecast of "about $5200," you will probably gain more respect from critical readers.

Report the results fairly We have all heard statements such as, "It is easy to lie with statistics." It is true that the *same* data can often be analyzed and reported by two different analysts to support diametrically opposite points of view. Certain results can be omitted, the axes of certain charts can be distorted, important assumptions can be ignored, and so on. This is partly a statistical issue and partly an ethical issue. There is not necessarily anything wrong with two competent analysts using different statistical methods to arrive at different conclusions. For example, in a case where gender discrimination in salary has been charged, honest statisticians might very well disagree as to the legitimacy of the charges, depending on how they analyze the data. The world is not always black and white, and statistical analysts often find themselves in the gray areas. However, you are ethically obligated to report your results as fairly as possible. You should not *deliberately* try to lie with statistics.

Get advice from an expert Even if you have read and understood every word in this book, you are still not an expert in statistics. You know a lot of useful techniques, but there are many specific details and nuances of statistical analysis that we have not had time to cover. A good example is violation of assumptions. At several places we have discussed how to *detect* violations of assumptions, but we have usually not discussed possible remedies because they require advanced methods. If you become stuck on how to write a specific part of your report because you lack the statistical knowledge, don't be afraid to consult someone with more statistical expertise. For example, try e-mailing former instructors. They might be flattered that you remember them and value their knowledge—and they can probably provide the information you need.

A.3 EXAMPLES OF STATISTICAL REPORTS

Because many of you probably learn better from *examples* of report writing than from lists of suggestions, we now present several example reports. Each of these is based on a statistical analysis we performed in a previous chapter. (We embellish these with details that were not given earlier to bring them more alive.) Again, our reports represent just one possible style of writing, and other styles might be equally good or even better. But we have attempted to follow the suggestions listed in the previous section. In particular, we have strived for clarity, conciseness, and precision—and the final reports you see here are the result of much editing!

EXAMPLE	A.1

This example is adapted from Example 3.9. I am working for the Spring Mills Company, and my boss, Sharon Sanders, has asked me to report on the accounts receivable problem our company is currently experiencing. My task is to describe data on our customers, analyze the magnitude of interest lost because of late payments from our customers, and suggest a solution for remedying the problem. Ms. Sanders knows basic statistics, but she might need a refresher on the meaning of box plots. ■

SPRING MILLS COMPANY
ZANESVILLE, OHIO

To: Sharon Sanders
From: Chris Albright
Subject: Report on accounts receivable
Date: July 6, 2008

EXECUTIVE SUMMARY

Our company produces and distributes a wide variety of manufactured goods. Due to this variety, we have a large number of customers. We have classified our customers as small, medium, or large depending on the amount of business they do with us. Recently, we have had problems with accounts receivable. We are not getting paid as promptly as we would like, and we sense that it is costing our company a good deal of money in potential interest. You assigned me to investigate the magnitude of the problem and to suggest a strategy for fixing it. This report discusses my findings.

DATA SET

I collected data on 280 customer accounts. The breakdown by size is: 150 small customers, 100 medium customers, and 30 large customers. For each account, my data set includes the number of days since the customer was originally billed (Days) and the amount the customer currently owes (Amount). If necessary, we can identify any of these accounts by name, although specific names do not appear in this report. The data and my analysis are in the file **Accounts Receivable.xlsx**. I have attached this file to my report in case you want to see further details.

SOFTWARE

My analysis was performed entirely in Excel 2007, using the StatTools add-in where necessary.

ANALYSIS

Given the objectives of the analysis, my analysis is broken down by customer size. Exhibit I shows summary statistics for the Days and Amount for each customer size. (Small, medium, and large are coded throughout as 1, 2, and 3. For example, Days1 refers to the Days variable for small customers). We see, not surprisingly, that larger customers tend to owe larger amounts. The median amounts for small, medium, and large customers are $250, $470, and $1395, and the mean amounts follow a similar pattern. In contrast, medium and large companies tend to delay payments about equally long (median days delayed about 19–20), whereas small companies tend to delay only about half this long. The standard deviations in this exhibit indicate some variation across companies of any size, although this variation is considerably smaller for the amounts owed by small companies.

Graphical comparisons of these different size customers appear in Exhibits 2 and 3. Each of these shows side-by-side box plots (The first of Days, the second of Amount) for easy visual comparison. (For any box plot, recall that the box contains the middle 50% of the observations, the line and the dot inside the box represent the median and mean, and individual points outside the box represent extreme observations.) These box plots graphically confirm the patterns we observed in Exhibit I.

Exhibits 1–3 describe the variables Days and Amount individually, but they do not indicate whether there is a relationship between them. Do our customers who owe large amounts tend to delay longer? To investigate this, I created scatterplots of Amount versus Days for each customer size. The scatterplot for small customers (not shown) indicates no relationship whatsoever; the correlation between Days and Amount is a negligible −0.044. However, the scatterplots for medium and large customers both indicate a fairly strong positive relationship. We show the scatterplot for medium-size customers in Exhibit 4. (The one for large customers is similar, only with many fewer points.) The correlation is fairly large, 0.612, and the upward sloping (and reasonably linear) pattern is clear: the larger the delay, the larger the amount owed—or vice versa.

Exhibit A.1   Summary Measures for Different Size Customers

	A	B	C	D
		Days(1)	Days(2)	Days(3)
7				
8	One Variable Summary	Data Set #2	Data Set #2	Data Set #2
9	Mean	9.800	20.550	19.233
10	Std. Dev.	3.128	6.622	6.191
11	Median	10.000	20.000	19.000
12	Minimum	2.000	8.000	3.000
13	Maximum	17.000	39.000	32.000
14	Count	150	100	30
15				
16		Amount(1)	Amount(2)	Amount(3)
17	One Variable Summary	Data Set #2	Data Set #2	Data Set #2
18	Mean	254.53	481.90	1454.33
19	Std. Dev.	49.28	99.15	293.89
20	Median	250.00	470.00	1395.00
21	Minimum	140.00	280.00	930.00
22	Maximum	410.00	750.00	2220.00
23	Count	150	100	30

Exhibit A.2   Box Plots of Days by Different Size Customers

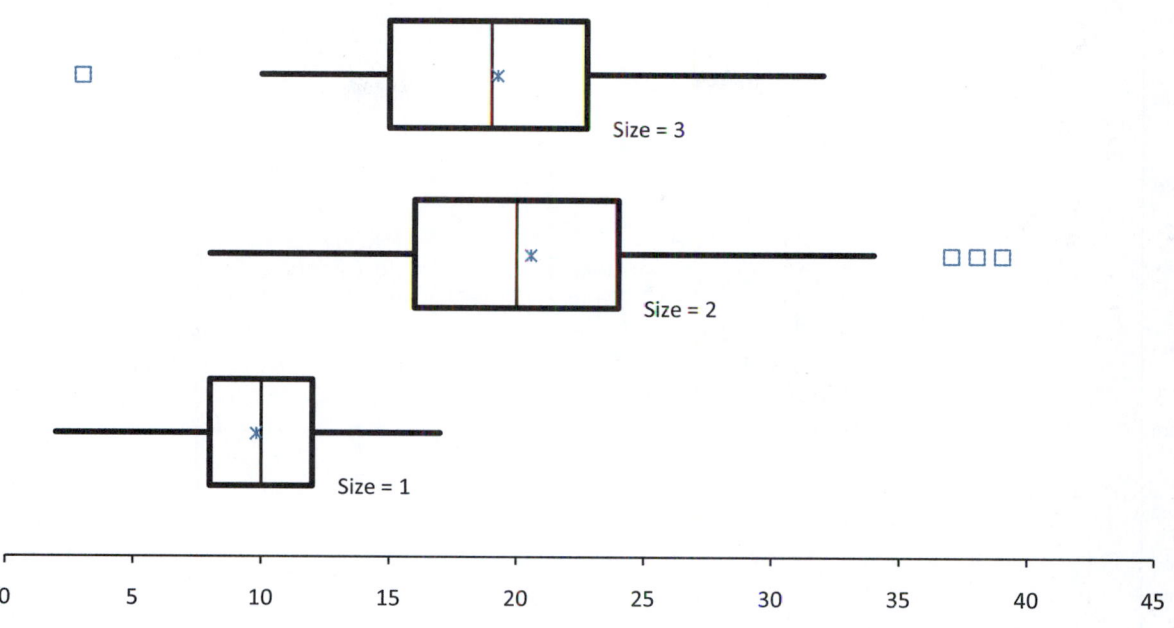

Box Plot of Comparison of Days

Size = 3

Size = 2

Size = 1

0   5   10   15   20   25   30   35   40   45

Exhibit A.3   Box Plots of Amount by Different Size Customers

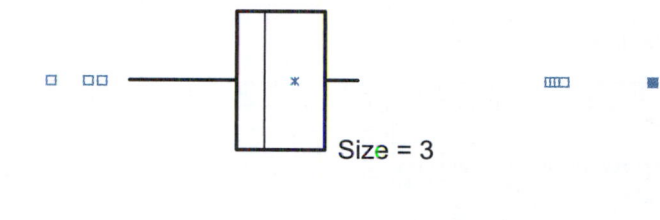

Boxplot of Comparison of Amount

Size = 3

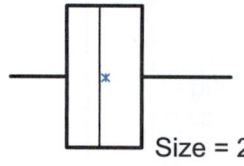

Size = 2

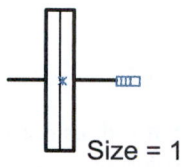

Size = 1

0   500   1000   1500   2000   2500

Exhibit A.4 Scatterplot of Amount versus Days for Medium Customers

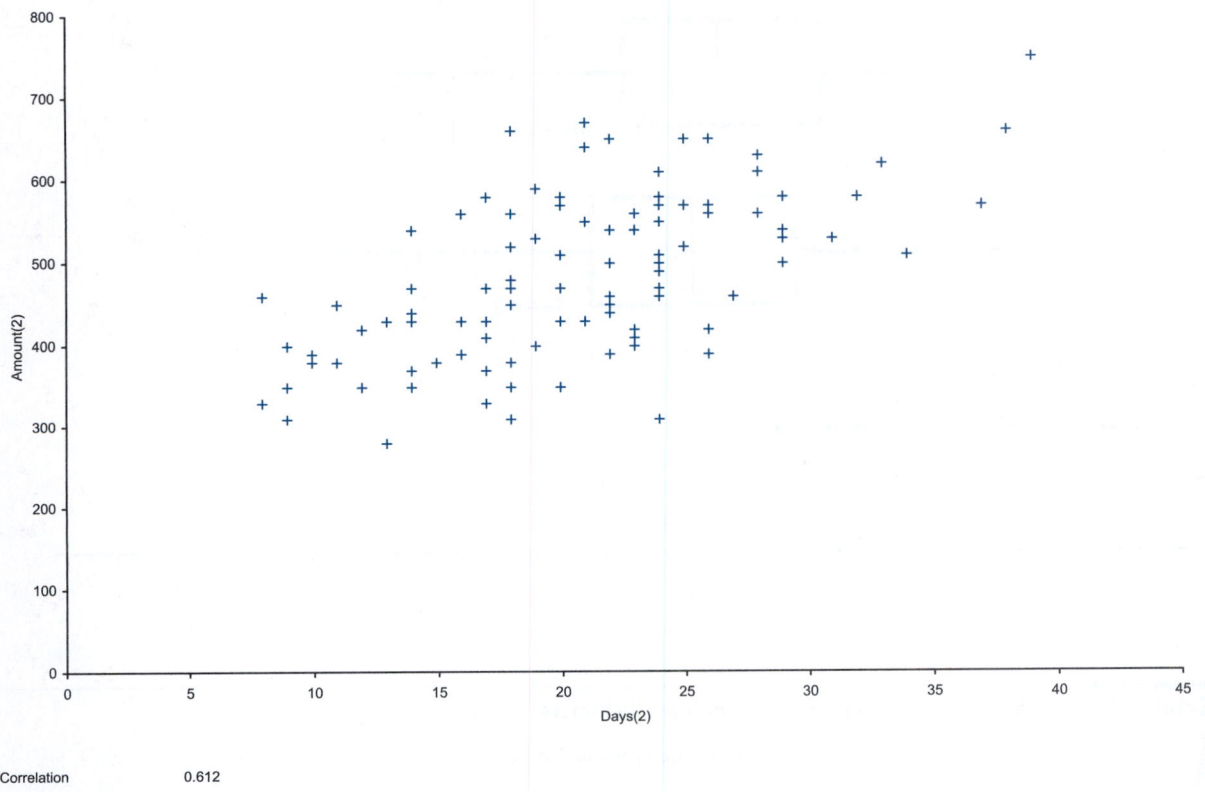

Scatterplot of Amount(2) vs Days(2)

Correlation   0.612

Exhibit A.5 Table of Lost Interest

	A	B	C	D	E	F	G	H	I
1	Interest Lost								
2									
3	Summary measures for selected variables								
4		Lost1	Lost2	Lost3					
5	Sum	$122.68	$338.65	$287.25					
6									
7	Annual interest rate		12%						
8									
9	Days1	Amount1	Lost1	Days2	Amount2	Lost2	Days3	Amount3	Lost3
10	7	$180.00	$0.41	17	$470.00	$2.63	19	$1,330.00	$8.31
11	8	$210.00	$0.55	22	$540.00	$3.91	20	$1,400.00	$9.21
12	10	$210.00	$0.69	28	$560.00	$5.16	14	$1,550.00	$7.13
13	8	$150.00	$0.39	24	$470.00	$3.71	15	$1,460.00	$7.20
14	9	$300.00	$0.89	26	$650.00	$5.56	23	$2,030.00	$15.35
15	5	$240.00	$0.39	29	$530.00	$5.05	19	$1,520.00	$9.49
16	4	$330.00	$0.43	21	$550.00	$3.80	15	$1,330.00	$6.56
17	10	$290.00	$0.95	33	$620.00	$6.73	17	$1,520.00	$8.50
18	5	$240.00	$0.39	16	$430.00	$2.26	21	$1,390.00	$9.60
19	13	$270.00	$1.15	27	$460.00	$4.08	24	$1,590.00	$12.55

The analysis to this point describes our customer population, but it does not directly answer our main concerns: How much potential interest are we losing and what can we do about it? The analysis in Exhibit 5 and accompanying pie chart in Exhibit 6 address the first of these questions. To create Exhibit 5, I assumed that we can earn an annual rate of 12% on excess cash. Then for each customer, I calculated the interest lost by not having a payment made for a certain number of days. (These calculations are shown for only a few of the customers.) Then I summed these lost interest amounts to obtain the totals in row 5 and created a pie chart from the sums in row 5 (expressed as percentages of the total).

The message from the pie chart is fairly clear. We do not need to worry about our many small customers; the interest we are losing from them is relatively small. However, we might want to put some pressure on the medium and large customers. I would suggest targeting the large customers first, especially those with large amounts due. There are fewer of them, so that we can concentrate our efforts more easily. Also, remember that amounts due and days delayed are positively correlated for the large customers. Therefore, the accounts with large amounts due are where we are losing the most potential interest.

Attachment: **Accounts Receivable.xlsx**

Exhibit A.6

Pie Chart of Lost Interest

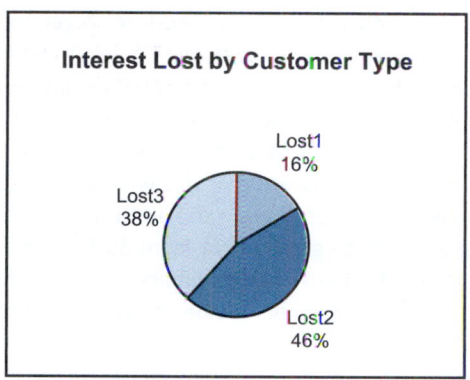

EXAMPLE **A.2**

This example is adapted from Example 9.9. I am a student in a required MBA statistics course. For the statistical inference part of the course, each student has been assigned to gather data in a real setting that can be used to find a suitably narrow confidence interval for a population parameter. Although the instructor, Rob Jacobs, certainly knows statistics well, he has asked us to include explanations of relevant statistical concepts in our reports, just to confirm that *we* know what we are talking about. Professor Jacobs has made it clear that he does not want a lot of "padding." He wants reports that are short and to the point. ■

Report on Confidence Intervals for Professor Rob Jacobs
Managerial Statistics, S540 – Spring semester, 2008
Submitted by Wayne Winston

EXECUTIVE SUMMARY

This report summarizes my findings on potential differences between husbands and wives in their ratings of automobile presentations. I chose this topic because my uncle manages a Honda dealership in town, and he enabled me to gain access to the data for this report. The report contains the following: (1) an explanation of the overall study, (2) a rationale for the sample size I chose, (3) the data, (4) the statistical methodology, and (5) a summary of my results.

THE STUDY

We tend to associate automobiles with males—horsepower, dual cams, and V-6 engines are macho terms. I decided to investigate whether husbands, when shopping for new cars with their wives, tend to react more favorably to salespeople's presentations than their wives. (My bias that this is true is bolstered by the fact that all salespeople I have seen, including all of those in this study, are men.) To test this, I asked a sample of couples at the Honda dealership to rate the sales presentation they had just heard on a 1 to 10 scale, 10 being the most favorable. The husbands and wives were asked to give independent ratings. I then used these data to calculate a confidence interval for the mean *difference* between the husbands' and wives' ratings. If my initial bias was correct, this confidence interval should be predominantly positive.

THE SAMPLE SIZE

Before I could conduct the study, I had to choose a sample size: the number of couples to sample. The eventual sample was based on two considerations: the time I could devote to the study and the length of the confidence interval I desired. For the latter consideration, I used StatTools's sample size determination procedure to get an estimate of the required sample size. This procedure requests a confidence level (I chose the usual 95% level), a desired confidence interval half-length, and a standard deviation of the differences. I suspected that most of the differences (husband rating minus wife rating) would be from -1 to $+3$, so I (somewhat arbitrarily) chose a desired half-length of 0.25 and guessed a standard deviation of 0.75. StatTools reported that this would require a sample size of 35 couples. I decided that this was reasonable, given the amount of time I could afford, so I used this sample size and proceeded to gather data from 35 husbands and wives. Of course, I realized that if the *actual* standard deviation of differences turned out to be larger than my guess, then my confidence interval would not be as narrow as I specified.

THE DATA

The data I collected includes a husband and a wife rating for each of the 35 couples in the sample. Exhibit 1 presents data for the first few couples, together with several summary statistics for the entire data set. As the sample means and medians indicate, husbands do tend to rate presentations somewhat higher than their wives, but this comparison of means and medians is only preliminary. The statistical *inference* is discussed next.

STATISTICAL METHODOLOGY

My goal is to compare two means: the mean rating of husbands and the mean rating of wives. There are two basic statistical methods for comparing two means: the two-sample method and the paired-sample method. I chose the latter. The two-sample method assumes that the observations from the two samples are *independent*. Although I asked each husband–wife pair to evaluate the presentation independently, I suspected that husbands and wives, by the very fact that they live together and tend to think alike, would tend to give positively correlated ratings. The data confirmed this. The correlation between the husband and wife ratings was a fairly large and positive 0.44. When data come in natural pairs and are positively correlated, then the paired-sample method for comparing means is preferred. The reason is that it takes advantage of the positive correlation to provide a narrower confidence interval than the two-sample method.

RESULTS

To obtain the desired confidence interval, I used StatTools's paired-sample procedure. This calculates the "husband minus wife" differences and then analyzes these differences. Exhibit 2 contains the StatTools output. The summary measures at the top of this output provide one more indication that husbands react, on average, more favorably to presentations than their wives. The mean difference is about 1.6 rating points. A graphical illustration of this difference appears in Exhibit 3, which includes a box plot of the "husband minus wife" differences. We see that the vast majority of the differences are positive.

Exhibit A.1   Data and Summary Measures

	A	B	C	D	E	F	G
3	Pair	Husband	Wife			Husband	Wife
4	1	6	3		One Variable Summary	Data Set #1	Data Set #1
5	2	7	8		Mean	6.914	5.286
6	3	8	5		Std. Dev.	1.222	1.792
7	4	6	4		Median	7.000	5.000
8	5	8	5		Count	35	35
9	6	7	6				
10	7	8	5				
11	8	6	7				
12	9	7	8				
13	10	7	5				

Exhibit A.2   Paired-sample Output from StatTools

	A	B	C	D	E	F
1	Sales presentation ratings					
2						
3	Pair	Husband	Wife			
4	1	6	3		Conf. Intervals (Paired-Sample)	Husband - Wife
5	2	7	8		Sample Size	35
6	3	8	5		Sample Mean	1.629
7	4	6	4		Sample Std Dev	1.664
8	5	8	5		Confidence Level	95.0%
9	6	7	6		Degrees of Freedom	34
10	7	8	5		Lower Limit	1.057
11	8	6	7		Upper Limit	2.200
12	9	7	8			
35	32	5	1			
36	33	7	5			
37	34	7	4			
38	35	10	5			

The right section of Exhibit 2 contains the statistical inference, including the 95% confidence interval for the mean difference. This interval extends from approximately 1 to 2.2. To understand how it is formed, the method first calculates the standard error (not shown) of the sample mean difference. This is the standard deviation of the differences divided by the square root of the sample size. Then it goes out approximately two standard errors on either side of the sample mean difference to form the limits of the confidence interval.

Because the confidence interval includes only positive values (and the lower limit is not even close to 0), there is little doubt that husbands, on average, react more positively to sales presentations than their wives. Note, though, that the confidence interval is not nearly as narrow as I specified in the sample size section. This is because the standard deviation of differences turned out to be considerably larger than I guessed (1.66 versus 0.75). If I really wanted a narrower confidence interval, I would need a considerably larger sample. Given that I have essentially proved my conjecture that the mean difference is positive, however, a larger sample does not appear to be necessary.

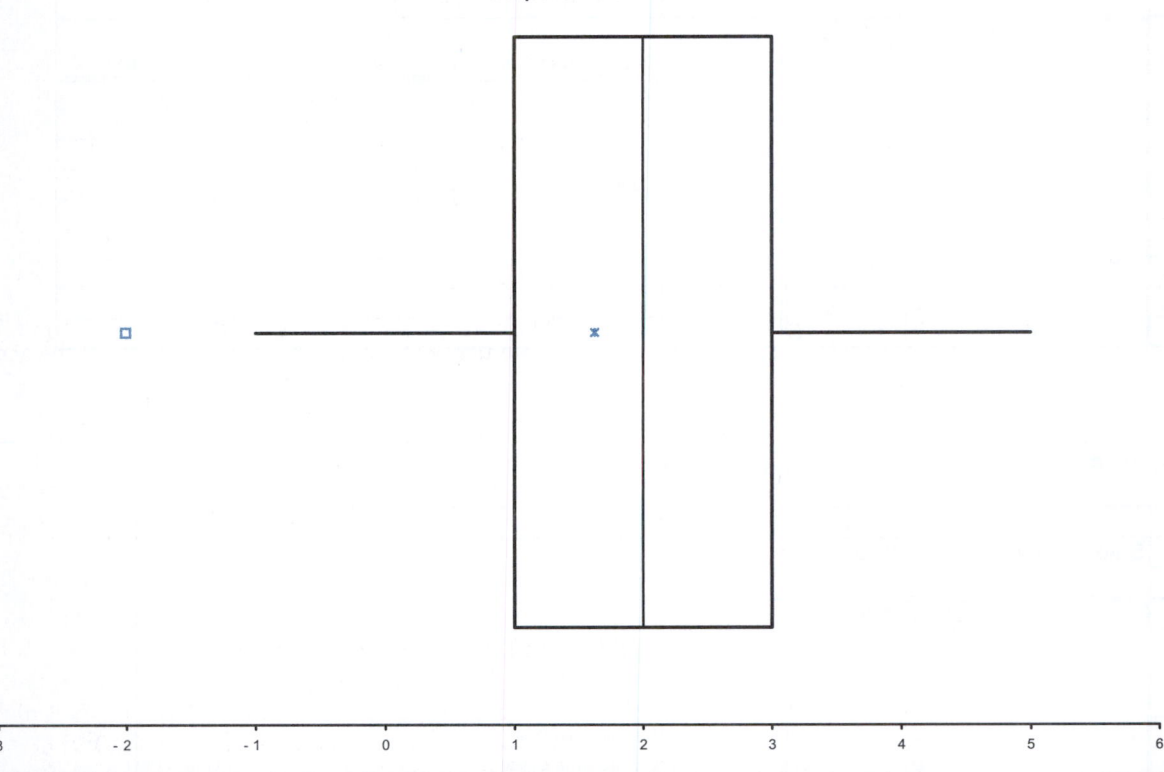

Boxplot of Difference

- 3   - 2   - 1   0   1   2   3   4   5   6

EXAMPLE	A.3

This example is adapted from Example 11.2. I am a statistical consultant, and I have been hired by the Bendrix Company, a manufacturing company, to analyze its overhead data. The company has supplied me with historical monthly data from the past three years on overhead expenses, machine hours, and the number of production runs. My task is to develop a method for forecasting overhead expenses in future months, given estimates of the machine hours and number of production runs that are expected in these months. My contact, Dave Clements, is in the company's finance department. He obtained an MBA degree about 10 years ago, and he vaguely remembers some of the statistics he learned at that time. However, he does not profess to be an expert. The more I can write my report in laymen's terms, the more he will appreciate it. ■

CHRISTOPHER J. ZAPPE STATISTICAL CONSULTING SERVICES BLOOMINGTON, INDIANA

To: Dave Clements, financial manager
Subject: Forecasting overhead
Date: July 20, 2008

Dave, here is the report you requested. (See also the attached Excel XP file, **Overhead Costs.xlsx**, that contains the details of my analysis. By the way, it was done with the help of the StatTools add-in for Excel. If you plan to do any further statistical analysis, I would strongly recommend purchasing this add-in.) As I explain in this report, regression analysis is the best-suited statistical methodology for your situation. It fits an equation to historical data, it uses this equation to forecast future values of overhead, and it provides a measure of accuracy of these forecasts. I believe you will be able to "sell" this analysis to your colleagues. The theory behind regression analysis is admittedly complex, but the outputs I provide are quite intuitive, even to nonstatisticians.

OBJECTIVES AND DATA

To ensure that we are on the same page, I will briefly summarize my task. You supplied me with Bendrix monthly data for the past 36 months on three variables: Overhead (total overhead expenses during the month), MachHrs (number of machine hours used during the month), and ProdRuns (number of separate production runs during the month). You suspect that Overhead is directly related to MachHrs and ProdRuns, and you want me to quantify this relationship so that you can forecast *future* overhead expenses on the basis of (estimated) future values of MachHrs and ProdRuns. Although you did not state this explicitly in your requirements, I assume that you would also like a measure of the accuracy of the forecasts.

STATISTICAL METHODOLOGY

Fortunately, there is a natural methodology for solving your problem: regression analysis. Regression analysis was developed specifically to quantify the relationship between a single *dependent* variable and one or more *explanatory* variables (assuming that there is a relationship to quantify). In your case, the dependent variable is Overhead, the explanatory variables are MachHrs and ProdRuns, and from a manufacturing perspective, there is every reason to believe that Overhead is related to MachHrs and ProdRuns. The outcome of the regression analysis is a regression equation that can be used to forecast future values of Overhead and provide a measure of the accuracy of these forecasts. There are a lot of calculations involved in regression analysis, but statistical software such as StatTools takes care of these calculations easily, allowing you to focus on the interpretation of the results.

PRELIMINARY ANALYSIS OF THE DATA

Before diving into the regression analysis itself, it is always a good idea to check graphically for relationships between the variables. The best type of chart for your problem is a scatterplot, which shows the relationship between any pair of variables. The scatterplots in Exhibits 1 and 2 illustrate how Overhead varies with MachHrs and with ProdRuns. In both charts the points follow a reasonably linear pattern from bottom left to upper right. That is, Overhead tends to increase linearly with MachHrs and with ProdRuns, which is probably what you suspected. The correlations below these plots indicate the strength of the linear relationships. The magnitudes of these correlations, 0.632 and 0.521, are fairly large. (The maximum possible correlation is 1.0.) They provide hope that regression analysis will yield reasonably accurate forecasts of overhead expenses.

Before moving to the regression analysis, there are two other charts you should consider. First, you ought to check whether there is a relationship between the two explanatory variables, MachHrs and ProdRuns. If the correlation between these variable is high (negative or positive), then you have a phenomenon called *multicollinearity*. This is not necessarily bad, but it complicates the interpretation of the regression equation. Fortunately, as Exhibit 3 indicates, there is virtually no relationship between MachHrs and ProdRuns, so multicollinearity is not a problem for you.

You should also check the time series nature of your overhead data. For example, if your overhead expenses are trending upward over time, or if there is a seasonal pattern to your expenses, then MachHrs and ProdRuns, by themselves, would probably not be adequate to forecast future values of Overhead. However, as illustrated in Exhibit 4, a time series graph of Overhead indicates no obvious trends or seasonal patterns.

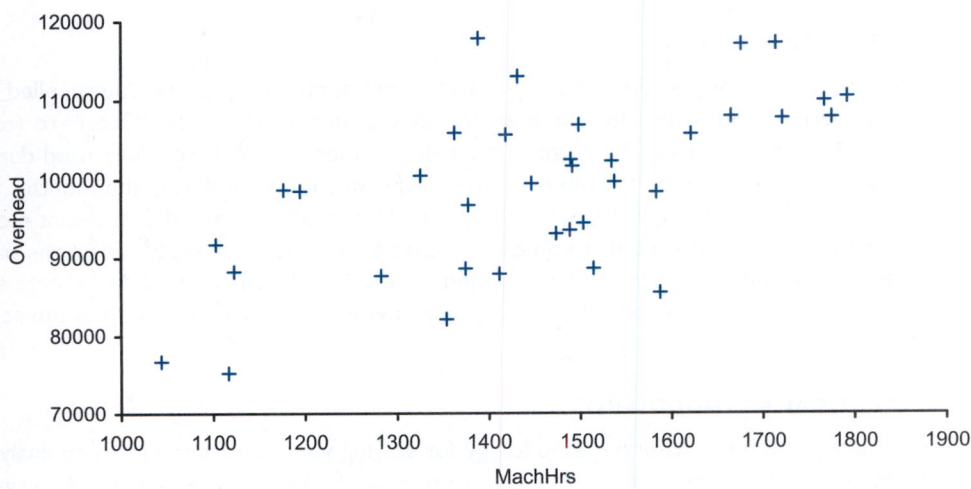

Correlation   0.632

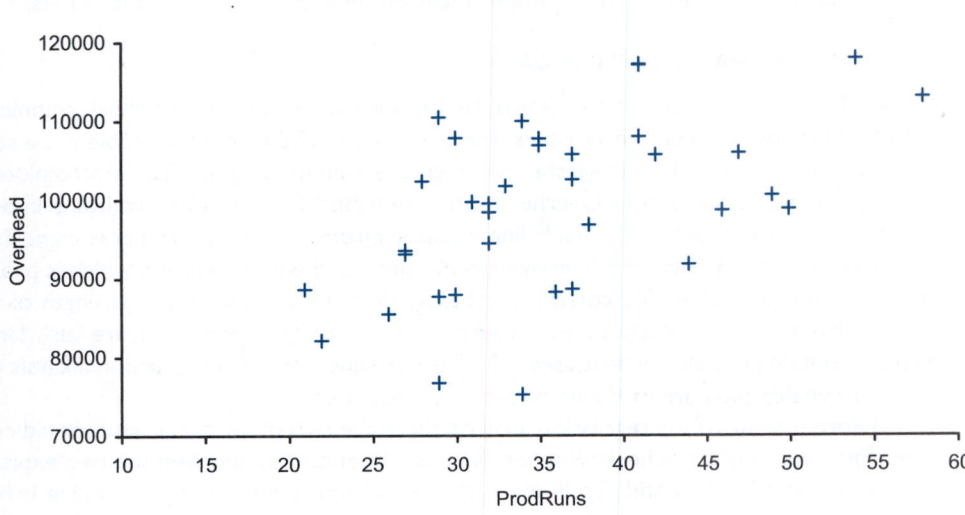

Correlation   0.521

REGRESSION ANALYSIS

The plots in Exhibits 1–4 provide some confidence that regression analysis for Overhead, using MachHrs and ProdRuns as the explanatory variables, will yield useful results. Therefore, I used StatTools's multiple regression procedure to estimate the regression equation. As you may know, the regression output from practically any software package,

Exhibit A.3   Scatterplot of MachHrs versus ProdRuns

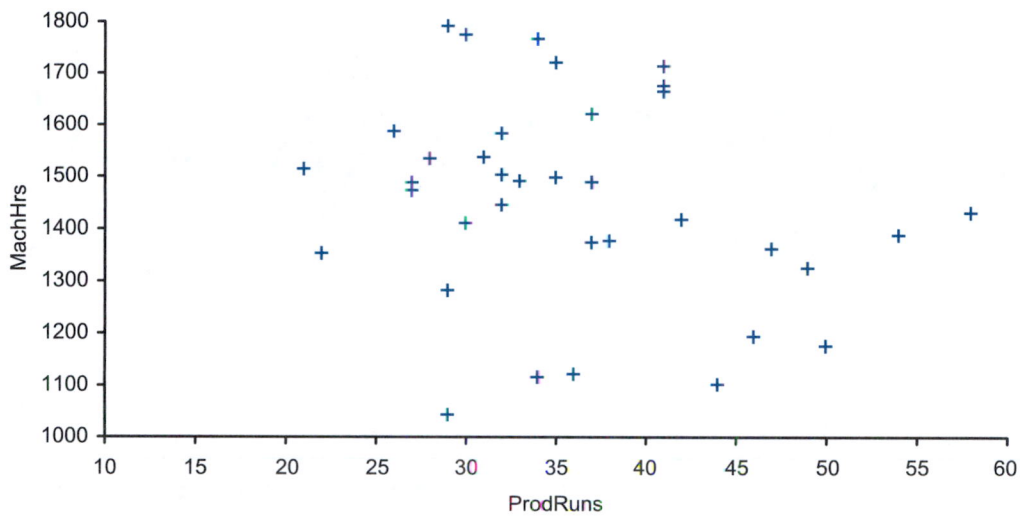

Scatterplot of MachHrs vs ProdRuns

Correlation   -0.229

including StatTools, can be a bit intimidating. For this reason, I report only the most relevant outputs. (You can see the rest in the Excel file if you like.) The estimated regression equation is

Forecasted Overhead = 3997 + 43.54MachHrs + 883.62ProdRuns

Two important summary measures in any regression analysis are R-square and the standard error of estimate. Their values for this analysis are 93.1% and $4109.

Now let's turn to interpretation. The two most important values in the regression equation are the coefficients of MachHrs and ProdRuns. For each extra machine hour your company uses, the regression equation predicts that an extra $43.54 in overhead will be incurred. Similarly, each extra production run is predicted to add $883.62 to overhead. Of course, these values should be considered approximate only, but they provide a sense of how much extra machine hours and extra production runs add to overhead. (Don't spend too much time trying to interpret the constant term, 3997. Its primary use is to get the forecasts to the correct "level.")

The R-square value indicates that 93.1% of the variation in overhead expenses you observed during the past 36 months can be "explained" by the values of MachHrs and ProdRuns your company used. Alternatively, only 6.9% of the variation in overhead has not been explained. To explain this remaining variation, you would probably need data on one or more *other* relevant variables. However, 93.1% is quite good. In statistical terms, you have a good fit.

For forecasting purposes, the standard error of estimate is even more important than R-square. It indicates the approximate magnitude of forecast errors you can expect when you base your forecasts on the regression equation. This standard error can be interpreted much like a standard deviation. Specifically, there is about a 68% chance that a forecast will be off by no more than one standard error, and there is about a 95% chance that a forecast will be off by no more than two standard errors.

Time Series of Overhead

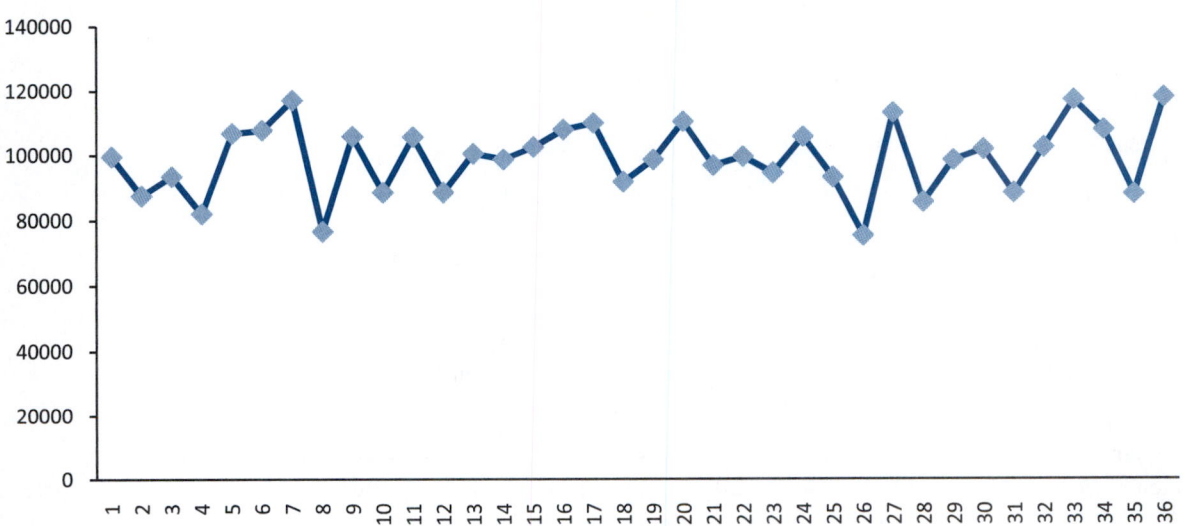

Month

FORECASTING

Your forecasting job is now quite straightforward. Suppose, for example, that you expect 1525 machine hours and 45 production runs next month. (These values are in line with your historical data.) Then you simply plug these values into the regression equation to obtain the forecasted overhead:

Forecasted overhead = 3997 + 43.54(1525) + 883.62(45) = $101,158

Given the standard error of estimate of $4109, you can be about 68% confident that this forecast will be off by no more than $4109 on either side, and you can be about 95% confident that it will be off by no more than $8218 on either side. Of course, I'm sure you know better than to take any of these values too literally, but I believe this level of forecasting accuracy should be useful to your company.

One last recommendation I have is to update the analysis as time moves on. As you observe future values of the variables, incorporate them into the data set (and remove old values if you believe they are obsolete), and rerun the regression analysis. You can do this easily with the same Excel file I have attached.

If you have any questions, feel free to call me at any time. You have my number.

A.4   CONCLUSION

Many people believe that statistical analysis is heavy-duty number crunching and little else. As many of our former students have told us, however, this is definitely not true. They continually testify to the importance of written reports (and oral presentations) in their jobs. In fact, we believe that many of you will be judged more by the quality of your *writing* (and speaking) than by the quality of your quantitative analysis. Therefore, keep the suggestions and examples in this chapter handy—you might need them more than you realize. Just remember that well-designed studies and careful statistical analysis are often worthless unless they are communicated clearly and effectively to the audience that needs them.

Aarvik, O., and P. Randolph. "The Application of Linear Programming to the Determination of Transmission Line Fees in an Electrical Power Network." *Interfaces* 6 (1975): 17–31.

Albright, S.C. "A Statistical Analysis of Hitting Streaks in Baseball." *Journal of the American Statistical Association* 88, no. 424 (1993): 1175–1196.

———. *VBA for Modelers*. Belmont, CA: Duxbury Press, 2001.

Altman, E. *Handbook of Corporate Finance*. New York: Wiley, 1986.

Appleton, D., J. French, and M. Vanderpump. "Ignoring a Covariate: An Example of Simpson's Paradox." *The American Statistician* 50 (1996): 340–341.

Armstrong, S. "Forecasting by Extrapolation: Conclusions from 25 Years of Research." *Interfaces* 14, no. 6 (1984): 52–66.

———. *Long-Range Forecasting*. New York: Wiley, 1985.

———. "Research on Forecasting: A Quarter-Century Review, 1960–1984." *Interfaces* 16, no. 1 (1986): 89–103.

Arntzen, B., G. Brown, T. Harrison, and L. Trafton. "Global Supply Chain Management at Digital Equipment Corporation." *Interfaces* 25, no. 1 (1995): 69–93.

Babich, P. "Customer Satisfaction: How Good Is Good Enough?" *Quality Progress* 25 (1992): 65–68.

Balson, W., J. Welsh, and D. Wilson. "Using Decision Analysis and Risk Analysis to Manage Utility Environmental Risk." *Interfaces* 22, no. 6 (1992): 126–139.

Barnett, A. "Genes, Race, IQ, and *The Bell Curve*." *ORMS Today* 22, no. 1 (1994): 18–24.

Bean, J., C. Noon, and G. Salton. "Asset Divestiture at Homart Development Company." *Interfaces* 17, no. 1 (1987): 48–65.

———, C. Noon, S. Ryan, and G. Salton. "Selecting Tenants in a Shopping Mall." *Interfaces* 18, no. 2 (1988): 1–10.

Benninga, S. *Numerical Methods in Finance*. Cambridge, MA: MIT Press, 1989.

Black, F., and M. Scholes. "The Pricing of Options and Corporate Liabilities." *Journal of Political Economy* 81 (1973): 637–654.

Blyth, C. "On Simpson's Paradox and the Sure-Thing Principle." *Journal of the American Statistical Association* 67 (1972): 364–366.

Borison, A. "Oglethorpe Power Corporation Decides about Investing in a Major Transmission System." *Interfaces* 25, no. 2 (1995): 25–36.

Boykin, R. "Optimizing Chemical Production at Monsanto." *Interfaces* 15, no. 1 (1985): 88–95.

Brigandi, A., D. Dargon, M. Sheehan, and T. Spencer. "AT&T's Call Processing Simulator (CAPS) Operational Design for Inbound Call Centers." *Interfaces* 24, no. 1 (1994): 6–28.

Brinkley, P., D. Stepto, J. Haag, K. Liou, K. Wang, and W. Carr. "Nortel Redefines Factory Information Technology: An OR-Driven Approach." *Interfaces* 28, no. 1 (1988): 37–52.

Brown, G., et al. "Real-Time Wide Area Dispatch of Mobil Tank Trucks." *Interfaces* 17, no. 1 (1987): 107–120.

Cawley, J., and P. Sommers, "Voting Irregularities in the 1995 Referendum on Quebec Sovereignty." *Chance* 9, no. 4 (Fall 1996): 29–30.

Cebry, M., A. DeSilva, and F. DiLisio. "Management Science in Automating Postal Operations: Facility and Equipment Planning in the United States Postal Service." *Interfaces* 22, no. 1 (1992): 110–130.

Charnes, A., and L. Cooper. "Generalization of the Warehousing Model." *Operational Research Quarterly* 6 (1955): 131–172.

Cox, J., S. Ross, and M. Rubenstein. "Option Pricing: A Simplified Approach." *Journal of Financial Economics* 7 (1979): 229–263.

Dantzig, G. "The Diet Problem." *Interfaces* 20, no. 4 (1990): 43–47.

Deming, E., *Out of the Crisis*. Cambridge, MA: MIT Center for Advanced Engineering Study, 1986.

DeWitt, C., L. Lasdon, A. Waren, D. Brenner, and S. Melhem. "OMEGA: An Improved Gasoline Blending System for Texaco." *Interfaces* 19, no. 1 (1989): 85–101.

Eaton, D., et al. "Determining Emergency Medical Service Vehicle Deployment in Austin, Texas." *Interfaces* 15, no. 1 (1985): 96–108.

Efroymson, M., and T. Ray. "A Brand-Bound Algorithm for Plant Location." *Operations Research* 14 (1966): 361–368.

Engemann, K., and H. Miller. "Operations Risk Management at a Major Bank." *Interfaces* 22, no. 6 (1992): 140–149.

Eppen, G., K. Martin, and L. Schrage. "A Scenario Approach to Capacity Planning." *Operations Research* 37, no. 4 (1989): 517–527.

Fabian, T. "A Linear Programming Model of Integrated Iron and Steel Production." *Management Science* 4 (1958): 415–449.

Feinstein, C. "Deciding Whether to Test Student Athletes for Drug Use." *Interfaces* 20, no. 3 (1990): 80–87.

Fitzsimmons, J., and L. Allen. "A Warehouse Location Model Helps Texas Comptroller Select Out-of-State Audit Offices." *Interfaces* 13, no. 5 (1983): 40–46.

GeneHunter. Ward Systems Group, Frederick, Maryland, 1995.

Glover, F., G. Jones, D. Karney, D. Klingman, and J. Mote. "An Integrated Production, Distribution, and Inventory System." *Interfaces* 9, no. 5 (1979): 21–35.

———, et al. "The Passenger-Mix Problem in the Scheduled Airlines." *Interfaces* 12 (1982): 873–880.

Graddy, K. "Do Fast-Food Chains Price Discriminate on the Race and Income Characteristics of an Area?" *Journal of Business & Economic Statistics* 15, no. 4 (1997): 391–401.

Grossman, S., and O. Hart. "An Analysis of the Principal Agent Problem." *Econometrica* 51 (1983): 7–45.

Hauser, J., and S. Gaskin. "Application of the Defender Consumer Model." *Marketing Science* 3, no. 4 (1984): 327–351.

Herrnstein, R., and C. Murray. *The Bell Curve.* New York: The Free Press, 1994.

Hertz, D. "Risk Analysis in Capital Investment." *Harvard Business Review* 42 (Jan.–Feb. 1964): 96–108.

Hess, S. "Swinging on the Branch of a Tree: Project Selection Applications." *Interfaces* 23, no. 6 (1993): 5–12.

Holmer, M. "The Asset-Liability Management Strategy System at Fannie Mae." *Interfaces* 24, no. 3 (1994): 3–21.

Hoppensteadt, F., and C. Peskin. *Mathematics in Medicine and the Life Sciences.* New York: Springer-Verlag, 1992.

Howard, R. "Decision Analysis: Practice and Promise." *Management Science* 34, no. 6 (1988): 679–695.

———. "Heathens, Heretics, and Cults: The Religious Spectrum of Decision Aiding." *Interfaces* 22, no. 6 (1992): 15–27.

Huerter, J., and W. Swart. "An Integrated Labor-Management System for Taco Bell." *Interfaces* 28, no. 1 (1998): 75–91.

Kauffman, J., B. Matsik, and K. Spencer. *Beginning SQL Programming.* Birmingham, UK: Wrox Press Ltd, 2001.

Kelly, J. "A New Interpretation of Information Rate." *Bell System Technical Journal* 35 (1956): 917–926.

Kimes, S., and J. Fitzsimmons. "Selecting Profitable Hotel Sites at La Quinta Motor Inns." *Interfaces* 20, no. 2 (1990): 12–20.

Kirkwood, C. "An Overview of Methods for Applied Decision Analysis." *Interfaces* 22, no. 6 (1992): 28–39.

Klingman, D., N. Phillips, D. Steiger, and W. Young. "The Successful Deployment of Management Science throughout Citgo Petroleum Corporation." *Interfaces* 17, no. 1 (1987): 4–25.

Kovar, M. "Four Million Adolescents Smoke: Or Do They?" *Chance* 13, no. 2 (2000): 10–14.

Krajewski, L., L. Ritzman, and P. McKenzie. "Shift Scheduling in Banking Operations: A Case Application." *Interfaces* 10, no. 2 (1980): 1–8.

Krumm, F., and C. Rolle. "Management and Application of Decision and Risk Analysis in DuPont." *Interfaces* 22, no. 6 (1992): 84–93.

Lancaster, L. "The Evolution of the Diet Model in Managing Food Systems." *Interfaces* 22, no. 5 (1992): 59–68.

Lanzenauer, C., E. Harbauer, B. Johnston, and D. Shuttleworth. "RRSP Flood: LP to the Rescue." *Interfaces* 17, no. 4 (1987): 27–40.

LeBlanc, L., J. Hill, G. Greenwell, and A. Czesnat. "Nu-kote's Spreadsheet Linear Programming Models for Optimizing Transportation." *Interfaces* 34, no. 2, (2004): 139–146.

Levy, P., and S. Lemeshow. *Sampling of Populations: Methods and Applications,* 3rd ed. New York: Wiley, 1999.

Littlechild, S. "Marginal Pricing with Joint Costs." *Economic Journal* 80 (1970): 323–334.

Love, R., and J. Hoey. "Management Science Improves Fast Food Operations." *Interfaces* 20, no. 2 (1990): 21–29.

Magoulas, K., and D. Marinos-Kouris. "Gasoline Blending LP." *Oil and Gas Journal* (July 1988): 44–48.

Marcus, A. "The Magellan Fund and Market Efficiency." *Journal of Portfolio Management* (Fall 1990): 85–88.

Martin, C., D. Dent, and J. Eckhart. "Integrated Production, Distribution, and Inventory Planning at Libbey-Owens-Ford." *Interfaces* 23, no. 3 (1993): 68–78.

McDaniel, S., and L. Kinney. "Ambush Marketing Revisited: An Experimental Study of Perceived Sponsorship Effects on Brand Awareness, Attitude Toward the Brand, and Purchase Intention." *Journal of Promotion Management* 3 (1996): 141–167.

Mellichamp, J., D. Miller, and O. Kwon. "The Southern Company Uses a Probability Model for Cost Justification of Oil Sample Analysis." *Interfaces* 23, no. 3 (1993): 118–124.

Miser, H., "Avoiding the Corrupting Lie of a Poorly Stated Problem." *Interfaces* 23, no. 6 (1993): 114–119.

Morrison, D., and R. Wheat. "Pulling the Goalie Revisited." *Interfaces* 16, no. 6 (1984): 28–34.

Mulvey, J. "Reducing the U.S. Treasury's Taxpayer Data Base by Optimization." *Interfaces* 10 (1980): 101–111.

Norton, R. "A New Tool to Help Managers." *Fortune* (May 30, 1994): 135–140.

Oliff, M., and E. Burch. "Multiproduct Production Scheduling at Owens-Corning Fiberglass." *Interfaces* 15, no. 5 (1985): 25–34.

Pankratz, A. *Forecasting with Dynamic Regression Models.* New York: Wiley, 1991.

Pass, S. "Digging for Value in a Mountain of Data." *ORMS Today* 24, no. 5 (1997): 24–28.

Peterson, R., and E. Silver. *Decision Systems for Inventory Management and Production Planning.* 2nd ed. New York: Wiley, 1985.

Press, S.J. "Sample-Audit Tax Assessment for Businesses: What's Fair?" *Journal of Business & Economic Statistics* 13, no. 3 (1995): 357–359.

Ramsey, F., and D. Schafer. *The Statistical Sleuth: A Course in Methods of Data Analysis.* Belmont, CA: Duxbury Press, 1997.

Reichheld, F. *The Loyalty Effect.* Harvard Business School Press, 1996.

Robichek, A., D. Teichroew, and M. Jones. "Optimal Short-Term Financing Decisions." *Management Science* 12 (1965): 1–36.

Robinson, P., L. Gao, and S. Muggenborg. "Designing an Integrated Distribution System at DowBrands, Inc." *Interfaces* 23, no. 3 (1993): 107–117.

Rohn, E. "A New LP Approach to Bond Portfolio Management." *Journal of Financial and Quantitative Analysis* 22 (1987): 439–467.

Rothstein, M. "Hospital Manpower Shift Scheduling by Mathematical Programming." *Health Services Research* (1973).

Salkin, H., and C. Lin. "Aggregation of Subsidiary Firms for Minimal Unemployment Compensation Payments via Integer Programming." *Management Science* 25 (1979): 405–408.

Schindler, S., and T. Semmel. "Station Staffing at Pan American World Airways." *Interfaces* 23, no. 3 (1993): 91–106.

Schnarrs, S., and J. Bavuso. "Extrapolation Models on Very Short-Term Forecasts." *Journal of Business Research* 14 (1986): 27–36.

Silver, E., D. Pyke, and R. Peterson. *Inventory Management and Production Planning and Scheduling.* 3rd ed., New York: Wiley, 1998.

Simonoff, J., and I. Sparrow. "Predicting Movie Grosses: Winners and Losers, Blockbusters and Sleepers." *Chance* 13, no. 3 (2000): 15–24.

Smith, S. "Planning Transistor Production by Linear Programming." *Operations Research* 13 (1965): 132–139.

Sonderman, D., and P. Abrahamson. "Radiotherapy Design Using Mathematical Programming." *Operations Research* 33, no. 4 (1985): 705–725.

Stanley, T., and W. Danko. *The Millionaire Next Door.* Atlanta, GA: Longstreet Press, 1996.

Strong, R. "LP Solves Problem: Eases Duration Matching Process." *Pension and Investment Age* 17, no. 26 (1989): 21.

Swart, W., and L. Donno. "Simulation Modeling Improves Operations, Planning and Productivity of Fast-Food Restaurants." *Interfaces* 11, no. 6 (1981): 35–47.

Ulvila, J. "Postal Automation (ZIP+4) Technology: A Decision Analysis." *Interfaces* 17, no. 2 (1987): 1–12.

Volkema, R. "Managing the Process of Formulating the Problem." *Interfaces* 25, no. 3 (1995): 81–87.

Walkenbach, J. *Microsoft Excel 2000 Bible.* Foster City, CA: IDG Books Worldwide, Inc., 1999.

Walker, W. "Using the Set Covering Problem to Assign Fire Companies to Firehouses." *Operations Research* 22 (1974): 275–277.

Westbrooke, I. "Simpson's Paradox: An Example in a New Zealand Survey of Jury Composition." *Chance* 11, no. 2 (1998): 40–42.

Westerberg, C., B. Bjorklund, and E. Hultman. "An Application of Mixed Integer Programming in a Swedish Steel Mill." *Interfaces* 7, no. 2 (1977): 39–43.

Winston, W.L. *Operations Research: Applications and Algorithms.* 4th ed. Belmont, California: Duxbury Press, 2003.

Zahavi, J. "Franklin Mint's Famous AMOS." *ORMS Today* 22, no. 5 (1995): 18–23.

Zangwill, W. "The Limits of Japanese Production Theory." *Interfaces* 22, no. 5 (1992): 14–25.